Customer Support I

Plunkett's InfoTech Industry Almanac 2011

Please register your book immediately...

if you did not purchase it directly from Plunkett Research, Ltd. This will enable us to fulfill your requests for assistance. Also, it will enable us to notify you of future editions.

Your purchase includes access to Book Data and Exports online

As a book purchaser, you can register for free, 1-year, 1-seat online access to the latest data for your book's industry trends, statistics and company profiles. This includes tools to export company data. We are migrating from our former CD-ROMs, for supplemental data and export tools, to the web. Simply send us this registration form, and we will send you a user name and password. In this manner, you will have access to our continual updates during the year. Certain restrictions apply.

_____ YES, please register me as a purchaser of the book.
I did not buy it directly from Plunkett Research, Ltd.

_____ YES, please register me for free online access. I am the actual, original purchaser. (Proof of purchase may be required.)

Customer Name _____

Title_____

Organization _____

Address_____

City_____State_____Zip_____

Country (if other than USA) _____

Phone_____Fax _____

E-mail _____

Return to: ## Plunkett Research, Ltd.

Attn: Registration
P.O. Drawer 541737, Houston, TX 77254-1737 USA
713.932.0000 · Fax 713.932.7080 · www.plunkettresearch.com
customersupport@plunkettresearch.com

* Purchasers of used books are not eligible to register. Use of online access is subject to the terms of the end user license agreement.

PLUNKETT'S INFOTECH INDUSTRY ALMANAC 2011

The Only Comprehensive Guide to InfoTech Companies and Trends

Jack W. Plunkett

Published by:
Plunkett Research, Ltd., Houston, Texas
www.plunkettresearch.com

PLUNKETT'S INFOTECH INDUSTRY ALMANAC 2011

Editor and Publisher:
Jack W. Plunkett

Executive Editor and Database Manager:
Martha Burgher Plunkett

Senior Editors and Researchers:
Michael Esterheld
Addie K. FryeWeaver
Christie Manck

Editors, Researchers and Assistants:
Kalonji Bobb
Elizabeth Braddock
Austin Bunch
Michelle Dotter
Jeremy Faulk
Andrew Olsen
Jill Steinberg
Suzanne Zarosky

Enterprise Accounts Manager
Emily Hurley

Information Technology Manager:
Wenping Guo

E-Commerce Managers:
Alejandra Avila
Kelly Burke

Video & Graphics Manager:
Geoffrey Trudeau

Special Thanks to:
Cellular Telecommunications & Internet Association (CTIA)
Forrester Research, Inc.
International Data Corporation (IDC)
International Telecommunications Union
InternetWordStats
Semiconductor Industry Association
U.S. Census Bureau
U.S. Department of Labor, *Bureau of Labor Statistics*
U.S. Federal Communications Commission
U.S. International Trade Administration

Plunkett Research, Ltd.
P. O. Drawer 541737, Houston, Texas 77254, USA
Phone: 713.932.0000   Fax: 713.932.7080   www.plunkettresearch.com

Published by:
Plunkett Research, Ltd.
P. O. Drawer 541737
Houston, Texas 77254-1737

Phone: 713.932.0000
Fax: 713.932.7080
Internet: www.plunkettresearch.com

ISBN13 # 978-1-59392-191-0
(eBook Edition # 978-1-59392-534-5)

Disclaimer of liability
for use and results of use:

PLUNKETT'S
INFOTECH INDUSTRY
ALMANAC 2011

CONTENTS

Continued on the next page

Continued from previous page

A Short InfoTech Industry Glossary

10-K: An annual report filed by publicly held companies. It provides a comprehensive overview of the company's business and its finances. By law, it must contain specific information and follow a given form, the "Annual Report on Form 10-K." The U.S. Securities and Exchange Commission requires that it be filed within 90 days after fiscal year end. However, these reports are often filed late due to extenuating circumstances. Variations of a 10-K are often filed to indicate amendments and changes. Most publicly held companies also publish an "annual report" that is not on Form 10-K. These annual reports are more informal and are frequently used by a company to enhance its image with customers, investors and industry peers.

802.11a (Wi-Fi5): A faster wireless network standard than 802.11b ("Wi-Fi"). 802.11a operates in the 5-GHz band at speeds of 54 Mbps. This standard may be affected by weather and is not as suitable for outdoor use. 802.11 standards are set by the IEEE (Institute of Electrical and Electronics Engineers).

802.11b (Wi-Fi): An extremely popular, Wi-Fi short-range wireless connection standard created by the IEEE (Institute of Electrical and Electronics Engineers). It operates at 11 Mbps and can be used to connect computer devices to each other. 802.11b competes with the Bluetooth standard. Its range is up to 380 feet, but 150 feet or so may be more practical in some installations.

802.11g: A recent addition to the series of 802.11 specifications for Wi-Fi wireless networks, 802.11g provides data transfer at speeds of up to 54 Mbps in the 2.4-GHz band. It can easily exchange data with 802.11b-enabled devices, but at much higher speed. 802.11g equipment, such as wireless access points, will be able to provide simultaneous WLAN connectivity for both 802.11g and 802.11b equipment. The 802.11 standards are set by the IEEE (Institute of Electrical and Electronics Engineers).

802.11n (MIMO): Multiple Input Multiple Output antenna technology. MIMO is a new standard in the series of 802.11 Wi-Fi specifications for wireless networks. It has the potential of providing data transfer speeds of 100 to perhaps as much as 500 Mbps. 802.11n also boasts better operating distances than current networks. MIMO uses spectrum more efficiently without any loss of reliability. The technology is based on several different antennas all tuned to the same channel, each transmitting a different signal. MIMO will be widely used as an enhancement to WiMAX networks.

802.15: See "Ultrawideband (UWB)." For 802.15.1, see "Bluetooth."

802.15.1: See "Bluetooth."

802.16 (WiMAX): An advanced wireless standard with significant speed and distance capabilities, WiMAX is officially known as the 802.16 standard. Using microwave technologies, it has the theoretical potential to broadcast at distances up to 30 miles and speeds of up to 70 Mbps. The mid-term goal of the WiMAX industry is to offer 15 Mbps speed for mobile WiMAX (802.16e) users and 40 Mbps for fixed WiMAX (802.16d) users. (The 802.XX standards are set by the IEEE (Institute of Electrical and Electronics Engineers).

Access Network: The network that connects a user's telephone equipment to the telephone exchange.

Active Server Page (ASP): A web page that includes one or more embedded programs, usually written in Java or Visual Basic code. See "Java."

Active X: A set of technologies developed by Microsoft Corporation for sharing information across different applications.

ADM: The application, development and maintenance of software.

ADN: See "Advanced Digital Network (ADN)."

Advanced Digital Network (ADN): See "Integrated Digital Network (IDN)."

AI: See "Artificial Intelligence (AI)."

Ajax: Asynchronous JavaScript and XML. It is a technology that enables web page data to update within a browser on a continuous basis, thus updating the page on the fly. This means that applications that reside on the Internet, such as instant messaging, can appear to run so quickly that they seem like programs that are local to a user's computer. An example is Google Inc.'s Google Maps, launched in 2005. During that year, Microsoft also announced services that will run via Ajax.

Analog: A form of transmitting information characterized by continuously variable quantities. Digital transmission, in contrast, is characterized by discrete bits of information in numerical steps. An analog signal responds to changes in light, sound, heat and pressure.

Analog IC (Integrated Circuit): A semiconductor that processes a continuous wave of electrical signals based on real-world analog quantities such as speed, pressure, temperature, light, sound and voltage.

Analytics: With regard to software, the programs that analyze data for noteworthy trends. For example, retailers use analytics to track sales and inventory data for positive or negative trends over time.

ANSI: American National Standards Institute. Founded in 1918, ANSI is a private, non-profit organization that administers and coordinates the U.S. voluntary standardization and conformity assessment system. Its mission is to enhance both the global competitiveness of U.S. business and the quality of U.S. life by promoting and facilitating voluntary consensus standards and conformity assessment systems, and safeguarding their integrity. See www.ansi.org.

Antitrust Legislation: A set of laws that foster a competitive environment preventing unreasonable restraint of trade or unfair trade practices such as price-fixing. In the United States, antitrust laws originated with the Sherman Antitrust Act of 1890.

APAC: Asia Pacific Advisory Committee. A multi-country committee representing the Asia and Pacific region.

API: See "Application Program Interface (API)."

Applets: Small, object-based applications written in Java that net browsers can download from the Internet on an as-needed basis. These may be software, accessories (such as spell checkers or calculators), information-packed databases or other items. See "Object Technology."

Application Program Interface (API): A set of protocols, routines and tools used by computer programmers as a way of setting common definitions regarding how one piece of software communicates with another.

Application Service Provider (ASP): A web site that enables utilization of software and databases that reside permanently on a service company's remote web server, rather than having to be downloaded to the user's computer. Advantages include the ability for multiple remote users to access the same tools over the Internet and the fact that the ASP provider is responsible for developing and maintaining the software. (ASP is also an acronym for "active server page," which is not related.) For the latest developments in ASP, see "Software as a Service (SaaS)."

Applications: Computer programs and systems that allow users to interface with a computer and that collect, manipulate, summarize and report data and information.

Applied Research: The application of compounds, processes, materials or other items discovered during basic research to practical uses. The goal is to move discoveries along to the final development phase.

Apps: See "Applications."

Archie: This software tool can be used to find files stored on anonymous FTP sites, as long as the user knows the file name or a sub-string of the file name that is being searched for. See "File Transfer Protocol (FTP)."

ARPANet: Advanced Research Projects Agency Network. The forefather of the Internet, ARPANet was developed during the latter part of the 1960s by the United States Department of Defense.

Artificial Intelligence (AI): The use of computer technology to perform functions normally associated with human intelligence, such as reasoning, learning and self-improvement.

ASCII: American Standard Code for Information Exchange. There are 128 standard ASCII codes that represent all Latin letters, numbers and punctuation. Each ASCII code is represented by a seven-digit binary number, such as 0000000 or 0000111. This code is accepted as a standard throughout the world.

ASEAN: Association of Southeast Asian Nations. A regional economic development association established in 1967 by five original member countries: Indonesia, Malaysia, Philippines, Singapore, and Thailand. Brunei joined on 8 January 1984, Vietnam on 28 July 1995, Laos and Myanmar on 23 July 1997, and Cambodia on 30 April 1999.

ASP: See "Application Service Provider (ASP)."

Asymmetrical Digital Subscriber Line (ADSL): High-speed technology that enables the transfer of data over existing copper phone lines, allowing more bandwidth downstream than upstream.

Asynchronous Communications: A stream of data routed through a network as generated instead of in organized message blocks. Most personal computers use this format to send data.

Asynchronous Transfer Mode (ATM): A digital switching and transmission technology based on high speed. ATM allows voice, video and data signals to be sent over a single telephone line at speeds from 25 million to 1 billion bits per second (bps). This digital ATM speed is much faster than traditional analog phone lines, which allow no more than 2 million bps. See "Broadband."

ATCA: Advanced Telecommunications Computing Architecture. It is a set of standards widely used in telecommunications equipment due to the rapid growth of VOIP. ATCA technology increases performance and reliability by optimizing the architecture specifically for communications servers by eliminating proprietary communications port specifications.

Backbone: Traditionally, the part of a communications network that carries the heaviest traffic; the high-speed line or series of connections that forms a large pathway within a network or within a region. The combined networks of AT&T, MCI and other large telecommunications companies make up the backbone of the Internet.

Back-Office: Generally considered to include such areas as accounting, human resources, call centers, financial transaction processing. A back-office application is a software program designed to handle back-office tasks. Also, see "Business Process Outsourcing (BPO)."

Bandwidth: The data transmission capacity of a network, measured in the amount of data (in bits and bauds) it can transport in one second. A full page of text is about 15,000 to 20,000 bits. Full-motion, full-screen video requires about 10 million bits per second, depending on compression.

Barriers to Outsourcing: Forms of resistance to outsourcing, which may include loss of control, quality issues, flexibility and customer and labor backlash.

Basic Research: Attempts to discover compounds, materials, processes or other items that may be largely or entirely new and/or unique. Basic research may start with a theoretical concept that has yet to be proven. The goal is to create discoveries that can be moved along to applied research. Basic research is sometimes referred to as "blue sky" research.

Baud: Refers to how many times the carrier signal in a modem switches value per second or how many bits a modem can send and receive in a second.

Beam: The coverage and geographic service area offered by a satellite transponder. A global beam effectively covers one-third of the earth's surface. A spot beam provides a very specific high-powered downlink pattern that is limited to a particular geographical area to which it may be steered or pointed.

Binhex: A means of changing non-ASCII (or non-text) files into text/ASCII files so that they can be used, for example, as e-mail.

Bit: A single digit number, either a one or a zero, which is the smallest unit of computerized data.

Bits Per Second (Bps): An indicator of the speed of data movement.

Blog (Web Log): A web site consisting of a personal journal, news coverage, special-interest content or other data that is posted on the Internet, frequently updated and intended for public viewing by anyone who might be interested in the author's thoughts. Short for "web log," blog content is frequently distributed via RSS (Real Simple Syndication). Blog content has evolved to include video files (VLOGs) and audio files (Podcasting) as well as text. Also, see "Real Simple Syndication (RSS)," "Video Blog (VLOG)," "Moblog"; "Podcasting," and "User-Generated Content (UGC)."

Bluetooth: An industry standard for a technology that enables wireless, short-distance infrared connections between devices such as cell phone headsets, Palm Pilots or PDAs, laptops, printers and Internet appliances.

BPM: See "Business Process Management (BPM)."

BPO: See "Business Process Outsourcing (BPO)."

Bps: See "Bits Per Second (Bps)."

Branding: A marketing strategy that places a focus on the brand name of a product, service or firm in order to increase the brand's market share, increase sales, establish credibility, improve satisfaction, raise the profile of the firm and increase profits.

BRIC: An acronym representing Brazil, Russia, India and China. The economies of these four countries are seen as some of the fastest growing in the world. A 2003 report by investment bank Goldman Sachs is often credited for popularizing the term; the report suggested that by 2050, BRIC economies will likely outshine those countries which are currently the richest in the world.

Broadband: The high-speed transmission range for telecommunications and computer data. Broadband refers to any transmission at 2 million bps (bits per second) or higher (much higher than analog speed). A broadband network can carry voice, video and data all at the same time. Internet users enjoying broadband access typically connect to the Internet via DSL line, cable modem or T1 line. Several wireless methods now offer broadband as well.

Browser: A program that allows a user to read Internet text or graphics and to navigate from one page to another. The most popular browsers are Microsoft Internet Explorer and Netscape Navigator. Firefox is an open source browser introduced in 2005 that is rapidly gaining popularity.

B-to-B, or B2B: See "Business-to-Business."

B-to-C, or B2C: See "Business-to-Consumer."

B-to-E, or B2E: See "Business-to-Employee."

B-to-G, or B2G: See "Business-to-Government."

Buffer: A location for temporarily storing data being sent or received. It is usually located between two devices that have different data transmission rates.

Business Process Management (BPM): Refers to tools and processes that automate, monitor and accelerate business functions (processes). BPM software, for example, can be used to seamlessly connect key employees to key software applications in an automated fashion. BPM may automate such routine support functions as human resources tasks, accounting tasks and back-office tasks.

Business Process Outsourcing (BPO): The process of hiring another company to handle business activities. BPO is one of the fastest-growing segments in the offshoring sector. Services include human resources management, billing and purchasing and call centers, as well as many types of customer service or marketing activities, depending on the industry involved. Also, see "Knowledge Process Outsourcing (KPO)."

Business-to-Business: An organization focused on selling products, services or data to commercial customers rather than individual consumers. Also known as B2B.

Business-to-Consumer: An organization focused on selling products, services or data to individual consumers rather than commercial customers. Also known as B2C.

Business-to-Employee: A corporate communications system, such as an intranet, aimed at conveying information from a company to its employees. Also known as B2E.

Business-to-Government: An organization focused on selling products, services or data to government units rather than commercial businesses or consumers. Also known as B2G.

Byte: A set of eight bits that represent a single character.

Cable Modem: An interface between a cable television system and a computer or router. Most cable modems are external devices that connect to the PC through a standard 10Base-T Ethernet card and twisted-pair wiring. External Universal Serial Bus (USB) modems and internal PCI modem cards are also available.

Caching: A method of storing data in a temporary location closer to the user so that it can be retrieved quickly when requested.

CAD: See "Computer-Aided Design (CAD)."

CAE: See "Computer-Aided Engineering (CAE)."

Call Automation: Part of the telephone equipment revolution, including voice mail, automated sending and receiving of faxes and the ability for customers to place orders and gather information using a touch-tone telephone to access sophisticated databases. See "Voice Mail."

CAM: See "Computer-Aided Manufacturing (CAM)."

CANDA: See "Computer-Assisted New Drug Application (CANDA)."

Capability Maturity Model (CMM): A global process management standard for software development established by the Software Engineering Institute at Carnegie Mellon University.

Capacitor: An electronic circuit device for temporary storage of electrical energy.

Captive Offshoring: Used to describe a company-owned offshore operation. For example, Microsoft owns and operates significant captive offshore research and development centers in China and elsewhere that are offshore from Microsoft's U.S. home base. Also see "Offshoring."

Carrier: In communications, the basic radio, television or telephony center of transmit signal. The carrier in an analog signal is modulated by varying volume or shifting frequency up or down in relation to the incoming signal. Satellite carriers operating in the analog mode are usually frequency-modulated.

CASE: See "Computer-Assisted Software Engineering (CASE)."

CATV: Cable television.

CDMA: See "Code Division Multiple Access (CDMA)."

Cell: In telecommunications, a geographic unit of a wireless phone system. Regions are divided into small cells, each equipped with a low-powered radio transmitter. When a mobile phone moves from one cell to another, phone calls are handed off.

Central Processing Unit (CPU): The part of a computer that interprets and executes instructions. It is composed of an arithmetic logic unit, a control unit and a small amount of memory.

CGI: See "Common Gateway Interface (CGI)."

CGI-BIN: The frequently used name of a directory on a web server where CGI programs exist.

Channel Definition Format (CDF): Used in Internet-based broadcasting. With this format, a channel serves as a web site that also sends an information file about that specific site. Users subscribe to a channel by downloading the file.

CIS: See "Commonwealth of Independent States (CIS)."

Click Through: In advertising on the Internet, click through refers to how often viewers respond to an ad by clicking on it. Also known as click rate.

Client/Server: In networking, a way of running a large computer setup. The server is the host computer that acts as the central holding ground for files, databases and application software. The clients are all of the PCs connected to the network that share data with the server. This represents a vast change from past networks, which were connected to expensive, complicated "mainframe" computers.

Cloud Computing: A computing method that uses a cluster of multiple computers networked together, often based on open standards. Cloud networks can consist of hundreds or even thousands of computers. They have the ability to run a broad set of applications by using "virtual" server technology to host middleware that is thus distributed across the cloud. Both Google and IBM are boosters of this technology, and Google's entire search infrastructure is based on the use of tens of thousands of small, inexpensive servers clustered together in its data centers as "clouds." Sometimes referred to as "utility computing."

CMM: See "Capability Maturity Model (CMM)."

CMOS: Complementary Metal Oxide Semiconductor; the technology used in making modern silicon-based microchips.

Coaxial Cable: A type of cable widely used to transmit telephone and broadcast traffic. The distinguishing feature is an inner strand of wires surrounded by an insulator that is in turn surrounded by another conductor, which serves as the ground. Cable TV wiring is typically coaxial.

Code Division Multiple Access (CDMA): A cellular telephone multiple-access scheme whereby stations use spread-spectrum modulations and orthogonal codes to avoid interfering with one another. IS-95 (also known as CDMAOne) is the 2G CDMA standard. CDMA2000 is the 3G standard. CDMA in the 1xEV-DO standard offers data transfer speeds up to 2.4 Mbps. CDMA 1xRTT is a slower standard offering speeds of 144 kbps.

Codec: Hardware or software that converts analog to digital and digital to analog (in both audio and video formats). Codecs can be found in digital telephones, set-top boxes, computers and videoconferencing equipment. The term is also used to refer to the compression of digital information into a smaller format.

Co-Location: Refers to the hosting of computer servers at locations operated by service organizations. Co-location is offered by firms that operate specially designed co-location centers with high levels of security, extremely high-speed telecommunication lines for Internet connectivity and reliable backup electrical power systems in case of power failure, as well as a temperature-controlled environment for optimum operation of computer systems.

Commerce Chain Management (CCM): Refers to Internet-based tools to facilitate sales, distribution, inventory management and content personalization in the e-commerce industry. Also see "Supply Chain."

Commoditization: The process whereby a good or service is deemed essentially the same by consumers, leading to price being almost the exclusive competitive factor.

Common Gateway Interface (CGI): A set of guidelines that determines the manner in which a web server receives and sends information to and from software on the same machine.

Commonwealth of Independent States (CIS): An organization consisting of 11 former members of the Soviet Union: Russia, Ukraine, Armenia, Moldova, Georgia, Belarus, Kazakhstan, Uzbekistan, Azerbaijan, Kyrgyzstan and Tajikistan. It was created in 1991. Turkmenistan recently left the Commonwealth as a permanent member, but remained as an associate member. The Commonwealth seeks to coordinate a variety of economic and social policies, including taxation, pricing, customs and economic regulation, as well as to promote the free movement of capital, goods, services and labor.

Communications Satellite Corporation (COMSAT): Serves as the U.S. Signatory to INTELSAT and INMARSAT.

Competitive Local Exchange Carrier (CLEC): A newer company providing local telephone service that competes against larger, traditional firms known as ILECs (incumbent local exchange carriers).

Compression: A technology in which a communications signal is squeezed so that it uses less bandwidth (or capacity) than it normally would. This saves storage space and shortens transfer time. The original data is decompressed when read back into memory.

Computed Tomography (CT): An imaging method that uses x-rays to create cross-sectional pictures of the body. The technique is frequently referred to as a "CAT Scan." A patient lies on a narrow platform while the machine's x-ray beam rotates around him or her. Small detectors inside the scanner measure the amount of x-rays that make it through the part of the body being studied. A computer takes this information and uses it to create several individual images, called slices. These images can be stored, viewed on a monitor, or printed on film. Three-dimensional models of organs can be created by stacking the individual slices together. The newest machines are capable of operating at 256 slice levels, creating very high resolution images in a short period of time.

Computer-Aided Design (CAD): A tool used to provide three-dimensional, on-screen design for everything from buildings to automobiles to clothing. It generally runs on workstations.

Computer-Aided Engineering (CAE): The use of computers to assist with a broad spectrum of engineering design work, including conceptual and analytical design.

Computer-Aided Manufacturing (CAM): The use of computers to assist with manufacturing processes, thereby increasing efficiency and productivity.

Computer-Assisted New Drug Application (CANDA): An electronic submission of a new drug application (NDA) to the FDA.

Computer-Assisted Software Engineering (CASE): The application of computer technology to systems development activities, techniques and methodologies. Sometimes referred to as "computer-aided systems engineering."

Consumer Price Index (CPI): A measure of the average change in consumer prices over time in a fixed market basket of goods and services, such as food, clothing and housing. The CPI is calculated by the U.S. Federal Government and is considered to be one measure of inflation.

Content Aggregator: A content aggregator collects content and distributes it to subscribers, network operators or other content companies.

Contract Manufacturer: A company that manufactures products that will be sold under the brand names of its client companies. For example, a large number of consumer electronics, such as laptop computers, are manufactured by contract manufacturers for leading brand-name computer companies such as Dell. Many other types of products are made under contract manufacturing, from apparel to pharmaceuticals. Also see "Original Equipment Manufacturer (OEM)" and "Original Design Manufacturer (ODM)."

Contract Manufacturing: See "Contract Manufacturer."

Cookie: A piece of information sent to a web browser from a web server that the browser software saves and then sends back to the server upon request. Cookies are used by web site operators to track the actions of users returning to the site.

Cost Per Click (CPC): Online advertising that is billed on a response basis. An advertiser sells a banner ad and is paid by the number of users who click on the ad.

Cost Per Thousand (CPM): A charge for advertising calculated on a fixed amount multiplied by the number of users who view an ad, computed in thousands.

CPC: See "Cost Per Click (CPC)."

CPM: See "Cost Per Thousand (CPM)."

CPU: See "Central Processing Unit (CPU)."

CT: See "Computed Tomography (CT)."

Customer Relationship Management (CRM): Refers to the automation, via sophisticated software, of business processes involving existing and prospective customers. CRM may cover aspects such as sales (contact management and contact history), marketing (campaign management and telemarketing) and customer service (call center history and field service history). Well known providers of CRM software include Salesforce, which delivers via a Software as a Service model (see "Software as a Service (Saas)"), Microsoft and Siebel, which as been acquired by Oracle.

Cyberspace: Refers to the entire realm of information available through computer networks and the Internet.

Dark Fiber: A reference to fiber optic bandwidth that is not being utilized.

Data Base Management System (DBMS): A software system used to store, retrieve and manipulate data in an organized fashion. Usually consists of dictionary, manipulation, security and access components.

Data Over Cable Service Interface Specification (DOCSIS): A set of standards for transferring data over cable television. DOCSIS 3.0 will enable very high-speed Internet access that may eventually reach 160 Mbps.

Datanets: Private networks of land-based telephone lines, satellites or wireless networks that allow corporate users to send data at high speeds to remote locations while bypassing the speed and cost constraints of traditional telephone lines.

DBMS: See "Data Base Management System (DBMS)."

Decompression: See "Compression."

Demand Chain: A similar concept to a supply chain, but with an emphasis on the end user.

Dendrimer: A type of molecule that can be used with small molecules to give them certain desirable characteristics. Dendrimers are utilized in technologies for electronic displays. See "Organic LED (OLED)."

Development: The phase of research and development (R&D) in which researchers attempt to create new products from the results of discoveries and applications created during basic and applied research.

Dial-Up Access: The connection of a computer or other device to a network through a modem and a public telephone network. The only difference between dial-up access and a telephone connection is that computers are at each end of the connection rather than people. Dial-up access is slower than DSL, cable modem and other advanced connections.

Digital: The transmission of a signal by reducing all of its information to ones and zeros and then regrouping them at the reception end. Digital transmission vastly improves the carrying capacity of the spectrum while reducing noise and distortion of the transmission.

Digital Local Telephone Switch: A computer that interprets signals (dialed numbers) from a telephone caller and routes calls to their proper destinations. A digital switch also provides a variety of calling features not available in older analog switches, such as call waiting.

Digital Rights Management (DRM): Restrictions placed on the use of digital content by copyright holders and hardware manufacturers. DRM for Apple, Inc.'s iTunes, for example, allows downloaded music to be played only on Apple's iPod player and iPhones, per agreement with music production companies Universal Music Group, SonyBMG, Warner Music and EMI.

Digital Signal Processor: A chip that converts analog signals such as sound and light into digital signals.

Digital Subscriber Line (DSL): A broadband (high-speed) Internet connection provided via telecommunications systems. These lines are a cost-effective means of providing homes and small businesses with relatively fast Internet access. Common variations include ADSL and SDSL. DSL competes with cable modem access and wireless access.

Digital Video Disc (DVD): Similar to music CDs, these discs can store more than seven times as much data. (DVDs store 4.7 gigabytes of data, compared to 650 megabytes on a CD.) They are commonly used to store full-length motion pictures.

Digital Video Recorder (DVR): A device that records video files, typically television programming including movies, in digital format to be replayed at a later time. The most commonly known DVR is the TiVo. DVRs encode video as MPEG files and save them onto a hard drive. DVRs are also known as PVRs (Personal Video Recorders).

Direct Broadcast Satellite (DBS): A high-powered satellite authorized to broadcast television programming directly to homes. Home subscribers use a dish and a converter to receive and translate the TV signal. An example is the DirecTV service. DBS operates in the 11.70- to 12.40-GHz range.

Disaster Recovery: A set of rules and procedures that allow a computer site to be put back in operation after a disaster has occurred. Moving backups off-site constitutes the minimum basic precaution for disaster recovery. The remote copy is used to recover data if the local storage is inaccessible after a disaster.

Discrete Semiconductor: A chip with one diode or transistor.

Disk Mirroring: A data redundancy technique in which data is recorded identically on multiple separate disk drives at the same time. When the primary disk is off-line, the alternate takes over, providing continuous access to data. Disk mirroring is sometimes referred to as RAID.

Distributed Internet applications Architecture (DNA): A current Microsoft project, also known as Windows DNA, that is dependent on Active Directory and is designed to provide secure delivery of software components over the Internet and intranets.

Domain: A name that has server records associated with it. See "Domain Name."

Domain (Top-Level): Either an ISO country code or a common domain name such as .com, .org or .net.

Domain Name: A unique web site name registered to a company, organization or individual (e.g., plunkettresearch.com).

DS-1: A digital transmission format that transmits and receives information at a rate of 1,544,000 bits per second.

DSL: See "Digital Subscriber Line (DSL)."

Duplicate Host: A single host name that maps to duplicate IP addresses.

DVD: See "Digital Video Disc (DVD)."

DVR: See "Digital Video Recorder (DVR)."

Dynamic HTML: Web content that changes with each individual viewing. For example, the same site could appear differently depending on geographic location of the reader, time of day, previous pages viewed or the user's profile.

Dynamic Random Access Memory (DRAM): A type of memory that stores each bit of data in a circuit that must be refreshed with power periodically. DRAM can reach very high densities since it has a simple structure designed to hold data for short periods of time.

E-Commerce: The use of online, Internet-based sales methods. The phrase is used to describe both business-to-consumer and business-to-business sales.

Electronic Data Interchange (EDI): An accepted standard format for the exchange of data between various companies' networks. EDI allows for the transfer of e-mail as well as orders, invoices and other files from one company to another.

Electronic Health Record (EHR): Refers to digital patient records in the health care industry.

Electronic News Production System (ENPS): A content management software application designed by broadcasters for use in television newsrooms. Introduced in 1997, the application addresses nearly all newsroom activities, including scripting, messaging, archiving, news wire management and text searching of news feeds.

Electronic Paper Display (EPD): A term used to describe a recently developed type of high contrast, flexible display. The displays use low amounts of power and can be viewed in bright sunlight and at any angle. They are well suited for use as screens on mobile devices and may have broad applications in outdoor advertising.

E-Mail (eMail): The use of software that allows the posting of messages (text, audio or video) over a network. E-mail can be used on a LAN, a WAN or the Internet, as well as via online services or wireless devices that are Internet enabled. It can be used to send a message to a single recipient or may be broadcast to a large group of people at once.

EMEA: The region comprised of Europe, the Middle East and Africa.

Enterprise Application: A major software tool intended to manage data over an extremely large corporate or government user base (e.g., SAP, Oracle).

Enterprise Resource Planning (ERP): An integrated information system that helps manage all aspects of a business, including accounting, ordering and human resources, typically across all locations of a major corporation or organization. ERP is considered to be a critical tool for management of large organizations. Suppliers of ERP tools include SAP and Oracle.

ePub: ePub, short for electronic publication, is an open standard for the publication of eBooks. The ePub standard was adopted by the International Digital Publishing Forum.

ERP: See "Enterprise Resource Planning (ERP)."

Ethernet: The standard format on which local area network equipment works. Abiding by Ethernet standards allows equipment from various manufacturers to work together.

EU: See "European Union (EU)."

EU Competence: The jurisdiction in which the EU can take legal action.

European Community (EC): See "European Union (EU)."

European Union (EU): A consolidation of European countries (member states) functioning as one body to facilitate trade. Previously known as the European Community (EC), the EU expanded to include much of Eastern Europe in 2004, raising the total number of member states to 25. In 2002, the EU launched a unified currency, the Euro. See europa.eu.int.

Expert Systems: A practical development of AI that requires creation of a knowledge base of facts and rules furnished by human experts and uses a defined set of rules to access this information in order to suggest solutions to problems. See "Artificial Intelligence (AI)."

Extensible Markup Language (XML): A programming language that enables designers to add extra functionality to documents that could not otherwise be utilized with standard HTML coding. XML was developed by the World Wide Web Consortium. It can communicate to various software programs the actual meanings contained in HTML documents. For example, it can enable the gathering and use of information from a large number of databases at once and place that information into one web site window. XML is an important protocol to web services. See "Web Services."

Extranet: A computer network that is accessible in part to authorized outside persons, as opposed to an intranet, which uses a firewall to limit accessibility.

Fabless: A method of operation used by a product supplier that does not have its own fabrication or manufacturing facilities. This phrase is often used to describe certain semiconductor firms that design chips but rely on outside, contract manufacturers for their actual fabrication.

Facilities Management: The management of a company's physical buildings and/or information systems on an outsourced basis.

FAQ: See "Frequently Asked Questions (FAQ)."

FDDI: See "Fiber Distributed Data Interface (FDDI)."

Federal Communications Commission (FCC): The U.S. Government agency that regulates broadcast television and radio, as well as satellite transmission, telephony and all uses of radio spectrum.

Femtosecond: One a billionth of one millionth of a second.

Ferroelectric Memory: A technology that creates memory for digital devices, such as cell phones, that retains data even when the power for the device is turned off. While flash memory does the same thing, ferroelectric memory stores data much faster and uses much less power.

Fiber Distributed Data Interface (FDDI): A token ring passing scheme that operates at 100 Mbps over fiber-optic lines with a built-in geographic limitation of 100 kilometers. This type of connection is faster than both Ethernet and T-3 connections. See "Token Ring."

Fiber Optics (Fibre Optics): A type of telephone and data transmission cable that can handle vast amounts of voice, data and video at once by carrying them along on beams of light via glass or plastic threads embedded in a cable. Fiber optics are rapidly replacing older copper wire technologies. Fiber optics offer much higher speeds and the ability to handle extremely large quantities of voice or data transmissions at once.

Fiber to the Home (FTTH): Refers to the extension of a fiber-optic system through the last mile so that it touches the home or office where it will be used. This can provide high speed Internet access at speeds of 15 to 100 Mbps, much faster than typical T1 or DSL line. FTTH is now commonly installed in new communities where telecom infrastructure is being built for the first time. Another phrase used to describe such installations is FTTP, or Fiber to the Premises.

Fiber to the Node (FTTN): Refers to the extension of a fiber-optic system through the last mile so that it touches a central neighborhood junction close to the home or office where it will be used. The remaining distance is covered by existing copper phone line that uses DSL (digital subscriber line) technology to speed data transfer.

Field Emission Display (FED): A self-luminescent display that can be extremely thin, draw very low power, and be very bright from all angles and in all types of light. The latest FEDs are based on carbon nanotubes. Samsung is a leader in this field. Early applications include high-end television and computer monitors.

File Server: A computer that is modified to store and transfer large amounts of data to other computers. File servers often receive data from mainframes and store it for transfer to other, smaller computers, or from small computers to mainframes.

File Transfer Protocol (FTP): A widely used method of transferring data and files between two Internet sites.

FinFET: A class of transistor used in semiconductors that has a fin-shaped area that points away from the plane of silicon in which the transistor is embedded. The angle affords greater density and insulation, resulting in the possibility of a chip as small as 22-nanometers.

Firewall: Hardware or software that keeps unauthorized users from accessing a server or network. Firewalls are designed to prevent data theft and unauthorized web site manipulation by "hackers."

Flash Memory: A solid state memory device commonly used in USB "thumb" drives and in certain mobile settings.

FRAM: Ferroelectric random access memory. It is a memory chip technology that utilizes magnetic charges, rather than traditional electrical charges.

Frame Relay: An accepted standard for sending large amounts of data over phone lines and private datanets. The term refers to the way data is broken down into standard-size "frames" prior to transmission.

Frequency: The number of times that an alternating current goes through its complete cycle in one second. One cycle per second is referred to as one hertz; 1,000 cycles per second, one kilohertz; 1 million cycles per second, one megahertz; and 1 billion cycles per second, one gigahertz.

Frequency Band: A term for designating a range of frequencies in the electromagnetic spectrum.

Frequently Asked Questions (FAQ): Answers inquiries about a given topic. Generally, FAQs come in the form of a help file or a hypertext document.

Front-Office Application: A computer program tailored to the needs of the customer relations portions of a business, such as sales and marketing.

FTP: See "File Transfer Protocol (FTP)."

FTTC: Fiber to the curb. See "Fiber to the Home (FTTH)."

FTTP: Fiber to the premises. See "Fiber to the Home (FTTH)."

Fuzzy Logic: Recognizes that some statements are not just "true" or "false," but also "more or less certain" or "very unlikely." Fuzzy logic is used in artificial intelligence. See "Artificial Intelligence (AI)."

Gateway: A device connecting two or more networks that may use different protocols and media. Gateways translate between the different networks and can connect locally or over wide area networks.

GDP: See "Gross Domestic Product (GDP)."

Geofencing: The practice of setting virtual boundaries around a physical location and targeting mobile device users within those areas for a variety of purposes including search and rescue, advertising and social interaction.

Geological Information System (GIS): A computer software system which captures, stores, updates, manipulates, analyzes, and displays all forms of geographically referenced information.

Geostationary: A geosynchronous satellite angle with zero inclination, making a satellite appear to hover over one spot on the earth's equator.

Gigabyte: A gigabytye is 1,024 megabytes.

Gigahertz (GHz): One billion cycles per second. See "Frequency."

Global Positioning System (GPS): A satellite system, originally designed by the U.S. Department of Defense for navigation purposes. Today, GPS is in wide use for consumer and business purposes, such as navigation for drivers, boaters and hikers. It utilizes satellites orbiting the earth at 10,900 miles to enable users to pinpoint precise locations using small, electronic wireless receivers.

Global System for Mobile Communications (GSM): The standard cellular format used throughout Europe, making one type of cellular phone usable in every nation on the continent and in the U.K. In the U.S., Cingular and T-Mobile also run GSM networks. The original GSM, introduced in 1991, has transfer speeds of only 9.6 kbps. GSM EDGE offers 2.75G data transfer speeds of up to 473.6 kbps. GSM GPRS offers slower 2.5G theoretical speeds of 144 kbps.

Globalization: The increased mobility of goods, services, labor, technology and capital throughout the world. Although globalization is not a new development, its pace has increased with the advent of new technologies, especially in the areas of telecommunications, finance and shipping.

GPS: See "Global Positioning System (GPS)."

Graphic Interchange Format (GIF): A widely used format for image files.

Gross Domestic Product (GDP): The total value of a nation's output, income and expenditures produced with a nation's physical borders.

Gross National Product (GNP): A country's total output of goods and services from all forms of economic activity measured at market prices for one calendar year. It differs from Gross Domestic Product (GDP) in that GNP includes income from investments made in foreign nations.

Groupware: A type of software that enables various people on a network to contribute to one document at the same time, sharing ideas, molding the final product and monitoring its progress along the way. Groupware is a new way of group "thinking" without physical meetings. Lotus Notes pioneered this market.

GSM: See "Global System for Mobile Communications (GSM)."

Handheld Devices Markup Language (HDML): A text-based markup language designed for display on a smaller screen (e.g., a cellular phone, PDA or pager). Enables the mobile user to send, receive and redirect e-mail as well as access the Internet (HDML-enabled web sites only).

Haptics: A technology in which a user of electronics, wireless devices and electronic games experiences unique sensations from a video game interface or a touchscreen, such as one might find on a smartphone. Advanced touchscreens using haptics can enable the user to feel the sensation of clicks on an icon, vibrations and other types of touch sensations.

HDMI: See "High-Definition Multi-Media Interface (HDMI)."

HDML: See "Handheld Devices Markup Language (HDML)."

HDSL: See "High-Data-Rate Digital Subscriber Line (HDSL)."

Helper Applications: Applications that allow the user to view or play downloadable files.

Hertz: A measure of frequency equal to one cycle per second. Most radio signals operate in ranges of megahertz or gigahertz.

HFC: Hybrid Fiber Coaxial. A type of cable system.

High-Data-Rate Digital Subscriber Line (HDSL): High-data-rate DSL, delivering up to T1 or E1 speeds.

High-Definition Multi-Media Interface (HDMI): An industry-standard interface to conduct uncompressed, all-digital audio and video signals into high definition entertainment components including HDTV. The goal is to enable consumer entertainment devices to display high quality, high-definition content. HDMI is backward-compatible with earlier DVI equipment, so that HDMI can HDMI equipment can display video received from DVI products.

HIPAA: The Health Insurance Portability and Accountability Act of 1996, which demands that all billing and patient data must be exchanged electronically between care givers and insurance payers. A major focus of HIPAA requirements is the protection of patient data privacy.

Hit: On the Internet, a single request from a web browser for something from a web server, e.g., a request for text or graphics on a web page. Hits are often confused with unique users when counting traffic on an Internet site. A unique user is one visitor during one website access period. That user is likely to make multiple hits during one visit, as he or she goes to various pages within a site. Each switch to a new page constitutes a hit.

Holographic Optical Disk: A disk drive that not only stores data on its surface, but also in volume throughout the depth and breadth of the disk.

Hosting: Maintaining a computer application for a third party. Hosting may include databases, web sites and proprietary applications.

HTML: See "Hypertext Markup Language (HTML)."

HTTP: See "Hypertext Transfer Protocol (HTTP)."

Hyperlink: On the Internet, an element in a web page that links to another page or to another place in the same document. Generally, the user clicks on the hyperlink in order to follow it.

Hypertext Markup Language (HTML): A language for coding text for viewing on the World Wide Web. HTML is unique because it enables the use of hyperlinks from one site to another, creating a web.

Hypertext Transfer Protocol (HTTP): The protocol used most frequently on the World Wide Web to move hypertext files between clients and servers on the Internet.

ICANN: The Internet Corporation for Assigned Names and Numbers. ICANN acts as the central coordinator for the Internet's technical operations.

IDN: See "Integrated Digital Network (IDN)."

IEEE: The Institute of Electrical and Electronic Engineers. The IEEE sets global technical standards and acts as an authority in technical areas including computer engineering, biomedical technology, telecommunications, electric power, aerospace and consumer electronics, among others. www.ieee.org.

ILEC: See "Incumbent Local Exchange Carrier (ILEC)."

IM: See "Instant Messaging (IM)."

Impressions: In Internet advertising, the total number of times an ad is displayed on a web page. Impressions are not the same as "hits," which count the number of times each page or element in a page is retrieved. Since a single complicated page on a web site could consist of five or more individual elements, including graphics and text, one viewer calling up that page would register multiple hits but just a single impression.

Incumbent Local Exchange Carrier (ILEC): A traditional telephone company that was providing local service prior to the establishment of the Telecommunications Act of 1996, when upstart companies (CLECs, or competitive local exchange carriers) were enabled to compete against the ILECS and were granted access to their system wiring.

Information Technology (IT): The systems, including hardware and software, that move and store voice, video and data via computers and telecommunications.

Infrastructure: 1) The equipment that comprises a system. 2) Public-use assets such as roads, bridges, sewers and other assets necessary for public accommodation and utilities. 3) The underlying base of a system or network.

Infrastructure (Telecommunications): The entity made up of all the cable and equipment installed in the worldwide telecommunications market. Most of today's telecommunications infrastructure is connected by copper and fiber-optic cable, which represents a huge capital investment that telephone companies would like to continue to utilize in as many ways as possible.

Initial Public Offering (IPO): A company's first effort to sell its stock to investors (the public). Investors in an up-trending market eagerly seek stocks offered in many IPOs because the stocks of newly public companies that seem to have great promise may appreciate very rapidly in price, reaping great profits for those who were able to get the stock at the first offering. In the United States, IPOs are regulated by the SEC (U.S. Securities Exchange Commission) and by the state-level regulatory agencies of the states in which the IPO shares are offered.

INMARSAT: The International Maritime Satellite Organization. INMARSAT operates a network of satellites used in transmissions for all types of international mobile services, including maritime, aeronautical and land mobile.

Insourcing: A unique and increasingly popular business method. It is similar to "outsourcing," in that it is a continuing business service or process provided to a company by an outside organization. The intent is to enable the client company to focus on its core strengths, while hiring outside firms to provide other needs such as warehouse, call center or human resources management. However, with insourcing, the services provider moves into or near the client company's facility and sets up shop. For example, ARAMARK has a business unit that will set up and manage an employee cafeteria within a client company's facility. (Occasionally, the term "insourcing" has also been used to describe the creation of jobs in America by foreign firms.) Also see "Third-Party Logistics (3PL)."

Installed Base: Products previously sold and currently in use by the end-customer.

Instant Messaging (IM): A type of e-mail that is viewed and then deleted. IM is used between opt-in networks of people for leisure or business purposes.

Integrated Circuit (IC): Another name for a semiconductor, an IC is a piece of silicon on which thousands (or millions) of transistors have been combined.

Integrated Digital Network (IDN): A network that uses both digital transmission and digital switching.

Integrated Services Digital Networks (ISDN): Internet connection services offered at higher speeds than standard "dial-up" service. While ISDN was considered to be an advanced service at one time, it has been eclipsed by much faster DSL, cable modem and T1 line service.

Intelligent Transportation Systems (ITS): Include a broad number of information technologies that can provide an electronic communications link to cars and trucks, enabling drivers to be alerted to road hazards, delays, construction and accidents. At the same time, ITS can transmit driving directions and a wealth of additional driving-related information. ITS enables automated drive-through toll collection and truck pre-clearance along highways and at bridge and tunnel crossings. ITS technologies are likewise in use at border stations, points of entry and customs checkpoints, especially in the NAFTA zone.

INTELSAT: The International Telecommunications Satellite Organization. INTELSAT operates a network of 20 satellites, primarily for international transmissions, and provides domestic services to some 40 countries.

Interactive TV (ITV): Allows two-way data flow between a viewer and the cable TV system. A user can exchange information with the cable system—for example, by ordering a product related to a show he/she is watching or by voting in an interactive survey.

Interactive Video On Demand (IVOD): An extension of VOD that offers many of the functions typically provided by VCRs, such as pause, fast forward and fast rewind. Through a set-top box, the IVOD customer can browse, select and purchase products; avoid or select advertisements; and investigate additional details about news events.

Interexchange Carrier (IXC or IEC): Any company providing long-distance phone service between LECs and LATAs. See "Local Exchange Carrier (LEC)" and "Local Access and Transport Area (LATA)."

Interface: Refers to (1) a common boundary between two or more items of equipment or between a terminal and a communication channel, (2) the electronic device that interconnects two or more devices or items of equipment having similar or dissimilar characteristics or (3) the electronic device placed between a terminal and a communication channel to protect the network from the hazard of excess voltage levels.

International Telecommunications Union (ITU): The international body responsible for telephone and computer communications standards describing interface techniques and practices. These standards include those that define how a nation's telephone and data systems connect to the worldwide communications network.

Internet: A global computer network that provides an easily accessible way for hundreds of millions of users to send and receive data electronically when appropriately connected via computers or wireless devices. Access is generally through HTML-enabled sites on the World Wide Web. Also known as the Net.

Internet Appliance: A non-PC device that connects users to the Internet for specific or general purposes. A good example is an electronic game machine with a screen and Internet capabilities. It is anticipated that many types of Internet appliances will be of common use in homes in the near future.

Internet Protocol (IP): A set of tools and/or systems used to communicate across the World Wide Web.

Internet Protocol Television (IPTV): Television delivered by Internet-based means such as fiber to the home (FTTH) or a very high speed DSL. Microsoft is a leading provider of advanced IPTV software. SBC and BT are two leading telecom firms that are using Microsoft's new software to offer television services over high speed Internet lines.

Internet Service Provider (ISP): A company that sells access to the Internet to individual subscribers. Leading examples are MSN and AOL.

Internet Telephony: See "Voice Over Internet Protocol (VOIP)."

Internet2: An advanced networking consortium lead by the U.S. research and education community that develops and deploys cutting edge network applications.

Intranet: A network protected by a firewall for sharing data and e-mail within an organization or company. Usually, intranets are used by organizations for internal communication.

IP Number/IP Address: A number or address with four parts that are separated by dots. Each machine on the Internet has its own IP (Internet protocol) number, which serves as an identifier.

IP VOD: See "VOD-Over-IP."

IPTV: See "Internet Protocol Television (IPTV)."

ISDN: See "Integrated Services Digital Networks (ISDN)."

ISO 9000, 9001, 9002, 9003: Standards set by the International Organization for Standardization. ISO 9000, 9001, 9002 and 9003 are the highest quality certifications awarded to organizations that meet exacting standards in their operating practices and procedures.

IT: See "Information Technology (IT)."

IT-Enabled Services (ITES): The portion of the Information Technology industry focused on providing business services, such as call centers, insurance claims processing and medical records transcription, by utilizing the power of IT, especially the Internet. Most ITES functions are considered to be back-office procedures. Also, see "Business Process Outsourcing (BPO)."

ITES: See "IT-Enabled Services (ITES)."

ITV: See "Interactive TV (ITV)."

Java: A programming language developed by Sun Microsystems that allows web pages to display interactive graphics. Any type of computer or operating systems can read Java.

Joint Photographic Experts Group (JPEG): A widely used format for digital image files.

Just-in-Time (JIT) Delivery: Refers to a supply chain practice whereby manufacturers receive components on or just before the time that they are needed on the assembly line, rather than bearing the cost of maintaining several days' or weeks' supply in a warehouse. This adds greatly to the cost-effectiveness of a manufacturing plant and puts the burden of warehousing and timely delivery on the supplier of the components.

Ka-Band: The frequency range from 18 to 31 GHz. The spectrum allocated for satellite communications is 30 GHz for the up-link and 20 GHz for the downlink.

Kbps: One thousand bits per second.

Kilobyte: 1,000 (or 1,024) bytes.

Kilohertz (kHz): A measure of frequency equal to 1,000 Hertz.

Knowledge Management (KM): Includes techniques and technologies that help users find their way through existing information. Also defined as capturing and growing knowledge as employees in an organization interact with customers, partners and products.

Knowledge Process Outsourcing (KPO): The use of outsourced and/or offshore workers to perform business tasks that require judgment and analysis. Examples include such professional tasks as patent research, legal research, architecture, design, engineering, market research, scientific research, accounting and tax return preparation. Also, see "Business Process Outsourcing (BPO)."

LAC: An acronym for Latin America and the Caribbean.

Large-Scale Integration (LSI): The placement of thousands of electronic gates on a single chip. This makes the manufacture of powerful computers possible.

LATA: See "Local Access and Transport Area (LATA)."

LDCs: See "Least Developed Countries (LDCs)."

Leased Line: A phone line that is rented for use in continuous, long-term data connections.

Least Developed Countries (LDCs): Nations determined by the U.N. Economic and Social Council to be the poorest and weakest members of the international community. There are currently 50 LDCs, of which 34 are in Africa, 15 are in Asia Pacific and the remaining one (Haiti) is in Latin America. The top 10 on the LDC list, in descending order from top to 10th, are Afghanistan, Angola, Bangladesh, Benin, Bhutan, Burkina Faso, Burundi, Cambodia, Cape Verde and the Central African Republic. Sixteen of the LDCs are also Landlocked Least Developed Countries (LLDCs) which present them with additional difficulties often due to the high cost of transporting trade goods. Eleven of the LDCs are Small Island Developing States (SIDS), which are often at risk of extreme weather phenomenon (hurricanes, typhoons, Tsunami); have fragile ecosystems; are often dependent on foreign energy sources; can have high disease rates for HIV/AIDS and malaria; and can have poor market access and trade terms.

LEC: See "Local Exchange Carrier (LEC)."

Light Emitting Diode (LED): A small tube containing material that emits light when exposed to electricity. The color of the light depends upon the type of material. The LED was first developed in 1962 at the University of Illinois at Urbana-Champaign. LEDs are important to a wide variety of industries, from wireless telephone handsets to signage to displays for medical equipment, because they provide a very high quality of light with very low power requirements. They also have a very long useful life and produce very low heat output when. All of these characteristics are great improvements over a conventional incandescent bulb. Several advancements have been made in LED technology. See "Organic LED (OLED)," "Polymer Light Emitting Diode (PLED)," "Small Molecule Organic Light Emitting Diode (SMOLED)" and "Dendrimer."

LINUX: An open, free operating system that is shared readily with millions of users worldwide. These users continuously improve and add to the software's code. It can be used to operate computer networks and Internet appliances as well as servers and PCs.

Liquid Crystal Display (LCD): A digital screen composed of liquid crystal cells that change luminosity when exposed to an electric field. The newest LCDs have a higher resolution and use less power than conventional displays.

Lithography: In the manufacture of semiconductors and MEMS (microelectromechanical systems), lithography refers to the transfer of a pattern of photosensitive material by exposing it to light or radiation. The photosensitive material changes physical properties when exposed to a source of radiation. Typically, a mask is employed that creates a desired pattern by blocking out light to some areas. Using this process to deposit materials on a substrate, integrated circuits can be manufactured.

LMDS: Local Multipoint Distribution Service. A fixed, wireless, point-to-multipoint technology designed to distribute television signals.

Local Access and Transport Area (LATA): An operational service area established after the breakup of AT&T to distinguish local telephone service from long-distance service. The U.S. is divided into over 160 LATAs.

Local Area Network (LAN): A computer network that is generally within one office or one building. A LAN can be very inexpensive and efficient to set up when small numbers of computers are involved. It may require a network administrator and a serious investment if hundreds of computers are hooked up to the LAN. A LAN enables all computers within the office to share files and printers, to access common databases and to send e-mail to others on the network.

Local Exchange Carrier (LEC): Any local telephone company, i.e., a carrier, that provides ordinary phone service under regulation within a service area. Also see "Incumbent Local Exchange Carrier (ILEC)" and "Competitive Local Exchange Carrier (CLEC)."

Location Based Advertising (LBA): The ability for advertisers and information providers to push information to mobile consumers based on their locations. For example, GPS equipped cell phones have the potential to alert consumers on the go to nearby restaurants, entertainment attractions, and special sale events at retailers.

LSI: See "Large-Scale Integration (LSI)."

M2M: See "Machine-to-Machine (M2M)."

Machine-to-Machine (M2M): Refers to the transmission of data from one device to another, typically through wireless means such as Wi-Fi or cellular. For example, a Wi-Fi network might be employed to control several machines in a household from a central computer. Such machines might include air conditioning and entertainment systems. Wireless sensor networks (WSNs) will be a major growth factor in M2M communications, in everything from factory automation to agriculture and transportation. In logistics and retailing, M2M can refer to the use of RFID tags to transmit information. See "Radio Frequency Identification (RFID)."

Magnetoresistive Random Access Memory (MRAM): A non-volatile computer memory technology in which data is stored by magnetic storage elements, as opposed to traditional electric charge or current flows. MRAM speed is faster than both DRAM and Flash memory.

Mainframe Computer: One of the largest types of computer, usually capable of serving many users simultaneously, with exceptional processing speed.

MAN: See "Metropolitan Area Network (MAN)."

Managed Service Provider (MSP): An outsourcer that deploys, manages and maintains the back-end software and hardware infrastructure for Internet businesses.

Manufacturing Resource Planning (MRP II): A methodology that supports effective planning with regard to all resources of a manufacturing company, linking MRP with sales and operations planning, production planning and master production scheduling.

Maquila (Maquiladora): A production plant, located in Mexico near the U.S.-Mexican border, that manufactures components but does not perform final assembly of completed products. The U.S. allows duty-free import of these components, which then undergo final assembly at a U.S. plant. Also see "Original Equipment Manufacturer (OEM)."

Market Segmentation: The division of a consumer market into specific groups of buyers based on demographic factors.

Marketing: Includes all planning and management activities and expenses associated with the promotion of a product or service. Marketing can encompass advertising, customer surveys, public relations and many other disciplines. Marketing is distinct from selling, which is the process of sell-through to the end user.

Mbps (Megabits per second): 1 million bits transmitted per second.

M-Commerce: Mobile e-commerce over wireless devices.

Media Object Server (MOS): An XML-based protocol designed to transfer information between newsroom automation systems and other systems, including media servers. The MOS protocol allows various devices to be controlled from a central device or piece of software, which limits the need to have operators stationed at multiple locations throughout the news studio.

Media Oriented Systems Transport (MOST): A standard adopted in 2004 by the Consumer Electronics Association for the integration of or interface with consumer electronics (such as iPods) into entertainment systems in automobiles.

Megabytes: 1 million bytes, or 1,024 kilobytes.

Megahertz (MHz): A measure of frequency equal to 1 million Hertz.

Memristor: A fourth fundamental circuit element in electrical engineering. A memristor may make it possible to develop computer systems with memories that retain data after the system is powered down, have no need for a booting process when powered on, consume less power and associate information in a manner similar to the human brain. Memristor is short for memory resistor.

Merchandising: Any marketing method utilized to foster sales growth.

Mesh Network: A network that uses multiple Wi-Fi repeaters or "nodes" to deploy a wireless Internet access network. Typically, a mesh network is operated by the users themselves. Each user installs a node at his or her locale, and plugs the node into his/her local Internet access, whether DSL, cable or satellite. Other users within the mesh can access all other nodes as needed, or as they travel about. A mesh network can provide access to an apartment complex, an office building, a campus or an entire city. Meraki is a leading node brand in this sector.

Metropolitan Area Network (MAN): A data and communications network that operates over metropolitan areas and recently has been expanded to nationwide and even worldwide connectivity of high-speed data networks. A MAN can carry video and data.

Microprocessor: A computer on a digital semiconductor chip. It performs math and logic operations and executes instructions from memory. (Also known as a central processing unit or CPU.)

Microwave: Line-of sight, point-to-point transmission of signals at high frequency. Microwaves are used in data, voice and all other types of information transmission. The growth of fiber-optic networks has tended to curtail the growth and use of microwave relays.

MID: See "Mobile Internet Device (MID)."

Middleware: Software that interprets requests between applications. Also used to describe software that helps an application communicate with an underlying operating system. Generally, middleware integrates various types of systems by acting as a conversion or translation layer.

Millions of Instructions per Second (MIPS): A unit used to compare relative computing power, measured in millions. For example, 25 MIPS is 25 million machine instructions per second.

MIME: See "Multipurpose Internet Mail Extensions (MIME)."

MIMO (Multiple Input Multiple Output): See "802.11n (MIMO)."

MIPS: See "Millions of Instructions per Second (MIPS)."

MMS: See "Multimedia Messaging System (MMS)."

Mobile Internet Device (MID): A small, personal, portable device that connects wirelessly to the Internet. Intel is a leading proponent of new devices that are mobile and convenient, and that enjoy powerful chips with long battery life.

Moblog: Mobile blog. This is a blog created by cell phone or other mobile device. It often consists largely of photos taken by a cell phone's built-in camera. Also, see "Blog (Web Log)."

Modem: A device that allows a computer to be connected to a phone line, which in turn enables the computer to receive and exchange data with other machines via the Internet.

Modulator: A device that modulates a carrier. Modulators are found in broadcasting transmitters and satellite transponders. The devices are also used by cable TV companies to place a baseband video television signal onto a desired VHF or UHF channel. Home video tape recorders also have built-in modulators that enable the recorded video information to be played back using a television receiver tuned to VHF channel 3 or 4.

Molecular Memory: A technology that utilizes nanowires or nanotubes to create ultra-dense memory chips that feature lower power consumption. An additional benefit may be reduced semiconductor fabrication costs.

MOS: See "Media Object Server (MOS)."

MOST: See "Media Oriented Systems Transport (MOST)."

MP3: A subsystem of MPEG used to compress sound into digital files. It is the most commonly used format for downloading music and audio books. MP3 compresses music significantly while retaining CD-like quality. MP3 players are personal, portable devices used for listening to music and audio book files. See "MPEG."

MPEG, MPEG-1, MPEG-2, MPEG-3, MPEG-4: Moving Picture Experts Group. It is a digital standard for the compression of motion or still video for transmission or storage. MPEGs are used in digital cameras and for Internet-based viewing.

MRAM: See "Magnetoresistive Random Access Memory (MRAM)."

MSP: See "Managed Service Provider (MSP)."

Multicasting: Sending data, audio or video simultaneously to a number of clients. Also known as broadcasting.

Multimedia: Refers to a presentation using several different media at once. For example, an encyclopedia in CD-ROM format is generally multimedia because it features written text, video and sound in one package.

Multimedia Messaging System (MMS): See "Text Messaging."

Multipoint Distribution System (MDS): A common carrier licensed by the FCC to operate a broadcast-like omni-directional microwave transmission facility within a given city. MDS carriers often pick up satellite pay-TV programming and distribute it, via their local MDS transmitter, to specially installed antennas and receivers.

Multipurpose Internet Mail Extensions (MIME): A widely used method for attaching non-text files to e-mails.

NAFTA: See "North American Free Trade Agreement (NAFTA)."

NAND: An advanced type of flash memory chip. It is popular for use in consumer electronics such as MP3 players and digital cameras.

Nanosecond (NS): A billionth of a second. A common unit of measure of computer operating speed.

Nanotechnology: The science of designing, building or utilizing unique structures that are smaller than 100 nanometers (a nanometer is one billionth of a meter). This involves microscopic structures that are no larger than the width of some cell membranes.

Near Video On Demand (NVOD): An alternative method of VOD television programming delivery. NVOD delivers only a small portion of the ordered programming to the customer before playback. This initial download serves as a buffer while the rest of the programming is viewed directly off the provider's server. In contrast, traditional VOD typically involves the delivery of the entire ordered programming to the customer for playback from the customer's hard drive.

Nearfield Communication (NFC): A short-range wireless connectivity standard that enables communication between devices that are touching or brought within several centimeters of each other. NFC is used to transfer data from one PDA to another and to enable cell phones to act as smart payment cards when waived before point-of-sale terminals.

Near-Shoring: Near-shoring is a variation on offshoring in which certain business operations, software development, support services, etc. are outsourced to locations that are closer to the home country. Near-shoring aims to achieve results similar to those of offshoring in general (such as labor cost savings), while at the same time taking advantage of the relative proximity to maintain outsourced operations in areas that share, for example, cultural heritage, common languages, common time zone, etc. Near-shored operations can be easier to monitor, since the costs and time involved in travelling to such sites are kept at a minimum. Examples might include a firm in the U.K. outsourcing to Eastern Europe, or a U.S. or Canadian corporation outsourcing to Mexico or Latin America.

Netbook: A low-priced, lightweight, laptop personal computer capable of basic tasks such as Internet browsing and email.

Network: In computing, a network is created when two or more computers are connected. Computers may be connected by wireless methods, using such technologies as 802.11b, or by a system of cables, switches and routers.

Network Information Center (NIC): Any organization responsible for supplying information about a network.

Network Numbers: The first portion of an IP address, which identifies the network to which hosts in the rest of the address are connected.

Network Personal Video Recording (nPVR): See "Server-Based SVOD Programming."

Network Storage: See "Network-Based VOD."

Network-Based VOD: Involves a television content provider storing either all or most of its programming content at its location, usually on its servers. Network-based VOD is more typical of cable TV than satellite TV.

Neural Networks: Computer architecture that enables redundancy and self-repair of communications paths and supports high traffic loads through routing decisions.

New Media: A wide array of digital communication technologies, including Internet development tools and services, desktop and portable personal computers, workstations, servers, audio/video compression and editing equipment, graphics hardware and software, high-density storage services and video conferencing systems.

NIC: See "Network Information Center (NIC)."

Node: Any single computer connected to a network or a junction of communications paths in a network.

North American Free Trade Agreement (NAFTA): A trade agreement signed in December 1992 by U.S. President George H. W. Bush, Canadian Prime Minister Brian Mulroney and Mexican President Carlos Salinas de Gortari. The agreement eliminates tariffs on most goods originating in and traveling between the three member countries. It was approved by the legislatures of the three countries and had entered into force by January 1994. When it was created, NAFTA formed one of the largest free-trade areas of its kind in the world.

nPVR: See "Network Personal Video Recording (nPVR)."

NRAM: A carbon nanotube-based technology for memory chips that can be manufactured in extremely small size.

NS: See "Nanosecond (NS)."

NTIA: National Telecommunications and Information Administration. A unit of the Department of Commerce that addresses U.S. government telecommunications policy, standards setting and radio spectrum allocation. www.ntia.doc.gov

NVOD: See "Near Video On Demand (NVOD)."

Object Technology: By merging data and software into "objects," a programming system becomes object-oriented. For example, an object called "weekly inventory sold" would have the data and programming needed to construct a flow chart. Some new programming systems–including Java–contain this feature. Object technology is also featured in many Microsoft products. See "Java."

OC3, up to OC768: Very high-speed data lines that run at speeds from 155 to 39,813.12 Mbps.

ODM: See "Original Design Manufacturer (ODM)."

OECD: See "Organisation for Economic Co-operation and Development (OECD)."

OEM: See "Original Equipment Manufacturer (OEM)."

Offshoring: The rapidly growing tendency among U.S., Japanese and Western European firms to send knowledge-based and manufacturing work overseas. The intent is to take advantage of lower wages and operating costs in such nations as China, India, Hungary and Russia. The choice of a nation for offshore work may be influenced by such factors as language and education of the local workforce, transportation systems or natural resources. For example, China and India are graduating high numbers of skilled engineers and scientists from their universities. Also, some nations are noted for large numbers of workers skilled in the English language, such as the Philippines and India. Also see "Captive Offshoring" and "Outsourcing."

OLED: See "Organic LED (OLED)."

Onshoring: The opposite of "offshoring." Providing or maintaining manufacturing or services within or nearby a company's domestic location. Sometimes referred to as reshoring.

Open Source (Open Standards): A software program for which the source code is openly available for modification and enhancement as various users and developers see fit. Open software is typically developed as a public collaboration and grows in usefulness over time. See "LINUX."

Operating System (OS): The software that allows applications like word processors or web browsers to run on a computer. For example, Windows 2000 is an operating system.

Optical Character Recognition (OCR): An industry-wide classification system for coding information onto merchandise. It enables retailers to record information on each SKU when it is sold and to transmit that information to a computer. This is accomplished through computerized cash registers that include bar-code scanners (called point-of-sale terminals).

Optical Fiber (Fibre): See "Fiber Optics (Fibre Optics)."

Organic LED (OLED): A type of electronic display based on the use of organic materials that produce light when stimulated by electricity. Also see "Polymer," "Polymer Light Emitting Diode (PLED)," "Small Molecule Organic Light Emitting Diode (SMOLED)" and "Dendrimer."

Organic Polymer: See "Polymer."

Organisation for Economic Co-operation and Development (OECD): A group of more than 30 nations that are strongly committed to the market economy and democracy. Some of the OECD members include Japan, the U.S., Spain, Germany, Australia, Korea, the U.K., Canada and Mexico. Although not members, Estonia, Israel and Russia are invited to member talks; and Brazil, China, India, Indonesia and South Africa have enhanced engagement policies with the OECD. The Organisation provides statistics, as well as social and economic data; and researches social changes, including patterns in evolving fiscal policy, agriculture, technology, trade, the environment and other areas. It publishes over 250 titles annually; publishes a corporate magazine, the OECD Observer; has radio and TV studios; and has centers in Tokyo, Washington, D.C., Berlin and Mexico City that distributed the Organisation's work and organizes events.

Original Design Manufacturer (ODM): A contract manufacturer that offers complete, end-to-end design, engineering and manufacturing services. ODMs design and build products, such as consumer electronics, that client companies can then brand and sell as their own. For example, a large percentage of laptop computers, cell phones and PDAs are made by ODMs. Also see "Original Equipment Manufacturer (OEM)" and "Contract Manufacturer."

Original Equipment Manufacturer (OEM): A company that manufactures a product or component for sale to a customer that will integrate the component into a final product or assembly. The OEM's customer will distribute the end product or resell it to an end user. For example, a personal computer made under a brand name by a given company may contain various components, such as hard drives, graphics cards or speakers, manufactured by several different OEM "vendors," but the firm doing the final assembly/manufacturing process is the final manufacturer. Also see "Original Design Manufacturer (ODM)" and "Contract Manufacturer."

OS: See "Operating System (OS)."

Outsourcing: The hiring of an outside company to perform a task otherwise performed internally by the company, generally with the goal of lowering costs and/or streamlining work flow. Outsourcing contracts are generally several years in length. Companies that hire outsourced services providers often prefer to focus on their core strengths while sending more routine tasks outside for others to perform. Typical outsourced services include the running of human resources departments, telephone call centers and computer departments. When outsourcing is performed overseas, it may be referred to as offshoring. Also see "Offshoring."

P2P: See "Peer-to-Peer (P2P)."

Packet Switching: A higher-speed way to move data through a network, in which files are broken down into smaller "packets" that are reassembled electronically after transmission.

Passive Optical Network (PON): A telecommunications network that brings high speed fiber optic cable all the way (or most of the way) to the end user. Also, see "Fiber to the Home (FTTH)."

PBX: A central telephone system within a large business office used to route incoming and outgoing calls to various employees and onto long-distance networks. PBX functions are typically enhanced by the application of computer functions, such as voice mail and call forwarding.

PC: See "Personal Computer (PC)."

PCMCIA: Personal Computer Memory Card International Association.

PDA: See "Personal Digital Assistant (PDA)."

Peer-to-Peer (P2P): Refers to a connection between computers that creates equal status between the computers. P2P can be used in an office or home to create a simple computer network. However, P2P more commonly refers to networks of computers that share information online. For example, peer-to-peer music sharing networks enable one member to search the hard drives of other members to locate music files and then download those files. These systems can be used for legal purposes. Nonetheless, they became notorious as systems that enable members to collect music and videos for free, circumventing copyright and other legal restrictions. At one time Napster was widely known as a P2P music system that enabled users to circumvent copyright.

Perpendicular Magnetic Recording (PMR): A technology for data recording on hard disks capable of delivering up to 10 times the storage density of traditional (longitudinal) recording on the same recording media. PMR is estimated to allow information densities of up to 1,000 GB per square inch (in comparison to 100 to 200 GB per square inch for longitudinal recording).

Personal Communication Service (PCS): A type of cellular mobile telephone service.

Personal Computer (PC): An affordable, efficient computer meant to be used by one person and is often connected to a local area network (LAN) for communication with a group of PCs in an office or home.

Personal Digital Assistant (PDA): A handheld or pocket-size device containing address and calendar information, as well as e-mail, games and other features. A Blackberry is a PDA.

Personal Television (PTV): Television programming that has been manipulated to a viewer's personal taste. For example, the TiVo service allows viewers to eliminate commercials, watch programming stored in memory or watch selected real-time moments in slow motion.

Personal Video Recorder (PVR): See "Digital Video Recorder (DVR)."

Personalized VOD Entertainment: A VOD service that automatically detects household television viewing interests by monitoring the channel-surfing behavior of residents. The system uses this viewing data to select programming relevant to the household. The service can also deliver custom VOD libraries to PVRs.

Petabyte: 1,024 terabytes, or about one million gigabytes.

Petaflop: A measure of computing speed equal to 1 quadrillion floating point operations per second.

Phase Change Memory (PCM): A memory chip technology that stores data by causing material to alter from a crystalline phase to a disordered phase. It has the potential to be vastly faster than flash memory while consuming far less power.

PHP: Personal Home Page, or PHP Hypertext Preprocessor. A software programming language. It is in the category of scripting languages, which means that the code within a PHP program is interpreted by other software when needed.

PLED: See "Polymer Light Emitting Diode (PLED)."

PLM: See "Product Lifecyle Management (PLM)."

Plug-In: Any small piece of software that adds extra functions to a larger piece of software.

PMR: See "Perpendicular Magnetic Recording (PMR)."

Podcasting: The creation of audio files as webcasts. The name comes from the ability of these files to be used on iPods and portable MP3 players. They can also be listened to on personal computers. Podcasts can be anything from unique radio-like programming to sales pitches to audio press releases. Audio RSS (Real Simple Syndication) enables the broadcast of these audio files to appropriate parties. Also see "Real Simple Syndication (RSS)," "Video Blog (VLOG)" and "Blog (Web Log)."

Point-to-Point Protocol (PPP): A protocol that enables a computer to use the combination of a standard telephone line and a modem to make TCP/IP connections.

P-OLED: See "Polymer Light Emitting Diode (PLED)."

Polymer: An organic or inorganic substance of many parts. Most common polymers, such as polyethylene and polypropylene, are organic. Organic polymers consist of molecules from organic sources (carbon compounds). Polymer means many parts. Generally, a polymer is constructed of many structural units (smaller, simpler molecules) that are joined together by a chemical bond. Some polymers are natural. For example, rubber is a natural polymer. Scientists have developed ways to manufacture synthetic polymers from organic materials. Plastic is a synthetic polymer.

Polymer Light Emitting Diode (PLED): An advanced technology that utilizes plastics (polymers) for the creation of electronic displays (screens). It is based on the use of organic polymers which emit light when stimulated with electricity. They are solution processable, which means they can be applied to substrates via ink jet printing. Also referred to as P-OLEDs.

POP: An acronym for both "Point of Presence" and "Post Office Protocol." Point of presence refers to a location that a network can be connected to (generally used to count the potential subscriber base of a cellular phone system). Post office protocol refers to the way in which e-mail software obtains mail from a mail server.

Port: An interface (or connector) between the computer and the outside world. The number of ports on a communications controller or front-end processor determines the number of communications channels that can be connected to it. The number of ports on a computer determines the number of peripheral devices that can be attached to it.

Portal: A comprehensive web site that is designed to be the first site seen when a computer logs on to the web. Portal sites are aimed at broad audiences with common interests and often have links to e-mail usage, a search engine and other features. Yahoo! and msn.com are portals.

Positioning: The design and implementation of a merchandising mix, price structure and style of selling to create an image of the retailer, relative to its competitors, in the customer's mind.

Powerline: A method of networking computers, peripherals and appliances together via the electrical wiring that is built in to a home or office. Powerline competes with 802.11b and other wireless networking methods.

PPP: See "Purchasing Power Parity (PPP) or Point-to-Point Protocol (PPP)."

Product Lifecycle: The prediction of the life of a product or brand. Stages are described as Introduction, Growth, Maturity and finally Sales Decline.

Product Lifecycle Management (PLM): See "Product Lifecycle."

Protocol: A set of rules for communicating between computers. The use of standard protocols allows products from different vendors to communicate on a common network.

PTV: See "Personal Television (PTV)."

Public Switched Telephone Network (PSTN): A term that refers to the traditional telephone system.

Purchasing Power Parity (PPP): Currency conversion rates that attempt to reflect the actual purchasing power of a currency in its home market, as opposed to examining price levels and comparing an exchange rate. PPPs are always given in the national currency units per U.S. dollar.

PVR: See "Personal Video Recorder (PVR)."

QoS: See "Quality of Service (QoS)."

Quality of Service (QoS): The improvement of the flow of broadband information on the Internet and other networks by raising the data flow level of certain routes and restricting it on others. QoS levels are supported on robust, high-bandwidth technologies such as 4G.

Quantum Computing: A technology that uses the unique abilities of quantum systems, to be in multiple states at once. Such superpositions would allow the computer to perform many different computations simultaneously. This is a merger of physics (and its laws of quantum mechanics) with computer science. Quantum computing works quantum bits, also known as qubits. The laws of quantum mechanics differ radically from the laws of traditional physics. Eventually, quantum computers incredible processing speeds may become feasible.

Qubit: The basic unit of information in a quantum computer. A qubit can exist not only in a state corresponding to 0 or 1 as in a binary bit, but also in states corresponding to a blend or superposition of these states. See "Quantum Computing."

R&D: Research and development. Also see "Applied Research" and "Basic Research."

Radio Frequency Identification (RFID): A technology that applies a special microchip-enabled tag to an individual item or piece of merchandise or inventory. RFID technology enables wireless, computerized tracking of that inventory item as it moves through the supply chain from factory to transport to warehouse to retail store or end user. Also known as radio tags.

RAM: See "Random Access Memory (RAM)."

Random Access Memory (RAM): Computer memory used to hold programs and data temporarily.

RDF: See "Resource Description Framework (RDF)."

Real Audio: A helper software application that enables the user to hear real-time audio via the Internet.

Real Simple Syndication (RSS): Uses XML programming language to let web logs and other data be broadcast to appropriate web sites and users. Formerly referred to as RDF Site Summary or Rich Site Summary, RSS also enables the publisher to create a description of the content and its location in the form of an RSS document. Also useful for distributing audio files. See "Podcasting."

Real Time: A system or software product specially designed to acquire, process, store and display large amounts of rapidly changing information almost instantaneously, with microsecond responses as changes occur.

Recommendation-Based VOD: See "Personalized VOD Entertainment."

Regional Bell Operating Company (RBOC): Former Bell system telephone companies (or their successors), created as a result of the breakup of AT&T by a Federal Court decree on December 31, 1983 (e.g., Bell Atlantic, now part of Verizon).

Request for Bids (RFB): A bid, sent by a firm that requires products or outsourced services, outlining all requirements to various bidding companies. Proposing companies are asked to place a bid based on the requested goods or services.

Request for Qualifications (RFQ): A proposal that asks companies to submit qualifications to provide goods or perform a described level of service. It is used to screen who is qualified to respond to an RFB. See "Request for Bids (RFB)."

Reshoring: See "Onshoring."

Resource Description Framework (RDF): A software concept that integrates many different software applications using XML as a syntax for the exchange of data. It is a core concept for development of the Semantic Web, an enhanced World Wide Web envisioned by W3C, the global organization that oversees development of the web. RDF may be useful for the syndication of news or the aggregation of all types of data for specific uses.

Return on Investment (ROI): A measure of a company's profitability, expressed in percentage as net profit (after taxes) divided by total dollar investment.

RFID: See "Radio Frequency Identification (RFID)."

Router: An electronic device that enables networks to communicate with each other. For example, the local area network (LAN) in an office connects to a router to give the LAN access to an Internet connection such as a T1 or DSL. Routers can be bundled with several added features, such as firewalls.

RSS: See "Real Simple Syndication (RSS)."

Ruby: An open source programming language first released in Japan in 1995. It is an object-oriented scripting language. "Ruby on Rails" is a framework that enables very rapid web site development. See www.rubyonrails.org.

Saas: See "Software as a Service (Saas)."

SACD: See "Super Audio Compact Disc (SACD)."

SAN: See "Storage Area Network (SAN)."

Satellite Broadcasting: The use of Earth-orbiting satellites to transmit, over a wide area, TV, radio, telephony, video and other data in digitized format.

Scalable: Refers to a network that can grow and adapt as customer needs increase and change. Scalable networks can easily manage increasing numbers of workstations, servers, user workloads and added functionality.

SCSI: See "Small Computer System Interface (SCSI)."

SDSL: See "Digital Subscriber Line (DSL)."

Semantic Web: An initiative started by the World Wide Web Consortium (W3C) that is focused on improving the way users access databases and online content by adding semantic metadata to content that will clearly define the relationships between data. Users will get much better search results, and web site developers will be able to create pages that update results and content based on related data on-the-fly. Data will automatically be shared across applications and across organizations.

Semiconductor: A generic term for a device that controls electrical signals. It specifically refers to a material (such as silicon, germanium or gallium arsenide) that can be altered either to conduct electrical current or to block its passage. Carbon nanotubes may eventually be used as semiconductors. Semiconductors are partly responsible for the miniaturization of modern electronic devices, as they are vital components in computer memory and processor chips. The manufacture of semiconductors is carried out by small firms, and by industry giants such as Intel and Advanced Micro Devices.

Serial Line Internet Protocol (SLIP): The connection of a traditional telephone line, or serial line, and modem to connect a computer to an Internet site.

Server: A computer that performs and manages specific duties for a central network such as a LAN. It may include storage devices and other peripherals. Competition within the server manufacturing industry is intense among leaders Dell, IBM, HP and others.

Server-Based SVOD Programming: Programming that is delivered directly to the customer's TV from where it is stored on the content provider's servers. In contrast, non-server-based SVOD (satellite TV) needs a storage device at the customer's location (such as a PVR or DVR) to store and play VOD content for the viewer's TV. Server-based SVOD surpasses non-server-based SVOD in its ability to simultaneously send or receive more than one video stream to or from the customer.

Service Level Agreement (SLA): A detail in a contract between a service provider and the client. The agreement specifies the level of service that is expected during the service contract term. For example, computer or Internet service contracts generally stipulate a maximum amount of time that a system may be unusable.

Service Oriented Architecture (SOA): Business application software that is designed in such a way that it can be constructed by using modules ("services") with specific tasks that can communicate with each other. Leading firms including IBM, Microsoft and SAP are offering software tools that can be used to create SOA business applications.

Set-Top Box: Sits on top of a TV set and provides enhancement to cable TV or other television reception. Typically a cable modem, this box may enable interactive enhancements to television viewing. For example, a cable modem is a set-top box that enables Internet access via TV cable. See "Cable Modem."

Shareware: Software that is available for users to download for free from the Internet, usually with the expectation that they will register or pay for the software if they continue to use it. Many shareware programs are set to expire after a period of time.

Shockwave: An authoring tool that allows multimedia presentations to appear on the Internet. Shockwave enables interactive graphics, sound and animation to be viewed on the web.

Short Messaging System (SMS): See "Text Messaging."

Silicon Photonics: Lightwave technology based on silicon chips. The technology utilizes lasers on silicon chips to increase chip speeds.

Simple Mail Transfer Protocol (SMTP): The primary form of protocol used in the transference of e-mail.

Simple Network Management Protocol (SNMP): A set of communication standards for use between computers connected to TCP/IP networks.

Simple Object Access Protocol (SOAP): A method for applications to communicate with each other using HTTP web protocols. SOAP is an important protocol in web services.

Six Sigma: A quality enhancement strategy designed to reduce the number of products coming from a manufacturing plant that do not conform to specifications. Six Sigma states that no more than 3.4 defects per million parts is the goal of high-quality output. Motorola invented the system in the 1980s in order to enhance its competitive position against Japanese electronics manufacturers.

SLIP: See "Serial Line Internet Protocol (SLIP)."

Slugs: Small graphical icons that are frequently used in order to establish a visual language. They often function as buttons, such as sound slugs, which inform the user of the size of a sound file and, when clicked, download the file.

Small Computer System Interface (SCSI): A dominant, international standard interface used by UNIX servers and many desktop computers to connect to storage devices; a physical connection between devices.

Small Molecule Organic Light Emitting Diode (SMOLED): A type of organic LED that relies on expensive manufacturing methods. Newer technologies are more promising. See "Polymer" and "Polymer Light Emitting Diode (PLED)."

SMDS: See "Switched Multimegabit Data Service (SMDS)."

SMOLED: See "Small Molecule Organic Light Emitting Diode (SMOLED)."

SOA: See "Service Oriented Architecture (SOA)."

SOAP: See "Simple Object Access Protocol (SOAP)."

SoC: See "System on a Chip (SoC)."

Social Media (Social Networks): Sites on the Internet that feature user generated content (UGC). Such media include wikis, blogs and specialty web sites such as MySpace.com, Facebook, YouTube, Yelp and Friendster.com. Social media are seen as powerful online tools because all or most of the content is user-generated.

Software as a Service (SaaS): Refers to the practice of providing users with software applications that are hosted on remote servers and accessed via the Internet. Excellent examples include the CRM (Customer Relationship Management) software provided in SaaS format by Salesforce. An earlier technology that operated in a similar, but less sophisticated, manner was called ASP or Application Service Provider.

Spam: A term used to refer to generally unwanted, solicitous, bulk-sent e-mail. In recent years, significant amounts of government legislation have been passed in an attempt to limit the use of spam. Also, many types of software filters have been introduced in an effort to block spam on the receiving end. In addition to use for general advertising purposes, spam may be used in an effort to spread computer viruses or to commit financial or commercial fraud.

Spintronics: Electronic devices that exploit the spin of electrons, not just their charge. These solid state devices are also known as magnetoelectronics. Such devices are smaller, more versatile and more robust at a much lower power than conventional electronics. Other names for this technology include: quantum spintronics, magnetoelectronics, spin electronics.

SQL: See "Structured Query Language (SQL)."

SRDF: See "Symmetrix Remote Data Facility (SRDF)."

Storage Area Network (SAN): Links host computers to advanced data storage systems.

Streaming Media: One-way audio and/or video that is compressed and transmitted over a data network. The media is viewed or heard almost as soon as data is fed to the receiver; there is usually a buffer period of a few seconds.

Structured Query Language (SQL): A language set that defines a way of organizing and calling data in a computer database. SQL is becoming the standard for use in client/server databases.

Subsidiary, Wholly-Owned: A company that is wholly controlled by another company through stock ownership.

Super Audio Compact Disc (SACD): A technology that offers high-resolution digital audio.

Supply Chain: The complete set of suppliers of goods and services required for a company to operate its business. For example, a manufacturer's supply chain may include providers of raw materials, components, custom-made parts and packaging materials.

Switch: A network device that directs packets of data between multiple ports, often filtering the data so that it travels more quickly.

Switched Multimegabit Data Service (SMDS): A method of extremely high-speed transference of data.

Symmetrix Remote Data Facility (SRDF): A high-performance, host-independent business solution that enables users to maintain a duplicate copy of all or some of their data at a remote site.

Synchronous Optical Network Technology (SONET): A mode of high-speed transmission meant to take full advantage of the wide bandwidth in fiber-optic cables.

System on a Chip (SoC): A chip capable of performing multiple functions, which may include an operating system and several applications embedded into one chip. SoCs are commonly used in devices such as cellphones.

T1: A standard for broadband digital transmission over phone lines. Generally, it can transmit at least 24 voice channels at once over copper wires, at a high speed of 1.5 Mbps. Higher speed versions include T3 and OC3 lines.

T3: Transmission over phone lines that supports data rates of 45 Mbps. T3 lines consist of 672 channels, and such lines are generally used by Internet service providers. They are also referred to as DS3 lines.

Tagging: A method of describing web sites with simple words so that links can be grouped by categories and easily found again in the future for access. Also, groups of tagged links can be shared for viewing by others. See http://del.icio.us.

TCP/IP: Transmission Control Protocol/Internet Protocol. The combination of a network and transport protocol developed by ARPANet for internetworking IP-based networks.

TDMA: See "Time Division Multiple Access (TDMA)."

Telecommunications: Systems of hardware and software used to carry voice, video and/or data between locations. This includes telephone wires, satellite signals, cellular links, coaxial cable and related devices.

Telnet: A terminal emulation program for TCP/IP networks like the Internet, which runs on a computer and connects to a particular network. Directions entered on a computer that is connected using Telnet will be read and followed just as if they had been entered on the server itself. Through Telnet, users are able to control a server and communicate with other servers on the same network at the same time. Telnet is commonly used to control web servers remotely.

Terabyte: A measure of data equal to 1,024 gigabytes, or about 1 trillion bytes of data.

Teraflop: A measure of computing speed equal to 1 trillion floating-point operations per second.

Text Messaging: The transmission of very short, text messages in a format similar to e-mail. Generally, text messaging is used as an additional service on cell phones. The format has typically been SMS (Short Messaging System), but a newer standard is evolving: MMS (Multimedia Messaging System). MMS can transmit pictures, sound and video as well as text.

Thin Client: In server applications, an application designed to be especially small so that the bulk of the data processing occurs on the server.

Third-Party Logistics (3PL): A specialist firm in logistics, which may provide a variety of transportation, warehousing and logistics-related services to buyers or sellers. These tasks were previously performed in-house by the customer. When 3PL services are provided within the client's own facilities, it can also be referred to as insourcing.

Time Division Multiple Access (TDMA): A 2G digital service for relatively large users of international public-switched telephony, data, facsimile and telex. TDMA also refers to a method of multiplexing digital signals that combines a number of signals passing through a common point by transmitting them sequentially, with each signal sent in bursts at different times. TDMA is sometimes referred to as IS-136 or D-AMPS.

Time Shifting: Services that allow viewers to digitally record television programs for playback at a later, more convenient time. Such services include video-on-demand (VOD) and personal TV services. Time shifting will eventually make up a significant portion of all television viewing.

Token Ring: A local area network architecture in which a token, or continuously repeating frame, is passed sequentially from station to station. Only the station possessing the token can communicate on the network.

Transaction Authority Markup Language (XAML): A computer programming code (developer language) created by Microsoft as part of its effort to launch the operating system code named Longhorn to facilitate the processing of online transactions.

Transistor: A device used for amplification or switching of electrical current.

Ubiquitous Computing: The concept of computers as an integral, invisible part of life. The opposite of virtual reality in that computers merge into the human world rather than requiring humans to conform to computer methods; also known as embodied virtuality, smart environment and ambient intelligence.

U-Commerce (U Commerce): Ubiquitous Commerce, Universal Commerce or Ultimate Commerce (ubiquitous meaning ever-present), depending on whom you ask. It describes the concept that buyers and sellers have the potential to interact anywhere, anytime thanks to the use of wireless devices, such as cell phones, by buyers to connect with sellers via the Internet where orders can be placed online and payments can be made via credit card or PayPal. The Association for Information Systems states that the qualities of U-Commerce include ubiquity, uniqueness, universality and unison.

UDDI: See "Universal Description, Discovery and Integration (UDDI)."

Ultrashort Pulse Laser (USP): A technology that utilizes ultrafast lasers that pulse on and off at almost immeasurable speed. Scientists estimate that USP flashes once every femtosecond, which is a billionth of a millionth of a second. USP destroys atoms by knocking out electrons, which causes no rise in temperature in surrounding atoms as is associated with traditional lasers. Potential applications include vastly improved laser surgery, scanning for explosives, gemstone verification and processing donated human tissue for transplantation.

Ultrawideband (UWB): A means of low-power, limited-range wireless data transmission that takes advantage of bandwidth set aside by the FCC in 2002. UWB encodes signals in a dramatically different way, sending digital pulses in a relatively secure manner that will not interfere with other wireless systems that may be operating nearby. It has the potential to deliver very large amounts of data to a distance of about 230 feet, even through doors and other obstacles, and requires very little power. Speeds are scalable from approximately 100 Mbps to 2Gbps. UWB works on the 802.15.3 IEEE specification.

Unified Communications: The use of advanced technology to replace traditional telecommunications infrastructure such as PBX, fax and even the desktop telephone. Special software operating on a local or remote server enables each office worker to have access, via the desktop PC, to communications tools that include VOIP phone service, email, voice mail, fax, instant messaging (IM), collaborative calendars and schedules, contact information such as address books, audio conferencing and video conferencing.

Uniform Resource Locator (URL): The address that allows an Internet browser to locate a homepage or web site.

Universal Description, Discovery and Integration (UDDI): A vital protocol used in web services. UDDI enables businesses to create a standard description of their activities so that they can be searched for appropriately by automatic software tools.

Universal Memory: Future-generation digital memory storage systems that would be ultradense and run on extremely low power needs. Potentially, universal memory could replace today's flash memory, RAM and many other types of memory. The technology may be based on the use of vast numbers of tiny carbon nanotubes resulting in the storage of trillions of bits of data per square centimeter.

Universal Serial Bus (USB): A connection port to computers and other devices. USB has become a standard receptacle to connect to mice, cameras, printers and other peripherals. USB 1.1 could achieve data transfer speeds of about 12Mbps. The newer USB 2.0 standard us a very high speed specification with the potential to read 480 Mbps.

UNIX: A multi-user, multitasking operating system that runs on a wide variety of computer systems, from PCs to mainframes.

URL: See "Uniform Resource Locator (URL)."

USB: See "Universal Serial Bus (USB)."

User Generated Content (UGC): Data contributed by users of interactive web sites. Such sites can include wikis, blogs, entertainment sites, shopping sites or social networks such as Facebook. UGC data can also include such things as product reviews, photos, videos, comments on forums, and how-to advice. Also see "Social Media (Social Networks)."

Utility Computing: See "Cloud Computing."

UWB: See "Ultrawideband (UWB)."

Value Added Tax (VAT): A tax that imposes a levy on businesses at every stage of manufacturing based on the value it adds to a product. Each business in the supply chain pays its own VAT and is subsequently repaid by the next link down the chain; hence, a VAT is ultimately paid by the consumer, being the last link in the supply chain, making it comparable to a sales tax. Generally, VAT only applies to goods bought for consumption within a given country; export goods are exempt from VAT, and purchasers from other countries taking goods back home may apply for a VAT refund.

VDSL: Very high-data-rate digital subscriber line, operating at data rates from 55 to 100 Mbps.

Vendor: Any firm, such as a manufacturer or distributor, from which a retailer obtains merchandise.

Very Small Aperture Terminal (VSAT): A small Earth station terminal, generally 0.6 to 2.4 meters in size, that is often portable and primarily designed to handle data transmission and private-line voice and video communications.

Video Blog (VLOG): The creation of video files as webcasts. VLOGs can be viewed on personal computers and wireless devices that are Internet-enabled. They can include anything from unique TV-like programming to sales pitches to music videos, news coverage or audio press releases. Online video is one of the fastest-growing segments in Internet usage. Leading e-commerce companies such as Microsoft, through its MSN service, Google and Yahoo!, as well as mainstream media firms such as Reuters, are making significant investments in online video services. Real Simple Syndication (RSS) enables the broadcasting of these files to appropriate parties. Also see "Real Simple Syndication (RSS)," "Podcasting" and "Blog (Web Log)."

Video On Demand (VOD): A system that allows customers to request programs or movies over cable or the Internet. Generally, the customer can select from an extensive list of titles. In some cases, a set-top device can be used to digitally record a broadcast for replay at a future date.

Virtual Private Network (VPN): Cordons off part of a public network to create a private LAN.

Virtual Server: A technology in which one server is operated as though it were several servers. The one, or "host" server, runs an application known as a "hypervisor" which creates one or more virtual machines. Virtualized servers often run as many as eight different software applications each, opposed to only one application on standard servers. The result is much higher efficiency and the need for fewer total servers.

Virtual Storage Access Method (VSAM): A data storage and retrieval mechanism designed to maintain large quantities of data on external disks or drums on computers designed for virtual storage systems.

Virtualization (in servers): See "Virtual Server."

VLOG: See Video Blog (VLOG)."

VOD: See Video On Demand (VOD)."

VOD-Over-IP: VOD (video on demand) television viewing that is distributed via the Internet.

Voice Mail: A sophisticated electronic telephone answering service that utilizes a computer. Voice mail enables users to receive faxes and phone messages and to access those messages from remote sites.

Voice Over Internet Protocol (VOIP): The ability to make telephone calls and send faxes over IP-based data networks, i.e., real-time voice between computers via the Internet. Leading providers of VOIP service include independent firms Skype and Vonage. However, all major telecom companies, such as SBC are planning or offering VOIP service. VOIP can offer greatly reduced telephone bills to users, since toll charges, certain taxes and other fees can be bypassed. Long-distance calls can pass to anywhere in the world using VOIP. Over the mid-term, many telephone handsets, including cellular phones, will have the ability to detect wireless networks offering VOIP connections and will switch seamlessly between landline and VOIP or cellular and VOIP as needed.

VOIP: See "Voice Over Internet Protocol (VOIP)."

VPN: See "Virtual Private Network (VPN)."

VSAM: See "Virtual Storage Access Method (VSAM)."

WAN: See "Wide Area Network (WAN)."

WAP: See "Wireless Access Protocol (WAP)."

Web 2.0: Generally refers to the evolving system of advanced services available via the Internet. These services include collaborative sites that enable multiple users to create content such as wikis, sites such as photo-sharing services that share data among large or small groups and sites such as Friendster and MySpace that enable consumers to form groups of people with similar interests. Common features of Web 2.0 are tagging, social networks and folksonomies.

Web Ontology Language (OWL): A markup language that is related to RDF. See "Resource Description Framework (RDF)" and "Semantic Web."

Web Page: A document on the World Wide Web that is identified by a URL.

Web Services: Self-contained modular applications that can be described, published, located and invoked over the World Wide Web or another network. Web services architecture evolved from object-oriented design and is geared toward e-business solutions. Microsoft Corporation is focusing on web services with its .NET initiative. Also see "Extensible Markup Language (XML)."

Web Services Description Language (WSDL): An important protocol to web services that describes the web service being offered.

Web Site: A specific domain name location on the World Wide Web. Each site contains a homepage and usually consists of additional documents.

Weblog: See "Blog (Web Log)."

Webmaster: Any individual who runs a web site. Webmasters generally perform maintenance and upkeep.

Website Meta-Language (WML): A free HTML generation toolkit for the Unix operating system.

Wide Area Network (WAN): A regional or global network that provides links between all local area networks within a company. For example, Ford Motor Company might use a WAN to enable its factory in Detroit to talk to its sales offices in New York and Chicago, its plants in England and its buying offices in Taiwan. Also see "Local Area Network (LAN)."

WiDi (Wireless Display): A technology that is primarily used to connect television sets to a computer and thus to the Internet, wirelessly. In that manner, a laptop, PC or other device can access a movie or video which will be beamed to the TV set for viewing. Intel is a major proponent of WiDi.

Wi-Fi: A popular phrase that refers to 802.11b and other 802.11 specifications. See "802.11b (Wi-Fi)."

Wi-Fi5: A popular phrase that refers to 802.11a. See "802.11a (Wi-Fi5)."

Wiki: A web site that enables large or small groups of users to create and co-edit data. The best known example is Wikipedia, a high traffic web site that presents a public encyclopedia that is continuously written and edited by a vast number of volunteer contributors and editors who include both experts and enthusiasts in various subjects. Also, see "User Generated Content (UGC)."

WiMAX (802.16): A wireless standard with exceptional speed and distance capabilities, officially known as the 802.16 standard. See "802.16 (WiMAX)." Wi-Fi stands for "World Interoperability for Microwave Access."

Wireless: Transmission of voice, video or data by a cellular telephone or other wireless device, as opposed to landline, telephone line or cable. It includes Wi-Fi, WiMAX and other local or long-distance wireless methods.

Wireless Access Protocol (WAP): A technology that enables the delivery of World Wide Web pages in a smaller format readable by screens on cellular phones.

Wireless Cable: A pay television service that delivers multiple programming services to subscribers equipped with special antennae and tuners. It is an alternative to traditional, wired cable TV systems.

Wireless LAN (WLAN): A wireless local area network. WLANs frequently operate on 802.11-enabled equipment (Wi-Fi).

WLAN: See "Wireless LAN (WLAN)."

WML: See "Website Meta-Language (WML)."

Workstation: A high-powered desktop computer, usually used by engineers.

World Trade Organization (WTO): One of the only globally active international organizations dealing with the trade rules between nations. Its goal is to assist the free flow of trade goods, ensuring a smooth, predictable supply of goods to help raise the quality of life of member citizens. Members form consensus decisions that are then ratified by their respective parliaments. The WTO's conflict resolution process generally emphasizes interpreting existing commitments and agreements, and discovers how to ensure trade policies to conform to those agreements, with the ultimate aim of avoiding military or political conflict.

World Wide Web: A computer system that provides enhanced access to various sites on the Internet through the use of hyperlinks. Clicking on a link displayed in one document takes you to a related document. The World Wide Web is governed by the World Wide Web

Consortium, located at www.w3.org. Also known as the web.

WSDL: See "Web Services Description Language (WSDL)."

WTO: See "World Trade Organization (WTO)."

XAML: See "Transaction Authority Markup Language (XAML)."

INTRODUCTION

PLUNKETT'S INFOTECH INDUSTRY ALMANAC, the twelfth edition of our guide to the InfoTech field, is designed as a general source for researchers of all types.

For purposes of this book, we define "InfoTech" as any technology that moves or manages voice, data or video—whether that movement be via wireless methods, the Internet, satellite, fiber optics, computer network or emerging methods. Computer hardware, software, network equipment, consulting services and the firms that manufacture or provide products/services in these fields are heavily featured.

The data and areas of interest covered are intentionally broad, ranging from the various aspects of the InfoTech industry, to emerging technology, to an in-depth look at the major firms (which we call "THE INFOTECH 500") within the many segments that make up the InfoTech industry.

This reference book is designed to be a general source for researchers. It is especially intended to assist with market research, strategic planning, employment searches, contact or prospect list creation and financial research, and as a data resource for executives and students of all types.

PLUNKETT'S INFOTECH INDUSTRY ALMANAC takes a rounded approach for the general reader. This book presents a complete overview of the InfoTech field (see "How To Use This Book").
For example, the changes in supercomputers, wireless access and data storage are covered in exacting detail, along with easy-to-use tables on all facets of InfoTech in general: from growth in the number of Internet users worldwide to U.S. computer equipment shipments.

THE INFOTECH 500 is our unique grouping of the biggest, most successful corporations in all segments of the InfoTech industry. Tens of thousands of pieces of information, gathered from a wide variety of sources, have been researched and are presented in a unique form that can be easily understood. This section includes thorough indexes to THE INFOTECH 500, by geography, industry, sales, brand names, subsidiary names and many other topics. (See Chapter 4.)

Especially helpful is the way in which PLUNKETT'S INFOTECH INDUSTRY ALMANAC enables readers who have no business background to readily compare the financial records and growth plans of InfoTech companies and major industry groups. You'll see the mid-term financial record of each firm, along with the impact of earnings, sales and strategic plans on each company's potential to fuel growth, to serve new markets and to provide investment and employment opportunities.

No other source provides this book's easy-to-understand comparisons of growth, expenditures, technologies, corporations and many other items of great importance to people of all types who may be studying this, one of the most exciting industries in the world today.

By scanning the data groups and the unique indexes, you can find the best information to fit your personal research needs. The major companies in InfoTech are profiled and then ranked using several different groups of specific criteria. Which firms are the biggest employers? Which companies earn the most profits? These things and much more are easy to find.

In addition to individual company profiles, an overview of information technology and its trends is provided. This book's job is to help you sort through easy-to-understand summaries of today's trends in a quick and effective manner.

Whatever your purpose for researching the InfoTech field, you'll find this book to be a valuable guide. Nonetheless, as is true with all resources, this volume has limitations that the reader should be aware of:

- Financial data and other corporate information can change quickly. A book of this type can be no more current than the data that was available as of the time of editing. Consequently, the financial picture, management and ownership of the firm(s) you are studying may have changed since the date of this book. For example, this almanac includes the most up-to-date sales figures and profits available to the editors as of early 2011. That means that we have typically used corporate financial data as of mid-2010.

- Corporate mergers, acquisitions and downsizing are occurring at a very rapid rate. Such events may have created significant change, subsequent to the publishing of this book, within a company you are studying.

- Some of the companies in THE INFOTECH 500 are so large in scope and in variety of business endeavors conducted within a parent organization, that we have been unable to completely list all subsidiaries, affiliations, divisions and activities within a firm's corporate structure.

- This volume is intended to be a general guide to a vast industry. That means that researchers should look to this book for an overview and, when conducting in-depth research, should contact the specific corporations or industry associations in question for the very latest changes and data. Where possible, we have listed contact names, toll-free telephone numbers and Internet site addresses for the companies, government agencies and industry associations involved so that the reader may get further details without unnecessary delay.

- Tables of industry data and statistics used in this book include the latest numbers available at the time of printing, generally through mid-2010. In a few cases, the only complete data available was for earlier years.

- We have used exhaustive efforts to locate and fairly present accurate and complete data. However, when using this book or any other source for business and industry information, the reader should use caution and diligence by conducting further research where it seems appropriate. We wish you success in your endeavors, and we trust that your experience with this book will be both satisfactory and productive.

Jack W. Plunkett
Houston, Texas
February 2011

HOW TO USE THIS BOOK

The two primary sections of this book are devoted first to the InfoTech industry as a whole and then to the "Individual Data Listings" for THE INFOTECH 500. If time permits, you should begin your research in the front chapters of this book. Also, you will find lengthy indexes in Chapter 4 and in the back of the book.

THE INFOTECH INDUSTRY

Glossary: A short list of InfoTech industry terms.

Chapter 1: Major Trends Affecting the InfoTech Industry. This chapter presents an encapsulated view of the major trends that are creating rapid changes in the InfoTech industry today.

Chapter 2: InfoTech Industry Statistics. This chapter presents in-depth statistics ranging from an industry overview to computer industry indicators to the growing use of broadband and much more.

Chapter 3: Important InfoTech Industry Contacts – Addresses, Telephone Numbers and Internet Sites. This chapter covers contacts for important government agencies, InfoTech organizations and trade groups. Included are numerous important Internet sites.

THE INFOTECH 500

Chapter 4: THE INFOTECH 500: Who They Are and How They Were Chosen. The companies compared in this book (the actual count is 501) were carefully selected from the InfoTech industry, largely in the United States. 156 of the firms are based outside the U.S. For a complete description, see THE INFOTECH 500 indexes in this chapter.

Individual Data Listings:

Look at one of the companies in THE INFOTECH 500's Individual Data Listings. You'll find the following information fields:

Company Name:

The company profiles are in alphabetical order by company name. If you don't find the company you are seeking, it may be a subsidiary or division of one of the firms covered in this book. Try looking it up in the Index by Subsidiaries, Brand Names and Selected Affiliations in the back of the book.

Ranks:

Industry Group Code: An NAIC code used to group companies within like segments. (See Chapter 4 for a list of codes.)

Ranks Within This Company's Industry Group: Ranks, within this firm's segment only, for annual sales and annual profits, with 1 being the highest rank.

Business Activities:

A grid arranged into six major industry categories and several sub-categories. A "Y" indicates that the firm operates within the sub-category. A complete Index by Industry is included in the beginning of Chapter 4.

Types of Business:

A listing of the primary types of business specialties conducted by the firm.

Brands/Divisions/Affiliations:

Major brand names, operating divisions or subsidiaries of the firm, as well as major corporate affiliations—such as another firm that owns a significant portion of the company's stock. A complete Index by Subsidiaries, Brand Names and Selected Affiliations is in the back of the book.

Contacts:

The names and titles up to 27 top officers of the company are listed, including human resources contacts.

Address:

The firm's full headquarters address, the headquarters telephone, plus toll-free and fax numbers where available. Also provided is the World Wide Web site address.

Financials:

Annual Sales (2010 or the latest fiscal year available to the editors, plus up to four previous years): These are stated in thousands of dollars (add three zeros if you want the full number). This figure represents consolidated worldwide sales from all operations. 2010 figures may be estimates.

Annual Profits (2010 or the latest fiscal year available to the editors, plus up to four previous years): These are stated in thousands of dollars (add three zeros if you want the full number). This figure represents consolidated, after-tax net profit from all operations. 2010 figures may be estimates.

Stock Ticker, International Exchange, Parent Company: When available, the unique stock market symbol used to identify this firm's common stock for trading and tracking purposes is indicated. Where appropriate, this field may contain "private" or "subsidiary" rather than a ticker symbol. If the firm is a publicly-held company headquartered outside of the U.S., its international ticker and exchange are given. If the firm is a subsidiary, its parent company is listed.

Total Number of Employees: The approximate total number of employees, worldwide, as of the end of 2010 (or the latest data available to the editors).

Apparent Salaries/Benefits:

(The following descriptions generally apply to U.S. employers only.) A "Y" in appropriate fields indicates "Yes."

Due to wide variations in the manner in which corporations report benefits to the U.S. Government's regulatory bodies, not all plans will have been uncovered or correctly evaluated during our effort to research this data. Also, the availability to employees of such plans will vary according to the qualifications that employees must meet to become eligible. For example, some benefit plans may be available only to salaried workers—others only to employees who work more than 1,000 hours yearly. Benefits that are available to employees of the main or parent company may not be available to employees of the subsidiaries. In addition, employers frequently alter the nature and terms of plans offered.

NOTE: Generally, employees covered by wealth-building benefit plans do not *fully* own ("vest in") funds contributed on their behalf by the employer until as many as five years of service with that employer have passed. All pension plans are voluntary—that is, employers are not obligated to offer pensions.

Pension Plan: The firm offers a pension plan to qualified employees. In this case, in order for a "Y" to appear, the editors believe that the employer offers a defined benefit or cash balance pension plan (see discussions below).The type and generosity of these plans vary widely from firm to firm. Caution: Some employers refer to plans as "pension" or "retirement" plans when they are actually 401(k) savings plans that require a contribution by the employee.

- Defined Benefit Pension Plans: Pension plans that do not require a contribution from the employee are infrequently offered. However, a few companies, particularly larger employers in high-profit-margin industries, offer defined benefit pension plans where the employee is guaranteed to receive a set pension benefit upon retirement. The amount of the benefit is determined by the years of service with the company and the employee's salary during the later years of employment. The longer a person works for the employer, the higher the retirement benefit. These defined benefit plans are funded entirely by the employer. The benefits, up to a reasonable limit, are guaranteed by the Federal Government's Pension Benefit Guaranty Corporation. These plans are not portable—if you leave the company, you cannot transfer your benefits into a different plan. Instead, upon retirement you will receive the benefits that vested during your service with the company. If your employer offers a pension plan, it must give you a summary plan description within 90 days of the date you join the plan. You can also request a summary annual report of the plan, and once every 12 months you may request an individual benefit statement accounting of your interest in the plan.

- Defined Contribution Plans: These are quite different. They do not guarantee a certain amount of pension benefit. Instead, they set out circumstances under which the employer will make a contribution to a plan on your behalf. The most common example is the 401(k) savings plan. Pension benefits are not guaranteed under these plans.

- Cash Balance Pension Plans: These plans were recently invented. These are hybrid plans—part defined benefit and part defined contribution. Many employers have converted their older defined benefit plans into cash balance plans. The employer makes deposits (or credits a given amount of money) on the employee's behalf, usually based on a percentage of pay. Employee accounts grow based on a predetermined interest benchmark, such as the interest rate on Treasury Bonds. There are some advantages to these plans, particularly for younger workers: a) The benefits, up to a reasonable limit, are guaranteed by the Pension Benefit Guaranty Corporation. b) Benefits are portable—they can be moved to another plan when the employee changes companies. c) Younger workers and those who spend a shorter number of years with an employer may receive higher benefits than they would under a traditional defined benefit plan.

ESOP Stock Plan (Employees' Stock Ownership Plan): This type of plan is in wide use. Typically, the plan borrows money from a bank and uses those funds to purchase a large block of the corporation's stock. The corporation makes contributions to the plan over a period of time, and the stock purchase loan is eventually paid off. The value of the plan grows significantly as long as the market price of the stock holds up. Qualified employees are allocated a share of the plan based on their length of service and their level of salary. Under federal regulations, participants in ESOPs are allowed to diversify their account holdings in set percentages that rise as the employee ages and gains years of service with the company. In this manner, not all of the employee's assets are tied up in the employer's stock.

Savings Plan, 401(k): Under this type of plan, employees make a tax-deferred deposit into an account. In the best plans, the company makes annual matching donations to the employees' accounts, typically in some proportion to deposits made by the employees themselves. A good plan will match one-half of employee deposits of up to 6% of wages. For example, an employee earning $30,000 yearly might deposit $1,800 (6%) into the plan. The company will match one-half of the employee's deposit, or $900. The plan grows on a tax-deferred basis, similar to an IRA. A very generous plan will match 100% of employee deposits. However, some plans do not call for the employer to make a matching deposit at all. Other plans call for a matching contribution to be made at the discretion of the firm's board of directors. Actual terms of these plans vary widely from firm to firm. Generally, these savings plans allow employees to deposit as much as 15% of salary into the plan on a tax-deferred basis. However, the portion that the company uses to calculate its matching deposit is generally limited to a maximum of 6%. Employees should take care to diversify the holdings in their 401(k) accounts, and most people should seek professional guidance or investment management for their accounts.

Stock Purchase Plan: Qualified employees may purchase the company's common stock at a price below its market value under a specific plan. Typically, the employee is limited to investing a small percentage of wages in this plan. The discount may range from 5 to 15%. Some of these plans allow for deposits to be made through regular monthly payroll deductions. However, new accounting rules for corporations, along with other factors, are leading many companies to curtail these plans—dropping the discount allowed, cutting the maximum yearly stock purchase or otherwise making the plans less generous or appealing.

Profit Sharing: Qualified employees are awarded an annual amount equal to some portion of a company's profits. In a very generous plan, the pool of money awarded to employees would be 15% of profits. Typically, this money is deposited into a long-term retirement account. Caution: Some employers refer to plans as "profit sharing" when they are actually 401(k) savings plans. True profit sharing plans are rarely offered.

Highest Executive Salary: The highest executive salary paid, typically a 2010 amount (or the latest year available to the editors) and typically paid to the Chief Executive Officer.

Highest Executive Bonus: The apparent bonus, if any, paid to the above person.

Second Highest Executive Salary: The next-highest executive salary paid, typically a 2010 amount (or the latest year available to the editors) and typically paid to the President or Chief Operating Officer.

Second Highest Executive Bonus: The apparent bonus, if any, paid to the above person.

Other Thoughts:

Apparent Women Officers or Directors: It is difficult to obtain this information on an exact basis, and employers generally do not disclose the data in a public way. However, we have indicated what our best efforts reveal to be the apparent number of women who either are in the posts of corporate officers or sit on the board of directors. There is a wide variance from company to company.

Hot Spot for Advancement for Women/Minorities: A "Y" in appropriate fields indicates "Yes." These are firms that appear either to have posted a substantial number of women and/or minorities to high posts or that appear to have a good record of going out of their way to recruit, train, promote and retain women or minorities. (See the Index of Hot Spots For Women and Minorities in the back of the book.) This information may change frequently and can be difficult to obtain and verify. Consequently, the reader should use caution and conduct further investigation where appropriate.

Growth Plans/ Special Features:

Listed here are observations regarding the firm's strategy, hiring plans, plans for growth and product development, along with general information regarding a company's business and prospects.

Locations:

A "Y" in the appropriate field indicates "Yes."

Primary locations outside of the headquarters, categorized by regions of the United States and by international locations. A complete index by locations is also in the front of this chapter.

Chapter 1

MAJOR TRENDS AFFECTING THE INFOTECH INDUSTRY

Major Trends Affecting the InfoTech Industry:

1) Introduction to the InfoTech Industry
2) Hot Fields Within the InfoTech Sector
3) Memory and Storage Needs Soar While Miniaturization Lowers Prices
4) Small, Cheap Computers and Netbooks Sell/Apple's iPad Makes a Splash
5) India and China PC Markets Targeted by Manufacturers
6) Supercomputing Hits 2.57 Petaflops
7) New Chips Provide Higher Speeds and Lighter Weights/Consume Less Power
8) Open Source Systems and Software are Backed by Major Software Firms
9) Cloud Computing, Software as a Service (SaaS) Point the Way to the Future
10) Wi-Fi Accelerates
11) WiMAX Extends Wireless Range Far Beyond Wi-Fi
12) MIMO (802.11n) Enhances WiMAX, the High-Speed Wireless Wave
13) Bluetooth Provides Wireless Connectivity to Millions of Cellphones and Other Devices
14) Ultrawideband (UWB) Offers Sizzling Short-Range Speed
15) Broadband Market Nears 1 Billion Users
16) Fiber-to-the-Home Gains Traction
17) Multimedia Hub Homes Slowly Become a Reality/TVs Are Internet Ready
18) Information Technology and Health Care

19) U.S. Broadband Connections Rank Behind Other Nations
20) Many Industry Sectors Seek Consulting and Outsourcing Income, Competing with Pure Consultancies
21) The Future: Pervasive Computing, Complete Mobility Will Be Standard
22) Nanotechnology Will Create Powerful Semiconductors in the Near Future
23) Nanotechnology Holds the Key to the Ultra-dense Molecular Memory of the Future
24) Virtualization of Servers Leads to Data Center Efficiency
25) Breakthrough Achieved in Quantum Computing

1)   Introduction to the InfoTech Industry

The technology breakthrough that enabled the modern computer occurred over 60 years ago, when researchers at Bell Laboratories in New Jersey created the first working transistor on December 16, 1947. William Shockley, John Bardeen and Walter Brattain received a well-deserved Nobel Prize in Physics in 1956 for their groundbreaking work in transistors.

What started with one transistor has grown at an astonishing rate. The Semiconductor Industry Association estimated that in 2008, a total of 6 quintillion transistors were manufactured (that's a six followed by 18 zeros). In 2011, an amount equal to 1,000 million transistors will be manufactured for each person on Earth. To see this growth in transistors in action, consider the steady evolution of Intel's semiconductors. In 1978, its wildly popular 8086 processor contained 29,000 transistors. The first Pentium processor was introduced by Intel in 1993, with 3.1 million transistors. In 2007, each of Intel's Zeon Quad-Core processors contained 820 million transistors. In February 2010, the company launched its newest Itanium chip with 2 billion transistors.

The worldwide market for information and communications technologies and services (ICT, which is the broadest view of InfoTech activities of all types) will total more than $4 trillion in 2011. Industry association WITSA expects ICT growth of 8.7% globally during 2011. (For the latest trends in ICT revenues on a global basis, see WITSA, the World Information Technology and Services Alliance, www.witsa.org.)

The boom years in IT spending are far from over, as investments that were deferred during the Great Recession are now coming online. In addition, advances in technologies, along with renewed growth in global trade of all types will continue to fuel demand for everything from consulting and systems integration to hardware and software. Investments in equipment and services will continue to follow evolving technological trends, with more emphasis on mobile computing, cloud-based systems, better network equipment and servers, along with better security.

Emerging markets are of extreme importance to the IT sector. Developing countries now account for more than one-half of all sales of PCs, and for about 70% of unit sales of cell phones. The number of cell phone subscribers worldwide is soaring, standing at 5.3 billion by the beginning of 2011, and expected to grow to as many as 5.8 billion in 2013. Low prices for equipment and services are fueling this boom in the Third World. China has grown to be one of the top markets worldwide for IT expenditures. Nonetheless, WITSA expects the Americas region to remain the largest ICT market, with 34.6% of the global market in 2013.

Worldwide sales of semiconductors increased dramatically to $300.5 billion in 2010, up 32.8% over the previous year, according to the Semiconductor Industry Association, thanks to a significant rebound as the recession ended. The organization projects further growth of 6.0% in 2011 and 3.4% in 2012.

Global personal computer (PC) shipments rebounded significantly during 2010, up 13.6% to 346.2 million according to analysts at IDC. However, for 2011 and 2012, growth in PCs will be hampered by a booming market in tablets and other mobile computing devices. In fact, when analyzing the direction of the IT market today, it's important to think one word: mobile. Analysts at Gartner predict that the number of smartphones in use will surpass the number of PCs by 2013. However, that prediction doesn't count all types of mobile devices. When you add in platforms such as iPads and netbooks connected wirelessly to the Internet, the shift to mobile computing is even more pronounced. It isn't that the PC is dead, but the PC is being relegated to a lessened status. The Pew Center's surveys show that 59% of Americans accessed the Internet via their cellphones in 2010. This pattern is being repeated around the world.

The InfoTech industry is a truly globalized sector. Research, development and manufacturing of components and completed systems have grown quickly in the labs and manufacturing plants of India, China, Taiwan, Korea, the Philippines and Indonesia, among other lands. Computer services continue to move offshore quickly, particularly to the tech centers of India. Asian PC brands are gaining strength, including Acer and Lenovo. Meanwhile, the leading global brands (HP and Dell, in that order) have much of their equipment manufactured in state of the art factories in Asia.

While the 1970s and 1980s will be remembered as the "Information Age," and the 1990s will undoubtedly be singled out in history as the beginning of the "Internet Age," the first decades of the 21st Century may become the "Broadband Age" or, even better said, the "Convergence Age." A few years back, the advent of the networked computer was truly revolutionary in terms of information processing, data sharing and data storage. In the '90s, the Internet was even more revolutionary in terms of communications and furthering the progress of data sharing, from the personal level to the global enterprise level.

Today, broadband sources such as Fiber-to-the-premises, Wi-Fi and cable modems provide high-speed access to information and media, creating an "always-on" environment for many users. The current move towards mobile computing will accelerate this environment of 24/7 constant access to data and communications. The result is a widespread convergence of entertainment, telephony and computerized information: data, voice and video, delivered to a rapidly evolving array of Internet appliances, wireless devices and desktop computers. This will fuel the next era of growth. Broadband access has been installed in enough U.S. households and businesses (more than 100 million) to create a true mass market, fueling demand for new Internet-delivered services, information and entertainment. Growth in broadband subscriptions worldwide is very strong. Analysts at In-Stat estimate that there were 763 million broadband subscribers worldwide by the end of 2010 (both fixed and wireless), and that the number will surpass one billion by 2013.

The advent of the Convergence Age is leading to a steady evolution in the way we access and utilize software applications, including the recent soaring growth of cloud computing.

Major innovations due to the Convergence Age:

1) On the consumer side, widespread access to fast Internet lines has created a boom in user-generated content (such as Flikr, YouTube and Wikipedia); games; social networking (such as Facebook and MySpace); as well as TV, radio and movies delivered via the Internet (such as Netflix's movie download service).
2) On the business side, the Convergence Age is leading to rapid adoption of Software as a Service. That is, the delivery of sophisticated software applications by remote servers that are accessed via the Internet, as opposed to software that is installed locally by its users (such as Salesforce and Microsoft's Windows Live).
3) On the technology side, the Convergence Age is leading to booming growth in computing power that is distributed over large numbers of small servers, now referred to as "cloud computing."
4) Mobile computing is soaring worldwide, taking advantage of the three trends listed above.

Source: Plunkett Research, Ltd.

The promise of the Convergence Age—the delivery of an entire universe of information and entertainment to PCs and mobile devices, on-demand with the click of a mouse—is now at hand. Consumers are swarming to new and enhanced products and services, such as the iPad and the iPhone. Over the next five to ten years, significant groundbreaking products will be introduced in areas such as high-density storage, artificial intelligence, optical switches and networking technologies, and advances will be made in quantum computing.

The InfoTech revolution continues in the office as well as in the home. The U.S. workforce totals about 150 million people. A vast segment of the workforce uses a computer of some type on the job daily, in every conceivable application—from factory workers managing computer-driven machinery, to receptionists answering computerized telephone systems, to cashiers ringing up sales at Wal-Mart on registers that are tied into vast computerized databases. This is the InfoTech revolution at work, moving voice, video and data through the air and over phone lines, driving productivity ahead at rates that we do not yet know how to calculate. Our ability to utilize technology effectively is finally catching up to our ability to create the technologies themselves. We're finding more and more uses for computers with increased processing speed, increased memory capacity, interfaces that are friendly and easy-to-use and software created to speed up virtually every task known to man. Cheaper, faster chips, bigger storage capability and more powerful software will continue to enter the market at blinding speed.

InfoTech continues to create new efficiency-creating possibilities on a continual basis. Now, RFID (radio frequency ID tagging, a method of digitally identifying and tracking each individual item of merchandise) promises to revolutionize logistics and drive InfoTech industry revenues even higher.

The health care industry is undergoing a technology revolution of its own. Patient records are finally going digital in standardized formats, and RFID is starting to make hospital inventories more manageable.

For businesses, the stark realities of global competition are fueling investments in InfoTech. Demands from customers for better service, lower prices, higher quality and more depth of inventory are mercilessly pushing companies to achieve efficient re-stocking, higher productivity and faster, more thorough information management. These demands will continue to intensify, partly because of globalization.

The solutions are rising from InfoTech channels: vast computer networks that speed information around the globe; e-mail, instant messaging, collaboration software and improved systems for real-time communication between branches, customers and headquarters; software with the power to call up answers to complex questions by delving deep into databases; satellites that are beginning to clutter the skies; and clear fiber-optic cables that carry tens of thousands of streams of data across minuscule beams of light. Businesses are paving the paths to their futures with dollars invested in InfoTech because: 1) substantial productivity gains are possible; 2) the relative cost of the technology itself has plummeted while its power has multiplied; and 3) competitive pressures leave them no choice.

2) Hot Fields Within the InfoTech Sector

- Computer security remains at or near the top in concerns among technology consumers and manufacturers alike. Whether it's security when conducting online banking and purchasing or security in using e-mail and online collaboration, technology users are fed up with being hacked, spammed, cheated and abused by fraud. Now, security is a growing concern for social media networks, cell phones and cloud computing.
- Supercomputers—Advances in technology have created sizzling new computer systems for research.
- Electronic games—Exciting new hardware, software and interactive online game playing continue to fuel global sales in this sector. Microsoft's new Kinect for Xbox and Nintendo's 3D gaming will accelerate the marketplace.
- Advertising on the Internet—Booming advertising methods include paid search engine placement. Google, Yahoo! and other leading search sites have completely revolutionized the advertising industry.
- Home networks—Especially Wi-Fi, coupled with media center PCs, will continue to be adopted. The biggest advancement here will be Internet-connected TVs and advanced on-demand delivery services such as movies downloaded from Netflix.
- Voice recognition—Advanced software to enable a user to "speak" to a computer as a form of data entry.
- Mobile computing—Faster 3G cell phone networks combined with smartphones such as the iPhone are making mobile computing the platform of choice for consumer entertainment and communications, including text messaging. 4G networks will expand quickly.
- Tablets—Apple scored an incredible success with its revolutionary iPad, adding a new layer of products to mobile computing.
- RFID—Radio frequency ID tags are revolutionizing tracking inventories and shipments of all types. As of 2010, costs were finally becoming reasonable, which will enable widespread implementation. New, advanced standards will address the concerns of users.
- Denser, faster, more energy-efficient chips continue to be announced. As of 2010, Intel was building 2 billion transistor chips using 32-nanometer technology. Nanotechnology will soon lead to

dramatic increases in chip density while making chips extremely energy efficient.
- Open operating systems—Operating systems such as Linux are booming because they are reliable, inexpensive, versatile and continuously improving.
- Fiber-to-the-premises (FTTP)—Fiber-optic cable installed all the way through to the living room is becoming standard in new housing communities.
- Mass market broadband—More than 100 million U.S. homes and businesses now have broadband. The price of bandwidth will remain a tremendous bargain. The global broadband market is already nearing 800 million subscribers and will soon reach 1 billion.
- Cloud computing—Clusters of thousands of inexpensive servers power vast data centers for search, storage and data sharing.
- Software as a Service (Saas)—Software for business or consumer use that is accessed via the Internet rather than installed on your local computer.
- Web services—Including Microsoft's .NET and XML in general, combined with advanced software tools, are revolutionizing the way users are able to call up, share and analyze data of all types.
- Video-conferencing and online collaboration—Businesses use online methods to cut down on the expense of travel and attendance at conferences. Methods for conducting virtual meetings are rapidly being adopted by larger corporations.
- Flash memory—Flash drives are now large enough in capacity and low enough in price to replace hard drives in some uses. Flash memory has no moving parts and can be very reliable in mobile settings. Now, there is widespread use of flash instead of hard drives in notebook computers.
- Digital health care records technologies.

Sites with the latest information on worldwide markets in InfoTech:
Gartner, www.gartner.com
Forrester Research, www.forrester.com
International Data Corporation, www.idc.com
Yankee Group, www.yankeegroup.com

Sites with the latest statistics on Internet usage:
ClickZ, www.clickz.com and click Stats.
Emarketer, www.emarketer.com
International Telecommunication Union, www.itu.int
Nielsen, www.nielsen-online.com
Pew Internet & American Life, www.pewinternet.org

3)   Memory and Storage Needs Soar While Miniaturization Lowers Prices

The unstoppable trend of miniaturization is fueling tremendous product innovation. This trend generally leads to better, faster products at lower prices. It also leads to devices that use less energy. Miniaturization interacts perfectly with the trend of convergence—where voice, video, data, telephony, entertainment and more are converging for use on digital devices. Convergence means that technology consumers, whether for business or personal use, need vastly higher amounts of memory and storage. Think, for example, of the exponentially growing number of pixels contained in a photo made by a digital camera. Or consider the fact that music and video files have become digital and portable at a rapid pace. On the corporate end, paperwork, customer files, vital intellectual property and more have become digitized and must be stored for current or archival access.

The prime enabler of this trend has been miniaturization. For example, it's easy to buy a 1-terabyte magnetic disk drive for as little as $85 today. That drive, with all its storage capacity, is the same physical size, if not smaller, than drives of a couple of years ago, which had significantly less capacity.

Meanwhile, mobility is a major factor. Flash memory, a silent, low-power-consumption device with no moving parts, has become a standard medium.

Seagate Technology, Inc. (www.seagate.com), one of the largest makers of disk drives in the world, launched a hybrid drive for notebook PCs in 2006 that combined 160 gigabytes of disk storage with 256 megabytes of flash memory. When the PC starts up (boots), the operating system loads data from the flash memory first. The combination greatly prolongs battery life. In 2009, Seagate introduced its Constellation ES hard drive with up to 2 terabytes in capacity.

Miniaturization coupled with the growing need for storage will mean endless opportunities for new products and new profits. By late 2007, Toshiba Corp. proved the ability to manufacture hard drives that store up to 228 gigabytes of data per square inch. By 2009, demonstrations of up to 800 gigabytes per square inch had been made. This kind of density is possible due to PMR or perpendicular magnetic recording. PMR records data in an up and down pattern rather than the traditional horizontal method. These micro-drives are perfect for today's mobile devices. By 2009, Hitachi was utilizing ultrahigh density to offer 2.5 inch notebook or netbook drives from 120 GB to 500 GB.

On a larger scale, storage needs are growing constantly, both for consumers who want to store an ever-growing stash of digitized photos, videos and music on their mobile devices and PCs, and for corporate and government systems, where the amount of data on hand in enterprise systems is growing at a sizzling rate. Large organizations find they have much greater needs than earlier estimated for digital storage. Included in the data are such items as growing customer data, long-term e-mail archives, financial records and in-depth human resources records.

In addition, 2009 saw the emergence of phase change memory, a memory chip technology that stores data by causing material to alter from a crystalline phase to a disordered phase. Tiny, precisely timed heat pulses are beamed at a substance similar to glass. As the substance cools, it forms a highly conductive crystalline latticework that can be read by measuring when the cell conducts electricity and when it doesn't. It has the potential to be vastly faster than flash memory while consuming far less power. Numonyx and Samsung began shipping phase change chips as of 2009.

Nanotechnology will enable ever-increasing levels of storage on smaller and smaller devices. IBM researchers, for example, are working on a project called Millipede, a nanomechanical system that etches microscopic indentations on a polymer surface, resulting in storage of roughly 25 million printed pages in a unit about the size of a postage stamp. Also, 45-nanometer manufacturing technology was launched in the semiconductor manufacturing industry in 2007, one-half the size of 2005's standard. (The nanometer scale refers to the smallest circuits created during the chip's fabrication.) Commercial production of 45-nanometer technology chips began in 2008 by IBM and AMD. Intel commercialized 32-nanometer chip production in 2009, and announced plans to refresh its entire line of server products with the new chips in 2010. An upcoming generation of chips at Intel will shrink to 15-nanometer size, the width of a few atoms.

Another storage wonder is the holographic optical disk. This kind of disk not only stores data on its surface, but also in volume throughout the depth and breadth of the disk. InPhase Technologies is a leader in this field and already has 300-gigabyte to 1.6 terabyte hard drives called Tapestry on the market that can transfer data at a rate of 20 megabytes per second.

The next wave in memory and storage may well abandon the use of transistors and rely instead on ions (which are charged particles manipulated by the addition or subtraction of electrons on the nuclear level). California-based startup Unity Semiconductor has built prototypes using the technology, trademarked CMOx, which promises to store four times the amount of data as current flash memory chips of the same size and record data between five and ten times faster. Unity, which has a technology development partnership with chip firm Micron Technology, does not expect to commercialize the new technology until 2012 at the earliest.

A Brief History of the PC

1971   Intel introduces the first microprocessor, the 4004.

1975   The Altair 8800 microcomputer is introduced by MITS.

1976   Popular hardware enters the market, but software is lacking. Apple introduces the Apple II personal computer. Commodore introduces the PET. Radio Shack enters the market with the TRS-80.

1977   Software becomes more exciting. VisiCalc, the first spreadsheet, hits the market.

1981   IBM finally enters the market with the IBM PC, based on a Microsoft operating system called DOS.

1982   Clones compatible with the IBM PC enter the market. Since IBM did not require exclusive access to MS DOS, clones are able to compete effectively. Compaq is born, rapidly becoming a $1-billion company. The concept of portable PCs is introduced, an idea that later evolves into the notebook computer.

1983   Software takes a great leap forward when Lotus Development introduces Lotus 1-2-3.

1984   A cult is born when Apple introduces the Macintosh. Dell Computer is launched by a college student in Austin, Texas.

1990   Microsoft introduces Windows 3.0.

1993   Mosaic is born, the first graphics-based web browser. The Internet is ready to surge. Intel's Pentium processor is launched, with 3.1 million transistors.

1994   Online directory giant Yahoo! is launched by two Stanford University students. Version 1.0 of open software Linux is released.

1995   Amazon.com is launched. The MP3 audio format is developed. Netscape, maker of the first widely used Internet browser, goes public.

1996   eBay is launched. The Palm Pilot PDA is introduced. Microsoft introduces the Internet Explorer browser.

1998   Apple introduces the iMac.

1999   Napster is created. Soon it has 60 million users and accounts for 4% of all traffic on the Internet. By 2001, Napster is forced to cease operations.

2002   HP merges with Compaq.

2003   64-bit chips are put on the market. Wi-Fi and other wireless technologies advance and proliferate. Notebooks become lighter, faster and more energy-efficient.

2004   Open systems, such as Linux and Mozilla, move ahead broadly, gaining widespread acceptance over a wide variety of platforms.

2005   Storage, security and portability top the needs of technology buyers and users. Broadband users at home and at the office now create a vast mass market. Intel's Pentium D processor uses 291 million transistors to hit 3.2 GHz.

2006   Worldwide PC shipments reach more than 240 million units. The first commercial installations of WiMAX are launched. Globally, there are more than 1 billion Internet users, including 80 million homes and businesses in the U.S.

2007   Seagate Technologies and Hitachi announce the first one terabyte hard drives for PCs (1,024 GB). Flash drives begin to replace hard drives in notebook computers.

2008   Seagate Technologies unveils the first 1.5-terabyte desktop and half-terabyte notebook hard drives.

2009   Numonyx and Samsung begin shipping phase change chips.

2010   Apple launches the wildly popular iPad tablet computer.

Source: Plunkett Research, Ltd.

---

4) Small, Cheap Computers and Netbooks Sell/Apple's iPad Makes a Splash

Sales of laptop computers surpassed sales of desktop models for the first time in 2008, according to California-based research firm iSuppli Corporation. After a global slump in computer sales of all types due to the recession of 2008 and 2009,

PC shipments rebounded in the fourth quarter of 2010, rising 15% on a global basis from the same quarter in 2009, and 24% in the U.S. Consumers who want to make a lower total investment, including those in less developed nations, offer a sizeable growth market for netbooks and other smaller computers. Another market for lower-priced PCs exists in less affluent homes and in situations where a second or third computer is needed for a household to take care of children's needs or other situations.

Certainly, this trend was a consideration in Apple's early 2005 announcement of the Mac mini, a powerful unit that was still available as of early 2011 for a starting price of $699. Aiming squarely at the home entertainment market, Apple has gained market share with this breakthrough, from buyers who want to utilize Apple's famed iLife multimedia software to manage music, video and photo files. Dell's low-end PCs offer tremendous power and features starting at about $249 after rebates in early 2011. Powerful notebook computers are available from many different manufactures in the $350 to $700 range (after rebates).

Small, lightweight laptops called netbooks are low-cost alternatives to full blown PCs or laptops. Netbooks typically offer small screens of 10 inches or less, weigh about three pounds, have no optical drive and run on inexpensive processors which sell for about $35 to $40, compared to as much as $150 for a traditional laptop chip. Users can perform basic tasks such as Internet browsing and e-mail, but lack the ability to perform graphics-intense tasks such as playing videos. Netbooks cost between $250 and $500, and although less than 1 million units were sold worldwide in 2007 (according to NPD Group's Display Search), 33.3 million sold in 2009, with 39.7 million projected for 2010. Top netbook makers include Acer, Asus, HP, Micro-Star International and Dell. Not only do netbooks capitalize on cheaper processors, they also benefit from less expensive displays and software. According to IDC, netbook makers buy simplified Windows operating systems for between $15 and $25 per unit, which is less than half the cost of the cheapest Windows system for laptops.

Meanwhile, now that nearly 2 billion people worldwide are accessing the Internet, a large question looms over makers of PCs and software: how to enable the next billion users? To find the answer, many organizations are attempting to create mass market, Internet-enabled PCs in the $150 to $400 price range for use in underdeveloped countries. Their intent lies somewhere between entrepreneurism and altruism. These innovators see low-priced PCs as a way to bridge the digital divide and bring the myriad blessings of the Internet, from distance education to health information to entertainment, into homes and schools worldwide where very limited budgets rule.

Intel Corp. launched a low-cost PC for children called the Classmate PC. In addition to the machines, the firm provides free training to teachers involved in the programs in countries around the world. More importantly, Intel launched the Intel World Ahead Program, focusing on developing nations, with the promotion of WiMAX for the rapid deployment of broadband networks, along with widespread distribution of low-cost PCs, and advancement of teacher training and other educational programs. Over a five-year period, the goal is to train 10 million teachers in the use of technology while encouraging the use of the Internet by 1 billion new users, including students. Intel is putting significant money and muscle behind this idea. It is donating 100,000 PCs to classrooms in developing nations as part of its $1 billion overall commitment. In 2009, Intel launched an updated, second-generation version of the Classmate PC with up to 16GB of flash memory. As of late 2009, Intel had sold almost 2 million Classmate PCs.

A slightly different vision of bringing Internet access and personal computing to the world's low-income masses continues to be pushed by Nicholas Negroponte, a visionary who was the founder of MIT's well-respected Media Lab. Negroponte originally supported the idea of "Crank It," a small, very clever notebook, running on electricity provided by a hand crank similar to that used by emergency radio receivers. Crank It was hoped to be distributed in large quantities for about $100 U.S. each, complete with a revolutionary color monitor that can be manufactured at unusually low cost. The Crank It model was scrapped in 2007 in favor of the AMD XO laptop which costs about $200.

Negroponte and the MIT Media Lab launched a research initiative in this effort, and a nonprofit association, One Laptop per Child (OLPC), was created to further the cause. The goal was to deliver millions of the laptops to school children in developing nations. As of early 2010, OLPC had sold only 1.4 million units largely in Peru, Uruguay and North America as part of a donation program, far less than the projected 100 million to 150 million. The association hopes to boost sales through a partnership with Microsoft in which the software giant will provide its Windows operating system for only $3 per unit. This is a significant departure from the previous Linux open system used in OLPC machines. While OLPC never reached the huge sales goals it had set for itself, it was clearly instrumental in building momentum in this sector, and was very successful in launching a global dialogue on the potential of delivering the digital age to the world's remotest schools at modest cost.

Negroponte's latest and perhaps most ambitious venture is the development of a $75 touchscreen tablet computer to be used in the OLPC initiative. Called the XO-3, the rugged, waterproof unit is half the thickness of an iPhone and is made of unbreakable plastic and uses open source software. Expected to be ready for release by 2012, the design of the unit is available to any interested hardware makers (such as Taiwan's contract manufacturer Quanta and chip maker Marvell).

Yet another twist on low-cost computers is NComputing Co.'s network-based computing terminal. It's a device that taps into a PC that is somewhere else (whether across the room or across the country). With no hard drive or processor, the device, which is also called a "thin client," uses the Internet to access files and programs stored on another computer. Retail prices start at about $150 for the simplest model, the L130, and go up to about $199 for the L300, which features a USB memory port. Additional users who access computers remotely can do so for as little as $70. As of early 2011, NComputing reported over 2.5 million seats sold in over 140 countries.

A promising player in the low-cost PC market is Taiwan's Asus, formerly ASUStek, which released its two-pound, $340 laptops called Eee PCs in Taiwan in October 2007. The following month, the Eee PC arrived in the U.S. and Europe, selling for $300. Today's Eee line of PCs range from a seven-inch, two-gigabyte unit with 512 megabytes of memory called the Eee PC 2G Surf to a 12-inch, 250 gigabyte unit with 2 gigabytes of memory called the Eee PC 1215T. The company expected to sell 20 million notebook computers in 2010.

The decline in the cost of flash memory is one factor that makes low-cost PCs feasible. PCs that have a low enough initial cost might be given away by Internet service providers as a way to encourage consumers to sign up for monthly Internet access charges. Or, a portion of their costs might be subsidized by governments seeking to enhance lifestyle and education levels. In order to distribute the hundreds of millions of PCs envisioned by the projects described above, significant levels of cooperation will be required by governments in the nations where the machines would be deployed.

In early 2010, Apple unveiled its long-anticipated iPad. The 9.7-inch touch screen unit is a multimedia tablet computer that combines the music and video capabilities of the wildly successful iPod, wireless e-mail and game applications of the iPhone and a digital reader that goes head-to-head with Amazon's Kindle. Entry level models sell for $499, and higher-end models with 3-G wireless capacity are priced at up to $829. The iPad uses Apple's A4 chip instead of one produced by Intel or Qualcomm, and the firm is expected to use the chip in future models of the iPhone. Although far from a low-cost computer, the iPad has a good start on revolutionizing the PC market to the same extent that the iPod altered the music industry and the iPhone impacted the cellphone industry. By August 2010, Apple had sold more than 3 million units. More than 20,000 third-party apps have been written specifically for use on iPads, in addition to the more than 200,000 iPhone apps the units can also run.

Competition for the iPad is coming from a variety of PC manufacturers including Dell, Samsung, Motorola and Acer. Dell released the Streak in the U.K. and the U.S. in 2010. Streak is a smaller (5-inch screen) tablet computer than the iPad but offers the ability to make cellular calls. It's cheaper also, priced at $199 with a two-year AT&T contract, runs on Google's Android operating system and has about 70,000 third-party apps available from the Android Market store. Meanwhile, Samsung's Galaxy Tab unit sells for $400 with a two-year wireless data contract.

Sales of tablet devices (which includes the iPad and its competitors) are forecast to rise sharply in 2011, but still remain a small part of the overall computer/cellphone market. Research firm iSuppli estimated global tablet sales in 2010 of 18 million units, and expected unit sales to rise in 2011 to 61 million. This is in comparison to an estimated 132 million desktop PCs, 204 million mobile PCs and 247 million smartphones shipped in 2010.

5) India and China PC Markets Targeted by Manufacturers

As of mid-2010, InternetWorldStats reported that there were approximately 1.97 billion PC users worldwide. Many PC manufacturers are looking to sell to the next 1 billion, who are likely to be in India, China and other emerging nations. The rapid growth of the middle classes in those countries points to an increasingly important consumer and business market.

PC sales in India were in the 8 to 9 million units per year range during 2008 and 2009, a very modest number for a nation of more than 1 billion residents. Research firm IDC estimated overall PC sales in 2010 at 10 million units.

IDC reported that for the entire Asia-Pacific region (excluding Japan) in 2010, PC sales rose 19% over 2009 to reach 107 million units. As of late 2010, about 66% of the Chinese population still did not have access to the Internet, so the growth potential there is huge. Sales of tablet computers and smartphones are particularly strong in China.

The players in the Asia Pacific region are led by China's Lenovo Group, Inc. (with a 20.2% market share in 2010) followed by HP and Dell, according to global market intelligence firm IDC. Taiwan-based Acer and Asus are also prominent with regard to market share. The Chinese government's 2009 economic stimulus plans offered rural residents subsidies worth 13% off the price of electronics made by participating manufacturers such as Lenovo.

The government in China is backing an initiative to develop chips domestically, instead of relying on those made by Intel and AMD. The Institute of Computing Technology developed the Loongson or Dragon chip which powered a computer as early as 2006 (the chip is manufactured by China's Lemote). Loongson doesn't use the standard x86 chip design so it is incapable of running Microsoft Windows without software emulation. Instead, Lemote is relying on open source operating environments and software.

PCs sold in both China and India tend to be low in cost. Lenovo launched 15 PC models in 2009, priced as low as $365. Dell, Inc. announced plans in late 2010 to invest more than $100 billion over 10 years to broaden operations in China. Intel is spending $1 billion in a five-year project to improve Internet access, as well as educating teachers and students in computer use, in India, China and other developing countries. Intel has already trained hundreds of thousands of teachers in China and India on PC and Internet use.

6) Supercomputing Hits 2.57 Petaflops

The claim to the title of the world's fastest computer is a moving target. The title was briefly held by the Japanese, when in March 2002, NEC unveiled the Earth Simulator. The Earth Simulator is the size of four tennis courts, took four years to build and cost almost $350 million.

How was NEC able to produce such a massively expensive computer? It convinced the Japanese Government to subsidize the project. NEC's goal was to advance scientists' understanding of the world's climates by producing a computer that performs better weather simulations and modeling than traditional weather-related systems. The Earth Simulator was built from the bottom up using a technique called vector computing, a concept in which a computer executes one instruction at a time, but does so on multiple data simultaneously. This technique was used by computer pioneer Seymour Cray, who built the first supercomputer in the early '70s.

Internet Search Tip: The Top Supercomputers in the World

For a complete list of the world's fastest supercomputers and details about recent developments, see: Top 500 Supercomputer Sites, www.top500.org. This site is presented by experts at the University of Mannheim, Germany; the University of Tennessee; and the National Energy Research Scientific Computing Center (U.S.).

For the past several years in the U.S., the focus of supercomputing has been on the linking of clusters of commodity processors designed for everyday applications. These are known as parallel configurations. In contrast, the Japanese focus has been on specialized, massive single architectures developed for the high-performance market.

The commodity approach utilized in the U.S. has enjoyed many measures of success. Americans have understood the need to work on new, advanced systems in order to avoid falling behind in areas where strong computing matters most, such as simulating complex systems like weather on the macroscopic end, and biotechnology projects like protein folding on the microscopic end. Simulation capability is vital for national security (for example, where simulations take the place of underground testing for weapons of mass destruction) and the advancement of basic science.

In late 2004, IBM launched the BlueGene/L, a machine that surpassed rivals made by Japanese firms. When IBM first conceived the BlueGene line, it was seen as a tremendous tool for genetic research. IBM also realized that BlueGene would have myriad additional uses. BlueGene/L sits at the Lawrence Livermore National Laboratory (operated in Livermore, California, by the University of California for the U.S. Department of Energy's

National Nuclear Security Administration). In late 2004, the machine set a world record by scoring a speed of 92 teraflops. That's equal to 92 trillion floating-point calculations each second (more than twice the speed of Earth Simulator's 41 teraflops—the world record of only two and a half years earlier). Better still, by late 2005, the BlueGene at Lawrence Livermore Labs hit 280.6 teraflops, tripling its initial speed. In late 2007, BlueGene still held the top spot among supercomputers, having been expanded so that it achieved a benchmark performance of 478.2 teraflops per second.

In 2008, the leader in supercomputing was a $133 million IBM system at Los Alamos national Laboratory that's nicknamed Roadrunner. It clocked 1.105 petaflops (a petaflop represents 1 quadrillion floating-point operations per second). The Roadrunner was surpassed in 2009 by Jaguar, the Cray XT5 supercomputer at Oak Ridge National Laboratory, which clocked 1.75 petaflops.

Some of the world's fastest supercomputers, including the Roadrunner, utilize technology that is the result of the IBM/Toshiba joint venture that created the "Cell." Built on designs from IBM's Power processor, the Cell contains multiple processing cores and can act like more than one chip at any given time. Because of its potential power, Cell is being touted as the equivalent of a supercomputer on a single chip. It was initially launched as the processor in Sony's PlayStation 3 game machine, which was introduced in the U.S. in November 2006. The Roadrunner system uses an advanced version of Cell technology. IBM is also using Cell technology to power server computers. The units are priced between $25,000 and $35,000 and will run typically on Linux operating systems.

China pulled in front in late 2010 with the Tianhe-1A system at the National Superconductor Center in Tianjin. It reached 2.57 petaflops. Instead of relying on Cell technology, the Tianhe-1A utilizes GPUs (graphics processing units) with chips made by Intel rival Nvidia to speed computation. China is gaining ground on other countries in the high performance computing race. Up until recently, there were no supercomputers in China on the list of the top 500 fastest machines in the world. As of November 2010, Chinese systems occupied the number one and number three positions, with 42 in all included in the top 500. The U.S. remains the leader in the number of supercomputers with 275 of the top 500 (as reported by research group Top500).

Of the top 10 supercomputers in the world as of 2010, four are located at U.S. Department of Energy facilities and five are located in the U.S. Number two was the Jaguar, a Cray system located at Oak Ridge National Laboratory, with number three in China, the Nebulae, at the National Supercomputing Centre in Shenzhen. Fourth is the TSUBAME 2.0 at the Tokyo Institute of Technology followed by the Hopper, a Cray system at a Department of Energy lab in Berkeley, California.

Government and corporate customers alike will benefit from this race. While aerospace and biotech researchers want enhanced computing power for breakthrough research, government agencies may be able to benefit from supercomputers for such areas as studying weather and climate change as well as for defense needs. Additionally, major manufacturers in such areas as automobiles and health imaging equipment see supercomputers as a tool for improved product engineering and faster time-to-market.

7) New Chips Provide Higher Speeds and Lighter Weights/Consume Less Power

The highest benchmark for semiconductor technology as of early 2011 is 32-nanometer chips. Prior to 2007, most manufacturers were building chips using 90-nanometer wafers. Intel's leap to 45-nanometer technology in 2007 approximately doubled the number of transistors that fit within a given space on a chip. The nanometer measurement refers to the smallest average feature on a chip. The smaller the measurement, the more transistors can be incorporated into a chip of given size. A nanometer is one billionth of a meter.

A significant component in the smaller chip is Intel's use of a unique new insulating material. One of the biggest hurdles in developing the next generation of chips has been the tendency of transistors to suffer a leakage of current as their insulators get thinner and thinner. Intel appears to have solved that problem. The resulting chip is much more powerful and features significant energy savings over previous technology. Intel's 32-nanometer chips can house about 2 billion transistors per processor, which makes graphics capabilities inherent in entertainment devices exponentially higher. After a few delays, Intel launched this new chip within its Itanium line in February 2010. Intel pushed 32-nanometer chip adoption across the board in 2010 and plans to continue on into 2011. The new chips, along with a return to new hardware and software investments by individual and corporate consumers after the global recession, resulted in a record year for Intel in 2010. An upcoming generation of chips at Intel will shrink to 15-nanometer size, the width of a few atoms.

In September 2009, IBM announced the successful development of a prototype, next-generation 32-nanometer chip using silicon-on-insulator technology. It has also fabricated test chips of eDRAM memory in 32-nanometer scale. In early 2010, IBM launched its Power7 chip for servers, which it states is four times faster than the previous IBM generation. The chip holds 1.2 billion transistors and features very high utilization of multiple cores along with low power consumption. The chip will be particularly advantageous in mid-range servers.

Intel also announced a major breakthrough in late 2006 regarding the creation of lasers on computer chips. The company, working with the University of California, Santa Barbara, created the world's first electrically-driven hybrid silicon laser. The device is a silicon chip with a layer of light-emitting Indium Phosphide. The combination unites the speed afforded by using lasers with the low cost advantages of silicon. The new chips may offer new levels of data communication speed at far lower costs. The laser is an integral part of silicon photonics, which is lightwave technology based on silicon chips. Silicon photonics opens the door for needs such as full-length movie downloads from the Internet without increasing bandwidth.

Big news in chips relating to the supercomputer market is on the horizon. In mid-2010, Intel announced plans for a new class of chips using technology from a cancelled Intel project codenamed Larrabee. The new chips, called Knight's Corner, combine features of the abandoned Larrabee graphics chip for PCs with designs for a single-chip cloud computer. Knight's Corner chips will offer in excess of 50 processor cores, compared to hundreds of cores used in Nvidia and AMD chips. Knight's Corner chips will be based on 22-nanometer technology.

8) Open Source Systems and Software are Backed by Major Software Firms

Long-term commercial operating systems such as Windows and UNIX continue to face serious competition from Linux. The increasingly popular Linux, originally launched by a Finn named Linus Torvalds, is a free and open operating system spreading through corporate data centers like wildfire.

The phrase "open source" is used to denote the fact that the vital programming, or source code, underlying the software is open to all programmers at no cost. This makes it easy for a programmer to adopt or modify the code for his or her own purposes and then to share any changes or improvements with the programming community. Many companies that were previously contracting with Microsoft or Sun for costly operating software packages have replaced them with far less expensive Linux operating systems.

According to the International Data Corporation (IDC), worldwide revenue from Linux rose 20.4% to $1.7 billion in the first quarter of 2010 compared to the same quarter in 2009. As of early 2010, Linux servers represented 16.2% of all server revenue. For the period from 2008 to 2013, a compound annual growth rate of 16.9% is expected. A significant number of government and corporate offices worldwide are switching to Linux in an effort to save costs. It's an uphill battle, however, since Microsoft's Windows XP, Vista or Windows 7 was still loaded on 95.2% of the world's PCs in 2009 (according to Gartner), while Linux is used on only 2%. Gartner projects Windows market share to drop to 94.4% by year end 2014.

As an open system, Linux is constantly improved and enhanced by the global community of people who use it. That is, software developers are free to add improvements to the basic code, and they do so on a regular basis. The longer the software is in use, the stronger and more bug-free it becomes. Meanwhile, the use of the software is free of charge to users who want to adopt it. Since software spending represents about 20% of the total IT market, this is a truly revolutionary concept that has broad implications for the entire IT industry.

Early versions of Linux, developed by a group of amateur and professional volunteers, were difficult to manage at best, and little, if any, technical support was available. Linux got a big boost when a start-up called Red Hat began selling technical support and documentation services. This step made corporate users more comfortable in making the switch to Linux, and Red Hat developed a significant revenue stream for itself. Another boost came with the global tech business slowdown in the early 2000s. Economic imperatives have forced IT managers to get the most for their technology budgets, and Linux is less expensive to implement. Lately, in addition to lower initial cost, many IT managers have found speed advantages, better security or other operating advantages to Linux. The recent global economic recession made Linux even more attractive to IT managers looking for ways to cut costs.

Major Open Source Software Products

Database
    MySQL
    PostgreSQL
Browser
    Firefox
    Google Chrome
E-Mail
    Novell Evolution, formerly Ximian
        Evolution (group e-mail)
    Bynari (e-mail server)
    Zimbra Collaboration Suite (now owned by
        VMware)
Operating System
    Linux
GUI
    Gnome
Word Processor and Office Tools
    Open Office
    IBM Lotus Symphony
Web Site Software
    Apache OFBiz
Web Content Management
    Dotnetnuke
    Alfresco
    Drupal
    Joomla

For in-depth information, visit: www.opensource.org
Source: Plunkett Research, Ltd.

One of the biggest open-software successes is Apache, used by about two-thirds of all web sites worldwide. Apache manages the interaction between a web site and the viewer's browser. This software is managed by The Apache Software Foundation (www.apache.org).

Another big open source success is MySQL (www.mysql.com), a sequel server-type database that has been adopted by some of the largest enterprises in the world. According to MySQL, more than 100 million copies of its software have been downloaded or distributed since its inception. Several thousand companies (including Google, Inc.) pay the MySQL organization a small fee for support and for the right to incorporate MySQL's code into their own software products.

The Zimbra Collaboration Suite, which was acquired by Yahoo! in September 2007 and acquired again by VMware in 2010, is an open source e-mail system cobbled together by computer enthusiasts from Silicon Valley and beefed up by techies in their spare time in Rochester, New York, and Denver, Colorado. By early 2010, Zimbra had about 55 million mailboxes, after posting mailbox growth of 86% in fiscal 2009.

To sum up, open source software is big, really big. Major software firms are rapidly getting behind the open source movement. Sun Microsystems shares much of the technology underlying its Java software designed to run servers. IBM, Oracle, SAP and Intel are all involved in Linux in one way or another. IBM is embracing open systems in many ways. For example, it has hundreds of engineers working on the open Linux code. IBM also contributes code to the Apache server software. These efforts by IBM, Sun and others are part of a growing effort by the legacy software firms to attract and build deep relationships with those coders and IT managers who see open systems as vital assets. Even Microsoft opened portions of code for its immensely popular Office software in 2008.

IBM, Sony and Phillips, three of the world's largest makers of IT equipment, joined in the creation of the Open Invention Network (OIN, www.openinventionnetwork.com). Other founding participants were Red Hat, Inc. and Novell, Inc. Patents and intellectual property rights for Linux applications are donated on a voluntary basis to the OIN by supporters who are able to do so. Use of these assets is available, royalty-free, to anyone who agrees to OIN's regulations.

A landmark agreement occurred in November 2006 when Microsoft and Novell, Inc. signed a pact in which Microsoft offers sales support for Suse Linux, the version of the open source operating system offered by Novell. Microsoft also agreed not to file patent infringement charges against Suse Linux users while Novell promised not to sue Windows users through 2012. Moreover, the two companies built a joint research facility in Cambridge, Massachusetts, where software combinations are designed and tested and support for new technologies is provided. The Microsoft-Novell agreement came on the heels of database management software company Oracle's announcement of its intentions to sell its support of Red Hat's version of Linux (which undercuts Red Hat's support and maintenance business). Meanwhile, Sun Microsystems offers its Java programming language available as free, open source software.

IBM has free open source software called IBM Lotus Symphony. Lotus Symphony competes with Microsoft's Office programs and its availability is a major step towards corporate customers' adoption of open source systems. In addition, IBM is partnering with Google in its desktop productivity programs called Google Pack. The collaboration illustrates a broader trend towards faster, automatic transfer of information between organizations and businesses. By 2015, IBM plans for software sales to account for as much as half of its pretax profit, up from about one-third in 2003. The company is expected to invest up to $20 billion between 2011 and 2015 on acquiring software companies to reach this goal.

There is no stopping the open source trend, and over the long term it could have serious negative effects on the revenues of mainstream software firms such as Microsoft and Oracle. Eventually, open source systems will move far beyond the PC and server arena. For example, the International Computer Science Institute (Berkeley, California) is boosting free, open source software for routers that send data through corporate networks. The eXtensible Open Router Platform (XORP) hopes to reduce costs and enhance networks. If successful, the project could be a direct attack on manufacturers that achieve a great deal of their revenues from expensive router products. Mainstream firms are fighting back by attempting to acquire open source start ups. For example, Oracle acquired Innobase and Sleepycat.

One of the most exciting open source products is Firefox, an Internet browser that is a direct challenge to the dominant browser, Microsoft's Internet Explorer. Another open system rapidly growing in popularity is a framework for web sites called dotnetnuke (www.dotnetnuke.com). By the beginning of 2010, this platform had 758,600 users.

Google is expected to make a major impact in the open systems war against Microsoft's dominance, with the release of Google's Chrome operating system, scheduled for sometime in 2011 (not to be confused with Google's Chrome web browser which launched in 2008). The operating system will use Linux as its core, and hopes to offer web browsing at higher speeds and greater security than what Microsoft offers. Google is betting on a major shift away from software loaded onto PCs to using applications online, and is designing Chrome to offer the speed and power to make it possible. See "Cloud Computing, Software as a Service (SaaS) Point the Way to the Future" in this chapter.

Plunkett's Law of Open Systems:
Closed, proprietary systems may succeed initially, due to early developers' advantage in launching revolutionary technologies (BetaMax, Windows, Macintosh, etc.). However, when a mass market exists, open, competitive systems will launch and may evolve to be extremely successful due to collaboration, flexibility, lower costs and potentially broader choices for the end user (MP3, Linux, Firefox, etc.).

Source: Plunkett Research, Ltd.

---

9) Cloud Computing, Software as a Service (SaaS) Point the Way to the Future

Many InfoTech industry observers consider cloud computing and similar remotely-based software strategies to be steps toward the future of computing and data access. There is a definite trend toward downplaying the role of software that is installed on the desktop, relying more on Internet-based applications. This trend is called Software as a Service (SaaS). In fact, Sun Microsystem's famous positioning line, "The network is the computer," pretty well sums up this trend, a thought that "uses the Internet as the computing platform of the future." Microsoft and other leading manufacturers are quickly enhancing their own suites of Internet-based applications.

Cloud computing is quickly gaining traction. Sometimes referred to as "utility computing," cloud computing uses a cluster of multiple computers networked together, often based on open standards. Cloud networks can consist of hundreds or even thousands of computers. They have the ability to run a broad set of applications by using "virtual" server technology to host middleware that is thus distributed across the cloud. Both Google and IBM are boosters of this technology, and Google's entire search infrastructure is based on the use of tens of thousands of small, inexpensive servers clustered together in its data centers as "clouds."

Over the long term, the result of these efforts will be a wide variety of software that is accessed only via the Internet instead of the desktop. Some software will be accessed for free, but many rich software applications will be rented to the user by subscription or by fees based on the amount of time used. PCs and mobile computers may evolve into radically different systems that are better suited to serve the needs of users via SaaS. The sharing of data will continue to simplify in nature. Business models and profit streams will be altered as a result. New systems and business models will emerge in step with the spread of broadband access. Despite the practical problems facing these new technologies, nothing less than the future of the local server and personal computing itself is at stake here.

Revenue on a global basis for cloud computing services was expected to rise by 17% to $68.3 billion in 2010, according to Gartner, Inc. By 2014, global revenue is expected to more than double to $148.8 billion.

Google has the jump on the rest of the industry with regard to cloud computing. By 2008, Google was already running some the largest and most efficient data centers in the world. The company took a further step for capitalizing on those servers through the 2008 launch of its open system web browser called Chrome. The free browser allows users to run separate applications on separate tabs, while Google displays targeted ads. In 2011, the firm plans to take a giant leap with the release of the Chrome operating system, a Linux-based open system environment designed to offer the speed and power necessary to fully utilize SaaS.

Meanwhile, Microsoft has invested a reported $3 billion in a landmark cloud computing project called the Azure Service Platform. A radical departure from Microsoft's historic positioning of the PC as the host for software applications such as word processors, spreadsheets and e-mail, Azure offers a host of web-hosted applications and is compatible with Windows Vista, Windows 7 and XP. Although still in the very early stages (some predict that it will take Microsoft between five and ten years to make a major shift to cloud computing) Coca-Cola Enterprises, Nokia and Ingersoll-Rand were all running e-mail on Microsoft servers as of late 2008. By mid-2010, Dell, Inc., Fujitsu Ltd. and Hewlett-Packard Co. were selling Azure as part of their data center lineup of products.

Microsoft took a further step toward web computing with its own major SaaS initiative, called Windows Live. This package provides consumers with Internet-based software providing e-mail (Hotmail), instant messenger, a personal calendar, digital photo management, video management and much more. The firm launched a Web version of its popular Office suite in 2009 that competes head-to-head with Google Docs. Microsoft also built a 707,000-square-foot, 100-megawatt data center in Chicago.

In late 2008, IBM launched its Virtual Linux Desktop that runs on a backroom server. Billed as a "Microsoft Free Desktop," it ranges in price from $59 to $289 per user, which could save between $500 and $800 per year per user compared to licenses for Microsoft's Vista operating system and the Office suite of applications and tools.

Salesforce, a customer relationship management (CRM) software leader, has achieved great success by selling Internet-based access to its tools. NetSuite is another major provider of Internet-based applications. Its offering for businesses includes CRM, enterprise resource planning (ERP), accounting, e-commerce and much more, all on a subscription basis. Among the advantages of SaaS are no software to purchase and no software to install or maintain.

Amazon is miles ahead of most in cloud computing. Since it must operate immense server capacity anyway, Amazon decided in early 2006 to offer cloud computing services on those servers to outside parties. "Amazon Web Services" (AWS) have been extremely popular. Using AWS requires no long-term contract or up-front investment. Charges are reasonable and usage-based (about 15 cents per gigabyte per month in the U.S.). Remote servers, remote storage and the "Amazon SimpleDB" database are among the most popular offerings. In early 2011, Amazon announced that it will use its massive computer network to offer a bulk e-mail service to businesses, a software-as-a-service offering that will threaten competing email firms.

The list of companies embracing cloud computing is growing at a blistering pace. Avon is shifting the management of its 6 million sales representatives from meetings and phone calls to smartphones and PCs connecting to a cloud system. Coca-Cola's 12,000 store merchandisers now use smartphones to access data on cloud systems regarding store inventories and displays. Genentech sales reps now use smartphone apps to research customer questions and access customer management programs while in the field. IDC reported that in 2009, $17 billion was spent on cloud computing IT, compared to $359 billion on non-cloud IT expenditures. In 2013, the firm forecasts $44 billion in cloud spending and $416 billion in non-cloud.

10) Wi-Fi Accelerates

While cellular phone companies are investing billions of dollars in technologies to give their subscribers enhanced services such as 3G and 4G mobile Internet access, new technologies have caught on that offer wireless Internet alternatives. Wi-Fi, short for "wireless fidelity" and sometimes referred to as WLAN (wireless local area network), has become a vital wireless tool throughout much of the world.

Wi-Fi offers a wireless connection at speeds of up to 54 megabits per second (Mbps), nearly 1,000 times the speed of dial-up and much faster than cellular phones. On the fixed end, each network is tied into an Internet connection that can be very high-speed. Wi-Fi enabled devices, like notebook computers or PDAs, provide mobile access to the Internet and therefore to information, entertainment and e-mail, and VOIP telephony. Wi-Fi networks are easy and inexpensive to set up. The signal utilizes public domain, unlicensed radio spectrum. Operators typically build them in high-traffic areas, such as coffee shops, fast food restaurants, airports, hotels, bookstores, shopping malls and other public places. For example, Starbucks coffee shops offer Wi-Fi connections. Select McDonald's restaurants offer Wi-Fi, and thousands of leading hotels provide Wi-Fi to guests. AT&T, Inc. now operates more than 125,000 hotspots around the globe.

Many consumers are finding Wi-Fi a convenient way to access the Internet from multiple points throughout their homes, and organizations are also using Wi-Fi to connect their networks as an alternative to, or in addition to, their wired local area networks. For example, students on the Dartmouth College campus utilize Wi-Fi access from any place at the school—dorm rooms, the student union, the library or even outside on the lawn. The Dartmouth Wi-Fi network (one of the first on college campuses) consists of hundreds of antennas placed in more than 150 buildings. The college relies on the system for telephone, intercom, video surveillance, on-campus cable TV programming and control of thermostats.

However, Wi-Fi technology does have its problems. Wi-Fi networks typically have a very limited local range (typically about 150 feet) and do not usually offer the far-reaching, roaming mobility of cellular phone connections. (On the other hand, a network of closely spaced Wi-Fi systems could efficiently offer mobile phone service in a limited area, such as a densely populated downtown.) In a noteworthy breakthrough in 2008, Intel created a longer-range Wi-Fi network by modifying a router's software so that signals can travel up to about 62 miles (100 kilometers). The Rural Connectivity Platform coordinates sending and receiving antennas, scheduling time slots for signals when coming or going. By 2010, inexpensive adapters were available from a number of manufacturers that help extend Wi-Fi ranges to as much as 1,000 feet.

In technical terms, Wi-Fi is described according to its range and speed. Common types of Wi-Fi include 802.11b and the faster 802.11g, but several other specifications exist. (The numbers refer to specifications set by the global engineering organization Institute of Electrical and Electronics Engineers, or IEEE.) Some Wi-Fi specifications offer higher speeds or other advantages. Semiconductor manufacturers are building chips that can communicate at different frequencies, making them able to connect to various levels of Wi-Fi networks.

Many telephone equipment manufacturers are focused on new technologies that allow consumers' phones to automatically switch between VOIP via Wi-Fi, at home or at the office, and cellular when away from home base, much in the same way that many cellular phones currently switch between digital and analog service. This is becoming especially useful in corporate environments where office workers can use their cellphones on both cellular networks and office Wi-Fi networks. Landline phones could be eliminated, which would be a boon for wireless firms such as T-Mobile USA and Verizon, but a potential problem for traditional telecom firms since it would negatively impact the landline business. Wi-Fi in the workplace is a growing market, spurring startups such as SpiderCloud Wireless, Inc., a Silicon Valley hardware manufacturer that has developed technology to better manage Wi-Fi systems for higher performance. ABI Research estimated global revenue from in-building wireless installations would reach more than $6 billion in 2010, up from approximately $2.2 billion in 2005.

Computer manufacturers and makers of digital devices of all types are now making Wi-Fi antennas standard equipment on items such as notebook computers. These devices can alert their owners when they come within range of a Wi-Fi network (a "hotspot"). The owner can then log in and go online. While some networks are offered as a free service, many others require a fee of some sort.

One of the most aggressive builders of Wi-Fi networks is Boingo (www.boingo.com). Charging $9.95 monthly for unlimited connect time, the firm is developing a system of thousands of such networks worldwide. As of early 2010, Boingo had negotiated over 125,000 locations around the world for its wireless connection service. The firm's locations include more than 500 airports, hotels, restaurants and other places, such as convention centers.

Spanish startup FON has built one of the largest Wi-Fi networks in the world by encouraging its subscribers to purchase a $40 router or install FON software on their existing cable modems. Once done, "FONero" households are part of a network of more than 1.5 million registered members as of early 2010. FON joined with mobile software development firm JoikuSpot to offer Wi-Fi hotspot software for mobile phones called FonSpot. The software enables a laptop or other Wi-Fi device to connect to the Internet using a compatible mobile phone as a secure Internet gateway.

11) WiMAX Extends Wireless Range Far Beyond Wi-Fi

A standard known as Worldwide Interoperability for Microwave Access, or WiMAX (802.16), is adding considerable fuel to the wireless fire. WiMAX has the capability to deliver extremely fast Internet connections to wireless devices, such as notebooks and mobile VOIP telephones, with each WiMAX antenna having about a 30-mile theoretical maximum broadcast range, but practical ranges will be shorter, particularly for mobile use. Theoretical WiMAX speeds can reach up to 144 Mbps, but initial industry commercial goals are for 15 Mbps speed for mobile devices and 40 Mbps for fixed devices. Due to its long range, WiMAX has tremendous potential as an alternative to traditional cellular telephone service. WiMAX also makes sense for delivery of intelligent transportation systems (ITS) to cars and trucks as they travel down the highway, if mobile WiMAX can be perfected. ITS has the potential to provide a wide range of communications and services to motorists, such as alerting drivers to traffic congestion, accidents, construction and other obstacles ahead and enabling drivers to find restaurants, hotels, rest areas, filling stations and other possible stops.

For WiMAX to move ahead, technical standards had to be set and adopted. The IEEE 802.16e Mobile WirelessMAN Standard for metropolitan area networks became official in December 2005, opening the door for the deployment of WiMAX networks the world over. Also, the European Commission Decision 2008 set another milestone when it stipulated that 3400 to 3800 MHz frequencies be used for WiMAX in Europe. It requires European Member States to move rapidly to make the spectrum range available for use for fixed, nomadic and mobile electronic communications networks. In addition, the security issues of this long-range system must be met. The fact that hackers could sit miles away from a

target is a looming problem. Finally, there is the issue of licensing. While Wi-Fi uses unlicensed radio spectrum, WiMAX uses licensed spectrum. The costs and regulatory issues involved in setting up WiMAX systems will be a barrier to entry, requiring more sophisticated startup efforts than Wi-Fi.

In November 2005, 13 carriers worldwide deployed the first fixed WiMAX networks in countries such as France, Mexico, Finland, Ukraine and Guatemala. Intel introduced its first WiMAX PC cards in late 2006, which enable notebook computers to connect with WiMAX networks. In May 2007, Sprint Nextel announced a plan to build a mobile WiMAX network large enough to serve 100 million users. The WiMAX Forum reported in 2009 that the Mobile WirelessMAN standard was being deployed in more than 135 countries by more than 460 operators.

WiMAX hit a milestone in 2008 when Clearwire Communications and Sprint Nextel agreed to combine their wireless broadband businesses. The company, now called Clearwire Corporation (www.clear.com), amassed funding from Intel, Google, Comcast, Time Warner Cable and Bright House Networks to develop nationwide mobile WiMAX networks. Comcast and other partners invested billions of dollars in Clearwire in recent years. In 2009, the firm extended its "Clear" network to over two dozen additional markets across the U.S.; the company hoped to cover 120 million people with this network by the end of 2010. By 2017, Clearwire hopes to be generating $17.5 billion in annual revenues.

Clearwire describes its Clear service as a "4G mobile Internet wireless network." In early 2011, packages that offered a combination of fixed and mobile access were available for $60 monthly. Base home Internet service is available for $35 monthly. At these prices, Clear may prove to be highly competitive with other forms of broadband, particularly if service quality is good.

> **Internet Research Tip: WiMAX Forum**
> For the latest information on WiMAX, see the WiMAX Forum, www.wimaxforum.org.

Comcast offers two "Internet 2go" plans. They utilize a combination of Comcast's 12 Mbps cable system, Clearwire's network and Sprint Nextel's 3G or 4G network where Clearwire is not available. A 3G package is available starting at $25 per month with a 12-month contract, and 4G service is available starting at $40 per month with a 12-month contract.

The service was initially launched in Portland, Oregon, with a growing list of cities across the U.S. as of early 2011. This pricing may prove irresistible to users who are currently paying separate bills for home Internet access from one provider and mobile Internet access for their laptops or netbooks from another. The savings could be significant.

Meanwhile, WiMAX faces significant competition from another advanced wireless technology, long term evolution (LTE). Clearwire is keeping its options open. In mid-2010, it announced that it had revised its agreement with Intel, which owns a significant investment in Clearwire, whereby Clearwire became free to include LTE in its 4G network. This enables Clearwire to rent space on its network to other operators who might prefer LTE over WiMAX.

Meraki and Do-it-Yourself Mesh Networks for the Masses

A mesh network uses multiple Wi-Fi repeaters or "nodes" to deploy a wireless Internet access network. Typically, a mesh network is operated by the users themselves. Each user installs a node at his or her locale, and plugs the node into his or her local Internet access, whether DSL, cable or satellite. Other users within the mesh can access all other nodes as needed, or as they travel about. A mesh network can provide access to an apartment complex, an office building, a campus or an entire city. As of early 2011, the firm provided network services to more than 15,000 organizations in excess of 140 countries. Meraki is a leading node brand in this sector, www.meraki.com.

---

12) MIMO (802.11n) Enhances WiMAX, the High-Speed Wireless Wave

Wi-Fi has been a popular method of setting up wireless computer networks, not only in the home, but also in office and institutional environments. However, Wi-Fi standards to date may not offer the data transfer speeds required by network managers. The major leap in wireless technology is 802.11n (Multiple Input Multiple Output antenna technology—also known as "MIMO"). It has the potential to provide theoretical data transfer speeds as high as 500 Mbps (although hardware manufacturers say that practical speeds will likely average around 150 Mbps). This high speed means that MIMO could compete with traditional LANs, offering a true wireless alternative to wired local area networks in the office environment. 802.11n also boasts better operating distances than current Wi-Fi networks.

MIMO uses spectrum more efficiently without any loss of reliability. The technology is based on several different antennas all tuned to the same channel, each transmitting a different signal. Industry standards and technical specifications for MIMO were tentatively set by the IEEE as of June 2006, and were quickly adopted by pioneer chip makers including Broadcom Corp., Marvell Technology Group Ltd. and Atheros Communications, Inc.

In June 2008, big news rocked the wireless world when the WiMAX Forum announced official certification for several products using MIMO in the 2.5 GHz band. This band is important for numerous reasons, including the fact that WiMAX network pioneer Clearwire used this spectrum for its nationwide rollout. By late 2008, the WiMAX Forum began testing products for certification in the 3.5 GHz band. The Forum further reported that more than 100 products using WiMAX were certified by the end of 2008, with another 99 certified in 2009. The WiMAX Forum projected that by the end of 2010, more than 800 million people worldwide would have access to next-generation WiMAX networks. By 2011, the Forum hoped to have more than 1,000 certified mobile WiMAX products available around the world.

13) Bluetooth Provides Wireless Connectivity to Millions of Cellphones and Other Devices

Bluetooth is a wireless technology aimed at enabling a host of different devices, such as desktop PCs, notebooks, PDAs, printers and cameras, to communicate effortlessly with one another, without the need for cables or setting up network protocols. While limited in range to only about 30 feet (compared to Wi-Fi's 150 feet), Bluetooth is particularly useful for enabling personal electronics to communicate with each other or with PCs. Bluetooth requires little power and is therefore excellent for use in battery-powered devices such as cellphones. Analysts estimate that there are more than 1 billion Bluetooth-enabled devices in the world, with another 13 million sold each week.

Internet Research Tip: Bluetooth

The Bluetooth Special Interest Group, (www.bluetooth.com) is an organization consisting of thousands of manufacturers that are currently using Bluetooth or that plan to use it in the near future.

In addition to short range, the development of Bluetooth usage is regulated by its speed limitations.

First-generation Bluetooth transmits data at speeds up to one megabit per second (Mbps). The latest generation transmits at speeds up to three Mbps. However, Bluetooth remains vastly slower than rival Ultrawideband.

Complex devices that use a combination of Bluetooth with UWB or Wi-Fi have become common. The extremely popular Nintendo Wii game playing console utilizes a Bluetooth chip manufactured by Broadcom in its remote control unit, while utilizing Wi-Fi to enable the Wii to surf the Internet and to interact with other game players online. Also, delivery giant UPS uses tens of thousands of scanner/data capture devices that utilize a combination of Bluetooth and Wi-Fi. These hand-held scanners are used in UPS package sorting facilities worldwide. The Bluetooth segment enables a lightweight, handheld scanning wand to communicate to a mobile data capture computer worn by a worker. The data capture device uses Wi-Fi to transfer data to the facility's computer network.

Currently, the most conspicuous use of Bluetooth is in wireless headsets worn by cellular phone users. Other popular uses include communication from wireless PC keyboards and mice to PCs, from MP3 music players to wireless headphones, as well as from notebook computers and other portable devices to printers. Bluetooth is also widely used in new automobiles as a way for cellphones, iPods and other devices to connect with communication and entertainment systems built into dashboards. Other uses within the automobile include communication between notebooks and mobile Internet access systems, and even car-to-car communication is possible between nearby automobiles.

Bluetooth 3.0 was launched in April 2009. It exponentially increased data transmission speeds. Operating in the 6 to 9 GHz range, version 3.0 is hoped to eliminate concerns of interference from wireless networks and other devices as found in the 2.4 GHz range used by Bluetooth 2.0. Data transfer speeds may reach as high as 50 Mbps at very close range, and 12.5 Mbps at 10 meters range. This means that very fast streaming video and other advanced applications will be possible.

In mid-2010, Bluetooth 4.0 was officially adopted by the Bluetooth Special Interest Group (SIG), effectively giving manufacturers the green light to use the new technology. The new, low-energy version offers ultra-low peak, average and idle mode power consumption and has the ability to run for years on standard coin-cell batteries. Analysts at West Technology Research Solutions

anticipate that 4.0 will be utilized in almost half of all wireless sensor network (WSN) devices in 2015.

Sony is focusing on an advanced Bluetooth technology that it dubs TransferJet, with transfer speeds that were hoped to reach 560 Mbps (in early 2010, Sony launched the first laptop with TransferJet that offered speeds of only 40 Mbps). Sony's TransferJet-equipped devices can communicate with each other simply by being a little more than an inch apart. The Japanese firm heads the TransferJet Consortium, which consisted of 18 companies as of early 2010, including Casio Computer Co., JVC Kenwood Holdings, Nikon Corporation, NTT DoCoMo, Inc. and Toshiba Corporation. The organization's mission is to set specifications for conformance and interoperability so that the technology can be commercialized.

New developments using Bluetooth are launched continually. At the 2011 Consumer Electronics Show (CES) in Las Vegas, a $3,700, 65" 3D TV made by Vizio was named the best Bluetooth device due to the clear connection between viewer's 3D glasses and the set.

14) Ultrawideband (UWB) Offers Sizzling Short-Range Speed

Ultrawideband (UWB) is a means of low-power, short-range wireless data transmission with extremely high-speed potential. Originally, UWB was developed for military purposes. Today, in the business and consumer arena, it can take advantage of bandwidth set aside by the FCC in 2002. UWB encodes signals in a dramatically different way, sending digital pulses in a relatively secure manner that will not interfere with other wireless systems that may be operating nearby. It has the potential to deliver very large amounts of data to a distance of about 230 feet, even through doors and other obstacles, and requires very little power. Speeds are scalable from approximately 50 Mbps to 2Gbps. UWB works on the 802.15.3 IEEE specification.

Prototypes of UWB-enabled devices were displayed first at the 2005 Consumer Electronics Show in Las Vegas and at other early 2005 trade conferences. Chipmakers Intel and Freescale Semiconductor, formerly part of Motorola, were early competitors in this field. UWB-enabled products have been slowly entering the market. Samsung launched a UWB phone for VOIP in 2006. Eventually, personal devices such as cellphones and MP3 music players with UWB capabilities may be on the market in large quantity.

The WiMedia Alliance (www.wimedia.org) published its own WiMedia UWB specifications, and it certified several UWB-enabled platforms, thereby enhancing the ability of manufacturers to incorporate UWB into their products. (In 2009, the WiMedia Alliance handed off UWB specification development to the Bluetooth Special Interest Group, the Wireless USB Promoter Group and the USB Implementers forum.) In 2010, the WiMedia Alliance launched Version 1.5 of its WiMedia Common Radio Platform Specification, which increases download speeds to 1,024 Mbps from 480 Mbps. The upgrade targets the needs of streaming video, which is the current focus of the Alliance.

There is much promise for the eventual use of UWB. It offers vastly faster speeds than Bluetooth 1.0 and Bluetooth 2.0, a wireless connection method that is already in wide use. However, Bluetooth 3.0 is so fast that it is proving to be serious competition to UWB. Nonetheless, UWB is so fast that it could become a favorite within the home or office for wireless transmission of such data as streaming video or stored TV programming. It could potentially transfer an entire feature-length movie in MPEG-4 format from a media center PC to a portable device in a few seconds. While UWB devices may seem pricey at first, rapidly increasing volume will lower prices over a short period of time. Wisair, Multispectral Solutions Inc. (a unit of Zebra Enterprise Solutions), OMRON and MeshDynamics were among firms already offering chipsets based on UWB as early as 2007.

It should be noted that wireless USB (Universal Serial Bus) platforms are also being developed with the goal of replacing wired connections to USB ports. Intel and other leading manufacturers are involved in this effort. This technology is sometimes referred to as W-USB.

15)   Broadband Market Nears 1 Billion Users

By late 2010, broadband connections in the U.S. reached an estimated 100 million homes and businesses by wireline (DSL), satellite or cable, according to Plunkett Research estimates. Fueling this growth has been intense price competition between cable and DSL providers, with monthly service now starting as low as $12.99 (for new customers for the first year) in some markets. The Internet is now reaching a vast U.S. market.

In addition, approximately 75 million mobile wireless subscriptions enabled customers to reach the Internet via their cellphones, iPads and other mobile devices in the U.S. Big improvements in the devices,

such as iPhones, and access, such as 3G, 4G and Clear's WiMax networks, are fueling this growth. In addition, most major e-commerce, news and entertainment sites have carefully designed their web pages to perform reasonably well on the "third screen," that is, cellphones.

Globally, industry observers estimated the number of broadband users at about 750 million by the end of 2010, and that number will soon exceed 1 billion. Much of that growth is being fueled by 3G cellphone services in major markets in Europe and Asia.

While the era of declining access costs is largely over, Internet access speeds continue to increase dramatically. In America, for example, as of early 2010 AT&T was offering 6 Mbps download speed and about 1 Mbps upload starting at $29.95 per month for its Elite service. (There are also packages with slower speeds that cost as little as $19.95 per month.) Cablevision offered sizzling 30 Mbps download and 5 Mbps upload at reasonable prices. Comcast offered 20 Mbps downloads with 4 Mbps uploads at $57.95 monthly under the PowerBoost Blast! plan. Verizon's FiOS plan offered excellent speed to price ratios, with a 15 Mbps download and 5 Mbps upload package starting at $49.99 monthly. FiOS's fastest packages offer 50 Mbps download and 20 Mbps upload. As of 2010, all the leading cable companies in America have their sights on utilizing new cable technology called Docsis 3.0 (Data Over Cable Service Interface Specifications) to offer download speeds of up to 100 Mbps, potentially rising to 160 Mbps and perhaps even 250 Mbps in the future). This is fast enough to enable a household to download a full-length HD movie in a couple of minutes.

While the adoption of broadband by Americans has reached major proportions, the FCC estimates that about 4% of U.S. homes do not have access to fast Internet service, primarily because they live in rural locations where DSL or cable are not available. There are additional problems in U.S. broadband distribution. While it is challenging to make an objective comparison of broadband availability from one nation to the next, America consistently ranks poorly in such studies. A study released in October 2009, funded by Cisco and conducted by the Said Business School at the University of Oxford in conjunction with the Universidad de Oviedo, ranked the United States 15th, behind Lithuania, in "Broadband Leadership." The study evaluated such metrics as percent of households with broadband and broadband quality.

In March 2010, FCC chairman Julius Genachowski published a proposal, the *National Broadband Plan*. He not only proposes to solve the problems of rural Internet access, he also has a plan called "100 Squared." His thought is to increase Internet services in America so that 100 million homes would enjoy 100 megabit download speed and 50 megabit upload speed by 2020 (compared to an average of about 3 or 4 megabits broadband download speed, and relatively slow upload speed, as of 2009). Docsis 3.0 will be the door to that future, and cable currently is the leader. The DSL providers will be scrambling to catch up.

What will widespread use of fast Internet access mean to consumers? The opportunities for new or enhanced products and services are endless, and the amount of entertainment, news, commerce and personal services designed to take advantage of broadband will continue to grow rapidly. For example, education support and classes via broadband is rapidly growing into a major industry. The most telling statistic may be the long-term rapid growth of the University of Phoenix and the other schools owned by Phoenix-based Apollo Group, Inc. While courses are also taught in person by this firm, it is largely an institution of online learning, and its enrollment by 2009 had grown to 420,000 students. Meanwhile, online learning has become mainstream throughout much of higher education. In *Online Nation: Five Years of Growth in Online Learning,* authors I.E. Allen and J. Seaman found that 19.8% (3.48 million) of college and vocational school students throughout America took at least one college course online in 2006. The National Alliance for Public Charter Schools reports there were 217 virtual charter schools in the U.S. in the 2009-10 school year, plus 132 hybrid virtual/brick and mortar charter schools.

Broadband in the home is essential for everyday activities ranging from children's homework to shopping to managing financial accounts, from renewing a driver's license to filing an insurance claim. Online entertainment and information options, already vast, will grow daily. Some online services will seem indispensable, and always-on will become the accepted standard. The quality of streaming video and audio will be clear and reliable, making music and movie downloads extremely fast, and allowing Internet telephone users to see their parties on the other end as if they were in the same room. Consumers will accept pay-per-view or pay-per-use service offerings because of their convenience and moderate cost. A significant portion of today's radio,

television and movie entertainment will migrate to the web.

> **Plunkett's Law of Convergence:**
> Online consumer usage grows exponentially as broadband access prices decline and more and more Internet devices are adopted—fixed and mobile. This increases demand for new online products and leads to increased offerings of high-value online services and entertainment at reasonable prices.

16) Fiber-to-the-Home Gains Traction

The major telephone firms are looking for ways to increase revenues through enhanced services while retaining their customer bases. One such way is through the delivery of ultra-high-speed Internet access, combined with enhanced entertainment and telephone options, by installing true fiber-to-the-home (FTTH) networks.

Under traditional service, homes are served by copper wires, which are limited to relatively slow service. However, old-fashioned copper networks are not up to the demands of today's always-on Internet consumers. Fiber-optic cable might be used in trunk lines to connect regions and cities to each other at the switch and network level, but speed drops significantly once the service hits local copper lines.

Things are much more advanced in major markets today. In AT&T's project, fiber is being brought into special hubs in existing neighborhoods. From those hubs, enhanced services are delivered into the home with advanced technologies on short, final runs of copper wire. Speeds can reach nearly 25 Mbps in many markets.

FTTH, in contrast, delivers fiber-optic cable all the way from the network to the local switch directly to the living room—with this system, Internet delivery speeds and the types of entertainment and data delivered can be astounding.

In 2005, Verizon announced a $23 billion, multi-year FTTH program that would make it the U.S. leader in FTTH. Verizon's FTTH (called FiOS) promises exceptional speeds, with 50 Mbps download speed now available in some areas. In November 2007, Verizon announced that it had increased the maximum upload speeds for FiOS to 20 Mbps. By 2010, Verizon had already passed 15.4 million homes and offices with FiOS capability. FiOS Internet access subscriptions totaled more than 3.88 million in 2010 (with 3.3 million of them utilizing FiOS television service as well as Internet access).

AT&T is also investing heavily in fiber. It has a network construction program underway that promises to pass fiber-optic cable close to 18 million U.S. homes over the midterm.

The Fiber-to-the-Home Council (www.ftthcouncil.org) tracks FTTH trends. According to the FTTH Councils of Asia-Pacific, Europe and North America, there were more than 6 million U.S. households with fiber to the home in 2010, up from 1.01 million connections in September 2006.

In many cases, FTTH has been provided by local government or by subdivision developers who are determined to provide leading-edge connectivity as a value-added feature to new homes. The council's analysis showed extremely high participation rates among residents who had very high-speed broadband available to them. Generally, residents are subscribing to advanced services at a rate of 40% to 75%. A good example of a connected community is Jackson, Tennessee. There, the local energy authority (JEA) built a 658-mile fiber-optic network that serves 26,000 homes.

FTTH technologies, though expensive, may save the Bells from being trampled by the cable companies. Fiber-optic networks can give consumers extremely fast Internet connections. Such ultra-high-speeds will also allow consumers to download movies in seconds and make videoconferencing a meaningful reality for businesses. (Additional fiber terms used in the industry include FTTP for Fiber-to-the-premises and FTTO for fiber-to-the-office.)

FTTH has been far more widely adopted in South Korea, Hong Kong, Japan and Taiwan. Collectively, they accounted for more than 38.9 million of the world's roughly 50 million fiber-to-the-home connections as of mid-2010, according to the FTTH Councils of Asia-Pacific, Europe and North America. Specifically, South Korea had almost 54% of its households connected to fiber, Japan almost 36%, Hong Kong 34% and Taiwan at 25%. The U.S. ranked 10th in the world, almost 7% market penetration behind several Scandinavian nations.

17) Multimedia Hub Homes Slowly Become a Reality/TVs Are Internet Ready

Computer software and hardware companies have growing stakes in entertainment, and consumers are keenly interested in using a home PC to control all of a household's entertainment. Microsoft has spent many years and billions of dollars on the development of its home entertainment strategy, resulting in its Windows Media Center applications.

The software, combined with appropriate PCs, plays and records television shows, manages music video and personal photo files, plays music files and burns CDs and DVDs, which can all be done by remote control with the right equipment. Today's version, which is part of the Windows 7 operating system, includes Internet radio among its many other entertainment features.

Designing computers to serve as electronic hubs of digital homes, routing music, movies, TV programming, e-mail and news between the web and PCs, television set-top boxes, stereo speakers and other gadgets, has long been the goal of Microsoft, as well as Sony, HP, Apple and Digeo (which was acquired by Arris Group, Inc. in 2009) to name a few. Intel is also at the forefront of PC-controlled home entertainment, investing in ever-more-powerful chips capable of generating high-definition video images suitable for many video uses, including cutting-edge projection TVs. In 2010, Intel launched Wireless Display Technology, or "WiDi," which eliminates the need for connecting cables between PCs and TVs.

Home entertainment centers now connect components such as TVs, sound systems, cable or satellite set-top boxes and, increasingly, PCs. On the fixed end, a home's network is tied to an Internet connection. Internet access for advanced entertainment is delivered by the consumer's choice of DSL, cable modem or satellite dish. The faster the download speed the better. In an increasing number of new neighborhoods, access is achieved by true fiber-to-the-home (FTTH) networks capable of delivery at blazing speeds, enabling such media as video-on-demand and interactive TV. Verizon, Comcast and AT&T are among the leaders in this field in the U.S.

Home entertainment networks are likely to include Wi-Fi. An additional option is ultrawideband (UWB) wireless, which can be used to beam data at up to 480 megabits per second across distances of up to 30 feet. UWB makes it possible to place that new plasma TV on a wall that doesn't have a cable outlet. UWB combined with coax has the potential to complete the multimedia home, making it possible to enjoy entertainment literally anywhere in the house—even in the backyard. Yet another approach is HomePlug technology, which relies on a home's existing electrical outlets and wiring to distribute digital signals and Internet access. An "AV2" specification for HomePlug is expected in 2011, which may offer high speeds based on MIMO technology to improve performance.

Until recently, Microsoft's Media Center software claimed only a small percentage of the home computer market, as many consumers initially refused to watch video programming on computer monitors. Today, the latest operating system and improved monitors offer significantly enhanced TV quality, compatible with hardware featuring multiple TV tuners that receive up to three signals. Microsoft's Windows 7 continues to offer enhancements. Viewers can watch one program while recording another. The greatest breakthrough, however, is the release of the Media Center Extender, utilizing home Wi-Fi systems, as the missing link that beams content from a PC to TVs in up to five additional rooms. For U.S. customers, the Windows 7 version includes support for digital cable service. In addition, Windows Media Center enables users to archive their favorite programs to video DVDs, and the system is optimized for HD and widescreen environments.

Computer industry giants, including Dell and Hewlett-Packard, have been quick to join the party with their own versions of Media Center PC hardware. Competitors include Alienware (see www.alienware.com) and Niveus Media.

Apple, Inc. has a secure place in the home media center arena thanks to its industry-changing iPod. Apple is hoping to have the same success with Apple TV. The moderately priced (reduced to $99 from its first release $229) Apple TV unit acts as an interface between a consumer's television, computer and iPod or other Apple devices. For example, Apple TV sends digital entertainment that is stored on your computer directly to your TV. This is becoming increasingly important since widescreen home TVs are now standard equipment in many living rooms, and these widescreens are vastly superior to computer monitors for watching videos. Also, the Apple TV unit sends home videos, movies, TV shows and photos from your iPods to TVs. The new cheaper unit relies on streaming movies and TV shows available for rent via Apple's iTunes store, with TV episodes available from Fox, ABC, ABC Family, Disney Channel and BBC America for 99 cents each and movie rentals for $4.99 each. The company also has an agreement with Netflix, enabling its subscribers to view content from its library of titles. Apple expected to top 1 million in unit sales by the end of 2010.

Entertainment-Enabled Macs and PCs

Consumers now have the ability to manage virtually all of their home entertainment options via personal computer or Apple's Macintosh computers. For example, Microsoft's Windows Media Center running on a fully featured entertainment PC from makers such as Dell or Sony can offer:

- Television access, which can be connected to cable, antenna or satellite
- Electronic games
- Internet access
- Communication, including VOIP telephony and e-mail
- DVR (digital video recording of TV programs)
- Music recording, storage and management in formats such as MP3 or WMA, as well as conversion of music CDs into MP3 files
- Recording and playing of CDs and DVDs
- Multiple picture frames on one screen
- Digital photography management, including editing of still and video
- Integration with a wireless home network
- Internet-based radio

As of 2010, growing numbers of televisions were built with Internet connectivity. Research firm iSuppli estimated that more than 25% of HDTVs shipped in 2010 would be Internet-ready. Previously, TVs had to connect to the web via game consoles, PCs or specialized boxes such as those offered by Roku (www.roku.com) or Vudu (www.vudu.com). This trend will accelerate quickly.

This brings up an important question: where will TV viewers of the future get their programming? Cable and satellite subscriptions are expensive. Broadcast TV is free, as is a lot of Internet-based programming, although online content is likely to become more and more subscription supported. At the same time, online delivery of rented movies is now mainstream, led by technology at Netflix, with competition from iTunes, Hulu.com (with its HuluPlus subscription service) and many other sites.

18)   Information Technology and Health Care

According to the Pew Internet & American Life Project, 79% of Internet users in the U.S. search for health care information. Studies by other firms have shown that nearly one-half of people seeking online health information do so to research information on a specific disease, while many others are interested in educational services, prescription drug information, fitness and alternative medicine. About 90% of those who searched for health care information online indicated that what they found seemed reliable.

Internet Research Tip:
According to The Medical Library Association (www.mlanet.org), the top 10 most useful web sites for health care information are:
National Cancer Institute, www.cancer.gov
Centers for Disease Control and Prevention (CDC), www.cdc.gov
FamilyDoctor.org, www.familydoctor.org
Health Finder, www.healthfinder.gov , a service of the U.S. Dept. of Health & Human Services
HIV InSite, http://hivinsite.ucsf.edu
KidsHealth, www.kidshealth.org
Mayo Clinic, www.mayoclinic.com
MEDLINEplus, www.nlm.gov/medlineplus
NIH SeniorHealth, http://nihseniorhealth.gov
NOAH: New York Online Access to Health, www.noah-health.org

Internet Research Tip—Checking a Web Site's Accuracy Rating:
When researching health care web sites, look for the seal of approval from the Health on the Net Foundation (www.hon.ch), a nonprofit organization based in Geneva, Switzerland. Founded in 1995 at the behest of international medical experts, the foundation approves medical web sites that meet or exceed its guidelines.

The Internet is also radically transforming the relationship between doctor and patient, since patients can obtain information previously not available from traditional resources. Consumers are now demanding the information necessary to help them make educated decisions regarding medical care. The Internet has allowed patients to walk into their doctors' offices with information in their hands that doctors didn't know about or simply wouldn't supply in the past. Patients can obtain straightforward information from the Internet about their diseases. This empowerment forces physicians to treat the patient more like a partner. It is a fundamental shift of knowledge from physician to patient. E-mail discussions between patient and doctor are growing in popularity. Blue Cross Blue Shield of Florida is offering thousands of physicians the option to be paid for consulting with patients online, via a secure web site.

Internet Research Tip—Getting Hospital Ratings Online:
Patients and concerned family members can now use any of several web sites to check on the quality of hospitals before checking in for treatment. Available data typically includes patient outcomes, fees and whether the latest in technology is available. For patients needing specialized care, this knowledge can be a real windfall. WebMD Health Services, at www.webmdhealthservices.com, (formerly Subimo) gets high marks for its ease of use. It sells subscriptions to major employers and health plans, whose members can then log in. Other sites include HealthGrades, www.healthgrades.com, Medicare's Hospital Compare at www.hospitalcompare.hhs.gov and United Healthcare's www.myUHC.com, designed to be used by the millions of patients who are covered by United's health plans.

Useful Internet sites can aid patients in finding a specialist, checking to see how a local hospital measures up and obtaining information about prescription drugs. For example, the American Medical Association offers a searchable database called DoctorFinder (https://extapps.ama-assn.org/doctorfinder/recaptcha.do) with information on doctors' educations and specialties. RxList (www.rxlist.com) allows visitors to search for a drug by generic or brand name, learn about its potential side effects, become familiar with warnings and read about clinical studies. One of the most promising health care sites is Medscape.com (www.medscape.com), where consumers can access information on topics ranging from AIDS to women's health.

The Internet is also becoming a source of information for health care insurance matters. SmartMedicalConsumer (www.smartmedicalconsumer.com) is a free tool offered by SmartMC LLC that organizes medical bills into summaries that flag billing errors and make working with insurance companies easier.

In addition, the Internet is becoming a useful tool for medical professionals. For example, a surgeon can obtain clinical information relevant to surgical practice, both from general professional sites and through specialty and sub-specialty sites. The surgeon can also follow links to other sites offering information on updated techniques or research and educational opportunities. Online discussion groups are growing in popularity; these forums are useful for physicians with similar interests who wish to share information. Another exciting development is live surgeries that can be viewed via webcams. Surgeons and students all over the world can watch and learn from surgical procedures from the comfort of their own homes or offices.

A promising service for diabetics has been developed through the combined efforts of the American Diabetes Association and the insurance group Kaiser Permanente. Together they launched a web site for people with diabetes that suggests customized treatment plans. It is based on a complex software program, developed at a cost of several million dollars, that models health care outcomes based on specified criteria such as medication, diet, demographics and exercise. The software accesses a massive database containing years of patient data. The web site, Diabetes PHD, www.diabetes.org/living-with-diabetes/complications/diabetes-phd/, could prove a model for web sites for dozens of other diseases and the patients who suffer from them.

Another Internet innovation that assists diabetes patients is the ability for physicians to monitor glucose levels online. Medem, Inc. launched an online service that saves diabetes patients from multiple office visits to check blood-glucose levels, while giving physicians the ability to evaluate patients' blood sugar levels more frequently. The tool links patients' glucose meters to their computers, then transmits information from those meters to a secure server via the Internet. The firm also offers the Health Care Notification Network (HCNN) that delivers urgent patient alerts such as medication and device recalls, warnings and label changes to health care providers online.

Physicians are increasingly turning to the Internet to prescribe medications. Surescripts, LLC, a consortium that runs an electronic prescription network, claims that there were 191 million e-prescriptions made in 2009, up from 2008's 68 million and about 12% of 2009's 1.63 billion original prescriptions, excluding refills. Prescriptions are transmitted through secured Internet networks directly to pharmacies. Surescripts estimates that about 62% of independent drug stores and almost all pharmacy chains are equipped to receive and process e-prescriptions. The software and hardware necessary to outfit a doctor's office to submit prescriptions this way runs about $1,000 to $1,750 per doctor. The programs available to doctors not only list available medications (including prices and the availability of generics), they also flag potential problems with other medications the patient may already be taking. The Center for Medicare and

Medicaid Services (CMS) pays participating doctors a bonus and will begin penalizing physicians who do not adopt e-prescriptions starting in 2012.

RFID Inventory Systems: RFID (radio frequency identification) will be a huge breakthrough in hospital inventory management. RFID systems are based on the placement of microchips in product packaging. These chips, continuously broadcasting product identification data, are used with special sensors in handheld devices or on shelves that alert a central inventory management system about product usage and the need to restock inventory. From loading docks to stockroom shelves to the hospital floor, radio frequency readers will wirelessly track the movement of each and every item, replacing bar codes. These systems will lead to fewer out-of-stock situations and the elimination of costly manual inventory counts.

Johns Hopkins hospital adopted RFID in order to track bags of intravenous fluid, one of the thousands of possible applications that could save the medical industry much of the estimated $75 billion a year currently lost due to mistakes in the prescription, storage and delivery of drugs. RFID chips and the scanners that look after them are rapidly becoming smaller and cheaper and will be steadily adopted for more and more items in hospitals and pharmacies as costs fall. Beyond the monetary savings through better inventory control, RFID systems could save some of the many people who die every year due to errors in prescription drug delivery.

RFID tags implanted in the wristbands worn by hospital patients will also reduce patient identification mistakes, thereby reducing instances of errors in treatment. Data gathered electronically from RFID systems will be integrated with enterprise-wide computer systems throughout the hospital.

The U.S. pharmaceutical industry, with the cooperation of the FDA, began voluntary use of RFID tags on containers of prescription drugs in 2005. The FDA is relying on a nonprofit group, GS1 (formerly EPCglobal, www.gs1.org), in Lawrenceville, New Jersey, to set standards for the tags, which have the potential to cut down on stolen drugs, counterfeiting of drugs, drug-related fraud and the dispensing of the wrong drugs. If early use of these tags proves satisfactory, use on all drug containers could become mandatory over the mid-term.

Advanced Information Technology and Medical Records Technology: There is a strong movement in the United States, the U.K., Canada and elsewhere to implement widespread use of electronic health records (EHRs). A major goal in this movement is to create Continuity of Care Records (CCRs), which would ensure that a patient's health history could be utilized seamlessly by hospitals, primary care physicians and specialists.

In 2009, the U.S. federal government authorized a $787 billion economic stimulus bill which included $19 billion to be spent by hospitals and physicians on the installation of EHRs. Hospitals will receive up to several million, depending upon their size, while individual physicians can receive up to $44,000. A 500-bed hospital, for example, is eligible as of 2011 for $6 million in federal funds to be used for digital health records. Hospitals and practices that do not adopt electronic records by 2015 will suffer cuts in Medicare reimbursements (that same 500-bed hospital would lose as much as $3.2 million in Medicare funding, according to PricewaterhouseCoopers). As of late 2010, only 20% of the U.S.' 5,708 hospitals had electronic records, according to Forrester Research. The research firm estimates that U.S. health care technology spending could reach more than $28 billion by 2013.

Technology firms both large and small are fiercely competing to develop systems that will fill the electronic bill. Ingenix, from UnitedHealth Group, and NextGen Healthcare, from Quality Systems, Inc., got a leg up on the competition by securing preferred designation from the American Medical Association (AMA) in 2010.

A growing number of other companies are hoping to cash in on the EHR movement. Dell, for example, plans to partner with hospitals to offer web-based EHRs, with Dell providing the necessary software, hardware and services. GE already has an EHR product called Centricity, and is adapting it to an Internet-based version. GE has even developed a Stimulus Simplicity Program with deferred payments and zero-percent financing from GE Capital. Meanwhile, Microsoft offers Amalga which takes a different tack. Instead of having doctors simply enter new patient data, Amalga scans existing data from a variety of hospitals and clinics to compile a complete patient history. IBM is partnering with Aetna to launch a cloud computing system that will track patient, lab and claims data, and assist physicians with measuring their care against national quality standards. Humana tapped athenahealth, Inc. to provide an EHR system for its members. The firm is subsidizing implementation costs, covering about 85% of the $4,000 per installation. Humana is also rewarding doctors who meet standards such as

dispensing generics and promoting wellness programs.

Many smaller technology firms already have systems on the market that keep patient records, manage prescriptions, schedule appointments, report test results and provide secure e-mail links between patients and their doctors and caregivers. For example, Epic Systems Corporation, a Wisconsin-based medical software firm, developed MyChart, which is already in use by major clinics and hospitals in the U.S. including the Baylor Clinic, the Cleveland Clinic, Kelsey-Seybold and the University of Pennsylvania Health System.

Proponents of EHRs estimate that they could significantly reduce medical errors, save lives and cut billions in medical spending a year—as much as $80 billion to $160 billion annually—in shortened hospital stays, reduced nursing time, savings on unnecessary drugs (or drugs that could dangerously react to medications already prescribed for a patient) and the reduction of redundant lab tests and paperwork. Physicians, caregivers and researchers could also benefit enormously by tracking clinical data nationwide and learning which treatments are most effective in any given situation.

Opponents to the adoption of the EHRs voice concerns about privacy, since database security breaches have occurred time and time again. Others, including legislators and physicians, argue that digitizing medical data is only one step to fixing a national health care system that is in crisis.

Microsoft and Google both offer free online medical records programs. Microsoft's HealthVault launched in October 2007 and Google Health debuted in May 2008. Both programs offer users the ability to store and manage personal medical data online. Data includes all manner of information including appointments, diagnoses, test results, prescription records and exercise logs. In mid-2010, Microsoft launched HealthVault in the U.K.

The programs offer patients the ability to control their own medical data, a radical departure from the need to request releases of medical records from one health care provider and send them to another. From the physician's perspective, clearly organized complete medical records supplied by the patient can streamline care, lessen costs and promote better diagnoses and treatments.

However, the programs' links to third parties, such as companies that supply medication information and reminders, cause concern among some observers over the possibility of disclosing private and extremely personal information. The programs are not currently covered by the Health Insurance Portability and Accountability Act (HIPAA) which bans the release of information without a patients' consent. Microsoft and Google claim that vendors must disclose how they use data from the programs, but valid concerns remain since medical information is highly sensitive. Issues such as mental illness, genetic predispositions and paternity tests are but a few of the medical conditions and procedures that should not be of public record. Watch for new developments as Microsoft and Google wrestle with privacy issues.

Developments in the U.K.'s public health system will likely spur the American effort to digitize medical records and patient care. In December 2003, England's National Health Service (NHS) announced plans for a $17 billion project to wire every hospital, doctor's office and clinic. The British government supplied $3.9 billion for a three-year period from 2004 to 2007, to be followed by another $13 billion. The program has hit a number of snags, especially regarding software development and privacy concerns. In addition, costs have risen to a projected $23.3 billion and the target date for completion has been extended until 2014-2015. When it is complete, information on each and every one of the 50 million patients registered in the U.K. national system will reside in a central database. Appointments and referrals will be scheduled online, and doctors' orders and prescriptions will be transmitted automatically to other caregivers and pharmacies. The system could serve as the electronic records and digitized patient care model for the rest of the world.

In Canada, another ambitious technical initiative is underway. The Canadian government is investing in health information projects including telemedicine, EHR, electronic prescription systems, laboratory information systems and diagnostic imaging systems. The goal is to link 50% of the country's medical community. Eventually, all Canadian health records may be digital. As of March 2010, Infoway (a federally funded nonprofit agency) had received $2.1 billion since its inception in 2001 in federal funding for EHR system development throughout the country.

Several major electronic medical claims processors have been established in the U.S. A pioneer was WebMD. Capario (formerly MedAvant Healthcare Solutions) also provides electronic processing services. The company was initially a coalition by Aetna, Anthem, Cigna, Heath Net, Oxford, PacifiCare and WellPoint Health Systems called MedUnite. Growth in health care transaction processing is still far from over. Billions of

transactions occur every year in the U.S., including prescription processing, insurance claims and so on.

The computer industry is also struggling to convert physicians to the use of PCs and Internet devices. For example, there are dozens of competing platforms attempting to get doctors to use wireless Palm-type devices or personal digital assistants (PDAs) to prescribe medications. This practice reduces medical errors, since electronic orders are easily legible and can be checked for conflicts with other medications currently taken by the patient. The PDAs check and notify physicians of drugs not covered by insurance or those to which a patient is allergic. Some systems can transmit physicians' orders directly to a local server, which then generates faxes to pharmacies or clinics. To eliminate fraud, doctors submit electronic signatures for verification, and drug store systems check for recognized fax numbers.

As hospitals and other major health care providers scramble to digitize, concerns about the quality of patient care have been voiced. As a result, caregivers and insurers have combined forces to monitor the changes brought about by the technological boom. The Leapfrog Group, a coalition of over 170 companies and private organizations that provides health care benefits, was created to improve, among other things, the flow of patient data and benchmarks for patient outcomes at hospitals. Leapfrog has set exacting standards for the health system to strive for in the creation and utilization of digital data. "Leapfrog compliance" is a catch phrase among hospitals, which are rated on the organization's web site (www.leapfroggroup.org) with regard to compliance issues such as computerized prescription order systems and statistics on staffing and medical procedure success rates.

In addition to Leapfrog, 22 electronics and health care companies banded together to help make high-tech medical tools work better together. This organization, the Continua Health Alliance (www.continuaalliance.org), includes partners such as GE Healthcare, IBM, Panasonic, Philips, Samsung, Cisco Systems, Intel and Medtronic. As of late 2010, the alliance boasted more than 200 member companies.

Many medical innovations are becoming widespread. For example, "med carts" equipped with computers and bar code scanners allow nurses to scan patients' identifying wristbands to verify identity and medication orders, improving safety and efficiency. These carts are evolving to use RFID instead of bar codes. In addition, examination and operating rooms are now often equipped with wireless laptops that transmit on-the-spot notes and evaluations for each patient to a central information system.

Remote Patient Monitoring: Visicu, Inc., a Baltimore, Maryland medical information technology company, offers an ICU remote monitoring system called eICU. The system is a combination of software, video and audio feeds and real-time patient vital statistics that hooks patients in ICUs in multiple hospitals to central monitoring facilities manned by ICU specialists. A specialist at the central location mans a standing desk outfitted with five monitors that display patient data, including real-time video and audio for up to 120 ICU beds at a time. The system ranks patients according to their conditions and flags gravely ill patients in red so that their progress can be more easily monitored. Indications such as changes in blood pressure alert the specialist who then contacts the nurse or physician on duty to treat the patient accordingly.

While 250 hospitals and 40 health systems in the U.S. utilized eICU as of mid-2010, the number of remotely monitored ICU beds is still relatively small. Cost is one factor, since a system for one ICU costs about $228,000, and insurance and Medicare do not reimburse hospitals for the technology. However, hospitals that do have eICU have experienced significant cost savings since the system cuts the average ICU stay from 4.4 days to 3.6 by lowering the instances of complications such as pneumonia and infections (these conditions generally occur when patients are not closely monitored by ICU specialists). The Leapfrog Group estimates that 54,000 patients per year could be saved if every U.S. ICU were monitored by specialists. Without technology such as eICU, 25,000 specialists would be needed to staff ICUs sufficiently, while there are only 6,000 such specialists currently licensed to practice.

Other remote monitoring systems are allowing patients to be monitored at home or at out-of-the-way care facilities. For example, American Telecare, Inc.'s CareTone Telephonic Stethoscope checks for heart, lung and bowel sounds using a small stethoscope, a phone line and two-way video stations. Cardiocom LLC's Telescale is a telemonitoring device integrated with an electronic scale. The patient steps onto the scale and answers questions using a touch pad about his or her symptoms. The answers and the patient's weight are communicated via two-way messaging to the consulting physician, who is alerted if there is any deterioration in the patient's health. The system also sends alerts back to

the patient for follow-up visits or care plan adjustments. Other remote monitoring systems include WellPoint, Inc.'s Anthem, a wireless scale and blood-pressure cuff, and a new system from Humana (set to launch in early 2011) that tracks cardiac patients' vital signs and links them via video chat to a nurse when necessary.

A twist on remote monitoring is CardioMEMS, Inc.'s implantable sensor device. It measures pulmonary artery pressure and transmits data to a secure web site for doctors and nurses. This system, as with all remote monitoring devices, is designed to alert physicians and their staffs when patients truly need care and cut down on routine office visits.

Market research company Datamonitor projects that the U.S. telemedicine market will grow from $900 million in 2007 to $6 billion by 2012. Significant investment in new telemedicine technology is being made. Cisco Systems is partnering with major insurer UnitedHealth Group to build an open network that uses Cisco's video-conferencing, broadband and other networking products. In April 2009, Intel and GE announced plans to invest $250 million through 2014 in remote technology to care for the elderly and chronically ill in their homes.

Computer Modeling: In recent times, impressive advances in computer modeling have lead to accurate mapping of very complex systems, including weather, planetary orbits and molecular interaction. Health care is another natural application of these capabilities. Everything from genes to bodily systems could be mapped by computers, allowing scientists to learn more about the complex interactions within the human body. The technology for mapping genes has now been around for quite awhile, but the technology for mapping other biological entities has been sadly absent. However, many scientists have now realized the benefits that could be gained from advanced mapping of the body and all the processes that go on within it. Think of all the innovations computer modeling has brought to the automobile industry, which can now design a car in a matter of months, predict how the car will perform in crashes, how it will react to wind resistance and how it will wear down over time. Now imagine a similar instance in health care: being able to model a complete human body, predict where things might go wrong, or determine how it will react to certain chemicals. Drug development and diagnosis are two obvious areas where health care might benefit from computer modeling.

One of the most promising uses of modeling is in analyzing patient care outcomes to project the best possible treatment for specific diseases and ailments. Patient records are kept in increasingly powerful databases, which can be analyzed to find the history of treatment outcomes. For the first time, payors such as HMOs and insurance companies have vast amounts of data available to them, including answers to questions such as:

- Which procedures and surgeries do and do not bring the desired results?
- Which physicians and hospitals have the highest and lowest rates of cure (or of untimely deaths of patients)?
- What is the average length of stay required for the treatment and recovery of patients undergoing various surgeries?
- How long should it take for the rehabilitation of a patient with a worker's compensation claim for a specific type of injury?

This knowledge will soon be essentially unlimited, and the result will be higher efficiency and increased use of the most effective treatment and rehabilitation regimens.

Scientists at Oxford in England, as well as at the University of California, San Diego and several other universities, have been developing models of the heart, liver and other organs, hoping to eventually build a complete model of the human body. The project to model the heart intends to mimic everything from chemical reactions up through cellular reactions, all coming together to make an almost perfect model of the heart. In this way, scientists can construct a "normal" heart, and then compare it to images of irregular or diseased hearts, in order to find out what goes wrong and, possibly, how to repair it. Novartis, a leading drug manufacturer, is already using a model of the heart to predict how the heart will react to different drugs, hoping to come up with a compound that can keep hearts healthy or heal them after a heart attack.

Internet Research Tip—Body Computer Modeling:
There are now several companies that are working on modeling human systems:
Immersion Corporation, San Jose, CA
    www.immersion.com/medical (simulation of the human body for training and education)
Insilicomed, La Jolla, CA
    www.insilicomed.com (biological models)
Epix Pharmaceuticals, Lexington, MA
    www.epixpharma.com (drug discovery)

---

19) U.S. Broadband Connections Rank Behind Other Nations

Global research firm Strategy Analytics reported in mid-2010 that, based on a variety of factors, the U.S. ranks 23rd on the list of 57 OECD nations in Internet access speeds, adoption and costs. As of early 2010, the Federal Communications Commission (FCC) reported that approximately 4% of U.S. households, in rural locations, were not located near access to high-speed Internet service.

The Information Technology and Innovation Foundation (ITIF) pointed out, in a May 2008 publication, "Explaining International Broadband Leadership," that America faces several unique circumstances. For example, the fact that Americans tend to live in low-density housing spread out over a wide area means that telecom wires run a longer distance to reach most Americans, incurring a higher capital cost. It is easy to visualize this difference when comparing U.S. homes to those of Singapore or South Korea, where families tend to live in very high-density, high-rise buildings offering ease of wiring. Likewise, tax policies, government incentives or subsidies, and focus on short-term return on telecom investment as opposed to long-term return may vary from nation-to-nation.

Up until recently, the U.S. Government had never adopted an aggressive broadband policy, despite rosy statements about the information superhighway by various politicians. In other nations, including South Korea, the government has accelerated and even subsidized broadband deployment with a goal of delivering the highest level of services possible to further such social goals as high-quality support for telemedicine, education, public services and industrial development. Instead of building broadband systems on one seamless standard, U.S. cable companies and telephone companies are battling for dominance with their two separate systems. WiMAX entrepreneurs are launching competing services that further muddy the scene if they feel they can beat the incumbent cable and phone offerings.

Relief with regard to broadband in the U.S. has been arriving continuously in recent months, as cable and telecom firms continue to roll out higher speeds at reasonable prices. Municipal governments such as the city of Chattanooga, Tennessee, are also working to promote broadband access (with mixed success). Its city-owned electric utility has been offering high-speed Internet service to downtown customers since 2003, and launched a $240 million fiber network offering TV, Internet and phone service to 170,000 customers in 2009.

A study released in October 2009, funded by Cisco and conducted by the Said Business School at the University of Oxford in conjunction with the Universidad de Oviedo, ranked the United States 15th, behind Lithuania, in "Broadband Leadership." On a brighter note, a study by the French business school INSEAD on behalf of the World Economic Forum in early 2008 concluded that the U.S. ranked fourth in the world behind Denmark, Sweden and Switzerland in Internet infrastructure. The study took 68 variables into account to measure market factors, political and regulatory environments and technology infrastructure in addition to bandwidth capacity and data transmission speeds.

As part of the $787 billion U.S. government stimulus package approved in 2009, $7.2 billion is promised for investment in broadband infrastructure. The burden for dispersing the funds lies with the FCC, which must complete a plan for providing faster, reliable Internet access to all Americans as well as regulating the services provided by Internet access firms.

Goals for the FCC plan include at least 100 million U.S. homes having affordable Internet access with download speeds of at least 100 Mbps and upload speeds of at least 50 Mbps. Additionally, every American community should have affordable access to at least one gigabit per second broadband service in institutions such as schools, hospitals and government buildings. Another goal is for every American to be able to use broadband to track his or her real-time energy consumption.

20) Many Industry Sectors Seek Consulting and Outsourcing Income, Competing with Pure Consultancies

While the traditional leading firms in the consulting industry were busy in the early 2000s restructuring, picking up acquisitions or distancing themselves from the accounting profession, aggressive competitors surfaced that created significant challenges. That is, leading manufacturers and service companies of many types now believe that they can achieve significant growth by offering consulting services. These consulting services are frequently offered in conjunction with complementary business offerings. For example, manufacturers of complex machinery or components may offer consulting services to enable clients to best determine what to order and how or where to use the products. Engineering firms often provide consulting

services that enable clients to best determine what types of projects to launch and what such projects will entail—far in advance of actual engineering services.

At the same time, a great deal of new competition has emerged in the information technology (IT) field. Manufacturers of computer hardware and software watched enviously as upstart IT consultancies grew at soaring rates during the boom of the 1990s. While these IT consulting firms were growing and charging top rates for their services, many computer industry manufacturers saw their prices per unit sold dropping rapidly due to intense global competition among hardware and software firms. Adding consulting and/or outsourcing services to their offerings gives hardware and software firms an opportunity to build stable repeat revenue on top of their manufacturing revenue bases, and they have a built-in clientele of existing customers and end users.

These new consulting practices take many forms. In the IT field, they are frequently packaged with the provision of outsourcing services—that is, contract management of a corporation's entire computing department. In other cases, new practices may consist primarily of pre-purchase design of a new facility or computer installation, followed by installation, ramp-up, training and continuing support.

This is big business, and it's a huge change in the consulting industry. For example, value-added services, including consulting and outsourcing, account for more than one-half of IBM's $95.8 billion in annual (2009) revenues. The unit, called IBM Global Services, is growing at a rapid clip by targeting small and medium-sized businesses through regional resellers, in addition to supplying consulting services directly to large firms. Sun Microsystems, Oracle, Dell, HP, SAP and the other major hardware and software firms all have their eyes on increased services revenues, including consulting—either through wholly-owned subsidiaries or through partnerships with consulting firms.

An interesting twist to this trend is HP's consulting activity. HP's IT consulting activity expanded on a dramatic scale when it acquired global technology services company EDS in August 2008. The $13.9 billion purchase was a big boost to HP's Services unit's revenues, which totaled $40.1 billion in 2009, compared to $26.2 billion in 2008 and only $19.6 billion in 2007. (HP's total revenue for 2008 was $118.4 billion, while 2009 revenue was $114.6 billion). HP created a new business group called EDS which operates out of the acquired firm's existing offices in Plano, Texas. EDS operates as part of HP Services.

The global economic recession of 2008-09 took its toll on consultancies, including those providing IT services. According to technology contract analysts at TPI, the amount spent on new services contracts fell from a high of approximately $90 billion in 2005 to $74.5 billion in 2009. New business is there, seeing as TPI reports that the number of new services contracts awarded each year almost doubled between 2000 and 2009. However, the contracts themselves were less valuable, and competition among consultancies continues to intensify. For 2010, TPI reported 422 outsourcing contracts, valued at $15 billion, expected to expire. The number of new global contracts was expected to rise throughout 2010 due to the improving economy in many nations.

21) The Future: Pervasive Computing, Complete Mobility Will Be Standard

The recent release of the Apple iPad and the continued enhancement of smartphones have set the stage for the decline of the importance of the desktop PC and even the reasonably portable laptop PC. Mobility, miniaturization, fast wireless connections, easy access to data and entertainment via apps, and long-lasting batteries reign supreme in this trend, which will accelerate broadly in 2011-12.

In the U.S., MIT Project Oxygen (www.oxygen.lcs.mit.edu) has been attempting for several years to define the nature of personal computing for the near future. It began in the Massachusetts Institute of Technology's Laboratory for Computer Science. The intent of this initiative is to conceptualize new user interfaces that will create natural, constant utilization of information technology. The project states its goal as designing a new system that will be: pervasive—it must be everywhere; embedded—it must live in our world, sensing and affecting it; nomadic—users must be free to move around according to their needs; and always on—it must never shut down or reboot. That sounds very much like an Internet-enabled smartphone.

The Project Oxygen initiative is centered on harnessing speech recognition and video recognition technologies that will have developed to the point that computer data receptors can be embedded in the walls surrounding us, responding to our spoken commands and actions. (This theory is exemplified in Microsoft's "Kinect" add-on for its Xbox electronic game machine. Kinect responds to the user's hand or body gestures as commands, thanks to a sophisticated, built-in camera and related software.)

As envisioned in Project Oxygen, a portable interface device would provide an ultimate array of personal functions, sort of like the ultimate smart phone. Meanwhile, stationary computers would manage communications with the user in a continuous, seamless fashion. Interfaces would include cameras and microphones that enable the user to communicate with this massive computing power via voice, motion or the handheld unit. The user's routine needs and tasks would be tended to automatically. For example, the user would be recognized when entering a room, and the room's systems would be adjusted to suit the user's profile. In keeping with the web services trend of Internet-based applications, most of this system's functions would operate by downloading software from the Internet on an as-needed basis. The emphasis on cloud computing that is growing today will be a boost to this vision. While a few of the goals of Project Oxygen have yet to be realized in today's mobile computing devices, it's clear that technology trends are stampeding in the right direction for this always-on future.

The advantages of the original iPad over a desktop PC are clear: It's lightweight, it's portable, it boots up instantly, and you can use it to access the Internet virtually anywhere there is Wi-Fi, and also over cellphone networks on the higher-priced model. The disadvantage? There's no keyboard. This means it isn't suitable for major efforts in document creation, spreadsheet data entry, etc.

The future of computers may well be in tablets like the iPad, but the future of tablets lies in easy-to-use docking stations that quickly enable tablets to use large monitors and keyboards. One attempt at solving this need is the Motorola Xoom. Based on an update of the popular Android cellphone operating system (Android 3.0 "Honeycomb," designed to work well with the larger screens found on tablets), and intended to work seamlessly with Verizon's 3G cellular network, the Xoom can be easily dropped into a desktop dock that adds the utility of speakers, three USB ports, battery charging, and a Bluetooth wireless keyboard.

Another major project, a joint effort of several institutions, is PlanetLab (www.planet-lab.org). Its purpose is to give the Internet an upgrade, making it smarter, faster and safer. The project involves setting up numerous networked "nodes" that are connected to the existing Internet, over 1,088 of which PlanetLab has already installed at 503 sites worldwide. These nodes will perform several duties in overseeing the Internet, including scanning and squashing viruses and worms before they have a chance to infect PCs; routing and rerouting bandwidth as necessary to get the maximum efficiency out of existing networks; and recognizing different users so anyone can set up their own preferences and software at any computer terminal instantly; as well as many other functions.

22) Nanotechnology Will Create Powerful Semiconductors in the Near Future

Silicon, the traditional material for semiconductors, is running out of gas. For years, the process of making faster semiconductors has required a complicated and expensive streamlining of manufacturing techniques for traditional silicon-based chips, with semiconductors becoming faster and faster while manufacturing facilities become more and more expensive. This process has followed the far-seeing prediction made by former Intel CEO Gordon Moore in 1965 that the number of transistors that could fit on a chip (which translates into processing speed) would double approximately every 18 months. This prediction came to be called "Moore's Law," and it has held true, more or less, for more than 40 years.

However, our refinement of today's silicon semiconductors faces immense challenges as more transistors are packed on each chip. This is because the circuitry will become so small that it will be unable to conduct electrical currents in an efficient and effective manner using traditional materials. Scientists have already seen this daunting phenomenon in labs, where excess heat and inefficient conductivity via tiny wires create chaos. Nanotechnology, using carbon tubes to create semiconductors, promises to solve these problems, making it possible to construct components for computer circuitry atom by atom, creating the ultimate in miniaturization.

In late 2005, global semiconductor industry associations cooperated to publish the International Technology Roadmap for Semiconductors (see http://public.itrs.net/). The latest executive summary of the roadmap was published in December 2010. Nanoscale solutions to future semiconductor restraints are widely discussed in the forecast. While today's smallest transistors may be only a few molecules across, and millions of transistors are clustered on the most powerful chips, industry leaders now envision transistors and nanoswitches as small as a single molecule or perhaps a single electron. Nanotubes and micro-engineered organic materials are the most promising materials of the chip industry's future.

To get an idea of how fast these potential semiconductors could be, compare them with today's semiconductors. Technology of recent years restricted the densest semiconductors to storing about 4 billion bits of data at once. Researchers at IBM's Almaden Research Center announced in March 2006 that they had successfully constructed a basic electric circuit on a single nanotube. In 2007, IBM announced the development of "Air Gap" technology, a self-assembly science that creates insulating vacuums around nanoscale wires in chips. This single breakthrough has the ability to reduce a microprocessor's power consumption by 15% or increase its performance by 35%.

Also in 2007, Hewlett-Packard Co. (HP) announced a startling breakthrough that promised to increase the number of transistors that can be placed on programmable chips by a factor of eight. By using nanowires in a crisscross pattern to create circuits for storing data or functioning as minute switches, chips become more efficient and save on energy consumption.

In 2008, a team of researchers at HP Labs announced the development of a switching memristor, a fourth basic element in integrated circuits that theoretically could enable the development of computers that power on and off like an electric light. Memristor is slang for memory resistor, a concept that opens the door to energy efficient computing systems with memories that continue to hold data even after the system powers down. As of 2009, Samsung, Micron Technology and Unity Semiconductor were also working on memristor technologies. HP reported an important advance in memristor technology in early 2010. The firm developed a three-dimensional array which allows memristors to be stacked in the thousands, making a new class of ultradense computing devices possible. In addition, the stacking ability mimics the design of the human brain, potentially enabling computers to work in analog as well as digital formats.

Intel researchers are studying the possibility of scaling down chips to as little as five nanometers by 2020. The firm is committed to a new class of transistors named FinFETs, so called due to an area of the transistor that is shaped like a fish fin. The "fin" points vertically away from the plane of silicon in which the transistor is embedded affording greater density and better insulation. The result is a 22-nanometer chip which may be available commercially in 2011. Intel announced plans to invest $2.7 billion between 2011 and 2013 to upgrade its plant in southern Israel where production of 22-nanometer chips is slated to begin in December of 2011. In addition to Intel, IBM is also working on the technology.

A networking breakthrough was made in 2010 when Fujitsu announced the world's first quantum dot laser capable of 25 gigabits per second (Gbps) of data transmission. The technology may be used in IEEE's new 100 Gbps Ethernet standard. Fujitsu has spun off QD Laser to focus on commercializing the laser.

23) Nanotechnology Holds the Key to the Ultra-dense Molecular Memory of the Future

"Universal memory" is a phrase used to describe future-generation digital memory storage systems that would be ultra-dense and run on extremely low power needs. Potentially, universal memory could replace today's flash memory, RAM and many other types of memory. The technology is based on the use of vast numbers of tiny carbon nanotubes or nanowires, resulting in the storage of trillions of bits of data per square centimeter. Early potential uses may include memory for cell phones, digital cameras and MP3 players.

Such molecular memory technology should eventually lead to the replacement of hard drives with such chips and to the development of computers and other devices that have nearly instant boot up. Zettacore www.zettacore.com and Nantero www.nantero.com are among the firms that have made strides in this field. Nantero, a pioneer in fabricating nanotube-based semiconductor products, calls its technology "NRAM." Nantero is collaborating with SVTC Technologies to accelerate the development of commercial applications for nanotube-based electronics. Specifically, the firms are working together on cylindrical carbon molecules (CNTs), which have excellent potential for semiconductor, nanotechnology and optics applications. As of early 2010, Nantero offered microelectronic-grade carbon nanotubes on a commercial scale through licensee Brewer Science. Applications for the new nanotubes include bio-sensor and infrared detectors as well as touch screen displays.

In February 2010, Samsung announced the creation of the first dynamic random access memory (DRAM) chip manufactured in the 30 nanometer class. The chip, which offers significant improvement in power consumption over the previous generations, can be used in servers, desktop PCs, laptops and mobile devices. It represents a

doubling of manufacturing cost-efficiency compared to 50 or 60 nanometer technology.

Researchers at the University of California at Berkeley are finding that memory chips based on nanotubes and iron particles have the possibility of storing data for a billion years or more. The tiny dimensions of the tube actually safeguard it from friction as electrons move repeatedly through the tube. It may take a billion years or more for the nanotube to "wear out."

SPOTLIGHT: Zettacore, Inc.

Zettacore, Inc. (www.zettacore.com), based in Denver, Colorado, is one of the leading companies developing molecular memory, or computer chips that use individual molecules to store bits of information. The main benefit of Zettacore's technology is that it is being designed to operate with existing technology, allowing the company to step directly into the broader commercial market once it begins manufacturing. The benefits of molecular memory include ultra-dense memory with extremely low power consumption, along with reduced semiconductor fabrication costs. The firm recently raised $21 million in financing, which will be used to bring its molecular memory chips to the commercial market.

---

24) Virtualization of Servers Leads to Data Center Efficiency

Many network administrators are running out of room to add more servers to their data centers. Meanwhile, their need to run applications, such as advanced databases, customer relationship management (CRM) software or enterprise-wide management information tools, is growing. IT managers have learned that their existing servers, in many cases, are running at only 5% to 10% capacity. Traditionally, servers were set up to run only one application at a time on one server, due to a fear that an effort to run multiple applications could lead to server failure.

Today, however, the relatively new concept of virtualization enables network administrators to create multiple "virtual" servers on one machine. Consequently, one server may be running eight or more applications, boosting capacity utilization to 60% or more. This eliminates the need to install additional servers. Space in the data center is optimized, equipment costs are lowered, and energy use is lowered. A leader in this technology is VMware, Inc. of Palo Alto, California, www.vmware.com, a former subsidiary of EMC.

Competitor Citrix Systems in Fort Lauderdale, Florida, is VMware's main competitor.

The partition of one server into several "virtual" servers is a software process. Multiple virtual servers, and even multiple operating systems or applications, can be running on one physical server at the same time. The software technology involved in virtualization oversees the physical server's complete component setup, including the CPU, RAM, disk drives and network controllers. Virtualization software sits on top of the physical server's operating system, dynamically allocating resources into several virtual servers at once while avoiding potential conflicts.

By the end of 2010, Gartner projected that one-half of all server-based computing would be on virtual machines. A growing number of manufacturers are shifting their focus from standard servers and PCs to virtual thin clients (stripped-down desktop computers that are primarily keyboards and monitors, with little to no software stored onboard) that relay data from users to virtual servers. Wyse Technology, based in San Jose, California, switched from building computer terminals to thin clients in 2005. Prices for Wyse's thin clients run between $50 and $200, although they may be given to clients free of charge when they purchase service contracts (a business model similar to that for cellphones).

25) Breakthrough Achieved in Quantum Computing

Quantum computing is a technology that uses the unique abilities of quantum systems to be in multiple states at once. Such superpositions would allow the computer to perform many different computations simultaneously. This is a merger of physics (and its laws of quantum mechanics) with computer science. Quantum computing uses quantum bits, also known as qubits, as the fundamental unit of data. Qubits differ vastly from data in traditional computing in that they are not binary. The laws of quantum mechanics differ radically from the laws of traditional physics. A qubit can exist not only in a state corresponding to 0 or 1 as in a binary bit, but also in states corresponding to a blend or superposition of these states. Qubits have the potential to enable the computer to perform calculations at speeds that may not be attained by traditional computers. This technology has immense potential applications in such areas as mathematical modeling, research, cryptography, genetics and the management of extremely large databases.

An important breakthrough occurred in Canada in late 2007 when D-Wave Systems unveiled the first practical quantum computer. D-Wave Systems' 16-qubit processor, called Orion, is capable of pattern-matching applications such as searching through a database of molecules as well as scheduling applications such as assigning seats on airlines. By 2008, the system processor had reached 28 qubits. The limitation of the Orion is that it must be submerged in a vat of liquid helium cooled to -273 degrees Celsius (-523 degrees Fahrenheit or just above absolute zero) in order to function.

In 2009, physicists at the University of California at Santa Barbara demonstrated the ability to electrically manipulate the quantum states of electrons held on defects in diamond crystals. This manipulation takes place at speeds measured in gigahertz. The result is a boon to the development of quantum computers, which could use electron spins to perform high speed computations.

Two breakthroughs were made in quantum computing in 2010. Researchers at University College, London developed a way to utilize silicon, rather than far more rare and expensive materials, to manipulate molecules necessary to the process. They also managed to raise working temperatures from -273 degrees Celsius to -269 degrees. Meanwhile, researchers at Australian National University in Canberra expanded quantum memory by manipulating light. Photons are trapped in bunches using tiny chambers, thereby increasing the amount of quantum information held without corruption or destruction. Although quantum computing is still many years away from practical applications, these two breakthroughs mean that the science is a bit closer to realization.

Chapter 2

INFOTECH INDUSTRY STATISTICS

Contents:

InfoTech Industry Overview

Worldwide InfoTech Market:	Amount	Unit	Date	Source
Worldwide Spending on IT	1.58	Tril. US$	2010	Forrester
Projection	1.69	Tril. US$	2011	Forrester
Worldwide Spending on IT Services	782	Bil. US$	2010	Gartner, Inc.
Projection	818	Bil. US$	2011	Gartner, Inc.
Worldwide Software Spending	280	Bil. US$	2009	PRE
Projection	308	Bil. US$	2010	PRE
Worldwide PC Shipments	346	Mil. Units	2010	IDC
Worldwide Semiconductor Sales	300.5	Bil. US$	2010*	SIA
Worldwide Electronic Game Industry Revenues	45.0	Bil. US$	2010	PRE
Worldwide Broadband Internet Subs. (incl. wireless)	763.0	Mil.	2010	In-Stat
Internet Users, Worldwide	1.97	Bil.	Jun-10	IWS
Worldwide Cell Phone Subscribers	5.3	Bil.	2010	ITU
Projection	5.8	Bil.	2013	Portio Research
Worldwide Cell Phone Handset Shipments	1,300.0	Mil. Units	2010	PRE

U.S. InfoTech Market:	Amount	Unit	Date	Source
U.S. Information Technology Spending	702.4	Bil. US$	2010	PRE
Computer Services	337.0	Bil. US$	2010	PRE
Software	164.2	Bil. US$	2010	PRE
Hardware	201.2	Bil. US$	2010	PRE
Electronic Game Industry (Hardware & Software), U.S.	18.6	Bil. US$	2010	NPD Group
Number of Cellular Phone Subscribers, U.S.	292.8	Mil.	Jun-10	CTIA
Number of High Speed Internet Subscribers in the U.S., Home & Business (Excluding Cellular)	100.0	Mil.	Dec-10	PRE
Wired Telecommunications Carriers Revenues	176.5	Bil. US$	2010	PRE
Annualized Wireless Revenues	155.8	Bil. US$	Jun-10	CTIA
Wireless Carrier Industry Direct Jobs	235	Thous.	Jun-10	CTIA
Cellular Population Penetration	93	%	Jun-10	CTIA
Value of U.S. Computer & Electronics Exports	139.1	Bil. US$	Sep-10	Census
Value of U.S. Computer & Electronics Imports	233.9	Bil. US$	Sep-10	Census

* Figure is an estimate.

Forrester = Forrester Research, Inc.   IDC = International Data Corporation

CTIA = Cellular Telecommunications Industry Association   FCC = U.S. Federal Communications Commission

PRE = Plunkett Research Estimate   ITU = International Telecommunications Union

SIA = Semiconductor Industry Association   IWS = InternetWorldStats

U.S. InfoTech Industry Quarterly Revenue: 2009-2010

(In Millions of US$)

NAICS Code[1]	Kind of business	2010			2009	% of Total[2]
		3Q*	2Q	1Q	4Q	
5112	Software publishers	37,262	38,685	36,062	41,371	100.0
	Government	2,747	2,935	2,549	2,888	7.4
	Business	30,908	31,601	29,306	33,573	82.9
	Households consumers & individuals	3,607	4,149	4,207	4,910	9.7
516, 5181, 519	Internet publishing & broadcasting, Internet service providers & web search portals & other information services	16,670	16,350	15,892	16,547	100.0
	Government	2,081	2,240	2,220	2,051	12.5
	Business	11,244	10,829	10,604	11,044	67.5
	Households consumers & individuals	3,345	3,281	3,068	3,452	20.1
5171	Wired telecommunications carriers	43,654	44,251	44,413	46,049	100.0
	Government	1,568	1,604	1,658	1,628	3.6
	Business	23,320	22,673	22,929	23,392	53.4
	Households consumers & individuals	18,766	19,974	19,826	21,029	43.0
5172	Wireless telecommunications carriers (except satellite)	50,629	49,066	48,811	48,649	100.0
5182	Data processing, hosting & related services	21,677	21,146	20,323	20,431	100.0
	Government	2,409	2,459	2,248	S	11.1
	Business	18,093	17,553	16,946	17,246	83.5
	Households consumers & individuals	S	S	S	S	S

Notes: Estimates have not been adjusted for seasonal variation, holiday or trading-day differences, or price changes. Estimates are based on data from the Quarterly Services Survey and have been adjusted using results of the 2007 Service Annual Survey. All estimates are based on the 2002 North American Industry Classification System (NAICS). Sector totals and subsector totals may include data for kinds of business not shown. Detail percents may not add to 100 percent due to rounding.

S = Estimate does not meet publication standards because of high sampling variability (coefficient of variation is greater than 30%) or poor response quality (total quantity response rate is less than 50%). Unpublished estimates derived from this table by subtraction are subject to these same limitations and should not be attributed to the U.S. Census Bureau.

[1] For a full description of the NAICS codes used in this table, see www.census.gov/epcd/www/naics.html.

[2] Percentages for class of customer using 3rd quarter 2010 numbers.

* Preliminary estimate.

Source: U.S. Census Bureau
Plunkett Research, Ltd.
www.plunkettresearch.com

Data Processing, Hosting & Related Services, U.S.: Estimated Revenue & Expenses, 2006-2009

(In Millions of US$; Latest Year Available)	2009	2008	2007	2006	09/08
NAICS Code: 5182					% Chg.
Total Operating Revenue	**80,151**	**77,663**	**72,588**	**70,081**	**3.2**
Data processing, IT infrastructure processing & hosting services	N/A	39,784	36,969	36,824	7.6
Business process management services	N/A	19,933	18,313	19,691	8.8
Data management services	N/A	7,357	7,091	7,036	3.8
Application service provisioning	N/A	7,844	6,810	6,338	15.2
Web site hosting services	N/A	S	S	2,529	S
Collocation services	N/A	S	S	S	S
Other operating revenue	N/A	37,879	35,619	33,256	6.3
IT design & development services	N/A	S	6,337	6,309	S
IT technical support services	N/A	1,726	1,406	1,419	22.8
IT technical consulting services	N/A	1,930	1,882	1,550	2.6
Information & document transformation services	N/A	4,028	3,508	3,397	14.8
Software publishing	N/A	2,740	2,229	1,961	22.9
Reselling services for computer hardware & software, retail	N/A	S	2,155	2,081	S
All other operating revenue	N/A	19,208	18,101	16,538	6.1
Total Operating Expenses	**N/A**	**64,411**	**60,061**	**54,446**	**7.2**

Notes: Estimates are based on data from the 2008 Service Annual Survey and administrative data. Estimates for 2007 and prior years have been revised to reflect historical corrections to individual responses. Dollar volume estimates are published in millions of dollars; consequently, results may not be additive. Estimates have been adjusted using results of the 2002 Economic Census. They cover taxable and tax-exempt firms and are not adjusted for price changes. The introduction and appendixes give information on confidentiality protection, sampling error, nonsampling error, sample design, and definitions. Links to this information on the Internet may be found at www.census.gov/svsd/www/cv.html. Appendix A, Tables A-3.4.3 & 3.6.1 (expenses) provide estimated measures of sampling variability.

S = Estimate does not meet publication standards because of high sampling variability (coefficient of variation is greater than 30%) or poor response quality (total quantity response rate is less than 50%). Unpublished estimates derived from this table by subtraction are subject to these same limitations and should not be attributed to the U.S. Census Bureau. For a description of publication standards and the total quantity response rate, see http://www.census.gov/quality/S20-0_v1.0_Data_Release.pdf.

Source: U.S. Census Bureau

Plunkett Research, Ltd.

www.plunkettresearch.com

Estimated Quarterly U.S. Retail Sales, Total & E-Commerce:
1st Quarter 2002-3rd Quarter 2010

(In Millions of US$; Not Seasonally Adjusted, Holiday & Trading-Day Differences; Does Not Include Food Services)

Quarter	Retail Sales in US$ Mil.		E-commerce as a Percent of Total Retail Sales	Percent Change Over Previous Quarter	
	Total	E-commerce*		Total Sales	E-commerce
1st Quarter 2002	717,302	9,721	1.4	-13.4	-10.8
2nd Quarter 2002	790,486	10,192	1.3	10.2	4.8
3rd Quarter 2002	792,657	10,882	1.4	0.3	6.8
4th Quarter 2002	833,877	14,322	1.7	5.2	31.6
1st Quarter 2003	741,233	12,506	1.7	-11.1	-12.7
2nd Quarter 2003	819,940	13,142	1.6	10.6	5.1
3rd Quarter 2003	831,222	14,098	1.7	1.4	7.3
4th Quarter 2003	875,437	18,115	2.1	5.3	28.5
1st Quarter 2004	795,916	16,399	2.1	-9.1	-9.5
2nd Quarter 2004	871,970	16,711	1.9	9.6	1.9
3rd Quarter 2004	873,695	17,650	2.0	0.2	5.6
4th Quarter 2004	938,213	22,798	2.4	7.4	29.2
1st Quarter 2005	836,952	20,402	2.4	-10.8	-10.5
2nd Quarter 2005	932,713	21,218	2.3	11.4	4.0
3rd Quarter 2005	940,880	22,469	2.4	0.9	5.9
4th Quarter 2005	987,085	28,386	2.9	4.9	26.3
1st Quarter 2006	897,180	25,749	2.9	-9.1	-9.3
2nd Quarter 2006	987,406	26,187	2.7	10.1	1.7
3rd Quarter 2006	978,211	27,158	2.8	-0.9	3.7
4th Quarter 2006	1,018,775	35,351	3.5	4.1	30.2
1st Quarter 2007	923,997	30,743	3.3	-9.3	-13.0
2nd Quarter 2007	1,016,136	32,043	3.2	10.0	4.2
3rd Quarter 2007	1,002,312	32,446	3.2	-1.4	1.3
4th Quarter 2007	1,062,803	42,112	4.0	6.0	29.8
1st Quarter 2008	953,358	34,543	3.6	-10.3	-18.0
2nd Quarter 2008	1,032,919	34,567	3.3	8.3	0.1
3rd Quarter 2008	1,006,551	33,479	3.3	-2.6	-3.1
4th Quarter 2008	966,329	39,301	4.1	-4.0	17.4
1st Quarter 2009	839,625	32,125	3.8	-13.1	-18.3
2nd Quarter 2009	919,646	32,769	3.6	9.5	2.0
3rd Quarter 2009	926,265	34,031	3.7	0.7	3.9
4th Quarter 2009	985,649	45,199	4.6	6.4	32.8
1st Quarter 2010	896,741	36,680	4.1	-9.0	-18.8
2nd Quarter 2010*	989,229	37,385	3.8	10.3	1.9
3rd Quarter 2010*	980,226	38,843	4.0	-0.9	3.9

[R] Revised Estimate. [P] Preliminary Estimate

* E-commerce sales are sales of goods and services over the Internet, an extranet, Electronic Data Interchange (EDI) or other online system. Payment may or may not be made online.

Source: U.S. Census Bureau
Plunkett Research, Ltd.
www.plunkettresearch.com

Top Ten Suppliers & Destinations of U.S. Computers & Electronic Products: 2004-September 2010

(NAICS Code 443; Value in Millions of US$)

Exports	2004	2005	2006	2007	2008	2009	2010*
World Total	163,207	168,708	185,833	187,047	190,282	160,628	139,071
Mexico	24,479	23,410	25,435	23,046	24,603	24,955	23,887
Canada	23,049	24,977	25,111	25,526	25,335	21,209	18,237
China	7,781	8,852	12,587	13,271	13,884	12,530	11,210
Hong Kong	7,168	7,124	7,092	7,232	7,049	6,708	5,926
Malaysia	7,364	7,077	8,130	7,015	8,043	5,975	5,902
Japan	10,530	9,918	10,641	9,577	8,771	7,197	5,791
Germany	7,114	7,545	8,750	9,316	8,738	7,057	5,552
Singapore	7,098	7,070	7,813	8,178	8,072	5,549	5,262
Brazil	2,895	3,414	4,047	4,834	5,779	5,237	4,891
Netherlands	5,863	6,770	6,730	7,157	7,195	5,646	4,548

Imports	2004	2005	2006	2007	2008	2009	2010*
World Total	249,131	270,732	295,846	305,754	300,114	266,612	233,890
China	64,019	79,683	95,791	105,521	107,891	103,356	94,229
Mexico	32,989	33,711	39,518	45,410	44,779	42,542	38,561
Malaysia	28,201	27,844	27,416	25,854	22,704	15,943	14,087
Japan	21,995	27,131	29,078	24,728	21,942	16,000	12,828
South Korea	19,572	15,169	14,434	14,778	16,153	14,978	12,289
Taiwan	15,778	15,507	17,653	16,830	15,448	13,233	12,061
Thailand	6,659	8,363	9,012	9,244	9,407	7,639	6,728
Canada	6,797	7,261	8,135	9,004	8,955	7,050	5,905
Germany	9,034	10,317	9,783	9,787	9,387	7,513	5,301
Singapore	10,337	9,607	9,881	9,055	6,789	4,751	4,558

* Year to date as of September 2010.

Source: U.S. International Trade Administration
Plunkett Research, Ltd.
www.plunkettresearch.com

Value of Computers & Electronic Products Manufacturers' Shipments, Inventories & Orders by Industry, U.S.: 2003-November 2010

(In Millions of US$)

Total	2003	2004	2005	2006	2007	2008	2009
Shipments[1]	351,930	364,751	373,175	391,922	403,866	390,695	355,872
New Orders[1]	287,010	296,103	296,312	336,825	342,001	320,681	295,690

Year to Date: November 2010*

	Shipments[1]	New Orders[1]	Inventories[2]	Unfilled Orders[2]
Computers & Electronic Products	360,608	295,502	46,007	123,087
Computers	47,746	48,020	2,101	5,645
Computer storage devices	7,034	N/A	1,068	29,143
Other peripheral equipment	11,417	N/A	1,419	N/A
Nondefense comm. equipment	32,472	31,483	6,169	21,918
Defense comm. equipment	5,948	5,840	2,221	6,147
Audio & video equipment	4,504	N/A	360	N/A
Electronic components	42,677	43,513	7,890	11,648
Nondefense search & navigation equipment	11,631	11,380	3,858	8,151
Defense search & navigation equipment	32,384	31,967	3,467	39,907
Electromedical, measuring & control instruments	94,546	95,265	12,072	29,671

[1] Shipments and new orders are the totals for the period and are adjusted for trading-day and calendar-month variations.

[2] Inventories and unfilled orders are seasonally adjusted but not adjusted for trading-day and calendar-month variations.

* Preliminary estimates as of November. Data on new and unfilled orders are not available for the semiconductor industry. Estimates for new orders and unfilled orders exclude semiconductor industry data. Inventories for semiconductor industry data are included in computers and electronic products, but are not shown separately.

Source: U.S. Census Bureau

Plunkett Research, Ltd.

www.plunkettresearch.com

Exports, Imports & Trade Balance of Computers & Electronic Products, U.S.: 2005-September 2010

(In Millions of US$)

Exports	NAICS Code	2005	2006	2007	2008	2009	Sep. 2010*
Computers & Electronic Products	334	168,708	185,833	187,047	190,282	160,628	139,071
Computer Equipment	3341	45,369	47,475	45,883	44,823	37,975	31,770
Communications Equipment	3342	18,643	20,686	24,519	27,422	23,908	20,227
Audio & Video Equipment	3343	6,937	7,941	8,464	8,153	7,792	6,915
Semiconductors & Other Electronic Components	3344	62,941	70,293	66,817	66,870	51,711	47,936
Navigational, Measuring, Medical & Control Instruments	3345	32,518	37,372	39,870	41,758	38,283	31,644
Magnetic & Optical Media	3346	2,301	2,065	1,493	1,255	959	578

Imports	NAICS Code	2005	2006	2007	2008	2009	Sep. 2010*
Computers & Electronic Products	334	270,732	295,846	305,754	300,114	266,612	233,890
Computer Equipment	3341	78,385	83,781	83,582	77,740	70,192	64,865
Communications Equipment	3342	47,131	50,930	66,718	71,714	67,414	57,572
Audio & Video Equipment	3343	40,922	47,105	48,398	48,030	41,779	31,370
Semiconductors & Other Electronic Components	3344	68,524	75,543	65,359	60,815	52,228	51,029
Navigational, Measuring, Medical & Control Instruments	3345	31,322	33,814	38,962	39,756	33,471	28,027
Magnetic & Optical Media	3346	4,449	4,672	2,736	2,059	1,528	1,027

Trade Balance	NAICS Code	2005	2006	2007	2008	2009	Sep. 2010*
Computers & Electronic Products	334	-102,024	-110,013	-118,707	-109,832	-105,985	-94,818
Computer Equipment	3341	-33,016	-36,306	-37,699	-32,916	-32,217	-33,095
Communications Equipment	3342	-28,488	-30,244	-42,199	-44,291	-43,505	-37,345
Audio & Video Equipment	3343	-33,985	-39,163	-39,933	-39,877	-33,988	-24,455
Semiconductors & Other Electronic Components	3344	-5,583	-5,250	1,459	6,055	-517	-3,092
Navigational, Measuring, Medical & Control Instruments	3345	1,196	3,557	909	2,002	4,812	3,617
Magnetic & Optical Media	3346	-2,148	-2,607	-1,243	-804	-569	-449

* Year to data as of September 2010.

Source: Foreign Trade Division, U.S. Census Bureau

Plunkett Research, Ltd.

www.plunkettresearch.com

Internet Access Technologies Compared

(In Millions of Bits per Second - Mbps)

Type of Access	Maximum Data Rate (In Mbps)	Characteristics
Dialup		
Dialup	.0288, .0336, .056	Analog modems that require dialup connection. Slowest method of Internet access.
ISDN	.064, .128	Integrated Services Digital Network. Digital access that requires dialup connection.
Wired Broadband		
ADSL	1.5 - 24 Downstream .5 - 3.5 Upstream	Asymmetrical Digital Subscriber Line. Data transfer speed downstream is different from speed upstream. Ideal for web surfing and home use.
SDSL	2.3	Symmetric Digital Subscriber Line. Downstream and upstream data transfer rates are similar. Ideal for businesses because of synchronous speed and high-speed router capabilities.
VDSL	55 - 100 Downstream 2.3 - 16 Upstream	Very High bit-Rate DSL. Offers much higher data rates than ADSL, allowing providers to offer high bandwidth services (such as AT&T's U-verse).
Cable Modem	4 - 16 Downstream .384 - 20 Upstream	Shared network service. Typically has greater bandwidth capabilities than DSL.
FTTx	15 to 50 Downstream 5 to 30 Upstream	Fiber to the x (Home, Node, Premises, etc). A rapidly growing method that takes fiber optic directly into the home or business. Numbers stated here are for Verizon FiOS service in mid-2009.
T1/DS1	1.544	Ideal for businesses with high bandwidth requirements.
T3/DS3	44.736	Equivalent to 30 T1 circuits.
E1 (Europe)	2.048	European version of T1.
E3 (Europe)	34.368	European version of T3.
OC3	155.52	High-speed access. Uses optical fiber technology.
OC12	622.08	Offers higher speed access than OC3. Uses optical fiber technology.
OC48	2,488.32	Offers one of the fastest data rates. Uses optical fiber technology. Extremely expensive to setup and maintain.
OC768	39,813.12	Network line used by AT&T, Cisco and others.
Wireless Broadband		
802.15.3 (UWB)	100 - 2,000	UWB stands for ultrawideband. It is useful for high-speed, short distance data transfer.
802.11a (Wi-Fi)	54	High-speed, broadband access to wireless local area networks (WLAN) with the Internet.
802.11b (Wi-Fi)	11	Offers higher bandwidth range than 802.11a.
802.11g (Wi-Fi)	54	Provides greater data transmission rate than 802.11b.
802.11n (MIMO)	100 - 500	Faster data transmission rates and broader area coverage than other 802.11 technologies. Used as an enhancement to WiMAX networks.
802.15 (Bluetooth) versions 1.0 - 2.0	1 - 3	Useful for high-speed, short distance data transfer.
802.15 Bluetooth version 3.0	24	Bluetooth 3.0 offers high speed data transfer at short range of up to 10 meters.
802.16 (WiMax)	15 - 70	Has the potential to be useful for distances of up to 30 miles.
Satellite	.128 - 5	Offers interactive broadband services via satellite. Limited upstream capabilities.

Note: 1 Mbps = 1,000 Kbps

Number of Business & Residential High Speed Internet Lines, U.S.: 2003-2010

Types of Technology[1]	Dec-03	Dec-04	Dec-05	Dec-06	Dec-07	Dec-08[2]	Dec-09	Dec-10[P]
ADSL	9,509,442	13,817,280	19,515,000	25,413,000	29,449,000	30,198,000	30,971,000	44,000,000
SDSL	N/A	N/A	369,000	345,000	293,000	241,000	225,000	N/A
Other Wireline	N/A	N/A	373,000	545,000	605,000	705,000	716,000	N/A
Cable Modem	16,446,322	21,357,400	26,558,000	31,982,000	36,507,000	40,273,000	43,128,000	50,000,000
Fiber	116,390	159,653	298,000	894,000	1,849,000	2,884,000	3,975,000	4,500,000
Satellite	N/A	N/A	427,000	572,000	791,000	938,000	1,116,000	N/A
Fixed Wireless	N/A	N/A	257,000	483,000	707,000	486,000	525,000	N/A
Power Line & Other	N/A	N/A	5,000	5,000	5,000	5,000	5,000	N/A
Total Fixed	26,072,154	35,334,333	47,803,000	60,238,000	70,206,000	75,729,000	80,662,000	100,000,000
Mobile Wireless	N/A	N/A	N/A	N/A	N/A	25,040,000	52,486,000	75,000,000
Total Lines	27,744,342	37,352,520	50,930,000	82,525,000	121,222,000	100,770,000	133,148,000	175,000,000

Note: High-speed lines are connections to end-user locations that deliver services at speeds exceeding 200 kbps in at least one direction. Advanced services lines, which are a subset of high-speed lines, are connections that deliver services at speeds exceeding 200 kbps in both directions. Line counts presented in this report are not adjusted for the number of persons at a single end-user location who have access to, or who use, the Internet-access services that are delivered over the high-speed connection to that location. For data through December 2004, only those providers with at least 250 lines per state were required to file.

[1] The mutually exclusive types of technology are, respectively: Asymmetric digital subscriber line (ADSL) technologies, which provide speeds in one direction greater than speeds in the other direction; symmetric digital subscriber line (SDSL) technologies; traditional wireline technologies "other" than ADSL and SDSL, including traditional telephone company high-speed services that provide equivalent functionality, and also Ethernet service if delivered to the subscriber's location over copper (as opposed to optical fiber) plant; cable modem, including the typical hybrid fiber-coax (HFC) architecture of upgraded cable TV systems; optical fiber to the subscriber's premises (e.g., Fiber-to-the-Home, or FTTH); satellite and fixed and mobile terrestrial wireless systems, which use radio spectrum to communicate with a radio transmitter; and electric power line.

[2] Reporting instructions for mobile wireless changed between the December 2007 and the December 2008 data, resulting in a one-time decrease in the reported number of high-speed mobile wireless Internet access service connections, and a decrease in the overall number of reported high speed Internet subscribers. Earlier reported data included all subscribers whose mobile devices were capable of sending or receiving data at speeds above 200 kbps. Starting with the December 2008 data, results include only those wireless customers whose current subscription plan includes data transfer to and from Internet sites through the mobile device (and exclude mobile-specific applications such as text messaging and ringtone downloading).

P = Plunkett Research estimate. NA = Not available.

Source: U.S. Federal Communications Bureau (FCC)
Plunkett Research, Ltd.
www.plunkettresearch.com

Computer Industry Employment by Business Type, U.S.: 2005-Oct. 2010

(Annual Estimates in Thousands of Employed Workers, Not Seasonally Adjusted)

NAICS Code[1]	Industry Sector	2005	2006	2007	2008	2009	2010*
Manufacturing							
334	Computer & electronic products	1,316.4	1,307.5	1,272.5	1,244.2	1,136.3	1,101.9
3341	Computer & peripheral equipment	205.1	196.2	186.2	183.2	166.0	162.3
334111	Electronic computers	111.0	105.3	100.1	100.4	92.0	90.2
334112	Computer storage devices	31.0	31.0	27.1	26.1	20.8	19.7
334113 334119	Computer terminals & other computer peripheral equip.	63.1	59.9	58.9	56.7	53.2	52.4
3342	Communications equipment	141.4	136.2	128.1	127.3	121.4	123.3
3343	Audio & video equipment	32.4	31.4	29.7	26.9	22.9	20.5
3344	Semiconductors & electronic components	452.0	457.9	447.5	431.8	377.0	368.4
334412	Bare printed circuit boards	59.7	57.6	55.4	49.8	40.9	39.9
334413	Semiconductors & related devices	222.9	229.2	218.1	207.8	185.4	184.1
334418	Printed circuit assemblies	53.0	53.8	55.1	55.7	49.4	49.9
334419	Electronic connectors & misc. electronic components	116.4	117.3	118.9	118.6	101.3	94.5
3345	Electronic instruments	441.0	444.5	443.2	441.0	421.3	403.1
3346	Magnetic media manufacturing & reproduction	44.5	41.5	37.9	34.0	27.8	24.3
Wholesale and retail trade							
42343	Computer & software wholesale	241.3	246.7	248.3	243.5	221.0	213.5
44312, 3	Computer, software, camera & photography supply stores	167.0	158.0	152.3	143.0	122.4	124.4
Information							
5112	Software publishers	237.9	244.0	255.3	263.6	256.2	257.4
517	Telecommunications	1,071.3	1,047.6	1,030.6	1,019.4	974.8	918.4
518	Data processing, hosting & related services	262.5	263.2	267.8	260.3	250.0	244.3
51913	Internet publishing & broadcasting & web search portals	67.2	69.1	72.9	80.6	82.6	91.1
Professional and business services							
5415	Computer systems design & related services	1,195.2	1,284.6	1,372.1	1,439.6	1,426.3	1,480.9
541511	Custom computer programming services	524.6	563.9	598.4	629.3	616.2	645.8
541512	Computer systems design services	511.2	561.5	611.3	643.8	653.5	678.4
541513	Computer facilities management services	56.2	56.4	57.7	57.1	52.8	48.3
541519	Other computer-related services	103.3	102.9	104.8	109.4	103.8	108.4
Other services							
811212	Computer & office machine repair	44.3	43.5	42.1	42.9	40.0	43.4

[1] For a full description of the NAICS codes used in this table, see www.census.gov/epcd/www/naics.html.

* As of October.

Source: U.S. Bureau of Labor Statistics

Plunkett Research, Ltd.

www.plunkettresearch.com

InfoTech Employment, U.S.: 1997-2010

(In Thousands of Employed Workers; Annual Average)

	Software Publishers (5112)	Data Processing, Hosting & Related Services (518)	Computer & Peripheral Manufacture (3341)	Communications Equipment Manufacture (3342)	Semiconductor & Component Manufacture (3344)
1997	195.2	268.4	316.7	235.0	639.8
1998	214.9	282.8	322.1	237.4	649.8
1999	235.0	307.1	310.1	228.7	630.5
2000	260.6	315.7	301.9	238.6	676.3
2001	268.9	316.8	286.2	225.4	645.4
2002	253.3	303.9	250.0	179.0	524.5
2003	238.9	280.0	224.0	149.2	461.1
2004	235.9	267.1	210.0	143.0	454.1
2005	237.9	262.5	205.1	141.4	452.0
2006	244.0	263.2	196.2	136.2	457.9
2007	255.3	267.8	186.2	128.1	447.5
2008	263.6	260.3	183.2	127.3	431.8
2009	256.2	250.0	166.0	121.4	377.0
2010*	259.4	246.3	160.2	121.3	365.9

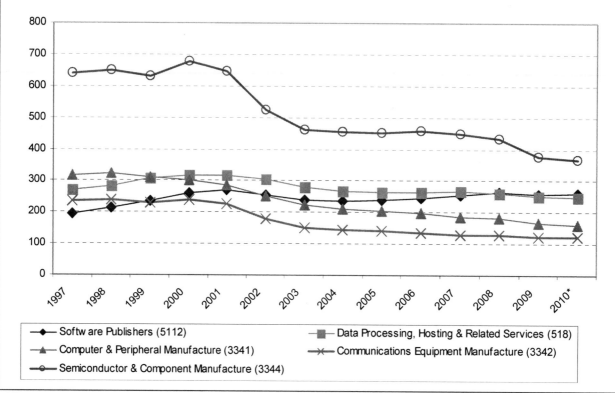

* Preliminary estimate. The figure for Software Publishers is as of November, not seasonally adjusted.

Source: U.S. Bureau of Labor Statistics

Plunkett Research, Ltd.

www.plunkettresearch.com

Chapter 3

IMPORTANT INFOTECH INDUSTRY CONTACTS

Addresses, Telephone Numbers and Internet Sites

Contents:

I.	Aerospace & Defense Industry Associations
II.	Canadian Government Agencies-General
III.	Canadian Government Agencies-InfoTech
IV.	Canadian Government Agencies-Scientific
V.	Careers-Computers/Technology
VI.	Careers-First Time Jobs/New Grads
VII.	Careers-General Job Listings
VIII.	Careers-Job Reference Tools
IX.	Chinese Government Agencies-Science & Technology
X.	Computer & Electronics Industry Associations
XI.	Computer & Electronics Industry Resources
XII.	Computer Education & Training
XIII.	Consulting Industry Associations
XIV.	Corporate Information Resources
XV.	Economic Data & Research
XVI.	Electronic Health Records/Continuity of Care Records
XVII.	Engineering Indices
XVIII.	Engineering, Research & Scientific Associations
XIX.	Game Industry Associations
XX.	Industry Research/Market Research
XXI.	Internet & Online Business Resources
XXII.	Internet Industry Associations
XXIII.	Internet Industry Resources
XXIV.	Internet Usage Statistics
XXV.	Licensing Associations
XXVI.	Manufacturing Associations-Machinery & Technology
XXVII.	MBA Resources
XXVIII.	Outsourcing Industry Resources
XXIX.	Patent Organizations
XXX.	Patent Resources
XXXI.	Payment, E-Commerce and Data Interchange Technology
XXXII.	Privacy & Consumer Matters
XXXIII.	Research & Development, Laboratories
XXXIV.	RFID Associations
XXXV.	RFID Resources
XXXVI.	Science & Technology Resources
XXXVII.	Software Industry Associations
XXXVIII.	Software Industry Resources
XXXIX.	Stocks and Financial Markets Data
XL.	Supercomputing
XLI.	Technology Law Associations
XLII.	Technology Transfer Associations
XLIII.	Telecommunications Industry Associations
XLIV.	Telecommunications Resources
XLV.	Telecommunications-VoIP Resources
XLVI.	Temporary Staffing Firms
XLVII.	Trade Associations-General
XLVIII.	Trade Associations-Global
XLIX.	Trade Resources
L.	Transportation Industry Associations
LI.	U.S. Government Agencies
LII.	Wireless & Cellular Industry Associations
LIII.	Wireless & Cellular Industry Resources

I. Aerospace & Defense Industry Associations

Aerospace Industries Association
1000 Wilson Blvd., Ste. 1700
Arlington, VA 22209-3928 US
Phone: 703-358-1000
E-mail Address: *globalcustomerservice@ihs.com*
Web Address: www.aia-aerospace.org
The Aerospace Industries Association represents the
nation's leading manufacturers and suppliers of civil,
military, and business aircraft, helicopters, unmanned
aerial vehicles, space systems, aircraft engines, missiles,
materiel, and related components, equipment, services, and
information technology.

Defense MicroElectronics Activity (DMEA)
4234 54th St.
McClellan, CA 95652-2100 US
Phone: 916-231-1568
Fax: 916-231-2868
Web Address: www.dmea.osd.mil
Defense MicroElectronics Activity (DMEA) was
established by the Department of Defense to provide a
broad spectrum of microelectronics services.

II. Canadian Government Agencies-General

Canadian Intellectual Property Office (CIPO)
Place du Portage, 50 Victoria St.
Rm. C-114
Gatineau, QC K1A 0C9 Canada
Phone: 819-934-0544
Fax: 819-953-7620
Toll Free: 866-997-1936
E-mail Address: *info@crc.gc.ca*
Web Address: www.cipo.gc.ca
The Canadian Intellectual Property Office (CIPO) is the
agency responsible for the administration and processing
of intellectual property in Canada.

III. Canadian Government Agencies-InfoTech

Institute for Information Technology (IIT)
46 Dineen Dr.
Fredericton, NB E3B 9W4 Canada
Phone: 506-444-0393
Toll Free: 506-452-3859
E-mail Address: *Lorna.Brown@nrc-cnrc.gc.ca*
Web Address: www.iit-iti.nrc-cnrc.gc.ca
The IIT, a member of Canada's National Research Council,
focuses its research and development activities on
information and telecommunications technologies.

IV. Canadian Government Agencies-Scientific

Institute for Microstructural Sciences (IMS)
Montreal Rd., Bldg. M-50

Ottawa, ON K1A 0R6 Canada
Phone: 613-949-9679
Fax: 613-957-8734
E-mail Address: *micha.hage-badr@nrc-cnrc.gc.ca*
Web Address: www.ims-ism.nrc-cnrc.gc.ca
The Institute for Microstructural Sciences (IMS) is a
branch of Canada's National Research Council (NRC) that
focuses its research on the information and
telecommunications technology sector.

V. Careers-Computers/Technology

ComputerJobs.com, Inc.
280 Interstate N. Cir. SE, Ste. 300
Atlanta, GA 30339-2411 US
Toll Free: 800-850-0045
E-mail Address: *michael@marketingmax.com*
Web Address: www.computerjobs.com
ComputerJobs.com, Inc. is an employment web site that
offers users a link to computer-related job opportunities
organized by skill and market.

Dice
4101 NW Urbandale Dr.
Urbandale, IA 50322 US
Phone: 515-280-1144
Fax: 515-280-1452
Toll Free: 877-386-3323
Web Address: www.dice.com
Dice provides free employment services for IT jobs. The
site includes advanced job searches by geographic location
and category, availability announcements and resume
postings, as well as employer profiles, a recruiter's page
and career links. Dice is owned by Dice Holdings, Inc., a
publicly traded company.

**Institute for Electrical and Electronics Engineers
(IEEE) Job Site**
445 Hoes Ln.
Piscataway, NJ 08855-1331 US
Phone: 732-981-0060
Toll Free: 800-678-4333
E-mail Address: *candidatejobsite@ieee.org*
Web Address: careers.ieee.org
The Institute for Electrical and Electronics Engineers
(IEEE) Job Site provides a host of employment services
for technical professionals, employers and recruiters. The
site offers job listings by geographic area, a resume bank
and links to employment services.

Pencom Systems, Inc.
152 Remsen St.
New York, NY 11201 US
Phone: 718-923-1111
Fax: 718-923-6066
E-mail Address: *tom@pencom.com*
Web Address: www.pencom.com

Pencom Systems, Inc., an open systems recruiting company, offers a web site geared toward high-technology and scientific professionals, featuring an interactive salary survey, career advisor, job listings and technology resources.

VI.   Careers-First Time Jobs/New Grads

Alumni-Network Recruitment Corporation
Phone: 905-465-2547
E-mail Address: *karen@alumni-network.com*
Web Address: www.alumni-network.com
Alumni-Network Recruitment Corporation is a professional search and recruiting firm, specializing in ERP, E-Commerce and Engineering.

Black Collegian Online (The)
140 Carondelet St.
New Orleans, LA 70130 US
Phone: 504-523-0154
Web Address: www.black-collegian.com
The Black Collegian Online features listings for job and internship opportunities, as well as other tools for students of color; it is the web site of The Black Collegian Magazine, published by IMDiversity, Inc. The site includes a list of the top 100 minority corporate employers and an assessment of job opportunities.

CollegeGrad.com, Inc.
234 E. College Ave., Ste. 200
State College, PA 16801 US
Phone: 262-375-6700
Toll Free: 1-800-991-4642
Web Address: www.collegegrad.com
CollegeGrad.com, Inc. offers in-depth resources for college students and recent grads seeking entry-level jobs.

Job Web
62 Highland Ave.
c/o Nat'l Association of Colleges & Employers (NACE)
Bethlehem, PA 18017-9085 US
Phone: 610-868-1421
Fax: 610-868-0208
Toll Free: 800-544-5272
E-mail Address: *editors@jobweb.com*
Web Address: www.jobweb.com
Job Web, owned and sponsored by National Association of Colleges and Employers (NACE), displays job openings and employer descriptions. The site also offers a database of career fairs, searchable by state or keyword, with contact information.

MBAjobs.net
Fax: 413-556-8849
E-mail Address: *contact@mbajobs.net*
Web Address: www.mbajobs.net
MBAjobs.net is a unique international service for MBA students and graduates, employers, recruiters and business

schools. The MBAjobs.net service is provided by WebInfoCo.

MonsterTRAK
11845 W. Olympic Blvd., Ste. 500
Los Angeles, CA 90064 US
Toll Free: 800-999-8725
E-mail Address: *trakstudent@monster.com*
Web Address: www.college.monster.com
MonsterTRAK provides information about internships and entry-level jobs.

National Association of Colleges and Employers (NACE)
62 Highland Ave.
Bethlehem, PA 18017-9085 US
Phone: 610-868-1421
Fax: 610-868-0208
Toll Free: 800-544-5272
E-mail Address: *mcollins@naceweb.org*
Web Address: www.naceweb.org
The National Association of Colleges and Employers (NACE) is a premier U.S. organization representing college placement offices and corporate recruiters who focus on hiring new grads.

VII.   Careers-General Job Listings

Career Exposure, Inc.
805 SW Broadway, Ste. 2250
Portland, OR 97205 US
Phone: 503-221-7779
Fax: 503-221-7780
E-mail Address: *lisam@mackenzie-marketing.com*
Web Address: www.careerexposure.com
Career Exposure, Inc. is an online career center and job placement service, with resources for employers, recruiters and job seekers.

CareerBuilder, Inc.
200 N. LaSalle St., Ste. 1100
Chicago, IL 60601 US
Phone: 773-527-3600
Toll Free: 800-638-4212
Web Address: www.careerbuilder.com
CareerBuilder, Inc. focuses on the needs of companies and also provides a database of job openings. The site has 1.5 million jobs posted by 300,000 employers, and receives an average 23 million unique visitors monthly. The company also operates online career centers for 150 newspapers, 1,000 partners and other online portals such as America Online. Resumes are sent directly to the company, and applicants can set up a special e-mail account for job-seeking purposes. CareerBuilder is primarily a joint venture between three newspaper giants: The McClatchy Company (which recently acquired former partner Knight Ridder), Gannett Co., Inc. and Tribune Company. In 2007,

Microsoft acquired a minority interest in CareerBuilder, allowing the site to ally itself with MSN.

CareerOneStop
Toll Free: 877-348-0502
E-mail Address: *info@careeronestop.org*
Web Address: www.careeronestop.org
CareerOneStop is operated by the employment commissions of various state agencies. It contains job listings in both the private sector and in government. CareerOneStop is sponsored by the U.S. Department of Labor. It includes a wide variety of useful career resources and workforce information.

HotJobs
45 W. 18th St., Fl. 6
New York, NY 10011 US
Phone: 646-351-5300
Web Address: www.hotjobs.yahoo.com
HotJobs, designed for experienced professionals, employers and job seekers, is a Monster-owned site that provides company profiles, a resume posting service and a resume workshop. The site allows posters to block resumes from being viewed by certain companies and provides a notification service of new jobs.

JobCentral
9002 N. Purdue Rd., Quad III, Ste. 100
c/o DirectEmployers Association, Inc.
Indianapolis, IN 46268 US
Phone: 317-874-9000
Fax: 317-874-9100
Toll Free: 866-268-6206
E-mail Address: *info@jobcentral.com*
Web Address: www.jobcentral.com
JobCentral, operated by the nonprofit DirectEmployers Association, Inc., links users directly to hundreds of thousands of job opportunities posted on the sites of participating employers, thus bypassing the usual job search sites. This saves employers money and allows job seekers to access many more job opportunities.

LaborMarketInfo
800 Capitol Mall, MIC 83
c/o Employment Dev. Dept., Labor Market Info. Div.
Sacramento, CA 95814 US
Phone: 916-262-2162
Fax: 916-262-2352
Toll Free: 800-480-3287
Web Address: www.labormarketinfo.edd.ca.gov
LaborMarketInfo, formerly the California Cooperative Occupational Information System, is geared to providing job seekers and employers a wide range of resources, namely the ability to find, access and use labor market information and services. It provides demographical statistics for employment on both a local and regional level, as well as career searching tools for California

residents. The web site is sponsored by California's Employment Development Office.

Recruiters Online Network
947 Essex Ln.
Medina, OH 44256 US
Phone: 888-364-4667
Fax: 888-237-8686
E-mail Address: *info@recruitersonline.com*
Web Address: www.recruitersonline.com
The Recruiters Online Network provides job postings from thousands of recruiters, Careers Online Magazine, a resume database, as well as other career resources.

True Careers, Inc.
Web Address: www.truecareers.com
True Careers, Inc. offers job listings and provides an array of career resources. The company also offers a search of over 2 million scholarships. It is partnered with CareerBuilder.com, which powers its career information and resume posting functions.

USAJOBS
1900 E St. NW
Washington, DC 20415 US
Phone: 202-606-1800
Web Address: usajobs.opm.gov
USAJOBS, a program of the U.S. Office of Personnel Management, is the official job site for the U.S. Federal Government. It provides a comprehensive list of U.S. government jobs, allowing users to search for employment by location; agency; type of work, using the Federal Government's numerical identification code, the General Schedule (GS) Series; or by senior executive positions. It also has a special veterans' employment section; an information center, offering resume and interview tips and other useful information such as hiring trends and a glossary of Federal terms; and allows users to create a profile and post a resume.

Wall Street Journal - CareerJournal
200 Liberty St.
New York, NY 10281 US
Phone: 212-416-2000
Toll Free: 800-568-7625
E-mail Address: *onelinejournal@wsj.com*
Web Address: cj.careercast.com/careers/jobsearch
The Wall Street Journal's CareerJournal, an executive career site, features a job database with thousands of available positions; career news and employment related articles; and advice regarding resume writing, interviews, networking, office life and job hunting.

VIII.   Careers-Job Reference Tools

NewsVoyager
4401 Wilson Blvd., Ste. 900
Arlington, VA 22203-1867 US

Phone: 571-366-1000
Fax: 571-366-1195
E-mail Address: *sally.clarke@naa.org*
Web Address: www.newsvoyager.com
NewsVoyager, a service of the Newspaper Association of America (NAA), links individuals to local, national and international newspapers. Job seekers can search through thousands of classified sections.

Vault.com, Inc.
75 Varick St., Fl. 8
New York, NY 10013 US
Phone: 212-366-4212
E-mail Address: *feedback@staff.vault.com*
Web Address: www.vault.com
Vault.com, Inc. is a comprehensive career web site for employers and employees, with job postings and valuable information on a wide variety of industries. Vault gears many of its features toward MBAs. The site has been recognized by Forbes and Fortune Magazines.

IX.   Chinese Government Agencies-Science & Technology

China Ministry of Science and Technology (MOST)
15B Fuxing Rd.
Beijing, 100862 China
Web Address: www.most.gov.cn
The China Ministry of Science and Technology (MOST) has information and links to its various departments including the Departments of Personnel; Social Development; Rural Science and Technology; Basic Research; and High and New Technology Development and Industrialization.

X.   Computer & Electronics Industry Associations

AeA
5201 Great America Pkwy., Ste. 400
Santa Clara, CA 95054 US
Phone: 408-987-4200
Fax: 408-987-4298
Toll Free: 800-284-4232
E-mail Address: *csc@aeanet.org*
Web Address: www.aeanet.org
AeA, formerly the American Electronics Association, is a trade association which represents thousands of U.S. electronics firms, including electronic systems and component manufacturers, suppliers and end users. It also publishes the annual AeA Directory with geographic and product indexes.

Armed Force Communications and Electronics Association
4400 Fair Lakes Ct.
Fairfax, VA 22033-3899 US
Phone: 703-631-6100
Fax: 703-631-6160

Toll Free: 800-336-4583
Web Address: www.afcea.org
AFCEA is an organization where government and industry leaders can meet to exchange ideas, discuss current problems and identify future requirements in the disciplines of communications, electronics, intelligence and information systems.

Asian-Oceanian Computing Industry Organization (ASOCIO)
2-45 Aomi, Koto-ku
c/o JISA, 17th Fl., Time 24 Bldg.
Tokyo, 135-8073 Japan
Phone: 81-3-5500-2706
Fax: 81-3-5500-2630
E-mail Address: *lucas@jisa.or.jp*
Web Address: www.asocio.org
The Asian-Oceanian Computing Industry Organization's (ASOCIO) objective is to develop the computing society and industry in the region.

Association for Computing Machinery (ACM)
2 Penn Plz., Ste. 701
New York, NY 10121-0701 US
Phone: 212-626-0500
Fax: 212-944-1318
Toll Free: 800-342-6626
E-mail Address: *acmhelp@acm.org.*
Web Address: www.acm.org
The Association for Computing Machinery (ACM) is dedicated to advancing the arts, sciences and applications of computing and information technology. ACM's online Digital Library serves the computing profession with publication and various career resources.

Association for Information Systems (AIS)
Computer Information Systems Dept., J. Mack Robinson College of Bus.
Georgia State University, 35 Broad St., Ste. 917
Atlanta, GA 30303 US
Phone: 404-413-7444
Fax: 404-413-7443
E-mail Address: *office@aisnet.org*
Web Address: www.aisnet.org
The Association for Information Systems (AIS) is an organization for information system researchers and educators working in colleges and universities worldwide. Its website offers substantial resources regarding computer systems research and new developments.

Association of Information Technology Professionals (AITP)
401 N. Michigan Ave., Ste. 2400
Chicago, IL 60611-4267 US
Phone: 312-245-1070
Fax: 312-673-6659
Toll Free: 800-224-9371
E-mail Address: *aitp_hq@aitp.org*

Web Address: www.aitp.org
The Association of Information Technology Professionals (AITP) is a 9,000 member trade organization that provides training and education through partnerships within the information technology industry.

Association of the Computer and Multimedia Industry of Malaysia (PIKOM)
1106 & 1107, Block B, Phileo Damansara II
No. 15, Jalan 16/11
Petaling Jaya, Selangor Darul Ehsan 46350 Malaysia
Phone: 603-7955-2922
Fax: 603-7955-2933
E-mail Address: *info@pikom.org.my*
Web Address: www.pikom.org.my
The Association of the Computer and Multimedia Industry of Malaysia, or, in Malay, Persatuan Industri Komputer dan Multimedia Malaysia (PIKOM), is the national association representing the information and communications technology (ICT) industry in Malaysia.

Business Technology Association (BTA)
12411 Wornall Rd., Ste. 200
Kansas City, MO 64145 US
Phone: 816-303-4082
Fax: 816-941-4838
Toll Free: 800-505-2821
E-mail Address: *info@bta.org*
Web Address: www.bta.org
The Business Technology Association (BTA) is an organization for resellers and dealers of business technology products. Its site offers buying groups, message boards, legal advice, news on industry trends and live chats.

Canadian Advanced Technology Alliances (CATAAlliance)
388 Albert St., Fl. 2
Ottawa, Ontario K1R 5B2 Canada
Phone: 613-236-6550
Fax: 613-236-8189
E-mail Address: *info@cata.ca*
Web Address: www.cata.ca
The Canadian Advanced Technology Alliances (CATAAlliance) is one of Canada's leading trade organizations for the research, development and technology sectors.

China Electronic Components Association (CECA)
No. 22 Shijingshan Rd.
Rm. 1508, Wanshang Blgd.
Beijing, 100043 China
Phone: 86-10-6863-8969
Fax: 86-10-6863-7639
E-mail Address: *zhangjing@chinaceca.com*
Web Address: english.chinaceca.com
The China Electronic Components Association (CECA) acts as the representative of the Chinese electronics components industry. Its web site provides consultation services and research reports on components for a wide variety of markets.

China Electronic Enterprises Association (CEEA)
No.15 Cuiweizhongli, Wanshou Rd.
Haidian District
Beijing, 100036 China
Phone: 86-10-6825-6060
Fax: 86-10-6825-7314
E-mail Address: *qh@ceea.org.cn*
Web Address: www.ceea.org.cn/bar/english/index.htm
The China Electronic Enterprises Association (CEEA) is a nonprofit organization for enterprises engaged in research, development, production, sales and provision of services in the following markets; consumer electronic product manufacturers; electronic elements & equipment manufacturers; telecommunications; information technology and broadcasting.

Computer & Communications Industry Association (CCIA)
900 17th St. NW, Ste. 1100
Washington, DC 20006 US
Phone: 202-783-0070
Fax: 202-783-0534
E-mail Address: *ccia@ccianet.org*
Web Address: www.ccianet.org
The Computer & Communications Industry Association (CCIA) is a nonprofit membership organization for companies and senior executives representing the computer, Internet, information technology (IT) and telecommunications industries.

Computer Technology Industry Association (CompTIA)
1815 S. Meyers Rd., Ste. 300
Oakbrook Terrace, IL 60181-5228 US
Phone: 630-678-8300
Fax: 630-678-8384
E-mail Address: *information@comptia.org*
Web Address: www.comptia.org
The Computer Technology Industry Association (CompTIA) is the leading association representing the international technology community. Its goal is to provide a unified voice, global advocacy and leadership, and to advance industry growth through standards, professional competence, education and business solutions.

Electronic Industries Alliance (EIA)
2500 Wilson Blvd., Ste. 500
Arlington, VA 22201 US
Phone: 703-907-7500
E-mail Address: *kschweers@eia.org*
Web Address: www.eia.org
The Electronic Industries Alliance (EIA) is a trade organization which represents more than 1,300 electronics firms, including governmental information technology

associations and telecommunications, electronic components and consumer electronics manufacturers. The EIA consists of an alliance between the following trade organizations: The Electronic Components, Assemblies & Materials Association (ECA); the Telecommunications Industry Association (TIA); the JEDEC Solid State Technology Association (JEDEC); and the Government Electronics and Information Technology Association (GEIA).

Electronic Industries Association of India (ELCINA)
422 Okhla Industrial Estate
ELCINA House
New Delhi, 110020 India
Phone: 91-11-2692-4597
Fax: 91-11-2692-3440
E-mail Address: elcina@vsnl.com
Web Address: www.elcina.com
The Electronic Industries Association of India (ELCINA) is an organization for the promotion of electronic hardware manufacturing through active representation and advice to the Indian government.

Electronics and Computer Software Export Promotion Council (ESC)
Opp. Asiad Village, Fl. 3, PHD House
New Delhi, 110016 India
Phone: 91-11-2696-5103
Fax: 91-11-2685-3412
E-mail Address: esc@vsnl.net
Web Address: www.escindia.in
The Electronics and Computer Software Export Promotion Council (ESC) represents the info-communication technology industry through electronics and IT trade facilitation.

Electronics Technicians Association (ETA)
5 Depot St.
Greencastle, IN 46135 US
Phone: 765-653-8262
Fax: 765-653-4287
Toll Free: 800-288-3824
E-mail Address: eta@eta-i.org
Web Address: www.eta-i.org
The Electronics Technicians Association (ETA) is a nonprofit professional association for electronics technicians. The firm provides recognized professional credentials for electronics technicians.

European Electronic Component Manufacturers Association (EECA)
Blvd. Auguste Reyers 80
Diamant Bldg. - Bd. A.
Brussels, 1030 Belgium
Phone: 32-2-706-86-00
Fax: 32-2-706-86-05
E-mail Address: secretariat.gen@eeca.be
Web Address: www.eeca.org

The EECA is comprised of four more specific industry associations: the European Semiconductor Industry Association (ESIA); the European Display Industry Association (EDIA); the European Passive Components Industry Association (EPCIA); and the European Packaging and Interconnection Industry Association (EPIA).

Federation of Malaysia Manufacturers (FMM)
Wisma FMM No. 3, Persiaran Dagang, PJU 9
Bandar Sri Damansara
Kuala Lumpur, 52200 Malaysia
Phone: 603-6276-1211
Fax: 603-6274-1266
E-mail Address: webmaster@fmm.org.my
Web Address: www.fmm.org.my
The Federation of Malaysian Manufacturers is an economic organization for the electrical and electronics industry in Malaysia.

Federation of Thai Electrical, Electronics and Allied Industries Club (FTI)
60 New Rachadapisek Rd., Klongtoey, Fl. 4, Zone C
Queen Sirikit National Convention Ctr.
Bangkok, 10110 Thailand
Phone: 66-2-345-1000
Fax: 66-2-345-1296-99
E-mail Address: information@off.fti.or.th
Web Address: www.fti.or.th/FTI Project/GroupCallEng.aspx
The Federation of Thai Electrical, Electronics and Allied Industries Club (FTI) represents manufacturers and related firms in these industries within Thailand.

German Association for Information Technology, Telecom and New Media (BITKOM)
Bundersverband Informationswirtschaft
Telekommunikation und neue Medien
Albrechtstr. 10A
Berlin-Mitte, 10117 Germany
Phone: 49-30-27576-0
Fax: 49-30-27576-400
E-mail Address: bitkom@bitkom.org
Web Address: www.bitkom.org
German Association for Information Technology, Telecom and New Media (BITKOM) represents information technology and telecommunications specialists and companies.

German Electrical and Electronic Manufacturers' Association (ZVEI)
Zentralverband Elektrotechnik- und Elektronikindustrie
Lyoner StraBe 9
Frankfurt am Main, 60528 Germany
Phone: (49)69-6302-0
Fax: (49)69-6302-317
E-mail Address: info@zvei.org
Web Address: www.zvei.org

The German Electrical and Electronic Manufacturers' Association (ZVEI) represents its members interests at the national and international level.

German Society for Information Science and Practive (DGI)
DGI e.V.
Hanauer LandstraBe 151-153
Frankfurt am Main, 60314
Phone: (069) 43 03 13
Fax: (069) 49 09 09 6
E-mail Address: *mail@dgi-info.de*
Web Address: www.dgd.de
The German Society for Information Science and Practive (DGI) represents individuals and corporations and those interested in information processing, retreival and presentation.

Global Semiconductor Alliance (GSA)
5430 LBJ Fwy, 3 Lincoln Ctr., Ste. 280
Dallas, TX 75240 US
Phone: 972-866-7579
Fax: 972-239-2292
E-mail Address: *jshelton@fsa.org*
Web Address: www.gsaglobal.org
The Global Semiconductor Alliance (GSA), formerly the Fabless Semiconductor Association (FSA), represents semiconductor manufacturers that do not have fabrication plants. GSA's mission is to positively impact the growth and investment return for fabless companies (those without fabrication plants) and their partners.

Hong Kong Electronic Industries Association (HKEIA)
Rm. 1201, 12/F, Harbor Crystal Ctr.
100 Granville Rd., Tsimshatsui E., Kowloon
Hong Kong, China
Phone: 852-2778-8328
Fax: 852-2788-2200
E-mail Address: *hkeia@hkeia.org*
Web Address: www.hkeia.org
Hong Kong Electronic Industries Association Limited (HKEIA) is a non-profit trade organization dedicated to the betterment of the electronics industry.

Hong Kong Green Manufacturing Alliance
4/F Hankow Ctr.
5-15 Hankow Rd., Tsimshatsui
Kowloon, Hong Kong, China
Phone: 852-2732-3108
Fax: 852-2721-3494
E-mail Address: *info@hkeama.org*
Web Address: www.gma.org.hk
The Hong Kong Green Manufacturing Alliance seeks to promote and assist members in compliance of all EU or other national legislation regarding the collection and treatment of end-of-life electrical and electronic products and parts and other hazardous substances related to the industry.

Indian Electrical & Electronics Manufacturers Association (IEEMA)
501 Kakad Chambers
132 Dr. Annie Besant Rd., Worli
Mumbai, 400018 India
Phone: 91-22-2493-0532
Fax: 91-22-2493-2705
E-mail Address: *mumbai@ieema.org*
Web Address: www.ieema.org
The Indian Electrical & Electronics Manufacturers Association (IEEMA) represents all sectors of the electrical and allied products businesses of the Indian electrical industry.

Information Technology Association of Canada (ITAC)
5090 Explorer Dr., Ste. 801
Mississauga, Ontario L4W 4T9 Canada
Phone: 905-602-8345
Fax: 905-602-8346
E-mail Address: *jgrosse@itac.ca*
Web Address: www.itac.ca
The Information Technology Association of Canada (ITAC) seeks to promote the contribution of the IT, software, computer and telecommunications industry in Canada.

Information Technology Industry Council (ITI)
1250 Eye St. NW, Ste. 200
Washington, DC 20005 US
Phone: 202-737-8888
Fax: 202-638-4922
Web Address: www.itic.org
The Information Technology Industry Council (ITI) is a premier group of the nation's leading high-tech companies and widely recognized as one of the tech industry's most effective lobbying organization in Washington, in various foreign capitals, and the WTO.

Information Technology Management Association (Singapore)
78 Shenton Way, 26-02
079120 Singapore
E-mail Address: *Vincent.wong@accenture.com*
Web Address: www.itma.org.sg
Information Technology Management Association represents members in the field of information technology management in Singapore.

Institute for Interconnecting and Packaging Electronic Circuits (IPC)
3000 Lakeside Dr., Ste. 309 S
Bannockburn, IL 60015 US
Phone: 847-615-7100
Fax: 847-615-7105
E-mail Address: *SharonStarr@ipc.org*
Web Address: www.ipc.org

The Institute for Interconnecting and Packaging Electronic Circuits (IPC) is a trade association for participants in the global electronic interconnect industry.

International Disk Drive Equipment and Materials Association (IDEMA)

1136 Jacklin Rd.
Milpitas, CA 95035 US
Phone: 408-719-0082
Fax: 408-719-0087
E-mail Address: *awhitlock@idema.org*
Web Address: www.idema.org
The International Disk Drive Equipment and Materials Association (IDEMA) is a not-for-profit trade association that represents its members on issues concerning the hard drive industry worldwide.

International Microelectronics and Packaging Society (IMAPS)

611 2nd St. NE
Washington, DC 20002 US
Phone: 202-548-4001
Fax: 202-548-6115
E-mail Address: *imaps@imaps.org*
Web Address: www.imaps.org
The International Microelectronics and Packaging Society (IMAPS) is dedicated to the advancement and growth of the use of microelectronics and electronic packaging through professional and public education and the dissemination of information.

International Technology Roadmap for Semiconductors (ITRS)

E-mail Address: *linda.wilson@sematech.org*
Web Address: www.itrs.net
The International Technology Roadmap for Semiconductors, known throughout the world as the ITRS, is the fifteen-year assessment of the semiconductor industry's future technology requirements. These future needs drive present-day strategies for world-wide research and development among manufacturers' research facilities, universities, and national labs. It is sponsored by the five leading chip manufacturing regions in the world: Europe, Japan, Korea, Taiwan, and the United States.

Japan Business Federation (Nippon Keidanren)

1150 Connecticut Ave. NW, Ste. 1050
Washington, D.C. 20036 US
Phone: 202-293-8430
Fax: 202-293-8438
Web Address: www.keidanren-usa.org
Japan Business Federation (Nippon Keidanren) is an amalgamation of Japan Federation of Economic Organizations and Japan Federation of Employers' Associations. The group focuses on the technological development of Japanese industry and the promotion of trade.

Japan Electronics and Information Technology Industries Association (JEITA)

Chiyoda First Bldg. S. Wing, 3-2-1
Nishi-Kanda, Chiyoda-ku
Tokyo, Chiyoda-ku 101-0065 Japan
Phone: 81-33-518-6532
Fax: 81-33-295-8727
E-mail Address: *S-miyagi@jeita.or.jp*
Web Address: www.jeita.or.jp/english
Japan Electronics and Information Technology Industries Association (JEITA) promotes the manufacturing and international trade and consumption of electronics and electronic components in Japan.

Korea Association of Information and Telecommunications (KAIT)

NO. 1678-2, 2nd Fl. Dong-Ah Villat 2 Town
Seocho-dong, Seocho-gu
Seoul, 137-070 Korea
Phone: 82-2-580-0580
Fax: 82-2-580-0599
E-mail Address: *webmaster@kait.or.kr*
Web Address: www.kait.or.kr/eng
The KAIT was created to develop and promote the InfoTech, computer, consumer electronics, wireless, software and telecommunications sectors in Korea.

Korea Electronics Association (KEA)

1599 Sangam-dong
Mapo-Gu
Seoul, 135-080 Korea
Phone: 82-2-6388-6000
Fax: 82-2-6388-6009
E-mail Address: *webmaster@gokea.org*
Web Address: www.gokea.org
The Korea Electronics Association (KEA) is an organization for professionals in the electronics industry.

Korea Semiconductor Industry Association (KSIA)

107 Yangjae-Dong Seocho-Ku
5F Dong-IL Bldg.
Seoul, 137-130 Korea
Phone: 82-2-570-5232
Fax: 82-2-577-1719
E-mail Address: *steve@ksia.or.kr*
Web Address: www.ksia.or.kr
The Korean Semiconductor Industry Association (KSIA) represents the interests of Korean semiconductor manufacturers.

Korean Display Equipment Material Industry Association (KODEMIA)

Sunil Bldg. 6F
Yangjae-dong 125-7, Seocho-gu
Seoul, 137-130 Korea
Phone: 82-2-572-5859
Fax: 82-2-572-7118
E-mail Address: *hsy@kodemia.or.kr*

Web Address: www.kodemia.or.kr
KODEMIA is the national trade organization representing about 80 member companies in the Korean display panel industry including manufacturers and suppliers.

Manufacturers' Association for Information Technology (MAIT)

Opp. Asian Games Vlg., Fl. 4, PHD House
New Delhi, 110-016 India
Phone: 91-11-2685-5487
Fax: 91-11-2685-1321
E-mail Address: *mait@vsnl.com*
Web Address: www.mait.com
The Manufacturers' Association for Information Technology (MAIT) is an organization that focuses on the promotion of the hardware, training, design/R&D and the associated services sectors of the Indian IT industry.

National Electrical Manufacturers Association (NEMA)

1300 N. 17th St., Ste. 1752
Rosslyn, VA 22209 US
Phone: 703-841-3200
Fax: 703-841-5900
E-mail Address: *communications@nema.org*
Web Address: www.nema.org
The National Electrical Manufacturers Association (NEMA) develops standards for the electrical manufacturing industry and promotes safety in the manufacture and use of electrical products.

Network Professionals Association (NPA)

1401 Hermes Ln.
San Diego, CA 92154 US
Fax: 888-672-6720
Toll Free: 888-672-6720
Web Address: www.npanet.org
The Network Professionals Association (NPA) is a self-regulating, nonprofit association of network computing professionals that sets standards of technical expertise and professionalism.

North American Chinese Semiconductor Association (NACSA)

P.O. Box 61086
Sunnyvale, CA 94088 US
E-mail Address: *info@nasca.com*
Web Address: www.nacsa.com
The North American Chinese Semiconductor Association (NACSA), founded in Silicon Valley in 1996, is dedicated to the advancement of Chinese professionals in high-tech and related industries, including chip design, chip manufacture, system manufacture, equipment manufacture and software.

Retail Solutions Providers Association (RSPA)

4115 Taggart Creek Rd.
Charlotte, NC 28208 US

Phone: 704-357-3124
Fax: 704-357-3127
E-mail Address: *JFinizio@GoRSPA.org*
Web Address: www.gorspa.org
The Retail Solutions Providers Association (RSPA) is a trade association composed of businesses involved in the purchase, resale, enhancement, installation and maintenance of point-of-sale systems to and for end users.

SEMATECH

2706 Montopolis Dr.
Austin, TX 78741 US
Phone: 512-356-3500
E-mail Address: *media.relations@sematech.org*
Web Address: www.sematech.org
SEMATECH is an international consortium of semiconductor manufacturing companies. The researches advanced technology and manufacturing effectiveness in the semiconductor industry, working to decrease time between innovation and manufacturing.

Semiconductor & Electronics Industries in the Philippines, Inc. (SEIPI)

RCBC Plz., Ayala Ave.
Unit 902, Twr. 2
Makati City, 1200 Philippines
Phone: 632-844-9028
Fax: 632-844-9037
E-mail Address: *philippine.electronics@seipi.org.ph*
Web Address: www.seipi.org.ph
The SEIPI Foundation is an organization of foreign and local semiconductor and electronics companies in the Philippines.

Semiconductor Equipment and Materials International (SEMI)

3081 Zanker Rd.
San Jose, CA 95134 US
Phone: 408-943-6900
Fax: 408-428-9600
E-mail Address: *semihq@semi.org*
Web Address: www.wps2a.semi.org
Semiconductor Equipment and Materials International (SEMI) is a trade association serving the global semiconductor equipment, materials and flat-panel display industries.

Semiconductor Equipment Association of Japan (SEAJ)

3 Rokubancho Chiyoda-Tu
6F Rokubancho SK Bldg.
Tokyo, 102-0085 Japan
Phone: 03-3261-8260
Fax: 03-3261-8263
Web Address: www.seaj.or.jp
The Semiconductor Equipment Association of Japan (SEAJ) represents the semiconductor manufacturing equipment industry in Japan. The association is an

organization of semiconductor manufacturing and flat panel display (FPD) manufacturing equipment manufacturers.

Semiconductor Industry Association (SIA)
181 Metro Dr., Ste. 450
San Jose, CA 95110 US
Phone: 408-436-6600
Fax: 408-436-6646
E-mail Address: mailbox@sia-online.org
Web Address: www.sia-online.org
The Semiconductor Industry Association (SIA) is a trade association representing the semiconductor industry in the U.S. Through its coalition of 95 companies, SIA represents more than 85% of semiconductor production in the U.S. The coalition aims to advance the competitiveness of the chip industry and shape public policy on issues particular to the industry.

Shenzhen Electronics Industries Association (SZEIA)
Huaqiang Rd.
831-835 SEG-Kangle Bldg.
Shenzhen, 518031 China
Phone: 86-755-83354641
Fax: 86-755-8321-5103
E-mail Address: szseia@szeia.com
Web Address: www.szeia.com
The Shenzhen Electronics Industries Association (SZEIA) is one of China's primary organizations for the electronics industry.

Singapore Computer Society
53/53A Neil Rd.
088891 Singapore
Phone: 65-6226-2567
Fax: 65-6226-2569
E-mail Address: scs.secretariat@scs.org.sg
Web Address: www.scs.org.sg
The Singapore Computer Society is the membership society for infocom professionals in Singapore.

Storage Network Industry Association (SNIA)
500 Sansome St., Ste. 504
San Francisco, CA 94111 US
Phone: 415-402-0006
Fax: 415-402-0009
E-mail Address: lesley.bakker@snia.org
Web Address: www.snia.org
The Storage Network Industry Association (SNIA) is a trade associated dedicated to viability of storage networks within the IT industry. SNIA sponsors technical work groups, produces the Storage Networking Conference series and maintains a Technology Center in Colorado Springs, Colorado.

Surface Mount Technology Association (SMTA)
5200 Willson Rd., Ste. 215
Edina, MN 55424 US
Phone: 952-920-7682
Fax: 952-926-1819
E-mail Address: tom_forsythe@kyzen.com
Web Address: www.smta.org
The Surface Mount Technology Association (SMTA) is an international network of professionals whose careers encompass electronic assembly technologies, microsystems, emerging technologies and associated business operations.

Taiwan Electrical and Electronic Manufacturers' Association (TEEMA)
Min Chuan E. Rd.
Prince Financial Ctr., 6F, No. 109, Sec. 6
Taipei, 114 Taiwan
Phone: 886-2-8792-6666
Fax: 886-2-8792-6088
Web Address: www.teema.org.tw
The Taiwan Electrical and Electronic Manufacturers' Association (TEEMA) works as an intermediary between its members and the government to help the industry to succeed.

Taiwan Semiconductor Industry Association (TSIA)
195 Sec. 4, Chung Hsing Rd.
Rm. 1246, Bldg. 51
Chutung, Hsinchu 310 Taiwan
Phone: 886-3-5913560
Fax: 886-3-5820056
E-mail Address: candy@tsia.org.tw
Web Address: www.tsia.org.tw
The TSIA is Taiwan's national trade organization, containing more than 140 member companies that represent all aspects of the semiconductor industry.

Technology Association of America (TAA)
1401 Wilson Blvd., Ste. 1100
Arlington, VA 22209 US
Phone: 703-522-5055
Fax: 703-525-2279
Web Address: www.itaa.org
The Technology Association of America (TAA) is a merger between the AeA (formerly the American Electronics Association) and the Information Technology Association of America (ITAA). The TAA is a nationwide nonprofit trade association that represents all segments of the technology industry.

USB Implementers Forum (USB-IF)
E-mail Address: admin@usb.org
Web Address: www.usb.org
USB Implementers Forum, Inc. is a nonprofit corporation founded by the group of companies that developed the Universal Serial Bus specification. The USB-IF was formed to provide a support organization and forum for the advancement and adoption of Universal Serial Bus technology. The Forum facilitates the development of high-quality compatible USB peripherals (devices), and

promotes the benefits of USB and the quality of products
that have passed compliance testing. Some of the many
activities that the USB-IF supports include USB
compliance workshops and USB compliance test
development.

Vietnam Electronic Industries Association (VEIA)
11B Phan Huy Chu, Hoan Kiem
Ha Noi, Vietnam
Phone: 84-4-933-2845
Fax: 84-4-933-2846
E-mail Address: *veia-vn@hn.vnn.vn*
Web Address: www.VEIA.org.vn
Vietnam Electronic Industries Association (VEIA) is the
representative body for the electronic businesses in
Vietnam.

**World Information Technology and Services Alliance
(WITSA)**
8300 Boone Blvd., Ste. 450
Vienna, VA 22182-2633 US
Phone: 571-265-5964
Fax: 703-893-1269
E-mail Address: *ahalvorsen@witsa.org*
Web Address: www.witsa.org
The World Information Technology and Services Alliance
(WITSA) is a consortium of over 60 information
technology (IT) industry associations from economies
around the world. WITSA members represent over 90
percent of the world IT market. Founded in 1978 and
originally known as the World Computing Services
Industry Association, WITSA is an advocate in
international public policy issues affecting the creation of a
robust global information infrastructure.

XI. Computer & Electronics Industry Resources

Centre for Development of Advanced Computing
Gulmohar Cross Rd. 9
Maharashtra
Mumbai, 400 049 India
Phone: 91-22-2620-1606
Fax: 91-22-2621-0139
Web Address: www.cdac.in
The Centre for Development of Advanced Computing is a
research and development institution created for the
design, development and deployment information
technology solutions for economic and human
advancement.

**Computer Professionals for Social Responsibility
(CPSR)**
P.O. Box 20046
Stanford, CA 94309 US
Phone: 650-989-1294
E-mail Address: *office@cpsr.org*
Web Address: www.cpsr.org

Computer Professionals for Social Responsibility (CPSR)
is a global organization promoting the responsible use of
computer technology. CPSR is a public interest alliance of
computer scientists and others concerned about the impact
of computer technology on society.

Department of Information Technology (India)
Electronics Niketan
6 CGO Complex, Lodhi Rd.
New Delhi, 110003 India
Phone: 011-24369903
Fax: 011-24366259
E-mail Address: *sansad@mit.gov.in*
Web Address: www.mit.gov.in
The Department of Information Technology, a part of the
Ministry of Communications & Information Technology
(MIT) of the Government of India, is charged with
promoting the information technology and
communications industries.

EETimes
Phone: 516-562-5623
E-mail Address: *jyoshida@cmp.com*
Web Address: www.eetimes.com
The EETimes is an online magazine devoted to electronic
engineers in the semiconductor, systems and software
design fields.

**Information Technology and Innovation Foundation
(ITIF)**
1250 I St. NW, Ste. 200
Washington, DC 20005 US
Phone: 202-449-1351
Fax: 202-638-4922
E-mail Address: *mail@innovationpolicy.org*
Web Address: www.itif.org
Information Technology and Innovation Foundation (ITIF)
is a non-partisan research and educational institute – a
think tank – whose mission is to formulate and promote
public policies to advance technological innovation and
productivity internationally, in Washington, and in the
States. Recognizing the vital role of technology in ensuring
American prosperity, ITIF focuses on innovation,
productivity, and digital economy issues.

ISWorld Net Singapore
Web Address: www.fba.nus.edu.sg
ISWorld Net Singapore contains directories, research
centers, projects, associations, materials, conferences and
other information pertaining to information technology and
computing in Singapore.

XII. Computer Education & Training

Association of Macintosh Trainers (AMT)
117 Portland Ave. S., Ste. 302
Minneapolis, MN 55401 US
E-mail Address: *info@mactrainers.com*

Web Address: www.mactrainers.com
The Association of Macintosh Trainers (AMT) offers a web site where consultants and designers can improve their Macintosh computer skills.

XIII. Consulting Industry Associations

National Association of Computer Consultant Businesses (NACCB)
1420 King St., Ste. 610
Alexandria, VA 22314 US
Phone: 703-838-2050
Fax: 703-838-3610
E-mail Address: *staff@naccb.org*
Web Address: www.naccb.org
The National Association of Computer Consultant Businesses (NACCB) is the only national association exclusively devoted to representing and developing relationships among companies that specialize in providing highly skilled computer professionals to clients in need of technical support and IT services.

Software Contractors' Guild
3 Country Club Dr., Ste. 303
Manchester, NH 03102 US
E-mail Address: *admin@scguild.com*
Web Address: www.scguild.com
Software Contractors' Guild puts businesses in touch with consultants.

XIV. Corporate Information Resources

bizjournals.com
120 W. Morehead St., Ste. 400
Charlotte, NC 28202 US
Web Address: www.bizjournals.com
Bizjournals.com is the online media division of American City Business Journals, the publisher of dozens of leading city business journals nationwide. It provides access to research into the latest news regarding companies small and large.

Business Wire
44 Montgomery St., Fl. 39
San Francisco, CA 94104 US
Phone: 415-986-4422
Fax: 415-788-5335
Toll Free: 800-227-0845
Web Address: www.businesswire.com
Business Wire offers news releases, industry- and company-specific news, top headlines, conference calls, IPOs on the Internet, media services and access to tradeshownews.com and BW Connect On-line through its informative and continuously updated web site.

Edgar Online, Inc.
50 Washington St., Fl. 11
Norwalk, CT 06854 US

Phone: 203-852-5666
Fax: 203-852-5667
Toll Free: 800-416-6651
Web Address: www.edgar-online.com
Edgar Online, Inc. is a gateway and search tool for viewing corporate documents, such as annual reports on Form 10-K, filed with the U.S. Securities and Exchange Commission.

PR Newswire Association LLC
810 7th Ave., Fl. 32
New York, NY 10019 US
Phone: 201-360-6700
Toll Free: 800-832-5522
E-mail Address: *information@prnewswire.com*
Web Address: www.prnewswire.com
PR Newswire Association LLC provides comprehensive communications services for public relations and investor relations professionals ranging from information distribution and market intelligence to the creation of online multimedia content and investor relations web sites. Users can also view recent corporate press releases. The Association is owned by United Business Media plc.

Silicon Investor
100 W. Main
P.O. Box 29
Freeman, MO 64746 US
E-mail Address: *admin_dave@techstocks.com*
Web Address: siliconinvestor.advfn.com
Silicon Investor is focused on providing information about technology companies. The company's web site serves as a financial discussion forum and offers quotes, profiles and charts.

XV. Economic Data & Research

Economic and Social Research Council (ESRC)
Polaris House
North Star Avenue
Swindon, SN2 1UJ UK
Phone: 01793 413000
Fax: 01793 413001
Web Address: www.esrc.ac.uk
The Economic and Social Research Council (ESRC) funds research and training in social and economic issues. It is an independent organization, established by Royal Charter. The group focuses on six research areas: economic affairs, education and human development, environment and planning, government and law, industry and employment and social affairs.

Eurostat
Phone: 32-2-299-9696
Toll Free: 80-0-6789-1011
Web Address: www.epp.eurostat.ec.europa.eu
Eurostat is the European Union's service that publishes a wide variety of comprehensive statistics on European

industries, populations, trade, agriculture, technology, environment and other matters.

India Brand Equity Foundation (IBEF)
249-F Sector 18
Udyog Vihar Phase IV
Gurgaon, Haryana 122015 India
Phone: 91-124-4014060
Fax: 91-124-4013873
E-mail Address: *ceo@ibef.org*
Web Address: www.ibef.org
India Brand Equity Foundation (IBEF) is a public-private partnership between the Ministry of Commerce and Industry, Government of India, and the Confederation of Indian Industry. The Foundation's primary objective is to build positive economic perceptions of India globally. It aims to effectively present the India business perspective and leverage business partnerships in a globalizing market-place.

National Bureau of Statistics (China)
57, Yuetan Nanjie, Sanlihe
Xicheng District
Beijing, 100826 China
Fax: 86-10-68782000
E-mail Address: *info@stats.gov.cn*
Web Address: www.stats.gov.cn/english
The National Bureau of Statistics of China provides statistics and economic data regarding China's economic and social issues.

Organization for Economic Co-operation and Development (OECD)
2 rue André Pascal
Cedex 16
Paris, F-75775 France
Phone: 33-145-24-8200
Fax: 33-145-24-8500
Web Address: www.oecd.org
The Organization for Economic Co-operation and Development (OECD) publishes detailed economic, government, population, social and trade statistics on a country-by-country basis for over 30 nations representing the world's largest economies. Sectors covered range from industry, labor, technology and patents, to health care, environment and globalization.

Statistics Bureau, Director-General for Policy Planning
19-1 Wakamatsu-cho
Shinjuku-ku
Tokyo, 162-8668 Japan
Phone: 81-3-5273-2020
Web Address: www.stat.go.jp/english
The Statistics Bureau and the Director-General for Policy Planning of Japan play the central role in the official statistical system in producing and disseminating basic official statistics, and coordinating statistical work under the Statistics Act and other legislation.

Statistics Canada
150 Tunney's Pasture Driveway
Ottawa, ON K1A 0T6 Canada
Phone: 613-951-8116
Fax: 613-951-0581
Toll Free: 800-263-1136
Web Address: www.statcan.gc.ca
A complete portal to Canadian economic data and statistics.

STAT-USA/Internet
STAT-USA, HCHB, U.S. Dept. of Commerce
Rm. 4885
Washington, DC 20230 US
Phone: 202-482-1986
Fax: 202-482-2164
Toll Free: 800-782-8872
E-mail Address: *statmail@esa.doc.gov*
Web Address: www.stat-usa.gov
STAT-USA/Internet offers daily economic news, statistical releases and databases relating to export and trade, as well as the domestic economy. It is provided by STAT-USA, which is an agency in the Economics & Statistics Administration of the U.S. Department of Commerce. The site mainly consists of two main databases, the State of the Nation (SOTN), which focuses on the current state of the U.S. economy; and the Global Business Opportunities (GLOBUS) & the National Trade Data Bank (NTDB), which deals with U.S. export opportunities, global political/socio-economic conditions and other world economic issues.

The Centre for European Economic Research (ZEW)
Wirtschaftsforschung GmbH
Postfach 10 34 43
Mannheim, D-68034 Germany
Phone: 49(0)621-1235-01
Fax: 49(0)621-1235-224
E-mail Address: *info@zew.de*
Web Address: www.zew.de/en
Zentrum fur Europaische, The Centre for European Economic Research (ZEW), distinguishes itself in the analyses of internationally comparative data in the European context and in the creation of databases which are important as a basis for scientific research. The institute maintains a special library relevant to economic research and provides external parties with selected data for the purpose of scientific research. ZEW also offers public events and seminars concentrating on banking, business and other economic-political topics.

XVI.	Electronic Health Records/Continuity of Care Records

American Health Information Management Association (AHIMA)
233 N. Michigan Ave., Fl. 21
Chicago, IL 60601-5800 US

Phone: 312-233-1100
Fax: 312-233-1090
E-mail Address: *info@ahima.org*
Web Address: www.ahima.org
The American Health Information Management
Association (AHIMA) is a professional association that
consists health information management professionals who
work throughout the health care industry.

XVII. Engineering Indices

Engineering Library
Cornell University
Carpenter Hall
Ithaca, NY 14853 US
Phone: 607-255-5933
Fax: 607-255-0278
E-mail Address: *engranswers@cornell.edu*
Web Address: www.astech.library.cornell.edu/ast/engr
Cornell University's Engineering Library web site has a
number of resources concerning engineering research.

XVIII. Engineering, Research & Scientific Associations

Agency For Science, Technology And Research (A*STAR)
1 Fusionopolis Way
20-10 Connexis N. Twr.
138632 Singapore
Phone: 65-6826-6111
Fax: 65-6777-1711
Web Address: www.a-star.edu.sg
The Agency For Science, Technology And Research
(A*STAR) of Singapore comprises the Biomedical
Research Council (BMRC), the Science and Engineering
Research Council (SERC), Exploit Technologies Pte Ltd
(ETPL), the A*STAR Graduate Academy (A*GA) and the
Corporate Planning and Administration Division (CPAD).
Both Councils fund the A*STAR public research institutes
which conducts research in specific niche areas in science,
engineering and biomedical science.

American National Standards Institute (ANSI)
1819 L St. NW, Fl. 6
Washington, DC 20036 US
Phone: 202-293-8020
Fax: 202-293-9287
E-mail Address: *info@ansi.org*
Web Address: www.ansi.org
The American National Standards Institute (ANSI) is a
private, nonprofit organization that administers and
coordinates the U.S. voluntary standardization and
conformity assessment system. Its mission is to enhance
both the global competitiveness of U.S. business and the
quality of life by promoting and facilitating voluntary
consensus standards and conformity assessment systems
and safeguarding their integrity.

American Society for Engineering Education (ASEE)
1818 North St. NW, Ste. 600
Washington, DC 20036-2479 US
Phone: 202-331-3500
Fax: 202-265-8504
E-mail Address: *publicaffairs@asee.org*
Web Address: asee.org
The American Society for Engineering Education (ASEE)
is dedicated to promoting and improving engineering and
technology education.

Association for Electrical, Electronic & Information Technologies (VDE)
Stresemannallee 15
Frankfurt am Main, 60596 Germany
Phone: 49(0)69 6308 284
Fax: 49(0)69 96315215
E-mail Address: *presse@vde.com*
Web Address: www.vde.com
The Association for Electrical, Electronic & Information
Technologies (VDE) is an organization with roughly
34,000 members representing one of the largest technical
associations in Europe.

Broadcast Technological Society (BTS) of the Institute of Electrical & Electronics Engineers, Inc.
445 Hoes Ln.
Piscataway, NJ 08854 US
Phone: 732-562-3906
Fax: 732-981-1769
E-mail Address: *bts@ieee.org*
Web Address:
www.ieee.org/organizations/society/bt/index.html
The Broadcast Technological Society (BTS) is the arm of
the Institute of Electrical & Electronics Engineers (IEEE)
devoted to devices, equipment, techniques and systems
related to broadcast technology.

China Association for Science and Technology (CAST)
3 Fuxing Rd.
Beijing, 100863 China
Phone: 8610-68571898
Fax: 8610-68571897
E-mail Address: *english@cast.org.cn*
Web Address: english.cast.org.cn
The China Association for Science and Technology
(CAST) is the largest national non-governmental
organization of scientific and technological workers in
China. The association has 167 member organizations in
the field of engineering, science and technology.

Chinese Academy of Sciences (CAS)
52 Sanlihe Rd.
Beijing, 100864 China
Phone: 86-10-68597289
Fax: 86-10-68512458
E-mail Address: *bulletin@mail.casipm.ac.cn*
Web Address: english.cas.ac.cn

By 2010, the Chinese Academy of Sciences (CAS) plans on maintaining roughly 80 national institutes for science and technological innovation each with distinctive features with roughly thirty planned for internationally acknowledged, high-level research.

Community Research and Development Information Service (CORDIS)
Office for Official Publications of the European Union Communities
2 rue Mercier
Luxembourg, L-2985 Luxembourg
Phone: 352-2929-42210
E-mail Address: *helpdesk@cordis.europa.eu*
Web Address: cordis.europa.eu
The Community Research and Development Information Service (CORDIS) provides information about research and development sponsored and supported by the European Union. It is managed by the Office for Official Publications of the European Union Communities (Publications Office).

Engineer's Club (The) (TEC)
1737 Silverwood Dr.
San Jose, CA 95124 US
Phone: 408-316-0488
E-mail Address: *tec@engineers.com*
Web Address: www.engineers.com/index.htm
The Engineer's Club (TEC) provides resources and web sites for engineers and technical professionals, including an online forum.

Federation of Technology Industries (FHI)
Federatie Van Technologiebranches
Dodeweg 6B
AK LEUSDEN, 3832 Netherlands
Phone: (033) 465 75 07
Fax: (033) 461 66 38
E-mail Address: *info@fhi.nl*
Web Address: federatie.fhi.nl
The Federation of Technology Industries (FHI) is the Dutch trade organization representing industrial electronics, industry automation, laboratory technology and medical technolgy.

IEEE Communications Society (ComSoc)
3 Park Ave., Fl. 17
New York, NY 10016 US
Phone: 212-705-8900
Fax: 212-705-8999
E-mail Address: *society@comsoc.org*
Web Address: www.comsoc.org
The IEEE Communications Society (ComSoc) is composed of industry professionals with a common interest in advancing communications technologies.

Indian Institute Of Technology - Roorkee
Roorkee

Uttarakhand, 247 667 India
Phone: 91-1332-285311
E-mail Address: *regis@iitr.ernet.in*
Web Address: www.iitr.ac.in
Indian Institute of Technology - Roorkee is among the foremost institutes in higher technological education and engineering in India for basic and applied research.

Industrial Research Institute (IRI)
2200 Clarendon Blvd., Ste. 1102
Arlington, VA 22201 US
Phone: 703-647-2580
Fax: 703-647-2581
E-mail Address: *information@iriinc.org*
Web Address: www.iriinc.org
The Industrial Research Institute (IRI) is a nonprofit organization of over 200 leading industrial companies, representing industries such as aerospace, automotive, chemical, computers and electronics, which carry out industrial research efforts in the U.S. manufacturing sector. IRI helps members improve research and development capabilities.

Institute of Electrical and Electronics Engineers (IEEE)
3 Park Ave., Fl. 17
New York, NY 10016-5997 US
Phone: 212-419-7900
Fax: 212-752-4929
E-mail Address: *ieeeusa@ieee.org*
Web Address: www.ieee.org
The Institute of Electrical and Electronics Engineers (IEEE) is a nonprofit, technical professional association of more than 375,000 individual members in approximately 160 countries. The IEEE sets global technical standards and acts as an authority in technical areas ranging from computer engineering, biomedical technology and telecommunications, to electric power, aerospace and consumer electronics.

Institution of Engineering and Technology (The) (IET)
Michael Faraday House
Stevenage
Herts, SG1 2AY UK
Phone: 44-1438-313-311
Fax: 44-1438-765-526
E-mail Address: *postmaster@theiet.org*
Web Address: www.theiet.org
The Institution of Engineering and Technology (IET) is an innovative international organization for electronics, electrical, manufacturing and IT professionals.

International Electrotechnical Commission (IEC)
3, rue de Varembe
P.O. Box 131
Geneva 20, CH-1211 Switzerland
Phone: 41-22-919-02-11
Fax: 41-22-919-03-00

E-mail Address: *info@iec.ch*
Web Address: www.iec.ch
The International Electrotechnical Commission (IEC), based in Switzerland, promotes international cooperation on all questions of standardization and related matters in electrical and electronic engineering.

International Standards Organization (ISO)
1 ch. de la Voie-Creuse
Case Postale 56
Geneva 20, CH-1211 Switzerland
Phone: 41-22-749-01-11
Fax: 41-22-733-34-30
E-mail Address: *central@iso.org*
Web Address: www.iso.org
The International Standards Organization (ISO) is a global consortium of national standards institutes from 157 countries. The established International Standards are designed to make products and services more efficient, safe and clean.

Japan Science and Technology Agency (JST)
Kawaguchi Ctr. Bldg.
4-1-8 Honcho, Kawaguchi-shi
Saitama, 332-0012 Japan
Phone: 81-48-226-5601
Fax: 81-48-226-5651
E-mail Address: *www-admin@tokyo.jst.go.jp*
Web Address: www.jst.go.jp/EN
The Japan Science and Technology Agency (JST) aims to act as a core organization for implementation of the nation's science and technology policies by conducting research and development with particular emphasis on new technological needs.

Optical Society of America (OSA)
2010 Massachusetts Ave. NW
Washington, DC 20036-1023 US
Phone: 202-223-8130
Fax: 202-223-1096
E-mail Address: *info@osa.org*
Web Address: www.osa.org
The Optical Society of America (OSA) is an interdisciplinary society offering synergy between all components of the optics industry, from basic research to commercial applications such as fiber-optic networks. It has a membership group of over 14,000 individuals from over 81 countries. Members include scientists, engineers, educators, technicians and business leaders.

Research in Germany, German Academic Exchange Service (DAAD)
Kennedyallee 50
Bonn, 53175 Germany
Phone: 49(0)228 882 - 0
Fax: 49(0)228 882 - 660
Web Address: www.research-in-germany.de
The Research in Germany portal, German Academic Exchange Service (DAAD), is an information platform and contact point for those looking to find out more about Germany's research landscape and its latest research achievements. The portal is an initiative of the Federal Ministry of Education and Research.

Royal Society (The)
6-9 Carlton House Ter.
London, SW1Y 5AG UK
Phone: 44-20-7451-2500
Fax: 44-20-7930-2170
E-mail Address: *info@royalsociety.org*
Web Address: www.royalsoc.ac.uk
The Royal Society is the UK's leading scientific organization. It operates as a national academy of science, supporting scientists, engineers, technologists and research. On its website, you will find a wealth of data about the research and development initiatives of its fellows and foreign members.

Virginia Center for Innovative Technology
2214 Rock Hill Rd., Ste. 600
Herndon, VA 20170-4228 US
Phone: 703-689-3000
Fax: 703-689-3041
E-mail Address: *hconnors@cit.org*
Web Address: www.cit.org
The Virginia Center for Innovative Technology is a nonprofit organization designed to enhance the research and development capability of Virginia's major research universities.

World Federation of Engineering Organizations
Maison de l'UNESCO 1
rue Miollis
Paris, Cedex 15 F-75732 France
Phone: 33-1-45-68-48-46
Fax: 33-1-45-68-48-65
E-mail Address: *tl.fmoi@unesco.org*
Web Address: www.wfeo.org
World Federation of Engineering Organizations (WFEO) is an international non-governmental organization that represents major engineering professional societies in over 90 nations. It has several standing committees including engineering and the environment, technology, communications, capacity building, education, energy and women in engineering.

XIX.   Game Industry Associations

ELSPA (UK Interactive Entertainment Association)
167 Wardour Street
London, W1F 8WP UK
Phone: 020 7534 0580
Fax: 020 7534 0581
E-mail Address: *info@elspa.com*

Web Address: www.elspa.com
The UK Interactive Entertainment Association operating as ELSPA is the UK's leading videogames trade body. Membership includes almost all major companies involved with the publishing and development of videogames in the UK.

Entertainment Software Association (ESA)
575 7th St. NW, Ste. 300
Washington, DC 20004 US
E-mail Address: *esa@theesa.com*
Web Address: www.theesa.com
The Entertainment Software Association (ESA) serves the business and public affairs needs of companies that publish video and computer games for consoles, personal computers and the Internet. The ESA owns the E3 Media & Business Summit, a major invitation-only annual trade show for the video game industry.

Hong Kong Digital Entertainment Industry Support Centre
100 Cyberport Rd.
Unit 403, IT St. Cyberport 3
Hong Kong, Hong Kong China
Phone: 3166-3777
Fax: 2788-5770
E-mail Address: *hkde_enquiry@hkde.org*
Web Address: www.hkde.org
The Hong Kong Digital Entertainment Industry Support Centre comprises three major sectors in Hong Kong, namely entertainment software, computer animation, and digital effects in the production of videos and films. The center supports the development of professionals in the field of animation, design, and programming as well as promotes traditional industries through business development, marketing and branding.

International Game Developers Association (IGDA)
19 Mantua Rd.
Mt. Royal, NJ 08061 US
Phone: 856-423-2990
Fax: 856-423-3420
E-mail Address: *contact@igda.org*
Web Address: www.igda.org
The International Game Developers Association (IGDA) represents members who produce video games. The firm promotes professional development and advocates issues which affect the game developer community.

TIGA (The Independent Game Developers Association Limited)
One London Mall, Fl. 6
London, EC2Y 5EB UK
Phone: 44 (0) 845 0941095
E-mail Address: *info@tiga.org*
Web Address:
TIGA is the trade association representing the UK's games industry. Its members include independent games

developers, in-house publisher owned developers, outsourcing companies, technology businesses and universities.

XX. Industry Research/Market Research

Forrester Research
400 Technology Sq.
Cambridge, MA 02139 US
Phone: 617-613-6000
Fax: 617-613-5200
Toll Free: 866-367-7378
Web Address: www.forrester.com
Forrester Research identifies and analyzes emerging trends in technology and their impact on business. Among the firm's specialties are the financial services, retail, health care, entertainment, automotive and information technology industries.

Gartner, Inc.
56 Top Gallant Rd.
Stamford, CT 06904-7700 US
Phone: 203-964-0096
E-mail Address: *tom.mccall@gartner.com*
Web Address: www.gartner.com
Gartner, Inc. provides thought leadership and strategic consulting services to more than 9,000 organizations worldwide.

MarketResearch.com
11200 Rockville Pike, Ste. 504
Rockville, MD 20852 US
Phone: 240-747-3000
Fax: 240-747-3004
Toll Free: 800-298-5699
E-mail Address: *customerservice@marketresearch.com*
Web Address: www.marketresearch.com
MarketResearch.com is a leading broker for professional market research and industry analysis. Users are able to search the company's database of research publications including data on global industries, companies, products and trends.

Plunkett Research, Ltd.
P.O. Drawer 541737
Houston, TX 77254-1737 US
Phone: 713-932-0000
Fax: 713-932-7080
E-mail Address: *customersupport@plunkettresearch.com*
Web Address: www.plunkettresearch.com
Plunkett Research, Ltd. is a leading provider of market research, industry trends analysis and business statistics. Since 1985, it has served clients worldwide, including corporations, universities, libraries, consultants and government agencies. At the firm's web site, visitors can view product information and pricing and access a great deal of basic market information on industries such as

financial services, infotech, e-commerce, health care and biotech.

Yankee Group (The)
800 Boylston St.
Prudential Twr., 27th Fl.
Boston, MA 02199-8106 US
Phone: 617-598-7200
E-mail Address: *info@yankeegroup.com*
Web Address: www.yankeegroup.com
The Yankee Group provides research and consulting services focusing on global communications, wireless, Internet and e-business markets and technologies.

XXI. Internet & Online Business Resources

InternetNews.com
Web Address: www.internetnews.com
InternetNews.com offers real-time business news specifically designed for Internet technology managers. News categories include hardware, software, mobility, content, networking and search.

XXII. Internet Industry Associations

Asia & Pacific Internet Association (APIA)
c/o PIKOM 1107 Block B Phileo Damansara II
15 Jalan 16/11 Petaling Jaya
Selangor Darul Ehsan, 46350 Malaysia
Phone: 603-7955-2933
E-mail Address: *apia-sec@apia.org*
Web Address: www.apia.org
Asia & Pacific Internet Association (APIA) is a nonprofit trade association whose aim is to promote the business interests of the Internet-related service industry in the Asia Pacific region. The site contains a list of organizations, standards, regional Internet registries and related Asia Pacific organizations.

China Internet Network Information Center
4 South 4th St., Zhongguancun
Haidian District
Beining, 100190 China
Phone: 86-10-58813000
Fax: 86-10-58812666
E-mail Address: *service@cnnic.cn*
Web Address: www.cnnic.cn
The China Internet Network Information Center compiles Internet information and databases regarding the Internet community and facilitates the development and application of Internet resources and relevant technologies in China.

Cooperative Association for Internet Data Analysis (CAIDA)
9500 Gilman Dr., Mail Stop 0505
La Jolla, CA 92093-0505 US
Phone: 858-534-5000
E-mail Address: *info@caida.org*

Web Address: www.caida.org
The Cooperative Association for Internet Data Analysis (CAIDA) works to promote an atmosphere of greater cohesion on the Internet. Member organizations come from the government, commercial and research sectors. CAIDA is located at the San Diego Supercomputer Center (SDSC) on the campus of the University of California, San Diego (UCSD).

Federation of Internet Service Providers of the Americas (FISPA)
124 W. John St.
Matthews, NC 28105 US
Phone: 704-844-2540
Fax: 704-844-2728
E-mail Address: *communications@fispa.org*
Web Address: www.fispa.org
The Federation of Internet Service Providers of the Americas (FISPA) encourages discussion, education and collective buying power for organizations involved in providing Internet access, web hosting, web design and other Internet products and services.

International Academy of Digital Arts and Sciences (IADAS)
19 W. 21st St., Ste. 602
New York, NY 10010 US
Phone: 212-675-4890
E-mail Address: *dmdavies@iadas.net*
Web Address: www.iadas.net
The International Academy of Digital Arts and Sciences (IADAS) is dedicated to the progress of new media worldwide. It runs The Webby Awards, honoring web sites for technological and creative achievements.

Internet Alliance
1111 19th St. NW, Ste. 1100
Washington, DC 20035-5782 US
Phone: 202-861-2476
E-mail Address: *emilyh@internetalliance.org*
Web Address: www.internetalliance.org
The Internet Alliance strives to assist the Internet industry in becoming the most important mass-market medium of the 21st century.

Internet Law & Policy Forum (ILPF)
2440 Western Ave., Ste. 709
Seattle, WA 98121 US
Phone: 206-727-0700
Fax: 206-374-2263
E-mail Address: *admin@ilpf.org*
Web Address: www.ilpf.org
The Internet Law & Policy Forum (ILPF) is dedicated to the sustainable global development of the Internet through legal and public policy initiatives. It is an international nonprofit organization whose member companies develop and deploy the Internet in every aspect of business today.

Internet Society (ISOC)
1775 Wiehle Ave., Ste. 102
Reston, VA 20190-5108 US
Phone: 703-439-2120
Fax: 703-326-9881
E-mail Address: *isoc@isoc.org*
Web Address: www.isoc.org
The Internet Society (ISOC) is a nonprofit organization
that provides leadership in public policy issues that
influence the future of the Internet. The organization is the
home of groups that maintain infrastructure standards for
the Internet, such as the Internet Engineering Task Force
(IETF) and the Internet Architecture Board (IAB).

Internet Systems Consortium, Inc. (ISC)
950 Charter St.
Redwood City, CA 94063 US
Phone: 650-423-1300
Fax: 650-423-1355
E-mail Address: *info@isc.org*
Web Address: www.isc.org
The Internet Systems Consortium, Inc. (ISC) is a nonprofit
organization with extensive expertise in the development,
management, maintenance and implementation of Internet
technologies.

NetCoalition
400 N. Capitol St. NW, Ste. 585
Washington, DC 20001 US
Phone: 202-347-8099
Fax: 202-783-6620
E-mail Address: *ginny@netcoalition.com*
Web Address: www.netcoalition.com
NetCoalition serves as a leading discussion forum for
exchanging ideas about the Internet.

**Organization for the Advancement of Structured
Information Standards (OASIS)**
630 Boston Rd., Ste. M-102
Billerica, MA 01821 US
Phone: 978-667-5115
Fax: 978-667-5114
E-mail Address: *info@oasis-open.org*
Web Address: www.oasis-open.org
The Organization for the Advancement of Structured
Information Standards (OASIS) is a consortium which
drives the development and adoption of e-business
standards. It produces Web services standards, along with
standards for security, e-business, and standardization
efforts in the public sector and for application-specific
markets. Founded in 1993, OASIS has more than 5,000
participants representing over 600 organizations and
individual members in 100 countries.

Texas Internet Service Providers Association (TISPA)
Web Address: www.tispa.org
Texas Internet Service Providers Association (TISPA) is a
nonprofit organization that advocates and supports an

open, competitive marketplace for Internet service in the
state of Texas. The group's website offers additional ISP
(Internet service providers), anti-spam resources, content
filter information, FCC information, access to other
Internet service groups and information on the Broadband
Scandal eBook.

US Internet Service Provider Association (US ISPA)
700 12th St. NW, Ste. 700E
Washington, DC 20005 US
Phone: 202-904-2351
E-mail Address: *kdean@usispa.org*
Web Address: www.usispa.org
US Internet Service Provider Association (US ISPA) is a
leading provider of technical, business, policy and
regulatory support to ISPs (Internet service providers).

World Wide Web Consortium (W3C)
32 Vassar St.
Rm. 32-G515
Cambridge, MA 02139 US
Phone: 617-253-2613
Fax: 617-258-5999
E-mail Address: *ij@w3.org*
Web Address: www.w3.org
The World Wide Web Consortium (W3C) develops
technologies and standards to enhance the performance
and utility of the World Wide Web. The W3C is hosted by
three different organizations: the European Research
Consortium for Informatics and Mathematics (ERICM)
handles inquiries about the W3C in the EMEA region;
Keio University handles W3C's Japanese and Korean
correspondence; and the Computer Science & Artificial
Intelligence Lab (CSAIL) at MIT handles all other
countries, include Australia and the U.S.

XXIII.   Internet Industry Resources

American Registry for Internet Numbers (ARIN)
3635 Concorde Pkwy., Ste. 200
Chantilly, VA 20151-1130 US
Phone: 703-227-0660
Fax: 703-227-0676
E-mail Address: *hostmaster@arin.net*
Web Address: www.arin.net
The American Registry for Internet Numbers (ARIN) is a
nonprofit organization that administers and registers
Internet protocol (IP) numbers. The organization also
develops policies and offers educational outreach services.

Berkman Center for Internet & Society
23 Everett St.
Harvard Law School, 2nd Fl.
Cambridge, MA 02138 US
Phone: 617-495-7547
Fax: 617-495-7641
E-mail Address: *cyber@law.harvard.edu*
Web Address: cyber.law.harvard.edu

The Berkman Center for Internet & Society focuses on the exploration of the development and inner-workings of laws pertaining to the Internet. The center offers Internet courses, conferences, advising and advocacy.

CommerceNet
169 University Ave.
Palo Alto, CA 94301 US
Phone: 650-289-4040
Fax: 650-289-4041
E-mail Address: *info@commerce.net*
Web Address: www.commerce.net
CommerceNet, an entrepreneurial research institute, is also an industry consortium for companies using, promoting and building electronic commerce solutions on the Internet.

Congressional Internet Caucus Advisory Committee (ICAC)
1634 Eye St. NW, Ste. 1107
Washington, DC 20006 US
Phone: 202-638-4370
Fax: 202-637-0968
E-mail Address: *arodway@netcaucus.org*
Web Address: www.netcaucus.org
The Congressional Internet Caucus Advisory Committee (ICAC) works to educate the public and a bipartisan group of over 170 members of the U.S. House and Senate about Internet-related policy issues.

Internet Assigned Numbers Authority (IANA)
4676 Admiralty Way, Ste. 330
Marina del Rey, CA 90292-6601 US
Phone: 310-823-9358
Fax: 310-823-8649
E-mail Address: *iana@iana.org*
Web Address: www.iana.org
The Internet Assigned Numbers Authority (IANA) serves as the central coordinator for the assignment of parameter values for Internet protocols. IANA is operated by the Internet Corporation for Assigned Names and Numbers (ICANN).

Internet Education Foundation
1634 I St. NW, Ste. 1100
Washington, DC 20006 US
Phone: 202-638-4370
Fax: 202-637-0968
E-mail Address: *tim@neted.org*
Web Address: www.neted.org
The Internet Education Foundation is a nonprofit organization dedicated to educating the public and policymakers about the potential of the global Internet to promote democracy, communications and commerce.

InterNIC
E-mail Address: *webmaster@internic.net*
Web Address: www.internic.net

InterNIC provides public information regarding Internet domain name registration services.

National Informatics Centre (NIC)
Lodhi Rd.
A-Block, CGO Complex
New Dehli, 110 003 India
Fax: 91-11-24362628
Web Address: www.home.nic.in
The Department of Information Technology provides support to India's governmental bodies through the applications of information technology and technological activities.

OASIS UDDI
P.O. Box 455
Billerica, MA 01821 US
Phone: 978-667-5115
Fax: 978-667-5114
E-mail Address: *info@oasis-open.org*
Web Address: uddi.xml.org
The web site of OASIS UDDI, an international technology consortium, provides information about UDDI, the Universal Description, Discovery and Integration protocol, a critical component of web services. The web site is structured as a community forum hosted by OASIS.

TechWeb
600 Harrison St., Fl. 6
San Francisco, CA 94107 US
Phone: 415-947-6000
E-mail Address: *svaughan@techweb.com*
Web Address: www.techweb.com
TechWeb is a web site that offers news and information concerning the cell phone, software, Internet and hardware technology fields. The site is a product of InformationWeek, a division of CMP Technology, which is itself a subsidiary of United Business Media.

TelecomWeb: The Telecom Intelligence Group
Phone: 973-602-0114
Toll Free: 888-707-5809
E-mail Address: *moneill@telecomweb.com*
Web Address: www.telecomweb.com
TelecomWeb: The Telecom Intelligence Group is an Internet source for business news, market research and competitive analysis on the global communications industry. The web site provides information about broadband, wireless, pricing, enterprise, policy and fiber optics.

XXIV. Internet Usage Statistics

Pew Internet & American Life Project
1615 L St. NW, Ste. 700
Washington, DC 20036 US
Phone: 202-419-4500
Fax: 202-419-4505

E-mail Address: *data@pewinternet.org*
Web Address: www.pewinternet.org
The Pew Internet & American Life Project, an initiative of the Pew Research Center, produces reports that explore the impact of the Internet on families, communities, work and home, daily life, education, health care and civic and political life.

XXV. Licensing Associations

Licensing Executives Society (U.S.A. and Canada), Inc.
1800 Diagonal Rd., Ste. 280
Alexandria, VA 22314 US
Phone: 703-836-3106
Fax: 703-836-3107
E-mail Address: *info@les.org*
Web Address: www.lesusacanada.org
Licensing Executives Society (U.S.A. and Canada), Inc., established in 1965, is a professional association composed of about 5,000 members who work in fields related to the development, use, transfer, manufacture and marketing of intellectual property. Members include executives, lawyers, licensing consultants, engineers, academic researchers, scientists and government officials. The society is part of the larger Licensing Executives Society International, Inc. (same headquarters address), with a worldwide membership of some 12,000 members in 30 national societies, representing approximately 80 countries.

XXVI. Manufacturing Associations-Machinery & Technology

National Center for Manufacturing Sciences (NCMS)
3025 Boardwalk Dr.
Ann Arbor, MI 48108-3230 US
Fax: 734-995-1150
Toll Free: 800-222-6267
Web Address: www.ncms.org
The National Center for Manufacturing Sciences (NCMS) is a nonprofit membership organization dedicated to advancing the global competitiveness of North American industry through collaboration.

XXVII. MBA Resources

MBA Depot
Phone: 512-499-8728
Web Address: www.mbadepot.com
MBA Depot is an online community for MBA professionals.

XXVIII. Outsourcing Industry Resources

CIO Outsourcing Center
492 Old Connecticut Path
Framingham, MA 01701-9208 US
Phone: 508-872-0080
Fax: 508-879-6063
E-mail Address: *info@cio.com*
Web Address: www.cio.com/topic/1513/Outsourcing
CIO Outsourcing Center, a feature on CIO.com, provides data for chief information officers about technology outsourcing. CIO.com and the Outsourcing Center are products of CXO Media Inc., which is itself a division of International Data Group.

Information Week Outsourcing Center
600 Community Dr.
InformationWeek
Manhasset, NY 11030 US
Phone: 516-562-5000
Fax: 516-562-5036
E-mail Address: *bevans@techweb.com*
Web Address: www.informationweek.com/outsourcing/
Information Week Outsourcing Center, a feature of InformationWeek.com, provides news and information about the technology outsourcing industry. InformationWeek is a division of CMP Technology, which is itself a subsidiary of United Business Media (UBM).

XXIX. Patent Organizations

European Patent Office
Av. de Cortenbergh 60
Brussels, 1000 Belgium
Phone: 32-2-274-15-90
Web Address: www.epo.org
The European Patent Office (EPO) provides a uniform application procedure for individual inventors and companies seeking patent protection in up to 38 European countries. It is the executive arm of the European Patent Organization and is supervised by the Administrative Council.

U.S. Patent and Trademark Office (PTO)
P. O. Box 1450
Office of Public Affairs
Alexandria, VA 22313-1450 US
Phone: 571-272-1000
Fax: 571-273-8300
Toll Free: 800-786-9199
E-mail Address: *usptoinfo@uspto.gov*
Web Address: www.uspto.gov
The U.S. Patent and Trademark Office (PTO) administers patent and trademark laws for the U.S. and enables registration of patents and trademarks.

XXX. Patent Resources

Patent Law for Non-Lawyers
E-mail Address: *info@thinkbiotech.com*
Web Address: www.dnapatent.com/law
Patent Law for Non-Lawyers is an informative site detailing the patent process in the fields of biotechnology

and engineering. The site assumes a working knowledge of the industry.

XXXI. Payment, E-Commerce and Data Interchange Technology

Center for Research in Electronic Commerce
McCombs School of Business
Austin, TX 78712-0201 US
Phone: 512-471-5921
Fax: 512-471-7725
E-mail Address: *abw@uts.cc.utexas.edu*
Web Address: cism.mccombs.utexas.edu
The Center for Research in Electronic Commerce at the University of Texas is a leading research institution in generating critical knowledge and understanding in the fields of information systems and management, electronic commerce and the digital economy.

Data Interchange Standards Association (DISA)
7600 Leesburg Pike, Ste. 430
Falls Church, VA 22043 US
Phone: 703-970-4480
Fax: 703-970-4488
E-mail Address: *info@disa.org*
Web Address: www.disa.org
The Data Interchange Standards Association (DISA) is a leading nonprofit organization that supports the development and use of electronic business interchange standards in e-commerce.

Financial Services Technology Consortium (FSTC)
44 Wall St., Fl. 12
New York, NY 10005 US
Phone: 212-461-7116
Fax: 646-349-3629
Web Address: www.fstc.org
The Financial Services Technology Consortium (FSTC) sponsors project-oriented collaborative research and development on inter-bank technical projects affecting the entire financial services industry. Particular emphasis is placed on payment systems and services and the leveraging of new technologies that help banks cement customer relationships, boost operational efficiency and expand market reach.

Global Business Dialogue on Electronic Commerce (GBDe)
Phone: 301-523-0891
Fax: 301-654-4054
E-mail Address: *gbde@wcore.com*
Web Address: www.gbd-e.org
The Global Business Dialogue on electronic commerce (GBDe) is a company-led response to the need for strengthened international coordination with regard to worldwide electronic commerce. The steering committee includes CEOs from 24 international companies, such as Hitachi, Fujitsu, Microsoft, NEC and Sybase.

International Center for Electronic Commerce (ICEC)
Technology Innovation Center of KAIST
Seoul Campus, 207-43, Cheongryang
Seoul, 130-012 Korea
Phone: 65-6-828-0230
E-mail Address: *icec@icec.net*
Web Address: www.icec.net
The International Center for Electronic Commerce (ICEC), based in Korea, is involved in the development of next-generation electronic commerce technologies and management schemes and establishing an international research consortium of e-commerce-related companies. It is part of the Graduate School of Management of the Korean Advanced Institute of Science & Technology (KAIST).

RosettaNet
1009 Lenox Dr., Ste. 202
Princeton Pike Corporate Ctr.
Lawrenceville, NJ 08648 US
Phone: 609-620-0200
Fax: 609-620-1200
Web Address: www.rosettanet.org
RosettaNet, a subsidiary of GS1 US, is a nonprofit organization whose mission is to develop e-business process standards that serve as a frame of reference for global trading networks. The organization's standards provide a common language for companies within the global supply chain.

XXXII. Privacy & Consumer Matters

Better Business Bureau Online (BBBO)
4200 Wilson Blvd., Ste. 800
Arlington, VA 22203 US
Phone: 703-276-0100
Fax: 703-525-8277
E-mail Address: *hcherico@cbbb.bbb.org*
Web Address: www.bbbonline.org
The Better Business Bureau Online (BBBO) is the online version of the Better Business Bureau, an organization that attempts to foster high standards of customer service and online privacy.

Electronic Frontier Foundation (EFF)
454 Shotwell St.
San Francisco, CA 94110-1914 US
Phone: 415-436-9333
Fax: 415-436-9993
E-mail Address: *information@eff.org*
Web Address: www.eff.org
The Electronic Frontier Foundation (EFF) is a nonprofit, non-partisan organization that strives to protect free speech, children and privacy, as well as to help form legislation affecting the Internet.

Electronic Privacy Information Center (EPIC)
1718 Connecticut Ave. NW, Ste. 200

Washington, DC 20009 US
Phone: 202-483-1140
Fax: 202-483-1248
Web Address: www.epic.org
The Electronic Privacy Information Center (EPIC) is
public interest research center, established to focus public
attention on emerging civil liberties issues and to protect
privacy, the First Amendment and constitutional values.

Federal Trade Commission-Privacy
600 Pennsylvania Ave. NW
Washington, DC 20580 US
Toll Free: 877-382-4357
Web Address: www.ftc.gov/privacy
Federal Trade Commission-Privacy is responsible for
many aspects of business-to-consumer and business-to-
business trade and regulation.

Internet Crime Complaint Center (IC3)
Web Address: www.ic3.gov
The Internet Crime Complaint Center (IC3) is a joint
venture between the FBI and the National White Collar
Crime Center. It provides a central collection point for
Internet crime complaints, which are then sent on to the
appropriate government agency. At the IC3 website,
consumers may file a complaint online. IC3 accepts
Internet crime complaints either from the person who
believes they were defrauded, or from third parties.

Privacy International
6-8 Amwell St.
Clerkenwell
London, EC1R 1UQ UK
Phone: 44-208-123-7933
E-mail Address: *privacyint@privacy.org*
Web Address: www.privacyinternational.org
Privacy International is a government and business
watchdog, alerting individuals to wiretapping and national
security activities, medical privacy infringement, police
information systems and the use of ID cards, video
surveillance and data matching.

TRUSTe
55 2nd St., Fl. 2
San Francisco, CA 94105 US
Phone: 415-520-3400
Fax: 415-520-3420
E-mail Address: *dotorg@truste.org*
Web Address: www.truste.org
TRUSTe, a nonprofit agency, formed an alliance with all
major portal sites to launch the Privacy Partnership
campaign, a consumer education program designed to raise
the awareness of Internet privacy issues. The organization
works to meet the needs of business web sites while
protecting user privacy.

XXXIII.   Research & Development, Laboratories

Applied Research Laboratories (ARL)
Applied Research Laboratories
University of Texas at Austin, 10000 Burnet Rd.
Austin, TX 78758 US
Phone: 512-835-3200
Fax: 512-835-3259
E-mail Address: *WebContactUs@arlut.utexas.edu*
Web Address: www.arlut.utexas.edu
Applied Research Laboratories (ARL) at the University of
Texas at Austin provides research programs dedicated to
improving the military capability of the United States in
applications of acoustics, electromagnetic and information
technology.

Council of Scientific & Industrial Research (CSIR)
2 Rafi Marg
Anusandhan Bhawan
New Delhi, 110 001 India
Phone: 011-23710618
Fax: 011-23713011
E-mail Address: *itweb@csir.res.in*
Web Address: www.csir.res.in
The Council of Scientific & Industrial Research (CSIR) is
a government-funded organization that promotes research
and development initiatives in India. It operates in the
fields of energy, biotechnology, space, science and
technology.

Electronics and Telecommunications Research Institute (ETRI)
138 Gajeongno
Yuseong-gu
Daejeon, 305-700 Korea
Phone: 82-42-860-6114
E-mail Address: *khchong@etri.re.kr*
Web Address: www.etri.re.kr
Established in 1976, ETRI is a nonprofit government-
funded research organization that promotes technological
excellence. The research institute has successfully
developed information technologies such as TDX-
Exchange, High Density Semiconductor Microchips, Mini-
Super Computer (TiCOM), and Digital Mobile
Telecommunication System (CDMA). ETRI's focus is on
information technologies, robotics, telecommunications,
digital broadcasting and future technology strategies.

Helmholtz Association
AhrstraBe 45
Bonn, 53175 Germany
Phone: 49 228 30818-0
Fax: 49 228 30818-30
E-mail Address: *org@helmholtz.de*
Web Address: www.helmholtz.de/en
The Helmholtz Association is a community of 16
scientific-technical and biological-medical research
centers. Helmholtz Centers perform top-class research in

strategic programs in six core fields: energy, earth and environment, health, key technologies, structure of matter, aeronautics, space and transport.

Institute for Telecommunication Sciences (ITS)
325 Broadway
Boulder, CO 80305-3328 US
Phone: 303-497-5216
E-mail Address: *info@its.bldrdoc.gov*
Web Address: www.its.bldrdoc.gov
The Institute for Telecommunication Sciences (ITS) is the research and engineering branch of the National Telecommunications and Information Administration (NTIA), a division of the U.S. Department of Commerce (DOC).

Leibniz Association of German Research Institutes (WGL)
Postfach 12 01 69, D-53043
Eduard-Pfluger-Str. 55
Bonn, D-53113 Germany
Phone: 49-228-30815-0
Fax: 49-228-30815-55
E-mail Address: *wgl@wgl.de*
Web Address: www.leibniz-gemeinschaft.de
The Leibniz Association of German Research Institutes (WGL) is a research organization that comprises over 80 institutes. WGL works on international interdisciplinary research and acts as a bridge between traditional research and customer oriented applications. The association focuses on scientific excellence and social relevance.

Max Planck Society (MPG)
P.O. Box 10 10 62
Munchen, 80084 Germany
Phone: 49 (89) 2108 - 0
Fax: 49 (89) 2108 - 1111
Web Address: www.mpg.de
The Max Planck Society (MPG) currently maintains 80 institutes, research units, and working groups that are devoted to basic research in the natural sciences, life sciences, social sciences, and the humanities. Max Planck Institutes work largely in an interdisciplinary setting and in close cooperation with universities and research institutes in Germany and abroad.

National Research Council Canada (NRC)
1200 Montreal Rd., Bldg. M-58
Ottawa, ON K1A 0R6 Canada
Phone: 613-993-9101
Fax: 613-952-9907
Toll Free: 877-672-2672
E-mail Address: *info@nrc-cnrc.gc.ca*
Web Address: www.nrc-cnrc.gc.ca
National Research Council Canada (NRC) is a government organization of 20 research institutes that carry out multidisciplinary research with partners in industries and sectors key to Canada's economic development.

National Science Council of Taiwan (NSC)
106 HoPing E. Rd., Sec. 2
Taipei, 10622 Taiwan
Phone: 886-2-27377992
Fax: 886-2-27377566
Web Address: www.nsc.gov.tw
The National Science Council of Taiwan oversees government funding of research and development as well as national technology programs.

SRI International
333 Ravenswood Ave.
Menlo Park, CA 94025-3493 US
Phone: 650-859-2000
E-mail Address: *ellie.javadi@sri.com*
Web Address: www.sri.com
SRI International is a nonprofit organization offering a wide range of services, including engineering services, information technology, pure and applied physical sciences, product development, pharmaceutical discovery, biopharmaceutical discovery and policy issues. SRI conducts research for commercial and governmental customers.

The Fraunhofer-Gesellschaft (FhG)
Fraunhofer-Gesellschaft zur Forderung der angewandten Forschung e.V.
Postfach 20 07 33
Munchen, 80007 Germany
Phone: 49-89-1205-0
Fax: 49-89-1205-7531
Web Address: www.fraunhofer.de
The Fraunhofer-Gesellschaft (FhG) institute focuses on research in health, security, energy, communication, the environment and mobility. FhG includes over 80 research units in 40 locations in Germany. Two-thirds of its projects are derived from industry contracts.

XXXIV. RFID Associations

Association for Automatic Identification and Mobility (AIM)
125 Warrendale-Bayle Rd., Ste. 100
Warrendale, PA 15086 US
Phone: 724-934-4470
Fax: 724-934-4495
E-mail Address: *diana@aimglobal.org*
Web Address: www.aimglobal.org
The Association for Automatic Identification and Mobility (AIM) is a global trade organization dedicated to accelerating the growth and use of RFID and other automated identification and data capture/collection (AIDC) technologies and services. Its more than 900 members are manufacturers or service providers of RFID, bar code, card, biometrics and electronic article surveillance technologies.

EPCglobal Inc.
Rue Royale 29
Brussels, 1000 Belgium
Phone: 32 2 229 18 80
Fax: 32 2 217 43 47
E-mail Address: *info@gs1belu.org*
Web Address: www.epcglobalinc.org
EPCglobal Inc. is a global standards organization for the
Electronic Product Code (EPC), which supports the use of
RFID. It was initially developed by the Auto-ID Center, an
academic research project at the Massachusetts Institute of
Technology (MIT). Today, offices and affiliates of
EPCglobal are based in nearly every nation of the world.
The nonprofit organization is a joint venture between GS1,
formerly known as EAN International, and GS1 US,
formerly known as the Uniform Code Council. (Also see
GS1 US (UCC) under Logistics and Supply Chain
Associations.)

XXXV.   RFID Resources

InformationWeek - RFIDinsights
600 Community Dr.
Manhasset, NY 11030 US
Phone: 516-562-5000
Fax: 516-562-5036
E-mail Address: *bevans@techweb.com*
Web Address: www.rfidinsights.com
The RFIDinsights section of the InformationWeek web site
is devoted to news, opinions and resources relating to radio
frequency identification (RFID). Sponsored by
InformationWeek, a weekly news publication, the site also
provides a best practices page of news stories about the
implementation of RFID at major corporations.

RFID.org
125 Warrendale-Bayne Rd., Ste. 100
Warrendale, PA 15086 US
Phone: 724-934-4470
Fax: 724-934-4495
E-mail Address: *diana@aimglobal.org*
Web Address: www.aimglobal.org/technologies/rfid/
RFID.org is a link to news, events, case studies and
commentary relating to radio frequency identification
(RFID) technologies and applications. The site is
sponsored by the global branch of the Association for
Automatic Identification and Mobility (AIM GLOBAL).

RFiDa.com
Phone: 609-680-0518
E-mail Address: *webmaster@rfida.com*
Web Address: www.rfida.com
RFiDa.com is a web site devoted to trends, technology,
applications and news relating to radio frequency
identification (RFID). The site includes comprehensive
knowledge bases and reference guides.

XXXVI.   Science & Technology Resources

Technology Review
1 Main St., Fl. 7
Cambridge, MA 02142 US
Phone: 617-475-8000
Fax: 617-475-8042
Toll Free: 800-877-5230
Web Address: www.technologyreview.com
Technology Review, an MIT enterprise, publishes tech
industry news, covers innovation and writes in-depth
articles about research, development and cutting-edge
technologies.

XXXVII.   Software Industry Associations

Apache Software Foundation
1901 Munsey Dr.
Forest Hill, MD 21050-2747 US
Phone: 979-273-1755
Fax: 410-803-2258
E-mail Address: *apache@apache.org*
Web Address: www.apache.org
One of the largest open software successes, Apache is used
by about two-thirds of all web sites worldwide. Apache's
software manages the interaction between a web site and
the viewer's browser.

Association of Shareware Professionals (ASP)
P.O. Box 1522
Martinsville, IN 46151 US
Phone: 765-349-4740
Fax: 815-301-3756
E-mail Address: *president@asp-shareware.org*
Web Address: www.asp-shareware.org
The Association of Shareware Professionals (ASP)
promotes the try-before-you-buy software industry.

Business Software Alliance (BSA)
1150 18th St. NW, Ste. 700
Washington, DC 20036 US
Phone: 202-872-5500
Fax: 202-872-5501
E-mail Address: *software@bsa.org*
Web Address: www.bsa.org
The Business Software Alliance (BSA) is a leading global
software industry association. BSA educates consumers
regarding software management, copyright protection,
cyber security, trade, e-commerce and other Internet-
related issues.

Colorado Software & Internet Association (CSIA)
1625 Broadway, Ste. 950
Denver, CO 80202 US
Phone: 303-592-4070
E-mail Address: *info@coloradotechnology.org*
Web Address: www.coloradosoftware.org

The Colorado Software & Internet Association (CSIA) promotes the software industry in Colorado through networking and organization.

European Software Institute (ESI)
Parque Tecnologico de Zamudio 204
Zamudio, Bizkaia E-48170 Spain
Phone: 34-94-420-95-19
Fax: 34-94-420-94-20
E-mail Address: *info@esi.es*
Web Address: www.esi.es
European Software Institute (ESI) is a nonprofit foundation launched as an initiative of the European Commission, with the support of leading European companies working in the information technology field.

Information Systems Security Association, Inc. (ISSA)
9220 SW Barbur Blvd., Ste. 119-333
Portland, OR 97219 US
Phone: 206-388-4584
Fax: 206-299-3366
Toll Free: 866-349-5818
E-mail Address: *editor@issa.org*
Web Address: www.issa.org
The Information Systems Security Association, Inc. (ISSA) is an international not-for-profit organization of information security professionals.

Initiative for Software Choice (ISC)
Phone: 703-812-1333
Fax: 703-812-1337
Web Address: www.softwarechoice.org
The Initiative for Software Choice (ISC) is a global initiative which is dedicated to protecting an environment in which competing software markets can develop without government pressures or mandates. ISC is part of The Computing Technology Industry Association, Inc. (CompTIA).

Irish Software Association (ISA)
Confederation House
84-86 Lower Baggot St.
Dublin, 2 Ireland
Phone: 353-1-605-1582
Fax: 353-1-638-1582
E-mail Address: *patricia.keogh@ibec.ie*
Web Address: www.software.ie
The Irish Software Association (ISA) promotes the interests of IT services and software companies in Ireland. It helps software companies grow and become competitive internationally.

Korea Software Industry Association (KOSA)
Daeyoung B/D 5F, 9-1
Samsung-dong, Gangnam-gu
Seoul, Korea
Phone: 822-2188-6940-3
Fax: 822-2188-6901-2
E-mail Address: *Kosainfo@sw.or.kr*
Web Address: english.sw.or.kr
The KOSA is Korea's nonprofit trade organization representing more than 800 member companies in the software industry.

Linux Foundation (The)
1796 18th St., Ste. C
San Francisco, CA 94107 US
Phone: 415-723-9709
E-mail Address: *info@linux-foundation.org*
Web Address: www.linux-foundation.org
The Linux Foundation, founded in 2007 by the merger of Open Source Development Labs (OSDL) and the Free Standards Group, is a nonprofit organization that standardizes, protects and promotes the work of Linux creator Linus Torvalds. It provides necessary services and resources to make and keep open source software competitive with closed platforms. The Foundation is supported by a global consortium of global open source IT industry leaders, and has facilities in the United States and Japan.

National Association of Software and Service Companies of India (NASSCOM)
International Youth Ctr.
Teen Murti Marg, Chanakyapuri
New Delhi, 110 021 India
Phone: 202-944-1973
Fax: 202-944-1970
E-mail Address: *in_pr@nasscom.in*
Web Address: www.nasscom.org
The National Association of Software and Service Companies (NASSCOM) is the trade body and chamber of commerce for the IT software and services industry in India. The association's 1,200 members consist of corporations located around the world involved in software development, software services, software products, IT-enabled/BPO services and e-commerce. Collectively, its members employ over 2 million people.

New Mexico Technology Council (NMTC)
P.O. Box 31278
Santa Fe, NM 87594-1278 US
Phone: 505-830-8414
E-mail Address: *heather.lovato@tig.com*
Web Address: www.nmtechcouncil.org
The New Mexico Technology Council (NMTC) represents the interests of the software industry in New Mexico.

Object Management Group (OMG)
140 Kendrick St.
Bldg. A, Ste. 300
Needham, MA 02494 US
Phone: 781-444-0404
Fax: 781-444-0320
E-mail Address: *info@omg.org*
Web Address: www.omg.org

The Object Management Group (OMG) is a not-for-profit organization devoted to the interoperability of enterprise software.

Singapore Infocomm Technology Federation (SiTF)
55/55A Neil Rd.
088892 Singapore
Phone: 65-6325-9700
Fax: 65-6325-4993
E-mail Address: *info@sitf.org.sg*
Web Address: sitf.org.sg
Singapore Infocomm Technology Federation (SiTF) is a infocom industry association that has eight chapters: Best Sourcing, Digital Media, eGovernment, eLearning, Security & Governance, Singapore Enterprise, Service-Oriented Architecture and Wireless.

Software & Information Industry Association (SIIA)
1090 Vermont Ave. NW, Fl. 6
Washington, DC 20005-4095 US
Phone: 202-289-7442
Fax: 202-289-7097
Web Address: www.siia.net
The Software & Information Industry Association (SIIA) is a principal trade association for the software and digital content industry.

Software Association of Oregon (SAO)
111 SW 5th Ave.
US Bank Twr., Ste. 120
Portland, OR 97204 US
Phone: 503-228-5401
Fax: 503-228-5411
E-mail Address: *info@sao.org*
Web Address: www.sao.org
The Software Association of Oregon (SAO) promotes the growth of Oregon's software industry.

Washington Technology Industry Association
2200 Alaskan Way, Ste. 390
Seattle, WA 98121 US
Phone: 206-448-3033
E-mail Address: *info@washingtontechnology.org*
Web Address: www.wsa.org
The Washington Technology Industry Association promotes and helps coordinate the software industry in the state of Washington.

XXXVIII.   Software Industry Resources

Software Engineering Institute (SEI)-Carnegie Mellon
4500 Fifth Ave.
Pittsburgh, PA 15213-2612 US
Phone: 412-268-5800
Fax: 412-268-6257
Toll Free: 888-201-4479
E-mail Address: *customer-relations@sei.cmu.edu*
Web Address: www.sei.cmu.edu

The Software Engineering Institute (SEI) is a federally funded research and development center at Carnegie Mellon University, sponsored by the U.S. Department of Defense through the Office of the Under Secretary of Defense for Acquisition, Technology, and Logistics [OUSD (AT&L)]. The SEI's core purpose is to help users make measured improvements in their software engineering capabilities.

XXXIX.   Stocks and Financial Markets Data

SiliconValley.com
2527 Camino Ramon, Ste. 300, c/o Bay Area News Group
San Ramon, CA 94583 US
Phone: 408-920-5888
E-mail Address: *jmead@mercurynews.com*
Web Address: www.siliconvalley.com
SiliconValley.com, run by San Jose Mercury News, offers an excellent summary of current financial news and information in the field of technology.

XL.   Supercomputing

Top 500 Supercomputer Sites
Prometeus GmbH
Fliederstr. 2
Waibstadt-Daisbach, D-74915 Germany
Phone: 49-7261-913-160
E-mail Address: *info@top500.org*
Web Address: www.top500.org
The Top 500 project was started in 1993 to provide a reliable basis for tracking and detecting trends in high-performance computing. Twice a year, a list of the sites operating the 500 most powerful computer systems is assembled and released. The Linpack benchmark is used as a performance measure for ranking the computer systems. The list contains a variety of information including system specifications and major application areas. The Top 500 web site is promoted by Prometeus GmbH.

XLI.   Technology Law Associations

International Technology Law Association (ITechLaw)
401 Edgewater Pl., Ste. 600
Wakefield, MA 01880 US
Phone: 781-876-8877
Fax: 781-224-1239
E-mail Address: *office@itechlaw.org*
Web Address: www.itechlaw.org
The International Technology Law Association (ITechLaw) offers information concerning Internet and converging technology law. It represents lawyers in the field of technology law.

XLII.   Technology Transfer Associations

Association of University Technology Managers (AUTM)
111 Deer Lake Rd., Ste. 100
Deerfield, IL 60015 US
Phone: 847-559-0846
Fax: 847-480-9282
E-mail Address: *info@autm.net*
Web Address: www.autm.net
The Association of University Technology Managers (AUTM) is a nonprofit professional association whose members belong to over 350 research institutions, universityies, teaching hospitals, government agencies and corporations from 45 countries. The association's mission is to advance the field of technology transfer, and enhance members' ability to bring academic and nonprofit research to people around the world.

The State Science and Technology Institute
5015 Pine Creek Dr.
Westerville, OH 43081 US
Phone: 614-901-1690
Fax: 614-901-1696
Web Address: www.ssti.org
The State Science and Technology Institute (SSTI) is a national nonprofit group that serves as a resource for technology-based economic development. In addition to the information on its web site, the Institute publishes a free weekly digest of news and issues related to technology-based economic development efforts, as well as a members-only publication listing application information, eligibility criteria and submission deadlines for a variety of funding oportunities, federal and otherwise.

XLIII.   Telecommunications Industry Associations

Asia-Pacific Telecommunity
Chaengwattana Rd.
12/49 Soi 5
Bangkok, 10210 Thailand
Phone: 66-2-573-0044
Fax: 66-2-573-7479
Web Address: www.aptsec.org
The APT is a unique organization of governments, telecom service providers, manufacturers of communication equipment, research & development organizations and other stakeholders active in the field of communication and information technology. APT serves as the focal organization for communication and information technology in the Asia Pacific region.

CompTel
900 17th St. NW, Ste. 400
Washington, DC 20006 US
Phone: 202-296-6650
Fax: 202-296-7585
E-mail Address: *mboles@comptel.org*
Web Address: www.comptel.org
CompTel is a trade organization representing voice, data and video communications service providers and their supplier partners. Members are supported through education, networking, policy advocacy and trade shows.

European Information Communications Technology Association (EICTA)
EICTA 20
Rue Joseph II
Brussels, B-1000 Belgium
Phone: 32-2-609-53-10
Fax: 32-2-609-53-39
E-mail Address: *info@eicta.org*
Web Address: www.eicta.org
The European Information Communications Technology Association (EICTA) is dedicated to improving the business environment for the European information and communications technology and consumer electronics sector.

European Telecommunications Standards Institute (ETSI)
ETSI Secretariat
650, route des Lucioles
Sophia-Antipolis Cedex, 06921 France
Phone: 33-4-92-94-42-00
Fax: 33-4-93-65-47-16
E-mail Address: *helpdesk@etsi.org*
Web Address: www.etsi.org
The European Telecommunications Standards Institute (ETSI) is a nonprofit organization whose mission is to produce the telecommunications standards that will be used throughout Europe.

International Federation for Information Processing (IFIP)
Hofstrasse 3
Laxenburg, A-2361 Austria
Phone: 43-2236-73616
Fax: 43-2236-73616 9
E-mail Address: *ifip@ifip.org*
Web Address: www.ifip.or.at
The International Federation for Information Processing (IFIP) is a multinational, apolitical organization in information & communications technologies and sciences recognized by United Nations and other world bodies. It represents information technology societies from 56 countries or regions, covering all 5 continents with a total membership of over half a million.

Pacific Telecommunications Council (PTC)
2454 S. Beretania St., Ste. 302
Honolulu, HI 96826 US
Phone: 808-941-3789
Fax: 808-944-4874
E-mail Address: *info@ptc.org*
Web Address: www.ptc.org

The Pacific Telecommunications Council (PTC), through a network of members extending across more than 50 nations, promotes the development and use of telecommunications and information and communications technologies to enhance the lives of people living in the Pacific hemisphere.

Telecommunications Industry Association (TIA)
2500 Wilson Blvd., Ste. 300
Arlington, VA 22201 US
Phone: 703-907-7700
Fax: 703-907-7727
E-mail Address: twalsh@tiaonline.org
Web Address: www.tiaonline.org
The Telecommunications Industry Association (TIA) is a leading trade association in the information, communications and entertainment technology industry. TIA focuses on market development, trade promotion, trade shows, domestic and international advocacy, standards development and enabling e-business.

Voice On the Net (VON) Coalition, Inc.
1718 M St. NW, PMB 336
Washington, DC 20036 US
Phone: 202-387-5282
Fax: 202-387-5319
E-mail Address: beverly321@gmail.com
Web Address: www.von.org
Voice On the Net (VON) Coalition, Inc. is an organization is an advocate for the IP telephony industry. The VON Coalition supports that the IP industry should remain free of governmental regulations. It also serves to educate consumers and the media on Internet communications technologies.

XLIV.   Telecommunications Resources

Center for Democracy and Technology
1634 I St. NW, Ste. 1100
Washington, DC 20006 US
Phone: 202-637-9800
Fax: 202-637-0968
Web Address: www.cdt.org
The Center for Democracy and Technology works to promote democratic values and constitutional liberties in the digital age. With expertise in law, technology, and policy, CDT seeks practical solutions to enhance free expression and privacy in global communications technologies.

Department of Telecommunication-Gov. of India
Sanchar Bhavan
20 Ashoka Rd.
New Delhi, 110 001 India
Phone: 24369191
Fax: 24362333
E-mail Address: MOCIT@nic.
Web Address: www.dot.gov.in

The Government of India's Department of Telecommunication website provides information, directories, guidelines, news and information related to the telecom, Internet, wifi and wireless communication. In addition, included are policy, licensing and coordination matters relating to telegraphs, telephones, wireless, data, facsimile and telematic services and other like forms of communications.

Infocomm Development Authority of Singapore (IDA)
8 Temasek Blvd.
14-00 Suntec Twr. 3
038998 Singapore
Phone: 65-6211-0888
Fax: 65-6211-2222
E-mail Address: info@ida.gov.sg
Web Address: www.ida.com
The goal of the Infocomm Development Authority of Singapore (IDA) is to actively seek opportunities to grow the infocom industry in both the domestic and international markets.

International Customer Management Institute (ICMI)
P.O. Box 6177
Annapolis, MD 21401-0177 US
Phone: 410-267-0700
Fax: 410-267-0962
Toll Free: 800-672-6177
E-mail Address: icmi@incoming.com
Web Address: www.incoming.com
International Customer Management Institute (ICMI) is a leader in call center consulting, training, publications and membership services. As a member of the CMP Media family, it offers clients a wide variety of membership services, including its publication, CallCenter Magazine, and an online knowledge center.

Ministry of Information Communications and the Arts, Singapore
140 Hill St., 02-02 MICA Bldg.
179369 Singapore
Phone: 65-6270-7988
Fax: 65-6837-9480
E-mail Address: mica@mica.gov.sg
Web Address: app.mica.gov.sg
Ministry of Information Communications and the Arts, Singapore, encompasses the development of Singapore as an infocom hub.

The International Communications Project
Intercomms Unit 2 Marine Action
Birdhill Industrial Estate
Birdhill, Co Tipperary Ireland
Phone: 353-86-108-3932
Fax: 353-61-749801
E-mail Address: robert.alcock@intercomms.net
Web Address: www.intercomms.net

International Communications (InterComms) is an authoritative policy, strategy and reference publication for the international telecommunications industry.

Total Telecom
Terrapinn Ltd., Wren House
43 Hatton Garden
London, EC1N 8EL UK
Phone: 44-20-7092-1215
Fax: 44-20-7242-4303
E-mail Address: *info@totaltele.com*
Web Address: www.totaltele.com
Total Telecom offers information, news and articles on the telecommunications industry in the U.K. and worldwide through its Total Telecom Online web site and the Total Telecom Magazine. Total Telecom is owned by Terrapinn Ltd.

XLV.   Telecommunications-VoIP Resources

VOIP News
514 Bryant St.
San Francisco, CA 94107 US
Toll Free: 877-864-7275
E-mail Address: *feedback@voip-news.com*
Web Address: www.voip-news.com
VoIP News provides extensive news and information about the VoIP industry, including FAQs, comparison guides, buyer's guides, a dictionary of terms, case studies, vendor directories and resources for providers, users and technicians.

XLVI.   Temporary Staffing Firms

Allegis Group
7301 Parkway Dr.
Hanover, MD 21076 US
Phone: 410-579-4800
Fax: 410-540-7556
Toll Free: 877-388-3823
Web Address: www.allegisgroup.com
The Allegis Group provides technical, professional and industrial recruiting and staffing services. Allegis specializes in information technology staffing services. The firm operates in the United Kingdom, Germany and The Netherlands as Aerotek and TEKsystems, and in India as Allegis Group India. Aerotek provides staffing solutions for aviation, engineering, automotive and scientific personnel markets.

CDI Corporation
1717 Arch St., Fl. 35
Philadelphia, PA 19103-2768 US
Phone: 215-569-2200
Fax: 215-569-1300
Toll Free: 800-996-7566
Web Address: www.cdicorp.com

CDI Corporation specializes in engineering and information technology staffing services. Company segments include CDI IT Solutions, specializing in information technology; CDI Engineering Solutions, specializing in engineering outsourcing services; AndersElite Limited, operating in the United Kingdom and Australia; and MRINetwork, specializing in executive recruitment.

Glotel, Inc.
30 S. Wacker Dr., Ste. 2800
Chicago, IL 60606 US
Phone: 312-612-7480
Fax: 312-715-0756
E-mail Address: *chicago@glotelinc.com*
Web Address: www.glotel.com
Glotel is a global technology staffing and managed projects solutions company specializing in the placement of contract and permanent personnel within all areas of technology. Glotel has a network of 19 offices throughout Europe, the U.S. and Asia-Pacific.

Harvey Nash
1680 Rte. 23 N, Ste. 300
Wayne, NJ 07470 US
Phone: 973-646-2100
Fax: 973-696-3985
E-mail Address: *info@harveynash.com*
Web Address: www.harveynash.com
Harvey Nash provides professional recruitment, interim executive leadership services and outsourcing services. The firm specializes in information technology staffing on a permanent and contract basis in US, UK and Europe. It also offers outsourcing services including offshore software development services, information technology systems management, workforce risk management and managed services for network administration.

Robert Walters PLC
55 Strand
London, WC2N 5WR UK
Phone: 44 (0) 20 7379 3333
Fax: 44 (0) 20 7509 8714
E-mail Address: *london@robertwalters.com*
Web Address: www.robertwalters.com
Robert Walters PLC is a professional recruitment specialist, outsourcing and human resource consultant. The firm provides services for the temporary, contract and permanent placement of individuals in the sectors of finance, operations, legal, information technology, marketing and administration support. It has offices in 17 countries including the US.

Volt Information Sciences, Inc.
560 Lexington Ave., Fl. 15
New York, NY 10022 US
Phone: 212-704-2400
Web Address: www.volt.com

Volt Information Sciences, Inc. maintains 300 temporary staffing offices in North America and in the U.K.

XLVII. Trade Associations-General

BUSINESSEUROPE
168 Ave. de Cortenbergh
Brussels, 1000 Belgium
Phone: 32-0-2-237-65-11
Fax: 32-0-2-231-14-45
E-mail Address: *main@businesseurope.eu*
Web Address: www.businesseurope.eu
BUSINESSEUROPE is a major European trade federation that operates in a manner similar to a chamber of commerce. Its members are the central national business federations of the 34 countries throughout Europe from which they come. Companies cannot become direct members of BUSINESSEUROPE, though there is a support group which offers the opportunity for firms to encourage BUSINESSEUROPE objectives in various ways.

Federation of Hong Kong Industries
5-15 Hankow Rd., Tsimshatsui
4/F. Hankow Ctr.
Kowloon, Hong Kong, China
Phone: 2732-3188
Fax: 2721-3494
E-mail Address: *fhki@fhki.org.hk*
Web Address: www.industryhk.org
The Federation of Hong Kong Industries promotes the trade, investment advancement and development of opportunities of the industrial and business communities of Hong Kong. The website hosts a trade enquiry on products and services.

Pacific Economic Cooperation Council (PECC)
29 Heng Mui Keng Terrace
119 620 Singapore
Phone: 65-6737-9823
Fax: 65-6737-9824
E-mail Address: *info@pecc.org*
Web Address: www.pecc.org
The Pacific Economic Cooperation Council (PECC) aims to serve as a regional forum for cooperation and policy coordination to promote economic development in the Asia-Pacific region.

The Associated Chambers of Commerce and Industry of India (ASSOCHAM)
1 Community Ctr. Zamrudpur, Kailash Colony
New Delhi, 110 048 India
Phone: 46550555
Fax: 46536481
E-mail Address: *assocham@nic.in*
Web Address: www.assocham.org
The Associated Chambers of Commerce and Industry of India (ASSOCHAM) has a membership of more than 300 chambers and trade associations and serves members from all over India.

XLVIII. Trade Associations-Global

World Trade Organization (WTO)
Centre William Rappard
Rue de Lausanne 154
Geneva 21, CH-1211 Switzerland
Phone: 41-22-739-51-11
Fax: 41-22-731-42-06
E-mail Address: *enquiries@wto.og*
Web Address: www.wto.org
The World Trade Organization (WTO) is a global organization dealing with the rules of trade between nations. To become a member, nations must agree to abide by certain guidelines. Membership increases a nation's ability to import and export efficiently.

XLIX. Trade Resources

SPRING Singapore
2 Bukit Merah Central
159835 Singapore
Phone: 65-6278-6666
Fax: 65-6278-6667
Web Address: www.spring.gov.sg
SPRING Singapore is a enterprise development agency for growing innovative companies. It works with partners to help small and medium enterprises with financing; capabilities and management development; technology and innovation; and access to markets.

L. Transportation Industry Associations

ITS America (Intelligent Transportation Society of America)
1100 17th St. NW, Ste. 1200
Washington, DC 20036 US
Phone: 202-484-4847
Fax: 202-484-3483
Toll Free: 800-374-8472
E-mail Address: *info@itsa.org*
Web Address: www.itsa.org
ITS America (Intelligent Transportation Society of America) is a nonprofit organization made up of members interested in furthering intelligent transportation systems.

LI. U.S. Government Agencies

Bureau of Economic Analysis (BEA)
1441 L St. NW
Washington, DC 20230 US
Phone: 202-606-9900
E-mail Address: *customerservice@bea.gov*
Web Address: www.bea.gov

The Bureau of Economic Analysis (BEA), an agency of the U.S. Department of Commerce, is the nation's economic accountant, preparing estimates that illuminate key national, international and regional aspects of the U.S. economy.

Bureau of Labor Statistics (BLS)
2 Massachusetts Ave. NE
Washington, DC 20212-0001 US
Phone: 202-691-5200
Web Address: stats.bls.gov
The Bureau of Labor Statistics (BLS) is the principal fact-finding agency for the Federal Government in the field of labor economics and statistics. It is an independent national statistical agency that collects, processes, analyzes and disseminates statistical data to the American public, U.S. Congress, other federal agencies, state and local governments, business and labor. The BLS also serves as a statistical resource to the Department of Labor.

FCC-VoIP Division
445 12th St. SW
Washington, DC 20554 US
Fax: 866-418-0232
Toll Free: 888-225-5322
E-mail Address: *fccinfo@fcc.gov*
Web Address: www.fcc.gov/voip
The VoIP division of the Federal Communications Commission (FCC) is dedicated to the promotion and regulation of the VoIP (Voice over Internet Protocol) industry. VoIP allows users to call from their computer over the Internet to regular telephone numbers.

Federal Communications Commission (FCC)
445 12th St. SW
Washington, DC 20554 US
Fax: 866-418-0232
Toll Free: 888-225-5322
E-mail Address: *fccinfo@fcc.gov*
Web Address: www.fcc.gov
The Federal Communications Commission (FCC) is an independent U.S. government agency established by the Communications Act of 1934, and is responsible for regulating interstate and international communications by radio, television, wire, satellite and cable.

Federal Communications Commission (FCC)-Wireless Telecommunications Bureau
445 12th St. SW
Washington, DC 20554 US
Fax: 888-225-5322
Toll Free: 888-225-5322
E-mail Address: *fccinfo@fcc.gov*
Web Address: wireless.fcc.gov
The Federal Communications Commission (FCC)-Wireless Telecommunications Bureau handles nearly all FCC domestic wireless telecommunications programs and policies, including cellular and PCS phones, pagers and two-way radios. The bureau also regulates the use of radio spectrum for businesses, aircraft/ship operators and individuals.

National Institute of Standards and Technology (NIST)
100 Bureau Dr.
Stop 1070
Gaithersburg, MD 20899-1070 US
Phone: 301-975-6478
E-mail Address: *inquiries@nist.gov*
Web Address: www.nist.gov
The National Institute of Standards and Technology (NIST) is an agency of the U.S. Department of Commerce's Technology Administration. It works with various industries to develop and apply technology, measurements and standards.

National Telecommunications and Information Administration (NTIA)
1401 Constitution Ave. NW
Herbert C. Hoover Bldg.
Washington, DC 20230 US
Phone: 202-482-2000
Fax: 202-219-2077
E-mail Address: *bforbes@ntia.doc.gov*
Web Address: www.ntia.doc.gov
The National Telecommunications and Information Administration (NTIA), an agency of the U.S. Department of Commerce, is the Executive Branch's principal voice on domestic and international telecommunications and information technology issues.

Office of Electronic Government and Technology
1800 F. St. NW
U.S. General Services Administration
Washington, DC 20405 US
Phone: 202-501-3473
E-mail Address: *john.ray@gsa.gov*
Web Address: www.estrategy.gov
The Office of Electronic Government and Technology's mission is to develop a policy framework to support e-commerce, to help government agencies find and use the best e-commerce tools and to spread the most promising ideas across the government. The Office is part of the U.S. General Services Administration (GSA).

Office of Technology and Electronic Commerce (OTEC)
1401 Constitution Ave. NW
International Trade Administration
Washington, DC 20230 US
Phone: 202-482-2000
E-mail Address: *OTEC@mail.doc.gov*
Web Address:
web.ita.doc.gov/ITI/itiHome.nsf/(HotNews)/HotNews
The Office of Technology and Electronic Commerce (OTEC) supports the growth and competitiveness of the U.S. telecommunications industry in the area of foreign

trade. It focuses on electronic commerce, information technology, microelectronics, instrumentation and telecommunications. OTEC is a division of the International Trade Administration (ITA) of the U.S. Department of Commerce (DOC).

U.S. Census Bureau
4600 Silver Hill Rd.
Washington, DC 20233-8800 US
Phone: 301-763-4636
Fax: 301-457-3670
Toll Free: 800-923-8282
E-mail Address: *pio@census.gov*
Web Address: www.census.gov
The U.S. Census Bureau is the official collector of data about the people and economy of the U.S. Founded in 1790, it provides official social, demographic and economic information.

U.S. Department of Commerce (DOC)
1401 Constitution Ave. NW
Washington, DC 20230 US
Phone: 202-482-2000
E-mail Address: *cgutierrez@doc.gov*
Web Address: www.commerce.gov
The U.S. Department of Commerce (DOC) regulates trade and provides valuable economic analysis of the economy.

U.S. Department of Labor (DOL)
200 Constitution Ave. NW
Frances Perkins Bldg.
Washington, DC 20210 US
Toll Free: 866-487-2365
Web Address: www.dol.gov
The U.S. Department of Labor (DOL) is the government agency responsible for labor regulations. This site provides tools to help citizens find out whether companies are complying with family and medical-leave requirements.

U.S. Securities and Exchange Commission (SEC)
100 F St. NE
Washington, DC 20549 US
Phone: 202-551-6000
Toll Free: 888-732-6585
E-mail Address: *publicinfo@sec.gov*
Web Address: www.sec.gov
The U.S. Securities and Exchange Commission (SEC) is a nonpartisan, quasi-judicial regulatory agency responsible for administering federal securities laws. These laws are designed to protect investors in securities markets and ensure that they have access to disclosure of all material information concerning publicly traded securities. Visitors to the web site can access the EDGAR database of corporate financial and business information.

U.S. Trade Representative (USTR)
600 17th St. NW
Washington, DC 20508 US

Phone: 202-395-7360
E-mail Address: *contactustr@ustr.eop.gov*
Web Address: www.ustr.gov
The U.S. Trade Representative (USTR) is the nation's chief trade negotiator and the principal trade policy advisor to the President.

LII.   Wireless & Cellular Industry Associations

Bluetooth Special Interest Group (SIG)
500 108th Ave. NE, Ste. 250
Bellevue, WA 98004 US
Phone: 425-691-3535
E-mail Address: *webmaster@bluetooth.com*
Web Address: www.bluetooth.com
The Bluetooth Special Interest Group (SIG) is a trade association comprised of leaders in the telecommunications, computing, automotive, industrial automation and network industries that is driving the development of Bluetooth wireless technology, a low cost short-range wireless specification for connecting mobile devices and bringing them to market.

Broadband Wireless Association (BWA)
54 Mancetter Rd.
Atherstone, Warwickshire CV9 1NY UK
Phone: 44-7968-845016
Fax: 44-1827-716299
E-mail Address: *slowe@broadband-wireless.org*
Web Address: www.broadband-wireless.org
The Broadband Wireless Association (BWA) provides representation, news and information for the European broadband wireless industry.

Canada Wireless Telecommunications Association (CWTA)
130 Albert St., Ste. 1110
Ottawa, ON K1P 5G4 Canada
Phone: 613-233-4888
Fax: 613-233-2032
E-mail Address: *info@cwta.ca*
Web Address: www.cwta.ca
The Canada Wireless Telecommunications Association (CWTA) seeks to be the pre-eminent source of input to government policy and public opinion on behalf of the wireless communications industry in Canada, in order to create and maintain a positive economic environment for the wireless industry.

CDMA Development Group (CDG)
575 Anton Blvd., Ste. 560
Costa Mesa, CA 92626 US
Phone: 714-545-5211
Fax: 714-545-4601
Toll Free: 888-800-2362
E-mail Address: *cdg@cdg.org*
Web Address: www.cdg.org

The CDMA Development Group (CDG) is composed of the world's leading code division multiple access (CDMA) service providers and manufacturers that have joined together to lead the adoption and evolution of CDMA wireless systems around the world.

Global System for Mobile Communication Association (GSMA)
71 High Holborn
1st Fl., Mid City Pl.
London, WC1V 6EA UK
Phone: 44-020-7759-2300
Fax: 44-020-7759-2301
E-mail Address: *info@gsm.org*
Web Address: www.gsmworld.com
The Global System for Mobile Communications Association (GSMA) is a global trade association representing more than 740 GSM mobile phone operators from 219 countries.

Hong Kong Wireless Technology Industry Association
100 Cyberport Rd, IT St.
Cyberport 3, Unit 403
Hong Kong, Hong Kong China
Phone: 852-2370-3130
Fax: 852-8208-8782
E-mail Address: *contact@hkwtia.org*
Web Address: www.hkwtia.org
Hong Kong Wireless Technology Industry Association (WTIA), which was established in 2001, is a nonprofit trade association registered in Hong Kong to provide a platform for the wireless-related business to work together to benefit the industry development and growth.

Open Mobile Alliance (OMA)
4330 La Jolla Village Dr., Ste. 110
San Diego, CA 92122 US
Phone: 415-265-7204
Fax: 858-623-0743
E-mail Address: *sjones@omaorg.org*
Web Address: www.openmobilealliance.org
The Open Mobile Alliance (OMA) facilitates global user adoption of mobile data services by specifying market driven mobile service enablers that ensure service interoperability across devices, geographies, service providers, operators and networks, while allowing businesses to compete through innovation and differentiation.

Personal Communications Industry Association (PCIA)
901 N. Washington St., Ste. 600
Alexandria, VA 22314 US
Fax: 703-836-1608
Toll Free: 800-759-0300
E-mail Address: *durcsakc@pcia.com*
Web Address: www.pcia.com
The Personal Communications Industry Association (PCIA) is an association of companies that own and operate tower, rooftop and other kinds of wireless broadcasting and telecommunications equipment.

Portable Computer and Communications Association (PCCA)
P.O. Box 680
Hood River, OR 97031 US
Phone: 541-490-5140
Fax: 419-410-8447
E-mail Address: *pcca@pcca.org*
Web Address: www.pcca.org
The Portable Computer and Communications Association (PCCA) exists to provide a forum for disparate computer and communications industries to meet, learn about each other and collaborate on the union of these industries.

Rural Cellular Association (RCA)
1650 Tysons Blvd., Ste. 1500
McLean, VA 22102 US
Phone: 703-883-0303
Toll Free: 800-722-1872
E-mail Address: *eric.peterson@rca-usa.org*
Web Address: www.rca-usa.org
The Rural Cellular Association (RCA) represents rural telecommunications providers in the United States before state and federal legislators. It primarily focuses on two-way wireless providers with a subscriber base less than 500,000.

Wi-Fi Alliance
3925 W. Braker Ln.
Austin, TX 78759 US
Phone: 512-305-0790
Fax: 512-305-0791
E-mail Address: *info@wi-fi.org*
Web Address: www.wi-fi.org
The Wi-Fi Alliance is a nonprofit group that promotes wireless interoperability via Wi-Fi (802.11 standards). It also provides consumers with current information about Wi-Fi systems.

WiMAX Forum
15220 NW Greenbrier Pkwy., Ste. 310
Beaverton, OR 97006 US
Phone: 503-924-2922
Fax: 503-924-3063
Web Address: www.wimaxforum.org
The WiMAX Forum supports the implementation and standardization of long-range wireless Internet connections. It is a nonprofit organization dedicated to the promotion and certification of interoperability and compatibility of broadband wireless products.

WiMedia Alliance, Inc.
2400 Camino Ramon, Ste. 375
San Ramon, CA 94583 US
Phone: 925-275-6661
Fax: 925-886-3809

E-mail Address: *scrumb@inventures.com*
Web Address: www.wimedia.org
WiMedia Alliance, Inc. is an open, nonprofit wireless
industry association that promotes the adoption and
standardization of ultrawideband (UWB) worldwide for
use in the PC, CE and mobile market segments.

Wireless Communications Alliance (WCA)
1639 Lewiston Dr.
Sunnyvale, CA 94087 US
Toll Free: 888-351-6701
E-mail Address: *pr@wca.org*
Web Address: www.wca.org
The Wireless Communications Alliance (WCA) is a
nonprofit business association for companies and
organizations working with wireless technologies. It
promotes networking, education and the exchange of
information amongst its members.

**Wireless Communications Association International
(WCA)**
1333 H St. NW, Ste. 700 W
Washington, DC 20005-4754 US
Phone: 202-452-7823
Fax: 202-452-0041
E-mail Address: *susan@wcai.com*
Web Address: www.wcai.com
The Wireless Communications Association International
(WCA) is the principal nonprofit trade association
representing the wireless broadband industry.

Wireless LAN Association (WLANA)
E-mail Address: *customercare@cwnp.com*
Web Address: www.wlana.org
The Wireless LAN Association (WLANA) is a nonprofit
educational trade association composed of the thought
leaders and technology innovators in the WLAN
technology industry. It provides information about wireless
local area applications, issues and trends and serves as a
resource to customers and prospects of wireless local area
and personal area products, as well as to industry press and
analysts.

LIII.   Wireless & Cellular Industry Resources

Wi-Fi Planet
23 Old Kings Hwy. S.
Jupitermedia Corporation
Darien, CT 06820 US
Phone: 203-662-2800
Fax: 203-655-4686
E-mail Address: *info@jupitermedia.com*
Web Address: www.wi-fiplanet.com
Wi-Fi Planet is a web site devoted to 802.11 wireless
networking protocols. The site features daily news,
reviews, tutorials, forums and event and product listings.
Wi-Fi Planet is a product of JupiterOnlineMedia, a
division of Jupitermedia Corporation.

Wireless Design Online
5340 Fryling Rd., Ste. 101
Erie, PA 16510 US
Phone: 215-675-1800
E-mail Address: *info@wirelessdesignonline.com*
Web Address: www.wirelessdesignonline.com
Wireless Design Online is an Internet source of cutting-
edge technical information for the wireless industry.

Wireless Week
6041 S. Syracuse Way, Ste. 310
Greenwood Village, CO 80111 US
Phone: 973-920-7783
E-mail Address: *holly.hoffer@advantagemedia.com*
Web Address: www.wirelessweek.com
Wireless Week is a weekly magazine covering the wireless
industry.

Chapter 4

THE INFOTECH 500:
WHO THEY ARE AND HOW THEY WERE CHOSEN

Includes Indexes by Company Name, Industry & Location, And a Complete Table of Sales, Profits and Ranks

The companies chosen to be listed in PLUNKETT'S INFOTECH INDUSTRY ALMANAC comprise a unique list. THE INFOTECH 500 (the actual count is 501 companies) were chosen specifically for their dominance in the many facets of the InfoTech industry in which they operate. Complete information about each firm can be found in the "Individual Profiles," beginning at the end of this chapter. These profiles are in alphabetical order by company name.

THE INFOTECH 500 companies are from all parts of the United States, Canada, Europe, Asia/Pacific and beyond. Essentially, THE INFOTECH 500 includes companies that are deeply involved in the technologies, services and trends that keep the entire industry forging ahead.

Simply stated, THE INFOTECH 500 contains 501 of the largest, most successful, fastest growing firms in InfoTech and related industries in the world. To be included in our list, the firms had to meet the following criteria:

1) Generally, these are corporations based in the U.S., however, the headquarters of 156 firms are located in other nations.

2) Prominence, or a significant presence, in InfoTech, InfoTech-based services, equipment and supporting fields. (See the following Industry Codes section for a complete list of types of businesses that are covered).

3) The companies in THE INFOTECH 500 do not have to be exclusively in the InfoTech field.

4) Financial data and vital statistics must have been available to the editors of this book, either directly from the company being written about or from outside sources deemed reliable and accurate by the editors. A small number of companies that we would like to have included are not listed because of a lack of sufficient, objective data.

INDUSTRY LIST, WITH CODES

This book refers to the following list of unique industry codes, based on the 2007 NAIC code system (NAIC is used by many analysts as a replacement for older SIC codes because NAIC is more specific to today's industry sectors, see www.census.gov/NAICS). Companies profiled in this book are given a primary NAIC code, reflecting the main line of business of each firm.

Energy

Manufacturing, Electrical
33591   Battery Manufacturing

InfoTech

Computers & Electronics Manufacturing
33411   Computer Networking & Related Equipment, Manufacturing
334111   Computer Hardware, Manufacturing
334112   Computer Storage Equipment & Misc Parts, Manufacturing
334119   Computer Accessories, Monitors, Printers Manufacturing
334310   Audio & Video Equipment, Consumer Electronics
33441   Semiconductors (Microchips)/Integrated Circuits/Components, Manufacturing
334419   Contract Electronics Manufacturing
3345   Instrument Manufacturing, including Measurement, Control, Test & Navigational
Computers & Electronics, Distribution
423430   Computer & Telecommunications Equipment Distribution
Software
5112   Computer Software
511201   Computer Software, Accounting, Banking & Financial

511210A   Computer Software, Supply Chain & Logistics
511210B   Computer Software, Network Management, System Testing, & Storage
511210C   Computer Software, Telecom, Communications & VOIP
511210D   Computer Software, Healthcare & Biotechnology
511210E   Computer Software, Security & Anti-Virus
511210F   Computer Software, Multimedia, Graphics & Publishing
511210G   Computer Software, Games & Entertainment
511210H   Computer Software, Business Management & ERP
511210I   Computer Software, Operating Systems, Languages & Development Tools
511210J   Computer Software, Data Base & File Management
511210K   Computer Software, Sales & Customer Relationship Management
511210L   Computer Software, Content & Document Management
511210M   Computer Software, E-Commerce & Web Analytics
511210N   Computer Software, Product Lifecycle, Engineering, Design & CAD
511210P   Computer Software, Educational & Training
Information & Data Processing Services
518210   Data Processing Services
Information Services-Professional
541512   Consulting--Computer, Telecommunications & Internet
541513   Computer Programming & Software Design

Internet

519130   Internet Publishing & Web Search Portals

Manufacturing

Machinery & Manufacturing Equipment
333295   Semiconductor Manufacturing Equipment
333313   Business Machines, Manufacturing
Electrical Equipment, Appliances, Tools
335   Electrical Equipment, Manufacturing
335313   Electrical Switches, Sensors, Microelectronics, Optomechanicals

Services

Consulting & Professional Services
541330   Engineering Services
541910   Market Research

Telecommunications

Telecommunications Equipment

3342	Communications Equipment, Manufacturing
334210	Telecommunications Equipment Manufacturing
334220	Radio & Wireless Communication, Manufacturing

INDEX OF RANKINGS WITHIN INDUSTRY GROUPS

Company	Industry Code	2009 Sales (U.S. $ thousands)	Sales Rank	2009 Profits (U.S. $ thousands)	Profits Rank
Audio & Video Equipment, Consumer Electronics					
LG ELECTRONICS INDIA PVT	334310				
PANASONIC CORPORATION	334310	85,729,000	3	-4,183,620	8
PINNACLE SYSTEMS INC	334310				
PIONEER CORPORATION	334310	6,022,370	7	1,408,170	2
ROYAL PHILIPS ELECTRONICS	334310	33,389,000	4	611,000	3
SAMSUNG ELECTRONICS CO	334310	123,691,000	1	8,587,090	1
SANYO ELECTRIC CO LTD	334310	18,067,918	6	-951,286	5
SHARP CORPORATION	334310	31,432,600	5	-1,388,960	7
SONY CORPORATION	334310	86,711,870	2	-1,109,850	6
VIDEOCON INDUSTRIES LTD	334310	2,263,400	8	111,520	4
Battery Manufacturing					
SIMPLO TECHNOLOGY CO LTD	33591				
Business Machines, Manufacturing					
IKON OFFICE SOLUTIONS INC	333313				
RICOH COMPANY LTD	333313	21,395,000	1	70,450	2
XEROX CORP	333313	15,179,000	2	485,000	1
Communications Equipment, Manufacturing					
BLONDER TONGUE LABORATORIES INC	3342	29,034	7	75	4
CALAMP CORP	3342	98,370	6	-49,665	6
FLUKE NETWORKS	3342				
HARRIS CORPORATION	3342	5,005,000	2	37,900	2
L-3 COMMUNICATIONS HOLDINGS INC	3342	15,615,000	1	911,000	1
PLANTRONICS INC	3342	674,590	3	-64,899	7
SONUS NETWORKS INC	3342	227,496	4	-4,932	5
TELEX COMMUNICATIONS INC	3342				
ZOOM TECHNOLOGIES INC	3342	189,056	5	6,243	3
Computer & Telecommunications Equipment Distribution					
ANIXTER INTERNATIONAL INC	423430	4,982,400	8	-29,300	13
ARROW ELECTRONICS INC	423430	14,684,101	4	123,512	2
AVNET INC	423430	16,229,900	3	-1,129,700	14
BLACK BOX CORPORATION	423430	999,548	14	45,309	7
CDW CORPORATION	423430	8,000,000	5		
COMPUCOM SYSTEMS INC	423430				
DIGITAL CHINA HOLDINGS LTD	423430	5,442,020	7	82,430	5
GTSI CORP	423430	761,870	15	5,456	10
INGRAM MICRO INC	423430	29,515,446	1	202,138	1
INSIGHT ENTERPRISES INC	423430	4,136,905	9	33,574	9
PC CONNECTION INC	423430	1,569,656	12	-1,222	12
PC MALL INC	423430	1,138,061	13	3,357	11
REDINGTON (INDIA) LTD	423430	2,784,650	10	35,090	8
SCANSOURCE INC	423430	1,847,969	11	47,688	6
SYNNEX CORP	423430	7,719,197	6	92,088	4
TECH DATA CORP	423430	24,080,484	2	117,278	3

Company	Industry Code	2009 Sales (U.S. $ thousands)	Sales Rank	2009 Profits (U.S. $ thousands)	Profits Rank
Computer Accessories, Monitors, Printers Manufacturing					
AU OPTRONICS CORP	334119	11,374,400	4	-847,360	23
BENQ CORPORATION	334119				
BOE TECHNOLOGY GROUP CO	334119	947,900	15	7,540	15
CANON INC	334119	34,440,000	1	1,412,800	1
CHICONY ELECTRONICS CO	334119	1,857,710	14	114,700	7
CHIMEI INNOLUX CORPORATION	334119	5,630,700	7	-81,940	20
DATALOGIC SCANNING INC	334119				
DIGITECH SYSTEMS CO LTD	334119	104,120	23	21,780	13
ELECTRONICS FOR IMAGING	334119	401,108	20	-2,171	16
ELITEGROUP COMPUTER SYSTEMS CO LTD	334119	2,525,930	12	28,190	12
IMMERSION CORP	334119	27,725	24	-28,279	18
INTERMEC INC	334119	658,205	18	-11,843	17
LEXMARK INTERNATIONAL INC	334119	3,879,900	8	145,900	4
LG DISPLAY CO LTD	334119	18,502,800	2	953,680	2
LITE-ON TECHNOLOGY CORP	334119	6,407,000	6	242,830	3
LOGITECH INTERNATIONAL SA	334119	2,208,832	13	107,032	8
MICRO-STAR INTERNATIONAL	334119	2,830,720	10	8,310	14
MOLEX INC	334119	2,581,841	11	-321,287	22
NVIDIA CORP	334119	3,424,859	9	-30,041	19
PRINTRONIX INC	334119				
PULSE ELECTRONICS CORP	334119	398,803	21	-193,837	21
SEIKO EPSON CORPORATION	334119	12,109,700	3	-1,200,960	24
SHIN ZU SHING CO LTD	334119	242,050	22	49,670	9
SYNAPTICS INC	334119	473,302	19	48,079	10
TANDBERG	334119	902,600	16	122,200	6
TPV TECHNOLOGY LTD	334119	8,032,000	5	141,200	5
TXCOM-AXIOHM	334119				
ZEBRA TECHNOLOGIES CORP	334119	803,585	17	47,104	11
Computer Hardware, Manufacturing					
ACER INC	334111	18,178,400	10	359,570	6
ADEPT TECHNOLOGY INC	334111	41,536	31	-13,068	19
AISINO CORPORATION INC	334111	1,136,300	20	92,600	9
APPLE INC	334111	42,905,000	7	8,235,000	1
ASUSTEK COMPUTER (ASUS)	334111	19,313,000	9	395,020	5
CASIO COMPUTER CO LTD	334111	5,762,590	13	-257,510	24
COGNEX CORP	334111	175,727	28	-4,869	17
CONCURRENT COMPUTER	334111	71,640	30	-14,477	20
CRAY INC	334111	284,047	27	-604	16
DELL INC	334111	61,101,000	4	2,478,000	4
DIEBOLD INC	334111	2,718,292	15	32,254	11
DRS TECHNOLOGIES INC	334111				
FUJITSU LIMITED	334111	52,204,400	5	-1,250,190	27
FUJITSU TECHNOLOGY SOLUTIONS (HOLDING) BV	334111				
GATEWAY INC	334111				
GERBER SCIENTIFIC INC	334111	498,940	24	2,236	15

Company	Industry Code	2009 Sales (U.S. $ thousands)	Sales Rank	2009 Profits (U.S. $ thousands)	Profits Rank
HCL INFOSYSTEMS LIMITED	334111	2,674,180	16	55,730	10
HEWLETT-PACKARD CO (HP)	334111	114,552,000	1	7,660,000	2
HITACHI LTD	334111	103,003,801	2	-8,109,571	31
KRONOS INC	334111				
LENOVO GROUP LIMITED	334111	14,901,400	11	-226,400	23
MELLANOX TECHNOLOGIES	334111	116,044	29	12,886	14
MICROS SYSTEMS INC	334111	907,725	21	96,292	8
MITAC INTERNATIONAL CORP	334111	1,974,730	17	18,700	12
NANYA TECHNOLOGY CORP	334111	1,324,680	18	-642,720	25
NCR CORPORATION	334111	4,612,000	14	-30,000	21
NEC CORPORATION	334111	45,478,800	6	-3,200,280	29
NINTENDO CO LTD	334111	19,933,000	8	3,025,680	3
PALM INC	334111	735,872	22	-732,188	26
POSITIVO INFORMATICA SA	334111				
RADISYS CORP	334111	304,273	26	-42,567	22
SMART MODULAR TECHNOLOGIES INC	334111	441,317	25	-11,403	18
SUN MICROSYSTEMS INC	334111	11,449,000	12	-2,234,000	28
SUPER MICRO COMPUTER INC	334111	505,609	23	16,107	13
TOSHIBA CORPORATION	334111	72,732,800	3	-3,755,040	30
TRANSCEND INFORMATION INC	334111	1,185,150	19	149,840	7
Computer Networking & Related Equipment, Manufacturing					
ASANTE NETWORKS INC	33411				
AVY PRECISION TECHNOLOGY	33411	123,910	14	20,520	5
CISCO SYSTEMS INC	33411	36,117,000	1	6,134,000	1
DIGI INTERNATIONAL INC	33411	165,928	12	4,083	12
D-LINK CORPORATION	33411	961,450	3	15,860	6
ECHELON CORP	33411	103,338	15	-32,034	14
EMULEX CORP	33411	378,222	8	7,544	10
ENTERASYS NETWORKS INC	33411				
EXTREME NETWORKS INC	33411	335,559	9	2,815	13
FINISAR CORPORATION	33411	497,058	6	-260,343	16
FORCE10 NETWORKS INC	33411				
FORTINET INC	33411	252,115	10	60,179	4
INTERACTIVE INTELLIGENCE	33411	131,418	13	8,640	9
JUNIPER NETWORKS INC	33411	3,315,900	2	115,200	2
NETGEAR INC	33411	686,595	4	9,333	8
NETWORK EQUIPMENT TECHNOLOGIES INC	33411	65,788	16	-53,503	15
QLOGIC CORP	33411	633,862	5	108,789	3
RIVERBED TECHNOLOGY INC	33411	394,146	7	7,085	11
SONICWALL INC	33411	200,575	11	13,154	7
Computer Programming & Software Design					
ACCENTURE PLC	541513	23,170,968	3	1,589,963	2
AFFILIATED COMPUTER SERVICES INC	541513	6,523,164	8	349,943	9
ARGON ST INC	541513	366,076	25	23,691	20
ATOS ORIGIN SA	541513	6,832,650	7	42,250	19
CAPGEMINI	541513	11,373,200	5	241,840	12
CDG GROUP	541513				

Company	Industry Code	2009 Sales (U.S. $ thousands)	Sales Rank	2009 Profits (U.S. $ thousands)	Profits Rank
CGI GROUP INC	541513	3,825,160	14	303,180	10
CIBER INC	541513	1,037,700	22	14,958	21
COGNIZANT TECHNOLOGY SOLUTIONS CORP	541513	3,278,663	15	534,963	7
COMPUTER SCIENCES CORPORATION (CSC)	541513	16,739,900	4	1,115,200	5
CSK CORPORATION	541513	2,236,420	17	-1,752,780	23
EMDEON INC	541513	918,448	24	14,003	22
GETRONICS NV	541513	2,787,460	16	82,410	15
HCL TECHNOLOGIES LTD	541513	2,232,140	18	287,950	11
IBM GLOBAL SERVICES	541513	55,000,000	2		
IBM INDIA PVT LTD	541513				
INDRA SISTEMAS SA	541513				
INFOSYS TECHNOLOGIES LTD	541513	4,663,000	12	1,281,000	3
INTERNATIONAL BUSINESS MACHINES CORP (IBM)	541513	95,758,000	1	13,425,000	1
ITAUTEC SA	541513				
KEANE INC	541513	1,200,000	20		
LOGICA PLC	541513	5,703,020	10	61,780	16
POMEROY IT SOLUTIONS	541513				
SAIC INC	541513	10,070,000	6	452,000	8
SRA INTERNATIONAL INC	541513	1,540,556	19	58,000	17
TATA CONSULTANCY SERVICES (TCS)	541513	6,015,700	9	1,136,700	4
TECH MAHINDRA LIMITED	541513	979,020	23	222,460	13
TELVENT GIT SA	541513	1,039,480	21	51,580	18
UNISYS CORP	541513	4,597,700	13	189,300	14
WIPRO LTD	541513	5,004,000	11	677,000	6
Computer Software, Accounting, Banking & Financial					
ACI WORLDWIDE INC	511201	405,755	5	19,626	4
BANCTEC INC	511201				
GUIDEWIRE SOFTWARE INC	511201				
INDUSTRIAL & FINANCIAL SYSTEMS (IFS) AB	511201				
INTUIT INC	511201	3,109,000	2	447,000	1
JACK HENRY & ASSOCIATES	511201	745,593	4	103,102	2
MISYS PLC	511201	1,109,220	3	13,140	5
S1 CORPORATION	511201	238,927	6	30,423	3
SUNGARD DATA SYSTEMS INC	511201	5,508,000	1	-576,000	6
Computer Software, Business Management & ERP					
ALLEN SYSTEMS GROUP INC	511210H				
ATTACHMATE CORPORATION	511210H				
BMC SOFTWARE INC	511210H	1,871,900	5	238,100	4
CA INC (CA TECHNOLOGIES)	511210H	4,271,000	3	671,000	3
CDC SOFTWARE CORP	511210H	240,787	12	-1,020	10
CITRIX SYSTEMS INC	511210H	1,614,088	6	191,017	5
COGNOS INC	511210H				
COMPUWARE CORP	511210H	1,090,455	8	139,647	7
EPICOR SOFTWARE CORP	511210H	409,624	10	-1,238	12

Company	Industry Code	2009 Sales (U.S. $ thousands)	Sales Rank	2009 Profits (U.S. $ thousands)	Profits Rank
INDUSTRIAL DEFENDER INC	511210H				
INFOR GLOBAL SOLUTIONS	511210H				
NETSUITE INC	511210H	165,540	15	-23,304	14
ORACLE CORP	511210H	23,252,000	1	5,593,000	1
PAR TECHNOLOGY CORP	511210H	223,048	13	-5,186	13
PEGASYSTEMS INC	511210H	264,013	11	32,212	9
QLIK TECHNOLOGIES INC	511210H				
SAP AG	511210H	14,499,400	2	2,374,900	2
SAS INSTITUTE INC	511210H	2,200,000	4		
SYBASE INC	511210H	1,170,569	7	164,059	6
TIBCO SOFTWARE INC	511210H	621,388	9	62,302	8
ULTIMATE SOFTWARE GROUP	511210H	196,579	14	-1,142	11
Computer Software, Content & Document Management					
AUTONOMY CORP PLC	511210L	739,688	3	191,551	1
NUANCE COMMUNICATIONS	511210L	950,352	1	-12,202	3
OPEN TEXT CORP	511210L	785,665	2	56,938	2
ROVI CORPORATION	511210L	483,911	4	-52,951	4
STERLING COMMERCE INC	511210L				
Computer Software, Data Base & File Management					
EMBARCADERO TECHNOLOGIES INC	511210J				
TERADATA CORPORATION	511210J	1,709,000	1	254,000	1
Computer Software, E-Commerce & Web Analytics					
ART TECHNOLOGY GROUP INC	511210M	179,382	2	16,796	1
BROADVISION INC	511210M	30,961	3	3,734	2
COREMETRICS INC	511210M				
FIRECLICK INC	511210M				
GSI COMMERCE INC	511210M	1,004,215	1	-11,028	3
ICROSSING INC	511210M				
MARKETLIVE INC	511210M				
Computer Software, Educational & Training					
INSTRUCTIVISION INC	511210P				
PLATO LEARNING INC	511210P	65,183	3	957	2
RENAISSANCE LEARNING INC	511210P	121,513	2	-19,923	3
SKILLSOFT PLC	511210P	328,494	1	50,789	1
Computer Software, Electronic Games & Entertainment					
ACTIVISION BLIZZARD INC	511210G	4,279,000	2	-26,000	2
ATARI INC	511210G	180,370	7	-293,430	6
BIOWARE CORP	511210G				
ELECTRONIC ARTS INC	511210G	4,212,000	3	-1,088,000	8
GIGAMEDIA LTD	511210G	159,581	8	-55,880	3
KONAMI CORP	511210G	3,153,527	4	110,699	1
LUCASARTS ENTERTAINMENT	511210G				
SEGA SAMMY HOLDINGS INC	511210G	4,630,230	1	-246,860	5
TAKE-TWO INTERACTIVE SOFTWARE INC	511210G	968,488	5	-137,930	4
THQ INC	511210G	829,963	6	-431,112	7
Computer Software, General					
OPERA SOFTWARE ASA	5112	95,160	2	4,800	2

Company	Industry Code	2009 Sales (U.S. $ thousands)	Sales Rank	2009 Profits (U.S. $ thousands)	Profits Rank
SOFTWARE AG	5112	1,140,130	1	189,710	1
SYMPHONY TECHNOLOGY GROUP	5112				
Computer Software, Healthcare & Biotechnology					
ALLSCRIPTS HEALTHCARE SOLUTIONS INC	511210D	548,439	2	26,022	3
CEGEDIM SA	511210D	1,161,910	1	72,710	1
DATATRAK INTERNATIONAL INC	511210D				
ECLINICALWORKS	511210D	100,000	4		
EPIC SYSTEMS CORPORATION	511210D				
MEDICAL INFORMATION TECHNOLOGY INC	511210D				
QUALITY SYSTEMS INC	511210D	245,515	3	46,119	2
TRIZETTO GROUP INC	511210D				
Computer Software, Multimedia, Graphics & Publishing					
ADOBE SYSTEMS INC	511210F	2,945,853	1	386,508	1
AVID TECHNOLOGY INC	511210F	628,970	3	-68,355	4
CHYRON CORP	511210F	25,614	5	-3,117	3
COREL CORPORATION	511210F				
MEDIAPLATFORM INC	511210F				
QUARK INC	511210F				
REALNETWORKS INC	511210F	862,264	2	-212,264	6
SCENE7 INC	511210F				
SIMTROL INC	511210F	591	6	-2,674	2
SONIC SOLUTIONS	511210F	67,478	4	-118,123	5
Computer Software, Network Management, System Testing, & Storage					
AM NETWORKS INC	511210B				
BROCADE COMMUNICATIONS SYSTEMS INC	511210B	1,952,926	2	-76,585	8
F5 NETWORKS INC	511210B	653,079	4	91,535	2
NETSCOUT SYSTEMS INC	511210B	267,604	5	20,048	4
NETWORK ENGINES INC	511210B	148,722	6	-3,198	6
NOVELL INC	511210B	862,185	3	-212,736	9
OPNET TECHNOLOGIES INC	511210B	122,879	7	4,732	5
RADWARE LTD	511210B	108,900	8	-5,900	7
ROCKET SOFTWARE	511210B				
SOLARWINDS	511210B	62,378	9	29,509	3
TELCORDIA TECHNOLOGIES	511210B				
VMWARE INC	511210B	2,023,937	1	197,098	1
Computer Software, Operating Systems, Languages & Development Tools					
ACCESS CO LTD	511210I	354,210	5	5,400	5
BORLAND SOFTWARE CORP	511210I				
MICROSOFT CORP	511210I	58,437,000	1	14,569,000	1
NEXPRISE INC	511210I				
PHOENIX TECHNOLOGIES LTD	511210I	67,697	7	-75,272	6
PROGRESS SOFTWARE CORP	511210I	494,137	4	32,755	4
QUEST SOFTWARE INC	511210I	695,236	2	70,359	3
RED HAT INC	511210I	652,572	3	78,721	2
ROGUE WAVE SOFTWARE INC	511210I				

Company	Industry Code	2009 Sales (U.S. $ thousands)	Sales Rank	2009 Profits (U.S. $ thousands)	Profits Rank
SERENA SOFTWARE INC	511210I	260,237	6	-339,506	7
WIND RIVER SYSTEMS INC	511210I				
Computer Software, Product Lifecycle, Engineering, Design & CAD					
ANSYS INC	511210N	516,885	9	116,391	5
AUTODESK INC	511210N	2,315,200	1	183,600	3
CADENCE DESIGN SYSTEMS	511210N	852,600	5	-149,900	10
DASSAULT SYSTEMES SA	511210N	1,684,250	2	228,420	1
GSE SYSTEMS INC	511210N	40,060	10	-797	8
INTERGRAPH CORP	511210N	770,400	7	188,600	2
MENTOR GRAPHICS CORP	511210N	789,101	6	-88,802	9
MSCSOFTWARE CORP	511210N				
NATIONAL INSTRUMENTS CORP	511210N	676,594	8	17,085	7
NAVTEQ CORPORATION	511210N				
PARAMETRIC TECHNOLOGY	511210N	938,185	4	31,522	6
SIEMENS PLM SOFTWARE	511210N				
SYNOPSYS INC	511210N	1,360,045	3	167,681	4
Computer Software, Sales & Customer Relationship Management					
ACXIOM CORP	511210K	1,276,573	2	37,504	5
AMDOCS LTD	511210K	2,862,607	1	326,176	1
ASPECT SOFTWARE INC	511210K				
ASTEA INTERNATIONAL INC	511210K	20,103	8	-899	8
CHEETAHMAIL INC	511210K				
CICERO INC	511210K	2,498	11	-1,280	9
CSG SYSTEMS INTERNATIONAL	511210K	500,717	4	43,333	4
FORESEE RESULTS INC	511210K				
LIVEPERSON INC	511210K	87,490	7	7,763	6
MICROS-RETAIL	511210K				
MICROSTRATEGY INC	511210K	377,788	5	74,837	2
PITNEY BOWES SOFTWARE	511210K				
RESPONSYS INC	511210K				
RIGHTNOW TECHNOLOGIES INC	511210K	152,700	6	5,900	7
SALESFORCE.COM INC	511210K	1,076,769	3	43,428	3
SELECTICA INC	511210K	16,445	10	-8,422	10
SPSS INC	511210K				
SUPPORT.COM INC	511210K	17,495	9	-14,577	11
TRILOGY INC	511210K				
Computer Software, Security & Anti-Virus					
AHNLAB INC	511210E	61,880	11	12,670	5
ARCSIGHT INC	511210E	136,168	8	9,913	7
BLUE COAT SYSTEMS INC	511210E	444,745	6	-8,508	10
CHECK POINT SOFTWARE TECHNOLOGIES LTD	511210E	924,417	5	357,523	1
COMMTOUCH SOFTWARE LTD	511210E	12,929	12	5,160	9
ENTRUST INC	511210E				
INTERNET SECURITY SYSTEMS	511210E				
MCAFEE INC	511210E	1,927,332	2	173,420	4
RSA SECURITY INC	511210E				
SAFENET INC	511210E				

Company	Industry Code	2009 Sales (U.S. $ thousands)	Sales Rank	2009 Profits (U.S. $ thousands)	Profits Rank
SOURCEFIRE INC	511210E	103,465	9	8,878	8
SYMANTEC CORP	511210E	6,149,854	1	-6,728,870	12
TREND MICRO INC	511210E	1,171,570	3	214,478	3
VASCO DATA SECURITY INTERNATIONAL INC	511210E	101,695	10	12,632	6
VERISIGN INC	511210E	1,030,619	4	249,239	2
WATCHGUARD TECHNOLOGIES	511210E				
WEBSENSE INC	511210E	262,907	7	-10,697	11
Computer Software, Supply Chain & Logistics					
AMERICAN SOFTWARE INC	511210A	78,024	6	3,016	5
ARIBA INC	511210A	338,972	3	8,193	4
ASPEN TECHNOLOGY INC	511210A	311,580	4	52,924	1
BRAVOSOLUTION SPA	511210A				
ELCOM INTERNATIONAL INC	511210A				
JDA SOFTWARE GROUP INC	511210A	385,800	2	26,339	2
MANHATTAN ASSOCIATES INC	511210A	246,667	5	16,562	3
MODUSLINK GLOBAL SOLUTIONS INC	511210A	1,008,554	1	-193,452	6
VENTYX INC	511210A				
Computer Software, Telecom, Communications & VOIP					
COMVERSE TECHNOLOGY INC	511210C				
CRITICAL PATH INC	511210C				
LOGMELN INC	511210C	74,408	4	8,797	2
OPENTV CORP	511210C	120,012	3	6,242	3
OPENWAVE SYSTEMS INC	511210C	191,698	2	-85,876	5
SEACHANGE INTERNATIONAL	511210C	201,836	1	9,974	1
SPANLINK COMMUNICATIONS	511210C				
TELECA AB	511210C				
ULTICOM INC	511210C	53,047	5	-3,136	4
VICORP GROUP PLC	511210C				
Computer Storage Equipment & Misc. Parts, Manufacturing					
AMPEX CORP	334112				
DATA ROBOTICS INC	334112				
DOT HILL SYSTEMS CORP	334112	234,383	10	-13,625	6
EMC CORP	334112	14,025,910	1	1,123,971	1
IMATION CORP	334112	1,649,500	6	-42,200	9
IOMEGA CORP	334112				
ISILON SYSTEMS INC	334112	123,911	12	-18,873	8
LEXAR MEDIA INC	334112				
MOSER BAER INDIA LIMITED	334112	537,350	9	-79,040	10
NETAPP INC	334112	3,406,393	5	64,600	4
NIDEC CORPORATION	334112	6,245,119	4	288,639	3
OCZ TECHNOLOGY GROUP INC	334112	155,982	11	-11,724	5
OVERLAND STORAGE INC	334112	105,621	13	-18,028	7
QUANTUM CORP	334112	808,972	8	-358,264	11
SEAGATE TECHNOLOGY PLC	334112	9,805,000	2	-3,125,000	13
SPANSION	334112	1,630,573	7	-514,059	12
WESTERN DIGITAL CORP	334112	7,453,000	3	470,000	2

Company	Industry Code	2009 Sales (U.S. $ thousands)	Sales Rank	2009 Profits (U.S. $ thousands)	Profits Rank
Consulting--Computer, Telecommunications & Internet					
ALTRAN TECHNOLOGIES SA	541512	1,907,120	5	-101,630	7
ANALYSTS INTERNATIONAL	541512	143,165	7	-15,907	6
CACI INTERNATIONAL INC	541512	2,730,162	2	89,698	3
DIMENSION DATA HOLDINGS	541512	3,973,100	1	135,200	1
GROUPE STERIA SCA	541512	2,193,980	3	64,880	4
MANTECH INTERNATIONAL	541512	2,020,334	4	111,764	2
PC-WARE INFORMATION TECHNOLOGIES AG	541512	1,202,920	6	11,710	5
Data Processing, Hosting & Related Services					
AKAMAI TECHNOLOGIES INC	518210	859,773	1	145,913	1
CORESITE REALTY CORP	518210				
DIGITAL RIVER INC	518210	403,766	2	53,042	2
EASYLINK SERVICES INTERNATIONAL CORPORATION	518210	85,365	5	-11,512	4
NAVISITE INC	518210	125,379	3	-15,111	5
RIGHTSCALE INC	518210				
SERVEPATH	518210				
WEB.COM GROUP INC	518210	106,489	4	2,609	3
WYSE TECHNOLOGY INC	518210				
Electrical Equipment, Manufacturing					
DIODES INC	335	434,357	4	9,848	4
HOSIDEN CORPORATION	335	4,892,320	3	149,840	2
MITSUBISHI ELECTRIC CORP	335	40,461,900	2	134,320	3
SAMSUNG ELECTRO-MECHANICS	335				
SIEMENS AG	335	113,842,000	1	3,404,080	1
SIEMENS LIMITED	335				
TII NETWORK TECHNOLOGIES	335	27,437	5	73	5
Electrical Switches, Sensors, Microelectronics, Optomechanicals					
ALPS ELECTRIC CO LTD	335313	5,790,360	1	-752,690	1
Electronic Component Manufacturing/Contract Manufacturing					
ACCTON TECHNOLOGY CORP	334419	535,040	16	20,340	11
BENCHMARK ELECTRONICS	334419	2,089,253	13	53,895	8
CELESTICA INC	334419	6,092,200	8	55,000	7
COMPAL ELECTRONICS INC	334419	20,955,900	4	596,060	4
CTS CORP	334419	498,982	17	-34,050	17
FLEXTRONICS INTERNATIONAL	334419	30,948,575	2	-6,135,518	22
FOXCONN INTERNATIONAL HOLDINGS LTD	334419	7,213,600	7	38,600	10
FOXCONN TECHNOLOGY CO	334419	4,832,000	10	195,150	5
HON HAI PRECISION INDUSTRY COMPANY LTD	334419	61,960,200	1	2,393,580	1
HTC CORP	334419	4,483,860	12	701,600	2
INVENTEC CORPORATION	334419	13,788,700	5	142,920	6
JABIL CIRCUIT INC	334419	11,684,538	6	-1,165,212	21
KEY TRONIC CORP	334419	184,924	20	1,063	15
LABARGE INC	334419	273,368	19	10,338	12
PLEXUS CORP	334419	1,616,622	14	46,327	9

Company	Industry Code	2009 Sales (U.S. $ thousands)	Sales Rank	2009 Profits (U.S. $ thousands)	Profits Rank
QISDA CORPORATION	334419	4,636,940	11	-55,830	19
QUANTA COMPUTER INC	334419	25,353,000	3	626,420	3
SANMINA-SCI CORPORATION	334419	5,177,481	9	-136,222	20
SIGMATRON INTERNATIONAL	334419	133,745	22	1,956	14
SMTC CORP	334419	179,509	21	-3,595	16
TTM TECHNOLOGIES INC	334419	582,476	15	4,857	13
VIASYSTEMS GROUP INC	334419	496,447	18	-54,717	18
Engineering Services					
VSE CORP	541330	1,014,639	1	24,024	1
Instrument Manufacturing, including Measurement, Control, Test & Navigational					
BHARAT ELECTRONICS LIMITED	3345				
GARMIN LTD	3345	2,946,440	1	703,950	1
SPECTRIS	3345	1,275,060	3	68,130	3
TEKTRONIX INC	3345				
TOMTOM NV	3345	1,806,050	2	105,940	2
TRIMBLE NAVIGATION LTD	3345	1,126,259	4	63,446	4
Internet Publishing & Web Search Portals					
ASK.COM	519130				
BUZZ TECHNOLOGIES INC	519130				
GOOGLE INC	519130	23,650,563	1	6,520,448	1
LIMELIGHT NETWORKS INC	519130	131,663	3	34,890	3
YAHOO! INC	519130	6,460,315	2	605,289	2
Market Research					
FORRESTER RESEARCH INC	541910	233,352	2	19,770	2
GARTNER INC	541910	1,139,800	1	82,964	1
Radio & Wireless Communication, Manufacturing					
LG ELECTRONICS INC	334220	65,780,900	1	1,855,860	2
LG ELECTRONICS USA INC	334220				
NOKIA CORPORATION	334220	55,759,100	2	1,212,210	3
PROXIM WIRELESS CORP	334220	29,700	5	-7,400	5
RESEARCH IN MOTION (RIM)	334220	11,065,186	4	1,892,616	1
TELEFON AB LM ERICSSON (ERICSSON)	334220	28,758,200	3	511,440	4
Semiconductor Manufacturing Equipment & Services					
ADVANCED SEMICONDUCTOR ENGINEERING INC	333295	2,716,120	2	213,550	2
ADVANTEST CORPORATION	333295	780,332	8	-762,517	12
AMKOR TECHNOLOGY INC	333295	2,179,109	3	156,283	3
AMTECH SYSTEMS INC	333295	52,973	13	-1,589	5
APPLIED MATERIALS INC	333295	5,013,607	1	-305,327	10
ARM HOLDINGS PLC	333295	470,290	10	62,350	4
ATMI INC	333295	254,704	12	-6,660	6
KLA TENCOR CORP	333295	1,520,216	5	-523,368	11
LAM RESEARCH CORP	333295	1,115,946	6	-302,148	9
NOVELLUS SYSTEMS INC	333295	639,194	9	-85,235	8
PHOTRONICS INC	333295	361,353	11	-41,910	7
SEMICONDUCTOR MANUFACTURING INTERNATIONAL	333295	1,070,387	7		

Company	Industry Code	2009 Sales (U.S. $ thousands)	Sales Rank	2009 Profits (U.S. $ thousands)	Profits Rank
SILICONWARE PRECISION INDUSTRIES CO LTD	333295	1,855,856	4	275,112	1
Semiconductors (Microchips)/Integrated Circuits/Components, Manufacturing					
ADVANCED MICRO DEVICES INC (AMD)	33441	5,403,000	7	293,000	10
ALTERA CORP	33441	1,195,413	27	251,062	12
ANALOG DEVICES INC	33441	2,014,908	21	247,772	14
ARTERIS INC	33441				
ATHEROS COMMUNICATIONS	33441	542,468	39	46,407	29
ATMEL CORP	33441	1,217,345	26	-109,498	45
AVX CORPORATION	33441	1,389,613	25	80,846	24
BROADCOM CORP	33441	4,490,323	10	65,261	27
CIRRUS LOGIC INC	33441	174,642	50	3,475	33
CONEXANT SYSTEMS INC	33441	208,427	47	-18,808	37
CYPRESS SEMICONDUCTOR	33441	667,786	38	-150,424	46
DIGITAL ANGEL CORP	33441	49,463	54	-12,430	36
DSP GROUP INC	33441	212,186	45	-8,436	35
ELPIDA MEMORY INC	33441	3,625,810	13	-1,959,070	54
ESS TECHNOLOGY INC	33441				
FREESCALE SEMICONDUCTOR	33441	3,508,000	15	748,000	6
GEMALTO NV	33441	2,225,640	19	154,458	16
GLOBALFOUNDRIES	33441				
HOYA CORP	33441	4,897,220	8	270,730	11
INFINEON TECHNOLOGIES AG	33441	4,428,000	11	-982,000	51
INNOVEX INC	33441				
INPHI CORPORATION	33441				
INTEL CORP	33441	35,127,000	1	4,369,000	1
INTERDIGITAL INC	33441	297,404	44	87,256	22
INTERNATIONAL RECTIFIER	33441	740,419	37	-247,417	48
KEMET CORP	33441	804,385	34	-285,209	49
LATTICE SEMICONDUCTOR	33441	194,420	48	-6,957	34
LINEAR TECHNOLOGY CORP	33441	968,498	30	313,510	9
LSI CORPORATION	33441	2,219,159	20	-47,719	40
MACRONIX INTERNATIONAL CO	33441	847,170	33	179,810	15
MARVELL TECHNOLOGY GROUP	33441	2,950,563	17	147,242	17
MAXIM INTEGRATED PRODUCTS	33441	1,646,015	23	10,455	32
MEDIATEK INC	33441	3,977,670	12	1,263,970	5
MEMC ELECTRONIC MATERIALS	33441	1,163,600	28	-68,300	42
MICROCHIP TECHNOLOGY INC	33441	903,297	32	248,820	13
MICRON TECHNOLOGY INC	33441	4,803,000	9	-1,882,000	53
MINDSPEED TECHNOLOGIES	33441	126,552	52	-25,114	38
MULTI-FINELINE ELECTRONIX	33441	764,432	36	46,068	30
NAN YA PCB CORP	33441				
NATIONAL SEMICONDUCTOR	33441	1,460,400	24	73,300	25
NOVATEK MICROELECTRONICS	33441	930,200	31	138,380	18
NXP SEMICONDUCTORS NV	33441				
PMC-SIERRA INC	33441	496,139	40	46,877	28
POWERCHIP TECHNOLOGY	33441	1,123,020	29	-648,490	50
QUALCOMM INC	33441	10,416,000	3	1,592,000	3

Company	Industry Code	2009 Sales (U.S. $ thousands)	Sales Rank	2009 Profits (U.S. $ thousands)	Profits Rank
RAMBUS INC	33441	113,007	53	-92,186	43
RDA MICROELECTRONICS INC	33441				
RENESAS ELECTRONICS CORP	33441				
ROHM CO LTD	33441	3,397,960	16	105,397	20
SANDISK CORP	33441	3,566,806	14	519,390	7
SIGMA DESIGNS INC	33441	209,160	46	26,423	31
SILICON LABORATORIES INC	33441	441,020	41	73,092	26
SKYWORKS SOLUTIONS INC	33441	802,577	35	94,983	21
STANDARD MICROSYSTEMS CORPORATION	33441	325,496	43	-49,409	41
STMICROELECTRONICS NV	33441	8,465,000	5	-1,131,000	52
TAIWAN SEMICONDUCTOR MANUFACTURING CO (TSMC)	33441	9,366,340	4	2,825,580	2
TEXAS INSTRUMENTS INC (TI)	33441	10,427,000	2	1,470,000	4
TOKYO ELECTRON LIMITED	33441	5,504,560	6	81,720	23
UNITED MICROELECTRONICS	33441	2,894,370	18	122,690	19
VARIAN SEMICONDUCTOR EQUIPMENT ASSOCIATES INC	33441	362,081	42	-37,998	39
VIA TECHNOLOGIES INC	33441	193,820	49	-97,580	44
VITESSE SEMICONDUCTOR	33441	168,177	51	-194,041	47
XILINX INC	33441	1,825,184	22	375,640	8
Telecommunications Equipment Manufacturing					
ADC TELECOMMUNICATIONS	334210	990,200	7	-452,900	12
ADTRAN INC	334210	484,185	10	74,221	3
ALCATEL-LUCENT	334210	21,723,000	2	-722,000	14
AVAYA INC	334210	4,500,000	3		
AVIAT NETWORKS INC	334210	679,900	8	-355,000	11
BEETEL TELETECH LIMITED	334210				
BELDEN INC	334210	1,415,262	5	1,641	5
CIENA CORP	334210	652,629	9	-581,154	13
ECI TELECOM LTD	334210				
FUJITSU NETWORK COMMUNICATIONS INC	334210				
HARMONIC INC	334210	319,566	14	-24,139	7
HUAWEI TECHNOLOGIES CO	334210	21,788,100	1	2,671,130	1
ITI LIMITED	334210	371,130	13	-145,800	9
JDS UNIPHASE CORPORATION	334210	1,283,300	6	-909,500	15
SAGEM TELECOMMUNICATIONS	334210				
SYMMETRICOM INC	334210	219,746	15	-45,757	8
TEKELEC	334210	469,261	11	47,402	4
TELLABS INC	334210	1,526,000	4	114,000	2
UTSTARCOM INC	334210	386,344	12	-225,688	10
WESTELL TECHNOLOGIES INC	334210	185,916	16	-16,594	6

ALPHABETICAL INDEX

COMVERSE TECHNOLOGY INC
CONCURRENT COMPUTER CORP
CONEXANT SYSTEMS INC
COREL CORPORATION
COREMETRICS INC
CORESITE REALTY CORP
CRAY INC
CRITICAL PATH INC
CSG SYSTEMS INTERNATIONAL INC
CSK CORPORATION
CTS CORP
CYPRESS SEMICONDUCTOR CORP
DASSAULT SYSTEMES SA
DATA ROBOTICS INC
DATALOGIC SCANNING INC
DATATRAK INTERNATIONAL INC
DELL INC
DIEBOLD INC
DIGI INTERNATIONAL INC
DIGITAL ANGEL CORP
DIGITAL CHINA HOLDINGS LIMITED
DIGITAL RIVER INC
DIGITECH SYSTEMS CO LTD
DIMENSION DATA HOLDINGS PLC
DIODES INC
D-LINK CORPORATION
DOT HILL SYSTEMS CORP
DRS TECHNOLOGIES INC
DSP GROUP INC
EASYLINK SERVICES INTERNATIONAL
CORPORATION
ECHELON CORP
ECI TELECOM LTD
ECLINICALWORKS
ELCOM INTERNATIONAL INC
ELECTRONIC ARTS INC
ELECTRONICS FOR IMAGING INC
ELITEGROUP COMPUTER SYSTEMS CO LTD
ELPIDA MEMORY INC
EMBARCADERO TECHNOLOGIES INC
EMC CORP
EMDEON INC
EMULEX CORP
ENTERASYS NETWORKS INC
ENTRUST INC
EPIC SYSTEMS CORPORATION
EPICOR SOFTWARE CORP
ESS TECHNOLOGY INC
EXTREME NETWORKS INC
F5 NETWORKS INC
FINISAR CORPORATION
FIRECLICK INC
FLEXTRONICS INTERNATIONAL LTD
FLUKE NETWORKS
FORCE10 NETWORKS INC
FORESEE RESULTS INC
FORRESTER RESEARCH INC
FORTINET INC

FOXCONN INTERNATIONAL HOLDINGS LTD
FOXCONN TECHNOLOGY CO LTD
FREESCALE SEMICONDUCTOR INC
FUJITSU LIMITED
FUJITSU NETWORK COMMUNICATIONS INC
FUJITSU TECHNOLOGY SOLUTIONS (HOLDING)
BV
GARMIN LTD
GARTNER INC
GATEWAY INC
GEMALTO NV
GERBER SCIENTIFIC INC
GETRONICS NV
GIGAMEDIA LTD
GLOBALFOUNDRIES
GOOGLE INC
GROUPE STERIA SCA
GSE SYSTEMS INC
GSI COMMERCE INC
GTSI CORP
GUIDEWIRE SOFTWARE INC
HARMONIC INC
HARRIS CORPORATION
HCL INFOSYSTEMS LIMITED
HCL TECHNOLOGIES LTD
HEWLETT-PACKARD CO (HP)
HITACHI LTD
HON HAI PRECISION INDUSTRY COMPANY LTD
HOSIDEN CORPORATION
HOYA CORP
HTC CORP
HUAWEI TECHNOLOGIES CO LTD
IBM GLOBAL SERVICES
IBM INDIA PVT LTD
ICROSSING INC
IKON OFFICE SOLUTIONS INC
IMATION CORP
IMMERSION CORP
INDRA SISTEMAS SA
INDUSTRIAL & FINANCIAL SYSTEMS (IFS) AB
INDUSTRIAL DEFENDER INC
INFINEON TECHNOLOGIES AG
INFOR GLOBAL SOLUTIONS
INFOSYS TECHNOLOGIES LTD
INGRAM MICRO INC
INNOVEX INC
INPHI CORPORATION
INSIGHT ENTERPRISES INC
INSTRUCTIVISION INC
INTEL CORP
INTERACTIVE INTELLIGENCE
INTERDIGITAL INC
INTERGRAPH CORP
INTERMEC INC
INTERNATIONAL BUSINESS MACHINES CORP
(IBM)
INTERNATIONAL RECTIFIER CORP
INTERNET SECURITY SYSTEMS INC

INTUIT INC
INVENTEC CORPORATION
IOMEGA CORP
ISILON SYSTEMS INC
ITAUTEC SA
ITI LIMITED
JABIL CIRCUIT INC
JACK HENRY & ASSOCIATES INC
JDA SOFTWARE GROUP INC
JDS UNIPHASE CORPORATION
JUNIPER NETWORKS INC
KEANE INC
KEMET CORP
KEY TRONIC CORP
KLA TENCOR CORP
KONAMI CORP
KRONOS INC
L-3 COMMUNICATIONS HOLDINGS INC
LABARGE INC
LAM RESEARCH CORP
LATTICE SEMICONDUCTOR CORP
LENOVO GROUP LIMITED
LEXAR MEDIA INC
LEXMARK INTERNATIONAL INC
LG DISPLAY CO LTD
LG ELECTRONICS INC
LG ELECTRONICS INDIA PVT LTD
LG ELECTRONICS USA INC
LIMELIGHT NETWORKS INC
LINEAR TECHNOLOGY CORP
LITE-ON TECHNOLOGY CORP
LIVEPERSON INC
LOGICA PLC
LOGITECH INTERNATIONAL SA
LOGMELN INC
LSI CORPORATION
LUCASARTS ENTERTAINMENT COMPANY LLC
MACRONIX INTERNATIONAL CO LTD
MANHATTAN ASSOCIATES INC
MANTECH INTERNATIONAL CORP
MARKETLIVE INC
MARVELL TECHNOLOGY GROUP LTD
MAXIM INTEGRATED PRODUCTS INC
MCAFEE INC
MEDIAPLATFORM INC
MEDIATEK INC
MEDICAL INFORMATION TECHNOLOGY INC
MELLANOX TECHNOLOGIES LTD
MEMC ELECTRONIC MATERIALS INC
MENTOR GRAPHICS CORP
MICROCHIP TECHNOLOGY INC
MICRON TECHNOLOGY INC
MICROS SYSTEMS INC
MICROSOFT CORP
MICROS-RETAIL
MICRO-STAR INTERNATIONAL
MICROSTRATEGY INC
MINDSPEED TECHNOLOGIES INC

MISYS PLC
MITAC INTERNATIONAL CORP
MITSUBISHI ELECTRIC CORPORATION
MODUSLINK GLOBAL SOLUTIONS INC
MOLEX INC
MOSER BAER INDIA LIMITED
MSCSOFTWARE CORP
MULTI-FINELINE ELECTRONIX
NAN YA PCB CORP
NANYA TECHNOLOGY CORPORATION
NATIONAL INSTRUMENTS CORP
NATIONAL SEMICONDUCTOR CORP
NAVISITE INC
NAVTEQ CORPORATION
NCR CORPORATION
NEC CORPORATION
NETAPP INC
NETGEAR INC
NETSCOUT SYSTEMS INC
NETSUITE INC
NETWORK ENGINES INC
NETWORK EQUIPMENT TECHNOLOGIES INC
NEXPRISE INC
NIDEC CORPORATION
NINTENDO CO LTD
NOKIA CORPORATION
NOVATEK MICROELECTRONICS CORP
NOVELL INC
NOVELLUS SYSTEMS INC
NUANCE COMMUNICATIONS INC
NVIDIA CORP
NXP SEMICONDUCTORS NV
OCZ TECHNOLOGY GROUP INC
OPEN TEXT CORP
OPENTV CORP
OPENWAVE SYSTEMS INC
OPERA SOFTWARE ASA
OPNET TECHNOLOGIES INC
ORACLE CORP
OVERLAND STORAGE INC
PALM INC
PANASONIC CORPORATION
PAR TECHNOLOGY CORPORATION
PARAMETRIC TECHNOLOGY CORP
PC CONNECTION INC
PC MALL INC
PC-WARE INFORMATION TECHNOLOGIES AG
PEGASYSTEMS INC
PHOENIX TECHNOLOGIES LTD
PHOTRONICS INC
PINNACLE SYSTEMS INC
PIONEER CORPORATION
PITNEY BOWES SOFTWARE INC
PLANTRONICS INC
PLATO LEARNING INC
PLEXUS CORP
PMC-SIERRA INC
POMEROY IT SOLUTIONS

POSITIVO INFORMATICA SA
POWERCHIP TECHNOLOGY CORP
PRINTRONIX INC
PROGRESS SOFTWARE CORP
PROXIM WIRELESS CORP
PULSE ELECTRONICS CORPORATION
QISDA CORPORATION
QLIK TECHNOLOGIES INC
QLOGIC CORP
QUALCOMM INC
QUALITY SYSTEMS INC
QUANTA COMPUTER INC
QUANTUM CORP
QUARK INC
QUEST SOFTWARE INC
RADISYS CORP
RADWARE LTD
RAMBUS INC
RDA MICROELECTRONICS INC
REALNETWORKS INC
RED HAT INC
REDINGTON (INDIA) LTD
RENAISSANCE LEARNING INC
RENESAS ELECTRONICS CORP
RESEARCH IN MOTION LTD (RIM)
RESPONSYS INC
RICOH COMPANY LTD
RIGHTNOW TECHNOLOGIES INC
RIGHTSCALE INC
RIVERBED TECHNOLOGY INC
ROCKET SOFTWARE
ROGUE WAVE SOFTWARE INC
ROHM CO LTD
ROVI CORPORATION
ROYAL PHILIPS ELECTRONICS NV
RSA SECURITY INC
S1 CORPORATION
SAFENET INC
SAGEM TELECOMMUNICATIONS
SAIC INC
SALESFORCE.COM INC
SAMSUNG ELECTRO-MECHANICS
SAMSUNG ELECTRONICS CO LTD
SANDISK CORP
SANMINA-SCI CORPORATION
SANYO ELECTRIC COMPANY LTD
SAP AG
SAS INSTITUTE INC
SCANSOURCE INC
SCENE7 INC
SEACHANGE INTERNATIONAL INC
SEAGATE TECHNOLOGY PLC
SEGA SAMMY HOLDINGS INC
SEIKO EPSON CORPORATION
SELECTICA INC
SEMICONDUCTOR MANUFACTURING
INTERNATIONAL
SERENA SOFTWARE INC

SERVEPATH
SHARP CORPORATION
SHIN ZU SHING CO LTD
SIEMENS AG
SIEMENS LIMITED
SIEMENS PLM SOFTWARE
SIGMA DESIGNS INC
SIGMATRON INTERNATIONAL INC
SILICON LABORATORIES INC
SILICONWARE PRECISION INDUSTRIES CO LTD
SIMPLO TECHNOLOGY CO LTD
SIMTROL INC
SKILLSOFT PLC
SKYWORKS SOLUTIONS INC
SMART MODULAR TECHNOLOGIES INC
SMTC CORP
SOFTWARE AG
SOLARWINDS
SONIC SOLUTIONS
SONICWALL INC
SONUS NETWORKS INC
SONY CORPORATION
SOURCEFIRE INC
SPANLINK COMMUNICATIONS
SPANSION
SPECTRIS
SPSS INC
SRA INTERNATIONAL INC
STANDARD MICROSYSTEMS CORPORATION
STERLING COMMERCE INC
STMICROELECTRONICS NV
SUN MICROSYSTEMS INC
SUNGARD DATA SYSTEMS INC
SUPER MICRO COMPUTER INC
SUPPORT.COM INC
SYBASE INC
SYMANTEC CORP
SYMMETRICOM INC
SYMPHONY TECHNOLOGY GROUP
SYNAPTICS INC
SYNNEX CORP
SYNOPSYS INC
TAIWAN SEMICONDUCTOR MANUFACTURING CO
LTD (TSMC)
TAKE-TWO INTERACTIVE SOFTWARE INC
TANDBERG
TATA CONSULTANCY SERVICES (TCS)
TECH DATA CORP
TECH MAHINDRA LIMITED
TEKELEC
TEKTRONIX INC
TELCORDIA TECHNOLOGIES
TELECA AB
TELEFON AB LM ERICSSON (ERICSSON)
TELEX COMMUNICATIONS INC
TELLABS INC
TELVENT GIT SA
TERADATA CORPORATION

TEXAS INSTRUMENTS INC (TI)
THQ INC
TIBCO SOFTWARE INC
TII NETWORK TECHNOLOGIES INC
TOKYO ELECTRON LIMITED
TOMTOM NV
TOSHIBA CORPORATION
TPV TECHNOLOGY LTD
TRANSCEND INFORMATION INC
TREND MICRO INC
TRILOGY INC
TRIMBLE NAVIGATION LTD
TRIZETTO GROUP INC (THE)
TTM TECHNOLOGIES INC
TXCOM-AXIOHM
ULTICOM INC
ULTIMATE SOFTWARE GROUP INC
UNISYS CORP
UNITED MICROELECTRONICS CORP
UTSTARCOM INC
VARIAN SEMICONDUCTOR EQUIPMENT
ASSOCIATES INC
VASCO DATA SECURITY INTERNATIONAL INC
VENTYX INC
VERISIGN INC
VIA TECHNOLOGIES INC
VIASYSTEMS GROUP INC
VICORP GROUP PLC
VIDEOCON INDUSTRIES LTD
VITESSE SEMICONDUCTOR CORP
VMWARE INC
VSE CORP
WATCHGUARD TECHNOLOGIES INC
WEB.COM GROUP INC
WEBSENSE INC
WESTELL TECHNOLOGIES INC
WESTERN DIGITAL CORP
WIND RIVER SYSTEMS INC
WIPRO LTD
WYSE TECHNOLOGY INC
XEROX CORP
XILINX INC
YAHOO! INC
ZEBRA TECHNOLOGIES CORP
ZOOM TECHNOLOGIES INC

INDEX OF HEADQUARTERS LOCATION BY U.S. STATE

To help you locate members of the firms geographically, the city and state of the headquarters of each company are in the following index.

ALABAMA
ADTRAN INC; Huntsville
INTERGRAPH CORP; Madison

ARIZONA
AMKOR TECHNOLOGY INC; Chandler
AMTECH SYSTEMS INC; Tempe
AVNET INC; Phoenix
ICROSSING INC; Scottsdale
INSIGHT ENTERPRISES INC; Tempe
JDA SOFTWARE GROUP INC; Scottsdale
LIMELIGHT NETWORKS INC; Tempe
MICROCHIP TECHNOLOGY INC; Chandler

ARKANSAS
ACXIOM CORP; Little Rock

CALIFORNIA
ACTIVISION BLIZZARD INC; Santa Monica
ADEPT TECHNOLOGY INC; Pleasanton
ADOBE SYSTEMS INC; San Jose
ADVANCED MICRO DEVICES INC (AMD); Sunnyvale
ALTERA CORP; San Jose
AMPEX CORP; Redwood City
APPLE INC; Cupertino
APPLIED MATERIALS INC; Santa Clara
ARCSIGHT INC; Cupertino
ARIBA INC; Sunnyvale
ARTERIS INC; Sunnyvale
ASANTE NETWORKS INC; Fremont
ASK.COM; Oakland
ATHEROS COMMUNICATIONS INC; Santa Clara
ATMEL CORP; San Jose
AUTODESK INC; San Rafael
BLUE COAT SYSTEMS INC; Sunnyvale
BROADCOM CORP; Irvine
BROADVISION INC; Redwood City
BROCADE COMMUNICATIONS SYSTEMS INC; San Jose
CADENCE DESIGN SYSTEMS INC; San Jose
CALAMP CORP; Oxnard
CISCO SYSTEMS INC; San Jose
CONEXANT SYSTEMS INC; Newport Beach
COREMETRICS INC; San Mateo
CYPRESS SEMICONDUCTOR CORP; San Jose
DATA ROBOTICS INC; Santa Clara
DSP GROUP INC; San Jose
ECHELON CORP; San Jose
ELECTRONIC ARTS INC; Redwood City
ELECTRONICS FOR IMAGING INC; Foster City

EMBARCADERO TECHNOLOGIES INC; San Francisco
EMULEX CORP; Costa Mesa
EPICOR SOFTWARE CORP; Irvine
ESS TECHNOLOGY INC; Fremont
EXTREME NETWORKS INC; Santa Clara
FINISAR CORPORATION; Sunnyvale
FIRECLICK INC; San Diego
FORCE10 NETWORKS INC; San Jose
FORTINET INC; Sunnyvale
GATEWAY INC; Irvine
GLOBALFOUNDRIES; Milpitas
GOOGLE INC; Mountain View
GUIDEWIRE SOFTWARE INC; San Mateo
HARMONIC INC; Sunnyvale
HEWLETT-PACKARD CO (HP); Palo Alto
IMMERSION CORP; San Jose
INGRAM MICRO INC; Santa Ana
INTEL CORP; Santa Clara
INTERNATIONAL RECTIFIER CORP; El Segundo
INTUIT INC; Mountain View
IOMEGA CORP; San Diego
JDS UNIPHASE CORPORATION; Milpitas
JUNIPER NETWORKS INC; Sunnyvale
KLA TENCOR CORP; Milpitas
LAM RESEARCH CORP; Fremont
LEXAR MEDIA INC; Fremont
LINEAR TECHNOLOGY CORP; Milpitas
LSI CORPORATION; Milpitas
LUCASARTS ENTERTAINMENT COMPANY LLC;
San Francisco
MARKETLIVE INC; Petaluma
MARVELL TECHNOLOGY GROUP LTD; Santa Clara
MAXIM INTEGRATED PRODUCTS INC; Sunnyvale
MCAFEE INC; Santa Clara
MEDIAPLATFORM INC; Beverly Hills
MELLANOX TECHNOLOGIES LTD; Sunnyvale
MINDSPEED TECHNOLOGIES INC; Newport Beach
MSCSOFTWARE CORP; Santa Ana
MULTI-FINELINE ELECTRONIX; Anaheim
NATIONAL SEMICONDUCTOR CORP; Santa Clara
NETAPP INC; Sunnyvale
NETGEAR INC; San Jose
NETSUITE INC; San Mateo
NETWORK EQUIPMENT TECHNOLOGIES INC;
Fremont
NEXPRISE INC; Carlsbad
NOVELLUS SYSTEMS INC; San Jose
NVIDIA CORP; Santa Clara
OCZ TECHNOLOGY GROUP INC; San Jose
OPENTV CORP; San Francisco
OPENWAVE SYSTEMS INC; Redwood City
ORACLE CORP; Redwood Shores
OVERLAND STORAGE INC; San Diego
PALM INC; Sunnyvale
PC MALL INC; Torrance
PHOENIX TECHNOLOGIES LTD; Milpitas
PINNACLE SYSTEMS INC; Mountain View
PLANTRONICS INC; Santa Cruz

PMC-SIERRA INC; Santa Clara
PRINTRONIX INC; Irvine
PROXIM WIRELESS CORP; Milpitas
QLOGIC CORP; Aliso Viejo
QUALCOMM INC; San Diego
QUALITY SYSTEMS INC; Irvine
QUANTUM CORP; San Jose
QUEST SOFTWARE INC; Aliso Viejo
RAMBUS INC; Sunnyvale
RESPONSYS INC; San Bruno
RIGHTSCALE INC; Santa Barbara
RIVERBED TECHNOLOGY INC; San Francisco
ROVI CORPORATION; Santa Clara
SALESFORCE.COM INC; San Francisco
SANDISK CORP; Milpitas
SANMINA-SCI CORPORATION; San Jose
SCENE7 INC; San Francisco
SELECTICA INC; San Jose
SERENA SOFTWARE INC; Redwood City
SERVEPATH; San Francisco
SIGMA DESIGNS INC; Milpitas
SMART MODULAR TECHNOLOGIES INC; Newark
SONIC SOLUTIONS; Novato
SONICWALL INC; San Jose
SPANSION; Sunnyvale
SUN MICROSYSTEMS INC; Santa Clara
SUPER MICRO COMPUTER INC; San Jose
SUPPORT.COM INC; Redwood City
SYBASE INC; Dublin
SYMANTEC CORP; Mountain View
SYMMETRICOM INC; San Jose
SYMPHONY TECHNOLOGY GROUP; Palo Alto
SYNAPTICS INC; Santa Clara
SYNNEX CORP; Fremont
SYNOPSYS INC; Mountain View
THQ INC; Agoura Hills
TIBCO SOFTWARE INC; Palo Alto
TRIMBLE NAVIGATION LTD; Sunnyvale
TTM TECHNOLOGIES INC; Santa Ana
VERISIGN INC; Mountain View
VITESSE SEMICONDUCTOR CORP; Camarillo
VMWARE INC; Palo Alto
WEBSENSE INC; San Diego
WESTERN DIGITAL CORP; Lake Forest
WIND RIVER SYSTEMS INC; Alameda
WYSE TECHNOLOGY INC; San Jose
XILINX INC; San Jose
YAHOO! INC; Sunnyvale

COLORADO
CIBER INC; Greenwood Village
CORESITE REALTY CORP; Denver
CSG SYSTEMS INTERNATIONAL INC; Englewood
DOT HILL SYSTEMS CORP; Longmont
QUARK INC; Denver
ROGUE WAVE SOFTWARE INC; Boulder
TRIZETTO GROUP INC (THE); Greenwood Village

CONNECTICUT
ATMI INC; Danbury
GARTNER INC; Stamford
GERBER SCIENTIFIC INC; South Windsor
PHOTRONICS INC; Brookfield
XEROX CORP; Norwalk

FLORIDA
ALLEN SYSTEMS GROUP INC; Naples
CITRIX SYSTEMS INC; Fort Lauderdale
HARRIS CORPORATION; Melbourne
JABIL CIRCUIT INC; St. Petersburg
TECH DATA CORP; Clearwater
ULTIMATE SOFTWARE GROUP INC; Weston
WEB.COM GROUP INC; Jacksonville

GEORGIA
AMERICAN SOFTWARE INC; Atlanta
CONCURRENT COMPUTER CORP; Duluth
EASYLINK SERVICES INTERNATIONAL
CORPORATION; Norcross
INFOR GLOBAL SOLUTIONS; Alpharetta
INTERNET SECURITY SYSTEMS INC; Atlanta
MANHATTAN ASSOCIATES INC; Atlanta
NCR CORPORATION; Duluth
S1 CORPORATION; Norcross
SIMTROL INC; Norcross
VENTYX INC; Atlanta

IDAHO
MICRON TECHNOLOGY INC; Boise

ILLINOIS
ALLSCRIPTS HEALTHCARE SOLUTIONS INC;
Chicago
ANIXTER INTERNATIONAL INC; Glenview
CDW CORPORATION; Vernon Hills
MOLEX INC; Lisle
NAVTEQ CORPORATION; Chicago
SIGMATRON INTERNATIONAL INC; Elk Grove
Village
SPSS INC; Chicago
TELLABS INC; Naperville
VASCO DATA SECURITY INTERNATIONAL INC;
Oakbrook Terrace
WESTELL TECHNOLOGIES INC; Aurora
ZEBRA TECHNOLOGIES CORP; Vernon Hills

INDIANA
CTS CORP; Elkhart
INTERACTIVE INTELLIGENCE; Indianapolis

KANSAS
GARMIN LTD; Olathe

KENTUCKY
LEXMARK INTERNATIONAL INC; Lexington

POMEROY IT SOLUTIONS; Hebron

MARYLAND
CIENA CORP; Linthicum
GSE SYSTEMS INC; Sykesville
MICROS SYSTEMS INC; Columbia
OPNET TECHNOLOGIES INC; Bethesda
SAFENET INC; Belcamp
SOURCEFIRE INC; Columbia

MASSACHUSETTS
AKAMAI TECHNOLOGIES INC; Cambridge
ANALOG DEVICES INC; Norwood
ART TECHNOLOGY GROUP INC; Cambridge
ASPECT SOFTWARE INC; Chelmsford
ASPEN TECHNOLOGY INC; Burlington
AVID TECHNOLOGY INC; Burlington
COGNEX CORP; Natick
ECLINICALWORKS; Westborough
ELCOM INTERNATIONAL INC; Norwood
EMC CORP; Hopkinton
ENTERASYS NETWORKS INC; Andover
FORRESTER RESEARCH INC; Cambridge
INDUSTRIAL DEFENDER INC; Foxborough
KEANE INC; Boston
KRONOS INC; Chelmsford
LOGMELN INC; Woburn
MEDICAL INFORMATION TECHNOLOGY INC;
Westwood
MODUSLINK GLOBAL SOLUTIONS INC; Waltham
NAVISITE INC; Andover
NETSCOUT SYSTEMS INC; Westford
NETWORK ENGINES INC; Canton
NOVELL INC; Waltham
NUANCE COMMUNICATIONS INC; Burlington
PARAMETRIC TECHNOLOGY CORP; Needham
PEGASYSTEMS INC; Cambridge
PROGRESS SOFTWARE CORP; Bedford
ROCKET SOFTWARE; Newton
RSA SECURITY INC; Bedford
SEACHANGE INTERNATIONAL INC; Acton
SKYWORKS SOLUTIONS INC; Woburn
SONUS NETWORKS INC; Westford
VARIAN SEMICONDUCTOR EQUIPMENT
ASSOCIATES INC; Gloucester

MICHIGAN
COMPUWARE CORP; Detroit
FORESEE RESULTS INC; Ann Arbor

MINNESOTA
ADC TELECOMMUNICATIONS INC; Eden Prairie
ANALYSTS INTERNATIONAL CORP; Minneapolis
DIGI INTERNATIONAL INC; Minnetonka
DIGITAL ANGEL CORP; S. St. Paul
DIGITAL RIVER INC; Eden Prairie
IMATION CORP; Oakdale
INNOVEX INC; Plymouth

PLATO LEARNING INC; Bloomington
SPANLINK COMMUNICATIONS; Minneapolis
TELEX COMMUNICATIONS INC; Burnsville

MISSOURI
BELDEN INC; St. Louis
JACK HENRY & ASSOCIATES INC; Monett
LABARGE INC; St. Louis
MEMC ELECTRONIC MATERIALS INC; St. Peters
VIASYSTEMS GROUP INC; St. Louis

MONTANA
RIGHTNOW TECHNOLOGIES INC; Bozeman

NEW HAMPSHIRE
PC CONNECTION INC; Merrimack
SKILLSOFT PLC; Nashua

NEW JERSEY
AVAYA INC; Basking Ridge
BLONDER TONGUE LABORATORIES INC; Old
Bridge
COGNIZANT TECHNOLOGY SOLUTIONS CORP;
Teaneck
DRS TECHNOLOGIES INC; Parsippany
INSTRUCTIVISION INC; Pine Brook
LG ELECTRONICS USA INC; Englewood Cliffs
TELCORDIA TECHNOLOGIES; Piscataway
ULTICOM INC; Mt. Laurel

NEW YORK
ACI WORLDWIDE INC; New York
ARROW ELECTRONICS INC; Melville
ATARI INC; New York
CA INC (CA TECHNOLOGIES); Islandia
CHEETAHMAIL INC; New York
CHYRON CORP; Melville
COMVERSE TECHNOLOGY INC; New York
IBM GLOBAL SERVICES; Armonk
INTERNATIONAL BUSINESS MACHINES CORP
(IBM); Armonk
L-3 COMMUNICATIONS HOLDINGS INC; New York
LIVEPERSON INC; New York
PAR TECHNOLOGY CORPORATION; New Hartford
PITNEY BOWES SOFTWARE INC; Troy
STANDARD MICROSYSTEMS CORPORATION;
Hauppauge
TAKE-TWO INTERACTIVE SOFTWARE INC; New
York
TII NETWORK TECHNOLOGIES INC; Edgewood

NORTH CAROLINA
AVIAT NETWORKS INC; Morrisville
CICERO INC; Cary
LENOVO GROUP LIMITED; Morrisville
RED HAT INC; Raleigh
SAS INSTITUTE INC; Cary

TEKELEC; Morrisville

OHIO
DATATRAK INTERNATIONAL INC; Mayfield Heights
DIEBOLD INC; North Canton
MICROS-RETAIL; Cleveland
STERLING COMMERCE INC; Dublin
TERADATA CORPORATION; Dayton

OREGON
DATALOGIC SCANNING INC; Eugene
LATTICE SEMICONDUCTOR CORP; Hillsboro
MENTOR GRAPHICS CORP; Wilsonville
RADISYS CORP; Hillsboro
TEKTRONIX INC; Beaverton

PENNSYLVANIA
AM NETWORKS INC; Quakertown
ANSYS INC; Canonsburg
ASTEA INTERNATIONAL INC; Horsham
BLACK BOX CORPORATION; Lawrence
GSI COMMERCE INC; King of Prussia
IKON OFFICE SOLUTIONS INC; Malvern
INTERDIGITAL INC; King of Prussia
PULSE ELECTRONICS CORPORATION; Trevose
QLIK TECHNOLOGIES INC; Radnor
SUNGARD DATA SYSTEMS INC; Wayne
UNISYS CORP; Blue Bell

SOUTH CAROLINA
AVX CORPORATION; Myrtle Beach
KEMET CORP; Simpsonville
SCANSOURCE INC; Greenville

TENNESSEE
EMDEON INC; Nashville

TEXAS
AFFILIATED COMPUTER SERVICES INC; Dallas
BANCTEC INC; Irving
BENCHMARK ELECTRONICS INC; Angleton
BMC SOFTWARE INC; Houston
BORLAND SOFTWARE CORPORATION; Austin
CIRRUS LOGIC INC; Austin
COMPUCOM SYSTEMS INC; Dallas
DELL INC; Round Rock
DIODES INC; Dallas
ENTRUST INC; Dallas
FREESCALE SEMICONDUCTOR INC; Austin
FUJITSU NETWORK COMMUNICATIONS INC;
Richardson
NATIONAL INSTRUMENTS CORP; Austin
SIEMENS PLM SOFTWARE; Plano
SILICON LABORATORIES INC; Austin
SOLARWINDS; Austin
TEXAS INSTRUMENTS INC (TI); Dallas
TRILOGY INC; Austin

VIRGINIA
ARGON ST INC; Fairfax
CACI INTERNATIONAL INC; Arlington
COMPUTER SCIENCES CORPORATION (CSC); Falls Church
GTSI CORP; Herndon
MANTECH INTERNATIONAL CORP; Fairfax
MICROSTRATEGY INC; Vienna
SAIC INC; McLean
SRA INTERNATIONAL INC; Fairfax
VSE CORP; Alexandria

WASHINGTON
ATTACHMATE CORPORATION; Seattle
CRAY INC; Seattle
F5 NETWORKS INC; Seattle
FLUKE NETWORKS; Everett
INTERMEC INC; Everett
ISILON SYSTEMS INC; Seattle
KEY TRONIC CORP; Spokane
MICROSOFT CORP; Redmond
REALNETWORKS INC; Seattle
WATCHGUARD TECHNOLOGIES INC; Seattle

WISCONSIN
EPIC SYSTEMS CORPORATION; Verona
PLEXUS CORP; Neenah
RENAISSANCE LEARNING INC; Wisconsin Rapids

INDEX OF NON-U.S. HEADQUARTERS LOCATION BY COUNTRY

BRAZIL
ITAUTEC SA; Sao Paulo
POSITIVO INFORMATICA SA; Curitiba

CANADA
BIOWARE CORP; Edmonton
CELESTICA INC; Toronto
CGI GROUP INC; Montreal
COGNOS INC; Ottawa
COREL CORPORATION; Ottawa
OPEN TEXT CORP; Waterloo
RESEARCH IN MOTION LTD (RIM); Waterloo
SMTC CORP; Markham

CHINA
AISINO CORPORATION INC; Beijing
BOE TECHNOLOGY GROUP CO LTD; Beijing
CDC SOFTWARE CORP; Hong Kong
DIGITAL CHINA HOLDINGS LIMITED; Hong Kong
FOXCONN INTERNATIONAL HOLDINGS LTD; Shenzhen
HUAWEI TECHNOLOGIES CO LTD; Shenzhen
RDA MICROELECTRONICS INC; Shanghai
SEMICONDUCTOR MANUFACTURING INTERNATIONAL; Shanghai
TPV TECHNOLOGY LTD; Harbour City, Tsim Sha Tsui, Kowloon
UTSTARCOM INC; Beijing
ZOOM TECHNOLOGIES INC; Beijing

FINLAND
NOKIA CORPORATION; Espoo

FRANCE
ALCATEL-LUCENT; Paris
ALTRAN TECHNOLOGIES SA; Levallois-Perret
ATOS ORIGIN SA; Bezons
CAPGEMINI; Paris
CEGEDIM SA; Boulogne-Billancourt
DASSAULT SYSTEMES SA; Velizy-Villacoublay
GROUPE STERIA SCA; Issy-les Moulineaux Cedex 9
SAGEM TELECOMMUNICATIONS; Paris
TXCOM-AXIOHM; Le Plessis Robinson

GERMANY
INFINEON TECHNOLOGIES AG; Neubiberg
PC-WARE INFORMATION TECHNOLOGIES AG; Leipzig
SAP AG; Walldorf
SIEMENS AG; Munich
SOFTWARE AG; Darmstadt

INDIA
BEETEL TELETECH LIMITED; New Delhi
BHARAT ELECTRONICS LIMITED; Bangalore
HCL INFOSYSTEMS LIMITED; Noida
HCL TECHNOLOGIES LTD; Noida
IBM INDIA PVT LTD; Bangalore
INFOSYS TECHNOLOGIES LTD; Bangalore
ITI LIMITED; Bangalore
LG ELECTRONICS INDIA PVT LTD; Greater Noida
MOSER BAER INDIA LIMITED; New Delhi
REDINGTON (INDIA) LTD; Chennai
SIEMENS LIMITED; Mumbai
TATA CONSULTANCY SERVICES (TCS); Mumbai
TECH MAHINDRA LIMITED; Pune
VIDEOCON INDUSTRIES LTD; Paithan
WIPRO LTD; Bangalore

IRELAND
ACCENTURE PLC; Dublin
SEAGATE TECHNOLOGY PLC; Dublin

ISRAEL
CHECK POINT SOFTWARE TECHNOLOGIES LTD;
Tel Aviv
COMMTOUCH SOFTWARE LTD; Netanya
ECI TELECOM LTD; Petah Tikva
RADWARE LTD; Tel Aviv

ITALY
BRAVOSOLUTION SPA; Milan

JAPAN
ACCESS CO LTD; Tokyo
ADVANTEST CORPORATION; Tokyo
ALPS ELECTRIC CO LTD; Tokyo
CANON INC; Tokyo
CASIO COMPUTER CO LTD; Tokyo
CSK CORPORATION; Tokyo
ELPIDA MEMORY INC; Tokyo
FUJITSU LIMITED; Tokyo
HITACHI LTD; Tokyo
HOSIDEN CORPORATION; Osaka
HOYA CORP; Tokyo
KONAMI CORP; Tokyo
MITSUBISHI ELECTRIC CORPORATION; Tokyo
NEC CORPORATION; Tokyo
NIDEC CORPORATION; Kyoto
NINTENDO CO LTD; Kyoto
PANASONIC CORPORATION; Osaka
PIONEER CORPORATION; Kanagawa
RENESAS ELECTRONICS CORP; Tokyo
RICOH COMPANY LTD; Tokyo
ROHM CO LTD; Kyoto
SANYO ELECTRIC COMPANY LTD; Moriguchi City
SEGA SAMMY HOLDINGS INC; Tokyo
SEIKO EPSON CORPORATION; Nagano
SHARP CORPORATION; Osaka

SONY CORPORATION; Tokyo
TOKYO ELECTRON LIMITED; Tokyo
TOSHIBA CORPORATION; Tokyo
TREND MICRO INC; Tokyo

KOREA
AHNLAB INC; Seoul
DIGITECH SYSTEMS CO LTD; Geonggi-Do
LG DISPLAY CO LTD; Seoul
LG ELECTRONICS INC; Seoul
SAMSUNG ELECTRO-MECHANICS; Suwon
SAMSUNG ELECTRONICS CO LTD; Seoul

NORWAY
OPERA SOFTWARE ASA; Oslo
TANDBERG; Lysaker

SINGAPORE
FLEXTRONICS INTERNATIONAL LTD; Singapore
INPHI CORPORATION; Singapore

SOUTH AFRICA
DIMENSION DATA HOLDINGS PLC; Johannesburg

SPAIN
INDRA SISTEMAS SA; Madrid
TELVENT GIT SA; Madrid

SWEDEN
INDUSTRIAL & FINANCIAL SYSTEMS (IFS) AB;
Linkoping
TELECA AB; Malmo
TELEFON AB LM ERICSSON (ERICSSON); Stockholm

SWITZERLAND
LOGITECH INTERNATIONAL SA; Romanel-sur-
Morges
STMICROELECTRONICS NV; Plan-Les-Ouates

TAIWAN
ACCTON TECHNOLOGY CORP; Hsinchu
ACER INC; Taipei
ADVANCED SEMICONDUCTOR ENGINEERING INC;
Kaohsiung
ASUSTEK COMPUTER INC (ASUS); Taipei
AU OPTRONICS CORP; Hsinchu
AVY PRECISION TECHNOLOGY INC; Taipei
BENQ CORPORATION; Taipei
CHICONY ELECTRONICS CO LTD; Taipei
CHIMEI INNOLUX CORPORATION; Jhunan Township
COMPAL ELECTRONICS INC; Taipei
D-LINK CORPORATION; Taipei
ELITEGROUP COMPUTER SYSTEMS CO LTD; Taipei
FOXCONN TECHNOLOGY CO LTD; Taipei
GIGAMEDIA LTD; Taipei
HON HAI PRECISION INDUSTRY COMPANY LTD;
Taipei Country

HTC CORP; Taoyuan
INVENTEC CORPORATION; Taipei
LITE-ON TECHNOLOGY CORP; Taipei
MACRONIX INTERNATIONAL CO LTD; Hsinchu
MEDIATEK INC; Hsinchu
MICRO-STAR INTERNATIONAL; Taipei
MITAC INTERNATIONAL CORP; Kuei Shan Hsiang
NAN YA PCB CORP; Taoyuan
NANYA TECHNOLOGY CORPORATION; Taoyuan
NOVATEK MICROELECTRONICS CORP; Hsinchu
POWERCHIP TECHNOLOGY CORP; Hsinchu
QISDA CORPORATION; Taoyuan
QUANTA COMPUTER INC; Tao Yuan Shien
SHIN ZU SHING CO LTD; Shulin City
SILICONWARE PRECISION INDUSTRIES CO LTD;
Taichung
SIMPLO TECHNOLOGY CO LTD; Hsin Chu Hsien
TAIWAN SEMICONDUCTOR MANUFACTURING CO
LTD (TSMC); Hsinchu
TRANSCEND INFORMATION INC; Taipei
UNITED MICROELECTRONICS CORP; Hsinchu
VIA TECHNOLOGIES INC; New Taipei City

THAILAND
BUZZ TECHNOLOGIES INC; Phuket
CDG GROUP; Chongnonsee, Yannawa, Bangkok

THE NETHERLANDS
FUJITSU TECHNOLOGY SOLUTIONS (HOLDING)
BV; Maarssen
GEMALTO NV; Amsterdam
GETRONICS NV; Zoetermeer
NXP SEMICONDUCTORS NV; Eindhoven
ROYAL PHILIPS ELECTRONICS NV; Amsterdam
TOMTOM NV; Amsterdam

UNITED KINGDOM
AMDOCS LTD; St. Peter Port
ARM HOLDINGS PLC; Cambridge
AUTONOMY CORP PLC; Cambridge
CRITICAL PATH INC; Dublin
LOGICA PLC; Reading
MISYS PLC; London
SPECTRIS; Egham
VICORP GROUP PLC; Berkshire

INDEX BY REGIONS OF THE U.S.
WHERE THE FIRMS HAVE LOCATIONS

WEST
ACCENTURE PLC
ACCESS CO LTD
ACCTON TECHNOLOGY CORP
ACER INC
ACTIVISION BLIZZARD INC
ACXIOM CORP
ADEPT TECHNOLOGY INC
ADOBE SYSTEMS INC
ADTRAN INC
ADVANCED MICRO DEVICES INC (AMD)
ADVANCED SEMICONDUCTOR ENGINEERING INC
ADVANTEST CORPORATION
AFFILIATED COMPUTER SERVICES INC
AKAMAI TECHNOLOGIES INC
ALCATEL-LUCENT
ALLEN SYSTEMS GROUP INC
ALLSCRIPTS HEALTHCARE SOLUTIONS INC
ALPS ELECTRIC CO LTD
ALTERA CORP
ALTRAN TECHNOLOGIES SA
AM NETWORKS INC
AMDOCS LTD
AMKOR TECHNOLOGY INC
AMPEX CORP
ANALOG DEVICES INC
ANALYSTS INTERNATIONAL CORP
ANIXTER INTERNATIONAL INC
ANSYS INC
APPLE INC
APPLIED MATERIALS INC
ARCSIGHT INC
ARGON ST INC
ARIBA INC
ARM HOLDINGS PLC
ARROW ELECTRONICS INC
ART TECHNOLOGY GROUP INC
ARTERIS INC
ASANTE NETWORKS INC
ASK.COM
ASPECT SOFTWARE INC
ASTEA INTERNATIONAL INC
ASUSTEK COMPUTER INC (ASUS)
ATHEROS COMMUNICATIONS INC
ATMEL CORP
ATTACHMATE CORPORATION
AUTODESK INC
AUTONOMY CORP PLC
AVAYA INC
AVIAT NETWORKS INC
AVID TECHNOLOGY INC
AVX CORPORATION
BELDEN INC
BENCHMARK ELECTRONICS INC
BENQ CORPORATION

BLACK BOX CORPORATION
BLUE COAT SYSTEMS INC
BMC SOFTWARE INC
BORLAND SOFTWARE CORPORATION
BROADCOM CORP
BROADVISION INC
BROCADE COMMUNICATIONS SYSTEMS INC
CA INC (CA TECHNOLOGIES)
CACI INTERNATIONAL INC
CADENCE DESIGN SYSTEMS INC
CALAMP CORP
CAPGEMINI
CDW CORPORATION
CELESTICA INC
CGI GROUP INC
CHECK POINT SOFTWARE TECHNOLOGIES LTD
CHEETAHMAIL INC
CHICONY ELECTRONICS CO LTD
CHIMEI INNOLUX CORPORATION
CIBER INC
CIENA CORP
CIRRUS LOGIC INC
CISCO SYSTEMS INC
CITRIX SYSTEMS INC
COGNEX CORP
COGNIZANT TECHNOLOGY SOLUTIONS CORP
COMMTOUCH SOFTWARE LTD
COMPAL ELECTRONICS INC
COMPUCOM SYSTEMS INC
COMPUTER SCIENCES CORPORATION (CSC)
COMPUWARE CORP
COMVERSE TECHNOLOGY INC
CONEXANT SYSTEMS INC
COREL CORPORATION
COREMETRICS INC
CORESITE REALTY CORP
CRAY INC
CRITICAL PATH INC
CSG SYSTEMS INTERNATIONAL INC
CTS CORP
CYPRESS SEMICONDUCTOR CORP
DATA ROBOTICS INC
DATALOGIC SCANNING INC
DELL INC
DIGI INTERNATIONAL INC
DIGITAL RIVER INC
DIMENSION DATA HOLDINGS PLC
DIODES INC
D-LINK CORPORATION
DOT HILL SYSTEMS CORP
DRS TECHNOLOGIES INC
DSP GROUP INC
ECHELON CORP
ECI TELECOM LTD
ECLINICALWORKS
ELECTRONIC ARTS INC
ELECTRONICS FOR IMAGING INC
ELITEGROUP COMPUTER SYSTEMS CO LTD

ELPIDA MEMORY INC
EMBARCADERO TECHNOLOGIES INC
EMC CORP
EMULEX CORP
EPICOR SOFTWARE CORP
ESS TECHNOLOGY INC
EXTREME NETWORKS INC
F5 NETWORKS INC
FINISAR CORPORATION
FIRECLICK INC
FLEXTRONICS INTERNATIONAL LTD
FLUKE NETWORKS
FORCE10 NETWORKS INC
FORRESTER RESEARCH INC
FORTINET INC
FOXCONN INTERNATIONAL HOLDINGS LTD
FUJITSU LIMITED
FUJITSU NETWORK COMMUNICATIONS INC
GARMIN LTD
GARTNER INC
GATEWAY INC
GLOBALFOUNDRIES
GOOGLE INC
GSI COMMERCE INC
GUIDEWIRE SOFTWARE INC
HARMONIC INC
HARRIS CORPORATION
HCL TECHNOLOGIES LTD
HEWLETT-PACKARD CO (HP)
HITACHI LTD
HON HAI PRECISION INDUSTRY COMPANY LTD
HOSIDEN CORPORATION
HOYA CORP
HUAWEI TECHNOLOGIES CO LTD
ICROSSING INC
IKON OFFICE SOLUTIONS INC
IMMERSION CORP
INDUSTRIAL & FINANCIAL SYSTEMS (IFS) AB
INDUSTRIAL DEFENDER INC
INFINEON TECHNOLOGIES AG
INFOR GLOBAL SOLUTIONS
INFOSYS TECHNOLOGIES LTD
INGRAM MICRO INC
INNOVEX INC
INPHI CORPORATION
INSIGHT ENTERPRISES INC
INTEL CORP
INTERACTIVE INTELLIGENCE
INTERGRAPH CORP
INTERMEC INC
INTERNATIONAL BUSINESS MACHINES CORP
(IBM)
INTERNATIONAL RECTIFIER CORP
INTUIT INC
INVENTEC CORPORATION
IOMEGA CORP
ISILON SYSTEMS INC
JABIL CIRCUIT INC

JACK HENRY & ASSOCIATES INC
JDA SOFTWARE GROUP INC
JDS UNIPHASE CORPORATION
JUNIPER NETWORKS INC
KEANE INC
KEY TRONIC CORP
KLA TENCOR CORP
KONAMI CORP
KRONOS INC
L-3 COMMUNICATIONS HOLDINGS INC
LAM RESEARCH CORP
LATTICE SEMICONDUCTOR CORP
LEXAR MEDIA INC
LG DISPLAY CO LTD
LG ELECTRONICS USA INC
LIMELIGHT NETWORKS INC
LINEAR TECHNOLOGY CORP
LITE-ON TECHNOLOGY CORP
LOGITECH INTERNATIONAL SA
LSI CORPORATION
LUCASARTS ENTERTAINMENT COMPANY LLC
MACRONIX INTERNATIONAL CO LTD
MANTECH INTERNATIONAL CORP
MARKETLIVE INC
MARVELL TECHNOLOGY GROUP LTD
MAXIM INTEGRATED PRODUCTS INC
MCAFEE INC
MEDIAPLATFORM INC
MELLANOX TECHNOLOGIES LTD
MEMC ELECTRONIC MATERIALS INC
MENTOR GRAPHICS CORP
MICROCHIP TECHNOLOGY INC
MICRON TECHNOLOGY INC
MICROS SYSTEMS INC
MICROSOFT CORP
MICRO-STAR INTERNATIONAL
MICROSTRATEGY INC
MINDSPEED TECHNOLOGIES INC
MITAC INTERNATIONAL CORP
MITSUBISHI ELECTRIC CORPORATION
MODUSLINK GLOBAL SOLUTIONS INC
MOLEX INC
MOSER BAER INDIA LIMITED
MSCSOFTWARE CORP
MULTI-FINELINE ELECTRONIX
NANYA TECHNOLOGY CORPORATION
NATIONAL INSTRUMENTS CORP
NATIONAL SEMICONDUCTOR CORP
NAVISITE INC
NCR CORPORATION
NEC CORPORATION
NETAPP INC
NETGEAR INC
NETSCOUT SYSTEMS INC
NETSUITE INC
NETWORK EQUIPMENT TECHNOLOGIES INC
NEXPRISE INC
NIDEC CORPORATION

NINTENDO CO LTD
NOKIA CORPORATION
NOVELL INC
NOVELLUS SYSTEMS INC
NUANCE COMMUNICATIONS INC
NVIDIA CORP
OCZ TECHNOLOGY GROUP INC
OPEN TEXT CORP
OPENTV CORP
OPENWAVE SYSTEMS INC
OPERA SOFTWARE ASA
OPNET TECHNOLOGIES INC
ORACLE CORP
OVERLAND STORAGE INC
PALM INC
PANASONIC CORPORATION
PAR TECHNOLOGY CORPORATION
PARAMETRIC TECHNOLOGY CORP
PC MALL INC
PEGASYSTEMS INC
PHOENIX TECHNOLOGIES LTD
PHOTRONICS INC
PINNACLE SYSTEMS INC
PIONEER CORPORATION
PITNEY BOWES SOFTWARE INC
PLANTRONICS INC
PLEXUS CORP
PMC-SIERRA INC
PRINTRONIX INC
PROGRESS SOFTWARE CORP
PROXIM WIRELESS CORP
PULSE ELECTRONICS CORPORATION
QLIK TECHNOLOGIES INC
QLOGIC CORP
QUALCOMM INC
QUALITY SYSTEMS INC
QUANTUM CORP
QUARK INC
QUEST SOFTWARE INC
RADISYS CORP
RAMBUS INC
REALNETWORKS INC
RED HAT INC
RENAISSANCE LEARNING INC
RENESAS ELECTRONICS CORP
RESEARCH IN MOTION LTD (RIM)
RESPONSYS INC
RICOH COMPANY LTD
RIGHTNOW TECHNOLOGIES INC
RIGHTSCALE INC
RIVERBED TECHNOLOGY INC
ROCKET SOFTWARE
ROGUE WAVE SOFTWARE INC
ROHM CO LTD
ROVI CORPORATION
ROYAL PHILIPS ELECTRONICS NV
RSA SECURITY INC
S1 CORPORATION

SAFENET INC
SAIC INC
SALESFORCE.COM INC
SAMSUNG ELECTRO-MECHANICS
SAMSUNG ELECTRONICS CO LTD
SANDISK CORP
SANMINA-SCI CORPORATION
SANYO ELECTRIC COMPANY LTD
SAP AG
SAS INSTITUTE INC
SCENE7 INC
SEACHANGE INTERNATIONAL INC
SEAGATE TECHNOLOGY PLC
SEGA SAMMY HOLDINGS INC
SEIKO EPSON CORPORATION
SELECTICA INC
SEMICONDUCTOR MANUFACTURING
INTERNATIONAL
SERENA SOFTWARE INC
SERVEPATH
SHARP CORPORATION
SIEMENS AG
SIEMENS PLM SOFTWARE
SIGMA DESIGNS INC
SIGMATRON INTERNATIONAL INC
SILICON LABORATORIES INC
SILICONWARE PRECISION INDUSTRIES CO LTD
SKYWORKS SOLUTIONS INC
SMART MODULAR TECHNOLOGIES INC
SMTC CORP
SOFTWARE AG
SONIC SOLUTIONS
SONICWALL INC
SONY CORPORATION
SPANLINK COMMUNICATIONS
SPANSION
SPECTRIS
SPSS INC
SRA INTERNATIONAL INC
STANDARD MICROSYSTEMS CORPORATION
STERLING COMMERCE INC
STMICROELECTRONICS NV
SUN MICROSYSTEMS INC
SUNGARD DATA SYSTEMS INC
SUPER MICRO COMPUTER INC
SUPPORT.COM INC
SYBASE INC
SYMANTEC CORP
SYMMETRICOM INC
SYMPHONY TECHNOLOGY GROUP
SYNAPTICS INC
SYNNEX CORP
SYNOPSYS INC
TAIWAN SEMICONDUCTOR MANUFACTURING CO
LTD (TSMC)
TATA CONSULTANCY SERVICES (TCS)
TECH DATA CORP
TECH MAHINDRA LIMITED

TEKTRONIX INC
TELCORDIA TECHNOLOGIES
TELECA AB
TELEFON AB LM ERICSSON (ERICSSON)
TELLABS INC
TELVENT GIT SA
TERADATA CORPORATION
TEXAS INSTRUMENTS INC (TI)
THQ INC
TIBCO SOFTWARE INC
TOKYO ELECTRON LIMITED
TOSHIBA CORPORATION
TRANSCEND INFORMATION INC
TREND MICRO INC
TRIMBLE NAVIGATION LTD
TRIZETTO GROUP INC (THE)
TTM TECHNOLOGIES INC
UNISYS CORP
UNITED MICROELECTRONICS CORP
UTSTARCOM INC
VARIAN SEMICONDUCTOR EQUIPMENT
ASSOCIATES INC
VENTYX INC
VERISIGN INC
VIA TECHNOLOGIES INC
VIASYSTEMS GROUP INC
VITESSE SEMICONDUCTOR CORP
VMWARE INC
VSE CORP
WATCHGUARD TECHNOLOGIES INC
WEB.COM GROUP INC
WEBSENSE INC
WESTERN DIGITAL CORP
WIND RIVER SYSTEMS INC
WIPRO LTD
WYSE TECHNOLOGY INC
XEROX CORP
XILINX INC
YAHOO! INC
ZEBRA TECHNOLOGIES CORP

SOUTHWEST
ACCENTURE PLC
ACI WORLDWIDE INC
ACTIVISION BLIZZARD INC
ADOBE SYSTEMS INC
ADTRAN INC
ADVANCED MICRO DEVICES INC (AMD)
ADVANCED SEMICONDUCTOR ENGINEERING INC
ADVANTEST CORPORATION
AFFILIATED COMPUTER SERVICES INC
AKAMAI TECHNOLOGIES INC
ALCATEL-LUCENT
ALLEN SYSTEMS GROUP INC
ALLSCRIPTS HEALTHCARE SOLUTIONS INC
ALPS ELECTRIC CO LTD
ALTERA CORP
ALTRAN TECHNOLOGIES SA

AM NETWORKS INC
AMDOCS LTD
AMKOR TECHNOLOGY INC
AMTECH SYSTEMS INC
ANALOG DEVICES INC
ANALYSTS INTERNATIONAL CORP
ANIXTER INTERNATIONAL INC
ANSYS INC
APPLE INC
APPLIED MATERIALS INC
ARCSIGHT INC
ARGON ST INC
ARIBA INC
ARM HOLDINGS PLC
ARROW ELECTRONICS INC
ASPEN TECHNOLOGY INC
ATMEL CORP
ATMI INC
ATOS ORIGIN SA
ATTACHMATE CORPORATION
AVIAT NETWORKS INC
AVNET INC
BANCTEC INC
BELDEN INC
BENCHMARK ELECTRONICS INC
BIOWARE CORP
BLACK BOX CORPORATION
BLUE COAT SYSTEMS INC
BMC SOFTWARE INC
BORLAND SOFTWARE CORPORATION
BROADCOM CORP
BROCADE COMMUNICATIONS SYSTEMS INC
CA INC (CA TECHNOLOGIES)
CACI INTERNATIONAL INC
CADENCE DESIGN SYSTEMS INC
CAPGEMINI
CDC SOFTWARE CORP
CDW CORPORATION
CELESTICA INC
CGI GROUP INC
CHECK POINT SOFTWARE TECHNOLOGIES LTD
CIBER INC
CIENA CORP
CIRRUS LOGIC INC
CISCO SYSTEMS INC
CITRIX SYSTEMS INC
COGNIZANT TECHNOLOGY SOLUTIONS CORP
COMPAL ELECTRONICS INC
COMPUCOM SYSTEMS INC
COMPUTER SCIENCES CORPORATION (CSC)
COMPUWARE CORP
COMVERSE TECHNOLOGY INC
COREMETRICS INC
CTS CORP
DATATRAK INTERNATIONAL INC
DELL INC
DIGI INTERNATIONAL INC
DIMENSION DATA HOLDINGS PLC

DIODES INC
DRS TECHNOLOGIES INC
ELECTRONIC ARTS INC
ELECTRONICS FOR IMAGING INC
ELPIDA MEMORY INC
EMULEX CORP
ENTRUST INC
F5 NETWORKS INC
FINISAR CORPORATION
FLEXTRONICS INTERNATIONAL LTD
FLUKE NETWORKS
FORCE10 NETWORKS INC
FORRESTER RESEARCH INC
FORTINET INC
FOXCONN INTERNATIONAL HOLDINGS LTD
FREESCALE SEMICONDUCTOR INC
FUJITSU LIMITED
FUJITSU NETWORK COMMUNICATIONS INC
GARTNER INC
GEMALTO NV
GLOBALFOUNDRIES
GOOGLE INC
HARRIS CORPORATION
HCL TECHNOLOGIES LTD
HEWLETT-PACKARD CO (HP)
HITACHI LTD
HON HAI PRECISION INDUSTRY COMPANY LTD
HOYA CORP
HUAWEI TECHNOLOGIES CO LTD
ICROSSING INC
IKON OFFICE SOLUTIONS INC
IMATION CORP
INDUSTRIAL & FINANCIAL SYSTEMS (IFS) AB
INFOR GLOBAL SOLUTIONS
INFOSYS TECHNOLOGIES LTD
INGRAM MICRO INC
INSIGHT ENTERPRISES INC
INTEL CORP
INTERGRAPH CORP
INTERMEC INC
INTERNATIONAL BUSINESS MACHINES CORP (IBM)
INTERNATIONAL RECTIFIER CORP
INTUIT INC
INVENTEC CORPORATION
JABIL CIRCUIT INC
JACK HENRY & ASSOCIATES INC
JDA SOFTWARE GROUP INC
JDS UNIPHASE CORPORATION
JUNIPER NETWORKS INC
KEANE INC
KEY TRONIC CORP
KLA TENCOR CORP
KRONOS INC
L-3 COMMUNICATIONS HOLDINGS INC
LABARGE INC
LAM RESEARCH CORP
LG ELECTRONICS USA INC

LIMELIGHT NETWORKS INC
LINEAR TECHNOLOGY CORP
LITE-ON TECHNOLOGY CORP
LOGICA PLC
LOGITECH INTERNATIONAL SA
MANTECH INTERNATIONAL CORP
MAXIM INTEGRATED PRODUCTS INC
MCAFEE INC
MEMC ELECTRONIC MATERIALS INC
MENTOR GRAPHICS CORP
MICROCHIP TECHNOLOGY INC
MICROS SYSTEMS INC
MICROSOFT CORP
MICROSTRATEGY INC
MITAC INTERNATIONAL CORP
MITSUBISHI ELECTRIC CORPORATION
MODUSLINK GLOBAL SOLUTIONS INC
MSCSOFTWARE CORP
MULTI-FINELINE ELECTRONIX
NATIONAL INSTRUMENTS CORP
NATIONAL SEMICONDUCTOR CORP
NAVISITE INC
NEC CORPORATION
NETSCOUT SYSTEMS INC
NETSUITE INC
NIDEC CORPORATION
NOKIA CORPORATION
NOVELL INC
NOVELLUS SYSTEMS INC
NVIDIA CORP
OPEN TEXT CORP
OPNET TECHNOLOGIES INC
ORACLE CORP
PARAMETRIC TECHNOLOGY CORP
PC CONNECTION INC
PEGASYSTEMS INC
PHOTRONICS INC
PITNEY BOWES SOFTWARE INC
PMC-SIERRA INC
PROGRESS SOFTWARE CORP
QLIK TECHNOLOGIES INC
QLOGIC CORP
QUALCOMM INC
QUALITY SYSTEMS INC
QUANTUM CORP
QUEST SOFTWARE INC
RED HAT INC
RESEARCH IN MOTION LTD (RIM)
RICOH COMPANY LTD
RIGHTNOW TECHNOLOGIES INC
RIVERBED TECHNOLOGY INC
ROCKET SOFTWARE
ROHM CO LTD
ROVI CORPORATION
ROYAL PHILIPS ELECTRONICS NV
S1 CORPORATION
SAIC INC
SAMSUNG ELECTRO-MECHANICS

SAMSUNG ELECTRONICS CO LTD
SANMINA-SCI CORPORATION
SANYO ELECTRIC COMPANY LTD
SAP AG
SAS INSTITUTE INC
SCANSOURCE INC
SEAGATE TECHNOLOGY PLC
SEIKO EPSON CORPORATION
SERVEPATH
SIEMENS AG
SIEMENS PLM SOFTWARE
SILICON LABORATORIES INC
SILICONWARE PRECISION INDUSTRIES CO LTD
SMART MODULAR TECHNOLOGIES INC
SOFTWARE AG
SOLARWINDS
SONUS NETWORKS INC
SPANSION
SPECTRIS
SPSS INC
SRA INTERNATIONAL INC
STANDARD MICROSYSTEMS CORPORATION
STERLING COMMERCE INC
STMICROELECTRONICS NV
SUN MICROSYSTEMS INC
SUNGARD DATA SYSTEMS INC
SYBASE INC
SYNNEX CORP
SYNOPSYS INC
TANDBERG
TATA CONSULTANCY SERVICES (TCS)
TECH DATA CORP
TECH MAHINDRA LIMITED
TEKELEC
TEKTRONIX INC
TELCORDIA TECHNOLOGIES
TELECA AB
TELEFON AB LM ERICSSON (ERICSSON)
TELEX COMMUNICATIONS INC
TELLABS INC
TELVENT GIT SA
TEXAS INSTRUMENTS INC (TI)
THQ INC
TOKYO ELECTRON LIMITED
TOSHIBA CORPORATION
TRILOGY INC
TRIMBLE NAVIGATION LTD
TRIZETTO GROUP INC (THE)
ULTICOM INC
UNISYS CORP
VARIAN SEMICONDUCTOR EQUIPMENT
ASSOCIATES INC
VERISIGN INC
VIA TECHNOLOGIES INC
VIASYSTEMS GROUP INC
VITESSE SEMICONDUCTOR CORP
VMWARE INC
VSE CORP

WEB.COM GROUP INC
WEBSENSE INC
WIND RIVER SYSTEMS INC
WIPRO LTD
XEROX CORP
XILINX INC

MIDWEST
ACCENTURE PLC
ACI WORLDWIDE INC
ACTIVISION BLIZZARD INC
ACXIOM CORP
ADC TELECOMMUNICATIONS INC
ADEPT TECHNOLOGY INC
ADTRAN INC
ADVANCED MICRO DEVICES INC (AMD)
AFFILIATED COMPUTER SERVICES INC
AKAMAI TECHNOLOGIES INC
ALCATEL-LUCENT
ALLEN SYSTEMS GROUP INC
ALLSCRIPTS HEALTHCARE SOLUTIONS INC
ALPS ELECTRIC CO LTD
ALTERA CORP
ALTRAN TECHNOLOGIES SA
AM NETWORKS INC
AMDOCS LTD
ANALOG DEVICES INC
ANALYSTS INTERNATIONAL CORP
ANIXTER INTERNATIONAL INC
ANSYS INC
APPLE INC
ARIBA INC
ARM HOLDINGS PLC
ARROW ELECTRONICS INC
ART TECHNOLOGY GROUP INC
ASK.COM
ASPECT SOFTWARE INC
ASUSTEK COMPUTER INC (ASUS)
ATMEL CORP
ATMI INC
ATOS ORIGIN SA
AUTONOMY CORP PLC
AVID TECHNOLOGY INC
BELDEN INC
BENCHMARK ELECTRONICS INC
BLACK BOX CORPORATION
BMC SOFTWARE INC
BRAVOSOLUTION SPA
BROADCOM CORP
BROCADE COMMUNICATIONS SYSTEMS INC
CA INC (CA TECHNOLOGIES)
CACI INTERNATIONAL INC
CADENCE DESIGN SYSTEMS INC
CALAMP CORP
CANON INC
CAPGEMINI
CDW CORPORATION
CGI GROUP INC

CHECK POINT SOFTWARE TECHNOLOGIES LTD
CIBER INC
CIENA CORP
CISCO SYSTEMS INC
CITRIX SYSTEMS INC
COGNEX CORP
COGNIZANT TECHNOLOGY SOLUTIONS CORP
COMPUCOM SYSTEMS INC
COMPUTER SCIENCES CORPORATION (CSC)
COMPUWARE CORP
COMVERSE TECHNOLOGY INC
CONCURRENT COMPUTER CORP
CORESITE REALTY CORP
CRAY INC
CSG SYSTEMS INTERNATIONAL INC
CTS CORP
CYPRESS SEMICONDUCTOR CORP
DATATRAK INTERNATIONAL INC
DELL INC
DIGI INTERNATIONAL INC
DIGITAL ANGEL CORP
DIGITAL RIVER INC
DIMENSION DATA HOLDINGS PLC
DIODES INC
DOT HILL SYSTEMS CORP
DRS TECHNOLOGIES INC
ECHELON CORP
ELECTRONIC ARTS INC
ELECTRONICS FOR IMAGING INC
EMDEON INC
EPIC SYSTEMS CORPORATION
EPICOR SOFTWARE CORP
F5 NETWORKS INC
FLEXTRONICS INTERNATIONAL LTD
FORESEE RESULTS INC
FORTINET INC
FREESCALE SEMICONDUCTOR INC
FUJITSU LIMITED
GARMIN LTD
GARTNER INC
GATEWAY INC
GOOGLE INC
GSI COMMERCE INC
HARRIS CORPORATION
HCL TECHNOLOGIES LTD
HEWLETT-PACKARD CO (HP)
HITACHI LTD
HON HAI PRECISION INDUSTRY COMPANY LTD
HOSIDEN CORPORATION
HOYA CORP
ICROSSING INC
IKON OFFICE SOLUTIONS INC
IMATION CORP
INDUSTRIAL & FINANCIAL SYSTEMS (IFS) AB
INFINEON TECHNOLOGIES AG
INFOR GLOBAL SOLUTIONS
INFOSYS TECHNOLOGIES LTD
INGRAM MICRO INC

INNOVEX INC
INSIGHT ENTERPRISES INC
INTEL CORP
INTERACTIVE INTELLIGENCE
INTERGRAPH CORP
INTERMEC INC
INTERNATIONAL BUSINESS MACHINES CORP
(IBM)
INTERNATIONAL RECTIFIER CORP
INTUIT INC
JABIL CIRCUIT INC
JACK HENRY & ASSOCIATES INC
JDA SOFTWARE GROUP INC
JDS UNIPHASE CORPORATION
JUNIPER NETWORKS INC
KEANE INC
KLA TENCOR CORP
KRONOS INC
L-3 COMMUNICATIONS HOLDINGS INC
LABARGE INC
LAM RESEARCH CORP
LATTICE SEMICONDUCTOR CORP
LEXMARK INTERNATIONAL INC
LG ELECTRONICS USA INC
LIMELIGHT NETWORKS INC
LINEAR TECHNOLOGY CORP
LSI CORPORATION
MANHATTAN ASSOCIATES INC
MAXIM INTEGRATED PRODUCTS INC
MCAFEE INC
MEMC ELECTRONIC MATERIALS INC
MENTOR GRAPHICS CORP
MICROCHIP TECHNOLOGY INC
MICROS SYSTEMS INC
MICROSOFT CORP
MICROS-RETAIL
MICROSTRATEGY INC
MITSUBISHI ELECTRIC CORPORATION
MODUSLINK GLOBAL SOLUTIONS INC
MOLEX INC
MSCSOFTWARE CORP
NATIONAL INSTRUMENTS CORP
NATIONAL SEMICONDUCTOR CORP
NAVISITE INC
NAVTEQ CORPORATION
NCR CORPORATION
NEC CORPORATION
NETWORK EQUIPMENT TECHNOLOGIES INC
NIDEC CORPORATION
NOKIA CORPORATION
NOVELL INC
NOVELLUS SYSTEMS INC
NVIDIA CORP
OPEN TEXT CORP
ORACLE CORP
PANASONIC CORPORATION
PARAMETRIC TECHNOLOGY CORP
PC CONNECTION INC

PC MALL INC
PEGASYSTEMS INC
PITNEY BOWES SOFTWARE INC
PLATO LEARNING INC
PLEXUS CORP
PMC-SIERRA INC
POMEROY IT SOLUTIONS
PROGRESS SOFTWARE CORP
QLIK TECHNOLOGIES INC
QLOGIC CORP
QUALCOMM INC
QUALITY SYSTEMS INC
QUANTUM CORP
QUEST SOFTWARE INC
RADISYS CORP
RAMBUS INC
RED HAT INC
RENAISSANCE LEARNING INC
RENESAS ELECTRONICS CORP
RESEARCH IN MOTION LTD (RIM)
RESPONSYS INC
RICOH COMPANY LTD
RIGHTNOW TECHNOLOGIES INC
RIVERBED TECHNOLOGY INC
ROHM CO LTD
ROVI CORPORATION
ROYAL PHILIPS ELECTRONICS NV
SAFENET INC
SAIC INC
SAMSUNG ELECTRO-MECHANICS
SAMSUNG ELECTRONICS CO LTD
SANMINA-SCI CORPORATION
SAP AG
SAS INSTITUTE INC
SCANSOURCE INC
SEACHANGE INTERNATIONAL INC
SEAGATE TECHNOLOGY PLC
SEGA SAMMY HOLDINGS INC
SERVEPATH
SHARP CORPORATION
SIEMENS AG
SIEMENS PLM SOFTWARE
SIGMATRON INTERNATIONAL INC
SKYWORKS SOLUTIONS INC
SMTC CORP
SONY CORPORATION
SPANLINK COMMUNICATIONS
SPECTRIS
SPSS INC
SRA INTERNATIONAL INC
STERLING COMMERCE INC
STMICROELECTRONICS NV
SUN MICROSYSTEMS INC
SUNGARD DATA SYSTEMS INC
SYBASE INC
SYNNEX CORP
SYNOPSYS INC
TATA CONSULTANCY SERVICES (TCS)

TECH DATA CORP
TEKELEC
TELEFON AB LM ERICSSON (ERICSSON)
TELEX COMMUNICATIONS INC
TELLABS INC
TELVENT GIT SA
TERADATA CORPORATION
TEXAS INSTRUMENTS INC (TI)
TRIMBLE NAVIGATION LTD
TRIZETTO GROUP INC (THE)
TTM TECHNOLOGIES INC
TXCOM-AXIOHM
ULTICOM INC
ULTIMATE SOFTWARE GROUP INC
UNISYS CORP
VASCO DATA SECURITY INTERNATIONAL INC
VIASYSTEMS GROUP INC
VMWARE INC
VSE CORP
WESTELL TECHNOLOGIES INC
WIND RIVER SYSTEMS INC
WIPRO LTD
XEROX CORP
ZEBRA TECHNOLOGIES CORP

SOUTHEAST
ACCENTURE PLC
ACI WORLDWIDE INC
ACTIVISION BLIZZARD INC
ACXIOM CORP
ADTRAN INC
ADVANCED MICRO DEVICES INC (AMD)
AFFILIATED COMPUTER SERVICES INC
AKAMAI TECHNOLOGIES INC
ALCATEL-LUCENT
ALLEN SYSTEMS GROUP INC
ALLSCRIPTS HEALTHCARE SOLUTIONS INC
ALPS ELECTRIC CO LTD
ALTERA CORP
AM NETWORKS INC
AMDOCS LTD
AMERICAN SOFTWARE INC
ANALOG DEVICES INC
ANALYSTS INTERNATIONAL CORP
ANIXTER INTERNATIONAL INC
ANSYS INC
APPLE INC
ARCSIGHT INC
ARGON ST INC
ARIBA INC
ARROW ELECTRONICS INC
ASPECT SOFTWARE INC
ATMEL CORP
AVAYA INC
AVIAT NETWORKS INC
AVID TECHNOLOGY INC
AVX CORPORATION
BELDEN INC

BENCHMARK ELECTRONICS INC
BENQ CORPORATION
BLACK BOX CORPORATION
BMC SOFTWARE INC
BORLAND SOFTWARE CORPORATION
BROADCOM CORP
BROCADE COMMUNICATIONS SYSTEMS INC
CA INC (CA TECHNOLOGIES)
CACI INTERNATIONAL INC
CADENCE DESIGN SYSTEMS INC
CALAMP CORP
CANON INC
CAPGEMINI
CASIO COMPUTER CO LTD
CGI GROUP INC
CHECK POINT SOFTWARE TECHNOLOGIES LTD
CIBER INC
CIENA CORP
CISCO SYSTEMS INC
CITRIX SYSTEMS INC
COGNEX CORP
COMMTOUCH SOFTWARE LTD
COMPUCOM SYSTEMS INC
COMPUTER SCIENCES CORPORATION (CSC)
COMPUWARE CORP
COMVERSE TECHNOLOGY INC
CONCURRENT COMPUTER CORP
CONEXANT SYSTEMS INC
CORESITE REALTY CORP
DELL INC
DIEBOLD INC
DIMENSION DATA HOLDINGS PLC
DRS TECHNOLOGIES INC
EASYLINK SERVICES INTERNATIONAL
CORPORATION
ECLINICALWORKS
ELECTRONIC ARTS INC
ELECTRONICS FOR IMAGING INC
EMDEON INC
FLEXTRONICS INTERNATIONAL LTD
FLUKE NETWORKS
FORTINET INC
FOXCONN INTERNATIONAL HOLDINGS LTD
GARTNER INC
GOOGLE INC
GSE SYSTEMS INC
GSI COMMERCE INC
HARRIS CORPORATION
HCL TECHNOLOGIES LTD
HEWLETT-PACKARD CO (HP)
HITACHI LTD
HOYA CORP
IKON OFFICE SOLUTIONS INC
IMATION CORP
INDRA SISTEMAS SA
INDUSTRIAL & FINANCIAL SYSTEMS (IFS) AB
INDUSTRIAL DEFENDER INC
INFOR GLOBAL SOLUTIONS

INFOSYS TECHNOLOGIES LTD
INGRAM MICRO INC
INTEL CORP
INTERGRAPH CORP
INTERMEC INC
INTERNATIONAL BUSINESS MACHINES CORP (IBM)
INTERNET SECURITY SYSTEMS INC
INTUIT INC
ITAUTEC SA
JABIL CIRCUIT INC
JACK HENRY & ASSOCIATES INC
JDA SOFTWARE GROUP INC
JDS UNIPHASE CORPORATION
JUNIPER NETWORKS INC
KEANE INC
KRONOS INC
L-3 COMMUNICATIONS HOLDINGS INC
LABARGE INC
LG ELECTRONICS USA INC
LIMELIGHT NETWORKS INC
LINEAR TECHNOLOGY CORP
LITE-ON TECHNOLOGY CORP
LIVEPERSON INC
LOGICA PLC
LOGITECH INTERNATIONAL SA
MANHATTAN ASSOCIATES INC
MANTECH INTERNATIONAL CORP
MAXIM INTEGRATED PRODUCTS INC
MCAFEE INC
MENTOR GRAPHICS CORP
MICROCHIP TECHNOLOGY INC
MICROS SYSTEMS INC
MICROSOFT CORP
MICROSTRATEGY INC
MITSUBISHI ELECTRIC CORPORATION
MODUSLINK GLOBAL SOLUTIONS INC
MOLEX INC
NATIONAL INSTRUMENTS CORP
NATIONAL SEMICONDUCTOR CORP
NCR CORPORATION
NOKIA CORPORATION
NOVELL INC
NVIDIA CORP
OPEN TEXT CORP
OPENWAVE SYSTEMS INC
ORACLE CORP
PANASONIC CORPORATION
PAR TECHNOLOGY CORPORATION
PARAMETRIC TECHNOLOGY CORP
PC CONNECTION INC
PC MALL INC
PEGASYSTEMS INC
PITNEY BOWES SOFTWARE INC
PLANTRONICS INC
POMEROY IT SOLUTIONS
PROGRESS SOFTWARE CORP
QUALCOMM INC

QUALITY SYSTEMS INC
QUANTUM CORP
QUARK INC
QUEST SOFTWARE INC
RADISYS CORP
RED HAT INC
RESEARCH IN MOTION LTD (RIM)
RICOH COMPANY LTD
ROCKET SOFTWARE
ROHM CO LTD
ROYAL PHILIPS ELECTRONICS NV
SAIC INC
SAMSUNG ELECTRONICS CO LTD
SANMINA-SCI CORPORATION
SANYO ELECTRIC COMPANY LTD
SAP AG
SAS INSTITUTE INC
SCANSOURCE INC
SEGA SAMMY HOLDINGS INC
SEIKO EPSON CORPORATION
SERVEPATH
SHARP CORPORATION
SIEMENS AG
SIEMENS PLM SOFTWARE
SIMTROL INC
SOFTWARE AG
SONY CORPORATION
SPSS INC
SRA INTERNATIONAL INC
STERLING COMMERCE INC
STMICROELECTRONICS NV
SUN MICROSYSTEMS INC
SUNGARD DATA SYSTEMS INC
SYBASE INC
SYNNEX CORP
SYNOPSYS INC
TATA CONSULTANCY SERVICES (TCS)
TECH DATA CORP
TECH MAHINDRA LIMITED
TELCORDIA TECHNOLOGIES
TELEFON AB LM ERICSSON (ERICSSON)
TELVENT GIT SA
TERADATA CORPORATION
TEXAS INSTRUMENTS INC (TI)
TRIMBLE NAVIGATION LTD
ULTIMATE SOFTWARE GROUP INC
VENTYX INC
VMWARE INC
VSE CORP
WEB.COM GROUP INC
WIND RIVER SYSTEMS INC
WIPRO LTD
XEROX CORP
ZEBRA TECHNOLOGIES CORP

NORTHEAST
ACCENTURE PLC
ACI WORLDWIDE INC

ACTIVISION BLIZZARD INC
ACXIOM CORP
ADEPT TECHNOLOGY INC
ADOBE SYSTEMS INC
ADVANCED MICRO DEVICES INC (AMD)
ADVANCED SEMICONDUCTOR ENGINEERING INC
ADVANTEST CORPORATION
AFFILIATED COMPUTER SERVICES INC
AKAMAI TECHNOLOGIES INC
ALCATEL-LUCENT
ALLEN SYSTEMS GROUP INC
ALLSCRIPTS HEALTHCARE SOLUTIONS INC
ALPS ELECTRIC CO LTD
ALTERA CORP
ALTRAN TECHNOLOGIES SA
AM NETWORKS INC
AMDOCS LTD
AMKOR TECHNOLOGY INC
AMTECH SYSTEMS INC
ANALOG DEVICES INC
ANALYSTS INTERNATIONAL CORP
ANIXTER INTERNATIONAL INC
ANSYS INC
APPLE INC
ARCSIGHT INC
ARGON ST INC
ARIBA INC
ARM HOLDINGS PLC
ARROW ELECTRONICS INC
ART TECHNOLOGY GROUP INC
ASK.COM
ASPECT SOFTWARE INC
ASPEN TECHNOLOGY INC
ASTEA INTERNATIONAL INC
ATARI INC
ATMEL CORP
ATMI INC
ATTACHMATE CORPORATION
AUTODESK INC
AUTONOMY CORP PLC
AVAYA INC
AVIAT NETWORKS INC
AVID TECHNOLOGY INC
AVX CORPORATION
BELDEN INC
BENCHMARK ELECTRONICS INC
BIOWARE CORP
BLACK BOX CORPORATION
BLONDER TONGUE LABORATORIES INC
BLUE COAT SYSTEMS INC
BMC SOFTWARE INC
BRAVOSOLUTION SPA
BROADCOM CORP
BROADVISION INC
BROCADE COMMUNICATIONS SYSTEMS INC
CA INC (CA TECHNOLOGIES)
CACI INTERNATIONAL INC
CADENCE DESIGN SYSTEMS INC

CANON INC
CAPGEMINI
CASIO COMPUTER CO LTD
CDW CORPORATION
CEGEDIM SA
CGI GROUP INC
CHECK POINT SOFTWARE TECHNOLOGIES LTD
CHEETAHMAIL INC
CHYRON CORP
CIBER INC
CICERO INC
CIENA CORP
CISCO SYSTEMS INC
CITRIX SYSTEMS INC
COGNEX CORP
COGNIZANT TECHNOLOGY SOLUTIONS CORP
COGNOS INC
COMPUCOM SYSTEMS INC
COMPUTER SCIENCES CORPORATION (CSC)
COMPUWARE CORP
COMVERSE TECHNOLOGY INC
CONEXANT SYSTEMS INC
COREL CORPORATION
CORESITE REALTY CORP
CTS CORP
DASSAULT SYSTEMES SA
DELL INC
DIGI INTERNATIONAL INC
DIMENSION DATA HOLDINGS PLC
DIODES INC
DRS TECHNOLOGIES INC
EASYLINK SERVICES INTERNATIONAL
CORPORATION
ECI TELECOM LTD
ECLINICALWORKS
ELCOM INTERNATIONAL INC
ELECTRONIC ARTS INC
ELECTRONICS FOR IMAGING INC
ELPIDA MEMORY INC
EMC CORP
EMDEON INC
EMULEX CORP
ENTERASYS NETWORKS INC
ENTRUST INC
EPICOR SOFTWARE CORP
EXTREME NETWORKS INC
F5 NETWORKS INC
FLEXTRONICS INTERNATIONAL LTD
FLUKE NETWORKS
FORRESTER RESEARCH INC
FORTINET INC
FUJITSU LIMITED
FUJITSU NETWORK COMMUNICATIONS INC
GARTNER INC
GATEWAY INC
GEMALTO NV
GERBER SCIENTIFIC INC
GETRONICS NV

GLOBALFOUNDRIES
GOOGLE INC
GSE SYSTEMS INC
GSI COMMERCE INC
GTSI CORP
HARRIS CORPORATION
HCL TECHNOLOGIES LTD
HEWLETT-PACKARD CO (HP)
HITACHI LTD
HON HAI PRECISION INDUSTRY COMPANY LTD
HOYA CORP
HUAWEI TECHNOLOGIES CO LTD
IBM GLOBAL SERVICES
ICROSSING INC
IKON OFFICE SOLUTIONS INC
INDRA SISTEMAS SA
INDUSTRIAL DEFENDER INC
INFINEON TECHNOLOGIES AG
INFOR GLOBAL SOLUTIONS
INFOSYS TECHNOLOGIES LTD
INGRAM MICRO INC
INSTRUCTIVISION INC
INTEL CORP
INTERACTIVE INTELLIGENCE
INTERDIGITAL INC
INTERGRAPH CORP
INTERMEC INC
INTERNATIONAL BUSINESS MACHINES CORP
(IBM)
INTERNATIONAL RECTIFIER CORP
INTUIT INC
JABIL CIRCUIT INC
JACK HENRY & ASSOCIATES INC
JDA SOFTWARE GROUP INC
JDS UNIPHASE CORPORATION
JUNIPER NETWORKS INC
KEANE INC
KEMET CORP
KLA TENCOR CORP
KRONOS INC
L-3 COMMUNICATIONS HOLDINGS INC
LABARGE INC
LAM RESEARCH CORP
LATTICE SEMICONDUCTOR CORP
LENOVO GROUP LIMITED
LG ELECTRONICS USA INC
LIMELIGHT NETWORKS INC
LINEAR TECHNOLOGY CORP
LIVEPERSON INC
LOGICA PLC
LOGMELN INC
MANTECH INTERNATIONAL CORP
MAXIM INTEGRATED PRODUCTS INC
MCAFEE INC
MEDIAPLATFORM INC
MEDIATEK INC
MEDICAL INFORMATION TECHNOLOGY INC
MEMC ELECTRONIC MATERIALS INC

MENTOR GRAPHICS CORP
MICROCHIP TECHNOLOGY INC
MICRON TECHNOLOGY INC
MICROS SYSTEMS INC
MICROSOFT CORP
MICROS-RETAIL
MICROSTRATEGY INC
MINDSPEED TECHNOLOGIES INC
MISYS PLC
MITSUBISHI ELECTRIC CORPORATION
MODUSLINK GLOBAL SOLUTIONS INC
MOLEX INC
NATIONAL INSTRUMENTS CORP
NATIONAL SEMICONDUCTOR CORP
NAVISITE INC
NCR CORPORATION
NEC CORPORATION
NETAPP INC
NETSCOUT SYSTEMS INC
NETSUITE INC
NETWORK ENGINES INC
NETWORK EQUIPMENT TECHNOLOGIES INC
NIDEC CORPORATION
NOKIA CORPORATION
NOVELL INC
NOVELLUS SYSTEMS INC
NUANCE COMMUNICATIONS INC
NVIDIA CORP
NXP SEMICONDUCTORS NV
OPEN TEXT CORP
OPENWAVE SYSTEMS INC
OPNET TECHNOLOGIES INC
ORACLE CORP
PANASONIC CORPORATION
PAR TECHNOLOGY CORPORATION
PARAMETRIC TECHNOLOGY CORP
PC CONNECTION INC
PEGASYSTEMS INC
PHOENIX TECHNOLOGIES LTD
PHOTRONICS INC
PITNEY BOWES SOFTWARE INC
PLANTRONICS INC
PLEXUS CORP
PMC-SIERRA INC
POMEROY IT SOLUTIONS
PROGRESS SOFTWARE CORP
PROXIM WIRELESS CORP
PULSE ELECTRONICS CORPORATION
QLIK TECHNOLOGIES INC
QLOGIC CORP
QUALCOMM INC
QUALITY SYSTEMS INC
QUANTUM CORP
QUARK INC
QUEST SOFTWARE INC
RADWARE LTD
RAMBUS INC
RED HAT INC

RENESAS ELECTRONICS CORP
RESEARCH IN MOTION LTD (RIM)
RESPONSYS INC
RICOH COMPANY LTD
RIGHTNOW TECHNOLOGIES INC
RIVERBED TECHNOLOGY INC
ROCKET SOFTWARE
ROHM CO LTD
ROVI CORPORATION
ROYAL PHILIPS ELECTRONICS NV
RSA SECURITY INC
S1 CORPORATION
SAFENET INC
SAIC INC
SAMSUNG ELECTRONICS CO LTD
SANMINA-SCI CORPORATION
SANYO ELECTRIC COMPANY LTD
SAP AG
SAS INSTITUTE INC
SCANSOURCE INC
SEACHANGE INTERNATIONAL INC
SEAGATE TECHNOLOGY PLC
SEIKO EPSON CORPORATION
SERENA SOFTWARE INC
SERVEPATH
SHARP CORPORATION
SIEMENS AG
SIEMENS PLM SOFTWARE
SILICON LABORATORIES INC
SKILLSOFT PLC
SKYWORKS SOLUTIONS INC
SMART MODULAR TECHNOLOGIES INC
SOFTWARE AG
SONUS NETWORKS INC
SONY CORPORATION
SOURCEFIRE INC
SPANLINK COMMUNICATIONS
SPECTRIS
SPSS INC
SRA INTERNATIONAL INC
STANDARD MICROSYSTEMS CORPORATION
STERLING COMMERCE INC
STMICROELECTRONICS NV
SUN MICROSYSTEMS INC
SUNGARD DATA SYSTEMS INC
SYBASE INC
SYMMETRICOM INC
SYNNEX CORP
SYNOPSYS INC
TAKE-TWO INTERACTIVE SOFTWARE INC
TANDBERG
TATA CONSULTANCY SERVICES (TCS)
TECH DATA CORP
TECH MAHINDRA LIMITED
TEKELEC
TEKTRONIX INC
TELCORDIA TECHNOLOGIES
TELEFON AB LM ERICSSON (ERICSSON)

TELLABS INC
TELVENT GIT SA
TEXAS INSTRUMENTS INC (TI)
TII NETWORK TECHNOLOGIES INC
TOKYO ELECTRON LIMITED
TOMTOM NV
TOSHIBA CORPORATION
TRANSCEND INFORMATION INC
TRIMBLE NAVIGATION LTD
TRIZETTO GROUP INC (THE)
TTM TECHNOLOGIES INC
ULTICOM INC
UNISYS CORP
VARIAN SEMICONDUCTOR EQUIPMENT
ASSOCIATES INC
VASCO DATA SECURITY INTERNATIONAL INC
VENTYX INC
VERISIGN INC
VIASYSTEMS GROUP INC
VITESSE SEMICONDUCTOR CORP
VMWARE INC
VSE CORP
WEB.COM GROUP INC
WIND RIVER SYSTEMS INC
WIPRO LTD
XEROX CORP
ZEBRA TECHNOLOGIES CORP
ZOOM TECHNOLOGIES INC

INDEX OF FIRMS WITH
INTERNATIONAL OPERATIONS

COREL CORPORATION
COREMETRICS INC
CRAY INC
CRITICAL PATH INC
CSK CORPORATION
CTS CORP
CYPRESS SEMICONDUCTOR CORP
DASSAULT SYSTEMES SA
DATA ROBOTICS INC
DATALOGIC SCANNING INC
DATATRAK INTERNATIONAL INC
DELL INC
DIEBOLD INC
DIGI INTERNATIONAL INC
DIGITAL ANGEL CORP
DIGITAL CHINA HOLDINGS LIMITED
DIGITAL RIVER INC
DIGITECH SYSTEMS CO LTD
DIMENSION DATA HOLDINGS PLC
DIODES INC
D-LINK CORPORATION
DOT HILL SYSTEMS CORP
DRS TECHNOLOGIES INC
DSP GROUP INC
EASYLINK SERVICES INTERNATIONAL
CORPORATION
ECHELON CORP
ECI TELECOM LTD
ELCOM INTERNATIONAL INC
ELECTRONIC ARTS INC
ELECTRONICS FOR IMAGING INC
ELITEGROUP COMPUTER SYSTEMS CO LTD
ELPIDA MEMORY INC
EMBARCADERO TECHNOLOGIES INC
EMC CORP
EMULEX CORP
ENTERASYS NETWORKS INC
ENTRUST INC
EPIC SYSTEMS CORPORATION
EPICOR SOFTWARE CORP
ESS TECHNOLOGY INC
EXTREME NETWORKS INC
F5 NETWORKS INC
FINISAR CORPORATION
FLEXTRONICS INTERNATIONAL LTD
FLUKE NETWORKS
FORCE10 NETWORKS INC
FORRESTER RESEARCH INC
FORTINET INC
FOXCONN INTERNATIONAL HOLDINGS LTD
FOXCONN TECHNOLOGY CO LTD
FREESCALE SEMICONDUCTOR INC
FUJITSU LIMITED
FUJITSU TECHNOLOGY SOLUTIONS (HOLDING)
BV
GARMIN LTD
GARTNER INC
GATEWAY INC

GEMALTO NV
GERBER SCIENTIFIC INC
GETRONICS NV
GIGAMEDIA LTD
GLOBALFOUNDRIES
GOOGLE INC
GROUPE STERIA SCA
GSE SYSTEMS INC
GSI COMMERCE INC
GUIDEWIRE SOFTWARE INC
HARMONIC INC
HARRIS CORPORATION
HCL INFOSYSTEMS LIMITED
HCL TECHNOLOGIES LTD
HEWLETT-PACKARD CO (HP)
HITACHI LTD
HON HAI PRECISION INDUSTRY COMPANY LTD
HOSIDEN CORPORATION
HOYA CORP
HTC CORP
HUAWEI TECHNOLOGIES CO LTD
IBM GLOBAL SERVICES
IBM INDIA PVT LTD
IKON OFFICE SOLUTIONS INC
IMATION CORP
IMMERSION CORP
INDRA SISTEMAS SA
INDUSTRIAL & FINANCIAL SYSTEMS (IFS) AB
INDUSTRIAL DEFENDER INC
INFINEON TECHNOLOGIES AG
INFOR GLOBAL SOLUTIONS
INFOSYS TECHNOLOGIES LTD
INGRAM MICRO INC
INNOVEX INC
INPHI CORPORATION
INSIGHT ENTERPRISES INC
INTEL CORP
INTERACTIVE INTELLIGENCE
INTERDIGITAL INC
INTERGRAPH CORP
INTERMEC INC
INTERNATIONAL BUSINESS MACHINES CORP
(IBM)
INTERNATIONAL RECTIFIER CORP
INTUIT INC
INVENTEC CORPORATION
IOMEGA CORP
ISILON SYSTEMS INC
ITAUTEC SA
ITI LIMITED
JABIL CIRCUIT INC
JDA SOFTWARE GROUP INC
JDS UNIPHASE CORPORATION
JUNIPER NETWORKS INC
KEANE INC
KEMET CORP
KEY TRONIC CORP
KLA TENCOR CORP

KONAMI CORP
KRONOS INC
L-3 COMMUNICATIONS HOLDINGS INC
LAM RESEARCH CORP
LATTICE SEMICONDUCTOR CORP
LENOVO GROUP LIMITED
LEXAR MEDIA INC
LEXMARK INTERNATIONAL INC
LG DISPLAY CO LTD
LG ELECTRONICS INC
LG ELECTRONICS INDIA PVT LTD
LIMELIGHT NETWORKS INC
LINEAR TECHNOLOGY CORP
LITE-ON TECHNOLOGY CORP
LIVEPERSON INC
LOGICA PLC
LOGITECH INTERNATIONAL SA
LOGMELN INC
LSI CORPORATION
MACRONIX INTERNATIONAL CO LTD
MANHATTAN ASSOCIATES INC
MANTECH INTERNATIONAL CORP
MARVELL TECHNOLOGY GROUP LTD
MAXIM INTEGRATED PRODUCTS INC
MCAFEE INC
MEDIATEK INC
MELLANOX TECHNOLOGIES LTD
MEMC ELECTRONIC MATERIALS INC
MENTOR GRAPHICS CORP
MICROCHIP TECHNOLOGY INC
MICRON TECHNOLOGY INC
MICROS SYSTEMS INC
MICROSOFT CORP
MICROS-RETAIL
MICRO-STAR INTERNATIONAL
MICROSTRATEGY INC
MINDSPEED TECHNOLOGIES INC
MISYS PLC
MITAC INTERNATIONAL CORP
MITSUBISHI ELECTRIC CORPORATION
MODUSLINK GLOBAL SOLUTIONS INC
MOLEX INC
MOSER BAER INDIA LIMITED
MSCSOFTWARE CORP
MULTI-FINELINE ELECTRONIX
NAN YA PCB CORP
NANYA TECHNOLOGY CORPORATION
NATIONAL INSTRUMENTS CORP
NATIONAL SEMICONDUCTOR CORP
NAVISITE INC
NAVTEQ CORPORATION
NCR CORPORATION
NEC CORPORATION
NETAPP INC
NETGEAR INC
NETSCOUT SYSTEMS INC
NETSUITE INC
NETWORK ENGINES INC

NETWORK EQUIPMENT TECHNOLOGIES INC
NIDEC CORPORATION
NINTENDO CO LTD
NOKIA CORPORATION
NOVATEK MICROELECTRONICS CORP
NOVELL INC
NOVELLUS SYSTEMS INC
NUANCE COMMUNICATIONS INC
NVIDIA CORP
NXP SEMICONDUCTORS NV
OCZ TECHNOLOGY GROUP INC
OPEN TEXT CORP
OPENTV CORP
OPENWAVE SYSTEMS INC
OPERA SOFTWARE ASA
ORACLE CORP
OVERLAND STORAGE INC
PALM INC
PANASONIC CORPORATION
PAR TECHNOLOGY CORPORATION
PARAMETRIC TECHNOLOGY CORP
PC MALL INC
PC-WARE INFORMATION TECHNOLOGIES AG
PEGASYSTEMS INC
PHOENIX TECHNOLOGIES LTD
PHOTRONICS INC
PIONEER CORPORATION
PITNEY BOWES SOFTWARE INC
PLANTRONICS INC
PLEXUS CORP
PMC-SIERRA INC
POMEROY IT SOLUTIONS
POSITIVO INFORMATICA SA
POWERCHIP TECHNOLOGY CORP
PRINTRONIX INC
PROGRESS SOFTWARE CORP
PROXIM WIRELESS CORP
PULSE ELECTRONICS CORPORATION
QISDA CORPORATION
QLIK TECHNOLOGIES INC
QLOGIC CORP
QUALCOMM INC
QUANTA COMPUTER INC
QUANTUM CORP
QUARK INC
QUEST SOFTWARE INC
RADISYS CORP
RADWARE LTD
RAMBUS INC
RDA MICROELECTRONICS INC
REALNETWORKS INC
RED HAT INC
REDINGTON (INDIA) LTD
RENAISSANCE LEARNING INC
RENESAS ELECTRONICS CORP
RESEARCH IN MOTION LTD (RIM)
RESPONSYS INC
RICOH COMPANY LTD

RIGHTNOW TECHNOLOGIES INC
RIGHTSCALE INC
RIVERBED TECHNOLOGY INC
ROCKET SOFTWARE
ROGUE WAVE SOFTWARE INC
ROHM CO LTD
ROVI CORPORATION
ROYAL PHILIPS ELECTRONICS NV
RSA SECURITY INC
S1 CORPORATION
SAFENET INC
SAGEM TELECOMMUNICATIONS
SAIC INC
SALESFORCE.COM INC
SAMSUNG ELECTRO-MECHANICS
SAMSUNG ELECTRONICS CO LTD
SANDISK CORP
SANMINA-SCI CORPORATION
SANYO ELECTRIC COMPANY LTD
SAP AG
SAS INSTITUTE INC
SCANSOURCE INC
SEACHANGE INTERNATIONAL INC
SEAGATE TECHNOLOGY PLC
SEGA SAMMY HOLDINGS INC
SEIKO EPSON CORPORATION
SELECTICA INC
SEMICONDUCTOR MANUFACTURING
INTERNATIONAL
SERENA SOFTWARE INC
SERVEPATH
SHARP CORPORATION
SHIN ZU SHING CO LTD
SIEMENS AG
SIEMENS LIMITED
SIEMENS PLM SOFTWARE
SIGMA DESIGNS INC
SIGMATRON INTERNATIONAL INC
SILICON LABORATORIES INC
SILICONWARE PRECISION INDUSTRIES CO LTD
SIMPLO TECHNOLOGY CO LTD
SKILLSOFT PLC
SKYWORKS SOLUTIONS INC
SMART MODULAR TECHNOLOGIES INC
SMTC CORP
SOFTWARE AG
SOLARWINDS
SONIC SOLUTIONS
SONICWALL INC
SONUS NETWORKS INC
SONY CORPORATION
SOURCEFIRE INC
SPANSION
SPECTRIS
SPSS INC
SRA INTERNATIONAL INC
STANDARD MICROSYSTEMS CORPORATION
STERLING COMMERCE INC

STMICROELECTRONICS NV
SUN MICROSYSTEMS INC
SUNGARD DATA SYSTEMS INC
SUPER MICRO COMPUTER INC
SUPPORT.COM INC
SYBASE INC
SYMANTEC CORP
SYMMETRICOM INC
SYNAPTICS INC
SYNNEX CORP
SYNOPSYS INC
TAIWAN SEMICONDUCTOR MANUFACTURING CO
LTD (TSMC)
TAKE-TWO INTERACTIVE SOFTWARE INC
TANDBERG
TATA CONSULTANCY SERVICES (TCS)
TECH DATA CORP
TECH MAHINDRA LIMITED
TEKELEC
TEKTRONIX INC
TELCORDIA TECHNOLOGIES
TELECA AB
TELEFON AB LM ERICSSON (ERICSSON)
TELLABS INC
TELVENT GIT SA
TERADATA CORPORATION
TEXAS INSTRUMENTS INC (TI)
THQ INC
TIBCO SOFTWARE INC
TOKYO ELECTRON LIMITED
TOMTOM NV
TOSHIBA CORPORATION
TPV TECHNOLOGY LTD
TRANSCEND INFORMATION INC
TREND MICRO INC
TRILOGY INC
TRIMBLE NAVIGATION LTD
TTM TECHNOLOGIES INC
TXCOM-AXIOHM
ULTICOM INC
ULTIMATE SOFTWARE GROUP INC
UNISYS CORP
UNITED MICROELECTRONICS CORP
UTSTARCOM INC
VARIAN SEMICONDUCTOR EQUIPMENT
ASSOCIATES INC
VASCO DATA SECURITY INTERNATIONAL INC
VENTYX INC
VERISIGN INC
VIA TECHNOLOGIES INC
VIASYSTEMS GROUP INC
VICORP GROUP PLC
VIDEOCON INDUSTRIES LTD
VITESSE SEMICONDUCTOR CORP
VMWARE INC
VSE CORP
WATCHGUARD TECHNOLOGIES INC
WEB.COM GROUP INC

WEBSENSE INC
WESTELL TECHNOLOGIES INC
WESTERN DIGITAL CORP
WIND RIVER SYSTEMS INC
WIPRO LTD
WYSE TECHNOLOGY INC
XEROX CORP
XILINX INC
YAHOO! INC
ZEBRA TECHNOLOGIES CORP
ZOOM TECHNOLOGIES INC

Individual Profiles
On Each Of
THE INFOTECH 500

ACCENTURE PLC

www.accenture.com

Industry Group Code: 541513 Ranks within this company's industry group: Sales: 3 Profits: 2

Hardware:	Software:	Telecommunications:	Electronic Publishing:	Equipment:	Specialty Services:	
Computers:	Consumer:	Local:	Online Service:	Telecom:	Consulting:	Y
Accessories:	Corporate:	Long Distance:	TV/Cable or Wireless:	Communication:	Contract Manufacturing:	
Network Equipment:	Telecom:	Cellular:	Games:	Distribution:	Processing:	
Chips/Circuits:	Internet:	Internet Service:	Financial Data:	VAR/Reseller:	Staff/Outsourcing:	Y
Parts/Drives:				Satellite Srv./Equip.:	Specialty Services:	

TYPES OF BUSINESS:

Technology Consulting Services
Computer Operations Outsourcing
Supply Chain Management
Technology Research
Software Development
Human Resources Consulting
Management Consulting
Research & Development

BRANDS/DIVISIONS/AFFILIATES:

Accenture Mobility Operated Services
CadenceQuest Inc
Acceria

CONTACTS: Note: Officers with more than one job title may be intentionally listed here more than once.

Peter Nanterme, CEO
Johan Deblaere, COO
Pamela J. Craig, CFO
Roxanne Taylor, Chief Mktg. Officer
Jill B. Smart, Chief Human Resources Officer
Kevin M. Campbell, CTO
Gianfranco Casati, Group CEO-Prod.
Julie Spellman Sweet, General Counsel/Corp. Sec./Compliance Officer
Karl-Heinz Floether, Chief Strategy & Corp. Dev. Officer
Roxanne Taylor, Chief Comm. Officer
David P. Rowland, Sr. VP-Finance
Karl-Heinz Floether, Group CEO-Systems Integration, Tech. & Delivery
Martin I. Cole, Group CEO-Comm. & High Tech.
Adrian Lajtha, Chief Leadership Officer
Sander van 't Noordende, Group CEO-Resources
William D. Green, Chmn.
Diego Visconti, Chmn.-Int'l, Strategic Countries

Phone: 353-1-646-2000	Fax:
Toll-Free:	
Address: 1 Grand Canal Square, Grand Canal Harbor, Dublin, 2 Ireland	

GROWTH PLANS/SPECIAL FEATURES:

Accenture plc is a leading provider of management consulting, technology and outsourcing services, with operations in over 200 cities in 53 countries. The firm delivers services through five operating groups, which together comprise 20 industry groups. The operating groups are communications and high-tech; financial services; health and public service; products; and resources. Accenture's communications and high-tech group offers technology, consulting and systems integration to the electronics, communications and media industries. Its financial services group provides consulting and outsourcing strategies to the insurance, capital markets and banking industries. Finally, its health and public service group works with local, state, provincial and national governments in the areas of defense; revenue; human services; health; justice; and postal and education authorities. Accenture's products group serves the automotive; life sciences; consumer goods; industrial equipment; retail; and transportation and travel services industries. The company's resources group works with the chemicals; energy; natural resources; and utilities industries. Accenture also offers management consulting services including customer relationship management; supply chain management; human performance; finance and performance management; and strategy. The firm's systems integration and technology services include systems integration consulting, such as information management services and cloud computing; technology consulting, such as enterprise architecture and infrastructure consulting; and IT outsourcing. Accenture offers outsourcing for business processes, applications and infrastructure needs. The company also offers global mobility services through its Accenture Mobility Operated Services. Clients include AT&T; Microsoft; Sony; Bank of America; and the U.S. Department of Commerce. In June 2010, the company acquired CadenceQuest, Inc., which specializes in retail consumer data. In July 2010, the firm purchased Acceria, a French business process firm.

Accenture offers its employees flexible work arrangements and ongoing training and development resources.

FINANCIALS: Sales and profits are in thousands of dollars—add 000 to get the full amount. 2010 Note: Financial information for 2010 was not available for all companies at press time.

2010 Sales: $23,094,078	2010 Profits: $2,060,459	**U.S. Stock Ticker: ACN**
2009 Sales: $23,170,968	2009 Profits: $1,589,963	Int'l Ticker: Int'l Exchange:
2008 Sales: $25,313,826	2008 Profits: $1,691,751	Employees: 204,000
2007 Sales: $21,452,747	2007 Profits: $1,243,148	Fiscal Year Ends: 8/31
2006 Sales: $18,228,366	2006 Profits: $973,329	Parent Company:

SALARIES/BENEFITS:

Pension Plan:	ESOP Stock Plan:	Profit Sharing:	Top Exec. Salary: $1,250,000	Bonus: $3,040,000
Savings Plan:	Stock Purch. Plan: Y		Second Exec. Salary: $1,189,500	Bonus: $1,986,465

OTHER THOUGHTS:

Apparent Women Officers or Directors: 6
Hot Spot for Advancement for Women/Minorities: Y

LOCATIONS: ("Y" = Yes)

West:	Southwest:	Midwest:	Southeast:	Northeast:	International:
Y	Y	Y	Y	Y	Y

Note: Financial information, benefits and other data can change quickly and may vary from those stated here.

ACCESS CO LTD

www.access-company.com

Industry Group Code: 511210I Ranks within this company's industry group: Sales: 5 Profits: 5

Hardware:	Software:		Telecommunications:	Electronic Publishing:	Equipment:	Specialty Services:
Computers:	Consumer:	Y	Local:	Online Service:	Telecom:	Consulting:
Accessories:	Corporate:	Y	Long Distance:	TV/Cable or Wireless:	Communication:	Contract Manufacturing:
Network Equipment:	Telecom:	Y	Cellular:	Games:	Distribution:	Processing:
Chips/Circuits:	Internet:		Internet Service:	Financial Data:	VAR/Reseller:	Staff/Outsourcing:
Parts/Drives:					Satellite Srv./Equip.:	Specialty Services:

TYPES OF BUSINESS:

Web Browser Technologies
Web Browsers-Mobile Devices
Software Development

BRANDS/DIVISIONS/AFFILIATES:

NetFront
JV2-Lite2 Wireless Edition
Java2 Platform
ELSE INTUITION
ACCESS NetFront Browser v4 1
Bluetooth
ACCESS Systems Americas, Inc.
Hipix

CONTACTS: *Note: Officers with more than one job title may be intentionally listed here more than once.*

Tomihisa Kamada, CEO
Toshiya Yasui, COO/Exec. VP
Tomihisa Kamada, Pres.
Nobuya Murofushi, CFO/Sr. VP
Kiyoyasu Oishi, Sr. VP-Mktg.
Toshiya Yasui, Sr. VP-Human Resources
Kunihiro Ishiguro, CIO
Kunihiro Ishiguro, CTO
Koichi Narasaki, Chief Strategy Officer
Kunihiro Ishiguro, CTO-IP Infusion, Inc.
Koichi Narasaki, CEO-IP Infusion, Inc.

Phone: 81-3-5259-3511	Fax: 81-3-5259-3544

Toll-Free:

Address: Hirata Bldg. 2-8-16 Sarugaku-cho, Chiyoda-ku, Tokyo, 101-0064 Japan

GROWTH PLANS/SPECIAL FEATURES:

Access Co. Ltd. is a software development firm offering web browser, protocol stack and mobile operating systems manufacturing based in Tokyo, Japan. The firm's primary products, the NetFront family of offerings, are Internet browsers designed for embedded applications and capable of being used in many different kinds of mobile devices including mobile phones, digital TVs, set-top boxes, PDAs, web phones, game consoles, e-mail terminals and automobile telematics systems. The NetFront products are key to Access' vision of bringing the Internet to the individual at any time, anywhere and from any device. Its most recent NetFront browser is ACCESS NetFront Browser v4.1. The ACCESS Linux Platform provides application window management, device memory management and navigation models for mobile products. It also includes a suite of media applications for music, photos and video. The Garnet OS platform offers a wide selection of hardware devices designed for managing mobile information, entertainment and communications. Additionally, the company offers Java platforms for mobile phones including the JV-Lite2 Wireless Edition and the Java2 Platform; and ELSE INTUITION, a mobile platform jointly developed by the company and Emblaze Mobile, Ltd. The firm's well known Bluetooth or AVE-Blue protocol stack is designed for embedded systems. When used in combination with Access' NetFront browser, it simplifies the development of wireless network connected devices such as automobile infotainment devices. Subsidiary ACCESS Systems Americas, Inc. (formerly PalmSource, Inc.) is an operating system that powers phones and mobile devices and develops software for mobile phones. In February 2010, NetFront became compatible with the Android product platform. In December 2010, Access Co. partnered with hipix rich format technology developer Human Monitoring, Ltd. to offer hipix on the NetFront platform.

FINANCIALS: Sales and profits are in thousands of dollars—add 000 to get the full amount. 2010 Note: Financial information for 2010 was not available for all companies at press time.

2010 Sales: $	2010 Profits: $	**U.S. Stock Ticker:**
2009 Sales: $354,210	2009 Profits: $5,400	**Int'l Ticker: 4813** Int'l Exchange: Tokyo-TSE
2008 Sales: $324,790	2008 Profits: $8,760	Employees:
2007 Sales: $248,000	2007 Profits: $-152,300	Fiscal Year Ends: 12/31
2006 Sales: $164,100	2006 Profits: $26,500	Parent Company:

SALARIES/BENEFITS:

Pension Plan:	ESOP Stock Plan:	Profit Sharing:	Top Exec. Salary: $	Bonus: $
Savings Plan: Y	Stock Purch. Plan:		Second Exec. Salary: $	Bonus: $

OTHER THOUGHTS:

Apparent Women Officers or Directors:
Hot Spot for Advancement for Women/Minorities:

LOCATIONS: ("Y" = Yes)

West:	Southwest:	Midwest:	Southeast:	Northeast:	International:
Y					Y

ACCTON TECHNOLOGY CORP

www.accton.com

Industry Group Code: 334419 Ranks within this company's industry group: Sales: 16   Profits: 11

Hardware:	Software:	Telecommunications:	Electronic Publishing:	Equipment:	Specialty Services:	
Computers:	Consumer:	Local:	Online Service:	Telecom:	Consulting:	
Accessories:	Corporate:	Long Distance:	TV/Cable or Wireless:	Communication:	Contract Manufacturing:	
Network Equipment:	Telecom:	Cellular:	Games:	Distribution:	Processing:	
Chips/Circuits:	Internet:	Internet Service:	Financial Data:	VAR/Reseller:	Staff/Outsourcing:	
Parts/Drives:				Satellite Srv./Equip.:	Specialty Services:	Y

TYPES OF BUSINESS:

Contract Electronics Manufacturing
Technical & Communications Outsourcing
IP Network Switches
Semiconductors & Chipsets
Wireless Hardware
Online Portal
VoIP Hardware
Consumer Electronics

BRANDS/DIVISIONS/AFFILIATES:

Accton Wireless Broadband
SMC Networks
Arcadyan
Acute Corporation
Vodtel
EdgeCore
Mototech
EdgeCore Networks

CONTACTS: Note: Officers with more than one job title may be intentionally listed here more than once.

An-Jye Haung, Pres.
Meen-Ron Lin, CFO
Luen-Ruey Lu, Vice Chmn.
Kuo-Tai Chiou, Sr. VP
Samuel Chang, Sr. VP
Chi-Hsiang Yu, Sr. VP
An-Jye Haung, Chmn.

Phone: 886-3-577-0270	Fax: 886-3-578-0764
Toll-Free:	
Address: 1 Creation Rd. III, Science-Based Industrial Park, Hsinchu, 300 Taiwan	

GROWTH PLANS/SPECIAL FEATURES:

Accton Technology Corp., based in Taiwan, provides outsourced communications equipment manufacturing services for original equipment manufactures (OEM) and original design manufacturers (ODM) and data communication for both personal and business needs. The firm's primary focus is Ethernet technology; however, the company's offers a variety of products including broadband products, network switches, network hubs, network cards and wireless products. These products are marketed under the Edge-core and SMC Networks brand names. Accton's numerous subsidiaries include Acute Corporation, a designer of semiconductors; Vodtel, a Voice over Internet Protocol (VOIP) hardware producer; Edge-Core, a provider of an integrated service platform; Accton Wireless Broadband Corp. or AWB, a provider of wireless infrastructure technology and advanced technology integration; and Mototech, a global ODM specialist in the broadband and data networking market. It also owns E-charity, an Internet platform for charitable works in Taiwan; url.com.tw, a Chinese-language online entertainment portal; and the Accton Arts Foundation, which encourages and funds artistic expression in and near science parks and corporations. Accton has operations in San Jose and Boston in the U.S.; Shanghai and Taiwan in China; the U.K.; and Japan. The company has plans to continue to expand its market reach within Europe, South America, China and India. In January 2010, the company formed a joint venture with Viettel Telcom to expand into the Vietnamese market. In February 2010, Accton announced it had formed an additional joint venture with LG-Nortel. The new company, Edgecore Networks, will offer data and voice solutions for North American businesses.

Accton offers employees a 10 month maternity leave and a three day paternity leave; a $3,000 salary incentive to encourage marriage; on-site child care; two month leave with pay for employees who have seven years of continuous service; birthday coupons; rooftop gardens; on-site coffee shops; and a health care center for employee use.

FINANCIALS: Sales and profits are in thousands of dollars—add 000 to get the full amount. 2010 Note: Financial information for 2010 was not available for all companies at press time.

2010 Sales: $	2010 Profits: $	U.S. Stock Ticker:
2009 Sales: $535,040	2009 Profits: $20,340	Int'l Ticker: 2345 Int'l Exchange: Taipei-TPE
2008 Sales: $461,130	2008 Profits: $4,340	Employees:
2007 Sales: $474,900	2007 Profits: $-7,800	Fiscal Year Ends: 12/31
2006 Sales: $469,160	2006 Profits: $ 690	Parent Company:

SALARIES/BENEFITS:

Pension Plan:	ESOP Stock Plan:	Profit Sharing:	Top Exec. Salary: $	Bonus: $
Savings Plan:	Stock Purch. Plan:		Second Exec. Salary: $	Bonus: $

OTHER THOUGHTS:

Apparent Women Officers or Directors:
Hot Spot for Advancement for Women/Minorities:

LOCATIONS: ("Y" = Yes)

West:	Southwest:	Midwest:	Southeast:	Northeast:	International:
Y					Y

ACER INC

www.acer.com.tw

Industry Group Code: 334111 Ranks within this company's industry group: Sales: 10 Profits: 6

Hardware:		Software:		Telecommunications:	Electronic Publishing:	Equipment:		Specialty Services:	
Computers:	Y	Consumer:	Y	Local:	Online Service:	Telecom:		Consulting:	
Accessories:	Y	Corporate:	Y	Long Distance:	TV/Cable or Wireless:	Communication:		Contract Manufacturing:	
Network Equipment:		Telecom:		Cellular:	Games:	Distribution:	Y	Processing:	
Chips/Circuits:		Internet:		Internet Service:	Financial Data:	VAR/Reseller:		Staff/Outsourcing:	
Parts/Drives:	Y					Satellite Srv./Equip.:		Specialty Services:	

TYPES OF BUSINESS:

Computer Equipment Distribution
PCs & Accessories
Components
Software

BRANDS/DIVISIONS/AFFILIATES:

Clear.fi
Aspire
Veriton
E-Ten
HiTRUST
Lottery Technology Services
TWP
Gateway Inc

CONTACTS: Note: Officers with more than one job title may be intentionally listed here more than once.

J. T. Wang, CEO
Gianfranco Lanci, Pres.
J. T. Wang, Chmn.

Phone: 886-2-6696-1234	Fax: 886-2-8991-1031
Toll-Free:	
Address: 7F, 137, Sector 2 Chien Kuo North Road, Taipei, 221 Taiwan	

GROWTH PLANS/SPECIAL FEATURES:

Acer, Inc. is a part of the Pan Acer Group that offers products under the brand names of Acer, Gateway, Packard Bell and eMachines. The company is one of the world's top PC manufacturers with a presence in over 100 countries. The company markets a full scope of branded IT products including PCs, servers, monitors, handheld devices, storage devices and projectors. The firm also supplies multiple brands of components, software and 3C products throughout China, Africa, the Middle East and Europe. Acer markets under several main brand names: Aspire, its consumer desktop and notebook PC brand name; TravelMate, its notebook-only brand name; Predator, its line of gaming PCs, and Veriton, its line of commercial PCs targeted for business users and MIS managers. The company's latest computer line is the Acer Aspire Timeline series, which are ultraportable netbooks featuring an 8.9-inch screen, WiFi connectivity and up to an eight-hour battery life. Models are available with features such as solid state hard drives, 3G connectivity (through a partnership with AT&T), a choice of Linux or Windows operating systems and a wide range of colors. The firm also offers flat screen LCD TVs, desktop monitors and projectors. Acer's Clear.fi technology allows consumers to link multiple devices over a single home network. The company has several subsidiaries, including Weblink, HiTRUST, Lottery Technology Services, E-Ten, TWP, Sertek and Apacer.

FINANCIALS: Sales and profits are in thousands of dollars—add 000 to get the full amount. 2010 Note: Financial information for 2010 was not available for all companies at press time.

2010 Sales: $	2010 Profits: $	**U.S. Stock Ticker:**
2009 Sales: $18,178,400	2009 Profits: $359,570	**Int'l Ticker: 2353** Int'l Exchange: Taipei-TPE
2008 Sales: $16,650,000	2008 Profits: $428,800	Employees:
2007 Sales: $14,070,000	2007 Profits: $310,170	Fiscal Year Ends: 12/31
2006 Sales: $11,320,000	2006 Profits: $313,470	Parent Company:

SALARIES/BENEFITS:

Pension Plan: Y	ESOP Stock Plan:	Profit Sharing:	Top Exec. Salary: $	Bonus: $
Savings Plan:	Stock Purch. Plan:		Second Exec. Salary: $	Bonus: $

OTHER THOUGHTS:

Apparent Women Officers or Directors:
Hot Spot for Advancement for Women/Minorities:

LOCATIONS: ("Y" = Yes)

West:	Southwest:	Midwest:	Southeast:	Northeast:	International:
Y					Y

Note: Financial information, benefits and other data can change quickly and may vary from those stated here.

ACI WORLDWIDE INC

www.aciworldwide.com

Industry Group Code: 511201 Ranks within this company's industry group: Sales: 5 Profits: 4

Hardware:	Software:		Telecommunications:	Electronic Publishing:	Equipment:	Specialty Services:	
Computers:	Consumer:		Local:	Online Service:	Telecom:	Consulting:	
Accessories:	Corporate:	Y	Long Distance:	TV/Cable or Wireless:	Communication:	Contract Manufacturing:	
Network Equipment:	Telecom:		Cellular:	Games:	Distribution:	Processing:	Y
Chips/Circuits:	Internet:		Internet Service:	Financial Data:	VAR/Reseller:	Staff/Outsourcing:	
Parts/Drives:					Satellite Srv./Equip.:	Specialty Services:	

TYPES OF BUSINESS:

Computer Software-Electronic Funds Transfer
Information Management Solutions
Electronic Banking & Smart Card Solutions
International Payments & Message Processing Software

BRANDS/DIVISIONS/AFFILIATES:

ACI Enterprise Banker
ACI Global Banker
ACI Proactive Risk Manager
ACI Automated Case Management

CONTACTS: Note: Officers with more than one job title may be intentionally listed here more than once.

Philip G. Heasley, CEO
J. Ronald Totaro, COO
Philip G. Heasley, Pres.
Scott Behrens, CFO/VP
Charles H. Linberg, CTO
Louis Blatt, Chief Prod. Officer
Dennis Byrnes, General Counsel/Sr. VP/Sec.
David N. Norem, Sr. VP-Global Customer Oper.
Craig Maki, Chief Corp. Dev. Officer
Tony Scotto, Chief Dev. Officer/VP
Harlan F. Seymour, Chmn.
Ralph Dangelmaier, Pres., Global Markets & Svcs.

Phone: 646-348-6700	Fax: 212-470-4000
Toll-Free:	
Address: 120 Broadway, Ste. 3350, New York, NY 10271 US	

GROWTH PLANS/SPECIAL FEATURES:

ACI Worldwide, Inc. develops, markets, installs and supports software products and services focused on facilitating electronic payments. Generally, ACI's products address three primary market segments: retail banking, including debit and credit card issuers; wholesale banking, including corporate cash management and treasury management operations; and retailers. Its product lines are divided into four categories: Initiate, Manage, Secure and Operate. Initiate products are designed around the initiation of payments through online banking systems, and include the products ACI Enterprise Banker, which is used as an Internet-based business banking product with electronic payment initiation capability and information reporting; and ACI Global Banker, which serves corporate cash management, trade finance, reporting and data exchange needs. The Manage segment serves retail payment engines, which are designed to route electronic payment transactions from transaction generators to the acquiring institutions so that they can be authorized for payment; back office services, which are card issuing and merchant management services; and wholesale payment engines, which focus on global, super-regional and regional financial institutions that provide treasury management services to large corporations. The products in the Secure division, such as ACI Proactive Risk Manager and ACI Automated Case Management, work to protect against fraud and money laundering. The Operate products work to support and augment the products in the Initiate, Manage and Secure divisions, and offer services such as legacy product support, automated data streams, protected monitoring and simulation services. In addition to its own products, it also distributes or acts as a sales agent for software developed by third parties. The majority of ACI's products are sold and supported through three distribution networks: the Americas, Europe/Middle East/Africa (EMEA) and Asia/Pacific.

FINANCIALS: Sales and profits are in thousands of dollars—add 000 to get the full amount. 2010 Note: Financial information for 2010 was not available for all companies at press time.

2010 Sales: $	2010 Profits: $	**U.S. Stock Ticker: ACIW**
2009 Sales: $405,755	2009 Profits: $19,626	**Int'l Ticker:** Int'l Exchange:
2008 Sales: $417,653	2008 Profits: $10,582	Employees: 2,114
2007 Sales: $366,218	2007 Profits: $-9,131	Fiscal Year Ends: 9/30
2006 Sales: $347,902	2006 Profits: $55,365	Parent Company:

SALARIES/BENEFITS:

Pension Plan:	ESOP Stock Plan:	Profit Sharing:	Top Exec. Salary: $575,000	Bonus: $762,613
Savings Plan: Y	Stock Purch. Plan: Y		Second Exec. Salary: $335,000	Bonus: $445,270

OTHER THOUGHTS:

Apparent Women Officers or Directors: 1
Hot Spot for Advancement for Women/Minorities:

LOCATIONS: ("Y" = Yes)

West:	Southwest:	Midwest:	Southeast:	Northeast:	International:
	Y	Y	Y	Y	Y

ACTIVISION BLIZZARD INC

www.activisionblizzard.com

Industry Group Code: 511210G Ranks within this company's industry group: Sales: 2 Profits: 2

Hardware:	Software:		Telecommunications:	Electronic Publishing:		Equipment:	Specialty Services:	
Computers:	Consumer:	Y	Local:	Online Service:		Telecom:	Consulting:	
Accessories:	Corporate:		Long Distance:	TV/Cable or Wireless:		Communication:	Contract Manufacturing:	
Network Equipment:	Telecom:		Cellular:	Games:	Y	Distribution:	Processing:	
Chips/Circuits:	Internet:		Internet Service:	Financial Data:		VAR/Reseller:	Staff/Outsourcing:	
Parts/Drives:						Satellite Srv./Equip.:	Specialty Services:	Y

TYPES OF BUSINESS:

Video Games
Logistics Services

BRANDS/DIVISIONS/AFFILIATES:

Activision Publishing, Inc.
Blizzard Entertainment, Inc.
Vivendi SA
World of Warcraft (WoW)
Guitar Hero
Call of Duty
StarCraft
Diablo

CONTACTS: *Note: Officers with more than one job title may be intentionally listed here more than once.*

Robert A. Kotick, CEO
Thomas Tippl, COO
Robert A. Kotick, Pres.
Thomas Tippl, CFO
Brian Hodous, Chief Customer Officer
Ann Weiser, Chief Human Resources Officer
Chris Walther, Chief Legal Officer
George Rose, Chief Public Policy Officer
Michael Griffith, CEO/Pres., Activision Publishing, Inc.
Michael Morhaime, CEO/Pres., Blizzard Entertainment
Jean-Bernard Levy, Chmn.

Phone: 310-255-2000	Fax:
Toll-Free:	
Address: 3100 Ocean Park Blvd., Santa Monica, CA 90405 US	

GROWTH PLANS/SPECIAL FEATURES:

Activision Blizzard, Inc. is a leading international publisher and developer of subscription-based massively multiplayer online role-playing games (MMORPGs) and other PC-based computer games; interactive entertainment software; and peripherals for a variety of game genres. The company was formed with the merger of Vivendi Games, owner of Blizzard Entertainment and its popular game World of Warcraft, and Activision, a leading publisher of interactive entertainment. World of Warcraft has over 12 million subscribers worldwide. Activision and Blizzard persist as separate brands within the company, which organizes its business into the following segments: Activision Publishing; Blizzard Entertainment, Inc. and its subsidiaries; Activision Blizzard Distribution. Activision Publishing publishes interactive entertainment software and peripherals, including certain studios, assets and titles previously included in Vivendi Games' Sierra Entertainment operating segment. Blizzard Entertainment, Inc. and its subsidiaries publish traditional games and MMORPGs. Activision Blizzard Distribution handles the distribution of interactive entertainment software and hardware products. Some of the company's most popular products include Guitar Hero, Call of Duty and Tony Hawk, as well as Spider-Man, James Bond, TRANSFORMERS, StarCraft, Diablo and Warcraft franchise games, including World of Warcraft. Activision Blizzard maintains operations throughout North America, Europe and Asia.

The firm offers its employees medical, dental, vision, life and AD&D insurance; a 401(k) plan; a college savings plan for family members; an employee assistance program; tuition reimbursement; group legal insurance; discounts at the company store; and gym membership discounts.

FINANCIALS: Sales and profits are in thousands of dollars—add 000 to get the full amount. 2010 Note: Financial information for 2010 was not available for all companies at press time.

2010 Sales: $	2010 Profits: $	**U.S. Stock Ticker:** ATVI
2009 Sales: $4,279,000	2009 Profits: $-26,000	**Int'l Ticker:** Int'l Exchange:
2008 Sales: $3,026,000	2008 Profits: $-233,000	Employees: 7,000
2007 Sales: $1,349,000	2007 Profits: $179,000	Fiscal Year Ends: 12/31
2006 Sales: $1,018,000	2006 Profits: $121,000	Parent Company:

SALARIES/BENEFITS:

Pension Plan:	ESOP Stock Plan:	Profit Sharing:	Top Exec. Salary: $953,654	Bonus: $2,167,250
Savings Plan: Y	Stock Purch. Plan:		Second Exec. Salary: $726,423	Bonus: $664,417

OTHER THOUGHTS:

Apparent Women Officers or Directors: 1
Hot Spot for Advancement for Women/Minorities:

LOCATIONS: ("Y" = Yes)

West:	Southwest:	Midwest:	Southeast:	Northeast:	International:
Y	Y	Y	Y	Y	Y

ACXIOM CORP

www.acxiom.com

Industry Group Code: 511210K Ranks within this company's industry group: Sales: 2 Profits: 5

Hardware:	Software:	Telecommunications:	Electronic Publishing:	Equipment:	Specialty Services:
Computers:	Consumer:	Local:	Online Service:	Telecom:	Consulting: Y
Accessories:	Corporate: Y	Long Distance:	TV/Cable or Wireless:	Communication:	Contract Manufacturing:
Network Equipment:	Telecom:	Cellular:	Games:	Distribution:	Processing: Y
Chips/Circuits:	Internet:	Internet Service:	Financial Data:	VAR/Reseller:	Staff/Outsourcing: Y
Parts/Drives:				Satellite Srv./Equip.:	Specialty Services: Y

TYPES OF BUSINESS:

Consumer Data Management
Consumer Databases
Consulting and Analytics
Risk Mitigation Services
CDI Technology
Consumer Privacy Solutions

BRANDS/DIVISIONS/AFFILIATES:

PersonicX
InfoBase-X
Acxiom Access-X Express
Acxiom Information Security Services (AISS)
GoDigital

CONTACTS: *Note: Officers with more than one job title may be intentionally listed here more than once.*

John A. Meyer, CEO
John A. Adams, COO/Exec. VP
John A. Meyer, Pres.
Christopher W. Wolf, CFO/Exec. VP
Tim Suther, Chief Mktg. Officer/Sr. VP
Cindy K. Childers, Sr. VP-Human Resources
Chuck Howland, VP-IT
John Costanza, VP-Prod. Mgmt.
Jerry C. Jones, Chief Legal Officer/Sr. VP
Shawn M. Donovan, Sr. VP-Sales, Markets & Consulting
Cameron Thompson, Group Managing Dir.-Healthcare
Michael Durham, Chmn.
Barry Adams, Dir.-Bus. Dev., Asia

Phone: 501-342-1000	Fax: 501-342-3913
Toll-Free: 800-322-9466	
Address: 601 E. 3rd St., Little Rock, AR 72201 US	

GROWTH PLANS/SPECIAL FEATURES:

Acxiom Corp. is a customer information management firm that assists its marketers in managing audiences, personalizing consumer experiences and creating profitable relationships. Its operations are divided into two segments: Information Services and Information Products. The Information Services unit develops and sells industry-tailored solutions through the integration of products, services and consulting. Its services include the design and creation of marketing databases and data warehouses; data integration and customer-recognition systems; marketing applications; list processing; and information technology services. This division includes the customer data integration (CDI), multichannel marketing services, infrastructure management and consulting services business lines. CDI solutions analyze prospects and customers, while the multichannel marketing unit designs, plans and manages campaigns; tracks results; and assists clients in improving business through e-mail, search marketing and personalizing web sites. Infrastructure management services include IT outsourcing, network management and other services, such as IT security. Consulting and analytics solutions include diagnostic software, analytic consulting and other professional services to support existing customer information. The Information Products segment, consisting of the consumer insights, risk mitigation and background screening product lines, develops and sells global data products. These include InfoBase-X, a database of U.S. telephone and consumer data; products that customize InfoBase-X such as PersonicX, which divides InfoBase into 70 segments based on demographics and consumer behavior; Acxiom Access-X Express, a data management tool for InfoBase; and others. Acxiom Information Security Services (AISS) provides criminal, civil and driving record background searches. Acxiom's clients include finance, insurance, information services, direct marketing, publishing, retail and telecommunications companies. In March 2010, the company opened the China Global Service Center in Nantong. In May 2010, it acquired a controlling interest in South American firm GoDigital.

Employees are offered health, dental and vision insurance; a health savings account; flexible spending account; an employee assistance program; short-and long-term disability; life insurance; pet insurance; and education and adoption assistance.

FINANCIALS: Sales and profits are in thousands of dollars—add 000 to get the full amount. 2010 Note: Financial information for 2010 was not available for all companies at press time.

2010 Sales: $1,099,235	2010 Profits: $44,549	**U.S. Stock Ticker: ACXM**
2009 Sales: $1,276,573	2009 Profits: $37,504	**Int'l Ticker:** Int'l Exchange:
2008 Sales: $1,384,079	2008 Profits: $-7,780	Employees: 6,400
2007 Sales: $1,390,511	2007 Profits: $67,873	Fiscal Year Ends: 3/31
2006 Sales: $1,328,773	2006 Profits: $61,775	Parent Company:

SALARIES/BENEFITS:

Pension Plan:	ESOP Stock Plan:	Profit Sharing:	Top Exec. Salary: $647,500	Bonus: $
Savings Plan: Y	Stock Purch. Plan: Y		Second Exec. Salary: $462,500	Bonus: $

OTHER THOUGHTS:

Apparent Women Officers or Directors: 1
Hot Spot for Advancement for Women/Minorities:

LOCATIONS: ("Y" = Yes)

West:	Southwest:	Midwest:	Southeast:	Northeast:	International:
Y		Y	Y	Y	Y

ADC TELECOMMUNICATIONS INC

www.adc.com

Industry Group Code: 334210 Ranks within this company's industry group: Sales: 7   Profits: 12

Hardware:		Software:		Telecommunications:	Electronic Publishing:	Equipment:		Specialty Services:	
Computers:		Consumer:		Local:	Online Service:	Telecom:	Y	Consulting:	Y
Accessories:		Corporate:	Y	Long Distance:	TV/Cable or Wireless:	Communication:		Contract Manufacturing:	
Network Equipment:	Y	Telecom:	Y	Cellular:	Games:	Distribution:		Processing:	
Chips/Circuits:		Internet:		Internet Service:	Financial Data:	VAR/Reseller:		Staff/Outsourcing:	
Parts/Drives:						Satellite Srv./Equip.:		Specialty Services:	

TYPES OF BUSINESS:

Telecommunications Equipment
Networking Systems
Broadband Connectivity Products
Equipment Services
Systems Integration

BRANDS/DIVISIONS/AFFILIATES:

Tyco Electronics, Ltd.
Tyco International, Ltd.

CONTACTS: Note: Officers with more than one job title may be intentionally listed here more than once.

Alan Clarke, Pres.
Harold G. Barksdale, Sec./VP
Eric J. Resch, VP-Tax
Mario Calastri, VP/Assistant Treas.
Michael Soland, VP/Assistant Treas.
Driscoll Nina, VP
Richard J. Suminski, VP

Phone: 952-938-8080	Fax:
Toll-Free: 800-366-3891	
Address: 13625 Technology Dr., Eden Prairie, MN 55344 US	

GROWTH PLANS/SPECIAL FEATURES:

ADC Telecommunications, Inc., a subsidiary of Tyco Electronics, Ltd., is a leading provider of global broadband communications network infrastructure products and services. The firm's products enable the delivery of high-speed Internet, data, video and voice communications over wireline, wireless, cable, enterprise and broadcast networks. The company operates in three business segments: global connectivity solutions, network solutions and professional services. Global connectivity solutions is the company's largest segment, accounting for 75.3% of ADC's revenue. ADC's connectivity devices are used in wireline, wireless, cable, enterprise and broadcast communications networks over fiber-optic, copper, coaxial and wireless media. These products provide the physical interconnections between network components or access points into networks. These devices include DSX and DDF products, FTTX products, fiber distribution panels and frames, structured cabling products and broadcast and entertainment products. ADC's network solutions segment (9.8% of revenue) offers both in-building and outdoor wireless coverage/capacity solutions, which provide coverage and capacity for wireless network operators, such as mobile telephone services, national and regional carriers and neutral host facility providers. The company's professional services segment (14.9% of revenue) helps operators plan, deploy and maintain Internet, data, video and voice communication networks, and supports technology lifecycle operations such as network design, build-out, turn-up and testing. ADC serves the broadband, cable TV, entertainment, broadcast, private and government, manufacturing, telecommunications and wireless service industries. Recently, ADC sold a portion of its network solutions business, the GSM base station and switching technology unit, to Altobridge. In December 2010, the company was acquired by Tyco Electronics, Ltd., a subsidiary of Tyco International, Ltd.

FINANCIALS: Sales and profits are in thousands of dollars—add 000 to get the full amount. 2010 Note: Financial information for 2010 was not available for all companies at press time.

2010 Sales: $1,156,600	2010 Profits: $78,500	U.S. Stock Ticker: Subsidiary
2009 Sales: $990,200	2009 Profits: $-452,900	Int'l Ticker: Int'l Exchange:
2008 Sales: $1,442,600	2008 Profits: $-40,100	Employees: 9,300
2007 Sales: $1,276,700	2007 Profits: $106,300	Fiscal Year Ends: 10/31
2006 Sales: $1,231,900	2006 Profits: $65,700	Parent Company: TYCO INTERNATIONAL LTD

SALARIES/BENEFITS:

Pension Plan:	ESOP Stock Plan:	Profit Sharing:	Top Exec. Salary: $767,831	Bonus: $1,466,365
Savings Plan:	Stock Purch. Plan:		Second Exec. Salary: $349,936	Bonus: $445,361

OTHER THOUGHTS:

Apparent Women Officers or Directors: 2
Hot Spot for Advancement for Women/Minorities: Y

LOCATIONS: ("Y" = Yes)

West:	Southwest:	Midwest:	Southeast:	Northeast:	International:
		Y			Y

ADEPT TECHNOLOGY INC

www.adept.com

Industry Group Code: 334111 Ranks within this company's industry group: Sales: 31   Profits: 19

Hardware:		Software:		Telecommunications:	Electronic Publishing:	Equipment:	Specialty Services:	
Computers:		Consumer:		Local:	Online Service:	Telecom:	Consulting:	
Accessories:	Y	Corporate:	Y	Long Distance:	TV/Cable or Wireless:	Communication:	Contract Manufacturing:	Y
Network Equipment:		Telecom:		Cellular:	Games:	Distribution:	Processing:	
Chips/Circuits:		Internet:		Internet Service:	Financial Data:	VAR/Reseller:	Staff/Outsourcing:	
Parts/Drives:	Y					Satellite Srv./Equip.:	Specialty Services:	Y

TYPES OF BUSINESS:

Factory Automation Systems
Factory Automation Software
Industrial Robotics
Machine Vision Systems

BRANDS/DIVISIONS/AFFILIATES:

Adept ActiveV
Cobra
Adept Quattro
Viper
Adept Python
MobileRobots, Inc.
InMoTx

CONTACTS: Note: Officers with more than one job title may be intentionally listed here more than once.

John Dulchinos, CEO
John Dulchinos, Pres.
Lisa Cummins, CFO
Lisa Cummins, Sec.
Dave Pap Rocki, VP-Worldwide Oper.
Joachim Melis, VP-Bus. & Dev.
Lisa Cummins, VP-Finance
Michael P. Kelly, Chmn.
Joachim Melis, Gen. Mgr.-Adept Europe

Phone: 925-245-3400	Fax: 925-960-0452
Toll-Free: 800-292-3378	
Address: 5960 Inglewood Dr, Pleasanton, CA 94588 US	

GROWTH PLANS/SPECIAL FEATURES:

Adept Technology, Inc. designs, manufactures and sells intelligent robotics systems. It produces factory automation components and systems for the fiber optic, telecommunications, industrial tooling, packaging, life science, alternative energy, automotive electronics and semiconductor industries worldwide. The company operates in two business segments: Robotics, accounting for 83% of the firm's 2010 revenue; and Services & Support, 17%. The Robotics segment offers intelligent motion controls systems; production automation software, including vision-guidance and application software; and robot mechanisms. Adept intelligent automation product lines include industrial robots, configurable linear modules, machine controllers for robot mechanisms and other flexible automation equipment, machine vision and systems and applications software. The company's AIM software simplifies the integration, programming and operation of robot, vision and flexible feeder applications with a user-friendly interface. The ActiveV software allows users real-time control of robots with industry-standard computers running operating systems such as Windows Vista, enabling the integration of robotic systems into existing computer networks. Its most widely deployed robots are the Cobra family, which are 4-axis SCARA (Selective Compliance Assembly Robot Arm) robot mechanisms, designed for assembly and material handling tasks. Other robots include Quattro parallel robots, Viper 6-axis articulated robots, Modular Adept Python single axis mechanisms and mobile robots. The Services & Support segment provides spare parts for existing systems, consultation, technical support and training courses in the use of Adept's products. The firm markets and sells its products worldwide through more than 200 systems integrators, a direct sales force and original equipment manufacturers (OEMs). In June 2010, the firm acquired MobileRobots, Inc., which develops autonomous robot and automated guided vehicle technologies. In January 2011, it agreed to acquire InMoTx, a provider of robotic technology to the food processing market.

FINANCIALS: Sales and profits are in thousands of dollars—add 000 to get the full amount. 2010 Note: Financial information for 2010 was not available for all companies at press time.

2010 Sales: $51,627	2010 Profits: $-1,428	U.S. Stock Ticker: ADEP
2009 Sales: $41,536	2009 Profits: $-13,068	Int'l Ticker: Int'l Exchange:
2008 Sales: $60,783	2008 Profits: $3,636	Employees: 163
2007 Sales: $48,688	2007 Profits: $-11,513	Fiscal Year Ends: 6/30
2006 Sales: $57,637	2006 Profits: $ 538	Parent Company:

SALARIES/BENEFITS:

Pension Plan:	ESOP Stock Plan:	Profit Sharing:	Top Exec. Salary: $241,154	Bonus: $
Savings Plan:	Stock Purch. Plan: Y		Second Exec. Salary: $201,385	Bonus: $

OTHER THOUGHTS:

Apparent Women Officers or Directors: 1
Hot Spot for Advancement for Women/Minorities:

LOCATIONS: ("Y" = Yes)

West:	Southwest:	Midwest:	Southeast:	Northeast:	International:
Y		Y		Y	Y

ADOBE SYSTEMS INC

www.adobe.com

Industry Group Code: 511210F Ranks within this company's industry group: Sales: 1 Profits: 1

Hardware:	Software:		Telecommunications:	Electronic Publishing:	Equipment:	Specialty Services:
Computers:	Consumer:	Y	Local:	Online Service:	Telecom:	Consulting:
Accessories:	Corporate:	Y	Long Distance:	TV/Cable or Wireless:	Communication:	Contract Manufacturing:
Network Equipment:	Telecom:		Cellular:	Games:	Distribution:	Processing:
Chips/Circuits:	Internet:		Internet Service:	Financial Data:	VAR/Reseller:	Staff/Outsourcing:
Parts/Drives:					Satellite Srv./Equip.:	Specialty Services:

TYPES OF BUSINESS:

Computer Software-Desktop & Publishing
Document Management Software
Photo Editing & Management Software
Graphic Design Software

BRANDS/DIVISIONS/AFFILIATES:

Adobe Acrobat
Adobe Flash Player
Adobe Photoshop
Adobe Creative Suite
Adobe Air
Day Software Holding AG
Omniture Inc
Adobe LiveCycle

CONTACTS: Note: Officers with more than one job title may be intentionally listed here more than once.

Shantanu Narayen, CEO
Shantanu Narayen, Pres.
Mark Garrett, CFO/Exec. VP
Ann Lewnes, Sr. VP-Global Mktg.
Donna Morris, Sr. VP-Human Resources
Gerri Martin-Flickinger, CIO/Sr. VP
Kevin Lynch, CTO
Karen Cottle, General Counsel/Sr. VP/Corp. Sec.
Matthew Thompson, Sr. VP-Worldwide Field Oper.
Paul Weiskopf, Sr. VP-Corp. Dev.
David Wadhwani, Sr. VP/Gen. Mgr.-Creative & Interactive Solutions
Christine Castro, VP-Corp. Comm.
Mike Saviage, VP-Investor Rel.
John E. Warnock, Co-Chmn.
Naresh Gupta, Sr. VP-Print & Classic Publishing Solutions Unit
John Loiacono, Sr. VP/Gen. Mgr.-Digital Media Solutions Bus. Unit
Charles M. Geschke, Co-Chmn.
Naresh Gupta, Managing Dir.-R&D, India

Phone: 408-536-6000	Fax: 408-537-6000
Toll-Free: 800-833-6687	
Address: 345 Park Ave., San Jose, CA 95110-2704 US	

GROWTH PLANS/SPECIAL FEATURES:

Adobe Systems, Inc. is one of the largest software companies in the world. It offers a line of creative, business, web and mobile software and services used by creative professionals, knowledge workers, consumers, original equipment manufacturers, developers and enterprises for creating, managing, delivering, optimizing and engaging with content across multiple operating systems, devices and media. The company operates in six segments: creative solutions; knowledge worker; enterprise; Omniture; platform; and print and publishing. The creative solutions segment focuses primarily on professional creative clients such as graphic designers, production artists, web designers, photographers and prepress professionals. Products include Adobe After Effects Professional, Adobe Creative Suite, Adobe Photoshop and Adobe Dreamweaver. The knowledge worker segment focuses on knowledge clients such as accountants, attorneys, architects, educators, engineers and stock analysts. This segment includes the Adobe Acrobat family of products. The enterprise segment provides server-based Customer Experience Management Solutions, including collaboration, data capture, information assurance, document output, process management and content services, to corporate and government customers. Products include Adobe LiveCycle and Adobe Connect. The Omniture segment, created when Adobe acquired web analytics company Omniture, Inc., provides online business optimization products and services. The platform segment includes client and developer technologies, such as Adobe Flash Player, Adobe AIR and Adobe ColdFusion. Finally, the print and publishing segment addresses market opportunities ranging from technical and business publishing to legacy type printing. In 2010, the firm opened three new data centers in North America, Asia and Europe. In October 2010, Adobe acquired Day Software Holding AG, an Enterprise Content Management (ECM) company. In December 2010, the company announced a strategic alliance with Deloitte Consulting related to enterprise systems.

The firm offers its employees life, disability, medical, dental, vision and prescription drug insurance; health care and dependent care reimbursement accounts; adoption assistance; an assistance program; product discounts; and a 401(k).

FINANCIALS: Sales and profits are in thousands of dollars—add 000 to get the full amount. 2010 Note: Financial information for 2010 was not available for all companies at press time.

2010 Sales: $3,800,000	2010 Profits: $774,680	U.S. Stock Ticker: ADBE
2009 Sales: $2,945,853	2009 Profits: $386,508	Int'l Ticker: Int'l Exchange:
2008 Sales: $3,579,889	2008 Profits: $871,814	Employees: 8,660
2007 Sales: $3,157,881	2007 Profits: $723,807	Fiscal Year Ends: 11/30
2006 Sales: $2,575,300	2006 Profits: $505,809	Parent Company:

SALARIES/BENEFITS:

Pension Plan:	ESOP Stock Plan:	Profit Sharing:	Top Exec. Salary: $875,000	Bonus: $
Savings Plan: Y	Stock Purch. Plan:		Second Exec. Salary: $510,000	Bonus: $

OTHER THOUGHTS:

Apparent Women Officers or Directors: 5
Hot Spot for Advancement for Women/Minorities: Y

LOCATIONS: ("Y" = Yes)

West:	Southwest:	Midwest:	Southeast:	Northeast:	International:
Y	Y			Y	Y

Note: Financial information, benefits and other data can change quickly and may vary from those stated here.

ADTRAN INC
www.adtran.com

Industry Group Code: 334210 Ranks within this company's industry group: Sales: 10   Profits: 3

Hardware:	Software:	Telecommunications:	Electronic Publishing:	Equipment:		Specialty Services:
Computers:	Consumer:	Local:	Online Service:	Telecom:	Y	Consulting:
Accessories:	Corporate:	Long Distance:	TV/Cable or Wireless:	Communication:		Contract Manufacturing:
Network Equipment: Y	Telecom: Y	Cellular:	Games:	Distribution:		Processing:
Chips/Circuits:	Internet:	Internet Service:	Financial Data:	VAR/Reseller:		Staff/Outsourcing:
Parts/Drives:				Satellite Srv./Equip.:		Specialty Services:

TYPES OF BUSINESS:
Carrier Networks
Enterprise Networks

BRANDS/DIVISIONS/AFFILIATES:
Total Access 500
Total Reach
Total Access 300
NetVanta

CONTACTS: Note: Officers with more than one job title may be intentionally listed here more than once.
Thomas R. Stanton, CEO
James E. Matthews, CFO
Kevin W. Schneider, CTO
James E. Matthews, Corp. Sec.
Michael Foliano, Sr. VP-Global Oper.
Tammie Dodson, Contact-Public Rel.
Gayle Ellis, Contact-Investor Rel.
James E. Matthews, Sr. VP-Finance/Treas.
Jay Wilson, Sr. VP/Gen. Mgr.-Carrier Networks Div.
Rick Schansman, Sr. VP/Gen Mgr.-Enterprise Networks Div.
Thomas R. Stanton, Chmn.

Phone: 256-963-8000	Fax: 256-963-8030
Toll-Free: 800-923-8726	
Address: 901 Explorer Blvd., Huntsville, AL 35806 US	

GROWTH PLANS/SPECIAL FEATURES:
ADTRAN, Inc. designs, manufactures, markets and services network access solutions for communications networks for use across IP, Asynchronous Transfer Mode (ATM) and Time Division Multiplexed (TDM) architectures. The company's products are used to enable voice, data, video and Internet communications across copper, fiber and wireless networks; to deploy new broadband networks; and to upgrade slower, established networks. ADTRAN operates in two segments: carrier networks, which accounts for about 77% of net sales, and enterprise networks, about 23% of sales. The carrier networks division caters to service providers with products that deliver voice, data and video services from their equipment to a customer's premises. The enterprise networks division provides products used by enterprise customers to construct voice, data and video networks within an enterprise customer's site or between distributed sites. ADTRAN sells over 1,700 high-speed network access and communications devices. All of the company's products are used to link end-user subscribers to a local service provider, called last mile access products. Products fall into three categories: carrier systems, business networking and loop access. Carrier systems include broadband access and optical access product lines, as well as the Total Access 500 multi-service access and aggregation platform. The business networking category includes Integrated Access Devices (IADs), Optical Network Terminals (ONTs) and Internetworking products such as IP Business Gateways and the NetVanta product line, which includes multi-service routers, managed Ethernet switches and IP phone products. The loop access category includes products such as Digital Data Service (DDS), Integrated Services Digital Network (Total Reach) products and High bit-rate Digital Subscriber Line (HDSL) products, including Total Access 3000 HDSL.

Employees are offered medical, dental and vision insurance; life insurance; short- and long-term disability coverage; flexible spending accounts; an employee assistance program; on-site medical services; a 401(k) plan; educational assistance; and computer purchase assistance.

FINANCIALS: Sales and profits are in thousands of dollars—add 000 to get the full amount. 2010 Note: Financial information for 2010 was not available for all companies at press time.
2010 Sales: $	2010 Profits: $	U.S. Stock Ticker: ADTN
2009 Sales: $484,185	2009 Profits: $74,221	Int'l Ticker: Int'l Exchange:
2008 Sales: $500,676	2008 Profits: $78,581	Employees: 1,606
2007 Sales: $476,778	2007 Profits: $76,335	Fiscal Year Ends: 12/31
2006 Sales: $472,708	2006 Profits: $78,333	Parent Company:

SALARIES/BENEFITS:
Pension Plan:	ESOP Stock Plan:	Profit Sharing:	Top Exec. Salary: $471,290	Bonus: $
Savings Plan: Y	Stock Purch. Plan:		Second Exec. Salary: $434,941	Bonus: $

OTHER THOUGHTS:
Apparent Women Officers or Directors: 2
Hot Spot for Advancement for Women/Minorities:

LOCATIONS: ("Y" = Yes)
West:	Southwest:	Midwest:	Southeast:	Northeast:	International:
Y	Y	Y	Y		Y

ADVANCED MICRO DEVICES INC (AMD)
www.amd.com

Industry Group Code: 33441 Ranks within this company's industry group: Sales: 7 Profits: 10

Hardware:		Software:		Telecommunications:	Electronic Publishing:	Equipment:	Specialty Services:
Computers:	Y	Consumer:		Local:	Online Service:	Telecom:	Consulting:
Accessories:		Corporate:		Long Distance:	TV/Cable or Wireless:	Communication:	Contract Manufacturing:
Network Equipment:		Telecom:		Cellular:	Games:	Distribution:	Processing:
Chips/Circuits:	Y	Internet:		Internet Service:	Financial Data:	VAR/Reseller:	Staff/Outsourcing:
Parts/Drives:						Satellite Srv./Equip.:	Specialty Services:

TYPES OF BUSINESS:
Microprocessors
Semiconductors
Chipsets
Wafer Manufacturing
Multimedia Graphics

BRANDS/DIVISIONS/AFFILIATES:
GLOBALFOUNDRIES, Inc.
Advanced Technology Investment Company
West Coast Hitech L.P.
Broadcom Corp.
Qualcomm, Inc.
ATI Technologies Inc.

CONTACTS: Note: Officers with more than one job title may be intentionally listed here more than once.
Thomas Seifert, Interim CEO
Robert J. Rivet, COO
Thomas Seifert, CFO/Sr. VP
Nigel Dessau, Chief Mktg. Officer/Sr. VP
Allen Sockwell, Sr. VP-Human Resources/Chief Talent Officer
Amhed Mahmoud, CIO/Sr. VP
Chekib Akrout, Sr. VP-Tech. Group
Rick Bergman, Sr. VP/Gen. Mgr.-Prod. Div.
Robert J. Rivet, Chief Admin. Officer
Thomas M. McCoy, Exec. VP-Legal Affairs
Marty Seyer, Corp. Strategy Officer/Sr. VP
Thomas M. McCoy, Exec. VP-Corp. & Public Affairs
Emilio Ghilardi, Chief Sales Officer/Sr. VP
Bruce L. Claflin, Chmn.

Phone: 408-749-4000	Fax:
Toll-Free:	
Address: 1 AMD Pl., Sunnyvale, CA 94088 US	

GROWTH PLANS/SPECIAL FEATURES:
Advanced Micro Devices, Inc. (AMD) is a global semiconductor company that provides processing products for the computing, graphics and consumer electronics markets. It supplies x86 microprocessors for the commercial and consumer markets; embedded microprocessors for commercial, commercial client and consumer markets; chipsets for desktop and notebook PCs, professional workstations and servers; and graphics, video and multimedia products for desktop and notebook computers, including home media PCs and professional workstations, servers and technology for game consoles. AMD has operations across the U.S., Canada, South and Central America, Europe, Africa, the Middle East and the Asia Pacific region. The company operates through three segments: Computing Solutions; Graphics; and Foundry. AMD's Computing Solutions segment encompasses microprocessors, chipsets and embedded processors. The Graphics segment consists of graphics, video and multimedia products, as well as royalties from the sale of game consoles that incorporate the firm's graphics technology. The Foundry segment consists of the operations of GLOBALFOUNDRIES, Inc., a manufacturing joint venture whose operations include front end wafer manufacturing and related activities. The firm's products include the Phenom line of processors for desktop PCs; Radeon graphic products for Desktop PCs; Crossfire chipsets; FirePro professional graphics products; Opteron, Athlon and Turion embedded processors; and the Fusion line of accelerated processing units (APUs).

FINANCIALS: Sales and profits are in thousands of dollars—add 000 to get the full amount. 2010 Note: Financial information for 2010 was not available for all companies at press time.

2010 Sales: $	2010 Profits: $	U.S. Stock Ticker: AMD
2009 Sales: $5,403,000	2009 Profits: $293,000	Int'l Ticker: Int'l Exchange:
2008 Sales: $5,808,000	2008 Profits: $-3,098,000	Employees: 13,400
2007 Sales: $5,858,000	2007 Profits: $-3,379,000	Fiscal Year Ends: 12/31
2006 Sales: $5,627,000	2006 Profits: $-166,000	Parent Company:

SALARIES/BENEFITS:

Pension Plan:	ESOP Stock Plan:	Profit Sharing:	Top Exec. Salary: $792,685	Bonus: $45,000
Savings Plan: Y	Stock Purch. Plan:		Second Exec. Salary: $596,258	Bonus: $24,375

OTHER THOUGHTS:
Apparent Women Officers or Directors: 1
Hot Spot for Advancement for Women/Minorities:

LOCATIONS: ("Y" = Yes)

West:	Southwest:	Midwest:	Southeast:	Northeast:	International:
Y	Y	Y	Y	Y	Y

Note: Financial information, benefits and other data can change quickly and may vary from those stated here.

ADVANCED SEMICONDUCTOR ENGINEERING INC

www.aseglobal.com

Industry Group Code: 333295 Ranks within this company's industry group: Sales: 2   Profits: 2

Hardware:		Software:	Telecommunications:	Electronic Publishing:	Equipment:	Specialty Services:	
Computers:		Consumer:	Local:	Online Service:	Telecom:	Consulting:	
Accessories:		Corporate:	Long Distance:	TV/Cable or Wireless:	Communication:	Contract Manufacturing:	Y
Network Equipment:		Telecom:	Cellular:	Games:	Distribution:	Processing:	
Chips/Circuits:	Y	Internet:	Internet Service:	Financial Data:	VAR/Reseller:	Staff/Outsourcing:	
Parts/Drives:					Satellite Srv./Equip.:	Specialty Services:	Y

TYPES OF BUSINESS:
Semiconductor Manufacturing
Semiconductor Packaging Services
Design & Testing Services

BRANDS/DIVISIONS/AFFILIATES:
ASE Group
Universal Scientific Industrial Co Ltd
ASE Electronics
Hung Ching
ISE Labs Inc

CONTACTS: *Note: Officers with more than one job title may be intentionally listed here more than once.*
Jason C.S. Chang, CEO
Tien Wu, COO
Richard H.P. Chang, Pres./Vice Chmn.
Joseph Tung, CFO/VP
Allen Kan, Mgr.-Investor Rel.
Raymond Lo, Pres., ASE Test Taiwan/Gen. Mgr.-Kaohsiung
Tien Wu, CEO-ISE Labs, Inc.
Cheng-Jung Wei, Pres., Universal Scientific Industrial Co.
Samuel Liu, CEO-Universal Scientific Industrial Co.
Jason C.S. Chang, Chmn.
Ung Bae, Pres., ASE Korea

Phone: 886-7-361-7131	Fax: 886-7-361-3094
Toll-Free:	
Address: 26 Chin 3rd Rd., Nantze Export Processing Zone, Kaohsiung, Taiwan	

GROWTH PLANS/SPECIAL FEATURES:
Advanced Semiconductor Engineering, Inc. (ASE) is a leading provider of semiconductor packaging, also called assembly, which is the process of turning bare semiconductors into finished semiconductors, and semiconductor testing services. ASE semiconductor assembly products are available in a variety of formats, including dual-in-line packages, quad packages, ball-grid arrays (BGAs), pin grid arrays (PGAs), chip scale packages (CSPs), system-in-package (SiPs), 3D packages, wafer bumping, flip chips and lead-free packages. These assemblies are used to connect the integrated circuit, or die, to the printed circuit board, protecting the die and facilitating electrical connections and heat dissipation. ASE provides services at all stages of the semiconductor manufacturing process except circuit design and wafer fabrication. Its service capabilities include front-end engineering testing, which is the testing of prototypes that takes place before volume production, including software development, electrical verification, reliability analysis and failure analysis; wafer probing, testing each chip on a wafer for defects packaging; and final testing, which makes sure that the product is functional before being sent to customers or assembled into electronic products. Company affiliates and subsidiaries include Universal Scientific Industrial Co. Ltd., which provides design manufacturing services from board design to systems assembly; ASE Electronics, a supplier of substrates and packaging material; Hung Ching, a company engaged in the development and management of commercial, residential and industrial real estate properties in Taiwan; and U.S.-based ISE Labs, Inc., a front-end engineering test firm. The firm's semiconductors are used in communications, computers, consumer electronics, industrial, automotive and other applications. ASE has operations in Taiwan, South Korea, Japan, Hong Kong, Singapore and Malaysia, as well as the Americas and Europe. In February 2010, the firm acquired full control of Universal Scientific Industrial Co. In May 2010, it broke ground on a new manufacturing facility in Taiwan.

FINANCIALS: Sales and profits are in thousands of dollars—add 000 to get the full amount. 2010 Note: Financial information for 2010 was not available for all companies at press time.

2010 Sales: $	2010 Profits: $	**U.S. Stock Ticker: ASX**
2009 Sales: $2,716,120	2009 Profits: $213,550	Int'l Ticker: 2311 Int'l Exchange: Taipei-TPE
2008 Sales: $2,779,400	2008 Profits: $181,310	Employees: 29,538
2007 Sales: $2,977,540	2007 Profits: $358,050	Fiscal Year Ends: 12/31
2006 Sales: $3,081,400	2006 Profits: $534,400	Parent Company:

SALARIES/BENEFITS:
Pension Plan:	ESOP Stock Plan:	Profit Sharing:	Top Exec. Salary: $	Bonus: $
Savings Plan:	Stock Purch. Plan:		Second Exec. Salary: $	Bonus: $

OTHER THOUGHTS:
Apparent Women Officers or Directors:
Hot Spot for Advancement for Women/Minorities:

LOCATIONS: ("Y" = Yes)
West:	Southwest:	Midwest:	Southeast:	Northeast:	International:
Y	Y			Y	Y

ADVANTEST CORPORATION

www.advantest.co.jp

Industry Group Code: 333295 **Ranks within this company's industry group:** Sales: 8 Profits: 12

Hardware:		Software:		Telecommunications:		Electronic Publishing:		Equipment:		Specialty Services:	
Computers:		Consumer:		Local:		Online Service:		Telecom:		Consulting:	
Accessories:	Y	Corporate:		Long Distance:		TV/Cable or Wireless:		Communication:		Contract Manufacturing:	
Network Equipment:		Telecom:		Cellular:		Games:		Distribution:		Processing:	
Chips/Circuits:	Y	Internet:		Internet Service:		Financial Data:		VAR/Reseller:		Staff/Outsourcing:	
Parts/Drives:								Satellite Srv./Equip.:		Specialty Services:	Y

TYPES OF BUSINESS:

Electronics Testing Equipment
Semiconductor & Component Test Systems
Mechatronics
Service & Other

BRANDS/DIVISIONS/AFFILIATES:

Advantest Finance Inc
Advantest Laboratories Ltd
Advantest Manufacturing Inc
Japan Engineering Inc
Advantest (Europe) GmbH
Advantest America Inc
Credence Systems GmbH

CONTACTS: *Note: Officers with more than one job title may be intentionally listed here more than once.*

Haruo Matsuno, CEO
Haruo Matsuno, Pres.
Hiroyasu Sawai, Sr. VP-Mktg. & Sales
Yoshiaki Yoshida, VP-New Concept Prod. Initiative
Shinichiro Kuroe, Managing Exec. Officer-Tech. Dev.
Hideaki Imada, Sr. VP-Prod.
Yuichi Kurita, Sr. VP-Admin.
Yuichi Kurita, Sr. VP-Corp. Planning
Masao Shimizu, Sr. VP-System Solutions
Yasuhiro Kawata, Sr. VP-Quality Assurance
Toshio Maruyama, Chmn.
R. Keith Lee, Pres./CEO-Advantest America, Inc.

Phone: 81-3-3214-7500	Fax:
Toll-Free:	
Address: Shin-Marunouchi Ctr. Bldg., 1-6-2, Marunouchi, Tokyo, 100-0005 Japan	

GROWTH PLANS/SPECIAL FEATURES:

Advantest Corporation is a leading manufacturer of electronics and semiconductor testing equipment. The company has three business segments: semiconductor and component test systems; mechatronics systems; and services, support and other. The semiconductor and component test system segment provides customers with test system products for the semiconductor industry and the electronic component industry. The segment's products include test systems for memory semiconductors and non-memory conductors. Test systems for non-memory conductors are divided into test systems for system-on-chip (SoC) semiconductors, LCD driver integrated circuits and semiconductors for use in car electronics. The mechatronics division focuses on peripheral devices such as test handlers, device interfaces and operations related to nanotechnology. The third segment consists of comprehensive customer solutions provided in connection with the first two segments, along with support services and an equipment leasing business. The firm has 14 Japanese subsidiaries and 16 overseas subsidiaries, including Advantest Laboratories Ltd.; Advantest Finance, Inc.; Advantest Manufacturing, Inc.; Japan Engineering Co., Ltd.; Advantest (Europe) GmbH; and Advantest America, Inc. In 2009, sales to Japan accounted for 23% of the firm's net sales; the rest of Asia represented 64%, while sales in the Americas and Europe were 9% and 4%, respectively.

The company offers U.S. employees a 401(k) plan; medical, dental and vision plans; flexible spending accounts; a bonus plan; and an employee assistance program.

FINANCIALS: Sales and profits are in thousands of dollars—add 000 to get the full amount. 2010 Note: Financial information for 2010 was not available for all companies at press time.

2010 Sales: $572,066	2010 Profits: $-123,108	**U.S. Stock Ticker:** ATE
2009 Sales: $780,332	2009 Profits: $-762,517	**Int'l Ticker:** 6857 Int'l Exchange: Tokyo-TSE
2008 Sales: $1,824,204	2008 Profits: $165,186	Employees: 3,151
2007 Sales: $1,990,784	2007 Profits: $301,194	Fiscal Year Ends: 3/31
2006 Sales: $2,161,590	2006 Profits: $352,209	Parent Company:

SALARIES/BENEFITS:

Pension Plan:	ESOP Stock Plan:	Profit Sharing:	Top Exec. Salary: $	Bonus: $
Savings Plan: Y	Stock Purch. Plan:		Second Exec. Salary: $	Bonus: $

OTHER THOUGHTS:

Apparent Women Officers or Directors:
Hot Spot for Advancement for Women/Minorities:

LOCATIONS: ("Y" = Yes)

West:	Southwest:	Midwest:	Southeast:	Northeast:	International:
Y	Y			Y	Y

Note: Financial information, benefits and other data can change quickly and may vary from those stated here.

AFFILIATED COMPUTER SERVICES INC

www.acs-inc.com

Industry Group Code: 541513 Ranks within this company's industry group: Sales: 8 Profits: 9

Hardware:	Software:	Telecommunications:	Electronic Publishing:	Equipment:	Specialty Services:	
Computers:	Consumer:	Local:	Online Service:	Telecom:	Consulting:	Y
Accessories:	Corporate:	Long Distance:	TV/Cable or Wireless:	Communication:	Contract Manufacturing:	
Network Equipment:	Telecom:	Cellular:	Games:	Distribution:	Processing:	Y
Chips/Circuits:	Internet:	Internet Service:	Financial Data:	VAR/Reseller:	Staff/Outsourcing:	Y
Parts/Drives:				Satellite Srv./Equip.:	Specialty Services:	Y

TYPES OF BUSINESS:

IT Consulting
Loan Processing Services
Systems Integration
Human Resources Services
IT Outsourcing
Business Process Outsourcing

BRANDS/DIVISIONS/AFFILIATES:

Xerox Corp
Buck Consultants
e-Services Group International
Anix
Pharm/DUR Inc.
ExcellerateHRO, LLP
TMS Health
Spur Information Solutions

CONTACTS: Note: Officers with more than one job title may be intentionally listed here more than once.

Lynn Blodgett, CEO
Tom Blodgett, COO
Lynn Blodgett, Pres.
Kevin Kyser, CFO/Exec. VP
Tracy Tolbert, Exec. VP-Sales
Lora Villarreal, Chief People Officer/Exec. VP
Chris Leach, Chief Info. Security Officer
Tom Blodgett, Exec. VP-Commercial Oper.
John Rexford, Exec. VP-Corp. Dev.
Rebecca Scholl, Sr. VP-Corp. Mktg. & Comm.
Ann Vezina, Exec. VP/Pres., Enterprise Solutions & Svcs.
Connie Harvey, Exec. VP/Pres., Healthcare Payer & Insurance
Derrell James, Exec. VP/Pres., IT Outsourcing Solutions
David Amoriell, Exec. VP/Pres., Transportation Solutions

Phone: 214-841-6111	Fax: 214-823-9369
Toll-Free:	
Address: 2828 N. Haskell Ave., Dallas, TX 75204 US	

GROWTH PLANS/SPECIAL FEATURES:

Affiliated Computer Services, Inc. (ACS), a subsidiary of Xerox Corp., provides business process outsourcing and IT services to commercial and government clients. The company operates in two segments: commercial and government. Through the commercial segment, ACS provides business process outsourcing, systems integration services and consulting services to a variety of commercial clients. The commercial segment is focused on markets including communications and consumer goods; healthcare; higher education; transportation; consumer goods and services; and financial services. Its solutions for the commercial segment include IT services; human capital management; finance and accounting; customer care; transaction processing; payment services; and commercial education. Services in the government market include technology and business process based services with a focus on transaction processing, child support payment processing, electronic toll collection, traffic violations processing, program management services (such as Medicaid fiscal agent services) and student loan processing and servicing. ACS serves customers in over 100 countries from more than 425 offices worldwide. Through subsidiary Buck Consultants the firm provides human resources consulting services to corporations. Among its acquisitions in 2009 were e-Services Group International; Anix; and Pharm/DUR Inc. In 2010, it acquired several other IT and consulting services companies, including ExcellerateHRO, LLP in August; TMS Health in October; and Spur Information Solutions in November. In February 2010, Xerox Corporation completed its acquisition of ACS for $6.4 billion.

FINANCIALS: Sales and profits are in thousands of dollars—add 000 to get the full amount. 2010 Note: Financial information for 2010 was not available for all companies at press time.

2010 Sales: $	2010 Profits: $	**U.S. Stock Ticker: Subsidiary**
2009 Sales: $6,523,164	2009 Profits: $349,943	**Int'l Ticker:** Int'l Exchange:
2008 Sales: $6,160,550	2008 Profits: $329,010	Employees: 74,000
2007 Sales: $5,772,479	2007 Profits: $253,090	Fiscal Year Ends: 6/30
2006 Sales: $5,353,661	2006 Profits: $358,806	Parent Company: XEROX CORP

SALARIES/BENEFITS:

Pension Plan:	ESOP Stock Plan:	Profit Sharing:	Top Exec. Salary: $1,013,491	Bonus: $1,228,555
Savings Plan: Y	Stock Purch. Plan:		Second Exec. Salary: $845,769	Bonus: $821,100

OTHER THOUGHTS:

Apparent Women Officers or Directors: 4
Hot Spot for Advancement for Women/Minorities: Y

LOCATIONS: ("Y" = Yes)

West:	Southwest:	Midwest:	Southeast:	Northeast:	International:
Y	Y	Y	Y	Y	Y

AHNLAB INC

global.ahnlab.com

Industry Group Code: 511210E Ranks within this company's industry group: Sales: 11 Profits: 5

Hardware:	Software:		Telecommunications:	Electronic Publishing:	Equipment:	Specialty Services:	
Computers:	Consumer:	Y	Local:	Online Service:	Telecom:	Consulting:	Y
Accessories:	Corporate:	Y	Long Distance:	TV/Cable or Wireless:	Communication:	Contract Manufacturing:	
Network Equipment:	Telecom:		Cellular:	Games:	Distribution:	Processing:	
Chips/Circuits:	Internet:		Internet Service:	Financial Data:	VAR/Reseller:	Staff/Outsourcing:	Y
Parts/Drives:					Satellite Srv./Equip.:	Specialty Services:	

TYPES OF BUSINESS:

Information Protection Software
Computer Network Security Consulting
Personalized Software Development
Mobile Device Software Protection

BRANDS/DIVISIONS/AFFILIATES:

TrusGuard
V3 Product Family
V3 Net
V3 NetGroup
V3 Internet Security 7.0 Platinum Enterprise
V3 VirusWall
SiteGuard
AhnLab HackShield Pro

CONTACTS: Note: Officers with more than one job title may be intentionally listed here more than once.

Hongsun Kim, CEO
Charles Ahn, Chmn.

Phone: 82-2-2186-6000	Fax: 82-2-2186-6100
Toll-Free:	
Address: Yongdungpo-Gu, Yeouido-Dong 12 CCCM Bldg., 6 Fl., Seoul, 150-869 Korea	

GROWTH PLANS/SPECIAL FEATURES:

Ahnlab, Inc. is a Korean company that specializes in developing information security software products. In addition to security software development, the company offers clients security consulting services. The firm offers the V3 family of products, which includes anti-virus solutions preserving the safety of all information environments that viruses can infiltrate. This family is comprised of the V3Net series for file servers; the V3NetGroup series for groupware servers; and the V3VirusWall series, which are gateway anti-virus solutions. Ahnlab also develops mobile device protection software and personalized information-protection software packages aimed at small- and medium-sized businesses, educational bodies and large corporations, such as the V3 Internet Security 7.0 Platinum Enterprise. The company's TrusGuard series consists of network security appliances. Its AOS (AhnLab Online Security) service provides a complete defense system to protect users from online threats. Specific tools within AOS include an anti-keylogger, anti-virus and anti-spyware, a robust firewall and a secure browser. Other online protection tolls include AhnLab HackShield Pro, which is designed especially for online gamers and detects hacking activity in real time; and the SiteGuard service, which blocks risk containing web sites. AhnLab also offers outsourced IT security through its AhnLab MSS (managed security services). Consulting services focus on checking security risks and operate through AhnLab Security Engineering Methodology (ASEM) and AhnLab Security Audit Consulting (ASAC). Ahnlab maintains partnerships all over the world, including S&F Scout and Wise Network in the U.S.; Damage Control S.A. de C.V. in Mexico; IPSteel in France; PT Tekhan Indo Mas in Indonesia; E-Plus Mutli Media Pte Ltd. in Singapore; Ingenuity in Malaysia; and LogicToken Limited in Hong Kong.

FINANCIALS: Sales and profits are in thousands of dollars—add 000 to get the full amount. 2010 Note: Financial information for 2010 was not available for all companies at press time.

2010 Sales: $	2010 Profits: $	**U.S. Stock Ticker:**
2009 Sales: $61,880	2009 Profits: $12,670	Int'l Ticker: 053800 Int'l Exchange: Seoul-KRX
2008 Sales: $58,060	2008 Profits: $7,880	Employees: 6,013
2007 Sales: $41,480	2007 Profits: $12,210	Fiscal Year Ends: 12/31
2006 Sales: $32,090	2006 Profits: $10,780	Parent Company:

SALARIES/BENEFITS:

Pension Plan:	ESOP Stock Plan:	Profit Sharing:	Top Exec. Salary: $	Bonus: $
Savings Plan:	Stock Purch. Plan:		Second Exec. Salary: $	Bonus: $

OTHER THOUGHTS:

Apparent Women Officers or Directors:
Hot Spot for Advancement for Women/Minorities:

LOCATIONS: ("Y" = Yes)

West:	Southwest:	Midwest:	Southeast:	Northeast:	International:
					Y

AISINO CORPORATION INC

www.aisino.com

Industry Group Code: 334111   Ranks within this company's industry group: Sales: 20   Profits: 9

Hardware:		Software:		Telecommunications:	Electronic Publishing:	Equipment:	Specialty Services:	
Computers:		Consumer:		Local:	Online Service:	Telecom:	Consulting:	
Accessories:	Y	Corporate:	Y	Long Distance:	TV/Cable or Wireless:	Communication:	Contract Manufacturing:	
Network Equipment:		Telecom:		Cellular:	Games:	Distribution:	Processing:	
Chips/Circuits:		Internet:		Internet Service:	Financial Data:	VAR/Reseller:	Staff/Outsourcing:	
Parts/Drives:						Satellite Srv./Equip.:	Specialty Services:	Y

TYPES OF BUSINESS:
Information Security Products
Digital Media Equipment
Printer Terminal Equipment

BRANDS/DIVISIONS/AFFILIATES:
Aisino Bill Master
Aisino Finance & Taxation Security Card

CONTACTS: Note: Officers with more than one job title may be intentionally listed here more than once.
Zhennan Liu, Pres.
Qiujia Pan, CFO
Yumin Wang, Corp. Sec.
Jiangning Chen, Deputy Pres.
Zhennan Liu, Chmn.

Phone: 86-10-8889-6666	Fax: 86-10-8889-6888
Toll-Free:	
Address: No. 18A, Xingshikou St., Haidian District, Beijing, 100097 China	

GROWTH PLANS/SPECIAL FEATURES:

Aisino Corporation, Inc., founded in 2000, is a developer of information security technologies. It provides software and solutions that protect and secure electronic governmental affairs, including its golden tax business and its Jindun business. The golden tax suite of products integrates processes related to the submission and collection of enterprise taxes. These include an online collection system, taxation enforcement management, general invoice control and an anti-counterfeit tax-control group of products. The Jindun business provides a system of integrated products for the acquisition of social and population information, such as the fingerprint IC card anti-cheat system, which utilizes communication capture and test paper barcode technology for fingerprint examination. Additionally, the Jindun business offers integrated security products focused on the maintenance of public security. For enterprises the firm combines its IT services with enterprise management software, value-added applications and application system integration. Specific value-added application products include Aisino Bill Master, a universal bill printing software, and the Aisino Finance & Taxation Security Card, which acts as a multifunctional computer, providing security and virus protection and upgrade features. The firm's gold card business products include ticket systems, which provide management for ticket operations; and the online highway non-stop collection system solution, which transmits voice, image and data information by using IP over SDH and TCP/IP protocol group technology. Other products within the gold card business include a general PDA smart card and a toll collection card box. Aisino also offers a variety of digital media, PC and terminal equipment, including set top boxes, servers and bill printers.

FINANCIALS: Sales and profits are in thousands of dollars—add 000 to get the full amount. 2010 Note: Financial information for 2010 was not available for all companies at press time.

2010 Sales: $	2010 Profits: $	U.S. Stock Ticker:
2009 Sales: $1,136,300	2009 Profits: $92,600	Int'l Ticker: 600271 Int'l Exchange: Singapore-SIN
2008 Sales: $867,310	2008 Profits: $80,940	Employees:
2007 Sales: $705,530	2007 Profits: $68,830	Fiscal Year Ends: 12/31
2006 Sales: $	2006 Profits: $	Parent Company:

SALARIES/BENEFITS:

Pension Plan:	ESOP Stock Plan:	Profit Sharing:	Top Exec. Salary: $	Bonus: $
Savings Plan:	Stock Purch. Plan:		Second Exec. Salary: $	Bonus: $

OTHER THOUGHTS:
Apparent Women Officers or Directors:
Hot Spot for Advancement for Women/Minorities:

LOCATIONS: ("Y" = Yes)

West:	Southwest:	Midwest:	Southeast:	Northeast:	International:
					Y

AKAMAI TECHNOLOGIES INC

www.akamai.com

Industry Group Code: 518210 Ranks within this company's industry group: Sales: 1 Profits: 1

Hardware:	Software:		Telecommunications:	Electronic Publishing:	Equipment:	Specialty Services:	
Computers:	Consumer:		Local:	Online Service:	Telecom:	Consulting:	
Accessories:	Corporate:	Y	Long Distance:	TV/Cable or Wireless:	Communication:	Contract Manufacturing:	
Network Equipment:	Telecom:	Y	Cellular:	Games:	Distribution:	Processing:	
Chips/Circuits:	Internet:	Y	Internet Service:	Financial Data:	VAR/Reseller:	Staff/Outsourcing:	
Parts/Drives:					Satellite Srv./Equip.:	Specialty Services:	Y

TYPES OF BUSINESS:

Online Information Service-Streaming Content
e-Business Software
Web Analytics
Online Content Distribution Support Services

BRANDS/DIVISIONS/AFFILIATES:

Velocitude LLC

CONTACTS: Note: Officers with more than one job title may be intentionally listed here more than once.

Paul Sagan, CEO
David Kenny, Pres.
J. D. Sherman, CFO
Robert W. Hughes, Exec. VP-Global Sales, Svcs. & Mktg.
Debra L. Canner, Sr. VP-Human Resources
Tom Leighton, Chief Scientist
Michael M. Afergan, CTO
Chris Schoettle, Exec. VP-Prod.
Harald Prokop, Sr. VP-Eng.
Melanie Haratunian, General Counsel/Sr. VP/Corp. Sec.
Robert Blumofe, Sr. VP-Oper. & Networks
Robert Wood, Chief Dev. Officer/VP
George Conrades, Chmn.

Phone: 617-444-3000	Fax: 617-444-3001
Toll-Free: 877-425-2624	
Address: 8 Cambridge Ctr., Cambridge, MA 02142-1401 US	

GROWTH PLANS/SPECIAL FEATURES:

Akamai Technologies, Inc. is a software and Internet content company that provides enterprise and government clients with e-business infrastructure services, enabling them to deliver web content and applications such as ads, video and other content at higher speeds and with greater reliability. Akamai's cloud-based distribution network is one of the largest in the world, consisting of 60,000 servers within 900 networks in over 70 countries, handling tens of billions of web interactions each day. Service offerings are broadly grouped into five areas: Application Performance Solutions; Digital Asset Solutions; Advertising Decision Solutions; Dynamic Site Solutions; and Other Solutions. Application Performance Solutions are designed to improve the performance of dynamic applications used by enterprises to connect with their employees, suppliers and customers, with a particular focus on portal applications and other web-based systems. Digital Asset Solutions allow customers to execute large file management and distribution strategies while improving end-user experience and reducing the costs associated with Internet-related infrastructure. Advertising Decision Solutions specialize in helping advertisers reach their target audiences online. Dynamic Site Solutions help to accelerate business-to-consumer web sites that integrate rich, collaborative content and applications within their online architecture, allowing for greater process optimization as well as localization and customization of content. Other solutions consist of Site Intelligence Offerings and Custom Solutions. Site Intelligence Offerings encompass network data feeds and web site analytics, giving clients real time access to data regarding the performance of their sites. Custom Solutions include a range of individualized services, such as facilitating content delivery behind firewalls and supporting mission-critical applications relying on intranets. In June 2010, Akamai acquired Velocitude, LLC, which specializes in delivering content to mobile devices.

Akamai offers its employees medical, dental and vision coverage; short- and long-term disability; a 401(k) plan; life and AD&D insurance; and an employee stock purchase plan, among other benefits.

FINANCIALS: Sales and profits are in thousands of dollars—add 000 to get the full amount. 2010 Note: Financial information for 2010 was not available for all companies at press time.

2010 Sales: $	2010 Profits: $	U.S. Stock Ticker: AKAM
2009 Sales: $859,773	2009 Profits: $145,913	Int'l Ticker: Int'l Exchange:
2008 Sales: $790,924	2008 Profits: $212,264	Employees: 1,750
2007 Sales: $636,406	2007 Profits: $100,967	Fiscal Year Ends: 12/31
2006 Sales: $428,672	2006 Profits: $57,401	Parent Company:

SALARIES/BENEFITS:

Pension Plan:	ESOP Stock Plan:	Profit Sharing:	Top Exec. Salary: $536,113	Bonus: $1,018,691
Savings Plan: Y	Stock Purch. Plan:		Second Exec. Salary: $428,453	Bonus: $571,863

OTHER THOUGHTS:

Apparent Women Officers or Directors: 4
Hot Spot for Advancement for Women/Minorities: Y

LOCATIONS: ("Y" = Yes)

West:	Southwest:	Midwest:	Southeast:	Northeast:	International:
Y	Y	Y	Y	Y	Y

ALCATEL-LUCENT

www.alcatel-lucent.com

Industry Group Code: 334210 Ranks within this company's industry group: Sales: 2 Profits: 14

Hardware:		Software:		Telecommunications:		Electronic Publishing:		Equipment:		Specialty Services:	
Computers:		Consumer:		Local:		Online Service:		Telecom:	Y	Consulting:	Y
Accessories:	Y	Corporate:	Y	Long Distance:		TV/Cable or Wireless:		Communication:	Y	Contract Manufacturing:	
Network Equipment:	Y	Telecom:	Y	Cellular:		Games:		Distribution:		Processing:	
Chips/Circuits:		Internet:		Internet Service:		Financial Data:		VAR/Reseller:		Staff/Outsourcing:	Y
Parts/Drives:								Satellite Srv./Equip.:	Y	Specialty Services:	Y

TYPES OF BUSINESS:

Telecommunications Equipment Manufacturer
Telecommunications Software & Information Systems
Digital Switching Equipment
Optical Networking Equipment
Communications Convergence Solutions
Wireless Access & Transmission Equipment
Network Management
Consulting Services

BRANDS/DIVISIONS/AFFILIATES:

Genesys Telecommunications Laboratories
Bell Labs
Optism Mobile Advertising Solution
ProgrammableWeb
OpenPlug
Alcatel-Lucent Wireless Network Optimization

CONTACTS: Note: Officers with more than one job title may be intentionally listed here more than once.

Ben Verwaayen, CEO
Paul Tufano, CFO/Exec. VP
Stephen Carter, Chief Mktg. Officer/Exec. VP
Pierre Barnabe, Exec. VP-Human Resources & Transformation
Robin Dargue/Exec. VP, Head-IT Transformation & Business
Steve Reynolds, General Counsel
John Dickson, Head-Oper.
Stephen Carter, Chief Strategy & Comm. Officer
Gabrielle Gauthey, Sr. VP-Public Affairs
Rajeev Singh-Molares, Pres., Asia Pacific
Robert Vrij, Exec. VP/Pres., Americas
Jeong Kim, Exec. VP/Pres., Bell Labs
Vivek Mohan, Exec. VP/Pres., Svcs.
Philippe Camus, Chmn.
Adolfo Hernandez, Exec. VP/Pres., EMEA

Phone: 33-1-40-76-10-10	Fax:
Toll-Free: 800-252-2835	
Address: 3rd Ave. Octave Greard, Paris, 75007 France	

GROWTH PLANS/SPECIAL FEATURES:

Alcatel-Lucent provides solutions that enable service providers, enterprises and governments worldwide to deliver voice, data and video communication services to end-users. A leader in fixed, mobile and converged broadband networking, Internet Protocol (IP) and optics technologies, applications and services, Alcatel-Lucent offers end-to-end solutions that enable communications services for residential, business and mobile customers in over 130 countries. The company has four reporting segments: Applications Software, Carrier, Enterprise and Services. The Applications Software group develops software solutions related to digital home management, IP and broadcast messaging, digital media and subscriber data management. This segment also includes subsidiary Genesys Telecommunications Laboratories, which provides contact center management software. The Carrier product group offers IP, wireless, wireline and optics products and solutions for service providers. The Enterprise business group offers secure, real-time communication products for businesses, industries and the public sector. The Services business group supports some of the world's largest service providers with consultation, integration, migration and transformation, deployment and maintenance services for communication networks. Alcatel-Lucent runs Bell Laboratories, a leading communications technology research and development laboratory. Bell Laboratories also develops prototype devices and conducts research in areas such as digital networking and signal processing, communications satellites and cellular telephony. In April 2010, the company introduced Optism Mobile Advertising Solution which aids mobile operators in the development of new business and furthers advertiser's targeted audiences through permission based marketing. In June 2010, the firm acquired online destination ProgrammableWeb. In September 2010, Alcatel-Lucent acquired OpenPlug, an applications development and mobile software provider. In October 2010, the firm opened a new regional delivery center in Bangalore, India. In November 2010, the firm released the Alcatel-Lucent Wireless Network Optimization solution, a series of software products that offer consolidation, assessment, consulting and optimization services for mobile data and voice networks.

FINANCIALS: Sales and profits are in thousands of dollars—add 000 to get the full amount. 2010 Note: Financial information for 2010 was not available for all companies at press time.

2010 Sales: $	2010 Profits: $	U.S. Stock Ticker: ALU
2009 Sales: $21,723,000	2009 Profits: $-722,000	Int'l Ticker: ALU Int'l Exchange: Paris-Euronext
2008 Sales: $22,033,000	2008 Profits: $-6,710,830	Employees: 78,373
2007 Sales: $24,350,000	2007 Profits: $-4,810,000	Fiscal Year Ends: 12/31
2006 Sales: $16,410,600	2006 Profits: $-175,040	Parent Company:

SALARIES/BENEFITS:

Pension Plan:	ESOP Stock Plan:	Profit Sharing:	Top Exec. Salary: $	Bonus: $
Savings Plan:	Stock Purch. Plan:		Second Exec. Salary: $	Bonus: $

OTHER THOUGHTS:

Apparent Women Officers or Directors: 2
Hot Spot for Advancement for Women/Minorities: Y

LOCATIONS: ("Y" = Yes)

West:	Southwest:	Midwest:	Southeast:	Northeast:	International:
Y	Y	Y	Y	Y	Y

ALLEN SYSTEMS GROUP INC

www.asg.com

Industry Group Code: 511210H Ranks within this company's industry group: Sales: Profits:

Hardware:	Software:		Telecommunications:	Electronic Publishing:	Equipment:	Specialty Services:	
Computers:	Consumer:		Local:	Online Service:	Telecom:	Consulting:	Y
Accessories:	Corporate:	Y	Long Distance:	TV/Cable or Wireless:	Communication:	Contract Manufacturing:	
Network Equipment:	Telecom:		Cellular:	Games:	Distribution:	Processing:	
Chips/Circuits:	Internet:		Internet Service:	Financial Data:	VAR/Reseller:	Staff/Outsourcing:	
Parts/Drives:					Satellite Srv./Equip.:	Specialty Services:	

TYPES OF BUSINESS:

Software-Enterprise Productivity
e-Commerce Business Solutions
Consulting Services

BRANDS/DIVISIONS/AFFILIATES:

ASG-MedAppz
ASG Federal, Inc.
CTG Healthcare Solutions

CONTACTS: Note: Officers with more than one job title may be intentionally listed here more than once.

Arthur L. Allen, CEO
Derek Eckelman, COO
Arthur L. Allen, Pres.
Ernest J. Schneidmann, CFO/Exec. VP
Joseph Garabed, Sr. VP-Worldwide Sales
Tom Romnios, Exec VP-Global Human Resources
Alan Bolt, CIO/Exec. VP
John Connor, CTO
Derek Eckelman, General Counsel/Exec. VP
Richard Vance, Exec. VP-Oper.
John Connor, Sr. VP-Bus. Dev.
Tony Perri, VP-Corp. Comm. & Mktg.
Jim Bladich, Sr. VP-Sales Oper.

Phone: 239-435-2200	Fax: 239-263-3692
Toll-Free: 800-932-5536	
Address: 1333 3rd Ave. S., Naples, FL 34102 US	

GROWTH PLANS/SPECIAL FEATURES:

Allen Systems Group, Inc. (ASG) provides enterprise software and professional services in the metadata management, security management, applications management, operations management, content management, information and data management, performance management and infrastructure management markets. All products the company offers are developed in-house or acquired through company acquisitions. The company operates over 75 offices worldwide. Its customers represent a variety of industries, including financial and brokerage services, government, insurance, health care, retail, education, telecommunications, technology and manufacturing. ASG's professional services include configuration, installation and customization to assist clients' transition to e-business. The company's consultants aid clients in understanding business strategy, identifying business issues and then determining how software can be implemented to overcome such issues. Through ASG Federal, Inc., the firm supports the IT requirements of the Federal Government with network systems performance capabilities and metadata management solutions. ASG provides all levels of support for its products during business hours and emergency support during non-business hours. The company's clients include American Express; General Electric; Coca-Cola; HSBC; Verizon; Wells Fargo; Lockheed Martin; Sony; Procter & Gamble; and Toyota. In March 2010, the firm established a partnership with healthcare IT consulting firm CTG Healthcare Solutions to aid in the deployment of ASG's software-as-a-service (SaaS) electronic medical record solution, ASG-MedAppz.

ASG offers its employees a comprehensive health benefit and insurance plan, an employee assistance program, flexible spending and dependent care accounts, computer-based and classroom training through ASG University, tuition reimbursement and external management and technical seminars.

FINANCIALS: Sales and profits are in thousands of dollars—add 000 to get the full amount. 2010 Note: Financial information for 2010 was not available for all companies at press time.

2010 Sales: $	2010 Profits: $	**U.S. Stock Ticker: Private**
2009 Sales: $	2009 Profits: $	**Int'l Ticker:** Int'l Exchange:
2008 Sales: $	2008 Profits: $	Employees:
2007 Sales: $	2007 Profits: $	Fiscal Year Ends: 12/31
2006 Sales: $	2006 Profits: $	Parent Company:

SALARIES/BENEFITS:

Pension Plan:	ESOP Stock Plan:	Profit Sharing:	Top Exec. Salary: $	Bonus: $
Savings Plan: Y	Stock Purch. Plan:		Second Exec. Salary: $	Bonus: $

OTHER THOUGHTS:

Apparent Women Officers or Directors:
Hot Spot for Advancement for Women/Minorities:

LOCATIONS: ("Y" = Yes)

West:	Southwest:	Midwest:	Southeast:	Northeast:	International:
Y	Y	Y	Y	Y	Y

Note: Financial information, benefits and other data can change quickly and may vary from those stated here.

ALLSCRIPTS HEALTHCARE SOLUTIONS INC   www.allscripts.com

Industry Group Code: 511210D Ranks within this company's industry group: Sales: 2 Profits: 3

Hardware:	Software:		Telecommunications:	Electronic Publishing:	Equipment:	Specialty Services:	
Computers:	Consumer:		Local:	Online Service:	Telecom:	Consulting:	Y
Accessories:	Corporate:	Y	Long Distance:	TV/Cable or Wireless:	Communication:	Contract Manufacturing:	
Network Equipment:	Telecom:		Cellular:	Games:	Distribution:	Processing:	
Chips/Circuits:	Internet:		Internet Service:	Financial Data:	VAR/Reseller:	Staff/Outsourcing:	
Parts/Drives:					Satellite Srv./Equip.:	Specialty Services:	

TYPES OF BUSINESS:

Prescription Management Software
Interactive Education Services
Clinical Software
Electronic Records Systems
Care Management Software

BRANDS/DIVISIONS/AFFILIATES:

Allscripts- Misys Healthcare Solutions, Inc.
Eclipsys Corporation

CONTACTS: Note: Officers with more than one job title may be intentionally listed here more than once.

Glen E. Tullman, CEO
Eileen McPartland, COO
Lee Shapiro, Pres.
Bill Davis, CFO
Dan Michelson, Chief Mktg. Officer/Exec. VP
Diane Adams, Exec. VP-Culture & Talent
John Gomez, Pres., Prod. Strategy & Dev.
Joe Carey, Chief of Staff
Kent Alexander, General Counsel/Exec. VP
Laurie McGraw, Chief Client Officer
Jeff Surges, Pres., Sales
Philip Pead, Chmn.

Phone: 312-506-1200	Fax: 312-506-1201
Toll-Free: 800-654-0889	
Address: 222 Merchandise Mart Plz., Ste. 2024, Chicago, IL 60654 US	

GROWTH PLANS/SPECIAL FEATURES:

Allscripts Healthcare Solutions, Inc. provides clinical software, connectivity and information solutions that physicians and healthcare providers use to improve delivery of services. Its business groups are designed to deliver timely information connecting physicians to each other and to the broader healthcare community, and to contribute to healthcare by improving both the quality and efficiency of care. The software and related services segment of the company's business provides clinical software solutions, including electronic health record, electronic prescribing and document imaging solutions. The information services segment, through the physicians' interactive business unit, provides clinical education and information solutions for physicians and patients, along with physician-patient connectivity solutions through a partnership with Medem, Inc. The prepackaged medications segment provides prepackaged medication fulfillment solutions, which includes both medications and software for dispensing and inventory control. TouchWorks Electronic Health Record (EHR) is a point-of-care clinical solution for small to mid-size physician practices that provides e-prescribing and related functions. The TouchWorks EHR solution is delivered online via the physician's PDA (personal digital assistant) to a nearby pharmacy. TouchWorks PM, meanwhile, is a practice management system helping to streamline activities such as patient scheduling, electronic remittances, electronic claims submission and electronic statement production. Allscripts also operates a prepackaged medications segment that provides point-of-care medication and medical supply management solutions for physicians. In March 2009, the company announced that it would sell its medication services business to A-S Medication Solutions for approximately $26 million. In September 2010, the company merged with Eclipsys Corp.

FINANCIALS: Sales and profits are in thousands of dollars—add 000 to get the full amount. 2010 Note: Financial information for 2010 was not available for all companies at press time.

2010 Sales: $704,502	2010 Profits: $62,870	U.S. Stock Ticker: MDRX
2009 Sales: $548,439	2009 Profits: $26,022	Int'l Ticker: Int'l Exchange:
2008 Sales: $383,771	2008 Profits: $25,399	Employees: 2,428
2007 Sales: $379,693	2007 Profits: $3,854	Fiscal Year Ends: 5/31
2006 Sales: $227,969	2006 Profits: $11,895	Parent Company:

SALARIES/BENEFITS:

Pension Plan:	ESOP Stock Plan:	Profit Sharing:	Top Exec. Salary: $291,667	Bonus: $394,000
Savings Plan: Y	Stock Purch. Plan: Y		Second Exec. Salary: $197,916	Bonus: $347,000

OTHER THOUGHTS:

Apparent Women Officers or Directors: 3
Hot Spot for Advancement for Women/Minorities: Y

LOCATIONS: ("Y" = Yes)

West:	Southwest:	Midwest:	Southeast:	Northeast:	International:
Y	Y	Y	Y	Y	

Note: Financial information, benefits and other data can change quickly and may vary from those stated here.

ALPS ELECTRIC CO LTD   www.alps.com

Industry Group Code: 335313 Ranks within this company's industry group: Sales: 1   Profits: 1

Hardware:		Software:	Telecommunications:	Electronic Publishing:	Equipment:	Specialty Services:
Computers:		Consumer:	Local:	Online Service:	Telecom:	Consulting:
Accessories:		Corporate:	Long Distance:	TV/Cable or Wireless:	Communication:	Contract Manufacturing:
Network Equipment:		Telecom:	Cellular:	Games:	Distribution:	Processing:
Chips/Circuits:		Internet:	Internet Service:	Financial Data:	VAR/Reseller:	Staff/Outsourcing:
Parts/Drives:	Y				Satellite Srv./Equip.:	Specialty Services:

TYPES OF BUSINESS:
Electronic Components Manufacturing
Automotive Parts Manufacturing

BRANDS/DIVISIONS/AFFILIATES:
Haptic Commander
GlidePoint
Avnet Electronics Marketing
Alps Green Device

CONTACTS: *Note: Officers with more than one job title may be intentionally listed here more than once.*
Masataka Kataoka, Pres.
Toshihiro Kuriyama, Chief Dir.-Tech
Junichi Umehara, Chief Dir.-Admin.
Yozo Yasuoka, Sr. Managing Dir.
Nobuhiko Komeya, Managing Dir.
Seishi Kai, Managing Dir.
Junichi Umehara, Dir.

Phone: 81-3-3726-1211	Fax: 81-2-3278-1741
Toll-Free:	
Address: 1-7 Yukigaya Otsuka-cho, Ota-Ku, Tokyo, 145-8501 Japan	

GROWTH PLANS/SPECIAL FEATURES:

Alps Electric Co., Ltd. is primarily engaged in the manufacture and sale of electronic components, specializing in electronics development and miniaturization. Alps operates via its three divisions: Automotive Division; the Home, Mobile and Industry Division; and the Mechatronics, Materials and Process Division. The Automotive Products Division develops on-board electronics and safety and comfort systems for automotive applications. One of its propriety systems, the Haptic Commander unit, incorporates modules to control various switches, air-conditioning units and passive keyless entry systems. The Home, Mobile and Industry Division consists of the electronic components used in the development of human-to-machine input and output devices, such as keyboards, remote controls, touch sensors, printers and power-saving LCDs. The firm's GlidePoint device is used primarily in the touch pads of laptop PCs and uses electrostatic detection technology to detect the movement of a fingertip. GlidePoint is additionally used in the touch pads of TV remote control units and mobile phone sensor keys. The Mechatronics, Materials and Process Division manufactures human-to-machine interface components, such as switches, variable resistors, sensors and connectors, which are used in automotive components; information and communication devices; and home appliances. The company is composed of over 82 subsidiary and affiliate companies that fall under three primary company headings; Alps Logistics, Company, Ltd., which consists of over 25 companies; Alpine Electronics, Inc., which consists of over 28 companies; and Alps Electronic, Company, Ltd., which consists of over 23 companies. In March 2010, the company announced a joint venture with the Innovation Network Corp. of Japan. The new company, Alps Green Device, will focus on providing power supply devices.

FINANCIALS: Sales and profits are in thousands of dollars—add 000 to get the full amount. 2010 Note: Financial information for 2010 was not available for all companies at press time.

2010 Sales: $	2010 Profits: $	U.S. Stock Ticker: APELY.PK
2009 Sales: $5,790,360	2009 Profits: $-752,690	Int'l Ticker: 6770 Int'l Exchange: Tokyo-TSE
2008 Sales: $6,926,600	2008 Profits: $44,200	Employees:
2007 Sales: $7,081,300	2007 Profits: $49,200	Fiscal Year Ends: 3/31
2006 Sales: $7,096,100	2006 Profits: $188,700	Parent Company:

SALARIES/BENEFITS:

Pension Plan:	ESOP Stock Plan:	Profit Sharing:	Top Exec. Salary: $	Bonus: $
Savings Plan:	Stock Purch. Plan:		Second Exec. Salary: $	Bonus: $

OTHER THOUGHTS:
Apparent Women Officers or Directors:
Hot Spot for Advancement for Women/Minorities:

LOCATIONS: ("Y" = Yes)

West:	Southwest:	Midwest:	Southeast:	Northeast:	International:
Y	Y	Y	Y	Y	Y

ALTERA CORP

www.altera.com

Industry Group Code: 33441 Ranks within this company's industry group: Sales: 27   Profits: 12

Hardware:	Software:		Telecommunications:	Electronic Publishing:	Equipment:	Specialty Services:
Computers:	Consumer:		Local:	Online Service:	Telecom:	Consulting:
Accessories:	Corporate:	Y	Long Distance:	TV/Cable or Wireless:	Communication:	Contract Manufacturing:
Network Equipment:	Telecom:		Cellular:	Games:	Distribution:	Processing:
Chips/Circuits: Y	Internet:		Internet Service:	Financial Data:	VAR/Reseller:	Staff/Outsourcing:
Parts/Drives:					Satellite Srv./Equip.:	Specialty Services:

TYPES OF BUSINESS:

Programmable Logic Devices
Development System Software
System-On-A-Programmable-Chip (SOPC) Devices
CMOS Semiconductor PDLs

BRANDS/DIVISIONS/AFFILIATES:

HardCopy
Avalon Microelectronics Inc

CONTACTS: Note: Officers with more than one job title may be intentionally listed here more than once.

John P. Daane, CEO
John P. Daane, Pres.
Ronald J. Pasek, CFO
Danny Biran, Sr. VP-Mktg.
Kevin H. Lyman, VP-Human Resources
Misha Burich, Sr. VP-R&D
William Y. Hata, VP-Eng.
Katherine Schuelke, General Counsel/VP/Corp. Sec.
William Y. Hata, VP-World Oper.
Lance Lissner, Sr. VP-Bus. Dev.
Scott Wylie, VP-Investor Rel.
Ronald J. Pasek, Sr. VP-Finance
John P. Daane, Chmn.
George A. Papa, Sr. VP-Worldwide Sales

Phone: 408-544-7000	Fax: 408-954-8186
Toll-Free: 800-767-3753	
Address: 101 Innovation Dr., San Jose, CA 95134 US	

GROWTH PLANS/SPECIAL FEATURES:

Altera Corp. is a world leader in system-on-a-programmable-chip (SOPC) technology. The company designs, manufactures and markets high-performance, high-density programmable logic devices (PLDs), HardCopy devices, pre-defined design building blocks known as intellectual property cores and associated development tools. The company has several worldwide office locations in areas that include the U.S., Malaysia, the U.K. and Canada. Founded in 1983, Altera was one of the first suppliers of complementary metal oxide semiconductor (CMOS) PLDs and is currently a global leader in this market. The company's PLDs consist of field-programmable arrays and complex programmable logic devices, which are semiconductor integrated circuits, manufactured as standard chips that its customers program to perform desired logic functions within their electronic systems. The firm offers a broad range of general-purpose PLDs that present unique features as well as differing densities and performance specifications for implementing particular applications. Programmable logic's primary advantage is that it allows for quicker design cycles, meeting customers' needs for quick time-to-market. Altera's HardCopy devices allow its customers to move from a PLD to a low-cost, high-volume, non-programmable implementation of their designs. The company operates in a wide variety of industries, such as telecommunications, data communication, electronic data processing, computer and storage products and industrial applications. In December 2010, the company acquired Avalon Microelectronics, Inc., which specializes in optical transport network technology.

Employees are offered medical, dental and vision coverage; an employee assistance program; life insurance; short and long-term disability; flexible spending account; a 401(k) plan; a retirement plan; accidental death and dismemberment coverage; business travel accident insurance; employee stock purchase plan; and educational reimbursement.

FINANCIALS: Sales and profits are in thousands of dollars—add 000 to get the full amount. 2010 Note: Financial information for 2010 was not available for all companies at press time.

2010 Sales: $	2010 Profits: $	**U.S. Stock Ticker:** ALTR
2009 Sales: $1,195,413	2009 Profits: $251,062	**Int'l Ticker:** Int'l Exchange:
2008 Sales: $1,367,224	2008 Profits: $359,651	Employees: 2,551
2007 Sales: $1,263,548	2007 Profits: $290,023	Fiscal Year Ends: 12/31
2006 Sales: $1,285,535	2006 Profits: $323,236	Parent Company:

SALARIES/BENEFITS:

Pension Plan: Y	ESOP Stock Plan:	Profit Sharing:	Top Exec. Salary: $700,027	Bonus: $520,000
Savings Plan: Y	Stock Purch. Plan: Y		Second Exec. Salary: $375,014	Bonus: $175,000

OTHER THOUGHTS:

Apparent Women Officers or Directors: 1
Hot Spot for Advancement for Women/Minorities:

LOCATIONS: ("Y" = Yes)

West:	Southwest:	Midwest:	Southeast:	Northeast:	International:
Y	Y	Y	Y	Y	Y

Note: Financial information, benefits and other data can change quickly and may vary from those stated here.

ALTRAN TECHNOLOGIES SA

www.altran.com

Industry Group Code: 541512 Ranks within this company's industry group: Sales: 5 Profits: 7

Hardware:	Software:	Telecommunications:	Electronic Publishing:	Equipment:	Specialty Services:	
Computers:	Consumer:	Local:	Online Service:	Telecom:	Consulting:	Y
Accessories:	Corporate:	Long Distance:	TV/Cable or Wireless:	Communication:	Contract Manufacturing:	
Network Equipment:	Telecom:	Cellular:	Games:	Distribution:	Processing:	
Chips/Circuits:	Internet:	Internet Service:	Financial Data:	VAR/Reseller:	Staff/Outsourcing:	
Parts/Drives:				Satellite Srv./Equip.:	Specialty Services:	

TYPES OF BUSINESS:

Consulting-Technology & Engineering
Research
Management Consulting
Automotive Consulting
Motor Sports Consulting

BRANDS/DIVISIONS/AFFILIATES:

Altran Foundation
Altran Technologies Korea
Altran Europe
Acsience
Altran GmbH & Co KG
Altran India
Altran Solutions Corp
Apax Partners, Inc

CONTACTS: Note: Officers with more than one job title may be intentionally listed here more than once.

Yves de Chaisemartin, CEO
Gerald Berge, CFO
Pascal Brier, VP
Frederic Grard, VP
Cyril Roger, VP
Yves de Chaisemartin, Chmn.
Patrick Dauga, Exec. Dir.-Americas

Phone: 33-1-46-17-46-17	Fax: 33-1-46-17-46-18
Toll-Free:	
Address: 2 rue Paul Vaillant-Couturier, Levallois-Perret, 92300 France	

GROWTH PLANS/SPECIAL FEATURES:

Altran Technologies SA, based in France, is a leader in global technology consulting, structured around three business segments and six practice focuses. The three business segments are technology and innovation consulting, accounting for nearly half of the firm's revenues; organization and information systems consulting, accounting for a third of revenues; and strategy and management consulting, representing the remainder of annual revenues. The six practice areas are aerospace and defense; automotive and transports; energy and industry; financial services; healthcare; and telecoms and media. The company derives roughly 43% of its revenues from activities in France, but it has operations in approximately 26 countries that include Brazil, Japan, Germany, India and many locations in the U.S. The majority of Altran's business is done with companies in the aerospace, automotive and telecommunications fields, but it also works with companies in the banking, energy, electronics and biotechnology industries. The company operates research laboratories in Cambridge, U.K. and Boston, Massachusetts. Altran works on an integral basis with companies, assisting them in areas such as the development and implementation of science and technology and the design of new products, as well as by providing advice on how to streamline business and manufacturing through the use of technology. The private equity firm Apax Partners, Inc. owns a controlling stake in the company. Altran is an official partner in the Solar Impulse project, which is currently developing a solar-powered aircraft capable of long-range flight. In April 2010, the Solar Impulse prototype plane remained in the air for over 90 minutes.

FINANCIALS: Sales and profits are in thousands of dollars—add 000 to get the full amount. 2010 Note: Financial information for 2010 was not available for all companies at press time.

2010 Sales: $	2010 Profits: $	U.S. Stock Ticker: ALTKF.PK
2009 Sales: $1,907,120	2009 Profits: $-101,630	Int'l Ticker: ALT Int'l Exchange: Paris-Euronext
2008 Sales: $2,234,170	2008 Profits: $15,440	Employees: 17,149
2007 Sales: $2,154,690	2007 Profits: $29,250	Fiscal Year Ends: 12/31
2006 Sales: $2,347,700	2006 Profits: $5,900	Parent Company:

SALARIES/BENEFITS:

Pension Plan:	ESOP Stock Plan:	Profit Sharing:	Top Exec. Salary: $	Bonus: $
Savings Plan: Y	Stock Purch. Plan:		Second Exec. Salary: $	Bonus: $

OTHER THOUGHTS:

Apparent Women Officers or Directors:
Hot Spot for Advancement for Women/Minorities:

LOCATIONS: ("Y" = Yes)

West:	Southwest:	Midwest:	Southeast:	Northeast:	International:
Y	Y	Y		Y	Y

AM NETWORKS INC

www.amcomm.com

Industry Group Code: 511210B Ranks within this company's industry group: Sales: Profits:

Hardware:		Software:		Telecommunications:		Electronic Publishing:	Equipment:	Specialty Services:
Computers:		Consumer:		Local:		Online Service:	Telecom:	Consulting:
Accessories:		Corporate:	Y	Long Distance:		TV/Cable or Wireless:	Communication:	Contract Manufacturing:
Network Equipment:	Y	Telecom:		Cellular:		Games:	Distribution:	Processing:
Chips/Circuits:		Internet:		Internet Service:		Financial Data:	VAR/Reseller:	Staff/Outsourcing:
Parts/Drives:							Satellite Srv./Equip.:	Specialty Services:

TYPES OF BUSINESS:

Software-Communications Networks
Fiber-Optic Infrastructure Products
Network Monitoring Systems

BRANDS/DIVISIONS/AFFILIATES:

NeST Group
Nestronix Inc
Omni2000
OmniStat
FiberSentinel
WaveSense

CONTACTS: *Note: Officers with more than one job title may be intentionally listed here more than once.*

C. Kamnitsis, Pres.
Michael Staples, CFO
Robert Addis, Dir.-Applications Eng.
Abraham Chandy, Dir.-Oper.
Bret A. Matz, Gen. Mgr./VP
Javad Hassan, Chmn.-NeST Group

Phone: 215-538-8700	Fax: 215-538-8789
Toll-Free: 800-248-9004	
Address: 1900 AM Dr., Quakertown, PA 18951 US	

GROWTH PLANS/SPECIAL FEATURES:

AM Networks, Inc., a member of the NeST Group of Companies, provides an array of products and services for the broadband industry. These products include fiber-optic infrastructure products, custom software/firmware and network monitoring solutions. The company provides monitoring solutions for a variety of network aspects, including power, fiber optics, radio frequency (RF) and signal quality. AM manufactures passive optical components, sub-assemblies and distribution equipment for deployment in fiber-optic broadband infrastructures; and utilizes advanced fiber fusing processes and ISO 9000 quality fiber termination procedures to produce optical tree coupler/splitters for FTTH. AM Networks also supplies the broadband industry with value-add optical sub-assemblies, including various LGX modules and rack-mount distribution enclosures. Its turnkey remote fiber test systems are capable of monitoring dark and active fiber links across a network operator's entire system; these include the Omni2000, a multi-user, multi-server system that consolidates an array of remote monitoring equipment into a single management platform. The firm's OmniStat network monitoring system provides remote monitoring capabilities for nearly 300 types of HFC network equipment. In connection with Nestronix, Inc., it also provides the FiberSentinel Fiber Tap Detection and Elimination System, which detects and shuts down intrusions into high-security connections, reroutes traffic and notifies the network operator. WaveSense, FiberSentinel's core technology, is capable of identifying, differentiating and characterizing eight different optical event types. AM Networks systems are in use in 30 countries across five continents, supporting over 500,000 network transponders, 300,000 plant miles and monitoring over 400 broadband data communications/HFC networks. The company maintains sales offices in North America, as well as in the U.K., India, the United Arab Emirates, Japan and Spain. Dubai, India and Japan; and operates an overseas development facility and a manufacturing plant in India. The firm's global partner companies include Vector; Scientific-Atlanta; C-COR; Alpha Technologies; Motorola, Inc.; Trispec Communications; and Multilink.

FINANCIALS: Sales and profits are in thousands of dollars—add 000 to get the full amount. 2010 Note: Financial information for 2010 was not available for all companies at press time.

2010 Sales: $	2010 Profits: $	**U.S. Stock Ticker: Subsidiary**
2009 Sales: $	2009 Profits: $	**Int'l Ticker:** Int'l Exchange:
2008 Sales: $	2008 Profits: $	Employees:
2007 Sales: $9,800	2007 Profits: $	Fiscal Year Ends: 3/31
2006 Sales: $	2006 Profits: $	Parent Company: NEST TECHNOLOGIES INC

SALARIES/BENEFITS:

Pension Plan:	ESOP Stock Plan:	Profit Sharing:	Top Exec. Salary: $	Bonus: $
Savings Plan:	Stock Purch. Plan:		Second Exec. Salary: $	Bonus: $

OTHER THOUGHTS:

Apparent Women Officers or Directors:
Hot Spot for Advancement for Women/Minorities:

LOCATIONS: ("Y" = Yes)

West:	Southwest:	Midwest:	Southeast:	Northeast:	International:
Y	Y	Y	Y	Y	Y

AMDOCS LTD

www.amdocs.com

Industry Group Code: 511210K Ranks within this company's industry group: Sales: 1 Profits: 1

Hardware:	Software:		Telecommunications:	Electronic Publishing:	Equipment:	Specialty Services:	
Computers:	Consumer:		Local:	Online Service:	Telecom:	Consulting:	
Accessories:	Corporate:	Y	Long Distance:	TV/Cable or Wireless:	Communication:	Contract Manufacturing:	
Network Equipment:	Telecom:		Cellular:	Games:	Distribution:	Processing:	
Chips/Circuits:	Internet:		Internet Service:	Financial Data:	VAR/Reseller:	Staff/Outsourcing:	Y
Parts/Drives:					Satellite Srv./Equip.:	Specialty Services:	Y

TYPES OF BUSINESS:

Software-Customer Services & Business Operations
Customer Relationship Management Software
Billing Management Software
Directory Publishing Systems
Technical & Support Services
Managed Services

BRANDS/DIVISIONS/AFFILIATES:

Amdocs CES
MX Telecom
Longshine Technology

CONTACTS: Note: Officers with more than one job title may be intentionally listed here more than once.

Eli Gelman, CEO
Eli Gelman, Pres.
Tamar Rapaport-Dagim, CFO/Sr. VP
Thomas G. O'Brien, Sec.
James Liang, Chief Strategy Officer/Sr. VP
Elizabeth Grausam, VP-Investor Rel.
Thomas G. O'Brien, Treas.
Brian Shepherd, Sr. VP/Head-Broadband Cable & Satellite Group
Ayal Shiran, Sr. VP/Head-Customer Bus. Group
Bruce K. Anderson, Chmn.
Anshoo Gaur, Pres., Amdocs Dev. Center India Pvt., Ltd.

Phone: 44-314-2128328	Fax: 44-314-2127500
Toll-Free:	
Address: Tower Hill House, Ste. 5, Le Bordage, St. Peter Port, Guernsey GY1 3QT UK	

GROWTH PLANS/SPECIAL FEATURES:

Amdocs, Ltd. provides software products and services primarily to tier one and tier two communications companies worldwide, offering an integrated approach to customer management to service providers in over 60 countries. Its product offerings are based on its proprietary Amdocs CES (Customer Experience Systems) software portfolio. At its core, the Amdocs CES is an open, service-orientated architecture that is intended to provide the functionality, scalability, modularity and adaptability required by service providers. To this end, the firm's solutions consist of billing and customer relationship management (CRM) systems, revenue management, network planning and resource management and directory sales and publishing systems for publishers of both traditional and Internet-based directories, as well as system implementation, integration, support and maintenance services. The firm also offers managed services, which include modernization and consolidation, operation of data centers, purchase and management of hardware assets, billing operations and application support. Additionally, Amdocs offers solutions bundles and packs for industry specific issues. The solutions provided by the company are designed to support a variety of lines of business, including wireline, cable and satellite. It also supports a range of communications services, including video, data, Internet protocol, electronic and mobile commerce. The company has recently begun to focus its solutions and services on providers in emerging markets, including Latin America, India and Southeast Asia. In March 2010, it acquired MX Telecom, expanding its position in the global mobile payments and services market. As part of a realignment of focus in China, in April 2010, the firm sold a controlling interest in Longshine Technology, a custom services developer for telecom and utilities companies in China.

The company offers its employees medical, dental and vision; prescription drug coverage; life insurance; AD&D coverage; flexible spending accounts; short and long term disability; commuting and parking subsidies; a 401(k) plan; and domestic partner coverage.

FINANCIALS: Sales and profits are in thousands of dollars—add 000 to get the full amount. 2010 Note: Financial information for 2010 was not available for all companies at press time.

2010 Sales: $2,984,223	2010 Profits: $343,906	U.S. Stock Ticker: DOX
2009 Sales: $2,862,607	2009 Profits: $326,176	Int'l Ticker: Int'l Exchange:
2008 Sales: $3,162,096	2008 Profits: $378,906	Employees:
2007 Sales: $2,836,173	2007 Profits: $364,937	Fiscal Year Ends: 9/30
2006 Sales: $2,480,050	2006 Profits: $318,636	Parent Company:

SALARIES/BENEFITS:

Pension Plan: Y	ESOP Stock Plan:	Profit Sharing:	Top Exec. Salary: $	Bonus: $
Savings Plan:	Stock Purch. Plan: Y		Second Exec. Salary: $	Bonus: $

OTHER THOUGHTS:

Apparent Women Officers or Directors: 1
Hot Spot for Advancement for Women/Minorities:

LOCATIONS: ("Y" = Yes)

West:	Southwest:	Midwest:	Southeast:	Northeast:	International:
Y	Y	Y	Y	Y	Y

AMERICAN SOFTWARE INC   www.amsoftware.com

Industry Group Code: 511210A Ranks within this company's industry group: Sales: 6   Profits: 5

Hardware:	Software:		Telecommunications:	Electronic Publishing:	Equipment:	Specialty Services:	
Computers:	Consumer:		Local:	Online Service:	Telecom:	Consulting:	Y
Accessories:	Corporate:	Y	Long Distance:	TV/Cable or Wireless:	Communication:	Contract Manufacturing:	
Network Equipment:	Telecom:		Cellular:	Games:	Distribution:	Processing:	
Chips/Circuits:	Internet:		Internet Service:	Financial Data:	VAR/Reseller:	Staff/Outsourcing:	Y
Parts/Drives:					Satellite Srv./Equip.:	Specialty Services:	

TYPES OF BUSINESS:

Computer Software-Supply Chain Management
Enterprise Resource Planning Software
E-Commerce Software
Consulting Services
IT Staffing

BRANDS/DIVISIONS/AFFILIATES:

Logility, Inc.
American Software ERP
New Generation Computing
Proven Method (The)
American Software USA, Inc.
American Software UK, Ltd.
Demand Management, Inc.
Optiant, Inc.

CONTACTS: Note: Officers with more than one job title may be intentionally listed here more than once.

James C. Edenfield, CEO
James C. Edenfield, Pres.
Vince Klinges, CFO
James. R. McGuone, General Counsel/Sec.
Pat McManus, Contact-Investor Rel.
James C. Edenfield, Treas.
J. Michael Edenfield, Exec. VP/CEO-Logility, Inc.
Jeffery W. Coombs, Exec. VP/COO-American Software USA, Inc.
Thomas L. Newberry, Chmn.

Phone: 404-264-5296	Fax: 404-264-5206
Toll-Free: 800-726-2946	
Address: 470 E. Paces Ferry Rd., Atlanta, GA 30305 US	

GROWTH PLANS/SPECIAL FEATURES:

American Software, Inc. develops and markets enterprise management software, as well as collaborative supply chain products and applications. The company has three major business segments: supply chain management (SCM), enterprise resource planning (ERP) and IT consulting. The SCM segment consists of Logility, Inc., a wholly-owned subsidiary, which develops collaborative supply chain software to deliver supply chain planning, inventory optimization, manufacturing, and transportation and logistics applications. This software is designed to help customers streamline and optimize the forecasting, production, distribution and management of products between trading partners. The ERP segment consists of two companies: American Software ERP and New Generation Computing (NGC). American Software ERP specializes in the provision of purchasing and materials management, customer order processing, financial, e-commerce, flow manufacturing and traditional manufacturing applications. NGC provides industry-specific business software to both retailers and manufacturers in the apparel, sewn products and furniture industries. This software assists customers in lowering operating costs, reducing supply chain time, meeting complex customer requirements and reducing production costs. The IT consulting segment consists of The Proven Method, an IT staffing and consulting services firm owned by American Software. Services include project management, staff augmentation and infrastructure and consulting services. The company also provides support for its software products, such as software enhancements, documentation, updates, customer education, consulting, systems integration services and maintenance. Additional subsidiaries of the company include American Software Research and Development Corporation; American Software U.K., Ltd.; American Software USA, Inc.; and Demand Management, Inc. In March 2010, American Software acquired Optiant, Inc., a developer of supply chain optimization systems.

FINANCIALS: Sales and profits are in thousands of dollars—add 000 to get the full amount. 2010 Note: Financial information for 2010 was not available for all companies at press time.

2010 Sales: $75,276	2010 Profits: $5,704	**U.S. Stock Ticker: AMSWA**	
2009 Sales: $78,024	2009 Profits: $3,016	**Int'l Ticker:** Int'l Exchange:	
2008 Sales: $89,001	2008 Profits: $6,533	Employees: 291	
2007 Sales: $84,367	2007 Profits: $8,433	Fiscal Year Ends: 4/30	
2006 Sales: $76,630	2006 Profits: $5,019	Parent Company:	

SALARIES/BENEFITS:

Pension Plan:	ESOP Stock Plan:	Profit Sharing:	Top Exec. Salary: $512,500	Bonus: $165,939
Savings Plan:	Stock Purch. Plan:		Second Exec. Salary: $305,000	Bonus: $391,401

OTHER THOUGHTS:

Apparent Women Officers or Directors:
Hot Spot for Advancement for Women/Minorities:

LOCATIONS: ("Y" = Yes)

West:	Southwest:	Midwest:	Southeast:	Northeast:	International:
			Y		Y

AMKOR TECHNOLOGY INC

www.amkor.com

Industry Group Code: 333295 Ranks within this company's industry group: Sales: 3   Profits: 3

Hardware:		Software:		Telecommunications:		Electronic Publishing:	Equipment:	Specialty Services:	
Computers:		Consumer:		Local:		Online Service:	Telecom:	Consulting:	
Accessories:		Corporate:		Long Distance:		TV/Cable or Wireless:	Communication:	Contract Manufacturing:	
Network Equipment:		Telecom:		Cellular:		Games:	Distribution:	Processing:	
Chips/Circuits:	Y	Internet:		Internet Service:		Financial Data:	VAR/Reseller:	Staff/Outsourcing:	
Parts/Drives:							Satellite Srv./Equip.:	Specialty Services:	Y

TYPES OF BUSINESS:

Semiconductors-Packaging & Testing
Semiconductor Design
Turnkey Solutions

BRANDS/DIVISIONS/AFFILIATES:

Nakaya Microdevices Corporation
Toshiba Corporation

CONTACTS: *Note: Officers with more than one job title may be intentionally listed here more than once.*

Kenneth T. Joyce, CEO
Kenneth T. Joyce, Pres.
Joanne Solomon, CFO/Exec. VP
Mike Lamble, VP-Worldwide Sales
Jooho Kim, Head-Worldwide Mfg.
Gil C. Tily, Chief Admin. Officer/Exec. VP
Gil C. Tily, General Counsel/Corp. Sec./Exec. VP
Jim Fusaro, Exec. VP-Assembly & Test Bus. Unit
James J. Kim, Chmn.
Jooho Kim, Pres., Amkor Technology Korea

Phone: 480-821-5000	Fax: 480-821-8276
Toll-Free:	
Address: 1900 South Price Rd., Chandler, AZ 85286 US	

GROWTH PLANS/SPECIAL FEATURES:

Amkor Technology, Inc. is one of the world's largest subcontractors of semiconductor packaging and test services. The firm offers a range of integrated services, including the final procedures necessary to prepare semiconductor devices for further use. Headquartered in the U.S., the company also has production capabilities in China, Japan, Korea, the Philippines, France, Singapore and Taiwan. The company operates in two segments: packaging and testing. Packaging includes dicing of a semiconductor wafer into separate chips, die bonding, wire bonding and encapsulation of the chip in protective plastic. The testing segment offers turnkey packaging and test solutions including semiconductor wafer bump, wafer probe, wafer backgrind, package design, final test, strip test, system level test, assembly, test and drop shipment and other test-related services. The semiconductors packaged and tested by the firm become components in electrical systems used in computing, wireless, communications, storage, consumer, commercial, industrial, medical, defense and automotive applications. Amkor offers over 1,000 different package types and sizes, and packages are increasingly custom designed for specific chips and specific end-market applications. The company provides customers with leading-edge packaging technologies, including dual and quad leadframe, 2D and 3D thin substrate, flip chip, ball grid array, system-in-package and wafer level solutions. Amkor also offers an extensive range of test engineering services for radio frequency (RF) applications, as well as RF/wireless semiconductor device test development services. The company's customer base consists of more than 200 companies, including many of the world's largest semiconductor companies. The firm maintains a joint venture with Nakaya Microdevices Corporation and Toshiba Corporation that provides semiconductor assembly and final testing services in Japan.

The company offers its employees benefits including an employee assistance program, flexible spending accounts, tuition reimbursement, profit sharing, medical and dental insurance, direct deposit and travel insurance.

FINANCIALS: Sales and profits are in thousands of dollars—add 000 to get the full amount. 2010 Note: Financial information for 2010 was not available for all companies at press time.

2010 Sales: $	2010 Profits: $	**U.S. Stock Ticker:** AMKR
2009 Sales: $2,179,109	2009 Profits: $156,283	**Int'l Ticker:** Int'l Exchange:
2008 Sales: $2,658,602	2008 Profits: $-456,695	Employees: 18,200
2007 Sales: $2,739,445	2007 Profits: $219,864	Fiscal Year Ends: 12/31
2006 Sales: $2,728,560	2006 Profits: $170,084	Parent Company:

SALARIES/BENEFITS:

Pension Plan:	ESOP Stock Plan:	Profit Sharing: Y	Top Exec. Salary: $581,539	Bonus: $
Savings Plan: Y	Stock Purch. Plan:		Second Exec. Salary: $526,346	Bonus: $

OTHER THOUGHTS:

Apparent Women Officers or Directors: 1
Hot Spot for Advancement for Women/Minorities:

LOCATIONS: ("Y" = Yes)

West:	Southwest:	Midwest:	Southeast:	Northeast:	International:
Y	Y			Y	Y

AMPEX CORP

www.ampex.com

Industry Group Code: 334112 Ranks within this company's industry group: Sales: Profits:

Hardware:		Software:		Telecommunications:	Electronic Publishing:	Equipment:	Specialty Services:
Computers:		Consumer:	Y	Local:	Online Service:	Telecom:	Consulting:
Accessories:	Y	Corporate:	Y	Long Distance:	TV/Cable or Wireless:	Communication:	Contract Manufacturing:
Network Equipment:		Telecom:		Cellular:	Games:	Distribution:	Processing:
Chips/Circuits:		Internet:		Internet Service:	Financial Data:	VAR/Reseller:	Staff/Outsourcing:
Parts/Drives:						Satellite Srv./Equip.:	Specialty Services:

TYPES OF BUSINESS:

Digital Image Processors
Computer Storage Equipment
Scanning Recording Devices
Tape-Based Storage Products

BRANDS/DIVISIONS/AFFILIATES:

Ampex Data Systems Corp.
Hillside Capital, Inc.
Ampex Great Britain Ltd.
Ampex Japan Ltd.

CONTACTS: *Note: Officers with more than one job title may be intentionally listed here more than once.*

D. Gordon Strickland, CEO
D. Gordon Strickland, Pres.
Christopher Lake, CFO/VP/Treas.
Joel D. Talcott, Corp. Sec./VP
Ramon C. H. Venema, VP/Controller
Larry Chiarella, Pres, Ampex Data Systems
D. Gordon Strickland, Chmn.

Phone: 650-367-4111	Fax: 650-367-4669
Toll-Free:	
Address: 1228 Douglas Ave., Redwood City, CA 94063-3199 US	

GROWTH PLANS/SPECIAL FEATURES:

Ampex Corp. develops and licenses visual information technology, specializing in hardware and software related to the electronic storage, processing and retrieval of data, particularly images. In addition, the company holds patents covering digital image-processing, data compression and recording technologies. Ampex's primary source of revenue is the licensing of its technologies, which are used in camera phones, digital cameras, still cameras, digital video camcorders and DVD recorders. Through subsidiary Ampex Data Systems, the firm develops and incorporates technology in the design and manufacture of high-performance data storage products, principally used in defense applications to gather digital images and other data from aircraft, satellites and submarines. These products are also used in flight and sensor test applications. Ampex leverages its research and development activities through its licensing division, which licenses the company's products to manufacturers of consumer electronics products. The company's licensing segment handles the licensing of intellectual property. Ampex has developed many innovative early breakthrough technologies, including the videotape recorder and slow-motion instant replay. Additional wholly-owned subsidies include Ampex Great Britain Ltd., which provides services for the company's customers in Europe and the Middle East. Ampex Japan Ltd. manufactures products and provides services to the company's customers throughout Japan. Hillside Capital, Inc. owns a majority stake in the company.

FINANCIALS: Sales and profits are in thousands of dollars—add 000 to get the full amount. 2010 Note: Financial information for 2010 was not available for all companies at press time.

2010 Sales: $	2010 Profits: $	**U.S. Stock Ticker: Private**
2009 Sales: $	2009 Profits: $	Int'l Ticker: Int'l Exchange:
2008 Sales: $	2008 Profits: $	Employees:
2007 Sales: $41,476	2007 Profits: $ 904	Fiscal Year Ends: 12/31
2006 Sales: $35,921	2006 Profits: $-3,948	Parent Company: HILLSIDE CAPITAL INC

SALARIES/BENEFITS:

Pension Plan:	ESOP Stock Plan:	Profit Sharing:	Top Exec. Salary: $	Bonus: $
Savings Plan:	Stock Purch. Plan:		Second Exec. Salary: $	Bonus: $

OTHER THOUGHTS:

Apparent Women Officers or Directors:
Hot Spot for Advancement for Women/Minorities:

LOCATIONS: ("Y" = Yes)

West:	Southwest:	Midwest:	Southeast:	Northeast:	International:
Y					Y

Note: Financial information, benefits and other data can change quickly and may vary from those stated here.

AMTECH SYSTEMS INC

www.amtechsystems.com

Industry Group Code: 333295 **Ranks within this company's industry group:** Sales: 13   Profits: 5

Hardware:		Software:	Telecommunications:	Electronic Publishing:	Equipment:	Specialty Services:	
Computers:		Consumer:	Local:	Online Service:	Telecom:	Consulting:	
Accessories:		Corporate:	Long Distance:	TV/Cable or Wireless:	Communication:	Contract Manufacturing:	Y
Network Equipment:		Telecom:	Cellular:	Games:	Distribution:	Processing:	
Chips/Circuits:	Y	Internet:	Internet Service:	Financial Data:	VAR/Reseller:	Staff/Outsourcing:	
Parts/Drives:					Satellite Srv./Equip.:	Specialty Services:	Y

TYPES OF BUSINESS:

Semiconductor Manufacturing Equipment
Diffusion Furnace Systems
Wafer Polishing Systems
Machinery Support & Maintenance Services

BRANDS/DIVISIONS/AFFILIATES:

Bruce Technologies, Inc.
Tempress Systems, Inc.
PR Hoffman Machine Products, Inc.
R2D Automation SAS

CONTACTS: Note: Officers with more than one job title may be intentionally listed here more than once.

Jong S. Whang, CEO
Fokko Pentinga, Pres.
Bradley C. Anderson, CFO/VP-Finance
Bradley C. Anderson, Sec.
Robert T. Hass, Chief Acct. Officer

Phone: 480-967-5146	Fax: 480-968-3763
Toll-Free:	
Address: 131 S. Clark Dr., Tempe, AZ 85281 US	

GROWTH PLANS/SPECIAL FEATURES:

Amtech Systems, Inc. is a supplier of horizontal diffusion furnace systems that are used in photovoltaic and semiconductor manufacturing. The company conducts operations via its four primary subsidiaries: Tempress Systems, Inc.; P.R. Hoffman Machine Products, Inc.; Bruce Technologies, Inc.; and RD2 Automation SAS. The company separates operations into two segments: the solar and semiconductor segment and the polishing supplies segment. The company's solar and semiconductor segment operates through subsidiaries Bruce Technologies and Tempress Systems. Bruce Technologies produces horizontal batch furnaces under the brand names of the Bruce Diffusion Furnace, APEX and Amtech Automation. Tempress Systems develops and manufactures horizontal and vertical diffusion furnace systems; in addition to producing and supplying application equipment for the photovoltaic, semiconductor, hybrid and nanotechnology industries. The company conducts its polishing supplies segment through P.R. Hoffman Machine Products and RD2 Automation. P.R Hoffman develops and sells lapping carriers, polishing templates, gears, double sided lapping and machines to high-tech companies throughout the world. RD2 Automation manufactures and sells silicon wafers, as well as selling and producing handling equipment. RD2's products are used by the solar and semiconductor industries for ID readers and solar cell transfer systems. The company's automation products help to reduce the amount of human handling of the silicon wafers, thereby reducing exposure to particle sources during the loading and unloading of the process tubes. Amtech's main market for it products are companies involved in semiconductor wafer manufacturing and semiconductor integrated circuit manufacturing. The company also finds a demand from manufacturers of optical components and solar cells and research and development facilities. Additionally, research institutes and universities make use of the company's products.

FINANCIALS: Sales and profits are in thousands of dollars—add 000 to get the full amount. 2010 Note: Financial information for 2010 was not available for all companies at press time.

2010 Sales: $120,019	2010 Profits: $9,563	**U.S. Stock Ticker:** ASYS
2009 Sales: $52,973	2009 Profits: $-1,589	**Int'l Ticker:** Int'l Exchange:
2008 Sales: $80,296	2008 Profits: $2,857	Employees: 360
2007 Sales: $45,984	2007 Profits: $2,417	Fiscal Year Ends: 9/30
2006 Sales: $40,445	2006 Profits: $1,318	Parent Company:

SALARIES/BENEFITS:

Pension Plan:	ESOP Stock Plan:	Profit Sharing:	Top Exec. Salary: $339,231	Bonus: $420,000
Savings Plan:	Stock Purch. Plan:		Second Exec. Salary: $247,509	Bonus: $211,568

OTHER THOUGHTS:

Apparent Women Officers or Directors:
Hot Spot for Advancement for Women/Minorities:

LOCATIONS: ("Y" = Yes)

West:	Southwest:	Midwest:	Southeast:	Northeast:	International:
	Y			Y	Y

ANALOG DEVICES INC

www.analog.com

Industry Group Code: 33441 Ranks within this company's industry group: Sales: 21 Profits: 14

Hardware:		Software:		Telecommunications:		Electronic Publishing:	Equipment:		Specialty Services:	
Computers:		Consumer:		Local:		Online Service:	Telecom:		Consulting:	
Accessories:		Corporate:		Long Distance:		TV/Cable or Wireless:	Communication:		Contract Manufacturing:	
Network Equipment:		Telecom:		Cellular:		Games:	Distribution:		Processing:	
Chips/Circuits:	Y	Internet:		Internet Service:		Financial Data:	VAR/Reseller:		Staff/Outsourcing:	
Parts/Drives:							Satellite Srv./Equip.:		Specialty Services:	

TYPES OF BUSINESS:

Integrated Circuits-Analog & Digital
MEMS Products
DSP Products
Accelerometers & Gyroscopes

BRANDS/DIVISIONS/AFFILIATES:

CONTACTS: Note: Officers with more than one job title may be intentionally listed here more than once.

Jerald G. Fishman, CEO
Jerald G. Fishman, Pres.
David Zinsner, CFO/VP-Finance
Emre Onder, VP-Mktg.
William Matson, VP-Human Resources
Samuel H. Fuller, VP-R&D
Peter Forte, CIO
Samuel H. Fuller, CTO
John Hassett, VP-Worldwide Mfg.
Margaret K. Seif, General Counsel/VP/Sec.
Mark Smrtic, VP-Foundry Oper.
Keith Rutherford, VP-Comm. Bus. Dev.
John Hussey, VP-Corp. Comm.
Seamus Brennan, Chief Acct. Officer/Corp. Controller
Thomas Wessel, VP-European Sales & Mktg.
Pat O'Doherty, VP-Healthcare
David Robertson, VP-Analog Tech.
Ray Stata, Chmn.
Howard Cheng, VP-Asia
Gerry Dundon, VP-Planning & Supply Chain Logistics

Phone: 781-329-4700	Fax: 781-326-8703
Toll-Free: 800-262-5643	
Address: 3 Technology Way, Norwood, MA 02062 US	

GROWTH PLANS/SPECIAL FEATURES:

Analog Devices, Inc. (ADI) designs, manufactures and markets a broad line of high-performance analog, mixed-signal and digital signal processing (DSP) integrated circuits (ICs). The company's products are divided into analog and digital products. Its analog products are then divided into converters; amplifiers and radio frequency (RF); power management and reference; and other analog. Converters translate real-world analog signals into digital data, and vice-versa. Amplifiers are used to condition analog signals and minimize noise, while RF products are designed to operate as wireless devices. Power management products include any device that can be plugged into a wall outlet or run on battery, such as converters, battery chargers, charge pumps and regulators. Other analog products include microelectromechanical devices (MEMS), such as accelerometers, as well as anything else that uses analog technology. ADI's digital signal processor (DSP) products are typically preprogrammed to execute software for applications such as wireless telecommunications or image processing. Its principal products are used in a wide variety of electronic equipment, including industrial process control, factory automation systems, smart munitions, base stations, central office equipment, wireless telephones, computers, cars, CAT scanners, digital cameras and DVD players. The company's product portfolio includes several thousand analog ICs, with as many as several hundred customers per design. ADI's analog technology base also includes an advanced IC technology known in the industry as surface micromachining, which is used to produce micro-electromechanical systems (MEMS) semiconductor products. ADI's customers include Dell, Alcatel, Lucent, Ericsson, Siemens, Sony, Philips, Ford and Volkswagen. The firm has manufacturing facilities in the U.S., Ireland and the Philippines.

The company offers its employees medical, dental and vision coverage; life insurance; dependant and health care spending accounts; a retirement plan; and an education assistance plan.

FINANCIALS: Sales and profits are in thousands of dollars—add 000 to get the full amount. 2010 Note: Financial information for 2010 was not available for all companies at press time.

2010 Sales: $2,761,503	2010 Profits: $712,084	**U.S. Stock Ticker: ADI**
2009 Sales: $2,014,908	2009 Profits: $247,772	**Int'l Ticker:** Int'l Exchange:
2008 Sales: $2,582,931	2008 Profits: $786,284	Employees: 8,500
2007 Sales: $2,464,721	2007 Profits: $496,907	Fiscal Year Ends: 10/31
2006 Sales: $2,250,100	2006 Profits: $549,482	Parent Company:

SALARIES/BENEFITS:

Pension Plan: Y	ESOP Stock Plan:	Profit Sharing:	Top Exec. Salary: $930,935	Bonus: $635,900
Savings Plan:	Stock Purch. Plan:		Second Exec. Salary: $398,580	Bonus: $570,498

OTHER THOUGHTS:

Apparent Women Officers or Directors: 1
Hot Spot for Advancement for Women/Minorities:

LOCATIONS: ("Y" = Yes)

West:	Southwest:	Midwest:	Southeast:	Northeast:	International:
Y	Y	Y	Y	Y	Y

Note: Financial information, benefits and other data can change quickly and may vary from those stated here.

ANALYSTS INTERNATIONAL CORP

www.analysts.com

Industry Group Code: 541512 Ranks within this company's industry group: Sales: 7 Profits: 6

Hardware:	Software:	Telecommunications:	Electronic Publishing:	Equipment:	Specialty Services:	
Computers:	Consumer:	Local:	Online Service:	Telecom:	Consulting:	Y
Accessories:	Corporate:	Long Distance:	TV/Cable or Wireless:	Communication:	Contract Manufacturing:	
Network Equipment:	Telecom:	Cellular:	Games:	Distribution:	Processing:	
Chips/Circuits:	Internet:	Internet Service:	Financial Data:	VAR/Reseller:	Staff/Outsourcing:	Y
Parts/Drives:				Satellite Srv./Equip.:	Specialty Services:	Y

TYPES OF BUSINESS:

IT Consulting
Custom Software Development
Staffing Services-IT & Software Engineering
Outsourcing Services

BRANDS/DIVISIONS/AFFILIATES:

CONTACTS: Note: Officers with more than one job title may be intentionally listed here more than once.

Brittany McKinney, Interim CEO
Brittany McKinney, Interim Pres.
Randy Strobel, CFO/Sr. VP
Robert E. Woods, General Counsel/Corp. Sec./Sr. VP
Joe Himmelberg, VP-National Field Oper.
Chris Cain, Sr. VP-Western & Eastern Regions
Douglas C. Neve, Chmn.

Phone: 952-835-5900	Fax: 952-897-4555
Toll-Free: 800-800-5044	
Address: 3601 W. 76th St., Minneapolis, MN 55435-3000 US	

GROWTH PLANS/SPECIAL FEATURES:

Analysts International Corp. (AIC) is a diversified information technology consulting and services firm, which offers customers two major services: information technology (IT) consulting and IT staffing. The vast majority of AIC's revenues come from clients in the U.S., mostly Fortune 500 companies, but the firm also has a small presence in Canada and the U.K. AIC offers its clients a full range of IT consulting and software services, including custom software development under company project management, supplemental IT and software engineering staffing and single-source staffing of programmers and other software professionals through its managed services group. Some of AIC's largest clients are Bank of America; Chevron/Texaco; IBM; and Lexmark International, Inc. AIC offers a range of services, including the following: staffing services, which provides IT professionals to large companies; technology integration, which helps companies acquire and integrate hardware and software; outsourcing services; and advisory services, which provide training in methodologies and processes for the use of new technology. The firm has acquired, integrated and sold several subsidiaries in the past few years; most recently, the company sold its Medical Concept Staffing and value added reseller subsidiaries.

AIC offers its employees medical, dental and vision coverage; life and AD&D insurance; flexible spending accounts; a 401(k) plan; an employee stock purchase plan; auto and home insurance; and a legal plan.

FINANCIALS: Sales and profits are in thousands of dollars—add 000 to get the full amount. 2010 Note: Financial information for 2010 was not available for all companies at press time.

2010 Sales: $	2010 Profits: $	U.S. Stock Ticker: ANLY
2009 Sales: $143,165	2009 Profits: $-15,907	Int'l Ticker: Int'l Exchange:
2008 Sales: $284,203	2008 Profits: $-10,134	Employees:
2007 Sales: $359,670	2007 Profits: $-16,212	Fiscal Year Ends: 12/31
2006 Sales: $346,987	2006 Profits: $-1,060	Parent Company:

SALARIES/BENEFITS:

Pension Plan:	ESOP Stock Plan:	Profit Sharing:	Top Exec. Salary: $467,308	Bonus: $
Savings Plan: Y	Stock Purch. Plan: Y		Second Exec. Salary: $275,000	Bonus: $

OTHER THOUGHTS:

Apparent Women Officers or Directors: 2
Hot Spot for Advancement for Women/Minorities: Y

LOCATIONS: ("Y" = Yes)

West:	Southwest:	Midwest:	Southeast:	Northeast:	International:
Y	Y	Y	Y	Y	Y

ANIXTER INTERNATIONAL INC

www.anixter.com

Industry Group Code: 423430 Ranks within this company's industry group: Sales: 8   Profits: 13

Hardware:	Software:	Telecommunications:	Electronic Publishing:	Equipment:		Specialty Services:
Computers:	Consumer:	Local:	Online Service:	Telecom:		Consulting:
Accessories:	Corporate:	Long Distance:	TV/Cable or Wireless:	Communication:		Contract Manufacturing:
Network Equipment:	Telecom:	Cellular:	Games:	Distribution:	Y	Processing:
Chips/Circuits:	Internet:	Internet Service:	Financial Data:	VAR/Reseller:		Staff/Outsourcing:
Parts/Drives:				Satellite Srv./Equip.:		Specialty Services:

TYPES OF BUSINESS:

Wire & Cable Distribution
C Class Inventory Component Distribution
Connectivity Parts Distribution

BRANDS/DIVISIONS/AFFILIATES:

Total Supply Solutions Limited
Eurofast SAS
World Class Wire & Cable Inc

CONTACTS: *Note: Officers with more than one job title may be intentionally listed here more than once.*

Robert J. Eck, CEO
Robert J. Eck, Pres.
Dennis J. Letham, CFO/Exec. VP-Finance
Rodney Smith, VP-Human Resources
John A. Dul, General Counsel/VP/Sec.
Rodney A. Shoemaker, Treas./VP
Terrance A. Faber, VP/Controller
Philip F. Meno, VP-Taxes
Nancy C. Ross-Dronzek, VP-Internal Audit
Ted A. Dosch, Sr. VP-Global Finance
Samuel Zell, Chmn.

Phone: 224-521-8000	Fax: 224-521-8100
Toll-Free: 800-264-9837	
Address: 2301 Patriot Blvd., Glenview, IL 60026 US	

GROWTH PLANS/SPECIAL FEATURES:

Anixter International, Inc. is a leading global distributor of data, voice, video and security network communication products and one of the largest North American distributors of specialty wire and cable products. With nearly 300 sales and warehouse locations in 52 countries, the firm sells over 450,000 products, such as transmission media (copper and fiber optic cable) and connectivity, support, supply and security surveillance products, as well as C-class inventory components (small parts used in manufacturing such as nuts and bolts) to original equipment manufacturers (OEMs). These products, used to connect personal computers, peripheral equipment, mainframe equipment, security equipment and various networks to each other, are incorporated into enterprise networks, physical security networks, central switching offices, web hosting sites and remote transmission sites. In addition, Anixter provides industrial wire and cable products, including electrical and electronic wire and cable, control and instrumentation cable and coaxial cable, used in a wide variety of maintenance, repair and construction-related applications. It also supplies a wide variety of electrical and electronic wire and cable products, fasteners and other small components used by OEMs. Subsidiaries include Total Supply Solutions Limited, a U.K.-based fastener distributor; Eurofast SAS, an aerospace fastener distributor; and World Class Wire & Cable, Inc.

The company offers its employees medical, dental and vision; a 401(k) plan; life insurance; short and long term disability coverage; and an employee assistance program.

FINANCIALS: Sales and profits are in thousands of dollars—add 000 to get the full amount. 2010 Note: Financial information for 2010 was not available for all companies at press time.

2010 Sales: $	2010 Profits: $	U.S. Stock Ticker: AXE
2009 Sales: $4,982,400	2009 Profits: $-29,300	Int'l Ticker: Int'l Exchange:
2008 Sales: $6,136,600	2008 Profits: $187,900	Employees: 7,811
2007 Sales: $5,852,900	2007 Profits: $245,500	Fiscal Year Ends: 12/31
2006 Sales: $4,938,600	2006 Profits: $209,300	Parent Company:

SALARIES/BENEFITS:

Pension Plan:	ESOP Stock Plan:	Profit Sharing:	Top Exec. Salary: $630,000	Bonus: $243,750
Savings Plan: Y	Stock Purch. Plan:		Second Exec. Salary: $530,000	Bonus: $178,125

OTHER THOUGHTS:

Apparent Women Officers or Directors: 1
Hot Spot for Advancement for Women/Minorities:

LOCATIONS: ("Y" = Yes)

West:	Southwest:	Midwest:	Southeast:	Northeast:	International:
Y	Y	Y	Y	Y	Y

Note: Financial information, benefits and other data can change quickly and may vary from those stated here.

ANSYS INC
www.ansys.com

Industry Group Code: 511210N **Ranks within this company's industry group:** Sales: 9 Profits: 5

Hardware:	Software:		Telecommunications:	Electronic Publishing:	Equipment:	Specialty Services:	
Computers:	Consumer:		Local:	Online Service:	Telecom:	Consulting:	Y
Accessories:	Corporate:	Y	Long Distance:	TV/Cable or Wireless:	Communication:	Contract Manufacturing:	
Network Equipment:	Telecom:		Cellular:	Games:	Distribution:	Processing:	
Chips/Circuits:	Internet:		Internet Service:	Financial Data:	VAR/Reseller:	Staff/Outsourcing:	
Parts/Drives:					Satellite Srv./Equip.:	Specialty Services:	Y

TYPES OF BUSINESS:
Software-Engineering, Design & Testing
MEMS Design Software

BRANDS/DIVISIONS/AFFILIATES:
ANSYS DesignModeler
ANSYS 12.0
ANSYS AUTODYN
ANSYS FLUENT
Nexxim
Siwave
ANSYS Workbench
ANSYS Engineering Knowledge Manager

CONTACTS: *Note: Officers with more than one job title may be intentionally listed here more than once.*
James E. Cashman, III, CEO
James E. Cashman, III, Pres.
Maria T. Shields, CFO/VP
Joshua Fredberg, VP-Mktg.
Elaine V. Keim, VP-Human Resources
Sheila S. DiNardo, General Counsel/VP/Sec.
Brian C. Drew, VP/Gen. Mgr.-Central Dev. Unit
Joseph S. Solecki, VP-Physics Bus. Unit
Shane R. Emswiler, VP/Gen. Mgr.-Electronics Bus. Unit
Peter J. Smith, Chmn.
Joseph C. Fairbanks, VP-Worldwide Sales & Support

Phone: 724-746-3304	Fax: 724-514-9494
Toll-Free: 866-267-9724	
Address: 275 Technology Dr., Canonsburg, PA 15317 US	

GROWTH PLANS/SPECIAL FEATURES:
ANSYS, Inc. develops, markets and supports engineering simulation software and technologies. The company's software enables users to analyze designs directly on the desktop, providing a platform for efficient product development, from design to final-stage testing and validation. ANSYS distributes its products through a network of channel partners in more than 40 countries and through its own direct sales offices in over 60 strategic locations worldwide. The company's products are used in many industries, including aerospace, electronics, automotive, energy, manufacturing, biomedical and defense. ANSYS' software can be divided into several product lines. ANSYS Workbench enables customers to simulate engineering designs using computer-aided design (CAD) technology. Multiphysics Solutions provides simulations of structural, thermal, fluid dynamics, acoustic and electromagnetic simulation and the ability to mix these forces for complex simulations. Fluid Dynamics Solutions simulates the motion of liquids and gasses. The Explicit Dynamics product suite simulates short, high deformation, large strain, fracture or complete material failure applications. The Electromagnetics product suite provides electromagnetic field simulation software used by electrical engineers to design high-performance electronic and electromechanical products. The company's system and circuit simulation technology provides schematic capture, layout and design management capabilities that allow engineers to simulate high-speed and high-power electronic circuits coupled to virtual physical models of components of other systems. The ANSYS Engineering Knowledge Manager application tracks simulation data and maintains an archival backup. The firm also offers software for the academic, high-performance computing and geometry interfaces. In addition, ANSYS offers consulting, implementation and training services to aid customers in the adoption of simulation technology. The firm's product names include ANSYS CFX, ANSYS FLUENT, Nexxim, ANSYS DesignModeler, ANSYS 12.0, ANSYS AUTODYN and Slwave.

ANSYS offers its employees medical, dental and vision coverage; a 401(k) plan; an employee stock purchase plan; tuition reimbursements; adoption assistance; short- and long-term disability; and flexible spending accounts.

FINANCIALS: Sales and profits are in thousands of dollars—add 000 to get the full amount. 2010 Note: Financial information for 2010 was not available for all companies at press time.
2010 Sales: $	2010 Profits: $	U.S. Stock Ticker: ANSS
2009 Sales: $516,885	2009 Profits: $116,391	Int'l Ticker: Int'l Exchange:
2008 Sales: $478,339	2008 Profits: $111,671	Employees: 1,600
2007 Sales: $385,340	2007 Profits: $82,392	Fiscal Year Ends: 12/31
2006 Sales: $263,640	2006 Profits: $14,156	Parent Company:

SALARIES/BENEFITS:
| Pension Plan: | ESOP Stock Plan: | Profit Sharing: | Top Exec. Salary: $510,000 | Bonus: $500,000 |
| Savings Plan: Y | Stock Purch. Plan: | | Second Exec. Salary: $240,000 | Bonus: $199,360 |

OTHER THOUGHTS:
Apparent Women Officers or Directors: 4
Hot Spot for Advancement for Women/Minorities: Y

LOCATIONS: ("Y" = Yes)
West:	Southwest:	Midwest:	Southeast:	Northeast:	International:
Y	Y	Y	Y	Y	Y

APPLE INC

Industry Group Code: 334111 Ranks within this company's industry group: Sales: 7 Profits: 1

www.apple.com

Hardware:		Software:		Telecommunications:		Electronic Publishing:		Equipment:		Specialty Services:	
Computers:	Y	Consumer:	Y	Local:		Online Service:	Y	Telecom:		Consulting:	
Accessories:	Y	Corporate:	Y	Long Distance:		TV/Cable or Wireless:		Communication:		Contract Manufacturing:	
Network Equipment:		Telecom:		Cellular:		Games:		Distribution:		Processing:	
Chips/Circuits:		Internet:		Internet Service:		Financial Data:		VAR/Reseller:		Staff/Outsourcing:	
Parts/Drives:								Satellite Srv./Equip.:		Specialty Services:	

TYPES OF BUSINESS:

Computer Hardware-PCs
Software
Computer Accessories
Retail Stores
Portable Music Players
Online Music Sales and Video Rentals
Cellular Phones
Home Entertainment Software & Systems

BRANDS/DIVISIONS/AFFILIATES:

iLife
iPad
iTunes
Mac OS X
MacBook Air
iPod
iPhone
Safari

CONTACTS: Note: Officers with more than one job title may be intentionally listed here more than once.

Steve P. Jobs, CEO
Timothy D. Cook, COO
Peter Oppenheimer, CFO/Sr. VP
Philip W. Schiller, Sr. VP-Worldwide Prod. Mktg.
Bob Mansfield, Sr. VP-Mac Hardware Eng.
Bruce Sewell, General Counsel/Sr. VP
Ronald B. Johnson, Sr. VP-Retail
Jonathan Ive, Sr. VP-Industrial Design
Bertrand Serlet, Sr. VP-Software Eng.
Scott Forstall, Sr. VP-iPhone Software
Bill Campbell, Chmn.

Phone: 408-996-1010	Fax: 408-996-0275
Toll-Free: 800-692-7753	
Address: 1 Infinite Loop, Cupertino, CA 95014 US	

GROWTH PLANS/SPECIAL FEATURES:

Apple, Inc. designs, manufactures and markets personal computers, portable digital music players and mobile communication devices; and sells a variety of related software, services, peripherals and networking solutions. The company's hardware products include the MacBook, MacBook Air and MacBook Pro notebook computers; Mac Pro and iMac desktop computers; Mac minis; and Xserve servers and Xserve RAID Storage Systems. The firm's Mac products feature Intel microprocessors, Mac OS X Leopard operating systems and iLife software. Software products include Mac OS X; iLife '09; iWork '09; Logic Studio; and FileMaker Pro. Additional products include the iSight digital video cameras; the iPod line of portable digital music players and accessories; the iPhone, with touch controls, phone, iPod, and Internet services; Final Cut Studio, a high-definition video production suite of applications; and the iTunes digital entertainment management software for MP3 music files, television shows and movies. The iPhone is available in over 80 countries through individual carrier distribution deals. Peripheral products are sold directly to end-users through its retail and online stores and include printers, storage devices, computer memory, digital video and still camera and other computing products and supplies. Apple's roughly 300 retail stores have been a tremendous success. In 2009, Apple opened 26 new stores, including 12 stores in the U.S. and 14 stores internationally. The firm opened 44 new stores in 2010. In September 2009, the firm introduced an updated version of the iPod classic; updated the third-generation iPod shuffle; and introduced the iPod nano, a flash-memory-based iPod, which includes a video camera, microphone, speaker, iTunes tagging, a built-in FM radio with live pause functionality and a built-in pedometer. In January 2010, the firm introduced the iPad tablet computer. In June 2010, Apple launched the iPhone 4, which features FaceTime, a Retina display and a five megapixel camera.

FINANCIALS: Sales and profits are in thousands of dollars—add 000 to get the full amount. 2010 Note: Financial information for 2010 was not available for all companies at press time.

2010 Sales: $65,225,000	2010 Profits: $14,013,000	U.S. Stock Ticker: AAPL
2009 Sales: $42,905,000	2009 Profits: $8,235,000	Int'l Ticker: Int'l Exchange:
2008 Sales: $37,491,000	2008 Profits: $6,119,000	Employees: 49,400
2007 Sales: $24,006,000	2007 Profits: $3,496,000	Fiscal Year Ends: 9/30
2006 Sales: $19,315,000	2006 Profits: $1,989,000	Parent Company:

SALARIES/BENEFITS:

Pension Plan:	ESOP Stock Plan:	Profit Sharing:	Top Exec. Salary: $800,400	Bonus: $800,000
Savings Plan: Y	Stock Purch. Plan: Y		Second Exec. Salary: $700,398	Bonus: $700,000

OTHER THOUGHTS:

Apparent Women Officers or Directors: 1
Hot Spot for Advancement for Women/Minorities:

LOCATIONS: ("Y" = Yes)

West:	Southwest:	Midwest:	Southeast:	Northeast:	International:
Y	Y	Y	Y	Y	Y

APPLIED MATERIALS INC

www.appliedmaterials.com

Industry Group Code: 333295 Ranks within this company's industry group: Sales: 1   Profits: 10

Hardware:		Software:		Telecommunications:	Electronic Publishing:	Equipment:	Specialty Services:
Computers:		Consumer:		Local:	Online Service:	Telecom:	Consulting:
Accessories:		Corporate:	Y	Long Distance:	TV/Cable or Wireless:	Communication:	Contract Manufacturing:
Network Equipment:		Telecom:		Cellular:	Games:	Distribution:	Processing:
Chips/Circuits:	Y	Internet:		Internet Service:	Financial Data:	VAR/Reseller:	Staff/Outsourcing:
Parts/Drives:						Satellite Srv./Equip.:	Specialty Services:

TYPES OF BUSINESS:

Semiconductor Manufacturing Equipment
Solar Cells
Photovoltaics (PV)
Global Services
Semiconductor Equipment Manufacturing
Display Technology Equipment
Solar Product Manufacturing
Automation Software

BRANDS/DIVISIONS/AFFILIATES:

Nanomanufacturing Technologies
Silicon Systems Group
Sokudo Company
SunFab
Brooks Software
Semitool, Inc.

CONTACTS: *Note: Officers with more than one job title may be intentionally listed here more than once.*

Michael R. Splinter, CEO
Michael R. Splinter, Pres.
George S. Davis, CFO/Exec. VP
Mary Humiston, VP-Global Human Resources
Ron Kifer, CIO
Mark R. Pinto, CTO
Manfred Kerschbaum, Chief of Staff/Sr. VP
Joseph J. Sweeney, General Counsel/Corp. Sec./Sr. VP
Charlie Pappis, Gen. Mgr.-Applied Global Svcs.
Chris Bowers, VP-Corp. Initiatives
Randhio Thakur, PH.D., Exec. VP/Gen. Mgr.-Silicon Systems
Michael R. Splinter, Chmn.
Joseph Flanagan, VP-Supply Chain

Phone: 408-727-5555	Fax: 408-748-9943
Toll-Free:	
Address: 3050 Bowers Ave., Santa Clara, CA 95054-3299 US	

GROWTH PLANS/SPECIAL FEATURES:

Applied Materials, Inc. (AMI), a global leader in the semiconductor industry, provides solutions for the global semiconductor, flat panel display, solar and related industries, with a portfolio of equipment, service and software products. The firm serves approximately 12,600 people in 11 principle regions including Canada, China, Europe, India, Israel, Japan, Korea, Malaysia, Singapore, Taiwan and the U.S. AMI operates in four reportable segments: Silicon; Applied Global Services; Display; and Energy and Environmental Solutions. The Silicon segment, operated by Silicon Systems Group develops, manufactures and sells a wide range of manufacturing equipment used to fabricate semiconductor chips or integrated circuits. Most chips are built on a silicon wafer base and include a variety of circuit components, such as transistors and other devices, that are connected by multiple layers of wiring (interconnects). The Applied Global Services segment provides products and services designed to improve the performance and productivity and reduce environmental impact of the fab operations of semiconductor, LCD and solar PV manufacturers. The Display segment designs, manufactures, sells and services equipment to fabricate thin film transistor LCDs for televisions, computer displays and other consumer-oriented electronic applications. The Energy and Environmental Solutions segment provides manufacturing solutions for the generation and conservation of energy. AMI's solutions utilize Nanomanufacturing Technology, or the production of ultra-small structures, including the engineering of thin layers of film onto substrates. In April 2010, Applied Materials opened a Singapore Operations Center, its first manufacturing facility in Asia. It is located in Changi North Industrial Park and will manufacture advanced semiconductor equipment as well as support Applied's worldwide supply chain operations and other corporate functions.

Employees are offered medical insurance; flexible spending accounts; adoption benefits; an employee assistance program; health appraisals; health and fitness education; a 401(k) plan; a stock purchase plan; credit union membership; and tuition reimbursement.

FINANCIALS: Sales and profits are in thousands of dollars—add 000 to get the full amount. 2010 Note: Financial information for 2010 was not available for all companies at press time.

2010 Sales: $9,548,667	2010 Profits: $937,866	**U.S. Stock Ticker: AMAT**
2009 Sales: $5,013,607	2009 Profits: $-305,327	**Int'l Ticker:** Int'l Exchange:
2008 Sales: $8,129,240	2008 Profits: $960,746	Employees: 13,045
2007 Sales: $9,734,856	2007 Profits: $1,710,196	Fiscal Year Ends: 10/31
2006 Sales: $9,167,014	2006 Profits: $1,516,663	Parent Company:

SALARIES/BENEFITS:

Pension Plan:	ESOP Stock Plan:	Profit Sharing:	Top Exec. Salary: $814,154	Bonus: $
Savings Plan: Y	Stock Purch. Plan: Y		Second Exec. Salary: $493,477	Bonus: $

OTHER THOUGHTS:

Apparent Women Officers or Directors: 2
Hot Spot for Advancement for Women/Minorities: Y

LOCATIONS: ("Y" = Yes)

West:	Southwest:	Midwest:	Southeast:	Northeast:	International:
Y	Y				Y

Note: Financial information, benefits and other data can change quickly and may vary from those stated here.

ARCSIGHT INC

www.arcsight.com

Industry Group Code: 511210E **Ranks within this company's industry group:** Sales: 8 Profits: 7

Hardware:	Software:		Telecommunications:	Electronic Publishing:	Equipment:	Specialty Services:	
Computers:	Consumer:		Local:	Online Service:	Telecom:	Consulting:	Y
Accessories:	Corporate:	Y	Long Distance:	TV/Cable or Wireless:	Communication:	Contract Manufacturing:	
Network Equipment:	Telecom:		Cellular:	Games:	Distribution:	Processing:	
Chips/Circuits:	Internet:		Internet Service:	Financial Data:	VAR/Reseller:	Staff/Outsourcing:	
Parts/Drives:					Satellite Srv./Equip.:	Specialty Services:	Y

TYPES OF BUSINESS:

IT & Network Security Products & Services
IT Support Services
Regulation Compliance

BRANDS/DIVISIONS/AFFILIATES:

ArcSight Security Information and Event Management
ArcSight ESM
ArcSight Identity View
ArcSight Compliance
ArcSight Logger
ArcSight Connectors
ArcSight Express
Hewlett-Packard Co (HP)

CONTACTS: Note: Officers with more than one job title may be intentionally listed here more than once.

Tom Reilly, CEO
Tom Reilly, Pres.
Stewart Grierson, CFO
Reed Henry, Sr. VP-Mktg.
Gail Boddy, VP-Human Resources
Hugh Njemanze, Exec. VP-R&D
Bruce Burroughs, CIO/VP
Hugh Njemanze, CTO
Bob Pratt, VP-Prod. Mgmt.
Haiyan Song, VP-Eng.
Tram Phi, General Counsel/Corp. Sec.
Kevin Mosher, Sr. VP-Worldwide Field Oper.
Jeff Scheel, Sr. VP-Bus. Dev.
Joni Kahn, Sr. VP-Support & Svcs.
Prescott Winter, CTO-Public Sector
Laura Menicucci, VP-Customer Support
Hector Aguilarmacias, VP-Software Dev.
Tim Durnford, VP/Country Mgr.-Canada

Phone: 408-864-2600	Fax: 408-342-1615
Toll-Free: 888-415-2778	
Address: 5 Results Way, Cupertino, CA 95014 US	

GROWTH PLANS/SPECIAL FEATURES:

ArcSight, Inc. provides security management and compliance solutions for businesses and government agencies. The company assists its clients in complying with corporate and government regulatory policies; as well as controlling risk in the form of rapid identification of compliance violations, cyber-security attacks, policy breaches and insider threats. Its primary security platform, the ArcSight Security Information and Event Management (SIEM) Platform, mitigates the potential risks posed by cyber-theft, cyber-warfare, cyber-espionage and cyber-fraud, from both internal and external threat factors. The SIEM platform is able to integrate into the existing IT infrastructure of businesses and government agencies. Once integrated, the principle components of the SIEM platform are the company's event security management products, which provide a centralized delivery system that alerts customers with real-time status updates and activity messages. ArcSight's products collect, analyze and correlate massive numbers of events from security point solutions, and provide analytics and reports tailored to specific compliance and security initiatives, as well as appliances that streamline event log collection, storage, analysis and reporting. The company offers several different products including the ArcSight ESM, ArcSight Identity View, ArcSight Compliance, ArcSight Logger, ArcSight Connectors and the ArcSight Express. Additionally, ArcSight has strategic partnerships with several companies including Deloitte; IBM; Cisco; McAfee; Oracle; and Wipro Technologies. The company has offices located in California, Texas, Georgia, Massachusetts, and international locations in Asia, Canada, Europe and the Middle East. In October 2010, the firm was acquired by Hewlett-Packard Co. (HP) for $1.5 billion.

FINANCIALS: Sales and profits are in thousands of dollars—add 000 to get the full amount. 2010 Note: Financial information for 2010 was not available for all companies at press time.

2010 Sales: $181,384	2010 Profits: $28,387	U.S. Stock Ticker: Subsidiary
2009 Sales: $136,168	2009 Profits: $9,913	Int'l Ticker: Int'l Exchange:
2008 Sales: $101,545	2008 Profits: $-2,009	Employees: 512
2007 Sales: $69,833	2007 Profits: $- 257	Fiscal Year Ends: 4/30
2006 Sales: $	2006 Profits: $	Parent Company: HEWLETT-PACKARD CO (HP)

SALARIES/BENEFITS:

Pension Plan:	ESOP Stock Plan:	Profit Sharing:	Top Exec. Salary: $375,000	Bonus: $337,500
Savings Plan:	Stock Purch. Plan:		Second Exec. Salary: $300,000	Bonus: $225,000

OTHER THOUGHTS:

Apparent Women Officers or Directors: 4
Hot Spot for Advancement for Women/Minorities: Y

LOCATIONS: ("Y" = Yes)

West:	Southwest:	Midwest:	Southeast:	Northeast:	International:
Y	Y		Y	Y	Y

Note: Financial information, benefits and other data can change quickly and may vary from those stated here.

ARGON ST INC

www.argonst.com

Industry Group Code: 541513 Ranks within this company's industry group: Sales: 25 Profits: 20

Hardware:		Software:		Telecommunications:		Electronic Publishing:		Equipment:		Specialty Services:	
Computers:		Consumer:		Local:		Online Service:		Telecom:	Y	Consulting:	
Accessories:		Corporate:	Y	Long Distance:		TV/Cable or Wireless:		Communication:	Y	Contract Manufacturing:	Y
Network Equipment:	Y	Telecom:	Y	Cellular:		Games:		Distribution:		Processing:	
Chips/Circuits:		Internet:		Internet Service:		Financial Data:		VAR/Reseller:		Staff/Outsourcing:	
Parts/Drives:	Y							Satellite Srv./Equip.:	Y	Specialty Services:	Y

TYPES OF BUSINESS:

Systems Engineering & Development
Defense & Intelligence Systems
Defense Simulation Tools
Imaging Systems
Communications Technology
Consulting
Engineering

BRANDS/DIVISIONS/AFFILIATES:

Boeing Company (The)

CONTACTS: Note: Officers with more than one job title may be intentionally listed here more than once.

Terry L. Collins, CEO
Kerry M. Rowe, COO
Kerry M. Rowe, Pres.
Robert S. Tamaru, VP-Tech.
Stanford K. Harmon, VP-Oper. Support
Robert S. Tamaru, VP-Strategic Dev.
Michael J. Hettmann, VP-Reconnaissance Systems
James Ross, VP-National Programs
Jay R. Grove, VP-Network Systems
W. Joseph Carlin, Sr. VP-Info. Dominance

Phone: 703-322-0881	Fax: 703-322-0885
Toll-Free:	
Address: 12701 Fair Lakes Cir., Ste. 800, Fairfax, VA 22033 US	

GROWTH PLANS/SPECIAL FEATURES:

Argon ST, Inc., a unit of Boeing's Network & Space Systems division, is a systems engineering, development and services company. The firm provides full-service C4ISR systems (command, control, communications, computers, intelligence, surveillance and reconnaissance) and combat systems, which address several markets including maritime defense; ground systems; airborne reconnaissance; network systems and security; and tactical communications. Argon serves a wide range of defense and intelligence customers as well as commercial enterprises. The company develops and services hardware and software in four areas: sensors, systems, networks and services. Argon designs and produces signals intelligence (SIGNINT) sensors that seek, exploit, identify, and locate the environment for RF energy, underwater sound, light, heat, and complex phenomena. Its systems support a range of different applications, including reconnaissance, communication, navigation, geo-location and threat warning, among others. Argon's network capabilities include system-of-systems and network-of-networks engineering that support wireless networks, mobile ad hoc networks, interference-resistant technologies and satellite communications. Through services such as information analysis and fusion, integration, engineering and manufacturing, the firm helps clients complete tasks. In August 2010, Boeing Co. acquired Argon for $782 million and, as a result, Argon became a wholly-owned subsidiary of Boeing.

The firm offers employees medical and dental coverage; life and disability insurance; a 401(k); a discount stock purchase plan; education assistance; an adoption program; and paid time off.

FINANCIALS: Sales and profits are in thousands of dollars—add 000 to get the full amount. 2010 Note: Financial information for 2010 was not available for all companies at press time.

2010 Sales: $	2010 Profits: $	U.S. Stock Ticker: Subsidiary
2009 Sales: $366,076	2009 Profits: $23,691	Int'l Ticker: Int'l Exchange:
2008 Sales: $340,934	2008 Profits: $20,273	Employees: 1,063
2007 Sales: $282,209	2007 Profits: $14,702	Fiscal Year Ends: 9/30
2006 Sales: $258,835	2006 Profits: $19,395	Parent Company: BOEING COMPANY (THE)

SALARIES/BENEFITS:

Pension Plan:	ESOP Stock Plan:	Profit Sharing:	Top Exec. Salary: $473,722	Bonus: $
Savings Plan: Y	Stock Purch. Plan: Y		Second Exec. Salary: $382,034	Bonus: $

OTHER THOUGHTS:

Apparent Women Officers or Directors:
Hot Spot for Advancement for Women/Minorities:

LOCATIONS: ("Y" = Yes)

West:	Southwest:	Midwest:	Southeast:	Northeast:	International:
Y	Y		Y	Y	Y

ARIBA INC

www.ariba.com

Industry Group Code: 511210A Ranks within this company's industry group: Sales: 3   Profits: 4

Hardware:	Software:		Telecommunications:	Electronic Publishing:	Equipment:	Specialty Services:	
Computers:	Consumer:		Local:	Online Service:	Telecom:	Consulting:	Y
Accessories:	Corporate:	Y	Long Distance:	TV/Cable or Wireless:	Communication:	Contract Manufacturing:	
Network Equipment:	Telecom:		Cellular:	Games:	Distribution:	Processing:	
Chips/Circuits:	Internet:		Internet Service:	Financial Data:	VAR/Reseller:	Staff/Outsourcing:	
Parts/Drives:					Satellite Srv./Equip.:	Specialty Services:	Y

TYPES OF BUSINESS:

Computer Software-Transaction Processing
Procurement & Logistics Solutions
Business Process Software
Consulting Services

BRANDS/DIVISIONS/AFFILIATES:

Procuri, Inc.
Tradex Technologies, Inc
Surplus Records, Inc.
Alliente, Inc.
Quadrem

CONTACTS: Note: Officers with more than one job title may be intentionally listed here more than once.

Robert M. Calderoni, CEO
Kent Parker, COO
Kevin S. Costello, Pres.
Ahmed Rubaie, CFO/Exec. VP
Tim Minahan, Chief Mktg. Officer
Matthew Zack, Sr. VP-Human Resources
Bhaskar Himatsingka, CTO
Matthew Zack, Sr. VP-Corp. Dev.
Bob Solomon, Sr. VP/Gen. Mgr.-Ariba Network Bus. Unit.
Daryl T. Rolley, Sr. VP/Gen. Mgr.-Ariba, North America & Asia
Greg Spray, Sr. VP-Solutions Mgmt.
Robert M. Calderoni, Chmn.
Michael J. Arenth, VP/Gen. Mgr.-Ariba, Europe

Phone: 650-390-1000	Fax: 650-390-1100
Toll-Free:	
Address: 807 11th Ave., Sunnyvale, CA 94089 US	

GROWTH PLANS/SPECIAL FEATURES:

Ariba, Inc. provides its clients with spend management software and solutions that allow for the efficient procurement of all required non-payroll goods and services. Its products and services enhance the visibility of spending activities across a clinet's suppliers, divisions and purchased goods or services. The company currently has office locations in 22 countries, operating in three geographic segments: North America; Europe, Middle East, and Africa; and Asia-Pacific. The company's software applications are provided as software-as-a-service (SaaS) and can integrate with all major business applications. Ariba's collaborative business commerce solutions combine SaaS technology with web-based communities and a global network of trading partners. For buyers Ariba provides a wide range of spend analysis solutions, including contract management, procurement analytics and supplier management. Its contract management solutions for buyers allow customers to streamline and automate the entire contract process. For procurement and expense activities, it offers applications and services for requisitioning and procurement across all kinds of spending. Supplier management solutions enable companies to identify and assess new sources of supply. Services for sellers include supplier sales and marketing programs; network catalog, order and invoice collaboration; and supply chain finance and payment management applications. The company's subsidiaries include Procuri, Inc., a provider of on-demand supply management solutions; Tradex Technologies, Inc, which provides marketplace systems; Surplus Records, Inc., a surplus directory of tools and industrial equipment; and Alliente, Inc., an e-business procurement service. In November 2010, the firm agreed to acquire Quadrem, a provider of on-demand supply management software. In the same month, it also finalized the sale of its sourcing services and business process outsourcing (BPO) services assets to Accenture.

The company offers its employees medical, dental and vision; a 401(k) plan; employee stock purchase plan; and flexible spending account.

FINANCIALS: Sales and profits are in thousands of dollars—add 000 to get the full amount. 2010 Note: Financial information for 2010 was not available for all companies at press time.

2010 Sales: $361,146	2010 Profits: $16,386	**U.S. Stock Ticker: ARBA**
2009 Sales: $338,972	2009 Profits: $8,193	**Int'l Ticker:** Int'l Exchange:
2008 Sales: $328,060	2008 Profits: $-41,062	Employees: 1,804
2007 Sales: $301,667	2007 Profits: $-14,977	Fiscal Year Ends: 9/30
2006 Sales: $296,016	2006 Profits: $-47,801	Parent Company:

SALARIES/BENEFITS:

Pension Plan:	ESOP Stock Plan: Y	Profit Sharing:	Top Exec. Salary: $675,000	Bonus: $1,350,000
Savings Plan: Y	Stock Purch. Plan:		Second Exec. Salary: $500,000	Bonus: $559,450

OTHER THOUGHTS:

Apparent Women Officers or Directors:
Hot Spot for Advancement for Women/Minorities:

LOCATIONS: ("Y" = Yes)

West:	Southwest:	Midwest:	Southeast:	Northeast:	International:
Y	Y	Y	Y	Y	Y

Note: Financial information, benefits and other data can change quickly and may vary from those stated here.

ARM HOLDINGS PLC
www.arm.com

Industry Group Code: 333295 Ranks within this company's industry group: Sales: 10 Profits: 4

Hardware:		Software:	Telecommunications:	Electronic Publishing:	Equipment:	Specialty Services:	
Computers:		Consumer:	Local:	Online Service:	Telecom:	Consulting:	
Accessories:		Corporate:	Long Distance:	TV/Cable or Wireless:	Communication:	Contract Manufacturing:	Y
Network Equipment:	Y	Telecom:	Cellular:	Games:	Distribution:	Processing:	
Chips/Circuits:	Y	Internet:	Internet Service:	Financial Data:	VAR/Reseller:	Staff/Outsourcing:	
Parts/Drives:					Satellite Srv./Equip.:	Specialty Services:	

TYPES OF BUSINESS:
Semiconductors Manufacturing

BRANDS/DIVISIONS/AFFILIATES:
ARM7
ARM Securcore
ARM9
ARM11
ARM Cortex
Streamline Performance Analyzer

CONTACTS: Note: Officers with more than one job title may be intentionally listed here more than once.
Warren East, CEO
Graham Budd, COO
Tudor Brown, Pres.
Tim Score, CFO
Ian Drew, Exec. VP-Mktg.
Bill Parsons, Exec. VP-Human Resources
Mike Muller, CTO
Phil David, General Counsel
Thomas P. Lantzsch, Exec. VP-Corp. Dev.
Ian Thornton, VP-Investor Rel.
Mike Inglis, Exec. VP/Gen Mgr.-Processor Div.
Simon Segars, Exec. VP/Gen. Mgr.-Physical IP Div.
John Cornish, Exec. VP/Gen. Mgr.-System Design Div.
Lance Howarth, VP/Gen. Mgr.-Media Processing Div.
Doug Dunn, Chmn.
Antonio Viana, Exec. VP-Worldwide Sales

Phone: 44-01223-400400	Fax: 44-01223-400700
Toll-Free:	
Address: 110 Fulbourn Rd., Cambridge, CB1 9NJ UK	

GROWTH PLANS/SPECIAL FEATURES:
ARM Holdings plc is a designer of microprocessors, physical IP and related technology and software. The firm also sells development tools intended to enhance the cost-effectiveness, performance and energy-efficiency of high-volume embedded applications. ARM Holdings licenses and sells development tools directly to systems companies and provides support services to its systems firms, licensees and other systems designers. In addition, the company licenses and sells its products and technology to international electronics firms; these firms then manufacture and market application-specific integrated circuits, microprocessors and application-specific standard processors that utilize ARM Holdings' technology to systems companies. These system companies use the firm's technology in a wide array of products, including cellular phones, PC peripherals and digital televisions. ARM Holdings offers several different microprocessor cores, including the low power ARM7, its most widely licensed product; ARM Securcore, a series aimed at the security and smart card industry; ARM9, a microprocessor series ranging from 150-250 Megahertz (MHz); ARM11, a family of microprocessors ranging from 300-600 MHz; and ARM Cortex, designed to address the need of applications processors running complex operating systems, running Real Time Operating Systems and low-cost microcontroller markets. The firm's physical IP products include memory components that support 2-128 bits; Standard cell libraries, which map the logic functions of a design to the physical functions of the design; interface/high-speed interface components that utilize each integrated circuit manufacturer's unique electrostatic discharge requirements, process rules and pad pitch; and silicon on insulator products, designed to perform better and operate at a lower power level than standard semiconductors. Based in the U.K., the company operates primarily in the U.S., Europe and Asia Pacific. In November 2010, ARM Holdings released Linux application optimization product Streamline Performance Analyzer.

ARM Holdings offers employees life and medical insurance; patent bonuses; equity; and flexible vacation and leave.

FINANCIALS: Sales and profits are in thousands of dollars—add 000 to get the full amount. 2010 Note: Financial information for 2010 was not available for all companies at press time.
2010 Sales: $	2010 Profits: $	U.S. Stock Ticker: ARMH
2009 Sales: $470,290	2009 Profits: $62,350	Int'l Ticker: ARM Int'l Exchange: London-LSE
2008 Sales: $478,020	2008 Profits: $69,710	Employees: 1,710
2007 Sales: $414,420	2007 Profits: $56,370	Fiscal Year Ends: 12/31
2006 Sales: $	2006 Profits: $	Parent Company:

SALARIES/BENEFITS:
Pension Plan:	ESOP Stock Plan:	Profit Sharing:	Top Exec. Salary: $704,564	Bonus: $486,418
Savings Plan: Y	Stock Purch. Plan:		Second Exec. Salary: $611,204	Bonus: $432,330

OTHER THOUGHTS:
Apparent Women Officers or Directors: 2
Hot Spot for Advancement for Women/Minorities: Y

LOCATIONS: ("Y" = Yes)
West:	Southwest:	Midwest:	Southeast:	Northeast:	International:
Y	Y	Y		Y	Y

ARROW ELECTRONICS INC

www.arrow.com

Industry Group Code: 423430 Ranks within this company's industry group: Sales: 4 Profits: 2

Hardware:		Software:		Telecommunications:	Electronic Publishing:	Equipment:		Specialty Services:	
Computers:		Consumer:		Local:	Online Service:	Telecom:		Consulting:	Y
Accessories:	Y	Corporate:	Y	Long Distance:	TV/Cable or Wireless:	Communication:		Contract Manufacturing:	
Network Equipment:	Y	Telecom:		Cellular:	Games:	Distribution:	Y	Processing:	
Chips/Circuits:	Y	Internet:		Internet Service:	Financial Data:	VAR/Reseller:	Y	Staff/Outsourcing:	
Parts/Drives:						Satellite Srv./Equip.:		Specialty Services:	Y

TYPES OF BUSINESS:

Electronic Components-Distributor
Computer Products-Distributor
Technical Support Services
Supply Chain Services
Design Services
Materials Planning
Assembly Services
Inventory Management

BRANDS/DIVISIONS/AFFILIATES:

Arrow Enterprise Computing Solutions
Arrow North American Components (NAC)
Converge
Verical, Inc.
Sphinx Group Ltd.
Intechra
Diasa Informatica
Nu Horizons Electronics

CONTACTS: Note: Officers with more than one job title may be intentionally listed here more than once.

Michael J. Long, CEO
Michael J. Long, Pres.
Paul J. Reilly, CFO/Exec. VP-Finance
John P. McMahon, Sr. VP-Human Resources
Peter S. Brown, General Counsel/Corp. Sec./Sr. VP
Paul J. Reilly, Exec. VP-Oper.
M. Catherine Morris, Chief Strategy Officer/Sr. VP
John Hourigan, Dir.-Corp. Comm.
Michael Taunton, Treas./VP
Peter T. Kong, Pres., Arrow Global Components
Andrew S. Bryant, Pres., Arrow Enterprise Computing Solutions
Vinnie Vellucci, Pres., Arrow North American Components
Michael J. Long, Chmn.
Simon Yu, Pres., Arrow Asia-Pacific Components

Phone: 631-847-2000	Fax: 631-847-2222
Toll-Free: 877-237-8621	
Address: 50 Marcus Dr., Melville, NY 11747-4210 US	

GROWTH PLANS/SPECIAL FEATURES:

Arrow Electronics, Inc. is a global provider of products, services and solutions to industrial and commercial users of electronic components of enterprise computing software. The company offers more than 450,000 products to its clients in the electronic industry products and solutions in materials planning, programming, assembly services and online supply chain tools and design. Arrow serves as a supply channel partner for over 900 suppliers and 125,000 original equipment manufacturers, contract manufacturers and commercial customers through a global network of over 250 locations in 51 countries and territories. Its operations are divided into two segments: enterprise computing solutions, representing 34% of 2009 sales; and global components, 66%. The enterprise computing solutions segment distributes enterprise IT products, such as servers, software and storage devices, to value added retailers (VARs) in North America, Middle East, Africa and Europe. This segment consists primarily of Arrow Enterprise Computing Solutions (ECS), which offers services in North America, Africa and Europe. Additionally, Arrow NAC provides enterprise solutions for contract, aerospace and defense manufacturers. The global components segment, consisting primarily of Arrow North American Components, Arrow EMEA and Arrow Asia/Pacific, distributes electronics components and related products. Its sales are comprised of semiconductors; passive, electro-mechanical and interconnect products such as capacitors, resistors, potentiometers, power supplies, relays, switches, and connectors; and computing, memory and other products. In 2010, Arrow made a number of acquisitions, including Converge and Verical, Inc. in April; Sphinx Group Ltd. in June; and Intechra and Diasa Informatica in December. In March 2010, Arrow ECS established a professional services business unit to offer technical and educational support to clients in North America. In January 2011, it acquired Nu Horizons Electronics.

Employee benefits include a 401(k); an employee stock ownership program; medical, dental and vision coverage; a domestic partner program; an employee assistance program; tuition assistance; volunteer grants; scholarships; and an employee referral program.

FINANCIALS: Sales and profits are in thousands of dollars—add 000 to get the full amount. 2010 Note: Financial information for 2010 was not available for all companies at press time.

2010 Sales: $	2010 Profits: $	**U.S. Stock Ticker: ARW**
2009 Sales: $14,684,101	2009 Profits: $123,512	**Int'l Ticker:** Int'l Exchange:
2008 Sales: $16,761,009	2008 Profits: $-613,739	Employees: 11,300
2007 Sales: $15,984,992	2007 Profits: $407,792	Fiscal Year Ends: 12/31
2006 Sales: $13,577,112	2006 Profits: $388,331	Parent Company:

SALARIES/BENEFITS:

Pension Plan:	ESOP Stock Plan: Y	Profit Sharing:	Top Exec. Salary: $1,057,692	Bonus: $1,485,000
Savings Plan: Y	Stock Purch. Plan:		Second Exec. Salary: $666,186	Bonus: $1,198,313

OTHER THOUGHTS:

Apparent Women Officers or Directors: 1
Hot Spot for Advancement for Women/Minorities:

LOCATIONS: ("Y" = Yes)

West:	Southwest:	Midwest:	Southeast:	Northeast:	International:
Y	Y	Y	Y	Y	Y

ART TECHNOLOGY GROUP INC

www.atg.com

Industry Group Code: 511210M Ranks within this company's industry group: Sales: 2 Profits: 1

Hardware:	Software:		Telecommunications:		Electronic Publishing:	Equipment:	Specialty Services:	
Computers:	Consumer:		Local:		Online Service:	Telecom:	Consulting:	Y
Accessories:	Corporate:	Y	Long Distance:		TV/Cable or Wireless:	Communication:	Contract Manufacturing:	
Network Equipment:	Telecom:		Cellular:		Games:	Distribution:	Processing:	
Chips/Circuits:	Internet:		Internet Service:		Financial Data:	VAR/Reseller:	Staff/Outsourcing:	
Parts/Drives:						Satellite Srv./Equip.:	Specialty Services:	

TYPES OF BUSINESS:

Software-Web Development & E-Commerce
Consulting Services
Application Development
Design Services
Training & Support Services

BRANDS/DIVISIONS/AFFILIATES:

eStara
OnDemand
Click to Call
Click to Chat
Call Tracking
InstantService
ATG LiveStore
Oracle Corp

CONTACTS: Note: Officers with more than one job title may be intentionally listed here more than once.

Robert D. Burke, CEO
Robert D. Burke, Pres.
Julie M. B. Bradley, CFO
Nina McIntyre, Chief Mktg. Officer/Sr. VP
Patricia O'Neill, Sr. VP-Human Resources
Kenneth Z. Volpe, Sr. VP-Tech.
Kenneth Z. Volpe, Sr. VP-Prod.
David McEvoy, General Counsel/VP
Drew Reynolds, Sr. VP-Corp. Dev.
Lou Frio, Sr. VP-Svcs.
Daniel C. Regis, Chmn.
Barry E. Clark, Sr. VP-Worldwide Sales

Phone: 617-386-1000	Fax: 617-386-1111
Toll-Free:	
Address: 1 Main St., Cambridge, MA 02142 US	

GROWTH PLANS/SPECIAL FEATURES:

Art Technology Group, Inc. (ATG) provides software solutions and support services that help businesses to develop and manage personalized web sites. ATG's products capture/maintain information about customers' personal preferences, online activity and transaction history, and use this information to provide more contextual content. Through its eStara subsidiary, the company provides OnDemand services for multi-channel interaction. Its Click to Call and Click to Chat services provide online businesses with proactive conversion solutions for enhancing online sales and support. eStara solutions allow customers to converse with a sales person or customer care agent by clicking a button on a web site, e-mail, banner ad or directory listing, and eStara's Call Tracking solutions allow advertisers to track the source of each in-bound call as well as information about callers. ATG also offers its Adaptive Scenario Engine (ASE), meant to improve sales by creating personal profiles for customers and determining the efficacy of online marketing strategies. ASE also provides the tools for improving web site content and presentation. ATG provides clients with related services such as support, education and professional services. The company's primary clients are medium-sized to large companies with high numbers of online customers. In 2009, the firm introduced ATG LiveStore, an on-demand program that expatiates the delivery of e-commerce sites for mid-sized and enterprise level merchants. In January 2010, the firm acquired InstantService, a Washington-based provider of live chat services for approximately $17 million. In January 2011, Oracle acquired Art Technology Group, Inc. for $1.1 billion.

ATG offers its employees educational reimbursement; an employee assistance program; charitable contributions match; medical, dental and vision insurance; life/disability insurance; domestic partner benefits; and on-site fitness and wellness programs.

FINANCIALS: Sales and profits are in thousands of dollars—add 000 to get the full amount. 2010 Note: Financial information for 2010 was not available for all companies at press time.

2010 Sales: $	2010 Profits: $	**U.S. Stock Ticker: Subsidiary**
2009 Sales: $179,382	2009 Profits: $16,796	**Int'l Ticker:** Int'l Exchange:
2008 Sales: $164,641	2008 Profits: $3,799	Employees: 545
2007 Sales: $137,060	2007 Profits: $-4,187	Fiscal Year Ends: 12/31
2006 Sales: $103,232	2006 Profits: $9,695	Parent Company: ORACLE CORP

SALARIES/BENEFITS:

Pension Plan:	ESOP Stock Plan:	Profit Sharing:	Top Exec. Salary: $400,000	Bonus: $300,000
Savings Plan: Y	Stock Purch. Plan: Y		Second Exec. Salary: $250,000	Bonus: $117,000

OTHER THOUGHTS:

Apparent Women Officers or Directors: 5
Hot Spot for Advancement for Women/Minorities: Y

LOCATIONS: ("Y" = Yes)

West:	Southwest:	Midwest:	Southeast:	Northeast:	International:
Y		Y		Y	Y

ARTERIS INC

www.arteris.com

Industry Group Code: 33441 Ranks within this company's industry group: Sales: Profits:

Hardware:	Software:	Telecommunications:	Electronic Publishing:	Equipment:	Specialty Services:
Computers:	Consumer:	Local:	Online Service:	Telecom:	Consulting:
Accessories:	Corporate:	Long Distance:	TV/Cable or Wireless:	Communication:	Contract Manufacturing:
Network Equipment:	Telecom:	Cellular:	Games:	Distribution:	Processing:
Chips/Circuits: Y	Internet:	Internet Service:	Financial Data:	VAR/Reseller:	Staff/Outsourcing:
Parts/Drives:				Satellite Srv./Equip.:	Specialty Services:

TYPES OF BUSINESS:
Network-On-A-Chip Technology

BRANDS/DIVISIONS/AFFILIATES:
FlexNoC
FlexWay
NoC Solution

CONTACTS: Note: Officers with more than one job title may be intentionally listed here more than once.
K. Charles Janac, CEO
K. Charles Janac, Pres.
Kurt Shuler, Dir.-Mktg.
Philippe Martin, CTO
Philippe Boucard, Sr. Dir.-IP Dev.
David Martens, VP-Sales, Americas, Korea, Taiwan & China
K. Charles Janac, Chmn.
Michel Telera, VP-Sales, EMEA & Asia

Phone: 408-470-7300	Fax: 408-470-7301
Toll-Free:	
Address: 111 W. Evelyn Ave., Ste. 101, Sunnyvale, CA 94086 US	

GROWTH PLANS/SPECIAL FEATURES:
Arteris, Inc. is a designer and developer of network-on-chip (NoC) technology. The company's products are designed to alleviate problems in modern device architecture due to more intellectual property (IP) blocks in a single system-on-chip (SoC). Traditional designs require shared communication between various IP blocks, such as graphics modules and MPEG decoders. This results in an inefficient design, extraneous wiring and added heat buildup. NoC technology is designed to share resources based on a layered data approach, which allows packet routing and information flow to be handled more intelligently. Arteris offers three primary products: the FlexNoC, the FlexWay and the NoC Solution. The FlexNoC is designed to maximize low latency and high throughput requirements. The FlexWay emphasizes scalability for users concerned with future needs. The NoC Solution specializes in high performance requirements, such as advanced processors or video technology. The company's technology is utilized in several different industries, including mobile phones, video equipment, automotive parts, consumer electronics and application-specific integrated circuits (ASICs).

FINANCIALS: Sales and profits are in thousands of dollars—add 000 to get the full amount. 2010 Note: Financial information for 2010 was not available for all companies at press time.

2010 Sales: $	2010 Profits: $	U.S. Stock Ticker: Private
2009 Sales: $	2009 Profits: $	Int'l Ticker: Int'l Exchange:
2008 Sales: $	2008 Profits: $	Employees:
2007 Sales: $	2007 Profits: $	Fiscal Year Ends:
2006 Sales: $	2006 Profits: $	Parent Company:

SALARIES/BENEFITS:
Pension Plan:	ESOP Stock Plan:	Profit Sharing:	Top Exec. Salary: $	Bonus: $
Savings Plan:	Stock Purch. Plan:		Second Exec. Salary: $	Bonus: $

OTHER THOUGHTS:
Apparent Women Officers or Directors:
Hot Spot for Advancement for Women/Minorities:

LOCATIONS: ("Y" = Yes)
West:	Southwest:	Midwest:	Southeast:	Northeast:	International:
Y					Y

Note: Financial information, benefits and other data can change quickly and may vary from those stated here.

ASANTE NETWORKS INC

www.asante.com

Industry Group Code: 33411 Ranks within this company's industry group: Sales: Profits:

Hardware:		Software:		Telecommunications:		Electronic Publishing:	Equipment:	Specialty Services:
Computers:		Consumer:		Local:		Online Service:	Telecom:	Consulting:
Accessories:		Corporate:	Y	Long Distance:		TV/Cable or Wireless:	Communication:	Contract Manufacturing:
Network Equipment:	Y	Telecom:	Y	Cellular:		Games:	Distribution:	Processing:
Chips/Circuits:		Internet:		Internet Service:		Financial Data:	VAR/Reseller:	Staff/Outsourcing:
Parts/Drives:							Satellite Srv./Equip.:	Specialty Services:

TYPES OF BUSINESS:

Networking Equipment
Hubs, Adapters & Switches
Web-Based Network Management Software

BRANDS/DIVISIONS/AFFILIATES:

IntraCore
FriendlyNET
SmartBridge
Asante Talk

CONTACTS: Note: Officers with more than one job title may be intentionally listed here more than once.

John Hwang, CEO
Michael Handelman, CFO
Feng Juang, Chmn.

Phone: 408-435-8388	Fax: 510-438-6790
Toll-Free: 877-262-0324	
Address: 47436 Fremont Blvd., Fremont, CA 94538 US	

GROWTH PLANS/SPECIAL FEATURES:

Asante Networks, Inc., the communication division of UIC Corporation, develops network switching, Internet camera and wireless router products for the consumer, enterprise and corporation, small medium business (SMB) and SOHO (small office, home office) markets. The firm provides hardware and software products to over 20 million users. Asante's products are sold through two main product lines: IntraCore and FriendlyNET. The IntraCore line targets enterprise customers and Internet Service Providers (ISPs) with Layer 2 and 3 switches for managed workgroups, Gigabit Ethernet, high-capacity fiber optic backbones and chassis-based multimedia for multi-service networks that support all applications and data types. The FriendlyNET line provides networking products for small offices, homes, schools and prepress markets. This line consists of cable/DSL routers, wireless network products, KVM switches and the GX5 and GX6 series of Gigabit Ethernet switches. Additional products include uplink connectors, such as GBIC and SFP module products, and Asante Talk, a device for connecting Ethernet Macs to share files or printers. In March 2010, the firm announced the release of the Asante SmartBridge, an IP-based, B2B and B2C Intelligent Switch.

FINANCIALS: Sales and profits are in thousands of dollars—add 000 to get the full amount. 2010 Note: Financial information for 2010 was not available for all companies at press time.

			U.S. Stock Ticker: Subsidiary
2010 Sales: $	2010 Profits: $		Int'l Ticker: Int'l Exchange:
2009 Sales: $	2009 Profits: $		Employees:
2008 Sales: $	2008 Profits: $		Fiscal Year Ends: 9/30
2007 Sales: $	2007 Profits: $		Parent Company: UIC CORPORATION
2006 Sales: $	2006 Profits: $		

SALARIES/BENEFITS:

Pension Plan:	ESOP Stock Plan:	Profit Sharing:	Top Exec. Salary: $	Bonus: $
Savings Plan:	Stock Purch. Plan:		Second Exec. Salary: $	Bonus: $

OTHER THOUGHTS:

Apparent Women Officers or Directors:
Hot Spot for Advancement for Women/Minorities:

LOCATIONS: ("Y" = Yes)

West:	Southwest:	Midwest:	Southeast:	Northeast:	International:
Y					Y

ASK.COM

www.ask.com

Industry Group Code: 519130 Ranks within this company's industry group: Sales: Profits:

Hardware:	Software:		Telecommunications:	Electronic Publishing:		Equipment:	Specialty Services:
Computers:	Consumer:		Local:	Online Service:	Y	Telecom:	Consulting:
Accessories:	Corporate:	Y	Long Distance:	TV/Cable or Wireless:		Communication:	Contract Manufacturing:
Network Equipment:	Telecom:		Cellular:	Games:		Distribution:	Processing:
Chips/Circuits:	Internet:	Y	Internet Service:	Financial Data:		VAR/Reseller:	Staff/Outsourcing:
Parts/Drives:						Satellite Srv./Equip.:	Specialty Services:

TYPES OF BUSINESS:

Online Portal-Search Engine
Natural Language Search Software
Advertising Services
Corporate Analytics Software

BRANDS/DIVISIONS/AFFILIATES:

Ask Jeeves
Ask for Kids
Bloglines
Ask Sponsored Listings
Dictionary.com
Thesaurus.com
Reference.com

CONTACTS: Note: Officers with more than one job title may be intentionally listed here more than once.

Doug Leeds, Pres.
Jared Cluff, Sr. VP-Mktg.
Angela Loeffler, VP-Human Resources
Scott Kim, CTO
Tony Gentile, Sr. VP-Prod. Mgmt.
Edward Ferguson, General Counsel/Sr. VP
Shravan Goli, Pres., Dictionary.com
Valerie Combs, VP-Corp. Comm.
Jeff Spitzer, Global Controller/VP
Shane McGilloway, Sr. VP-Search Mktg. & Optimization
Tomasz Imielinski, Exec. VP-Tech.
Scott Garell, Pres., Ask Networks
Cesar Mascaraque, Managing Dir.-Ask Jeeves (U.K.)

Phone: 510-985-7400	Fax: 510-985-7412
Toll-Free:	
Address: 555 12th St., Ste. 500, Oakland, CA 94607 US	

GROWTH PLANS/SPECIAL FEATURES:

Ask.com, a subsidiary of IAC/InterActiveCorp., offers users information retrieval products through various web sites, portals and downloadable applications. Its brands include Ask.com, Ask for Kids and Bloglines. Ask.com, an Internet search engine, uses a unique algorithm technology called ExpertRank, which provides search results by identifying the most authoritative sites on the Internet rather than the most popular. Ask.com sites are available in seven countries including the U.S., Germany, Spain, Italy, Japan, the Netherlands and the U.K. Ask for Kids is a child-friendly means for children to search for information online. Ask for Kids is structured as a learning and edutainment destination site, which combines human editorial judgment and age-appropriate feature content. Bloglines is a free online service for searching, subscribing, publishing and sharing RSS feeds and blogs. Bloglines is a pioneer in bringing RSS (Really Simple Syndication) feeds and rich content to mainstream Internet users. The site offers news feed and blog articles, images as well as audio and video. Blogline is available in nine different languages. Ask Sponsored Listings is a SME (Search Engine Marketing) platform that assists advertisers in reaching target audiences. IAC generates revenue both by syndicating search results and ad products and offering advertisers a variety of targeted tools for promoting their products. Other sites in the Ask Network include Dictionary.com, Thesaurus.com and Reference.com. In November 2010, the company announced plans to shift from an internet search engine to its original format, under Ask Jeeves, a question and answer service. Consequently, the firm will lay off 130 employees and close its offices in Edison, New Jersey and Hangzhou, China. All other employees will be moved to company headquarters in Oakland, California.

The company offers its employees medical, dental and vision; a 401(k) matching plan; tuition assistance; matching charitable contributions program; subsidized parking and commuting plan; an employee discount program; and discounted gym memberships.

FINANCIALS: Sales and profits are in thousands of dollars—add 000 to get the full amount. 2010 Note: Financial information for 2010 was not available for all companies at press time.

2010 Sales: $	2010 Profits: $	**U.S. Stock Ticker: Subsidiary**
2009 Sales: $	2009 Profits: $	**Int'l Ticker:** Int'l Exchange:
2008 Sales: $	2008 Profits: $	Employees:
2007 Sales: $	2007 Profits: $	Fiscal Year Ends: 12/31
2006 Sales: $	2006 Profits: $	Parent Company: IAC/INTERACTIVECORP

SALARIES/BENEFITS:

Pension Plan:	ESOP Stock Plan:	Profit Sharing:	Top Exec. Salary: $	Bonus: $307,070
Savings Plan: Y	Stock Purch. Plan:		Second Exec. Salary: $	Bonus: $

OTHER THOUGHTS:

Apparent Women Officers or Directors: 2
Hot Spot for Advancement for Women/Minorities:

LOCATIONS: ("Y" = Yes)

West:	Southwest:	Midwest:	Southeast:	Northeast:	International:
Y		Y		Y	Y

ASPECT SOFTWARE INC
www.aspect.com

Industry Group Code: 511210K Ranks within this company's industry group: Sales: Profits:

Hardware:	Software:		Telecommunications:	Electronic Publishing:	Equipment:	Specialty Services:	
Computers:	Consumer:		Local:	Online Service:	Telecom:	Consulting:	
Accessories:	Corporate:	Y	Long Distance:	TV/Cable or Wireless:	Communication:	Contract Manufacturing:	
Network Equipment:	Telecom:	Y	Cellular:	Games:	Distribution:	Processing:	
Chips/Circuits:	Internet:		Internet Service:	Financial Data:	VAR/Reseller:	Staff/Outsourcing:	Y
Parts/Drives:					Satellite Srv./Equip.:	Specialty Services:	Y

TYPES OF BUSINESS:
Software-Customer Service Request Processing
Call Center Automation Systems
IT Services

BRANDS/DIVISIONS/AFFILIATES:
Seamless Customer Service
Streamlined Collections
Productive Workforce
Optimized Collections
Aspect Unified IP
PerformanceEdge
Quilogy, Inc.

CONTACTS: Note: Officers with more than one job title may be intentionally listed here more than once.
James D. Foy, CEO
James D. Foy, Pres.
Michael J. Provenzano, III, CFO
Laurie Cairns, Sr. VP-Mktg.
Gary Barnett, Exec. VP-R&D
Jamie Ryan, CIO/Sr. VP-IT
Gary Barnett, CTO
Gwen Braygreen, Sr. VP-Aspect Tech. Svcs. & Continuing Eng.
David Reibel, General Counsel/Sr. VP
Andrew Bezaitis, Sr. VP-Corp. Dev.
Aleassa Schambers, Corp. Contact
Michael J. Provenzano, III, Exec. VP-Finance
Kevin Schwartz, Exec. VP-Global Professional Svcs.
David Herzog, VP-Customer Experience
Mike Sheridan, Exec. VP-Worldwide Sales

Phone: 978-250-7900	Fax: 978-244-7410
Toll-Free:	
Address: 300 Apollo Dr., Chelmsford, MA 01824 US	

GROWTH PLANS/SPECIAL FEATURES:
Aspect Software, Inc. is a leading provider of contact servers for managing dynamic customer transactions across wired and wireless communication channels. It was created from the merger of Aspect Communications Corporation and Concerto Software, Inc. The firm's products are divided into two categories: unified communications (UC) applications and contact center platform products. Aspect offers such UC applications as Seamless Customer Service, which coordinates self-service and live agent calls; Streamlined Collections, which automates early stage collections efforts and enhances past due account targeting; Productive Workforce, to improve resource utilization; and Optimized Collections, a solution for improving debtor contact productivity. Its contact center products include Aspect Unified IP and PerformanceEdge. Aspect Unified IP offers inbound, outbound and multi-channel contact, multimedia recording, quality monitoring and quality management services. Aspect offers PerformanceEdge, a contact center optimization suite that combines many different management tools, including workforce management; campaign management; performance management; recording and quality management; and coaching and eLearning. In addition to software products, the company offers IT services, including Microsoft UC Services, UC RapidStart and UC Strategy and Business Case Services, to aid in the implementation of advanced network processes. Aspect serves clients in more than 50 countries in customer service, sales and telemarketing, collections and outsourcing, both in-house and at outsourced contact centers. Some of its clients include Microsoft Corporation; Merck & Co., Inc.; General Electric; AT&T Wireless Services; Blue Cross and Blue Shield Association; Air France; Alaska Airlines; and Ticketmaster. In January 2010, the company acquired IT services firm Quilogy, Inc. In December 2010, it opened technical support and software production and distribution offices in Galway, Ireland.

FINANCIALS: Sales and profits are in thousands of dollars—add 000 to get the full amount. 2010 Note: Financial information for 2010 was not available for all companies at press time.
2010 Sales: $	2010 Profits: $	U.S. Stock Ticker: Private
2009 Sales: $	2009 Profits: $	Int'l Ticker: Int'l Exchange:
2008 Sales: $	2008 Profits: $	Employees:
2007 Sales: $600,000	2007 Profits: $	Fiscal Year Ends: 12/31
2006 Sales: $	2006 Profits: $	Parent Company:

SALARIES/BENEFITS:
Pension Plan:	ESOP Stock Plan:	Profit Sharing:	Top Exec. Salary: $	Bonus: $
Savings Plan:	Stock Purch. Plan:		Second Exec. Salary: $	Bonus: $

OTHER THOUGHTS:
Apparent Women Officers or Directors: 2
Hot Spot for Advancement for Women/Minorities: Y

LOCATIONS: ("Y" = Yes)
West:	Southwest:	Midwest:	Southeast:	Northeast:	International:
Y		Y	Y	Y	Y

ASPEN TECHNOLOGY INC

www.aspentec.com

Industry Group Code: 511210A Ranks within this company's industry group: Sales: 4   Profits: 1

Hardware:	Software:		Telecommunications:	Electronic Publishing:	Equipment:	Specialty Services:
Computers:	Consumer:		Local:	Online Service:	Telecom:	Consulting:
Accessories:	Corporate:	Y	Long Distance:	TV/Cable or Wireless:	Communication:	Contract Manufacturing:
Network Equipment:	Telecom:		Cellular:	Games:	Distribution:	Processing:
Chips/Circuits:	Internet:		Internet Service:	Financial Data:	VAR/Reseller:	Staff/Outsourcing:
Parts/Drives:					Satellite Srv./Equip.:	Specialty Services:

TYPES OF BUSINESS:

Computer Software-Manufacturing Automation
Decision Support Software
Support Services
Petroleum & Chemical Process Software

BRANDS/DIVISIONS/AFFILIATES:

aspenONE
Aspen Dynamics
aspenONE V7
Aspen InfoPlus.21
Aspen DMCplus
Aspen PIMS
Aspen Plus
Aspen HYSYS

CONTACTS: Note: Officers with more than one job title may be intentionally listed here more than once.

Mark E. Fusco, CEO
Mark E. Fusco, Pres.
Mark Sullivan, CFO/Exec. VP
Manolis Kotzabasakis, Sr. VP-Sales & Strategy
Joanna Nikka, Sr. VP-Human Resources
Willie K. Chan, Sr. VP-R&D
Frederic G. Hammond, General Counsel/Sr. VP/Sec.
Antonio Pietri, Exec. VP-Field Oper.
Richard Packwood, Sr. VP-Bus. Dev.
Blair Wheeler, Sr. VP-Mktg.
Michele Triponey, Sr. VP-Global Customer Support & Training
Henry Lau, Sr. VP/Managing Dir.-Asia-Pacific
Jamie Hintlian, VP/Gen. Mgr.-Pharmaceuticals
Stephen M. Jennings, Chmn.
John Hague, Sr. VP/Managing Dir.-Middle East & North Africa

Phone: 781-221-6400	Fax: 781-221-6410
Toll-Free:	
Address: 200 Wheeler Rd., Burlington, MA 01803 US	

GROWTH PLANS/SPECIAL FEATURES:

Aspen Technology, Inc. is a leading provider of software and services for the process industries. The company's decision support software and services enable its customers to automate, integrate and optimize complex engineering, manufacturing and supply chain functions. Customers use Aspen's e-business products to automate and synchronize collaborations with suppliers, customers and other trading partners over the Internet. These products enable customers to increase their competitiveness and profitability by improving manufacturing efficiency, responsiveness and product quality. The firm is also active in process modeling and chemical engineering. Its products include Aspen HYSYS and Aspen Plus for process simulation and optimization; Aspen DMCplus for advanced process control; Aspen PIMS for advanced planning and scheduling; aspenONE V7 for process engineering; and Aspen InfoPlus.21 for plant information management. The company provides industry solutions under the aspenONE brand name for the oil and gas, petroleum, chemicals, special chemicals, pharmaceutical and consumer goods markets. Additionally, it provides customer support services and customer training for its products. The company has over 30 offices located in 28 countries and a customer base of over 1,500 leading process manufacturers in the chemicals, refining, construction and energy industries.

Employees are offered medical, vision and dental insurance; dependent care and health care reimbursement programs; a 401(k) plan; tuition reimbursement; life insurance; short-and long-term disability coverage; auto and homeowner insurance group rates; and travel accident insurance.

FINANCIALS: Sales and profits are in thousands of dollars—add 000 to get the full amount. 2010 Note: Financial information for 2010 was not available for all companies at press time.

2010 Sales: $166,344	2010 Profits: $-107,445	**U.S. Stock Ticker:** AZPN
2009 Sales: $311,580	2009 Profits: $52,924	**Int'l Ticker:** Int'l Exchange:
2008 Sales: $311,613	2008 Profits: $24,946	Employees: 1,289
2007 Sales: $341,029	2007 Profits: $45,518	Fiscal Year Ends: 6/30
2006 Sales: $293,148	2006 Profits: $12,823	Parent Company:

SALARIES/BENEFITS:

Pension Plan:	ESOP Stock Plan:	Profit Sharing:	Top Exec. Salary: $500,000	Bonus: $896,000
Savings Plan: Y	Stock Purch. Plan:		Second Exec. Salary: $300,000	Bonus: $224,000

OTHER THOUGHTS:

Apparent Women Officers or Directors: 3
Hot Spot for Advancement for Women/Minorities: Y

LOCATIONS: ("Y" = Yes)

West:	Southwest:	Midwest:	Southeast:	Northeast:	International:
	Y			Y	Y

ASTEA INTERNATIONAL INC

www.astea.com

Industry Group Code: 511210K Ranks within this company's industry group: Sales: 8 Profits: 8

Hardware:	Software:		Telecommunications:	Electronic Publishing:	Equipment:	Specialty Services:	
Computers:	Consumer:		Local:	Online Service:	Telecom:	Consulting:	Y
Accessories:	Corporate:	Y	Long Distance:	TV/Cable or Wireless:	Communication:	Contract Manufacturing:	
Network Equipment:	Telecom:		Cellular:	Games:	Distribution:	Processing:	
Chips/Circuits:	Internet:		Internet Service:	Financial Data:	VAR/Reseller:	Staff/Outsourcing:	
Parts/Drives:					Satellite Srv./Equip.:	Specialty Services:	Y

TYPES OF BUSINESS:
Software-Field Service & Customer Relationship Management
Service Lifecycle Management Solutions
Mobile Field Force Automation

BRANDS/DIVISIONS/AFFILIATES:
Astea International Japan Inc
Astea Alliance
FieldCentrix Enterprise

CONTACTS: Note: Officers with more than one job title may be intentionally listed here more than once.
Zack B. Bergreen, CEO
John Tobin, Pres.
Fredric Etskovitz, CFO
Debbie Geiger, VP-Mktg.
Frederic Etskovitz, Treas.
Steve Scott, Gen. Mgr.-APAC
Tommy Swider, Sr. VP-Professional Svcs., North America
Hideo Yamazaki, Managing Dir.-Japan
John Roache, VP-Sales, North America
Zack B. Bergreen, Chmn.
Ian Evans, Managing Dir.-EMEA

Phone: 215-682-2500	Fax: 215-682-2515
Toll-Free: 800-347-7334	
Address: 240 Gibraltar Rd., Horsham, PA 19044-2306 US	

GROWTH PLANS/SPECIAL FEATURES:
Astea International, Inc. develops, markets and supports service management software. The firm's software is licensed to companies that sell and service equipment, or that sell and deliver professional services. Its products help to automate enterprise business processes for purposes of operational efficiency improvement, cost containment, revenue enhancement and the expansion of management's awareness of operational performance through analytical reporting. Astea markets its products to a wide range of industries, including imaging systems; information technology; retail systems; industrial controls and instrumentation; facilities management; medical devices and diagnostic systems; and telecommunications. The Astea Alliance service management suite helps provide start-to-finish software products for companies by optimizing business processes for contact centers; order processing; business intelligence for financial and operational benefits; field service management; depot repair; logistics; professional services; and sales and marketing. The firm's FieldCentrix Enterprise is a service management program that runs on a wide range of mobile devices and features add-ons such as workforce optimization capabilities, a web-based customer self-service portal and equipment-centric functionality. The company maintains facilities in the U.S. in Pennsylvania and California and internationally in Israel, the U.K, Japan, the Netherlands and Australia. It also operates in South Africa through a distribution partnership with Fullcircle Technologies. Astea's partners include Honeywell, Infomill, MCA Solutions, L&T Infotech, Microsoft Corp., Panorama Software, NAVTEQ and ITOCHU Techno-Solutions Corporation. The firm's software is developed on the Microsoft .NET platform. The firm recently incorporated a new subsidiary, Astea International Japan, Inc., which provides professional services, sales and customer support to Tokyo-based service companies.

FINANCIALS: Sales and profits are in thousands of dollars—add 000 to get the full amount. 2010 Note: Financial information for 2010 was not available for all companies at press time.

2010 Sales: $	2010 Profits: $	U.S. Stock Ticker: ATEA
2009 Sales: $20,103	2009 Profits: $- 899	Int'l Ticker: Int'l Exchange:
2008 Sales: $23,851	2008 Profits: $-3,135	Employees: 158
2007 Sales: $30,370	2007 Profits: $2,765	Fiscal Year Ends: 12/31
2006 Sales: $18,182	2006 Profits: $-7,084	Parent Company:

SALARIES/BENEFITS:
Pension Plan:	ESOP Stock Plan:	Profit Sharing:	Top Exec. Salary: $242,895	Bonus: $
Savings Plan:	Stock Purch. Plan:		Second Exec. Salary: $194,316	Bonus: $6,613

OTHER THOUGHTS:
Apparent Women Officers or Directors: 1
Hot Spot for Advancement for Women/Minorities:

LOCATIONS: ("Y" = Yes)
West:	Southwest:	Midwest:	Southeast:	Northeast:	International:
Y				Y	Y

Note: Financial information, benefits and other data can change quickly and may vary from those stated here.

ASUSTEK COMPUTER INC (ASUS)

www.asus.com

Industry Group Code: 334111 Ranks within this company's industry group: Sales: 9 Profits: 5

Hardware:		Software:		Telecommunications:		Electronic Publishing:		Equipment:		Specialty Services:	
Computers:	Y	Consumer:		Local:		Online Service:		Telecom:	Y	Consulting:	
Accessories:	Y	Corporate:		Long Distance:		TV/Cable or Wireless:		Communication:	Y	Contract Manufacturing:	
Network Equipment:	Y	Telecom:		Cellular:		Games:		Distribution:		Processing:	
Chips/Circuits:		Internet:		Internet Service:		Financial Data:		VAR/Reseller:		Staff/Outsourcing:	
Parts/Drives:	Y							Satellite Srv./Equip.:		Specialty Services:	

TYPES OF BUSINESS:

Computer Manufacturing
Computer Components & Accessories
Networking Devices
Wireless Communication Products
Smart Phones
Personal Computers
Computer Monitors

BRANDS/DIVISIONS/AFFILIATES:

ASUS
Eee PC
Pegatron Holding

CONTACTS: Note: Officers with more than one job title may be intentionally listed here more than once.

Jerry Shen, CEO
Jerry Shen, Pres.
Jonney Shih, Chief Branding Officer
Jonathan Tsang, Vice Chmn.
Jonney Shih, Chmn.

Phone: 886-02-28943447	Fax: 886-02-28926140
Toll-Free:	
Address: No. 150, Li-Te Rd., Peitou, Taipei, 112 Taiwan	

GROWTH PLANS/SPECIAL FEATURES:

ASUSTeK Computer, Inc. participates in the 3C industry (computing, consumer electronics and communications). The company manufactures PCs, monitors, mobile phones, networking equipment, notebook computers, storage devices, PC components, PDAs and server equipment, generally under the ASUS brand. One of the company's latest and more successful products, the Eee PC, is 8-inch solid-state minimalist laptop PC featuring built-in Wi-Fi connectivity, Intel processors and Linux/Windows XP compatibility. In partnership with Garmin, the firm manufactures the Garmin-Asus M10 smartphone, incorporating advanced GPS technology. The firm also produces commercial desk tops, commercial notebooks and servers and workstations. Additionally, the company manufactures PC components such as barebones; graphic cards; motherboards; multi-media products such as audio cards, digital media players and TV tuners; and DVD and Blu-ray drives. In 2010, the firm spun off its contract manufacturing and motherboard business as a free standing company, Pegatron Holding. This will enable ASUSTeK to concentrate on its ASUS branded computers, servers and accessories business.

FINANCIALS: Sales and profits are in thousands of dollars—add 000 to get the full amount. 2010 Note: Financial information for 2010 was not available for all companies at press time.

2010 Sales: $	2010 Profits: $	U.S. Stock Ticker:
2009 Sales: $19,313,000	2009 Profits: $395,020	Int'l Ticker: 2357 Int'l Exchange: Taipei-TPE
2008 Sales: $20,401,670	2008 Profits: $578,320	Employees:
2007 Sales: $22,660,800	2007 Profits: $828,700	Fiscal Year Ends: 12/31
2006 Sales: $16,807,000	2006 Profits: $576,600	Parent Company:

SALARIES/BENEFITS:

Pension Plan:	ESOP Stock Plan:	Profit Sharing:	Top Exec. Salary: $	Bonus: $
Savings Plan:	Stock Purch. Plan:		Second Exec. Salary: $	Bonus: $

OTHER THOUGHTS:

Apparent Women Officers or Directors:
Hot Spot for Advancement for Women/Minorities:

LOCATIONS: ("Y" = Yes)

West:	Southwest:	Midwest:	Southeast:	Northeast:	International:
Y		Y			Y

ATARI INC

www.atari.com

Industry Group Code: 511210G Ranks within this company's industry group: Sales: 7 Profits: 6

Hardware:		Software:		Telecommunications:		Electronic Publishing:		Equipment:		Specialty Services:	
Computers:		Consumer:	Y	Local:		Online Service:	Y	Telecom:		Consulting:	
Accessories:		Corporate:		Long Distance:		TV/Cable or Wireless:		Communication:		Contract Manufacturing:	
Network Equipment:		Telecom:		Cellular:		Games:	Y	Distribution:		Processing:	
Chips/Circuits:		Internet:		Internet Service:		Financial Data:		VAR/Reseller:		Staff/Outsourcing:	
Parts/Drives:								Satellite Srv./Equip.:		Specialty Services:	

TYPES OF BUSINESS:
Computer Software-Video Games
Educational Software

BRANDS/DIVISIONS/AFFILIATES:
Atari S.A.
Infogrames Entertainment S.A.
Test Drive
Alone in the Dark
Roller Coaster Tycoon
Unreal
Dungeons & Dragons
Hasbro, Inc.

CONTACTS: *Note: Officers with more than one job title may be intentionally listed here more than once.*
Jim Wilson, Pres.
Pierre Hintze, VP-Prod. Dev.
Anthony Jacobson, VP-Bus. Dev.
Jim Lapin, CEO-Atari S.A.
Jim Wilson, Deputy CEO-Atari S.A.
Thom Kozik, VP
John Burns, VP/Gen. Mgr.-Europe

Phone: 212-726-6500	Fax:
Toll-Free:	
Address: 417 Fifth Ave., New York, NY 10016 US	

GROWTH PLANS/SPECIAL FEATURES:
Atari, Inc., a subsidiary of French software publisher Atari S.A. (formerly Infogrames Entertainment S.A.), is a publisher and distributor of interactive entertainment. It publishes and distributes video game software for most major gaming consoles, as well as personal computer (PC) platforms. It also publishes and sublicenses games for wireless, Internet and other evolving platforms. Atari's products extend across most major video game genres, including action, adventure, strategy, role-playing and racing. The company's products are based on intellectual properties that it has created internally and owns, or that have been licensed to it by third parties. Atari's properties include popular franchises such as Driver, Unreal, V-Rally, Roller Backyard, Roller Coaster Tycoon, Alone in the Dark and Test Drive. The company also publishes software based on key theme licenses, including The Matrix, Terminator, Mission: Impossible, Dragon Ball Z, Men In Black, Superman, Godzilla, Arthur & the Minimoys and Dungeons & Dragons. In addition, Atari holds an exclusive worldwide license on 10 Hasbro intellectual properties including Dungeons & Dragons, Monopoly, Scrabble, Risk, Game of Life, Clue, Yatzhee, Battleship, Boggle and Simon.

FINANCIALS: Sales and profits are in thousands of dollars—add 000 to get the full amount. 2010 Note: Financial information for 2010 was not available for all companies at press time.

2010 Sales: $153,000	2010 Profits: $-25,650	**U.S. Stock Ticker:** Subsidiary
2009 Sales: $180,370	2009 Profits: $-293,430	**Int'l Ticker:** Int'l Exchange:
2008 Sales: $80,100	2008 Profits: $-23,600	Employees:
2007 Sales: $122,285	2007 Profits: $-69,711	Fiscal Year Ends: 3/31
2006 Sales: $206,796	2006 Profits: $-68,986	Parent Company: ATARI SA

SALARIES/BENEFITS:
Pension Plan:	ESOP Stock Plan:	Profit Sharing:	Top Exec. Salary: $	Bonus: $
Savings Plan:	Stock Purch. Plan:		Second Exec. Salary: $	Bonus: $

OTHER THOUGHTS:
Apparent Women Officers or Directors:
Hot Spot for Advancement for Women/Minorities:

LOCATIONS: ("Y" = Yes)
West:	Southwest:	Midwest:	Southeast:	Northeast:	International:
				Y	

Note: Financial information, benefits and other data can change quickly and may vary from those stated here.

ATHEROS COMMUNICATIONS INC

www.atheros.com

Industry Group Code: 33441 Ranks within this company's industry group: Sales: 39 Profits: 29

Hardware:		Software:	Telecommunications:	Electronic Publishing:	Equipment:	Specialty Services:
Computers:		Consumer:	Local:	Online Service:	Telecom:	Consulting:
Accessories:		Corporate:	Long Distance:	TV/Cable or Wireless:	Communication:	Contract Manufacturing:
Network Equipment:	Y	Telecom:	Cellular:	Games:	Distribution:	Processing:
Chips/Circuits:	Y	Internet:	Internet Service:	Financial Data:	VAR/Reseller:	Staff/Outsourcing:
Parts/Drives:					Satellite Srv./Equip.:	Specialty Services:

TYPES OF BUSINESS:
Wireless Chip Manufacturing
Semiconductor Systems

BRANDS/DIVISIONS/AFFILIATES:
Super G
Super AG
XSPAN
Intellon Corporation

CONTACTS: Note: Officers with more than one job title may be intentionally listed here more than once.
Craig H. Barratt, CEO
Craig H. Barratt, Pres.
Jack R. Lazar, CFO
Reynette Au, VP-Mktg. & Alliances
William J. McFarland, CTO
Richard G. Bahr, VP-Eng.
Adam H. Tachner, General Counsel/VP
Hing Chu, VP-Oper.
Jack R. Lazar, VP-Corp. Dev.
Molly Mulloy, Sr. Mgr.-Corp. Comm.
David Allen, Dir.-Investor Rel.
David D. Torre, Chief Acct. Officer/VP
Gary L. Szilagyi, VP-Worldwide Sales/Gen. Mgr.-Computing & Consumer
Amir Faintuch, VP/Gen. Mgr.-Mobile
Ben Naskar, VP/Gen. Mgr.-Networking
John L. Hennessy, Chmn.
Jason Zheng, VP-Asia Pacific

Phone: 408-773-5200	Fax: 408-773-9940
Toll-Free:	
Address: 5480 Great America Pkwy., Santa Clara, CA 95054 US	

GROWTH PLANS/SPECIAL FEATURES:
Atheros Communications, Inc. develops semiconductor system technologies for wireless communications products such as computing and networking equipment, digital entertainment, broadband access and mobile devices. The firm combines its wireless systems expertise with high-performance radio frequency (RF), mixed-signal and digital semiconductor design to create integrated chipsets for complementary metal-oxide semiconductor (CMOS) processes. The company also provides a portfolio of products that range from entry-level wireless networking products for homes and small offices to sophisticated wireless infrastructure systems-on-chip with advanced network management capabilities for the enterprise market. These wireless system technologies are used in a variety of applications in the personal computer (PC), enterprise access, small office and branch office networking, home networking, hotspot, wireless broadband, voice, mobile computing devices and consumer electronics markets. Atheros currently provides five basic types of semiconductors: radio-on-a-chip (RoC), consisting of one or more CMOS radio transmitters and receivers; MAC + Baseband, consisting of low frequency analog circuits and data converters integrated through a digital interface; stand-alone network processing unit (NPU) chips, supporting a variety of clock speeds and network interfaces; wireless system-on-a-chip (WiSoC); and integrated single chip offerings, which are designed to include substantially all necessary digital and analog circuitry within a single chip structure. The company's chipsets can be incorporated into WLAN devices to provide end users extended range, longer battery life and network management tools that reduce the overall cost of operating wireless networks. The firm's trademarks include Align, AMP, ETHOS, FYX, ROCm and XSPAN. During 2009, Hon Hai Precision Industry Co. Ltd., a Taiwan-based electronic products manufacturer, and Nintendo Co., Ltd., respectively accounted for 17% and 13% of the firm's annual revenues. In December 2009, Atheros completed its $244 million acquisition of U.S.-based Intellon Corporation, a fabless semiconductor company specializing in powerline communications (PLC) technologies. In January 2011, the firm agreed to be acquired by technology company, Qualcomm, Inc. for $3.1 billion.

FINANCIALS: Sales and profits are in thousands of dollars—add 000 to get the full amount. 2010 Note: Financial information for 2010 was not available for all companies at press time.

2010 Sales: $	2010 Profits: $	**U.S. Stock Ticker: ATHR**
2009 Sales: $542,468	2009 Profits: $46,407	**Int'l Ticker:** Int'l Exchange:
2008 Sales: $472,396	2008 Profits: $18,872	Employees: 1,302
2007 Sales: $416,960	2007 Profits: $39,980	Fiscal Year Ends: 12/31
2006 Sales: $301,691	2006 Profits: $18,678	Parent Company:

SALARIES/BENEFITS:

Pension Plan:	ESOP Stock Plan:	Profit Sharing:	Top Exec. Salary: $284,167	Bonus: $241,542
Savings Plan:	Stock Purch. Plan:		Second Exec. Salary: $283,333	Bonus: $514,375

OTHER THOUGHTS:
Apparent Women Officers or Directors: 3
Hot Spot for Advancement for Women/Minorities: Y

LOCATIONS: ("Y" = Yes)

West:	Southwest:	Midwest:	Southeast:	Northeast:	International:
Y					Y

Note: Financial information, benefits and other data can change quickly and may vary from those stated here.

ATMEL CORP

www.atmel.com

Industry Group Code: 33441 Ranks within this company's industry group: Sales: 26   Profits: 45

Hardware:		Software:		Telecommunications:		Electronic Publishing:	Equipment:		Specialty Services:	
Computers:		Consumer:		Local:		Online Service:	Telecom:		Consulting:	
Accessories:		Corporate:		Long Distance:		TV/Cable or Wireless:	Communication:		Contract Manufacturing:	
Network Equipment:		Telecom:		Cellular:		Games:	Distribution:		Processing:	
Chips/Circuits:	Y	Internet:		Internet Service:		Financial Data:	VAR/Reseller:		Staff/Outsourcing:	
Parts/Drives:							Satellite Srv./Equip.:		Specialty Services:	

TYPES OF BUSINESS:

Semiconductor Manufacturing
Non-Volatile Memory & Logic Integrated Circuits
Mixed-Signal Semiconductors
RF Semiconductors
Microcontrollers
Military & Aerospace Products

BRANDS/DIVISIONS/AFFILIATES:

MeshNetics ZigBee
maXTouch
VaultIC
UWB Media Access Controller (The)
ATR4252 IC
AT32UC3L AVR32
ATtiny87
AT90SO

CONTACTS: *Note: Officers with more than one job title may be intentionally listed here more than once.*

Steven Laub, CEO
Walter Lifsey, COO/Exec. VP
Steven Laub, Pres.
Stephen Cumming, CFO
Alf-Egil Bogen, VP-Corp. Mktg.
Jing Liao, VP-Global Human Resources
Tom Wasilczyk, CIO/VP-IT
Tom Roff, VP-Worldwide Mfg.
Scott Wornow, Chief Legal Officer/Sr. VP
Walter Lifsey, Exec. VP-Worldwide Oper.
Robert Pursel, Dir.-Investor Rel.
Stephen Cumming, VP-Finance
Rod Erin, VP-Memory, Automotive & Advanced Prod. Bus. Units
Tsung-Ching Wu, Exec. VP
Robert Valiton, VP-Global Sales Oper.
Peter Jones, VP-Microcontroller & Touch Bus. Unit
David Sugishita, Chmn.
Yang Chiah Yee, VP-Sales, APAC & Japan

Phone: 408-441-0311	Fax: 408-436-4314
Toll-Free:	
Address: 2325 Orchard Pkwy., San Jose, CA 95131 US	

GROWTH PLANS/SPECIAL FEATURES:

Atmel Corp. designs, manufactures and markets semiconductor integrated circuit (IC) products. These products include non-volatile memory, advanced logic, mixed-signal and radio frequency (RF) components. The company produces a full range of chips including application-specific ICs, memory, microcontrollers and programmable logic. Atmel Corporation's semiconductors are used in applications in a variety of markets, including industrial, multimedia, security, automotive, imaging, military and aerospace. The firm operates through four business segments: application specific integrated circuit (ASIC); microcontrollers; nonvolatile memories; and RF and automotive. The ASIC segment, which accounts for approximately 26% of the firm's revenues, provides semi-custom, single customer integrated circuits for the telecommunications, consumer, banking and military markets. The microcontrollers unit (38% of revenues) offers a variety of proprietary and standard microcontrollers, which mostly contain embedded nonvolatile memory; and military and aerospace application specific products. The nonvolatile memories division (24% of revenues) provides serial and parallel interface programmable read only memories and serial and parallel flash memories for use in a variety of applications. The RF and automotive segment (12% of revenues) includes radio frequency and analog circuits for the telecommunications, automotive and industrial markets. Atmel Corporation operates sales offices in over 60 countries and owns over 30 design centers throughout the world. Recently released products of the firm include the UWB Media Access Controller, an ultra wideband evaluation kit; the AT697 Revision F, a radiation-hardened processor; the 32-bit AT32UC3L AVR32 microcontroller; the ATtiny87 8-bit microcontroller; VaultIC security modules; the ATR4252 IC active antenna IC; the maXTouch series of capacitive touchscreen controller solutions; and AT90SO microcontrollers. In June 2010, the company sold its French wafer fabrication business to LFoundry GmbH. In September 2010, Atmel Corporation sold its French and U.K. Smart Card operations to INSIDE Contactless S.A. for roughly $32 million.

FINANCIALS: Sales and profits are in thousands of dollars—add 000 to get the full amount. 2010 Note: Financial information for 2010 was not available for all companies at press time.

2010 Sales: $	2010 Profits: $	U.S. Stock Ticker: ATML
2009 Sales: $1,217,345	2009 Profits: $-109,498	Int'l Ticker: Int'l Exchange:
2008 Sales: $1,566,763	2008 Profits: $-27,209	Employees: 5,600
2007 Sales: $1,639,237	2007 Profits: $47,885	Fiscal Year Ends: 12/31
2006 Sales: $1,670,887	2006 Profits: $14,650	Parent Company:

SALARIES/BENEFITS:

Pension Plan:	ESOP Stock Plan:	Profit Sharing:	Top Exec. Salary: $686,760	Bonus: $790,391
Savings Plan: Y	Stock Purch. Plan: Y		Second Exec. Salary: $476,983	Bonus: $310,294

OTHER THOUGHTS:

Apparent Women Officers or Directors:
Hot Spot for Advancement for Women/Minorities:

LOCATIONS: ("Y" = Yes)

West:	Southwest:	Midwest:	Southeast:	Northeast:	International:
Y	Y	Y	Y	Y	Y

Note: Financial information, benefits and other data can change quickly and may vary from those stated here.

ATMI INC

www.atmi.com

Industry Group Code: 333295   Ranks within this company's industry group: Sales: 12   Profits: 6

Hardware:		Software:		Telecommunications:		Electronic Publishing:		Equipment:		Specialty Services:	
Computers:		Consumer:		Local:		Online Service:		Telecom:		Consulting:	
Accessories:		Corporate:		Long Distance:		TV/Cable or Wireless:		Communication:		Contract Manufacturing:	
Network Equipment:		Telecom:		Cellular:		Games:		Distribution:		Processing:	
Chips/Circuits:	Y	Internet:		Internet Service:		Financial Data:		VAR/Reseller:		Staff/Outsourcing:	
Parts/Drives:								Satellite Srv./Equip.:		Specialty Services:	Y

TYPES OF BUSINESS:

Equipment-Semiconductor Manufacturing
Semiconductor Materials
Materials Packaging & Delivery Systems
Outsourced Services
Research & Development

BRANDS/DIVISIONS/AFFILIATES:

Safe Delivery Source
Integrity PadReactor
ATMI Austar LifeSciences Limited
Artelis SA
Accudose
JetMixer
NOWTrak
TX-4

CONTACTS: *Note: Officers with more than one job title may be intentionally listed here more than once.*

Doug Neugold, CEO
Doug Neugold, Pres.
Tim Carlson, CFO/Exec. VP
Kathy Mincieli, Sr. VP-Human Resources
Kevin Laing, CIO/Sr. VP
Lawrence A. Dubois, CTO/Sr. VP
Ellen Harmon, Chief Legal Officer/Exec. VP/Sec.
Paul Hohlstein, Sr. VP-Oper.
Dan Sharkey, Exec. VP-Bus. Dev.
Tim Carlson, Treas.
Tod Higinbotham, Exec. VP/Gen. Mgr.-Microelectronics
Mario Philips, Sr. VP/Gen. Mgr.-ATMI LifeSciences
Ellen Harmon, Chief Compliance Officer
Doug Neugold, Chmn.
Paul Hohlstein, Sr. VP-Supply Chain

Phone: 203-794-1100	Fax: 203-792-8040
Toll-Free: 800-766-2681	
Address: 7 Commerce Dr., Danbury, CT 06810 US	

GROWTH PLANS/SPECIAL FEATURES:

ATMI, Inc. provides materials, materials packaging and materials delivery systems for use in microelectronics devices. The firm's products include frontend semiconductor performance materials; high-purity materials packaging; sub-atmospheric pressure gas delivery systems for safe handling and delivery of toxic and hazardous gases to semiconductor process equipment; and dispensing systems that allow for the reliable introduction of low volatility liquids and solids to microelectronics and biopharmaceutical processes. Products created using the firm's materials are used in the information technology, automotive, life sciences, communications and consumer products industries. The company provides a broad range of ultra-high-purity semiconductor materials and semiconductor materials packaging and delivery systems. The firm's Safe Delivery Source product line uses absorbent materials for the transport of highly pressurized gases used in semiconductor manufacturing. Its other brands include AutoClean, Accudose, ErgoNOW, LevTech, JetMixer, NOWTrak and TX-4. ATMI also conducts venture activities and government-funded research and development. The firm owns 30% interest in Shanghai-based Anji Microelectronics, a developer of semiconductor materials; the two companies share resources and efforts in the development and marketing of their products. The company owns or leases seven facilities in the U.S., as well as locations in China, Japan, South Korea, Taiwan and Belgium. ATMI plans to continue its growth through product line expansion and by leveraging its core technology to create new high growth product lines, including growing its leadership position in advanced interconnect applications. In April 2010, the company launched Integrity PadReactor, a disposable bioreactor that can accommodate between 20 and 1,000 liters. In October 2010, the firm, through ATMI Austar LifeSciences Limited (a joint venture with Austar) opened a new manufacturing facility in China. In November 2010, the company acquired Artelis S.A., a Belgian biotechnology firm.

Employees are offered life, disability, medical and dental coverage; a 401(k); education assistance plans; adoption assistance; and stock purchase plans.

FINANCIALS: Sales and profits are in thousands of dollars—add 000 to get the full amount. 2010 Note: Financial information for 2010 was not available for all companies at press time.

2010 Sales: $	2010 Profits: $	**U.S. Stock Ticker: ATMI**
2009 Sales: $254,704	2009 Profits: $-6,660	**Int'l Ticker:** Int'l Exchange:
2008 Sales: $339,063	2008 Profits: $33,327	Employees: 761
2007 Sales: $364,088	2007 Profits: $40,359	Fiscal Year Ends: 12/31
2006 Sales: $325,913	2006 Profits: $39,961	Parent Company:

SALARIES/BENEFITS:

Pension Plan:	ESOP Stock Plan:	Profit Sharing: Y	Top Exec. Salary: $494,000	Bonus: $115,000
Savings Plan: Y	Stock Purch. Plan: Y		Second Exec. Salary: $316,000	Bonus: $55,000

OTHER THOUGHTS:

Apparent Women Officers or Directors: 3
Hot Spot for Advancement for Women/Minorities: Y

LOCATIONS: ("Y" = Yes)

West:	Southwest:	Midwest:	Southeast:	Northeast:	International:
	Y	Y		Y	Y

ATOS ORIGIN SA

www.atosorigin.com

Industry Group Code: 541513 Ranks within this company's industry group: Sales: 7 Profits: 19

Hardware:	Software:		Telecommunications:	Electronic Publishing:	Equipment:	Specialty Services:	
Computers:	Consumer:		Local:	Online Service:	Telecom:	Consulting:	Y
Accessories:	Corporate:	Y	Long Distance:	TV/Cable or Wireless:	Communication:	Contract Manufacturing:	
Network Equipment:	Telecom:		Cellular:	Games:	Distribution:	Processing:	
Chips/Circuits:	Internet:		Internet Service:	Financial Data:	VAR/Reseller:	Staff/Outsourcing:	Y
Parts/Drives:					Satellite Srv./Equip.:	Specialty Services:	Y

TYPES OF BUSINESS:

IT Consulting
Business Process Outsourcing
Payment Solutions
e-Commerce Consulting
Supply Chain Management
Customer Relationship Management
Product Lifecycle Management
Web Design

BRANDS/DIVISIONS/AFFILIATES:

Atos Consulting
Atos WorldGrid
Bank Card Company
Banksys

CONTACTS: Note: Officers with more than one job title may be intentionally listed here more than once.

Thierry Breton, CEO
Michel-Alain Proch, CFO
Jean-Marie Simon, Head-Human Resources
Philippe Mareine, Gen. Sec.
Charles Dehelly, Sr. VP-Oper.
Marc-Henri Desportes, Head-Bus. Dev. & Strategy
Didier Dhennin, CEO-Atos Worldline
Eric Grall, Head-Global Managed Svcs.
Winfied Holz, CEO-Germany & Central Europe
Herve Payan, Head-Global Consulting
Thierry Breton, Chmn.
Gilles Grapinet, Sr. Exec. VP-Global Functions
Eric Guilhou, Sr. Exec. VP-Purchasing

Phone: 33-1-73-260-0000	Fax:
Toll-Free:	
Address: River Ouest 80, Quai Voltaire, Bezons, 95877 France	

GROWTH PLANS/SPECIAL FEATURES:

Atos Origin SA is an international consulting firm that performs information technology (IT) services for its clients. The firm conducts operations in three primary business lines: consulting, systems integration and managed operations. The consulting segment operates through subsidiary Atos Consulting, which provides enterprise services, strategy development and technology consulting to its clients. The systems integration business is designed to help companies obtain the maximum value out of an existing IT infrastructure. It also implements software from SAP, Oracle and Siebel and provides custom software operations. The managed operations division provides technology outsourcing services for clients, including datacenters, desktop support and other network related business. This segment also provides business process outsourcing services. The company's Atos WorldGrid subsidiary assists energy and utility companies with outsourced services, such as billing, meter management, maintenance, geolocation and other communications. By an agreement with the International Olympic Committee, Atos Origin will provide IT support for the Olympic Games in Vancouver, London, Sochi and Rio de Janeiro. Its role is to assume primary responsibility for IT consulting, systems integration, operations management, information security and software applications development at the Olympic events. Other subsidiaries include Banksys and Bank Card Company. In August 2010, the company acquired Venture Infotek, an Indian payment processing company.

FINANCIALS: Sales and profits are in thousands of dollars—add 000 to get the full amount. 2010 Note: Financial information for 2010 was not available for all companies at press time.

2010 Sales: $	2010 Profits: $	U.S. Stock Ticker:
2009 Sales: $6,832,650	2009 Profits: $42,250	Int'l Ticker: ATO Int'l Exchange: Paris-Euronext
2008 Sales: $7,494,330	2008 Profits: $30,120	Employees: 49,036
2007 Sales: $9,251,500	2007 Profits: $76,200	Fiscal Year Ends: 12/31
2006 Sales: $8,527,100	2006 Profits: $-417,800	Parent Company:

SALARIES/BENEFITS:

Pension Plan:	ESOP Stock Plan:	Profit Sharing:	Top Exec. Salary: $	Bonus: $1,008,406
Savings Plan:	Stock Purch. Plan:		Second Exec. Salary: $	Bonus: $

OTHER THOUGHTS:

Apparent Women Officers or Directors:
Hot Spot for Advancement for Women/Minorities:

LOCATIONS: ("Y" = Yes)

West:	Southwest:	Midwest:	Southeast:	Northeast:	International:
	Y	Y			Y

ATTACHMATE CORPORATION

www.attachmate.com

Industry Group Code: 511210H Ranks within this company's industry group: Sales: Profits:

Hardware:	Software:		Telecommunications:	Electronic Publishing:	Equipment:	Specialty Services:
Computers:	Consumer:		Local:	Online Service:	Telecom:	Consulting:
Accessories:	Corporate:	Y	Long Distance:	TV/Cable or Wireless:	Communication:	Contract Manufacturing:
Network Equipment:	Telecom:	Y	Cellular:	Games:	Distribution:	Processing:
Chips/Circuits:	Internet:		Internet Service:	Financial Data:	VAR/Reseller:	Staff/Outsourcing:
Parts/Drives:					Satellite Srv./Equip.:	Specialty Services:

TYPES OF BUSINESS:

Software-Web User Information
Systems Management Software
Security Software
VoIP Software

BRANDS/DIVISIONS/AFFILIATES:

NetIQ Corporation
NetIQ Security Manager
Reflection Suite
Novell Inc

CONTACTS: Note: Officers with more than one job title may be intentionally listed here more than once.

Jeff Hawn, CEO
Charles Sansbury, COO
Charles Sansbury, CFO
Kathleen Ownes, VP-North American Sales
Jennifer Shettleroe, VP-Global Prod. Dev. & Tech. Support
Eric Varness, VP-Prod. & Mktg.
Bob Flynn, Pres./Gen. Mgr.-Host Connectivity Solutions Bus.
Jay Gardner, Pres./Gen. Mgr.-NetIQ Bus.
Edwin Bowman, Gen. Mgr.-Latin America
Jeff Hawn, Chmn.
Ton Musters, VP/Gen. Mgr.-EMEA

Phone: 206-217-7100	Fax: 206-217-7515
Toll-Free: 800-872-2829	
Address: 1500 Dexter Ave. N., Seattle, WA 98109 US	

GROWTH PLANS/SPECIAL FEATURES:

Attachmate Corporation is a provider of enterprise management, integration and security for Internet-based systems, which include web servers, intranets and extranets. Its products are designed to enable organizations to centrally manage and administer multiple Internet-based systems across their enterprises, regardless of the quantity or geographic locations of servers supporting those systems. The company operates in over 60 countries, and is owned by private equity groups Golden Gate Capital, Francisco Partners and Thoma Cressey Equity Partners. The firm offers products in the categories of terminal emulation, systems and security management, enterprise fraud management, legacy modernization, secure communications, Unisys mainframe systems and airlines and travel industry software. Attachmate's primary product, the Reflection Suite, is a terminal emulation product that allows users of varying operating system to transfer files amongst each other in one graphical user interface. Supported operating systems include Linux, UNIX, OpenVMS and IBM. Through the NetIQ, a recently acquired affiliate, the company offers the Security Manager Suite and related applications; the firm also offers privacy and security software to protect against viruses, worms, spam, hackers and employee misuse of company resources. The company's customers include Sharp Electronics; Pentagon Federal Credit Union; AT&T; Raytheon; Motorola; and the Kansas Department of Human Resources. In November 2010, the firm agreed to buy software developer Novell, Inc. for $2.2 billion.

The company offers employees a variety of health plan options, incentive plans, life insurance and exercise facilities at the majority of its offices.

FINANCIALS: Sales and profits are in thousands of dollars—add 000 to get the full amount. 2010 Note: Financial information for 2010 was not available for all companies at press time.

2010 Sales: $	2010 Profits: $	**U.S. Stock Ticker: Private**
2009 Sales: $	2009 Profits: $	**Int'l Ticker:** Int'l Exchange:
2008 Sales: $	2008 Profits: $	Employees:
2007 Sales: $	2007 Profits: $	Fiscal Year Ends: 6/30
2006 Sales: $	2006 Profits: $	Parent Company: GOLDEN GATE CAPITAL

SALARIES/BENEFITS:

Pension Plan:	ESOP Stock Plan:	Profit Sharing:	Top Exec. Salary: $	Bonus: $
Savings Plan: Y	Stock Purch. Plan:		Second Exec. Salary: $	Bonus: $

OTHER THOUGHTS:

Apparent Women Officers or Directors:
Hot Spot for Advancement for Women/Minorities:

LOCATIONS: ("Y" = Yes)

West:	Southwest:	Midwest:	Southeast:	Northeast:	International:
Y	Y			Y	Y

Note: Financial information, benefits and other data can change quickly and may vary from those stated here.

AU OPTRONICS CORP

www.auo.com

Industry Group Code: 334119 Ranks within this company's industry group: Sales: 4 Profits: 23

Hardware:		Software:		Telecommunications:		Electronic Publishing:	Equipment:	Specialty Services:
Computers:		Consumer:		Local:		Online Service:	Telecom:	Consulting:
Accessories:	Y	Corporate:		Long Distance:		TV/Cable or Wireless:	Communication:	Contract Manufacturing:
Network Equipment:		Telecom:		Cellular:		Games:	Distribution:	Processing:
Chips/Circuits:	Y	Internet:		Internet Service:		Financial Data:	VAR/Reseller:	Staff/Outsourcing:
Parts/Drives:							Satellite Srv./Equip.:	Specialty Services:

TYPES OF BUSINESS:

Liquid Crystal Display Panels
Information Technology Displays
Television Displays
Consumer Product Displays
Solar Module Production

BRANDS/DIVISIONS/AFFILIATES:

AUO Energy (Suzhou) Corp.
AFPD Pte.

CONTACTS: Note: Officers with more than one job title may be intentionally listed here more than once.

Lai-Juh Chen, CEO
Lai-Juh Chen, Pres.
Andy Yang, CFO
Michael Tsai, VP/Gen. Mgr.-IT, Display Bus. Group
Fang-Chen Luo, CTO/VP
T. K. Wu, VP/Gen. Mgr.-Consumer Prod., Display Bus.
Shih-Kun Chen, VP-Global Solar Mfg.
Fwu-Chyi Hsiang, Exec. VP-Global Oper. Unit
Paul Peng, Exec. VP-Display Bus. Oper.
James Chen, VP-Solar Bus.
Frank Ko, VP/Gen. Mgr.-TV Display Bus.
Yong-Hong Lu, VP-AUO Tech. Center
Li Kunyao, Chmn.
K. P. Chu, VP-Supply Chain Mgmt.

Phone: 886-3-500-8899	Fax: 886-3-563-7608
Toll-Free:	
Address: 1 Li-Hsin Rd. 2, Hsinchu Science Park, Hsinchu, 30078 Taiwan	

GROWTH PLANS/SPECIAL FEATURES:

AU Optronics Corp. (AUO), based in Taiwan, designs, manufactures, assembles and markets thin-film transistor liquid crystal display (TFT-LCD) panels used in various electronics such as laptops, cellular phones, digital cameras and LCD televisions, among others. AUO's screens are bought by original equipment manufacturers (OEMs) and companies that design and assemble products based on customer specifications. The company organizes its display manufacturing into three market channels: TV displays, information technology displays and consumer product displays. The TV display segment consists primarily of cover applications for LCD televisions, which typically includes display panels with sizes of 19-65 inches. The information technology segment includes applications for notebook and desktop computers, which range in size from 8.9-24 inches. The consumer products display segment covers applications for audio-video and mobile device displays, such as mobile phones, automobile displays, digital camcorders and digital photo frames. These display panels range from 1.2-10.4 inches. The company also produces curved-screen displays for mobile-device technology; along with image and fingerprint scanning technology for mobile devices. Recently, the company expanded into the solar energy market, manufacturing multi-crystalline solar modules through AUO Energy (Suzhou) Corp. In March 2010, the firm agreed to acquire AFPD Pte., a subsidiary of Toshiba Mobile Display Co. that manufactures LCD panels. In May 2010, it established a joint venture solar cell manufacturing plant with SunPower Corp. in Malaysia. In December 2010, it received certification to sell its EcoDuo solar module on the British market. Throughout 2010, the company made a number of joint venture investments for TFT-LCD module production, including one with TPV Technology Limited for a plant in Brazil.

The company offers its employees an on-site wellness center that is staffed by licensed nurses; a profit sharing program; an on-site fitness center; staff discount and subsidies at the on-sight cafeteria, convenience store, bakery and coffee shop; and subsidized travel and entertainment discounts.

FINANCIALS: Sales and profits are in thousands of dollars—add 000 to get the full amount. 2010 Note: Financial information for 2010 was not available for all companies at press time.

2010 Sales: $	2010 Profits: $	U.S. Stock Ticker: AUO
2009 Sales: $11,374,400	2009 Profits: $-847,360	Int'l Ticker: 2409 Int'l Exchange: Taipei-TPE
2008 Sales: $12,520,800	2008 Profits: $638,000	Employees:
2007 Sales: $14,810,000	2007 Profits: $1,740,000	Fiscal Year Ends: 12/31
2006 Sales: $8,993,764	2006 Profits: $279,024	Parent Company:

SALARIES/BENEFITS:

Pension Plan:	ESOP Stock Plan:	Profit Sharing: Y	Top Exec. Salary: $	Bonus: $
Savings Plan:	Stock Purch. Plan:		Second Exec. Salary: $	Bonus: $

OTHER THOUGHTS:

Apparent Women Officers or Directors:
Hot Spot for Advancement for Women/Minorities:

LOCATIONS: ("Y" = Yes)

West:	Southwest:	Midwest:	Southeast:	Northeast:	International:
					Y

AUTODESK INC

www.autodesk.com

Industry Group Code: 511210N **Ranks within this company's industry group:** Sales: 1 Profits: 3

Hardware:	Software:		Telecommunications:	Electronic Publishing:	Equipment:	Specialty Services:
Computers:	Consumer:	Y	Local:	Online Service:	Telecom:	Consulting:
Accessories:	Corporate:	Y	Long Distance:	TV/Cable or Wireless:	Communication:	Contract Manufacturing:
Network Equipment:	Telecom:		Cellular:	Games:	Distribution:	Processing:
Chips/Circuits:	Internet:		Internet Service:	Financial Data:	VAR/Reseller:	Staff/Outsourcing:
Parts/Drives:					Satellite Srv./Equip.:	Specialty Services:

TYPES OF BUSINESS:

Computer Software-Design & Drafting
Computer Assisted Design Software
Mapping & Infrastructure Management Technology
Film & Media Production Software

BRANDS/DIVISIONS/AFFILIATES:

AutoCAD
AutoCAD LT
Moldflow Corp
Dynamite SIM
Dynamite VSP
Autodesk Revit
Illuminate Labs
Autodesk Inventor

CONTACTS: Note: Officers with more than one job title may be intentionally listed here more than once.

Carl Bass, CEO
Carl Bass, Pres.
Mark Hawkins, CFO/Exec. VP
Chris Bradshaw, Chief Mktg. Officer/Sr. VP
Jan Becker, Sr. VP-Human Resources
Jay Bhatt, Sr. VP-Eng., Architecture, & Construction
Pascal Di Fronzo, General Counsel/Sr. VP/Corp. Sec.
Moonhie Chin, Sr. VP-Oper.
Moonhie Chin, Sr. VP-Strategic Planning
Jan Becker, Sr. VP-Corp. Real Estate
Marc Petit, Sr. VP-Media & Entertainment
Amar Hanspal, Sr. VP-Platform Solutions & Emerging Bus.
Robert Kross, Sr. VP-Mfg. Industry Group

Phone: 415-507-5000	Fax: 415-507-5100
Toll-Free:	
Address: 111 McInnis Pkwy., San Rafael, CA 94903 US	

GROWTH PLANS/SPECIAL FEATURES:

Autodesk, Inc. is a 2D and 3D design software and services company. The firm offers products and solutions to customers in the architectural, manufacturing, geospatial mapping, engineering, construction and digital media markets. The company provides a broad range of integrated and interoperable design software, Internet services, wireless development platforms and point-of-location applications. Autodesk is organized into four operating segments: Platform Solutions and Emerging Business (PSEB); Manufacturing Solutions; Architecture, Engineering and Construction (AEC); and Media & Entertainment. The PSEB segment accounts for roughly 36% of revenues; Manufacturing Solutions, 23%; and AEC, 30%. All three of these divisions sell software products and services to professionals who design, build, manage and own building projects. The principal products sold by these segments are AutoCAD and AutoCAD LT (2D design products), as well as such 3D model products as AutoCAD Civil 3D, Autodesk Moldflow, Autodesk Revit and Autodesk Inventor. The Media & Entertainment segment, accounting for 11% of Autodesk's revenues, sells products to post-production facilities and creative professionals for projects such as feature films, interactive game production and interactive web streaming. The firm's products are sold both directly to customers and through resellers and distributors. The company also sells mapping and infrastructure management technologies to public and private users. Autodesk products are available in 20 languages and are utilized by over 10 million users and 800,000 firms worldwide. Autodesk's recent acquisitions include Moldflow Corp., a plastic component performance prediction and optimization software specialist; and certain analysis technology assets of BOSS International, Inc. In January 2010, the firm acquired Dynamite SIM and Dynamite VSP visualization software products from 3AM Solutions. In May 2010, the company launched its Autodesk Education Suit of six products designed to help students learn core design and engineering skills. In July 2010, Autodesk acquired game lighting technology developer Illuminate Labs.

FINANCIALS: Sales and profits are in thousands of dollars—add 000 to get the full amount. 2010 Note: Financial information for 2010 was not available for all companies at press time.

2010 Sales: $1,713,700	2010 Profits: $58,000	**U.S. Stock Ticker:** ADSK
2009 Sales: $2,315,200	2009 Profits: $183,600	**Int'l Ticker:** Int'l Exchange:
2008 Sales: $2,171,900	2008 Profits: $356,200	Employees: 6,800
2007 Sales: $1,839,800	2007 Profits: $289,700	Fiscal Year Ends: 1/31
2006 Sales: $1,537,200	2006 Profits: $333,600	Parent Company:

SALARIES/BENEFITS:

Pension Plan:	ESOP Stock Plan:	Profit Sharing:	Top Exec. Salary: $825,000	Bonus: $810,000
Savings Plan: Y	Stock Purch. Plan: Y		Second Exec. Salary: $440,000	Bonus: $592,281

OTHER THOUGHTS:

Apparent Women Officers or Directors: 3
Hot Spot for Advancement for Women/Minorities: Y

LOCATIONS: ("Y" = Yes)

West:	Southwest:	Midwest:	Southeast:	Northeast:	International:
Y				Y	Y

Note: Financial information, benefits and other data can change quickly and may vary from those stated here.

AUTONOMY CORP PLC
www.autonomy.com

Industry Group Code: 511210L Ranks within this company's industry group: Sales: 3 Profits: 1

Hardware:	Software:		Telecommunications:	Electronic Publishing:	Equipment:	Specialty Services:
Computers:	Consumer:		Local:	Online Service:	Telecom:	Consulting:
Accessories:	Corporate:	Y	Long Distance:	TV/Cable or Wireless:	Communication:	Contract Manufacturing:
Network Equipment:	Telecom:		Cellular:	Games:	Distribution:	Processing:
Chips/Circuits:	Internet:		Internet Service:	Financial Data:	VAR/Reseller:	Staff/Outsourcing:
Parts/Drives:					Satellite Srv./Equip.:	Specialty Services:

TYPES OF BUSINESS:
Data Management Software
Speech & Pattern Recognition Technology
Intelligent Search Software

BRANDS/DIVISIONS/AFFILIATES:
ZANTAZ
Virage
Cardiff
etalk
Meridio
Interwoven Inc
Vidient Systems, Inc.
CA Technologies

CONTACTS: Note: Officers with more than one job title may be intentionally listed here more than once.
Mike Lynch, CEO
Andrew M. Kanter, COO
Sushovan Hussain, CFO
Nicole Eagan, Chief Mktg. Officer
Peter Menell, Chief Research Officer
Eloy Avila, CTO
Ian Black, Head-Global Oper., Autonomy Group
Joel Scott, COO-Autonomy Inc., US
Stouffer Egan, CEO-Autonomy Inc., US
David Humphrey, Managing Dir.-Virage Security & Surveillance

Phone: 44-1223-448-000	Fax: 44-1223-448-001
Toll-Free:	
Address: Cambridge Business Park, Cowley Rd., Cambridge, CB4 OWZ UK	

GROWTH PLANS/SPECIAL FEATURES:
Autonomy Corp. plc is a leader in infrastructure software for the enterprise and provides Meaning Based Computing (MBC) software, which offers software to cope with unstructured information such as documents, e-mails, telephone conversations and multimedia. The Autonomy group of companies includes ZANTAZ, a leader in the archiving, e-Discovery and Proactive Information Risk Management (IRM) markets; Cardiff, which provides Intelligent Document solutions; etalk, a provider of contact center products; Virage, a provider of rich media management and security and surveillance technology; and Meridio, which provides records management software. Autonomy designs software to recognize the relationships that exist between disconnected information for greater ease of use and efficiency using sophisticated pattern-matching algorithms. This software can understand and rank the most important concepts within documents, web pages and e-mails and thereby process them automatically for different applications in a variety of ways. Autonomy's speech recognition technology enables organizations to make sense of large volumes of enterprise and web information in text, e-mail, voice and voice forms, allowing users to obtain relevant broadcast information to support business decisions and increase efficiency. End-user applications for Autonomy's software include information access technology, pan-enterprise search, information governance, end-to-end e-Discovery and archiving, records management, business process management, customer interaction solutions and video and audio analysis. The firm serves companies in the e-commerce, energy and utilities, financial services, investigative, manufacturing, media, pharmaceutical and professional services industries. Among the company's subsidiaries are Autonomy Services Gmb H; Autonomy Systems Ltd; Autonomy Systems Singapore Pte Ltd; Autonomy France Sarl; Autonomy Belgium BVBA and Autonomy Netherlands BV. In January 2010, Autonomy formed a strategic partnership with Vidient Systems, Inc to develop and market intelligent video surveillance solutions. In June 2010, the company announced its intention to acquire CA Technologies Information Governance business, including CA Records Manager and CA Message Manager.

FINANCIALS: Sales and profits are in thousands of dollars—add 000 to get the full amount. 2010 Note: Financial information for 2010 was not available for all companies at press time.

2010 Sales: $	2010 Profits: $	U.S. Stock Ticker: AUTNF.PK
2009 Sales: $739,688	2009 Profits: $191,551	Int'l Ticker: AU Int'l Exchange: London-LSE
2008 Sales: $503,229	2008 Profits: $131,749	Employees: 1,200
2007 Sales: $304,300	2007 Profits: $62,500	Fiscal Year Ends: 12/31
2006 Sales: $250,682	2006 Profits: $39,085	Parent Company:

SALARIES/BENEFITS:
Pension Plan:	ESOP Stock Plan:	Profit Sharing:	Top Exec. Salary: $	Bonus: $
Savings Plan:	Stock Purch. Plan:		Second Exec. Salary: $	Bonus: $

OTHER THOUGHTS:
Apparent Women Officers or Directors: 1
Hot Spot for Advancement for Women/Minorities:

LOCATIONS: ("Y" = Yes)
West:	Southwest:	Midwest:	Southeast:	Northeast:	International:
Y		Y		Y	Y

AVAYA INC

www.avaya.com

Industry Group Code: 334210 Ranks within this company's industry group: Sales: 3 Profits:

Hardware:		Software:		Telecommunications:	Electronic Publishing:	Equipment:	Specialty Services:	
Computers:		Consumer:		Local:	Online Service:	Telecom:	Consulting:	Y
Accessories:		Corporate:	Y	Long Distance:	TV/Cable or Wireless:	Communication:	Contract Manufacturing:	
Network Equipment:	Y	Telecom:	Y	Cellular:	Games:	Distribution:	Processing:	
Chips/Circuits:		Internet:		Internet Service:	Financial Data:	VAR/Reseller:	Staff/Outsourcing:	
Parts/Drives:						Satellite Srv./Equip.:	Specialty Services:	

TYPES OF BUSINESS:

Telecommunications Systems
Telecommunications Software
Consulting Services
Networking Systems & Software
Network Maintenance, Management & Security Services
Systems Planning & Integration

BRANDS/DIVISIONS/AFFILIATES:

Sierra Holdings Corp.
LifeSize Communications Inc
Nortel Enterprise Solutions
Avaya Aura Contact Center Suite
Silver Lake Partners
TPG Inc
Konftel
Avaya Government Solutions

CONTACTS: Note: Officers with more than one job title may be intentionally listed here more than once.

Kevin Kennedy, CEO
Kevin Kennedy, Pres.
Anthony Massetti, CFO/Sr. VP
Joel Hackney, Sr. VP-Global Sales & Mktg./Pres., Field Oper.
Roger Gaston, Sr. VP-Human Resources
Stephen J. Gold, CIO/Sr. VP
Pamela F. Craven, Chief Admin. Officer
Jim Chirico, Exec. VP-Bus. Oper.
Mohamad Ali, Sr. VP-Corp. Dev. & Strategy
Jay Barta, Contact-Corp. Comm.
Kevin MacKay, Controller/Chief Acct. Officer/VP
Chris Formant, Sr. VP/Pres., Avaya Gov't Solutions
Steven J. Bandrowczak, VP/Gen. Mgr.-Data Solutions
Alan Baratz, Sr. VP/Pres., Global Comm. Solutions
Tom Mitchell, Sr. VP-Channel Integration
Joachim Heel, Sr. VP/Pres., Avaya Global Svcs.

Phone: 908-953-6000	Fax: 908-953-7609
Toll-Free: 866-462-8292	
Address: 211 Mt. Airy Rd., Basking Ridge, NJ 07920 US	

GROWTH PLANS/SPECIAL FEATURES:

Avaya, Inc. is a leading global provider of unified communications solutions, contact center solutions, data networking and related services for businesses of all sizes and government organizations. Avaya is a subsidiary of Sierra Holdings Corp., which is owned by private equity firms Silver Lake Partners and TPG Inc. Avaya operates in three business segments: Global Communications Solutions, Data Networking and Avaya Global Services. The Global Communications Solutions segment provides unified communications services, including centralized call control, communications support tools, messaging platforms and audio/video conferencing solutions; contact center solutions, including the Avaya Aura Contact Center Suite; and small and medium enterprise (SME) enterprise communications solutions, targeting enterprises with up to 250 employees. The Data Networking business segment offers a portfolio of integrated networking solutions, encompassing Ethernet switching, routers, Virtual Private Network appliances, wireless networking, access control and unified management solutions, as well as the Avaya Virtual Enterprise Network Architecture, an end-to-end virtualization strategy solution. Finally, the Avaya Global Services segment offers product support, integration and professional and managed services to assist with the evaluation, planning, design, implementation, support, management and optimization of enterprise communications networks. Customers of Avaya include government organizations and enterprises in the financial services, manufacturing, media and communications, professional services, health care and education industries. Recently, the company acquired Nortel's Enterprise Solutions unit. In March 2010, the firm announced a partnership with LifeSize Communications, Inc. to establish interoperability between the Avaya Aura platform and LifeSize HD video conferencing systems. In August 2010, the firm sold its 59.13% stake in AGC Networks, Ltd. In December 2010, Avaya announced plans to invest $165 million over three years in research and development facilities in Ontario, Canada. In January 2011, the company acquired Konftel, an audio collaboration technology developer, for approximately $15 million.

FINANCIALS: Sales and profits are in thousands of dollars—add 000 to get the full amount. 2010 Note: Financial information for 2010 was not available for all companies at press time.

2010 Sales: $	2010 Profits: $	U.S. Stock Ticker: Private
2009 Sales: $4,500,000	2009 Profits: $	Int'l Ticker: Int'l Exchange:
2008 Sales: $4,300,000	2008 Profits: $	Employees: 15,500
2007 Sales: $5,100,000	2007 Profits: $	Fiscal Year Ends: 9/30
2006 Sales: $5,148,000	2006 Profits: $201,000	Parent Company: SILVER LAKE PARTNERS

SALARIES/BENEFITS:

Pension Plan:	ESOP Stock Plan:	Profit Sharing:	Top Exec. Salary: $1,153,846	Bonus: $44,363
Savings Plan:	Stock Purch. Plan:		Second Exec. Salary: $559,615	Bonus: $314,546

OTHER THOUGHTS:

Apparent Women Officers or Directors: 1
Hot Spot for Advancement for Women/Minorities:

LOCATIONS: ("Y" = Yes)

West:	Southwest:	Midwest:	Southeast:	Northeast:	International:
Y			Y	Y	Y

Note: Financial information, benefits and other data can change quickly and may vary from those stated here.

AVIAT NETWORKS INC

www.aviatnetworks.com

Industry Group Code: 334210 Ranks within this company's industry group: Sales: 8 Profits: 11

Hardware:	Software:	Telecommunications:	Electronic Publishing:	Equipment:		Specialty Services:
Computers:	Consumer:	Local:	Online Service:	Telecom:	Y	Consulting:
Accessories:	Corporate:	Long Distance:	TV/Cable or Wireless:	Communication:	Y	Contract Manufacturing:
Network Equipment:	Telecom: Y	Cellular:	Games:	Distribution:		Processing:
Chips/Circuits:	Internet:	Internet Service:	Financial Data:	VAR/Reseller:		Staff/Outsourcing:
Parts/Drives:				Satellite Srv./Equip.:		Specialty Services:

TYPES OF BUSINESS:

Wireless Transmission Systems
Network Management Services
Network Operations Centers

BRANDS/DIVISIONS/AFFILIATES:

Harris Stratex Networks, Inc.
NetBoss XT
Telsima Corporation
Zain Nigeria

CONTACTS: Note: Officers with more than one job title may be intentionally listed here more than once.

Harald J. Braun, CEO
Heinz H. Stumpe, COO/Sr. VP
Harald J. Braun, Pres.
Thomas L. Cronan, CFO/Sr. VP
Shaun McFall, Chief Mktg. Officer/Sr. VP
Mimi Gigoux, Chief Human Resources Officer/VP
Paul A. Kennard, CTO/Sr. VP
Meena Elliot, General Counsel/Corp. Sec./VP
J. Russell Mincey, Corp. Controller/Chief Acct. Officer/VP
Carol A. Goudy, Corp. Treas./Assistant Sec.
Michael Pangia, Chief Sales Officer/Sr. VP
Charles D. Kissner, Chmn.

Phone: 919-767-3230	Fax: 919-767-3233
Toll-Free:	
Address: 637 Davis Dr., Research Triangle Park, Morrisville, NC 27560 US	

GROWTH PLANS/SPECIAL FEATURES:

Aviat Networks, Inc., formerly Harris Stratex Networks, is a leading global independent supplier of turnkey wireless network solutions and comprehensive network management software, including advanced Internet Protocol (IP) network migration solutions. Aviat operates through two business segments: North America and international. The firm serves all global markets, including telephone service providers, private network operators, government agencies, transportation and utility companies, public safety agencies and broadcast system operators. Aviat's products include broadband wireless access base stations, point-to-point digital microwave radio systems for access, backhaul, trunking and license-exempt applications, supporting new network deployments, network expansion and capacity upgrades. Aviat also offers a comprehensive suite of network-related professional services, such as network design and planning, including network system engineering and optimization; deployment and integration, including field installation; Network Management Software and Operating System Software (NMS/OSS) integration, including the NetBoss XT product line of enterprise management software for telecom, wireless and wireline, government and other network owners; managed network services, including the management of networks through 24-hour-a-day, seven-day-a-week network operations centers (NOC); maintenance and support; customer support; and training. In March 2009, the firm acquired Telsima Corporation, a developer and provider of WiMAX Forum Certified products for broadband wireless networks. In September 2009, Aviat partnered with Zain Nigeria, a provider of mobile service in 24 Middle Eastern and African countries, to establish a new NOC in Lagos, Nigeria. In January 2010, the company changed its name to Aviat Networks.

FINANCIALS: Sales and profits are in thousands of dollars—add 000 to get the full amount. 2010 Note: Financial information for 2010 was not available for all companies at press time.

2010 Sales: $	2010 Profits: $	U.S. Stock Ticker: AVNW
2009 Sales: $679,900	2009 Profits: $-355,000	Int'l Ticker: Int'l Exchange:
2008 Sales: $718,400	2008 Profits: $-11,900	Employees: 1,521
2007 Sales: $507,900	2007 Profits: $-17,900	Fiscal Year Ends: 6/30
2006 Sales: $357,500	2006 Profits: $-35,800	Parent Company:

SALARIES/BENEFITS:

Pension Plan:	ESOP Stock Plan:	Profit Sharing:	Top Exec. Salary: $695,000	Bonus: $200,000
Savings Plan:	Stock Purch. Plan:		Second Exec. Salary: $378,447	Bonus: $54,194

OTHER THOUGHTS:

Apparent Women Officers or Directors: 2
Hot Spot for Advancement for Women/Minorities: Y

LOCATIONS: ("Y" = Yes)

West:	Southwest:	Midwest:	Southeast:	Northeast:	International:
Y	Y		Y	Y	Y

AVID TECHNOLOGY INC

www.avid.com

Industry Group Code: 511210F Ranks within this company's industry group: Sales: 3 Profits: 4

Hardware:		Software:		Telecommunications:	Electronic Publishing:	Equipment:	Specialty Services:
Computers:		Consumer:		Local:	Online Service:	Telecom:	Consulting:
Accessories:	Y	Corporate:	Y	Long Distance:	TV/Cable or Wireless:	Communication:	Contract Manufacturing:
Network Equipment:	Y	Telecom:		Cellular:	Games:	Distribution:	Processing:
Chips/Circuits:		Internet:		Internet Service:	Financial Data:	VAR/Reseller:	Staff/Outsourcing:
Parts/Drives:	Y					Satellite Srv./Equip.:	Specialty Services:

TYPES OF BUSINESS:

Film Editing Systems
Digital Audio Equipment
Network & Storage Products
Asset Management Products
Musical Score Electronic Publishing Products

BRANDS/DIVISIONS/AFFILIATES:

Media Composer
NewsCutter
iNews Instinct
Pinnacle Studio
Dazzle
Avid Interplay
Blue Order
Euphonix

CONTACTS: Note: Officers with more than one job title may be intentionally listed here more than once.

Gary G. Greenfield, CEO
Kirk Arnold, COO
Gary G. Greenfield, Pres.
Ken Sexton, CFO/Exec. VP
Ron Greenburg, Sr. VP-Worldwide Mktg.
Ed Raine, VP-Human Resources
Jerry Kelly, CIO/VP
Paul Senechal, VP-Tech.
Ken Sexton, Chief Admin. Officer
Paige Parsi, General Counsel/Corp. Sec./VP
Kirk Arnold, Exec. VP-Customer Oper.
Glover Lawrence, VP-Corp. Dev.
Amy Peterson, Contact-Corp. Comm.
Tom Fitzsimmons, Dir.-Investor Rel.
Jason G. Burke, Chief Acct. Officer/VP-Finance
Beth Martinko, VP-Customer Success
Chris Gahagan, Sr. VP-Prod.
Martin Vann, Sr. VP-Worldwide Sales/Professional Svcs.
Gary G. Greenfield, Chmn.
Paul Senechal, VP-Supply

Phone: 978-640-6789	Fax: 978-640-3366
Toll-Free:	
Address: 75 Network Dr., Burlington, MA 01803 US	

GROWTH PLANS/SPECIAL FEATURES:

Avid Technology, Inc. is a leading provider of digital media content-creation products. Avid's customers include film, video, audio and broadcast professionals, artists, individual hobbyists and clients in the education, government and commercial markets. The company is organized into two business units: video and audio. Its video products and services are divided into four categories: professional video-editing solutions, including Media Composer, a television program editing program, and NewsCutter and iNews Instinct, designed for news production; consumer video-editing software including Pinnacle Studio and Dazzle, which are designed for consumers and entry-level videographers; broadcast newsroom systems, including graphics, ingest, play-to-air and automation device control equipment used to accelerate broadcast production; and storage and workflow software and systems, including Avid Interplay, a production asset management solution for post-production and broadcast customers. The firm's audio business segment divides its products into six categories. Digital audio software and workstation solutions are used for music and sound creation, recording, editing, signal processing and integrated surround mixing in audio production applications. Control surfaces oversee ICON (Integrated Console System), a large-format digital mixing console. Audio interfaces focus on audio recording creation. Live systems products include the VENUE product line, used in live sound reinforcement for concerts, theater performances and other public address events. The final two categories are desktop and studio monitors and other software, such as Sebelius, used to electronically create, edit and publish musical scores. In March 2010, Avid acquired Blue Order, a media archive solutions company. In April 2010, the firm acquired Euphonix, a digital audio console and media controller solutions company.

The company offers its employees healthcare and life insurance; short and long-term disability coverage; flexible spending accounts; a 401(k) plan; a stock purchase plan; and education assistance and employee assistance programs.

FINANCIALS: Sales and profits are in thousands of dollars—add 000 to get the full amount. 2010 Note: Financial information for 2010 was not available for all companies at press time.

2010 Sales: $	2010 Profits: $	**U.S. Stock Ticker:** AVID
2009 Sales: $628,970	2009 Profits: $-68,355	**Int'l Ticker:** Int'l Exchange:
2008 Sales: $844,901	2008 Profits: $-198,177	Employees:
2007 Sales: $929,570	2007 Profits: $-7,979	Fiscal Year Ends: 1/31
2006 Sales: $910,578	2006 Profits: $-42,927	Parent Company:

SALARIES/BENEFITS:

Pension Plan:	ESOP Stock Plan:	Profit Sharing:	Top Exec. Salary: $882,692	Bonus: $
Savings Plan: Y	Stock Purch. Plan: Y		Second Exec. Salary: $603,802	Bonus: $

OTHER THOUGHTS:

Apparent Women Officers or Directors: 5
Hot Spot for Advancement for Women/Minorities: Y

LOCATIONS: ("Y" = Yes)

West:	Southwest:	Midwest:	Southeast:	Northeast:	International:
Y		Y	Y	Y	Y

Note: Financial information, benefits and other data can change quickly and may vary from those stated here.

AVNET INC

www.avnet.com

Industry Group Code: 423430 Ranks within this company's industry group: Sales: 3 Profits: 14

Hardware:	Software:	Telecommunications:	Electronic Publishing:	Equipment:		Specialty Services:	
Computers:	Consumer:	Local:	Online Service:	Telecom:		Consulting:	
Accessories:	Corporate:	Long Distance:	TV/Cable or Wireless:	Communication:		Contract Manufacturing:	
Network Equipment:	Telecom:	Cellular:	Games:	Distribution:	Y	Processing:	
Chips/Circuits:	Internet:	Internet Service:	Financial Data:	VAR/Reseller:		Staff/Outsourcing:	
Parts/Drives:				Satellite Srv./Equip.:		Specialty Services:	Y

TYPES OF BUSINESS:

Components-Distributor
Marketing Services
Supply Chain Advisory Services

BRANDS/DIVISIONS/AFFILIATES:

Avnet Technology Solutions
Avnet Electronics Marketing
Avnet Logistics
Tallard Technologies SA
Bell Microproducts Inc
Broadband Integrated Resources Ltd
Eurotone Electric Ltd
itX Group Ltd

CONTACTS: *Note: Officers with more than one job title may be intentionally listed here more than once.*

Roy Vallee, CEO
Rick Hamada, COO
Ray Sadowski, CFO/Sr. VP
Harley Feldberg, Pres., Avnet Electronics Mktg. Global
MaryAnn Miller, Chief Human Resources Officer/VP
Steve Phillips, CIO/Sr. VP
David Birk, General Counsel/Sr. VP
Steve Church, Chief Bus. Dev. & Process Officer
Al Maag, Chief Comm. Officer/VP
Vincent Keenan, Investor Rel.
Phil Gallagher, Pres., Avnet Technology Solutions Global
Steve Church, Chief Operational Excellence Officer
Jim Smith, Pres., Avnet Logistics
Patrick Zammit, Pres., Avnet Electronics Mktg., EMEA
Roy Vallee, Chmn.
Graeme Watt, Pres., Avnet Technology Solutions, EMEA

Phone: 480-643-2000	Fax: 480-643-7370
Toll-Free: 800-409-1483	
Address: 2211 S. 47th St., Phoenix, AZ 85034 US	

GROWTH PLANS/SPECIAL FEATURES:

Avnet, Inc. is one of the world's largest value-added distributors of electronic components, enterprise computer and storage products, software and embedded subsystems. The company operates through two divisions, Technology Solutions and Electronics Marketing, which operate throughout the Americas, Europe, the Middle East, Africa, Asia and Australia. The firm connects more than 300 suppliers to over 100,000 original equipment manufacturers (OEMs), electronic manufacturing services (EMS) providers, original design manufacturers (ODMs) and value-added resellers (VARs) that design and build the electronic equipment for end-market use, as well as to other industrial customers. Additionally, the firm provides engineering design, materials management and logistics services, system integration and configuration and supply chain services. The Electronics Marketing division markets and sells semiconductors and interconnect, passive and electromechanical devices (IP&E) to a customer base whose end-markets include automotive, communications, computer hardware and peripheral, industrial and manufacturing, medical equipment, military and aerospace. The Technology Solutions division markets and sells servers, data storage, software and related services to resellers and mid to high-end users, as well as focusing on the worldwide OEM market. Avnet generated 44% of its 2010 revenues in the Americas, 25% in the Asia/Pacific region and 31% in the Europe/Middle East/Africa region. In July 2010, the company acquired Tallard Technologies SA, a value-added distributor in Latin America, and Bell Microproducts, Inc., a global distributor. In October 2010, the firm purchased Broadband Integrated Resources, Ltd., which specializes in broadband and cable repair, and Eurotone Electric, Ltd., a Chinese renewable energy company. In January 2011, Avnet acquired itX Group, Ltd., an Australian information technology company.

Employees are offered medical, dental and vision insurance; flexible spending accounts; life and AD&D insurance; travel accident insurance; a pension plan; a 401(k) savings plan; an employee stock purchase plan; short- and long-term disability; and tuition reimbursement, among others.

FINANCIALS: Sales and profits are in thousands of dollars—add 000 to get the full amount. 2010 Note: Financial information for 2010 was not available for all companies at press time.

2010 Sales: $19,160,200	2010 Profits: $410,400	**U.S. Stock Ticker: AVT**
2009 Sales: $16,229,900	2009 Profits: $-1,129,700	**Int'l Ticker:** Int'l Exchange:
2008 Sales: $17,952,700	2008 Profits: $499,100	Employees: 14,200
2007 Sales: $15,681,100	2007 Profits: $393,100	Fiscal Year Ends: 6/30
2006 Sales: $14,253,630	2006 Profits: $204,547	Parent Company:

SALARIES/BENEFITS:

Pension Plan: Y	ESOP Stock Plan: Y	Profit Sharing:	Top Exec. Salary: $1,050,000	Bonus: $2,359,240
Savings Plan: Y	Stock Purch. Plan:		Second Exec. Salary: $610,000	Bonus: $1,235,792

OTHER THOUGHTS:

Apparent Women Officers or Directors: 3
Hot Spot for Advancement for Women/Minorities: Y

LOCATIONS: ("Y" = Yes)

West:	Southwest:	Midwest:	Southeast:	Northeast:	International:
	Y				Y

AVX CORPORATION

www.avxcorp.com

Industry Group Code: 33441 Ranks within this company's industry group: Sales: 25 Profits: 24

Hardware:		Software:		Telecommunications:		Electronic Publishing:		Equipment:		Specialty Services:	
Computers:		Consumer:		Local:		Online Service:		Telecom:		Consulting:	Y
Accessories:		Corporate:		Long Distance:		TV/Cable or Wireless:		Communication:		Contract Manufacturing:	Y
Network Equipment:		Telecom:		Cellular:		Games:		Distribution:		Processing:	
Chips/Circuits:	Y	Internet:		Internet Service:		Financial Data:		VAR/Reseller:	Y	Staff/Outsourcing:	
Parts/Drives:	Y							Satellite Srv./Equip.:		Specialty Services:	

TYPES OF BUSINESS:

Electronic Equipment-Capacitors
Passive Electronic Components
Connector Products
Electronic Components Reselling
Product Design
Contract Manufacturing

BRANDS/DIVISIONS/AFFILIATES:

Kyocera Corp
Kyocera Elco Connectors
American Technical Ceramics Corp

CONTACTS: Note: Officers with more than one job title may be intentionally listed here more than once.

John S. Gilbertson, CEO
John S. Gilbertson, Pres.
Kurt Cummings, CFO/VP
C. Marshall Jackson, Exec. VP-Sales & Mktg.
Kathleen M. Kelly, VP-Human Resources
Carl Eggerding, CTO/VP
John Lawing, VP-Advanced Prod.
Kurt Cummings, Corp. Sec.
Kurt Cummings, Treas.
Peter Venuto, VP-Sales
Peter Collis, VP-Tantalum Prod.
Keith Thomas, VP/Pres., Kyocera Electronic Devices
John Sarvis, VP-Ceramic Prod.
John S. Gilbertson, Chmn.

GROWTH PLANS/SPECIAL FEATURES:

AVX Corporation is an international supplier of a broad line of passive electronic components and related products. The firm has 19 manufacturing facilities in 10 countries and research and development facilities in the U.S., the U.K., the Czech Republic, France and Israel. The business is divided into three segments based on the company's five product lines: Passive Components, which include ceramic, tantalum and advanced components; Kyocera Electronic Devices Resale, which sells passive electronic components manufactured by Kyocera Corp., a Japanese semiconductor packager; and Connectors, which consists primarily of Elco automotive, telecom and memory connectors manufactured by AVX. The company's products include a full line of multi-layered ceramic and solid tantalum capacitors, and passive components such as film, capacitors, high-energy/voltage power capacitors and non-linear resistors. In addition to its standard products, the company works with customers to design, produce and manufacture advanced passive component products that meet the specifications of particular applications. AVX sells its products to customers in a broad array of industries, including telecommunications, information technology hardware, automotive electronics, medical devices and instrumentation, industrial instrumentation, military and aerospace electronic systems and consumer electronics. The firm's primary customers are original equipment manufacturers (OEMs) and contract equipment manufacturers. The company is 72%-owned by Kyocera Corp. AVX Corporation owns American Technical Ceramics Corp., a manufacturer of high-performance electronic components.

Phone: 843-448-9411	Fax: 843-448-7139
Toll-Free:	
Address: 801 17th Ave. S., Myrtle Beach, SC 29577 US	

FINANCIALS: Sales and profits are in thousands of dollars—add 000 to get the full amount. 2010 Note: Financial information for 2010 was not available for all companies at press time.

2010 Sales: $1,304,966	2010 Profits: $142,858	U.S. Stock Ticker: AVX
2009 Sales: $1,389,613	2009 Profits: $80,846	Int'l Ticker: Int'l Exchange:
2008 Sales: $1,619,275	2008 Profits: $149,473	Employees: 10,600
2007 Sales: $1,498,495	2007 Profits: $153,865	Fiscal Year Ends: 3/31
2006 Sales: $1,333,208	2006 Profits: $81,752	Parent Company:

SALARIES/BENEFITS:

Pension Plan: Y	ESOP Stock Plan:	Profit Sharing:	Top Exec. Salary: $706,000	Bonus: $54,400
Savings Plan:	Stock Purch. Plan:		Second Exec. Salary: $334,000	Bonus: $26,200

OTHER THOUGHTS:

Apparent Women Officers or Directors:
Hot Spot for Advancement for Women/Minorities:

LOCATIONS: ("Y" = Yes)

West:	Southwest:	Midwest:	Southeast:	Northeast:	International:
Y			Y	Y	Y

AVY PRECISION TECHNOLOGY INC

www.avy.com.tw

Industry Group Code: 33411 Ranks within this company's industry group: Sales: 14 Profits: 5

Hardware:	Software:	Telecommunications:	Electronic Publishing:	Equipment:	Specialty Services:
Computers:	Consumer:	Local:	Online Service:	Telecom:	Consulting:
Accessories:	Corporate:	Long Distance:	TV/Cable or Wireless:	Communication:	Contract Manufacturing:
Network Equipment:	Telecom:	Cellular:	Games:	Distribution:	Processing:
Chips/Circuits:	Internet:	Internet Service:	Financial Data:	VAR/Reseller:	Staff/Outsourcing:
Parts/Drives: Y				Satellite Srv./Equip.:	Specialty Services:

TYPES OF BUSINESS:

Manufacturing-Aluminum & Plastic Electronic Equipment Cases

BRANDS/DIVISIONS/AFFILIATES:

AVY Co., Ltd.
DongGuan Cheng Guang Metal Products Co., Ltd.
DongGuang YingHua Precision Metal (LiaoBu)
AVY Precision Metal Components (Suzhou) Co., Ltd.
AVY Precision Electroplating (Suzhou) Co., Ltd.

CONTACTS: Note: Officers with more than one job title may be intentionally listed here more than once.

Mincheng Li, Gen. Mgr.
Jiongxiong Dong, Chmn.

Phone: 886-2-25472089	Fax: 886-2-25472909
Toll-Free:	
Address: 101 Fu Hsing North Rd., 10th Fl., Taipei, Taiwan	

GROWTH PLANS/SPECIAL FEATURES:

AVY Precision Technology, Inc. produces stamped and molded aluminum and plastic casings for consumer electronic products and related equipment. The company primarily produces casings for digital cameras; it also produces casings for mobile phones, scanners, car parts, MP3 players, PDAs, keyboards and electronic dictionaries. The company maintains manufacturing facilities both in Taiwan and mainland China; which are run either by the company or through one of its subsidiaries. These include AVY Co., Ltd., located in Taiwan; DongGuan Cheng Guang Metal Products Co., Ltd.; DongGuang YingHua Precision Metal (LiaoBu); AVY Precision Metal Components (Suzhou) Co., Ltd.; and AVY Precision Electroplating (Suzhou) Co., Ltd. The company's primary market areas are the U.S., Japan, Southeast Asia and Europe. In June 2010, the firm announced plans to list its AVY Precision Electroplating (Suzhou) Co., Ltd. subsidiary on the Taiwanese stock market.

The company offers its employees health insurance; two days off a week; disability insurance; bonuses for major festivals, birthdays and Labor Day; staff uniform provisions; educational assistance for employees and their children; and a marriage allowance.

FINANCIALS: Sales and profits are in thousands of dollars—add 000 to get the full amount. 2010 Note: Financial information for 2010 was not available for all companies at press time.

2010 Sales: $	2010 Profits: $	U.S. Stock Ticker:
2009 Sales: $123,910	2009 Profits: $20,520	Int'l Ticker: 5392 Int'l Exchange: Taipei-TPE
2008 Sales: $113,870	2008 Profits: $16,410	Employees: 4,700
2007 Sales: $74,995	2007 Profits: $	Fiscal Year Ends: 12/31
2006 Sales: $	2006 Profits: $	Parent Company:

SALARIES/BENEFITS:

Pension Plan:	ESOP Stock Plan:	Profit Sharing:	Top Exec. Salary: $	Bonus: $
Savings Plan:	Stock Purch. Plan:		Second Exec. Salary: $	Bonus: $

OTHER THOUGHTS:

Apparent Women Officers or Directors:
Hot Spot for Advancement for Women/Minorities:

LOCATIONS: ("Y" = Yes)

West:	Southwest:	Midwest:	Southeast:	Northeast:	International:
					Y

BANCTEC INC

www.banctec.com

Industry Group Code: 511201 Ranks within this company's industry group: Sales: Profits:

Hardware:		Software:		Telecommunications:	Electronic Publishing:	Equipment:	Specialty Services:	
Computers:		Consumer:		Local:	Online Service:	Telecom:	Consulting:	Y
Accessories:	Y	Corporate:	Y	Long Distance:	TV/Cable or Wireless:	Communication:	Contract Manufacturing:	
Network Equipment:		Telecom:		Cellular:	Games:	Distribution:	Processing:	Y
Chips/Circuits:		Internet:		Internet Service:	Financial Data:	VAR/Reseller:	Staff/Outsourcing:	Y
Parts/Drives:						Satellite Srv./Equip.:	Specialty Services:	

TYPES OF BUSINESS:

Software-Financial Transaction Processing
Network Management & Support Services
Check Processing Equipment
Document Management Software
Image Capture Software
Professional Services

BRANDS/DIVISIONS/AFFILIATES:

eFIRST
PayCourier
IntelliScan
CenterVision
X-Series
E-Series
Image Sentry
Beta Systems ECM Solutions GmbH

CONTACTS: Note: Officers with more than one job title may be intentionally listed here more than once.

J. Coley Clark, CEO
Jeff Cushman, CFO/Sr. VP
Mark D. Fairchild, CTO
Bob Robinson, General Counsel/Sec./VP
Michael D. Fallin, Sr. VP/Pres., Americas
J. Coley Clark, Chmn.
Mike Peplow, Sr. VP/Pres., EMEA

Phone: 972-821-4000	Fax: 972-821-4823
Toll-Free: 800-226-2832	
Address: 2701 E. Grauwyler Rd., Irving, TX 75061 US	

GROWTH PLANS/SPECIAL FEATURES:

BancTec, Inc. provides software that automates the capturing, processing and archiving of paper and electronic forms for governments, banks, utility, and insurance and telecommunications companies. The company is engaged in document retrieval and high volume document processing, as well as the processing and reparation of damaged checks. The firm is also involved in payment processing, mortgage origination, inbound mail processing, claims processing, explanation of benefits (EOB) processing, accounts payable (AP) automation; account origination; case management; revenue cycle management; image capture & archive; and backfile conversion. The company also offers consulting management services in areas such as treasury, risk management and working capital management. In addition, the firm offers multi-vendor services such as warranty repair and customer service. The company offers both hardware and software products. Its hardware products consist of document processors and scanners in the IntelliScan, X-Series and E-Series suites. The firm's software products include AP Master, for accounts payable automation; CenterVision, a global transactional content management platform; eFIRST Process, which streamlines business processes for large businesses; eFIRST Archive; for the storage and protection of documents; eFIRST Capture, a document distributor, retriever and processer; PayCourier, a payment processing software; PayCourier Archive, which stores an unlimited amount of payment data and images; Image Sentry, an image capture and exchange software; and IntelliScan, a provider of real-time identification of documents. BancTec has offices in 14 countries in North America and Europe and services companies in over 50 countries. In June 2010, the firm acquired Beta Systems ECM Solutions GmbH from German company Beta Systems Software AG.

FINANCIALS: Sales and profits are in thousands of dollars—add 000 to get the full amount. 2010 Note: Financial information for 2010 was not available for all companies at press time.

2010 Sales: $	2010 Profits: $	**U.S. Stock Ticker:** Private
2009 Sales: $	2009 Profits: $	**Int'l Ticker:** Int'l Exchange:
2008 Sales: $	2008 Profits: $	Employees:
2007 Sales: $390,000	2007 Profits: $	Fiscal Year Ends: 12/31
2006 Sales: $379,500	2006 Profits: $- 800	Parent Company:

SALARIES/BENEFITS:

Pension Plan:	ESOP Stock Plan:	Profit Sharing:	Top Exec. Salary: $	Bonus: $
Savings Plan:	Stock Purch. Plan:		Second Exec. Salary: $	Bonus: $

OTHER THOUGHTS:

Apparent Women Officers or Directors:
Hot Spot for Advancement for Women/Minorities:

LOCATIONS: ("Y" = Yes)

West:	Southwest:	Midwest:	Southeast:	Northeast:	International:
	Y				Y

BEETEL TELETECH LIMITED

www.beetel.in

Industry Group Code: 334210 **Ranks within this company's industry group:** Sales: Profits:

Hardware:	Software:	Telecommunications:	Electronic Publishing:	Equipment:		Specialty Services:	
Computers:	Consumer:	Local:	Online Service:	Telecom:		Consulting:	
Accessories:	Corporate:	Long Distance:	TV/Cable or Wireless:	Communication:	Y	Contract Manufacturing:	
Network Equipment:	Telecom:	Cellular:	Games:	Distribution:	Y	Processing:	
Chips/Circuits:	Internet:	Internet Service:	Financial Data:	VAR/Reseller:	Y	Staff/Outsourcing:	
Parts/Drives:				Satellite Srv./Equip.:		Specialty Services:	

TYPES OF BUSINESS:

Telecommunications Equipment Manufacturing
Telecommunications Equipment Distribution
Telecommunications Equipment Marketing

BRANDS/DIVISIONS/AFFILIATES:

Bharti Airtel Ltd
Bharti Teletech Ltd.
Bharti Learning Systems
Bharti AXA Life Insurance
FieldFresh Foods Ltd

CONTACTS: *Note: Officers with more than one job title may be intentionally listed here more than once.*

Vinod Sawhny, CEO
Prabhat Ummat, Chief Mktg. Officer
Sumant Sinha, Chief Human Resources Officer
Suresh Gupta, Chief Commercial Officer
Nafis Kazim, Head-B2B
Sanjeev Chhabra, Head-B2E
Sunil D Sharma, Head-B2C
Rakesh Bharti Mittal, Chmn.

Phone: 91-11-4170960005	Fax: 91-11-41709869
Toll-Free:	
Address: D-195 Okhla Industrial Area, Phase - I, New Delhi, 110 020 India	

GROWTH PLANS/SPECIAL FEATURES:

Beetel Teletech Limited (formerly Bharti Teletech Limited), a subsidiary of Bharti Airtel Ltd., manufactures, distributes and markets a wide array of mobile and telecommunications products, including well known brands such as Apple, BlackBerry, Transcend and audio/video conferencing products from Polycom. The firm manufactures its landline telephones for the retail market at its Goa and Ludhiana manufacturing plants, then exports these phones to approximately 30 countries on five continents throughout the world. Landline phone brands manufactured include Beetel brand for Airtel, BSNL/MTNL. The firm has a network of over 800 distributors and more than 40,000 dealers which cover nearly 4,000 towns and regions within India. The Beetel brand was the first to launch caller ID phones in India. The firm also owns and/or operates several organizations such as Bharti AXA Life Insurance, a joint venture between itself (74% stake) and AXA (26% stake), which offers various individual and group life insurance plans. Bharti Learning Systems, a wholly-owned subsidiary of Bharti Enterprises, offers end-to-end learning and skill- building solutions for the Bharti Group of companies, as well as several other large corporations. FieldFresh Foods, a joint venture with DMPL India Limited (owned by Del Monte Pacific Limited), manufactures processed fruits and vegetables and promotes world class standards for agricultural practices, progressive farming techniques and identification and adoption of appropriate technologies. In September 2010, Beetel entered the mobile handset market, launching a line of eight cellular phones available on the Indian market.

FINANCIALS: Sales and profits are in thousands of dollars—add 000 to get the full amount. 2010 Note: Financial information for 2010 was not available for all companies at press time.

2010 Sales: $	2010 Profits: $	U.S. Stock Ticker: Subsidiary	
2009 Sales: $	2009 Profits: $	Int'l Ticker: Int'l Exchange:	
2008 Sales: $	2008 Profits: $	Employees:	
2007 Sales: $	2007 Profits: $	Fiscal Year Ends:	
2006 Sales: $	2006 Profits: $	Parent Company: BHARTI AIRTEL LTD	

SALARIES/BENEFITS:

Pension Plan:	ESOP Stock Plan:	Profit Sharing:	Top Exec. Salary: $	Bonus: $
Savings Plan:	Stock Purch. Plan:		Second Exec. Salary: $	Bonus: $

OTHER THOUGHTS:

Apparent Women Officers or Directors:
Hot Spot for Advancement for Women/Minorities:

LOCATIONS: ("Y" = Yes)

West:	Southwest:	Midwest:	Southeast:	Northeast:	International:
					Y

BELDEN INC

www.belden.com

Industry Group Code: 334210 Ranks within this company's industry group: Sales: 5   Profits: 5

Hardware:		Software:	Telecommunications:	Electronic Publishing:	Equipment:		Specialty Services:	
Computers:		Consumer:	Local:	Online Service:	Telecom:	Y	Consulting:	
Accessories:	Y	Corporate:	Long Distance:	TV/Cable or Wireless:	Communication:		Contract Manufacturing:	
Network Equipment:		Telecom:	Cellular:	Games:	Distribution:		Processing:	
Chips/Circuits:		Internet:	Internet Service:	Financial Data:	VAR/Reseller:		Staff/Outsourcing:	
Parts/Drives:					Satellite Srv./Equip.:		Specialty Services:	

TYPES OF BUSINESS:

Cable & Wire Systems Manufacturing & Retail
Electronic Products
Broadcasting Equipment
Aerospace & Automotive Electronics
Enclosures

BRANDS/DIVISIONS/AFFILIATES:

LTK Wiring Co., Ltd.
Trapeze Networks Inc

CONTACTS: Note: Officers with more than one job title may be intentionally listed here more than once.

John S. Stroup, CEO
John S. Stroup, Pres.
Gray G. Benoist, CFO/VP-Finance
Steve Biegacki, VP-Global Sales & Mktg.
Kevin L. Bloomfield, General Counsel/Corp. Sec./VP
Christoph Gusenleitner, Exec. VP-Oper.
Gray G. Benoist, Chief Acct. Officer
Naresh Kumra, Exec. VP-Asia Pacific
Henk Derksen, VP-Financial Planning & Analysis/Treas.
John Norman, VP-EMEA Finance
Bryan C. Cressey, Chmn.
Christoph Gusenleitner, Exec. VP-EMEA & Global Connectivity

Phone: 314-854-8000	Fax: 314-854-8001
Toll-Free: 800-235-3361	
Address: 7701 Forsyth Blvd., Ste. 800, St. Louis, MO 63105 US	

GROWTH PLANS/SPECIAL FEATURES:

Belden, Inc. designs, manufactures and markets signal transmission products, including cable, connectivity and networking components. The firm's cables include copper cables, such as shielded and unshielded twisted pair cables, coaxial cables, stranded cables, and ribbon cables; fiber optic cables; and composite cables. The company operates in four segments: Belden Americas, wireless, EMEA and Asia Pacific. The Belden Americas segment, which generated approximately 54% of the firm's 2009 revenue, designs and provides cable products for use in the industrial, audio and video, security, networking and communications markets. It also provides connectivity, cable management products, cabinetry and tubing and sleeving products. The wireless segment, which generated about 4% of the firm's 2009 revenue, provides a suite of wireless local area network products principally for use in the healthcare and education markets, as well as the retail, manufacturing, logistics, financial, government, hospitality and enterprise markets. Through its Trapeze Networks brand, the firm offers indoor and outdoor WLAN products services. The company's EMEA segment, which generated approximately 24% of its 2009 revenue, provides industrial Ethernet switches and related equipment, both rail-mounted and rack-mounted, for factory automation; power generation and distribution; process automation; and large-scale infrastructure projects such as bridges, wind farms and airport runways. Belden's Asia Pacific segment, which generated approximately 18% of its 2009 revenue, includes the operations of its LTK Wiring Co. subsidiary, providing cable products principally within China. The firm markets its products primarily to distributors and OEMs throughout the Americas, Europe and Asia. Its manufacturing facilities are located in the U.S., Canada, Mexico, China and Europe with 57% of sales deriving from outside of the United States. In July 2009, the company ceased operations at its Leominster, Massachusetts plant.

FINANCIALS: Sales and profits are in thousands of dollars—add 000 to get the full amount. 2010 Note: Financial information for 2010 was not available for all companies at press time.

2010 Sales: $	2010 Profits: $	**U.S. Stock Ticker:** BDC
2009 Sales: $1,415,262	2009 Profits: $1,641	**Int'l Ticker:** Int'l Exchange:
2008 Sales: $2,005,890	2008 Profits: $-342,188	Employees: 6,200
2007 Sales: $2,032,841	2007 Profits: $137,123	Fiscal Year Ends: 12/31
2006 Sales: $1,495,811	2006 Profits: $65,935	Parent Company:

SALARIES/BENEFITS:

Pension Plan:	ESOP Stock Plan:	Profit Sharing:	Top Exec. Salary: $700,000	Bonus: $990,990
Savings Plan:	Stock Purch. Plan:		Second Exec. Salary: $400,000	Bonus: $387,090

OTHER THOUGHTS:

Apparent Women Officers or Directors: 3
Hot Spot for Advancement for Women/Minorities: Y

LOCATIONS: ("Y" = Yes)

West:	Southwest:	Midwest:	Southeast:	Northeast:	International:
Y	Y	Y	Y	Y	Y

BENCHMARK ELECTRONICS INC

www.bench.com

Industry Group Code: 334419 **Ranks within this company's industry group:** Sales: 13 Profits: 8

Hardware:		Software:		Telecommunications:	Electronic Publishing:	Equipment:	Specialty Services:	
Computers:	Y	Consumer:		Local:	Online Service:	Telecom:	Consulting:	
Accessories:		Corporate:	Y	Long Distance:	TV/Cable or Wireless:	Communication:	Contract Manufacturing:	Y
Network Equipment:		Telecom:		Cellular:	Games:	Distribution:	Processing:	
Chips/Circuits:	Y	Internet:		Internet Service:	Financial Data:	VAR/Reseller:	Staff/Outsourcing:	
Parts/Drives:						Satellite Srv./Equip.:	Specialty Services:	Y

TYPES OF BUSINESS:

Contract Electronics Manufacturing
Design & Engineering
Printed Circuit Boards

BRANDS/DIVISIONS/AFFILIATES:

Pemstar Inc

CONTACTS: Note: Officers with more than one job title may be intentionally listed here more than once.

Cary T. Fu, CEO
Gayla J. Delly, Pres.
Donald F. Adam, CFO
Kenneth S. Barrow, Sec.
Cary T. Fu, Chmn.

Phone: 979-849-6550	**Fax:** 979-848-5270
Toll-Free:	
Address: 3000 Technology Dr., Angleton, TX 77515 US	

GROWTH PLANS/SPECIAL FEATURES:

Benchmark Electronics, Inc. provides contract-manufacturing services for complex printed circuit boards and related electronics systems and subsystems. Benchmark primarily serves original equipment manufacturers (OEMs) of computers and related products for business enterprises; medical devices; industrial control equipment; testing and instrumentation products; and telecommunications equipment. The firm provides comprehensive and integrated design and manufacturing services, from initial product design to volume production and direct order fulfillment. In addition, the company offers specialized engineering services including advanced design, software development, industrial design, assembly automation, printed circuit board layout, prototyping and test development. Many of Benchmark's manufacturing services are provided on a turnkey basis, whereby it purchases customer-specified components from its suppliers, assembles the components on finished printed circuit boards, performs post-production testing and provides production process and testing documentation. Benchmark offers flexible, just-in-time delivery programs allowing product shipments to be closely coordinated with customer inventory requirements. The company offers its customers a range of traditional and more advanced manufacturing technologies, encompassing processes such as pin-through-hole, surface mount, chip-on-board, fine pitch, flip chip and ball grid array. The firm has manufacturing facilities in 10 countries worldwide, operating approximately 127 surface mount production lines, where electrical components are soldered directly onto printed circuit boards. Benchmark operates domestic facilities in Alabama, Arizona, California, Minnesota, New Hampshire, North Dakota, Oregon and Texas, totaling approximately 1.6 million square feet. Operations outside the U.S., totaling roughly 1.5 million square feet, include facilities in Brazil, China, Ireland, Malaysia, Mexico, the Netherlands, Romania, Singapore and Thailand, providing international customers with a combination of strategic regional locations and global procurement capabilities. Subsidiary Pemstar, Inc. is an electronics manufacturer headquartered in Rochester, Minnesota.

FINANCIALS: Sales and profits are in thousands of dollars—add 000 to get the full amount. 2010 Note: Financial information for 2010 was not available for all companies at press time.

2010 Sales: $	2010 Profits: $	**U.S. Stock Ticker:** BHE
2009 Sales: $2,089,253	2009 Profits: $53,895	**Int'l Ticker:** Int'l Exchange:
2008 Sales: $2,590,167	2008 Profits: $-135,632	Employees: 9,849
2007 Sales: $2,915,919	2007 Profits: $93,282	Fiscal Year Ends: 12/31
2006 Sales: $2,907,304	2006 Profits: $111,677	Parent Company:

SALARIES/BENEFITS:

Pension Plan:	ESOP Stock Plan:	Profit Sharing:	Top Exec. Salary: $700,000	Bonus: $933,800
Savings Plan: Y	Stock Purch. Plan:		Second Exec. Salary: $485,000	Bonus: $485,000

OTHER THOUGHTS:

Apparent Women Officers or Directors: 2
Hot Spot for Advancement for Women/Minorities:

LOCATIONS: ("Y" = Yes)

West:	Southwest:	Midwest:	Southeast:	Northeast:	International:
Y	Y	Y	Y	Y	Y

BENQ CORPORATION

www.benq.com

Industry Group Code: 334119 Ranks within this company's industry group: Sales: Profits:

Hardware:		Software:	Telecommunications:	Electronic Publishing:	Equipment:		Specialty Services:
Computers:	Y	Consumer:	Local:	Online Service:	Telecom:	Y	Consulting:
Accessories:	Y	Corporate:	Long Distance:	TV/Cable or Wireless:	Communication:		Contract Manufacturing:
Network Equipment:		Telecom:	Cellular:	Games:	Distribution:		Processing:
Chips/Circuits:		Internet:	Internet Service:	Financial Data:	VAR/Reseller:		Staff/Outsourcing:
Parts/Drives:					Satellite Srv./Equip.:		Specialty Services:

TYPES OF BUSINESS:

Manufacturing-Computer, Consumer Electronics & Comm. Equipment

BRANDS/DIVISIONS/AFFILIATES:

Joybook
Joybook Lite
nReader
AU Optronics Corporation
Qisda Corporation
Darfon Electronics Corporation
Daxin Materials Corp.
Darwin Precision Company

CONTACTS: *Note: Officers with more than one job title may be intentionally listed here more than once.*

Conway Lee, CEO
Conway Lee, Pres.
Peter Chen, Exec. VP/Gen. Mgr.-Tech. Prod. Center
Adams Lee, Pres., BenQ Europe
Tony Yang, Pres., BenQ China
Lars Yoder, Pres., BenQ America
Peter Tan, Pres., BenQ Latin America
K. Y. Lee, Chmn.
Adrian Chang, Pres., BenQ Asia Pacific

Phone: 886-2-2727-8899	Fax: 886-2-2797-9288
Toll-Free:	
Address: 16 Jihu Rd., Neihu, Taipei, 114 Taiwan	

GROWTH PLANS/SPECIAL FEATURES:

BenQ Corporation produces consumer electronics, communication devices and components. The company's primary products include LCD monitors, computers and mobile devices. BenQ has seven series of LCD monitors, comprising over 50 models of PC displays and LCD TVs. These monitors are generally designed to function with high-performance systems, such as next generation gaming consoles or high definition (HD) DVD players. BenQ's computers include notebooks, sold under the Joybook and Joybook Lite brands, and all-in-one desktops. BenQ's consumer electronics products comprise LCD displays, digital projectors, an e-book reader (the nReader) and digital cameras and camcorders. Lastly, the company's communications equipment consists of a mobile Internet device and several models of mobile phones. The MID S6 mobile Internet device is a compact handheld device with a 4.8-inch touch screen display that primarily supports web browsing and e-mails through wireless connectivity. The BenQ Group consists of several independent companies aside from BenQ Corp., including AU Optronics Corporation; Qisda Corporation; Darfon Electronics Corporation; Daxin Materials Corp.; and Darwin Precision Company.

FINANCIALS: Sales and profits are in thousands of dollars—add 000 to get the full amount. 2010 Note: Financial information for 2010 was not available for all companies at press time.

2010 Sales: $	2010 Profits: $	**U.S. Stock Ticker: BNQQF**	
2009 Sales: $	2009 Profits: $	**Int'l Ticker:** Int'l Exchange:	
2008 Sales: $	2008 Profits: $	Employees:	
2007 Sales: $	2007 Profits: $	Fiscal Year Ends: 12/31	
2006 Sales: $	2006 Profits: $	Parent Company:	

SALARIES/BENEFITS:

Pension Plan:	ESOP Stock Plan:	Profit Sharing:	Top Exec. Salary: $	Bonus: $
Savings Plan:	Stock Purch. Plan:		Second Exec. Salary: $	Bonus: $

OTHER THOUGHTS:

Apparent Women Officers or Directors:
Hot Spot for Advancement for Women/Minorities:

LOCATIONS: ("Y" = Yes)

West:	Southwest:	Midwest:	Southeast:	Northeast:	International:
Y			Y		Y

Note: Financial information, benefits and other data can change quickly and may vary from those stated here.

BHARAT ELECTRONICS LIMITED

www.bel-india.com

Industry Group Code: 3345 Ranks within this company's industry group: Sales: Profits:

Hardware:		Software:		Telecommunications:	Electronic Publishing:	Equipment:		Specialty Services:	
Computers:	Y	Consumer:		Local:	Online Service:	Telecom:	Y	Consulting:	Y
Accessories:	Y	Corporate:		Long Distance:	TV/Cable or Wireless:	Communication:	Y	Contract Manufacturing:	Y
Network Equipment:		Telecom:		Cellular:	Games:	Distribution:		Processing:	Y
Chips/Circuits:		Internet:		Internet Service:	Financial Data:	VAR/Reseller:		Staff/Outsourcing:	
Parts/Drives:						Satellite Srv./Equip.:		Specialty Services:	Y

TYPES OF BUSINESS:

Electronic Navigation & Communication Equipment

BRANDS/DIVISIONS/AFFILIATES:

BEL Optronic Devices Ltd
GEBE Private Limited
BEL-Multitone Ltd

CONTACTS: Note: Officers with more than one job title may be intentionally listed here more than once.

Ashwani Datt, Managing Dir.
M. Raghuveer, Dir.-Finance
H. Ramakrishna, Dir.-Mktg.
M. Shanmukh, Dir.-Human Resources
I.V. Sarma, Dir.-R&D
C. Prakash, Sec.
Ashwani Datt, Chmn.

Phone: 91-80-25039300	Fax: 91-80-25039305
Toll-Free:	
Address: Nagavara Outer Ring Rd., Bangalore, 560 045 India	

GROWTH PLANS/SPECIAL FEATURES:

Bharat Electronics Limited (BEL), established by the Indian government's Ministry of Defense, manufactures a multitude of electronics products and services to a variety of industries within India, as well as around the world. The firm produces defense, non-defense and systems/turnkey products. Defense products are geared toward military and government use, and include radars; naval systems; opto electronics; tank electronics; simulators; and communications products. Non-defense products address the needs of various industries such as TV/broadcasting and telecommunications. They include switching equipment, such as single base modules (SBM-VE) and remote line concentrators; electronic voting machines; electronic components, such as liquid crystal displays, power devices and integrated circuits and silicon detectors; telecom products, such as intermediate data rate equipment and digital loop carrier on optical fiber; TV and broadcast products; DTH; and the Amida Simputer, a handheld mobile computer. The system/turnkey products division offers system solutions to clients involved in activities such as map survey; radio path survey; traffic study; prediction of link performance; configuration planning; equipment identification and supplies; installation and commissioning; training; warranty support; annual maintenance contract; and integrated logistic support. Products offered include, but are not limited to, vehicle tracking and messaging systems; artillery command control communication systems; integrated secure digital communication networks; and police communication networks. Additionally, BEL provides several services to its customers such as software development, quality assurance facilities; contract manufacturing; design and manufacturing services; and semiconductor device packaging. The firm has one subsidiaries: BEL Optronic Devices Ltd, as well as two joint ventures: GE-BE Private Limited (joint venture between BEL and General Electric Medical Systems) and BEL-Multitone Ltd. (BEL and Multitone, UK).

FINANCIALS: Sales and profits are in thousands of dollars—add 000 to get the full amount. 2010 Note: Financial information for 2010 was not available for all companies at press time.

		U.S. Stock Ticker: Government-Owned
2010 Sales: $	2010 Profits: $	Int'l Ticker: Int'l Exchange:
2009 Sales: $	2009 Profits: $	Employees:
2008 Sales: $	2008 Profits: $	Fiscal Year Ends:
2007 Sales: $	2007 Profits: $	Parent Company:
2006 Sales: $	2006 Profits: $	

SALARIES/BENEFITS:

Pension Plan:	ESOP Stock Plan:	Profit Sharing:	Top Exec. Salary: $	Bonus: $
Savings Plan:	Stock Purch. Plan:		Second Exec. Salary: $	Bonus: $

OTHER THOUGHTS:

Apparent Women Officers or Directors: 1
Hot Spot for Advancement for Women/Minorities:

LOCATIONS: ("Y" = Yes)

West:	Southwest:	Midwest:	Southeast:	Northeast:	International:
					Y

Note: Financial information, benefits and other data can change quickly and may vary from those stated here.

BIOWARE CORP

www.bioware.com

Industry Group Code: 511210G Ranks within this company's industry group: Sales: Profits:

Hardware:	Software:		Telecommunications:	Electronic Publishing:		Equipment:	Specialty Services:
Computers:	Consumer:	Y	Local:	Online Service:		Telecom:	Consulting:
Accessories:	Corporate:		Long Distance:	TV/Cable or Wireless:		Communication:	Contract Manufacturing:
Network Equipment:	Telecom:		Cellular:	Games:	Y	Distribution:	Processing:
Chips/Circuits:	Internet:		Internet Service:	Financial Data:		VAR/Reseller:	Staff/Outsourcing:
Parts/Drives:						Satellite Srv./Equip.:	Specialty Services:

TYPES OF BUSINESS:
Computer Software/Games
E-commerce

BRANDS/DIVISIONS/AFFILIATES:
Electronic Arts, Inc.
Baldur's Gate
Neverwinter Nights
Star Wars: Knights of the Old Republic
Dragon Age: Origins
Mass Effect
Infinity Engine
BioWare Odyssey Engine

CONTACTS: Note: Officers with more than one job title may be intentionally listed here more than once.
Ray Muzyka, CEO/Gen. Mgr.
Greg Zeschuk, Pres./Gen. Mgr.-BioWare Austin
Aaryn Flynn, Gen. Mgr.-BioWare Edmonton
Mike Laidlaw, Dir.-Creative
Mark Darrah, Exec. Producer

Phone: 780-430-0164	Fax: 780-439-6374
Toll-Free:	
Address: 200, 4445 Calgary Trail, Edmonton, AB T6H 5R7 Canada	

GROWTH PLANS/SPECIAL FEATURES:
BioWare Corp., founded in 1996, is one of the most successful game developers in the world, selling hundreds of thousands, sometimes millions of units per title. It specializes in creating computer and console video games, mainly in the role playing game (RPG) format. Its first title, Shattered Steel, sold nearly 200,000 units. BioWare's best-selling game, Baldur's Gate, was followed by Baldur's Gate: Tales of the Sword Coast; Baldur's Gate II: Shadows of Amn; and Baldur's Gate II: Throne of Bhaal. Together, the Baldur's Gate series has sold almost 5 million copies. Other titles the company has released include Neverwinter Nights; Jade Empire; Mass Effect; and Star Wars: Knights of the Old Republic (KOTOR). Its newest games are Dragon Age: Origins, a fantasy RPG released in 2009; Sonic Chronicles: The Dark Brotherhood; and the critically acclaimed science fiction RPG Mass Effect 2. BioWare also licenses its game engine technology; games including Planescape: Torment and the Icewind Dale series were developed using BioWare's Infinity Engine; Neverwinter Nights 2 was powered by its Aurora Engine; and Star Wars: Knights of the Old Republic 2: The Sith Lords was made with the BioWare Odyssey Engine. The firm operates its own e-commerce site for its products at Store.bioware.com. It is currently collaborating with LucasArts to develop and publish a new massively multiplayer online (MMO) PC game called Star Wars: The Old Republic, partially building off the success of BioWare's original KOTOR game. Scheduled future releases include Dragon Age 2 (scheduled for release in March 2011), Mass Effect 3 (to be released in late 2011) and Mass Effect 2 for Playstation 3 (in January 2011). In March 2010, it released an expansion pack for its Dragon Age series. In June 2010, BioWare and FUNimation agreed to develop a feature length animated movie based on the Dragon Age franchise.

FINANCIALS: Sales and profits are in thousands of dollars—add 000 to get the full amount. 2010 Note: Financial information for 2010 was not available for all companies at press time.

2010 Sales: $	2010 Profits: $	**U.S. Stock Ticker: Subsidiary**
2009 Sales: $	2009 Profits: $	**Int'l Ticker:** Int'l Exchange:
2008 Sales: $	2008 Profits: $	Employees:
2007 Sales: $	2007 Profits: $	Fiscal Year Ends: 12/31
2006 Sales: $	2006 Profits: $	Parent Company: ELECTRONIC ARTS INC

SALARIES/BENEFITS:

Pension Plan:	ESOP Stock Plan:	Profit Sharing:	Top Exec. Salary: $	Bonus: $
Savings Plan:	Stock Purch. Plan:		Second Exec. Salary: $	Bonus: $

OTHER THOUGHTS:
Apparent Women Officers or Directors:
Hot Spot for Advancement for Women/Minorities:

LOCATIONS: ("Y" = Yes)

West:	Southwest:	Midwest:	Southeast:	Northeast:	International:
	Y			Y	Y

BLACK BOX CORPORATION

www.blackbox.com

Industry Group Code: 423430 Ranks within this company's industry group: Sales: 14 Profits: 7

Hardware:		Software:		Telecommunications:		Electronic Publishing:		Equipment:		Specialty Services:	
Computers:		Consumer:		Local:		Online Service:		Telecom:		Consulting:	Y
Accessories:	Y	Corporate:		Long Distance:		TV/Cable or Wireless:		Communication:		Contract Manufacturing:	Y
Network Equipment:	Y	Telecom:		Cellular:		Games:		Distribution:	Y	Processing:	
Chips/Circuits:		Internet:		Internet Service:		Financial Data:		VAR/Reseller:	Y	Staff/Outsourcing:	
Parts/Drives:	Y							Satellite Srv./Equip.:		Specialty Services:	Y

TYPES OF BUSINESS:

Networking Products, Distribution
Technical Network Services
Data & Voice Infrastructure
Custom Networking Products
Hotline Services
Security Products

BRANDS/DIVISIONS/AFFILIATES:

iCompel
Scottel Voice & Data, Inc.
Quanta Systems LLC
CBS Technologies Corp.
Nortel Customer Assurance Program

CONTACTS: Note: Officers with more than one job title may be intentionally listed here more than once.

Terry Blakemore, CEO
Terry Blakemore, Pres.
Michael McAndrew, CFO/VP
Michael McAndrew, Corp. Sec.
Michael McAndrew, Treas.
Rick Dinkins, Exec. VP-Air Force Programs
Jeff Murray, Sr. VP/Gen. Mgr.-Network Svcs., Federal Div.
Thomas G. Greig, Chmn.
Francis Wertheimber, Sr. VP-Pacific Rim & Far East

Phone: 724-746-5500	Fax: 724-746-0746
Toll-Free:	
Address: 1000 Park Dr., Lawrence, PA 15055-1018 US	

GROWTH PLANS/SPECIAL FEATURES:

Black Box Corporation is among the world's largest providers of dedicated network infrastructure services. Black Box offers one-source network infrastructure services for data networks, including design, installation, integration, monitoring and maintenance of voice, data and integrated communications systems. With more than 3,000 technical experts and 194 offices, Black Box serves more than 175,000 clients in 141 countries throughout the world. Through its Black Box catalog and web site, as well as on-site services offices, the company offers over 118,000 network infrastructure products and provides technical support for all of its solutions. The company's products includes cables, cabinets and racks, connectors, converters, line drivers, modems, switches, digital signage and multimedia, audio/video cables, monitors and displays, projectors, computer accessories, networking products, surge protectors, infrastructure hardware, adaptors, training systems, testers and tools, printer servers, media converters, power supplies and cabling and infrastructure. Additionally, the firm offers security products such as CCTV systems and related devices. Clients of Black Box range from small organizations to some of the world's largest corporations, encompassing the government, technology, retail, manufacturing, business services, banking, healthcare, distributors, education, real estate development and utilities industries. Approximately 60% of revenues are from large companies, 25% from small companies and 15% from medium-sized companies. Voice services account for about 62% of revenues; hotline services, 19%; and data services, 19%. Recent acquisitions include Quanta Systems LLC; CBS Technologies Corp.; and Scottel Voice & Data, Inc. In February 2009, the company launched iCompel, a group of products that include media players and appliances with a simplified content layout. In September 2009, Black Box launched the Nortel Customer Assurance Program (NCAP). In October 2009, the firm received a $37.7 million contract with Miami International Airport and Dade County's general aviation airports to provide telecommunications and network management services.

FINANCIALS: Sales and profits are in thousands of dollars—add 000 to get the full amount. 2010 Note: Financial information for 2010 was not available for all companies at press time.

2010 Sales: $961,393	2010 Profits: $34,503	U.S. Stock Ticker: BBOX
2009 Sales: $999,548	2009 Profits: $45,309	Int'l Ticker: Int'l Exchange:
2008 Sales: $1,016,742	2008 Profits: $39,233	Employees:
2007 Sales: $1,016,310	2007 Profits: $35,609	Fiscal Year Ends: 3/31
2006 Sales: $721,335	2006 Profits: $30,770	Parent Company:

SALARIES/BENEFITS:

Pension Plan:	ESOP Stock Plan:	Profit Sharing:	Top Exec. Salary: $526,731	Bonus: $330,000
Savings Plan:	Stock Purch. Plan:		Second Exec. Salary: $315,373	Bonus: $80,000

OTHER THOUGHTS:

Apparent Women Officers or Directors:
Hot Spot for Advancement for Women/Minorities:

LOCATIONS: ("Y" = Yes)

West:	Southwest:	Midwest:	Southeast:	Northeast:	International:
Y	Y	Y	Y	Y	Y

BLONDER TONGUE LABORATORIES INC　　www.blondertongue.com

Industry Group Code: 3342 Ranks within this company's industry group: Sales: 7 Profits: 4

Hardware:	Software:	Telecommunications:	Electronic Publishing:	Equipment:		Specialty Services:
Computers:	Consumer:	Local:	Online Service:	Telecom:	Y	Consulting:
Accessories:	Corporate:	Long Distance:	TV/Cable or Wireless:	Communication:	Y	Contract Manufacturing:
Network Equipment:	Telecom:	Cellular:	Games:	Distribution:		Processing:
Chips/Circuits:	Internet:	Internet Service:	Financial Data:	VAR/Reseller:		Staff/Outsourcing:
Parts/Drives:				Satellite Srv./Equip.:		Specialty Services:

TYPES OF BUSINESS:

Electronics Manufacturing
Telephony Products
Networking & Broadband Equipment
Receivers & Antennas
Cable TV Equipment
Microwave Products

BRANDS/DIVISIONS/AFFILIATES:

EdgeQAM Collection
HDE Encoder Collection
MDDA-860

CONTACTS: Note: Officers with more than one job title may be intentionally listed here more than once.

James A. Luksch, CEO
Robert J. Palle, Jr., COO/Exec. VP
Robert J. Palle, Jr., Pres.
Eric S. Skolnik, CFO/Sr. VP
Jeff Smith, VP-Sales & Service Mgmt.
Kant Mistry, CTO
Kant Mistry, VP-Eng.
Allen Horvath, VP-Mfg.
Robert J. Palle, Jr., Sec.
Emily M. Nikoo, Sr. VP-Oper.
Eric S. Skolnik, Treas.
Norman A. Westcott, Sr. VP-Oper. Svcs.
Nezam Nikoo, VP-Advanced Digital Tech.
James A. Luksch, Chmn.

Phone: 732-679-4000	Fax: 732-679-4353
Toll-Free: 800-523-6049	
Address: 1 Jake Brown Rd., Old Bridge, NJ 08857 US	

GROWTH PLANS/SPECIAL FEATURES:

Blonder Tongue Laboratories, Inc. designs, manufactures and supplies electronics and telecommunications systems equipment. Its customer base includes telecommunications service providers; the lodging/hospitality market; and the institutional market, including hospitals, prisons and schools. Four major categories define its products: analog video headend products, which generated 40% of 2009 revenue; digital transition headend products, 2%; digital video headend products, 24%; and distribution products, 17%. The analog video headend products allow operators to acquire, process and manipulate analog signals for further transmission. These products include antennas, satellite receivers, modulators, demodulators and equalizers. The headend is essentially the brain of an analog TV signal distribution system. Digital transition headend products are used in applications where service providers receive local off-air digital broadcast channels and/or digital channels from cable operators and have a need to continue providing an analog broadcast tier. Its products include demodulators, modulators and processors. Digital video headend products are used by operators to acquire, process and manipulate digital video signals. Its line of products includes the EdgeQAM Collection and HDE encoder collection, which includes a line of HD and SD MPEG-2 encoders and multiplexers. Lastly, the distribution products facilitate the transfer of signals from the headend to destinations in a home, apartment unit or other terminal location along a distribution network of fiber optic or coaxial cable. The firm's distribution products include line extenders, broadband amplifiers, directional taps, splitters and wall taps. Other products include high-speed data products, such as cable modems and cable modem termination systems; test products, including analog and digital QPSK analyzers and signal level meters; and fiber products, including optical transmitters, receivers, couplers and splitters. In June 2010, the company launched the MDDA-860, a digital product that allows service providers to select one digital off-air and/or digital cable signal and transcode it into an ASI stream for further multiplexing.

FINANCIALS: Sales and profits are in thousands of dollars—add 000 to get the full amount. 2010 Note: Financial information for 2010 was not available for all companies at press time.

2010 Sales: $	2010 Profits: $	**U.S. Stock Ticker: BDR**
2009 Sales: $29,034	2009 Profits: $ 75	**Int'l Ticker:**　Int'l Exchange:
2008 Sales: $35,320	2008 Profits: $- 411	Employees:　180
2007 Sales: $33,012	2007 Profits: $- 561	Fiscal Year Ends: 12/31
2006 Sales: $35,775	2006 Profits: $ 342	Parent Company:

SALARIES/BENEFITS:

Pension Plan:	ESOP Stock Plan:	Profit Sharing:	Top Exec. Salary: $425,938	Bonus: $
Savings Plan: Y	Stock Purch. Plan:		Second Exec. Salary: $333,343	Bonus: $

OTHER THOUGHTS:

Apparent Women Officers or Directors: 1
Hot Spot for Advancement for Women/Minorities:

LOCATIONS: ("Y" = Yes)

West:	Southwest:	Midwest:	Southeast:	Northeast:	International:
				Y	

BLUE COAT SYSTEMS INC

www.bluecoat.com

Industry Group Code: 511210E Ranks within this company's industry group: Sales: 6 Profits: 10

Hardware:	Software:		Telecommunications:	Electronic Publishing:	Equipment:	Specialty Services:
Computers:	Consumer:		Local:	Online Service:	Telecom:	Consulting:
Accessories:	Corporate:	Y	Long Distance:	TV/Cable or Wireless:	Communication:	Contract Manufacturing:
Network Equipment:	Telecom:		Cellular:	Games:	Distribution:	Processing:
Chips/Circuits:	Internet:		Internet Service:	Financial Data:	VAR/Reseller:	Staff/Outsourcing:
Parts/Drives:					Satellite Srv./Equip.:	Specialty Services:

TYPES OF BUSINESS:
WAN & Internet Security Applications
WAN Acceleration & Optimization Technology

BRANDS/DIVISIONS/AFFILIATES:
ProxySG Appliances
ProxyClient
ProxyAV Appliances
CacheFlow 5000
Blue Coat WebFilter
WebPulse
S7 Software Solutions Pvt. Ltd.
Packeteer Inc.

CONTACTS: Note: Officers with more than one job title may be intentionally listed here more than once.
Brian M. NeSmith, CEO
Brian M. NeSmith, Pres.
Gordon Brooks, CFO/Sr. VP
Kevin Biggs, Sr. VP-Worldwide Sales & Field Oper.
Jim Haar, CIO
Betsy E. Bayha, General Counsel/Sec./Sr. VP
Dave de Simone, Sr. VP-Corp. Oper.
Jim Vogt, Sr. VP/Gen. Mgr.-Cloud Svcs. Bus. Unit
John Shoop, VP-Worldwide Carrier Sales
David Hanna, Chmn.

Phone: 408-220-2200	Fax: 408-220-2250
Toll-Free: 866-302-2628	
Address: 420 N. Mary Ave., Sunnyvale, CA 94085-4121 US	

GROWTH PLANS/SPECIAL FEATURES:
Blue Coat Systems, Inc. offers business applications that secure and optimize WAN- (Wide Area Network) and Internet-based operations. It specializes in internally and externally hosted network applications with users spread across multiple locations. Blue Coat primarily serves medium and large enterprises in fields such as finance, government and healthcare. In general, the firm's technology has three applications: Secure Web Gateway Products, which provide protection from malware, spyware or other malicious threats; WAN Optimization Products, which deal with WAN acceleration and optimization for the delivery of internal, external, real-time and customized applications across distributed enterprises' networks; and Application Performance Monitoring Products, which enable distributed enterprises to discover, classify, prioritize and monitor applications, content and users. The company's products include the following. ProxySG Appliances serve as the hardware basis of both the Secure Web Gateway and WAN Optimization products. They are installed in directly at Internet gateways or at WAN entry or exit points. ProxyClient is a software application installed on desktops or laptops at remote locations that do not have a ProxySG Appliance and on computers used by mobile employees. It offers WAN optimization and security. The CacheFlow 5000 appliance focuses on the reduction of bandwidth consumption. ProxyAV Appliances offer inline threat protection and malware scanning designed to complement the ProxySG appliance. Blue Coat WebFilter works with the ProxySG appliance to block harmful or inappropriate content. WebPulse is a real-time cloud computing security service. In January 2010, the firm acquired a majority interest in S7 Software Solutions Pvt. Ltd., an India-based IT research and development company. In March 2010, Blue Coat opened a new WebPulse data center in Australia.

Blue Coat offers its employees medical, dental and vision insurance, flexible spending accounts, an employee assistance plan, educational assistance, business travel accident insurance and on-site fitness facilities.

FINANCIALS: Sales and profits are in thousands of dollars—add 000 to get the full amount. 2010 Note: Financial information for 2010 was not available for all companies at press time.

2010 Sales: $496,137	2010 Profits: $42,879	U.S. Stock Ticker: BCSI
2009 Sales: $444,745	2009 Profits: $-8,508	Int'l Ticker: Int'l Exchange:
2008 Sales: $305,439	2008 Profits: $32,568	Employees: 1,261
2007 Sales: $177,700	2007 Profits: $-7,198	Fiscal Year Ends: 4/30
2006 Sales: $141,722	2006 Profits: $2,940	Parent Company:

SALARIES/BENEFITS:
Pension Plan:	ESOP Stock Plan:	Profit Sharing: Y	Top Exec. Salary: $350,000	Bonus: $1,575
Savings Plan: Y	Stock Purch. Plan: Y		Second Exec. Salary: $325,400	Bonus: $101,463

OTHER THOUGHTS:
Apparent Women Officers or Directors: 2
Hot Spot for Advancement for Women/Minorities: Y

LOCATIONS: ("Y" = Yes)
West:	Southwest:	Midwest:	Southeast:	Northeast:	International:
Y	Y			Y	Y

BMC SOFTWARE INC

www.bmc.com

Industry Group Code: 511210H Ranks within this company's industry group: Sales: 5 Profits: 4

Hardware:	Software:		Telecommunications:	Electronic Publishing:	Equipment:	Specialty Services:	
Computers:	Consumer:		Local:	Online Service:	Telecom:	Consulting:	Y
Accessories:	Corporate:	Y	Long Distance:	TV/Cable or Wireless:	Communication:	Contract Manufacturing:	
Network Equipment:	Telecom:		Cellular:	Games:	Distribution:	Processing:	
Chips/Circuits:	Internet:		Internet Service:	Financial Data:	VAR/Reseller:	Staff/Outsourcing:	
Parts/Drives:					Satellite Srv./Equip.:	Specialty Services:	

TYPES OF BUSINESS:

Computer Software-Mainframe Related
Systems Management Software
e-Business Software
Consulting & Training Services

BRANDS/DIVISIONS/AFFILIATES:

BMC Atrium
GridApp Systems Inc

CONTACTS: Note: Officers with more than one job title may be intentionally listed here more than once.

Robert E. Beauchamp, CEO
Stephen B. Solcher, CFO/Sr. VP
John McMahon, Sr. VP-Worldwide Sales & Svcs.
Hollie Castro, Sr. VP-Admin.
Denise M. Clolery, General Counsel/Sr. VP/Corp. Sec.
Steve Goddard, Sr. VP-Bus. Oper.
Ken Berryman, Sr. VP-Strategy & Corp. Dev.
T. Cory Bleuer, Chief Acct. Officer/Controller/VP
William D. Miller, Pres., Mainframe Service Mgmt.
Robert E. Beauchamp, Chmn.

Phone: 713-918-8800	Fax: 713-918-8000
Toll-Free: 800-841-2031	
Address: 2101 Citywest Blvd., Houston, TX 77042 US	

GROWTH PLANS/SPECIAL FEATURES:

BMC Software, Inc. is one of the world's largest software vendors. The company provides system management, service management and automation solutions primarily for large companies. Its software products span mainframe and distributed systems, applications, databases and IT process management functions. The company operates in two software business segments: Enterprise Service Management (ESM) and Mainframe Service Management (MSM). The Enterprise Service Management (ESM) segment consists of the company's solutions and related professional services related to a variety of IT management issues, including service support, service assurance and service automation. Also included is the firm's BMC Atrium software package, which helps provide centralized coordination and execution of IT processes. The company's Mainframe Service Management (MSM) segment creates products that address IT challenges for mainframe systems management, data management and enterprise workload automation, with particular focus on streamlining mainframe operations in order to reduce costs and manage large amounts of data without affecting the availability of critical business applications. MSM products are organized into three areas: data and performance management, and enterprise scheduling and output management. The company also operates a professional services segment, consisting of a worldwide team of software consultants who provide implementation, integration, IT process design and re-engineering and education services related to its products. The company's customers include manufacturers, telecommunication companies, financial service providers, educational institutions, retailers, distributors, hospitals, service providers, government agencies and channel partners including resellers, distributors and system integrators. Approximately 16,000 companies worldwide use BMC products, including 90% of the Fortune 100 companies. In December 2010, the company acquired GridApp Systems, Inc., which specializes in cloud-based data applications.

FINANCIALS: Sales and profits are in thousands of dollars—add 000 to get the full amount. 2010 Note: Financial information for 2010 was not available for all companies at press time.

2010 Sales: $1,911,200	2010 Profits: $406,100	**U.S. Stock Ticker:** BMC
2009 Sales: $1,871,900	2009 Profits: $238,100	**Int'l Ticker:** Int'l Exchange:
2008 Sales: $1,731,600	2008 Profits: $313,600	Employees: 6,100
2007 Sales: $1,580,400	2007 Profits: $215,900	Fiscal Year Ends: 3/31
2006 Sales: $1,498,400	2006 Profits: $102,000	Parent Company:

SALARIES/BENEFITS:

Pension Plan:	ESOP Stock Plan:	Profit Sharing:	Top Exec. Salary: $950,000	Bonus: $1,326,675
Savings Plan:	Stock Purch. Plan:		Second Exec. Salary: $475,000	Bonus: $442,225

OTHER THOUGHTS:

Apparent Women Officers or Directors: 3
Hot Spot for Advancement for Women/Minorities: Y

LOCATIONS: ("Y" = Yes)

West:	Southwest:	Midwest:	Southeast:	Northeast:	International:
Y	Y	Y	Y	Y	Y

BOE TECHNOLOGY GROUP CO LTD

www.boe.com.cn

Industry Group Code: 334119 Ranks within this company's industry group: Sales: 15   Profits: 15

Hardware:		Software:		Telecommunications:	Electronic Publishing:	Equipment:	Specialty Services:
Computers:		Consumer:		Local:	Online Service:	Telecom:	Consulting:
Accessories:	Y	Corporate:		Long Distance:	TV/Cable or Wireless:	Communication:	Contract Manufacturing:
Network Equipment:		Telecom:		Cellular:	Games:	Distribution:	Processing:
Chips/Circuits:		Internet:		Internet Service:	Financial Data:	VAR/Reseller:	Staff/Outsourcing:
Parts/Drives:						Satellite Srv./Equip.:	Specialty Services:

TYPES OF BUSINESS:
Computer Monitors & LCD Displays

BRANDS/DIVISIONS/AFFILIATES:

CONTACTS: Note: Officers with more than one job title may be intentionally listed here more than once.
Chen Yanshun, Pres.
Sun Yun, CFO
Wang Yanjun, CIO
Feng Liqiong, Chief Counsel/Corp. Sec.
Su Zhiwen, Gen. Auditor
Han Goujian, VP
Song Ying, VP
Wang Jiaheng, VP
Liu Xiaodong, VP
Wang Dongsheng, Chmn.

Phone: 86-10-6431-8888	**Fax:** 86-10-6436-3965
Toll-Free:	
Address: No. 10 Jiuxianqiao Rd. Chaoyang District, Beijing, 100016 China	

GROWTH PLANS/SPECIAL FEATURES:

BOE Technology Group Co., Ltd. is a supplier of thin-film transistor-liquid crystal displays (TFT-LCDs). The company distributes its products domestically and to other Asian countries, Europe and the Americas. The firm operates in five business units: TFT-LCD Business for IT and TV Products; TFT-LCD Business for Mobile and Application Products; Back Light Products Business; Display System and Solutions Business; and Other Display Components and Parts Business. The TFT-LCD Business for IT and TV Products segment supplies monitor, notebook and TV products. TFT-LCD Business for Mobile and Application Products focuses on mobile electronic items smaller than 14.1 inches. Back Light Products Business includes CCFL and LED backlight products. The Display System and Solutions Business consists of high brightness LCD terminals, car LCD terminals, ruggedized LCD terminals and general LCD terminals. The Other Display Components and Parts Business segment involves CRT and VFP products, as well as other display components and materials. The company's Beijing facility has the capacity to produce approximately 100,000 G5 TFT-LCD units per month. Its Hefei facility can produce roughly 90,000 TFT-LCD G6 units. BOE currently produces the smart cards that are used in the Beijing transit system.

BOE offers its employees medical insurance.

FINANCIALS: Sales and profits are in thousands of dollars—add 000 to get the full amount. 2010 Note: Financial information for 2010 was not available for all companies at press time.

2010 Sales: $	2010 Profits: $	**U.S. Stock Ticker:** BTEGF
2009 Sales: $947,900	2009 Profits: $7,540	**Int'l Ticker:** 200725 Int'l Exchange: Shanghai-SHE
2008 Sales: $1,264,130	2008 Profits: $122,480	**Employees:** 12,906
2007 Sales: $	2007 Profits: $	**Fiscal Year Ends:** 12/31
2006 Sales: $	2006 Profits: $	**Parent Company:**

SALARIES/BENEFITS:

Pension Plan:	ESOP Stock Plan:	Profit Sharing:	Top Exec. Salary: $	Bonus: $
Savings Plan:	Stock Purch. Plan:		Second Exec. Salary: $	Bonus: $

OTHER THOUGHTS:
Apparent Women Officers or Directors: 4
Hot Spot for Advancement for Women/Minorities: Y

LOCATIONS: ("Y" = Yes)

West:	Southwest:	Midwest:	Southeast:	Northeast:	International:
					Y

BORLAND SOFTWARE CORPORATION

www.borland.com

Industry Group Code: 511210I Ranks within this company's industry group: Sales: Profits:

Hardware:	Software:		Telecommunications:	Electronic Publishing:	Equipment:	Specialty Services:
Computers:	Consumer:		Local:	Online Service:	Telecom:	Consulting:
Accessories:	Corporate:	Y	Long Distance:	TV/Cable or Wireless:	Communication:	Contract Manufacturing:
Network Equipment:	Telecom:		Cellular:	Games:	Distribution:	Processing:
Chips/Circuits:	Internet:		Internet Service:	Financial Data:	VAR/Reseller:	Staff/Outsourcing:
Parts/Drives:					Satellite Srv./Equip.:	Specialty Services:

TYPES OF BUSINESS:

Software-e-Business
Software Development Tools
Online Community for Software Developers

BRANDS/DIVISIONS/AFFILIATES:

Micro Focus International Plc
CaliberRM
SilkPerformer
SilkCentral
SilkTest
AppServer
VisiBroker

CONTACTS: Note: Officers with more than one job title may be intentionally listed here more than once.

Nigel Clifford, CEO-Micro Focus Int'l plc

Phone: 512-340-2200	Fax:
Toll-Free:	
Address: 8310 N. Capital of Texas Hwy., Bldg. 2, Ste. 100, Austin, TX 78731 US	

GROWTH PLANS/SPECIAL FEATURES:

Borland Software Corporation, a wholly-owned subsidiary of Micro Focus International Plc, is a provider of Open Application Lifecycle Management solutions. The company offers several software products that include CaliberRM, Together, Silk, StarTeam and Application Middleware. CaliberRM is an enterprise software application that is designed to facilitate user collaboration. Borland's Together software has visual modeling capabilities for architectural design that can be integrated with a client's existing applications. The Silk software suite provides quality control testing applications and includes the SilkCentral, SilkTest and SilkPerformer software. Its StarTeam platform is designed for high-performance, low-latency, transaction-intensive applications. The company's Application Middleware, comprised of VisiBroker and AppServer, is infrastructure software that integrates with J2EE and CORBA. The VisiBroker application integrates with a client's existing CORBA application to improve performance, while AppServer integrates with and optimizes J2EE applications. Its customers include a number of firms within the financial services, healthcare, hospitality, manufacturing, technology and government sectors. As a result of Borland's recent acquisition by Micro Focus International Plc, its professional and educational consulting services have been outsourced to Micro Focus and are no longer available through Borland.

FINANCIALS: Sales and profits are in thousands of dollars—add 000 to get the full amount. 2010 Note: Financial information for 2010 was not available for all companies at press time.

2010 Sales: $	2010 Profits: $	**U.S. Stock Ticker: Subsidiary**
2009 Sales: $	2009 Profits: $	**Int'l Ticker:** Int'l Exchange:
2008 Sales: $172,027	2008 Profits: $-215,722	Employees: 879
2007 Sales: $211,783	2007 Profits: $-59,205	Fiscal Year Ends: 4/30
2006 Sales: $304,660	2006 Profits: $-51,953	Parent Company: MICRO FOCUS INTERNATIONAL PLC

SALARIES/BENEFITS:

Pension Plan:	ESOP Stock Plan:	Profit Sharing:	Top Exec. Salary: $	Bonus: $
Savings Plan:	Stock Purch. Plan:		Second Exec. Salary: $	Bonus: $

OTHER THOUGHTS:

Apparent Women Officers or Directors:
Hot Spot for Advancement for Women/Minorities:

LOCATIONS: ("Y" = Yes)

West:	Southwest:	Midwest:	Southeast:	Northeast:	International:
Y	Y		Y		Y

Note: Financial information, benefits and other data can change quickly and may vary from those stated here.

BRAVOSOLUTION SPA   www.bravosolution.com

Industry Group Code: 511210A Ranks within this company's industry group: Sales: Profits:

Hardware:	Software:		Telecommunications:	Electronic Publishing:	Equipment:		Specialty Services:	
Computers:	Consumer:		Local:	Online Service:	Telecom:		Consulting:	Y
Accessories:	Corporate:	Y	Long Distance:	TV/Cable or Wireless:	Communication:		Contract Manufacturing:	
Network Equipment:	Telecom:		Cellular:	Games:	Distribution:		Processing:	
Chips/Circuits:	Internet:		Internet Service:	Financial Data:	VAR/Reseller:		Staff/Outsourcing:	
Parts/Drives:					Satellite Srv./Equip.:		Specialty Services:	Y

TYPES OF BUSINESS:

Supply Management Solutions
Software Solutions
Sourcing Management

BRANDS/DIVISIONS/AFFILIATES:

BravoSolution US
BravoSolution Spain
BravoSolution Italy
BravoSolution Benelux
BravoSolution UK
BravoSolution France

CONTACTS: *Note: Officers with more than one job title may be intentionally listed here more than once.*

Nader Sabbaghian, CEO
Jim Wetecamp, Sr. VP-Solution Strategy
Ezio Melzi, Managing Dir.-BravoSolution Italy
Marc Bergeron, Gen. Mgr.-BravoSolution U.S.
Susana Alvarez, Managing Dir.-BravoSolution Spain

Phone: 39-02-210-512-1	Fax: 39-02-210-512-240
Toll-Free:	
Address: 11 Via Rombon, Milan, 20134 Italy	

GROWTH PLANS/SPECIAL FEATURES:

BravoSolution spa, based in Milan, Italy, is a leading international provider of supply management solutions, designed to enhance the performance of a company's entire sourcing cycle and delivered through software, professional services and category solutions. BravoSolution serves over 400 clients in 30 countries through 12 offices located in China, France, Italy, Mexico, Spain, the Netherlands, the U.K. and the U.S. The firm offers over 200 active eSourcing platforms, delivered on-demand, with solutions geared toward increased process efficiency; decision support; cost reduction; improved process governance; and improved vendor relations for client companies. The firm divides its solutions into three categories: on-demand software solutions; strategic category solutions; and tailored strategic services. The on-demand suite of solutions includes program management, sourcing solutions, spend visibility, vendor management and contract management. Strategic category solutions include collaborative sourcing, a spending snapshot and full-service sourcing events. Tailored strategic services, also classified by BravoSolution as professional services, include strategic sourcing, change management, low-cost country sourcing, software implementation, spend analysis implementation and educational services, as well as cost reduction programs.

FINANCIALS: Sales and profits are in thousands of dollars—add 000 to get the full amount. 2010 Note: Financial information for 2010 was not available for all companies at press time.

2010 Sales: $	2010 Profits: $	U.S. Stock Ticker: Subsidiary
2009 Sales: $	2009 Profits: $	Int'l Ticker: Int'l Exchange:
2008 Sales: $	2008 Profits: $	Employees:
2007 Sales: $	2007 Profits: $	Fiscal Year Ends: 12/31
2006 Sales: $	2006 Profits: $	Parent Company: ITALCEMENTI GROUP (THE)

SALARIES/BENEFITS:

Pension Plan:	ESOP Stock Plan:	Profit Sharing:	Top Exec. Salary: $	Bonus: $
Savings Plan:	Stock Purch. Plan:		Second Exec. Salary: $	Bonus: $

OTHER THOUGHTS:

Apparent Women Officers or Directors: 1
Hot Spot for Advancement for Women/Minorities:

LOCATIONS: ("Y" = Yes)

West:	Southwest:	Midwest:	Southeast:	Northeast:	International:
		Y		Y	Y

BROADCOM CORP

www.broadcom.com

Industry Group Code: 33441 Ranks within this company's industry group: Sales: 10   Profits: 27

Hardware:	Software:	Telecommunications:	Electronic Publishing:	Equipment:	Specialty Services:
Computers:	Consumer:	Local:	Online Service:	Telecom:	Consulting:
Accessories:	Corporate:	Long Distance:	TV/Cable or Wireless:	Communication:	Contract Manufacturing:
Network Equipment:	Telecom:	Cellular:	Games:	Distribution:	Processing:
Chips/Circuits: Y	Internet:	Internet Service:	Financial Data:	VAR/Reseller:	Staff/Outsourcing:
Parts/Drives:				Satellite Srv./Equip.:	Specialty Services:

TYPES OF BUSINESS:

Integrated Circuits-Broadband Transmission
Communications Products
System-on-a-Chip Technology

BRANDS/DIVISIONS/AFFILIATES:

Dune Networks
Teknovus

CONTACTS: Note: Officers with more than one job title may be intentionally listed here more than once.

Scott A. McGregor, CEO
Scott A. McGregor, Pres.
Eric K. Brandt, CFO/Sr. VP
Thomas F. Lagatta, Exec. VP-Sales
Terri Timberman, Exec. VP-Human Resources
Kenneth E. Venner, CIO/Exec. VP-Corp. Svcs.
Henry Samueli, CTO
Neil Y. Kim, Exec. VP-Central Eng.
Arthur Chong, General Counsel/Sec./Sr. VP
Neil Y. Kim, Exec. VP-Oper.
Bob Marsocci, Corp. Comm.
Peter Andrew, Investor Rel.
Robert L. Tirva, Corp. Controller/Principal Acct. Officer/Sr. VP
Scott A. Bibaud, Exec. VP/Gen. Mgr.-Mobile Platforms Group
Daniel A. Marotta, Exec. VP/Gen. Mgr.-Broadband Comm. Group
Robert A. Rango, Exec. VP/Gen. Mgr.-Wireless Connectivity Group
Ravij Ramaswami, Exec. VP/Gen. Mgr.-Enterprise Networking Group
John E. Major, Chmn.

Phone: 949-926-5000	Fax: 949-926-5203
Toll-Free:	
Address: 5300 California Ave., Irvine, CA 92617 US	

GROWTH PLANS/SPECIAL FEATURES:

Broadcom Corp. is a developer of semiconductors for wired and wireless communications. The company's products enable the delivery of voice, video, data and multimedia to mobile devices, consumer electronics devices and business networking products. Broadcom produces system-on-a-chip (SoC) and software solutions for manufacturers of computing and networking equipment, consumer electronics, broadband access products and mobile devices. The firm's products target the broadband communications, enterprise networking and mobile and wireless markets. In the broadband communications market, products incorporating Broadcom's solutions include digital cable, satellite and Internet Protocol (IP) set-top boxes and media servers; cable and digital subscriber line (DSL) modems and residential gateways; high definition televisions (HDTVs); high definition Blu-ray Disc players; and digital video recorders (DVRs). In the enterprise networking markets, products incorporating the firm's solutions include servers; workstations; desktop and notebook computers; wireless infrastructures and wireless access points; switches, hubs and routers; network interface cards; optical networks; and virtual private networks and security appliances. In the mobile and wireless market, products incorporating Broadcom's solutions include wireless-enabled laptop and desktop computers; home broadband gateways; printers; Voice over Internet Protocol (VoIP) phones; handheld media devices; mobile Internet devices; personal navigation devices; TV-enabled mobile devices; and home gaming and entertainment systems. The mobile and wireless products account for approximately 38% of total revenues; the broadband communications products, 34%; enterprise networking products, 24%; and all other, 4%. In December 2009, the firm acquired Dune Networks, a developer of switch fabric products for data center networking applications. In March 2010, Broadcom acquired Teknovus, a developer and marketer of Ethernet Passive Optical Network (EPON) solutions.

Broadcom offers its employees health, dental and vision care; short and long-term disability coverage; a 401(k) plan; an Employee Stock Purchase Plan; credit union membership; and tuition reimbursement.

FINANCIALS: Sales and profits are in thousands of dollars—add 000 to get the full amount. 2010 Note: Financial information for 2010 was not available for all companies at press time.

2010 Sales: $	2010 Profits: $	**U.S. Stock Ticker:** BRCM
2009 Sales: $4,490,323	2009 Profits: $65,261	**Int'l Ticker:** Int'l Exchange:
2008 Sales: $4,658,125	2008 Profits: $214,794	Employees: 7,407
2007 Sales: $3,776,395	2007 Profits: $213,342	Fiscal Year Ends: 12/31
2006 Sales: $3,667,818	2006 Profits: $379,041	Parent Company:

SALARIES/BENEFITS:

Pension Plan:	ESOP Stock Plan:	Profit Sharing:	Top Exec. Salary: $682,500	Bonus: $1,242,150
Savings Plan: Y	Stock Purch. Plan: Y		Second Exec. Salary: $360,000	Bonus: $500,000

OTHER THOUGHTS:

Apparent Women Officers or Directors:
Hot Spot for Advancement for Women/Minorities:

LOCATIONS: ("Y" = Yes)

West:	Southwest:	Midwest:	Southeast:	Northeast:	International:
Y	Y	Y	Y	Y	Y

Note: Financial information, benefits and other data can change quickly and may vary from those stated here.

BROADVISION INC

www.broadvision.com

Industry Group Code: 511210M **Ranks within this company's industry group:** Sales: 3 Profits: 2

Hardware:	Software:		Telecommunications:	Electronic Publishing:	Equipment:	Specialty Services:	
Computers:	Consumer:		Local:	Online Service:	Telecom:	Consulting:	Y
Accessories:	Corporate:	Y	Long Distance:	TV/Cable or Wireless:	Communication:	Contract Manufacturing:	
Network Equipment:	Telecom:		Cellular:	Games:	Distribution:	Processing:	
Chips/Circuits:	Internet:		Internet Service:	Financial Data:	VAR/Reseller:	Staff/Outsourcing:	
Parts/Drives:					Satellite Srv./Equip.:	Specialty Services:	Y

TYPES OF BUSINESS:

Software-Web Site Tools
Human Resources Management Software
Content Management Software
Consulting & Support Services

BRANDS/DIVISIONS/AFFILIATES:

BroadVision Quicksiler
Clearvale
CLEAR
Commerce Agility Suite
Business Agility Suite
BroadVision OnDemand Ltd.

CONTACTS: *Note: Officers with more than one job title may be intentionally listed here more than once.*

Pehong Chen, CEO
Pehong Chen, Pres.
Shin-Yuan Tzou, CFO
Giovanni Rodriguez, Chief Mktg. Officer
James Wu, CTO
David Boyer, Sr. VP-Eng. & Tech. Support
Ling Wu, VP/Gen. Mgr.-Global Bus. Dev.
Gene Kuo, VP/Gen. Mgr.-Asia Pacific & Japan
Ralph Lentz, VP/Gen. Mgr.-Americas
Pehong Chen, Chmn.
Andrea Rubei, VP/Gen. Mgr.-EMEA

Phone: 650-331-1000	Fax: 650-542-5900
Toll-Free:	
Address: 1600 Seaport Blvd., Ste. 550, Redwood City, CA 94063 US	

GROWTH PLANS/SPECIAL FEATURES:

BroadVision, Inc. develops, markets and supports personalized e-business solutions. The firm provides a single, secure, high-performance framework on which customers can integrate personalization applications and agile toolsets and create e-commerce, portal solutions and Enterprise Social Networks. The company's software is designed to offer secure transaction processing, multi-platform availability, multilingual and multicurrency support, personalization and high scalability and configurability. The company offers several products, including its Business Agility Suite, which allows web managers to personalize web page content, including information, resources and business processes, based on the preferences of individual visitors to the site. The Commerce Agility Suite enables lead generation, sales execution, customer support and business-to-business and business-to-consumer channel management through a single solution. QuickSilver facilitates the creation of complex documents through its multiple format support, which includes HTML, PDF and Postscript formats. Clearvale is a cloud computing solution that allows customers to publicize, personalize, and socialize their communications and collaborations from any location. The firm also offers business consulting, implementation, migration and performance tuning and ongoing training and technical support services. The company's international business unit, BroadVision OnDemand, Ltd., is headquartered in Beijing, China; its principle product is CLEAR, an on-demand human resources management solution.

The firm offers its employees medical, dental, vision, life and workers' compensation insurance; flexible spending plans and an employee assistance program.

FINANCIALS: Sales and profits are in thousands of dollars—add 000 to get the full amount. 2010 Note: Financial information for 2010 was not available for all companies at press time.

2010 Sales: $	2010 Profits: $	**U.S. Stock Ticker:** BVSN
2009 Sales: $30,961	2009 Profits: $3,734	**Int'l Ticker:** Int'l Exchange:
2008 Sales: $35,903	2008 Profits: $-15,010	Employees: 219
2007 Sales: $50,018	2007 Profits: $17,278	Fiscal Year Ends: 12/31
2006 Sales: $51,984	2006 Profits: $15,016	Parent Company:

SALARIES/BENEFITS:

Pension Plan:	ESOP Stock Plan: Y	Profit Sharing:	Top Exec. Salary: $350,000	Bonus: $
Savings Plan: Y	Stock Purch. Plan:		Second Exec. Salary: $200,000	Bonus: $

OTHER THOUGHTS:

Apparent Women Officers or Directors:
Hot Spot for Advancement for Women/Minorities:

LOCATIONS: ("Y" = Yes)

West:	Southwest:	Midwest:	Southeast:	Northeast:	International:
Y				Y	Y

BROCADE COMMUNICATIONS SYSTEMS INC   www.brocade.com

Industry Group Code: 511210B **Ranks within this company's industry group:** Sales: 2   Profits: 8

Hardware:		Software:		Telecommunications:	Electronic Publishing:	Equipment:	Specialty Services:	
Computers:		Consumer:		Local:	Online Service:	Telecom:	Consulting:	Y
Accessories:		Corporate:	Y	Long Distance:	TV/Cable or Wireless:	Communication:	Contract Manufacturing:	
Network Equipment:	Y	Telecom:		Cellular:	Games:	Distribution:	Processing:	
Chips/Circuits:		Internet:		Internet Service:	Financial Data:	VAR/Reseller:	Staff/Outsourcing:	
Parts/Drives:						Satellite Srv./Equip.:	Specialty Services:	

TYPES OF BUSINESS:

Data Storage Equipment
Storage Area Networking (SAN) Equipment
SAN Management Software
IT Infrastructure Management Software

BRANDS/DIVISIONS/AFFILIATES:

Brocade DCX-4S Backbone
Brocade NetIron CER 2000
Brocade One

CONTACTS: *Note: Officers with more than one job title may be intentionally listed here more than once.*

Michael Klayko, CEO
Richard Deranleau, CFO
John McHugh, Chief Mktg. Officer/VP
Lisa McGill, VP-Human Resources
Raymond Lee, VP-IT
Dave Stevens, CTO
Parviz Ghalambor, VP-Eng.
Tyler Wall, General Counsel/Corp. Sec./VP
Raymond Lee, VP-Oper.
T. J. Grewal, VP-Corp. Dev.
Richard Deranleau, VP-Finance
Ian Whiting, Sr. VP-Worldwide Sales
Daniel Fairfax, VP-Global Svcs.
Jason Nolet, VP-Data Center & Enterprise Networking
Barbara Spicek, VP-Worldwide Channels
Dave House, Chmn.
Alberto Soto, Head-Sales, EMEA

Phone: 408-333-8000	Fax: 408-333-8101
Toll-Free:	
Address: 1745 Technology Dr., San Jose, CA 95110 US	

GROWTH PLANS/SPECIAL FEATURES:

Brocade Communication Systems, Inc. is a leading supplier of data center networking hardware and software products and services that help enterprises connect and manage their information. The company is organized into three operating units: Data Center, Global Services and Ethernet Products. The Data Center unit encompasses the Brocade family of Storage Area Network (SAN) infrastructure products and solutions, including directors, switches, routers, fabric-based software applications and distance/extension products. This segment also offers management applications and utilities to centralize data management. The firm's Global Services division offers services related to extended warranty, installation, consulting, break/fix maintenance, network management, telecommunications and related software maintenance and support revenue. The Ethernet Products segment offers Brocade's Open Systems Interconnection Reference Model (OSI) Layer 2-3 switches and routers, which enable efficient use of bandwidth-intensive network business applications and digital entertainment on wide area and local area networks; OSI Layer 4-7 switches, which allow enterprises and service providers to build highly available network infrastructures that efficiently direct the flow of traffic; and file area network products and associated management solutions. Brocade products and services are marketed, sold and supported worldwide through distribution partners, including original equipment manufacturers (OEMs), distributors, systems integrators, value-added resellers (VARs) and by Brocade directly. In February 2010, the company entered a strategic partnership with McAfee, Inc. to offer a broad set of network security products. In June 2010, it unveiled its new Brocade One, a unified network architecture that removes network layers and simplifies network management.

Brocade offers its employees an education reimbursement program, flexible spending accounts, an employee assistance program, a fitness center, paternity leave and medical, dental, vision, life and business travel accident insurance.

FINANCIALS: Sales and profits are in thousands of dollars—add 000 to get the full amount. 2010 Note: Financial information for 2010 was not available for all companies at press time.

2010 Sales: $	2010 Profits: $	**U.S. Stock Ticker:** BRCD
2009 Sales: $1,952,926	2009 Profits: $-76,585	**Int'l Ticker:** Int'l Exchange:
2008 Sales: $1,466,937	2008 Profits: $167,070	**Employees:** 4,070
2007 Sales: $1,236,863	2007 Profits: $76,872	**Fiscal Year Ends:** 10/31
2006 Sales: $750,592	2006 Profits: $67,629	**Parent Company:**

SALARIES/BENEFITS:

Pension Plan:	ESOP Stock Plan:	Profit Sharing:	Top Exec. Salary: $726,924	Bonus: $2,421,953
Savings Plan: Y	Stock Purch. Plan:		Second Exec. Salary: $387,693	Bonus: $645,854

OTHER THOUGHTS:

Apparent Women Officers or Directors: 2
Hot Spot for Advancement for Women/Minorities:

LOCATIONS: ("Y" = Yes)

West:	Southwest:	Midwest:	Southeast:	Northeast:	International:
Y	Y	Y	Y	Y	Y

BUZZ TECHNOLOGIES INC   www.12buzz.com

Industry Group Code: 519130 Ranks within this company's industry group: Sales: Profits:

Hardware:		Software:		Telecommunications:	Electronic Publishing:	Equipment:	Specialty Services:	
Computers:		Consumer:	Y	Local:	Online Service:	Telecom:	Consulting:	
Accessories:		Corporate:	Y	Long Distance:	TV/Cable or Wireless:	Communication:	Contract Manufacturing:	
Network Equipment:		Telecom:		Cellular:	Games:	Distribution:	Processing:	
Chips/Circuits:		Internet:	Y	Internet Service:	Financial Data:	VAR/Reseller:	Staff/Outsourcing:	
Parts/Drives:						Satellite Srv./Equip.:	Specialty Services:	Y

TYPES OF BUSINESS:

Internet Search Portal
Venture Capital
News
Technology Services

BRANDS/DIVISIONS/AFFILIATES:

Buzz Asia
BuzzTV
Ad Network
BangkokPost.com

GROWTH PLANS/SPECIAL FEATURES:

Buzz Technologies, Inc., based in Thailand, provides a search engine for general Internet, video and news searches. In addition, the company offers phone to phone Voice over Internet protocol (VoIP); free video e-mail with short message service (SMS); free to air satellite television to PCs; and news, entertainment and social networking properties. Buzz Technologies' Ad Network services thousands of publishers and advertisers across Asia. The firm is involved in venture capital across Asia, specifically in industries such as technology, mining, real estate, shipping, alternative energy and media/entertainment. The company's technology offerings are provided through 12buzz, an online casino and various mobile and software investments. Media and broadcasting services are offered through Buzz Asia, BuzzTV satellite television affiliates and industry journals. It also owns BangkokPost.com, the web site for the Bangkok Post newspaper.

CONTACTS: Note: Officers with more than one job title may be intentionally listed here more than once.

Shayne Heffernan, CEO
Panitan Santipet, CFO
Sutida Suwunnavid, Chmn.

Phone: 66-76-326-318	Fax: 66-76-326-319
Toll-Free:	
Address: 123/29 M.5 T. Cherngtalay A. Talang, Phuket, 83110 Thailand	

FINANCIALS: Sales and profits are in thousands of dollars—add 000 to get the full amount. 2010 Note: Financial information for 2010 was not available for all companies at press time.

2010 Sales: $	2010 Profits: $	U.S. Stock Ticker: BZTG.PK
2009 Sales: $	2009 Profits: $	Int'l Ticker: Int'l Exchange:
2008 Sales: $	2008 Profits: $	Employees:
2007 Sales: $	2007 Profits: $	Fiscal Year Ends:
2006 Sales: $	2006 Profits: $	Parent Company:

SALARIES/BENEFITS:

Pension Plan:	ESOP Stock Plan:	Profit Sharing:	Top Exec. Salary: $	Bonus: $
Savings Plan:	Stock Purch. Plan:		Second Exec. Salary: $	Bonus: $

OTHER THOUGHTS:

Apparent Women Officers or Directors: 1
Hot Spot for Advancement for Women/Minorities:

LOCATIONS: ("Y" = Yes)

West:	Southwest:	Midwest:	Southeast:	Northeast:	International:
					Y

CA INC (CA TECHNOLOGIES)   www.ca.com

Industry Group Code: 511210H Ranks within this company's industry group: Sales: 3   Profits: 3

Hardware:	Software:		Telecommunications:	Electronic Publishing:	Equipment:	Specialty Services:	
Computers:	Consumer:		Local:	Online Service:	Telecom:	Consulting:	Y
Accessories:	Corporate:	Y	Long Distance:	TV/Cable or Wireless:	Communication:	Contract Manufacturing:	
Network Equipment:	Telecom:		Cellular:	Games:	Distribution:	Processing:	
Chips/Circuits:	Internet:		Internet Service:	Financial Data:	VAR/Reseller:	Staff/Outsourcing:	
Parts/Drives:					Satellite Srv./Equip.:	Specialty Services:	

TYPES OF BUSINESS:

Computer Software-Diversified
Enterprise Management Software
Security Software
Storage Software
Application Development Software
Business Intelligence Software
Application Life Cycle Management
Consulting Services

BRANDS/DIVISIONS/AFFILIATES:

CA Technologies
CA Clarity
CA Wily Introscope
CA SiteMinder
Oblicore, Inc.
3Tera, Inc.
Nimsoft AS
Hyperformix

CONTACTS: Note: Officers with more than one job title may be intentionally listed here more than once.

William E. McCraken, CEO
Nancy E. Cooper, CFO/Exec. VP
George Fischer, Exec. VP-Worldwide Sales, Mktg. & Client Service
Andrew Goodman, Exec. VP-Worldwide Human Resources
Donald F. Ferguson, CTO/Exec. VP
Ajei S. Gopal, Exec. VP-Prod. & Tech.
Phillip J. Harrington, Chief Admin. Officer/Exec. VP-Risk
Amy Fliegelman Olli, General Counsel/Exec. VP
George Fischer, Exec. VP-Oper.
Jacob Lamm, Exec. VP-Strategy & Corp. Dev.
William L. Hughes, Chief Comm. Officer
David Dobson, Exec. VP-Customer Solutions
Thomas Kendra, Exec. VP-Enterprise Prod. & Solutions
Christopher O'Malley, Exec. VP-Cloud Prod. & Solutions
John Ruthven, Exec. VP-Growth & Emerging Markets
Arthur F. Weinbach, Chmn.

Phone: 631-342-6000	Fax: 631-342-6800
Toll-Free: 800-225-5224	
Address: 1 Computer Associates Plz., Islandia, NY 11749 US	

GROWTH PLANS/SPECIAL FEATURES:

CA, Inc. designs, markets and licenses computer software products under the CA Technologies brand. Its software allows businesses to run and manage critical aspects of their IT operations and data center managers and programmers to automate their daily functions. Offering integrated software products designed to operate with all major hardware platforms and operating systems, the firm seeks to unify and simplify complex IT environments. The company does not operate in separate business segments, but does maintain several focus areas relating to both mainframe and distributed IT environments, including infrastructure management; project and portfolio management; IT security management, including compliance and risk management; data center automation and virtualization; and cloud computing. A few examples of CA's brands and products include CA Clarity, an IT governance and project management offering; CA Wily Introscope, an infrastructure management software suite; CA Access Control and CA SiteMinder, IT security and threat management offerings; and CA Service Desk Manager, a service desk automation tool. CA is headquartered in the U.S., with over 150 offices in more than 45 countries. The company's customers include many large national and multi-national firms in a variety of industries, including banks, insurance companies and other financial service providers; governmental agencies; manufacturers; technology firms; retail companies; educational institutions and health care providers. In January 2010, the company acquired Oblicore, Inc. In March 2010, it acquired 3Tera, Inc. and Nimsoft AS. Additional acquisitions in 2010 include 4Base Technology in August; Arcot Systems, Inc. in October; and Hyperformix in November.

CA offers employees medical and dental coverage; life, disability and long-term care insurance; a 401(k) plan; flexible spending accounts; an adoption assistance program; a company match for charitable gifts; and an employee assistance program.

FINANCIALS: Sales and profits are in thousands of dollars—add 000 to get the full amount. 2010 Note: Financial information for 2010 was not available for all companies at press time.

2010 Sales: $4,353,000	2010 Profits: $771,000	**U.S. Stock Ticker: CA**
2009 Sales: $4,271,000	2009 Profits: $671,000	**Int'l Ticker:** Int'l Exchange:
2008 Sales: $4,277,000	2008 Profits: $479,000	Employees: 13,800
2007 Sales: $3,943,000	2007 Profits: $118,000	Fiscal Year Ends: 3/31
2006 Sales: $3,772,000	2006 Profits: $159,000	Parent Company:

SALARIES/BENEFITS:

Pension Plan:	ESOP Stock Plan:	Profit Sharing:	Top Exec. Salary: $1,114,584	Bonus: $1,542,507
Savings Plan: Y	Stock Purch. Plan: Y		Second Exec. Salary: $958,333	Bonus: $941,781

OTHER THOUGHTS:

Apparent Women Officers or Directors: 2
Hot Spot for Advancement for Women/Minorities: Y

LOCATIONS: ("Y" = Yes)

West:	Southwest:	Midwest:	Southeast:	Northeast:	International:
Y	Y	Y	Y	Y	Y

Note: Financial information, benefits and other data can change quickly and may vary from those stated here.

CACI INTERNATIONAL INC

www.caci.com

Industry Group Code: 541512 Ranks within this company's industry group: Sales: 2 Profits: 3

Hardware:	Software:		Telecommunications:	Electronic Publishing:	Equipment:	Specialty Services:	
Computers:	Consumer:		Local:	Online Service:	Telecom:	Consulting:	Y
Accessories:	Corporate:	Y	Long Distance:	TV/Cable or Wireless:	Communication:	Contract Manufacturing:	
Network Equipment:	Telecom:		Cellular:	Games:	Distribution:	Processing:	
Chips/Circuits:	Internet:		Internet Service:	Financial Data:	VAR/Reseller:	Staff/Outsourcing:	
Parts/Drives:					Satellite Srv./Equip.:	Specialty Services:	Y

TYPES OF BUSINESS:

Consulting-InfoTech Related
Engineering Simulation Software
Custom Software Engineering
Managed Network Services
Information Management Tools
Knowledge Management
Systems Integration
Radio Frequency Identification (RFID)

BRANDS/DIVISIONS/AFFILIATES:

CACI Limited
Institute for Quality Management, Inc.
Wexford Group International
Athena Innovative Solutions, Inc.
Dragon Development Corp.
Wide Area Workflow
CACI Research and Development Labs
CACI Vision & Solution Center

CONTACTS: Note: Officers with more than one job title may be intentionally listed here more than once.

Paul M. Cofoni, CEO
Paul M. Cofoni, Pres.
Thomas A. Mutryn, CFO/Exec. VP
H. Robert Boehm, Chief Human Resources Officer/Exec. VP
Deborah B. Dunie, CTO/Exec. VP
Steven H. Weiss, Exec. VP-Gov't Bus. Oper.
Ronald Schneider, Exec. VP-Bus. Dev.
Jody A. Brown, Exec. VP-Public Rel. & Bus. Comm.
David Dragics, Sr. VP-Investor Rel.
Thomas A. Mutryn, Treas.
William M. Fairl, Pres., U.S. Oper.
Randall C. Fuerst, COO-U.S. Oper.
Gregory R. Bradford, CEO-CACI Ltd.
Karl Johnson, Exec. VP-Missions Systems Group
J.P. London, Chmn.
Gregory R. Bradford, Pres., U.K. Oper.

Phone: 703-841-7800	Fax: 703-841-7882
Toll-Free:	
Address: 1100 N. Glebe Rd., Arlington, VA 22201 US	

GROWTH PLANS/SPECIAL FEATURES:

CACI International, Inc. is an information technology (IT) company that provides IT and network services to defense, intelligence and other government departments. Contracts with the U.S. government make up 96% of the company's revenue. The firm specializes in four areas: systems integration; engineering and logistics; managed network services; and knowledge management. CACI's domestic operations work through several joint ventures and subsidiaries, including Institute for Quality Management, Inc.; Wexford Group International; Athena Innovative Solutions, Inc; and Dragon Development Corp. Operations consist of providing data, information and knowledge management programs such as HighView Document Exploitation; business systems like the Wide Area Workflow solution; command, control, communications, computers, intelligence, surveillance and reconnaissance (C4ISR) programs such as Rapid Deployment Communications; and information assurance and cyber security; logistics information systems which utilize Radio Frequency Identification (RFID). International operations are conducted through subsidiary CACI Ltd., which is based in the U.K. and accounts for over 90% of the company's commercial revenue. The subsidiary focuses on business systems solutions; data, information and knowledge management; and enterprise IT and network services. The company also operates the CACI Vision & Solution Center, where customers can test IT solutions before installing them. In January 2010, the firm formed a strategic alliance with Riverbed Technology, expanding its networking, applications and storage offerings. In February 2010, CACI acquired SystemWare, Inc., which specializes in cybersecurity and operational security. In March 2010, the U.S. Navy awarded CACI with a $219 million contract to provide communications, intelligence, surveillance and IT services to the Space and Naval Warfare (SPAWAR) Systems.

Employees are offered medical, dental, vision, life and AD&D insurance; short- and long-term disability; a health care flexible spending account; a 401(k) plan with a company match; a discounted employee stock purchase plan; tuition reimbursement; technical training; an employee mobility program; a group legal plan; and an employee assistance program.

FINANCIALS: Sales and profits are in thousands of dollars—add 000 to get the full amount. 2010 Note: Financial information for 2010 was not available for all companies at press time.

2010 Sales: $3,149,131	2010 Profits: $106,515	U.S. Stock Ticker: CACI
2009 Sales: $2,730,162	2009 Profits: $89,698	Int'l Ticker: Int'l Exchange:
2008 Sales: $2,420,537	2008 Profits: $77,935	Employees: 13,100
2007 Sales: $1,937,972	2007 Profits: $78,532	Fiscal Year Ends: 6/30
2006 Sales: $1,755,324	2006 Profits: $84,840	Parent Company:

SALARIES/BENEFITS:

Pension Plan:	ESOP Stock Plan:	Profit Sharing:	Top Exec. Salary: $700,000	Bonus: $1,549,092
Savings Plan: Y	Stock Purch. Plan: Y		Second Exec. Salary: $515,000	Bonus: $581,446

OTHER THOUGHTS:

Apparent Women Officers or Directors: 2
Hot Spot for Advancement for Women/Minorities: Y

LOCATIONS: ("Y" = Yes)

West:	Southwest:	Midwest:	Southeast:	Northeast:	International:
Y	Y	Y	Y	Y	Y

Note: Financial information, benefits and other data can change quickly and may vary from those stated here.

CADENCE DESIGN SYSTEMS INC

www.cadence.com

Industry Group Code: 511210N Ranks within this company's industry group: Sales: 5   Profits: 10

Hardware:		Software:		Telecommunications:	Electronic Publishing:	Equipment:		Specialty Services:	
Computers:		Consumer:		Local:	Online Service:	Telecom:		Consulting:	Y
Accessories:		Corporate:	Y	Long Distance:	TV/Cable or Wireless:	Communication:		Contract Manufacturing:	
Network Equipment:	Y	Telecom:		Cellular:	Games:	Distribution:		Processing:	
Chips/Circuits:	Y	Internet:		Internet Service:	Financial Data:	VAR/Reseller:		Staff/Outsourcing:	
Parts/Drives:						Satellite Srv./Equip.:		Specialty Services:	Y

TYPES OF BUSINESS:

Software-Electronic Design Automation
Training & Support Services
Design & Methodology Services

BRANDS/DIVISIONS/AFFILIATES:

Incisive Functional Verification Platform
Encounter Digital IC Design Platform
Virtuoso Custom Design Platform
AllegroSystem Interconnect Platform
Denali Software, Inc.

CONTACTS: *Note: Officers with more than one job title may be intentionally listed here more than once.*

Lip-Bu Tan, CEO
Lip-Bu Tan, Pres.
Geoff Ribar, CFO/Sr. VP
John Bruggeman, Chief Mktg. Officer/Sr. VP
Tina Jones, Sr. VP-Global Human Resources
Chi-Ping Hsu, Sr. VP-R&D, Implementation Group
Jim Cowie, General Counsel/Corp. Sec./Sr. VP
Thomas Cooley, Sr. VP-Worldwide Field Oper.
Charlie Huang, Chief Strategy Officer/Sr. VP
Jennifer Jordan, Corp. VP-Investor Rel.
Craig Johnson, Corp. VP-Strategic Planning
Nimish Modi, Sr. VP-R&D, Front End Group
Sanjay Srivastava, Sr. VP-SoC Realization
John B. Shoven, Chmn.

Phone: 408-943-1234	Fax: 408-428-5001
Toll-Free: 800-746-6223	
Address: 2655 Seely Ave., San Jose, CA 95134-1931 US	

GROWTH PLANS/SPECIAL FEATURES:

Cadence Design Systems, Inc. (Cadence) is a leading provider of electronic design automation (EDA) software and hardware. Cadence licenses, sells and leases its hardware technology and provides design and methodology services throughout the world to help manage and accelerate electronic product development processes. Cadence combines its design technologies into platforms for four major design activities: functional verification, digital integrated circuit (IC) design, custom IC design and system interconnect. The four Cadence design platforms are Incisive, a program which verifies the function of a logic system; Encounter, a digital IC design program modeled to balance cost and function; Virtuoso, a custom circuit schematic program; and Allegro, a printed circuit board simulation and design system. The company additionally augments its platform product offerings with a set of design for manufacturing (DFM) products that service both the digital and custom IC design flows. Cadence offers a number of fee-based services, including Internet, classroom and custom educational courses; and engineering services and reusable design technologies to aid customers with the design of complex ICs. The company sells software using subscription and term licenses, as well as perpetual licenses for customers who prefer to have the right to use the technology continuously without time restriction. In June 2010, it acquired Denali Software, Inc., a provider of EDA software and intellectual property.

FINANCIALS: Sales and profits are in thousands of dollars—add 000 to get the full amount. 2010 Note: Financial information for 2010 was not available for all companies at press time.

2010 Sales: $	2010 Profits: $	**U.S. Stock Ticker: CDNS**
2009 Sales: $852,600	2009 Profits: $-149,900	**Int'l Ticker:** Int'l Exchange:
2008 Sales: $1,038,600	2008 Profits: $-1,856,700	Employees: 4,400
2007 Sales: $1,615,013	2007 Profits: $286,800	Fiscal Year Ends: 12/31
2006 Sales: $1,483,895	2006 Profits: $142,592	Parent Company:

SALARIES/BENEFITS:

Pension Plan:	ESOP Stock Plan:	Profit Sharing:	Top Exec. Salary: $531,692	Bonus: $11,765
Savings Plan: Y	Stock Purch. Plan: Y		Second Exec. Salary: $423,135	Bonus: $

OTHER THOUGHTS:

Apparent Women Officers or Directors: 1
Hot Spot for Advancement for Women/Minorities:

LOCATIONS: ("Y" = Yes)

West:	Southwest:	Midwest:	Southeast:	Northeast:	International:
Y	Y	Y	Y	Y	Y

CALAMP CORP

www.calamp.com

Industry Group Code: 3342 Ranks within this company's industry group: Sales: 6 Profits: 6

Hardware:	Software:	Telecommunications:	Electronic Publishing:	Equipment:		Specialty Services:	
Computers:	Consumer:	Local:	Online Service:	Telecom:	Y	Consulting:	
Accessories:	Corporate:	Long Distance:	TV/Cable or Wireless:	Communication:	Y	Contract Manufacturing:	
Network Equipment:	Telecom:	Cellular:	Games:	Distribution:		Processing:	
Chips/Circuits:	Internet:	Internet Service:	Financial Data:	VAR/Reseller:		Staff/Outsourcing:	
Parts/Drives:				Satellite Srv./Equip.:	Y	Specialty Services:	

TYPES OF BUSINESS:

Microwave Communications Equipment
Wireless Broadband Access Systems
Satellite Products

BRANDS/DIVISIONS/AFFILIATES:

California Amplifier, Inc.
CalAmp Products, Inc.
CalAmp DataCom, Inc.
California Amplifier SARL
CalAmp Wireless Networks Corporation
CalAmp Wireless Networks, Inc.

CONTACTS: Note: Officers with more than one job title may be intentionally listed here more than once.

Rick Gold, CEO
Michael J. Burdiek, COO
Michael J. Burdiek, Pres.
Rick Vitelle, CFO
Rick Vitelle, Corp. Sec.
Garo Sarkissian, VP-Corp. Dev.
Frank Perna Jr., Chmn.

Phone: 805-987-9000	Fax: 805-856-3869
Toll-Free:	
Address: 1401 N. Rice Ave., Oxnard, CA 93030 US	

GROWTH PLANS/SPECIAL FEATURES:

CalAmp Corp., formerly California Amplifier, Inc., is a provider of wireless communications products that enable access to information, data and entertainment content. The firm offers its products through two primary business segments, the Wireless DataCom division and the Satellite division. The Wireless DataCom segment is subdivided into two business lines. The Wireless Networks business line provides products and systems to state and local governmental entities and industrial, utility and transportation firms for use in applications where the ability to communicate with mobile personnel or to command and control remote assets is required. Fire, police and emergency medical services personnel use these multi-network wireless systems to communicate with dispatchers and back-office databases, while utilities, oil and gas, mining, rail and security companies utilize them to allow real-time monitoring and control of remote equipment. The Mobile Resource Management (MRM) business line, meanwhile, offers products mainly used by municipalities, vehicle financing companies and large enterprises for asset tracking, service delivery optimization, security monitoring and machine-to-machine communications. The Satellite division develops, manufactures and sells Direct Broadcast Satellite (DBS) outdoor consumer premise equipment (CPE) to the U.S. digital and HD satellite TV market. Its DBS equipment consists of reflector dish antennae and the outdoor electronics used to process satellite signals and transfer them to set-top boxes in the home. Its two primary customers are Echostar and DirecTV, which incorporate CalAmp's DBS equipment into their subscription systems. Subsidiaries of the company include CalAmp Products, Inc.; CalAmp DataCom, Inc.; CalAmp Wireless Networks Corporation; California Amplifier SARL, in France; and CalAmp Wireless Networks, Inc., in Canada. International offices are located in Canada, Mexico, the U.K., France and Israel.

CalAmp offers its employees benefits which include life insurance, disability insurance and health benefits, as well as a 401(k) plan.

FINANCIALS: Sales and profits are in thousands of dollars—add 000 to get the full amount. 2010 Note: Financial information for 2010 was not available for all companies at press time.

2010 Sales: $112,113	2010 Profits: $-10,851	U.S. Stock Ticker: CAMP
2009 Sales: $98,370	2009 Profits: $-49,665	Int'l Ticker: Int'l Exchange:
2008 Sales: $140,907	2008 Profits: $-84,149	Employees: 510
2007 Sales: $211,714	2007 Profits: $-31,188	Fiscal Year Ends: 2/28
2006 Sales: $196,908	2006 Profits: $14,562	Parent Company:

SALARIES/BENEFITS:

Pension Plan:	ESOP Stock Plan:	Profit Sharing:	Top Exec. Salary: $425,000	Bonus: $
Savings Plan: Y	Stock Purch. Plan:		Second Exec. Salary: $280,000	Bonus: $30,343

OTHER THOUGHTS:

Apparent Women Officers or Directors: 1
Hot Spot for Advancement for Women/Minorities:

LOCATIONS: ("Y" = Yes)

West:	Southwest:	Midwest:	Southeast:	Northeast:	International:
Y		Y	Y		Y

CANON INC
www.canon.com

Industry Group Code: 334119 Ranks within this company's industry group: Sales: 1   Profits: 1

Hardware:		Software:		Telecommunications:	Electronic Publishing:	Equipment:	Specialty Services:
Computers:		Consumer:	Y	Local:	Online Service:	Telecom:	Consulting:
Accessories:	Y	Corporate:		Long Distance:	TV/Cable or Wireless:	Communication:	Contract Manufacturing:
Network Equipment:		Telecom:	Y	Cellular:	Games:	Distribution:	Processing:
Chips/Circuits:		Internet:		Internet Service:	Financial Data:	VAR/Reseller:	Staff/Outsourcing:
Parts/Drives:						Satellite Srv./Equip.:	Specialty Services:

TYPES OF BUSINESS:
Business Machines-Copiers
Printers & Scanners
Semiconductor Production Equipment
Cameras, Film & Digital
Optics & Lenses
X-Ray Equipment
Fax Machines
Photovoltaic Cells

BRANDS/DIVISIONS/AFFILIATES:
Bubble Jet
Tokki Corporation
Hitachi Ltd
Canon Ecology Industry Inc
Canon Marketing Japan Inc
Canon Information Systems Co Ltd
Canon Singapore PTE Ltd
Canon Machinery, Inc.

CONTACTS: Note: Officers with more than one job title may be intentionally listed here more than once.
Fujio Mitarai, CEO
Tsuneji Uchida, COO
Tsuneji Uchida, Pres.
Toshizo Tanaka, CFO/Exec. VP
Kengo Uramoto, Group Exec.-Human Resources Mgmt.
Makoto Araki, Group Exec.-Info. & Comm. Systems
Toshiaki Ikoma, CTO/Exec. VP
Toshiaki Ikoma, CEO-Optical Prod. Oper.
Kunio Watanabe, Managing Dir.-Corp. Planning Dev.
Masahiro Haga, Group Exec.-Finance & Acct.
Toshizo Tanaka, Sr. Gen. Mgr.-Policy & Economy Research
Yoroku Adachi, Pres./CEO-Canon USA, Inc.
Yasuo Mitsuhashi, CEO-Peripheral Prod. Oper.
Fujio Mitarai, Chmn.
Ryoichi Bamba, Pres./CEO-Canon Europe Ltd.
Masahiro Osawa, Group Exec.-Global Procurement

Phone: 81-3-3758-2111	Fax: 81-3-5482-5135
Toll-Free:	
Address: 30-2, Shimomaruko 3-chome, Ohta-ku, Tokyo, 146-8501 Japan	

GROWTH PLANS/SPECIAL FEATURES:
Canon, Inc. manufactures copiers, printers, computer peripherals, digital and film cameras and semiconductor production equipment. The company operates in five segments: business information products; office imaging products; computer peripherals; cameras; and optical products and other products. The business information products group includes document scanners, electronic calculators and dictionaries and computer information products. The office imaging products segment manufactures, markets and services a wide range of monochrome-networked and personal-use multifunctional devices (MFDs), full-color copying machines and office color MFDs. The computer peripherals segment includes laser printers, inkjet printers and scanners. The next operating segment, cameras, consists of film and digital cameras, lenses and liquid crystal display (LCD) projectors. The company's flagship camera products are the Digital ELPH and the EOS Rebel cameras. Canon's last line of business, optical products and others, includes semiconductor exposure systems, broadcasting equipment, medical equipment and LCD exposure systems. These products include X-ray equipment; medical image recording equipment; semiconductor steppers and aligners; and television camera lenses. In March 2010, Nagasaki Canon Inc, a producer of compact digital cameras and digital single-lens reflex (SLR) cameras, began operations. In February 2010, Canon and Fujitsu Limited announced plans to join forces and offer cloud computing-based services. With this agreement, the two companies will combine Fujitsu's cloud-based IT management services with Canon's print management and operations technologies to offer customers various products. Also in 2010 the firm liquidated its subsidiary, SED, Inc., which was involved in Surface-conduction Electron-emitter Display technology. The same year, the company took Tokki Corporation and Canon Machinery, Inc. as wholly-owned subsidiaries.

Employees are offered medical, dental and vision insurance; flexible spending accounts; life insurance; an employee assistance program; and an educational assistance program.

FINANCIALS: Sales and profits are in thousands of dollars—add 000 to get the full amount. 2010 Note: Financial information for 2010 was not available for all companies at press time.

2010 Sales: $	2010 Profits: $	U.S. Stock Ticker: CAJ
2009 Sales: $34,440,000	2009 Profits: $1,412,800	Int'l Ticker: 7751 Int'l Exchange: Tokyo-TSE
2008 Sales: $44,990,780	2008 Profits: $3,397,231	Employees: 166,980
2007 Sales: $43,179,800	2007 Profits: $4,705,400	Fiscal Year Ends: 12/31
2006 Sales: $34,930,748	2006 Profits: $3,826,261	Parent Company:

SALARIES/BENEFITS:
Pension Plan: Y	ESOP Stock Plan:	Profit Sharing:	Top Exec. Salary: $	Bonus: $
Savings Plan:	Stock Purch. Plan: Y		Second Exec. Salary: $	Bonus: $

OTHER THOUGHTS:
Apparent Women Officers or Directors:
Hot Spot for Advancement for Women/Minorities:

LOCATIONS: ("Y" = Yes)
West:	Southwest:	Midwest:	Southeast:	Northeast:	International:
		Y	Y	Y	Y

CAPGEMINI

www.capgemini.com

Industry Group Code: 541513 Ranks within this company's industry group: Sales: 5 Profits: 12

Hardware:	Software:	Telecommunications:	Electronic Publishing:	Equipment:	Specialty Services:	
Computers:	Consumer:	Local:	Online Service:	Telecom:	Consulting:	Y
Accessories:	Corporate:	Long Distance:	TV/Cable or Wireless:	Communication:	Contract Manufacturing:	
Network Equipment:	Telecom:	Cellular:	Games:	Distribution:	Processing:	
Chips/Circuits:	Internet:	Internet Service:	Financial Data:	VAR/Reseller:	Staff/Outsourcing:	Y
Parts/Drives:				Satellite Srv./Equip.:	Specialty Services:	Y

TYPES OF BUSINESS:

Management Consulting
IT Consulting
Outsourcing Services
Professional Staffing Services
Design & Development Services

BRANDS/DIVISIONS/AFFILIATES:

SSS Holdings Corporation Ltd
Sonda SA
CPM Braxis SA
Thesys Technologies Private Ltd
Strategic Systems Solutions
Sonda Procwork

CONTACTS: Note: Officers with more than one job title may be intentionally listed here more than once.

Paul Hermelin, CEO
Nicolas Dufourcq, CFO
Philippe Grangeon, Dir.-Mktg.
Jeremy Roffe-Vidal, Dir.-Human Resources
Andy Mulholland, Dir.-Tech
Alain Donzeaud, Gen. Sec.
Serge Kampf, Chmn.

Phone: 33-1-47-54-50-00	Fax: 33-1-47-54-50-86
Toll-Free:	
Address: Place de l'Etoile, 11 rue de Tilsitt, Paris, 75017 France	

GROWTH PLANS/SPECIAL FEATURES:

Capgemini is one of the world's largest international management consulting and information technology (IT) services firms. Based in Paris, with offices in 35 countries, the firm's services are organized into four main divisions: outsourcing, 36.4% of total revenues; technology services, 40%; consulting, 6.7%; and local professional services, 16.9%. The outsourcing division offers applications management, infrastructure management and business process outsourcing. The technology division, which employs a large portion of Capgemini's workforce, provides application development, systems architecture design, systems integration and infrastructure services. The company's consulting division specializes in customer relationship management, finance, employee transformation, supply chain and organizational transformation. The local professional services division, operating under the Sogeti brand name, connects local professionals to companies in need of help in software development, applications management, hardware management and network management. Capgemini primarily earns revenues in France, 23.8%; the U.K. and Ireland, 22.1%; North America, 19%; and the Benelux countries, 16.7%. Operations are conducted in six main industry groups: manufacturing, retail and distribution, 27.5% of revenues; energy and utilities, 13%; financial services, 16.5%; public sector, 28.1%; telecommunications, media and entertainment, 8%; and other, 6.9%. Capgemini maintains alliances with top technology companies to provide accelerated systems development and integration services to its clients. The company has held technological partnerships with companies including Oracle; Microsoft; Sun Systems; IBM; Intel; Cisco Systems; and HP. The firm joined with Nokia and Oracle in creating the Managed Mobility Services Collaboration, aimed at providing cost-effective, scalable enterprise-wide mobility applications and services, including configuration, security and call center and asset management. In 2010, Capgemini acquired Strategic Systems Solutions, a global IT and business process outsourcing company; Sonda Procwork, a Latin American business process outsourcing company; CPM Braxis, a Brazilian IT services firm; and Thesys Technologies, an Indian IT services company.

FINANCIALS: Sales and profits are in thousands of dollars—add 000 to get the full amount. 2010 Note: Financial information for 2010 was not available for all companies at press time.

2010 Sales: $	2010 Profits: $	**U.S. Stock Ticker:**
2009 Sales: $11,373,200	2009 Profits: $241,840	**Int'l Ticker: CAPP** Int'l Exchange: Paris-Euronext
2008 Sales: $11,741,800	2008 Profits: $789,980	Employees: 90,516
2007 Sales: $11,732,300	2007 Profits: $664,600	Fiscal Year Ends: 12/31
2006 Sales: $12,243,000	2006 Profits: $465,900	Parent Company:

SALARIES/BENEFITS:

Pension Plan:	ESOP Stock Plan:	Profit Sharing:	Top Exec. Salary: $	Bonus: $
Savings Plan:	Stock Purch. Plan:		Second Exec. Salary: $	Bonus: $

OTHER THOUGHTS:

Apparent Women Officers or Directors:
Hot Spot for Advancement for Women/Minorities:

LOCATIONS: ("Y" = Yes)

West:	Southwest:	Midwest:	Southeast:	Northeast:	International:
Y	Y	Y	Y	Y	Y

CASIO COMPUTER CO LTD

www.casio.com

Industry Group Code: 334111 Ranks within this company's industry group: Sales: 13 Profits: 24

Hardware:		Software:		Telecommunications:		Electronic Publishing:		Equipment:		Specialty Services:	
Computers:	Y	Consumer:		Local:		Online Service:		Telecom:	Y	Consulting:	
Accessories:	Y	Corporate:		Long Distance:		TV/Cable or Wireless:		Communication:	Y	Contract Manufacturing:	
Network Equipment:	Y	Telecom:		Cellular:		Games:		Distribution:		Processing:	
Chips/Circuits:		Internet:		Internet Service:		Financial Data:		VAR/Reseller:		Staff/Outsourcing:	
Parts/Drives:	Y							Satellite Srv./Equip.:		Specialty Services:	

TYPES OF BUSINESS:

Electronics & Computer Manufacturing
Timepieces
Calculators
Cellular Phones
Electronic Music Instruments
LCDs
Digital Cameras
Factory Automation Equipment

BRANDS/DIVISIONS/AFFILIATES:

Yamagata Casio Co., Ltd.
Kofu Casio Co., Ltd.
Casio Techno Co., Ltd.
Casio America, Inc.
NEC Corporation
Hitachi Ltd

CONTACTS:
Note: Officers with more than one job title may be intentionally listed here more than once.
Kazuo Kashio, CEO
Kazuo Kashio, Pres.
Hiroshi Nakamura, Managing Dir./Chief Dir.-Sales
Tadashi Takasu, Mgr.-R&D
Yukio Kashio, Exec. VP
Fumitsune Murakami, Sr. Managing Dir.
Takatoshi Yamamoto, Managing Dir.
Akinori Takagi, Managing Dir.
Toshio Kashio, Chmn.

Phone: 03-5334-4111	Fax:
Toll-Free:	
Address: 6-2, Hon-machi 1-chome, Shibuya-ku, Tokyo, 151-8543 Japan	

GROWTH PLANS/SPECIAL FEATURES:

Casio Computer Co., Ltd. makes a wide range of consumer electronics products, timepieces, mobile network solutions (MNS), system equipment, electronic components and other equipment. Its consumer electronics products include calculators, electronic dictionaries, label printers, digital cameras and electronic musical instruments, such as keyboards. Timepieces include digital watches, analog watches and clocks. Casio's MNS products include cellular phones and handheld terminals, such as mobile PCs, inventory computers and PDAs. The firm's system equipment products include cash registers, office computers, data projectors and page printers. The electronic component business includes small LCDs for mobile devices, as well as bump processing services (a technology through which electrodes are formed for liquid crystal driver chips). Other products include molds and factory automation products. Consumer electronics account for approximately 37.8% of the firm's annual sales; MNS, 24.7%; timepieces, 18.2%; electronic components, 4.8%; system equipment, 8.2%; and others, 6.3%. Key Casio products include cell phones, calculators, electronic dictionaries, digital cameras and timepieces. The firm has several domestic subsidiaries, including Yamagata Casio Co., Ltd., which manufactures electronic timepieces, digital cameras and cell phones; Kofu Casio Co., Ltd., which manufactures LCDs and system equipment; and Casio Techno Co., Ltd., which provides customer service for the firm's products. Internationally, it has nine Asian subsidiaries, located in Taiwan, Hong Kong, China, India, Singapore and Thailand; five subsidiaries across the Americas, including firms in the U.S., Canada, Mexico and Brazil; and eight European subsidiaries, headquartered in the U.K., Germany, Russia, France, the Netherlands, Norway, Spain and Italy. The firm also maintains a joint venture with Hitachi, Ltd. focused on new mobile network technologies. In March 2010, Casio announced a joint venture with Hitachi and NEC Corporation to focus on integrating their respective mobile terminal business operations.

FINANCIALS:
Sales and profits are in thousands of dollars—add 000 to get the full amount. 2010 Note: Financial information for 2010 was not available for all companies at press time.

2010 Sales: $5,203,570	2010 Profits: $-254,970	**U.S. Stock Ticker:** CSIOY.PK
2009 Sales: $5,762,590	2009 Profits: $-257,510	**Int'l Ticker:** 6952 Int'l Exchange: Tokyo-TSE
2008 Sales: $6,930,760	2008 Profits: $135,580	Employees: 13,202
2007 Sales: $5,264,100	2007 Profits: $213,200	Fiscal Year Ends: 3/31
2006 Sales: $4,934,900	2006 Profits: $201,900	Parent Company:

SALARIES/BENEFITS:

Pension Plan:	ESOP Stock Plan:	Profit Sharing:	Top Exec. Salary: $	Bonus: $
Savings Plan:	Stock Purch. Plan:		Second Exec. Salary: $	Bonus: $

OTHER THOUGHTS:
Apparent Women Officers or Directors:
Hot Spot for Advancement for Women/Minorities:

LOCATIONS: ("Y" = Yes)

West:	Southwest:	Midwest:	Southeast:	Northeast:	International:
			Y	Y	Y

CDC SOFTWARE CORP

www.cdcsoftware.com

Industry Group Code: 511210H Ranks within this company's industry group: Sales: 12 Profits: 10

Hardware:	Software:		Telecommunications:	Electronic Publishing:	Equipment:	Specialty Services:	
Computers:	Consumer:		Local:	Online Service:	Telecom:	Consulting:	Y
Accessories:	Corporate:	Y	Long Distance:	TV/Cable or Wireless:	Communication:	Contract Manufacturing:	
Network Equipment:	Telecom:		Cellular:	Games:	Distribution:	Processing:	
Chips/Circuits:	Internet:		Internet Service:	Financial Data:	VAR/Reseller:	Staff/Outsourcing:	
Parts/Drives:					Satellite Srv./Equip.:	Specialty Services:	Y

TYPES OF BUSINESS:

Computer Software, Business Management
IT Services
Consulting Services

BRANDS/DIVISIONS/AFFILIATES:

CDC Front Office
CDC Manufacturing
CDC Supply Chain
CDC SaaS
CDC Solutions
CDC Solutions for Microsoft
Vitova Ltd.
TradeBeam, Inc.

CONTACTS: Note: Officers with more than one job title may be intentionally listed here more than once.

Peter Yip, CEO
Stephen Dexter, CFO
Jason Rushforth, Sr. VP-Worldwide Mktg.
Alan MacLamroc, CTO
Donald Novajosky, General Counsel/VP
Monish Bahl, Sr. VP-Bus. Dev.
Mark Sutcliffe, Pres, CDC Factory
Monish Bahl, Sr. VP-Mergers & Acquisitions
Jason Rushforth, Sr. VP-Global Strategic Alliances
Lee R. Reisterer, Sr. VP-Professional Svcs.
John Clough, Chmn.
Oscar Pierre, Sr. VP-Europe & Latin America Oper.
Niklas Ronnback, Sr. VP/Pres., CDC Supply Chain

Phone: 852-2903-7888	Fax: 852-2903-7887
Toll-Free:	
Address: 11/F, ING Tower 308 Des Voeux Rd. Central, Hong Kong, K3 00000 China	

GROWTH PLANS/SPECIAL FEATURES:

CDC Software Corp. provides enterprise software applications and services that include on-premise, cloud-based or hybrid deployment solutions, as well as application implementation, technical support and IT Consulting. CDC's product suites include CDC Front Office, CDC Back Office, CDC SaaS (Software as a Service) and CDC Plant/Shop Solutions. CDC Front Office Suite enables clients to manage all aspects of customer service relations; this suite includes the Pivotal CRM, c360, CDC Respond, Vitova Limited and CDC MarketFirst programs. CDC Back Office solutions are designed for multi-enterprise, multi-channel, multi-language and multi-currency order environments; this suite includes Supply Chain Execution, Platinum HRM, e-M-Power, CDC TradeBeam and Ross Enterprise applications, which are tailored to the needs of specific industries. The CDC SaaS suite allows clients to manage the e-commerce aspects of their business; this suite includes CDC eCommerce, eBizNET, CDC gomembers NFP/NGO, and Markbright. These applications manage transactions, streamline checkout, merchandise products and allow member based organizations to automate their planning process. Lastly, the company's CDC Plant/Shop Floor Solutions assists in the manufacturing side of the business, and includes applications CDC Factory and CDC Activplant. Additionally, the company offers consulting services that assists clients in software implementation and in streamlining methodologies. CDC also offers customers software training for all of their product suites; as well as global technical support accessible through self-service customer portals and multilingual customer support staffs. In April 2010, the company acquired a majority stake in Vitova Ltd, an Enterprise content management company based in China. In May 2010, CDC acquired TradeBeam, Inc., a provider of on-demand SaaS supply chain visibility and global trade management solutions.

The company offers its U.S. employee medical, dental and vision; AD&D insurance; short and long term disability; life insurance; an employee assistance program; and a flexible spending account.

FINANCIALS: Sales and profits are in thousands of dollars—add 000 to get the full amount. 2010 Note: Financial information for 2010 was not available for all companies at press time.

2010 Sales: $	2010 Profits: $	U.S. Stock Ticker: CDCS
2009 Sales: $240,787	2009 Profits: $-1,020	Int'l Ticker: Int'l Exchange:
2008 Sales: $230,899	2008 Profits: $23,091	Employees:
2007 Sales: $	2007 Profits: $	Fiscal Year Ends: 12/31
2006 Sales: $	2006 Profits: $	Parent Company:

SALARIES/BENEFITS:

Pension Plan:	ESOP Stock Plan:	Profit Sharing:	Top Exec. Salary: $	Bonus: $
Savings Plan: Y	Stock Purch. Plan:		Second Exec. Salary: $	Bonus: $

OTHER THOUGHTS:

Apparent Women Officers or Directors:
Hot Spot for Advancement for Women/Minorities:

LOCATIONS: ("Y" = Yes)

West:	Southwest:	Midwest:	Southeast:	Northeast:	International:
	Y				Y

CDG GROUP

www.cdg.co.th

Industry Group Code: 541513 Ranks within this company's industry group: Sales: Profits:

Hardware:	Software:	Telecommunications:	Electronic Publishing:	Equipment:	Specialty Services:	
Computers:	Consumer:	Local:	Online Service:	Telecom:	Consulting:	Y
Accessories:	Corporate:	Long Distance:	TV/Cable or Wireless:	Communication:	Contract Manufacturing:	
Network Equipment:	Telecom:	Cellular:	Games:	Distribution:	Processing:	
Chips/Circuits:	Internet:	Internet Service:	Financial Data:	VAR/Reseller:	Staff/Outsourcing:	Y
Parts/Drives:				Satellite Srv./Equip.:	Specialty Services:	Y

TYPES OF BUSINESS:

Information Technology Products & Services

BRANDS/DIVISIONS/AFFILIATES:

Control Data (Thailand) Ltd.
CDG Systems
Computer Peripherals and Supplies, Ltd.
ESRI

CONTACTS: Note: Officers with more than one job title may be intentionally listed here more than once.

Nart Liuchareon, CEO
Supavadee Phantumvanit, COO

Phone: 662-0-2678-0200	Fax: 662-0-2678-0321-3
Toll-Free:	
Address: CDG House 202 Nanglinchi Rd., Chongnonsee, Yannawa, Bangkok, 10120 Thailand	

GROWTH PLANS/SPECIAL FEATURES:

CDG Group is a Thailand-based IT company that offers a range of services, including computer facility management, technology support, consulting and outsourcing services. The group consists of five subsidiaries, including the flagship company Control Data (Thailand) Ltd., which specializes in information management, outsourcing systems and systems integration. Additionally, it is responsible for the production of Thailand's national identification card system. Other companies within the group include CDG Systems, a turnkey and general technology support provider; Computer Peripherals and Supplies, Ltd., which provides printing technologies and other services; and ESRI Co. Ltd., which specializes in GIS (Geographic Information Systems) software and solutions. The firm was originally a branch of the US-based Control Data Corporation, but was later spun off to become its own private company. It provides services to a variety of sectors, such as government, banking and academic institutions. Beyond IT services, CDG also operates as a technology reseller, featuring products from companies such as HP, Epson, Apple and Pearson NCS. The company is present throughout Thailand, with service centers in Bangkok and 76 provinces. The firm is allied with several international technology companies, such as Dell Computer, IBM, Microsoft and others. CDG recently expanded its services to other countries in Southeast Asia, with infrastructure projects for the Post and Telecommunications Corporation in Burma and extending an ESRI presence in Vietnam to provide GIS services.

FINANCIALS: Sales and profits are in thousands of dollars—add 000 to get the full amount. 2010 Note: Financial information for 2010 was not available for all companies at press time.

2010 Sales: $	2010 Profits: $	U.S. Stock Ticker: Private
2009 Sales: $	2009 Profits: $	Int'l Ticker: Int'l Exchange:
2008 Sales: $	2008 Profits: $	Employees:
2007 Sales: $	2007 Profits: $	Fiscal Year Ends:
2006 Sales: $	2006 Profits: $	Parent Company:

SALARIES/BENEFITS:

Pension Plan:	ESOP Stock Plan:	Profit Sharing:	Top Exec. Salary: $	Bonus: $
Savings Plan:	Stock Purch. Plan:		Second Exec. Salary: $	Bonus: $

OTHER THOUGHTS:

Apparent Women Officers or Directors: 1
Hot Spot for Advancement for Women/Minorities:

LOCATIONS: ("Y" = Yes)

West:	Southwest:	Midwest:	Southeast:	Northeast:	International:
					Y

CDW CORPORATION

www.cdw.com

Industry Group Code: 423430 **Ranks within this company's industry group:** Sales: 5 Profits:

Hardware:	Software:	Telecommunications:	Electronic Publishing:	Equipment:		Specialty Services:	
Computers:	Consumer:	Local:	Online Service:	Telecom:		Consulting:	
Accessories:	Corporate:	Long Distance:	TV/Cable or Wireless:	Communication:		Contract Manufacturing:	
Network Equipment:	Telecom:	Cellular:	Games:	Distribution:		Processing:	
Chips/Circuits:	Internet:	Internet Service:	Financial Data:	VAR/Reseller:	Y	Staff/Outsourcing:	
Parts/Drives:				Satellite Srv./Equip.:		Specialty Services:	

TYPES OF BUSINESS:

Computer Products, Direct Selling
Online Sales
Custom Installation & Repair-Computers

BRANDS/DIVISIONS/AFFILIATES:

CDW Government Inc
CDW Canada Inc
Providence Equity Partners LLC
Madison Dearborn Partners LLC
TKC Integration Services

CONTACTS: *Note: Officers with more than one job title may be intentionally listed here more than once.*

John A. Edwardson, CEO
Thomas E. Richards, COO
Thomas E. Richards, Pres.
Ann E. Ziegler, CFO/Sr. VP
Dennis G. Berger, Sr. VP/Chief Coworker Svcs. Officer
Jonathan J. Stevens, CIO/Sr. VP-Oper.
William T. Weaver, VP-Advanced Tech.
Matthew A. Troka, Sr. VP-Prod. & Partner Mgmt.
Christine A. Leahy, General Counsel/Sr. VP/Sec.
Anne B. Ireland, VP-Oper. & Sales Planning
Douglas E. Eckrote, Sr. VP-Strategic Solutions & Svcs.
Vicky Bunker, Head-Investor Rel.
Virginia L. Seggerman, Controller/VP
Christina V. Rother, Sr. VP-Sales, CDW LLC
James J. Lillis, VP-Systems Solutions
Maria M. Sullivan, VP-Small Bus.
Collin B. Kebo, VP-Financial Planning & Analysis
John A. Edwardson, Chmn.

Phone: 847-465-6000	Fax: 847-465-6800
Toll-Free: 800-750-4239	
Address: 200 N. Milwaukee Ave., Vernon Hills, IL 60061 US	

GROWTH PLANS/SPECIAL FEATURES:

CDW Corporation, owned by private equity firms Madison Dearborn Partners LLC and Providence Equity Partners, Inc., is one of the leading providers of multi-branded information technology products and services to business, government and education customers in the U.S. and Canada. The firm offers over 100,000 products from 1,300 leading technology brands, in addition to customized solution design and management, with focus areas including notebooks, desktops, printers, servers and storage, unified communications, security, wireless, power and cooling, networking, software licensing and mobility solutions. The company manages its inventory through a 450,000-square-foot distribution center in Vernon Hills, Illinois, and a 513,000-square-foot distribution center in Las Vegas, Nevada, which ship approximately 2,000 custom-configured systems daily. CDW offers customers free access to certified technicians for telephone support and complete custom installation and repair services via the company's configuration center, in addition to access to a database of frequently asked technical questions and direct links to manufacturers' tech support web sites. Its CDW Government, Inc. subsidiary provides specialized product offerings and services to federal, state and local governments, as well as the educational sector. CDW Canada, Inc. serves commercial and public sector customers in Canada. In February 2010, CDW Government announced an agreement with TKC Integration Services, a subsidiary of Qivliq LLC, to deliver server, desktop and collaboration software on a Microsoft platform to the U.S. Department of Energy.

The company offers its employees medical, dental and vision insurance; a 401(k) plan; a profit sharing plan; life and AD&D insurance; flexible spending accounts; tuition reimbursement; short- and long-term disability insurance; and an employee assistance program.

FINANCIALS: Sales and profits are in thousands of dollars—add 000 to get the full amount. 2010 Note: Financial information for 2010 was not available for all companies at press time.

2010 Sales: $	2010 Profits: $	U.S. Stock Ticker: Private
2009 Sales: $8,000,000	2009 Profits: $	Int'l Ticker: Int'l Exchange:
2008 Sales: $8,071,000	2008 Profits: $	Employees: 6,700
2007 Sales: $8,145,000	2007 Profits: $	Fiscal Year Ends: 12/31
2006 Sales: $6,785,473	2006 Profits: $266,080	Parent Company: MADISON DEARBORN PARTNERS LLC

SALARIES/BENEFITS:

Pension Plan:	ESOP Stock Plan:	Profit Sharing: Y	Top Exec. Salary: $	Bonus: $1,055,629
Savings Plan: Y	Stock Purch. Plan:		Second Exec. Salary: $	Bonus: $

OTHER THOUGHTS:

Apparent Women Officers or Directors: 7
Hot Spot for Advancement for Women/Minorities: Y

LOCATIONS: ("Y" = Yes)

West:	Southwest:	Midwest:	Southeast:	Northeast:	International:
Y	Y	Y		Y	Y

CEGEDIM SA

www.cegedim.fr

Industry Group Code: 511210D Ranks within this company's industry group: Sales: 1 Profits: 1

Hardware:	Software:		Telecommunications:	Electronic Publishing:	Equipment:	Specialty Services:
Computers:	Consumer:		Local:	Online Service:	Telecom:	Consulting:
Accessories:	Corporate:	Y	Long Distance:	TV/Cable or Wireless:	Communication:	Contract Manufacturing:
Network Equipment:	Telecom:		Cellular:	Games:	Distribution:	Processing:
Chips/Circuits:	Internet:		Internet Service:	Financial Data:	VAR/Reseller:	Staff/Outsourcing:
Parts/Drives:					Satellite Srv./Equip.:	Specialty Services:

TYPES OF BUSINESS:

Software - Development & Marketing
Databases
Pharmaceuticals Marketing & Tracking Software
Compliance Services

BRANDS/DIVISIONS/AFFILIATES:

Cegedim Dendrite
Dendrite International Inc
Santesurf
Cegedim Strategic Data
Cegers
Infopharm
InfoSante

CONTACTS: Note: Officers with more than one job title may be intentionally listed here more than once.

Jean-Claude Labrune, CEO
Karl Guenault, COO
Daniel Flis, Dir.-Comm.
J. E. Umiastowski, Chief Investor Rel. Officer
Pierre Marucchi, Managing Dir.
Laurent Labrune, CRM & Strategic Data
Alain Missoffe, Healthcare Professionals
Bruno Sarfati, Strategic Data
Jean-Claude Labrune, Chmn.

Phone: 33-1-49-09-22-00	Fax: 33-1-46-03-45-95
Toll-Free:	
Address: 127-137, rue d'Aguesseau, Boulogne-Billancourt, 92641 France	

GROWTH PLANS/SPECIAL FEATURES:

Cegedim S.A., formerly Dendrite International, Inc., is a developer of databases and software solutions for pharmaceutical companies, healthcare professionals, health insurance providers and France-based companies in virtually any market sector. The company operated through three divisions: healthcare professionals; customer relationship management (CRM) and strategic Data; and insurance and services. Cegedim's CRM and strategic data services serve pharmaceutical companies in over 80 countries. Through Cegedim Dendrite, the company develops databases that provide pharmaceutical companies with information regarding where their drugs are sold, who prescribes them and why the drugs are prescribed. Additional healthcare products and services include tools for optimizing information resources; report and analysis tools for office and hospital sales forces; strategic marketing, operational marketing and competition monitoring tools and studies; performance measurement and promotional spending auditing tools; and pharmacy order-taking tools. Sales force optimization services are offered through subsidiary Itops; market research studies are offered through subsidiary Cegedim Strategic Data; sales statistics are offered through subsidiaries Cegers, Infopharm and InfoSante; and prescription analysis is offered through Cegedim Customer Information. The healthcare professionals segment provides software products, information systems and consulting services for pharmacists, doctors and other healthcare professionals through subsidiaries Alliadis; Cegedim Rx; AGDF Cedegin RS; and In Practice Systems (INPS) to name a few. Subsidiary Santesurf provides a free and secure French intranet exclusively for healthcare professionals. Cegedim's insurance and services division provides outsourced human resources management, Internet hosting services, electronic bill payment, medical financial leasing, corporate databases, printing services and sample management. Subsidiaries in this sector include Cegedim Activ; Cetip; and iSante.

FINANCIALS: Sales and profits are in thousands of dollars—add 000 to get the full amount. 2010 Note: Financial information for 2010 was not available for all companies at press time.

2010 Sales: $	2010 Profits: $	U.S. Stock Ticker:
2009 Sales: $1,161,910	2009 Profits: $72,710	Int'l Ticker: CGM Int'l Exchange: Paris-Euronext
2008 Sales: $1,121,330	2008 Profits: $44,250	Employees: 8,600
2007 Sales: $995,010	2007 Profits: $58,340	Fiscal Year Ends: 12/31
2006 Sales: $868,600	2006 Profits: $60,700	Parent Company:

SALARIES/BENEFITS:

Pension Plan:	ESOP Stock Plan:	Profit Sharing:	Top Exec. Salary: $	Bonus: $
Savings Plan:	Stock Purch. Plan:		Second Exec. Salary: $	Bonus: $

OTHER THOUGHTS:

Apparent Women Officers or Directors:
Hot Spot for Advancement for Women/Minorities:

LOCATIONS: ("Y" = Yes)

West:	Southwest:	Midwest:	Southeast:	Northeast:	International:
				Y	Y

Note: Financial information, benefits and other data can change quickly and may vary from those stated here.

CELESTICA INC

www.celestica.com

Industry Group Code: 334419 Ranks within this company's industry group: Sales: 8 Profits: 7

Hardware:		Software:		Telecommunications:		Electronic Publishing:		Equipment:		Specialty Services:	
Computers:		Consumer:		Local:		Online Service:		Telecom:		Consulting:	
Accessories:		Corporate:		Long Distance:		TV/Cable or Wireless:		Communication:		Contract Manufacturing:	Y
Network Equipment:		Telecom:		Cellular:		Games:		Distribution:		Processing:	
Chips/Circuits:	Y	Internet:		Internet Service:		Financial Data:		VAR/Reseller:		Staff/Outsourcing:	
Parts/Drives:								Satellite Srv./Equip.:		Specialty Services:	Y

TYPES OF BUSINESS:

Contract Electronics Manufacturing
Printed Circuit Assemblies
Manufacturing Support Services (ODM)
Product Design
Distribution Services
Regulatory Compliance Services

BRANDS/DIVISIONS/AFFILIATES:

Invec Solutions
Allied Panels Entwicklungs-und Produktions Gmbh
Green Services
CoreSim Technology

CONTACTS: Note: Officers with more than one job title may be intentionally listed here more than once.

Craig H. Muhlhauser, CEO
Craig H. Muhlhauser, Pres.
Paul Nicoletti, CFO/Exec. VP
Scott Smith, Exec. VP-Global Sales, Solutions & Mktg.
Betty DelBianco, Exec. VP-Human Resources
Mary Gendron, CIO/Sr. VP
John Peri, Exec. VP-Eng. & Electronics
Betty DelBianco, Chief Admin. Officer
Betty DelBianco, Chief Legal Officer/Corp. Sec.
Peter Lindgren, Sr. VP/Gen. Mgr.-Growth & Emerging Markets
Michael Sobolewski, Dir.-Bus. Dev. & Sales, Healthcare
Mike McCaughey, Sr. VP/Gen. Mgr.-Global Customer Bus. Units
Sandra Ketchen, VP-Healthcare
Nancy Duarte-Lonnroth, Dir.-Quality & Regulatory Affairs, Healthcare
Robert L. Crandall, Chmn.
Rob Sellers, Sr. VP-Customer Dev., Asia
John Peri, Exec. VP-Supply Chain Mgmt.

Phone: 416-448-5800	Fax: 416-448-4810
Toll-Free: 888-899-9998	
Address: 844 Don Mills Rd., Toronto, ON M3C 1V7 Canada	

GROWTH PLANS/SPECIAL FEATURES:

Celestica, Inc. is a provider of electronics manufacturing services (EMS). The company, based in Canada, operates a global network of approximately 20 manufacturing/design facilities and 10 specialized centers worldwide, with operations in Asia, Europe and the Americas. It provides a broad range of services to original equipment manufacturers (OEMs), including supply chain management; design; prototyping; product assembly and test; systems assembly; product assurance; failure analysis; logistics; and product upgrades and repair. Celestica primarily supports OEMs in the healthcare, alternative energy, communications, consumer, industrial, aerospace and defense sectors. The firm's objective is to assist its customers in overcoming manufacturing challenges related to cost, quality, time-to-market and rapidly changing technologies. It offers end-to-end services covering entire product lifecycles, from design to fulfillment and after-market services; Celestica refers to this strategy as Total Cost of Ownership. The firm's CoreSim Technology aims to help customers minimize design spins, get products ready for market faster and improve manufacturing yields. Additionally, the company offers Green Services, which help customers comply with various international environmental regulations. Celestica's clients have included over 100 OEMs, such as IBM; Avaya; Cisco Systems; Hewlett Packard; Motorola; Alcatel-Lucent; Research in Motion; and Sun Microsystems. Its products and services contribute to the completion of various end products, including networking, wireless, telecommunications and computing equipment; handheld communications devices; peripherals; storage devices; servers; medical products; audio-visual equipment, including flat-panel televisions; printers and related supplies; gaming products; aerospace and defense electronics such as in-flight entertainment and guidance systems; and a range of industrial electronic equipment. In January 2010, Celestica acquired Invec Solutions, a Scottish company that provides repair, warranty management and parts management services to consumer electronics and information technology firms. In August 2010, the company acquired Austrian medical engineering and manufacturing service firm Allied Panels Entwicklungs-und Produktions Gmbh.

FINANCIALS: Sales and profits are in thousands of dollars—add 000 to get the full amount. 2010 Note: Financial information for 2010 was not available for all companies at press time.

2010 Sales: $	2010 Profits: $	**U.S. Stock Ticker:** CLS	
2009 Sales: $6,092,200	2009 Profits: $55,000	**Int'l Ticker:** CLS **Int'l Exchange:** Toronto-TSX	
2008 Sales: $7,678,200	2008 Profits: $-720,500	**Employees:** 33,000	
2007 Sales: $8,070,400	2007 Profits: $-13,700	**Fiscal Year Ends:** 12/31	
2006 Sales: $8,811,700	2006 Profits: $-150,600	**Parent Company:**	

SALARIES/BENEFITS:

Pension Plan: Y	ESOP Stock Plan:	Profit Sharing:	Top Exec. Salary: $1,006,159	Bonus: $910,524
Savings Plan:	Stock Purch. Plan:		Second Exec. Salary: $515,154	Bonus: $365,403

OTHER THOUGHTS:

Apparent Women Officers or Directors: 3
Hot Spot for Advancement for Women/Minorities: Y

LOCATIONS: ("Y" = Yes)

West:	Southwest:	Midwest:	Southeast:	Northeast:	International:
Y	Y				Y

Note: Financial information, benefits and other data can change quickly and may vary from those stated here.

CGI GROUP INC

www.cgi.com

Industry Group Code: 541513 Ranks within this company's industry group: Sales: 14   Profits: 10

Hardware:	Software:		Telecommunications:	Electronic Publishing:	Equipment:	Specialty Services:	
Computers:	Consumer:		Local:	Online Service:	Telecom:	Consulting:	Y
Accessories:	Corporate:	Y	Long Distance:	TV/Cable or Wireless:	Communication:	Contract Manufacturing:	
Network Equipment:	Telecom:		Cellular:	Games:	Distribution:	Processing:	
Chips/Circuits:	Internet:		Internet Service:	Financial Data:	VAR/Reseller:	Staff/Outsourcing:	Y
Parts/Drives:					Satellite Srv./Equip.:	Specialty Services:	Y

TYPES OF BUSINESS:

IT Consulting
Systems Management Services
Systems Development & Integration
Business Process Outsourcing

BRANDS/DIVISIONS/AFFILIATES:

CGI Technologies and Solutions, Inc.
CGI Federal, Inc.
Stanley, Inc.

CONTACTS: Note: Officers with more than one job title may be intentionally listed here more than once.

Michael E. Roach, CEO
Michael E. Roach, Pres.
David Anderson, CFO/Exec. VP
Luc Pinard, Chief Tech. & Quality Officer/Exec. VP
Benoit Dube, Chief Legal Officer/Exec. VP
Claude Seguin, Sr. VP-Corp. Dev.
Andre Imbeau, Exec. Vice Chmn./Corp. Sec.
Nazzic Turner, Sr. VP/Gen. Mgr.-U.S. Enterprise Markets
George D. Schindler, Pres., CGI Federal
Robert D. Hannum, Jr., Sr. VP-U.S. East
Serge Godin, Exec. Chmn.
Donna Morea, Pres., U.S., Europe & Asia

Phone: 514-841-3200	Fax: 514-841-3299
Toll-Free:	
Address: 1130 Sherbrooke St. W., 7th Fl., Montreal, QC H3A 2M8 Canada	

GROWTH PLANS/SPECIAL FEATURES:

CGI Group, Inc., based in Canada, is one of the largest independent information technology (IT) services companies in the world, with more than 125 offices in 16 countries. The firm offers its services to clients in a variety of sectors, including financial services, telecommunications, government, healthcare, utilities, retail, distribution and manufacturing. The company offers its clients four primary types of services: systems integration and consulting, technology management, application management and business process services. CGI's systems integration and consulting segment provides a full range of IT management, consulting and implementation services that cover the entire enterprise environment. The company's technology management services allow clients to delegate partial or complete responsibility for their IT functions to the firm. CGI's application management services provide day-to-day maintenance and updating of a client's business applications. The firm's business process services help streamline client operations through management of back-office business processes and transactions. CGI's outsourcing contracts include services such as the following: development and integration of new projects and applications; application maintenance and support; technology management, including enterprise and end-user computing and network services; and business processing, including payroll services, document management and finance and administration services. The company has technology alliances with firms such as Bell, Microsoft, Oracle, SAP, Sun Microsystems and IBM. The firm maintains some 15 wholly-owned subsidiaries, most of which manage company activities in various world regions; subsidiary CGI Technologies and Solutions, Inc. oversees CGI's U.S. operations, while CGI Federal, Inc. offers IT services to the civilian, defense and intelligence sectors of the U.S. Federal Government. In August 2010, the company acquired Stanley, Inc., an IT service company that serves defense, intelligence and federal civilian government agencies.

CGI provides its employees with various benefits, including life and disability insurance; wellness programs; and counseling services.

FINANCIALS: Sales and profits are in thousands of dollars—add 000 to get the full amount. 2010 Note: Financial information for 2010 was not available for all companies at press time.

2010 Sales: $3,732,117	2010 Profits: $362,766	U.S. Stock Ticker: GIB
2009 Sales: $3,825,160	2009 Profits: $303,180	Int'l Ticker: GIB Int'l Exchange: Toronto-TSX
2008 Sales: $3,550,260	2008 Profits: $280,820	Employees:
2007 Sales: $3,481,360	2007 Profits: $227,330	Fiscal Year Ends: 9/30
2006 Sales: $2,962,550	2006 Profits: $124,830	Parent Company:

SALARIES/BENEFITS:

Pension Plan:	ESOP Stock Plan:	Profit Sharing: Y	Top Exec. Salary: $879,111	Bonus: $807,832
Savings Plan: Y	Stock Purch. Plan: Y		Second Exec. Salary: $879,111	Bonus: $666,454

OTHER THOUGHTS:

Apparent Women Officers or Directors: 3
Hot Spot for Advancement for Women/Minorities: Y

LOCATIONS: ("Y" = Yes)

West:	Southwest:	Midwest:	Southeast:	Northeast:	International:
Y	Y	Y	Y	Y	Y

CHECK POINT SOFTWARE TECHNOLOGIES LTD

www.checkpoint.com

Industry Group Code: 511210E Ranks within this company's industry group: Sales: 5 Profits: 1

Hardware:	Software:		Telecommunications:	Electronic Publishing:	Equipment:	Specialty Services:
Computers:	Consumer:		Local:	Online Service:	Telecom:	Consulting:
Accessories:	Corporate:	Y	Long Distance:	TV/Cable or Wireless:	Communication:	Contract Manufacturing:
Network Equipment:	Telecom:		Cellular:	Games:	Distribution:	Processing:
Chips/Circuits:	Internet:		Internet Service:	Financial Data:	VAR/Reseller:	Staff/Outsourcing:
Parts/Drives:					Satellite Srv./Equip.:	Specialty Services:

TYPES OF BUSINESS:

Software-Internet Security
Firewall Software
VPN Software
Support Services

BRANDS/DIVISIONS/AFFILIATES:

NGX
Pointsec
FireWall-1
VPN-1
ClusterXL
Check Point Power-1
Check Point Full Disk Encryption
Check Point Software Blades

CONTACTS: Note: Officers with more than one job title may be intentionally listed here more than once.

Gil Shwed, CEO
Tal Payne, CFO
Juliette Sultan, VP-Global Mktg.
Dorit Dor, VP-Prod.
John Slavitt, General Counsel
Amnon Bar-Lev, VP-Global Field Oper.
Gil Shwed, Chmn.

Phone: 972-3-753-4555	Fax: 972-3-575-9256
Toll-Free: 800-429-4391	
Address: 5 Ha'Solelim St., Tel Aviv, 67897 Israel	

GROWTH PLANS/SPECIAL FEATURES:

Check Point Software Technologies, Ltd. specializes in Internet security. The firm develops, markets and supports a range of network security, data security and management software and combined hardware/software products. Many of the company's network security solutions operate through its NGX platform, which provides a unified security architecture; central management and enforcement of security policy; and centralized, real-time security updates. Check Point also offers data security solutions through its Pointsec product line, which protects and encrypts sensitive corporate information stored on mobile devices such as smartphones and PDAs. The firm's Software Blades are flexible and independent security modules that allow customers to build custom-designed Check Point Security Gateway systems. The company's Open Platform for Security (OPSEC) framework allows customers to extend the capabilities of its products and services, enabling integration with leading hardware appliances and third-party security software applications. Check Point's products and services include firewall and virtual private network (VPN) gateways; firewall and VPN security appliances; dedicated security gateways; endpoint security; data security; security management; and enterprise based support, collaborative enterprise support and real-time security update subscription. Check Point's FireWall-1 product is a security suite that integrates access control, authentication, encryption, network address translation, content security and auditing. Check Point's VPN-1 product family establishes confidential communication channels for site-to-site, remote access and extranets. ClusterXL is an add-on module to VPN-1 and FireWall-1, allowing security administrators to run different modules in high-availability or load-sharing modes. Recent acquisitions include the security appliance operations of Nokia Corporation; the application database of Facetime Communications; and a data security startup firm, Liquid Machines.

FINANCIALS: Sales and profits are in thousands of dollars—add 000 to get the full amount. 2010 Note: Financial information for 2010 was not available for all companies at press time.

2010 Sales: $	2010 Profits: $	U.S. Stock Ticker: CHKP
2009 Sales: $924,417	2009 Profits: $357,523	Int'l Ticker: CPW Int'l Exchange: Frankfurt-Euronext
2008 Sales: $575,141	2008 Profits: $278,027	Employees: 225
2007 Sales: $730,877	2007 Profits: $281,064	Fiscal Year Ends: 12/31
2006 Sales: $575,141	2006 Profits: $278,027	Parent Company:

SALARIES/BENEFITS:

Pension Plan:	ESOP Stock Plan:	Profit Sharing:	Top Exec. Salary: $	Bonus: $
Savings Plan:	Stock Purch. Plan:		Second Exec. Salary: $	Bonus: $

OTHER THOUGHTS:

Apparent Women Officers or Directors: 3
Hot Spot for Advancement for Women/Minorities: Y

LOCATIONS: ("Y" = Yes)

West:	Southwest:	Midwest:	Southeast:	Northeast:	International:
Y	Y	Y	Y	Y	Y

CHEETAHMAIL INC
www.cheetahmail.com

Industry Group Code: 511210K Ranks within this company's industry group: Sales: Profits:

Hardware:	Software:		Telecommunications:	Electronic Publishing:	Equipment:	Specialty Services:	
Computers:	Consumer:		Local:	Online Service:	Telecom:	Consulting:	Y
Accessories:	Corporate:	Y	Long Distance:	TV/Cable or Wireless:	Communication:	Contract Manufacturing:	
Network Equipment:	Telecom:		Cellular:	Games:	Distribution:	Processing:	
Chips/Circuits:	Internet:		Internet Service:	Financial Data:	VAR/Reseller:	Staff/Outsourcing:	
Parts/Drives:					Satellite Srv./Equip.:	Specialty Services:	Y

TYPES OF BUSINESS:
E-Mail Marketing Services
Customer Analysis
Web Site Analysis & Services

BRANDS/DIVISIONS/AFFILIATES:
Experian Group Limited
SiteClarity

CONTACTS: Note: Officers with more than one job title may be intentionally listed here more than once.
Matthew Seeley, Pres.
Josh McBride, VP-Sales
Tushar Angre, VP-Oper.
Michael Bordash, VP-Dev.
Rachel Bergman, Sr. VP/Gen. Mgr.
Ben Isaacson, Privacy Leader
Steve Lomax, Managing Dir.-CheetahMail Europe

Phone: 212-809-0825	Fax: 212-863-4490
Toll-Free:	
Address: 29 Broadway, 6th. Fl., New York, NY 10006 US	

GROWTH PLANS/SPECIAL FEATURES:

Cheetahmail, Inc., a subsidiary of Experian Group Limited, provides clients with online marketing tools and strategies. The company's services are customized for a wide range of clients in industries such as financial services, retail, telecommunications, utilities, media, insurance, automotive, leisure, manufacturing and government sectors. The firm's services allow companies to understand and chart the demographics, behaviors, needs and interests of their customer base, with ready access and analysis of a customer list. This information enables clients to prudently market their products online. Cheetahmail clients include Barclays; Borders Books; Neiman Marcus; KLM; and Wyndham Hotels. Client companies are not allowed to use Cheetahmail to send commercial information to unsolicited e-mail addresses. Cheetahmail's web site business, SiteClarity, redesigns company web sites based on customer behavior information, in addition to offering assistance with software, security and other online issues. The firm maintains several offices in the U.S., the U.K., New Zealand, Australia, Spain, France, Germany, Ireland, Netherlands and South Africa.

Cheetahmail's employee benefits include comprehensive health coverage, an employee assistance program; tuition reimbursement; adoption assistance; and auto and home insurances.

FINANCIALS: Sales and profits are in thousands of dollars—add 000 to get the full amount. 2010 Note: Financial information for 2010 was not available for all companies at press time.

2010 Sales: $	2010 Profits: $	U.S. Stock Ticker: Subsidiary
2009 Sales: $	2009 Profits: $	Int'l Ticker: Int'l Exchange:
2008 Sales: $	2008 Profits: $	Employees:
2007 Sales: $10,100	2007 Profits: $	Fiscal Year Ends: 3/31
2006 Sales: $	2006 Profits: $	Parent Company: EXPERIAN GROUP LIMITED

SALARIES/BENEFITS:

Pension Plan:	ESOP Stock Plan:	Profit Sharing:	Top Exec. Salary: $	Bonus: $
Savings Plan: Y	Stock Purch. Plan: Y		Second Exec. Salary: $	Bonus: $

OTHER THOUGHTS:
Apparent Women Officers or Directors: 1
Hot Spot for Advancement for Women/Minorities:

LOCATIONS: ("Y" = Yes)

West:	Southwest:	Midwest:	Southeast:	Northeast:	International:
Y				Y	Y

CHICONY ELECTRONICS CO LTD

www.chicony.com.tw

Industry Group Code: 334119 Ranks within this company's industry group: Sales: 14   Profits: 7

Hardware:		Software:		Telecommunications:		Electronic Publishing:		Equipment:		Specialty Services:	
Computers:		Consumer:		Local:		Online Service:		Telecom:		Consulting:	
Accessories:	Y	Corporate:		Long Distance:		TV/Cable or Wireless:		Communication:		Contract Manufacturing:	Y
Network Equipment:		Telecom:		Cellular:		Games:		Distribution:		Processing:	
Chips/Circuits:		Internet:		Internet Service:		Financial Data:		VAR/Reseller:		Staff/Outsourcing:	
Parts/Drives:								Satellite Srv./Equip.:		Specialty Services:	

TYPES OF BUSINESS:
Computer Peripherals Manufacturing
Consumer Electronics Manufacturing

BRANDS/DIVISIONS/AFFILIATES:
Eagle
Panda
Dragon
Chicony Electronics GmbH
Chicony Electronics CEZ SRO
Chicony America Inc

CONTACTS: *Note: Officers with more than one job title may be intentionally listed here more than once.*
Maogui Lin, Gen. Mgr.
Lin Yuling, CFO
Jinzong Lu, Chief Mktg. Officer
Shaolong Chen, Gen. Mgr.-Germany Branch
Maogui Lin, Vice Chmn.
Kuntai Xu, Chmn.
Yaoqing Zhang, Gen. Mgr.-U.S. Branch

Phone: 886-02-2298-8120	Fax: 886-02-2298-8442
Toll-Free:	
Address: No. 25, Wu-Gong 6th. Rd., Wu-Ku Industrial Park, Taipei, Taiwan	

GROWTH PLANS/SPECIAL FEATURES:

Chicony Electronics Co. Ltd. is a Taiwan-based manufacturer of computers and computer peripherals. The company's product portfolio includes desktop and mobile keyboards, digital cameras, personal computer (PC) cameras and digital video cameras. Keyboard products include standard desktop models, cordless keyboards, multimedia keyboards, backlit keyboards, numeric keypads and wireless mice. Digital cameras include the company's Eagle 3 and Eagle 5 models. The firm's PC cameras include its Panda brand of notebook and desktop cameras. Chicony's handheld digital video cameras are marketed under its Dragon brand name. Chicony is a major supplier of power supplies and webcams for Microsoft's Xbox 360 video game console. The firm also provides keyboards, adaptors, webcam modules and other components for netbook computers produced by such companies as Asustek Computer, Acer, Hewlett-Packard (HP) and other international vendors. Subsidiaries of the company include Chicony Electronics GmbH, in Germany; Chicony Electronics CEZ S.R.O., in Czech Republic; and Chicony America Inc., in Irvine, California. Chicony also maintains sales offices in Japan, as well as manufacturing, marketing and sales offices in mainland China.

FINANCIALS: Sales and profits are in thousands of dollars—add 000 to get the full amount. 2010 Note: Financial information for 2010 was not available for all companies at press time.

2010 Sales: $	2010 Profits: $	**U.S. Stock Ticker:**
2009 Sales: $1,857,710	2009 Profits: $114,700	**Int'l Ticker: 2385** Int'l Exchange: Taipei-TPE
2008 Sales: $1,518,620	2008 Profits: $91,010	Employees:
2007 Sales: $1,286,120	2007 Profits: $84,390	Fiscal Year Ends: 12/31
2006 Sales: $	2006 Profits: $	Parent Company:

SALARIES/BENEFITS:

Pension Plan:	ESOP Stock Plan: Y	Profit Sharing:	Top Exec. Salary: $	Bonus: $
Savings Plan: Y	Stock Purch. Plan:		Second Exec. Salary: $	Bonus: $

OTHER THOUGHTS:
Apparent Women Officers or Directors:
Hot Spot for Advancement for Women/Minorities:

LOCATIONS: ("Y" = Yes)

West:	Southwest:	Midwest:	Southeast:	Northeast:	International:
Y					Y

CHIMEI INNOLUX CORPORATION   www.chimei-innolux.com

Industry Group Code: 334119 Ranks within this company's industry group: Sales: 7 Profits: 20

Hardware:	Software:	Telecommunications:	Electronic Publishing:	Equipment:	Specialty Services:
Computers:	Consumer:	Local:	Online Service:	Telecom:	Consulting:
Accessories:	Corporate:	Long Distance:	TV/Cable or Wireless:	Communication:	Contract Manufacturing:
Network Equipment:	Telecom:	Cellular:	Games:	Distribution:	Processing:
Chips/Circuits:	Internet:	Internet Service:	Financial Data:	VAR/Reseller:	Staff/Outsourcing:
Parts/Drives: Y				Satellite Srv./Equip.:	Specialty Services:

TYPES OF BUSINESS:

Computer Accessories-Flat-Panel LCDs
OLED Displays
LCD Televisions
Medical Display Panels
Color Filters

BRANDS/DIVISIONS/AFFILIATES:

Ningbo Chi Mei Optoelectronics Ltd.
Nanhai Chi Mei Optoelectronics Ltd.
iZ3D, LLC
Chi Mei Optoelectronics
TPO Displays Corp.
Innolux Display Corp.

CONTACTS: Note: Officers with more than one job title may be intentionally listed here more than once.

Hsing-Chien Tuan, CEO
Loreta Chen, Contact-Media Rel.
Katy Chang, Contact-Investor Rel.
Jyh-Chau Wang, Pres., Southern Taiwan Science Park Branch
Chin-Lung Ting, VP
Jeff Ting-Chen Hsu, VP
Micro Cheng-Hui Chao, VP
Ching-Siang Liao, Chmn.

Phone: 886-37-586-000	Fax: 886-37-586-600
Toll-Free:	
Address: No. 160 Kesyue Rd. Chu-Nan Site Hsinchu, Jhunan Township, Taiwan	

GROWTH PLANS/SPECIAL FEATURES:

Chimei Innolux Corporation manufactures thin-film transistor liquid-crystal display (TFT-LCD) flat-panel displays, used in notebook computers, desktop monitors and LCD TVs. The firm was formed in March 2010 from the merger of Chi Mei Optoelectronics, TPO Displays Corp. and Innolux Display Corp. Its flat-panel PC monitors come in 10 sizes, ranging from 15.6- to 27-inch models, while its notebook panels come in seven sizes, ranging from 10.1- 17.3-inch models. The firm's LCD TV panels come in 10 sizes ranging from the 18.5- to 55-inch models. CMO creates 10 medical display panels in seven sizes, from 18.1- 30-inch models, with four of the 10 panels offering color displays. The company's 20 special-application displays come in eight sizes, ranging from 7- to 15.4-inch models. These displays are often used gaming machines, kiosks, vehicle and avionics displays, cash registers and digital signage. Lastly, Chimei Innolux Corporation also offers 73 audio-visual (AV), automotive/avionic and mobile device displays, in sizes ranging from 1.36- to 12.3-inch models. The company also manufactures color filters and is currently developing organic light-emitting diode (OLED) displays. The firm operates 10 manufacturing facilities, primarily located near the company's headquarters, and six Taiwan-based sales offices. It has two subsidiaries on the Chinese mainland: Ningbo Chi Mei Optoelectronics Ltd.; and Nanhai Chi Mei Optoelectronics Ltd. Chimei Innolux Corporation also maintains five international subsidiaries, headquartered in Japan, Singapore, the U.S., the Netherlands and Germany. Additionally, the firm maintains a joint venture in the U.S. with Neurol Optics, LLC and Troika VC Fund called iZ3D, LLC. This joint venture develops and markets iZ3D products for the electronic entertainment market and for commercial and professional visualization applications.

The firm offers benefits including labor and health insurance; cash incentives for three annual festivals; and various recreational activities.

FINANCIALS: Sales and profits are in thousands of dollars—add 000 to get the full amount. 2010 Note: Financial information for 2010 was not available for all companies at press time.

2010 Sales: $	2010 Profits: $	U.S. Stock Ticker:
2009 Sales: $5,630,700	2009 Profits: $-81,940	Int'l Ticker: 3481 Int'l Exchange: Taipei-TPE
2008 Sales: $5,491,480	2008 Profits: $165,820	Employees:
2007 Sales: $5,724,400	2007 Profits: $106,300	Fiscal Year Ends: 12/31
2006 Sales: $4,806,600	2006 Profits: $241,400	Parent Company:

SALARIES/BENEFITS:

Pension Plan: Y	ESOP Stock Plan:	Profit Sharing: Y	Top Exec. Salary: $	Bonus: $
Savings Plan:	Stock Purch. Plan:		Second Exec. Salary: $	Bonus: $

OTHER THOUGHTS:

Apparent Women Officers or Directors: 2
Hot Spot for Advancement for Women/Minorities: Y

LOCATIONS: ("Y" = Yes)

West:	Southwest:	Midwest:	Southeast:	Northeast:	International:
Y					Y

CHYRON CORP

www.chyron.com

Industry Group Code: 511210F Ranks within this company's industry group: Sales: 5 Profits: 3

Hardware:		Software:		Telecommunications:	Electronic Publishing:	Equipment:	Specialty Services:
Computers:		Consumer:	Y	Local:	Online Service:	Telecom:	Consulting:
Accessories:	Y	Corporate:	Y	Long Distance:	TV/Cable or Wireless:	Communication:	Contract Manufacturing:
Network Equipment:		Telecom:		Cellular:	Games:	Distribution:	Processing:
Chips/Circuits:		Internet:		Internet Service:	Financial Data:	VAR/Reseller:	Staff/Outsourcing:
Parts/Drives:						Satellite Srv./Equip.:	Specialty Services:

TYPES OF BUSINESS:

Software-Video & Audio Presentations
Graphics Systems
Video & Audio Control & Automation Systems
Content Creation Software

BRANDS/DIVISIONS/AFFILIATES:

AXIS
Lyric
Lyric Pro
CAMIO
iSQ
WAPSTR
CodiStrator
Xclyps

CONTACTS: Note: Officers with more than one job title may be intentionally listed here more than once.

Michael I. Wellesley-Wesley, CEO
Kevin Prince, COO/Sr. VP
Michael I. Wellesley-Wesley, Pres.
Jerry Kieliszak, CFO/Sr. VP
Jerry Kieliszak, Sec.
Roger L. Ogden, Chmn.

Phone: 631-845-2000	Fax: 631-845-1267
Toll-Free:	
Address: 5 Hub Dr., Melville, NY 11747 US	

GROWTH PLANS/SPECIAL FEATURES:

Chyron Corp. develops, manufactures, markets and supports hardware and software products for video and audio production and post-production. The Graphics System/CG Family comprises real-time 2D/3D serial digital video graphics-processing platforms that integrate a Windows front end with real-time graphics processing for television character generator applications. The firm's AXIS Graphics software offers the ability to generate broadcast graphics online, eliminating the need for specialized systems or software. The company's other graphics systems brand names include HyperX3, LEX3, MicroX and SOLO2. Lyric and Lyric Pro, the firm's content creation and playback software systems, can support both standard definition (SD) and high definition (HD) channels without requiring an upgrade. Lyric drives all the firm's graphic software systems, and can be manipulated through the Lyric Enhancement Interface Framework (LEIF). The Chyron Application Library (CAL) allows users to create customized, real time, high-quality broadcast graphics applications for Chyron products. Chyron's Newsroom Integration and Asset Management offerings help news producers create and share visual content across a number of servers as well as allowing producers to control playback in real time with intuitive control. These products include the brand names CAMIO, iSQ (Intelligent Sequncer), iRB (Intelligent Rundown Builder), OMS (Order Management System), MOS2WAP and WAPSTR. The firm also offers dedicated systems such as CodiStrator, which offers real-time illustration features, such as those used by sports commentators, and XClyps, which allows control over graphics playout.

Chyron offers its employees medical and dental coverage; life insurance; short- and long-term disability; a 401(k) plan; and stock options.

FINANCIALS: Sales and profits are in thousands of dollars—add 000 to get the full amount. 2010 Note: Financial information for 2010 was not available for all companies at press time.

2010 Sales: $	2010 Profits: $	U.S. Stock Ticker: CHYR
2009 Sales: $25,614	2009 Profits: $-3,117	Int'l Ticker: Int'l Exchange:
2008 Sales: $34,337	2008 Profits: $17,815	Employees: 104
2007 Sales: $32,327	2007 Profits: $3,715	Fiscal Year Ends: 12/31
2006 Sales: $26,246	2006 Profits: $3,121	Parent Company:

SALARIES/BENEFITS:

Pension Plan: Y	ESOP Stock Plan:	Profit Sharing:	Top Exec. Salary: $455,175	Bonus: $21,420
Savings Plan: Y	Stock Purch. Plan: Y		Second Exec. Salary: $201,058	Bonus: $4,731

OTHER THOUGHTS:

Apparent Women Officers or Directors:
Hot Spot for Advancement for Women/Minorities:

LOCATIONS: ("Y" = Yes)

West:	Southwest:	Midwest:	Southeast:	Northeast:	International:
				Y	Y

Note: Financial information, benefits and other data can change quickly and may vary from those stated here.

CIBER INC

www.ciber.com

Industry Group Code: 541513 Ranks within this company's industry group: Sales: 22   Profits: 21

Hardware:	Software:	Telecommunications:	Electronic Publishing:	Equipment:	Specialty Services:	
Computers:	Consumer:	Local:	Online Service:	Telecom:	Consulting:	Y
Accessories:	Corporate:	Long Distance:	TV/Cable or Wireless:	Communication:	Contract Manufacturing:	
Network Equipment:	Telecom:	Cellular:	Games:	Distribution:	Processing:	
Chips/Circuits:	Internet:	Internet Service:	Financial Data:	VAR/Reseller:	Staff/Outsourcing:	Y
Parts/Drives:				Satellite Srv./Equip.:	Specialty Services:	Y

TYPES OF BUSINESS:

IT Consulting
Application Management Outsourcing
Application Development
Enterprise Integrations
Global Security Solutions

BRANDS/DIVISIONS/AFFILIATES:

CIBER International

CONTACTS: Note: Officers with more than one job title may be intentionally listed here more than once.

David C. Peterschmidt, CEO
Mac J. Slingerlend, Pres.
Peter H. Cheesbrough, CFO/Exec. VP
Robin Caputo, VP-Mktg.
Susan Keesen, General Counsel/VP
Robin Caputo, VP-Public Rel.
Gary Kohn, VP-Investor Rel.
Chris Loffredo, Chief Acct. Officer/VP
Scott Frock, VP-IT Outsourcing
Mike Townend, VP-Mktg., Ciber Europe & Asia Pacific
Marcia M. Kim, Pres., Federal Gov't Solutions Div.
Tony Hadzi, Exec. VP/Pres., CIBER North America
Bobby G. Stevenson, Chmn.
Terje Laugerud, Exec. VP/CEO-Ciber International

Phone: 303-220-0100	Fax: 303-220-7100
Toll-Free: 800-242-3799	
Address: 6363 S. Fiddler's Green Cir., Ste. 1400, Greenwood Village, CO 80111 US	

GROWTH PLANS/SPECIAL FEATURES:

CIBER, Inc. provides system integration and information technology (IT) consulting services. The company operates in five segments: custom solutions (formerly the commercial solutions and state and local solutions divisions); federal government solutions; international solutions; U.S. ERP (formerly known as enterprise solutions); and IT outsourcing. The custom solutions segment offers application portfolio management support to U.S.-based commercial, state and local government clients, including the analysis, design, development, testing, implementation and maintenance of business applications. The federal government division provides custom IT services and support, such as strategic staffing, security assessments, legacy modernization services, data warehousing solutions and help desk support to defense and civilian agencies. The international division, CIBER International, offers IT services and support to commercial and public sector concerns primarily in the Netherlands, the U.K., Germany, Norway, Sweden, Denmark and Finland. The U.S. ERP (Enterprise Resource Planning) division provides consulting services in the U.S. to support multi-package software from enterprise vendors including Oracle, SAP and Lawson, as well as several supply chain and education management products. The IT outsourcing division specializes in services including help desks, content hosting, software rollouts, security monitoring and server virtualization through datacenters around the world. CIBER has offices across the U.S. and in 18 countries abroad.

The company offer its employees medical, dental and vision insurance; disability insurance; life insurance; flexible spending accounts; adoption assistance; computer and software discounts; and tuition assistance.

FINANCIALS: Sales and profits are in thousands of dollars—add 000 to get the full amount. 2010 Note: Financial information for 2010 was not available for all companies at press time.

2010 Sales: $	2010 Profits: $	**U.S. Stock Ticker:** CBR
2009 Sales: $1,037,700	2009 Profits: $14,958	**Int'l Ticker:** Int'l Exchange:
2008 Sales: $1,191,567	2008 Profits: $26,884	Employees: 8,000
2007 Sales: $1,081,975	2007 Profits: $23,951	Fiscal Year Ends: 12/31
2006 Sales: $995,837	2006 Profits: $24,735	Parent Company:

SALARIES/BENEFITS:

Pension Plan:	ESOP Stock Plan:	Profit Sharing:	Top Exec. Salary: $630,000	Bonus: $232,200
Savings Plan: Y	Stock Purch. Plan: Y		Second Exec. Salary: $368,950	Bonus: $192,350

OTHER THOUGHTS:

Apparent Women Officers or Directors: 4
Hot Spot for Advancement for Women/Minorities: Y

LOCATIONS: ("Y" = Yes)

West:	Southwest:	Midwest:	Southeast:	Northeast:	International:
Y	Y	Y	Y	Y	Y

CICERO INC
www.ciceroinc.com

Industry Group Code: 511210K Ranks within this company's industry group: Sales: 11 Profits: 9

Hardware:	Software:		Telecommunications:	Electronic Publishing:	Equipment:	Specialty Services:	
Computers:	Consumer:		Local:	Online Service:	Telecom:	Consulting:	Y
Accessories:	Corporate:	Y	Long Distance:	TV/Cable or Wireless:	Communication:	Contract Manufacturing:	
Network Equipment:	Telecom:		Cellular:	Games:	Distribution:	Processing:	
Chips/Circuits:	Internet:		Internet Service:	Financial Data:	VAR/Reseller:	Staff/Outsourcing:	
Parts/Drives:					Satellite Srv./Equip.:	Specialty Services:	Y

TYPES OF BUSINESS:

Software-Business Integration
Technology Consulting Services
E-Mail Security Products
Customer Relationship Management Software

BRANDS/DIVISIONS/AFFILIATES:

Level 8 Systems, Inc.
Cicero Integrator
Cicero XM Integrator
Cicero XM Desktop
Cicero XM Enterprise
Cicero XM Studio
SOAdesk LLC

CONTACTS: Note: Officers with more than one job title may be intentionally listed here more than once.

John Broderick, CEO
John Broderick, CFO
Tony Castagno, CTO
James W. Hunt, Dir.-Prod. Dev.
John P. Broderick, Corp. Sec.
Neil Crane, Dir.-Prod. Strategy
Mike Garner, Chief Customer Officer
Hal Harris, Dir.-Professional Svcs.
Clint Babcock, Dir.-Pre-Sales & Partner Support
Alex Aversano, Dir.-Alliances
John Steffens, Chmn.

Phone: 919-380-5000	Fax: 919-380-5121
Toll-Free:	
Address: 8000 Regency Pkwy., Ste. 542, Cary, NC 27518 US	

GROWTH PLANS/SPECIAL FEATURES:

Cicero, Inc. (formerly Level 8 Systems, Inc.) is a global provider of patented business software that enables organizations to integrate new and existing information and processes at the desktop. The firm produces business integration software for contact centers, customer relationship management (CRM) and professionals in the financial, insurance, telecommunications, intelligence, security, governmental and law enforcement sectors. The Cicero software line is a business application integration program that maximizes end-user productivity, streamlines business operations and integrates systems and applications. The software provides automatic information sharing among all line-of-business applications and tools to leverage existing IT structures, and can interact with Windows applications, web pages, commercial software packages, legacy applications and Java applications. Its products include Cicero Integrator, a desktop program that connects various enterprise software applications; Cicero XM Integrator, which adds a customizable interface and other features; Cicero XM Desktop, which combines XM Integrator with scripting functions; Cicero XM Enterprise, which delivers communications, telephony and computer telephony integration capabilities including presence, IM and email to reduce the need for multiple contact center systems; and Cicero XM Studio, which allows non-IT staff to build and enhance back-end integrations, scripts, smart workflows and composite screens without any impact on underlying applications or business logic. Cicero provides technical support, training and consulting services across all of its operating segments. The firm's software operates in Windows 2000, XP, Vista and 7 environments. In January 2010, the company acquired SOAdesk, LLC, which develops customer care software for desktop users.

FINANCIALS: Sales and profits are in thousands of dollars—add 000 to get the full amount. 2010 Note: Financial information for 2010 was not available for all companies at press time.

2010 Sales: $	2010 Profits: $	U.S. Stock Ticker: CICN
2009 Sales: $2,498	2009 Profits: $-1,280	Int'l Ticker: Int'l Exchange:
2008 Sales: $3,452	2008 Profits: $- 823	Employees: 25
2007 Sales: $1,808	2007 Profits: $-1,975	Fiscal Year Ends: 12/31
2006 Sales: $ 972	2006 Profits: $-2,997	Parent Company:

SALARIES/BENEFITS:

Pension Plan:	ESOP Stock Plan:	Profit Sharing:	Top Exec. Salary: $175,000	Bonus: $25,000
Savings Plan:	Stock Purch. Plan:		Second Exec. Salary: $	Bonus: $

OTHER THOUGHTS:

Apparent Women Officers or Directors:
Hot Spot for Advancement for Women/Minorities:

LOCATIONS: ("Y" = Yes)

West:	Southwest:	Midwest:	Southeast:	Northeast:	International:
				Y	Y

CIENA CORP

www.ciena.com

Industry Group Code: 334210 Ranks within this company's industry group: Sales: 9   Profits: 13

Hardware:		Software:		Telecommunications:		Electronic Publishing:		Equipment:		Specialty Services:	
Computers:		Consumer:		Local:		Online Service:		Telecom:	Y	Consulting:	
Accessories:		Corporate:		Long Distance:		TV/Cable or Wireless:		Communication:	Y	Contract Manufacturing:	
Network Equipment:	Y	Telecom:		Cellular:		Games:		Distribution:		Processing:	
Chips/Circuits:		Internet:		Internet Service:		Financial Data:		VAR/Reseller:		Staff/Outsourcing:	
Parts/Drives:								Satellite Srv./Equip.:		Specialty Services:	

TYPES OF BUSINESS:

Communications Networking Equipment
Software & Support Services
Consulting Services
Switching Platforms
Packet Interworking Products
Access Products
Network & Service Management Tools

BRANDS/DIVISIONS/AFFILIATES:

ActivEdge 3000 Series
ActivEdge 5000 Series
ActivFlex 5400 Series
CoreDirector FS
ActivSpan 4200 Series
ActivSpan 5100/5200
ActivFlex 6500
Ciena One Software Suite

CONTACTS: Note: Officers with more than one job title may be intentionally listed here more than once.

Gary B. Smith, CEO
Gary B. Smith, Pres.
James E. Moylan, Jr., CFO/Sr. VP-Finance
Thomas Mock, Sr. VP-Corp. Mktg.
Randall Harris, Sr. VP-Global Human Resources
Stephen B. Alexander, CTO/Sr. VP-Tech.
Stephen B. Alexander, Sr. VP-Prod.
David M. Rothenstein, General Counsel/Sr. VP/Corp. Sec.
Michael G. Aquino, Sr. VP-Global Field Oper.
James Frodsham, Chief Strategy Officer/Sr. VP
Andrew Petrik, Controller/VP
Philippe Morin, Sr. VP-Global Prod. Group
Patrick H. Nettles, Chmn.
Rick Dodd, Sr. VP-Global Mktg.

Phone: 410-694-5700	Fax: 410-694-5750
Toll-Free: 800-921-1144	
Address: 1201 Winterson Rd., Linthicum, MD 21090 US	

GROWTH PLANS/SPECIAL FEATURES:

Ciena Corp. is a provider of communications networking equipment, software and services that support the transport, switching, aggregation and management of voice, video and data traffic. Its product portfolio includes a range of communications networking equipment and software that is utilized from the core of communications networks, from metropolitan network infrastructures to the network edge, where end users gain access to communications services. Products are offered in four major categories: carrier Ethernet service delivery devices, packet-optical switching devices, packet-optical transport devices and the Ciena One software suite. Carrier Ethernet service delivery devices are designed to provide intelligent access to high-speed Ethernet networks. Products in this category include the ActivEdge 3000 Series, the ActivEdge 5000 Series and the ActivFlex 5400 Series. Packet-optical switching devices are designed to provision and automate bandwidth to prevent slowdowns and overloads. Products in this category include the ActivFlex 5400 Series and the CoreDirector FS multiservice optical switch. Packet-optical transport devices are designed to provide scalable additions to an existing network. These products include the ActivSpan 4200 Series, the ActivSpan 5100/5200 and the ActivFlex 6500. The Ciena One software suite monitors and manages the functions of a network, including switching control and gateway management. Products include the On-Center Network and Services Management Suite and the CatenaView EMS voice, data and video operator. Ciena also offers consulting and technical implementation advice. The firm sells its communications networking equipment, software and services through direct sales efforts and channel relationships. The company services a wide variety of industries, including telecommunications, government, financial services, health care and education.

The company offers its employees medical, dental and vision insurance; short- and long-term disability insurance; flexible spending accounts; business travel accident and life insurance; stock options; a 401(k) plan; an employee stock purchase plan; an employee assistance program; and educational assistance.

FINANCIALS: Sales and profits are in thousands of dollars—add 000 to get the full amount. 2010 Note: Financial information for 2010 was not available for all companies at press time.

2010 Sales: $1,236,636	2010 Profits: $-333,514	**U.S. Stock Ticker: CIEN**
2009 Sales: $652,629	2009 Profits: $-581,154	**Int'l Ticker:** Int'l Exchange:
2008 Sales: $902,448	2008 Profits: $38,894	Employees: 4,201
2007 Sales: $779,769	2007 Profits: $82,788	Fiscal Year Ends: 10/31
2006 Sales: $564,056	2006 Profits: $ 595	Parent Company:

SALARIES/BENEFITS:

Pension Plan:	ESOP Stock Plan:	Profit Sharing:	Top Exec. Salary: $650,000	Bonus: $
Savings Plan: Y	Stock Purch. Plan: Y		Second Exec. Salary: $400,000	Bonus: $

OTHER THOUGHTS:

Apparent Women Officers or Directors: 1
Hot Spot for Advancement for Women/Minorities:

LOCATIONS: ("Y" = Yes)

West:	Southwest:	Midwest:	Southeast:	Northeast:	International:
Y	Y	Y	Y	Y	Y

CIRRUS LOGIC INC

www.cirrus.com

Industry Group Code: 33441 Ranks within this company's industry group: Sales: 50 Profits: 33

Hardware:	Software:		Telecommunications:	Electronic Publishing:	Equipment:	Specialty Services:
Computers:	Consumer:		Local:	Online Service:	Telecom:	Consulting:
Accessories:	Corporate:		Long Distance:	TV/Cable or Wireless:	Communication:	Contract Manufacturing:
Network Equipment:	Telecom:		Cellular:	Games:	Distribution:	Processing:
Chips/Circuits: Y	Internet:		Internet Service:	Financial Data:	VAR/Reseller:	Staff/Outsourcing:
Parts/Drives:					Satellite Srv./Equip.:	Specialty Services:

TYPES OF BUSINESS:

Integrated Circuits-Analog & Digital
DSP Chips
Audio Chips

BRANDS/DIVISIONS/AFFILIATES:

Cirrus
CobraNet
Apex Precision Power
SA303-IHZ (The)
SA53-IHZ (The)
CS5374 (The)

CONTACTS: Note: Officers with more than one job title may be intentionally listed here more than once.

Jason Rhode, CEO
Jason Rhode, Pres.
Thurman K. Case, CFO
Timothy R. Turk, VP-Worldwide Sales
Jo-Dee M. Benson, VP-Human Resources
Gregory Scott Thomas, General Counsel/Corp. Sec./VP
Jo-Dee M. Benson, VP-Corp. Comm.
Thurman K. Case, VP-Finance/Treas.
Greg Brennan, VP/Gen. Mgr.-Apex Precision Power Bus. Unit
Scott Anderson, Sr. VP/Gen. Mgr.-Mixed Signal Audio Div.
Lewis Venters, VP-Corp. Quality
Tom Stein, VP/Gen. Mgr.-Energy, Exploration & Lighting Div.
Michael L. Hackworth, Chmn.
Randy Carlson, VP-Supply Chain Mgmt.

Phone: 512-851-4000	Fax: 512-851-4977
Toll-Free: 800-888-5016	
Address: 2901 Via Fortuna, Austin, TX 78746 US	

GROWTH PLANS/SPECIAL FEATURES:

Cirrus Logic, Inc. is a developer of analog, high-precision and mixed-signal integrated circuits (ICs) for a broad range of audio and energy industries. The company also produces audio chips for high-volume audio, storage and communications applications providers. With regard to audio products, Cirrus Logic offers high-precision analog components, mixed-signal components and audio digital signal processor (DSP) products for consumer, professional and automotive entertainment markets. Cirrus Logic offers a broad line of products under the Cirrus Logic name as well as the Cirrus, Apex Precision Power and CobraNet brands. These brands allow system-level applications in mass storage (magnetic and optical), audio (professional, consumer and PC) and precision data conversion (16 bits and higher). These products include DSPs and CODECs for A/V receivers, DVD receivers, DVD recorders and portable players; analog-to-digital and digital-to-analog converters, CODECs and other components optimized for professional audio applications; embedded processor solutions; and automotive electronics components. Cirrus Logic's energy products include high-precision analog and mixed-signal components for energy-related applications, such as energy measurement, energy exploration and energy control systems; and board-level modules, ICs and hybrids for high-power pulse width modulation and power amplifier applications. The firm owns over 1,000 patents. It offers more than 700 products that serve over 2,500 end customers worldwide through both direct and distributor-based channel sales. Recent products introduced by the company include the SA303-IHZ and SA53-IHZ high current pulse width modulated ICs; and the CS5374, a low-noise marine streamer solution.

The firm offers its employees benefits including health, dental, vision, life and disability insurance; a 401(k) plan; health and dependent care reimbursement accounts; an employee stock option plan; paid time off and holidays; tuition reimbursement; and an employee assistance program.

FINANCIALS: Sales and profits are in thousands of dollars—add 000 to get the full amount. 2010 Note: Financial information for 2010 was not available for all companies at press time.

2010 Sales: $220,989	2010 Profits: $38,398	U.S. Stock Ticker: CRUS
2009 Sales: $174,642	2009 Profits: $3,475	Int'l Ticker: Int'l Exchange:
2008 Sales: $181,885	2008 Profits: $-5,846	Employees: 505
2007 Sales: $182,304	2007 Profits: $27,895	Fiscal Year Ends: 3/31
2006 Sales: $193,694	2006 Profits: $52,426	Parent Company:

SALARIES/BENEFITS:

Pension Plan:	ESOP Stock Plan:	Profit Sharing:	Top Exec. Salary: $390,000	Bonus: $193,971
Savings Plan: Y	Stock Purch. Plan: Y		Second Exec. Salary: $275,000	Bonus: $91,183

OTHER THOUGHTS:

Apparent Women Officers or Directors: 1
Hot Spot for Advancement for Women/Minorities:

LOCATIONS: ("Y" = Yes)

West:	Southwest:	Midwest:	Southeast:	Northeast:	International:
Y	Y				Y

CISCO SYSTEMS INC

www.cisco.com

Industry Group Code: 33411 Ranks within this company's industry group: Sales: 1 Profits: 1

Hardware:		Software:		Telecommunications:		Electronic Publishing:		Equipment:		Specialty Services:	
Computers:		Consumer:		Local:		Online Service:		Telecom:	Y	Consulting:	
Accessories:	Y	Corporate:	Y	Long Distance:		TV/Cable or Wireless:		Communication:	Y	Contract Manufacturing:	
Network Equipment:	Y	Telecom:	Y	Cellular:		Games:		Distribution:		Processing:	
Chips/Circuits:		Internet:		Internet Service:		Financial Data:		VAR/Reseller:		Staff/Outsourcing:	
Parts/Drives:	Y							Satellite Srv./Equip.:		Specialty Services:	Y

TYPES OF BUSINESS:

Computer Networking Equipment
Routers & Switches
Real-Time Conferencing Technology
Server Virtualization Software
Data Storage Products
Security Products
Teleconference Systems and Technology
Unified Communications Systems

BRANDS/DIVISIONS/AFFILIATES:

Scientific Atlanta Inc
Webex Communications Inc
Tandberg
Cisco United Communications
Flip Video
Unified Computing Systems

CONTACTS: *Note: Officers with more than one job title may be intentionally listed here more than once.*

John T. Chambers, CEO
Frank A. Calderoni, CFO/Exec. VP
Susan L. Bostrom, Chief Mktg. Officer/Exec. VP
Brian Schipper, Sr. VP-Human Resources
Gregory Akers, Sr. VP-R&D
Rebecca Jacoby, CIO/Sr. VP
Mark Chandler, General Counsel/Sr. VP-Legal Svcs./Sec.
Robert Lloyd, Exec. VP-Worldwide Oper.
Ned Hooper, Chief Strategy Officer/Sr. VP-Consumer Bus.
Blair Christie, Sr. VP-Global Corp. Comm.
Wim Elfrink, Chief Globalization Officer/Exec. VP-Cisco Svcs.
Wendy Bahr, Sr. VP-Global & Transformational Partnerships
Marthin De Beer, Sr. VP-Emerging Tech. Bus. Group
Randy Pond, Exec. VP-Oper., Processes & Systems
John T. Chambers, Chmn.
Edzard Overbeek, Pres., Asia Pacific & Japan

Phone: 408-526-4000	Fax: 408-526-4100
Toll-Free: 800-553-6387	
Address: 170 W. Tasman Dr., San Jose, CA 95134 US	

GROWTH PLANS/SPECIAL FEATURES:

Cisco Systems, Inc. designs, develops, manufactures and markets Internet protocol (IP)-based networking and other products related to the communications and information technology industries, and provides services associated with these products. The firm's products, which include routers, switches and advanced technologies, are installed at large enterprises, public institutions, telecommunications companies, commercial businesses and personal residences. Cisco divides its products into three categories: routing and switching; advanced technologies; and other products. The routing and switching category includes a variety of routers, from core network infrastructure for service providers and enterprises to access routers for branch offices and for telecommuters and consumers at home. The category also includes switching systems, which employ the use of Ethernet, Power over Ethernet, Fibre Channel over Ethernet, Packet over Synchronous Optical Network and Multiprotocol Label Switching. Its Ethernet switching applications include fixed-configuration switches for small and medium-sized businesses to modular switches for enterprises and service providers. The advanced technologies category includes application networking services; video systems; wireless technology products; home networking products, which includes adapters, gateways, modems and home network management software; security products, which include network security, physical and building security, virtual private networks (VPN), firewall and security management solutions; storage area networking products; and Cisco United Communications products, which integrate voice, video, data and mobile applications on fixed and mobile networks. The other products category insists of optical networking products, cable access, the Flip Video family of camcorder lines and service provider voice-over-IP (VoIP) services. Cisco's strategic push is now focused on Unified Computing Systems, which bundle server, storage and networking systems into one new product. Each of Cisco's new servers is capable of running hundreds of virtual servers by utilizing virtualization software. In addition to its product offerings, Cisco provides a range of product support services. The firm's business is divided by region into five segments: the U.S. and Canada, European Markets, Emerging Markets, Asia Pacific and Japan.

FINANCIALS: Sales and profits are in thousands of dollars—add 000 to get the full amount. 2010 Note: Financial information for 2010 was not available for all companies at press time.

2010 Sales: $40,040,000	2010 Profits: $7,767,000	**U.S. Stock Ticker: CSCO**
2009 Sales: $36,117,000	2009 Profits: $6,134,000	**Int'l Ticker:** Int'l Exchange:
2008 Sales: $39,540,000	2008 Profits: $8,052,000	Employees: 70,700
2007 Sales: $34,922,000	2007 Profits: $7,333,000	Fiscal Year Ends: 7/31
2006 Sales: $28,484,000	2006 Profits: $5,580,000	Parent Company:

SALARIES/BENEFITS:

Pension Plan:	ESOP Stock Plan:	Profit Sharing:	Top Exec. Salary: $815,385	Bonus: $1,600,000
Savings Plan:	Stock Purch. Plan:		Second Exec. Salary: $773,762	Bonus: $1,600,000

OTHER THOUGHTS:

Apparent Women Officers or Directors: 13
Hot Spot for Advancement for Women/Minorities: Y

LOCATIONS: ("Y" = Yes)

West:	Southwest:	Midwest:	Southeast:	Northeast:	International:
Y	Y	Y	Y	Y	Y

Note: Financial information, benefits and other data can change quickly and may vary from those stated here.

CITRIX SYSTEMS INC

www.citrix.com

Industry Group Code: 511210H **Ranks within this company's industry group:** Sales: 6 Profits: 5

Hardware:	Software:		Telecommunications:	Electronic Publishing:		Equipment:	Specialty Services:	
Computers:	Consumer:	Y	Local:	Online Service:	Y	Telecom:	Consulting:	Y
Accessories:	Corporate:	Y	Long Distance:	TV/Cable or Wireless:		Communication:	Contract Manufacturing:	
Network Equipment:	Telecom:		Cellular:	Games:		Distribution:	Processing:	
Chips/Circuits:	Internet:		Internet Service:	Financial Data:		VAR/Reseller:	Staff/Outsourcing:	
Parts/Drives:						Satellite Srv./Equip.:	Specialty Services:	

TYPES OF BUSINESS:

Computer Software-Application Server
Consulting Services
Training & Technical Support
Online Services

BRANDS/DIVISIONS/AFFILIATES:

XenApp
XenDesktop
XenServer
NetScaler
GoToMeeting
GoToAssist
GoToMyPC
Netviewer AG

CONTACTS: *Note: Officers with more than one job title may be intentionally listed here more than once.*

Mark B. Templeton, CEO
Mark B. Templeton, Pres.
David J. Henshall, CFO/Sr. VP
Wes R. Wasson, Chief Mktg. Officer/Sr. VP
David R. Friedman, Sr. VP-Human Resources
David R. Friedman, General Counsel
Frank Artale, VP-Bus. Dev.
Brett Caine, Sr. VP/Gen. Mgr.-Online Svcs. Div.
Al J. Monserrat, Sr. VP-Sales & Svcs.
Peter Levine, Sr. VP/Gen. Mgr.-Datacenter & Cloud Div.
Gordon Payne, Sr. VP/Gen. Mgr.-Desktop Div.
Michael Cristinziano, VP-Strategic Dev.
Thomas F. Bogan, Chmn.

Phone: 954-267-3000	Fax: 954-267-9319
Toll-Free: 800-424-8749	
Address: 851 W. Cypress Creek Rd., Fort Lauderdale, FL 33309 US	

GROWTH PLANS/SPECIAL FEATURES:

Citrix Systems, Inc. designs, develops and markets products that allow applications to be delivered, supported and shared on-demand with high performance, enhanced security and improved total cost of ownership. Citrix offers application delivery systems in four product groupings: desktop solutions; online services; datacenter and cloud solutions; and technical services. The firm's desktop solutions, XenApp and XenDesktop, reduce the complexity and cost of administering Windows-based applications and desktops in the enterprise. Citrix XenApp, an application virtualization tool, runs the business logic of applications on a central server, transmitting only screen pixels, keystrokes and mouse movements through an encrypted channel to users' computers. Desktop virtualization is achieved through Citrix XenDesktop, which streams desktop images through multiple virtual machines. The online services division includes products such as GoToMyPC, GoToMeeting, GoToAssist and GoToWebinar which are designed to provide web-based access to office resources for off-site locations. The datacenter and cloud solutions product group includes virtual infrastructure and application networking products. Virtual infrastructure includes the Citrix XenServer, a server virtualization solution that aggregates a pool of computing and storage resources. Citrix Essentials for XenServer adds capabilities such as lab automation, high availability, provisioning, workflow orchestration and seamless integration with storage systems to existing virtualization management systems. Application networking, through products including Citrix NetScalar, Citrix Access Gateway and Citrix Repeater, is designed to improve application performance, access datacenter resources in offsite locations, and deliver local area network-like performance over a wide area network. The technical services division provides consulting services, technical support and product training to support Citrix products. In December 2010, the firm agreed to acquire Netviewer AG.

Citrix offers its employees medical, dental, vision and life insurance; educational assistance; a 401(k) plan; a pension plan; stock options and an employee stock purchase plan; car allowances; an employee assistance plan; and onsite fitness centers.

FINANCIALS: Sales and profits are in thousands of dollars—add 000 to get the full amount. 2010 Note: Financial information for 2010 was not available for all companies at press time.

2010 Sales: $	2010 Profits: $	**U.S. Stock Ticker:** CTXS
2009 Sales: $1,614,088	2009 Profits: $191,017	**Int'l Ticker:** Int'l Exchange:
2008 Sales: $1,583,354	2008 Profits: $178,276	Employees: 4,816
2007 Sales: $1,391,942	2007 Profits: $214,483	Fiscal Year Ends: 12/31
2006 Sales: $1,134,319	2006 Profits: $182,997	Parent Company:

SALARIES/BENEFITS:

Pension Plan: Y	ESOP Stock Plan:	Profit Sharing:	Top Exec. Salary: $800,000	Bonus: $954,158
Savings Plan: Y	Stock Purch. Plan: Y		Second Exec. Salary: $435,000	Bonus: $325,107

OTHER THOUGHTS:

Apparent Women Officers or Directors:
Hot Spot for Advancement for Women/Minorities:

LOCATIONS: ("Y" = Yes)

West:	Southwest:	Midwest:	Southeast:	Northeast:	International:
Y	Y	Y	Y	Y	Y

COGNEX CORP

www.cognex.com

Industry Group Code: 334111 Ranks within this company's industry group: Sales: 28 Profits: 17

Hardware:		Software:		Telecommunications:	Electronic Publishing:	Equipment:	Specialty Services:	
Computers:	Y	Consumer:		Local:	Online Service:	Telecom:	Consulting:	
Accessories:	Y	Corporate:	Y	Long Distance:	TV/Cable or Wireless:	Communication:	Contract Manufacturing:	
Network Equipment:		Telecom:		Cellular:	Games:	Distribution:	Processing:	
Chips/Circuits:		Internet:		Internet Service:	Financial Data:	VAR/Reseller:	Staff/Outsourcing:	
Parts/Drives:						Satellite Srv./Equip.:	Specialty Services:	Y

TYPES OF BUSINESS:

Computer Hardware-Human Vision Replacement
Machine Vision Technology
Modular Vision Systems-Computers & Software
Surface Inspection Systems
Automotive Vision Technology

BRANDS/DIVISIONS/AFFILIATES:

In-Sight
DataMan
Checker
VisionPro

CONTACTS: Note: Officers with more than one job title may be intentionally listed here more than once.

Robert J. Shillman, CEO
Robert Willett, COO
Robert Willett, Pres.
Richard A. Morin, CFO
Richard A. Morin, Exec. VP-Admin.
Anthony J. Medaglia, Jr., Sec.
Robin Pratt, Sr. Mgr.-Corp. Comm.
Susan Conway, Dir.-Investor Rel.
Richard A. Morin, Exec. VP-Finance/Treas.
Thomas F. Nash, Pres., Surface Inspection Systems Div.
Robert J. Shillman, Chmn.

Phone: 508-650-3000	Fax: 508-650-3333
Toll-Free:	
Address: 1 Vision Dr., Natick, MA 01760-2059 US	

GROWTH PLANS/SPECIAL FEATURES:

Cognex Corp. develops, manufactures and markets systems used to automate manufacturing processes where vision is required. Machine vision is used for applications in which human vision is inadequate to meet requirements for feature size, accuracy or speed, or in instances where substantial cost savings are obtained through reduction of labor and improved quality. Cognex's systems are used in industries including semiconductors, electronics, automotive, consumer products, metals, plastics and paper. The company is divided into two divisions: the modular vision systems division (MVSD) and the surface inspection systems division (SISD). MVSD develops, manufactures and markets modular vision systems that are used to automate the manufacture of discrete items, such as semiconductor chips, cellular phones and light bulbs, by locating, identifying, inspecting and measuring them during the manufacturing process. MVSD generates approximately 79% of Cognex's revenue. SISD (21% of revenues) designs, develops, manufactures and markets surface inspection vision systems that are used to inspect the surfaces of materials processed in a continuous fashion, such as paper, metals, plastics and non-wovens, to ensure there are no flaws or defects on the surfaces. Cognex machine vision systems consist of two primary elements: a computer, which serves as a machine vision engine; and software that processes and analyzes images. When connected to a video camera, the machine vision system captures images and extracts information, which determines appropriate action for other equipment in the manufacturing process. The firm's machine vision products include In-Sight vision sensors; DataMan code verifiers, fixed-mount readers and handheld readers; Checker sensors; and VisionPro, an operator display panel.

Employees are offered life, AD&D, disability, long-term care, medical, dental and vision insurance; flexible spending accounts; credit union membership; stock options; tuition assistance; patent awards; product discounts; paid time off; and an employee assistance program.

FINANCIALS: Sales and profits are in thousands of dollars—add 000 to get the full amount. 2010 Note: Financial information for 2010 was not available for all companies at press time.

2010 Sales: $	2010 Profits: $	U.S. Stock Ticker: CGNX
2009 Sales: $175,727	2009 Profits: $-4,869	Int'l Ticker: Int'l Exchange:
2008 Sales: $242,680	2008 Profits: $27,275	Employees: 832
2007 Sales: $225,737	2007 Profits: $26,899	Fiscal Year Ends: 12/31
2006 Sales: $238,424	2006 Profits: $39,855	Parent Company:

SALARIES/BENEFITS:

Pension Plan:	ESOP Stock Plan:	Profit Sharing:	Top Exec. Salary: $255,981	Bonus: $
Savings Plan: Y	Stock Purch. Plan: Y		Second Exec. Salary: $249,623	Bonus: $

OTHER THOUGHTS:

Apparent Women Officers or Directors: 2
Hot Spot for Advancement for Women/Minorities:

LOCATIONS: ("Y" = Yes)

West:	Southwest:	Midwest:	Southeast:	Northeast:	International:
Y		Y	Y	Y	Y

Note: Financial information, benefits and other data can change quickly and may vary from those stated here.

COGNIZANT TECHNOLOGY SOLUTIONS CORP   www.cognizant.com

Industry Group Code: 541513 Ranks within this company's industry group: Sales: 15   Profits: 7

Hardware:	Software:	Telecommunications:	Electronic Publishing:	Equipment:	Specialty Services:	
Computers:	Consumer:	Local:	Online Service:	Telecom:	Consulting:	Y
Accessories:	Corporate:	Long Distance:	TV/Cable or Wireless:	Communication:	Contract Manufacturing:	
Network Equipment:	Telecom:	Cellular:	Games:	Distribution:	Processing:	
Chips/Circuits:	Internet:	Internet Service:	Financial Data:	VAR/Reseller:	Staff/Outsourcing:	Y
Parts/Drives:				Satellite Srv./Equip.:	Specialty Services:	

TYPES OF BUSINESS:

Consulting-IT & Systems
Outsourcing Services
Software Engineering

BRANDS/DIVISIONS/AFFILIATES:

PIPC Group (The)
Process Space
UBS India Service Centre Private Limited
Galileo Performance

CONTACTS: Note: Officers with more than one job title may be intentionally listed here more than once.

Fransisco D'Souza, CEO
Gordon J. Coburn, COO
Fransisco D'Souza, Pres.
Gordon J. Coburn, CFO
Gordon J. Coburn, Sec.
Rajeev Mehta, COO-Global Client Svcs.
Gordon J. Coburn, Treas.
John E. Klein, Chmn.
Chandra Sekaran, Pres./Managing Dir.-Global Delivery

Phone: 201-801-0233	Fax: 201-801-0243
Toll-Free: 888-937-3277	
Address: 500 Frank W. Burr Blvd., Teaneck, NJ 07666 US	

GROWTH PLANS/SPECIAL FEATURES:

Cognizant Technology Solutions Corp. specializes in custom IT design, development, integration and maintenance services. The firm provides these services primarily to Global 2000 companies located in the U.S., Europe and Asia. The company's core competencies include complex systems development; application maintenance; infrastructure management; enterprise software package implementation and maintenance; technology strategy consulting; data warehousing and business intelligence; application testing; and vertically-oriented business process outsourcing (V-BPO). Cognizant provides its IT services using an integrated on-site/offshore business model. This business model combines technical and account management teams located on-site at the customer location and offshore at dedicated development centers located primarily in India, Argentina, the U.S., the Philippines, China and Hungary. Cognizant operates in four business segments: financial services, which provides services to customers in the banking and insurance industries; healthcare, which provides services to healthcare and life science industries; manufacturing, retail and logistics, which provides services to those industries; and other, which covers communications, information services, media and high technology. The firm has developed proprietary methodologies for integrating on-site and offshore teams, including Cognizant's Process Space software engineering process, which is available to all on-site and offshore programmers. For most projects, Process Space is used as part of an initial assessment that allows the firm to define the scope and risks of the project and subdivide the project into smaller phases with frequent deliverables and feedback from customers. In late 2009, Cognizant acquired UBS India Service Centre Private Limited from UBS Group. In May 2010, the company acquired U.K.-based program management consulting firm The PIPC Group. In June 2010, the firm acquired French IT testing consulting services provider Galileo Performance.

FINANCIALS: Sales and profits are in thousands of dollars—add 000 to get the full amount. 2010 Note: Financial information for 2010 was not available for all companies at press time.

2010 Sales: $	2010 Profits: $	U.S. Stock Ticker: CTSH
2009 Sales: $3,278,663	2009 Profits: $534,963	Int'l Ticker: Int'l Exchange:
2008 Sales: $2,816,304	2008 Profits: $430,845	Employees: 78,400
2007 Sales: $2,135,577	2007 Profits: $350,133	Fiscal Year Ends: 12/31
2006 Sales: $1,424,267	2006 Profits: $232,795	Parent Company:

SALARIES/BENEFITS:

Pension Plan:	ESOP Stock Plan: Y	Profit Sharing:	Top Exec. Salary: $518,400	Bonus: $590,216
Savings Plan: Y	Stock Purch. Plan: Y		Second Exec. Salary: $466,560	Bonus: $531,195

OTHER THOUGHTS:

Apparent Women Officers or Directors: 1
Hot Spot for Advancement for Women/Minorities:

LOCATIONS: ("Y" = Yes)

West:	Southwest:	Midwest:	Southeast:	Northeast:	International:
Y	Y	Y		Y	Y

COGNOS INC

www.cognos.com

Industry Group Code: 511210H Ranks within this company's industry group: Sales: Profits:

Hardware:	Software:		Telecommunications:	Electronic Publishing:	Equipment:	Specialty Services:	
Computers:	Consumer:		Local:	Online Service:	Telecom:	Consulting:	Y
Accessories:	Corporate:	Y	Long Distance:	TV/Cable or Wireless:	Communication:	Contract Manufacturing:	
Network Equipment:	Telecom:		Cellular:	Games:	Distribution:	Processing:	
Chips/Circuits:	Internet:		Internet Service:	Financial Data:	VAR/Reseller:	Staff/Outsourcing:	
Parts/Drives:					Satellite Srv./Equip.:	Specialty Services:	

TYPES OF BUSINESS:

Business Intelligence Software
Performance Management Software

BRANDS/DIVISIONS/AFFILIATES:

International Business Machines Corp (IBM)
Cognos PowerPlay
Cognos Visualize
Cognos DecisionStream
Cognos NoticeCast
Cognos Performance Applications
Cognos ReportNet

GROWTH PLANS/SPECIAL FEATURES:

Cognos, Inc., a subsidiary of IBM, is a provider of business intelligence (BI) and financial performance management (FPM) software. The company develops, markets and supports an integrated BI platform that allows its clients to improve business performance by enabling effective decision-making at all levels of the organization through the consistent analysis and reporting of data from multiple perspectives. Cognos' software is designed to provide customers with the ability to effectively use data to make faster, more informed decisions in order to improve operational effectiveness, increase customer satisfaction, accelerate corporate response times and ultimately increase revenues and profits. The company offers BI and analytic application components, including IBM Cognos 10 and Cognos Express, application development tools, support and service. Additionally, the company's FPM software, Cognos TM1, allows users to effectively direct the full management cycle with planning, budgeting, consolidation, reporting, analysis and scorecarding capabilities.

CONTACTS: Note: Officers with more than one job title may be intentionally listed here more than once.

Phone: 613-738-1440	Fax: 613-738-0002
Toll-Free:	
Address: 3755 Riverside Dr., P.O. Box 9707, Station T, Ottawa, ON K1G 4K9 Canada	

FINANCIALS: Sales and profits are in thousands of dollars—add 000 to get the full amount. 2010 Note: Financial information for 2010 was not available for all companies at press time.

2010 Sales: $	2010 Profits: $	**U.S. Stock Ticker: Subsidiary**
2009 Sales: $	2009 Profits: $	**Int'l Ticker:** Int'l Exchange:
2008 Sales: $	2008 Profits: $	Employees:
2007 Sales: $979,264	2007 Profits: $115,697	Fiscal Year Ends: 2/28
2006 Sales: $877,500	2006 Profits: $108,576	Parent Company: INTERNATIONAL BUSINESS MACHINES CORP (IBM)

SALARIES/BENEFITS:

Pension Plan:	ESOP Stock Plan:	Profit Sharing:	Top Exec. Salary: $	Bonus: $
Savings Plan:	Stock Purch. Plan:		Second Exec. Salary: $	Bonus: $

OTHER THOUGHTS:

Apparent Women Officers or Directors:
Hot Spot for Advancement for Women/Minorities:

LOCATIONS: ("Y" = Yes)

West:	Southwest:	Midwest:	Southeast:	Northeast:	International:
				Y	Y

Note: Financial information, benefits and other data can change quickly and may vary from those stated here.

COMMTOUCH SOFTWARE LTD
www.commtouch.com

Industry Group Code: 511210E Ranks within this company's industry group: Sales: 12 Profits: 9

Hardware:	Software:		Telecommunications:	Electronic Publishing:	Equipment:	Specialty Services:
Computers:	Consumer:		Local:	Online Service:	Telecom:	Consulting:
Accessories:	Corporate:	Y	Long Distance:	TV/Cable or Wireless:	Communication:	Contract Manufacturing:
Network Equipment:	Telecom:		Cellular:	Games:	Distribution:	Processing:
Chips/Circuits:	Internet:	Y	Internet Service:	Financial Data:	VAR/Reseller:	Staff/Outsourcing:
Parts/Drives:					Satellite Srv./Equip.:	Specialty Services:

TYPES OF BUSINESS:
Software-Web Based E-Mail Filtering
Anti-Virus Software
URL Filtering Software

BRANDS/DIVISIONS/AFFILIATES:
Zero-Hour Virus Outbreak Protection
GlobalView Mail Reputation Services
Commtouch, Inc.
Command

CONTACTS: Note: Officers with more than one job title may be intentionally listed here more than once.
Ido Hadari, CEO
Amir Lev, Pres.
Ron Ela, CFO
Rebecca Steinberg Herson, VP-Mktg.
Amir Lev, CTO
Asaf Greiner, VP-Prod.
Ronen Rosenblatt, VP-Eng.
Gary Davis, General Counsel/VP/Corp. Sec.
Yossi Maslaton, VP-Network Oper. & Customer Svcs.
Ofer Tal, VP-Int'l Sales & Bus. Dev.
Gabriel Mizrahi, VP-Tech.
Lior Samuelson, Chmn.
Francois Depayras, VP-Sales & Bus. Dev., Americas

Phone: 972-9-863-6888	Fax: 972-9-863-6863
Toll-Free:	
Address: 4A Hatzoran St., P.O. Box 8511, Netanya, 42504 Israel	

GROWTH PLANS/SPECIAL FEATURES:
Commtouch Software, Ltd. is a provider of e-mail defense and URL filtering solutions to enterprise customers and original equipment manufacturer (OEM) distribution partners. Products include the company's real-time anti-spam Zero-Hour virus outbreak detection and GlobalView Mail Reputation services, as well as a URL filtering applications and various anti-spam add-on solutions. Commtouch offers its solutions to small, medium and large enterprises through a variety of third party distribution channels. Its software is also available for integration as add-on applications with security, content filtering, anti-virus and other filtering solutions through alliances and strategic technology partnerships. At the core of Commtouch's e-mail defense offerings is the firm's proprietary Recurrent Pattern Detection (RPD) technology which serves to analyze messages associated with mass e-mail outbreaks and direct the blocking of such e-mails, without the need to analyze individual messages. The firm offers a software development kit (SDK) comprised of multiple components and built on RPD technology; the kit enables third-party vendors to integrate Commtouch solutions into their own products, with specific applications including anti-virus software, content filtering solutions, firewall systems, security servers and other network appliances. The core of Commtouch's URL filtering solutions is composed of its in-the-cloud infrastructure, which analyzes various feeds from worldwide sources pertaining to URLs and provides a ranking of the URLs tailored to the needs of each individual customer. The URL filtering services analyze and categorize the source of URLs being accessed, with applications including the prevention of malicious software attacks as well as the restriction of employee access to non-business web sites from company computers. The firm's current marketing efforts are focused on potential new OEM customers, with business development being overseen from Commtouch's headquarters in Israel and by subsidiary Commtouch, Inc., located in Sunnyvale, California. In September 2010, it acquired the Command antivirus software division of Authentium, Inc.

FINANCIALS: Sales and profits are in thousands of dollars—add 000 to get the full amount. 2010 Note: Financial information for 2010 was not available for all companies at press time.

2010 Sales: $	2010 Profits: $	U.S. Stock Ticker: CTCH
2009 Sales: $12,929	2009 Profits: $5,160	Int'l Ticker: Int'l Exchange:
2008 Sales: $12,264	2008 Profits: $2,770	Employees: 72
2007 Sales: $3,925	2007 Profits: $-2,690	Fiscal Year Ends: 12/31
2006 Sales: $7,234	2006 Profits: $- 190	Parent Company:

SALARIES/BENEFITS:
Pension Plan:	ESOP Stock Plan:	Profit Sharing:	Top Exec. Salary: $	Bonus: $
Savings Plan: Y	Stock Purch. Plan: Y		Second Exec. Salary: $	Bonus: $

OTHER THOUGHTS:
Apparent Women Officers or Directors: 2
Hot Spot for Advancement for Women/Minorities: Y

LOCATIONS: ("Y" = Yes)
West:	Southwest:	Midwest:	Southeast:	Northeast:	International:
Y			Y		Y

Note: Financial information, benefits and other data can change quickly and may vary from those stated here.

COMPAL ELECTRONICS INC

www.compal.com

Industry Group Code: 334419 Ranks within this company's industry group: Sales: 4 Profits: 4

Hardware:		Software:	Telecommunications:	Electronic Publishing:	Equipment:	Specialty Services:
Computers:	Y	Consumer:	Local:	Online Service:	Telecom:	Consulting:
Accessories:	Y	Corporate:	Long Distance:	TV/Cable or Wireless:	Communication:	Contract Manufacturing:
Network Equipment:		Telecom:	Cellular:	Games:	Distribution:	Processing:
Chips/Circuits:		Internet:	Internet Service:	Financial Data:	VAR/Reseller:	Staff/Outsourcing:
Parts/Drives:					Satellite Srv./Equip.:	Specialty Services:

TYPES OF BUSINESS:

Contract Electronics Manufacturing
Personal Music Players
Monitors
Notebook Computers
LCD Televisions
Automotive Electronics

BRANDS/DIVISIONS/AFFILIATES:

Bizcom Electronics Inc
Compal Europe (UK) Limited
Auscom Engineering Inc
Sitronix Technology Corporation

CONTACTS: Note: Officers with more than one job title may be intentionally listed here more than once.

Ruicong Chen, Gen. Mgr.
Ray Chen, Pres.
Wenbin Xu, Managing Dir.
Wenzhong Shen, Exec. Deputy Gen. Mgr.
Shaozu Gong, Sr. Deputy Gen. Mgr.
Zongbin Weng, Sr. Deputy Gen. Mgr./Gen. Mgr.-Bus. Group
Shengxiong Xu, Chmn.

Phone: 886-2-8797-8588	Fax: 886-2-2658-6547
Toll-Free:	
Address: 581 Ruiguang Rd., Neihu, Taipei, 11492 Taiwan	

GROWTH PLANS/SPECIAL FEATURES:

Compal Electronics, Inc., headquartered in Taiwan, is one of the world's leading contract manufacturers of notebook computers, monitors, automotive electronics and consumer digital electronics. Compal specializes in manufacturing high-quality electronics marketed under its clients' brands. The company has established branches in China, Brazil, Poland and the U.S. Compal's in-house research and development groups enable it to produce innovative and high-quality products at a rapid pace, with the capability to process most orders in 48 hours. The firm's manufacturing facilities, the Ping-Cheng Factory in Taiwan and the Kunshan and Compal Factories in China, are state-of-the-art and are certified for ISO-9001 international quality standards and ISO-14001 and OHSAS 18000 international environmental standards. Compal makes a wide variety of products including notebook computers, LCD televisions, monitors and portable music players. Compal's subsidiaries include Bizcom Electronics, Inc.; Compal Europe (UK) Limited; and Auscom Engineering, Inc. In December 2010, the company formed a joint venture with Sitronix Technology Corporation to develop integrated chips for tablet PCs.

Compal offers its employees company trips, an onsite fitness center, shuttle services, a pension plan and health insurance.

FINANCIALS: Sales and profits are in thousands of dollars—add 000 to get the full amount. 2010 Note: Financial information for 2010 was not available for all companies at press time.

2010 Sales: $	2010 Profits: $	**U.S. Stock Ticker:**	
2009 Sales: $20,955,900	2009 Profits: $596,060	**Int'l Ticker: 2324** Int'l Exchange: Taipei-TPE	
2008 Sales: $11,937,700	2008 Profits: $372,550	Employees: 30,000	
2007 Sales: $11,730,000	2007 Profits: $270,000	Fiscal Year Ends: 12/31	
2006 Sales: $11,472,000	2006 Profits: $262,500	Parent Company:	

SALARIES/BENEFITS:

Pension Plan: Y	ESOP Stock Plan:	Profit Sharing: Y	Top Exec. Salary: $	Bonus: $
Savings Plan:	Stock Purch. Plan:		Second Exec. Salary: $	Bonus: $

OTHER THOUGHTS:

Apparent Women Officers or Directors:
Hot Spot for Advancement for Women/Minorities:

LOCATIONS: ("Y" = Yes)

West:	Southwest:	Midwest:	Southeast:	Northeast:	International:
Y	Y				Y

COMPUCOM SYSTEMS INC

www.compucom.com

Industry Group Code: 423430 Ranks within this company's industry group: Sales: Profits:

Hardware:	Software:	Telecommunications:	Electronic Publishing:	Equipment:		Specialty Services:	
Computers:	Consumer:	Local:	Online Service:	Telecom:		Consulting:	Y
Accessories:	Corporate:	Long Distance:	TV/Cable or Wireless:	Communication:		Contract Manufacturing:	
Network Equipment:	Telecom:	Cellular:	Games:	Distribution:	Y	Processing:	
Chips/Circuits:	Internet:	Internet Service:	Financial Data:	VAR/Reseller:	Y	Staff/Outsourcing:	Y
Parts/Drives:				Satellite Srv./Equip.:		Specialty Services:	Y

TYPES OF BUSINESS:

Computer Products, Distribution
Business Software Applications
Management Services
Consulting
IT Outsourcing

BRANDS/DIVISIONS/AFFILIATES:

Court Square Capital Partners
CompuCom Canada Co
CompuCom Federal Systems, Inc.

CONTACTS: Note: Officers with more than one job title may be intentionally listed here more than once.

James W. Dixon, CEO
Jeffrey E. Frick, COO
James W. Dixon, Pres.
Kevin A. Shank, Sr. VP-Sales & Delivery
Timothy Shea, Sr. VP-Human Resources
John Douglas, CIO
David W. Hall, CTO
Ed Anderson, Chief Strategy Officer
Timothy Shea, Sr. VP-Corp. Dev.
Jill Welch, Sr. VP/Gen. Mgr.-Application Svcs. Div.
William D. Barry, Sr. VP-Enterprise Sales
Phil Soper, Gen. Mgr.-Canada

Phone: 972-856-3600	Fax: 972-856-5395
Toll-Free: 800-225-1475	
Address: 7171 Forest Ln., Dallas, TX 75230-2306 US	

GROWTH PLANS/SPECIAL FEATURES:

CompuCom Systems, Inc. distributes desktop computer products, and provides network integration services, outsourcing and IT consulting for large corporate customers nationwide. The company is owned by the private equity firm Court Square Capital Partners. Its services can be divided into four categories: IT infrastructure, Hardware, Software and Application Services. The IT infrastructure segment, working under the company's trademark Integrated Infrastructure Management model, involves consulting, network integration and outsourcing operations. The hardware segment offers clients services in hardware procurement, configuration and deployment of IT hardware products. The software services segment consists of building client familiarity with various business applications, as well as effective company wide deployment of the applications. The application services segment includes client training, support, quality assurance and custom software for clients' projects. CompuCom is an authorized dealer of major distributed desktop computer products. It offers services for a wide variety of hardware and software, including Wintel-based personal computer products, certain Unix-based systems, servers, networking and storage products and peripherals. CompuCom also has several government contracts, mainly in Canada, through subsidiary CompuCom Canada Co. Through its subsidiary CompuCom Federal Systems, Inc., the firm provides services to government agencies including the North American Aerospace Defense Command (NORAD), the U.S. Navy, the U.S. Army Space Command and U.S. Air Force Space Command. The company also has relationships with state and local governments including Texas, California, North Carolina and Arizona.

The company offers its employees medical, dental and vision; a 401(k) plan; flexible spending accounts; life insurance; AD&D coverage; an employee assistance program; tuition assistance; group legal plan; home and auto insurance; an employee discount program; and pet insurance.

FINANCIALS: Sales and profits are in thousands of dollars—add 000 to get the full amount. 2010 Note: Financial information for 2010 was not available for all companies at press time.

2010 Sales: $	2010 Profits: $	U.S. Stock Ticker: Private
2009 Sales: $	2009 Profits: $	Int'l Ticker: Int'l Exchange:
2008 Sales: $	2008 Profits: $	Employees:
2007 Sales: $2,100,000	2007 Profits: $	Fiscal Year Ends: 12/31
2006 Sales: $	2006 Profits: $	Parent Company: COURT SQUARE CAPITAL PARTNERS

SALARIES/BENEFITS:

Pension Plan:	ESOP Stock Plan:	Profit Sharing:	Top Exec. Salary: $	Bonus: $
Savings Plan: Y	Stock Purch. Plan:		Second Exec. Salary: $	Bonus: $

OTHER THOUGHTS:

Apparent Women Officers or Directors: 1
Hot Spot for Advancement for Women/Minorities:

LOCATIONS: ("Y" = Yes)

West:	Southwest:	Midwest:	Southeast:	Northeast:	International:
Y	Y	Y	Y	Y	Y

Note: Financial information, benefits and other data can change quickly and may vary from those stated here.

COMPUTER SCIENCES CORPORATION (CSC)

www.csc.com

Industry Group Code: 541513 Ranks within this company's industry group: Sales: 4 Profits: 5

Hardware:	Software:	Telecommunications:	Electronic Publishing:	Equipment:	Specialty Services:	
Computers:	Consumer:	Local:	Online Service:	Telecom:	Consulting:	Y
Accessories:	Corporate:	Long Distance:	TV/Cable or Wireless:	Communication:	Contract Manufacturing:	
Network Equipment:	Telecom:	Cellular:	Games:	Distribution:	Processing:	
Chips/Circuits:	Internet:	Internet Service:	Financial Data:	VAR/Reseller:	Staff/Outsourcing:	Y
Parts/Drives:				Satellite Srv./Equip.:	Specialty Services:	Y

TYPES OF BUSINESS:

IT Consulting
Credit Services
Customer Relationship Management
Business Process Reengineering
Management Consulting
Outsourcing
Supply Chain Management
Cloud Computing

BRANDS/DIVISIONS/AFFILIATES:

North American Public Sector
Business Solutions and Services
Global Outsourcing Services

CONTACTS: *Note: Officers with more than one job title may be intentionally listed here more than once.*

Michael W. Laphen, CEO
Michael W. Laphen, Pres.
Michael J. Mancuso, CFO/VP
Peter Allen, Pres., Global Mktg. & Sales
Nathan Siekierka, VP-Human Resources
Carlos C. Solari, VP-Cyber Tech. & Svcs.
William L. Deckelman, Jr., General Counsel/VP/Sec.
Randy E. Phillips, VP-Corp. Dev.
Chris Grandis, Dir.-Media Rel.
Bryan Brady, VP-Investor Rel.
Donald G. DeBuck, VP/Controller
Donald Purdy, Chief Cybersecurity Strategist
Michael W. Laphen, Chmn.

Phone: 703-876-1000	Fax:
Toll-Free:	
Address: 3170 Fairview Park Dr., Falls Church, VA 22042 US	

GROWTH PLANS/SPECIAL FEATURES:

Computer Sciences Corporation (CSC) is a leading global provider of information technology and business process outsourcing, consulting and systems integration services and other professional services, specializing in the application of complex information technology (IT). The company delivers its services within three broad service lines: North American Public Sector (NPS), Global Outsourcing Services (GOS) and Business Services and Solutions (BS&S). The NPS line of business provides a broad spectrum of IT services to the U.S. federal government, ranging from traditional systems integration and outsourcing to complex project management and technical services. Key offerings include enterprise modernization; telecommunications and networking; managed services; base and range operations; and training and simulation. The GOS line of business provides information systems outsourcing services to clients in a broad array of industries including aerospace and defense, automotive, chemical and natural resources, consumer goods, financial services, healthcare, manufacturing, retail and telecommunications. The BS&S line of business provides consulting and systems integration services; business process outsourcing and software maintenance services; credit reporting services, as well as professional technology staffing services in Australia and computer equipment repair and maintenance services in Asia. The company has major operations throughout North America, Europe and the Asia-Pacific region, including India. In August 2009, CSC acquired the Brazilian operations of BearingPoint, a management and technology consulting company. In April 2010, the firm started offering hosted video services as part of its suite of Unified Communications and Collaboration (UCC) services.

Employees are offered medical, dental and vision insurance; life and AD&D insurance; disability coverage; flexible spending accounts; a 401(k) plan; an employee assistance program; credit union membership; and educational assistance programs.

FINANCIALS: Sales and profits are in thousands of dollars—add 000 to get the full amount. 2010 Note: Financial information for 2010 was not available for all companies at press time.

2010 Sales: $16,128,000	2010 Profits: $834,000	U.S. Stock Ticker: CSC
2009 Sales: $16,739,900	2009 Profits: $1,115,200	Int'l Ticker:　Int'l Exchange:
2008 Sales: $16,499,500	2008 Profits: $544,600	Employees: 94,000
2007 Sales: $14,854,900	2007 Profits: $397,300	Fiscal Year Ends: 3/31
2006 Sales: $14,644,800	2006 Profits: $495,600	Parent Company:

SALARIES/BENEFITS:

Pension Plan:	ESOP Stock Plan:	Profit Sharing:	Top Exec. Salary: $1,057,692	Bonus: $2,142,400
Savings Plan: Y	Stock Purch. Plan:		Second Exec. Salary: $498,750	Bonus: $504,000

OTHER THOUGHTS:

Apparent Women Officers or Directors: 1
Hot Spot for Advancement for Women/Minorities:

LOCATIONS: ("Y" = Yes)

West:	Southwest:	Midwest:	Southeast:	Northeast:	International:
Y	Y	Y	Y	Y	Y

COMPUWARE CORP

www.compuware.com

Industry Group Code: 511210H Ranks within this company's industry group: Sales: 8 Profits: 7

Hardware:	Software:		Telecommunications:	Electronic Publishing:	Equipment:	Specialty Services:	
Computers:	Consumer:		Local:	Online Service:	Telecom:	Consulting:	Y
Accessories:	Corporate:	Y	Long Distance:	TV/Cable or Wireless:	Communication:	Contract Manufacturing:	
Network Equipment:	Telecom:		Cellular:	Games:	Distribution:	Processing:	
Chips/Circuits:	Internet:		Internet Service:	Financial Data:	VAR/Reseller:	Staff/Outsourcing:	Y
Parts/Drives:					Satellite Srv./Equip.:	Specialty Services:	

TYPES OF BUSINESS:

Computer Software-Mainframes
Distributed Systems Products
Client/Server Systems Consulting
File & Data Management
Product Application Management & Development
Software for UNIX Systems
IT Staffing Services

BRANDS/DIVISIONS/AFFILIATES:

Abend-AID
Xpediter
File-AID
Hiperstation
Covisint
Compuware Gomez
Uniface
Changepoint

CONTACTS: Note: Officers with more than one job title may be intentionally listed here more than once.

Peter Karmanos, Jr., CEO
Bob Paul, COO
Bob Paul, Pres.
Laura Fournier, CFO/Exec. VP
Paul Czarnik, CTO/Sr. VP
Denise Starr, Chief Admin. Officer
Daniel S. Follis, Jr., General Counsel/VP/Sec.
Laura Fournier, Treas.
Peter Karmanos, Jr., Chmn.

Phone: 313-227-7300	Fax: 313-227-7555
Toll-Free: 800-521-9353	
Address: 1 Campus Martius, Detroit, MI 48226 US	

GROWTH PLANS/SPECIAL FEATURES:

Compuware Corp. provides software products and professional services for the information technology departments of businesses. The company offers products and services in application development, integration, testing and performance management. Compuware's mainframe products focus on improving the productivity of developers and analysts in analysis, unit testing, functional testing, performance testing, defect removal, fault management, file and data management and application performance management in the OS/390 and z/OS series environments. Generally, the firm's strategy involves the purchase and marketing of external technologies alongside internal research and development efforts. The company's products are sold under the brand names File-AID, Abend-AID, Xpediter, Uniface, Gomez, Changepoint, Hiperstation, Vantage and Strobe. Compuware's distributed products focus on improving the productivity of the entire development team, including architects, developers, testers and operating analysts. These products support requirements management, application development, unit and functional testing and application performance analysis. Compuware's distributed products also help development teams in application profiling and rapid new application rollout, as well as in managing server and network application availability on multiple platforms including IBM z/Series (mainframe); Java; Microsoft and .NET; and UNIX. Subsidiary Covisint specifically addresses business-to-business and supply chain strategies. Compuware Gomez, another subsidiary, offers solutions aimed at optimizing the performance, availability, and quality of web and mobile applications. In September 2010, Covisint acquired clinical decision support and quality performance management firm DocSite.

The firm offers its employees life, AD&D, disability, medical, vision and dental insurance; group legal coverage; a global employee stock purchase plan; flexible spending accounts; a stock purchase plan; a 401(k) plan; an employee assistance program; and veterinary pet insurance.

FINANCIALS: Sales and profits are in thousands of dollars—add 000 to get the full amount. 2010 Note: Financial information for 2010 was not available for all companies at press time.

2010 Sales: $892,179	2010 Profits: $140,806	**U.S. Stock Ticker:** CPWR
2009 Sales: $1,090,455	2009 Profits: $139,647	**Int'l Ticker:** Int'l Exchange:
2008 Sales: $1,229,611	2008 Profits: $134,394	Employees: 4,336
2007 Sales: $1,213,002	2007 Profits: $158,092	Fiscal Year Ends: 3/31
2006 Sales: $1,205,361	2006 Profits: $142,960	Parent Company:

SALARIES/BENEFITS:

Pension Plan:	ESOP Stock Plan:	Profit Sharing:	Top Exec. Salary: $1,200,000	Bonus: $3,942,000
Savings Plan: Y	Stock Purch. Plan: Y		Second Exec. Salary: $550,000	Bonus: $1,806,750

OTHER THOUGHTS:

Apparent Women Officers or Directors: 4
Hot Spot for Advancement for Women/Minorities: Y

LOCATIONS: ("Y" = Yes)

West:	Southwest:	Midwest:	Southeast:	Northeast:	International:
Y	Y	Y	Y	Y	Y

COMVERSE TECHNOLOGY INC

www.cmvt.com

Industry Group Code: 511210C Ranks within this company's industry group: Sales: Profits:

Hardware:	Software:		Telecommunications:	Electronic Publishing:	Equipment:		Specialty Services:	
Computers:	Consumer:		Local:	Online Service:	Telecom:	Y	Consulting:	
Accessories:	Corporate:	Y	Long Distance:	TV/Cable or Wireless:	Communication:		Contract Manufacturing:	
Network Equipment:	Telecom:	Y	Cellular:	Games:	Distribution:		Processing:	
Chips/Circuits:	Internet:		Internet Service:	Financial Data:	VAR/Reseller:		Staff/Outsourcing:	
Parts/Drives:					Satellite Srv./Equip.:		Specialty Services:	Y

TYPES OF BUSINESS:

Computer Software-Telecommunications
Voice Messaging Systems
Call Management Systems
Signaling Software
Security & Business Intelligence Software
Mobile Roaming Technology & Services

BRANDS/DIVISIONS/AFFILIATES:

Comverse, Inc.
Total Communications
Verint Systems, Inc.
Ulticom, Inc.
Signalware
Starhome
Application Store

CONTACTS: Note: Officers with more than one job title may be intentionally listed here more than once.

Andre Dahan, CEO
Andre Dahan, Pres.
Stephen Swad, CFO/Exec. VP
John Bunyan, Chief Mktg. Officer/Sr. VP
Lance Miyamoto, Exec. VP-Global Human Resources
Lauren Wright, Sr. VP-Bus. Oper.
Dan Bodner, CEO/Pres., Verint Systems
Shawn Osborne, CEO/Pres., Uticom, Inc.
Eitan Achlow, CEO-Starhome
Charles Burdick, Chmn.

Phone: 212-739-1000	Fax:
Toll-Free:	
Address: 810 7th Ave., New York, NY 10019 US	

GROWTH PLANS/SPECIAL FEATURES:

Comverse Technology, Inc. (CTI), together with its subsidiaries, designs, develops, manufactures, markets and supports software, systems and related services for multimedia communication and information processing applications. The firm's products are used in a range of applications by wireless and wireline telecommunications network operators and service providers, call centers and other government, public and commercial organizations worldwide. Subsidiary Comverse, Inc. provides software, systems and services that enable network-based multimedia enhanced communication and converged billing services to over 500 communications service providers in 130 countries. These products, which make up the Total Communication portfolio, address advanced messaging solutions, personalized data and content-based solutions, and billing and account management. Comverse's services are compatible with a variety of deployment models, including in-network, hosted and managed services, and can also run in Voice over Internet Protocol (VoIP), circuit-switched and converged network systems. Through Verint Systems, Inc., CTI provides analytic software-based solutions for communications interception, networked video security and business intelligence. The company also owns a significant stake in Ulticom, Inc. provides service-enabling signaling software for wireline, wireless and Internet communications. Its Signalware family of products is used by equipment manufacturers, application developers and service providers to deploy infrastructure and enhanced services within the mobility, messaging, payment and location segments. Starhome, another partially-owned subsidiary develops, integrates and manages value-added services for mobile operators, especially advanced roaming services. In February 2009, the company launched the Application Store, which allows telecom carriers more efficient and cost-effective ways to provide new services to subscribers.

FINANCIALS: Sales and profits are in thousands of dollars—add 000 to get the full amount. 2010 Note: Financial information for 2010 was not available for all companies at press time.

2010 Sales: $	2010 Profits: $	U.S. Stock Ticker: CMVT.PK
2009 Sales: $	2009 Profits: $	Int'l Ticker: Int'l Exchange:
2008 Sales: $	2008 Profits: $	Employees:
2007 Sales: $	2007 Profits: $	Fiscal Year Ends: 1/31
2006 Sales: $1,588,554	2006 Profits: $-39,870	Parent Company:

SALARIES/BENEFITS:

Pension Plan:	ESOP Stock Plan:	Profit Sharing:	Top Exec. Salary: $	Bonus: $
Savings Plan:	Stock Purch. Plan:		Second Exec. Salary: $	Bonus: $

OTHER THOUGHTS:

Apparent Women Officers or Directors: 1
Hot Spot for Advancement for Women/Minorities:

LOCATIONS: ("Y" = Yes)

West:	Southwest:	Midwest:	Southeast:	Northeast:	International:
Y	Y	Y	Y	Y	Y

CONCURRENT COMPUTER CORP

www.ccur.com

Industry Group Code: 334111 Ranks within this company's industry group: Sales: 30 Profits: 20

Hardware:		Software:		Telecommunications:	Electronic Publishing:	Equipment:	Specialty Services:	
Computers:		Consumer:		Local:	Online Service:	Telecom:	Consulting:	
Accessories:		Corporate:	Y	Long Distance:	TV/Cable or Wireless:	Communication:	Contract Manufacturing:	
Network Equipment:	Y	Telecom:		Cellular:	Games:	Distribution:	Processing:	
Chips/Circuits:		Internet:		Internet Service:	Financial Data:	VAR/Reseller:	Staff/Outsourcing:	
Parts/Drives:						Satellite Srv./Equip.:	Specialty Services:	Y

TYPES OF BUSINESS:

Software-Real-Time & Video-on-Demand
Networking Systems Architecture
Operating Systems Software
Government Technology Services

BRANDS/DIVISIONS/AFFILIATES:

DataSuite
OI
iHawk
ImaGen
Campaign Director
RedHawk Linux
ReportOne
NightStar

CONTACTS: Note: Officers with more than one job title may be intentionally listed here more than once.

Dan Mondor, CEO
Dan Mandor, Pres.
Emory Berry, CFO
David King, Chief Mktg. Officer
Robert E. Chism, CTO
Andy Huang, VP-Eng.
Kirk L. Somers, General Counsel/Exec. VP
Emory Berry, VP-Oper.
David King, Sr. VP-Video Solutions
Paul Haddad, Sr. VP-Media Data & Advertising Solutions
Kirk L. Somers, Exec. VP-Corp. Affairs
Steve G. Nussrallah, Chmn.

Phone: 678-258-4000	Fax: 678-258-4300
Toll-Free: 877-978-7363	
Address: 4375 River Green Pkwy., Ste. 100, Duluth, GA 30096 US	

GROWTH PLANS/SPECIAL FEATURES:

Concurrent Computer Corp. (CCC) provides computer systems for the video market and the high performance, real-time market. Its business is divided into two segments: products and services. Its products fall into two categories: video and real time. CCC's video products consist of hardware and software as well as integration services sold to broadband companies that provide interactive, digital video. Its video products enable broadband users to stream video content to their digital subscribers. The customers are then able to control the video stream with familiar operations like pause, fast-forward and rewind. The company's video products support a variety of North American cable operators, including Cox Communications, Inc. and Time Warner, Inc. and include brand names such as DataSuite, Oi, Xi, Campaign Director and ReportOne. Its real time products consist of RedHawk Linux, iHawk hardware, SIMulation Workbench, NightStar, ImaGen, Power Hawk, and other real time operating systems and software development tools. These products provide a wide variety of companies with real-time computer systems for use in applications that require low latency response times such as simulation, image generation and data acquisition. These products are specifically designed for use with applications that acquire, process, store, analyze and display large amounts of rapidly changing data with microsecond response times. Its systems and software support applications in the military, aerospace, financial and automotive markets. The company also provides computer systems, equipment, spare parts and consulting services to U.S. government prime contractors and agencies of the U.S. government, including Boeing and Lockheed-Martin.

Employees are offered medical, vision and dental insurance; disability coverage; health care and dependent care flexible spending accounts; a 401(k) plan; an educational assistance program; life insurance; and an employee assistance program.

FINANCIALS: Sales and profits are in thousands of dollars—add 000 to get the full amount. 2010 Note: Financial information for 2010 was not available for all companies at press time.

2010 Sales: $60,421	2010 Profits: $-1,014	U.S. Stock Ticker: CCUR
2009 Sales: $71,640	2009 Profits: $-14,477	Int'l Ticker: Int'l Exchange:
2008 Sales: $70,816	2008 Profits: $ 265	Employees: 302
2007 Sales: $69,149	2007 Profits: $-12,171	Fiscal Year Ends: 6/30
2006 Sales: $71,612	2006 Profits: $-9,345	Parent Company:

SALARIES/BENEFITS:

Pension Plan:	ESOP Stock Plan:	Profit Sharing:	Top Exec. Salary: $370,000	Bonus: $54,500
Savings Plan: Y	Stock Purch. Plan:		Second Exec. Salary: $295,000	Bonus: $33,500

OTHER THOUGHTS:

Apparent Women Officers or Directors:
Hot Spot for Advancement for Women/Minorities:

LOCATIONS: ("Y" = Yes)

West:	Southwest:	Midwest:	Southeast:	Northeast:	International:
		Y	Y		Y

Note: Financial information, benefits and other data can change quickly and may vary from those stated here.

CONEXANT SYSTEMS INC

www.conexant.com

Industry Group Code: 33441 Ranks within this company's industry group: Sales: 47   Profits: 37

Hardware:		Software:		Telecommunications:		Electronic Publishing:		Equipment:		Specialty Services:	
Computers:		Consumer:		Local:		Online Service:		Telecom:	Y	Consulting:	
Accessories:		Corporate:	Y	Long Distance:		TV/Cable or Wireless:		Communication:	Y	Contract Manufacturing:	
Network Equipment:		Telecom:	Y	Cellular:		Games:		Distribution:		Processing:	
Chips/Circuits:	Y	Internet:		Internet Service:		Financial Data:		VAR/Reseller:		Staff/Outsourcing:	
Parts/Drives:								Satellite Srv./Equip.:		Specialty Services:	

TYPES OF BUSINESS:

Broadband Networking Equipment
Communications Semiconductor Products
Universal Access Products
Media Processing Products

BRANDS/DIVISIONS/AFFILIATES:

CONTACTS: Note: Officers with more than one job title may be intentionally listed here more than once.

D. Scott Mercer, CEO
Sailesh Chittipeddi, COO
Sailesh Chittipeddi, Pres.
Jean Hu, CFO
Christian Scherp, Exec. VP-Sales
Michael Vishny, Sr. VP-Human Resources
Mark D. Peterson, Chief Legal Officer/Sec./Sr. VP
Jean Hu, Sr. VP-Bus. Dev.
Scott L. Allen, Sr. VP-Comm.
Scott L. Allen, Sr. VP-Investor Rel.
Jean Hu, Treas.
Phil Pompa, Sr. VP-Prod. Mktg.
D. Scott Mercer, Chmn.

Phone: 949-483-4600	Fax:
Toll-Free: 888-855-4562	
Address: 4000 MacArthur Blvd., Newport Beach, CA 92660 US	

GROWTH PLANS/SPECIAL FEATURES:

Conexant Systems, Inc. designs, develops and sells semiconductor system products. Conexant provides mixed-signal and digital signal processing as well as standards-based communications protocol implementation solutions in four main product areas: imaging, audio, video and dial-up and embedded modems. The company provides imaging products for multifunction printers, fax platforms and connected frame segments. Its audio products include applications for high definition (HD) audio integrated circuits, HD audio codecs and speakers-on-a-chip solutions used in personal computers, peripheral sound products, notebook docking stations, voice over IP (VoIP) speakerphones, intercoms and surveillance products. The company's embedded modem products include applications for home automations, security systems, desktops, notebooks and set-top boxes. Conexant's video products include MPEG encoders and decoders, video decoders and demodulators.

The company offers employees medical, dental and vision insurance; life and AD&D insurance; disability coverage; flexible spending accounts; a 401(k) plan; adoption assistance; business travel accident insurance; educational assistance; and an employee assistance program.

FINANCIALS: Sales and profits are in thousands of dollars—add 000 to get the full amount. 2010 Note: Financial information for 2010 was not available for all companies at press time.

2010 Sales: $240,726	2010 Profits: $20,234	U.S. Stock Ticker: CNXT
2009 Sales: $208,427	2009 Profits: $-18,808	Int'l Ticker: Int'l Exchange:
2008 Sales: $331,504	2008 Profits: $-313,085	Employees: 596
2007 Sales: $360,703	2007 Profits: $-402,462	Fiscal Year Ends: 9/30
2006 Sales: $753,227	2006 Profits: $-122,591	Parent Company:

SALARIES/BENEFITS:

Pension Plan:	ESOP Stock Plan:	Profit Sharing:	Top Exec. Salary: $553,846	Bonus: $450,000
Savings Plan: Y	Stock Purch. Plan: Y		Second Exec. Salary: $375,000	Bonus: $343,579

OTHER THOUGHTS:

Apparent Women Officers or Directors: 1
Hot Spot for Advancement for Women/Minorities:

LOCATIONS: ("Y" = Yes)

West:	Southwest:	Midwest:	Southeast:	Northeast:	International:
Y			Y	Y	

Note: Financial information, benefits and other data can change quickly and may vary from those stated here.

COREL CORPORATION

www.corel.com

Industry Group Code: 511210F **Ranks within this company's industry group:** Sales: Profits:

Hardware:	Software:		Telecommunications:	Electronic Publishing:	Equipment:	Specialty Services:
Computers:	Consumer:	Y	Local:	Online Service:	Telecom:	Consulting:
Accessories:	Corporate:	Y	Long Distance:	TV/Cable or Wireless:	Communication:	Contract Manufacturing:
Network Equipment:	Telecom:		Cellular:	Games:	Distribution:	Processing:
Chips/Circuits:	Internet:		Internet Service:	Financial Data:	VAR/Reseller:	Staff/Outsourcing:
Parts/Drives:					Satellite Srv./Equip.:	Specialty Services:

TYPES OF BUSINESS:

Computer Software-Graphic Design
Word Processing Software
File Compression Software
Optical Disk Authoring Software
Media Playback Software

BRANDS/DIVISIONS/AFFILIATES:

Vector Capital
CorelPainter
WordPerfect Office
CorelDRAW
Corel DESIGNER
Intervideo Inc.
WinZip
WinDVD

CONTACTS: Note: Officers with more than one job title may be intentionally listed here more than once.

Kris Hagerman, CEO
Thomas P. Berquist, CFO
Shawn Cadeau, Sr. VP-Global Mktg.
Nathalie Parent, VP-Human Resources
Graham Brown, CTO
Eleanor B. Lacey, General Counsel
Kazuo Sakai, Sr. VP-APAC & Japan Oper.
Eleanor B. Lacey, Sr. VP-Bus. Dev.
Amanda Bedborough, Exec. VP-Global Sales
Jeremy Liang, Sr. VP-Digital Media Dev.
Kevin Thornton, Sr. VP-Americas Sales
Nick Davies, Sr. VP/Gen. Mgr.-Graphics & Productivity
Alexander Slusky, Chmn.
Kazuo Sakai, Pres., Corel Japan

Phone: 613-728-0826	Fax: 613-728-9790
Toll-Free: 877-572-6735	
Address: 1600 Carling Ave., Ottawa, ON K1Z 8R7 Canada	

GROWTH PLANS/SPECIAL FEATURES:

Corel Corporation is a Canadian-based global packaged technology company that specializes in graphics, productivity and digital media software, with an estimated installed base of over 100 million current users in over 75 countries. The company operates along two product lines: Graphics and Productivity and Digital Media. Its Graphics and Productivity products include the CorelDRAW Graphics Suite, a leading vector illustration, page layout, image editing and bitmap conversion software suite; Corel Painter, a digital painting and drawing software; CorelDESIGNER Technical Suite, a graphics application for creating and updating complex technical illustrations; WordPerfect Office, the firm's word-processing program, featuring Microsoft-compatible word processing, spreadsheet and presentation applications; iGrafx, a business process analysis, streamlining and optimization solutions; and WinZip, a compression utility. The firm's Digital Media portfolio includes Corel Paint Shop Photo, a digital image editing and management application; Digital Studio 2010, a software program designed for organizing and enhancing photos and video clips taken by point-and-shoot cameras; PhotoImpact, an image editing software with some digital art features; VideoStudio, its video editing and DVD authoring software; DVD Movie Factory and DVD Movie Writer, optical disc authoring software applications; and WinDVD software for DVD, video and Blu-ray Disc playback on personal computers. The company's products are sold through a scalable distribution platform comprised of international resellers, retailers, original equipment manufacturers, online providers and its global e-stores.

Employees of the firm are offered incentive programs including sales compensation plans, team bonus plans, and annual and quarterly incentive plans.

FINANCIALS: Sales and profits are in thousands of dollars—add 000 to get the full amount. 2010 Note: Financial information for 2010 was not available for all companies at press time.

2010 Sales: $	2010 Profits: $	U.S. Stock Ticker: Private
2009 Sales: $	2009 Profits: $	Int'l Ticker: CRE Int'l Exchange: Toronto-TSX
2008 Sales: $268,230	2008 Profits: $3,707	Employees: 1,040
2007 Sales: $250,500	2007 Profits: $-13,100	Fiscal Year Ends: 11/30
2006 Sales: $177,200	2006 Profits: $9,300	Parent Company: VECTOR CAPITAL

SALARIES/BENEFITS:

Pension Plan:	ESOP Stock Plan:	Profit Sharing: Y	Top Exec. Salary: $	Bonus: $
Savings Plan: Y	Stock Purch. Plan:		Second Exec. Salary: $	Bonus: $

OTHER THOUGHTS:

Apparent Women Officers or Directors: 3
Hot Spot for Advancement for Women/Minorities: Y

LOCATIONS: ("Y" = Yes)

West:	Southwest:	Midwest:	Southeast:	Northeast:	International:
Y				Y	Y

Note: Financial information, benefits and other data can change quickly and may vary from those stated here.

COREMETRICS INC

www.coremetrics.com

Industry Group Code: 511210M Ranks within this company's industry group: Sales: Profits:

Hardware:	Software:		Telecommunications:	Electronic Publishing:	Equipment:	Specialty Services:	
Computers:	Consumer:		Local:	Online Service:	Telecom:	Consulting:	
Accessories:	Corporate:	Y	Long Distance:	TV/Cable or Wireless:	Communication:	Contract Manufacturing:	
Network Equipment:	Telecom:		Cellular:	Games:	Distribution:	Processing:	
Chips/Circuits:	Internet:		Internet Service:	Financial Data:	VAR/Reseller:	Staff/Outsourcing:	
Parts/Drives:					Satellite Srv./Equip.:	Specialty Services:	Y

TYPES OF BUSINESS:

Software-Web Analytics
E-Mail Marketing & Surveys
Hosted Services

BRANDS/DIVISIONS/AFFILIATES:

LIVE Profiles
Online Analytics
LIVEmail
Coremetrics Search
Coremetrics Intelligent Offer
LIVEmark
SurfAid Analytics
International Business Machines Corp (IBM)

CONTACTS: Note: Officers with more than one job title may be intentionally listed here more than once.

Joe Davis, CEO
Shawn Farshchi, COO
Joe Davis, Pres.
Terry Schmid, CFO
Jeff Schmidt, VP-Worldwide Sales
John Payne, VP-Prod. Mgmt.
John Squire, Chief Strategy Officer
John Payne, Gen. Mgr.-Coremetrics Dallas
Richard Sheppard, VP/Gen. Mgr.-EMEA

Phone: 650-762-1400	Fax: 650-762-1499
Toll-Free: 877-721-2673	
Address: 1840 Gateway Dr., Ste. 320, San Mateo, CA 94404 US	

GROWTH PLANS/SPECIAL FEATURES:

Coremetrics, Inc., a subsidiary of IBM, provides web analytics and market optimization products. The firm's core offering consists of Lifetime Individual Visitor Experience (LIVE) Profiles, which provides a complete record of visitor interactions with client web sites, giving clients valuable insight into customer behavior including what they purchase and what they only browse through. The firm also offers products that compliment its LIVE Profiles, such as Coremetric Analytics. Coremetric Analytics helps companies utilize the data collected in LIVE Profiles to market accurately and effectively. It includes tools for marketing optimization, merchandising, content analysis, scenario analysis, profile mining, on-site search and multichannel analysis. Other products that complement LIVE Profiles include LIVEmail, which creates unique e-mails tailored to customer profiles; Coremetrics Search, informing businesses how customers get to their site from search engines like Google and Yahoo!; Coremetrics Intelligent Offer, making relevant product offers for cross-selling; LIVEmark, offering industry benchmarking; and other products. Additionally, the Scholarly Publishing solution, based on the SurfAid Analytics platform recently acquired by Coremetrics, delivers research friendly statistics to those writing in academic settings. Coremetrics' systems are typically delivered through third-party application providers including @Once, CheetahMail, Digital Impact, ForeSee Results and Responsys. In August 2010, the company was acquired by IBM.

FINANCIALS: Sales and profits are in thousands of dollars—add 000 to get the full amount. 2010 Note: Financial information for 2010 was not available for all companies at press time.

2010 Sales: $	2010 Profits: $	**U.S. Stock Ticker:** Subsidiary
2009 Sales: $	2009 Profits: $	**Int'l Ticker:** Int'l Exchange:
2008 Sales: $	2008 Profits: $	Employees:
2007 Sales: $16,900	2007 Profits: $	Fiscal Year Ends:
2006 Sales: $	2006 Profits: $	Parent Company: INTERNATIONAL BUSINESS MACHINES CORP (IBM)

SALARIES/BENEFITS:

Pension Plan:	ESOP Stock Plan:	Profit Sharing:	Top Exec. Salary: $	Bonus: $
Savings Plan:	Stock Purch. Plan:		Second Exec. Salary: $	Bonus: $

OTHER THOUGHTS:

Apparent Women Officers or Directors:
Hot Spot for Advancement for Women/Minorities:

LOCATIONS: ("Y" = Yes)

West:	Southwest:	Midwest:	Southeast:	Northeast:	International:
Y	Y				Y

CORESITE REALTY CORP

www.coresite.com

Industry Group Code: 518210 Ranks within this company's industry group: Sales: Profits:

Hardware:	Software:	Telecommunications:	Electronic Publishing:	Equipment:	Specialty Services:
Computers:	Consumer:	Local:	Online Service:	Telecom:	Consulting:
Accessories:	Corporate:	Long Distance:	TV/Cable or Wireless:	Communication:	Contract Manufacturing:
Network Equipment:	Telecom:	Cellular:	Games:	Distribution:	Processing:
Chips/Circuits:	Internet:	Internet Service:	Financial Data:	VAR/Reseller:	Staff/Outsourcing:
Parts/Drives:				Satellite Srv./Equip.:	Specialty Services: Y

TYPES OF BUSINESS:

Data Center Operation
Colocation Services
Peering Services

BRANDS/DIVISIONS/AFFILIATES:

Any2
Cage-to-Cabinet Colocation

CONTACTS: *Note: Officers with more than one job title may be intentionally listed here more than once.*

Thomas M. Ray, CEO
Thomas M. Ray, Pres.
Jeffrey Finnin, CFO
Chris Bair, Sr. VP-Sales
Lori Hossack, Dir.-Human Resources
Chuck Price, Sr. VP-IT
Dominic Tobin, Sr. VP-Oper.
David Dunn, Sr. VP-Strategy & Mktg.
Billie Haggard, Sr. VP-Data Centers
Rob Rockwood, Sr. VP-Acquisitions
Rob Sistek, Sr. VP-Capital Markets

Phone: 866-777-2673	Fax: 303-405-1011
Toll-Free:	
Address: 1050 17th St., Ste. 800, Denver, CO 80365 US	

GROWTH PLANS/SPECIAL FEATURES:

CoreSite Realty Corp., operating as a real estate investment trust (REIT), owns, operates, constructs and manages data centers and provides data center solutions. Through its data centers, the company assists clients, including corporations, cloud computing service providers, financial firms and government agencies, with improving business continuity and expanding their Information and Communication Technology (ICT) infrastructure. CoreSite offers three principal solutions: wholesale data centers, colocation and peering. The firm operates 11 wholesale data centers, which range from private data center suites to single-customer private data centers, and provide features such as dedicated UPS, cooling infrastructure, cooling towers and generator plants, depending on a customer's size. Through its colocation business, which it brands as Cage-to-Cabinet Colocation, the firm offers cages 5,000 square feet and larger up to single cabinets in managed data centers. This business also provides remote hands services, through which the company offers on-site technical assistance, equipment status relay and wiring services. CoreSite's peering services include both private, dedicated cross connections and the company's proprietary Internet exchange, Any2, which facilitates Internet traffic between Internet Service providers (ISPs) and content networks. CoreSite's data centers are located across the U.S. in New York City, Los Angeles, Boston, Chicago, Miami, San Francisco, San Jose, Santa Clara, northern Virginia and Washington, D.C. In February 2010, the company expanded its Boston data center. In September 2010, the firm completed its initial public offering (IPO) on the New York Stock Exchange.

FINANCIALS: Sales and profits are in thousands of dollars—add 000 to get the full amount. 2010 Note: Financial information for 2010 was not available for all companies at press time.

2010 Sales: $	2010 Profits: $	**U.S. Stock Ticker:** COR
2009 Sales: $	2009 Profits: $	**Int'l Ticker:** Int'l Exchange:
2008 Sales: $	2008 Profits: $	Employees:
2007 Sales: $	2007 Profits: $	Fiscal Year Ends: 12/31
2006 Sales: $	2006 Profits: $	Parent Company:

SALARIES/BENEFITS:

Pension Plan:	ESOP Stock Plan:	Profit Sharing:	Top Exec. Salary: $	Bonus: $
Savings Plan:	Stock Purch. Plan:		Second Exec. Salary: $	Bonus: $

OTHER THOUGHTS:

Apparent Women Officers or Directors: 1
Hot Spot for Advancement for Women/Minorities:

LOCATIONS: ("Y" = Yes)

West:	Southwest:	Midwest:	Southeast:	Northeast:	International:
Y		Y	Y	Y	

CRAY INC

www.cray.com

Industry Group Code: 334111 Ranks within this company's industry group: Sales: 27 Profits: 16

Hardware:		Software:		Telecommunications:	Electronic Publishing:	Equipment:		Specialty Services:	
Computers:	Y	Consumer:		Local:	Online Service:	Telecom:		Consulting:	
Accessories:		Corporate:	Y	Long Distance:	TV/Cable or Wireless:	Communication:		Contract Manufacturing:	Y
Network Equipment:		Telecom:		Cellular:	Games:	Distribution:		Processing:	
Chips/Circuits:	Y	Internet:		Internet Service:	Financial Data:	VAR/Reseller:		Staff/Outsourcing:	
Parts/Drives:						Satellite Srv./Equip.:		Specialty Services:	

TYPES OF BUSINESS:

Computer Hardware-Supercomputers
Custom Computers
Software Design

BRANDS/DIVISIONS/AFFILIATES:

Cray XE6
Cray XE6m
Cray XMT
Cray CX1000
Cray CX1
Cray Threadstorm

CONTACTS: Note: Officers with more than one job title may be intentionally listed here more than once.

Peter J. Ungaro, CEO
Peter J. Ungaro, Pres.
Brian C. Henry, CFO/Exec. VP
Paul Ciernia, VP-Sales Oper.
Linda J. Howitson, VP-Human Resources
Margaret A. (Peg) Williams, VP-R&D
Steve Scott, CTO/Sr. VP
Barry C. Bolding, VP-Prod. Div.
Charles A. Morreale, VP-Custom Eng.
Michael C. Piraino, General Counsel/VP/Corp. Sec.
Wayne J. Kugel, Sr. VP-Oper. & Customer Support
Larry Hoelzeman, VP-Americas Sales
Robert Pencek, Dir.-Intelligence Accounts
Ulla Thiel, VP-Europe
Andrew Wyatt, VP-Asia-Pacific South
Stephen C. Kiely, Chmn.
Mamoru Nakano, Pres., Cray Japan

Phone: 206-701-2000	Fax: 206-701-2500
Toll-Free: 877-272-9462	
Address: 901 5th Ave., Ste. 1000, Seattle, WA 98164 US	

GROWTH PLANS/SPECIAL FEATURES:

Cray, Inc. is a global leader in the design, development, marketing and servicing of high-performance computer (HPC) systems, more commonly known as supercomputers, for government, industry and academic institutions. The company manufactures a standard supercomputer product line, as well as designing and manufacturing customized computers. Its key product lines include the XE6, XE6m, XMT, CX1000 and CX1 supercomputers, all sold under the Cray brand name. Cray supercomputers feature an interconnection system that allows users to network dozens of processors with multiple cores. The Cray XE6 and XE6m lines are designed to support up to 192 AMD Opteron 6100 Series processors per cabinet. The Cray XMT utilizes a Cray Threadstorm processor and is compatible with up to 96 AMD Opteron CPUs per cabinet. The company's CX1000 technology line supports Intel Xeon 5600 processors and NVIDIA Tesla graphics processing units (GPUs). Offered in two configurations, the CX1 line are personal workstations that can operate using Microsoft Windows software and do not require machine room configurations. The firm sells its products primarily through a direct sales force that operates throughout the U.S., Canada, Europe, Japan and Asia-Pacific. In May 2010, the company launched the Cray XE6, its newest high-end supercomputer.

FINANCIALS: Sales and profits are in thousands of dollars—add 000 to get the full amount. 2010 Note: Financial information for 2010 was not available for all companies at press time.

2010 Sales: $	2010 Profits: $	**U.S. Stock Ticker:** CRAY
2009 Sales: $284,047	2009 Profits: $- 604	**Int'l Ticker:** Int'l Exchange:
2008 Sales: $282,853	2008 Profits: $-40,359	Employees: 872
2007 Sales: $186,153	2007 Profits: $-10,635	Fiscal Year Ends: 12/31
2006 Sales: $221,017	2006 Profits: $-12,070	Parent Company:

SALARIES/BENEFITS:

Pension Plan:	ESOP Stock Plan:	Profit Sharing:	Top Exec. Salary: $440,385	Bonus: $440,000
Savings Plan: Y	Stock Purch. Plan: Y		Second Exec. Salary: $349,038	Bonus: $132,600

OTHER THOUGHTS:

Apparent Women Officers or Directors: 3
Hot Spot for Advancement for Women/Minorities: Y

LOCATIONS: ("Y" = Yes)

West:	Southwest:	Midwest:	Southeast:	Northeast:	International:
Y		Y			Y

CRITICAL PATH INC

www.criticalpath.net

Industry Group Code: 511210C Ranks within this company's industry group: Sales: Profits:

Hardware:	Software:		Telecommunications:	Electronic Publishing:	Equipment:	Specialty Services:
Computers:	Consumer:		Local:	Online Service:	Telecom:	Consulting:
Accessories:	Corporate:	Y	Long Distance:	TV/Cable or Wireless:	Communication:	Contract Manufacturing:
Network Equipment:	Telecom:	Y	Cellular:	Games:	Distribution:	Processing:
Chips/Circuits:	Internet:		Internet Service:	Financial Data:	VAR/Reseller:	Staff/Outsourcing:
Parts/Drives:					Satellite Srv./Equip.:	Specialty Services:

TYPES OF BUSINESS:

Communications Software
Messaging Software
Identity Management Software
Professional Services

BRANDS/DIVISIONS/AFFILIATES:

Memova
Memova Messaging
Memova Mobile
Memova Anti-Abuse
Ilex

CONTACTS: Note: Officers with more than one job title may be intentionally listed here more than once.

Mark Palomba, CEO
Tim Noel, CFO
Donald Dew, CTO
Barry Twohig, Exec. VP-Eng.
Cristian Germani, Contact-Public Rel.
Mark Ferrer, Chmn.

Phone: 353-1241-5000	Fax: 353-1241-5170
Toll-Free: 877-441-7284	
Address: 42-47, Lower Mount St, Dublin, Ireland 2 UK	

GROWTH PLANS/SPECIAL FEATURES:

Critical Path, Inc. provides messaging services to consumers and service providers. The firm's solutions include its Memova product line and the company is divided into two segments Service Provider Solutions; and Enterprise and Government Solutions. The firm's Memova product line provides consumer-messaging services for mobile operators, broadband and fixed-line service providers. The Memova product line is comprised of Memova Mobile, a mobile e-mail and multimedia content solution; Memova Messaging, a platform for delivering e-mail and value-added messaging services; and Memova Anti-Abuse, a turnkey anti-spam and anti-virus solution. Some of the features in the Service Provider Solutions segment, the firm provides Universal Contacts, integrating a single contact list across e-mail, IM, text messaging, VoIP, video chat and different devices; Social Address Book, automatic contact updating software geared to facebook and other social networking sites; and Phone Backup, storing video, text, photos, contacts from cell phones that can be retrieved if the device is lost or damaged. Critical Path's Enterprise and Government Solutions include data management of phone directories; develops a security protocol with IT departments to develop identity authentication; Single-Sign On (SSO) functionalities; and managing corporate application data from human resources. The company additionally provides consulting, hosting, training and support services for its software. Critical Path's products have been deployed by over 200 service providers globally, including Vodafone; Telecom Italia; O2; Telefonica Moviles; Tiscali; SFR; Indosat; WIND; and ONO. The company has offices in Australia, Canada, France, Germany, Hong Kong, India, Indonesia, Ireland, Italy, Singapore, Spain, Sweden, Switzerland, U.S and the U.K. Recently, Critical Path sold its SuperNews Usenet access business to Giganews, Inc., a leading Usenet newsgroup services company. In September 2009, the firm launched its Identity and Access Management Suite. The company partnered with Ilex to develop this new software, which handles data and business process management, identity and access control.

FINANCIALS: Sales and profits are in thousands of dollars—add 000 to get the full amount. 2010 Note: Financial information for 2010 was not available for all companies at press time.

2010 Sales: $	2010 Profits: $	U.S. Stock Ticker: Private
2009 Sales: $	2009 Profits: $	Int'l Ticker: Int'l Exchange:
2008 Sales: $	2008 Profits: $	Employees:
2007 Sales: $44,014	2007 Profits: $-10,436	Fiscal Year Ends: 12/31
2006 Sales: $41,655	2006 Profits: $-10,966	Parent Company:

SALARIES/BENEFITS:

Pension Plan:	ESOP Stock Plan:	Profit Sharing:	Top Exec. Salary: $	Bonus: $
Savings Plan:	Stock Purch. Plan:		Second Exec. Salary: $	Bonus: $

OTHER THOUGHTS:

Apparent Women Officers or Directors:
Hot Spot for Advancement for Women/Minorities:

LOCATIONS: ("Y" = Yes)

West:	Southwest:	Midwest:	Southeast:	Northeast:	International:
Y					Y

Note: Financial information, benefits and other data can change quickly and may vary from those stated here.

CSG SYSTEMS INTERNATIONAL INC   www.csgsystems.com

Industry Group Code: 511210K Ranks within this company's industry group: Sales: 4 Profits: 4

Hardware:	Software:	Telecommunications:	Electronic Publishing:	Equipment:	Specialty Services:	
Computers:	Consumer:	Local:	Online Service:	Telecom:	Consulting:	Y
Accessories:	Corporate:	Long Distance:	TV/Cable or Wireless:	Communication:	Contract Manufacturing:	
Network Equipment:	Telecom:	Cellular:	Games:	Distribution:	Processing:	Y
Chips/Circuits:	Internet:	Internet Service:	Financial Data:	VAR/Reseller:	Staff/Outsourcing:	
Parts/Drives:				Satellite Srv./Equip.:	Specialty Services:	Y

TYPES OF BUSINESS:
Customer Care & Billing Services
Customer Relationship Management

BRANDS/DIVISIONS/AFFILIATES:
ComTec Inc
Prairie Interactive Messaging Inc
Dataprose Inc
Quaero Corporation
Intec Telecom Systems PLC

CONTACTS: Note: Officers with more than one job title may be intentionally listed here more than once.
Peter Kalan, CEO
Robert M. Scott, COO/Exec. VP
Peter Kalan, Pres.
Randy Wiese, CFO/Exec. VP
Michael Henderson, Exec. VP-Sales & Mktg.
Suzanne Broski, VP-Human Resources
Lonnie Mahrt, CIO/Sr. VP-Oper.
Ken Kennedy, CTO
Ken Kennedy, Sr. VP-Software Dev.
Joe Ruble, Chief Admin. Officer
Joe Ruble, General Counsel/Exec. VP
Bret C. Griess, Exec. VP-Oper.
Jerry Baker, Sr. VP-Bus. & New Market Dev.
Karen Eckmann, VP-Corp. Comm.
Liz Bauer, VP-Investor Rel.
Jay McCracken, Sr. VP-Strategic Bus. Units
Dwayne Ruffin, Sr. VP-Prod. Strategy
Sean Brown, Sr. VP-Prod. Mgmt.
Naras Eechambadi, Sr. VP-Quaero Customer Intelligence Solutions
Donald B. Reed, Chmn.

Phone: 303-796-2850	Fax: 303-804-4088
Toll-Free: 800-366-2744	
Address: 9555 Maroon Cir., Englewood, CO 80112 US	

GROWTH PLANS/SPECIAL FEATURES:

CSG Systems International, Inc. (CSG) provides customer care and billing services to the North American broadband and direct broadcast satellite markets. These services are geared towards targeting and acquiring potential customers; analyzing customer purchase patterns to recommend the most relevant product packages; managing back office processes; improving customer satisfaction; disseminating information to customers via preferred mediums; and streamlining customer service operations. Subsidiaries include ComTec, Inc., which provides statement production, electronic statement presentation hardware and software technologies, as well as plant capacities; Prairie Interactive Messaging, Inc., which provides inbound and outbound automated voice, text/SMS, e-mail, and fax messaging services to manage workforce communications, collections, lead generation, automated order capture, service outage notifications, and other key business functions; Quaero Corporation, a North Carolina-based customer service, analytics and marketing services provider; and Dataprose, Inc. a provider of direct mail services and statement presentment. CSG's largest customers are Comcast Corporation (24% of total 2009 revenues), DISH Network Corporation (18%), Time Warner, Inc. (14%) and Charter Communications, Inc. (9%). In November 2010, the company acquired Intec Telecom Systems PLC, a provider of billing software, for about $376 million.

The firm offers employees benefits including life, business travel accident, disability, medical, dental and vision insurance; a legal assistance plan; a long-term care plan; flexible spending accounts; a 401(k) savings plan; an employee stock purchase plan; adoption assistance; and educational assistance.

FINANCIALS: Sales and profits are in thousands of dollars—add 000 to get the full amount. 2010 Note: Financial information for 2010 was not available for all companies at press time.

2010 Sales: $	2010 Profits: $	U.S. Stock Ticker: CSGS
2009 Sales: $500,717	2009 Profits: $43,333	Int'l Ticker: Int'l Exchange:
2008 Sales: $472,057	2008 Profits: $31,771	Employees: 2,061
2007 Sales: $419,261	2007 Profits: $53,573	Fiscal Year Ends: 12/31
2006 Sales: $383,106	2006 Profits: $59,770	Parent Company:

SALARIES/BENEFITS:

Pension Plan:	ESOP Stock Plan:	Profit Sharing:	Top Exec. Salary: $500,000	Bonus: $570,240
Savings Plan: Y	Stock Purch. Plan: Y		Second Exec. Salary: $438,000	Bonus: $354,780

OTHER THOUGHTS:
Apparent Women Officers or Directors: 5
Hot Spot for Advancement for Women/Minorities: Y

LOCATIONS: ("Y" = Yes)

West:	Southwest:	Midwest:	Southeast:	Northeast:	International:
Y		Y			

CSK CORPORATION

www.csk.com

Industry Group Code: 541513 Ranks within this company's industry group: Sales: 17 Profits: 23

Hardware:	Software:	Telecommunications:	Electronic Publishing:	Equipment:	Specialty Services:	
Computers:	Consumer:	Local:	Online Service:	Telecom:	Consulting:	Y
Accessories:	Corporate:	Long Distance:	TV/Cable or Wireless:	Communication:	Contract Manufacturing:	
Network Equipment:	Telecom:	Cellular:	Games:	Distribution:	Processing:	
Chips/Circuits:	Internet:	Internet Service:	Financial Data:	VAR/Reseller:	Staff/Outsourcing:	Y
Parts/Drives:				Satellite Srv./Equip.:	Specialty Services:	Y

TYPES OF BUSINESS:

IT Services
Financial Services
Business Services

BRANDS/DIVISIONS/AFFILIATES:

CSI Solutions Corp
CSK System Management Corp
SuperSoft Corp
CSK Nearshore Systems Corp
CSK-IT Management Corp
CSK Systems Corp
CSK Holdings Corp

CONTACTS: Note: Officers with more than one job title may be intentionally listed here more than once.

Tatsuyasu Kumazaki, Managing Dir.
Takeshi Nakanishi, Pres.
Shunichi Ishimura, Pres., Bus. Svcs. Company
Tooru Tanihara, Pres., IT Mgmt. Company
Masahiko Suzuki, Pres., IT Solution Company
Akihiro Azuma, Chmn.

Phone: 81-3-6438-3901	Fax:
Toll-Free:	
Address: 2-26-1 Minami-Aoyama, Minato-ku, CSK Ayoma Bldg., Tokyo, 107-0062 Japan	

GROWTH PLANS/SPECIAL FEATURES:

CSK Corporation, formerly known as CSK Holdings Corporation, is an umbrella company that offers information technology (IT) services through over 30 subsidiaries. The subsidiaries fall under three main company groups: the Business Service Company, the IT Management Company and the IT Solution Company. The Business Service Company, which operates the CSK ServiceWare Corporation, primarily provides business process outsourcing services such as consulting, business process analysis, call center services, back office services and e-commerce operations. The IT Management Company supplies a variety of information technology services, such as data center service, on-site management, facility management, maintenance and infrastructure design. Companies within this group include CSI Solutions Corp. and CSK System Management Corp. The IT Solution Company provides information technology consulting, systems integration and other similar development services. Companies within this division include SuperSoft Corp. and CSK Nearshore Systems Corp. The firm also has a prepaid card services segment, which develops, sells and settles card systems. In April 2010, CSK sold its Cosmo Securities Co., Ltd. subsidiary to Iwai Securities Co., Ltd. In October 2010, the company merged with its CSK-IT Management Corporation and CSK Systems Corporation subsidiaries and renamed itself to CSK Corporation.

FINANCIALS: Sales and profits are in thousands of dollars—add 000 to get the full amount. 2010 Note: Financial information for 2010 was not available for all companies at press time.

2010 Sales: $2,061,340	2010 Profits: $-719,630	U.S. Stock Ticker:
2009 Sales: $2,236,420	2009 Profits: $-1,752,780	Int'l Ticker: 9737 Int'l Exchange: Tokyo-TSE
2008 Sales: $2,600,980	2008 Profits: $13,800	Employees:
2007 Sales: $2,669,190	2007 Profits: $94,180	Fiscal Year Ends: 3/31
2006 Sales: $2,411,500	2006 Profits: $308,700	Parent Company:

SALARIES/BENEFITS:

Pension Plan:	ESOP Stock Plan:	Profit Sharing:	Top Exec. Salary: $	Bonus: $
Savings Plan:	Stock Purch. Plan:		Second Exec. Salary: $	Bonus: $

OTHER THOUGHTS:

Apparent Women Officers or Directors:
Hot Spot for Advancement for Women/Minorities:

LOCATIONS: ("Y" = Yes)

West:	Southwest:	Midwest:	Southeast:	Northeast:	International:
					Y

CTS CORP

www.ctscorp.com

Industry Group Code: 334419 Ranks within this company's industry group: Sales: 17 Profits: 17

Hardware:		Software:		Telecommunications:		Electronic Publishing:		Equipment:		Specialty Services:	
Computers:		Consumer:		Local:		Online Service:		Telecom:		Consulting:	
Accessories:		Corporate:		Long Distance:		TV/Cable or Wireless:		Communication:		Contract Manufacturing:	Y
Network Equipment:		Telecom:		Cellular:		Games:		Distribution:		Processing:	
Chips/Circuits:		Internet:		Internet Service:		Financial Data:		VAR/Reseller:		Staff/Outsourcing:	
Parts/Drives:	Y							Satellite Srv./Equip.:		Specialty Services:	

TYPES OF BUSINESS:

Contract Electronics Manufacturing
Components & Sensors
Manufacturing & Assembly Services
Electronics Manufacturing Services
Supply Chain Services
Component Design Services (ODM)
Automotive Electronics

BRANDS/DIVISIONS/AFFILIATES:

Fordahl SA

CONTACTS: Note: Officers with more than one job title may be intentionally listed here more than once.

Vinod M. Khilnani, CEO
Vinod M. Khilnani, Pres.
Donna L. Belusar, CFO/Sr. VP
Bret A. Robertson, Sr. VP/Gen. Mgr.-CTS Electronics Mfg. Svcs.
Richard G. Cutter III, General Counsel/VP/Sec.
Matthew W. Long, Treas.
Donald R. Schroeder, Exec. VP/Gen. Mgr.-CTS Electronic Components
Vinod Khilnani, Chmn.

Phone: 574-293-7511	Fax: 574-293-6146
Toll-Free:	
Address: 905 West Blvd. N., Elkhart, IN 46514 US	

GROWTH PLANS/SPECIAL FEATURES:

CTS Corp. designs, manufactures and sells electronic components and provides electronic component design and supply chain services to major markets worldwide, focused primarily on the needs of original equipment manufacturers (OEMs). The firm's end markets include the automotive (accounting for approximately 27% of CTS' revenue), computer (6%), communications (21%), industrial (10%), medical (9%) and defense and aerospace (22%) and other markets (5%). The company operates manufacturing facilities in North America, Asia and Europe. CTS operates through two business segments: Components and Sensors; and Electronics Manufacturing Services (EMS). The Components and Sensors division consists of products that perform specific electronic functions for a given product family and are intended for use in customer assemblies. Products consist principally of automotive sensors and actuators used in commercial or consumer vehicles; electronic components used in communications infrastructure and computer markets; components used in computer and other high-speed applications, switches, resistor networks, and potentiometers used to serve multiple markets; and fabricated piezoelectric materials and substrates used primarily in medical, industrial and defense and aerospace markets. EMS includes the higher level assembly of electronic and mechanical components into a finished subassembly or assembly performed under a contract manufacturing agreement with an OEM or other contract manufacturer. Additionally, for some customers, the firm provides full turnkey manufacturing and completion including design, bill-of-material management, logistics and repair. Products from the EMS segment are principally sold in the communications, computer, medical, industrial, and defense and aerospace OEM markets. In January 2011, the company announced an agreement to buy Fordahl SA, a Switzerland-based designer of electronic components.

Employees are offered medical and dental coverage; life insurance and AD&D; a 401(k) plan; direct deposit; short- and long-term disability; health and dependent care reimbursement accounts; and tuition reimbursement.

FINANCIALS: Sales and profits are in thousands of dollars—add 000 to get the full amount. 2010 Note: Financial information for 2010 was not available for all companies at press time.

2010 Sales: $	2010 Profits: $	U.S. Stock Ticker: CTS
2009 Sales: $498,982	2009 Profits: $-34,050	Int'l Ticker:　　Int'l Exchange:
2008 Sales: $691,707	2008 Profits: $28,062	Employees: 4,316
2007 Sales: $685,945	2007 Profits: $23,947	Fiscal Year Ends: 12/31
2006 Sales: $655,614	2006 Profits: $24,197	Parent Company:

SALARIES/BENEFITS:

Pension Plan:	ESOP Stock Plan:	Profit Sharing:	Top Exec. Salary: $514,038	Bonus: $606,565
Savings Plan: Y	Stock Purch. Plan:		Second Exec. Salary: $322,463	Bonus: $76,101

OTHER THOUGHTS:

Apparent Women Officers or Directors: 2
Hot Spot for Advancement for Women/Minorities:

LOCATIONS: ("Y" = Yes)

West:	Southwest:	Midwest:	Southeast:	Northeast:	International:
Y	Y	Y		Y	Y

CYPRESS SEMICONDUCTOR CORP
www.cypress.com

Industry Group Code: 33441 Ranks within this company's industry group: Sales: 38 Profits: 46

Hardware:		Software:		Telecommunications:		Electronic Publishing:		Equipment:		Specialty Services:	
Computers:		Consumer:		Local:		Online Service:		Telecom:		Consulting:	
Accessories:	Y	Corporate:		Long Distance:		TV/Cable or Wireless:		Communication:		Contract Manufacturing:	
Network Equipment:		Telecom:		Cellular:		Games:		Distribution:		Processing:	
Chips/Circuits:	Y	Internet:		Internet Service:		Financial Data:		VAR/Reseller:		Staff/Outsourcing:	
Parts/Drives:	Y							Satellite Srv./Equip.:		Specialty Services:	

TYPES OF BUSINESS:
Integrated Circuits
MEMS Technology
Memory Chips
Optical Components
Network Equipment
Digital Imaging Hardware
Foundry Services

BRANDS/DIVISIONS/AFFILIATES:
Cypress Envirosystems
AgigaTech, Inc.
Cypress Foundry Solutions
CapSense
TrueTouch
RoboClock

CONTACTS: Note: Officers with more than one job title may be intentionally listed here more than once.
T. J. Rodgers, CEO
T. J. Rodgers, Pres.
Brad W. Buss, CFO
Chris Seams, Exec. VP-Mktg. & Sales
Thomas Surrette, Sr. VP-Human Resources
Paul Keswick, Exec. VP-IT
Cathal Phelan, CTO/Exec. VP
Paul Keswick, Exec. VP-New Prod. Dev.
Paul Keswick, Exec. VP-Eng.
Shahin Sharifzadeh, Exec. VP-Worldwide Mfg.
Brad W. Buss, Exec. VP-Admin.
Shahin Sharifzadeh, Exec. VP-Worldwide Oper.
Brad W. Buss, Exec. VP-Finance
Sabbas Daniel, Exec. VP-Quality
Dinesh Ramanathan, Exec. VP-Data Comm. Div.
Norm Taffe, Exec. VP-Consumer & Computation Div.
Dana Nazarian, Exec. VP-Memory & Imaging Div.
Eric A. Benhamou, Chmn.
Shahin Sharifzadeh, Pres., China Oper.

Phone: 408-943-2600	Fax: 408-943-4730
Toll-Free:	
Address: 198 Champion Ct., San Jose, CA 95134 US	

GROWTH PLANS/SPECIAL FEATURES:

Cypress Semiconductor Corp. is a provider of high-performance, mixed-signal, integrated circuit products for the data communications, telecommunications, computation, consumer products, automotive and industrial control markets. The company's Consumer and Computation Division is responsible for general-purpose timing, USB and programmable system on a chip (PSoC) products. PSoC products are used in various consumer applications such as digital still and video cameras, appliances, handheld devices, laptop computers and LCD monitors. Other products in this division include the CapSense and TrueTouch touch-sensing/touchscreen products, RoboClock clock buffers and CyFi low-power RF radio. Cypress' Data Communications Division focuses on communication products, peripheral controllers, dual-port interconnects, programmable logic devices and Power PSoC, as well as a line of switches, cable drivers and equalizers for the professional video market. The firm's Memory and Imaging Division consists of its memory business and image sensor business. Its memory business designs and manufactures static random access memories (SRAM) products and nonvolatile memories (nvSRAMs) which are used to store and retrieve data in networking, wireless infrastructure and handsets, computation, consumer, automotive, industrial and other electronic systems. Its memory products target a variety of markets including networking, telecommunications, wireless communications and consumer applications. Cypress' image sensor products are used in high-end industrial, medical and aeronautic applications. Its Emerging Technologies division includes Cypress Envirosystems, a subsidiary specializing in introducing new technologies to older industrial plants and buildings; AgigaTech, Inc., an nvSRAM company; its optical navigation systems (ONS); its China business unit; and Cypress Foundry Solutions, which provides certain foundry-related services and operates a silicon processing facility.

Cypress offers its employees access to the Stanford Instructional Network; credit union membership; an employee assistance program; a patent award program; a new product bonus program; flexible spending accounts; and medical, vision, AD&D, disability and travel accident insurance.

FINANCIALS: Sales and profits are in thousands of dollars—add 000 to get the full amount. 2010 Note: Financial information for 2010 was not available for all companies at press time.

2010 Sales: $	2010 Profits: $	U.S. Stock Ticker: CY
2009 Sales: $667,786	2009 Profits: $-150,424	Int'l Ticker: Int'l Exchange:
2008 Sales: $765,716	2008 Profits: $-284,876	Employees: 3,600
2007 Sales: $821,597	2007 Profits: $382,919	Fiscal Year Ends: 12/31
2006 Sales: $855,043	2006 Profits: $39,482	Parent Company:

SALARIES/BENEFITS:
Pension Plan:	ESOP Stock Plan:	Profit Sharing:	Top Exec. Salary: $594,221	Bonus: $536,952
Savings Plan:	Stock Purch. Plan: Y		Second Exec. Salary: $340,393	Bonus: $173,446

OTHER THOUGHTS:
Apparent Women Officers or Directors:
Hot Spot for Advancement for Women/Minorities:

LOCATIONS: ("Y" = Yes)
West:	Southwest:	Midwest:	Southeast:	Northeast:	International:
Y		Y			Y

Note: Financial information, benefits and other data can change quickly and may vary from those stated here.

DASSAULT SYSTEMES SA

www.3ds.com

Industry Group Code: 511210N Ranks within this company's industry group: Sales: 2 Profits: 1

Hardware:	Software:		Telecommunications:	Electronic Publishing:		Equipment:	Specialty Services:	
Computers:	Consumer:	Y	Local:	Online Service:	Y	Telecom:	Consulting:	Y
Accessories:	Corporate:	Y	Long Distance:	TV/Cable or Wireless:		Communication:	Contract Manufacturing:	
Network Equipment:	Telecom:		Cellular:	Games:		Distribution:	Processing:	
Chips/Circuits:	Internet:	Y	Internet Service:	Financial Data:		VAR/Reseller:	Staff/Outsourcing:	
Parts/Drives:						Satellite Srv./Equip.:	Specialty Services:	

TYPES OF BUSINESS:

Computer Software-Product Lifecycle Management
3D Imaging Software

BRANDS/DIVISIONS/AFFILIATES:

Enovia Matrixone Inc
CATIA
DELMIA
SIMULIA
ENOVIA
SolidWorks
3DVIA
Exalead

CONTACTS: Note: Officers with more than one job title may be intentionally listed here more than once.

Bernard Charles, CEO
Bernard Charles, Pres.
Thibault de Tersant, CFO/Sr. Exec. VP
Pascal Daloz, Exec. VP-Mktg.
Laurence Barthes, Chief People Officer/Exec. VP
Dominique Florack, Sr. Exec. VP-R&D
Laurence Barthes, CIO/Exec. VP
Dominique Florack, Sr. Exec. VP-Prod.
Pascal Daloz, Exec. VP-Strategy
Bruno Latchague, Exec. VP-PLM Enterprise Bus. Transformation
Etienne Droit, Exec. VP-PLM Value Selling
Lynne Wilson, CEO-3DVIA
Michel Tellier, CEO-ENOVIA
Charles Edelstenne, Chmn.
Philippe Forestier, Exec. VP-Global Affairs & Communities

Phone: 33-1-61-62-61-62	Fax: 33-1-70-73-43-63
Toll-Free:	
Address: 10 rue Marcel Dassault, Velizy-Villacoublay, 78140 France	

GROWTH PLANS/SPECIAL FEATURES:

Dassault Systemes S.A. is a global provider of product lifecycle management (PLM) software and 3D rendering software. The company's software applications and services enable businesses in a variety of industries to digitally define and simulate products. Its products facilitate the design, simulation and production of complex systems, such as cars, aircraft and dams, as well as the manufacturing facilities and systems used to produce them. Its applications are also employed to design and manufacture products for everyday life, from tableware and household appliances to jewelry. The company's services support industrial processes and provide a 3D vision of the entire lifecycle of products, from conception to maintenance. Its software brands include CATIA, which creates and simulates the digital product; DELMIA, which simulates manufacturing processes; SIMULIA for virtual testing; ENOVIA, for online global collaborative lifecycle management; and SolidWorks, a set of modeling tools for creating 3D designs. The most recent addition to Dassault's brand lineup, its 3DVIA platform, is dedicated to extending 3D content creation to new businesses and consumers by making 3D technology more accessible and user-friendly. Dassault Systemes provides PLM software to an array of industries, including automotive, aerospace, shipbuilding, industrial equipment, high-tech, electronics, consumer goods, life sciences, energy, construction and business services. PLM software aims to offer customers a competitive advantage in the market by reducing product introduction costs, managing supplier networks, extending design expertise globally and accelerating time to market. Dassault also maintains a strategic partnership with EuropaCorp plc to develop industrial and experiential 3D technologies for applications in cinema and marketing. In June 2010, Dassault acquired Paris-based Exalead, a developer of enterprise and web search software, for approximately $175 million. In December 2010, the company announced a strategic alliance with Thales S.A. to focus on PLM systems integration for defense, transportation and public sector clients in France.

FINANCIALS: Sales and profits are in thousands of dollars—add 000 to get the full amount. 2010 Note: Financial information for 2010 was not available for all companies at press time.

2010 Sales: $	2010 Profits: $	**U.S. Stock Ticker: DASTY.PK**
2009 Sales: $1,684,250	2009 Profits: $228,420	**Int'l Ticker: DSY** Int'l Exchange: Paris-Euronext
2008 Sales: $1,778,360	2008 Profits: $263,800	Employees: 7,834
2007 Sales: $1,677,100	2007 Profits: $237,820	Fiscal Year Ends: 12/31
2006 Sales: $1,528,300	2006 Profits: $237,200	Parent Company:

SALARIES/BENEFITS:

Pension Plan:	ESOP Stock Plan:	Profit Sharing:	Top Exec. Salary: $	Bonus: $
Savings Plan:	Stock Purch. Plan:		Second Exec. Salary: $	Bonus: $

OTHER THOUGHTS:

Apparent Women Officers or Directors: 2
Hot Spot for Advancement for Women/Minorities: Y

LOCATIONS: ("Y" = Yes)

West:	Southwest:	Midwest:	Southeast:	Northeast:	International:
				Y	Y

Note: Financial information, benefits and other data can change quickly and may vary from those stated here.

DATA ROBOTICS INC

www.drobo.com

Industry Group Code: 334112 Ranks within this company's industry group: Sales: Profits:

Hardware:		Software:		Telecommunications:	Electronic Publishing:	Equipment:	Specialty Services:
Computers:		Consumer:		Local:	Online Service:	Telecom:	Consulting:
Accessories:	Y	Corporate:		Long Distance:	TV/Cable or Wireless:	Communication:	Contract Manufacturing:
Network Equipment:	Y	Telecom:		Cellular:	Games:	Distribution:	Processing:
Chips/Circuits:		Internet:		Internet Service:	Financial Data:	VAR/Reseller:	Staff/Outsourcing:
Parts/Drives:						Satellite Srv./Equip.:	Specialty Services:

TYPES OF BUSINESS:

Network Storage Devices

BRANDS/DIVISIONS/AFFILIATES:

BeyondRAID
Drobo
DroboElite
DroboPro
Drobo S
DroboPro FS
Drobo FS

CONTACTS: *Note: Officers with more than one job title may be intentionally listed here more than once.*

Tom Buiocchi, CEO
Ezra Hookano, VP-Sales, Bus. Div.
Mark Herbert, Sr. VP-Eng.
Jeff Hoever, VP-Oper.
AJ Jennings, Sr. VP-Bus. Dev.
Danielle Murcray, VP-Finance
Julian Terry, Chief Architect
Sonya Andreae, VP-Support
Malissa King, VP-Sales, Prosumer Div.
Aneel Bhusri, Chmn.
Paul Thackeray, VP-Sales, EMEA

Phone: 408-567-3100	Fax: 408-567-3101
Toll-Free:	
Address: 1705 Wyatt Dr., Santa Clara, CA 95054-1524 US	

GROWTH PLANS/SPECIAL FEATURES:

Data Robotics, Inc. designs and produces data storage equipment. The company's technology is designed to implement redundant disks to ensure data integrity and security. The products are ideal for customers who wish to maintain their data but are unfamiliar with advanced RAID (redundant array of independent disks) configurations. The firm markets its products to three core groups: home and home office users; creative professionals; and businesses. The home and home office products include the Drobo and Drobo FS, which are primarily used as network storage and file backup systems. These products can support between four and five drives and can connect to networks through FireWire, USB or Gigabit Ethernet connections. The creative professional and prosumer (professional consumer) products include the DroboPro and Drobo S, which allow small businesses or professionals like photographers and videographers to backup and share data. These products support between five and eight drives and can connect through iSCSI (internet small computer system interface) or eSATA (external serial advanced technology attachment) ports. The DroboPro FS and DroboElite, which are the company's upper-tier products, are meant for small-to-medium businesses or business departments. These products support up to eight drives and can connect through dual Gigabit Ethernet or iSCSI ports. The devices can be networked into a simple SAN (storage area network) to provide community data protection. Data Robotics' BeyondRaid technology offers the benefits of RAID 5 and 6 configurations without the need to change network configurations. Users also have the ability to switch between single- and double-disk redundancy on the fly.

FINANCIALS: Sales and profits are in thousands of dollars—add 000 to get the full amount. 2010 Note: Financial information for 2010 was not available for all companies at press time.

2010 Sales: $	2010 Profits: $	U.S. Stock Ticker: Private
2009 Sales: $	2009 Profits: $	Int'l Ticker: Int'l Exchange:
2008 Sales: $	2008 Profits: $	Employees:
2007 Sales: $	2007 Profits: $	Fiscal Year Ends:
2006 Sales: $	2006 Profits: $	Parent Company:

SALARIES/BENEFITS:

Pension Plan:	ESOP Stock Plan:	Profit Sharing:	Top Exec. Salary: $	Bonus: $
Savings Plan:	Stock Purch. Plan:		Second Exec. Salary: $	Bonus: $

OTHER THOUGHTS:

Apparent Women Officers or Directors:
Hot Spot for Advancement for Women/Minorities:

LOCATIONS: ("Y" = Yes)

West:	Southwest:	Midwest:	Southeast:	Northeast:	International:
Y					Y

DATALOGIC SCANNING INC

www.scanning.datalogic.com

Industry Group Code: 334119 Ranks within this company's industry group: Sales: Profits:

Hardware:		Software:		Telecommunications:	Electronic Publishing:	Equipment:	Specialty Services:
Computers:		Consumer:		Local:	Online Service:	Telecom:	Consulting:
Accessories:	Y	Corporate:	Y	Long Distance:	TV/Cable or Wireless:	Communication:	Contract Manufacturing:
Network Equipment:		Telecom:		Cellular:	Games:	Distribution:	Processing:
Chips/Circuits:		Internet:		Internet Service:	Financial Data:	VAR/Reseller:	Staff/Outsourcing:
Parts/Drives:						Satellite Srv./Equip.:	Specialty Services:

TYPES OF BUSINESS:

Computer Accessories-Bar Code Scanners
Data Management Software
Portable Data Collection Terminals
Integrated Sorting Systems

BRANDS/DIVISIONS/AFFILIATES:

Datalogic SPA
Magellan
Gryphon
QuickScan
PowerScan
Magellan 3300HSi
Master B+
Master BB+

CONTACTS: Note: Officers with more than one job title may be intentionally listed here more than once.

William L. Parnell, CEO
William L. Parnell, Pres.
David L. Sullivan, Sr. VP-Worldwide Mktg., Sales & Svcs.
Rhone Lee, VP-Human Resources
Chet Galka, VP-Finance
Glen Feeley, VP-Americas
David Suarez, Dir.-Sales, Latin America
Matt Schler, Gen. Mgr.-Fixed Retail Scanning
Pietro Todescato, Gen. Mgr.-Handheld Scanning
Giulio Berzuini, VP-Sales & Mktg., EMEA
Brad West, VP-Supply Chain Oper.

Phone: 541-683-5700	Fax: 541-345-7140
Toll-Free: 800-695-5700	
Address: 959 Terry St., Eugene, OR 97402-9150 US	

GROWTH PLANS/SPECIAL FEATURES:

Datalogic Scanning, Inc., a subsidiary of Datalogic S.p.A., provides integrated bar code scanning and data management equipment for the retail supply chain. The firm made one of the first commercial bar code scanners in 1974. Datalogic Scanning does business in approximately 235 countries and regions and has sales/service offices in Asia-Pacific, Europe and the Americas. The firm's products primarily include high-performance POS (Point of Sale) on-counter and in-counter scanners; and industrial/general purpose handheld scanners. The company's on-counter scanners include the Diamond and Magellan lines. Datalogic Scanning's in-counter scanners consist of five Magellan lines, including the Magellan 8500Xt Scanner & Scanner/Scale. The firm's on-counter scanners combine several functions and innovations designed to increase cashier productivity, including one-step bar code scanning and electronic article surveillance tag deactivation; 3D scanning technology that scans five sides of an item simultaneously; regular software updates; and remote diagnostic capabilities. With regard to handheld scanners, Datalogic Scanning offers the PowerScan 7000, 8000, 8300 and 8500 lines for industrial needs; and the Gryphon, QuickScan, Touch and Heron lines for general uses (including linear and 2D decoding). Its mobile and wireless products allow retail employees to pre-scan items for customers in the checkout line to reduce checkout time; assist shoppers by providing detailed product information on the spot; and manage inventory more efficiently. The firm also offers the Master B+ and Master BB+ decoders, which allow customers to connect an array of input devices to over 2000 different terminals and PCs. In 2010, Datalogic Scanning introduced several new products, including Gryphon GBT4100, a linear imager for use in the healthcare, retail, light industrial and banking sectors; Gryphon L GD4300, which features the company's Green Spot Technology; and Magellan 3300HSi, an omni-directional, in-counter, single plane scanner that utilizes imaging technology.

FINANCIALS: Sales and profits are in thousands of dollars—add 000 to get the full amount. 2010 Note: Financial information for 2010 was not available for all companies at press time.

			U.S. Stock Ticker: Subsidiary
2010 Sales: $		2010 Profits: $	Int'l Ticker: Int'l Exchange:
2009 Sales: $		2009 Profits: $	Employees:
2008 Sales: $		2008 Profits: $	Fiscal Year Ends: 12/31
2007 Sales: $		2007 Profits: $	Parent Company: DATALOGIC SPA
2006 Sales: $		2006 Profits: $	

SALARIES/BENEFITS:

Pension Plan:	ESOP Stock Plan:	Profit Sharing:	Top Exec. Salary: $	Bonus: $152,208
Savings Plan:	Stock Purch. Plan:		Second Exec. Salary: $	Bonus: $

OTHER THOUGHTS:

Apparent Women Officers or Directors:
Hot Spot for Advancement for Women/Minorities:

LOCATIONS: ("Y" = Yes)

West:	Southwest:	Midwest:	Southeast:	Northeast:	International:
Y					Y

DATATRAK INTERNATIONAL INC

www.datatrak.net

Industry Group Code: 511210D Ranks within this company's industry group: Sales: Profits:

Hardware:	Software:		Telecommunications:	Electronic Publishing:	Equipment:	Specialty Services:	
Computers:	Consumer:		Local:	Online Service:	Telecom:	Consulting:	Y
Accessories:	Corporate:	Y	Long Distance:	TV/Cable or Wireless:	Communication:	Contract Manufacturing:	
Network Equipment:	Telecom:		Cellular:	Games:	Distribution:	Processing:	
Chips/Circuits:	Internet:		Internet Service:	Financial Data:	VAR/Reseller:	Staff/Outsourcing:	
Parts/Drives:					Satellite Srv./Equip.:	Specialty Services:	Y

TYPES OF BUSINESS:

Software-Clinical Trial Data Collection
Consulting Services

BRANDS/DIVISIONS/AFFILIATES:

DATATRAK eClinical
DATATRAK Safety Case Manager
eClinical Enterprise Manager
DATATRAK eTrain

CONTACTS: Note: Officers with more than one job title may be intentionally listed here more than once.

Laurence P. Birch, CEO
Laurence P. Birch, Pres.
Bill Coates, VP-Sales
Chris Wilke, CTO
Varnesh Sritharan, VP-Legal Affairs/Sec.
Bill Gluck, VP-Clinical & Consulting Svcs.

Phone: 440-443-0082	Fax: 440-442-3482
Toll-Free: 888-756-3282	
Address: 6150 Parkland Blvd., Ste. 100, Mayfield Heights, OH 44124 US	

GROWTH PLANS/SPECIAL FEATURES:

DATATRAK International, Inc. develops and markets electronic data capture (EDC) software that allows its customers to collect, review, transmit and store clinical trial data electronically. The firm's proprietary software suite, DATATRAK eClinical consists of DATATRAK Safety Case Manager, which obtains and manages individual case safety report (ICSR) data; the eClinical Enterprise Manager, which manages user lists and access to clinical trial information; and DATATRAK eTrain, a software training program, as well as EDC; clinical data management and interactive response technologies for the randomization and management of inventory. In addition to software products, the company offers a variety of professional services; hands-on training; a support center; a learning center with tutorials, manuals and guides; and hosting services.

The firm offers employees medical, dental and vision insurance; life insurance; disability coverage; and a 401(k) plan.

FINANCIALS: Sales and profits are in thousands of dollars—add 000 to get the full amount. 2010 Note: Financial information for 2010 was not available for all companies at press time.

2010 Sales: $	2010 Profits: $	**U.S. Stock Ticker: DATA**
2009 Sales: $	2009 Profits: $	Int'l Ticker: Int'l Exchange:
2008 Sales: $8,826	2008 Profits: $-16,797	Employees: 47
2007 Sales: $10,562	2007 Profits: $-10,854	Fiscal Year Ends: 12/31
2006 Sales: $17,690	2006 Profits: $-4,490	Parent Company:

SALARIES/BENEFITS:

Pension Plan:	ESOP Stock Plan:	Profit Sharing:	Top Exec. Salary: $220,000	Bonus: $
Savings Plan: Y	Stock Purch. Plan:		Second Exec. Salary: $173,538	Bonus: $

OTHER THOUGHTS:

Apparent Women Officers or Directors:
Hot Spot for Advancement for Women/Minorities:

LOCATIONS: ("Y" = Yes)

West:	Southwest:	Midwest:	Southeast:	Northeast:	International:
	Y	Y			Y

DELL INC
www.dell.com

Industry Group Code: 334111 Ranks within this company's industry group: Sales: 4   Profits: 4

Hardware:		Software:	Telecommunications:	Electronic Publishing:	Equipment:	Specialty Services:	
Computers:	Y	Consumer:	Local:	Online Service:	Telecom:	Consulting:	Y
Accessories:	Y	Corporate:	Long Distance:	TV/Cable or Wireless:	Communication:	Contract Manufacturing:	
Network Equipment:		Telecom:	Cellular:	Games:	Distribution:	Processing:	
Chips/Circuits:		Internet:	Internet Service:	Financial Data:	VAR/Reseller:	Staff/Outsourcing:	
Parts/Drives:					Satellite Srv./Equip.:	Specialty Services:	

TYPES OF BUSINESS:
Computer Hardware-PCs, Manufacturing
Direct Sales
Technical & Support Services
Online Music Service
Web Hosting Services
Printers & Accessories
Personal Music Players
Storage Devices

BRANDS/DIVISIONS/AFFILIATES:
OptiPlex
Dell Financial Servies L.P.
Inspiron
PowerEdge
Alienware
KACE
Latitude
Dell Precision

CONTACTS: Note: Officers with more than one job title may be intentionally listed here more than once.
Michael S.Dell, CEO
Brian T. Gladden, CFO/Sr. VP
Karen H. Quintos, Chief Mktg. Officer/Sr. VP
Steve H. Price, Sr. VP-Human Resources
Jeffrey W. Clark, Vice Chmn.-Tech.
Brad R. Anderson, Sr. VP-Enterprise Prod. Group
Lawrence P. Tu, General Counsel/Sr. VP
Jeffrey W. Clark, Vice Chmn.-Oper.
David L. Johnson, Sr. VP-Corp. Strategy
Paul D. Bell, Pres., Public
Stephen F. Schuckenbrock, Pres., Large Enterprise
Stephen Felice, Pres., Consumer, Small & Medium Bus.
Peter Altabef, Pres., Dell Svcs.
Michael S. Dell, Chmn.

Phone: 512-338-4400	Fax: 512-728-3653
Toll-Free: 800-289-3355	
Address: 1 Dell Way, Round Rock, TX 78682 US	

GROWTH PLANS/SPECIAL FEATURES:

Dell, Inc. designs, develops, manufactures, markets, sells and supports a wide range of computing products that in many cases are customized to individual customer requirements. The company's product categories include desktop PCs; servers and networking products; storage; mobility products; and software and peripherals. A few of Dell's products include OptiPlex desktop computers; Alienware, Latitude and Inspiron notebook computers; PowerEdge servers; Dell Precision workstation products; and PowerVault storage products. The company utilizes a direct selling strategy to bypass retailers and middlemen by selling products online directly to end users. The company has four operating segments: large enterprise; public; small and medium business; and consumer. The large enterprise segment includes large global and national corporate business customers. The public segment focuses customers such as educational institutions, government, health care and law enforcement agencies. The small and medium business segment focuses on providing simple, customized IT applications and services to small and medium-sized businesses. The consumer segment sells to customers through online at store dell.com, over the phone and through retail. The firm offers a variety of support services such as warranty services, proactive maintenance offerings, technical support and consulting services. Through Dell Financial Services L.P., a wholly-owned subsidiary of Dell, the company is able to offer or arrange various financial services for its business and consumer customers in the U.S. Through the company's ongoing research and development activities, it is able to stay competitive in the technology market. In 2010, the company acquired systems management appliance firm, KACE. Also in 2010 the firm agreed to acquire Software-as-a-Service (SaaS) integration company, Boomi.

The firm offers employees medical, dental and vision insurance; flexible spending accounts; life insurance; disability coverage; an employee assistance program; health and wellness programs; a 401(k) plan; discounts on Dell merchandise and other products and services from various vendors; auto and home insurance discounts; adoption assistance; and an educational assistance program

FINANCIALS: Sales and profits are in thousands of dollars—add 000 to get the full amount. 2010 Note: Financial information for 2010 was not available for all companies at press time.

2010 Sales: $52,902,000	2010 Profits: $1,433,000	**U.S. Stock Ticker:** DELL
2009 Sales: $61,101,000	2009 Profits: $2,478,000	**Int'l Ticker:** Int'l Exchange:
2008 Sales: $61,133,000	2008 Profits: $2,947,000	Employees: 96,000
2007 Sales: $57,420,000	2007 Profits: $2,583,000	Fiscal Year Ends: 1/31
2006 Sales: $55,788,000	2006 Profits: $3,602,000	Parent Company:

SALARIES/BENEFITS:

Pension Plan:	ESOP Stock Plan:	Profit Sharing:	Top Exec. Salary: $931,731	Bonus: $
Savings Plan: Y	Stock Purch. Plan:		Second Exec. Salary: $703,846	Bonus: $591,231

OTHER THOUGHTS:
Apparent Women Officers or Directors: 2
Hot Spot for Advancement for Women/Minorities:

LOCATIONS: ("Y" = Yes)

West:	Southwest:	Midwest:	Southeast:	Northeast:	International:
Y	Y	Y	Y	Y	Y

DIEBOLD INC

www.diebold.com

Industry Group Code: 334111 Ranks within this company's industry group: Sales: 15 Profits: 11

Hardware:		Software:		Telecommunications:	Electronic Publishing:	Equipment:	Specialty Services:
Computers:	Y	Consumer:		Local:	Online Service:	Telecom:	Consulting:
Accessories:		Corporate:	Y	Long Distance:	TV/Cable or Wireless:	Communication:	Contract Manufacturing:
Network Equipment:		Telecom:		Cellular:	Games:	Distribution:	Processing:
Chips/Circuits:		Internet:		Internet Service:	Financial Data:	VAR/Reseller:	Staff/Outsourcing:
Parts/Drives:						Satellite Srv./Equip.:	Specialty Services:

TYPES OF BUSINESS:

Computer Hardware-Automated Teller Machines
Self-Service Terminals
Security Systems
Technical Services
Software
Electronic Voting Machines

BRANDS/DIVISIONS/AFFILIATES:

Procomp Industria Eletronica LTDA

CONTACTS: Note: Officers with more than one job title may be intentionally listed here more than once.

Thomas W. Swidarski, CEO
Thomas W. Swidarski, Pres.
Bradley C. Richardson, CFO/Exec. VP
John M. Deignan, Chief Mktg. Officer/VP
Sheila M. Rutt, Chief Human Resources Officer/VP
Frank A. Natoli, CTO/VP
Warren W. Dettinger, General Counsel/VP
George S. Mayes, Jr., Exec. VP-Global Oper.
John D. Kristoff, Chief Comm. Officer/VP
Timothy J. McDannold, VP/Treas.
Charles E. Ducey, Exec. VP-North America Oper.
Joao Abud, Pres., Brazilian Div.
Chad F. Hesse, Sr. Corp. Counsel/Sec.
M. Scott Hunter, Chief Tax Officer/VP
John N. Lauer, Chmn.
James Chen, Exec. VP-Int'l Oper.
Linda M. Parcher, Chief Procurement Officer/VP

Phone: 330-490-4000	Fax: 330-490-3794
Toll-Free: 800-999-3600	
Address: 5995 Mayfair Rd., P.O. Box 3077, North Canton, OH 44720-8077 US	

GROWTH PLANS/SPECIAL FEATURES:

Diebold, Inc., incorporated in 1876, develops, manufactures, sells and services self-service transaction systems; electronic and physical security systems; software; and various products used to equip bank facilities and electronic voting terminals. The company's primary customers include banks and financial institutions, as well as public libraries, government agencies, utilities and various retail outlets in over 90 countries. The company provides two core segments: Self-service and security. The self-service segment primarily serves the banking industry by supplying automated teller machines (ATMs). Diebold provides the hardware, software and customer support for these systems. The security unit specializes in protecting customer assets. This division serves financial, retail, commercial and government customers with both physical and electronic systems. The products in this segment include vaults, safes, depositories, bullet-resistive items and other similar safety measures. The electronic applications include alarms, remote monitoring and identity confirmation measures like card verifiers and biometrics. Through its wholly-owned Brazilian subsidiary, Procomp Industria Eletronica LTDA, the company also provides election systems equipment, software, training, support and installation services for ballot casting equipment. In September 2009, the company sold its US Election Systems business to Election Systems & Software, Inc. In October 2009, the firm expanded its direct sales operations to Turkey. In February 2010, Diebold acquired Aurillion, a health care information company. In April 2010, it signed an outsourcing agreement to provide ATMs to Citibank's Russian operation.

Diebold offers its employees medical, dental, vision and prescription drug coverage; an employee stock purchase plan; educational assistance; a long-term disability plan; an employee assistance program; adoption assistance; baby benefits; flexible spending accounts; and a college scholarship program.

FINANCIALS: Sales and profits are in thousands of dollars—add 000 to get the full amount. 2010 Note: Financial information for 2010 was not available for all companies at press time.

2010 Sales: $	2010 Profits: $	U.S. Stock Ticker: DBD
2009 Sales: $2,718,292	2009 Profits: $32,254	Int'l Ticker: Int'l Exchange:
2008 Sales: $3,081,838	2008 Profits: $88,583	Employees: 16,397
2007 Sales: $2,888,351	2007 Profits: $39,541	Fiscal Year Ends: 12/31
2006 Sales: $2,920,974	2006 Profits: $104,552	Parent Company:

SALARIES/BENEFITS:

Pension Plan:	ESOP Stock Plan:	Profit Sharing:	Top Exec. Salary: $750,000	Bonus: $920,000
Savings Plan: Y	Stock Purch. Plan: Y		Second Exec. Salary: $353,720	Bonus: $260,160

OTHER THOUGHTS:

Apparent Women Officers or Directors: 3
Hot Spot for Advancement for Women/Minorities: Y

LOCATIONS: ("Y" = Yes)

West:	Southwest:	Midwest:	Southeast:	Northeast:	International:
			Y		Y

DIGI INTERNATIONAL INC

www.digi.com

Industry Group Code: 33411 Ranks within this company's industry group: Sales: 12 Profits: 12

Hardware:		Software:		Telecommunications:		Electronic Publishing:		Equipment:		Specialty Services:	
Computers:		Consumer:		Local:		Online Service:		Telecom:	Y	Consulting:	
Accessories:	Y	Corporate:	Y	Long Distance:		TV/Cable or Wireless:		Communication:	Y	Contract Manufacturing:	
Network Equipment:	Y	Telecom:	Y	Cellular:	Y	Games:		Distribution:		Processing:	
Chips/Circuits:	Y	Internet:		Internet Service:		Financial Data:		VAR/Reseller:		Staff/Outsourcing:	
Parts/Drives:								Satellite Srv./Equip.:		Specialty Services:	

TYPES OF BUSINESS:

Networking Equipment
Data Communications Hardware & Software
Local Area Networking Products
Wireless & Cellular Products-Backup Connectivity

BRANDS/DIVISIONS/AFFILIATES:

Digi
iDigi
Rabbit
Digi m-Trak
XBee
XBee Pro
ConnectCore X3 H
ConnectCore 3G

CONTACTS: Note: Officers with more than one job title may be intentionally listed here more than once.

Joseph T. Dunsmore, CEO
Joseph T. Dunsmore, Pres.
Steve Snyder, CFO/Sr. VP
Larry Kraft, Sr. VP-Sales & Mktg.
Tracy Roberts, VP-Human Resources
Joel Young, Sr. VP-R&D
Tracy Roberts, VP-IT
Joel Young, CTO
Steve Ericson, VP-Prod. Mgmt.
Jon A. Nyland, VP-Mfg. Oper.
Stephen E. Popovich, VP-Bus. Dev.
Subramanian Krishnan, Treas.
John Guargena, VP-Americas Sales
Curt Ahart, VP-Bus. Dev.
Joseph T. Dunsmore, Chmn.
Frederic Luu, VP-Sales & Mktg., EMEA

Phone: 952-912-3444	Fax: 952-912-4952
Toll-Free: 877-912-3444	
Address: 11001 Bren Rd. E., Minnetonka, MN 55343 US	

GROWTH PLANS/SPECIAL FEATURES:

Digi International, Inc. produces connectivity hardware and software products for multi-user environments, remote access and other data communications networks. Digi's offerings include products for industrial automation, building automation and security, out-of-band management (enabling immediate response in the case of catastrophic network failure), medical and healthcare, retail point-of-sale and office networking. The firm's products are divided into two categories: embedded and non-embedded. An embedded product is incorporated by a product developer into an electronic device, such as retail scanners or medical instruments. Embedded products include modules; chips; software and development tools; network interface cards; and various services. A non-embedded product is connected externally to a device or larger system to provide network connectivity or port expansion. Non-embedded products include cellular routers, gateways, wireless communications adapters; console servers; serial servers; USB connected products; and serial cards. The company's products and services are sold under the Digi, Rabbit, Digi m-Trak and iDigi brand names. Its products are available through approximately 280 distributors in more than 70 countries around the world. Recently introduced products include XBee and Xbee-PRO wireless connectivity modules, the ConnectCore 3G cellular module and the ConnectCore X3 H cellular gateway for harsh environments.

Employees are offered medical, dental and vision insurance; educational reimbursement; a 401(k) savings plan; an employee stock purchase plan; flexible spending accounts; a 529 college savings plan; an employee assistance program; life insurance; disability coverage; on-site exercise facilities and corporate discounts.

FINANCIALS: Sales and profits are in thousands of dollars—add 000 to get the full amount. 2010 Note: Financial information for 2010 was not available for all companies at press time.

2010 Sales: $	2010 Profits: $	U.S. Stock Ticker: DGII
2009 Sales: $165,928	2009 Profits: $4,083	Int'l Ticker: Int'l Exchange:
2008 Sales: $185,056	2008 Profits: $12,351	Employees: 634
2007 Sales: $173,263	2007 Profits: $19,773	Fiscal Year Ends: 12/31
2006 Sales: $144,663	2006 Profits: $11,113	Parent Company:

SALARIES/BENEFITS:

Pension Plan:	ESOP Stock Plan:	Profit Sharing:	Top Exec. Salary: $406,000	Bonus: $121,496
Savings Plan: Y	Stock Purch. Plan: Y		Second Exec. Salary: $234,000	Bonus: $56,111

OTHER THOUGHTS:

Apparent Women Officers or Directors: 1
Hot Spot for Advancement for Women/Minorities:

LOCATIONS: ("Y" = Yes)

West:	Southwest:	Midwest:	Southeast:	Northeast:	International:
Y	Y	Y		Y	Y

Note: Financial information, benefits and other data can change quickly and may vary from those stated here.

DIGITAL ANGEL CORP

www.digitalangel.com

Industry Group Code: 33441 Ranks within this company's industry group: Sales: 54   Profits: 36

Hardware:		Software:		Telecommunications:		Electronic Publishing:		Equipment:		Specialty Services:	
Computers:		Consumer:	Y	Local:		Online Service:		Telecom:		Consulting:	
Accessories:		Corporate:	Y	Long Distance:		TV/Cable or Wireless:		Communication:	Y	Contract Manufacturing:	
Network Equipment:		Telecom:		Cellular:		Games:		Distribution:		Processing:	
Chips/Circuits:	Y	Internet:		Internet Service:		Financial Data:		VAR/Reseller:		Staff/Outsourcing:	
Parts/Drives:								Satellite Srv./Equip.:		Specialty Services:	

TYPES OF BUSINESS:

Chips-Global Positioning & RFID
Personal Safeguard Technologies
RFID Products
Security Monitoring Systems
Consulting Services
Navigation & GPS Equipment
Search & Rescue Equipment

BRANDS/DIVISIONS/AFFILIATES:

Destron Fearing
Signature Industries Limited
Bio-Thermo
SARBE
Digital Angel International, Inc.

CONTACTS: Note: Officers with more than one job title may be intentionally listed here more than once.

Joseph J. Grillo, CEO
Parke Hess, COO
Lorraine M. Breece, CFO/VP
Patricia Petersen, General Counsel
David Sullivan, Pres., Destron Fearing
Brent C. Archer, Sr. VP-Supply Chain

Phone: 651-552-6301	Fax:
Toll-Free:	
Address: 490 Villaume Ave., S. St. Paul, MN 55075 US	

GROWTH PLANS/SPECIAL FEATURES:

Digital Angel Corp. (DAC) is a developer of global positioning satellite (GPS) and radio frequency identification (RFID) technology. The firm operates in two business segments: Animal Identification and Emergency Identification. The Animal Identification segment develops visual and electronic identification tags and implantable RFID microchips, primarily for identification, tracking and location of companion pets, livestock, horses, fish and wildlife, and more recently, for animal bio-sensing applications, such as temperature reading for companion pet and livestock applications. The company holds patents on its syringe-injectable microchip, which is individually programmed to store a unique, permanent 10-16 digit alphanumeric identification code. The microchip ranges from 8-28 millimeters in length and 2.1-3.5 millimeters in diameter. The Bio-Thermo implantable microchip product provides temperature readings of animals by passing an RFID handheld scanner over the animal of by having the animal walk through a portal scanner. Subsidiaries within the Animal Identification segment include Destron Fearing and Digital Angel International, Inc. The Emergency Identification segment provides emergency location and tracking of pilots, aircraft and maritime vehicles in remote locations, as well as sound horn alarms. Products include GPS enabled search and rescue equipment and intelligent communications devices for mobile data and radio applications. The company's SARBE brand serves commercial and military markets. Signature Industries Limited, the company's 98.5% owned subsidiary, also operates within this segment. In November 2009, the company sold its McMurdo unit in the U.K. In April 2010, the firm also sold its U.K. unit, Clifford & Snell.

FINANCIALS: Sales and profits are in thousands of dollars—add 000 to get the full amount. 2010 Note: Financial information for 2010 was not available for all companies at press time.

2010 Sales: $	2010 Profits: $	**U.S. Stock Ticker:** DIGA
2009 Sales: $49,463	2009 Profits: $-12,430	**Int'l Ticker:** Int'l Exchange:
2008 Sales: $62,260	2008 Profits: $-58,011	Employees: 244
2007 Sales: $77,794	2007 Profits: $-32,020	Fiscal Year Ends: 12/31
2006 Sales: $54,053	2006 Profits: $-27,209	Parent Company:

SALARIES/BENEFITS:

Pension Plan:	ESOP Stock Plan:	Profit Sharing: Y	Top Exec. Salary: $345,145	Bonus: $67,500
Savings Plan: Y	Stock Purch. Plan:		Second Exec. Salary: $189,242	Bonus: $22,680

OTHER THOUGHTS:

Apparent Women Officers or Directors: 2
Hot Spot for Advancement for Women/Minorities: Y

LOCATIONS: ("Y" = Yes)

West:	Southwest:	Midwest:	Southeast:	Northeast:	International:
		Y			Y

DIGITAL CHINA HOLDINGS LIMITED

www.digitalchina.com.hk

Industry Group Code: 423430 Ranks within this company's industry group: Sales: 7 Profits: 5

Hardware:	Software:		Telecommunications:	Electronic Publishing:	Equipment:		Specialty Services:	
Computers:	Consumer:		Local:	Online Service:	Telecom:		Consulting:	Y
Accessories:	Corporate:	Y	Long Distance:	TV/Cable or Wireless:	Communication:		Contract Manufacturing:	
Network Equipment:	Telecom:		Cellular:	Games:	Distribution:	Y	Processing:	
Chips/Circuits:	Internet:		Internet Service:	Financial Data:	VAR/Reseller:		Staff/Outsourcing:	
Parts/Drives:					Satellite Srv./Equip.:		Specialty Services:	Y

TYPES OF BUSINESS:

Computer & Telecommunications Equipment Distribution
Systems Integration
IT Services

BRANDS/DIVISIONS/AFFILIATES:

Digital China (Hefei) Co., Ltd.
Fuzhou Digital China Co., Ltd.
Changsha Digital China Co., Ltd.
Digiwin Group
Octopus China Investments Limited

CONTACTS: Note: Officers with more than one job title may be intentionally listed here more than once.

Guo Wei, CEO
Lin Yang, Pres.
Li Yan, VP-Human Resources
Xie Yun, CTO
Li Yan, VP/Head-Enterprise Planning Office
Tiang Hongtao, VP/Gen. Mgr.-Finance
Zhou Yibing, VP/Pres., Infrastructure Svcs. Bus. Unit
Li Jun, VP/Pres., Application Svcs. Bus. Unit
Hu Deqiang, VP-East & South China Bus.
Yan Guorong, Standing VP
Guo Wei, Chmn.
Shuai Yong, VP/Head-Supply Chain Svcs.

Phone: 852-3416-8000	Fax: 852-2805-5991
Toll-Free:	
Address: Ste. 2008, 20/F., Taikoo Pl., 979 King's Rd., Hong Kong, China	

GROWTH PLANS/SPECIAL FEATURES:

Digital China Holdings Limited is one of the largest systems integrators and distributors of IT products in China. Established in 1984, its pursuit is the technological advancement and digitization of China. Digital China operates in four segments: Services, which generates approximately 21% of revenues; Distribution, 30%; Supply Chain Services, 9%; and Systems, 40%. Serving the manufacturing, finance, government and telecommunications sectors, the Services segment offers consultations, systems integration, application software development and related training. Utilizing a network consisting of over 10,000 resellers and chain stores in China, Hong Kong and Macau, the Distribution segment offers general IT equipment from 20 international manufacturers, including data projectors; PC servers; accessories and peripherals; and notebook and desktop computers. The firm's Supply Chain Services business provides supply-chain consultancy and implementation services for manufacturers of IT and other high-value density manufacturers. Lastly, the Systems segment offers products for corporate users, including software, networking technologies, storage products and mainframe servers. It also offers hardware maintenance and training, as well as providing other technical services. Technology partners include Microsoft; General Electric Co.; Sony; NEC Corporation; Panasonic; Samsung; Adobe Systems, Inc.; Acer, Inc.; Hewlett-Packard; SAP AG; and Symantec Corp. Besides its Hong Kong headquarters, the firm has a secondary headquarters in Beijing; three logistics centers, in Guangzhou, Shanghai and Beijing; and regional centers in 19 cities throughout China. Subsidiaries of the firm include Digital China (Hefei) Co., Ltd.; Fuzhou Digital China Co., Ltd.; and Changsha Digital China Co., Ltd. In January 2010, the company announced a joint venture with Octopus China Investments Limited, a card services company, to develop technologies related to official identification cards issued to Chinese citizens by the government. In October 2010, it acquired a 30% stake in Digiwin Group, a Chinese provider of enterprise resources planning software and services.

FINANCIALS: Sales and profits are in thousands of dollars—add 000 to get the full amount. 2010 Note: Financial information for 2010 was not available for all companies at press time.

2010 Sales: $6,451,580	2010 Profits: $105,983	U.S. Stock Ticker:
2009 Sales: $5,442,020	2009 Profits: $82,430	Int'l Ticker: 0861 Int'l Exchange: Hong Kong-HKEX
2008 Sales: $4,531,400	2008 Profits: $51,570	Employees: 9,600
2007 Sales: $254,200	2007 Profits: $2,100	Fiscal Year Ends: 3/31
2006 Sales: $198,600	2006 Profits: $2,500	Parent Company:

SALARIES/BENEFITS:

Pension Plan:	ESOP Stock Plan:	Profit Sharing:	Top Exec. Salary: $	Bonus: $
Savings Plan:	Stock Purch. Plan:		Second Exec. Salary: $	Bonus: $

OTHER THOUGHTS:

Apparent Women Officers or Directors: 4
Hot Spot for Advancement for Women/Minorities: Y

LOCATIONS: ("Y" = Yes)

West:	Southwest:	Midwest:	Southeast:	Northeast:	International: Y

DIGITAL RIVER INC

www.digitalriver.com

Industry Group Code: 518210 Ranks within this company's industry group: Sales: 2 Profits: 2

Hardware:	Software:		Telecommunications:	Electronic Publishing:		Equipment:	Specialty Services:	
Computers:	Consumer:		Local:	Online Service:	Y	Telecom:	Consulting:	Y
Accessories:	Corporate:	Y	Long Distance:	TV/Cable or Wireless:		Communication:	Contract Manufacturing:	
Network Equipment:	Telecom:		Cellular:	Games:		Distribution:	Processing:	
Chips/Circuits:	Internet:		Internet Service:	Financial Data:		VAR/Reseller:	Staff/Outsourcing:	
Parts/Drives:						Satellite Srv./Equip.:	Specialty Services:	Y

TYPES OF BUSINESS:

E-Commerce Software
E-Commerce Outsourcing
Digital Software Delivery
Web Development
Marketing & Merchandising Services
Fraud Screening
Transaction Processing

BRANDS/DIVISIONS/AFFILIATES:

BlueHornet Networks, Inc.
MindVision, Inc.
DirectTrack, Inc.
Fireclick Inc
KeywordMax, Inc.
element 5, Inc.
fatfoogoo AG
Journey Education Marketing, Inc.

CONTACTS: Note: Officers with more than one job title may be intentionally listed here more than once.

Joel A. Ronning, CEO
Thomas Donnelly, CFO
Kevin L. Crudden, General Counsel/VP
Joel A. Ronning, Chmn.

Phone: 952-253-1234	Fax: 952-253-8497
Toll-Free:	
Address: 9625 W. 76th St., Ste. 150, Eden Prairie, MN 55344 US	

GROWTH PLANS/SPECIAL FEATURES:

Digital River, Inc. provides outsourced e-commerce services primarily in the software and high-tech products markets. Its primary offering is a suite of software that enables its clients to deliver software to customers digitally. Digital River's offerings include a complete range of services needed to conduct business online: Online store design, development and hosting; store merchandising and optimization; order management; fraud prevention screening; export controls and management; tax management; digital product delivery via download; physical product fulfillment; subscription management; e-mail marketing; web site optimization; web analytics; and CD production and delivery. The firm's operations are provided by eight international data centers which can be accessed by more than 180 countries around the world. Product fulfillment services are conducted through third party agencies on four continents. The firm also offers a number of services through its subsidiaries, including BlueHornet Networks, Inc., which is a provider of e-mail marketing services; MindVision, Inc., which provides software delivery tools and outsourced e-commerce services; DirectTrack, which offers affiliate marketing and tracking services; Fireclick, which specializes in web analytics; element 5, Inc., a provider of outsourcing services; and KeywordMax, which works in advertising. The company's client list includes firms covering a wide variety of industries, including Adobe Systems, Inc.; Aspyr Media, Inc.; Autodesk, Inc.; Canon Europa N.V.; Cyber Patrol, LLC; Eastman Kodak Company; Electronic Arts, Inc.; Lexmark, Inc.; Microsoft Corporation; Nuance Communications, Inc.; SanDisk Corporation; Symantec Corporation, and Trend Micro, Inc. In May 2010, Digital River acquired fatfoogoo AG, which specializes in e-commerce operations. In September 2010, the company purchased Journey Education Marketing, Inc., which resells software and other goods to educational institutions.

Digital River offers its employees medical, dental and vision coverage; a 401(k) plan; an employee stock purchase plan; short- and long-term disability; and life insurance.

FINANCIALS: Sales and profits are in thousands of dollars—add 000 to get the full amount. 2010 Note: Financial information for 2010 was not available for all companies at press time.

2010 Sales: $	2010 Profits: $	U.S. Stock Ticker: DRIV
2009 Sales: $403,766	2009 Profits: $53,042	Int'l Ticker: Int'l Exchange:
2008 Sales: $394,226	2008 Profits: $63,595	Employees: 1,335
2007 Sales: $349,275	2007 Profits: $70,814	Fiscal Year Ends: 12/31
2006 Sales: $307,632	2006 Profits: $60,810	Parent Company:

SALARIES/BENEFITS:

Pension Plan:	ESOP Stock Plan:	Profit Sharing:	Top Exec. Salary: $450,000	Bonus: $356,484
Savings Plan: Y	Stock Purch. Plan: Y		Second Exec. Salary: $300,000	Bonus: $190,125

OTHER THOUGHTS:

Apparent Women Officers or Directors: 1
Hot Spot for Advancement for Women/Minorities:

LOCATIONS: ("Y" = Yes)

West:	Southwest:	Midwest:	Southeast:	Northeast:	International:
Y		Y			Y

Note: Financial information, benefits and other data can change quickly and may vary from those stated here.

DIGITECH SYSTEMS CO LTD

www.digitechsys.co.kr

Industry Group Code: 334119 Ranks within this company's industry group: Sales: 23   Profits: 13

Hardware:		Software:		Telecommunications:		Electronic Publishing:		Equipment:		Specialty Services:	
Computers:		Consumer:		Local:		Online Service:		Telecom:		Consulting:	
Accessories:		Corporate:	Y	Long Distance:		TV/Cable or Wireless:		Communication:		Contract Manufacturing:	Y
Network Equipment:		Telecom:		Cellular:		Games:		Distribution:		Processing:	
Chips/Circuits:		Internet:		Internet Service:		Financial Data:		VAR/Reseller:		Staff/Outsourcing:	
Parts/Drives:	Y							Satellite Srv./Equip.:		Specialty Services:	

TYPES OF BUSINESS:

Manufacturing-Touch Screens
Touch Screen Controllers
Touch Screen Device Drivers

BRANDS/DIVISIONS/AFFILIATES:

CONTACTS: Note: Officers with more than one job title may be intentionally listed here more than once.

Hwan-yong Lee, CEO
Hwan-yong Lee, Pres.

Phone: 82-31-366-9300	Fax: 82-31-366-9328
Toll-Free:	
Address: 667-2 Ssangsong-Ri, Mado-Myeon, Geonggi-Do, 445-861 Korea	

GROWTH PLANS/SPECIAL FEATURES:

Digitech Systems Co. Ltd., established in 2000, primarily manufactures touch screens and associated hardware. Its products consist mainly of touch panels, such as for mobile devices, point-of-sale terminals, information kiosks, tablet PCs, automobile navigation systems, medical equipment, gaming machines, industrial terminals and ATMs; and touch controllers, the chips and boards that translate the analog touch signal into a digital computer signal. The firm also produces device drivers, the software that runs the touch devices. Its software supports Linux, Mac OS X and Microsoft platforms. The company's touch screens and associated hardware support both 4- and 5-wire resistive configurations, as well as EST and Mobile capacitive touch screens. These terms refer to how the touch screen reads the position finger or other pointing device. Resistive models work by pressing together different layers of glass and other substrates; when the two surfaces meet, a small electrical potential difference is generated, and its location is read by the machine and translated into an X-Y coordinate. Capacitive screens pass a very small current from the screen into the pointing device and use that signal to triangulate an X-Y coordinate. Digitech has two manufacturing plants, both located in the Gyeonggi province of Korea.

Benefits for Digitech employees include health, medical, unemployment and injury insurance; access to a company boarding house and company restaurant; commuter bus service; and a holiday gift.

FINANCIALS: Sales and profits are in thousands of dollars—add 000 to get the full amount. 2010 Note: Financial information for 2010 was not available for all companies at press time.

2010 Sales: $	2010 Profits: $	U.S. Stock Ticker:
2009 Sales: $104,120	2009 Profits: $21,780	Int'l Ticker: 091690 Int'l Exchange: Seoul-KRX
2008 Sales: $39,080	2008 Profits: $10,360	Employees:
2007 Sales: $36,910	2007 Profits: $11,070	Fiscal Year Ends: 12/31
2006 Sales: $	2006 Profits: $	Parent Company:

SALARIES/BENEFITS:

Pension Plan: Y	ESOP Stock Plan:	Profit Sharing:	Top Exec. Salary: $	Bonus: $
Savings Plan:	Stock Purch. Plan:		Second Exec. Salary: $	Bonus: $

OTHER THOUGHTS:

Apparent Women Officers or Directors:
Hot Spot for Advancement for Women/Minorities:

LOCATIONS: ("Y" = Yes)

West:	Southwest:	Midwest:	Southeast:	Northeast:	International:
					Y

DIMENSION DATA HOLDINGS PLC
www.dimensiondata.com

Industry Group Code: 541512 **Ranks within this company's industry group:** Sales: 1 Profits: 1

Hardware:	Software:		Telecommunications:	Electronic Publishing:	Equipment:	Specialty Services:	
Computers:	Consumer:		Local:	Online Service:	Telecom:	Consulting:	Y
Accessories:	Corporate:	Y	Long Distance:	TV/Cable or Wireless:	Communication:	Contract Manufacturing:	
Network Equipment:	Telecom:	Y	Cellular:	Games:	Distribution:	Processing:	
Chips/Circuits:	Internet:	Y	Internet Service:	Financial Data:	VAR/Reseller:	Staff/Outsourcing:	
Parts/Drives:					Satellite Srv./Equip.:	Specialty Services:	Y

TYPES OF BUSINESS:

IT Consulting
Network Integration Services
IT Security Services
Converged Communications Solutions
Data Center & Storage Solutions
Customer Interaction Solutions

BRANDS/DIVISIONS/AFFILIATES:

Express Data
Merchants
Plessey
Microsoft Corp.
Cisco Systems Inc.
Magenta Computacion S.A.
mvision
Nippon Telegraph and Telephone Corp (NTT)

CONTACTS: *Note: Officers with more than one job title may be intentionally listed here more than once.*

Brett William Dawson, CEO
Jason Goodall, COO
David Sherriffs, CFO
Connie de Lange, Group Exec.-Mktg.
Marilyn Rose Williams, Group Exec.-Human Resources
Etteinne Reinecke, CTO
Patrick Quarmby, Dir.-Corp. Finance
Bruce Watson, Group Exec.-Cisco Alliance
Andrew Briggs, Group Exec.-Sales
Bill Padfield, CEO-Datacraft Asia Ltd.
Stephen Joubert, Group Exec.-Global Solutions
Jeremy John Ord, Chmn.
Allan Cawood, CEO-Dimension Data, Middle East & Africa

Phone: 27-11-575-0000	Fax:
Toll-Free:	
Address: 57 Sloane St., Bryanston, Johannesburg, 2021 South Africa	

GROWTH PLANS/SPECIAL FEATURES:

Dimension Data Holdings plc is an information technology (IT) services and solutions provider. The firm serves the financial services, telecommunications, healthcare, manufacturing, government and education industries. The company operates in six segments: network integration; converged communications; security solutions; data centers and storage; customer interactive solutions (CIS); and Microsoft solutions. Network integration solutions include performance optimization, managed networks, Multiprotocol Label Switching (MPLS), secure network infrastructure assessment, wireless and mobility services and network and service management. The converged communications segment assists clients with the convergence of voice, video and data over Internet Protocol (IP) through telephony, enterprise mobility, collaboration and converged networks solutions. IT security solutions include perimeter security, intrusion management, adaptive security infrastructure and risk assessment. Data center and storage solutions address IT disruption risks through disaster recovery, managed storage, server and application monitoring and backup and recovery assessment, and also include data migration and archiving services. The CIS segment includes consulting, benchmarking, contact center integration, interaction management, workforce optimization and self-service solutions. Microsoft solutions include desktop lifecycle management, security management, unified communications and IP Telephony/Active Directory (IPAD) Connector services. Dimension Data is a Microsoft Gold Partner in 21 countries and a Global Cisco Gold Partner in 33 countries. The company is headquartered in South Africa with additional operations in 47 countries, and serves over 6,000 clients, including 79% of Global Fortune 100 and 63% of Global Fortune 500 companies. Dimension Data's subsidiaries include African company Plessey; Australian firm Express Data; Merchants, which operates in South Africa and the U.K.; and Singapore-based Datacraft. In April 2010, the firm acquired 51% ownership of Chilean systems integrator Magenta Computacion S.A. In September 2010, the company acquired managed video service provider mvision. In December 2010, Dimension Data was acquired by, and is now a subsidiary of, telecommunications group Nippon Telegraph and Telephone Corporation.

FINANCIALS: Sales and profits are in thousands of dollars—add 000 to get the full amount. 2010 Note: Financial information for 2010 was not available for all companies at press time.

2010 Sales: $	2010 Profits: $	**U.S. Stock Ticker:** Subsidiary
2009 Sales: $3,973,100	2009 Profits: $135,200	**Int'l Ticker:** DDT **Int'l Exchange:** London-LSE
2008 Sales: $4,510,600	2008 Profits: $118,400	**Employees:** 11,032
2007 Sales: $3,773,200	2007 Profits: $92,500	**Fiscal Year Ends:**
2006 Sales: $	2006 Profits: $	**Parent Company:** NIPPON TELEGRAPH AND TELEPHONE CORP (NTT)

SALARIES/BENEFITS:

Pension Plan:	ESOP Stock Plan:	Profit Sharing:	Top Exec. Salary: $	Bonus: $
Savings Plan:	Stock Purch. Plan:		Second Exec. Salary: $	Bonus: $

OTHER THOUGHTS:

Apparent Women Officers or Directors: 3
Hot Spot for Advancement for Women/Minorities: Y

LOCATIONS: ("Y" = Yes)

West:	Southwest:	Midwest:	Southeast:	Northeast:	International:
Y	Y	Y	Y	Y	Y

DIODES INC
www.diodes.com

Industry Group Code: 335 Ranks within this company's industry group: Sales: 4　Profits: 4

Hardware:		Software:		Telecommunications:		Electronic Publishing:	Equipment:		Specialty Services:	
Computers:		Consumer:	Y	Local:		Online Service:	Telecom:		Consulting:	
Accessories:	Y	Corporate:		Long Distance:		TV/Cable or Wireless:	Communication:		Contract Manufacturing:	
Network Equipment:		Telecom:		Cellular:		Games:	Distribution:		Processing:	
Chips/Circuits:	Y	Internet:		Internet Service:		Financial Data:	VAR/Reseller:		Staff/Outsourcing:	
Parts/Drives:	Y						Satellite Srv./Equip.:		Specialty Services:	

TYPES OF BUSINESS:
Semiconductor Manufacturing
Semiconductor Design
Semiconductor Marketing

BRANDS/DIVISIONS/AFFILIATES:
FabTech, Inc.
Shanghai Kaihong Electronics Co., Ltd.
Shanghai Kaihong Technology
DII Taiwan Co, Ltd.
Diodes Hong Kong, Ltd.
Diodes Zetex, Ltd.

CONTACTS: Note: Officers with more than one job title may be intentionally listed here more than once.
Keh-Shew Lu, CEO
Keh-Shew Lu, Pres.
Richard D. White, CFO/Treas.
Mark A. King, Sr. VP-Sales & Mktg.
Ed Tang, VP-Corp. Admin.
Richard D. White, Sec.
Joseph Liu, Sr. VP-Oper.
Hans Rohrer, Sr. VP-Bus. Dev.
Carl C. Wertz, VP-Investor Rel.
Carl C. Wertz, VP-Finance
Julie Holland, VP-Worldwide Analog Prod.
Francis Tang, VP-Worldwide Discrete Prod.
Raymond Soong, Chmn.
Colin Greene, Pres., Europe/VP-Europe Sales & Mktg.

Phone: 972-385-2810	Fax:
Toll-Free:	
Address: 15660 N. Dallas Parkway, Ste. 850, Dallas, TX 75248 US	

GROWTH PLANS/SPECIAL FEATURES:

Diodes, Inc. designs, manufactures and markets discrete and analogue semiconductor products. The semiconductors are found in a variety of end-user products in the consumer electronics, computing, industrial, communications and automotive sectors. These products include diodes; rectifiers; transistors; metal oxide semiconductor field-effect transistors (MOSFETs); protection devices; functional specific arrays; amplifiers and comparators; Hall effect and temperature sensors; power management devices (including light emitting diode drivers); DC-DC switching and linear voltage regulators; voltage references; special function devices (including USB power switch, load switch, voltage supervisor and motor controllers); and silicon wafers used to manufacture these products. Diodes' product line includes over 6,000 offerings. The company is a global supplier of electronic signal amplification and switching functions, which are basic building-block electronic components incorporated into almost every electronic device. The company conducts a number of operations through its subsidiaries, including FabTech, Inc., which is responsible for wafer fabrication, research and development, engineering and sales; Shanghai Kaihong Electronics Co., Ltd., which handles packaging, assembly, testing, research and development and engineering; Shanghai Kaihong Technology Electronics Company, Ltd., which also handles packaging, assembly, testing, research and development and engineering; DII Taiwan Corporation, Ltd., which handles only sales and marketing; Diodes Hong Kong, Ltd, which contains a logistical center and handles sales and marketing; and Diodes Zetex, Ltd., a U.K.-based semiconductor company. The company has over 250 customers worldwide, including original equipment manufacturers (OEMs). The firm also has approximately 90 distributor customers around the world, through which the firm indirectly serves over 10,000 customers.

FINANCIALS: Sales and profits are in thousands of dollars—add 000 to get the full amount. 2010 Note: Financial information for 2010 was not available for all companies at press time.

2010 Sales: $	2010 Profits: $	**U.S. Stock Ticker: DIOD**
2009 Sales: $434,357	2009 Profits: $9,848	**Int'l Ticker:**　Int'l Exchange:
2008 Sales: $432,785	2008 Profits: $30,529	Employees: 3,501
2007 Sales: $401,159	2007 Profits: $56,130	Fiscal Year Ends: 12/31
2006 Sales: $343,308	2006 Profits: $48,143	Parent Company:

SALARIES/BENEFITS:

Pension Plan:	ESOP Stock Plan:	Profit Sharing:	Top Exec. Salary: $343,000	Bonus: $780,000
Savings Plan: Y	Stock Purch. Plan: Y		Second Exec. Salary: $248,000	Bonus: $286,000

OTHER THOUGHTS:
Apparent Women Officers or Directors: 1
Hot Spot for Advancement for Women/Minorities:

LOCATIONS: ("Y" = Yes)

West:	Southwest:	Midwest:	Southeast:	Northeast:	International:
Y	Y	Y		Y	Y

Note: Financial information, benefits and other data can change quickly and may vary from those stated here.

D-LINK CORPORATION
www.dlink.com

Industry Group Code: 33411 Ranks within this company's industry group: Sales: 3 Profits: 6

Hardware:		Software:		Telecommunications:	Electronic Publishing:	Equipment:	Specialty Services:
Computers:		Consumer:	Y	Local:	Online Service:	Telecom:	Consulting:
Accessories:	Y	Corporate:	Y	Long Distance:	TV/Cable or Wireless:	Communication:	Contract Manufacturing:
Network Equipment:	Y	Telecom:		Cellular:	Games:	Distribution:	Processing:
Chips/Circuits:		Internet:		Internet Service:	Financial Data:	VAR/Reseller:	Staff/Outsourcing:
Parts/Drives:						Satellite Srv./Equip.:	Specialty Services:

TYPES OF BUSINESS:
Networking Equipment Manufacturing & Distribution
Broadband Products
Modems
Telephony Products
Security Products
Software
Switches & Routers
Media Converters

BRANDS/DIVISIONS/AFFILIATES:
DGS-3200

CONTACTS: Note: Officers with more than one job title may be intentionally listed here more than once.
Tony Tsao, CEO
Tony Tsao, Pres.
A.P. Chen, CFO
Tom Paterniti, VP-Bus. Dev.
John DiFrenna, VP-Channel Oper., U.S. & Mexico
Keith A. Karlsen, Exec. VP-D-Link Systems, Inc.
John Lee, Chmn.
Nick Tidd, CEO-D-Link North America
Tom Paterniti, VP-Dist.

Phone: 886-2-6600-0123	Fax: 886-2-6600-9898
Toll-Free:	
Address: 1F, No. 289 Sinhu 3rd Rd., Neihu District, Taipei, 114 Taiwan	

GROWTH PLANS/SPECIAL FEATURES:
D-Link Corporation is a leading global designer, developer, manufacturer and distributor of networking, broadband, digital, voice and data communications products for mass consumer and small- to medium-sized business market segments. The company is one of the largest networking hardware vendors in the distribution channel, including value-added resellers, online retailers, retail chains, service providers and direct market resellers. D-Link, which is based in Taiwan, has 174 offices located in 71 countries. Its products are sold through independent distributors worldwide, with emerging markets and the Asia Pacific region responsible for a majority (52%) of revenues. The firm manufactures ADSL broadband products; cable modems; wireless LAN; IP telephony products (VOIP); remote router and security products; network attached storage; LAN switches; print servers; LAN hubs; network management software; LAN cards and network kits; media converters; transceivers; KVM switches; home phone line networks; analog modems; USB devices; audio/video converters; broadband Internet video phones; and home plug power lines. D-Link holds the patents and copyrights on a number of technological platforms, including Application Specific Integrated Circuit (ASIC) computer chips, hardware technology designs and software applications. The company is also a key contributor to the Digital Living Network Alliance (DLNA), a group that works to maintain industry standards in consumer electronics. The company's client list includes Microsoft, T-Mobile, Honeywell, Quakecon, Yahoo and Pavlov Media, among several other corporate and government customers. In April 2009, D-Link introduced the DGS-3200 Managed Gigabit Switch, a power-saving technology that automatically reduces the power usage of unnecessary ports.

FINANCIALS: Sales and profits are in thousands of dollars—add 000 to get the full amount. 2010 Note: Financial information for 2010 was not available for all companies at press time.

		U.S. Stock Ticker:
2010 Sales: $	2010 Profits: $	Int'l Ticker: 2332 Int'l Exchange: Taipei-TPE
2009 Sales: $961,450	2009 Profits: $15,860	Employees: 2,087
2008 Sales: $1,087,000	2008 Profits: $100,200	Fiscal Year Ends: 12/31
2007 Sales: $1,249,800	2007 Profits: $75,600	Parent Company:
2006 Sales: $1,091,400	2006 Profits: $49,100	

SALARIES/BENEFITS:

Pension Plan:	ESOP Stock Plan:	Profit Sharing:	Top Exec. Salary: $	Bonus: $
Savings Plan:	Stock Purch. Plan:		Second Exec. Salary: $	Bonus: $

OTHER THOUGHTS:
Apparent Women Officers or Directors:
Hot Spot for Advancement for Women/Minorities:

LOCATIONS: ("Y" = Yes)

West:	Southwest:	Midwest:	Southeast:	Northeast:	International:
Y					Y

Note: Financial information, benefits and other data can change quickly and may vary from those stated here.

DOT HILL SYSTEMS CORP

www.dothill.com

Industry Group Code: 334112   Ranks within this company's industry group: Sales: 10   Profits: 6

Hardware:		Software:		Telecommunications:	Electronic Publishing:	Equipment:	Specialty Services:
Computers:		Consumer:		Local:	Online Service:	Telecom:	Consulting:
Accessories:		Corporate:	Y	Long Distance:	TV/Cable or Wireless:	Communication:	Contract Manufacturing:
Network Equipment:	Y	Telecom:		Cellular:	Games:	Distribution:	Processing:
Chips/Circuits:		Internet:		Internet Service:	Financial Data:	VAR/Reseller:	Staff/Outsourcing:
Parts/Drives:	Y					Satellite Srv./Equip.:	Specialty Services:

TYPES OF BUSINESS:

Data Storage & Backup Equipment
Storage Area Network Equipment
Storage Management Software

BRANDS/DIVISIONS/AFFILIATES:

R/Evolution
RAIDcore
RAIDar
AssuredCopy
AssuredSnap
Clover Communications Inc

CONTACTS: *Note: Officers with more than one job title may be intentionally listed here more than once.*

Dana W. Kammersgard, CEO
Dana W. Kammersgard, Pres.
Hanif I. Jamal, CFO/Sr. VP
Dave Zimmer, VP-Worldwide Channel Sales
Kenneth F. Day, CTO
James E. Kuenzel, Sr. VP-Eng.
Ernest Hafersat, Sr. VP-Worldwide Mfg.
Hanif I. Jamal, Corp. Sec.
Ernest Hafersat, Sr. VP-Oper.
Hanif I. Jamal, Treas.
Cooper Cowart, VP/Gen. Mgr.-HP Bus. Unit
Mike Flood, VP-Worldwide Quality & Consumer Support
Charles F. Christ, Chmn.
Garret Wein, VP-Worldwide OEM Sales
Ernest Hafersat, Sr. VP-Supply Base Mgmt.

Phone: 303-845-3200	Fax:
Toll-Free: 800-872-2783	
Address: 1351 S. Sunset St., Longmont, CO 80501 US	

GROWTH PLANS/SPECIAL FEATURES:

Dot Hill Systems Corp. is a provider of storage systems for organizations, performance networked storage and data management solutions in an open systems architecture. Dot Hill's storage solutions consist of integrated hardware and software products employing a modular system that allows customers to add capacity as needed. The company's hardware storage systems come in a variety of configurations, such as Fibre Channel, Small Computer Systems Interface (SCSI), Intranet SCSI (iSCSI), serial attached SCSI (SAS) and serial advanced technology attachment (SATA) technologies with direct attached storage (DAS) and storage area network (SAN) configurations. The firm's hardware product lines include the R/Evolution line; the AssuredSnap Solutions line; the Just a Bunch of Disks, or JBOD, line; and the SANnet line. Its product lines range from approximately 146 gigabyte (GB) to complete 108 terabyte (TB) storage systems. The firm's software products include network attached software (NAS); a web-based graphical user interface that allows customers to remotely control the firm's R/Evolution products; RAIDar, a program for configuring, monitoring, error reporting and running diagnostics on its 2730 RAID systems; RAIDcore, an internal server storage software; AssuredCopy, which provides volume back-ups; and AssuredSnap software, which works with the firm's AssuredSnap storage arrays to provide rollback and roll forward manipulation of point-in-time data snapshots. The company's customers consist of entry-level and midrange level businesses. The company recently completed the acquisition of Cloverleaf Communications, Inc., a software company specializing in heterogeneous storage virtualization and unified storage technologies.

FINANCIALS: Sales and profits are in thousands of dollars—add 000 to get the full amount. 2010 Note: Financial information for 2010 was not available for all companies at press time.

2010 Sales: $	2010 Profits: $	**U.S. Stock Ticker:** HILL
2009 Sales: $234,383	2009 Profits: $-13,625	**Int'l Ticker:** Int'l Exchange:
2008 Sales: $272,879	2008 Profits: $-25,765	Employees: 285
2007 Sales: $207,095	2007 Profits: $-60,228	Fiscal Year Ends: 12/31
2006 Sales: $239,217	2006 Profits: $-80,772	Parent Company:

SALARIES/BENEFITS:

Pension Plan:	ESOP Stock Plan: Y	Profit Sharing:	Top Exec. Salary: $367,500	Bonus: $50,000
Savings Plan: Y	Stock Purch. Plan:		Second Exec. Salary: $270,000	Bonus: $50,000

OTHER THOUGHTS:

Apparent Women Officers or Directors: 1
Hot Spot for Advancement for Women/Minorities:

LOCATIONS: ("Y" = Yes)

West:	Southwest:	Midwest:	Southeast:	Northeast:	International:
Y		Y			Y

DRS TECHNOLOGIES INC

www.drs.com

Industry Group Code: 334111 Ranks within this company's industry group: Sales: Profits:

Hardware:		Software:		Telecommunications:		Electronic Publishing:		Equipment:		Specialty Services:	
Computers:	Y	Consumer:		Local:		Online Service:		Telecom:		Consulting:	
Accessories:	Y	Corporate:		Long Distance:		TV/Cable or Wireless:		Communication:		Contract Manufacturing:	Y
Network Equipment:		Telecom:		Cellular:		Games:		Distribution:		Processing:	
Chips/Circuits:		Internet:		Internet Service:		Financial Data:		VAR/Reseller:		Staff/Outsourcing:	
Parts/Drives:	Y							Satellite Srv./Equip.:		Specialty Services:	Y

TYPES OF BUSINESS:

Computer Hardware & Systems
Aerospace & Defense Technology
Combat Control Systems
Communications Systems
Electro-Optical Systems
Power Generation, Conversion & Propulsion Equipment
Unmanned Vehicles
Data Storage Products

BRANDS/DIVISIONS/AFFILIATES:

C4I
RSTA
DRS/ATI OBVP
Allison Transmission, Inc.

CONTACTS: Note: Officers with more than one job title may be intentionally listed here more than once.

Mark S. Newman, CEO
Robert F. Mehmel, COO
Robert F. Mehmel, Pres.
Richard A. Schneider, CFO/Exec. VP
Andrea J. Mandel, Sr. VP-Human Resources
Allen H. Golland, CIO/Sr. VP
Michael W. Hansen, VP-Tech.
Mark A. Dorfman, General Counsel/Sec./Sr. VP
Robert Russo, Sr. VP-Oper.
Michael W. Hansen, VP-Strategy
Richard Goldberg, VP-Public Affairs & Comm.
Thomas P. Crimmins, Controller/Sr. VP
Phillip M. Balisle, Exec. VP-Washington Oper.
R.Alan Gross, Sr. VP-Compliance
Durwood W. Ringo Jr., Sr. VP-Gov't Rel.
Jason W. Rinsky, Sr. VP-Corp. Taxation
Mark S. Newman, Chmn.
Albert S. Moran Jr., VP-Strategic Supply Chain Initiatives

Phone: 973-898-1500	Fax: 973-898-4730
Toll-Free:	
Address: 5 Sylvan Way, Parsippany, NJ 07054 US	

GROWTH PLANS/SPECIAL FEATURES:

DRS Technologies, Inc. is a supplier of electronic defense products and systems, and military support services. The company develops and manufactures a range of products, from rugged computers and peripherals to systems and components, in the areas of communications, combat systems, data storage, digital imaging, electro-optics, flight safety and space. DRS sells its defense electronics systems to aerospace and defense contractors, all branches of the U.S. military, government intelligence agencies and international military forces. The firm operates through four divisions: the command, control, communications, computers and intelligence (C4I) division; the reconnaissance, surveillance and target acquisition (RSTA) division; the sustainment systems division; and the technical services division. The C4I group is a leading provider of naval computer workstations used to process and display integrated combat information. It produces surveillance, radar and tracking systems, acoustic signal processing and display equipment and combat control systems for U.S. and international military organizations. It also produces naval and industrial power generation, conversion, propulsion, distribution and control systems. The RSTA group is a leader in electro-optical infrared sighting; targeting and weapons guidance systems; high-performance focal plane arrays; and infrared uncooled sensors, assemblies and components. It also produces unmanned vehicles, air combat training, electronic warfare and network systems. The sustainment systems division offers products and services such as fuel and water distribution, mobile power conditioning systems and heavy equipment transporters. The technical service division offers engineering, logistical and other services. Additionally, DRS manufactures deployable flight incident recorders and emergency locator beacon systems. In August 2010, the firm introduced a new low cost EO/IR micro-gimbal compact infrared detector technological solution. In November 2010, the firm and Allison Transmission, Inc. partnered to develop the DRS/ATI OBVP system, a military vehicle solution that combines advanced power train technology and sufficient on-board power for crew survivability and force protection.

FINANCIALS: Sales and profits are in thousands of dollars—add 000 to get the full amount. 2010 Note: Financial information for 2010 was not available for all companies at press time.

2010 Sales: $	2010 Profits: $	U.S. Stock Ticker: Private
2009 Sales: $	2009 Profits: $	Int'l Ticker: Int'l Exchange:
2008 Sales: $3,295,384	2008 Profits: $165,769	Employees: 10,200
2007 Sales: $2,821,113	2007 Profits: $103,572	Fiscal Year Ends: 3/31
2006 Sales: $1,735,532	2006 Profits: $81,494	Parent Company:

SALARIES/BENEFITS:

Pension Plan:	ESOP Stock Plan:	Profit Sharing:	Top Exec. Salary: $936,250	Bonus: $1,258,300
Savings Plan: Y	Stock Purch. Plan:		Second Exec. Salary: $504,400	Bonus: $581,100

OTHER THOUGHTS:

Apparent Women Officers or Directors: 4
Hot Spot for Advancement for Women/Minorities: Y

LOCATIONS: ("Y" = Yes)

West:	Southwest:	Midwest:	Southeast:	Northeast:	International:
Y	Y	Y	Y	Y	Y

DSP GROUP INC

www.dspg.com

Industry Group Code: 33441 Ranks within this company's industry group: Sales: 45 Profits: 35

Hardware:		Software:	Telecommunications:	Electronic Publishing:	Equipment:		Specialty Services:	
Computers:		Consumer:	Local:	Online Service:	Telecom:	Y	Consulting:	
Accessories:		Corporate:	Long Distance:	TV/Cable or Wireless:	Communication:	Y	Contract Manufacturing:	
Network Equipment:		Telecom:	Cellular:	Games:	Distribution:		Processing:	
Chips/Circuits:	Y	Internet:	Internet Service:	Financial Data:	VAR/Reseller:		Staff/Outsourcing:	
Parts/Drives:					Satellite Srv./Equip.:		Specialty Services:	

TYPES OF BUSINESS:

Integrated Circuits-Digital Signal Processors
Speech Processors
RF Devices

BRANDS/DIVISIONS/AFFILIATES:

XpandR
XciteR Vega Firebird
XciteR DW
XceedR DE
XceedR DCX

CONTACTS: Note: Officers with more than one job title may be intentionally listed here more than once.

Ofer Elyakim, CEO
Boaz Edan, COO
Brian Robertson, Pres.
Dror Levy, CFO
Oz Zimmerman, VP-Mktg.
Tali Chen, VP-Human Resources
Eli Fogel, CTO/Sr. VP
Dror Levy, Corp. Sec.
Danny Hacohen, VP-Bus. Oper.
Dror Levy, VP-Finance
Avi Barel, VP-Sales
Lior Blanka, VP/Mgr.-Platform Div.
Ofer Ramon, VP/Mgr.-VLSI & RF Div.
Eliyahu Ayalon, Chmn.

Phone: 408-986-4300	Fax: 408-986-4323
Toll-Free:	
Address: 2580 N. 1st St., Ste. 460, San Jose, CA 95131 US	

GROWTH PLANS/SPECIAL FEATURES:

DSP Group, Inc. is a fabless semiconductor company and a global leader in the short-range wireless communication market, enabling home networking convergence for voice, video and data. DSP combines digital signal processing (DSP) technology with advanced complementary metal oxide semiconductor (CMOS) radio frequency (RF) devices, communications technologies and speech-processing algorithms. The company has developed several semiconductor devices for residential, enterprise and automotive wireless communications applications. These applications include digital 2.4GHz, DECT (1.9GHz), 5.8GHz and Bluetooth for voice, data and video communications, as well as products for digital voice recorders and MP3 applications. The company develops connected multimedia screen applications used in multimedia handsets, Wi-Fi video baby monitors, wireless digital picture frames and Internet radios. XpandR is the major product line in this segment. The firm also offers VoIP telephony services for both the home and the office. The XciteR product line, which separated into the Vega Firebird family and the DW family, provides embedded services for low-cost corded IP-phones to advanced cordless IP-phones with DECT handsets. The firm also provides cordless applications for the development of Wi-Fi Public Switched Telephone Network (PSTN) cordless phones; cordless headsets; and digital answering machine and digital video recorders (DVR). The XceedR suite of products, divided into the XceedR DE and the XceedR DCX families, consist of digital baseband processors and RF chips for low to mid-range and mid-to-high range cordless technologies. DSP sells its products primarily through distributors and representatives, as well as directly to original equipment manufacturers (OEMs) and original design manufacturers (ODMs). Export sales generate roughly 98% of DSP's total revenue.

FINANCIALS: Sales and profits are in thousands of dollars—add 000 to get the full amount. 2010 Note: Financial information for 2010 was not available for all companies at press time.

2010 Sales: $	2010 Profits: $	U.S. Stock Ticker: DSPG
2009 Sales: $212,186	2009 Profits: $-8,436	Int'l Ticker: Int'l Exchange:
2008 Sales: $305,800	2008 Profits: $-212,394	Employees: 446
2007 Sales: $248,788	2007 Profits: $-4,753	Fiscal Year Ends: 12/31
2006 Sales: $216,948	2006 Profits: $22,379	Parent Company:

SALARIES/BENEFITS:

Pension Plan:	ESOP Stock Plan:	Profit Sharing:	Top Exec. Salary: $330,000	Bonus: $100,000
Savings Plan:	Stock Purch. Plan:		Second Exec. Salary: $267,880	Bonus: $119,294

OTHER THOUGHTS:

Apparent Women Officers or Directors: 1
Hot Spot for Advancement for Women/Minorities:

LOCATIONS: ("Y" = Yes)

West:	Southwest:	Midwest:	Southeast:	Northeast:	International:
Y					Y

EASYLINK SERVICES INTERNATIONAL CORPORATION

www.easylink.com
Industry Group Code: 518210 Ranks within this company's industry group: Sales: 5 Profits: 4

Hardware:	Software:		Telecommunications:	Electronic Publishing:	Equipment:	Specialty Services:	
Computers:	Consumer:		Local:	Online Service:	Telecom:	Consulting:	
Accessories:	Corporate:	Y	Long Distance:	TV/Cable or Wireless:	Communication:	Contract Manufacturing:	
Network Equipment:	Telecom:		Cellular:	Games:	Distribution:	Processing:	Y
Chips/Circuits:	Internet:		Internet Service:	Financial Data:	VAR/Reseller:	Staff/Outsourcing:	
Parts/Drives:					Satellite Srv./Equip.:	Specialty Services:	

TYPES OF BUSINESS:

Transaction Management & Delivery Services
Document Management Services

BRANDS/DIVISIONS/AFFILIATES:

EasyLink Managed File Transfer
EDI Value Added Network
EDI Managed Services
EasyLink Desktop Messaging
EasyLink Production Messaging
EasyLink Workflow Services
EasyLink Document Capture Management Services

CONTACTS: *Note: Officers with more than one job title may be intentionally listed here more than once.*

Thomas J. Stallings, CEO
Glen E. Shipley, CFO
Kevin R. Maloney, Sr. VP-Global Sales & Mktg.
Glen E. Shipley, Sec.
Patrick A. Harper, Sr. VP-Worldwide Oper.
Joachim Braun, VP-Dev.
Teresa A. Deuel, Exec. VP-Worldwide Customer Support
Kim D. Cooke, Chmn.
Anthony Richardson, Pres., North Asia

Phone: 678-533-8000	Fax:
Toll-Free:	
Address: 6025 The Corners Pkwy., Ste. 100, Norcross, GA 30092 US	

GROWTH PLANS/SPECIAL FEATURES:

EasyLink Services International Corporation is a global provider of value added services that facilitate the electronic exchange of documents and information between enterprises, their trading communities and their customers. It delivers it services through a global Internet Protocol (IP) network, which hosts its applications on enterprise-class platforms that comprise server and network operations centers located worldwide. EasyLink's core services include electronic data interchange (EDI) services, fax services, telex services and other services that are integral to the movement of money, materials, products and people in the global economy including insurance claims, trade and travel confirmations, purchase orders, invoices, shipping notices and funds transfers. The firm operates through two segments: Supply Chain Messaging, which includes generated 50% of the firm's revenue for 2010 and includes all of its EDI and telex services; and On Demand Messaging, which generated 50% of its revenue and includes all fax, e-mail, document capture and management (DCM) and workflow services. EasyLink's Supply Chain Messaging products include EDI Value Added Network (VAN) for moving information regardless of file size, communication protocol or data format; EDI Managed Services, offering multiple EDI s ranging from meeting first time EDI requirements to complete outsourcing of the EDI function; EasyLink Managed File Transfer, an outsourced product that safely allows organizations to manage high-volume data exchanges; and a wide range of telex services. The firm's On Demand Messaging products include Production Messaging, a fully managed outsourced document delivery system; Desktop Messaging, an outsourced corporate faxing application that allows users to send and receive faxes exactly like e-mail; Workflow Services, a hosted application that integrates users' critical faxes with tailored process flows to improve communication efficiency, visibility and control; and Document Capture Management Services, which combines a global fax network and human quality checks to turn manual processes directly into data consumable by back office applications.

FINANCIALS: Sales and profits are in thousands of dollars—add 000 to get the full amount. 2010 Note: Financial information for 2010 was not available for all companies at press time.

2010 Sales: $81,443	2010 Profits: $15,757	U.S. Stock Ticker: ESIC
2009 Sales: $85,365	2009 Profits: $-11,512	Int'l Ticker: Int'l Exchange:
2008 Sales: $92,161	2008 Profits: $16,301	Employees: 282
2007 Sales: $21,870	2007 Profits: $2,736	Fiscal Year Ends: 7/31
2006 Sales: $19,771	2006 Profits: $2,976	Parent Company:

SALARIES/BENEFITS:

Pension Plan:	ESOP Stock Plan:	Profit Sharing:	Top Exec. Salary: $400,000	Bonus: $215,011
Savings Plan: Y	Stock Purch. Plan:		Second Exec. Salary: $250,000	Bonus: $134,382

OTHER THOUGHTS:

Apparent Women Officers or Directors: 1
Hot Spot for Advancement for Women/Minorities:

LOCATIONS: ("Y" = Yes)

West:	Southwest:	Midwest:	Southeast:	Northeast:	International:
			Y	Y	Y

ECHELON CORP

www.echelon.com

Industry Group Code: 33411 Ranks within this company's industry group: Sales: 15 Profits: 14

Hardware:		Software:	Telecommunications:	Electronic Publishing:	Equipment:	Specialty Services:
Computers:		Consumer:	Local:	Online Service:	Telecom:	Consulting:
Accessories:		Corporate:	Long Distance:	TV/Cable or Wireless:	Communication:	Contract Manufacturing:
Network Equipment:	Y	Telecom:	Cellular:	Games:	Distribution:	Processing:
Chips/Circuits:		Internet:	Internet Service:	Financial Data:	VAR/Reseller:	Staff/Outsourcing:
Parts/Drives:					Satellite Srv./Equip.:	Specialty Services:

TYPES OF BUSINESS:

Computer Networking Equipment-Energy Controls
Remote Appliance, Sensor & Equipment Controls
Remote Diagnostics
Municipal Transportation Networks
Automation Systems
Utility Grid Diagnostic Systems

BRANDS/DIVISIONS/AFFILIATES:

LonWorks
Pyxos
i.LON
LonWorks 2.0

CONTACTS: Note: Officers with more than one job title may be intentionally listed here more than once.

Ron Sege, CEO
Ron Sege, Pres.
Oliver Stanfield, CFO/Exec. VP
Linda Hanson, VP-Corp. Mktg.
Robert Dolin, CTO/VP
Robert Machlin, Sr. VP-Prod.
Kathleen Bloch, General Counsel/Sr. VP
Russell Harris, Sr. VP-Oper.
Anders Axelsson, Sr. VP-LWI Sales & Market Dev.
Michael Anderson, Sr. VP-NES Sales & Market Dev.
M. Kenneth Oshman, Exec. Chmn.

Phone: 408-938-5200	Fax: 540-790-3800
Toll-Free: 888-324-3566	
Address: 550 Meridian Ave., San Jose, CA 95126 US	

GROWTH PLANS/SPECIAL FEATURES:

Echelon Corp. is a provider of control network technology for automation systems. The company develops, markets and supports products and services that allow device manufacturers, integrators and end users to implement control networks in the building, industrial, transportation, utility, home and other automation markets. Services include building automation systems, system failure prediction, municipal transportation applications, remote diagnostics and home pay-per-use capabilities. Its line of products includes transceivers, concentrator products, control modules, routers, network interfaces, development tools and software tools and toolkits. Echelon devises these technologies for both Internet standards and for its LonWorks 2.0 control networking platform. Each device is also capable of communicating with other devices in its control network and taking actions based on information that it receives from them as well as allowing the integration of products or subsystems from multiple vendors. In the utility sector, Echelon operates its networked energy services (NES) system, which pinpoints power outages and can reduce stress on the grid, avoiding blackouts and brownouts. The Pyxos FT chip embedded control networking platform product is intended to reduce the cost of manufacturing, installing and maintaining a machine. For system integrators serving the street lighting, remote facility monitoring, and energy management markets, the firm has developed the i.LON Internet server family of products. The firm's transportation products use LonWorks systems and include products for railcars, light rail, buses, motor coaches, fire trucks, naval vessels, and aircraft.

The company offers its employees stock options; medical, dental and vision insurance; life and AD&D insurance; short- and long-term disability insurance; flexible spending accounts; and tuition reimbursement.

FINANCIALS: Sales and profits are in thousands of dollars—add 000 to get the full amount. 2010 Note: Financial information for 2010 was not available for all companies at press time.

2010 Sales: $	2010 Profits: $	U.S. Stock Ticker: ELON
2009 Sales: $103,338	2009 Profits: $-32,034	Int'l Ticker: Int'l Exchange:
2008 Sales: $134,047	2008 Profits: $-25,831	Employees: 325
2007 Sales: $137,577	2007 Profits: $-14,512	Fiscal Year Ends: 12/31
2006 Sales: $57,276	2006 Profits: $-24,440	Parent Company:

SALARIES/BENEFITS:

Pension Plan:	ESOP Stock Plan:	Profit Sharing:	Top Exec. Salary: $407,141	Bonus: $
Savings Plan: Y	Stock Purch. Plan: Y		Second Exec. Salary: $324,000	Bonus: $

OTHER THOUGHTS:

Apparent Women Officers or Directors: 4
Hot Spot for Advancement for Women/Minorities: Y

LOCATIONS: ("Y" = Yes)

West:	Southwest:	Midwest:	Southeast:	Northeast:	International:
Y		Y			Y

ECI TELECOM LTD

www.ecitele.com

Industry Group Code: 334210 Ranks within this company's industry group: Sales: Profits:

Hardware:	Software:	Telecommunications:		Electronic Publishing:	Equipment:		Specialty Services:
Computers:	Consumer:	Local:		Online Service:	Telecom:	Y	Consulting:
Accessories:	Corporate:	Long Distance:	Y	TV/Cable or Wireless:	Communication:		Contract Manufacturing:
Network Equipment:	Telecom:	Cellular:	Y	Games:	Distribution:		Processing:
Chips/Circuits:	Internet:	Internet Service:		Financial Data:	VAR/Reseller:		Staff/Outsourcing:
Parts/Drives:					Satellite Srv./Equip.:		Specialty Services:

TYPES OF BUSINESS:

Digital Communications Equipment Manufacturing
Optical Networking Equipment
Broadband Access Equipment
Data Encryption Services

BRANDS/DIVISIONS/AFFILIATES:

Swarth Group (The)
ECI 1Net
Hi-FOCuS
ShadeTree

CONTACTS: Note: Officers with more than one job title may be intentionally listed here more than once.

Rafi Maor, CEO
Rafi Maor, Pres.
Giora Bitan, CFO/Exec. VP
Aviel Tenenbaum, Exec. VP-Global Sales & Mktg.
Adi Bildner, VP-Human Resources
Arnie Taragin, General Counsel/Corp. VP
Hezi Basok, Exec. VP-Global Bus. Oper.
Sandra Welfeld, Dir.-Corp. Comm.
Eran Talmon, Gen. Mgr./Head-Global Svcs. Div.
Eyal Shaked, Exec. VP-Networks Solutions Div.
Shaul Shani, Chmn.

Phone: 972-3-926-6555	Fax: 972-3-926-6444
Toll-Free:	
Address: 30 Hasivim St., Petah Tikva, 49517 Israel	

GROWTH PLANS/SPECIAL FEATURES:

ECI Telecom, Ltd., based in Israel, provides advanced telecommunications solutions to carriers and service providers worldwide. ECI 1Net is the company's central Next-Generation Network (NGN), offering fully integrated network equipment, solutions and a suite of services for a variety of platforms. The key product components of 1Net include the 9000 series of Carrier Ethernet Switch Routers (CESR), aggregation switches and demarcation units; WDM/ROADM optical gear, built on the XDM packet-optical platform; Multi-Service Provisioning Platforms (MSPP), built around XDM and Broadgate products, which manage and monitor network transmissions; and Multi-Service Access Nodes (MSAN), built on the Hi-FOCuS platform. Hi-FOCuS supports a full range of video, voice and data services. Data security solutions include Aurora-G, an encryption solution that protects data transmission over Ethernet networks. ECI's data networking division maps, manufactures and markets broadband routers, enabling telecommunications companies to deliver Internet Protocol (IP)-based data, voice and video services. The company uses ShadeTree software, developed in-house, to handle its network routing. The firm's solutions are targeted at a number of market segments, including wireline operators, wireless carriers, cable multiple system operators (MSOs), energy and other utilities, carrier of carriers, transportation companies and government and defense clients.

FINANCIALS: Sales and profits are in thousands of dollars—add 000 to get the full amount. 2010 Note: Financial information for 2010 was not available for all companies at press time.

2010 Sales: $	2010 Profits: $	U.S. Stock Ticker: Private
2009 Sales: $	2009 Profits: $	Int'l Ticker: Int'l Exchange:
2008 Sales: $	2008 Profits: $	Employees:
2007 Sales: $	2007 Profits: $	Fiscal Year Ends: 12/31
2006 Sales: $656,342	2006 Profits: $22,095	Parent Company: SWARTH GROUP (THE)

SALARIES/BENEFITS:

Pension Plan: Y	ESOP Stock Plan:	Profit Sharing:	Top Exec. Salary: $	Bonus: $
Savings Plan: Y	Stock Purch. Plan:		Second Exec. Salary: $	Bonus: $

OTHER THOUGHTS:

Apparent Women Officers or Directors:
Hot Spot for Advancement for Women/Minorities:

LOCATIONS: ("Y" = Yes)

West:	Southwest:	Midwest:	Southeast:	Northeast:	International:
Y				Y	Y

ECLINICALWORKS
www.eclinicalworks.com

Industry Group Code: 511210D Ranks within this company's industry group: Sales: 4 Profits:

Hardware:	Software:		Telecommunications:	Electronic Publishing:	Equipment:	Specialty Services:	
Computers:	Consumer:		Local:	Online Service:	Telecom:	Consulting:	Y
Accessories:	Corporate:	Y	Long Distance:	TV/Cable or Wireless:	Communication:	Contract Manufacturing:	
Network Equipment:	Telecom:		Cellular:	Games:	Distribution:	Processing:	
Chips/Circuits:	Internet:		Internet Service:	Financial Data:	VAR/Reseller:	Staff/Outsourcing:	
Parts/Drives:					Satellite Srv./Equip.:	Specialty Services:	

TYPES OF BUSINESS:
Electronic Health Record Software
Electronic Prescription Filing
Patient Flow Management
Claims Submission & Management Software
Business Optimization Software

BRANDS/DIVISIONS/AFFILIATES:
Enterprise Business Optimizer
eClinicalWorks Electronic Health eXchange
eClinicalMobile
eClinicalMessenger
eClinicalWorks P2P

CONTACTS: Note: Officers with more than one job title may be intentionally listed here more than once.
Girish Kumar Navari, CEO
Healther Caouette, Contact-Media

Phone: 508-836-2700	Fax: 508-836-4466
Toll-Free: 866-888-6929	
Address: 112 Turnpike Rd., Westborough Executive Park, Westborough, MA 01581 US	

GROWTH PLANS/SPECIAL FEATURES:

eClinicalWorks is a private company operating in the ambulatory clinical systems market. The company primarily provides electronic medical record (EMR) and practice management (PM) tools for its clients, including physicians; large and small health systems; large and medium medical group practices, including Federally Qualified Health Centers (FQHCs) and Community Health Centers (CHCs); and small, solo provider practices. The firm's customer base consists of more than 40,000 providers in all 50 states, including greater than 500 hospitals and health systems. eClinicalWorks' EMR solution provides patient flow management, patient record access, registry reporting, electronic prescription request, referring physician communication and clinical data transfers. When used with the firm's PM system, this solution enables clients to review patient history, current medications, allergies and diagnostic tests; streamline medical billing management; check patient insurance eligibility; electronically submit and manage claims; and perform clinical and financial analyses through its Enterprise Business Optimizer (eBO) tool. Other tools include the eClinicalWorks Electronic Health eXchange (EHX), a community portal for increased hospital, physician and patient integration; eClinicalMobile, a mobile browser for checking schedules, electronically filing prescriptions, viewing patient history and checking lab results; eClinicalWorks P2P offers interoperability between practices that use eClinicalWorks and those that do not; and eClinicalMessenger, a Voice over Internet Protocol (VoIP)-based messaging service that enables physician/patient communication. The company also maintains a web-based patient portal allowing patients to access their physician's systems to view their own lab results and appointment information, as well as request prescription refills and communicate with doctors and nurses. In May 2010, the company announced a partnership with Intellidose to integrate Intellidose's IntrinsiQ chemotherapy management solution with eClinicalWorks' EMR solutions to provide oncology practices complete health information systems.

eClinicalWorks offers its employees health, dental, vision, life and disability insurance; business travel accident insurance; flexible spending accounts; and a 401(k) plan.

FINANCIALS: Sales and profits are in thousands of dollars—add 000 to get the full amount. 2010 Note: Financial information for 2010 was not available for all companies at press time.

2010 Sales: $	2010 Profits: $	U.S. Stock Ticker: Private
2009 Sales: $100,000	2009 Profits: $	Int'l Ticker: Int'l Exchange:
2008 Sales: $85,000	2008 Profits: $	Employees: 700
2007 Sales: $	2007 Profits: $	Fiscal Year Ends: 12/31
2006 Sales: $	2006 Profits: $	Parent Company:

SALARIES/BENEFITS:
Pension Plan:	ESOP Stock Plan:	Profit Sharing:	Top Exec. Salary: $	Bonus: $
Savings Plan: Y	Stock Purch. Plan:		Second Exec. Salary: $	Bonus: $

OTHER THOUGHTS:
Apparent Women Officers or Directors:
Hot Spot for Advancement for Women/Minorities:

LOCATIONS: ("Y" = Yes)
West:	Southwest:	Midwest:	Southeast:	Northeast:	International:
Y			Y	Y	

ELCOM INTERNATIONAL INC

www.elcom.com

Industry Group Code: 511210A **Ranks within this company's industry group: Sales: Profits:**

Hardware:	Software:		Telecommunications:	Electronic Publishing:	Equipment:	Specialty Services:	
Computers:	Consumer:		Local:	Online Service:	Telecom:	Consulting:	Y
Accessories:	Corporate:	Y	Long Distance:	TV/Cable or Wireless:	Communication:	Contract Manufacturing:	
Network Equipment:	Telecom:		Cellular:	Games:	Distribution:	Processing:	
Chips/Circuits:	Internet:		Internet Service:	Financial Data:	VAR/Reseller:	Staff/Outsourcing:	
Parts/Drives:					Satellite Srv./Equip.:	Specialty Services:	Y

TYPES OF BUSINESS:

E-Commerce Software Development

BRANDS/DIVISIONS/AFFILIATES:

Professional Electronic Commerce Online System
PECOS
eProcurement Scotl@nd

CONTACTS: Note: Officers with more than one job title may be intentionally listed here more than once.

Mark Stephenson, Global Head-Sales
Kevin Larnach, Exec. VP-Oper.
David Elliott, Dir.-Finance
William Lock, Chmn.

Phone: 781-440-4000	Fax: 781-762-1540
Toll-Free:	
Address: 10 Oceana Way, Ste. 102, Norwood, MA 02062 US	

GROWTH PLANS/SPECIAL FEATURES:

Elcom International, Inc. offers Internet-based remotely-hosted, integrated eProcurement and eMarketplace services. The company is able to provide rapid deployment and single point responsibility to its customers by remotely hosting its Professional Electronic Commerce Online System (PECOS) ePurchasing service. Over 100 organizations are currently using or accessing Elcom's service under this arrangement. In the U.K., Elcom has a contract with Capgemini UK Plc associated with the Scottish Executive's eProcurement Scotl@dnd service, where Elcom provides a Commerce Process Management system to agencies, councils and National Health Service of Scotland Trusts in Scotland. Elcom's professional service offerings include various consulting and supplier services to its clients, which range from implementation of PECOS and initial training and consulting, to interfacing data from PECOS into back-end computer systems, including Enterprise Resource Planning systems such as Oracle and SAP It has licensed a third-party dynamic trading system platform that performs auction, reverse auction and other electronic negotiation functions, which it offers as an optional functionality.

FINANCIALS: Sales and profits are in thousands of dollars—add 000 to get the full amount. 2010 Note: Financial information for 2010 was not available for all companies at press time.

2010 Sales: $	2010 Profits: $	U.S. Stock Ticker: ELCO.PK
2009 Sales: $	2009 Profits: $	Int'l Ticker: Int'l Exchange:
2008 Sales: $	2008 Profits: $	Employees:
2007 Sales: $	2007 Profits: $	Fiscal Year Ends: 12/31
2006 Sales: $2,546	2006 Profits: $-6,832	Parent Company:

SALARIES/BENEFITS:

Pension Plan:	ESOP Stock Plan:	Profit Sharing:	Top Exec. Salary: $	Bonus: $
Savings Plan:	Stock Purch. Plan:		Second Exec. Salary: $	Bonus: $

OTHER THOUGHTS:

Apparent Women Officers or Directors:
Hot Spot for Advancement for Women/Minorities:

LOCATIONS: ("Y" = Yes)

West:	Southwest:	Midwest:	Southeast:	Northeast:	International:
				Y	Y

ELECTRONIC ARTS INC

www.ea.com

Industry Group Code: 511210G Ranks within this company's industry group: Sales: 3 Profits: 8

Hardware:		Software:		Telecommunications:		Electronic Publishing:		Equipment:		Specialty Services:	
Computers:		Consumer:	Y	Local:		Online Service:		Telecom:		Consulting:	
Accessories:		Corporate:		Long Distance:		TV/Cable or Wireless:		Communication:		Contract Manufacturing:	
Network Equipment:		Telecom:		Cellular:	Y	Games:	Y	Distribution:		Processing:	
Chips/Circuits:		Internet:		Internet Service:		Financial Data:		VAR/Reseller:		Staff/Outsourcing:	
Parts/Drives:								Satellite Srv./Equip.:		Specialty Services:	

TYPES OF BUSINESS:

Computer Software-Video Games
Online Interactive Games
E-Commerce Sales
Mobile Games

BRANDS/DIVISIONS/AFFILIATES:

EA Games
EA Sports
EA Play
Madden NFL
NCAA Football
Pogo.com
Playfish
Chillingo Ltd

CONTACTS: Note: Officers with more than one job title may be intentionally listed here more than once.

John S. Riccitiello, CEO
John Schappert, COO
Eric Brown, CFO/Exec. VP
Gabrielle Toledano, Exec. VP-Human Resources
Stephen G. Bene, General Counsel/Sec./Sr. VP
Joel Linzner, Exec. VP-Bus. & Legal Affairs
Ken Barker, Chief Acct. Officer/Sr. VP
Peter Moore, Pres., EA Sports Label
Frank Gibeau, Pres., EA Games Label
Rod Humble, Pres., EA Play Label
Lawrence F. Probst, III, Chmn.

Phone: 650-628-1500	Fax: 650-628-1414
Toll-Free:	
Address: 209 Redwood Shores Pkwy., Redwood City, CA 94065-1175 US	

GROWTH PLANS/SPECIAL FEATURES:

Electronic Arts, Inc. (EA) develops, markets, publishes and distributes video game software. The company designs products for a number of platforms, including video game consoles such as the Sony PlayStation 3, Microsoft Xbox 360 and Nintendo Wii; handheld game systems, including PlayStation Portable (PSP), Nintendo DS and Apple iPod; personal computers (PCs); and mobile phones. The company operates in three segments: Labels, EA Interactive and the Global Publishing Organization. The firm's Labels include EA Games, EA Sports and EA Play. The EA Games label encompasses the largest percentage of the company's studios and development staff, focused on producing a diverse portfolio of action-adventure, role playing, racing and combat games, as well as massively-multiplayer online role-playing games (MMORPG) such as Warhammer Online. The EA Sports label produces a variety of sports-based video games, including the Madden NFL, Fight Night and NCAA Football franchises. The EA Play label develops games that are intended to be quick to learn and play, making them easily accessible for a wide audience. The EA Interactive segment produces Internet and mobile device games, and includes EA Mobile, which produces games specifically for mobile devices; Pogo, an online service with over 1.6 million subscribers; and Playfish, which creates free-to-play games for social networking platforms. The Global Publishing Organization develops, distributes and sells products created by the other divisions. The company operates in over 35 countries worldwide. In October 2010, the firm acquired Chillingo, Ltd., a publisher of independent mobile games. In November 2010, EA signed a five-year contract with Facebook that will enable the company to sell virtual goods on the social networking service.

EA offers its employees healthcare coverage; an employee assistance program; life insurance; travelers' insurance; car allowances; disability insurance; free or discounted EA games; access to gyms and in-company restaurants; charitable donation matching; bonus plans; and spot stock awards.

FINANCIALS: Sales and profits are in thousands of dollars—add 000 to get the full amount. 2010 Note: Financial information for 2010 was not available for all companies at press time.

2010 Sales: $3,654,000	2010 Profits: $-677,000	**U.S. Stock Ticker:** ERTS
2009 Sales: $4,212,000	2009 Profits: $-1,088,000	**Int'l Ticker:** Int'l Exchange:
2008 Sales: $3,665,000	2008 Profits: $-454,000	Employees: 7,800
2007 Sales: $3,091,000	2007 Profits: $76,000	Fiscal Year Ends: 3/31
2006 Sales: $2,951,000	2006 Profits: $236,000	Parent Company:

SALARIES/BENEFITS:

Pension Plan:	ESOP Stock Plan:	Profit Sharing:	Top Exec. Salary: $800,000	Bonus: $746,667
Savings Plan: Y	Stock Purch. Plan: Y		Second Exec. Salary: $713,764	Bonus: $

OTHER THOUGHTS:

Apparent Women Officers or Directors: 2
Hot Spot for Advancement for Women/Minorities: Y

LOCATIONS: ("Y" = Yes)

West:	Southwest:	Midwest:	Southeast:	Northeast:	International:
Y	Y	Y	Y	Y	Y

ELECTRONICS FOR IMAGING INC

www.efi.com

Industry Group Code: 334119 Ranks within this company's industry group: Sales: 20 Profits: 16

Hardware:		Software:		Telecommunications:		Electronic Publishing:		Equipment:		Specialty Services:	
Computers:		Consumer:	Y	Local:		Online Service:		Telecom:		Consulting:	
Accessories:	Y	Corporate:	Y	Long Distance:		TV/Cable or Wireless:		Communication:		Contract Manufacturing:	
Network Equipment:		Telecom:		Cellular:		Games:		Distribution:		Processing:	
Chips/Circuits:		Internet:		Internet Service:		Financial Data:		VAR/Reseller:		Staff/Outsourcing:	
Parts/Drives:								Satellite Srv./Equip.:		Specialty Services:	

TYPES OF BUSINESS:

Networking Equipment-Printing & Graphics
Print Management Applications & Software
Print Servers
Super-Wide Format Inkjet Printers

BRANDS/DIVISIONS/AFFILIATES:

Fiery
Splash
PressVu
UltraVu
MicroPress
VUTEk QS220
Digital StoreFront
EFI Mobile Client

CONTACTS: Note: Officers with more than one job title may be intentionally listed here more than once.

Guy Gecht, CEO
Fred Rosenzweig, Pres.
Vincent Pilette, CFO
Bryan Ko, Sec.
Jane Cedrone, Mgr.-Public Rel.
Gill Cogan, Interim Chmn.

Phone: 650-357-3500	Fax: 650-357-3907
Toll-Free: 800-875-7117	
Address: 303 Velocity Way, Foster City, CA 94404 US	

GROWTH PLANS/SPECIAL FEATURES:

Electronics for Imaging, Inc. (EFI) provides color digital print controllers, super-wide format printers and inks, and print management solutions for professional and enterprise printing. The company's main products include the Fiery, Splash and MicroPress brands of stand-alone print servers connected to digital copiers, which are embedded in digital copiers and desktop color laser printers. Once networked, EFI-powered printers and copiers are shared between work groups and departments to produce color and black/white documents. The firm also offers super-wide format digital inkjet printers used for billboard graphics, commercial photo labs and large sign shops. These products include the following series: PressVu, Jetrion, Rastek, UltraVu, VUTEk 3360, GS and QS. Additionally, the company provides software for the commercial printing and enterprise markets. Fiery XF and Colorproof XF offer color proofing solutions that increase workflow, power, and expandability; EFI management information systems collect, organize and present critical information to improve process control and profit potential; and Digital StoreFront and PrinterSite offer a web interface to manage print transactions between customer and printer. EFI also provides enterprise solutions that transform paper documents into electronic files for delivery or storage. The firm sells its products to original equipment manufacturers (OEMs) such as Canon; Fuji; Toshiba; Sharp; Xerox; and Konica Minolta. The company has offices across the U.S. and in Germany, Belgium and the Netherlands. In 2010, EFI released several new products, including VUTEk QS220, a direct-to-substrate, two-meter high-definition UV-curing flatbed printer; EFI Mobile Client, which allows customers monitor and proof their EFI printers' performance through iPhones, iPods and iPads; and software application PrintMe Connect for AirPrint, which allows for direct printing from iPhone, iPad and iPod touch iOS 4.2-enabled devices to the firm's Fiery-branded printers.

The firm offers employees medical, dental, vision and pet insurance; tuition assistance; stock ownership; paid time off; and assistance programs.

FINANCIALS: Sales and profits are in thousands of dollars—add 000 to get the full amount. 2010 Note: Financial information for 2010 was not available for all companies at press time.

2010 Sales: $	2010 Profits: $	U.S. Stock Ticker: EFII
2009 Sales: $401,108	2009 Profits: $-2,171	Int'l Ticker: Int'l Exchange:
2008 Sales: $560,380	2008 Profits: $-113,444	Employees: 2,021
2007 Sales: $620,586	2007 Profits: $26,843	Fiscal Year Ends: 12/31
2006 Sales: $564,611	2006 Profits: $- 183	Parent Company:

SALARIES/BENEFITS:

Pension Plan: Y	ESOP Stock Plan: Y	Profit Sharing:	Top Exec. Salary: $554,125	Bonus: $
Savings Plan: Y	Stock Purch. Plan:		Second Exec. Salary: $473,687	Bonus: $

OTHER THOUGHTS:

Apparent Women Officers or Directors: 1
Hot Spot for Advancement for Women/Minorities:

LOCATIONS: ("Y" = Yes)

West:	Southwest:	Midwest:	Southeast:	Northeast:	International:
Y	Y	Y	Y	Y	Y

ELITEGROUP COMPUTER SYSTEMS CO LTD   www.ecs.com.tw

Industry Group Code: 334119 Ranks within this company's industry group: Sales: 12   Profits: 12

Hardware:		Software:	Telecommunications:	Electronic Publishing:	Equipment:	Specialty Services:
Computers:	Y	Consumer:	Local:	Online Service:	Telecom:	Consulting:
Accessories:		Corporate:	Long Distance:	TV/Cable or Wireless:	Communication:	Contract Manufacturing:
Network Equipment:		Telecom:	Cellular:	Games:	Distribution:	Processing:
Chips/Circuits:		Internet:	Internet Service:	Financial Data:	VAR/Reseller:	Staff/Outsourcing:
Parts/Drives:	Y				Satellite Srv./Equip.:	Specialty Services:

TYPES OF BUSINESS:
Computer Hardware Manufacturing
PC Systems
Graphics Cards
Motherboards

BRANDS/DIVISIONS/AFFILIATES:
ECS A785GM-M
Black Series
NGTS2501GMU-F
U3N2
S6M2
Motherboard Intelligent BIOS II
ECS GeForce GT 240
H55H-MU

CONTACTS: *Note: Officers with more than one job title may be intentionally listed here more than once.*
Chaozong Zeng, Gen. Mgr.-ODM Bus.
Weizheng Wang, Gen. Mgr.-Channel Bus.
Wenyan Lin Guo, Chmn.

Phone: 866-2-2162-1177	Fax: 886-2-2797-0690
Toll-Free:	
Address: Ti Ding Blvd., No. 239, Sec. 2, Taipei, 11493 Taiwan	

GROWTH PLANS/SPECIAL FEATURES:
Elitegroup Computer Systems Co., Ltd. (ECS) is one of the world's leading makers of motherboards for PCs. The firm is publicly traded on the Taiwan Stock Exchange market. Headquartered in Taiwan, the company sells products through business partners and distributors in more than 60 countries worldwide, as well as through international branch offices in North and South America, Europe and across the Pacific Rim. ECS produces and markets a number of product lines, including Intel and AMD motherboards, phase-out mainboards, notebook computers, desktop PCs, wireless devices and graphics cards. The firm produces its hardware through two ISO 9001:2000 and ISO 14001:2004 certified manufacturing facilities located in Shenzhen, China with production capacities in excess of 2.5 million motherboards and 200,000 laptop computer systems per month. Some of the firm's other products include the ECS A785GM-M, a Micro ATX Black Series motherboard; the Motherboard Intelligent BIOS II tweaking utility for Black Series motherboards; the NGTS2501GMU-F graphics card; and the ECS GeForce GT 240 series graphics card. In January 2010, the company released the U3N2 and S6M2 expansion cards for USB 3.0 and SATA 6Gigabits per second external devices. In 2010, the firm introduced several products including the A890GXM Series motherboard; the Black Extreme P67H2-A motherboard; the Black Deluxe H67H2-M motherboard; the Black Series A890GXM-A2 motherboard; and the H55H-MU green-concept designed motherboard.

FINANCIALS: Sales and profits are in thousands of dollars—add 000 to get the full amount. 2010 Note: Financial information for 2010 was not available for all companies at press time.

2010 Sales: $	2010 Profits: $	**U.S. Stock Ticker:**
2009 Sales: $2,525,930	2009 Profits: $28,190	**Int'l Ticker:** 2331 Int'l Exchange: Taipei-TPE
2008 Sales: $2,815,880	2008 Profits: $10,155	**Employees:** 15,298
2007 Sales: $2,963,330	2007 Profits: $26,840	**Fiscal Year Ends:** 12/31
2006 Sales: $	2006 Profits: $	**Parent Company:**

SALARIES/BENEFITS:

Pension Plan:	ESOP Stock Plan:	Profit Sharing:	Top Exec. Salary: $	Bonus: $
Savings Plan:	Stock Purch. Plan:		Second Exec. Salary: $	Bonus: $

OTHER THOUGHTS:
Apparent Women Officers or Directors:
Hot Spot for Advancement for Women/Minorities:

LOCATIONS: ("Y" = Yes)

West:	Southwest:	Midwest:	Southeast:	Northeast:	International:
Y					Y

ELPIDA MEMORY INC

www.elpida.com

Industry Group Code: 33441 Ranks within this company's industry group: Sales: 13 Profits: 54

Hardware:		Software:		Telecommunications:		Electronic Publishing:	Equipment:		Specialty Services:
Computers:		Consumer:		Local:		Online Service:	Telecom:		Consulting:
Accessories:		Corporate:		Long Distance:		TV/Cable or Wireless:	Communication:		Contract Manufacturing:
Network Equipment:		Telecom:		Cellular:		Games:	Distribution:		Processing:
Chips/Circuits:	Y	Internet:		Internet Service:		Financial Data:	VAR/Reseller:		Staff/Outsourcing:
Parts/Drives:							Satellite Srv./Equip.:		Specialty Services:

TYPES OF BUSINESS:

Semiconductors (Microchips)
Integrated Circuits
Computer Components

BRANDS/DIVISIONS/AFFILIATES:

Rexchip Electronics Corporation
Tera Probe Inc
TeraPower Technology Inc
Powerchip Technology Corporation
ProMOS Technologies Inc
Winbond Electronics Corporation
Akita Elpida Memory Inc
Walton Advanced Engineering Inc

CONTACTS: Note: Officers with more than one job title may be intentionally listed here more than once.

Yukio Sakamoto, CEO
Shuichi Otsuka, COO
Yukio Sakamoto, Pres.
Yasuo Shirai, CFO
Oliver Chang, Chief Sales Officer
Takao Adachi, CTO-New Bus. Unit
Toshiaki Hagiwara, Chief Admin. Officer
Takehiro Fukuda, Dir.-Finance & Acct.
Hideki Gomi, CTO-DRAM Tech.
Akira Tsujimoto, Chief Quality Assurance Officer
Yasushi Takahashi, Head-Computing & AMD Div.
Yoshitaka Kinoshita, Head-Mobile & Digital Consumer Div.

Phone: 81-3-3281-1500	Fax: 81-3-3281-1776
Toll-Free:	

Address: Sumitomo Seimei Yaesu Bldg. 3F, 2-1 Yaesu 2-chome, Tokyo, 104-0028 Japan

GROWTH PLANS/SPECIAL FEATURES:

Elpida Memory, Inc. is a Japan-based manufacturer of Dynamic Random Access Memory (DRAM) silicon chips. It offers products including DDR3 SDRAM, Mobile RAM components, graphics DDR (GDDR) and high performance XDR DRAM. The company's operations are conducted in part through its 15 consolidated subsidiaries which handle development, front-end production, back-end production and sales. Development operations include The Development Center, which is involved in technology research and circuit design; the Hiroshima Development Center, a manufacturing concern; the Kansai Design Center and Tohoku Design Center DRAM chip designers; the Munich Design Center, a GDDR developer, the Milan Design Center new memory developer; and the Rexchip Technology Development Office, a 40 nanometer chip designer. Front-end process production bases are conducted through the Hiroshima Plant, which has a 130,000 monthly wafer production capacity; the Rexchip Electronics Corporation, which has an 80,000 monthly wafer production capacity; Tera Probe, Inc.; TeraPower Technology, Inc.; Powerchip Technology Corporation; ProMOS Technologies, Inc.; and Winbond Electronics Corporation. Back-end process production bases include Akita Elpida Memory, Inc., which develops MCP (multiple chip package), PoP (Package on Package) and other types of advanced packages; Powertech Technology Inc., a packager and tester of PC and server DRAM technology; and Walton Advanced Engineering, Inc., another packager and tester for digital consumer electronic goods. The firm operates sales offices in the U.S., Europe and Asia.

FINANCIALS: Sales and profits are in thousands of dollars—add 000 to get the full amount. 2010 Note: Financial information for 2010 was not available for all companies at press time.

2010 Sales: $5,678,150	2010 Profits: $37,510	U.S. Stock Ticker:
2009 Sales: $3,625,810	2009 Profits: $-1,959,070	Int'l Ticker: 6665 Int'l Exchange: Tokyo-TSE
2008 Sales: $4,047,120	2008 Profits: $-234,974	Employees:
2007 Sales: $4,170,000	2007 Profits: $450,000	Fiscal Year Ends: 3/31
2006 Sales: $2,054,200	2006 Profits: $-40,000	Parent Company:

SALARIES/BENEFITS:

Pension Plan:	ESOP Stock Plan:	Profit Sharing:	Top Exec. Salary: $	Bonus: $
Savings Plan:	Stock Purch. Plan:		Second Exec. Salary: $	Bonus: $

OTHER THOUGHTS:

Apparent Women Officers or Directors:
Hot Spot for Advancement for Women/Minorities:

LOCATIONS: ("Y" = Yes)

West:	Southwest:	Midwest:	Southeast:	Northeast:	International:
Y	Y			Y	Y

EMBARCADERO TECHNOLOGIES INC   www.embarcadero.com

Industry Group Code: 511210J   Ranks within this company's industry group: Sales: Profits:

Hardware:	Software:		Telecommunications:	Electronic Publishing:	Equipment:	Specialty Services:
Computers:	Consumer:		Local:	Online Service:	Telecom:	Consulting:
Accessories:	Corporate:	Y	Long Distance:	TV/Cable or Wireless:	Communication:	Contract Manufacturing:
Network Equipment:	Telecom:		Cellular:	Games:	Distribution:	Processing:
Chips/Circuits:	Internet:		Internet Service:	Financial Data:	VAR/Reseller:	Staff/Outsourcing:
Parts/Drives:					Satellite Srv./Equip.:	Specialty Services:

TYPES OF BUSINESS:
Software-Application & Database Management

BRANDS/DIVISIONS/AFFILIATES:
JBuilder
TurboRuby
Studio Software Architect
Schema Examiner
DB Optimizer XE
Blackfish SQL
ToolCloud

CONTACTS: Note: Officers with more than one job title may be intentionally listed here more than once.
Wayne D. Williams, CEO
Jim Lines, CFO
Michael Swindell, Sr. VP-Mktg.
Lorraine C. Gnecco, VP-Human Resources
Tony de la Lama, Sr. VP-Worldwide R&D
James Pitts, CTO
Michael Swindell, Sr. VP-Prod. Mgmt.
Michelle Chase, Contact-Media Rel.
Allen Lovett, VP-Sales, Americas
Jan Liband, VP-Mktg.
David Intersimone, VP-Developer Rel./Chief Evangelist
Nigel Brown, VP/Gen. Mgr.-Int'l

Phone: 415-834-3131	Fax: 415-434-1721
Toll-Free: 877-783-5332	
Address: 100 California St., 12th Fl., San Francisco, CA 94111 US	

GROWTH PLANS/SPECIAL FEATURES:

Embarcadero Technologies, Inc. is a technology company that addresses application and database lifecycle operations for corporate clients. Embarcadero designs and develops products for information transmission across databases. The products compress time frames and increase database performance and availability, allowing companies to more efficiently build, optimize and manage their databases and applications. The firm offers its products to more than 3 million users in 80 countries, with a client list that includes roughly 90 of the Fortune 100 companies. Products are offered in subgroups such as design and architecture tools; application development; database management and development; performance optimization; and embedded and workgroup database management systems. Examples of Embarcadero software include JBuilder, an application development tool for Java; TurboRuby, a development tool for Ruby environments; Studio Software Architect, a design tool and visualization program for use on the UML 2.0 specification; Schema Examiner, an automated error checking application for database developers; DB Optimizer XE, for SQL database profiling, monitoring and tuning; and Blackfish SQL, a managed, SQL-compliant embedded database management system. Major industry sectors served by Embarcadero include government, health care, financial services, food services, insurance, pharmaceuticals, education, research and technology, travel and utilities. International sales account for roughly a quarter of annual revenues, and the group maintains sales offices in North and South America, Europe and Asia. The firm also markets products through independent distributors in various countries worldwide. During 2010, the company rolled out its ToolCloud application, which allows users to manage Embarcadero applications and project lifecycles through an online web-based platform.

FINANCIALS: Sales and profits are in thousands of dollars—add 000 to get the full amount. 2010 Note: Financial information for 2010 was not available for all companies at press time.

2010 Sales: $	2010 Profits: $	U.S. Stock Ticker: Private	
2009 Sales: $	2009 Profits: $	Int'l Ticker: Int'l Exchange:	
2008 Sales: $	2008 Profits: $	Employees:	
2007 Sales: $	2007 Profits: $	Fiscal Year Ends: 12/31	
2006 Sales: $60,000	2006 Profits: $5,800	Parent Company: THOMA BRAVO LLC	

SALARIES/BENEFITS:
Pension Plan:	ESOP Stock Plan:	Profit Sharing:	Top Exec. Salary: $	Bonus: $
Savings Plan: Y	Stock Purch. Plan:		Second Exec. Salary: $	Bonus: $

OTHER THOUGHTS:
Apparent Women Officers or Directors: 1
Hot Spot for Advancement for Women/Minorities:

LOCATIONS: ("Y" = Yes)
West:	Southwest:	Midwest:	Southeast:	Northeast:	International:
Y					Y

EMC CORP

www.emc.com

Industry Group Code: 334112 Ranks within this company's industry group: Sales: 1   Profits: 1

Hardware:		Software:		Telecommunications:	Electronic Publishing:	Equipment:	Specialty Services:	
Computers:		Consumer:		Local:	Online Service:	Telecom:	Consulting:	Y
Accessories:	Y	Corporate:	Y	Long Distance:	TV/Cable or Wireless:	Communication:	Contract Manufacturing:	
Network Equipment:		Telecom:		Cellular:	Games:	Distribution:	Processing:	
Chips/Circuits:		Internet:		Internet Service:	Financial Data:	VAR/Reseller:	Staff/Outsourcing:	
Parts/Drives:	Y					Satellite Srv./Equip.:	Specialty Services:	

TYPES OF BUSINESS:

Computer Storage Equipment-Mainframe Disk Memory
Network Storage Systems
Management Protection Software
Consulting Services
Storage Management Services

BRANDS/DIVISIONS/AFFILIATES:

VMware Inc
RSA Security Inc
Captiva Software Corp
Greenplum Inc
Decho Corporation
Isilon Systems Inc
Bus-Tech Inc
Connectrix

CONTACTS: Note: Officers with more than one job title may be intentionally listed here more than once.

Joseph M. Tucci, CEO
Joseph M. Tucci, Pres.
David Goulden, CFO/Exec. VP
Jeremy Burton, Chief Mktg. Officer/Exec. VP
John T. (Jack) Mollen, Exec. VP-Human Resources
Sanjay Mirchandani, CIO/Sr. VP
Jeffrey M. Nick, CTO/Sr. VP
Paul T. Dacier, General Counsel/Exec. VP
Pat Gelsinger, COO/Pres., EMC Info. Infrastructure Prod.
Irina Simmons, Treas./Sr. VP
William J. Teuber, Jr., Vice Chmn.
Mark S. Lewis, Pres., Content Mgmt. & Archiving Div.
Howard D. Elias, COO/Pres., EMC Info. Infrastructure & Cloud Svcs
Joseph M. Tucci, Chmn.
Rainer Erlat, Pres., EMEA

Phone: 508-435-1000	Fax: 508-435-5222
Toll-Free:	
Address: 176 South St., Hopkinton, MA 01748-9103 US	

GROWTH PLANS/SPECIAL FEATURES:

EMC Corp., along with its subsidiaries, develops, delivers and supports systems, software and services for the storage, management and protection of electronic information. EMC operates in two business divisions: Information Infrastructure and VMware Virtual Infrastructure. The Information Infrastructure business is divided into three segments, Information Storage; Content Management and Archiving; and RSA Information Security. The information store segment provides a range of networked information storage systems, software and services to support customers' information storage and management strategies. Products include Celerra IP storage systems; Centera content addressed storage systems; Connectrix directors and switches; and LifeLine software for consumers and small and home office users. The segment also maintains Decho Corporation, combination of its Mozy, Inc. and Pi Corp. subsidiaries that is focused on personal information management. The content management and archiving segment helps customers optimize business processes and create, manage and archive information such as documents, e-mail, web pages, records and application data. Its products include the Documentum, Captiva and Document Sciences xPression families. The RSA Information Security segment offers products and services focused on information confidentiality. The RSA Data Security System combines product suites and services for comprehensive data protection, including loss prevention, encryption and key management. EMC Global Services offers consulting services, technology deployment managed services, customer support services, training and certification through more than 14,000 support-service professionals, as well as a global network of alliances and partners. The VMware Virtual Infrastructure division, represented by a majority stake in VMware, Inc. provides virtual infrastructure software from the desktop to the data center, supporting a range of operating systems. In June 2010, the company acquired Greenplum, Inc., which specializes in data storage. In November 2010, the firm acquired Bus-Tech, Inc. and Isilon Systems, Inc., which develop data storage and retrieval systems.

FINANCIALS: Sales and profits are in thousands of dollars—add 000 to get the full amount. 2010 Note: Financial information for 2010 was not available for all companies at press time.

2010 Sales: $	2010 Profits: $	**U.S. Stock Ticker: EMC**
2009 Sales: $14,025,910	2009 Profits: $1,123,971	Int'l Ticker: Int'l Exchange:
2008 Sales: $14,880,000	2008 Profits: $2,160,000	Employees: 43,200
2007 Sales: $13,230,205	2007 Profits: $1,665,668	Fiscal Year Ends: 12/31
2006 Sales: $11,155,090	2006 Profits: $1,227,601	Parent Company:

SALARIES/BENEFITS:

Pension Plan:	ESOP Stock Plan:	Profit Sharing:	Top Exec. Salary: $872,308	Bonus: $1,068,420
Savings Plan: Y	Stock Purch. Plan: Y		Second Exec. Salary: $609,673	Bonus: $655,684

OTHER THOUGHTS:

Apparent Women Officers or Directors: 1
Hot Spot for Advancement for Women/Minorities:

LOCATIONS: ("Y" = Yes)

West:	Southwest:	Midwest:	Southeast:	Northeast:	International:
Y				Y	Y

EMDEON INC

www.emdeon.com

Industry Group Code: 541513　Ranks within this company's industry group: Sales: 24　Profits: 22

Hardware:	Software:		Telecommunications:	Electronic Publishing:	Equipment:	Specialty Services:	
Computers:	Consumer:		Local:	Online Service:	Telecom:	Consulting:	Y
Accessories:	Corporate:	Y	Long Distance:	TV/Cable or Wireless:	Communication:	Contract Manufacturing:	
Network Equipment:	Telecom:		Cellular:	Games:	Distribution:	Processing:	
Chips/Circuits:	Internet:		Internet Service:	Financial Data:	VAR/Reseller:	Staff/Outsourcing:	
Parts/Drives:					Satellite Srv./Equip.:	Specialty Services:	Y

TYPES OF BUSINESS:
Healthcare Business & Administration Management

BRANDS/DIVISIONS/AFFILIATES:
EBS Master

CONTACTS: Note: Officers with more than one job title may be intentionally listed here more than once.
George I. Lazenby, IV, CEO
Bob A. Newport, Jr., CFO
Susan Byrd, VP-Human Resources
Franklin Baumann, Chief Medical Officer
Damien Creavin, CIO
Gregory T. Stevens, General Counsel/Sec./Exec. VP
Pat Coughlin, COO-Payment Svcs.
Frank Manzella, Sr. VP-Corp. Dev.
Sajid Khan, COO-eServices
Tommy Lewis, Sr. VP-Corp. Comm.
Tommy Lewis, Contact-Investor Rel.
J. Philip Hardin, Exec. VP-Provider Svcs.
Gary D. Stuart, Exec. VP-Payer Svcs.
Adam A. Hameed, Sr. VP-Data & Analytics Solutions
Mark Lyle, Sr. VP-Pharmacy Svcs.
Tracy L. Bahl, Exec. Chmn.

Phone: 615-932-3000	Fax:
Toll-Free:	
Address: 3055 Lebanon Pike, Ste. 1000, Nashville, TN 37214 US	

GROWTH PLANS/SPECIAL FEATURES:
Emdeon, Inc. acts as a holding company for EBS Master, through which it offers a suite of products and services that integrate and automate business and administrative functions used in the healthcare industry. The firm operates through three segments: payer services, provider services and pharmacy services. Payer services provide payment cycle solutions that facilitate healthcare administration activities. Provider services offer solutions for revenue cycle management patient billing and payment services and clinical exchange capabilities. Pharmacy services comprise the firm's solutions for prescription benefit claim filing, adjudication and management, as well as electronic prescriptions. The firm has established relationships with approximately 500,000 physicians, 81,000 dentists, 55,000 pharmacies, 5,000 hospitals and 1,200 payers. It processed 5.3 billion healthcare-related transactions during 2009, with recurring business accounting for more than 90% of its revenue. Besides processing transactions, Emdeon stores over 25 terabytes of historical claim data which it uses to drive services such as data analytics that its customers use to plan their businesses. Emdeon conducts all of its business through EBS Master and its subsidiaries. In January 2010, the firm acquired FutureVision Investment Group, L.L.C., a provider of outsourced services specializing in electronic data conversion and information management solutions. In March 2010, Emdeon agreed to acquire healthcare IT firm Healthcare Technology Management Services. In June 2010, Emdeon acquired Chapin Revenue Cycle Management, LLC, a leading provider of revenue cycle services to hospitals. In August 2010, the company formed a strategic relationship with Noridian Mutual Insurance Company to operate a printing facility in North Dakota and secure an experienced and highly reputable Medicare Administrative Contractor. In addition, Emdeon acquired license and reseller rights for Noridian's EXACT software, a comprehensive medical technology platform.

FINANCIALS: Sales and profits are in thousands of dollars—add 000 to get the full amount. 2010 Note: Financial information for 2010 was not available for all companies at press time.

2010 Sales: $	2010 Profits: $	**U.S. Stock Ticker: EM**
2009 Sales: $918,448	2009 Profits: $14,003	**Int'l Ticker:**　Int'l Exchange:
2008 Sales: $853,599	2008 Profits: $11,933	Employees: 2,100
2007 Sales: $808,537	2007 Profits: $17,276	Fiscal Year Ends: 12/31
2006 Sales: $	2006 Profits: $	Parent Company:

SALARIES/BENEFITS:

Pension Plan:	ESOP Stock Plan:	Profit Sharing:	Top Exec. Salary: $519,231	Bonus: $421,180
Savings Plan:	Stock Purch. Plan:		Second Exec. Salary: $311,538	Bonus: $285,905

OTHER THOUGHTS:
Apparent Women Officers or Directors: 2
Hot Spot for Advancement for Women/Minorities:

LOCATIONS: ("Y" = Yes)

West:	Southwest:	Midwest:	Southeast:	Northeast:	International:
		Y	Y	Y	

Note: Financial information, benefits and other data can change quickly and may vary from those stated here.

EMULEX CORP

www.emulex.com

Industry Group Code: 33411 Ranks within this company's industry group: Sales: 8 Profits: 10

Hardware:		Software:		Telecommunications:	Electronic Publishing:	Equipment:		Specialty Services:	
Computers:		Consumer:		Local:	Online Service:	Telecom:	Y	Consulting:	
Accessories:		Corporate:	Y	Long Distance:	TV/Cable or Wireless:	Communication:	Y	Contract Manufacturing:	
Network Equipment:	Y	Telecom:		Cellular:	Games:	Distribution:	Y	Processing:	
Chips/Circuits:		Internet:		Internet Service:	Financial Data:	VAR/Reseller:		Staff/Outsourcing:	
Parts/Drives:						Satellite Srv./Equip.:		Specialty Services:	

TYPES OF BUSINESS:

Networking Equipment-High-Performance Interfaces
High-Speed Fiber-Channel Products
Networking Software

BRANDS/DIVISIONS/AFFILIATES:

LightPulse
InSpeed
FibreSpy
ServerEngines Corp.

CONTACTS: Note: Officers with more than one job title may be intentionally listed here more than once.

Jim McCluney, CEO
Jeff Benck, COO
Jeff Benck, Pres.
Michael J. Rockenbach, CFO/Exec. VP
Susan Bowman, Sr. VP-Human Resources & Facilities
Dave Goff, CIO/VP
Randall Wick, General Counsel/Sr. VP
John Warwick, Sr. VP-Oper.
Raju Vegensa, Chief Strategist
Paul F. Folino, Chmn.
Jeff Hoogenboom, Sr. VP-Worldwide Sales

Phone: 714-662-5600	Fax: 714-241-0792
Toll-Free: 800-368-5391	
Address: 3333 Susan St., Costa Mesa, CA 92626 US	

GROWTH PLANS/SPECIAL FEATURES:

Emulex Corp. manufactures network convergence solutions that intelligently connect servers, storage and networks within data centers. The firm is a global supplier of storage networking host bus adapters (HBAs); converged network adapters (CNAs); network interface cards (NICs); mezzanine cards for blade servers; application specific integrated circuits (ASICs); embedded storage bridges, routers and switches; and input/output controllers. These products are electronic component parts assembled on internally designed printed circuit boards, which are sold as board-level products. Host server products include LightPulse HBAs, which connect servers and storage to networks using a variety of industry standard protocols. Embedded storage products include InSpeed and FibreSpy switches, which work to intelligently connect storage controllers to networks. Emulex's products are used by many different companies, including Cisco Systems, Inc.; Dell Inc.; Hewlett-Packard Company; Sun Microsystems, Inc.; Oracle America, Inc.; and International Business Machines Corporation (IBM). In August 2010, the company acquired ServerEngines Corp., a semiconductor design company, for about $78 million.

Emulex offers its employees medical and dental benefits; life insurance; short- and long-term disability; flexible spending accounts; a 401(k) plan; an employee stock purchase plan; education assistance; health club memberships; computer purchase discounts; and access to a credit union.

FINANCIALS: Sales and profits are in thousands of dollars—add 000 to get the full amount. 2010 Note: Financial information for 2010 was not available for all companies at press time.

2010 Sales: $399,150	2010 Profits: $23,620	U.S. Stock Ticker: ELX
2009 Sales: $378,222	2009 Profits: $7,544	Int'l Ticker: Int'l Exchange:
2008 Sales: $488,301	2008 Profits: $-7,071	Employees: 791
2007 Sales: $470,187	2007 Profits: $29,434	Fiscal Year Ends: 6/30
2006 Sales: $402,813	2006 Profits: $40,451	Parent Company:

SALARIES/BENEFITS:

Pension Plan:	ESOP Stock Plan:	Profit Sharing:	Top Exec. Salary: $603,827	Bonus: $752,552
Savings Plan: Y	Stock Purch. Plan: Y		Second Exec. Salary: $585,750	Bonus: $730,022

OTHER THOUGHTS:

Apparent Women Officers or Directors: 1
Hot Spot for Advancement for Women/Minorities:

LOCATIONS: ("Y" = Yes)

West:	Southwest:	Midwest:	Southeast:	Northeast:	International:
Y	Y			Y	Y

Note: Financial information, benefits and other data can change quickly and may vary from those stated here.

ENTERASYS NETWORKS INC

www.enterasys.com

Industry Group Code: 33411 Ranks within this company's industry group: Sales: Profits:

Hardware:		Software:		Telecommunications:	Electronic Publishing:	Equipment:	Specialty Services:
Computers:		Consumer:		Local:	Online Service:	Telecom:	Consulting:
Accessories:		Corporate:	Y	Long Distance:	TV/Cable or Wireless:	Communication:	Contract Manufacturing:
Network Equipment:	Y	Telecom:		Cellular:	Games:	Distribution:	Processing:
Chips/Circuits:		Internet:		Internet Service:	Financial Data:	VAR/Reseller:	Staff/Outsourcing:
Parts/Drives:						Satellite Srv./Equip.:	Specialty Services:

TYPES OF BUSINESS:

Networking Equipment
WAN & LAN Connectivity Products
Network Testing Equipment
Security Products
Switches & Routers
Wireless Networking Equipment
Support Services

BRANDS/DIVISIONS/AFFILIATES:

Matrix
XSR
RoamAbout
Dragon
Netsight
Siemens AG
Siemens Enterprise Communications Group
Gores Group LLC (The)

CONTACTS: Note: Officers with more than one job title may be intentionally listed here more than once.

Hamid Akhavan, CEO
Barry Cioe, VP-Mktg.
Dan Petlon, VP-IT & System Quality
Vala Afshar, VP-Global Tech. Svcs.
Barry Cioe, VP-Prod. Mgmt.
Dan Dulac, VP-Global Solutions Eng.
Jack Lyon, VP-Oper.
Padraig Hayes, VP-Finance/Controller
Chris Crowell, Gen. Mgr.
Mark Stone, Chmn.
Tony Walker, VP-Global Sales Oper.

Phone: 978-684-1000	Fax: 978-684-1658
Toll-Free:	
Address: 50 Minuteman Rd., Andover, MA 01810 US	

GROWTH PLANS/SPECIAL FEATURES:

Enterasys Networks, Inc. is the network infrastructure and security segment of Siemens Enterprise Communications Group. Through its Secure Networks platform, the company designs, develops, markets and supports switches; routers; wireless devices; virtual private networking; management software; and intrusion defense/security software and services. When linked to its multilayer Matrix switches, featuring advanced ASIC-based architecture, the firm's XSR security routers provide secure networks with both switches and routers sharing similar, complementary security and management features. Enterasys typically deploys routers in the center of a network, where security and traffic control are most important. The company's RoamAbout series of WLAN switches and access platforms provide connectivity to multiple users. The RoamAbout series also includes switch managers, which provide automated features and group settings for controlling multiple switches and access points. The Dragon and NetSight product lines offer dedicated security devices and products, including NetSight Inventory Manager, NetSight Automated Security Manager and Dragon Security Command Console. In addition to products, the company also provides pre-sales/post-sales support, a security response center, product manuals and other resources. In addition, Enterasys provides training in the company's products that range from self-paced tutorials to onsite courses and certification programs. Customers include commercial enterprises, governmental entities, educational institutions and the health care industry. In recent years, private equity firm The Gores Group, LLC, owner of Enterasys, acquired controlling interest in Siemens Enterprise Communications from Siemens AG (who maintains minority-ownership). As a result, Enterasys and another Gores Group company, SER Solutions, were merged into the new acquisition, forming the joint venture Siemens Enterprise Communications Group.

FINANCIALS: Sales and profits are in thousands of dollars—add 000 to get the full amount. 2010 Note: Financial information for 2010 was not available for all companies at press time.

2010 Sales: $	2010 Profits: $	U.S. Stock Ticker: Private
2009 Sales: $	2009 Profits: $	Int'l Ticker: Int'l Exchange:
2008 Sales: $	2008 Profits: $	Employees:
2007 Sales: $80,800	2007 Profits: $	Fiscal Year Ends: 12/31
2006 Sales: $	2006 Profits: $	Parent Company: GORES GROUP LLC (THE)

SALARIES/BENEFITS:

Pension Plan:	ESOP Stock Plan:	Profit Sharing:	Top Exec. Salary: $	Bonus: $175,000
Savings Plan:	Stock Purch. Plan:		Second Exec. Salary: $	Bonus: $

OTHER THOUGHTS:

Apparent Women Officers or Directors:
Hot Spot for Advancement for Women/Minorities:

LOCATIONS: ("Y" = Yes)

West:	Southwest:	Midwest:	Southeast:	Northeast:	International:
				Y	Y

Note: Financial information, benefits and other data can change quickly and may vary from those stated here.

ENTRUST INC

www.entrust.com

Industry Group Code: 511210E Ranks within this company's industry group: Sales: Profits:

Hardware:	Software:		Telecommunications:		Electronic Publishing:	Equipment:	Specialty Services:
Computers:	Consumer:		Local:		Online Service:	Telecom:	Consulting:
Accessories:	Corporate:	Y	Long Distance:		TV/Cable or Wireless:	Communication:	Contract Manufacturing:
Network Equipment:	Telecom:		Cellular:		Games:	Distribution:	Processing:
Chips/Circuits:	Internet:		Internet Service:	Y	Financial Data:	VAR/Reseller:	Staff/Outsourcing:
Parts/Drives:						Satellite Srv./Equip.:	Specialty Services:

TYPES OF BUSINESS:
Computer Software-Security
Digital Identification & Certificates

BRANDS/DIVISIONS/AFFILIATES:
Entrust IdentityGuard
Entrust TransactionGuard
Entrust GetAccess
Entrust Authority Security Manager
Entrust PKI
CygnaCom Solutions
Thoma Bravo LLC

CONTACTS: Note: Officers with more than one job title may be intentionally listed here more than once.
Bill Conner, CEO
Bill Conner, Pres.
David Wagner, CFO/Sr. VP
David Rockvam, Chief Mktg. Officer/Sr. VP
Eric Skinner, CTO
Bill Holtz, Sr. VP-Oper.
Lindsey Jones, Media Rel.
Peter Bello, Sr. VP/Gen. Mgr.-Sales & Svcs., Canada, APAC
Robert VanKirk, VP-U.S., Sales & Service
Michael E. McGrath, Chmn.
Neill Duff, Sr. VP/Gen. Mgr.-EMEA

Phone: 972-728-0447	Fax: 972-728-0440
Toll-Free: 888-690-2424	
Address: 5400 LBJ Freeway, 1 Lincoln Ctr., Ste. 1340, Dallas, TX 75240 US	

GROWTH PLANS/SPECIAL FEATURES:
Entrust, Inc. (Entrust) is a global provider of security applications that protect and secure digital identities and information. It designs, produces and sells security, policy and access management software products and related services for the purpose of securing digital identities and information. The company has sold its products and services to over 4,000 enterprise, government and consumer clients in 60 countries. These clients include Citibank; Expedia, Inc.; U.K. Ministry of Defense; NASA; the Bank of New Zealand; and the U.S. Department of State. The firm offers two platforms for securing digital identity: authentication and fraud monitoring, and public key/digital certificates infrastructure. The authentication and fraud platform features Entrust IdentityGuard, which secures and protects the digital identity of citizens, government agents, and corporate employees; Entrust TransactionGuard, which monitors transactions and seeks fraudulent behavior access patterns amid the massive volumes of data generated by transactional web sites; and Entrust GetAccess, a single sign-on solution that delivers a single entry and access point to web portal information and applications. The public key/digital certificates platform provides authentication, encryption and digital certificate capabilities to the enterprise and government marketplace. Utilizing Entrust Authority Security Manager and Entrust PKI, this division specializes in securing e-mail, network folder encryption, ePassport, strong authentication and document-signing. CygnaCom Solutions, a Virginia-based subsidiary, also focuses on public key infrastructure and cryptography. Entrust maintains offices international offices in Australia, Canada, China, Germany, India, Japan, Argentina and the U.K. In July 2009, the company was acquired by private equity firm Thoma Bravo, LLC.

The firm offers its employees medical and dental insurance, as well as an employee assistance plan.

FINANCIALS: Sales and profits are in thousands of dollars—add 000 to get the full amount. 2010 Note: Financial information for 2010 was not available for all companies at press time.

2010 Sales: $	2010 Profits: $	U.S. Stock Ticker: Private
2009 Sales: $	2009 Profits: $	Int'l Ticker: Int'l Exchange:
2008 Sales: $99,661	2008 Profits: $-1,027	Employees: 411
2007 Sales: $99,665	2007 Profits: $-6,190	Fiscal Year Ends: 12/31
2006 Sales: $95,183	2006 Profits: $-15,417	Parent Company: THOMA BRAVO LLC

SALARIES/BENEFITS:

Pension Plan:	ESOP Stock Plan:	Profit Sharing:	Top Exec. Salary: $500,000	Bonus: $445,000
Savings Plan:	Stock Purch. Plan:		Second Exec. Salary: $257,769	Bonus: $125,000

OTHER THOUGHTS:
Apparent Women Officers or Directors:
Hot Spot for Advancement for Women/Minorities:

LOCATIONS: ("Y" = Yes)

West:	Southwest:	Midwest:	Southeast:	Northeast:	International:
	Y			Y	Y

EPIC SYSTEMS CORPORATION

www.epicsystems.com

Industry Group Code: 511210D **Ranks within this company's industry group:** Sales: Profits:

Hardware:	Software:		Telecommunications:	Electronic Publishing:	Equipment:	Specialty Services:	
Computers:	Consumer:		Local:	Online Service:	Telecom:	Consulting:	
Accessories:	Corporate:	Y	Long Distance:	TV/Cable or Wireless:	Communication:	Contract Manufacturing:	
Network Equipment:	Telecom:		Cellular:	Games:	Distribution:	Processing:	
Chips/Circuits:	Internet:		Internet Service:	Financial Data:	VAR/Reseller:	Staff/Outsourcing:	Y
Parts/Drives:					Satellite Srv./Equip.:	Specialty Services:	

TYPES OF BUSINESS:

Health Industry Computer Software
Information Networks
Support Services

BRANDS/DIVISIONS/AFFILIATES:

Epicenter
EpicCare
Epic Europe B.V.
Community Library Exchange
Clinical Context Object Workgroup

CONTACTS: Note: Officers with more than one job title may be intentionally listed here more than once.

Phone: 608-271-9000	Fax: 608-271-7237
Toll-Free:	
Address: 1979 Milky Way, Verona, WI 53593 US	

GROWTH PLANS/SPECIAL FEATURES:

Epic Systems Corporation is a developer of health industry clinical, access and revenue software for mid-size and large medical groups, hospitals, academic facilities, children's organizations, multi-hospital systems and integrated healthcare organizations. All Epic software applications are designed to share a single database, called Epicenter, so that each viewer can access all available patient data through a single interface from anywhere in the organization. The firm's clinical software products include integrated inpatient and ambulatory systems under the EpicCare brand, as well as health information management tools and specialty information systems, including systems designed for cardiology, oncology, obstetrics, emergency care, operating room, anesthesia, intensive care, pharmacy, home care, radiology and clinical and public laboratory applications. Other products offer access services, including scheduling, inpatient and ambulatory registration, call management and nurse triage solutions; revenue cycle services, such as hospital and professional billing solutions; health plan and managed care administration systems; clinical and financial data repositories; enterprise reporting; patient medical record access systems; and connectivity solutions, including voice recognition, interfacing, patient monitoring devices and Clinical Context Object Workgroup compatibility. In conjunction with its software applications, the company provides extensive client services, including training, process engineering, tailoring of applications to the client's situation and access to network specialists who plan and implement the client's system. In addition, Epic hosts Community Library Exchange, an online collection of application tools and pre-made content that allows clients to share report and registration templates, custom forms, enterprise report formats and documentation shortcuts. The company has approximately 200 clients. Epic also operates in the Netherlands under Epic Europe B.V.

Employees of the firm are offered health insurance; life and disability insurance; a 401(k) plan; stock appreciation rights; flexible spending accounts; social gatherings; continuing education programs; personal computer loans; sabbaticals; frequent flyer miles; and life and disability insurance.

FINANCIALS: Sales and profits are in thousands of dollars—add 000 to get the full amount. 2010 Note: Financial information for 2010 was not available for all companies at press time.

2010 Sales: $	2010 Profits: $	U.S. Stock Ticker: Private
2009 Sales: $	2009 Profits: $	Int'l Ticker: Int'l Exchange:
2008 Sales: $	2008 Profits: $	Employees:
2007 Sales: $	2007 Profits: $	Fiscal Year Ends: 12/31
2006 Sales: $	2006 Profits: $	Parent Company:

SALARIES/BENEFITS:

Pension Plan:	ESOP Stock Plan:	Profit Sharing:	Top Exec. Salary: $	Bonus: $
Savings Plan: Y	Stock Purch. Plan:		Second Exec. Salary: $	Bonus: $

OTHER THOUGHTS:

Apparent Women Officers or Directors:
Hot Spot for Advancement for Women/Minorities:

LOCATIONS: ("Y" = Yes)

West:	Southwest:	Midwest:	Southeast:	Northeast:	International:
		Y			Y

EPICOR SOFTWARE CORP

www.epicor.com

Industry Group Code: 511210H Ranks within this company's industry group: Sales: 10 Profits: 12

Hardware:	Software:		Telecommunications:	Electronic Publishing:	Equipment:	Specialty Services:	
Computers:	Consumer:		Local:	Online Service:	Telecom:	Consulting:	Y
Accessories:	Corporate:	Y	Long Distance:	TV/Cable or Wireless:	Communication:	Contract Manufacturing:	
Network Equipment:	Telecom:		Cellular:	Games:	Distribution:	Processing:	
Chips/Circuits:	Internet:		Internet Service:	Financial Data:	VAR/Reseller:	Staff/Outsourcing:	
Parts/Drives:					Satellite Srv./Equip.:	Specialty Services:	

TYPES OF BUSINESS:

Software-Enterprise Resource Planning
Customer Relationship Management Software
Supply Chain Management Software
Consulting Services
Supplier Relationship Management Software

BRANDS/DIVISIONS/AFFILIATES:

Human Resource Systems Corp

CONTACTS: Note: Officers with more than one job title may be intentionally listed here more than once.

L. George Klaus, CEO
L. George Klaus, Pres.
Michael Pietrini, CFO/Exec. VP-Finance
Michael Pietrini, Exec. VP-Admin.
Russell Clark, Chief Acct. Officer/Sr. VP-Finance
L. George Klaus, Chmn.

Phone: 949-585-4000	Fax: 949-585-4091
Toll-Free: 800-999-6995	
Address: 18200 Von Karman Ave., Ste. 1000, Irvine, CA 92612 US	

GROWTH PLANS/SPECIAL FEATURES:

Epicor Software Corp. is a supplier of enterprise resource planning (ERP), customer relationship management (CRM) and supply chain management (SCM) software focused exclusively on mid-market companies. The firm designs, develops, markets and supports enterprise and e-business software for use by mid-sized companies, as well as divisions and subsidiaries of larger corporations worldwide. Epicor offers products for a variety of industries, including distribution, financial services, hospitality, retail, accounting, manufacturing and information technology services. Epicor's software is designed to help companies focus on their customers, suppliers, partners and employees through enterprise-wide management of resources and information. This software enables businesses to integrate their systems and operations with the Internet in order to incorporate a significant number of internationalized features to address global market opportunities, including support for national languages, multiple currencies and accounting for value-added taxation. Products are accompanied by a full range of consulting services designed to enable customers to integrate Epicor programs in a cost-effective, timely manner. The firm offers services in supplier relationship management, SCM and CRM. Its manufacturing products include ERP and e-business applications for make-to-order and mixed-mode manufacturers, primarily in the metal fabrication, capital equipment, electronics, consumer goods and aerospace industries. The company's products for service companies provide tools to improve staff utilization optimize resources and increase cash flow. The firm's hospitality and entertainment solutions are designed for the service industry, and other recreations and entertainment companies. Epicor's supplier relationship management tools include strategic sourcing and e-procurement applications. The company sells its products in over 150 countries and maintains offices in North America, Europe, Asia, Australia and Latin America. In December 2010, the firm acquired Human Resource Systems Corporation.

Epicor offers its employees medical, dental and vision coverage; pet insurance; life and AD&D insurance; short- and long-term disability; a 401(k) plan; an employee stock purchase plan; and tuition reimbursement.

FINANCIALS: Sales and profits are in thousands of dollars—add 000 to get the full amount. 2010 Note: Financial information for 2010 was not available for all companies at press time.

2010 Sales: $	2010 Profits: $	**U.S. Stock Ticker: EPIC**
2009 Sales: $409,624	2009 Profits: $-1,238	**Int'l Ticker:** Int'l Exchange:
2008 Sales: $487,879	2008 Profits: $-3,451	Employees: 2,539
2007 Sales: $429,832	2007 Profits: $39,075	Fiscal Year Ends: 12/31
2006 Sales: $384,096	2006 Profits: $23,818	Parent Company:

SALARIES/BENEFITS:

Pension Plan:	ESOP Stock Plan:	Profit Sharing:	Top Exec. Salary: $736,403	Bonus: $302,588
Savings Plan: Y	Stock Purch. Plan: Y		Second Exec. Salary: $311,218	Bonus: $91,229

OTHER THOUGHTS:

Apparent Women Officers or Directors:
Hot Spot for Advancement for Women/Minorities:

LOCATIONS: ("Y" = Yes)

West:	Southwest:	Midwest:	Southeast:	Northeast:	International:
Y		Y		Y	Y

ESS TECHNOLOGY INC

www.esstech.com

Industry Group Code: 33441   Ranks within this company's industry group: Sales: Profits:

Hardware:		Software:	Telecommunications:	Electronic Publishing:	Equipment:	Specialty Services:
Computers:		Consumer:	Local:	Online Service:	Telecom:	Consulting:
Accessories:		Corporate:	Long Distance:	TV/Cable or Wireless:	Communication:	Contract Manufacturing:
Network Equipment:		Telecom:	Cellular:	Games:	Distribution:	Processing:
Chips/Circuits:	Y	Internet:	Internet Service:	Financial Data:	VAR/Reseller:	Staff/Outsourcing:
Parts/Drives:	Y				Satellite Srv./Equip.:	Specialty Services:

TYPES OF BUSINESS:

Chips-Audio, Video & Modem
Digital-to-Analog Converters
TV Tuners

BRANDS/DIVISIONS/AFFILIATES:

Imperium Partners Group LLC
Phoenix
Vibratto-S
RadiX
Crescendo II

CONTACTS:
Note: Officers with more than one job title may be intentionally listed here more than once.

Robert L. Blair, CEO
Robert L. Blair, Pres.
John Marsh, CFO
Robert Wong, VP-Mktg. & Sales
Calto Wong, Dir.-Technical Mktg.

Phone: 510-492-1088	Fax: 510-492-1098
Toll-Free:	
Address: 48401 Fremont Blvd., Fremont, CA 94538 US	

GROWTH PLANS/SPECIAL FEATURES:

ESS Technology, Inc., owned by private equity firm Imperium Partners Group, LLC, designs, develops and markets highly integrated mixed-signal semiconductor, hardware, software and system solutions for audio and video applications in the consumer electronics, home and automotive market. The firm designs multimedia decoder and encoder chips for electronics such as DVD players and digital media players. The company separates its products into four categories: DVD, TV tuner, digital media player, digital-to-analog (DAC) converters and Soundbar. Its DVD products include the Phoenix system-on-chip devices and Vibratto-S single chip automotive DVD decoder. Its TV tuner products are comprised of RadiX TV Tuner, a highly integrated, multi-standard silicon TV tuner with fast channel locking time and low power consumption. Its single-chip digital media player is a high-performance audio/photo/video decoder designed to access high-resolution photos, high-quality music and high-bitrate videos from flash cards, memory cards, hard disks and USB storage devices. These chips can be incorporated into digital picture frames, hard-drive media players, digital signage and photo and video IP phones applications. The company's audio DAC products include the Sabre line of digital and analog converters and drivers designed to deliver clear audio in consumer applications such as Blu-ray players, audio pre-amplifiers and A/V receivers and professional applications such as recording systems, mixer consoles and digital audio workstations. The firm's Soundbar category consists of the Crescendo II family of products used for televisions and home theater systems. Customers of ESS's products include global consumer electronics manufacturers and distributors, such as Samsung, LGE, Sony, Sharp and others.

FINANCIALS: Sales and profits are in thousands of dollars—add 000 to get the full amount. 2010 Note: Financial information for 2010 was not available for all companies at press time.

2010 Sales: $	2010 Profits: $	U.S. Stock Ticker: Private
2009 Sales: $	2009 Profits: $	Int'l Ticker: Int'l Exchange:
2008 Sales: $	2008 Profits: $	Employees:
2007 Sales: $67,393	2007 Profits: $3,122	Fiscal Year Ends: 12/31
2006 Sales: $97,797	2006 Profits: $-44,094	Parent Company: IMPERIUM PARTNERS GROUP LLC

SALARIES/BENEFITS:

Pension Plan:	ESOP Stock Plan:	Profit Sharing:	Top Exec. Salary: $	Bonus: $
Savings Plan:	Stock Purch. Plan:		Second Exec. Salary: $	Bonus: $

OTHER THOUGHTS:

Apparent Women Officers or Directors:
Hot Spot for Advancement for Women/Minorities:

LOCATIONS: ("Y" = Yes)

West:	Southwest:	Midwest:	Southeast:	Northeast:	International:
Y					Y

EXTREME NETWORKS INC

www.extremenetworks.com

Industry Group Code: 33411 Ranks within this company's industry group: Sales: 9 Profits: 13

Hardware:		Software:		Telecommunications:		Electronic Publishing:		Equipment:		Specialty Services:	
Computers:		Consumer:		Local:		Online Service:		Telecom:		Consulting:	
Accessories:		Corporate:		Long Distance:		TV/Cable or Wireless:		Communication:		Contract Manufacturing:	
Network Equipment:	Y	Telecom:		Cellular:		Games:		Distribution:		Processing:	
Chips/Circuits:		Internet:		Internet Service:		Financial Data:		VAR/Reseller:		Staff/Outsourcing:	
Parts/Drives:								Satellite Srv./Equip.:		Specialty Services:	

TYPES OF BUSINESS:

Computer Networking & Related Equipment, Manufacturing
Switches
Security Appliances & Security Rules Engines
Network Management Software
Embedded Operating System Software

BRANDS/DIVISIONS/AFFILIATES:

SummitWM
Summit
BlackDiamond
Alpine
Sentriant Access Guard
Sentriant Network Guard
Epicenter

CONTACTS: Note: Officers with more than one job title may be intentionally listed here more than once.

Bob L. Corey, CEO
Bob L. Corey, CFO/Sr. VP
Paul Hooper, Chief Mktg. Officer
Suresh Gopalakrishnan, VP-Eng.
Diane C. Honda, General Counsel/Sec.
Frank Blohm, VP-Worldwide Oper./Chief Quality Officer
Greg Cross, Dir.-Public Rel.
Helmut Wilke, Sr. VP-Worldwide Sales
Mike Seaton, VP/Gen. Mgr.-Worldwide Svcs.
Gordon L. Stitt, Chmn.

Phone: 408-579-2800	Fax: 408-579-3000
Toll-Free: 888-257-3000	
Address: 3585 Monroe St., Santa Clara, CA 95051 US	

GROWTH PLANS/SPECIAL FEATURES:

Extreme Networks, Inc., together with its subsidiaries, is a leading provider of network infrastructure equipment for corporate, government, education and health care enterprises and metropolitan telecommunications service providers. The company uses application-specific integrated circuits (ASICs) and creates designs that are common and uniform across product lines. These products enable layer-three switching at wire-speed in each major area of a network. Extreme Networks has four main product lines: stackable Ethernet switching systems; modular Ethernet switching systems; wireless Ethernet controllers and access points; and centralized management software. The company's switching product lines includes BlackDiamond products, the Summit Series, and the Alpine line. The layer-three Summit, BlackDiamond and Alpine product lines share the same common hardware and operating system, enabling businesses to more easily build a network infrastructure. The Extreme Networks' wireless Ethernet controllers and access points segment offers the SummitWM family of wireless network controllers and associated Altitude access points to enable the deployment of nomadic and mobile converged network applications. The company's wireless access products are environmentally hardened to enable indoor and outdoor deployments while offering performance options including 802.11b/g to 802.11n. The centralized management software segment offers the Epicenter management software system, which provides central configuration, status and alerting capabilities for the company's switching technology, to enable customers to reduce the overall cost of network administration and operations. Electronic network security systems products include the Sentriant family of security systems, offering electronic protection for Ethernet networks from the initial connection and access by a user (the Sentriant Access Guard family) to ongoing network monitoring and detection of anomalies in behavior and communications (Sentriant Network Guard). In August 2009, the company acquired the software assets of Soapstone Networks, Inc.

Employees are offered medical, dental and vision insurance; disability coverage; life insurance; an employee assistance program; flexible spending accounts; educational assistance; employee discounts; and pet insurance.

FINANCIALS: Sales and profits are in thousands of dollars—add 000 to get the full amount. 2010 Note: Financial information for 2010 was not available for all companies at press time.

2010 Sales: $309,354	2010 Profits: $ 227	**U.S. Stock Ticker: EXTR**
2009 Sales: $335,559	2009 Profits: $2,815	**Int'l Ticker:** Int'l Exchange:
2008 Sales: $361,835	2008 Profits: $8,381	Employees: 740
2007 Sales: $342,834	2007 Profits: $-14,197	Fiscal Year Ends: 6/30
2006 Sales: $358,601	2006 Profits: $8,509	Parent Company:

SALARIES/BENEFITS:

Pension Plan:	ESOP Stock Plan:	Profit Sharing:	Top Exec. Salary: $494,099	Bonus: $
Savings Plan: Y	Stock Purch. Plan: Y		Second Exec. Salary: $347,813	Bonus: $4,000

OTHER THOUGHTS:

Apparent Women Officers or Directors: 1
Hot Spot for Advancement for Women/Minorities:

LOCATIONS: ("Y" = Yes)

West:	Southwest:	Midwest:	Southeast:	Northeast:	International:
Y				Y	Y

Note: Financial information, benefits and other data can change quickly and may vary from those stated here.

F5 NETWORKS INC

www.f5.com

Industry Group Code: 511210B Ranks within this company's industry group: Sales: 4 Profits: 2

Hardware:	Software:		Telecommunications:	Electronic Publishing:	Equipment:	Specialty Services:	
Computers:	Consumer:		Local:	Online Service:	Telecom:	Consulting:	
Accessories:	Corporate:	Y	Long Distance:	TV/Cable or Wireless:	Communication:	Contract Manufacturing:	
Network Equipment:	Telecom:		Cellular:	Games:	Distribution:	Processing:	
Chips/Circuits:	Internet:		Internet Service:	Financial Data:	VAR/Reseller:	Staff/Outsourcing:	
Parts/Drives:					Satellite Srv./Equip.:	Specialty Services:	Y

TYPES OF BUSINESS:

Server Software
Internet Traffic Management Solutions
Firewall Software
File Virtualization

BRANDS/DIVISIONS/AFFILIATES:

Application Security Manager
BIG-IP Controller
FirePass Controller
iControl Software
ARX
VIPRION
Enterprise Manager

CONTACTS: *Note: Officers with more than one job title may be intentionally listed here more than once.*

John McAdam, CEO
John McAdam, Pres.
Andy Reinland, CFO/Sr. VP
Dan Matte, Sr. VP-Mktg.
Karl Triebes, CTO
Karl Triebes, Sr. VP-Prod. Dev.
Jeffrey A. Christianson, General Counsel/Sr. VP
Edward J. Eames, Sr. VP-Bus. Oper.
Dan Matte, Sr. VP-Bus. Dev.
Alane Moran, Contact-Investor Rel.
John Rodriguez, Chief Acct. Officer/Sr. VP
Mark Anderson, Sr. VP-Worldwide Sales
Calvin Rowland, VP-Application Partner Programs
Gary Abad, VP-N. America Channel Sales
Erik Giesa, VP-Prod. Mktg. & Mgmt.
Alan J. Higginson, Chmn.

Phone: 206-272-5555	Fax: 206-272-5556
Toll-Free: 888-882-4447	
Address: 401 Elliott Ave. W., Ste. 500, Seattle, WA 98119 US	

GROWTH PLANS/SPECIAL FEATURES:

F5 Networks, Inc. provides application delivery networking products that improve the security, availability and performance of network applications. Its core products, the BIG-IP controller, FirePass controller, Application Security Manager firewall and iControl, help manage traffic to servers and network devices in a way that maximizes availability and throughput. BIG-IP products share a common full-proxy operating system that enables them to inspect and modify traffic flow to and from servers and has built-in functionality to secure, optimize and ensure the availability of application traffic. F5 Data Manager provides customers with expanded visibility into their file storage environments, allowing them to see statistics and graphical reporting relating to their data. The company's FirePass product provides Secure Socket Layer-Virtual Private Network (SSL-VPN) that allows enterprises to provide authorized users connected to the Internet with secure remote access to corporate networks and applications by leveraging standard Web browser technology. The Application Security Manager firewall provides content-based, application-level security against attacks. The iControl software interface products enable communication with one another and allow integration with third party products, including custom and commercial enterprise applications. Intelligent file virtualization manages file storage infrastructure through non-disruptive data migration, automated storage tiering, dynamic load balancing, and efficient data replication though the ARX product family. The company sells its products and services to large enterprise customers and service providers through a variety of channels, including distributors, value-added resellers and systems integrators. In February 2010, F5 opened two new support centers for its BIG-IP hardware in Beijing and Shanghai and expanded its manufacturing operations of BIG-IP hardware in China as well.

F5 Networks offers employees medical, dental and vision insurance as well as life and disability insurance; flexible spending accounts; and tuition assistance.

FINANCIALS: Sales and profits are in thousands of dollars—add 000 to get the full amount. 2010 Note: Financial information for 2010 was not available for all companies at press time.

2010 Sales: $881,972	2010 Profits: $151,153	**U.S. Stock Ticker: FFIV**
2009 Sales: $653,079	2009 Profits: $91,535	**Int'l Ticker:** Int'l Exchange:
2008 Sales: $650,173	2008 Profits: $74,331	Employees: 2,012
2007 Sales: $525,667	2007 Profits: $77,000	Fiscal Year Ends: 9/30
2006 Sales: $394,049	2006 Profits: $66,005	Parent Company:

SALARIES/BENEFITS:

Pension Plan:	ESOP Stock Plan:	Profit Sharing:	Top Exec. Salary: $595,606	Bonus: $448,654
Savings Plan: Y	Stock Purch. Plan: Y		Second Exec. Salary: $389,623	Bonus: $183,350

OTHER THOUGHTS:

Apparent Women Officers or Directors: 2
Hot Spot for Advancement for Women/Minorities:

LOCATIONS: ("Y" = Yes)

West:	Southwest:	Midwest:	Southeast:	Northeast:	International:
Y	Y	Y		Y	Y

FINISAR CORPORATION

www.finisar.com

Industry Group Code: 33411 Ranks within this company's industry group: Sales: 6 Profits: 16

Hardware:		Software:	Telecommunications:	Electronic Publishing:	Equipment:	Specialty Services:
Computers:		Consumer:	Local:	Online Service:	Telecom:	Consulting:
Accessories:		Corporate:	Long Distance:	TV/Cable or Wireless:	Communication:	Contract Manufacturing:
Network Equipment:	Y	Telecom:	Cellular:	Games:	Distribution:	Processing:
Chips/Circuits:		Internet:	Internet Service:	Financial Data:	VAR/Reseller:	Staff/Outsourcing:
Parts/Drives:					Satellite Srv./Equip.:	Specialty Services:

TYPES OF BUSINESS:

Optical Subsystems & Components
Network Test & Monitoring Systems
CML Transmitters

BRANDS/DIVISIONS/AFFILIATES:

Quadwire
WaveShaper
Laserwire
C.wire

CONTACTS: Note: Officers with more than one job title may be intentionally listed here more than once.

Eitan Gertel, CEO
Kurt Adzema, CFO
Todd Swanson, Sr. VP-Mktg. & Sales
Chris Brown, General Counsel/VP
Stephen K. Workman, Sr. VP-Corp. Dev.
Victoria McDonald, Sr. Mgr.-Corp. Comm.
Stephen K. Workman, Sr. VP-Investor Rel.
Joseph Young, Sr. VP/Gen. Mgr.-Optics Group
Stephen K. Workman, Sec.
Mark Colyar, Sr. VP/Gen. Mgr.
Jerry S. Rawls, Chmn.

Phone: 408-548-1000	Fax: 408-541-6138
Toll-Free:	
Address: 1389 Moffett Park Dr., Sunnyvale, CA 94089 US	

GROWTH PLANS/SPECIAL FEATURES:

Finisar Corporation is a provider of optical subsystems and components that connect local area networks (LANs), storage area networks (SANs), metropolitan area networks (MANs) and wide area networks (WANs). The company operates in two segments: optical subsystems and components; and network test systems. The firm's optical subsystems consist primarily of transceivers that provide the fundamental optical-electrical interface for connecting the equipment used in building the networks. These products rely on the use of digital semiconductor lasers in conjunction with integrated circuit design and novel packaging technology to provide means for transmitting and receiving digital signals over fiber optic cables using a wide range of network protocols, transmission speeds and physical configurations over distances of 230 feet to 124 miles. The firm's line of optical components consists primarily of packaged lasers and photo-detectors used in transceivers, primarily for LAN and SAN applications. The network test systems allow the generation and capture of data at high speeds; the filtration of data; and the identification of various types of intermittent errors and other network problems for SANs, LANs, wireless networks, voice-over-Internet protocol applications and newly emerging technologies including SAS and SATA. The firm's key product lines include the WaveShaper family of programmable optical processors and the Laserwire, Quadwire and C.wire brands of optical cables. Finisar sells its optical subsystems and component products to manufacturers of storage and networking equipment such as Brocade, Cisco Systems, EMC, Emulex, Hewlett-Packard Company, Huawei, McData, QLogic and Siemens. In July 2009, the company sold its network tool business to JDS Uniphase Corporation.

FINANCIALS: Sales and profits are in thousands of dollars—add 000 to get the full amount. 2010 Note: Financial information for 2010 was not available for all companies at press time.

2010 Sales: $629,880	2010 Profits: $14,131	U.S. Stock Ticker: FNSR
2009 Sales: $497,058	2009 Profits: $-260,343	Int'l Ticker: Int'l Exchange:
2008 Sales: $401,625	2008 Profits: $-79,013	Employees: 6,893
2007 Sales: $418,548	2007 Profits: $-45,399	Fiscal Year Ends: 4/30
2006 Sales: $364,293	2006 Profits: $-33,029	Parent Company:

SALARIES/BENEFITS:

Pension Plan:	ESOP Stock Plan:	Profit Sharing:	Top Exec. Salary: $438,881	Bonus: $
Savings Plan:	Stock Purch. Plan:		Second Exec. Salary: $344,548	Bonus: $

OTHER THOUGHTS:

Apparent Women Officers or Directors: 1
Hot Spot for Advancement for Women/Minorities:

LOCATIONS: ("Y" = Yes)

West:	Southwest:	Midwest:	Southeast:	Northeast:	International:
Y	Y				Y

FIRECLICK INC

www.fireclick.com

Industry Group Code: 511210M Ranks within this company's industry group: Sales: Profits:

Hardware:	Software:		Telecommunications:	Electronic Publishing:	Equipment:	Specialty Services:	
Computers:	Consumer:		Local:	Online Service:	Telecom:	Consulting:	
Accessories:	Corporate:	Y	Long Distance:	TV/Cable or Wireless:	Communication:	Contract Manufacturing:	
Network Equipment:	Telecom:		Cellular:	Games:	Distribution:	Processing:	
Chips/Circuits:	Internet:		Internet Service:	Financial Data:	VAR/Reseller:	Staff/Outsourcing:	
Parts/Drives:					Satellite Srv./Equip.:	Specialty Services:	Y

TYPES OF BUSINESS:

Software-Web Analytics
Hosted Application Services
Online Business Analysis
Internet Marketing Software

BRANDS/DIVISIONS/AFFILIATES:

Digital River, Inc.
Fireclick Advanced Warehouse Suite
Fireclick Advanced Marketing Suite
BlueHornet e-Marketing Suite 3.0

CONTACTS: Note: Officers with more than one job title may be intentionally listed here more than once.

Joel A. Ronning, CEO-Digital River, Inc.

Phone: 952-253-1234	Fax: 650-887-2983
Toll-Free:	
Address: 2355 Northside Dr., Ste. B250, San Diego, CA 92108 US	

GROWTH PLANS/SPECIAL FEATURES:

Fireclick, Inc., a wholly-owned subsidiary of Digital River, Inc., provides comprehensive web analytics software. It offers hosted application services that automatically gather and store data for online businesses, and measure web site traffic, customer behavior and the effectiveness of marketing campaigns and advertising. The company offers three product suites: Fireclick Advanced Warehouse, BlueHornet eMarketing Suite 3.0 (eMS 3.0) and Fireclick Advanced Marketing Suite. The Advanced Warehouse suite of tools allows customers to customize analytical reports utilizing a variety of recorded data displayed in a spreadsheet format using Fireclick Reporter or a graphical format using Fireclick Index. This suite also features the Site Index, a tool that allows customers to view real-time web analytics data in the context of their own web site, superimposing links with color-coded overlays, displaying click-through rates and revenue flow without needing to analyze a separate database. The BlueHornet eMS 3.0 gives customers a number of features including the following. Data Collection Tools focuses on permission based data collection on web pages. Data Management Tools offers data storage and grouping for easy accessibility. E-mail Creation Tools used to design e-mail marketing campaigns. A SPAM Rating Tool helps customers' e-mails bypass spam filters in their subscriber's inboxes. Event Triggered Messaging allows customers to send specific e-mails automatically on specific dates. Dynamic Content customizes offers, images and links to a subscriber's profile. The suite also offers real-time subscriber statistics reporting. The firm's Advanced Marketing Suite combines the Advanced Warehouse package with e-mail marketing solutions provided by BlueHornet and a keyword bid management solution powered by Digital River's KeywordMax. The company's customers include over 400 Internet retail sites. Fireclick's web site offers a free demo for portions of its software.

FINANCIALS: Sales and profits are in thousands of dollars—add 000 to get the full amount. 2010 Note: Financial information for 2010 was not available for all companies at press time.

2010 Sales: $	2010 Profits: $	**U.S. Stock Ticker: Subsidiary**
2009 Sales: $	2009 Profits: $	**Int'l Ticker:** Int'l Exchange:
2008 Sales: $	2008 Profits: $	Employees:
2007 Sales: $	2007 Profits: $	Fiscal Year Ends: 12/31
2006 Sales: $	2006 Profits: $	Parent Company: DIGITAL RIVER INC

SALARIES/BENEFITS:

Pension Plan:	ESOP Stock Plan:	Profit Sharing:	Top Exec. Salary: $	Bonus: $
Savings Plan:	Stock Purch. Plan:		Second Exec. Salary: $	Bonus: $

OTHER THOUGHTS:

Apparent Women Officers or Directors:
Hot Spot for Advancement for Women/Minorities:

LOCATIONS: ("Y" = Yes)

West:	Southwest:	Midwest:	Southeast:	Northeast:	International:
Y					

FLEXTRONICS INTERNATIONAL LTD

www.flextronics.com

Industry Group Code: 334419 Ranks within this company's industry group: Sales: 2 Profits: 22

Hardware:		Software:	Telecommunications:	Electronic Publishing:	Equipment:		Specialty Services:	
Computers:		Consumer:	Local:	Online Service:	Telecom:	Y	Consulting:	Y
Accessories:		Corporate:	Long Distance:	TV/Cable or Wireless:	Communication:	Y	Contract Manufacturing:	Y
Network Equipment:		Telecom:	Cellular:	Games:	Distribution:		Processing:	Y
Chips/Circuits:	Y	Internet:	Internet Service:	Financial Data:	VAR/Reseller:		Staff/Outsourcing:	
Parts/Drives:	Y				Satellite Srv./Equip.:		Specialty Services:	Y

TYPES OF BUSINESS:

Contract Electronics Manufacturing
Telecommunications Equipment Manufacturing
Engineering, Design & Testing Services
Logistics Services
Camera Modules
Medical Devices
LCD Displays
Original Design Manufacturing (ODM)

BRANDS/DIVISIONS/AFFILIATES:

CONTACTS: Note: Officers with more than one job title may be intentionally listed here more than once.

Michael M. McNamara, CEO
Paul Read, CFO
Paul Humphries, Exec. VP-Human Resources
Caroline Dowling, Pres., Retail Svcs.
Carrie L. Schiff, General Counsel/Sr. VP
Francois Barbier, Pres., Global Oper.
Paul Humphries, Exec. VP-Comm.
Sean Burke, Pres., Computing
Michael Clarke, Pres., Infrastructure
Dan Croteau, Pres., Medical
E.C. Sykes, Pres., Industrial
H. Raymond Bingham, Chmn.
John O'Sullivan, Pres., Global Svcs.

Phone: 65-6890-7188	Fax: 65-5431-888
Toll-Free:	
Address: 2 Changi S. Ln., Singapore, 486123 Singapore	

GROWTH PLANS/SPECIAL FEATURES:

Flextronics International, Ltd. is a leading global provider of vertically-integrated advanced electronics manufacturing services (EMS) to original equipment manufacturers (OEMs). Flextronics' services include printed circuit board and flexible circuit fabrication; systems assembly and manufacturing; logistics; after-sales services; design and engineering services; original design manufacturer services; and components design and manufacturing. The company manufactures high-density, multilayer and flexible printed circuit board (PCB) as well as rigid-flex circuit board. It manufactures PCBs on a low-volume, quick-turn basis, as well as on a high-volume production basis. Flextronics' assembly and manufacturing operations, which generate the majority of its revenues, include PCB assembly and assembly of systems and subsystems that incorporate PCBs and complex electromechanical components. The company's global logistics services include freight forwarding, warehousing/inventory management and outbound/e-commerce services. The firm's after-sales services include product repair, re-manufacturing and maintenance. Flextronics' design and engineering services include user interface and industrial design; mechanical engineering and tooling design; electronic system design; and PCB design. The company's components group designs and manufactures subsystem products for the electronics market, such as camera modules, power supplies, antennas, RF modules, MP3 players and digital cameras. The firm's total manufacturing capacity is approximately 27 million square feet in over 30 countries across four continents. The company's 2010 sales in Asia represented roughly 48% of sales, while the Americas represented 33% and Europe represented 19%. In May 2010, Flextronics announced plans to build a new power manufacturing facility in Ganzhou, China.

FINANCIALS: Sales and profits are in thousands of dollars—add 000 to get the full amount. 2010 Note: Financial information for 2010 was not available for all companies at press time.

2010 Sales: $24,110,733	2010 Profits: $18,594	U.S. Stock Ticker: FLEX
2009 Sales: $30,948,575	2009 Profits: $-6,135,518	Int'l Ticker: Int'l Exchange:
2008 Sales: $27,558,135	2008 Profits: $-681,383	Employees: 165,000
2007 Sales: $18,853,688	2007 Profits: $508,638	Fiscal Year Ends: 3/31
2006 Sales: $15,287,976	2006 Profits: $141,162	Parent Company:

SALARIES/BENEFITS:

Pension Plan:	ESOP Stock Plan:	Profit Sharing:	Top Exec. Salary: $1,250,000	Bonus: $2,942,814
Savings Plan: Y	Stock Purch. Plan:		Second Exec. Salary: $600,000	Bonus: $1,159,062

OTHER THOUGHTS:

Apparent Women Officers or Directors: 2
Hot Spot for Advancement for Women/Minorities:

LOCATIONS: ("Y" = Yes)

West:	Southwest:	Midwest:	Southeast:	Northeast:	International:
Y	Y	Y	Y	Y	Y

Note: Financial information, benefits and other data can change quickly and may vary from those stated here.

FLUKE NETWORKS

www.flukenetworks.com

Industry Group Code: 3342 Ranks within this company's industry group: Sales: Profits:

Hardware:		Software:		Telecommunications:	Electronic Publishing:	Equipment:	Specialty Services:
Computers:		Consumer:		Local:	Online Service:	Telecom:	Consulting:
Accessories:	Y	Corporate:	Y	Long Distance:	TV/Cable or Wireless:	Communication:	Contract Manufacturing:
Network Equipment:	Y	Telecom:	Y	Cellular:	Games:	Distribution:	Processing:
Chips/Circuits:		Internet:		Internet Service:	Financial Data:	VAR/Reseller:	Staff/Outsourcing:
Parts/Drives:						Satellite Srv./Equip.:	Specialty Services:

TYPES OF BUSINESS:

Computer Networking Equipment-Management Systems
Software
VoIP Software

BRANDS/DIVISIONS/AFFILIATES:

Visual Performance Manager
OptiView Network Analyzer
Xlink Analyzer
NetFlow Tracker
OptiView Link Analyzer
PfR Manager
LinkRunner Network Multimeter
LinkRunner Pro & Duo Network Multimeter

CONTACTS: Note: Officers with more than one job title may be intentionally listed here more than once.

David Coffin, Pres.
Jeff Lime, Sr. VP-Mktg.
Wayne Fuller, Exec. VP-Oper.
Chris Odell, Chmn.

Phone: 425-446-4519	Fax: 425-446-5043
Toll-Free: 800-283-5853	
Address: 6920 Seaway Blvd., Everett, WA 98203 US	

GROWTH PLANS/SPECIAL FEATURES:

Fluke Networks, a subsidiary of the Danahar Corp., creates systems for the testing, monitoring and analysis of telecommunication and enterprise networks. Additionally, the firm certifies the fiber and copper foundation of these networks. The company's products are divided into three groups: Datacom Cabling, IT Networking and Telecommunication Providers. Datacom Cabling services focus on certification, testing, troubleshooting tools, and network infrastructure installation. IT Networking's main focus is diagnostics, analysis, reporting, and application performance management. Telecommunication Providers offer carriers with tools for video qualification of their existing networks, access management, process improvement solutions and testing solutions. In 2009, Fluke Networks acquired both Airmagnet Inc., a performance, security and compliance solutions provider for wireless LANs, and ClearSight Networks, a network analysis tools provider for troubleshooting, real-time application monitoring, and protocol analysis. In September 2010, the company released OptiView Version 6, which integrates the ClearSight Analyzer solution into the company's Optiview portable analysis platform.

FINANCIALS: Sales and profits are in thousands of dollars—add 000 to get the full amount. 2010 Note: Financial information for 2010 was not available for all companies at press time.

2010 Sales: $	2010 Profits: $	U.S. Stock Ticker: Subsidiary
2009 Sales: $	2009 Profits: $	Int'l Ticker: Int'l Exchange:
2008 Sales: $	2008 Profits: $	Employees:
2007 Sales: $	2007 Profits: $	Fiscal Year Ends: 12/31
2006 Sales: $	2006 Profits: $	Parent Company: DANAHER CORP

SALARIES/BENEFITS:

Pension Plan:	ESOP Stock Plan:	Profit Sharing:	Top Exec. Salary: $	Bonus: $
Savings Plan:	Stock Purch. Plan:		Second Exec. Salary: $	Bonus: $

OTHER THOUGHTS:

Apparent Women Officers or Directors:
Hot Spot for Advancement for Women/Minorities:

LOCATIONS: ("Y" = Yes)

West:	Southwest:	Midwest:	Southeast:	Northeast:	International:
Y	Y		Y	Y	Y

FORCE10 NETWORKS INC

www.force10networks.com

Industry Group Code: 33411 Ranks within this company's industry group: Sales: Profits:

Hardware:	Software:	Telecommunications:	Electronic Publishing:	Equipment:	Specialty Services:
Computers:	Consumer:	Local:	Online Service:	Telecom:	Consulting:
Accessories:	Corporate: Y	Long Distance:	TV/Cable or Wireless:	Communication:	Contract Manufacturing:
Network Equipment: Y	Telecom:	Cellular:	Games:	Distribution:	Processing:
Chips/Circuits:	Internet:	Internet Service:	Financial Data:	VAR/Reseller:	Staff/Outsourcing:
Parts/Drives:				Satellite Srv./Equip.:	Specialty Services:

TYPES OF BUSINESS:
Ethernet Switches & Routers
Security Mechanisms

BRANDS/DIVISIONS/AFFILIATES:
ExaScale E-Series
S-Series
C-Series
Virtualization Framework
Force10 Management System
Turin Networks

CONTACTS: Note: Officers with more than one job title may be intentionally listed here more than once.
Henry Wasik, CEO
Ebrahim Abbasi, COO
Henry Wasik, Pres.
Bill Zerella, CFO
Arpit Joshipura, Chief Mktg. Officer
Mary Cole, VP-Human Resources
Leah Maher, General Counsel/VP
James Hanley, Pres., Field Oper.

Phone: 408-571-3500	Fax: 408-571-3550
Toll-Free: 866-571-2600	
Address: 350 Holger Way, San Jose, CA 95134-1362 US	

GROWTH PLANS/SPECIAL FEATURES:
Force10 Networks, Inc. (FTN) develops and manufactures resilient Ethernet switches and routers. The company's combination switcher-router devices come in two capacities: 1-gigabit and 10-gigabit. The ExaScale E-Series is the company's main line of these switch/routers. Units come in three chassis sizes, with six, seven or 14 line card slots, and with up to either 1,260 one-gigabit ports or 140 10-gigabit ports. The second product line, the C-Series, is designed for small- to medium-sized data centers and offers two different configurations at four or eight line card slots. The S-Series is a group of more compact switches/routers that assist to aggregate Ethernet traffic and increase network efficiency for data centers. The Force10 Management System, or FTMS, is a module designed to observe, analyze and regulate the functioning of FTN network devices. The firm's Virtualization Framework more easily manages virtualized environments through an advanced network virtualization and management software suite featuring enhanced architectural design elements. FTN offers worldwide assistance for all of its products. The company's customers include institutions or businesses that require organization for a large-volume Ethernet network, and have included telecommunications companies and service providers, research institutions and universities in over 60 countries. Headquartered in California, the company also has properties in the U.K., Brazil, Mexico, Spain, Malaysia, Hong Kong, Germany, the Netherlands, India, Japan, Australia and China. The firm recently merged with Turin Networks, a carrier ethernet, wireless backhaul and converged access systems provider; FTN was the surviving company.

FINANCIALS: Sales and profits are in thousands of dollars—add 000 to get the full amount. 2010 Note: Financial information for 2010 was not available for all companies at press time.

2010 Sales: $	2010 Profits: $	U.S. Stock Ticker: Private
2009 Sales: $	2009 Profits: $	Int'l Ticker: Int'l Exchange:
2008 Sales: $	2008 Profits: $	Employees:
2007 Sales: $	2007 Profits: $	Fiscal Year Ends: 10/31
2006 Sales: $	2006 Profits: $	Parent Company:

SALARIES/BENEFITS:
Pension Plan:	ESOP Stock Plan:	Profit Sharing:	Top Exec. Salary: $	Bonus: $
Savings Plan:	Stock Purch. Plan:		Second Exec. Salary: $	Bonus: $

OTHER THOUGHTS:
Apparent Women Officers or Directors: 2
Hot Spot for Advancement for Women/Minorities: Y

LOCATIONS: ("Y" = Yes)
West:	Southwest:	Midwest:	Southeast:	Northeast:	International:
Y	Y				Y

FORESEE RESULTS INC

www.foreseeresults.com

Industry Group Code: 511210K Ranks within this company's industry group: Sales: Profits:

Hardware:	Software:		Telecommunications:	Electronic Publishing:	Equipment:	Specialty Services:	
Computers:	Consumer:		Local:	Online Service:	Telecom:	Consulting:	Y
Accessories:	Corporate:	Y	Long Distance:	TV/Cable or Wireless:	Communication:	Contract Manufacturing:	
Network Equipment:	Telecom:		Cellular:	Games:	Distribution:	Processing:	
Chips/Circuits:	Internet:		Internet Service:	Financial Data:	VAR/Reseller:	Staff/Outsourcing:	
Parts/Drives:					Satellite Srv./Equip.:	Specialty Services:	Y

TYPES OF BUSINESS:

Online Survey Software
Support Services
Survey Design & Analysis

BRANDS/DIVISIONS/AFFILIATES:

CS SiteManager
CS SiteGov
American Consumer Satisfaction Index
Satisfaction Research Analysts

CONTACTS: Note: Officers with more than one job title may be intentionally listed here more than once.

Larry Freed, CEO
Larry Freed, Pres.
Jeff Blackman, CFO
Walter Rothschild, Chief Mktg. Officer
Mitchell Cohen, VP-Tech.
Drew Bennett, Sr. Dir.-Prod.
Eric Head, Sr. Dir.-Bus. Dev.
Dave Lewan, Sr. Dir.-Gov't & Public Sector Sales & Sales Oper.
Don Morrison, VP-Sales
Cia McCaffery, VP
Jeff Dwoskin, Sr. Dir.-Client Svcs.

Phone: 734-205-2600	Fax: 734-205-2601
Toll-Free: 800-621-2850	
Address: 2500 Green Rd., Ste. 400, Ann Arbor, MI 48105 US	

GROWTH PLANS/SPECIAL FEATURES:

ForeSee Results, Inc. acts as an index tool for companies interested in understanding consumers' relationships to company web sites. The firm develops software designed to measure customer satisfaction in a variety of areas through customer surveys, using the methodology of the American Consumer Satisfaction Index. Its CS SiteManager product is targeted to commercial entities, while CS SiteGov is targeted to governmental agencies. ForeSee's Satisfaction Research Analysts support companies by working with them to complete the survey and analysis process. The process is divided into three stages. The inline research survey development stage helps companies develop a customized survey and determine where on their site to place it. The implementation stage tests the survey in different surroundings and advises companies as to what type of survey to use. Finally, the continuous measurement stage helps to authenticate the accuracy of the results of the survey and establish other areas for possible analysis. ForeSee's products measure/project activity in four areas: the quality and navigating fluidity of a company's web site, the consumer's overall satisfaction with the company's service, the demographics and other characteristics of the company's consumer base and probable future customer behavior.

FINANCIALS: Sales and profits are in thousands of dollars—add 000 to get the full amount. 2010 Note: Financial information for 2010 was not available for all companies at press time.

2010 Sales: $	2010 Profits: $	U.S. Stock Ticker: Private	
2009 Sales: $	2009 Profits: $	Int'l Ticker: Int'l Exchange:	
2008 Sales: $	2008 Profits: $	Employees:	
2007 Sales: $3,900	2007 Profits: $	Fiscal Year Ends:	
2006 Sales: $	2006 Profits: $	Parent Company:	

SALARIES/BENEFITS:

Pension Plan:	ESOP Stock Plan:	Profit Sharing:	Top Exec. Salary: $	Bonus: $
Savings Plan:	Stock Purch. Plan:		Second Exec. Salary: $	Bonus: $

OTHER THOUGHTS:

Apparent Women Officers or Directors: 1
Hot Spot for Advancement for Women/Minorities:

LOCATIONS: ("Y" = Yes)

West:	Southwest:	Midwest:	Southeast:	Northeast:	International:
		Y			

Note: Financial information, benefits and other data can change quickly and may vary from those stated here.

FORRESTER RESEARCH INC

www.forrester.com

Industry Group Code: 541910 Ranks within this company's industry group: Sales: 2 Profits: 2

Hardware:	Software:	Telecommunications:	Electronic Publishing:		Equipment:	Specialty Services:	
Computers:	Consumer:	Local:	Online Service:	Y	Telecom:	Consulting:	Y
Accessories:	Corporate:	Long Distance:	TV/Cable or Wireless:		Communication:	Contract Manufacturing:	
Network Equipment:	Telecom:	Cellular:	Games:		Distribution:	Processing:	
Chips/Circuits:	Internet:	Internet Service:	Financial Data:		VAR/Reseller:	Staff/Outsourcing:	
Parts/Drives:					Satellite Srv./Equip.:	Specialty Services:	Y

TYPES OF BUSINESS:

Market Research
Consulting & Advisory
Workshops & Events

BRANDS/DIVISIONS/AFFILIATES:

RoleView
Forrester Wave (The)
Consumer Technographics Data & Services
Strategic Oxygen LLC
Forrester Leadership Boards
Giga Information Group, Inc.

CONTACTS: Note: Officers with more than one job title may be intentionally listed here more than once.

George F. Colony, CEO
Charles Rutstein, COO
Michael A. Doyle, CFO
Dwight Griesman, Chief Mktg. Officer
Elizabeth Lemons, Chief People Officer
George M. Orlov, CIO
George M. Orlov, CTO
Gail S. Mann, Chief Legal Officer/Sec.
Tom Pohlmann, Managing Dir.-IT Client Group
Mark R. Nemec, Managing Dir.-Tech. Industry Client Group
Dennis van Lingen, Managing Dir.-Mktg. & Strategy Client Group
Greg Nelson, Chief Sales Officer
George F. Colony, Chmn.
Dennis van Lingen, Chief EMEA Officer

Phone: 617-613-6000	Fax: 617-613-5200
Toll-Free: 866-367-7378	
Address: 400 Technology Sq., Cambridge, MA 02139 US	

GROWTH PLANS/SPECIAL FEATURES:

Forrester Research, Inc., an independent research firm, provides research and analysis related to technology change and its impact on changing business models, best practices, technology investments, implementation and customer trends. The firm's products and services are targeted to 19 specific roles at major companies, including senior management, business strategists and marketing and information technology professionals. Forrester's primary research product, RoleView, consists of a library of cross-linked documents that interconnects its reports, data, product rankings, best practices, evaluation tools and research archives. The product includes The Forrester Wave, which provides detailed analyses of vendors' technologies and services. Consulting services leverage RoleView to deliver customized research to assist clients in developing and executing technology and business strategy; informing critical decisions; and reducing business risk. The firm's data products and services focus on consumers' and business users' attitudes about and behavior toward technology, including ownership, future purchases and adoption trends. These products incorporate extensive survey research designed and analyzed by the company's staff. Forrester's data services include Consumer Technographics, which deliver survey-based data and quantitative research; and Business Data Services, an ongoing quantitative business technology research program. Forrester Leadership Boards provide executives and other employees with membership-directed research, industry-specific benchmark data, industry trends and best practices coverage and networking through event meetings and group audio-conferences. Subsidiary Giga Information Group, Inc. provides technology research, advice and personalized consulting services. Forrester also owns Strategic Oxygen LLC, which produces the Strategic Oxygen data-driven decision tool for tech marketers.

Forrester offers its employees medical, dental and vision insurance; employee assistance programs; flexible spending accounts; performance bonuses; travel assistance; backup childcare; and onsite massages, gym and piano lesions.

FINANCIALS: Sales and profits are in thousands of dollars—add 000 to get the full amount. 2010 Note: Financial information for 2010 was not available for all companies at press time.

2010 Sales: $	2010 Profits: $	**U.S. Stock Ticker: FORR**
2009 Sales: $233,352	2009 Profits: $19,770	**Int'l Ticker:** Int'l Exchange:
2008 Sales: $240,875	2008 Profits: $29,215	Employees:
2007 Sales: $212,056	2007 Profits: $18,943	Fiscal Year Ends: 12/31
2006 Sales: $181,473	2006 Profits: $16,171	Parent Company:

SALARIES/BENEFITS:

Pension Plan:	ESOP Stock Plan:	Profit Sharing:	Top Exec. Salary: $320,000	Bonus: $145,000
Savings Plan: Y	Stock Purch. Plan: Y		Second Exec. Salary: $308,000	Bonus: $78,759

OTHER THOUGHTS:

Apparent Women Officers or Directors: 3
Hot Spot for Advancement for Women/Minorities: Y

LOCATIONS: ("Y" = Yes)

West:	Southwest:	Midwest:	Southeast:	Northeast:	International:
Y	Y			Y	Y

Note: Financial information, benefits and other data can change quickly and may vary from those stated here.

FORTINET INC

www.fortinet.com

Industry Group Code: 33411 Ranks within this company's industry group: Sales: 10 Profits: 4

Hardware:	Software:		Telecommunications:	Electronic Publishing:	Equipment:	Specialty Services:	
Computers:	Consumer:	Y	Local:	Online Service:	Telecom:	Consulting:	
Accessories:	Corporate:	Y	Long Distance:	TV/Cable or Wireless:	Communication:	Contract Manufacturing:	
Network Equipment:	Telecom:		Cellular:	Games:	Distribution:	Processing:	
Chips/Circuits:	Internet:		Internet Service:	Financial Data:	VAR/Reseller:	Staff/Outsourcing:	
Parts/Drives:					Satellite Srv./Equip.:	Specialty Services:	Y

TYPES OF BUSINESS:

Software-Network Security
ASIC Network Security Appliances
Security Subscription Services

BRANDS/DIVISIONS/AFFILIATES:

FortiGate
FortiManager
FortiGuard
FortiMail
FortiDB
FortiWeb

CONTACTS: *Note: Officers with more than one job title may be intentionally listed here more than once.*

Ken Xie, CEO
Ken Xie, Pres.
Ken Goldman, CFO
Michael Valentine, VP-Americas Sales & Support
Sherry Pulvers, VP-Human Resources
Michael Xie, CTO
Michael Xie, VP-Eng.
John Whittle, General Counsel/VP
John Wittle, VP-Corp. Dev.
John Walecka, Chmn.
Patrice Perche, VP-Int'l Sales & Support

Phone: 408-235-7700	Fax: 408-235-7737
Toll-Free: 866-868-3678	
Address: 1090 Kifer Rd., Sunnyvale, CA 94086 US	

GROWTH PLANS/SPECIAL FEATURES:

Fortinet, Inc., with a presence in more than 30 countries, is a worldwide market leader in unified threat management security systems. The company specializes in protecting computers from web-based threats, such as viruses, worms, intrusions and inappropriate web content, among others, while ensuring that network performance is undisturbed. The company offers two brands of hardware products, FortiGate and FortiManager. FortiGate systems are network-based, application-specific integrated circuit (ASIC)-accelerated appliances. These are external modules that contain all the software and hardware necessary to protect the networks and consoles to which they are connected. Defensive tactics involve firewalls, the establishment of secure virtual private networks (VPNs), antivirus, antispam and antispyware applications, intrusion prevention systems (IPS), web filtering and traffic shaping. The FortiGate units are designed for a wide variety of customers with a variety of needs and so come with different capacities. The larger FortiGate-5000 series modules are marketed to service providers and large enterprises, while smaller versions, such as the Fortigate-50 series, are more suitable for smaller businesses or individual telecommuters. The company's FortiManager systems are external modules that centralize the management and updating of multiple FortiGate products. Fortinet's software offerings include FortiGuard, a suite of security software that includes antivirus, intrusion prevention and firewall capabilities; FortiMail, an e-mail antispam and security application; FortiWeb, an Internet application; and FortiDB, a database security suite. Typical Fortinet customers are educational and healthcare institutions, financial services enterprises, government agencies, IT firms, wireless service providers and VoIP companies.

Employees are offered medical, dental and vision insurance; life insurance; disability coverage; flexible spending accounts; a 401(k) plan; and discounted network security products.

FINANCIALS: Sales and profits are in thousands of dollars—add 000 to get the full amount. 2010 Note: Financial information for 2010 was not available for all companies at press time.

2010 Sales: $	2010 Profits: $	**U.S. Stock Ticker: FTNT**
2009 Sales: $252,115	2009 Profits: $60,179	**Int'l Ticker:** Int'l Exchange:
2008 Sales: $211,791	2008 Profits: $7,363	Employees: 1,223
2007 Sales: $	2007 Profits: $	Fiscal Year Ends: 12/31
2006 Sales: $	2006 Profits: $	Parent Company:

SALARIES/BENEFITS:

Pension Plan:	ESOP Stock Plan:	Profit Sharing:	Top Exec. Salary: $319,300	Bonus: $79,506
Savings Plan: Y	Stock Purch. Plan:		Second Exec. Salary: $309,000	Bonus: $79,750

OTHER THOUGHTS:

Apparent Women Officers or Directors: 2
Hot Spot for Advancement for Women/Minorities:

LOCATIONS: ("Y" = Yes)

West:	Southwest:	Midwest:	Southeast:	Northeast:	International:
Y	Y	Y	Y	Y	Y

FOXCONN INTERNATIONAL HOLDINGS LTD www.fih-foxconn.com

Industry Group Code: 334419 Ranks within this company's industry group: Sales: 7 Profits: 10

Hardware:		Software:		Telecommunications:		Electronic Publishing:		Equipment:		Specialty Services:	
Computers:		Consumer:	Y	Local:		Online Service:		Telecom:		Consulting:	
Accessories:	Y	Corporate:		Long Distance:		TV/Cable or Wireless:		Communication:		Contract Manufacturing:	Y
Network Equipment:	Y	Telecom:		Cellular:		Games:		Distribution:		Processing:	
Chips/Circuits:	Y	Internet:		Internet Service:		Financial Data:		VAR/Reseller:		Staff/Outsourcing:	
Parts/Drives:	Y							Satellite Srv./Equip.:		Specialty Services:	

TYPES OF BUSINESS:
Contract Electronics Manufacturing
Handset & Wireless Communications Manufacturing
Original Design Manufacturing (ODM) Services
Engineering Services
Assembly Services
Refurbishing Services
Outsourcing Services

BRANDS/DIVISIONS/AFFILIATES:
Hon Hai Precision Industry Company Ltd
Foxconn Technology Group

CONTACTS: Note: Officers with more than one job title may be intentionally listed here more than once.
Samuel Chin Wai Leung, CEO
Dai Feng Shuh, COO
Timo Harju, CFO/Exec. VP
Henry Chao Shan Ping, Dir.-Electronic Parts Prod. & Assembly
Tang Wan Mui, Corp. Sec.
Tom Chen Hsu Tang, VP-Bus. Dev.
Vincent Tong Wen Hsin, Dir.-Investor Rel.
Jonathan Hsu Chung Chand, Treas.
Pao Yi Hsin, VP
Ko Ming Chung, Dir.-Mechanical Prod.
Samuel Chin Wai Leung, Chmn.
Michael Smith, VP-Mexico Oper.

Phone: 852-267-24588	Fax: 852-267-24589
Toll-Free:	
Address: 2, 2nd Donghuan Rd., 10th Yousong Industrial Dist., Shenzhen, China	

GROWTH PLANS/SPECIAL FEATURES:
Foxconn International Holdings Ltd. is a holding company that provides handset and wireless equipment manufacturing services for the computer, communication and consumer electronics industries. Hon Hai Precision Industry Company Ltd owns the majority of the firm's shares. Operating primarily through its subsidiaries, the firm offers design services for product development, including industrial design, mechanical design, tooling design and software development; manufacturing and assembly, including magnesium alloy technology, high precision tooling technology, nanotechnology, material technology and optical display modules; and repairs and refurbishing services, including software upgrades, handset phasing, swap and unit recovery, accessory replacement and antennae swapping. The firm's vertically integrated structure consolidates all aspects of the product creation process, including tooling and process design; critical component manufacturing; casing and enclosure manufacturing; sub-assembly and testing; and system assembly and final testing. The firm has operations, manufacturing facilities and refurbishing centers across Asia, Mexico, the U.S. and Europe. Some of the firm's key clients are Sony Ericsson, Motorola and Apple.

FINANCIALS: Sales and profits are in thousands of dollars—add 000 to get the full amount. 2010 Note: Financial information for 2010 was not available for all companies at press time.

2010 Sales: $	2010 Profits: $	U.S. Stock Ticker:
2009 Sales: $7,213,600	2009 Profits: $38,600	Int'l Ticker: 2038 Int'l Exchange: Hong Kong-HKE
2008 Sales: $9,271,000	2008 Profits: $121,100	Employees: 118,702
2007 Sales: $10,732,300	2007 Profits: $721,400	Fiscal Year Ends:
2006 Sales: $10,381,200	2006 Profits: $718,000	Parent Company: HON HAI PRECISION INDUSTRY COMPANY LTD

SALARIES/BENEFITS:

Pension Plan:	ESOP Stock Plan:	Profit Sharing:	Top Exec. Salary: $	Bonus: $
Savings Plan:	Stock Purch. Plan:		Second Exec. Salary: $	Bonus: $

OTHER THOUGHTS:
Apparent Women Officers or Directors:
Hot Spot for Advancement for Women/Minorities:

LOCATIONS: ("Y" = Yes)

West:	Southwest:	Midwest:	Southeast:	Northeast:	International:
Y	Y		Y		Y

Note: Financial information, benefits and other data can change quickly and may vary from those stated here.

FOXCONN TECHNOLOGY CO LTD   www.foxconntech.com.tw

Industry Group Code: 334419 Ranks within this company's industry group: Sales: 10   Profits: 5

Hardware:		Software:		Telecommunications:	Electronic Publishing:	Equipment:		Specialty Services:	
Computers:	Y	Consumer:		Local:	Online Service:	Telecom:	Y	Consulting:	
Accessories:	Y	Corporate:		Long Distance:	TV/Cable or Wireless:	Communication:	Y	Contract Manufacturing:	Y
Network Equipment:	Y	Telecom:		Cellular:	Games:	Distribution:		Processing:	Y
Chips/Circuits:	Y	Internet:		Internet Service:	Financial Data:	VAR/Reseller:		Staff/Outsourcing:	
Parts/Drives:	Y					Satellite Srv./Equip.:		Specialty Services:	Y

TYPES OF BUSINESS:

Contract Electronics Manufacturing
Original Design Manufacturer (ODM)
Electronics Manufacturing & Design
Research and Engineering Services
Outsourcing

BRANDS/DIVISIONS/AFFILIATES:

Foxconn Electronics, Inc.
Hon Hai Precision Industry Co. Ltd.
Foxconn Technology Group

CONTACTS: *Note: Officers with more than one job title may be intentionally listed here more than once.*

Hsien Sheng Pai, Gen. Mgr.
Han Ming Lee, Chmn.

Phone: 886-2-2268-0970	Fax: 886-2-2268-7176
Toll-Free:	
Address: No. 66-1, Chung-shan Rd., Tucheng City, Taipei, 236 Taiwan	

GROWTH PLANS/SPECIAL FEATURES:

Foxconn Technology Co. Ltd., a worldwide leader in computer components manufacturing, is an original design manufacturer (ODM) and a provider of computer, communication and consumer electronic products. With its beginnings in 1974 as Hon Hai Precision Industry Co, Foxconn has become one of the world's leading exporters of electronics, with major clients including Apple, Cisco, Hewlett-Packard, Microsoft, Dell, Nintendo and Sony. The company's services include research and development, product design, assembly, processing and after-sales services. Foxconn develops strategic alliances with leading brands in the industries it serves, addressing the current needs of its customers while also conducting new product research to anticipate industry trends. The company groups its products and services under three broad categories: magnesium alloys, thermal modules and consumer electronics products. The magnesium alloy category includes the design and production of products made from magnesium alloys; the surface application of magnesium alloy to products such as portable computer enclosures; and magnesium alloy recycling. The thermal modules category includes heat insulating products as well as cooling systems for various product applications. The consumer electronic products category includes such products as mobile phones, computers and video game controllers. Foxconn is a leading international producer of mobile phones, with customers including Apple, Nokia, Sony Ericsson and others. Additionally, it produces a wide array of PC components and peripherals, including motherboards, graphic cards, chassis, card readers and power supplies.

Foxconn offers its employees an annual bonus program, a profit sharing plan, training programs, and comprehensive insurance. Its facilities in Taiwan include an on-site hospital, library and soccer field, as well as a gym and fitness center.

FINANCIALS: Sales and profits are in thousands of dollars—add 000 to get the full amount. 2010 Note: Financial information for 2010 was not available for all companies at press time.

2010 Sales: $	2010 Profits: $	**U.S. Stock Ticker: Subsidiary**
2009 Sales: $4,832,000	2009 Profits: $195,150	**Int'l Ticker: 2354** Int'l Exchange: Taipei-TPE
2008 Sales: $5,016,550	2008 Profits: $194,600	Employees:
2007 Sales: $4,238,510	2007 Profits: $283,770	Fiscal Year Ends: 12/31
2006 Sales: $	2006 Profits: $	Parent Company: HON HAI PRECISION INDUSTRY COMPANY LTD

SALARIES/BENEFITS:

Pension Plan:	ESOP Stock Plan:	Profit Sharing:	Top Exec. Salary: $	Bonus: $
Savings Plan:	Stock Purch. Plan:		Second Exec. Salary: $	Bonus: $

OTHER THOUGHTS:

Apparent Women Officers or Directors:
Hot Spot for Advancement for Women/Minorities:

LOCATIONS: ("Y" = Yes)

West:	Southwest:	Midwest:	Southeast:	Northeast:	International:
					Y

FREESCALE SEMICONDUCTOR INC   www.freescale.com

Industry Group Code: 33441 Ranks within this company's industry group: Sales: 15 Profits: 6

Hardware:		Software:		Telecommunications:		Electronic Publishing:		Equipment:		Specialty Services:	
Computers:		Consumer:		Local:		Online Service:		Telecom:	Y	Consulting:	
Accessories:		Corporate:		Long Distance:		TV/Cable or Wireless:		Communication:		Contract Manufacturing:	
Network Equipment:		Telecom:		Cellular:		Games:		Distribution:		Processing:	
Chips/Circuits:	Y	Internet:		Internet Service:		Financial Data:		VAR/Reseller:		Staff/Outsourcing:	
Parts/Drives:								Satellite Srv./Equip.:		Specialty Services:	

TYPES OF BUSINESS:

Semiconductor Manufacturing
Control System Components
Networking & Wireless Equipment Components

BRANDS/DIVISIONS/AFFILIATES:

Blackstone Group LP (The)
Carlyle Group (The)
Xtrinsic

CONTACTS: *Note: Officers with more than one job title may be intentionally listed here more than once.*

Rich Beyer, CEO
Alan Campell, CFO/Sr. VP
Henri Richard, Chief Sales & Mktg. Officer/Sr. VP
Michel Cadieux, Sr. VP-Human Resources & Security
Sam Coursen, CIO/VP
Ken Hansen, CTO/VP
Jonathan Greenberg, General Counsel/Sr. VP/Sec.
Vivek Mohindra, Sr. VP-Strategy & Bus. Transformation
Lisa T. Su, Sr. VP/Gen. Mgr.-Networking & Multimedia
Mitch Haws, VP-Investor Rel.
Reza Kazerounian, Sr. VP/Gen. Mgr.-Microcontroller Solutions
Rajeeva Lahri, Sr. VP-Prod. Planning & Global Back-End Oper.
Tom Deitrich, Sr. VP/Gen. Mgr.-Cellular Prod.
Rich Beyer, Chmn.
David M. Uze, VP/Gen. Mgr.-Japan
Alex Pepe, Sr. VP-Procurement & Global Front-End Oper.

Phone: 512-895-2000	Fax: 512-895-2652
Toll-Free: 800-521-6274	
Address: 6501 William Cannon Dr. W., Austin, TX 78735 US	

GROWTH PLANS/SPECIAL FEATURES:

Freescale Semiconductor, Inc., a semiconductor manufacturer, specializes in embedded processors. The company has three product lines: Microcontroller Solutions, which accounts for roughly 32% of sales; Networking and Multimedia, approximately 26%; and Radio Frequency (RF), Analog and Sensors, 23%. The remaining revenues are generated from cellular products and intellectual properties. Microcontroller Solutions products comprise microcontrollers, embedded microprocessors and digital signal processors. These products are primarily utilized in automotive systems, such as airbags; consumer products, including alarm systems; industrial products, such as manufacturing equipment; and computer peripherals, including keyboards. Networking and Multimedia products serve the wireless networking, industrial and consumer markets, including systems that transmit and process data and voice signals. Specific products include wireless infrastructure equipment, such as cellular base stations; network access equipment, such as voice and data routers; pervasive computing equipment, including gaming, networked storage and imaging devices; industrial equipment, such as automated vehicles and robotics; and mobile consumer applications, including portable media players and personal navigation devices. Lastly, RF, Analog and Sensors products comprise microcontrollers and microprocessors used to interface embedded systems with the outside world, such as in automotive, industrial, consumer, wireless and networking systems. The company is currently in the process of disposing of its cellular products business. The firm has 59 sales offices in 22 countries. The Americas represent 38% of product sales, with Europe, the Middle East and Africa (EMEA) accounting for 34%; Asia Pacific, 18%; and Japan, 8%. Freescale is owned by a consortium of private equity investors including The Blackstone Group and The Carlyle Group. In June 2010, the company introduced its Xtrinsic sensor family of products, designed for motion and touch applications.

The firm offers employees medical, dental and vision insurance; flexible spending accounts; life insurance; disability coverage; adoption assistance; a 401(k) plan; and bonus plans.

FINANCIALS: Sales and profits are in thousands of dollars—add 000 to get the full amount. 2010 Note: Financial information for 2010 was not available for all companies at press time.

2010 Sales: $	2010 Profits: $	**U.S. Stock Ticker: Private**
2009 Sales: $3,508,000	2009 Profits: $748,000	**Int'l Ticker:** Int'l Exchange:
2008 Sales: $5,226,000	2008 Profits: $-7,939,000	Employees: 22,900
2007 Sales: $5,722,000	2007 Profits: $-1,613,000	Fiscal Year Ends: 12/31
2006 Sales: $6,359,000	2006 Profits: $-1,994,000	Parent Company:

SALARIES/BENEFITS:

Pension Plan:	ESOP Stock Plan:	Profit Sharing:	Top Exec. Salary: $	Bonus: $
Savings Plan: Y	Stock Purch. Plan:		Second Exec. Salary: $	Bonus: $

OTHER THOUGHTS:

Apparent Women Officers or Directors: 1
Hot Spot for Advancement for Women/Minorities:

LOCATIONS: ("Y" = Yes)

West:	Southwest:	Midwest:	Southeast:	Northeast:	International:
	Y	Y			Y

Note: Financial information, benefits and other data can change quickly and may vary from those stated here.

FUJITSU LIMITED

www.fujitsu.com

Industry Group Code: 334111 Ranks within this company's industry group: Sales: 5 Profits: 27

Hardware:		Software:		Telecommunications:		Electronic Publishing:		Equipment:		Specialty Services:	
Computers:	Y	Consumer:	Y	Local:		Online Service:		Telecom:	Y	Consulting:	Y
Accessories:	Y	Corporate:	Y	Long Distance:		TV/Cable or Wireless:		Communication:	Y	Contract Manufacturing:	
Network Equipment:	Y	Telecom:	Y	Cellular:	Y	Games:		Distribution:		Processing:	
Chips/Circuits:	Y	Internet:		Internet Service:		Financial Data:		VAR/Reseller:		Staff/Outsourcing:	Y
Parts/Drives:	Y							Satellite Srv./Equip.:		Specialty Services:	

TYPES OF BUSINESS:

Computer Hardware Manufacturing
Telecommunications Equipment
IT Outsourcing & Consulting Services
Microelectronics
Appliances & Consumer Electronics
Nanotechnology Research
Software Products
Flash Memory Products

BRANDS/DIVISIONS/AFFILIATES:

Fujitsu Laboratories Ltd
Fujitsu Services Inc
Fujitsu Consulting
Fujitsu Network Communications Inc
Fujitsu Technology Solutions (Holding) BV
Fujitsu Semiconductor, Ltd.
Fujitsu Mobile-Phone Products Ltd
PFU Ltd.

CONTACTS:
Note: Officers with more than one job title may be intentionally listed here more than once.
Masami Yamamoto, Pres.
Kazuhiko Kato, CFO/Exec. VP
Masahiro Koezuka, Chief Strategy Officer/Exec. VP
Kazuo Ishida, Sr. Exec. VP
Masami Fujita, Sr. Exec. VP
Richard Christou, Sr. Exec. VP-Global Bus. Group
Michiyoshi Mazuka, Chmn.
Anthony Doye, Pres./CEO-Fujitsu America

Phone: 81-3-6252-2220	Fax: 81-03-6252-2783
Toll-Free:	
Address: Shiodome City Center, 1-5-2 Higashi-Shimbashi, Tokyo, 105-7123 Japan	

GROWTH PLANS/SPECIAL FEATURES:

Fujitsu Limited is a leading provider of IT products and services globally. The company has three business segments: Technology Solutions, representing 63% of annual revenue; Ubiquitous Product Solutions, 22%; and Device Solutions, 12% (a marginal 3% is generated from miscellaneous activities). The Technology Solutions group incorporates two branches: System Platform and Services. The System Platforms branch provides customers with network equipment to support their IT infrastructure and advanced network systems. This segment provides servers, storage systems software, network products, network management systems, optical transmission systems and mobile phone base stations. The Services branch a range of IT services, including system integration, installation, support, consulting, front-end technologies (ATMs, POS systems, etc.) outsourcing, network, maintenance, monitoring and system security. The Ubiquitous Product Solutions group provides PCs, peripherals and mobile phones and optical transceiver modules. The Device Solutions group provides logic LSI devices, semiconductor components and structural components. Sales within Japan represent roughly 68% of its annual total. The firm has approximately 540 subsidiaries, some of which include Fujitsu Laboratories, Ltd.; Fujitsu Services, Inc.; Fujitsu Consulting; Fujitsu Network Communications, Inc.; Fujitsu Technology Solutions (Holding) B.V.; Fujitsu Semiconductor, Ltd.; and Fujitsu Mobile-Phone Products, Ltd. In January 2010, Fujitsu agreed to acquire all the outstanding shares of PFU Ltd., a top image scanner company. In June 2010, it signed an agreement with Toshiba Corp. to merge their respective mobile phone businesses into a single entity controlled by Fujitsu. In September 2010, the company formed a strategic alliance with CA Technologies to develop cloud computing technologies. In November 2010, Fujitsu and Microsoft began a partnership to offer cloud computing services to clients in the U.K. through Microsoft's Windows Azure platform.

FINANCIALS:
Sales and profits are in thousands of dollars—add 000 to get the full amount. 2010 Note: Financial information for 2010 was not available for all companies at press time.

2010 Sales: $56,903,000	2010 Profits: $1,131,910	**U.S. Stock Ticker:** FJTSY
2009 Sales: $52,204,400	2009 Profits: $-1,250,190	**Int'l Ticker:** 6702 Int'l Exchange: Tokyo-TSE
2008 Sales: $53,308,650	2008 Profits: $481,070	Employees: 175,000
2007 Sales: $43,249,400	2007 Profits: $868,500	Fiscal Year Ends: 3/31
2006 Sales: $40,746,200	2006 Profits: $582,900	Parent Company:

SALARIES/BENEFITS:

Pension Plan:	ESOP Stock Plan:	Profit Sharing:	Top Exec. Salary: $	Bonus: $
Savings Plan:	Stock Purch. Plan:		Second Exec. Salary: $	Bonus: $

OTHER THOUGHTS:

Apparent Women Officers or Directors:
Hot Spot for Advancement for Women/Minorities:

LOCATIONS: ("Y" = Yes)

West:	Southwest:	Midwest:	Southeast:	Northeast:	International:
Y	Y	Y		Y	Y

FUJITSU NETWORK COMMUNICATIONS INC

www.fujitsu.com/us/services/telecom

Industry Group Code: 334210 Ranks within this company's industry group: Sales: Profits:

Hardware:	Software:	Telecommunications:	Electronic Publishing:	Equipment:		Specialty Services:	
Computers:	Consumer:	Local:	Online Service:	Telecom:	Y	Consulting:	Y
Accessories:	Corporate:	Long Distance:	TV/Cable or Wireless:	Communication:		Contract Manufacturing:	
Network Equipment:	Telecom:	Cellular:	Games:	Distribution:		Processing:	
Chips/Circuits:	Internet:	Internet Service:	Financial Data:	VAR/Reseller:		Staff/Outsourcing:	
Parts/Drives:				Satellite Srv./Equip.:		Specialty Services:	Y

TYPES OF BUSINESS:

Telecommunications Equipment & Software
Network Management Equipment
Consulting & Training Services
Life Cycle Maintenance Services
Electronics & Computer Equipment Manufacturing

BRANDS/DIVISIONS/AFFILIATES:

Fujitsu, Ltd.
LifeBook
PalmSecure
FLASHWAVE
PLASMAVISION
ECLIPSE
Intelec Geomatique
DMR

CONTACTS: Note: Officers with more than one job title may be intentionally listed here more than once.

Makoto Hamada, CEO
Makoto Hamada, Pres.
Doug Moore, Sr. VP-Mktg. & Sales
Takashi Wakabayashi, Exec. VP-Eng.
Hans Roering, Sr. VP-Mfg.
Hans Roering, Sr. VP-Oper.
Bill Erickson, Sr. VP-Planning & Dev.
George Chase, Exec. Advisor
Yozaburo Tajima, Exec. VP
Doug Moore, Sr. VP-Svcs.

Phone: 972-690-6000	Fax: 972-479-4647
Toll-Free: 800-777-3278	
Address: 2801 Telecom Pkwy., Richardson, TX 75082 US	

GROWTH PLANS/SPECIAL FEATURES:

Fujitsu Network Communications, Inc. (FNC), a subsidiary of Fujitsu, Ltd., designs and manufactures network management and telecommunications equipment for the service provider and cable TV markets in North America. The company's services include IT consulting and integration; IT infrastructure services; and telecommunications planning, deployment, maintenance and enhancement services. Its products include aggregation and transport devices, service access products and various types of software. The firm's brands include FLASHWAVE, a packet optical networking platform; NETSMART, which includes network management solutions; and the FSP 150 family, a Fiber Service Platform (FSP) that provides optical and Ethernet networking solutions for access, regional and metro core networks. The firm also provides network life cycle services to its customers targeting four areas: planning, deployment, maintenance and enhancement services. Planning includes network design, interoperability testing, fiber characterization, training and other solutions. Deployment services include engineering, furnishing and installation services; on-site configuration and turn-up or long-term testing; product and technology training offered both in-house and at corporate locations; and furnish material (FMAT), which is identifying and ordering materials for installing network equipment. Maintenance includes a 24-hour-a-day, year-round call center helpline, which is staffed by a team of technical support engineers; and training, software, product repair and replacement and other services. Enhancement services include a migration program that helps customers move data from its old systems to its new system; program and project management services to manage network migrations and other operations; and training services. In October 2009, the firm's FLASHWAVE Packet Optical Networking Platforms (ONPs) were selected by TELUS for its next-generation converged Packet/TDM optical network. In March 2010, FNC announced the addition of 3G 40Gbps optical interfaces to its FLASHWAVE 7500 platform.

FINANCIALS: Sales and profits are in thousands of dollars—add 000 to get the full amount. 2010 Note: Financial information for 2010 was not available for all companies at press time.

2010 Sales: $	2010 Profits: $	U.S. Stock Ticker: Subsidiary
2009 Sales: $	2009 Profits: $	Int'l Ticker: Int'l Exchange:
2008 Sales: $	2008 Profits: $	Employees:
2007 Sales: $543,400	2007 Profits: $	Fiscal Year Ends: 3/31
2006 Sales: $	2006 Profits: $	Parent Company: FUJITSU LIMITED

SALARIES/BENEFITS:

Pension Plan:	ESOP Stock Plan:	Profit Sharing:	Top Exec. Salary: $	Bonus: $
Savings Plan:	Stock Purch. Plan:		Second Exec. Salary: $	Bonus: $

OTHER THOUGHTS:

Apparent Women Officers or Directors:
Hot Spot for Advancement for Women/Minorities:

LOCATIONS: ("Y" = Yes)

West:	Southwest:	Midwest:	Southeast:	Northeast:	International:
Y	Y			Y	

Note: Financial information, benefits and other data can change quickly and may vary from those stated here.

FUJITSU TECHNOLOGY SOLUTIONS (HOLDING) BV ts.fujitsu.com

Industry Group Code: 334111 Ranks within this company's industry group: Sales: Profits:

Hardware:		Software:		Telecommunications:		Electronic Publishing:		Equipment:		Specialty Services:	
Computers:	Y	Consumer:		Local:		Online Service:		Telecom:		Consulting:	
Accessories:	Y	Corporate:	Y	Long Distance:		TV/Cable or Wireless:		Communication:		Contract Manufacturing:	
Network Equipment:	Y	Telecom:		Cellular:		Games:		Distribution:	Y	Processing:	
Chips/Circuits:		Internet:		Internet Service:		Financial Data:		VAR/Reseller:		Staff/Outsourcing:	
Parts/Drives:								Satellite Srv./Equip.:		Specialty Services:	Y

TYPES OF BUSINESS:

Computer Hardware-PCs & Laptops
Servers
Storage Devices
Monitors & Peripherals
Software Distribution
Support Services

BRANDS/DIVISIONS/AFFILIATES:

Fujitsu Limited
Fujitsu-Siemens Computer Holding Company

CONTACTS: Note: Officers with more than one job title may be intentionally listed here more than once.

Rolf Schwirz, CEO
Ralf Russ, CFO
Wolfgang Horak, Sr. VP-Sales, Southeastern Europe
Ralf Russ, CIO
Benno Zollner, VP-Service Oper. & Region Support Group
Ralf Russ, Chief Strategy Officer
Pierfilippo Roggero, Sr. VP-Sales, Southern & Western Europe
Hans-Dieter Wysuwa, Sr. VP-Corp. Channels
Satoru Hayashi, Chmn.
Niamh Spelman, Sr. VP-Sales, Emerging Markets
Heribert Goggerle, Exec. VP-Supply Oper.

Phone: 31-346-59-8111	Fax: 31-346-56-1298
Toll-Free:	
Address: Het Kwadrant 1, Maarssen, 3606 AZ The Netherlands	

GROWTH PLANS/SPECIAL FEATURES:

Fujitsu Technology Solutions (Holding) B.V., formerly Fujitsu-Siemens Computer Holding Company, manufactures and distributes electronics in the EMEA (Europe, Middle East, Africa) market. Originally founded as a 50/50 joint venture between Fujitsu Limited and Siemens AG, the firm became a wholly-owned subsidiary of Fujitsu in 2009. The move by Fujitsu is part of an increasing effort to diversify its revenue across sales channels outside of Japan. The company offers a complete line of IT products; from hardware, such as servers, PCs and notebooks, to solutions for dynamic IT environments, such as infrastructure virtualization and infrastructure-as-a-service solutions. It also licenses software from leading software developers, including Microsoft, Adobe, Novell, Oracle, IBM, Citrix, SAP and Symantec. Additionally, it offers financing, technical support and installation services for its products. It has production facilities in Germany and Japan, as well as sales and support offices in most major regions of Europe and India.

FINANCIALS: Sales and profits are in thousands of dollars—add 000 to get the full amount. 2010 Note: Financial information for 2010 was not available for all companies at press time.

2010 Sales: $	2010 Profits: $	U.S. Stock Ticker: Subsidiary
2009 Sales: $	2009 Profits: $	Int'l Ticker: Int'l Exchange:
2008 Sales: $	2008 Profits: $	Employees: 10,500
2007 Sales: $8,600,000	2007 Profits: $	Fiscal Year Ends: 3/31
2006 Sales: $7,000,000	2006 Profits: $	Parent Company: FUJITSU LIMITED

SALARIES/BENEFITS:

Pension Plan:	ESOP Stock Plan:	Profit Sharing:	Top Exec. Salary: $	Bonus: $
Savings Plan:	Stock Purch. Plan:		Second Exec. Salary: $	Bonus: $

OTHER THOUGHTS:

Apparent Women Officers or Directors: 1
Hot Spot for Advancement for Women/Minorities:

LOCATIONS: ("Y" = Yes)

West:	Southwest:	Midwest:	Southeast:	Northeast:	International:
					Y

GARMIN LTD

www.garmin.com

Industry Group Code: 3345 Ranks within this company's industry group: Sales: 1 Profits: 1

Hardware:	Software:	Telecommunications:	Electronic Publishing:	Equipment:		Specialty Services:
Computers:	Consumer:	Local:	Online Service:	Telecom:		Consulting:
Accessories:	Corporate:	Long Distance:	TV/Cable or Wireless:	Communication:	Y	Contract Manufacturing:
Network Equipment:	Telecom:	Cellular:	Games:	Distribution:		Processing:
Chips/Circuits:	Internet:	Internet Service:	Financial Data:	VAR/Reseller:		Staff/Outsourcing:
Parts/Drives:				Satellite Srv./Equip.:		Specialty Services:

TYPES OF BUSINESS:
Communications Equipment-GPS-Based
Aviation Electronics
Marine Electronics
Automotive Electronics
Recreation & Fitness Electronics
Navigational Equipment
Smart Phones
Cellular Phones

BRANDS/DIVISIONS/AFFILIATES:
Garmin International, Inc.
Garmin USA, Inc.
Digital Cyclone, Inc.
Garmin Australasia Pty Ltd.
Dynastream Innovations, Inc.
Garmin Singapore Pte. Ltd
Garmin China Co. Ltd.
Garmin (Europe) Ltd.

CONTACTS: Note: Officers with more than one job title may be intentionally listed here more than once.
Min Kao, CEO
Clifton A. Pemble, COO
Clifton A. Pemble, Pres.
Kevin Rauckman, CFO
Gary Kelley, VP-Mktg.
Laurie Minard, VP-Human Resources
Ed Link, VP-IT
Andrew Etkind, General Counsel/VP/Sec.
Brian Pokorny, VP-Oper.
Jon Cassat, VP-Comm.
Kerri R. Thurston, Mgr.-Investor Rel.
Kevin Rauckman, Treas.
Dan Bartel, VP-Worldwide Sales
Min Kao, Chmn.
Dan Bartel, Managing Dir.-Garmin Europe

Phone: 913-397-8200	Fax: 913-397-8282
Toll-Free:	
Address: 1200 E. 151st St., Olathe, KS 66062-3426 US	

GROWTH PLANS/SPECIAL FEATURES:

Garmin Ltd. designs, manufactures and markets navigation and communications equipment based on GPS (global positioning system) technology. The company markets its products to the aviation, marine, automotive, wireless, original equipment manufacturers (OEM) and general recreation and fitness industries. Its products are sold in approximately 100 countries through a network of 3,000 independent dealers, including retailers such as Best Buy; Amazon.com; Costco; Target; Wal-Mart; and Halford's. Garmin's aviation products include integrated cockpit systems that combine various navigational and communications systems such as autopilot; GPS and radar color displays; radio; transponders and receivers; satellite weather receivers; and air traffic information. Its marine products include chart plotters, depth sounders, fish finders, radar systems, handheld GPS devices and systems that integrate its various marine products. The automotive products include the nuvi line of personal travel assistants; the StreetPilot series of electronic maps; the zumo line of motorcycle-specific navigational aids; and other aids such as traffic receivers. Its wireless products include various GPS navigational devices for mobile phones, personal digital assistants (PDAs) and laptop computers. For the recreation and fitness industry, it offers products such as Approach, a golf course navigational aid; eTrex, a waterproof handheld system for hikers and boaters; GPSMAP, a chart plotter for marine use that can be upgraded with sonar capabilities; Foretrex, a small navigator which can be worn on the wrist for hands-free use; and Geko GPS receivers, offering handheld GPS coupled with Wide Area Augmentation System (WAAS) capabilities for even greater accuracy. In 2009, the firm announced plans to partner with computer maker Asustek to build a new line of enhanced cell phones to be branded Garmin-Asus.

Garmin offers employees benefits including tuition reimbursement; medical, dental and vision plans; life and disability insurance; a 401(k) plan; a discount stock purchase plan; and discounts on company products.

FINANCIALS: Sales and profits are in thousands of dollars—add 000 to get the full amount. 2010 Note: Financial information for 2010 was not available for all companies at press time.

2010 Sales: $	2010 Profits: $	**U.S. Stock Ticker: GRMN**
2009 Sales: $2,946,440	2009 Profits: $703,950	**Int'l Ticker:** Int'l Exchange:
2008 Sales: $3,494,077	2008 Profits: $732,848	Employees: 8,437
2007 Sales: $3,180,000	2007 Profits: $860,000	Fiscal Year Ends: 12/31
2006 Sales: $1,774,000	2006 Profits: $514,123	Parent Company:

SALARIES/BENEFITS:

Pension Plan:	ESOP Stock Plan:	Profit Sharing:	Top Exec. Salary: $500,503	Bonus: $ 203
Savings Plan: Y	Stock Purch. Plan: Y		Second Exec. Salary: $500,011	Bonus: $ 203

OTHER THOUGHTS:
Apparent Women Officers or Directors: 1
Hot Spot for Advancement for Women/Minorities:

LOCATIONS: ("Y" = Yes)

West:	Southwest:	Midwest:	Southeast:	Northeast:	International:
Y		Y			Y

GARTNER INC

www.gartner.com

Industry Group Code: 541910 Ranks within this company's industry group: Sales: 1 Profits: 1

Hardware:	Software:	Telecommunications:	Electronic Publishing:		Equipment:	Specialty Services:	
Computers:	Consumer:	Local:	Online Service:	Y	Telecom:	Consulting:	Y
Accessories:	Corporate:	Long Distance:	TV/Cable or Wireless:		Communication:	Contract Manufacturing:	
Network Equipment:	Telecom:	Cellular:	Games:		Distribution:	Processing:	
Chips/Circuits:	Internet:	Internet Service:	Financial Data:		VAR/Reseller:	Staff/Outsourcing:	
Parts/Drives:					Satellite Srv./Equip.:	Specialty Services:	Y

TYPES OF BUSINESS:

Research-Computer Hardware & Software
Industry Research
IT Symposia & Conferences
Measurement & Advisory Services

BRANDS/DIVISIONS/AFFILIATES:

Gartner Research
Gartner Consulting
Gartner Events
Gartner Symposium

CONTACTS: *Note: Officers with more than one job title may be intentionally listed here more than once.*

Eugene A. Hall, CEO
Christopher Lafond, CFO/Exec. VP
David Godfrey, Sr. VP-Global Sales
Robin Kranich, Sr. VP-Human Resources
Peter Sondergaard, Sr. VP-Research
Darko Hrelic, CIO/Sr. VP
Lewis Schwartz, General Counsel/Sr. VP/Corp. Sec.
Diane Julian, Sr. VP-Strategy
Alwyn Dawkins, Sr. VP-Gartner Events
Per Anders Waern, Sr. VP-Gartner Consulting
Ken Davis, Sr. VP-End-User Programs
Dale Kutnick, Sr. VP-Exec. Programs
James C. Smith, Chmn.

Phone: 203-964-0096	Fax:
Toll-Free:	
Address: 56 Top Gallant Rd., Stamford, CT 06904-7700 US	

GROWTH PLANS/SPECIAL FEATURES:

Gartner, Inc. is a research and advisory firm that offers independent research and analysis on IT, computer hardware, software, communications and related technology industries. It provides coverage of the IT industry to roughly 60,000 client organizations with consultants in 80 countries. The company operates in three segments: research, consulting and events. The research segment provides research content and advice for IT professionals, technology companies and the investment community in the form of reports and briefings, as well as peer networking services and membership programs designed specifically for CIOs and other senior executives. The consulting division consists primarily of consulting, measurement engagements and strategic advisory services (paid one-day analyst engagements known as SAS), which provide assessments of cost, performance, efficiency and quality focused on the IT industry. This division seeks to accomplish three major outcomes for its clients: applying IT to drive improvements in business performance; creating sustainable IT efficiency that ensures a constant return on IT investments; and strengthening the IT organization and operations to ensure high-value services to the client's lines of business and to enable the client to adapt to business changes. The events group consists of various symposia, conferences and exhibitions focused on the IT industry. The group offers a range of membership-only peer networking programs designed to bring together business executives and IT professionals in order to outline the key business drivers and best practices for the new economy. The segment also hosts events such as Gartner Symposium and other conferences on specialized topics such as outsourcing, mobile wireless, customer relationship management, application integration and business intelligence.

FINANCIALS: Sales and profits are in thousands of dollars—add 000 to get the full amount. 2010 Note: Financial information for 2010 was not available for all companies at press time.

2010 Sales: $	2010 Profits: $	U.S. Stock Ticker: IT
2009 Sales: $1,139,800	2009 Profits: $82,964	Int'l Ticker: Int'l Exchange:
2008 Sales: $1,279,065	2008 Profits: $103,871	Employees: 4,198
2007 Sales: $1,168,475	2007 Profits: $73,553	Fiscal Year Ends: 12/31
2006 Sales: $1,037,299	2006 Profits: $58,192	Parent Company:

SALARIES/BENEFITS:

Pension Plan:	ESOP Stock Plan:	Profit Sharing:	Top Exec. Salary: $724,065	Bonus: $724,065
Savings Plan: Y	Stock Purch. Plan: Y		Second Exec. Salary: $419,268	Bonus: $251,561

OTHER THOUGHTS:

Apparent Women Officers or Directors: 4
Hot Spot for Advancement for Women/Minorities: Y

LOCATIONS: ("Y" = Yes)

West:	Southwest:	Midwest:	Southeast:	Northeast:	International:
Y	Y	Y	Y	Y	Y

GATEWAY INC

www.gateway.com

Industry Group Code: 334111 Ranks within this company's industry group: Sales: Profits:

Hardware:		Software:		Telecommunications:		Electronic Publishing:		Equipment:		Specialty Services:	
Computers:	Y	Consumer:		Local:		Online Service:		Telecom:		Consulting:	
Accessories:	Y	Corporate:		Long Distance:		TV/Cable or Wireless:		Communication:		Contract Manufacturing:	
Network Equipment:		Telecom:		Cellular:		Games:		Distribution:	Y	Processing:	
Chips/Circuits:		Internet:		Internet Service:		Financial Data:		VAR/Reseller:		Staff/Outsourcing:	
Parts/Drives:								Satellite Srv./Equip.:		Specialty Services:	

TYPES OF BUSINESS:

Computer Hardware-Retail & Direct Selling
Computers & Accessories
Servers & Workstations
Notebook Computers
Support Services

BRANDS/DIVISIONS/AFFILIATES:

Acer Inc
eMachines Inc
BestBuy

CONTACTS: Note: Officers with more than one job title may be intentionally listed here more than once.

Gianfranco Lanci, Pres./CEO-Acer Inc.
J.T. Wang, Chmn.-Acer, Inc.

Phone: 949-471-7000	Fax: 949-471-7041
Toll-Free:	
Address: 7565 Irvine Center Dr., Irvine, CA 92618 US	

GROWTH PLANS/SPECIAL FEATURES:

Gateway, Inc., a subsidiary of Acer, Inc., is a leading direct marketer and retailer of personal computers and related products and services. The company offers desktop and portable personal computers, digital media personal computers, servers, workstations, peripheral products, third-party software and program services and support. Gateway's personal computers include a choice of varying clock-speed microprocessors, memory and storage capacities and other options, all specified by the customer, including everyone from individuals to large corporations. The company works directly with a broad range of suppliers to evaluate and implement the latest developments in personal computer technology. Gateway faces intense competition from other computer original equipment manufacturers (OEMs) and marketers such as Hewlett-Packard and Sony. The firm's main focus is in core PC business and convergence products. The company's subsidiary eMachines sells exclusively through third-party retailers, while the Gateway brand is sold to customers through a direct sales force, among other channels. The company markets its personal and professional equipment through its retail segment, supported significantly by BestBuy; and through its international channels in China, Canada, Mexico, Japan and the U.K. All of the company's manufacturing needs are taken care of by third-party original design manufacturers. In 2009, the firm introduced a number of notebooks and desktops including the firm's first 11.6-inch Netbook, EC Series Notebooks, the TC Series Notebook, and the Gateway One ZX Series, an all-in-one Desktop PC with multi-touch displays. In September 2010, the company introduced the NV59C66u notebook with features WiMAX capabilities.

FINANCIALS: Sales and profits are in thousands of dollars—add 000 to get the full amount. 2010 Note: Financial information for 2010 was not available for all companies at press time.

2010 Sales: $	2010 Profits: $	U.S. Stock Ticker: Subsidiary
2009 Sales: $	2009 Profits: $	Int'l Ticker: Int'l Exchange:
2008 Sales: $	2008 Profits: $	Employees:
2007 Sales: $	2007 Profits: $	Fiscal Year Ends: 12/31
2006 Sales: $3,980,800	2006 Profits: $9,600	Parent Company: ACER INC

SALARIES/BENEFITS:

Pension Plan:	ESOP Stock Plan:	Profit Sharing:	Top Exec. Salary: $	Bonus: $
Savings Plan: Y	Stock Purch. Plan:		Second Exec. Salary: $	Bonus: $

OTHER THOUGHTS:

Apparent Women Officers or Directors:
Hot Spot for Advancement for Women/Minorities:

LOCATIONS: ("Y" = Yes)

West:	Southwest:	Midwest:	Southeast:	Northeast:	International:
Y		Y		Y	Y

GEMALTO NV

www.gemalto.com

Industry Group Code: 33441 Ranks within this company's industry group: Sales: 19 Profits: 16

Hardware:		Software:		Telecommunications:		Electronic Publishing:	Equipment:		Specialty Services:	
Computers:		Consumer:	Y	Local:		Online Service:	Telecom:		Consulting:	Y
Accessories:	Y	Corporate:	Y	Long Distance:		TV/Cable or Wireless:	Communication:		Contract Manufacturing:	
Network Equipment:		Telecom:	Y	Cellular:		Games:	Distribution:		Processing:	
Chips/Circuits:		Internet:		Internet Service:		Financial Data:	VAR/Reseller:		Staff/Outsourcing:	
Parts/Drives:							Satellite Srv./Equip.:		Specialty Services:	

TYPES OF BUSINESS:

Computer Storage Equipment-Smart Cards
Smart Card Interfaces, Readers & Chipsets
Smart Card Software & Development Tools
Consulting, Training & Support Services
Online Security Programs

BRANDS/DIVISIONS/AFFILIATES:

JustAskGemalto.com
YuuWaa
Valimo Wireless Oy
Cinterion Wireless Modules GmbH
PH8
Protiva One4all

CONTACTS: *Note: Officers with more than one job title may be intentionally listed here more than once.*

Olivier Piou, CEO
Jacques Tierny, CFO
Paul Beverly, Exec. VP-Corp. Mktg.
Philippe Cabanettes, Exec. VP-Human Resources
Jean-Pierre Charlet, General Counsel/Exec. VP/Corp. Sec.
Claude Dahan, Exec. VP-Oper.
Martin McCourt, Exec. VP-Strategy, Mergers & Acquisitions
Jacques Seneca, Exec. VP-Security Bus. Unit
Philippe Vallee, Exec. VP-Telecomm. Bus. Unit
Philippe Cambriel, Exec. VP-Secure Transactions Bus. Unit
Christophe Pagezy, Exec. VP-Corp. Projects
Paul Beverly, Pres., North America

Phone: 31-20-562-06-80	Fax: 31-20-562-06-86
Toll-Free:	
Address: Barbara Strozzilaan 382, Amsterdam, 1083 HN The Netherlands	

GROWTH PLANS/SPECIAL FEATURES:

Gemalto N.V. is a leading global provider of digital security systems such as smart cards, payment terminals, card readers, online security programs, e-passports and subscriber identity module (SIM) cards. Gemalto serves the mobile telecommunications, public telephony, banking, retail, health care, transportation, identity, WLAN, pay-TV, e-government and access control markets. Smart cards are plastic cards approximately the size of credit cards that contain embedded microchips used to store and process information. The company's products conform to certification standards in every domain, including banking, JAVA GSM and telephony. Its products include YuuWaa, a solution for sharing, storing and backing up all types of multimedia data from a single interface; memory and microprocessor-based smart cards; identification and financial smart cards; cards with radio-frequency chips (RFID); electronic tags; traditional magnetic strip cards and smart card interfaces; readers and chipsets; as well as smart card software and development tools. The firm also offers consulting, training and support services. Gemalto maintains 18 production sites, 30 personalization centers, nine R&D centers and 77 sales and marketing offices around the world. Additionally, the firm operates JustAskGemalto.com, a site which provides the latest news and tips on digital security topics. In February 2010, Gemalto acquired mobile authentication company Valimo Wireless Oy. In June 2010, the company acquired industrial machine-to-machine (M2M) wireless communication module developer Cinterion Wireless Modules GmbH. In December 2010, Cinterion launched its new flagship product, PH8, an evolved high-speed packet access M2M solution. Also in December 2010, Gemalto released authentication solution Protiva One4all, which is specifically designed for trading floors with workstations that have more than one trading terminal.

FINANCIALS: Sales and profits are in thousands of dollars—add 000 to get the full amount. 2010 Note: Financial information for 2010 was not available for all companies at press time.

2010 Sales: $	2010 Profits: $	**U.S. Stock Ticker:**
2009 Sales: $2,225,640	2009 Profits: $154,458	**Int'l Ticker: AXL** Int'l Exchange: Paris-Euronext
2008 Sales: $2,238,260	2008 Profits: $203,840	Employees: 10,000
2007 Sales: $2,172,980	2007 Profits: $118,580	Fiscal Year Ends: 12/31
2006 Sales: $2,367,900	2006 Profits: $249,890	Parent Company:

SALARIES/BENEFITS:

Pension Plan:	ESOP Stock Plan:	Profit Sharing:	Top Exec. Salary: $	Bonus: $
Savings Plan:	Stock Purch. Plan:		Second Exec. Salary: $	Bonus: $

OTHER THOUGHTS:

Apparent Women Officers or Directors:
Hot Spot for Advancement for Women/Minorities:

LOCATIONS: ("Y" = Yes)

West:	Southwest:	Midwest:	Southeast:	Northeast:	International:
	Y			Y	Y

Note: Financial information, benefits and other data can change quickly and may vary from those stated here.

GERBER SCIENTIFIC INC

www.gerberscientific.com

Industry Group Code: 334111 Ranks within this company's industry group: Sales: 24 Profits: 15

Hardware:		Software:		Telecommunications:	Electronic Publishing:	Equipment:	Specialty Services:
Computers:		Consumer:		Local:	Online Service:	Telecom:	Consulting:
Accessories:	Y	Corporate:	Y	Long Distance:	TV/Cable or Wireless:	Communication:	Contract Manufacturing:
Network Equipment:		Telecom:		Cellular:	Games:	Distribution:	Processing:
Chips/Circuits:		Internet:		Internet Service:	Financial Data:	VAR/Reseller:	Staff/Outsourcing:
Parts/Drives:						Satellite Srv./Equip.:	Specialty Services:

TYPES OF BUSINESS:

Computer Hardware-Automated Manufacturing Systems
Computer-Aided Design Systems
Digital Imaging Equipment
Apparel & Flexible Materials Equipment

BRANDS/DIVISIONS/AFFILIATES:

Gerber Technology, Inc.
Gerber Scientific Products, Inc.
Gerber Innovations
Spandex Ltd.
EDGE FX
SOLARA ion
OMEGA 4.0
Yunique Solutions

CONTACTS: Note: Officers with more than one job title may be intentionally listed here more than once.

Marc T. Giles, CEO
Marc T. Giles, Pres.
Michael R. Elia, CFO/Exec. VP
Patricia L. Burmahl, Sr. VP-Global Human Resources
John R. Hancock, Sr. VP/Pres., Gerber Tech.
William V. Grickis, Jr., General Counsel/Sr. VP/Sec.
Thoman P. Finn, Sr. VP-Global Oper.
Stephen Lovass, Sr. VP/Pres., Gerber Scientific Products
Rodney Larson, Sr. VP/Pres., Spandex, Ltd.
Donald P. Aiken, Chmn.
James S. Arthurs, Sr. VP/Pres., Gerber Scientific, Asia Pacific

Phone: 860-644-1551	Fax: 860-643-7039
Toll-Free:	
Address: 83 Gerber Rd. W., South Windsor, CT 06074 US	

GROWTH PLANS/SPECIAL FEATURES:

Gerber Scientific, Inc. provides integrated computerized design and manufacturing equipment, software and related services for the following industries: sign-making and specialty graphics; and apparel and flexible materials. Gerber's sign making and specialty graphics products, produced through the subsidiaries Gerber Scientific Products (GSP), Gerber Innovations and Spandex Ltd., include digital imaging equipment; plotters and routers (cutting tools); digital print materials; and design software. Gerber Scientific products include, but are not limited to digital imaging equipment; inkjet printing; aftermarket supplies; distribution; laser templating, inspection, marking and engraving products; and raw materials. These products include the GERBER Solara ion, a wide-format ultraviolet inkjet printer for digital imaging markets; the GERBER EDGE FX, a thermal imaging system that uses heat and pressure to infuse durable resin pigments to more than 30 different printing material substrates, produces high-quality images, and dries instantly; and OMEGA 4.0, a design and production software package used for vinyl cutting, routing, thermal transfer printing and inkjet workflow improvements. Spandex offers technical knowledge, supplier relationships, supply chain infrastructure, and a wide array of products and support services. Gerber Innovations designs, manufactures, sells and services automated equipment for the die making, short run and sample making segments of the packaging industry, which it sells directly to end-use customers. Gerber Technology (GT) runs the apparel and flexible materials business. Products include product lifecycle management (PLM) software, plotters and single- or multi-ply cutting systems. In December 2010, the company sold its ophthalmic lens processing business unit Gerber Coburn to Coburn Technologies for approximately $19 million.

FINANCIALS: Sales and profits are in thousands of dollars—add 000 to get the full amount. 2010 Note: Financial information for 2010 was not available for all companies at press time.

2010 Sales: $458,355	2010 Profits: $-1,458	U.S. Stock Ticker: GRB
2009 Sales: $498,940	2009 Profits: $2,236	Int'l Ticker: Int'l Exchange:
2008 Sales: $594,298	2008 Profits: $14,504	Employees: 1,950
2007 Sales: $574,798	2007 Profits: $13,508	Fiscal Year Ends: 4/30
2006 Sales: $530,418	2006 Profits: $2,644	Parent Company:

SALARIES/BENEFITS:

Pension Plan:	ESOP Stock Plan:	Profit Sharing:	Top Exec. Salary: $490,385	Bonus: $
Savings Plan: Y	Stock Purch. Plan:		Second Exec. Salary: $302,885	Bonus: $

OTHER THOUGHTS:

Apparent Women Officers or Directors: 1
Hot Spot for Advancement for Women/Minorities:

LOCATIONS: ("Y" = Yes)

West:	Southwest:	Midwest:	Southeast:	Northeast:	International:
				Y	Y

GETRONICS NV

www.getronics.com

Industry Group Code: 541513 Ranks within this company's industry group: Sales: 16 Profits: 15

Hardware:	Software:	Telecommunications:	Electronic Publishing:	Equipment:	Specialty Services:	
Computers:	Consumer:	Local:	Online Service:	Telecom:	Consulting:	Y
Accessories:	Corporate: Y	Long Distance:	TV/Cable or Wireless:	Communication:	Contract Manufacturing:	
Network Equipment:	Telecom:	Cellular:	Games:	Distribution: Y	Processing:	
Chips/Circuits:	Internet:	Internet Service:	Financial Data:	VAR/Reseller:	Staff/Outsourcing:	Y
Parts/Drives:				Satellite Srv./Equip.:	Specialty Services:	Y

TYPES OF BUSINESS:

IT Consulting
Systems Integration
e-Commerce Support & Systems Development
Communication Technology Services
Technology Product Distribution

BRANDS/DIVISIONS/AFFILIATES:

Royal KPN NV
Getronics Workspace Alliance

CONTACTS: Note: Officers with more than one job title may be intentionally listed here more than once.

Erik van der Meijden, CEO
Jos Shoemaker, COO
Steven van Schilfgaarde, CFO
Peter Enneking, VP-Legal
Dave Baldwin, Gen. Mgr.-U.K. & Ireland

Phone: 31 88-661-0000	Fax:
Toll-Free:	
Address: Rontgenlaan 75, Zoetermeer, 2719 DX The Netherlands	

GROWTH PLANS/SPECIAL FEATURES:

Getronics NV, a subsidiary of Royal KPN NV, provides information and communication technology services to businesses. The company offers consulting in customer relations, applications integration, network management, security, telecommunications, technology integration, deployment and outsourcing to help clients increase productivity and reduce costs. Getronics organizes its services into the following categories: workspace management services, connectivity, datacenters and consultancy. The firm also distributes third-party computer and networking products. Getronics has customers in the financial services, manufacturing, media, retail, telecommunications and government industries, with a presence in over 100 countries. The firm manages approximately 2 million workspaces internationally and roughly 350,000 locations in the Netherlands. The company's recently launched Getronics Workspace Alliance, a partnership with several other companies (CompuCom, NTT DATA, Tecnocom, APX and ServiceOne) provide international organizations with global IT support and focus on workspace outsourcing.

FINANCIALS: Sales and profits are in thousands of dollars—add 000 to get the full amount. 2010 Note: Financial information for 2010 was not available for all companies at press time.

2010 Sales: $	2010 Profits: $	U.S. Stock Ticker: Subsidiary
2009 Sales: $2,787,460	2009 Profits: $82,410	Int'l Ticker: Int'l Exchange:
2008 Sales: $2,572,880	2008 Profits: $105,150	Employees:
2007 Sales: $649,540	2007 Profits: $30,610	Fiscal Year Ends: 12/31
2006 Sales: $3,737,000	2006 Profits: $5,900	Parent Company: ROYAL KPN NV

SALARIES/BENEFITS:

Pension Plan:	ESOP Stock Plan:	Profit Sharing:	Top Exec. Salary: $	Bonus: $
Savings Plan:	Stock Purch. Plan:		Second Exec. Salary: $	Bonus: $

OTHER THOUGHTS:

Apparent Women Officers or Directors:
Hot Spot for Advancement for Women/Minorities:

LOCATIONS: ("Y" = Yes)

West:	Southwest:	Midwest:	Southeast:	Northeast:	International:
				Y	Y

Note: Financial information, benefits and other data can change quickly and may vary from those stated here.

GIGAMEDIA LTD
www.gigamedia.com

Industry Group Code: 511210G Ranks within this company's industry group: Sales: 8 Profits: 3

Hardware:	Software:		Telecommunications:	Electronic Publishing:	Equipment:	Specialty Services:	
Computers:	Consumer:	Y	Local:	Online Service:	Telecom:	Consulting:	
Accessories:	Corporate:	Y	Long Distance:	TV/Cable or Wireless:	Communication:	Contract Manufacturing:	
Network Equipment:	Telecom:		Cellular:	Games:	Distribution:	Processing:	
Chips/Circuits:	Internet:	Y	Internet Service:	Financial Data:	VAR/Reseller:	Staff/Outsourcing:	Y
Parts/Drives:					Satellite Srv./Equip.:	Specialty Services:	

TYPES OF BUSINESS:
Online Gaming & Entertainment Software
Online Gaming Services

BRANDS/DIVISIONS/AFFILIATES:
Cambridge Entertainment Software Limited
Cambridge Interactive Development Corporation
Internet Media Licensing Limited
FunTown
Hoshin Gigamedia
T2CN
Spongebob Squarepants

CONTACTS: *Note: Officers with more than one job title may be intentionally listed here more than once.*
Arthur M. Wang, CEO
Thomas T. Hui, COO
Thomas T. Hui, Pres.
Quincy Tang, CFO
Lester Wong, General Counsel
John Lee, Chief Strategy Officer
Brad Miller, Dir.-Investor Rel.
John Huen, CEO-Gigamedia China
Michael Y. J. Ding, Chmn.
John Lee, Dir.-Int'l Bus.

Phone: 886-2-2656-8000	Fax:
Toll-Free:	
Address: 207 Tiding Blvd., Section 2, Taipei, Taiwan	

GROWTH PLANS/SPECIAL FEATURES:
Gigamedia Ltd. is a provider of gaming software and services to the online gaming industry, particularly the online poker and casino markets, and an operator of online games in China, including Taiwan, Hong Kong and Macau. The Taiwan-based holding company operates two principal businesses through its subsidiaries: gaming software and services; and online games. Through its gaming software and services business, the company develops and licenses online poker and casino gaming software and application services, primarily targeting continental European markets. Its gaming software and service business is operated by wholly-owned subsidiary, Cambridge Entertainment Software Limited (CESL), which provides software programs and application services through wholly-owned subsidiaries, Cambridge Interactive Development Corporation (CIDC) and Internet Media Licensing Limited (IMLL). Its online games division, operated by subsidiaries, FunTown, Hoshin Gigamedia and T2CN, operates a portfolio of online games and primarily targets online Greater China markets. FunTown is a leading online games operator in Asia and one of Taiwan's largest MahJong online game sites. T2CN is a leading online sports game operator in China and Hoshin Gigamedia owns the Taiwan-based operations of the firm's online games business. In May 2010, the company sold the sale of its 60% interest in its online gambling software business to Mangas Gaming. In June 2010, Gigamedia announced a partnership with MTV Networks to co-develop a massively multiplayer online game based on Nickelodeon cartoon character Spongebob Squarepants.

FINANCIALS: Sales and profits are in thousands of dollars—add 000 to get the full amount. 2010 Note: Financial information for 2010 was not available for all companies at press time.

2010 Sales: $	2010 Profits: $	**U.S. Stock Ticker: GIGM**
2009 Sales: $159,581	2009 Profits: $-55,880	**Int'l Ticker:** Int'l Exchange:
2008 Sales: $190,369	2008 Profits: $44,388	Employees: 835
2007 Sales: $151,714	2007 Profits: $38,890	Fiscal Year Ends: 12/31
2006 Sales: $	2006 Profits: $	Parent Company:

SALARIES/BENEFITS:
Pension Plan:	ESOP Stock Plan:	Profit Sharing:	Top Exec. Salary: $	Bonus: $
Savings Plan:	Stock Purch. Plan:		Second Exec. Salary: $	Bonus: $

OTHER THOUGHTS:
Apparent Women Officers or Directors: 1
Hot Spot for Advancement for Women/Minorities:

LOCATIONS: ("Y" = Yes)
West:	Southwest:	Midwest:	Southeast:	Northeast:	International:
					Y

Note: Financial information, benefits and other data can change quickly and may vary from those stated here.

GLOBALFOUNDRIES INC

www.globalfoundries.com

Industry Group Code: 33441 Ranks within this company's industry group: Sales:　　Profits:

Hardware:	Software:	Telecommunications:	Electronic Publishing:	Equipment:	Specialty Services:
Computers:	Consumer:	Local:	Online Service:	Telecom:	Consulting:
Accessories:	Corporate:	Long Distance:	TV/Cable or Wireless:	Communication:	Contract Manufacturing:
Network Equipment:	Telecom:	Cellular:	Games:	Distribution:	Processing:
Chips/Circuits: Y	Internet:	Internet Service:	Financial Data:	VAR/Reseller:	Staff/Outsourcing:
Parts/Drives:				Satellite Srv./Equip.:	Specialty Services:

TYPES OF BUSINESS:
Semiconductors

BRANDS/DIVISIONS/AFFILIATES:
Advanced Micro Devices Inc (AMD)
Advanced Technology Investment Co

CONTACTS: Note: Officers with more than one job title may be intentionally listed here more than once.
Doug Grose, CEO
Chia Song Hwee, COO
Robert Krakauer, CFO
Jim Kupec, Sr. VP-Worldwide Sales & Mktg.
Kathy Borneman, Sr. VP-Human Resources
Gregg Bartlett, Sr. VP-R&D
Baskara Rao Paidithali, VP-IT
Gregg Bartlett, Sr. VP-Process Tech.
Alexie Lee, General Counsel/VP
Kay Chai Ang, Sr. VP-300mm Fab Oper.
Jon Carvill, VP-Global Comm.
Mojy Chian, Sr. VP-Design Enablement
Ron Dickinson, VP-Bus. Process Mgmt.
Tony Tsai, VP-Quality & Reliability Assurance
Raj Kumar, Sr. VP-200mm Bus. Unit/Gen. Mgr.-Singapore
Leow Kim Keat, VP-Supply Chain Mgmt. & Global Procurement

Phone: 408-462-3900	Fax:
Toll-Free:	
Address: 840 N. McCarthy Blvd., Milpitas, CA 95035 US	

GROWTH PLANS/SPECIAL FEATURES:
GLOBALFOUNDRIES, Inc. (GFI) is a designer and manufacturer of semiconductor wafers. The company was once the manufacturing arm of Advanced Micro Devices, Inc. (AMD), which designs computer processors. The firm was recently spun off and is now a joint venture between AMD and the Advanced Technology Investment Company (ATIC). GFI aims to be a world leader in wafer fabrication and research as most chip designers outsource the expensive manufacturing operations to third parties. The company's services include leading edge-technologies, advanced technologies, base technologies, value-added modules and RFCMOS (radio frequency complementary metal-oxide-semiconductors). Its leading-edge technologies include systems-on-chip (SoC) production in sizes as small as 28 nanometers (nm), which allows a much higher chip density for high performance and low power processors. The firm has also developed better materials to cope with the increased heat that results from faster processors, such as strained silicon, high-k metal gates and immersion lithography. Its advanced technologies offerings include SoCs that are similarly small, but more mainstream. These products include SoCs smaller than 90 nanometers, which allow for complex processing in generic and low power varieties. GFI's base technologies include SoCs between the sizes of .13 and .6 micrometers (um), which are commonly found in consumer electronic, computing, communication and automotive products. The company's value added modules can mix and match additional technology to a base logic chip, including radio frequency, high voltage and non-volatile memory capabilities. Finally, the firm's RFCMOS modules allow the additions of Bluetooth, GPS, mobile phone, WiFI and WiMax capabilities to base electronics. GFI's extensive intellectual property portfolio allows clients to customize their products with developed and tested technologies. The company operates three 300 mm and four 200 mm wafer manufacturing facilities in locations around the world, including the U.S., Germany and Singapore.

FINANCIALS: Sales and profits are in thousands of dollars—add 000 to get the full amount. 2010 Note: Financial information for 2010 was not available for all companies at press time.

2010 Sales: $	2010 Profits: $	**U.S. Stock Ticker: Joint Venture**
2009 Sales: $	2009 Profits: $	**Int'l Ticker:**　　Int'l Exchange:
2008 Sales: $	2008 Profits: $	Employees:
2007 Sales: $	2007 Profits: $	Fiscal Year Ends: 12/31
2006 Sales: $	2006 Profits: $	Parent Company: ADVANCED MICRO DEVICES INC (AMD)

SALARIES/BENEFITS:
Pension Plan:	ESOP Stock Plan:	Profit Sharing:	Top Exec. Salary: $	Bonus: $
Savings Plan:	Stock Purch. Plan:		Second Exec. Salary: $	Bonus: $

OTHER THOUGHTS:
Apparent Women Officers or Directors: 2
Hot Spot for Advancement for Women/Minorities:

LOCATIONS: ("Y" = Yes)
West:	Southwest:	Midwest:	Southeast:	Northeast:	International:
Y	Y			Y	Y

Note: Financial information, benefits and other data can change quickly and may vary from those stated here.

GOOGLE INC

www.google.com

Industry Group Code: 519130 **Ranks within this company's industry group:** Sales: 1 Profits: 1

Hardware:	Software:	Telecommunications:	Electronic Publishing:	Equipment:	Specialty Services:
Computers:	Consumer:	Local:	Online Service:	Telecom:	Consulting:
Accessories:	Corporate:	Long Distance:	TV/Cable or Wireless:	Communication:	Contract Manufacturing:
Network Equipment:	Telecom:	Cellular: Y	Games:	Distribution:	Processing:
Chips/Circuits:	Internet:	Internet Service:	Financial Data:	VAR/Reseller:	Staff/Outsourcing:
Parts/Drives:				Satellite Srv./Equip.:	Specialty Services: Y

TYPES OF BUSINESS:

Search Engine-Internet
Paid Search Listing Advertising Services
News Site Search Service
Catalog Search Service
Shopping Site
Web Log Tool
Search and Advertising on Cell Phones

BRANDS/DIVISIONS/AFFILIATES:

Google Books
Google Maps
Google News
Gmail
YouTube LLC
Picasa
Chrome
Android

CONTACTS: Note: Officers with more than one job title may be intentionally listed here more than once.

Eric Schmidt, CEO
Patrick Pichette, CFO/Sr. VP
Alan Eustace, Sr. VP-Research
Sergey Brin, Pres., Tech./Co-Founder
Larry Page, Pres., Prod./Co-Founder
Alan Eustace, Sr. VP-Eng.
David C. Drummond, Chief Legal Officer
Shona Brown, Sr. VP-Bus. Oper.
Nikesh Arora, Chief Bus. Officer
Jonathan Rosenberg, Sr. VP-Prod. Mgmt.
David C. Drummond, Sr. VP-Corp. Dev.
Eric Schmidt, Chmn.

Phone: 650-253-0000	Fax: 650-253-0001
Toll-Free:	
Address: 1600 Amphitheatre Pkwy., Mountain View, CA 94043 US	

GROWTH PLANS/SPECIAL FEATURES:

Google, Inc. operates Google.com, one of the world's largest and most used search engines, which indexes the content of billions of Internet pages. While Google charges nothing for its search engine, it charges fees to other sites that use its search technology, and has a lucrative program that enables business clients to bid for ad space. Businesses use the AdWords program to promote their products and services. In addition, third-party websites that comprise the Google Network use the AdSense program to deliver ads that generate revenue and are relevant to search results. Additional services in this area include Google Images, a searchable index of images; Google Books, which contains digital editions of part or all of certain books; Google Scholar, an academic search tool; and Google News, which compiles a searchable list of news articles. The company's applications include office productivity and content sharing tools, such as Google Docs, Gmail, Blogger and YouTube. Client products mostly serve desktop needs, such as the Google Toolbar browser add-on, the Google Chrome browser, the Google Chrome OS operating system and the Picasa photo sharing service. Google's GEO services encompass the company's cartographical and other similar tools, including Google Maps, Google Local Search, Google Earth and Google SketchUp, a three dimensional modeling tool. Google Mobile operations include Android, a free and open source smart phone operating system, and related mobile applications. Additional service categories include Google Checkout, an online shopping and payment service, and Google Labs, an experimental testing service. Google provides its services in 112 different languages, with more than 50% of its searches coming from outside the U.S.

Employee benefits include medical, dental and vision insurance; a 401(k) plan flexible spending accounts; a college savings plan; adoption assistance; tuition reimbursement; free on-site lunches and dinners; recreation facilities; on-site dry cleaning; and oil change and car wash facilities.

FINANCIALS: Sales and profits are in thousands of dollars—add 000 to get the full amount. 2010 Note: Financial information for 2010 was not available for all companies at press time.

2010 Sales: $	2010 Profits: $	U.S. Stock Ticker: GOOG
2009 Sales: $23,650,563	2009 Profits: $6,520,448	Int'l Ticker: Int'l Exchange:
2008 Sales: $21,795,550	2008 Profits: $4,226,858	Employees: 19,835
2007 Sales: $16,593,986	2007 Profits: $4,203,720	Fiscal Year Ends: 12/31
2006 Sales: $10,604,917	2006 Profits: $3,077,446	Parent Company:

SALARIES/BENEFITS:

Pension Plan: Y	ESOP Stock Plan:	Profit Sharing:	Top Exec. Salary: $450,000	Bonus: $2,524,038
Savings Plan: Y	Stock Purch. Plan:		Second Exec. Salary: $450,000	Bonus: $3,214,738

OTHER THOUGHTS:

Apparent Women Officers or Directors: 1
Hot Spot for Advancement for Women/Minorities:

LOCATIONS: ("Y" = Yes)

West:	Southwest:	Midwest:	Southeast:	Northeast:	International:
Y	Y	Y	Y	Y	Y

GROUPE STERIA SCA

www.steria.com

Industry Group Code: 541512 Ranks within this company's industry group: Sales: 3 Profits: 4

Hardware:	Software:		Telecommunications:	Electronic Publishing:	Equipment:	Specialty Services:	
Computers:	Consumer:		Local:	Online Service:	Telecom:	Consulting:	
Accessories:	Corporate:	Y	Long Distance:	TV/Cable or Wireless:	Communication:	Contract Manufacturing:	
Network Equipment:	Telecom:		Cellular:	Games:	Distribution:	Processing:	
Chips/Circuits:	Internet:		Internet Service:	Financial Data:	VAR/Reseller:	Staff/Outsourcing:	
Parts/Drives:					Satellite Srv./Equip.:	Specialty Services:	Y

TYPES OF BUSINESS:

Information Technology Services

BRANDS/DIVISIONS/AFFILIATES:

Steria SA

CONTACTS: Note: Officers with more than one job title may be intentionally listed here more than once.

Francois Enaud, CEO
Laurent Lemaire, CFO
Johan Vermeule, Group Human Resources Dir.
Jurgen Sponnagle, VP/CEO-Central Europea, Spain & Scandinavia
Olivier Vallet, CEO-France
Jacques Bentz, Chmn.
Mukesh Aghi, CEO-India

Phone: 33-1-34-88-60-00	Fax: 33-1-34-88-69-69
Toll-Free:	
Address: 46 rue Camille Desmoulins, Issy-les Moulineaux Cedex 9, France	

GROWTH PLANS/SPECIAL FEATURES:

Groupe Steria SCA, operating through subsidiary Steria SA, is a provider of information technology (IT) services. The areas of business can be divided in three sections: transformation services, operation services and industrial delivery. Transformation services consist of IT transformation services; application development; business intelligence services; and Oracle consulting and installation services; and SAP consulting and management services. Operation services include application; data and infrastructure management; testing services; and finance and accounting, human resources and vertical business process outsourcing. The industrial delivery segment consists of the Global Delivery Unit, a group of production centers in Europe which coordinates managed service projects carried out by the company by supporting supervision two supervision centers in France and the U.K. The segment is also involved in onshore, near shore and offshore delivery. The firm has a presence in 16 countries around the world, including Austria, Belgium, China, Denmark, France, Germany, India, Luxemburg, Morocco, Norway, Poland, Singapore, Spain, Switzerland, Sweden and the U.K.

FINANCIALS: Sales and profits are in thousands of dollars—add 000 to get the full amount. 2010 Note: Financial information for 2010 was not available for all companies at press time.

2010 Sales: $	2010 Profits: $	U.S. Stock Ticker:
2009 Sales: $2,193,980	2009 Profits: $64,880	Int'l Ticker: RIA Int'l Exchange: Paris-Euronext
2008 Sales: $2,536,460	2008 Profits: $74,120	Employees: 18,393
2007 Sales: $2,034,400	2007 Profits: $71,830	Fiscal Year Ends: 12/31
2006 Sales: $	2006 Profits: $	Parent Company:

SALARIES/BENEFITS:

Pension Plan:	ESOP Stock Plan:	Profit Sharing:	Top Exec. Salary: $	Bonus: $
Savings Plan:	Stock Purch. Plan:		Second Exec. Salary: $	Bonus: $

OTHER THOUGHTS:

Apparent Women Officers or Directors:
Hot Spot for Advancement for Women/Minorities:

LOCATIONS: ("Y" = Yes)

West:	Southwest:	Midwest:	Southeast:	Northeast:	International:
					Y

GSE SYSTEMS INC

www.gses.com

Industry Group Code: 511210N Ranks within this company's industry group: Sales: 10 Profits: 8

Hardware:	Software:		Telecommunications:	Electronic Publishing:	Equipment:	Specialty Services:	
Computers:	Consumer:		Local:	Online Service:	Telecom:	Consulting:	
Accessories:	Corporate:	Y	Long Distance:	TV/Cable or Wireless:	Communication:	Contract Manufacturing:	
Network Equipment:	Telecom:		Cellular:	Games:	Distribution:	Processing:	
Chips/Circuits:	Internet:		Internet Service:	Financial Data:	VAR/Reseller:	Staff/Outsourcing:	
Parts/Drives:					Satellite Srv./Equip.:	Specialty Services:	Y

TYPES OF BUSINESS:

Software-Manufacturing Processes
Simulation Systems & Services
Engineering & Training Services
Security Systems & Services

BRANDS/DIVISIONS/AFFILIATES:

GSE-UNIS
EnVision Systems, Inc.
Xtreme Tools
TAS Holdings Limited
PEGASUS
SIMON
JADE
GSE Power Systems, Inc.

CONTACTS: Note: Officers with more than one job title may be intentionally listed here more than once.

James A. Eberle, CEO
Chin-Our Jerry Jen, Pres.
Jeffery G. Hough, CFO/Sr. VP
Jean-Marc Holt, Managing Dir.-GSE Power Systems AB
Gill R. Grady, Sr. VP
Charles W. Kelly, VP
George McCullough, VP
Jerome Feldman, Chmn.

Phone: 410-970-7800	Fax: 410-970-7997
Toll-Free: 800-638-7912	
Address: 1332 Londontown Blvd., Ste. 200, Sykesville, MD 21784 US	

GROWTH PLANS/SPECIAL FEATURES:

GSE Systems, Inc. is a global provider of real-time simulators used primarily in the nuclear power, fossil energy and chemical industries. The firm operates in four business units: nuclear, fossil, process and simulation centers. Both the nuclear and fossil units provide full scope simulators to train power plant operators, engineers and managers in their respective power industries. The process unit offers process simulators used to evaluate process design, control strategy development, hazard analysis, operating procedure validation, de-bottlenecking and optimization. Process simulators are used by the refining, specialty chemicals, nuclear processing, minerals, fermentation, pharmaceuticals, polymers, tobacco and brewing industries. The simulation centers segment is in the process of building simulation training centers in the United Arab Emirates, as well as in North America, Europe and Asia. Simulation product suites include JADE (Java Applications & Development Environment) for use in nuclear and fossil power plants; SIMON, a computer workstation system used for monitoring stability of boiling water reactor plants; Xtreme Tools, a purely Microsoft Windows-based modeling environment; and PEGASUS plant surveillance software. The firm's training services include development of drill guides, computer based training programs, specialized training materials, classroom simulation development and construction of turn-key facilities, including training programs and staff. GSE Systems' subsidiaries include GSE Power Systems, Inc.; GSE Power Systems, AB (located in Sweden); GSE Engineering Systems (Beijing) Co. Ltd.; and GSE Systems, Ltd. (located in the U.K.). It also owns 10% interest in Emirates Simulation Academy, LLC, a U.A.E. limited liability firm. In April 2010, the company acquired TAS Holdings Limited, an engineering firm that does business as TAS Engineering Consultants. In July 2010, GSE Systems and UNIS formed China-based simulation joint venture GSE-UNIS, which is 49% owned by GSE Systems. In January 2011, the firm acquired interactive multi-media tutorials and simulation model provider EnVision Systems, Inc.

FINANCIALS: Sales and profits are in thousands of dollars—add 000 to get the full amount. 2010 Note: Financial information for 2010 was not available for all companies at press time.

2010 Sales: $	2010 Profits: $	U.S. Stock Ticker: GVP
2009 Sales: $40,060	2009 Profits: $- 797	Int'l Ticker: Int'l Exchange:
2008 Sales: $29,004	2008 Profits: $- 690	Employees: 201
2007 Sales: $31,900	2007 Profits: $1,169	Fiscal Year Ends: 12/31
2006 Sales: $27,502	2006 Profits: $- 346	Parent Company:

SALARIES/BENEFITS:

Pension Plan:	ESOP Stock Plan:	Profit Sharing:	Top Exec. Salary: $272,500	Bonus: $
Savings Plan: Y	Stock Purch. Plan:		Second Exec. Salary: $225,000	Bonus: $

OTHER THOUGHTS:

Apparent Women Officers or Directors: 1
Hot Spot for Advancement for Women/Minorities:

LOCATIONS: ("Y" = Yes)

West:	Southwest:	Midwest:	Southeast:	Northeast:	International:
			Y	Y	Y

GSI COMMERCE INC

www.gsicommerce.com

Industry Group Code: 511210M Ranks within this company's industry group: Sales: 1 Profits: 3

Hardware:	Software:		Telecommunications:	Electronic Publishing:	Equipment:	Specialty Services:	
Computers:	Consumer:		Local:	Online Service:	Telecom:	Consulting:	Y
Accessories:	Corporate:	Y	Long Distance:	TV/Cable or Wireless:	Communication:	Contract Manufacturing:	
Network Equipment:	Telecom:		Cellular:	Games:	Distribution:	Processing:	
Chips/Circuits:	Internet:		Internet Service:	Financial Data:	VAR/Reseller:	Staff/Outsourcing:	
Parts/Drives:					Satellite Srv./Equip.:	Specialty Services:	Y

TYPES OF BUSINESS:

E-Commerce Consulting
Web Site Design Services
Managed Hosting Services
Customer Service Operations
Online Marketing
Merchandising Services
Order Fulfillment

BRANDS/DIVISIONS/AFFILIATES:

gsi interactive
e-Dialog Inc
ShipQuik
Retail Convergence, Inc.
VendorNet
RueLaLa.com
ShopRunner.com
SmartBargains.com

CONTACTS: Note: Officers with more than one job title may be intentionally listed here more than once.

Michael G. Rubin, CEO
Michael G. Rubin, Pres.
Michael R. Conn, CFO
Fiona Dias, Exec. VP-Mktg.
Jim Flanagan, Exec. VP-Human Resources
Jim Macintyre, Chief-eCommerce Tech.
Bob Liewald, Exec. VP-Merch.
Arthur H. Miller, General Counsel/Exec. VP
Robert Wuesthoff, Exec. VP-Global Oper.
Fiona Disa, Exec. VP-Strategy
Michael R. Conn, Exec. VP-Finance
Scott Hardy, Exec. VP-Bus. Mgmt.
Damon Mintzer, Exec. VP-Sales
Ronald C. Williamsion, Sr. VP-Customer Care
Steven Davis, Exec. VP/Pres., Rue La La
Michael G. Rubin, Chmn.

Phone: 610-491-7000	Fax:
Toll-Free:	
Address: 935 First Ave., King of Prussia, PA 19406 US	

GROWTH PLANS/SPECIAL FEATURES:

GSI Commerce, Inc. is a provider of e-commerce products and services that enable retailers, branded manufacturers, entertainment companies and professional sports organizations to operate e-commerce businesses both domestically and internationally. The company operates in three segments: e-commerce services, interactive marketing services and consumer engagement The e-commerce services segment delivers customized products and services to clients through an integrated e-commerce platform, which is made up of three components: technology, fulfillment and call center services. Technology services include an e-Commerce Engine, a software product that provides configurable features that enable the buying and selling of products online, such as product presentation, merchandising, shopping cart and checkout. The fulfillment component offers fulfillment and drop shipping services through sevenfulfillment centers (five in the U.S., one in Canada and one in Europe). Call center services are also provided through three customer care centers in the U.S. and one in the U.K. The interactive marketing services segment provides interactive marketing, online advertising and design services through its in-house digital marketing agency, TrueAction. The segment also offers e-mail marketing services through subsidiary, e-Dialog, Inc. The consumer engagement segment consists of exclusive membership shopping sites such as ShopRunner.com, RueLaLa.com and SmartBargains.com. The company also operates ShipQuik, a package-delivery program in partnership with UPS. In May 2010, GSI acquired Vendornet, a provider of multichannel ecommerce supply chain solutions.

Employees are offered medical, dental and vision insurance; flexible spending accounts; life insurance; disability coverage; an employee assistance program; auto and home insurance; pet insurance; and group legal insurance.

FINANCIALS: Sales and profits are in thousands of dollars—add 000 to get the full amount. 2010 Note: Financial information for 2010 was not available for all companies at press time.

2010 Sales: $	2010 Profits: $	**U.S. Stock Ticker:** GSIC
2009 Sales: $1,004,215	2009 Profits: $-11,028	**Int'l Ticker:** Int'l Exchange:
2008 Sales: $966,926	2008 Profits: $-16,923	Employees: 4,470
2007 Sales: $749,957	2007 Profits: $3,039	Fiscal Year Ends: 12/31
2006 Sales: $609,553	2006 Profits: $53,701	Parent Company:

SALARIES/BENEFITS:

Pension Plan:	ESOP Stock Plan:	Profit Sharing:	Top Exec. Salary: $474,000	Bonus: $
Savings Plan: Y	Stock Purch. Plan:		Second Exec. Salary: $444,158	Bonus: $296,474

OTHER THOUGHTS:

Apparent Women Officers or Directors: 2
Hot Spot for Advancement for Women/Minorities: Y

LOCATIONS: ("Y" = Yes)

West:	Southwest:	Midwest:	Southeast:	Northeast:	International:
Y		Y	Y	Y	Y

GTSI CORP

www.gtsi.com

Industry Group Code: 423430 **Ranks within this company's industry group:** Sales: 15 Profits: 10

Hardware:		**Software:**		**Telecommunications:**		**Electronic Publishing:**		**Equipment:**		**Specialty Services:**	
Computers:		Consumer:		Local:		Online Service:		Telecom:		Consulting:	Y
Accessories:		Corporate:	Y	Long Distance:		TV/Cable or Wireless:		Communication:		Contract Manufacturing:	
Network Equipment:		Telecom:		Cellular:		Games:		Distribution:	Y	Processing:	
Chips/Circuits:		Internet:		Internet Service:		Financial Data:		VAR/Reseller:		Staff/Outsourcing:	
Parts/Drives:								Satellite Srv./Equip.:		Specialty Services:	Y

TYPES OF BUSINESS:

Computer Equipment Distribution
IT Products & Services-Government Related
Technical Engineering & Support Services
Consulting Services
Financing

BRANDS/DIVISIONS/AFFILIATES:

CONTACTS:

Note: Officers with more than one job title may be intentionally listed here more than once.

Sterling Phillips, CEO
Peter Whitfield, CFO/Sr. VP
Todd Leto, Sr. VP-Sales & Mktg.
Bridget Atkinson, VP-Human Resources & Organizational Dev.
Paul Liberty, VP-Corp. Affairs
Paul Liberty, VP-Investor Rel.
John M. Toups, Chmn.
Mark Smith, VP-Supply Chain

Phone: 703-502-2000	**Fax:**
Toll-Free: 800-999-4874	
Address: 2553 Dulles View Dr., Ste. 100, Herndon, VA 20171 US	

GROWTH PLANS/SPECIAL FEATURES:

GTSI Corp. provides IT products and services to U.S. federal, state and local governments and to prime contractors who are working directly on government contracts. Sales to the federal government generate approximately 72% of the company's sales, while prime contractors account for 23% of its sales and state and local governments together account for 5%. Its services are directed at government needs, such as mobile evidence capture, unified communications, mobile clinical applications, green IT, virtualization and cloud computing. Services offered by GTSI include hardware integration; customer image propagation; automated system diagnostics and data capture; customer asset tagging; and complex configurations of various IT solutions, such as VoIP (Voice over Internet Protocol). The company's technology lifecycle management (TLM) methodology has three core elements: planning of the entire process of IT Infrastructure Optimization; ongoing Program Management of the lifecycle elements; and separating the acquisition necessities of IT Infrastructure Optimization from realities of three-year budget cycles and narrowly defined budget line items. GTSI's Solutions division consists of desktop virtualization; networking; data center services; cyber and physical security; and IT service management. GTSI's Services division is made up of professional services, integration services, support services and financial services. Professional services provide network infrastructure design, data management, enterprise computer, security and enterprise software. Integration services consist of engineering, integration, asset management and logistical support. Support services include problem resolution and cost of ownership reviews to minimize downtime and expenses. Financial services deal with budgetary concerns. Hardware generates approximately 65% of the company's total sales; software generates 24%, services generate 7% and financing generates 4%.

GTSI offers its employees tuition reimbursement; an employee assistance program; weight loss and smoking cessation programs; on-site gym, deli and massage; credit union membership; flexible spending accounts; adoption assistance; and medical, dental and vision insurance.

FINANCIALS:

Sales and profits are in thousands of dollars—add 000 to get the full amount. 2010 Note: Financial information for 2010 was not available for all companies at press time.

2010 Sales: $	2010 Profits: $	**U.S. Stock Ticker: GTSI**
2009 Sales: $761,870	2009 Profits: $5,456	**Int'l Ticker:** Int'l Exchange:
2008 Sales: $821,165	2008 Profits: $7,835	Employees: 615
2007 Sales: $723,465	2007 Profits: $-1,767	Fiscal Year Ends: 12/31
2006 Sales: $862,977	2006 Profits: $-3,014	Parent Company:

SALARIES/BENEFITS:

Pension Plan:	ESOP Stock Plan:	Profit Sharing:	Top Exec. Salary: $525,000	Bonus: $656,250
Savings Plan: Y	Stock Purch. Plan: Y		Second Exec. Salary: $340,000	Bonus: $318,750

OTHER THOUGHTS:

Apparent Women Officers or Directors: 1
Hot Spot for Advancement for Women/Minorities:

LOCATIONS: ("Y" = Yes)

West:	Southwest:	Midwest:	Southeast:	Northeast:	International:
				Y	

GUIDEWIRE SOFTWARE INC

www.guidewire.com

Industry Group Code: 511201 Ranks within this company's industry group: Sales: Profits:

Hardware:		Software:		Telecommunications:		Electronic Publishing:	Equipment:	Specialty Services:
Computers:		Consumer:		Local:		Online Service:	Telecom:	Consulting:
Accessories:		Corporate:	Y	Long Distance:		TV/Cable or Wireless:	Communication:	Contract Manufacturing:
Network Equipment:		Telecom:		Cellular:		Games:	Distribution:	Processing:
Chips/Circuits:		Internet:	Y	Internet Service:		Financial Data:	VAR/Reseller:	Staff/Outsourcing:
Parts/Drives:							Satellite Srv./Equip.:	Specialty Services:

TYPES OF BUSINESS:
Insurance Policy & Claims Management Software

BRANDS/DIVISIONS/AFFILIATES:
Guidewire PolicyCenter
Guidewire ClaimCenter
Guidewire BillingCenter
US Venture Partners
Bay Partners
Thunderhead
PartnerConnect

CONTACTS: Note: Officers with more than one job title may be intentionally listed here more than once.
John Raguin, CEO
Karen Blasing, CFO
Brian Desmond, VP-Mktg.
Ben Brantley, CTO
Jeremy Henrickson, VP-Prod. Dev.
Priscilla Hung, VP-Corp. Dev. & Alliances
Alex Naddaff, VP-Professional Svcs.
Marcus Ryu, VP-Prod. & Strategy
Dan Gordon, VP-Prod. Mgmt.
Pete Espinosa, VP-Worldwide Sales

Phone: 650-357-9100	Fax: 650-357-9101
Toll-Free:	
Address: 2211 Bridgepointe Pkwy., Ste. 200, San Mateo, CA 94404 US	

GROWTH PLANS/SPECIAL FEATURES:

Guidewire Software, Inc. provides web-based technology solutions to workers' compensation and property and casualty (P&C) insurers. The firm's software, The Guidewire Insurance Suite, runs operations such as policy administration, claims, underwriting and billing. The Guidewire Insurance Suite comprises three solutions: Guidewire PolicyCenter, Guidewire ClaimCenter and Guidewire BillingCenter. Guidewire PolicyCenter, a complete policy administration suite, is designed to aid clients in increasing premium revenues at lower loss cost and expense; improving overall underwriting accuracy and efficiency; and responding flexibly to business opportunities. Guidewire ClaimCenter, a comprehensive claims program, manages the new loss entry, investigation, settlement and recovery stages of the claims process. Guidewire BillingCenter, a complete billing solution, is designed to allow insurers to streamline the billing process; increase billing accuracy; implement more flexible billing models; reduce billing leakage; and optimize float. Guidewire Software maintains operations in the U.S., France, the U.K., Japan, Hong Kong, Canada and Australia. Some of the firm's main clients include Hastings Mutual Insurance Company, a regional insurance carrier; Canal Insurance, a line-of-business insurance specialist; CNA, which specializes in commercial insurance lines; and Amica Mutual Insurance, a personal insurance carrier. The company is owned by private investors such as U.S. Venture Partners and Bay Partners, as well as by Guidewire Software employees. In July 2009, the firm partnered with Thunderhead, a provider of document automation and multi-channel communications solutions, to offer Thunderhead's services to Guidewire Software P&C insurance clients. In May 2010, Guidewire Software introduced PartnerConnect, an invitation-only solution for use by strategic system integrator and regional consulting alliance partners.

FINANCIALS: Sales and profits are in thousands of dollars—add 000 to get the full amount. 2010 Note: Financial information for 2010 was not available for all companies at press time.

2010 Sales: $	2010 Profits: $	U.S. Stock Ticker: Private	
2009 Sales: $	2009 Profits: $	Int'l Ticker: Int'l Exchange:	
2008 Sales: $	2008 Profits: $	Employees:	
2007 Sales: $	2007 Profits: $	Fiscal Year Ends:	
2006 Sales: $	2006 Profits: $	Parent Company:	

SALARIES/BENEFITS:

Pension Plan:	ESOP Stock Plan:	Profit Sharing:	Top Exec. Salary: $	Bonus: $
Savings Plan:	Stock Purch. Plan:		Second Exec. Salary: $	Bonus: $

OTHER THOUGHTS:
Apparent Women Officers or Directors: 2
Hot Spot for Advancement for Women/Minorities: Y

LOCATIONS: ("Y" = Yes)

West:	Southwest:	Midwest:	Southeast:	Northeast:	International:
Y					Y

HARMONIC INC

www.harmonicinc.com

Industry Group Code: 334210 Ranks within this company's industry group: Sales: 14 Profits: 7

Hardware:	Software:	Telecommunications:	Electronic Publishing:	Equipment:		Specialty Services:	
Computers:	Consumer:	Local:	Online Service:	Telecom:	Y	Consulting:	Y
Accessories:	Corporate:	Long Distance:	TV/Cable or Wireless:	Communication:	Y	Contract Manufacturing:	
Network Equipment:	Telecom:	Cellular:	Games:	Distribution:		Processing:	
Chips/Circuits:	Internet:	Internet Service:	Financial Data:	VAR/Reseller:		Staff/Outsourcing:	
Parts/Drives:				Satellite Srv./Equip.:		Specialty Services:	

TYPES OF BUSINESS:

Networking Equipment
Video Stream Processing
Cable Edge & Access
Software

BRANDS/DIVISIONS/AFFILIATES:

CLEARcut Studio
MAXLink
PWRLink
METROLink
GIGALight
DiviCom
Scopus Video Networks Ltd

CONTACTS: Note: Officers with more than one job title may be intentionally listed here more than once.

Patrick Harshman, CEO
Patrick Harshman, Pres.
Carolyn V. Aver, CFO
Nimrod Ben-Natan, VP-Prod. Mktg. Solutions & Strategy
Peter E. Hillard, VP-Human Resources
Neven Haltmayer, VP-R&D
Charles Bonasera, VP-Oper.
Shahar Bar, VP-Corp. Dev.
Jim Marino, VP-N. America Sales
David Price, VP-Bus. Dev. & Mktg. Comm.
Shimon Shanor, VP-Strategic Markets
Raymond Tse, VP-APAC Sales
Lewis Solomon, Chmn.
Matthew Aden, VP-Worldwide Sales & Service

Phone: 408-542-2500	Fax: 408-542-2511
Toll-Free: 800-788-1330	
Address: 549 Baltic Way, Sunnyvale, CA 94089 US	

GROWTH PLANS/SPECIAL FEATURES:

Harmonic, Inc. designs, manufactures and sells video infrastructure products and system solutions that enable network operators to efficiently deliver broadcast and on-demand services that include digital video, video-on-demand (VOD), high definition television, and high-speed Internet access and telephony. The company's products fall into two categories: video processing solutions and edge and access products. Harmonic provides technical support services to its customers worldwide. Its video processing solutions provide broadband operators with the ability to acquire a variety of signals from different sources, in different protocols, and to organize, manage and distribute this content to maximize use of the available bandwidth. Its edge products enable cable operators to deliver customized broadcast or narrowcast on-demand services to their subscribers. The firm's access products, which consist mainly of optical transmission products, node platforms and return path products, allow cable operators to deliver video, data and voice services over their networks. Harmonic sells its products to various broadband communication companies, which include Cablevision Systems; Charter Communications; Comcast; Cox Communications; DIRECTV; Dish Network; ESPN; Time Warner Cable; Alliant; Insight Communications; Time Warner Cable; The Weather Channel; E!; and SingTel. In May 2010, Harmonic announced a definitive agreement to acquire Omneon, Inc., a provider of video production and playout solutions, for $247 million. Also in May 2010, the company introduced the PWRBlazer 3142E, a 4x4 scalable optical node that can deliver and support VOD, data and telephony services.

The firm offers its employees a 401(k) savings plan; an employee stock purchase plan; an employee referral bonus; flexible spending accounts; life and AD&D insurance; long-term care, travel and accident insurance; tuition reimbursement; a 529 college fund; credit union membership; flexible time off; an on-site fitness center; public transportation benefits; and medical, dental and vision insurance.

FINANCIALS: Sales and profits are in thousands of dollars—add 000 to get the full amount. 2010 Note: Financial information for 2010 was not available for all companies at press time.

2010 Sales: $	2010 Profits: $	**U.S. Stock Ticker: HLIT**
2009 Sales: $319,566	2009 Profits: $-24,139	Int'l Ticker: Int'l Exchange:
2008 Sales: $364,963	2008 Profits: $63,992	Employees:
2007 Sales: $311,204	2007 Profits: $23,421	Fiscal Year Ends: 12/31
2006 Sales: $247,684	2006 Profits: $1,007	Parent Company:

SALARIES/BENEFITS:

Pension Plan:	ESOP Stock Plan: Y	Profit Sharing:	Top Exec. Salary: $450,000	Bonus: $101,520
Savings Plan: Y	Stock Purch. Plan: Y		Second Exec. Salary: $431,269	Bonus: $46,530

OTHER THOUGHTS:

Apparent Women Officers or Directors: 1
Hot Spot for Advancement for Women/Minorities:

LOCATIONS: ("Y" = Yes)

West:	Southwest:	Midwest:	Southeast:	Northeast:	International:
Y					Y

HARRIS CORPORATION

www.harris.com

Industry Group Code: 3342 Ranks within this company's industry group: Sales: 2   Profits: 2

Hardware:	Software:	Telecommunications:	Electronic Publishing:	Equipment:		Specialty Services:
Computers:	Consumer:	Local:	Online Service:	Telecom:	Y	Consulting:
Accessories:	Corporate:	Long Distance:	TV/Cable or Wireless:	Communication:	Y	Contract Manufacturing:
Network Equipment:	Telecom:	Cellular:	Games:	Distribution:		Processing:
Chips/Circuits:	Internet:	Internet Service:	Financial Data:	VAR/Reseller:		Staff/Outsourcing:
Parts/Drives:				Satellite Srv./Equip.:		Specialty Services:

TYPES OF BUSINESS:

Communications Equipment Manufacturing
Wireless Communications Equipment
Broadcasting Equipment
Microwave Equipment

BRANDS/DIVISIONS/AFFILIATES:

Falcon III
Crucial Security Inc

CONTACTS: *Note: Officers with more than one job title may be intentionally listed here more than once.*

Howard L. Lance, CEO
Robert K. Henry, COO/Exec. VP
Howard L. Lance, Pres.
Gary L. McArthur, CFO/Sr. VP
Jeffrey S. Shuman, VP-Human Resources & Corp. Rel.
William H. Miller, Jr., CIO/VP-Info. Svcs.
R. Kent Buchanan, CTO
R. Kent Buchanan, VP-Eng.
Eugene S. Cavallucci, General Counsel/VP
Ricardo A. Navarro, VP-Corp. Dev.
Pamela Padgett, VP-Corp. Comm.
Pamela Padgett, VP-Investor Rel.
Lewis A. Schwartz, Principal Acct. Officer/VP
Daniel R. Pearson, Pres., Gov't Comm. Systems Div.
Wesley B. Covell, Pres., Defense Programs
Harris Morris, Jr., Pres., Broadcast Comm.
Peter Challan, VP-Gov't Rel.
Howard L. Lance, Chmn.
Leon Shivamber, Head-Int'l Bus. Dev.
Leon V. Shivamber, VP-Supply Chain Mgmt.

Phone: 321-727-9100	Fax:
Toll-Free: 800-442-7747	
Address: 1025 W. NASA Blvd., Melbourne, FL 32919-0001 US	

GROWTH PLANS/SPECIAL FEATURES:

Harris Corporation is an international communications and information technology company. The firm, along with its subsidiaries, provides sales and services to government and commercial markets in over 150 countries. Harris operates through three divisions: RF Communications, Government Communications Systems and Broadcast Communications. The RF Communications segment is a global supplier of secure radio communications products and systems for defense and government operations; and also performs advanced research, primarily for the U.S. Department of Defense and for international customers in government, defense and peacekeeping organizations. Its products include the Falcon III multiband manpack radio. The firm's Government Communications Systems segment designs, develops and supplies communications and information networks and equipment; develops integrated intelligence, surveillance and reconnaissance solutions; develops, designs and supports information systems for image and other data collection, processing, analysis, interpretation, display, storage and retrieval; offers enterprise IT and communications engineering, operations and support services; and conducts advanced research studies, primarily for various agencies of the U.S. government and other aerospace and defense companies. The Broadcast Communications segment serves the global digital and analog media markets, providing infrastructure and networking products and solutions; media and workflow solutions; and television and radio transmission equipment and systems. In April 2009, Harris opened a new facility in St. Louis, Missouri; acquired Crucial Security, Inc.; and agreed to acquire Tyco Electronics Wireless Systems from Tyco Electronics Ltd. In May 2009, the firm spun off its Harris Stratex Networks, Inc. subsidiary. In June 2009, the company acquired the Air Traffic Control operations of SolaCom Technologies, Inc.; and opened a new office in India. In February 2010, Harris acquired the land-based, situational awareness technology assets of OSI Geospatial, Inc.

The firm offers employees benefits including medical, dental and vision insurance; a 401(k); paid time off; tuition reimbursement; and health and dependent care spending accounts.

FINANCIALS: Sales and profits are in thousands of dollars—add 000 to get the full amount. 2010 Note: Financial information for 2010 was not available for all companies at press time.

2010 Sales: $5,206,100	2010 Profits: $561,600	**U.S. Stock Ticker: HRS**
2009 Sales: $5,005,000	2009 Profits: $37,900	**Int'l Ticker:** Int'l Exchange:
2008 Sales: $4,596,100	2008 Profits: $444,200	Employees: 15,800
2007 Sales: $3,737,900	2007 Profits: $480,400	Fiscal Year Ends: 6/30
2006 Sales: $3,474,800	2006 Profits: $237,900	Parent Company:

SALARIES/BENEFITS:

Pension Plan:	ESOP Stock Plan:	Profit Sharing:	Top Exec. Salary: $1,061,539	Bonus: $1,372,478
Savings Plan: Y	Stock Purch. Plan:		Second Exec. Salary: $568,173	Bonus: $603,272

OTHER THOUGHTS:

Apparent Women Officers or Directors: 3
Hot Spot for Advancement for Women/Minorities: Y

LOCATIONS: ("Y" = Yes)

West:	Southwest:	Midwest:	Southeast:	Northeast:	International:
Y	Y	Y	Y	Y	Y

Note: Financial information, benefits and other data can change quickly and may vary from those stated here.

HCL INFOSYSTEMS LIMITED

www.hclinfosystems.in

Industry Group Code: 334111 Ranks within this company's industry group: Sales: 16 Profits: 10

Hardware:		Software:		Telecommunications:		Electronic Publishing:		Equipment:		Specialty Services:	
Computers:	Y	Consumer:		Local:		Online Service:		Telecom:	Y	Consulting:	Y
Accessories:	Y	Corporate:		Long Distance:		TV/Cable or Wireless:		Communication:		Contract Manufacturing:	
Network Equipment:	Y	Telecom:		Cellular:		Games:		Distribution:	Y	Processing:	
Chips/Circuits:		Internet:		Internet Service:		Financial Data:		VAR/Reseller:	Y	Staff/Outsourcing:	
Parts/Drives:	Y							Satellite Srv./Equip.:		Specialty Services:	Y

TYPES OF BUSINESS:
Computer Hardware & Systems
IT Products and Services
Personal Computers

BRANDS/DIVISIONS/AFFILIATES:
HCL Digilife
Busybee
Beanstalk
Ezeebee
HCL Infocom Limited
HCL Security Limited
HCL Infinet Limited
Motorola Inc

CONTACTS: Note: Officers with more than one job title may be intentionally listed here more than once.
Ajai Chowdhry, CEO
J.V. Ramamurthy, COO
J.V. Ramamurthy, Pres.
Sandeep Kanwar, CFO/Exec. VP
George Paul, Exec. VP-Mktg.
Vivek Punekar, VP-Human Resources
George Paul, Exec. VP-R&D
Sushil Kumar Jain, Sec.
Rajendra Kumar, Exec. VP-Corp. Initiatives
M. Chandrasekaran, Sr. VP-Office Automation Prod. Bus.
Rajeev Asija, Exec. VP-Enterprise Solutions & Svcs.
Ajai Chowdhry, Chmn.
Hari Baskaran, Exec. VP-Dist. & Mktg. Svcs.

Phone: 91-120-252-6518	Fax: 91-120-255-0923
Toll-Free:	
Address: E-4,5 & 6, Sector 11, Noida, 201 301 India	

GROWTH PLANS/SPECIAL FEATURES:
HCL Infosystems Limited is a provider of information technology (IT) products and services, including PCs; servers; imaging equipment; voice and video products; networking products; TV and FM broadcasting technologies; computer peripherals; system integration services; consulting; and training services. The company operates in three segments: computer systems and related products and services; telecommunication and office automation; and Internet and related services. The first segment, accounting for approximately 28.4% of 2009 revenues, is focused on computer hardware; IT services, including system maintenance; facilities management; and system integration across a variety of industries. The second segment, with 71.2% of 2009 revenues, is focused on the distribution of telecommunication and office automation products, as well as related comprehensive maintenance and allied services. The third segment, with 0.4% of revenues, provides virtual private networks, Internet access and other connectivity services. The company has a network of roughly 65 HCL Digilife stores in large cities and over 500 service locations; its products are also sold through more than 93,000 retail outlets in over 10,000 cities and towns throughout India. HCL Digilife stores offer a range of consumer electronics products, some produced by the company and some offered through distribution partnerships with such brands as Apple, Kodak, Nokia and Microsoft. The company has four computer hardware manufacturing plants in India, including two in Puducherry, one in Chennai and one in Uttarakhand. Computers, under such brands as Infiniti, Busybee, Beanstalk and Ezeebee, are shipped to locations countrywide via a network of logistics support partners. Wholly-owned subsidiaries of the company include HCL Infocom Limited, HCL Security Limited and HCL Infinet Limited, an Internet service provider focused on corporate networking services. In December 2009, HCL announced a partnership with Motorola to develop a government radio network serving police forces, fire and rescue services, hospitals and public works agencies in India.

FINANCIALS: Sales and profits are in thousands of dollars—add 000 to get the full amount. 2010 Note: Financial information for 2010 was not available for all companies at press time.

2010 Sales: $	2010 Profits: $	U.S. Stock Ticker:
2009 Sales: $2,674,180	2009 Profits: $55,730	Int'l Ticker: 500179 Int'l Exchange: Bombay-BSE
2008 Sales: $2,671,860	2008 Profits: $66,030	Employees: 5,900
2007 Sales: $2,511,410	2007 Profits: $66,380	Fiscal Year Ends: 6/30
2006 Sales: $	2006 Profits: $	Parent Company:

SALARIES/BENEFITS:

Pension Plan:	ESOP Stock Plan:	Profit Sharing:	Top Exec. Salary: $	Bonus: $
Savings Plan:	Stock Purch. Plan:		Second Exec. Salary: $	Bonus: $

OTHER THOUGHTS:
Apparent Women Officers or Directors: 1
Hot Spot for Advancement for Women/Minorities:

LOCATIONS: ("Y" = Yes)

West:	Southwest:	Midwest:	Southeast:	Northeast:	International:
					Y

HCL TECHNOLOGIES LTD

www.hcltech.com

Industry Group Code: 541513 Ranks within this company's industry group: Sales: 18 Profits: 11

Hardware:	Software:		Telecommunications:	Electronic Publishing:	Equipment:	Specialty Services:	
Computers:	Consumer:		Local:	Online Service:	Telecom:	Consulting:	Y
Accessories:	Corporate:	Y	Long Distance:	TV/Cable or Wireless:	Communication:	Contract Manufacturing:	
Network Equipment:	Telecom:		Cellular:	Games:	Distribution:	Processing:	
Chips/Circuits:	Internet:		Internet Service:	Financial Data:	VAR/Reseller:	Staff/Outsourcing:	Y
Parts/Drives:					Satellite Srv./Equip.:	Specialty Services:	Y

TYPES OF BUSINESS:

IT Services
Application Engineering
Software Development
System Design & Integration
Business Process Outsourcing
IT Infrastructure Management Services

BRANDS/DIVISIONS/AFFILIATES:

CONTACTS: Note: Officers with more than one job title may be intentionally listed here more than once.

Vineet Nayar, CEO
Anil Chanana, CFO
Rahul Singh, Pres., Business Process Outsourcing Svcs.
Anant Gupta, Pres., Infrastructure Svcs. Div.
Shiv Nadar, Chmn.

Phone: 91-120-252-0917	Fax: 91-120-252-6907
Toll-Free:	
Address: A-10/11, Sector 3, Noida, 201301 India	

GROWTH PLANS/SPECIAL FEATURES:

HCL Technologies, Ltd., based in India, is a global IT services company providing software IT solutions, engineering and research and development services, remote infrastructure management services and business process outsourcing (BPO). With offices in 26 countries, HCL serves customers in the aerospace and defense, energy and utilities, healthcare, life sciences, semiconductors, transportation and logistics, automotive, financial services, software, media and entertainment, storage and server, travel and hospitality, consumer electronics, retail and consumer, government, industrial manufacturing and telecommunications industries. The firm operates in six business lines. The BPO division offers full process outsourcing and multiple process outsourcing solutions, including business generation and operations management. The Enterprise Application Services division provides business support and optimization services such as blue printing, development, deployment, global rollouts and application maintenance and support. The Custom Applications Development division provides application development, application management, application support, re-engineering, modernization, migration, legacy mainframe application and independent verification and validation. The Engineering and R&D Services division provides hardware product, embedded, mechanical and software product engineering services. The Enterprise Transformation Services division offers integrated business processes, technology, application and data services for business and technology transformation. Finally, the Infrastructure Management division is a leading IT services provider in India, offering end-user computing and datacenter, network, security, application operations and process and tools services.

FINANCIALS: Sales and profits are in thousands of dollars—add 000 to get the full amount. 2010 Note: Financial information for 2010 was not available for all companies at press time.

2010 Sales: $	2010 Profits: $	**U.S. Stock Ticker:**
2009 Sales: $2,232,140	2009 Profits: $287,950	**Int'l Ticker: 532281** Int'l Exchange: Bombay-BSE
2008 Sales: $2,299,300	2008 Profits: $319,660	Employees: 54,216
2007 Sales: $1,520,040	2007 Profits: $330,200	Fiscal Year Ends: 6/30
2006 Sales: $976,030	2006 Profits: $144,115	Parent Company:

SALARIES/BENEFITS:

Pension Plan:	ESOP Stock Plan:	Profit Sharing:	Top Exec. Salary: $	Bonus: $
Savings Plan:	Stock Purch. Plan:		Second Exec. Salary: $	Bonus: $

OTHER THOUGHTS:

Apparent Women Officers or Directors: 1
Hot Spot for Advancement for Women/Minorities:

LOCATIONS: ("Y" = Yes)

West:	Southwest:	Midwest:	Southeast:	Northeast:	International:
Y	Y	Y	Y	Y	Y

HEWLETT-PACKARD CO (HP)   www.hp.com

Industry Group Code: 334111 Ranks within this company's industry group: Sales: 1   Profits: 2

Hardware:		Software:		Telecommunications:	Electronic Publishing:	Equipment:	Specialty Services:	
Computers:	Y	Consumer:	Y	Local:	Online Service:	Telecom:	Consulting:	Y
Accessories:	Y	Corporate:	Y	Long Distance:	TV/Cable or Wireless:	Communication:	Contract Manufacturing:	
Network Equipment:		Telecom:		Cellular:	Games:	Distribution:	Processing:	
Chips/Circuits:		Internet:		Internet Service:	Financial Data:	VAR/Reseller:	Staff/Outsourcing:	Y
Parts/Drives:						Satellite Srv./Equip.:	Specialty Services:	

TYPES OF BUSINESS:

Computer Hardware-PCs
Computer Software
Printers & Supplies
Scanners
Outsourcing
Servers
Consulting
Managed Print Services

BRANDS/DIVISIONS/AFFILIATES:

HP StorageWorks
HP Labs (Hewlett-Packard Laboratories)
Electronic Data Systems Corp (EDS)
HP Mini
ArcSight Inc

CONTACTS: Note: Officers with more than one job title may be intentionally listed here more than once.

Leo Apotheker, CEO
Cathie Lesjak, CFO/Exec. VP
Michael Mendenhall, Chief Mktg. Officer/Sr. VP
Marcela Perez de Alonso, Exec. VP-Human Resources
Prith Banerjee, Sr. VP-Research/Dir.-HP Labs
Randall D. Mott, CIO/Exec. VP
Shane Robison, CTO/Exec. VP
Pete Bocian, Chief Admin. Officer/Exec. VP
Michael J. Holston, General Counsel/Exec. VP/Sec.
Shane Robison, Chief Strategy Officer
Todd Bradley, Exec. VP-Personal Systems Group
Ann M. Livermore, Exec. VP-Enterprise Bus.
Vyomesh Joshi, Exec. VP-Imaging & Printing Group
Don Grantham, Chief Sales Officer/Sr. VP
Ray Lane, Chmn.

Phone: 650-857-1501	Fax: 650-857-5518
Toll-Free:	
Address: 3000 Hanover St., Palo Alto, CA 94304-1185 US	

GROWTH PLANS/SPECIAL FEATURES:

Hewlett-Packard Co. (HP) is a global provider of products, technologies, software and services to customers ranging from individuals to large enterprises. Offerings span personal computing and other access devices; imaging and printing-related products and services; enterprise IT infrastructure; and multi-vendor services. The company operates in seven segments: Enterprise Storage and Servers (ESS); HP Services (HPS); HP Software; the Personal Systems Group (PSG); the Imaging and Printing Group (IPG); HP Financial Services (HPFS); and Corporate Investments. The ESS segment provides storage and server solutions such as HP StorageWorks, offering entry-level, mid-range and high-end arrays; storage area networks; network attached storage; storage management software; and virtualization technologies. The HPS segment provides a portfolio of multi-vendor IT services, including technology services; consulting and integration; and outsourcing services such as computer department outsourcing and managed print services. HPS also encompasses the operations of recently-acquired Electronic Data Systems Corporation (EDS), a technology services provider currently managing more than 1 million applications worldwide on behalf of a range of business and government clients. The HP Software segment provides business technology optimization software that allows customers to manage and automate their IT infrastructure, operations, applications, IT services and business processes. The PSG segment provides PCs, workstations, handheld computing devices, digital entertainment systems, calculators, software and services for the commercial and consumer markets. The IPG segment provides consumer and commercial printer hardware, printing supplies, printing media and scanning devices. The HPFS segment provides a broad range of financial life-cycle management services. The Corporate Investments segment includes the Hewlett-Packard Laboratories and certain business incubation projects. In May 2009, HP announced plans to eliminate 5,700 jobs in Europe, the Middle East and Africa over the next two years. In November 2009, the firm agreed to acquire 3Com Corp. for $2.7 billion. In April 2010, the firm agreed to acquire Palm, Inc. for approximately $1 billion. In October 2010, the company purchased security software developer, ArcSight, Inc. for $1.5 billion.

FINANCIALS: Sales and profits are in thousands of dollars—add 000 to get the full amount. 2010 Note: Financial information for 2010 was not available for all companies at press time.

2010 Sales: $	2010 Profits: $	**U.S. Stock Ticker: HPQ**	
2009 Sales: $114,552,000	2009 Profits: $7,660,000	**Int'l Ticker:** Int'l Exchange:	
2008 Sales: $118,364,000	2008 Profits: $8,329,000	Employees: 304,000	
2007 Sales: $104,286,000	2007 Profits: $7,264,000	Fiscal Year Ends: 10/31	
2006 Sales: $91,658,000	2006 Profits: $6,198,000	Parent Company:	

SALARIES/BENEFITS:

Pension Plan: Y	ESOP Stock Plan:	Profit Sharing:	Top Exec. Salary: $1,268,750	Bonus: $15,809,414
Savings Plan: Y	Stock Purch. Plan: Y		Second Exec. Salary: $743,125	Bonus: $6,151,355

OTHER THOUGHTS:

Apparent Women Officers or Directors: 5
Hot Spot for Advancement for Women/Minorities: Y

LOCATIONS: ("Y" = Yes)

West:	Southwest:	Midwest:	Southeast:	Northeast:	International:
Y	Y	Y	Y	Y	Y

Note: Financial information, benefits and other data can change quickly and may vary from those stated here.

HITACHI LTD

Industry Group Code: 334111 Ranks within this company's industry group: Sales: 2   Profits: 31

Hardware:		Software:		Telecommunications:	Electronic Publishing:	Equipment:		Specialty Services:	
Computers:	Y	Consumer:	Y	Local:	Online Service:	Telecom:	Y	Consulting:	Y
Accessories:	Y	Corporate:	Y	Long Distance:	TV/Cable or Wireless:	Communication:	Y	Contract Manufacturing:	
Network Equipment:		Telecom:	Y	Cellular:	Games:	Distribution:		Processing:	
Chips/Circuits:	Y	Internet:		Internet Service:	Financial Data:	VAR/Reseller:		Staff/Outsourcing:	Y
Parts/Drives:	Y					Satellite Srv./Equip.:		Specialty Services:	

TYPES OF BUSINESS:

Computer Hardware Manufacturing
Consumer Appliances & Electronics
Materials Manufacturing
Financial Services Products
Power & Industrial Systems
Medical & Scientific Equipment
Transportation Systems
Consulting Services

BRANDS/DIVISIONS/AFFILIATES:

Clarion Co Ltd
Hitachi Global Storage Technologies
Hitachi High Technologies America Inc
Hitachi Medical Corporation
Hitachi Medical Systems America
Hitachi Consulting

CONTACTS: Note: Officers with more than one job title may be intentionally listed here more than once.

Takashi Kawamura, CEO
Takashi Kawamura, Pres.
Kazuhiro Mori, Exec. VP
Hiroaki Nakanishi, Exec. VP
Takashi Hatchoji, Exec. VP
Nayoa Takahashi, Exec. VP
Takashi Kawamura, Chmn.

Phone: 81-3-3258-1111	Fax: 81-3-4564-2148
Toll-Free:	
Address: 6-6, Marunouchi 1-chome, Chiyoda-ku, Tokyo, 100-8280 Japan	

GROWTH PLANS/SPECIAL FEATURES:

Hitachi, Ltd. is a Japan-based electronics company. Hitachi divides its products and services into the following seven segments: Information and Telecommunications Systems; Electronic Devices; Power and Industrial Systems; Digital Media and Consumer Products; High Functional Materials and Components; Logistics and Services; and Financial Services. Its Information and Telecommunication Systems segment includes communications infrastructure hardware, hard drives and other storage products. This segment accounts for 21% of revenues. The Electronic Devices segment creates a wide variety of digital devices and accounts for 11% of revenues. The Power and Industrial Systems segment, accounting for 26% of revenues, offers products and services in support of nuclear, thermal and hydroelectric power systems; railway systems; elevators and escalators. The main customers of this segment are power companies. Hitachi's growth strategy in recent years includes higher emphasis on environmental protection and alternative energy development. It is working to expand its nuclear power systems business, and has partial ownership of several U.S. and Canadian companies engaged in the construction and operation of nuclear power plants. The Digital Media and Consumer Products segment produces flat-panel TVs, digital consumer electronics and home appliances. This segment accounts for 13% of revenues. The High Functional Materials and Components segment develops such products as specialty steels, magnetic materials, semiconductor materials, and synthetic resin products. This segment accounts for 15% of revenues. The Logistics and Services segment, with 10% of revenues, conducts a range of operations such as freight transport and warehousing. The Financial Services segment works on both corporate and client needs and accounts for 4% of revenues. Subsidiaries include Clarion Co., Ltd.; Hitachi Consulting; Hitachi Global Storage Technologies; Hitachi High Technologies America Inc; and Hitachi Medical Corporation. In February 2009, the company announced plans to establish a manufacturing facility and a rolling stock assembly in the U.K., with plans to assemble up to 30 vehicles monthly.

FINANCIALS: Sales and profits are in thousands of dollars—add 000 to get the full amount. 2010 Note: Financial information for 2010 was not available for all companies at press time.

2010 Sales: $109,058,000	2010 Profits: $-1,026,200	**U.S. Stock Ticker: HIT**
2009 Sales: $103,003,801	2009 Profits: $-8,109,571	**Int'l Ticker: 6501** Int'l Exchange: Tokyo-TSE
2008 Sales: $113,390,020	2008 Profits: $-587,060	Employees: 359,746
2007 Sales: $87,107,200	2007 Profits: $-278,800	Fiscal Year Ends: 3/31
2006 Sales: $80,209,000	2006 Profits: $316,270	Parent Company:

SALARIES/BENEFITS:

Pension Plan:	ESOP Stock Plan:	Profit Sharing:	Top Exec. Salary: $	Bonus: $
Savings Plan:	Stock Purch. Plan:		Second Exec. Salary: $	Bonus: $

OTHER THOUGHTS:

Apparent Women Officers or Directors: 1
Hot Spot for Advancement for Women/Minorities:

LOCATIONS: ("Y" = Yes)

West:	Southwest:	Midwest:	Southeast:	Northeast:	International:
Y	Y	Y	Y	Y	Y

HON HAI PRECISION INDUSTRY COMPANY LTD www.foxconn.com

Industry Group Code: 334419 Ranks within this company's industry group: Sales: 1 Profits: 1

Hardware:	Software:	Telecommunications:	Electronic Publishing:	Equipment:	Specialty Services:	
Computers:	Consumer:	Local:	Online Service:	Telecom:	Consulting:	
Accessories:	Corporate:	Long Distance:	TV/Cable or Wireless:	Communication:	Contract Manufacturing:	Y
Network Equipment:	Telecom:	Cellular:	Games:	Distribution:	Processing:	
Chips/Circuits:	Internet:	Internet Service:	Financial Data:	VAR/Reseller:	Staff/Outsourcing:	
Parts/Drives:				Satellite Srv./Equip.:	Specialty Services:	

TYPES OF BUSINESS:

Contract Electronics Manufacturing
Consumer Electronics & Components Manufacturing
Product Design Services
Cameras & Projectors
Optical Technology
Original Design Manufacturing (ODM)
Wireless Products Manufacturing
Solar Cell Manufacturing

BRANDS/DIVISIONS/AFFILIATES:

Foxconn International Holdings Ltd
eCMMS
Foxconn Technology Group

CONTACTS: Note: Officers with more than one job title may be intentionally listed here more than once.

Terry T.M. Gou, CEO
Terry T.M. Gou, Chmn.

Phone: 886-2-226-80970	Fax:
Toll-Free:	
Address: 2 Zihyou St., Tucheng City, Taipei Country, 236 Taiwan	

GROWTH PLANS/SPECIAL FEATURES:

Hon Hai Precision Industry Company Ltd., which does business under its registered trade name Foxconn Technology Group, is a technology manufacturer that focuses on joint-design and development, manufacturing, assembly and after-sales services for global communication, computer and customer-electronics firms. Foxconn is operated by a propriety business model called eCMMS (e-enabled Components, Modules, Moves and Services), and is one of the largest multinational electronics and computer components manufacturing service providers in the world. Its primary areas of focus are nanotechnology, wireless connectivity, heat transfer, green manufacturing processes and material sciences. The firm holds more than 15,000 patents worldwide. Some of Foxconn's most notable contract design and manufacturing products include the Mac Mini, iPod and iPhone for Apple, Inc.; branded motherboards for Intel Corp.; the Wii for Nintendo; the Xbox 360 for Microsoft; Motorola cell phones; and a variety of computers for retailers such as Dell and Hewlett Packard. Other non-branded products include computer cases, motherboards, graphics cards and other computer components that are primarily sold to corporate users. The firm has locations in Brazil, Australia, China, the U.K., France, the Czech Republic, India and CanadaIn February 2010, Hon Hai announced plans to build a $300 million solar cell and module plant in Taiwan. Also in February 2010, the company announced it had been awarded 1,859 patents by Taiwan's Intellectual Property Office. In March 2010, the company contracted with Matsushita of Japan to supply slim-type DVD drives. Also in March 2010, the company announced a partnership with Kinh Bac Unban Development Company, to invest in a high-tech complex in Hai Phong City, Vietnam. In April 2010, the company purchased a majority stake in a LCD TV plant in Slovakia from Sony Corp. Also in April 2010, the company announced that it would supply the components for the RIM BlackBerry tablet.

FINANCIALS: Sales and profits are in thousands of dollars—add 000 to get the full amount. 2010 Note: Financial information for 2010 was not available for all companies at press time.

2010 Sales: $	2010 Profits: $	U.S. Stock Ticker: Private
2009 Sales: $61,960,200	2009 Profits: $2,393,580	Int'l Ticker: Int'l Exchange:
2008 Sales: $61,685,100	2008 Profits: $1,743,620	Employees: 200,000
2007 Sales: $53,847,700	2007 Profits: $2,456,970	Fiscal Year Ends: 12/31
2006 Sales: $40,600,000	2006 Profits: $	Parent Company:

SALARIES/BENEFITS:

Pension Plan:	ESOP Stock Plan:	Profit Sharing:	Top Exec. Salary: $	Bonus: $
Savings Plan:	Stock Purch. Plan:		Second Exec. Salary: $	Bonus: $

OTHER THOUGHTS:

Apparent Women Officers or Directors:
Hot Spot for Advancement for Women/Minorities:

LOCATIONS: ("Y" = Yes)

West:	Southwest:	Midwest:	Southeast:	Northeast:	International:
Y	Y	Y		Y	Y

HOSIDEN CORPORATION

www.hosiden.co.jp

Industry Group Code: 335 Ranks within this company's industry group: Sales: 3 Profits: 2

Hardware:		Software:		Telecommunications:		Electronic Publishing:		Equipment:		Specialty Services:	
Computers:		Consumer:		Local:		Online Service:		Telecom:		Consulting:	
Accessories:	Y	Corporate:		Long Distance:		TV/Cable or Wireless:		Communication:	Y	Contract Manufacturing:	
Network Equipment:		Telecom:		Cellular:		Games:		Distribution:	Y	Processing:	
Chips/Circuits:	Y	Internet:		Internet Service:		Financial Data:		VAR/Reseller:		Staff/Outsourcing:	
Parts/Drives:								Satellite Srv./Equip.:		Specialty Services:	

TYPES OF BUSINESS:
Electronic Components Manufacturing

BRANDS/DIVISIONS/AFFILIATES:

CONTACTS: Note: Officers with more than one job title may be intentionally listed here more than once.
Kenji Furuhashi, CEO
Kenji Furuhashi, Pres.
Haremi Kitatani, VP
Yasuhiro Shigeno, Managing Dir.
Eiichi Ino, Managing Dir.

Phone: 81-72-993-1010	Fax: 81-72-994-5101
Toll-Free:	
Address: 4-33, Kitakyuhoji 1-chome, Yao-city, Osaka, 581-0071 Japan	

GROWTH PLANS/SPECIAL FEATURES:

Hosiden Corporation, founded in 1950, primarily manufactures electronics components. Its products are divided into the following seven categories. Hosiden's connectors include waterproof connectors; DIN circular connectors, which can be used to connect a mouse or keyboard to a PC; optical connectors, which are used to hook up digital audio equipment, including TVs, DVD players or set-top boxes; USB (universal serial bus) connectors; and integrated circuit (IC) card connectors, which are used to hook together the circuit boards within an electronic device. The firm provides plugs and jacks for DC power sources, headphones and communications equipment. The company's sockets consist of cathode ray tube (CRT) sockets, which are an internal component for CRT TVs. Hosiden's switches include various mechanical switches, such as slide switches and electrically driven switches such as touch panels, tactile push switches and remote control units. The firm's acoustic components include miniature speakers, headphones, microphones and Bluetooth modules. Its actuators primarily consist of DC solenoids, which are small electrical components that create a magnetic field. Lastly, Hosiden's liquid crystal displays (LCDs) comprise passive matrix LCD modules, including color LCDs. The firm's products are used in five main applications: Cell phones, notebook PCs, digital still cameras, car navigation systems and set-top boxes. Hosiden maintains 13 domestic sales offices, distribution centers and manufacturing facilities; as well as overseas subsidiaries with more than 22 sales offices and manufacturing facilities in Europe, Asia and the U.S. Electro-mechanical components generate the largest share (86.3%) of net sales, followed by acoustic components (8.3%), LCDs (3.2%) and applied equipment and others (2.2%).

FINANCIALS: Sales and profits are in thousands of dollars—add 000 to get the full amount. 2010 Note: Financial information for 2010 was not available for all companies at press time.

2010 Sales: $3,743,860	2010 Profits: $85,290	**U.S. Stock Ticker:**
2009 Sales: $4,892,320	2009 Profits: $149,840	**Int'l Ticker: 6804** Int'l Exchange: Tokyo-TSE
2008 Sales: $4,523,100	2008 Profits: $84,920	**Employees:**
2007 Sales: $3,372,480	2007 Profits: $32,720	**Fiscal Year Ends:** 3/31
2006 Sales: $	2006 Profits: $	**Parent Company:**

SALARIES/BENEFITS:

Pension Plan:	ESOP Stock Plan:	Profit Sharing:	Top Exec. Salary: $	Bonus: $
Savings Plan:	Stock Purch. Plan:		Second Exec. Salary: $	Bonus: $

OTHER THOUGHTS:
Apparent Women Officers or Directors:
Hot Spot for Advancement for Women/Minorities:

LOCATIONS: ("Y" = Yes)

West:	Southwest:	Midwest:	Southeast:	Northeast:	International:
Y		Y			Y

HOYA CORP

www.hoya.co.jp

Industry Group Code: 33441 Ranks within this company's industry group: Sales: 8 Profits: 11

Hardware:		Software:	Telecommunications:	Electronic Publishing:	Equipment:	Specialty Services:	
Computers:		Consumer:	Local:	Online Service:	Telecom:	Consulting:	
Accessories:		Corporate:	Long Distance:	TV/Cable or Wireless:	Communication:	Contract Manufacturing:	Y
Network Equipment:		Telecom:	Cellular:	Games:	Distribution:	Processing:	
Chips/Circuits:		Internet:	Internet Service:	Financial Data:	VAR/Reseller:	Staff/Outsourcing:	
Parts/Drives:	Y				Satellite Srv./Equip.:	Specialty Services:	Y

TYPES OF BUSINESS:

Semiconductor Manufacturing Equipment
Glass Semiconductor Components
Medical Equipment
Cameras
Optical Glass
Eyeglass Lenses
Laser & UV Light Sources

BRANDS/DIVISIONS/AFFILIATES:

Pentax
Eye City
Hoya Magnetics Singapore Pte. Ltd.
Hoya Candeo Optronics Corp.

CONTACTS: Note: Officers with more than one job title may be intentionally listed here more than once.

Hiroshi Suzuki, CEO
Hiroshi Hamada, COO/Exec. VP
Hiroshi Suzuki, Pres.
Kenji Ema, CFO/Exec. VP
Taro Hagiwara, CTO/Exec. VP
Naoji Ito, Mgr.-Corp. Comm.
Chris N. Japp, Pres., Hoya (Pentax) Lifecare Div.

Phone: 81-3-3952-1151	Fax: 81-3-3952-1314
Toll-Free:	
Address: 2-7-5 Naka-Ochiai, Shinjuku-ku, Tokyo, 161-8525 Japan	

GROWTH PLANS/SPECIAL FEATURES:

Hoya Corp., established in 1941, primarily manufactures optical products and glass information technology (IT) equipment. The firm operates in five divisions: Electro-Optics, which generates 35% of sales; Vision Care, 25%; Pentax, 26%; Health Care, 13%; and Photonics, 1%. The electro-optics division primarily produces mask blanks and photomasks (specialized glass plates) for semiconductor manufacturing; photomasks used in liquid crystal display (LCD) manufacturing; and glass discs used in hard drives. The vision care division produces eyeglass lenses for markets in Japan, Asia-Pacific, North America and Europe. The Pentax division is subdivided into three businesses: life care, imaging systems and optical components. The life care business manufactures medical equipment, including chromatography systems for sorting biopharmaceutical materials; endoscopic products for ear, nose and throat examinations; and special ceramics for bone replacement. The imaging systems business produces Pentax brand cameras. The optical components business offers components of lens modules used in digital cameras and DVD, CD and other optical drives. The health care division produces contact lenses and intraocular lenses (IOLs), which are used to treat cataracts. The division also operates a chain of contact lens stores called Eye City in Japan. The photonics division primarily produces laser and UV light sources, often used to manufacture LCD panels, semiconductors and digital cameras. Geographically, Japan generated 37% of 2010 sales; Europe, 20%; North America, 12%; and Asia and other areas, 31%. In February 2010, Hoya established a lens simulation center in Malaysia. In May 2010, the firm opened a second manufacturing facility for glass substrates for hard disk drives (HDD) in Vietnam. In June 2010, Hoya's subsidiary, Hoya Magnetics Singapore Pte Ltd., sold its hard disk glass media manufacturing operations to Western Digital Corporation. In October 2010, its specialty glass business for imaging sensors was spun off into a new subsidiary, Hoya Candeo Optronics Corp.

FINANCIALS: Sales and profits are in thousands of dollars—add 000 to get the full amount. 2010 Note: Financial information for 2010 was not available for all companies at press time.

2010 Sales: $4,813,840	2010 Profits: $440,900	U.S. Stock Ticker: HOCPY.PK
2009 Sales: $4,897,220	2009 Profits: $270,730	Int'l Ticker: 7741 Int'l Exchange: Tokyo-TSE
2008 Sales: $4,816,300	2008 Profits: $817,300	Employees:
2007 Sales: $3,900,900	2007 Profits: $833,900	Fiscal Year Ends: 3/31
2006 Sales: $3,442,300	2006 Profits: $756,200	Parent Company:

SALARIES/BENEFITS:

Pension Plan:	ESOP Stock Plan:	Profit Sharing:	Top Exec. Salary: $	Bonus: $
Savings Plan:	Stock Purch. Plan:		Second Exec. Salary: $	Bonus: $

OTHER THOUGHTS:

Apparent Women Officers or Directors:
Hot Spot for Advancement for Women/Minorities:

LOCATIONS: ("Y" = Yes)

West:	Southwest:	Midwest:	Southeast:	Northeast:	International:
Y	Y	Y	Y	Y	Y

HTC CORP

www.htc.com/tw

Industry Group Code: 334419 Ranks within this company's industry group: Sales: 12 Profits: 2

Hardware:	Software:	Telecommunications:	Electronic Publishing:	Equipment:		Specialty Services:	
Computers:	Consumer:	Local:	Online Service:	Telecom:		Consulting:	
Accessories:	Corporate:	Long Distance:	TV/Cable or Wireless:	Communication:	Y	Contract Manufacturing:	Y
Network Equipment:	Telecom:	Cellular:	Games:	Distribution:		Processing:	
Chips/Circuits:	Internet:	Internet Service:	Financial Data:	VAR/Reseller:		Staff/Outsourcing:	
Parts/Drives:				Satellite Srv./Equip.:		Specialty Services:	Y

TYPES OF BUSINESS:

Original Design Manufacturing
Mobile Computing & Communications Hardware
Cellular Phones & Smartphones
PDAs
Contract Manufacturing

BRANDS/DIVISIONS/AFFILIATES:

HTC USA Inc
HTC Advantage X7500
HTC FUZE
HTC S720
HTC P4000
T-Mobile G1
Touch Diamond

CONTACTS: *Note: Officers with more than one job title may be intentionally listed here more than once.*

Peter Chou, CEO
Fred Liu, COO
Horace Luke, Chief Innovation Officer
Cher Wang, Chmn.
Jason Mackenzie, VP-HTC America

Phone: 886-3-375-3252	Fax: 886-3-375-3251
Toll-Free:	
Address: 23 Xinghua Rd., Taoyuan, 330 Taiwan	

GROWTH PLANS/SPECIAL FEATURES:

HTC Corp., formerly High Tech Computer Corporation, specializes in designing and manufacturing mobile computing and communications hardware, including cell phones, smart phones and PDAs. The company operates as an original equipment manufacturer (OEM) by providing contract design as well as manufacturing services. The firm's customers include major mobile device brands and wireless service providers such as Cingular; T-Mobile; Sprint; Verizon; Orange, 02; Vodafone Telus; and NTT DoCoMo. The company is a hardware platform development partner with Microsoft for the Windows CE operating system and makes 80% of the mobile phones running off of the Windows OS. The firm also has partnerships with Intel, Texas Instruments, QUALCOMM, Sony and Citizen. Some of the company's products include the T-Mobile G1, which features the Google Android operating system; Touch Diamond; HTC FUZE; AT&T Tilt; HTC P4000 PDA phone; the T-Mobile Wing; the Dash; the HTC Advantage X7500 mobile office device, and the HTC S720 smartphone. The company has recently released a number of cell phones utilizing the Android operating system, including the Droid Eris, the HTC Magic and the G1.

FINANCIALS: Sales and profits are in thousands of dollars—add 000 to get the full amount. 2010 Note: Financial information for 2010 was not available for all companies at press time.

2010 Sales: $	2010 Profits: $	U.S. Stock Ticker:
2009 Sales: $4,483,860	2009 Profits: $701,600	Int'l Ticker: 2498 Int'l Exchange: Taipei-TPE
2008 Sales: $4,528,650	2008 Profits: $851,180	Employees: 8,249
2007 Sales: $3,650,000	2007 Profits: $890,000	Fiscal Year Ends: 12/31
2006 Sales: $3,202,894	2006 Profits: $774,060	Parent Company:

SALARIES/BENEFITS:

Pension Plan:	ESOP Stock Plan:	Profit Sharing:	Top Exec. Salary: $	Bonus: $
Savings Plan:	Stock Purch. Plan:		Second Exec. Salary: $	Bonus: $

OTHER THOUGHTS:

Apparent Women Officers or Directors: 1
Hot Spot for Advancement for Women/Minorities:

LOCATIONS: ("Y" = Yes)

West:	Southwest:	Midwest:	Southeast:	Northeast:	International:
					Y

HUAWEI TECHNOLOGIES CO LTD

www.huawei.com

Industry Group Code: 334210 Ranks within this company's industry group: Sales: 1 Profits: 1

Hardware:	Software:	Telecommunications:	Electronic Publishing:	Equipment:		Specialty Services:
Computers:	Consumer:	Local:	Online Service:	Telecom:		Consulting:
Accessories:	Corporate:	Long Distance:	TV/Cable or Wireless:	Communication:	Y	Contract Manufacturing:
Network Equipment:	Telecom:	Cellular:	Games:	Distribution:		Processing:
Chips/Circuits:	Internet:	Internet Service:	Financial Data:	VAR/Reseller:		Staff/Outsourcing:
Parts/Drives:				Satellite Srv./Equip.:		Specialty Services:

TYPES OF BUSINESS:

Communications Equipment
Network Equipment
Software
Wireless Handsets

BRANDS/DIVISIONS/AFFILIATES:

SmartAX MA5600T
Huawei Marine Networks
Seven Network Limited
Cyber Security Evaluation Center
4G RF

CONTACTS: Note: Officers with more than one job title may be intentionally listed here more than once.

Ren Zhengfei, CEO
Ren Zhengfei, Pres.
Yang Zhirong, Pres., Huawei Access Network Prod. Line
Philip Jiang, Pres., Huawei Latin America
Sun Yafang, Chmn.
William Xu, Pres., Huawei Europe

Phone: 86-755-2878-0808	Fax: 86-755-2878-9251
Toll-Free:	
Address: Bantian, Longgang District, Shenzhen, 518129 China	

GROWTH PLANS/SPECIAL FEATURES:

Huawei Technologies Co., Ltd. specializes in the research, development, manufacture and marketing of communications equipment. The company operates as a wholly-owned subsidiary of Shenzhen Huawei Investment & Holding, Co. It operates 100 branch offices worldwide, with its products deployed in over 100 countries, serving 1 billion users worldwide. The majority of the company's sales are generated internationally. Its products are divided into a number of categories, including data communications; digital media entertainment; storage and network security; voice evolution solutions; data communications; terminals; mobile core networks; GSM; CDMA2000; UMTS; IP BSS; WiMAX; optical network; and broadband access. The firm's components, mainly based on its proprietary ASIC chips, are used in products such as switching; integrated access networks; DSL; optical transport; videoconferencing; intelligent networks; network support; GSM and GPRS applications; routers; and LAN switches. The company devotes a minimum of 10% of its sales revenue to research and development activities. It has 14 research and development sites in the U.S. India, Sweden and Russia. Huawei has a joint venture, Huawei Marine Networks, with Global Marine Systems Limited that manufactures submarine cable. The company, along with Seven Network Limited, manages the first 4G wireless network in Australia. In April 2010, Huawei opened a research and development center in Ottawa, Ontario. In November 2010, the company announced an agreement to acquire 4G RF, a semiconductor company, from its parent company Option. In December 2010, the firm opened the Cyber Security Evaluation Center in Banbury, England. The center will provide analysis of security risks for telecom vendors worldwide.

FINANCIALS: Sales and profits are in thousands of dollars—add 000 to get the full amount. 2010 Note: Financial information for 2010 was not available for all companies at press time.

2010 Sales: $	2010 Profits: $	U.S. Stock Ticker: Private
2009 Sales: $21,788,100	2009 Profits: $2,671,130	Int'l Ticker: Int'l Exchange:
2008 Sales: $18,329,000	2008 Profits: $1,151,000	Employees:
2007 Sales: $12,840,000	2007 Profits: $957,000	Fiscal Year Ends: 12/31
2006 Sales: $8,504,000	2006 Profits: $512,000	Parent Company: SHENZHEN HUAWEI INVESTMENT & HOLDING CO

SALARIES/BENEFITS:

Pension Plan:	ESOP Stock Plan:	Profit Sharing:	Top Exec. Salary: $	Bonus: $
Savings Plan:	Stock Purch. Plan:		Second Exec. Salary: $	Bonus: $

OTHER THOUGHTS:

Apparent Women Officers or Directors: 1
Hot Spot for Advancement for Women/Minorities:

LOCATIONS: ("Y" = Yes)

West:	Southwest:	Midwest:	Southeast:	Northeast:	International:
Y	Y			Y	Y

IBM GLOBAL SERVICES

www.ibm.com/services

Industry Group Code: 541513 Ranks within this company's industry group: Sales: 2 Profits:

Hardware:	Software:	Telecommunications:	Electronic Publishing:	Equipment:	Specialty Services:	
Computers:	Consumer:	Local:	Online Service:	Telecom:	Consulting:	Y
Accessories:	Corporate:	Long Distance:	TV/Cable or Wireless:	Communication:	Contract Manufacturing:	
Network Equipment:	Telecom:	Cellular:	Games:	Distribution:	Processing:	
Chips/Circuits:	Internet:	Internet Service:	Financial Data:	VAR/Reseller:	Staff/Outsourcing:	Y
Parts/Drives:				Satellite Srv./Equip.:	Specialty Services:	Y

TYPES OF BUSINESS:

Computer Services & Consulting
IT Services
Computer Operations Outsourcing
Customer Relationship Management
Supply Chain Management
Financial Management
Human Capital Management

BRANDS/DIVISIONS/AFFILIATES:

International Business Machines Corp (IBM)
Global Technology Services
Global Business Services
IBM Cloud
IT Infrastructure Library

CONTACTS: *Note: Officers with more than one job title may be intentionally listed here more than once.*

Virginia M. Rometty, Sr. VP-Mktg. & Sales
Virginia M. Rometty, Sr. VP-Strategy
Martin J. Schroeter, Treas.
Frank Kern, Sr. VP
Andrew Stevens, Managing Partner-Global Bus. Svcs., Asia Pacific

Phone: 914-499-1900	Fax: 914-765-7382
Toll-Free: 800-426-4968	
Address: New Orchard Rd., Armonk, NY 10504 US	

GROWTH PLANS/SPECIAL FEATURES:

IBM Global Services, a subsidiary of IBM Corp., provides consulting services to businesses of all sizes. With operations in approximately 170 countries, the firm generates over half of IBM Corp.'s revenue. IBM Global Services operates in two segments: Global Technology Services (GTS) and Global Business Services (GBS). GTS offers strategic outsourcing services, business transformation outsourcing, integrated technology services and maintenance. GBS offers systems integration, consulting integration and application management services. IBM Global Services provides 11 types of information technology (IT) services. Its business continuity and resiliency services aid businesses in maintaining operations under non-ideal conditions; complying with industry and government regulations; and recovering from disastrous situations. The company's IT strategy and architecture services include the IT Infrastructure Library, a management tool that helps clients assess, plan and design their individual IT service governance and management capabilities; and middleware infrastructure planning, workshops and case building. IBM Global Services' integrated communications services aid businesses in the design, implementation and management of their communications and networking environments. Its end user services, which currently support roughly 4 million end user devices, aim to increase productivity for IT professionals. The company's middleware services include the IBM Cloud, a testing solution used to increase speed time and decrease operational costs. With regard to storage and data, the firm offers services including storage optimization/integration, information life cycle management and data mobility/management. It offers several types of security services, including solutions for mid-sized businesses, managed security, professional security and virtualization security solutions. IBM Global Services' offers comprehensive maintenance and technical support services for in-warranty and post-warranty IBM machines. Its server services include integration, optimization and management of IBM servers including IBM System i, IBM System x and IBM System z, as well as certain non-IBM servers. The firm also offers IT outsourcing and site services to IT facilities and data centers.

FINANCIALS: Sales and profits are in thousands of dollars—add 000 to get the full amount. 2010 Note: Financial information for 2010 was not available for all companies at press time.

2010 Sales: $	2010 Profits: $	U.S. Stock Ticker: Subsidiary
2009 Sales: $55,000,000	2009 Profits: $	Int'l Ticker: Int'l Exchange:
2008 Sales: $58,892,000	2008 Profits: $	Employees: 210,000
2007 Sales: $54,100,000	2007 Profits: $	Fiscal Year Ends: 12/31
2006 Sales: $48,300,000	2006 Profits: $	Parent Company: INTERNATIONAL BUSINESS MACHINES CORP (IBM)

SALARIES/BENEFITS:

Pension Plan:	ESOP Stock Plan:	Profit Sharing:	Top Exec. Salary: $	Bonus: $
Savings Plan:	Stock Purch. Plan:		Second Exec. Salary: $	Bonus: $

OTHER THOUGHTS:

Apparent Women Officers or Directors: 1
Hot Spot for Advancement for Women/Minorities:

LOCATIONS: ("Y" = Yes)

West:	Southwest:	Midwest:	Southeast:	Northeast:	International:
				Y	Y

IBM INDIA PVT LTD

www.ibm.com/in

Industry Group Code: 541513 Ranks within this company's industry group: Sales: Profits:

Hardware:	Software:		Telecommunications:	Electronic Publishing:	Equipment:	Specialty Services:	
Computers:	Consumer:		Local:	Online Service:	Telecom:	Consulting:	Y
Accessories:	Corporate:	Y	Long Distance:	TV/Cable or Wireless:	Communication:	Contract Manufacturing:	
Network Equipment:	Telecom:		Cellular:	Games:	Distribution:	Processing:	Y
Chips/Circuits:	Internet:		Internet Service:	Financial Data:	VAR/Reseller:	Staff/Outsourcing:	Y
Parts/Drives:					Satellite Srv./Equip.:	Specialty Services:	Y

TYPES OF BUSINESS:

Consulting Services
Technology Implementation Services
Business Process Outsourcing (BPO)

BRANDS/DIVISIONS/AFFILIATES:

International Bussiness Machines Corp (IBM)

CONTACTS: Note: Officers with more than one job title may be intentionally listed here more than once.

Shanker Annaswamy, Managing Dir.
Manish Gupta, Dir.-IBM Research, India
Prashanth Balarama, Mgr.-External Rel.

Phone: 91-80-406-83000	**Fax:** 91-80-406-84225
Toll-Free: 800-425-3333	
Address: 12 Subramanya Arcade, Bannerghatta Rd., Bangalore, India	

GROWTH PLANS/SPECIAL FEATURES:

IBM India Pvt. Ltd., a subsidiary of IBM Corp., provides consulting and technology services to businesses of all sizes in a wide range of industries.   IBM India offers a variety of services from human resources development and financial management to operations and supply chain optimization. Additionally, the company is a leader in Web 2.0 technologies. The Web 2.0 platform is a web technology and design platform that strives to enhance communications, creativity, secure information sharing, collaboration and functionality of the Internet.   This technology has lead to the development and evolution of social networking sites, video sharing sites and blogs. Other research areas include business analytics and optimization, human language technologies, software service technologies and mobile enabled emerging solutions.   Its services are rendered across a broad range of industry sectors that include aerospace and defense; automotive; chemicals and petroleum; consumer products and retail; energy and utilities; financial markets; government; healthcare and life sciences; higher education and research; media and entertainment; and telecommunications, travel and transportation. IBM India has also forged alliances with a several leading technology organizations, such as Cisco, Oracle and SAP, in an effort to combine and maximize resources to better handle client needs. The firm's employees and researchers have been recognized with five Nobel prizes, seven U.S. National Medals of Technology, five Nation Medals of Science and 21 memberships in the National Academy of Sciences.

FINANCIALS: Sales and profits are in thousands of dollars—add 000 to get the full amount. 2010 Note: Financial information for 2010 was not available for all companies at press time.

2010 Sales: $	2010 Profits: $	**U.S. Stock Ticker:** Subsidiary
2009 Sales: $	2009 Profits: $	**Int'l Ticker:** Int'l Exchange:
2008 Sales: $	2008 Profits: $	Employees: 85,000
2007 Sales: $	2007 Profits: $	Fiscal Year Ends: 12/31
2006 Sales: $	2006 Profits: $	Parent Company: INTERNATIONAL BUSINESS MACHINES CORP (IBM)

SALARIES/BENEFITS:

Pension Plan:	ESOP Stock Plan:	Profit Sharing:	Top Exec. Salary: $	Bonus: $
Savings Plan:	Stock Purch. Plan:		Second Exec. Salary: $	Bonus: $

OTHER THOUGHTS:

Apparent Women Officers or Directors:
Hot Spot for Advancement for Women/Minorities:

LOCATIONS: ("Y" = Yes)

West:	Southwest:	Midwest:	Southeast:	Northeast:	International:
					Y

Note: Financial information, benefits and other data can change quickly and may vary from those stated here.

ICROSSING INC

www.icrossing.com

Industry Group Code: 511210M Ranks within this company's industry group: Sales: Profits:

Hardware:	Software:		Telecommunications:	Electronic Publishing:	Equipment:	Specialty Services:	
Computers:	Consumer:		Local:	Online Service:	Telecom:	Consulting:	
Accessories:	Corporate:	Y	Long Distance:	TV/Cable or Wireless:	Communication:	Contract Manufacturing:	
Network Equipment:	Telecom:		Cellular:	Games:	Distribution:	Processing:	
Chips/Circuits:	Internet:		Internet Service:	Financial Data:	VAR/Reseller:	Staff/Outsourcing:	
Parts/Drives:					Satellite Srv./Equip.:	Specialty Services:	Y

TYPES OF BUSINESS:

Search Engine Marketing
Web Analytics Software

BRANDS/DIVISIONS/AFFILIATES:

Hearst Corporation (The)
iCrossing Marketing Platform

CONTACTS: Note: Officers with more than one job title may be intentionally listed here more than once.

Don Scales, CEO
Dave Johnson, COO
Don Scales, Pres.
Michael Jackson, CFO
Tari Haro, Chief Mktg. Officer
Maggie Luciano-Williams, Chief People Officer
Peter Randazzo, CTO
Adam Lavelle, Chief Strategy Officer
Christopher Wallace, VP-Media
Michael Jackson, Treas./Exec. VP
Patrick Bertermann, CEO-iCrossing GmbH
Arjo Ghosh, Chmn.-iCrossiing U.K.
Brian Powley, Pres., North America
Marlin Jackson, Exec. VP-Global Dev.
Richard Rosemblatt, Chmn.
Paul Doleman, CEO-iCrossing, U.K.

Phone: 480-505-5800	Fax: 480-505-5801
Toll-Free: 866-620-3780	
Address: 15169 N. Scottsdale Rd., Ste. C-400, Scottsdale, AZ 85254 US	

GROWTH PLANS/SPECIAL FEATURES:

ICrossing, Inc., a subsidiary of the Hearst Corporation, is a search engine marketing company. The firm offers planning services, development services and the iCrossing Marketing Platform. The company's planning services are offered for the areas of primary customer research; digital marketing strategy; competitive and market research; persona development; digital marketing strategy; integrated search marketing strategy; mobile marketing strategy; analytics and performance planning; marketing intelligence dashboarding; and social media and word-of-mouth strategy. ICrossing's development services include e-mail marketing; search engine marketing; mobile marketing and web site development; emerging media development; social media campaign development; and display and rich media advertising. The firm's iCrossing Marketing Platform offers clients data capture from campaign metrics, search sources and social networks in order to develop campaign and media spending strategies. The marketing platform also provides services such as bid and feeds management; SEO automation; display ad serving solutions; mobile advertising; and pixel-tracking and tagging, in addition to other tracking and measurement solutions. In June 2010, the firm was acquired by the Hearst Corporation.

FINANCIALS: Sales and profits are in thousands of dollars—add 000 to get the full amount. 2010 Note: Financial information for 2010 was not available for all companies at press time.

2010 Sales: $	2010 Profits: $	U.S. Stock Ticker: Subsidiary
2009 Sales: $	2009 Profits: $	Int'l Ticker: Int'l Exchange:
2008 Sales: $	2008 Profits: $	Employees:
2007 Sales: $	2007 Profits: $	Fiscal Year Ends: 12/31
2006 Sales: $	2006 Profits: $	Parent Company: HEARST CORPORATION (THE)

SALARIES/BENEFITS:

Pension Plan:	ESOP Stock Plan:	Profit Sharing:	Top Exec. Salary: $	Bonus: $
Savings Plan:	Stock Purch. Plan:		Second Exec. Salary: $	Bonus: $

OTHER THOUGHTS:

Apparent Women Officers or Directors: 1
Hot Spot for Advancement for Women/Minorities:

LOCATIONS: ("Y" = Yes)

West:	Southwest:	Midwest:	Southeast:	Northeast:	International:
Y	Y	Y		Y	

IKON OFFICE SOLUTIONS INC

www.ikon.com

Industry Group Code: 333313 Ranks within this company's industry group: Sales: Profits:

Hardware:	Software:	Telecommunications:	Electronic Publishing:	Equipment:		Specialty Services:	
Computers:	Consumer:	Local:	Online Service:	Telecom:		Consulting:	
Accessories:	Corporate:	Long Distance:	TV/Cable or Wireless:	Communication:		Contract Manufacturing:	
Network Equipment:	Telecom:	Cellular:	Games:	Distribution:	Y	Processing:	
Chips/Circuits:	Internet:	Internet Service:	Financial Data:	VAR/Reseller:		Staff/Outsourcing:	Y
Parts/Drives:				Satellite Srv./Equip.:		Specialty Services:	

TYPES OF BUSINESS:

Business Machine Distributor
Document Management Services
Document Management Software
Business Equipment Leasing
Managed Print Services Outsourcing

BRANDS/DIVISIONS/AFFILIATES:

IKON Financial Services
Ricoh Company Ltd
DataSource, Inc.

CONTACTS: Note: Officers with more than one job title may be intentionally listed here more than once.

Shiro Kondo, CEO
Shiro Kondo, Pres.
Wendy Pinckney, Contact-Media
Terrie Campbell, VP-Managed Document Svcs.
Masamitsu Sakurai, Chmn.

Phone: 610-296-8000	Fax: 610-408-7025
Toll-Free: 888-275-4566	
Address: 70 Valley Stream Pkwy., Malvern, PA 19355-0989 US	

GROWTH PLANS/SPECIAL FEATURES:

IKON Office Solutions, Inc., a wholly-owned subsidiary of Ricoh Americas Corporation, is an international document management service company and a distributor of equipment primarily made by Canon, Ricoh, Electronics for Imaging and Hewlett Packard. Its business service offerings include traditional copiers, printers, multi-functioning peripheral technologies and document management software, as well as other office equipment. The firm's document management software, primarily from companies such as Captaris, eCopy and Kofax, is designed to provide customized, document management solutions supported by the firm's enterprise services organization. IKON sells business machines and supplies through a large geographically oriented sales force with 400 locations in North America and Europe. Other services include professional services; a blend of on-site and off-site managed document management services; customized workflow solutions; and an expansive customer service network. Professional services help companies assess the efficiency of information processes, meet regulatory compliance requirements and automate manual tasks, thereby reducing document costs. On-site services include document production management, mailroom services management, facsimile service management, imaging and records management and general office support services. IKON also offers legal document services for law firms and law departments that include the accessing, controlling and disseminating of information. Through IKON Financial Services, the company leases its business equipment, as well as non-IKON furniture. In February 2010, the firm announced a partnership with Control Systems Copitrak, to provide tracking and charge back service for client related work to professionals in these following industries Legal, Architectural, Engineering, and Accounting. In February 2010, the company expanded its partnership with DataSource, Inc. DataSource will be utilizing IKON WebPrint for efficient and cost effective printing.

Employees of the firm receive dependent life insurance; flexible spending accounts; an employee assistance program; a monthly investment program designed to encourage employee stock ownership; tuition reimbursement; a national merit scholarship program for children of employees; and discounted auto and homeowners insurance.

FINANCIALS: Sales and profits are in thousands of dollars—add 000 to get the full amount. 2010 Note: Financial information for 2010 was not available for all companies at press time.

2010 Sales: $	2010 Profits: $	U.S. Stock Ticker: Subsidiary
2009 Sales: $	2009 Profits: $	Int'l Ticker: Int'l Exchange:
2008 Sales: $	2008 Profits: $	Employees:
2007 Sales: $4,168,300	2007 Profits: $114,500	Fiscal Year Ends: 9/30
2006 Sales: $4,228,200	2006 Profits: $106,200	Parent Company: RICOH COMPANY LTD

SALARIES/BENEFITS:

Pension Plan: Y	ESOP Stock Plan:	Profit Sharing:	Top Exec. Salary: $	Bonus: $
Savings Plan: Y	Stock Purch. Plan:		Second Exec. Salary: $	Bonus: $

OTHER THOUGHTS:

Apparent Women Officers or Directors: 2
Hot Spot for Advancement for Women/Minorities: Y

LOCATIONS: ("Y" = Yes)

West:	Southwest:	Midwest:	Southeast:	Northeast:	International:
Y	Y	Y	Y	Y	Y

IMATION CORP

www.imation.com

Industry Group Code: 334112   Ranks within this company's industry group: Sales: 6   Profits: 9

Hardware:		Software:	Telecommunications:	Electronic Publishing:	Equipment:		Specialty Services:	
Computers:		Consumer:	Local:	Online Service:	Telecom:		Consulting:	
Accessories:	Y	Corporate:	Long Distance:	TV/Cable or Wireless:	Communication:		Contract Manufacturing:	
Network Equipment:		Telecom:	Cellular:	Games:	Distribution:	Y	Processing:	
Chips/Circuits:		Internet:	Internet Service:	Financial Data:	VAR/Reseller:		Staff/Outsourcing:	
Parts/Drives:	Y				Satellite Srv./Equip.:		Specialty Services:	Y

TYPES OF BUSINESS:

Data Storage Products
Diskettes & Storage Tapes
Optical Storage Media
Imaging Systems
Hard Drives
Flash Memory Devices

BRANDS/DIVISIONS/AFFILIATES:

Imation
Memorex
TDK Life on Record
XtremeMac
Memcorp

CONTACTS: Note: Officers with more than one job title may be intentionally listed here more than once.

Mark E. Lucas, CEO
Mark E. Lucas, Pres.
Paul R. Zellar, CFO/Sr. VP
Subodh Kulkarni, CTO
John L. Sullivan, General Counsel/Sr. VP/Corp. Sec.
James C. Ellis, VP-Strategy, Mergers & Acquisitions
Linda W. Hart, Chmn.
Subodh Kulkarni, VP-Global Commercial Bus.

Phone: 651-704-4000	Fax: 888-704-4200
Toll-Free: 888-466-3456	
Address: 1 Imation Pl., Oakdale, MN 55128-3421 US	

GROWTH PLANS/SPECIAL FEATURES:

Imation Corp. develops, manufactures, sources, markets and distributes removable data storage media products (both optical and magnetic) for users of a broad array of digital information technologies in approximately 100 countries worldwide. The primary brand names under which it sells its products are Imation, Memorex, TDK Life on Record and XtremeMac. The firm offers a variety of products that capture, process, store, reproduce and distribute information and images for information-intensive markets, including enterprise computing, network servers, personal computing, graphic arts, medical imaging, photographic imaging, commercial and consumer markets. Imation divides its products into two segments: removable data storage products and accessories, and electronic products. Removable data storage products include Blu-ray, DVD and CD recordable media; 3.5 inch floppy diskettes; toner cartridges; external and removable hard disk drives (HDDs); solid state drives; tape cartridges; USB flash drives; and a wireless projection link. The company is a media supplier to the enterprise data center market, where organizations store, manage and protect mission-critical data. Through subsidiary Memcorp, the company also sells various consumer electronics products, such as flat panel displays and televisions, including LCD displays and digital picture frames; clock-radios; DVD players, karaoke systems; and MP3 players. Imation has recently been combining its global manufacturing and research & development functions into one operational unit to commercialize new products more rapidly.

Imation offers its employees medical, dental and vision coverage; short- and long-term disability; life and AD&D insurance; legal services; tuition reimbursement; a 401(k) plan; and a pension plan.

FINANCIALS: Sales and profits are in thousands of dollars—add 000 to get the full amount. 2010 Note: Financial information for 2010 was not available for all companies at press time.

2010 Sales: $	2010 Profits: $	**U.S. Stock Ticker: IMN**
2009 Sales: $1,649,500	2009 Profits: $-42,200	**Int'l Ticker:** Int'l Exchange:
2008 Sales: $1,981,000	2008 Profits: $-33,300	Employees: 1,210
2007 Sales: $1,895,800	2007 Profits: $-50,400	Fiscal Year Ends: 12/31
2006 Sales: $1,584,700	2006 Profits: $76,400	Parent Company:

SALARIES/BENEFITS:

Pension Plan: Y	ESOP Stock Plan:	Profit Sharing:	Top Exec. Salary: $720,014	Bonus: $875,448
Savings Plan: Y	Stock Purch. Plan:		Second Exec. Salary: $490,394	Bonus: $483,029

OTHER THOUGHTS:

Apparent Women Officers or Directors: 2
Hot Spot for Advancement for Women/Minorities: Y

LOCATIONS: ("Y" = Yes)

West:	Southwest:	Midwest:	Southeast:	Northeast:	International:
	Y	Y	Y		Y

IMMERSION CORP

www.immersion.com

Industry Group Code: 334119 Ranks within this company's industry group: Sales: 24 Profits: 18

Hardware:		Software:		Telecommunications:		Electronic Publishing:		Equipment:		Specialty Services:	
Computers:		Consumer:	Y	Local:		Online Service:		Telecom:	Y	Consulting:	
Accessories:	Y	Corporate:	Y	Long Distance:		TV/Cable or Wireless:		Communication:		Contract Manufacturing:	
Network Equipment:		Telecom:		Cellular:		Games:		Distribution:		Processing:	
Chips/Circuits:		Internet:		Internet Service:		Financial Data:		VAR/Reseller:		Staff/Outsourcing:	
Parts/Drives:								Satellite Srv./Equip.:		Specialty Services:	Y

TYPES OF BUSINESS:

Computer Hardware-Haptic Technology
Touch Simulation Systems
Medical Training Simulators
Video Game Technology
Automotive & Industrial Control Systems
Mobile Phone Technology

BRANDS/DIVISIONS/AFFILIATES:

AccuTouch
TouchSense
CathLabVR
LapVR
Virtual IV

CONTACTS: Note: Officers with more than one job title may be intentionally listed here more than once.

Victor Viegas, CEO
Victor Viegas, Pres.
Shum Mukherjee, CFO
Dennis Sheehan, VP-Mktg.
Janice Passarello, VP-Human Resources
Christophe Ramstein, CTO
Rob Lacroix, VP-Eng.
Anne Marie Peters, VP-Legal
Craig Vachon, Sr. VP/Gen. Mgr.-Touch Line Bus.
Craig Vacon, Chief Commercial Officer
Joseph LaValle, VP-Sales
Jack Saltich, Chmn.

Phone: 408-467-1900	Fax: 408-467-1901
Toll-Free:	
Address: 801 Fox Ln., San Jose, CA 95131 US	

GROWTH PLANS/SPECIAL FEATURES:

Immersion Corp. is a provider of haptic technologies that allow people to use their sense of touch when operating digital devices. It develops and manufactures or licenses a wide range of hardware and software technologies and products that focus primarily in the automotive, consumer electronics, gaming, and commercial and industrial devices and controls; medical simulation; and mobile communications. The company operates in two segments: medical and touch. The medical segment, accounting for 40% of revenue, develops simulation technologies that can be used for medical training and testing. The division has four medical simulation product lines: the Virtual IV system, which simulates needle-based procedures such as intravenous catheterization and phlebotomy; the Endoscopy AccuTouch system, which simulates endoscopic procedures; the CathLabVR system, which simulates endovascular interventions; and the LapVR system, which simulates minimally invasive procedures involving abdominal and pelvic organs. The touch segment, generating 60% of revenue, develops the TouchSense intellectual property for gaming products and rotary controls and touch screens appropriate for use in automobiles, as well as in mobile phones. In markets where its touch technologies are a small piece of a larger system, such as mobile phones and controls for automotive interfaces, Immersion licenses its technologies or software products to manufacturers who integrate them into their products and then sell their end products under their own brand names. In other markets, such as medical simulation, touch screen input devices and 3D computer-aided design, the company sells products manufactured in-house or by others under the Immersion brand. The company has over 700 issued or pending patents in the U.S. and internationally.

FINANCIALS: Sales and profits are in thousands of dollars—add 000 to get the full amount. 2010 Note: Financial information for 2010 was not available for all companies at press time.

2010 Sales: $	2010 Profits: $	**U.S. Stock Ticker: IMMR**
2009 Sales: $27,725	2009 Profits: $-28,279	Int'l Ticker: Int'l Exchange:
2008 Sales: $27,981	2008 Profits: $-50,990	Employees: 124
2007 Sales: $34,702	2007 Profits: $117,018	Fiscal Year Ends: 12/31
2006 Sales: $27,853	2006 Profits: $-10,424	Parent Company:

SALARIES/BENEFITS:

Pension Plan:	ESOP Stock Plan:	Profit Sharing:	Top Exec. Salary: $250,182	Bonus: $
Savings Plan:	Stock Purch. Plan:		Second Exec. Salary: $223,896	Bonus: $66,844

OTHER THOUGHTS:

Apparent Women Officers or Directors: 5
Hot Spot for Advancement for Women/Minorities: Y

LOCATIONS: ("Y" = Yes)

West:	Southwest:	Midwest:	Southeast:	Northeast:	International:
Y					Y

INDRA SISTEMAS SA

www.indracompany.com

Industry Group Code: 541513 Ranks within this company's industry group: Sales: Profits:

Hardware:		Software:		Telecommunications:		Electronic Publishing:		Equipment:		Specialty Services:	
Computers:		Consumer:		Local:		Online Service:		Telecom:		Consulting:	Y
Accessories:		Corporate:	Y	Long Distance:		TV/Cable or Wireless:		Communication:		Contract Manufacturing:	
Network Equipment:		Telecom:		Cellular:		Games:		Distribution:		Processing:	
Chips/Circuits:		Internet:		Internet Service:		Financial Data:		VAR/Reseller:		Staff/Outsourcing:	Y
Parts/Drives:								Satellite Srv./Equip.:		Specialty Services:	Y

TYPES OF BUSINESS:

Data Management
IT Consulting
Simulation & Training Technology
Aerospace & Defense

BRANDS/DIVISIONS/AFFILIATES:

Indra bmb
Europraxis
CARDplus
EDITRAN
MAPA
NETplus
Tramita
Indra Systems, Inc.

CONTACTS: *Note: Officers with more than one job title may be intentionally listed here more than once.*

Regino Moranchel, CEO
Javier de Andres, COO
Regino Moranchel, Pres.
Juan Carlos Baena, CFO
Tomas Contreras, Deputy Exec. VP-Human Resources
Pedro Ramon Y Cajal, Sec.
Rafael Gallego, Exec. VP-Oper.
Emma Fernandez, Sr. VP-Talent, Innovation & Strategy
Carlos Suarez Perez, Exec. VP-Defense
Santiago Roura, Exec. VP-Oper.
Javier Monzon, Chmn.
Emilio Diaz, Exec. VP-Int'l Oper.

Phone: 34-91-480-50-00	Fax: 34-91-480-50-80
Toll-Free:	
Address: Avenida de Bruselas 35, Madrid, 28108 Spain	

GROWTH PLANS/SPECIAL FEATURES:

Indra Sistemas SA is an IT company that provides products and services to a variety of industries. Indra operates in six markets: security and defense; transport and traffic; energy and industry; telecom and media; finance and insurance; and public administration and healthcare. The firm is organized into two segments: services and solutions. The services division involves the outsourcing of business processes and information systems carried out by subsidiary Indra bmb. The solutions unit focuses on obtaining, processing, transferring and presenting data such as hospital management and banking facilities, air defense systems and electronic intelligence systems. Within this segment, subsidiary Europraxis provides consulting on technological, operations and strategy issues. The company's products include CARDplus identification cards and related services; EDITRAN communications platforms; MAPA document management support; NETplus, an electronic funds transfer system; Tramita, for electronic file administration; and other custom applications. Its U.S. subsidiary, Indra Systems, Inc., provides automated test equipment and simulation and training technology for air, land and sea platforms, serving both military and commercial clients. In July 2010, Indra formed a joint venture with Proactiva Medio Ambiente to operate water control systems in Lima, Peru. In September 2010, the firm acquired the outstanding shares of Indra Espacio from Thales Alenia Space France.

FINANCIALS: Sales and profits are in thousands of dollars—add 000 to get the full amount. 2010 Note: Financial information for 2010 was not available for all companies at press time.

2010 Sales: $	2010 Profits: $	**U.S. Stock Ticker: ISMAF.PK**
2009 Sales: $	2009 Profits: $	**Int'l Ticker: IDR.MC** Int'l Exchange: Madrid-MCE
2008 Sales: $	2008 Profits: $	Employees:
2007 Sales: $	2007 Profits: $	Fiscal Year Ends: 12/31
2006 Sales: $	2006 Profits: $	Parent Company:

SALARIES/BENEFITS:

Pension Plan:	ESOP Stock Plan:	Profit Sharing:	Top Exec. Salary: $	Bonus: $
Savings Plan:	Stock Purch. Plan:		Second Exec. Salary: $	Bonus: $

OTHER THOUGHTS:

Apparent Women Officers or Directors: 4
Hot Spot for Advancement for Women/Minorities: Y

LOCATIONS: ("Y" = Yes)

West:	Southwest:	Midwest:	Southeast:	Northeast:	International:
			Y	Y	Y

INDUSTRIAL & FINANCIAL SYSTEMS AB (IFS)   www.ifsworld.com

Industry Group Code: 511201 **Ranks within this company's industry group: Sales: Profits:**

Hardware:	Software:		Telecommunications:	Electronic Publishing:	Equipment:	Specialty Services:
Computers:	Consumer:		Local:	Online Service:	Telecom:	Consulting:
Accessories:	Corporate:	Y	Long Distance:	TV/Cable or Wireless:	Communication:	Contract Manufacturing:
Network Equipment:	Telecom:		Cellular:	Games:	Distribution:	Processing:
Chips/Circuits:	Internet:		Internet Service:	Financial Data:	VAR/Reseller:	Staff/Outsourcing:
Parts/Drives:					Satellite Srv./Equip.:	Specialty Services:

TYPES OF BUSINESS:

Software Applications
Banking & Financial Software
Manufacturing Software
Application Service Provider

BRANDS/DIVISIONS/AFFILIATES:

IFS Applications
IFS Foundation1
IFS Defence Ltd
IFS Talk
IFS WikiHelp
IFS Communicator
360 Scheduling Ltd
IFS Retail

CONTACTS: Note: Officers with more than one job title may be intentionally listed here more than once.

Alastair Sorbie, CEO
Alastair Sorbie, Pres.
Paul Smith, CFO
Thomas Petersson, VP-Mktg.
Thomas Petersson, VP-Products
Fredrik vom Hofe, VP-Bus. Dev.
Anders Boos, Chmn.

Phone: 46-13-460-40-00	Fax: 46-13-460-40-01
Toll-Free:	
Address: Teknikringen 5, Linkoping, 581 15 Sweden	

GROWTH PLANS/SPECIAL FEATURES:

Industrial and Financial Systems AB (IFS), based in Sweden, is a global provider of component-based enterprise software for banking, financial and manufacturing companies. The company serves the automotive, aviation, rail and transit, telecommunications, energy and utilities, aerospace and defense, process and high-tech industries. IFS operates in more than 50 countries, and its software is used by more than 2,000 customers. The company does business in two areas: life cycle management, where it focuses on asset and product management, and midmarket ERP, in which it serves midsize distribution and manufacturing companies. The firm's software is based on IFS Foundation1, an innovative architecture that allows applications to be integrated piece-by-piece. This step-by-step methodology causes a minimum of disruption to operations. The IFS Applications platform consists of several enterprise application components available in 22 languages. The software is utilized in financials, human resources, sales and service, engineering, manufacturing, distribution, maintenance and business enabling. The company maintains strong, long-term partnerships with companies from a wide range of industries. Among IFS's collaborations is its 50-50 joint venture with BAE Systems called IFS Defence Ltd., which services the defense industry worldwide; and joint venture IFS Retail (with Dutch IT services provider Centric) which offers an IT solution for the international retail industry. In May 2010, the firm partnered with Italian IT firm Insirio S.p.A. to jointly market IT solutions to the oil and gas industry. In September 2010, the company acquired 360 Scheduling Ltd., a mobile workforce scheduling and optimization software provider. In October 2010, the firm launched proof of concept social media solutions IFS WikiHelp, IFS Talk and IFS Communicator.

FINANCIALS: Sales and profits are in thousands of dollars—add 000 to get the full amount. 2010 Note: Financial information for 2010 was not available for all companies at press time.

		U.S. Stock Ticker:
2010 Sales: $	2010 Profits: $	Int'l Ticker: IFS Int'l Exchange: Stockholm-SSE
2009 Sales: $	2009 Profits: $	Employees:
2008 Sales: $	2008 Profits: $	Fiscal Year Ends: 12/31
2007 Sales: $	2007 Profits: $	Parent Company:
2006 Sales: $322,300	2006 Profits: $35,900	

SALARIES/BENEFITS:

Pension Plan:	ESOP Stock Plan:	Profit Sharing:	Top Exec. Salary: $	Bonus: $
Savings Plan:	Stock Purch. Plan:		Second Exec. Salary: $	Bonus: $

OTHER THOUGHTS:

Apparent Women Officers or Directors: 2
Hot Spot for Advancement for Women/Minorities: Y

LOCATIONS: ("Y" = Yes)

West:	Southwest:	Midwest:	Southeast:	Northeast:	International:
Y	Y	Y	Y		Y

INDUSTRIAL DEFENDER INC

www.industrialdefender.com

Industry Group Code: 511210H Ranks within this company's industry group: Sales: Profits:

Hardware:		Software:		Telecommunications:		Electronic Publishing:		Equipment:		Specialty Services:	
Computers:		Consumer:		Local:		Online Service:		Telecom:		Consulting:	Y
Accessories:	Y	Corporate:	Y	Long Distance:		TV/Cable or Wireless:		Communication:		Contract Manufacturing:	
Network Equipment:		Telecom:		Cellular:		Games:		Distribution:		Processing:	
Chips/Circuits:		Internet:		Internet Service:		Financial Data:		VAR/Reseller:		Staff/Outsourcing:	
Parts/Drives:								Satellite Srv./Equip.:		Specialty Services:	Y

TYPES OF BUSINESS:

Digital Security Technology
Managed Security Services
Professional Services

BRANDS/DIVISIONS/AFFILIATES:

Cyber Risk Protection
Industrial Defender Managed Security Services
AutoAudit
Security Event Manager
Simple Network Management Protocol
Access Manager
Unified Threat Management

CONTACTS: Note: Officers with more than one job title may be intentionally listed here more than once.

Brian M. Ahern, CEO
Brian M. Ahern, Pres.
Jim Gennari, CFO
Tim Bridge, VP-Global Sales
Phil Dunbar, VP-R&D
John Shaw, Sr. VP-Tech.
John Shaw, Sr. VP-Prod.
Debra Griffith, Sr. VP-Corp. Dev.
T.C. Lau, VP-Professional Svcs.
Walter Sikora, VP-Security Solutions

Phone: 508-718-6700	Fax: 508-718-6701
Toll-Free:	
Address: 16 Chestnut St., Ste. 300, Foxborough, MA 02035 US	

GROWTH PLANS/SPECIAL FEATURES:

Industrial Defender, Inc. offers the Cyber Risk Protection integrated digital security suite, primarily serving industrial infrastructure businesses including electric utilities and transportation, chemical, water and oil and gas companies. The Cyber Risk Protection suite, based on its Defense-in-Depth technology platform and designed for new and legacy real-time process control and SCADA (Supervisory Control and Data Acquisition) systems, includes: UTM (Unified Threat Management), a device that includes firewall, antivirus, intrusion prevention and integrated virtual private network (VPN) capabilities; host intrusion detection software, which are computing asset protection components that are installed on host systems such as workstations and servers; a network intrusion detection system, which passively monitors all network traffic within the security perimeter; Security Event Manager, which centralizes critical security and performance information by integrating data and alerts from all Industrial Defender programs; Simple Network Management Protocol (SNMP) network device monitoring; AutoAudit, an automated compliance function; and Access Manager, which is designed to provide secure access and authentication from remote locations and substations. In addition to security, the company's products are designed to enable visibility, monitoring, patch, configuration and asset management. Aside from its Cyber Risk Protection suite, Industrial Defender also offers professional and consulting services, such as network architecture review, vulnerability assessment services and penetration testing services; and Industrial Defender Managed Security Services, which offers third-party digital security management services for clients, including real-time monitoring of multi-vendor control systems, network traffic, firewalls, routers and gateways. Since initial operation, the company has managed the digital security of 170 plants in 21 countries.

FINANCIALS: Sales and profits are in thousands of dollars—add 000 to get the full amount. 2010 Note: Financial information for 2010 was not available for all companies at press time.

2010 Sales: $	2010 Profits: $	U.S. Stock Ticker: Private	
2009 Sales: $	2009 Profits: $	Int'l Ticker:　Int'l Exchange:	
2008 Sales: $	2008 Profits: $	Employees:	
2007 Sales: $	2007 Profits: $	Fiscal Year Ends:	
2006 Sales: $	2006 Profits: $	Parent Company:	

SALARIES/BENEFITS:

Pension Plan:	ESOP Stock Plan:	Profit Sharing:	Top Exec. Salary: $	Bonus: $
Savings Plan:	Stock Purch. Plan:		Second Exec. Salary: $	Bonus: $

OTHER THOUGHTS:

Apparent Women Officers or Directors:
Hot Spot for Advancement for Women/Minorities:

LOCATIONS: ("Y" = Yes)

West:	Southwest:	Midwest:	Southeast:	Northeast:	International:
Y			Y	Y	Y

Note: Financial information, benefits and other data can change quickly and may vary from those stated here.

INFINEON TECHNOLOGIES AG

www.infineon.com

Industry Group Code: 33441 Ranks within this company's industry group: Sales: 11 Profits: 51

Hardware:	Software:	Telecommunications:	Electronic Publishing:	Equipment:		Specialty Services:	
Computers:	Consumer:	Local:	Online Service:	Telecom:	Y	Consulting:	
Accessories:	Corporate:	Long Distance:	TV/Cable or Wireless:	Communication:	Y	Contract Manufacturing:	
Network Equipment:	Telecom:	Cellular:	Games:	Distribution:		Processing:	
Chips/Circuits: Y	Internet:	Internet Service:	Financial Data:	VAR/Reseller:		Staff/Outsourcing:	
Parts/Drives:				Satellite Srv./Equip.:		Specialty Services:	

TYPES OF BUSINESS:

Semiconductor Manufacturing
Fiber-Optic Components
GPS Microchips
Embedded Memory Products
Broadband Components

BRANDS/DIVISIONS/AFFILIATES:

LS Power Semitech Co Ltd
Infineon Technologies Asia Pacific Pte Ltd
Infineon Technologies Japan KK
Infineon Technologies North America Corp
AUDO MAX
CoolMOS C6/E6
TDA5240
XMM 2138

CONTACTS: Note: Officers with more than one job title may be intentionally listed here more than once.

Peter Bauer, CEO
Reinhard Ploss, Exec. VP/Head-Oper.
Hermann Eul, Exec. VP-Mktg. & Sales
Thomas Marquardt, Global Head-Human Resources
Hermann Eul, Exec. VP-R&D
Hermann Eul, Exec. VP-Tech.
Max Dietrich Kley, Chmn.

Phone: 49-89-2346-5555	Fax: 49-89-2349-552-987
Toll-Free:	
Address: Am Campeon 1-12, Neubiberg, 85579 Germany	

GROWTH PLANS/SPECIAL FEATURES:

Infineon Technologies AG designs, develops, manufactures and markets semiconductors and complete system solutions. The company's business is organized into three principal operating segments: Chip Card and Security; Automotive; and Industrial and Multimarket. Infineon's Chip Card & Security segment designs, develops, manufactures and markets a wide range of security controllers and security memories for chip card and security applications. These products include security memory ICs in prepaid telecom cards, access and transportation cards; contact-based and contactless security microcontroller ICs for identification documents, payment cards, SIM cards and Pay-TV applications; Trusted Platform Module products in computers and networks; and RFID ICs for object identification. The Automotive segment designs, develops, manufactures and markets semiconductors safety management, powertrain applications and body and convenience systems. The company's Industrial and Multimarket division offers power modules, small signal semiconductors, discrete power semiconductors and power management ICs. These products are used in DC/DC power converters, lighting, industrial drives, uninterruptible power supplies, medical equipment, power generation, industrial automation and switched-mode power supplies. Infineon's subsidiaries include Infineon Technologies Asia Pacific Pte. Ltd.; Infineon Technologies Japan K.K.; and Infineon Technologies North America Corp. Through LS Power Semitech Co., Ltd., a joint venture with LS Industrial Systems, the company develops, produces and markets molded power modules for white good applications. Infineon owns 46% of the venture. In 2010, the firm released several new products, including XMM 2138, a platform that supports Dual-SIM mobile phones; CoolMOS C6/E6, a series of 650-volt metal oxide semiconductor field effect transistors (MOSFETS); TDA5240, TDA5235 and TDA5225 wireless control receivers; and AUDO MAX, a series of 32-bit microcontrollers for automotive powertrains and chassis. In August 2010, the firm agreed to sell its Wireless Solutions division to Intel for roughly $1.4 billion.

FINANCIALS: Sales and profits are in thousands of dollars—add 000 to get the full amount. 2010 Note: Financial information for 2010 was not available for all companies at press time.

2010 Sales: $	2010 Profits: $	**U.S. Stock Ticker: IFNNY**
2009 Sales: $4,428,000	2009 Profits: $-982,000	**Int'l Ticker: IFX** Int'l Exchange: Frankfurt-Euronext
2008 Sales: $6,084,000	2008 Profits: $-4,396,000	Employees: 26,464
2007 Sales: $10,923,000	2007 Profits: $-523,000	Fiscal Year Ends: 9/30
2006 Sales: $10,060,000	2006 Profits: $-340,000	Parent Company:

SALARIES/BENEFITS:

Pension Plan:	ESOP Stock Plan:	Profit Sharing:	Top Exec. Salary: $	Bonus: $
Savings Plan:	Stock Purch. Plan:		Second Exec. Salary: $	Bonus: $

OTHER THOUGHTS:

Apparent Women Officers or Directors:
Hot Spot for Advancement for Women/Minorities:

LOCATIONS: ("Y" = Yes)

West:	Southwest:	Midwest:	Southeast:	Northeast:	International:
Y		Y		Y	Y

INFOR GLOBAL SOLUTIONS
www.infor.com

Industry Group Code: 511210H Ranks within this company's industry group: Sales: Profits:

Hardware:	Software:		Telecommunications:	Electronic Publishing:	Equipment:	Specialty Services:	
Computers:	Consumer:		Local:	Online Service:	Telecom:	Consulting:	Y
Accessories:	Corporate:	Y	Long Distance:	TV/Cable or Wireless:	Communication:	Contract Manufacturing:	
Network Equipment:	Telecom:		Cellular:	Games:	Distribution:	Processing:	
Chips/Circuits:	Internet:		Internet Service:	Financial Data:	VAR/Reseller:	Staff/Outsourcing:	
Parts/Drives:					Satellite Srv./Equip.:	Specialty Services:	

TYPES OF BUSINESS:
Software-Manufacturing & Distribution
IT Consulting
Business Intelligence Software

BRANDS/DIVISIONS/AFFILIATES:
Bridgelogix
Qurius NV

CONTACTS: Note: Officers with more than one job title may be intentionally listed here more than once.
Charles Phillips, CEO
Raghavan Rajaji, CFO/Exec. VP
Duncan Angrove, Pres., Mktg.
Glenn Goldberg, Sr. VP-Human Resources
Soma Somasundaram, Sr. VP-Global Prod. Dev.
Gregory M. Giangiordano, General Counsel/Sr. VP/Corp. Sec.
Pam Murphy, Sr. VP-Corp. Oper.
Bruce Richardson, Chief Strategy Officer/Sr. VP
Kevin Samuelson, Sr. VP-Mergers & Acquisitions
Jim Byrnes, Sr. VP-Global Svcs.
Marylon McGinnis, Sr. VP-Global Support
C. James Schaper, Chmn.
Stephan Scholl, Exec. VP-Global Field Oper.

Phone: 678-319-8000	Fax: 678-319-8000
Toll-Free: 866-244-5479	
Address: 13560 Morris Rd., Ste. 4100, Alpharetta, GA 30004 US	

GROWTH PLANS/SPECIAL FEATURES:
Infor Global Solutions is a privately held provider of software and IT consulting tailor-made for the manufacturing, distribution and services market segments. The company's products are specifically engineered for a variety of industries, including the automotive, aerospace, chemicals, communications, financial services, food and beverage, hospitality, industrial, life sciences, paper, plastic fabrication, retail and building materials industries. The software designed at Infor addresses customer relationship management; enterprise asset management; enterprise resource planning; financial management; human capital management; service-oriented architecture; performance management; product lifecycle management; supply chain management; and workforce management. In addition to the production of this industry-specific software, Infor offers professional services including application consulting, education, application development, managed services and management consulting. The firm also implements some software in partnerships with other developers, such as IBM, Microsoft and Progress. Infor maintains over 70,000 customers worldwide and has support operations in over 100 countries, which are serviced through its direct offices in 36 countries in North America, Europe, Asia and Australia. Support and training is available in 20 languages. In June 2010, the firm acquired partner company, Bridgelogix, a developer of barcode data collection applications. In July 2010, the company acquired the enterprise resource planning (ERP) operations of its implementation partner, Qurius NV.

FINANCIALS: Sales and profits are in thousands of dollars—add 000 to get the full amount. 2010 Note: Financial information for 2010 was not available for all companies at press time.
2010 Sales: $ 2010 Profits: $ **U.S. Stock Ticker: Private**
2009 Sales: $ 2009 Profits: $ **Int'l Ticker:**   Int'l Exchange:
2008 Sales: $ 2008 Profits: $ Employees:
2007 Sales: $ 2007 Profits: $ Fiscal Year Ends: 6/30
2006 Sales: $2,080,000   2006 Profits: $ Parent Company:

SALARIES/BENEFITS:
Pension Plan: ESOP Stock Plan: Profit Sharing: Top Exec. Salary: $ Bonus: $
Savings Plan: Stock Purch. Plan: Second Exec. Salary: $ Bonus: $

OTHER THOUGHTS:
Apparent Women Officers or Directors: 3
Hot Spot for Advancement for Women/Minorities: Y

LOCATIONS: ("Y" = Yes)
West:	Southwest:	Midwest:	Southeast:	Northeast:	International:
Y	Y	Y	Y	Y	Y

Note: Financial information, benefits and other data can change quickly and may vary from those stated here.

INFOSYS TECHNOLOGIES LTD

www.infosys.com

Industry Group Code: 541513 Ranks within this company's industry group: Sales: 12 Profits: 3

Hardware:	Software:		Telecommunications:	Electronic Publishing:	Equipment:	Specialty Services:	
Computers:	Consumer:		Local:	Online Service:	Telecom:	Consulting:	Y
Accessories:	Corporate:	Y	Long Distance:	TV/Cable or Wireless:	Communication:	Contract Manufacturing:	
Network Equipment:	Telecom:		Cellular:	Games:	Distribution:	Processing:	
Chips/Circuits:	Internet:		Internet Service:	Financial Data:	VAR/Reseller:	Staff/Outsourcing:	Y
Parts/Drives:					Satellite Srv./Equip.:	Specialty Services:	Y

TYPES OF BUSINESS:

Consulting-IT & Systems
Software Development & Services
Business Process Outsourcing

BRANDS/DIVISIONS/AFFILIATES:

Finacle
Infosys Consulting
Infosys BPO
iEngage Digital Consumer Platform
Infosys Leadership Institute
Infosys Mexico
Infosys China
Flypp

CONTACTS:
Note: Officers with more than one job title may be intentionally listed here more than once.
S. Gopalakrishnan, CEO
S. D. Shibulal, COO
T. V. Mohandas Pai, Dir.-Human Resources
T. V. Mohandas Pai, Dir.-Research & Education
K. Dinesh, Head-Info. Systems
T. V. Mohandas Pai, Dir.-Admin.
K. Dinesh, Head-Quality, Productivity & Comm. Design Group
Srinath Batni, Head-Delivery Excellence
N. R. Narayana Murthy, Chmn.

Phone: 91-80-2852-0261	Fax: 91-80-2852-0362
Toll-Free:	
Address: Plot No. 44 & 97A, Electronics City, Hosur Rd., Bangalore, 560 100 India	

GROWTH PLANS/SPECIAL FEATURES:

Infosys Technologies, Ltd. provides IT and consulting services to clients worldwide. The company offers a range of customized software solutions including development, maintenance and reengineering, as well as e-commerce consulting through offices in roughly 33 countries. Infosys' applications perform a variety of business functions, such as automating bank operations and assisting with inventory, distribution and warehouse management. For example, Finacle, one of its software applications, is a universal banking solution that addresses the core banking, treasury, wealth management, consumer and corporate e-business, mobile banking and web-based cash management requirements of universal, retail, corporate, community and private banks. The firm's software is also used in the energy and utilities, engineering enterprises, financial services, health care, life sciences, manufacturing, retail, technology, telecommunications and transportation industries. Infosys provides consulting services in the U.S. through its American subsidiary Infosys Consulting. Other wholly-owned subsidiaries include Infosys Mexico, Infosys Australia, Infosys China and Infosys Sweden. In addition to consulting and IT services, the company provides business process outsourcing for the banking, securities and brokerage, insurance, telecommunications, finance and health care industries through Infosys BPO, a majority-owned subsidiary. Infosys also sets up dedicated offshore software development centers for large clients. Approximately 65.8% of company revenues are derived from clients in the U.S., and approximately 23% are derived from clients in Europe. The company also offers Flypp, an application platform that allows mobile service providers to offer digital customers an array of ready-to-use experiential applications for mobile devices. In June 2010, the company released iEngage Digital Consumer Platform.

Infosys offers employee training through the Infosys Leadership Institute. The company's InStep internship program is internationally recognized for attractive pay and assigning real-time projects to interns.

FINANCIALS:
Sales and profits are in thousands of dollars—add 000 to get the full amount. 2010 Note: Financial information for 2010 was not available for all companies at press time.

2010 Sales: $4,804,000	2010 Profits: $1,313,000	**U.S. Stock Ticker: INFY**
2009 Sales: $4,663,000	2009 Profits: $1,281,000	**Int'l Ticker: 500209** Int'l Exchange: Bombay-BSE
2008 Sales: $4,176,000	2008 Profits: $1,163,000	Employees: 113,800
2007 Sales: $3,090,000	2007 Profits: $850,000	Fiscal Year Ends: 3/31
2006 Sales: $2,152,000	2006 Profits: $555,000	Parent Company:

SALARIES/BENEFITS:

Pension Plan:	ESOP Stock Plan:	Profit Sharing:	Top Exec. Salary: $426,698	Bonus: $443,616
Savings Plan:	Stock Purch. Plan:		Second Exec. Salary: $332,995	Bonus: $412,639

OTHER THOUGHTS:

Apparent Women Officers or Directors: 1
Hot Spot for Advancement for Women/Minorities:

LOCATIONS: ("Y" = Yes)

West:	Southwest:	Midwest:	Southeast:	Northeast:	International:
Y	Y	Y	Y	Y	Y

Note: Financial information, benefits and other data can change quickly and may vary from those stated here.

INGRAM MICRO INC

www.ingrammicro.com

Industry Group Code: 423430 Ranks within this company's industry group: Sales: 1 Profits: 1

Hardware:	Software:	Telecommunications:	Electronic Publishing:	Equipment:		Specialty Services:	
Computers:	Consumer:	Local:	Online Service:	Telecom:		Consulting:	
Accessories:	Corporate:	Long Distance:	TV/Cable or Wireless:	Communication:		Contract Manufacturing:	
Network Equipment:	Telecom:	Cellular:	Games:	Distribution:	Y	Processing:	
Chips/Circuits:	Internet:	Internet Service:	Financial Data:	VAR/Reseller:	Y	Staff/Outsourcing:	
Parts/Drives:				Satellite Srv./Equip.:		Specialty Services:	Y

TYPES OF BUSINESS:

Microcomputers, Distribution
Networking Equipment
Software & Accessories Distribution
Supply Chain Management Services
Online Marketing Services

BRANDS/DIVISIONS/AFFILIATES:

Micro Logistics
Arete Sistemas
Arkenova Sistemas

CONTACTS: Note: Officers with more than one job title may be intentionally listed here more than once.

Gregory M.E. Spierkel, CEO
William D. Humes, CFO/Exec. VP
Lynn Jolliffe, Exec. VP-Human Resources
Mario Leone, CIO/Exec. VP
Larry C. Boyd, General Counsel/Sr. VP/Sec.
G. Sam Kamel, Sr. VP-Corp. Strategy
Ria M. Carlson, Sr. VP-Comm. & Brand Mgmt.
Shailendra Gupta, Sr. Exec. VP/Pres., Ingram Micro Asia-Pacific
Keith W. F. Bradley, Sr. Exec. VP/Pres., Ingram Micro North America
Eduardo Araujo, Sr. Exev. VP/Pres., Ingram Micro Latin America
Dale R. Laurance, Chmn.
Alain Maquet, Sr. VP/Pres., EMEA
Robert Gifford, Sr. Exec. VP-Global Logistics

Phone: 714-566-1000	Fax:
Toll-Free:	
Address: 1600 E. St. Andrew Pl., Santa Ana, CA 92705-4926 US	

GROWTH PLANS/SPECIAL FEATURES:

Ingram Micro, Inc. is a global distributor of technology products and supply chain management services. The company markets microcomputer hardware, networking equipment and software products to nearly 180,000 resellers in approximately 150 countries. Ingram provides a comprehensive inventory of hundreds of thousands of distinct items from nearly 1,300 suppliers. Its products are sold in four primary segments: IT Peripheral, Systems, Software and Networking. Peripherals include printers, scanners, displays, projectors, monitors, mass storage and tape. Systems products include servers, desktops, laptop computers and personal digital assistants. Software products include operating systems, entertainment software, security tools and business applications. Networking products include routers, switches, hubs, wireless networks, networking cards, video conferencing, storage area networks and software products such as business application, operating system, entertainment and security software. In terms of revenue, peripherals account for 40% to 45% of revenue, systems for 25% to 30%, software for 15% to 20% and networking products for 10% to 15%. In addition, the company offers components, such as processors, motherboards, hard drives and memory; supplies and accessories, including ink and toner supplies, paper, carrying cases and anti-glare screens; and consumer electronic products, such as cell phones, digital cameras, DVD players and televisions. Ingram also offers supply chain management services such as sales and marketing, customer care, financial services and logistics to suppliers and resellers. Its Micro Logistics division provides end-to-end order management and fulfillment, retail logistics merchandising, warehousing and storage, contract manufacturing, distribution center services, product procurement, reverse logistics, transportation management, marketing services and other outsourcing services. Through its web site, Ingram also offers online account management, a vast resource library and advanced marketing tools. In December 2010, the company acquired Arete Sistemas and Arkenova Sistemas, two Spanish wholesale providers.

Ingram Micro offers its employees medical, dental and vision coverage; a 401(k) plan; adoption assistance; tuition reimbursement; an employee assistance program; and product discounts.

FINANCIALS: Sales and profits are in thousands of dollars—add 000 to get the full amount. 2010 Note: Financial information for 2010 was not available for all companies at press time.

2010 Sales: $	2010 Profits: $	U.S. Stock Ticker: IM
2009 Sales: $29,515,446	2009 Profits: $202,138	Int'l Ticker: Int'l Exchange:
2008 Sales: $34,362,152	2008 Profits: $-394,921	Employees: 13,750
2007 Sales: $35,047,089	2007 Profits: $275,908	Fiscal Year Ends: 12/31
2006 Sales: $31,357,477	2006 Profits: $265,766	Parent Company:

SALARIES/BENEFITS:

Pension Plan:	ESOP Stock Plan:	Profit Sharing:	Top Exec. Salary: $850,000	Bonus: $1,807,950
Savings Plan: Y	Stock Purch. Plan:		Second Exec. Salary: $650,000	Bonus: $829,530

OTHER THOUGHTS:

Apparent Women Officers or Directors: 5
Hot Spot for Advancement for Women/Minorities: Y

LOCATIONS: ("Y" = Yes)

West:	Southwest:	Midwest:	Southeast:	Northeast:	International:
Y	Y	Y	Y	Y	Y

INNOVEX INC
www.innovexinc.com

Industry Group Code: 33441 Ranks within this company's industry group: Sales: Profits:

Hardware:	Software:	Telecommunications:	Electronic Publishing:	Equipment:	Specialty Services:
Computers:	Consumer:	Local:	Online Service:	Telecom:	Consulting:
Accessories:	Corporate:	Long Distance:	TV/Cable or Wireless:	Communication:	Contract Manufacturing:
Network Equipment:	Telecom:	Cellular:	Games:	Distribution:	Processing:
Chips/Circuits: Y	Internet:	Internet Service:	Financial Data:	VAR/Reseller:	Staff/Outsourcing:
Parts/Drives: Y				Satellite Srv./Equip.:	Specialty Services:

TYPES OF BUSINESS:
Flexible Circuits Manufacturer
Disk Drive Components
LCD Components
Copper Clad Polyimide Manufacturing

BRANDS/DIVISIONS/AFFILIATES:

CONTACTS: Note: Officers with more than one job title may be intentionally listed here more than once.
Randy Acres, CEO
Randy Acres, Pres.
Randy L Acres, CFO
Stephen S. Lai, Sr. VP-Worldwide Sales & Mktg.
Brian Dahmes, VP-Tech.
John Clark III, Chmn.

Phone: 763-383-4000	Fax: 763-383-4091
Toll-Free:	
Address: 3033 Campus Dr., Ste. E180, Plymouth, MN 55441 US	

GROWTH PLANS/SPECIAL FEATURES:
Innovex, Inc. is a leading worldwide provider of high-density flexible circuit-based electronic interconnect solutions to original equipment manufacturers (OEMs) in the electronics industry. The company provides flexible circuits for such applications as data storage devices, such as hard disk drives (HDDs) and tape drives; liquid crystal displays (LCDs) for mobile telecommunication devices; and printers. Innovex's manufacturing capabilities include photolithographic processes, circuit-finishing processes and flexible circuit assembly. Innovex's products encompass a range of flexible circuitry, including single-metal layer circuitry, largely for dynamic applications; double-metal layer, mainly for static or fold-to-fit applications; multi-layer flex, usually fitted flat and not formed; and flip-chip, SMD and BGA assemblies. Innovex also supplies flexible circuits to the telecommunications market that provide interfaces between LCDs and mobile communication devices. The company has its headquarters in Minnesota, although its main base of operation is in Chiang Mai, Northern Thailand. The firm also has offices in the U.K., Taiwan, Singapore, China and Korea.

FINANCIALS: Sales and profits are in thousands of dollars—add 000 to get the full amount. 2010 Note: Financial information for 2010 was not available for all companies at press time.

2010 Sales: $	2010 Profits: $	U.S. Stock Ticker: INVX.PK
2009 Sales: $	2009 Profits: $	Int'l Ticker: Int'l Exchange:
2008 Sales: $71,039	2008 Profits: $-28,001	Employees: 3,306
2007 Sales: $87,844	2007 Profits: $-32,147	Fiscal Year Ends: 9/30
2006 Sales: $173,144	2006 Profits: $-16,970	Parent Company:

SALARIES/BENEFITS:

Pension Plan:	ESOP Stock Plan:	Profit Sharing:	Top Exec. Salary: $305,937	Bonus: $
Savings Plan:	Stock Purch. Plan:		Second Exec. Salary: $290,769	Bonus: $

OTHER THOUGHTS:
Apparent Women Officers or Directors:
Hot Spot for Advancement for Women/Minorities:

LOCATIONS: ("Y" = Yes)

West:	Southwest:	Midwest:	Southeast:	Northeast:	International:
Y		Y			Y

INPHI CORPORATION

www.inphi-corp.com

Industry Group Code: 33441 Ranks within this company's industry group: Sales: Profits:

Hardware:		Software:		Telecommunications:		Electronic Publishing:		Equipment:		Specialty Services:	
Computers:		Consumer:		Local:		Online Service:		Telecom:		Consulting:	
Accessories:	Y	Corporate:		Long Distance:		TV/Cable or Wireless:		Communication:		Contract Manufacturing:	
Network Equipment:		Telecom:		Cellular:		Games:		Distribution:		Processing:	
Chips/Circuits:	Y	Internet:		Internet Service:		Financial Data:		VAR/Reseller:		Staff/Outsourcing:	
Parts/Drives:	Y							Satellite Srv./Equip.:		Specialty Services:	

TYPES OF BUSINESS:
Fabless Semiconductor Technology

BRANDS/DIVISIONS/AFFILIATES:
INPHI Design Center

CONTACTS: *Note: Officers with more than one job title may be intentionally listed here more than once.*
Young K. Sohn, CEO
Young K. Sohn, Pres.
John Edmunds, CFO/VP
Ron Torten, VP-Worldwide Sales
Gopal Raghavan, CTO
Norman Yeung, VP-Eng.
Atul Shingal, VP-Oper.
Loi Nguyen, VP-Corp. Comm.
Loi Nguyen, VP-Mktg., Networking & Multi-Markets
Paul Washkewicz, VP-Mktg., Computing & Storage
Lawrence Tse, VP-Eng., New Bus. Initiatives
Diosdado P. Banatao, Chmn.

Phone: 408-217-7300	Fax:
Toll-Free:	
Address: 1 Coleman St., #06-08 The Adelphi, Singapore, 179803 Singapore	

GROWTH PLANS/SPECIAL FEATURES:

INPHI Corporation is a fabless provider of high-speed analog semiconductor solutions. The firm offers its services to the communications and computing industries. The company's analog semiconductor solutions provide high signal integrity at leading-edge data speeds while reducing system power consumption. INPHI Corp.'s semiconductor solutions are designed to address bandwidth bottlenecks in networks, maximize throughput and minimize latency in computing environments and enable the rollout of next generation communications and computing infrastructures. Its solutions provide a vital high-speed interface between analog signals and digital information in high-performance systems such as telecommunications transport systems, enterprise networking equipment, datacenter and enterprise servers, storage platforms, test and measurement equipment and military systems. The firm provides 40G (gigabits per second) and 100G high-speed analog semiconductor solutions for the communications market and high-speed memory interface solutions for the computing market. The company is also supplies components for DDR2 and DDR3 memory modules, and has recently introduced the industry's first Isolation Memory Buffer. This component is essential to the development of load-reduced, dual-inline memory modules (LRDIMMS). LRDIMMS products are capable of delivering over four times the memory capacity and nearly double the bandwidth of standard memory modules. INPHI Corp. has a broad product portfolio with 17 product lines and more than 170 products. In April 2010, the firm opened an INPHI Design Center in the U.K. In June 2010, the company opened a new office in Singapore. INPHI Corp. became publicly traded in the U.S. in November 2010.

The firm offers its employees a 401(k), dental insurance, medical insurance and stock options.

FINANCIALS: Sales and profits are in thousands of dollars—add 000 to get the full amount. 2010 Note: Financial information for 2010 was not available for all companies at press time.

2010 Sales: $	2010 Profits: $	**U.S. Stock Ticker: IPHI**
2009 Sales: $	2009 Profits: $	**Int'l Ticker:** Int'l Exchange:
2008 Sales: $	2008 Profits: $	Employees:
2007 Sales: $	2007 Profits: $	Fiscal Year Ends: 12/31
2006 Sales: $	2006 Profits: $	Parent Company:

SALARIES/BENEFITS:

Pension Plan:	ESOP Stock Plan:	Profit Sharing:	Top Exec. Salary: $	Bonus: $
Savings Plan:	Stock Purch. Plan:		Second Exec. Salary: $	Bonus: $

OTHER THOUGHTS:
Apparent Women Officers or Directors:
Hot Spot for Advancement for Women/Minorities:

LOCATIONS: ("Y" = Yes)

West:	Southwest:	Midwest:	Southeast:	Northeast:	International:
Y					Y

INSIGHT ENTERPRISES INC

www.insight.com

Industry Group Code: 423430 Ranks within this company's industry group: Sales: 9 Profits: 9

Hardware:	Software:	Telecommunications:	Electronic Publishing:		Equipment:		Specialty Services:	
Computers:	Consumer:	Local:	Online Service:	Y	Telecom:		Consulting:	Y
Accessories:	Corporate:	Long Distance:	TV/Cable or Wireless:		Communication:		Contract Manufacturing:	
Network Equipment:	Telecom:	Cellular:	Games:		Distribution:	Y	Processing:	
Chips/Circuits:	Internet:	Internet Service:	Financial Data:		VAR/Reseller:	Y	Staff/Outsourcing:	Y
Parts/Drives:					Satellite Srv./Equip.:		Specialty Services:	

TYPES OF BUSINESS:

Computer & Electronic Products, Direct Selling
Online Sales
Supply Chain Services

BRANDS/DIVISIONS/AFFILIATES:

CONTACTS: *Note: Officers with more than one job title may be intentionally listed here more than once.*

Ken Lamneck, CEO
Ken Lamneck, Pres.
Glynis Bryan, CFO
Michael Guggemos, CIO
Steven R. Andrews, Chief Admin. Officer
Steven R. Andrews, General Counsel/Sec.
Stephen Speidel, Sr. VP-Oper.
Helen K. Johnson, Sr. VP-Investor Rel.
Helen K. Johnson, Treas.
David Olsen, Sr. VP/Corp. Controller/Principal Acct. Officer
Timothy A. Crown, Chmn.
Stuart A. Fenton, Pres., Insight EMEA & APAC

Phone: 480-902-1001	Fax: 480-902-1157
Toll-Free: 800-467-4448	
Address: 6820 South Harl Ave., Tempe, AZ 85283 US	

GROWTH PLANS/SPECIAL FEATURES:

Insight Enterprises, Inc. provides information technology (IT) products to businesses and government institutions globally. It sells products in three categories: hardware, software and services. The firm sells hardware, computer accessories and office equipment from manufacturers such as Hewlett-Packard, Cisco, Lenovo and IBM. These include computers, servers, printers, printer consumables, power management tools, hard drives, monitors and related accessories. Its software applications are offered to clients in three forms: licensing agreements with software publishers, boxed products and software as a service (SaaS) models. Software products include business, creativity, security and networking applications from Adobe, Microsoft and Symantec, among others, as well as operating systems and software licenses. Its service offerings in the U.S. and U.K., provided by company service personnel and service partners, include IT lifecycle services; software licensing and financing; procurement; pre-configuring systems; logistics planning; installation; IT maintenance services; and software asset management services. Insight is located in 22 countries, supporting clients in 190 countries. In 2009, sales of hardware accounted for roughly 50% of net sales; software, 44%; and services, approximately 6%. Geographically, North American sales represented 69%, while the EMEA region generated 28% and Asia-Pacific the remaining 3%.

Employees are offered medical, dental and vision insurance; life insurance; short-and long-term disability coverage; a 401(k) plan; flexible spending accounts; pet insurance; legal plans; auto and home insurance; tuition reimbursement; fitness center memberships; and adoption assistance.

FINANCIALS: Sales and profits are in thousands of dollars—add 000 to get the full amount. 2010 Note: Financial information for 2010 was not available for all companies at press time.

2010 Sales: $	2010 Profits: $	U.S. Stock Ticker: NSIT
2009 Sales: $4,136,905	2009 Profits: $33,574	Int'l Ticker: Int'l Exchange:
2008 Sales: $4,825,489	2008 Profits: $-239,727	Employees:
2007 Sales: $4,800,431	2007 Profits: $77,795	Fiscal Year Ends: 12/31
2006 Sales: $3,593,256	2006 Profits: $76,818	Parent Company:

SALARIES/BENEFITS:

Pension Plan:	ESOP Stock Plan:	Profit Sharing:	Top Exec. Salary: $513,461	Bonus: $829,963
Savings Plan: Y	Stock Purch. Plan:		Second Exec. Salary: $400,000	Bonus: $343,294

OTHER THOUGHTS:

Apparent Women Officers or Directors: 3
Hot Spot for Advancement for Women/Minorities: Y

LOCATIONS: ("Y" = Yes)

West:	Southwest:	Midwest:	Southeast:	Northeast:	International:
Y	Y	Y			Y

Note: Financial information, benefits and other data can change quickly and may vary from those stated here.

INSTRUCTIVISION INC

www.instructivision.com

Industry Group Code: 511210P Ranks within this company's industry group: Sales: Profits:

Hardware:	Software:		Telecommunications:	Electronic Publishing:	Equipment:	Specialty Services:	
Computers:	Consumer:	Y	Local:	Online Service:	Telecom:	Consulting:	
Accessories:	Corporate:		Long Distance:	TV/Cable or Wireless:	Communication:	Contract Manufacturing:	
Network Equipment:	Telecom:		Cellular:	Games:	Distribution:	Processing:	
Chips/Circuits:	Internet:		Internet Service:	Financial Data:	VAR/Reseller:	Staff/Outsourcing:	
Parts/Drives:					Satellite Srv./Equip.:	Specialty Services:	Y

TYPES OF BUSINESS:

Educational Multimedia Production
Educational Software, Books & Videos
Video Production Services
Homeschooling Materials

BRANDS/DIVISIONS/AFFILIATES:

Key It In
Math Made Easy
Frog Inside-Out (The)
Teaching Critical Thinking in Science
Study Skills for Success
Cults: Saying No Under Pressure
Conducting Effective Conferences with Parents
Boosting Student Motivation

CONTACTS: *Note: Officers with more than one job title may be intentionally listed here more than once.*

Rosemary Comras, Pres.
Rosemary Comras, Sec.
Rosemary Comras, Treas.
Rosemary Comras, Chmn.

Phone: 973-575-9992	Fax: 973-575-9134
Toll-Free: 888-551-5144	
Address: 16 Chapin Rd., Ste. 904, Pine Brook, NJ 07058 US	

GROWTH PLANS/SPECIAL FEATURES:

Instructivision, Inc. develops supplemental educational software, videotapes and related workbooks for schools and home schooling applications. Though it sells educational products to elementary and high schools throughout the U.S., the company focuses primarily on New Jersey. The firm specializes in test preparation products for college entrance exams and state assessment tests for New Jersey, Connecticut, Louisiana and Florida. It also provides an Interactive Online Test for students to practice their state assessment tests. Instructivision offers products that help students prepare for the SAT, ACT and GED; videos and programs to assist parents who wish to teach their children at home; and products designed to help teachers improve themselves in areas such as creative teaching and classroom discipline. In addition, the company produces educational software and books for other publishers under royalty agreements. These products include the Key It In math workbooks and Math Made Easy video series; a variety of science instructional and teaching skills videos, such as The Frog Inside-Out and Teaching Critical Thinking in Science; the Study Skills for Success computer software; and teacher in-service videos, such as Cults: Saying No Under Pressure (narrated by Charlton Heston), Conducting Effective Conferences with Parents and Boosting Student Motivation. Instructivision owns a video production studio and post-production facility where it creates its products.

FINANCIALS: Sales and profits are in thousands of dollars—add 000 to get the full amount. 2010 Note: Financial information for 2010 was not available for all companies at press time.

2010 Sales: $	2010 Profits: $	U.S. Stock Ticker: ISTC.PK
2009 Sales: $	2009 Profits: $	Int'l Ticker: Int'l Exchange:
2008 Sales: $	2008 Profits: $	Employees:
2007 Sales: $	2007 Profits: $	Fiscal Year Ends: 9/30
2006 Sales: $	2006 Profits: $	Parent Company:

SALARIES/BENEFITS:

Pension Plan:	ESOP Stock Plan:	Profit Sharing:	Top Exec. Salary: $	Bonus: $
Savings Plan:	Stock Purch. Plan:		Second Exec. Salary: $	Bonus: $

OTHER THOUGHTS:

Apparent Women Officers or Directors: 1
Hot Spot for Advancement for Women/Minorities:

LOCATIONS: ("Y" = Yes)

West:	Southwest:	Midwest:	Southeast:	Northeast:	International:
				Y	

INTEL CORP
www.intel.com

Industry Group Code: 33441 Ranks within this company's industry group: Sales: 1 Profits: 1

Hardware:		Software:		Telecommunications:	Electronic Publishing:	Equipment:		Specialty Services:	
Computers:		Consumer:	Y	Local:	Online Service:	Telecom:		Consulting:	
Accessories:	Y	Corporate:	Y	Long Distance:	TV/Cable or Wireless:	Communication:	Y	Contract Manufacturing:	
Network Equipment:	Y	Telecom:		Cellular:	Games:	Distribution:		Processing:	
Chips/Circuits:	Y	Internet:		Internet Service:	Financial Data:	VAR/Reseller:		Staff/Outsourcing:	
Parts/Drives:	Y					Satellite Srv./Equip.:		Specialty Services:	

TYPES OF BUSINESS:

Microprocessors
Semiconductors
Circuit Boards
Flash Memory Products
Software Development
Home Network Equipment
Digital Imaging Products
Healthcare Products

BRANDS/DIVISIONS/AFFILIATES:

Pentium
Dual Core
Numonyx B.V.
SpectraWatt Inc
NetEffect Inc.
UQ Communications
Wind River Systems, Inc.
Intel Research Labs

CONTACTS: *Note: Officers with more than one job title may be intentionally listed here more than once.*

Paul S. Otellini, CEO
Paul S. Otellini, Pres.
Stacy J. Smith, CFO/Sr. VP
Deborah S. Conrad, Chief Mktg. Officer/VP
Patricia Murray, Sr. VP/Dir.-Human Resources
Diane M. Bryant, Co-CIO/VP
Justin R. Rattner, CTO/VP/Dir.-Intel Labs
Robert J. Baker, Sr. VP/Gen. Mgr.-Mfg. & Tech. Group
Andy D. Bryant, Chief Admin. Officer/Exec. VP
A. Douglas Melamed, General Counsel/Sr. VP
Leslie S. Culbertson, VP/Dir.-Finance
John N. Johnson, Co-CIO/VP
Arvind Sodhani, Exec. VP/Pres., Intel Capital
William M. Holt, Sr. VP/Gen. Mgr.-Mfg. & Tech. Group
David Perlmutter, Exec. VP/Gen. Mgr.-Intel Architecture Group
Jane E. Shaw, Chmn.
Brain M. Krzanich, VP/Gen. Mgr.-Supply Chain & Mfg.

Phone: 408-765-8080	**Fax:**
Toll-Free:	
Address: 2200 Mission College Blvd., Santa Clara, CA 95054-1549 US	

GROWTH PLANS/SPECIAL FEATURES:

Intel Corp. is a global semiconductor chip maker that develops advanced integrated digital technology platforms for the computing and communications industries. It operates in nine segments: PC Client Group; Data Center Group; Embedded and Communications Group; Digital Home Group; Ultra-Mobility Group; NAND Solutions Group; Wind River Software Group; Software and Services Group; and Digital Health Group. The PC Client Group provides Intel architecture-based products and platforms for notebooks, netbooks and desktops. The Data Center Group delivers server, storage and workstation platforms. The Embedded Communications Group's products include solutions for applications through long life-cycle support, platform integration and software and architectural scalability. The Digital Home Group provides products for next-generation consumer electronics with interactive Internet content and traditional broadcast programming. The Ultra-Mobility Group offers energy-efficient Intel Atom processors and related chipsets designed for mobile Internet devices (MIDs) within the handheld market segment. The NAND Solutions Group produces flash memory products used in portable memory storage devices, digital camera memory cards and solid-state drives. The Wind River Software Group develops and licenses device software optimization products, including operating systems, for customers in the embedded and handheld market segments. The Software and Services Group promotes Intel architecture as the platform of choice for software applications and operating systems. Lastly, the Digital Health Group offers technology products for healthcare providers and for use in personal healthcare. The PC Client Group accounted for 75% of revenue in 2009; Data Center Group, 18%; Embedded Communications Group, Digital Home Group and Ultra-Mobility Group, 4%; and NAND Solutions Group, Wind River Software Group, Software and Services Group and Digital Health Group, 3%. In August 2010, the company agreed to acquire security-software company, McAfee, Inc. for $7.68 billion.

The firm offers its employees medical and dental coverage; life, AD&D and long-term disability insurance; on-site recreational facilities; an employee assistance program; flexible spending accounts; a stock purchase plan; a profit-sharing plan; a pension plan; and a 401(k) plan.

FINANCIALS: Sales and profits are in thousands of dollars—add 000 to get the full amount. 2010 Note: Financial information for 2010 was not available for all companies at press time.

2010 Sales: $	2010 Profits: $	**U.S. Stock Ticker: INTC**
2009 Sales: $35,127,000	2009 Profits: $4,369,000	**Int'l Ticker:** Int'l Exchange:
2008 Sales: $37,586,000	2008 Profits: $5,292,000	Employees: 79,800
2007 Sales: $38,334,000	2007 Profits: $6,976,000	Fiscal Year Ends: 12/31
2006 Sales: $35,382,000	2006 Profits: $5,044,000	Parent Company:

SALARIES/BENEFITS:

Pension Plan: Y	ESOP Stock Plan:	Profit Sharing: Y	Top Exec. Salary: $1,000,000	Bonus: $5,251,500
Savings Plan: Y	Stock Purch. Plan: Y		Second Exec. Salary: $500,000	Bonus: $1,857,300

OTHER THOUGHTS:

Apparent Women Officers or Directors: 8
Hot Spot for Advancement for Women/Minorities: Y

LOCATIONS: ("Y" = Yes)

West:	Southwest:	Midwest:	Southeast:	Northeast:	International:
Y	Y	Y	Y	Y	Y

INTERACTIVE INTELLIGENCE INC

www.inin.com

Industry Group Code: 33411 Ranks within this company's industry group: Sales: 13   Profits: 9

Hardware:	Software:		Telecommunications:	Electronic Publishing:	Equipment:	Specialty Services:
Computers:	Consumer:		Local:	Online Service:	Telecom:	Consulting:
Accessories:	Corporate:	Y	Long Distance:	TV/Cable or Wireless:	Communication:	Contract Manufacturing:
Network Equipment:	Telecom:		Cellular:	Games:	Distribution:	Processing:
Chips/Circuits:	Internet:		Internet Service:	Financial Data:	VAR/Reseller:	Staff/Outsourcing:
Parts/Drives:					Satellite Srv./Equip.:	Specialty Services:

TYPES OF BUSINESS:

Business Communication Software

BRANDS/DIVISIONS/AFFILIATES:

Global Software Services Inc
Customer Interaction Center
Messaging Interaction Center
Enterprise Interaction Center

CONTACTS: *Note: Officers with more than one job title may be intentionally listed here more than once.*

Donald E. Brown, CEO
Donald E. Brown, Pres.
Stephen R. Head, CFO
Joseph A. Staples, Chief Mktg. Officer
Michael D. Gagle, Chief Scientist
Stephen R. Head, VP-Admin.
Stephen R. Head, Corp. Sec.
William J. Gildea III, VP-Bus. Dev.
Stephen R. Head, VP-Finance/Treas.
Pamela J. Hynes, VP-Customer Service
Hans W. Heltzel, VP-Support & Professional Svcs.
Donald E. Brown, Chmn.
Gary R. Blough, Exec. VP-Worldwide Sales

Phone: 317-872-3000	Fax: 317-872-3000
Toll-Free: 800-267-1364	
Address: 7601 Interactive Way, Indianapolis, IN 46278 US	

GROWTH PLANS/SPECIAL FEATURES:

Interactive Intelligence, Inc. develops software applications for various business communication services. With more than 3,500 customers, the firm's primary markets are contact centers, enterprise IP telephony and enterprise messaging. For contact centers, the firm's products allow clients to intelligently route, monitor, record, track, and report on phone calls, as well as fax, e-mail and web interactions, whether in a single center or across multi-site contact center operations. Contact center applications also allow clients services including predictive dialing, workforce management and screen recording. The company's enterprise IP telephony solutions build off its success with contact center applications. It offers software solutions for various IP telephony applications, including multimedia queuing, mobile access and messaging, targeting enterprises with 100 to 5,000 users, especially those that rely on the Microsoft platform. The business process automation platform allows users to automate and unify phone calls, faxes, e-mails and web interactions. Interactive Intelligence's primary products include the Customer Interaction Center, which serves the contact center and enterprise IP telephony markets; the Enterprise Interaction Center, which serves the enterprise IP telephony market; and the Messaging Interaction Center. In October 2010, the firm acquired Global Software Services, Inc., a developer of debt collection software, for about $14 million.

Employees are offered health insurance; life insurance; disability coverage; flexible spending accounts; health savings accounts; an employee assistance program; tuition reimbursement; and adoption assistance.

FINANCIALS: Sales and profits are in thousands of dollars—add 000 to get the full amount. 2010 Note: Financial information for 2010 was not available for all companies at press time.

2010 Sales: $	2010 Profits: $	U.S. Stock Ticker: ININ
2009 Sales: $131,418	2009 Profits: $8,640	Int'l Ticker: Int'l Exchange:
2008 Sales: $121,406	2008 Profits: $4,338	Employees:
2007 Sales: $109,901	2007 Profits: $17,456	Fiscal Year Ends: 12/31
2006 Sales: $83,044	2006 Profits: $10,248	Parent Company:

SALARIES/BENEFITS:

Pension Plan:	ESOP Stock Plan:	Profit Sharing:	Top Exec. Salary: $350,000	Bonus: $500,107
Savings Plan: Y	Stock Purch. Plan: Y		Second Exec. Salary: $235,000	Bonus: $270,328

OTHER THOUGHTS:

Apparent Women Officers or Directors: 1
Hot Spot for Advancement for Women/Minorities:

LOCATIONS: ("Y" = Yes)

West:	Southwest:	Midwest:	Southeast:	Northeast:	International:
Y		Y		Y	Y

INTERDIGITAL INC

www.interdigital.com

Industry Group Code: 33441 Ranks within this company's industry group: Sales: 44 Profits: 22

Hardware:		Software:		Telecommunications:		Electronic Publishing:	Equipment:		Specialty Services:
Computers:		Consumer:		Local:		Online Service:	Telecom:	Y	Consulting:
Accessories:		Corporate:		Long Distance:		TV/Cable or Wireless:	Communication:		Contract Manufacturing:
Network Equipment:		Telecom:		Cellular:		Games:	Distribution:		Processing:
Chips/Circuits:	Y	Internet:		Internet Service:		Financial Data:	VAR/Reseller:		Staff/Outsourcing:
Parts/Drives:							Satellite Srv./Equip.:		Specialty Services:

TYPES OF BUSINESS:

Microchips-Voice & Data Transmission
Wireless Telephony Equipment
TDMA & CDMA Technology

BRANDS/DIVISIONS/AFFILIATES:

InterDigital Communications Corp
SlimChip
CDMA
TDMA
OFDMA
MIMO
3GPP Long Term Evolution

CONTACTS: Note: Officers with more than one job title may be intentionally listed here more than once.

William J. Merritt, CEO
William J. Merritt, Pres.
Scott A. McQuilkin, CFO
James J. Nolan, Exec. VP-R&D
Naresh Soni, CTO
Gary D. Isaacs, Chief Admin. Officer
Steven W. Sprecher, General Counsel/Corp. Sec.
Mark A. Lemmo, Exec. VP-Corp. Dev.
Janet M. Point, Exec. VP-Comm.
Janet M. Point, Exec. VP-Investor Rel.
Richard J. Brezski, Chief Acct. Officer
Brian G. Kiernan, Exec. VP-Standards
Lawrence F. Shay, Exec. VP-Intellectual Property
Steven T. Clontz, Chmn.

Phone: 610-878-7800	Fax: 610-878-7842
Toll-Free:	
Address: 781 3rd Ave., King of Prussia, PA 19406 US	

GROWTH PLANS/SPECIAL FEATURES:

InterDigital, Inc., formerly InterDigital Communications Corp., designs and develops advanced digital wireless technologies for use in digital cellular and wireless IEEE 802-related products. InterDigital offers licenses to its patents to equipment producers that manufacture, use and sell digital cellular and IEEE 802-related products. In addition, the firm develops solutions for improving bandwidth availability and network capacity; wireless security; and seamless connectivity and mobility across networks and devices. InterDigital primarily generates revenues from royalties received under its patent license agreements. To a lesser extent, the firm also generates revenues by licensing its technology solutions and providing related development support. InterDigital has a long history of developing cellular technologies including those related to code division multiple access (CDMA) and time division multiple access (TDMA), and more recently, orthogonal frequency-division multiple access (OFDMA) and multiple-input and multiple-output (MIMO) technologies. A number of its TDMA-based and CDMA-based inventions are being used in all 2G, 2.5G and 3G wireless networks and mobile terminal devices. InterDigital's patent portfolio consists of 1,242 U.S. patents, of which 187 were issued in 2009, and 5,996 non-U.S. patents, of which 1,048 were issued in 2009. The company is currently focusing its product development efforts on advanced cellular technologies, including 3G wideband code division multiple access (WCDMA) technologies.

Employees are offered short- and long-term cash and equity-based bonus/incentive compensation plans; a profit sharing plan; a 401(k) plan with a company match; medical, dental, vision and prescription insurance; short- and long-term disability insurance; life and AD&D insurance; flexible spending accounts; an employee stock purchase plan; a 529 college savings plan; an employee referral program; a tuition reimbursement and company-sponsored training program; an employee assistance program; and fitness and wellness programs.

FINANCIALS: Sales and profits are in thousands of dollars—add 000 to get the full amount. 2010 Note: Financial information for 2010 was not available for all companies at press time.

2010 Sales: $	2010 Profits: $	**U.S. Stock Ticker: IDCC**
2009 Sales: $297,404	2009 Profits: $87,256	**Int'l Ticker:** Int'l Exchange:
2008 Sales: $228,469	2008 Profits: $26,207	Employees: 299
2007 Sales: $234,232	2007 Profits: $20,004	Fiscal Year Ends: 12/31
2006 Sales: $480,466	2006 Profits: $225,222	Parent Company:

SALARIES/BENEFITS:

Pension Plan:	ESOP Stock Plan:	Profit Sharing: Y	Top Exec. Salary: $500,000	Bonus: $323,438
Savings Plan: Y	Stock Purch. Plan: Y		Second Exec. Salary: $328,900	Bonus: $137,727

OTHER THOUGHTS:

Apparent Women Officers or Directors: 1
Hot Spot for Advancement for Women/Minorities:

LOCATIONS: ("Y" = Yes)

West:	Southwest:	Midwest:	Southeast:	Northeast:	International:
				Y	Y

INTERGRAPH CORP

www.intergraph.com

Industry Group Code: 511210N Ranks within this company's industry group: Sales: 7 Profits: 2

Hardware:		Software:		Telecommunications:	Electronic Publishing:	Equipment:	Specialty Services:	
Computers:	Y	Consumer:		Local:	Online Service:	Telecom:	Consulting:	Y
Accessories:	Y	Corporate:	Y	Long Distance:	TV/Cable or Wireless:	Communication:	Contract Manufacturing:	
Network Equipment:	Y	Telecom:		Cellular:	Games:	Distribution:	Processing:	
Chips/Circuits:		Internet:		Internet Service:	Financial Data:	VAR/Reseller:	Staff/Outsourcing:	
Parts/Drives:						Satellite Srv./Equip.:	Specialty Services:	Y

TYPES OF BUSINESS:

Software-Mapping & Design
Geospatial Products
Servers & Workstations
Public Safety Solutions
Management Consulting
Imaging Software
Supply Chain Solutions
Technical Services

BRANDS/DIVISIONS/AFFILIATES:

Process, Power & Marine (PP&M)
Security, Government & Infrastructure (SG&I)
SmartPlant Enterprise
Marine Enterprise
Hexagon AB

CONTACTS: *Note: Officers with more than one job title may be intentionally listed here more than once.*

Ola Rollen, CEO
Steven Cost, CFO
Ed Porter, Exec. VP-Human Resources
Gerhard Sallinger, Pres., Process, Power & Marine
John K. Graham, Pres., Security, Gov't & Infrastructure

Phone: 256-730-2000	Fax: 256-730-2048
Toll-Free: 800-345-4856	
Address: 19 Interpro Rd., Madison, AL 35758 US	

GROWTH PLANS/SPECIAL FEATURES:

Intergraph Corp. provides mapping and design software and services for government agencies and private businesses in more than 60 countries. Intergraph's products allow customers to acquire, share and reuse design and mapping data over the Internet. The company operates through two business segments: Process, Power & Marine (PP&M) and Security, Government & Infrastructure (SG&I). PP&M provides services for the design, construction and operation of process and power plants, offshore platforms and ships. Intergraph's SmartPlant Enterprise provides a portfolio of applications for 3D modeling and visualization; information management; engineering and schematics; and materials management and project controls. The company's Marine Enterprise suite includes design and assembly; information management; engineering and schematics; and materials planning and procurement solutions. SG&I provides software and integration services for industries such as communications, defense, government, photogrammetry, public safety, transportation and utilities. Its communications business upgrades and installs network infrastructure for telecommunications interests around the world. The defense business provides motion capture software and geospatial intelligence services to government agencies. The company's government business serves information sharing and administration needs. The firm's photogrammetry services provide geospatial data and remote sensing for commercial and government entities, such as the U.S. Geological Survey. Its public safety business provides services for readiness planning; response management; incident investigation and resolution; and video enhancement and analysis. The transportation segment works to ease congestion concerns and maintain infrastructure asset databases. For utility and communications companies, Intergraph enables the use of digital models and diagrams of facilities and infrastructure to better maintain a service delivery network; prevent, detect and respond to outages; and effectively manage mobile workforces. The company also conducts business for the U.S. federal government and classified business through its subsidiary, Intergraph Government Solutions. In October 2010, the firm was acquired by Hexagon AB for $2.1 billion.

FINANCIALS: Sales and profits are in thousands of dollars—add 000 to get the full amount. 2010 Note: Financial information for 2010 was not available for all companies at press time.

2010 Sales: $	2010 Profits: $	U.S. Stock Ticker: Subsidiary
2009 Sales: $770,400	2009 Profits: $188,600	Int'l Ticker: Int'l Exchange:
2008 Sales: $808,400	2008 Profits: $152,100	Employees: 3,978
2007 Sales: $725,300	2007 Profits: $118,500	Fiscal Year Ends: 12/31
2006 Sales: $631,600	2006 Profits: $100,800	Parent Company: HEXAGON AB

SALARIES/BENEFITS:

Pension Plan:	ESOP Stock Plan:	Profit Sharing:	Top Exec. Salary: $	Bonus: $
Savings Plan: Y	Stock Purch. Plan:		Second Exec. Salary: $	Bonus: $

OTHER THOUGHTS:

Apparent Women Officers or Directors:
Hot Spot for Advancement for Women/Minorities:

LOCATIONS: ("Y" = Yes)

West:	Southwest:	Midwest:	Southeast:	Northeast:	International:
Y	Y	Y	Y	Y	Y

INTERMEC INC

www.intermec.com

Industry Group Code: 334119 Ranks within this company's industry group: Sales: 18   Profits: 17

Hardware:		Software:		Telecommunications:		Electronic Publishing:	Equipment:	Specialty Services:
Computers:	Y	Consumer:		Local:	Y	Online Service:	Telecom:	Consulting:
Accessories:	Y	Corporate:	Y	Long Distance:		TV/Cable or Wireless:	Communication:	Contract Manufacturing:
Network Equipment:		Telecom:		Cellular:	Y	Games:	Distribution:	Processing:
Chips/Circuits:		Internet:		Internet Service:		Financial Data:	VAR/Reseller:	Staff/Outsourcing:
Parts/Drives:							Satellite Srv./Equip.:	Specialty Services:

TYPES OF BUSINESS:

Computer Hardware-Bar Code Systems
Supply Chain Software & Services
RFID Products
Software
Mobile Computing Products

BRANDS/DIVISIONS/AFFILIATES:

UNOVA Inc
GATC Inc
Skynax

CONTACTS: Note: Officers with more than one job title may be intentionally listed here more than once.

Patrick J. Byrne, CEO
Patrick J. Byrne, Pres.
Robert J. Driessnack, CFO/Sr. VP
Jim McDonnell, Sr. VP-Global Sales
Jeanne Lyon, VP-Human Resources
Arvin Danielson, CTO
Janis L. Harwell, General Counsel/Sr. VP/Corp. Sec.
Janis L. Harwell, Sr. VP-Corp. Strategy
Earl Thompson, Sr. VP-Mobile Solutions Bus. Unit
Allen J. Lauer, Chmn.
Larry Klimczyk, VP-Intermec Global Solutions
Dennis Faerber, Sr. VP-Global Supply Chain Oper.

Phone: 425-348-2600	Fax: 425-267-2983
Toll-Free: 800-755-5505	
Address: 6001 36th Ave. W., Everett, WA 98203-1264 US	

GROWTH PLANS/SPECIAL FEATURES:

Intermec, Inc., formerly UNOVA, designs, develops, manufactures, integrates, sells, resells and services wired and wireless automated identification and data collection (AIDC) products, including radio frequency identification (RFID) products; mobile computing products; wired and wireless bar code printers; and label media products. The company's products are sold to customers domestically and internationally in market segments including industrial goods, consumer packaged goods, transportation, logistics, retail and the public sector, and in work applications such as manufacturing production, warehousing, field service, direct store delivery, in-transit visibility, store floor operations and RFID supply chain management. Intermec's bar code scanning products include wireless handheld computers and terminals; linear and area imagers incorporating active pixel technology; and badge and laser scanners. These products are able to read or collect data and move that data directly into standard enterprise resource planning systems, warehouse management systems and order fulfillment, transportation, logistics and other business applications. The company also manufactures rugged handheld computers for use in warehouses and industrial environments. The firm's mobile computing products include handheld and vehicle-mounted mobile computers and accessories and related services that facilitate local-area and wide-area wireless and wired data communications. These products typically contain multiple wireless technologies that can operate simultaneously in a mobile computer, allowing customers to communicate remotely with their field employees. Intermec's line of bar code printers ranges from low-cost, light-duty models to higher-cost industrial models that accommodate a number of printing widths, materials and label configurations. The company's RFID product line is focused on passive UHF technology and consists of RFID tags, readers, software and related equipment sold under the Intermec trade name. In October 2010, the firm acquired GATC, a Czech software development company, and its data management software Skynax.

Intermec offers its employees medical, dental and vision coverage; life and AD&D insurance; a 401(k) plan; and more.

FINANCIALS: Sales and profits are in thousands of dollars—add 000 to get the full amount. 2010 Note: Financial information for 2010 was not available for all companies at press time.

2010 Sales: $	2010 Profits: $	**U.S. Stock Ticker: IN**
2009 Sales: $658,205	2009 Profits: $-11,843	**Int'l Ticker:** Int'l Exchange:
2008 Sales: $890,883	2008 Profits: $35,462	Employees:
2007 Sales: $849,200	2007 Profits: $23,100	Fiscal Year Ends: 12/31
2006 Sales: $850,000	2006 Profits: $32,000	Parent Company:

SALARIES/BENEFITS:

Pension Plan:	ESOP Stock Plan:	Profit Sharing:	Top Exec. Salary: $610,731	Bonus: $
Savings Plan: Y	Stock Purch. Plan: Y		Second Exec. Salary: $309,376	Bonus: $

OTHER THOUGHTS:

Apparent Women Officers or Directors: 3
Hot Spot for Advancement for Women/Minorities: Y

LOCATIONS: ("Y" = Yes)

West:	Southwest:	Midwest:	Southeast:	Northeast:	International:
Y	Y	Y	Y	Y	Y

INTERNATIONAL BUSINESS MACHINES CORP (IBM) www.ibm.com

Industry Group Code: 541513 Ranks within this company's industry group: Sales: 1 Profits: 1

Hardware:		Software:		Telecommunications:	Electronic Publishing:	Equipment:		Specialty Services:	
Computers:	Y	Consumer:	Y	Local:	Online Service:	Telecom:	Y	Consulting:	Y
Accessories:	Y	Corporate:	Y	Long Distance:	TV/Cable or Wireless:	Communication:	Y	Contract Manufacturing:	
Network Equipment:	Y	Telecom:	Y	Cellular:	Games:	Distribution:	Y	Processing:	
Chips/Circuits:	Y	Internet:	Y	Internet Service:	Financial Data:	VAR/Reseller:		Staff/Outsourcing:	Y
Parts/Drives:	Y					Satellite Srv./Equip.:		Specialty Services:	Y

TYPES OF BUSINESS:

Computer Hardware
Supercomputers
Microelectronic Technology
Software Development
Networking Systems
IT Consulting & Outsourcing
Financial Services

BRANDS/DIVISIONS/AFFILIATES:

Intelliden, Inc.
Lombardi
Sterling Commerce
BigFix, Inc.
Unica Corporation
Storwize
Netezza Corporation
Datacap

CONTACTS: Note: Officers with more than one job title may be intentionally listed here more than once.

Samuel J. Palmisano, CEO
Samuel J. Palmisano, Pres.
Mark Loughridge, CFO/Sr. VP
Virginia M Rometty, Sr. VP-Mktg. & Sales
J. Randall MacDonald, Sr. VP-Human Resources
John E. Kelly, III, Sr. VP/Dir.-IBM Research
Linda S. Sanford, Sr. VP-IT & Enterprise On Demand Transformation
Robert C. Weber, General Counsel/Sr. VP-Legal & Regulatory Affairs
Virginia M Rometty, Sr. VP-Strategy
Jon C. Iwata, Sr. VP-Comm. & Mktg.
Linda S. Sanford, Sr. VP-IT & Enterprise On Demand Transformation
Michael E. Daniels, Sr. VP-Svcs.
Rodney C. Adkins, Sr. VP-IBM Systems and Tech Group.
Samuel J. Palmisano, Chmn.
R. Frankin Kern, Sr. VP-IBM Global Bus. Svcs.

Phone: 914-499-1900	Fax: 800-314-1092
Toll-Free: 800-426-4968	
Address: 1 New Orchard Rd., Armonk, NY 10504-1722 US	

GROWTH PLANS/SPECIAL FEATURES:

International Business Machines Corp. (IBM) produces computer hardware and software, with one of the largest technology consulting businesses in the world. It operates in five primary segments: global technology services; systems and technology; global business services; software; and global financing. The global technology services segment primarily includes IT infrastructure services and business process services. The systems and technology division provides IBM's clients with business solutions built on advanced computing power and storage capabilities. Offerings include servers and infrastructure storage products; microelectronics for IBM systems and for sale to original equipment manufacturers; and retail store solutions, such as network-connected cash registers to improve point-of-sale operations. The global business services segment primarily reflects professional services and application outsourcing services. Capabilities include consulting, systems integration and application management services. The software segment consists primarily of middleware and operating systems software. Middleware software enables clients to integrate systems, processes and applications across a standard software platform. Offerings include information management software; operating systems; and Tivoli software for infrastructure management, including security and storage management. The global financing division's capabilities include commercial financing, client financing and remarketing. IBM is active in over 170 countries worldwide; major markets include the U.S., Israel, Canada, Greece, Ireland, France, Germany, Italy, the U.K., Japan, Denmark, Sweden, Finland, the Netherlands, Portugal, Cyprus, Norway, Spain, Switzerland, Austria, Belgium, the Bahamas and the Caribbean region. In 2010, the firm acquired several companies, including IT solutions provider National Interest Security Company, LLC; data integrity software firm Initiate Systems, Inc.; cloud integration company Cast Iron Systems; IT infrastructure management provider BigFix, Inc.; former AT&T subsidiary Sterling Commerce; marketing firm Unica Corporation; the assets of Wilshire Credit Corporation; data compression technology firm Storwize; business analytics company Netezza Corporation; Canadian firm Clarity Systems; and software developers Lombardi, Intelliden, Inc., Coremetrics; BLADE Network Technologies, OpenPages, PSS Systems and Datacap.

FINANCIALS: Sales and profits are in thousands of dollars—add 000 to get the full amount. 2010 Note: Financial information for 2010 was not available for all companies at press time.

2010 Sales: $	2010 Profits: $	**U.S. Stock Ticker: IBM**
2009 Sales: $95,758,000	2009 Profits: $13,425,000	**Int'l Ticker:** Int'l Exchange:
2008 Sales: $103,600,000	2008 Profits: $12,300,000	Employees: 399,409
2007 Sales: $98,786,000	2007 Profits: $10,418,000	Fiscal Year Ends: 12/31
2006 Sales: $91,424,000	2006 Profits: $9,492,000	Parent Company:

SALARIES/BENEFITS:

Pension Plan:	ESOP Stock Plan:	Profit Sharing:	Top Exec. Salary: $1,800,000	Bonus: $4,750,000
Savings Plan: Y	Stock Purch. Plan: Y		Second Exec. Salary: $720,000	Bonus: $975,000

OTHER THOUGHTS:

Apparent Women Officers or Directors: 4
Hot Spot for Advancement for Women/Minorities: Y

LOCATIONS: ("Y" = Yes)

West:	Southwest:	Midwest:	Southeast:	Northeast:	International:
Y	Y	Y	Y	Y	Y

Note: Financial information, benefits and other data can change quickly and may vary from those stated here.

INTERNATIONAL RECTIFIER CORP

www.irf.com

Industry Group Code: 33441 Ranks within this company's industry group: Sales: 37 Profits: 48

Hardware:		Software:	Telecommunications:	Electronic Publishing:	Equipment:	Specialty Services:
Computers:		Consumer:	Local:	Online Service:	Telecom:	Consulting:
Accessories:		Corporate:	Long Distance:	TV/Cable or Wireless:	Communication:	Contract Manufacturing:
Network Equipment:		Telecom:	Cellular:	Games:	Distribution:	Processing:
Chips/Circuits:	Y	Internet:	Internet Service:	Financial Data:	VAR/Reseller:	Staff/Outsourcing:
Parts/Drives:					Satellite Srv./Equip.:	Specialty Services:

TYPES OF BUSINESS:

Semiconductors-Power Management
Analog Integrated Circuits
Chipsets

BRANDS/DIVISIONS/AFFILIATES:

DirectFET
DirectFET 2
IRF6708S2 (The)
IR3870M SupIRBuck
IRF6728M 30V (The)
iP2010
iP2011

CONTACTS: Note: Officers with more than one job title may be intentionally listed here more than once.

Oleg Khaykin, CEO
Michael Barrow, COO
Oleg Khaykin, Pres.
Ilan Daskal, CFO
Adam White, Sr. VP-Worldwide Sales
Henning Hauenstein, VP-Automotive Prod.
Jun Honda, Mgr.-Systems Eng., Energy Saving Prod. Bus. Unit
Timothy E. Bixler, General Counsel/VP/Sec.
David Jacquinod, Mgr.-Prod Mktg., Automotive Bus. Unit
Richard J. Dahl, Chmn.

Phone: 310-726-8000	Fax: 310-322-3332
Toll-Free:	
Address: 101 N. Sepulveda Blvd., El Segundo, CA 90245 US	

GROWTH PLANS/SPECIAL FEATURES:

International Rectifier Corp. is a designer, manufacturer and marketer of power management semiconductors. Its semiconductors address the core challenges of power management, power performance and power conservation by increasing system efficiency, allowing more compact end-products, improving features on electronic devices and prolonging battery life. Major products sold by the company include high-voltage integrated circuits (HVICs); low voltage analog and mixed signal integrated circuits (LVICs); metal oxide semiconductor field effect transistors (MOSFETs); digital integrated circuits (ICs); radiation-resistant power MOSFETs (RAD-Hard); insulated gate bipolar transistors (IGBTs); high-reliability DC-DC converters; power stage modules; and DC-DC converter type applications. Its products are used in a variety of applications, including telecommunications, automotive, industrial motors, consumer electronics, personal computers, household appliances, game consoles and networking applications. The company operates in six business segments: Power Management Devices, focusing on power supply, data processing and industrial and commercial battery-powered applications; Energy-Savings Products, focusing on energy-saving products such as variable-speed motion controls and advanced lighting products, as well as consumer applications such as plasma televisions; HiREL, focusing on high-reliability components for such applications as satellites, aircraft and submarines; Enterprise Power, focused on data center applications, notebooks, graphics cards and gaming consoles; Automotive Products, focused on products for use in automotive applications; and Intellectual Properties, focused on managing the firm's intellectual properties and technologies. The company has operations in 12 countries, including wafer fabrication and assembly facilities in California, Arizona, Minnesota, Massachusetts, Mexico, and Wales. In 2010, International Rectifier released several new products, including the IR3870M SupIRBuck integrated voltage regulator for general consumer electronics and point-of-load DC-DC converters; the AUIRF7739L2 and AUIRF7665S2 automotive DirectFET 2 power MOSFETs for the automotive industry; iP2010 and iP2011, Gallium Nitride-based power devices for multiphase and point-of-load applications; and the IRF6708S2 and IRF6728M 30V DirectFET MOSFET chipset for 19-volt input synchronous buck use.

FINANCIALS: Sales and profits are in thousands of dollars—add 000 to get the full amount. 2010 Note: Financial information for 2010 was not available for all companies at press time.

2010 Sales: $895,297	2010 Profits: $80,827	U.S. Stock Ticker: IRF
2009 Sales: $740,419	2009 Profits: $-247,417	Int'l Ticker: Int'l Exchange:
2008 Sales: $984,830	2008 Profits: $-62,642	Employees: 4,534
2007 Sales: $1,202,469	2007 Profits: $77,742	Fiscal Year Ends: 6/30
2006 Sales: $1,014,800	2006 Profits: $36,510	Parent Company:

SALARIES/BENEFITS:

Pension Plan:	ESOP Stock Plan:	Profit Sharing:	Top Exec. Salary: $750,000	Bonus: $
Savings Plan: Y	Stock Purch. Plan: Y		Second Exec. Salary: $350,000	Bonus: $

OTHER THOUGHTS:

Apparent Women Officers or Directors: 2
Hot Spot for Advancement for Women/Minorities:

LOCATIONS: ("Y" = Yes)

West:	Southwest:	Midwest:	Southeast:	Northeast:	International:
Y	Y	Y		Y	Y

Note: Financial information, benefits and other data can change quickly and may vary from those stated here.

INTERNET SECURITY SYSTEMS INC

www.iss.net

Industry Group Code: 511210E Ranks within this company's industry group: Sales: Profits:

Hardware:	Software:		Telecommunications:	Electronic Publishing:	Equipment:	Specialty Services:	
Computers:	Consumer:		Local:	Online Service:	Telecom:	Consulting:	Y
Accessories:	Corporate:	Y	Long Distance:	TV/Cable or Wireless:	Communication:	Contract Manufacturing:	
Network Equipment:	Telecom:		Cellular:	Games:	Distribution:	Processing:	
Chips/Circuits:	Internet:		Internet Service:	Financial Data:	VAR/Reseller:	Staff/Outsourcing:	
Parts/Drives:					Satellite Srv./Equip.:	Specialty Services:	Y

TYPES OF BUSINESS:

Software-Network Security
Outsourced Security Management Services
Consulting, Training & Research Services

BRANDS/DIVISIONS/AFFILIATES:

ISS Professional Security Services
International Business Machines Corp (IBM)
IBM X-Force

CONTACTS: Note: Officers with more than one job title may be intentionally listed here more than once.

Brian Truskowski, Gen. Mgr.
Samuel J. Palmisano, Chmn./CEO/Pres., IBM
Michael E. Daniels, Sr. VP-Global Tech. Svcs., IBM

Phone: 404-236-2600	Fax: 404-236-2626
Toll-Free: 800-536-7080	
Address: 6303 Barfield Rd., Atlanta, GA 30328 US	

GROWTH PLANS/SPECIAL FEATURES:

Internet Security Systems, Inc. (ISS), a business unit of IBM, manufactures security and information protection hardware and software. The firm's products provide preemptive protection for all levels of the IT infrastructure, including networks, servers and endpoint devices such as PCs and laptops. The company's software incorporates security technologies including intrusion prevention and detection systems; security management; desktop and server protection systems; Unified Threat Management (UTM) appliances; e-mail security; web content filtering; vulnerability management; and data security. The firm's security management solutions include managed security services, professional security services, medium-business security solutions, Payment Card Industry (PCI) compliance solutions and virtualization security solutions. ISS divides its solutions into two categories: consulting security services and managed security services. Consulting services, comprised of the ISS Professional Security Services suite, provides comprehensive, enterprise-wide security assessment, design and deployment services in the areas of security governance, privacy, threat mitigation, data security, identity and access management and education and training. Managed security services provide 24-hour information security services at a lower cost than maintaining in-house security resources. ISS also maintains a research and development team, IBM X-Force, which tests software vulnerabilities and studies viruses and other malware, exploits and active attacks, spam, phishing and malicious web content. Customers typically include companies in the banking, government, healthcare, retail and telecommunications industries.

ISS offers its employees benefits including medical, dental and vision coverage and group life insurance.

FINANCIALS: Sales and profits are in thousands of dollars—add 000 to get the full amount. 2010 Note: Financial information for 2010 was not available for all companies at press time.

2010 Sales: $	2010 Profits: $	U.S. Stock Ticker: Subsidiary
2009 Sales: $	2009 Profits: $	Int'l Ticker: Int'l Exchange:
2008 Sales: $	2008 Profits: $	Employees:
2007 Sales: $	2007 Profits: $	Fiscal Year Ends: 12/31
2006 Sales: $	2006 Profits: $	Parent Company: INTERNATIONAL BUSINESS MACHINES CORP (IBM)

SALARIES/BENEFITS:

Pension Plan:	ESOP Stock Plan:	Profit Sharing:	Top Exec. Salary: $	Bonus: $
Savings Plan: Y	Stock Purch. Plan: Y		Second Exec. Salary: $	Bonus: $

OTHER THOUGHTS:

Apparent Women Officers or Directors:
Hot Spot for Advancement for Women/Minorities:

LOCATIONS: ("Y" = Yes)

West:	Southwest:	Midwest:	Southeast: Y	Northeast:	International:

INTUIT INC

www.intuit.com

Industry Group Code: 511201 **Ranks within this company's industry group:** Sales: 2 Profits: 1

Hardware:	Software:		Telecommunications:	Electronic Publishing:		Equipment:	Specialty Services:
Computers:	Consumer:	Y	Local:	Online Service:	Y	Telecom:	Consulting:
Accessories:	Corporate:	Y	Long Distance:	TV/Cable or Wireless:		Communication:	Contract Manufacturing:
Network Equipment:	Telecom:		Cellular:	Games:		Distribution:	Processing:
Chips/Circuits:	Internet:		Internet Service:	Financial Data:		VAR/Reseller:	Staff/Outsourcing:
Parts/Drives:						Satellite Srv./Equip.:	Specialty Services:

TYPES OF BUSINESS:

Computer Software-Financial Management
Business Accounting Software
Consumer Finance Software
Tax Preparation Software
Online Financial Services

BRANDS/DIVISIONS/AFFILIATES:

QuickBooks
Intuit Health
Medfusion
Quicken
LaCerte
Intuit Real Estate Solutions
TurboTax
Mint.com

CONTACTS: *Note: Officers with more than one job title may be intentionally listed here more than once.*

Brad D. Smith, CEO
Brad D. Smith, Pres.
R. Neil Williams, CFO/Sr. VP
Caroline Donahue, Sr. VP-Sales & Channel Mktg.
Sherry Whiteley, Chief Human Resources Officer/Sr. VP
Ginny T. Lee, CIO/Sr. VP
Tayloe Stansbury, CTO/Sr. VP
Laura A. Fennell, General Counsel/Sr. VP/Corp. Sec.
Kris Halvorsen, Chief Innovation Officer/Sr. VP
Harry Pforzheimer, Chief Comm. Officer
Scott D. Cook, Chmn.-Exec. Committee
Nora Denzel, Sr. VP/Gen. Mgr.-Employee Mgmt. Solutions
Kiran Patel, Exec. VP/Gen. Mgr.-Small Bus. Group
Sasan Goodarzi, Pres., Intuit Financial Services
Bill Campbell, Chmn.
Alexander M. Lintner, Pres., Global Bus. Div.

Phone: 650-944-6000	Fax: 650-944-3699
Toll-Free: 800-446-8848	
Address: 2632 Marine Way, Mountain View, CA 94043 US	

GROWTH PLANS/SPECIAL FEATURES:

Intuit, Inc. is a provider of software and web-based services. The firm specializes in providing financial management and tax solutions to consumers; small and medium-sized businesses; financial institutions; and accounting professionals. The company has four business segments: Small Business Group; Tax; Accounting Professionals; Financial Services; Other Businesses. The Small Business Group includes three smaller divisions: Financial Management Solutions, Employee Management Solutions and Payment Solutions. Financial Management Solutions includes QuickBooks financial and business management software and services, technical support, financial supplies, as well as Intuit Websites, which provides website design and hosting services for small and medium-sized businesses. The Employee Management Solutions division provides payroll products and services for small businesses. Payment Solutions offers merchant services for small businesses, including credit and debit card processing, electronic check conversion and automated clearing house services. The Tax segment operates in two divisions: Consumer Tax, which includes TurboTax income tax preparation products and services for consumers and small businesses; and the Accounting Professionals division, which includes LaCerte and ProSeries professional tax products and services. The Financial Services segment consists of outsourced online services for banks and credit unions provided by Intuit Financial Services Business. Other Businesses includes Quicken personal finance products and services; Mint.com online personal finance services; Intuit Health online patient-to-provider communication solutions; and the company's businesses in Canada and the UK. In January 2010, the company sold Intuit Real Estate Solutions to Vista Equity Partners for approximately $128 million. In May 2010, Intuit acquired Medfusion, a North Carolina based patient-to-provider communications company, for approximately $91 million. In July 2010, the firm combined Medfusion with its Quicken Health Group to form a new business unit called Intuit Health.

FINANCIALS: Sales and profits are in thousands of dollars—add 000 to get the full amount. 2010 Note: Financial information for 2010 was not available for all companies at press time.

2010 Sales: $3,455,000	2010 Profits: $574,000	**U.S. Stock Ticker:** INTU
2009 Sales: $3,109,000	2009 Profits: $447,000	**Int'l Ticker:** Int'l Exchange:
2008 Sales: $2,993,000	2008 Profits: $476,762	Employees: 7,700
2007 Sales: $2,672,947	2007 Profits: $440,003	Fiscal Year Ends: 7/31
2006 Sales: $2,293,010	2006 Profits: $416,963	Parent Company:

SALARIES/BENEFITS:

Pension Plan:	ESOP Stock Plan:	Profit Sharing:	Top Exec. Salary: $800,000	Bonus: $1,428,000
Savings Plan: Y	Stock Purch. Plan: Y		Second Exec. Salary: $700,000	Bonus: $1,025,000

OTHER THOUGHTS:

Apparent Women Officers or Directors: 5
Hot Spot for Advancement for Women/Minorities: Y

LOCATIONS: ("Y" = Yes)

West:	Southwest:	Midwest:	Southeast:	Northeast:	International:
Y	Y	Y	Y	Y	Y

INVENTEC CORPORATION

www.inventec.com

Industry Group Code: 334419 Ranks within this company's industry group: Sales: 5 Profits: 6

Hardware:		Software:		Telecommunications:		Electronic Publishing:		Equipment:		Specialty Services:	
Computers:	Y	Consumer:		Local:		Online Service:		Telecom:		Consulting:	
Accessories:	Y	Corporate:		Long Distance:		TV/Cable or Wireless:		Communication:	Y	Contract Manufacturing:	Y
Network Equipment:	Y	Telecom:		Cellular:		Games:		Distribution:		Processing:	
Chips/Circuits:		Internet:		Internet Service:		Financial Data:		VAR/Reseller:		Staff/Outsourcing:	
Parts/Drives:								Satellite Srv./Equip.:		Specialty Services:	

TYPES OF BUSINESS:

Contract Electronics Manufacturing
Computers, Notebooks & Servers
Portable Electronics
Storage Devices
Software Products
Communications Products
Digital Home Products
Original Design Manufacturing (ODM)

BRANDS/DIVISIONS/AFFILIATES:

Inventec Appliances Corporation
Inventec Multimedia & Telecom Corporation
Inventec Besta Co., Ltd.
Inventec Micro-Electronics Corporation

CONTACTS: Note: Officers with more than one job title may be intentionally listed here more than once.

C.S. Chuang, Sr. Managing Dir.
Alexander Hsu, VP-Finance
Wang Chih-Cheng, Gen. Mgr.-Bus. Div.
Hanzhong Yang, Deputy Gen. Mgr.
Chao Chen, Exec. Deputy Gen. Mgr.
Shizhi Wen, Sr. Deputy Gen. Mgr.
Li Shiqin, Chmn.

Phone: 886-2-2881-0721	Fax: 886-2-2882-3605
Toll-Free:	
Address: 66 Hou-Kang St., Shin-Lin District, Taipei, 111 Taiwan	

GROWTH PLANS/SPECIAL FEATURES:

Inventec Corporation is a holding company that provides contract manufacturing services through four main subsidiaries: Inventec Appliances Corporation; Inventec Multimedia & Telecom Corporation; Inventec Besta Co., Ltd.; and Inventec Micro-Electronics Corporation. The company provides services primarily through its role as an original design manufacturer (ODM), in which it designs and produces products that are eventually sold under other company's brand names. Inventec's services can be divided into four primary categories: personal computing; software and services; mobile communications; and enterprise solutions. Personal computing products include portable notebook computers and mini-notebooks, mainstream consumer notebooks and multimedia and gaming notebooks offering larger screens, higher memory capacities and faster processing speeds. The software and services segment is largely focused on developing enhanced software applications for use in the firm's general portfolio of products, with most of its manpower devoted to research and development activities. This segment also produces dictionary and translation software, for both computers and mobile devices, marketed under the Dr. Eye brand name. The mobile communications segment focuses on expanding applications for communications technology, exploring new combined-use devices such as portable computers combined with the features of mobile phones to deliver single devices with broad applications across data, voice, text and video. This segment also manufactures smartphones, personal digital assistants (PDAs) and other mobile devices, as well as data cards for computers and mobile phones. The enterprise solutions segment offers products such as general and blade servers, large-scale memory storage devices and server management software. In March 2010, the company opened a computer manufacturing plant in Chongqing, China. Also in March 2010, the company unveiled its new mobile cargo data center, which is designed to take up to 20% less space then traditional servers.

Inventec offers its employees health insurance; travel insurance; and an educational allowances for employees and their children.

FINANCIALS: Sales and profits are in thousands of dollars—add 000 to get the full amount. 2010 Note: Financial information for 2010 was not available for all companies at press time.

2010 Sales: $	2010 Profits: $	**U.S. Stock Ticker:**
2009 Sales: $13,788,700	2009 Profits: $142,920	**Int'l Ticker: 2356** Int'l Exchange: Taipei-TPE
2008 Sales: $11,748,600	2008 Profits: $165,310	Employees:
2007 Sales: $7,247,370	2007 Profits: $170,880	Fiscal Year Ends: 9/30
2006 Sales: $7,152,030	2006 Profits: $170,890	Parent Company:

SALARIES/BENEFITS:

Pension Plan:	ESOP Stock Plan:	Profit Sharing:	Top Exec. Salary: $	Bonus: $
Savings Plan:	Stock Purch. Plan:		Second Exec. Salary: $	Bonus: $

OTHER THOUGHTS:

Apparent Women Officers or Directors:
Hot Spot for Advancement for Women/Minorities:

LOCATIONS: ("Y" = Yes)

West:	Southwest:	Midwest:	Southeast:	Northeast:	International:
Y	Y				Y

Note: Financial information, benefits and other data can change quickly and may vary from those stated here.

IOMEGA CORP
www.iomega.com

Industry Group Code: 334112 Ranks within this company's industry group: Sales: Profits:

Hardware:		Software:		Telecommunications:	Electronic Publishing:		Equipment:	Specialty Services:
Computers:		Consumer:		Local:	Online Service:	Y	Telecom:	Consulting:
Accessories:	Y	Corporate:	Y	Long Distance:	TV/Cable or Wireless:		Communication:	Contract Manufacturing:
Network Equipment:		Telecom:		Cellular:	Games:		Distribution:	Processing:
Chips/Circuits:		Internet:		Internet Service:	Financial Data:		VAR/Reseller:	Staff/Outsourcing:
Parts/Drives:	Y						Satellite Srv./Equip.:	Specialty Services:

TYPES OF BUSINESS:
Computer Storage Equipment-Disk Drives
Hard Drives
Zip Drives
Optical Drives
Data Storage Software
Online Storage Services

BRANDS/DIVISIONS/AFFILIATES:
EMC Retrospect 8.1
Iomega StorCenter
Iomega ScreenPlay
Iomega Micro Mini
iStorage Online
Iomega iConnect Wireless Data Station
REV drive
Iomega eGo Portable Hard Drive

CONTACTS: Note: Officers with more than one job title may be intentionally listed here more than once.
Peter Wharton, VP-Mktg.
Erny-Jay Mezas, VP-Americas Sales
Rajeev Mukul, VP-APAC & Japan Sales
John Palmer, VP-Enterprise Sales
Joseph M. Tucci, CEO/Pres., EMC Corp.
Joseph M. Tucci, Chmn.
Jan Jensen, VP-EMEA Sales

Phone: 858-314-7000	Fax: 858-314-7001
Toll-Free: 888-446-6342	
Address: 3721 Valley Ctr. Dr., Ste. 200, San Diego, CA 92130 US	

GROWTH PLANS/SPECIAL FEATURES:
Iomega Corp., a wholly-owned subsidiary of EMC Corp., designs, manufactures and markets removable data storage devices for home and office computers. The company's products are organized into three business categories: consumer products, business products and other products. The firm's consumer products line includes Zip drives, Iomega desktop hard disk drives (HDD), Iomega ScreenPlay multimedia drives and TV link, eGo and Super eGo portable hard drives, Iomega CD-RW drives, Iomega DVD-RW drives, Iomega REV 120GB Backup Drive, Iomega Media Xporter Drive, MiniMax HDD drives, Micro Mini USB flash drives and Iomega Floppy USB. Business products include REV drives; Iomega StorCenter network hard drives; REV-based Autoloader, which has one REV drive and holds 10 REV disks; Iomega Network Attached Storage (NAS) servers; OfficeScreen Managed Firewall and SSL virtual private network (VPN) Services; iStorage offsite remote storage; and aftermarket service plans. The other products category consists of license and patent fee income and products that have been discontinued or are otherwise immaterial, including Jaz disks and Iomega software products such as Iomega Automatic Backup. Iomega's products can be purchased as aftermarket products for PCs or as built-in features of PCs. In 2009, the firm introduced several new products including the Iomega iConnect Wireless Data Station; Iomega v.Clone software; Iomega StorCenter Pro ix4-100 and Pro ix4-200r NAS Rackmount Server; Iomega eGo Portable Hard Drive; and EMC Retrospect 8.1. In 2010, the firm introduced several new products including Iomega Skin, three uniquely designed and colored 500GB portable hard drives; and the StorCenter ix12-300r Network Storage, a rackmount storage device.

FINANCIALS: Sales and profits are in thousands of dollars—add 000 to get the full amount. 2010 Note: Financial information for 2010 was not available for all companies at press time.

2010 Sales: $	2010 Profits: $	U.S. Stock Ticker: Subsidiary
2009 Sales: $	2009 Profits: $	Int'l Ticker: Int'l Exchange:
2008 Sales: $	2008 Profits: $	Employees:
2007 Sales: $336,614	2007 Profits: $10,055	Fiscal Year Ends: 10/31
2006 Sales: $229,554	2006 Profits: $-8,843	Parent Company: EMC CORP

SALARIES/BENEFITS:

Pension Plan:	ESOP Stock Plan:	Profit Sharing:	Top Exec. Salary: $	Bonus: $
Savings Plan:	Stock Purch. Plan:		Second Exec. Salary: $	Bonus: $

OTHER THOUGHTS:
Apparent Women Officers or Directors: 1
Hot Spot for Advancement for Women/Minorities:

LOCATIONS: ("Y" = Yes)

West:	Southwest:	Midwest:	Southeast:	Northeast:	International:
Y					Y

ISILON SYSTEMS INC

www.isilon.com

Industry Group Code: 334112 Ranks within this company's industry group: Sales: 12   Profits: 8

Hardware:		Software:		Telecommunications:	Electronic Publishing:	Equipment:	Specialty Services:
Computers:	Y	Consumer:		Local:	Online Service:	Telecom:	Consulting:
Accessories:	Y	Corporate:	Y	Long Distance:	TV/Cable or Wireless:	Communication:	Contract Manufacturing:
Network Equipment:		Telecom:		Cellular:	Games:	Distribution:	Processing:
Chips/Circuits:	Y	Internet:		Internet Service:	Financial Data:	VAR/Reseller:	Staff/Outsourcing:
Parts/Drives:	Y					Satellite Srv./Equip.:	Specialty Services:

TYPES OF BUSINESS:
Clustered Storage Systems

BRANDS/DIVISIONS/AFFILIATES:
Isilon IQ
OneFS
Isilon IQ Accelerator
Isilon EX 6000
SyncIQ
SmartConnect
SnapshotIQ
SmartQuotas

CONTACTS: Note: Officers with more than one job title may be intentionally listed here more than once.
Sujal M. Patel, Pres.
Bill Richter, CFO
Eric Broderson, Sr. VP-Mktg.
Gwen E. Weld, VP-Human Resources & Organizational Dev.
Paul Rutherford, CTO
Brett Helsel, Sr. VP-Eng.
Keenan M. Conder, General Counsel/VP/Corp. Sec.
Mary Godwin, VP-Oper.
Eric Broderson, Sr. VP-Bus. Dev.
Bill Richter, VP-Finance
George Bennett, Sr. VP-Worldwide Field Oper.

Phone: 206-315-7602	Fax: 206-315-7501
Toll-Free: 877-247-4566	
Address: 3101 West Ave., Seattle, WA 98121 US	

GROWTH PLANS/SPECIAL FEATURES:
Isilon Systems, Inc., a subsidiary of EMC Corporation, is a provider of scale-out network attached storage (NAS) systems for digital content. The company's Isilon IQ storage systems comprise three or more nodes, each of which is a self-contained, rack-mountable device that contains industry standard hardware including disk drives, a central processing unit (CPU), memory chips and network interfaces. Isilon IQ is integrated with its proprietary OneFS operating system software, which unifies a cluster of nodes into a single shared resource. OneFS combines the three distinct layers of traditional storage architecture, which consist of a file system, a volume manager and a redundant array of independent disks (RAID), into a single unified software layer. Consequently, Isilon IQ nodes automatically work together to aggregate their collective computing power into a single, unified storage system that is designed to withstand the failure of any piece of hardware, including disks, switches or even entire nodes. The company's Isilon IQ Accelerator-x and Isilon EX 6000, EX 9000 and EX 12000 platform extension nodes optimize system performance. Isilon Systems also carries four related software applications that extend the capabilities and functionality of its systems: SyncIQ replication software; SmartQuotas provisioning and management software; SmartConnect load-balancing software; and SnapshotIQ protection software. The company has sold its clustered storage systems to over 1,200 customers across a wide range of industries. The firm sells its products both directly through its field sales force and indirectly through a channel partner program that includes over 210 resellers and distributors. In December 2010, Isilon was acquired by EMC Corporation, a provider of information infrastructure solutions.

FINANCIALS: Sales and profits are in thousands of dollars—add 000 to get the full amount. 2010 Note: Financial information for 2010 was not available for all companies at press time.

2010 Sales: $	2010 Profits: $	U.S. Stock Ticker: Subsidiary
2009 Sales: $123,911	2009 Profits: $-18,873	Int'l Ticker: Int'l Exchange:
2008 Sales: $114,422	2008 Profits: $-25,078	Employees:
2007 Sales: $88,998	2007 Profits: $-26,932	Fiscal Year Ends: 12/31
2006 Sales: $61,206	2006 Profits: $-25,988	Parent Company: EMC CORPORATION

SALARIES/BENEFITS:

Pension Plan:	ESOP Stock Plan:	Profit Sharing:	Top Exec. Salary: $250,865	Bonus: $160,161
Savings Plan:	Stock Purch. Plan:		Second Exec. Salary: $230,796	Bonus: $120,121

OTHER THOUGHTS:
Apparent Women Officers or Directors: 2
Hot Spot for Advancement for Women/Minorities:

LOCATIONS: ("Y" = Yes)

West:	Southwest:	Midwest:	Southeast:	Northeast:	International:
Y					Y

ITAUTEC SA

www.itautec.com.br

Industry Group Code: 541513 **Ranks within this company's industry group:** Sales: Profits:

Hardware:		Software:		Telecommunications:	Electronic Publishing:	Equipment:		Specialty Services:	
Computers:	Y	Consumer:	Y	Local:	Online Service:	Telecom:		Consulting:	
Accessories:		Corporate:	Y	Long Distance:	TV/Cable or Wireless:	Communication:		Contract Manufacturing:	
Network Equipment:		Telecom:		Cellular:	Games:	Distribution:	Y	Processing:	
Chips/Circuits:		Internet:		Internet Service:	Financial Data:	VAR/Reseller:	Y	Staff/Outsourcing:	
Parts/Drives:						Satellite Srv./Equip.:		Specialty Services:	

TYPES OF BUSINESS:

Information Technology

BRANDS/DIVISIONS/AFFILIATES:

InfoWay SM3322
InfoWay ST4254
InfoWay ST4262
InfoWay 3D
InfoWay Note W7415
InfoWay Note N8645
InfoWay Net W7020
Grupo Itausa - Investimentos Itau S.A.

CONTACTS: *Note: Officers with more than one job title may be intentionally listed here more than once.*

Mario Anseloni, CEO
Joao Batista Ribeiro, CFO/Exec. VP
Wilton R. da Silva, Exec. VP-Dev.
Denise Duarte Damiani, Exec. VP-Strategic & New Bus.
Mario Anseloni, Dir.-Investor Rel.
Jose Roberto Ferraz de Campos, Exec. VP
Claudio V. Filho, Exec. VP
Silvio Roberto Direito Passos, Exec. VP
Ricardo E. Setubal, Chmn.

Phone: 55-11-3543-3511 **Fax:** 55-11-3543-3509
Toll-Free:
Address: 2028 Paulista Ave., Sao Paulo, SP 01310-942 Brazil

GROWTH PLANS/SPECIAL FEATURES:

Itautec S.A. is a Brazilian firm that specializes in information technology (IT) products and services. The company is part of investment firm Grupo Itausa - Investimentos Itau S.A. Itautec's products include home products, such as desktops, laptops and netbooks; and products designed for businesses. Its desktop portfolio contains systems like the InfoWay SM3322, an entry-level system; the InfoWay ST4254, which has upgraded memory for enhanced video playback performance; the InfoWay ST4262, which specializes in media playback; and the InfoWay 3D, which was developed in partnership with NVIDIA to offer a three-dimensional experience. The firm's laptops include the InfoWay Note W7415 entry-level system, and the InfoWay Note N8645, which is upgraded for gaming. The company's netbook, the InfoWay Net W7020, is designed to offer both portability and functionality. Itautec's business products include computers, such as desktops, workstations, laptops, netbooks and servers; banking products, such as automatic teller machines (ATMs); retail machines, such as cashier touch screens, printers, cash registers, bar code readers and management software; self service products, including self checkout machines; management tools, such as payment, web access and security programs; and additional software, such as the Linux operating system. The company also offers outsourcing, logistics, training, technical support and customer service functions. Itautec operates internationally through subsidiaries in the U.S., Argentina, Mexico, Portugal and Spain. In Brazil, the firm operates a manufacturing facility and 37 offices.

FINANCIALS: Sales and profits are in thousands of dollars—add 000 to get the full amount. 2010 Note: Financial information for 2010 was not available for all companies at press time.

2010 Sales: $	2010 Profits: $	**U.S. Stock Ticker: Subsidiary**
2009 Sales: $	2009 Profits: $	**Int'l Ticker: ITEC3** Int'l Exchange: Sao Paulo-SAO
2008 Sales: $	2008 Profits: $	Employees:
2007 Sales: $	2007 Profits: $	Fiscal Year Ends: 12/31
2006 Sales: $	2006 Profits: $	Parent Company: ITAUSA INVESTIMENTOS ITAU SA

SALARIES/BENEFITS:

Pension Plan:	ESOP Stock Plan:	Profit Sharing:	Top Exec. Salary: $	Bonus: $
Savings Plan:	Stock Purch. Plan:		Second Exec. Salary: $	Bonus: $

OTHER THOUGHTS:

Apparent Women Officers or Directors:
Hot Spot for Advancement for Women/Minorities:

LOCATIONS: ("Y" = Yes)

West:	Southwest:	Midwest:	Southeast:	Northeast:	International:
			Y		Y

ITI LIMITED

www.itiltd-india.com

Industry Group Code: 334210   Ranks within this company's industry group: Sales: 13   Profits: 9

Hardware:	Software:	Telecommunications:	Electronic Publishing:	Equipment:		Specialty Services:	
Computers:	Consumer:	Local:	Online Service:	Telecom:	Y	Consulting:	
Accessories:	Corporate:	Long Distance:	TV/Cable or Wireless:	Communication:		Contract Manufacturing:	Y
Network Equipment:	Telecom:	Cellular:	Games:	Distribution:		Processing:	
Chips/Circuits:	Internet:	Internet Service:	Financial Data:	VAR/Reseller:		Staff/Outsourcing:	
Parts/Drives:				Satellite Srv./Equip.:		Specialty Services:	Y

TYPES OF BUSINESS:

Telecommunications Equipment Manufacturing
Telecommunications Infrastructure
Telecommunications Switching
Phone Call Transmission

BRANDS/DIVISIONS/AFFILIATES:

Center for Development of Telemetics

CONTACTS:
Note: Officers with more than one job title may be intentionally listed here more than once.

K.L. Dhingra, Managing Dir.
B.P. Gupta, Dir.-Finance
R.K. Agarwal, Dir.-Mktg.
K.K. Khurana, Dir.-Human Resources
Rachana Choudhary, Corp. Sec.
K.K. Gupta, Dir.-Prod.
K.L. Dhingra, Chmn.

Phone: 91-80-2561-4466	Fax: 91-80-2561-7525
Toll-Free:	
Address: ITI Bhavan, Dooravaninagar, Bangalore, 560 016 India	

GROWTH PLANS/SPECIAL FEATURES:

ITI Limited is an India-based telecommunications company and a wing of the Indian Government's Department of Telecommunications. The company offers a complete range of telecom products and services covering the spectrum of switching, transmission, access and subscriber premises equipment. ITI manufactures its mobile infrastructure equipment based on GSM (Global System for Mobile) technology. The firm also manufactures switching, transmission, broadband equipment, customer premises equipment, IT and convergence equipment, power plant, network management systems, SIM cards, banking automation equipment and non-conventional energy system products. ITI has a dedicated network systems business unit for carrying out network planning, engineering, implementation and maintenance services, as well as consultancy services. The company also carries out in-house research and development activities focused on specialized areas of encryption, network management, satellite, wireless, system engineering and IT and access products to provide customized solutions to the firm's various customers. ITI has manufacturing facilities in Bangalore, Naini, Rae Bareli, Mankapur, Palakkad and Srinagar. The company has regional offices in New Delhi, Bangalore, Kolkata, Lucknow, Mumbai, Chennai, Hyderabad, Bhubaneshwar, Bhopal, Ahmadabad and Kochi, and these locations are further supported by 36 area offices located throughout India. ITI has been involved recently in the construction of the Army Static Switched Communication Network (ASCON), a strategic communication network supporting the Indian Army. In December 2010, the company signed an agreement with the Center for Development of Telemetics, the other wing of the Department of Telecommunications, concerning C-DoT Gigabit Passive Optical Network products.

FINANCIALS: Sales and profits are in thousands of dollars—add 000 to get the full amount. 2010 Note: Financial information for 2010 was not available for all companies at press time.

2010 Sales: $998,940	2010 Profits: $-99,680	**U.S. Stock Ticker:**
2009 Sales: $371,130	2009 Profits: $-145,800	**Int'l Ticker: 523610** Int'l Exchange: Bombay-BSE
2008 Sales: $251,490	2008 Profits: $-78,200	Employees: 11,737
2007 Sales: $384,620	2007 Profits: $-88,430	Fiscal Year Ends: 3/31
2006 Sales: $	2006 Profits: $	Parent Company:

SALARIES/BENEFITS:

Pension Plan:	ESOP Stock Plan:	Profit Sharing:	Top Exec. Salary: $	Bonus: $
Savings Plan:	Stock Purch. Plan:		Second Exec. Salary: $	Bonus: $

OTHER THOUGHTS:

Apparent Women Officers or Directors:
Hot Spot for Advancement for Women/Minorities:

LOCATIONS: ("Y" = Yes)

West:	Southwest:	Midwest:	Southeast:	Northeast:	International:
					Y

JABIL CIRCUIT INC

www.jabil.com

Industry Group Code: 334419 Ranks within this company's industry group: Sales: 6 Profits: 21

Hardware:	Software:	Telecommunications:	Electronic Publishing:	Equipment:	Specialty Services:	
Computers:	Consumer:	Local:	Online Service:	Telecom:	Consulting:	
Accessories:	Corporate:	Long Distance:	TV/Cable or Wireless:	Communication:	Contract Manufacturing:	Y
Network Equipment:	Telecom:	Cellular:	Games:	Distribution:	Processing:	
Chips/Circuits:	Internet:	Internet Service:	Financial Data:	VAR/Reseller:	Staff/Outsourcing:	
Parts/Drives:				Satellite Srv./Equip.:	Specialty Services:	Y

TYPES OF BUSINESS:

Contract Electronics Manufacturing
Maintenance & Support Services
Custom Design Services

BRANDS/DIVISIONS/AFFILIATES:

GROWTH PLANS/SPECIAL FEATURES:

Jabil Circuit, Inc., with operations in 22 countries, is a provider of worldwide electronic manufacturing services. It provides electronics and mechanical design, production, product management and after-market services to companies in the aerospace, automotive, computing, consumer, defense, industrial, instrumentation, medical, networking, peripherals, storage and telecommunications industry. The company's business units are capable of providing customers with varying combinations of the following services: integrated design and engineering; component selection, sourcing and procurement; automate assembly; design and implementation of product testing; parallel global production; enclosure service; systems assembly, direct-order fulfillment and configure-to-order; and after-market services. The firm conducts its operations in facilities located in Austria, Belgium, Brazil, China, England, France, Germany, Hungary, India, Ireland, Italy, Japan, Malaysia, Mexico, The Netherlands, Poland, Russia, Scotland, Singapore, Taiwan, Ukraine, and the U.S. The largest customers include Cisco Systems, Inc.; EchoStar Corporation; Hewlett-Packard Company; International Business Machines Corporation (IBM); NetApp, Inc.; Nokia Corporation; Nokia Siemens Networks S.p.A.; Pace plc; Research in Motion Limited; and Royal Philips Electronics.

CONTACTS:
Note: Officers with more than one job title may be intentionally listed here more than once.

Timothy L. Main, CEO
Mark T. Mondello, COO
Timothy L. Main, Pres.
Forbes I. J. Alexander, CFO
William E. Peters, Sr. VP-Human Dev.
David Couch, CIO
Robert L. Paver, General Counsel/Corp. Sec.
Donald J. Myers, VP-Corp. Dev.
Beth A. Walters, VP-Comm.
Beth A. Walters, VP-Investor Rel.
Sergio A. Cadavrid, Treas.
John P. Lovato, CEO/Exec. VP-Consumer Div.
William D. Muir, Jr., CEO/Exec. VP-EMS Div.
Meheryar Dastoor, Controller
William D. Morean, Chmn.

Phone: 727-577-9749	**Fax:** 727-579-8529
Toll-Free:	
Address: 10560 Dr. Martin Luther King Jr. St. N., St. Petersburg, FL 33716 US	

FINANCIALS:
Sales and profits are in thousands of dollars—add 000 to get the full amount. 2010 Note: Financial information for 2010 was not available for all companies at press time.

2010 Sales: $13,409,411	2010 Profits: $168,840	**U.S. Stock Ticker:** JBL
2009 Sales: $11,684,538	2009 Profits: $-1,165,212	**Int'l Ticker:** Int'l Exchange:
2008 Sales: $12,779,703	2008 Profits: $133,892	**Employees:** 69,000
2007 Sales: $12,290,592	2007 Profits: $73,236	**Fiscal Year Ends:** 8/31
2006 Sales: $10,265,447	2006 Profits: $164,518	**Parent Company:**

SALARIES/BENEFITS:

Pension Plan:	ESOP Stock Plan:	Profit Sharing:	Top Exec. Salary: $1,000,000	Bonus: $524,103
Savings Plan:	Stock Purch. Plan:		Second Exec. Salary: $699,519	Bonus: $253,015

OTHER THOUGHTS:

Apparent Women Officers or Directors: 5
Hot Spot for Advancement for Women/Minorities: Y

LOCATIONS: ("Y" = Yes)

West:	Southwest:	Midwest:	Southeast:	Northeast:	International:
Y	Y	Y	Y	Y	Y

Note: Financial information, benefits and other data can change quickly and may vary from those stated here.

JACK HENRY & ASSOCIATES INC

www.jackhenry.com

Industry Group Code: 511201 Ranks within this company's industry group: Sales: 4 Profits: 2

Hardware:		Software:		Telecommunications:	Electronic Publishing:	Equipment:	Specialty Services:	
Computers:	Y	Consumer:		Local:	Online Service:	Telecom:	Consulting:	Y
Accessories:		Corporate:	Y	Long Distance:	TV/Cable or Wireless:	Communication:	Contract Manufacturing:	
Network Equipment:	Y	Telecom:		Cellular:	Games:	Distribution:	Processing:	
Chips/Circuits:		Internet:		Internet Service:	Financial Data:	VAR/Reseller:	Staff/Outsourcing:	
Parts/Drives:						Satellite Srv./Equip.:	Specialty Services:	

TYPES OF BUSINESS:

Software-Data Processing
Financial Services Software
Consulting Services
Hardware Sales

BRANDS/DIVISIONS/AFFILIATES:

Silverlake System
CIF 20/20
Core Director
Episys
Symitar
ProfitStars
iPay Technologies
Cruise

CONTACTS: Note: Officers with more than one job title may be intentionally listed here more than once.

John F. Prim, CEO
Tony L. Wormington, Pres.
Kevin D. Williams, CFO
Mark Forbis, CTO/VP
Janet E. Gray, Sec.
Kevin D. Williams, Treas.
Jerry D. Hall, Exec. VP/Vice Chmn.
Michael E. Henry, Chmn.

Phone: 417-235-6652	Fax: 417-235-4281
Toll-Free: 800-299-4222	
Address: 663 W. Hwy. 60, Monett, MO 65708 US	

GROWTH PLANS/SPECIAL FEATURES:

Jack Henry & Associates, Inc. (JHA) is a leading provider of integrated computer systems relating to data processing and management information for banks, credit unions and other financial institutions in the U.S. The company serves more than 11,200 financial institutions and corporate entities. It provides its products and services through three marketed brands: Jack Henry Banking, Symitar, Profit Stars and iPay Technologies. Jack Henry Banking currently supports over 1,500 commercial banks with information and transaction processing platforms that provide enterprise-wide automation. Its core banking software platforms include SilverLake, an IBM System i-based product designed for commercial-focused banks with assets ranging from $500 million to $30 million; CIF 20/20, an IBM-System i-based system that supports 780 banks ranging from new institutions to those with assets exceeding $2 billion; and Core Director, a Windows-based client/server system that serves more than 250 banks ranging from new institutions to banks with assets over $1 billion. The Symitar brand supports credit unions through its two core platforms: Episys, an IBM System p-based program designed for credit unions with more than $50 million in assets; and Cruise, a Window-based client/server system designed for credit unions with less than $50 million in assets. ProfitStars provides approximately 65 specialized products and services to over 9,600 financial services organizations. Products include business intelligence and management applications; retail delivery products; business banking systems; electronic funds transfer products; Internet banking products; risk management and protection programs; document imaging products; and professional services and education products. iPay Technologies provides electronic bill pay services. The firm also sells re-marketed hardware products that support its software, such as IBM Power Systems, Lenovo workstations, Dell Servers and Canon check scanners. In June 2010, the company completed its acquisition of iPay Technologies.

The firm offers employees medical, dental and vision insurance; flexible spending accounts; and education assistance.

FINANCIALS: Sales and profits are in thousands of dollars—add 000 to get the full amount. 2010 Note: Financial information for 2010 was not available for all companies at press time.

2010 Sales: $836,586	2010 Profits: $117,870	U.S. Stock Ticker: JKHY
2009 Sales: $745,593	2009 Profits: $103,102	Int'l Ticker: Int'l Exchange:
2008 Sales: $742,926	2008 Profits: $104,222	Employees: 4,528
2007 Sales: $666,467	2007 Profits: $104,681	Fiscal Year Ends: 6/30
2006 Sales: $590,877	2006 Profits: $89,923	Parent Company:

SALARIES/BENEFITS:

Pension Plan:	ESOP Stock Plan:	Profit Sharing:	Top Exec. Salary: $495,733	Bonus: $625,430
Savings Plan: Y	Stock Purch. Plan: Y		Second Exec. Salary: $408,484	Bonus: $394,094

OTHER THOUGHTS:

Apparent Women Officers or Directors: 1
Hot Spot for Advancement for Women/Minorities:

LOCATIONS: ("Y" = Yes)

West:	Southwest:	Midwest:	Southeast:	Northeast:	International:
Y	Y	Y	Y	Y	

JDA SOFTWARE GROUP INC

www.jda.com

Industry Group Code: 511210A Ranks within this company's industry group: Sales: 2 Profits: 2

Hardware:	Software:		Telecommunications:	Electronic Publishing:	Equipment:	Specialty Services:	
Computers:	Consumer:		Local:	Online Service:	Telecom:	Consulting:	Y
Accessories:	Corporate:	Y	Long Distance:	TV/Cable or Wireless:	Communication:	Contract Manufacturing:	
Network Equipment:	Telecom:		Cellular:	Games:	Distribution:	Processing:	
Chips/Circuits:	Internet:		Internet Service:	Financial Data:	VAR/Reseller:	Staff/Outsourcing:	
Parts/Drives:					Satellite Srv./Equip.:	Specialty Services:	

TYPES OF BUSINESS:

Retail Industry Software
Supply Chain Management Software
Consulting Services

BRANDS/DIVISIONS/AFFILIATES:

i2 Technologies Inc

CONTACTS:
Note: Officers with more than one job title may be intentionally listed here more than once.

Hamish Brewer, CEO
Hamish M. Brewer, Pres.
Peter S. Hathaway, CFO/Exec. VP
Jason Zintak, Exec. VP-Sales & Mktg.
Brian Boylan, Sr. VP-Human Resources
Aditya Srivastava, CTO/Sr. VP
David King, Sr. VP-Prod. Dev.
Kelly Thomas, Sr. VP-Mfg.
G. Michael Bridge, General Counsel/Sr. VP
Raghav Keshav, Chief Product Officer
Razat Gaurav, Sr. VP-EMEA
Duane Kotsen, Sr. VP-Implementation Svcs.
Tom Dziersk, Sr. VP-Americas
James D. Armstrong, Chmn.
Stephen McNulty, Regional VP-Asia Pacific
David Johnston, Sr. VP-Supply Chain

Phone: 480-308-3000	Fax: 480-308-3001
Toll-Free: 800-438-5301	
Address: 14400 N. 87th St., Scottsdale, AZ 85260-3649 US	

GROWTH PLANS/SPECIAL FEATURES:

JDA Software Group, Inc. is a leading provider of enterprise software products designed to enable planning, optimization and execution of supply chain processes. JDA organizes and manages its operations by type of customer across three reportable business segments: retail; manufacturing and distribution; and services industries. The retail segment includes all revenues related to applications and services sold to retail customers. The manufacturing and distribution segment includes all revenues related to applications sold to manufacturing and distribution companies, including process manufacturers, consumer goods manufacturers, life sciences companies, high tech organizations, oil and gas companies, automotive producers and other discrete manufacturers involved with government, aerospace and defense contracts. The services industry segment includes all revenues related to applications sold to customers in service industries such as travel, transportation, hospitality, media and telecommunications. It sells these products to manufacturers, wholesale/ distributors and retailers as well as government and aerospace defense contractors. JDA has licensed software to more than 6,000 companies worldwide. The company's products enable customers to collect, manage, organize and analyze information, as well as to interact with suppliers and customers over the Internet. Customers may select individual products and implement them on a stand-alone basis or they can implement various combinations of products to create an integrated system. The company also provides services through a single global organization, JDA Services, which include maintenance, consulting, implementation, training and managed services. In January 2010, JDA acquired i2 Technologies, Inc., a global provider of supply chain products, for approximately $600 million.

Employees of JDA are offered medical, dental and vision coverage; life insurance; and tuition reimbursement.

FINANCIALS:
Sales and profits are in thousands of dollars—add 000 to get the full amount. 2010 Note: Financial information for 2010 was not available for all companies at press time.

2010 Sales: $	2010 Profits: $	U.S. Stock Ticker: JDAS
2009 Sales: $385,800	2009 Profits: $26,339	Int'l Ticker: Int'l Exchange:
2008 Sales: $390,332	2008 Profits: $3,124	Employees: 1,718
2007 Sales: $373,575	2007 Profits: $26,522	Fiscal Year Ends: 12/31
2006 Sales: $277,467	2006 Profits: $- 446	Parent Company:

SALARIES/BENEFITS:

Pension Plan:	ESOP Stock Plan:	Profit Sharing:	Top Exec. Salary: $479,614	Bonus: $371,875
Savings Plan: Y	Stock Purch. Plan:		Second Exec. Salary: $316,219	Bonus: $318,750

OTHER THOUGHTS:

Apparent Women Officers or Directors:
Hot Spot for Advancement for Women/Minorities:

LOCATIONS: ("Y" = Yes)

West:	Southwest:	Midwest:	Southeast:	Northeast:	International:
Y	Y	Y	Y	Y	Y

Note: Financial information, benefits and other data can change quickly and may vary from those stated here.

JDS UNIPHASE CORPORATION

www.jdsu.com

Industry Group Code: 334210 Ranks within this company's industry group: Sales: 6 Profits: 15

Hardware:		Software:	Telecommunications:	Electronic Publishing:	Equipment:		Specialty Services:	
Computers:		Consumer:	Local:	Online Service:	Telecom:	Y	Consulting:	
Accessories:		Corporate:	Long Distance:	TV/Cable or Wireless:	Communication:	Y	Contract Manufacturing:	
Network Equipment:	Y	Telecom:	Cellular:	Games:	Distribution:		Processing:	
Chips/Circuits:		Internet:	Internet Service:	Financial Data:	VAR/Reseller:		Staff/Outsourcing:	
Parts/Drives:					Satellite Srv./Equip.:		Specialty Services:	

TYPES OF BUSINESS:

Telecommunications Equipment Manufacturing
Fiber Optic Products
Laser Products
Optical Test & Measurement Equipment
Photovoltaic Products

BRANDS/DIVISIONS/AFFILIATES:

CONTACTS: Note: Officers with more than one job title may be intentionally listed here more than once.

Thomas Waechter, CEO
Thomas Waechter, Pres.
David Vellequette, CFO/Exec. VP
Brett Hooper, VP-Human Resources
Judith Kay, VP-Exec. Oper.
Roy W. Bie, Sr. VP-Advanced Optical Tech. Bus.
David Heard, Pres., Test & Measurement Bus.
Alan Lowe, Exec. VP/Pres., Commercial Optical Prod. Bus.
Kevin Kennedy, Vice Chmn.
Martin A. Kaplan, Chmn.

Phone: 408-546-5000	Fax: 408-546-4300
Toll-Free:	
Address: 430 N. McCarthy Blvd., Milpitas, CA 95035 US	

GROWTH PLANS/SPECIAL FEATURES:

JDS Uniphase Corporation (JDSU) is a designer and manufacturer of products for fiber-optic communications. System manufacturers in the telecommunications, data communications and cable television industries, as well as original equipment manufacturers, deploy the company's fiber-optic components and modules to enable transmission of video, audio and text data. These products include transmitters, receivers, amplifiers, multiplexers, demultiplexers, add/drop modules, switches, optical performance monitors/couplers, splitters and circulators. JDSU's Communications Test and Measurement segment, which accounts for approximately 47% of revenues, offers products and services that enable the design, deployment, and maintenance of communication equipment and networks. The firm's Communications and Commercial Optical Products division (37% of revenues) offers optical communications products used by network equipment manufacturers for telecommunication and enterprise data communication applications. JDSU sells its communications products to the world's leading and emerging telecommunications, data communications and cable television systems providers. The segment also offers photovoltaic (PV) products including concentrated photovoltaic (CPV) cells and receivers for generating energy from sunlight, as well as fiber optic-based systems for delivering and measuring electrical power. The company's Advanced Optical Technologies segment (16% of revenues) applies its optical technologies for use in the display, security, medical/environmental, instrumentation, aerospace and defense markets. Specific product applications include computer-driven projectors, intelligent lightning systems, office equipment, security products and decorative surface treatments. JDSU also supplies laser products for biotechnology, graphic arts and imaging, semiconductor processing, materials processing and a variety of other laser-based applications. In May 2010, the company acquired the Network Solutions communications test business of Agilent Technologies, Inc. In October 2010, the firm opened a new facility in Suzhou, China for the manufacturing of high-precision optical coatings.

The company offers employees medical, dental and vision insurance; life insurance; disability coverage; flexible spending accounts; educational reimbursement; and an employee assistance program.

FINANCIALS: Sales and profits are in thousands of dollars—add 000 to get the full amount. 2010 Note: Financial information for 2010 was not available for all companies at press time.

2010 Sales: $1,363,900	2010 Profits: $-61,800	**U.S. Stock Ticker: JDSU**
2009 Sales: $1,283,300	2009 Profits: $-909,500	**Int'l Ticker:** Int'l Exchange:
2008 Sales: $1,512,000	2008 Profits: $-40,300	Employees: 4,700
2007 Sales: $1,396,800	2007 Profits: $-26,300	Fiscal Year Ends: 6/30
2006 Sales: $1,204,300	2006 Profits: $-151,200	Parent Company:

SALARIES/BENEFITS:

Pension Plan:	ESOP Stock Plan:	Profit Sharing:	Top Exec. Salary: $686,539	Bonus: $331,962
Savings Plan: Y	Stock Purch. Plan: Y		Second Exec. Salary: $416,827	Bonus: $151,161

OTHER THOUGHTS:

Apparent Women Officers or Directors: 2
Hot Spot for Advancement for Women/Minorities: Y

LOCATIONS: ("Y" = Yes)

West:	Southwest:	Midwest:	Southeast:	Northeast:	International:
Y	Y	Y	Y	Y	Y

Note: Financial information, benefits and other data can change quickly and may vary from those stated here.

JUNIPER NETWORKS INC

www.juniper.net

Industry Group Code: 33411 Ranks within this company's industry group: Sales: 2 Profits: 2

Hardware:		Software:		Telecommunications:		Electronic Publishing:		Equipment:		Specialty Services:	
Computers:		Consumer:		Local:		Online Service:		Telecom:		Consulting:	
Accessories:		Corporate:	Y	Long Distance:		TV/Cable or Wireless:		Communication:		Contract Manufacturing:	
Network Equipment:	Y	Telecom:	Y	Cellular:	Y	Games:		Distribution:		Processing:	
Chips/Circuits:		Internet:	Y	Internet Service:		Financial Data:		VAR/Reseller:		Staff/Outsourcing:	
Parts/Drives:								Satellite Srv./Equip.:		Specialty Services:	

TYPES OF BUSINESS:

Networking Equipment
IP Networking Systems
Internet Routers
Network Security Products
Internet Software
Intrusion Prevention
Application Acceleration

BRANDS/DIVISIONS/AFFILIATES:

Junos Platform
E-Series
J-Series
M-Series
T-Series
MX-Series
Junos Innovation Fund
Junos OS

CONTACTS: *Note: Officers with more than one job title may be intentionally listed here more than once.*

Kevin Johnson, CEO
Robyn Denholm, CFO/Exec. VP
Lauren P. Flaherty, Chief Mktg. Officer/Exec. VP
Steven Rice, Exec. VP-Human Resources
Pradeep Sindhu, CTO
Mitchell Gaynor, General Counsel/Sr. VP/Sec.
Michael Rose, Exec. VP- Oper., Service & Support
Luis Avila-Marco, Sr. VP-Corp. Dev. & Strategy
Cindy Ta, Contact-Media Rel.
Kathleen Bela, Contact-Investor Rel.
Gene Zamiska, VP-Finance/Controller
Stefan Dyckerhoff, Exec. VP/Gen. Mgr.-Infrastructure Prod. Group
David Yen, Exec. VP/Gen. Mgr.-Fabric & Switching Tech. Group
Mark Bauhaus, Exec. VP/Gen. Mgr.-Service Layer Tech. Bus. Group
Gerri Elliott, Exec. VP-Strategic Alliances
Scott Kriens, Chmn.
John Morris, Exec. VP-Worldwide Field Oper.

Phone: 408-745-2000	**Fax:** 408-745-2100
Toll-Free: 888-586-4737	
Address: 1194 N. Mathilda Ave., Sunnyvale, CA 94089-1206 US	

GROWTH PLANS/SPECIAL FEATURES:

Juniper Networks, Inc. is a provider of custom-designed Internet protocol (IP) networking platforms for Internet service providers, enterprises, governments and educational institutions. Its operations are organized into two segments: infrastructure and service layer technologies (SLT). The infrastructure segment primarily offers scalable router products used to control and direct network traffic. Product families offered by the firm include the M-Series, T-Series, E-Series, EX-Series and MX-Series. The SLT segment offers services that protect networks as well as maximize existing bandwidth and acceleration of applications across a distributed network. The SLT product families include firewall services, virtual private network systems, intrusion detection/prevention and application acceleration platforms. In addition, Junos Platform, the company's extended software portfolio, offers Junos Space, a network application platform; the Junos OS operating system; and Junos Pulse, an integrated, multi-service network client. The firm outsources manufacturing to companies including IBM, Flextronics, Celestica and Plexus. Juniper Networks maintains several strategic alliances with companies including IBM, Avaya, Ericsson, NEC and Motorola. The company's customers include wireline, wireless and cable ISPs; private enterprises; federal, state and local government agencies; and research and education institutions. The firm maintains sales offices in 47 countries worldwide. Juniper Networks owns over 500 issued or pending technology patents. In February 2010, the company launched $50 million corporate venture Junos Innovation Fund. In April 2010, Juniper Networks acquired video delivery specialist Ankeena Networks, Inc. In July 2010, the firm acquired software company SMobile Systems, Inc. In November 2010, the company acquired Internet video storage and delivery infrastructure firm Blackwave's intellectual property. In December 2010, Juniper Networks acquired virtualization security technology provider Altor Networks.

The firm offers its employees benefits including medical, dental and vision insurance; a 401(k); paid time off and holidays; and a stock purchase plan.

FINANCIALS: Sales and profits are in thousands of dollars—add 000 to get the full amount. 2010 Note: Financial information for 2010 was not available for all companies at press time.

2010 Sales: $	2010 Profits: $	**U.S. Stock Ticker:** JNPR
2009 Sales: $3,315,900	2009 Profits: $115,200	**Int'l Ticker:** Int'l Exchange:
2008 Sales: $3,572,376	2008 Profits: $511,749	Employees: 7,231
2007 Sales: $2,836,100	2007 Profits: $360,800	Fiscal Year Ends: 12/31
2006 Sales: $2,303,580	2006 Profits: $-1,001,437	Parent Company:

SALARIES/BENEFITS:

Pension Plan:	ESOP Stock Plan:	Profit Sharing:	Top Exec. Salary: $740,000	Bonus: $2,074,425
Savings Plan: Y	Stock Purch. Plan: Y		Second Exec. Salary: $481,250	Bonus: $224,984

OTHER THOUGHTS:

Apparent Women Officers or Directors: 7
Hot Spot for Advancement for Women/Minorities: Y

LOCATIONS: ("Y" = Yes)

West:	Southwest:	Midwest:	Southeast:	Northeast:	International:
Y	Y	Y	Y	Y	Y

KEANE INC

www.keane.com

Industry Group Code: 541513 Ranks within this company's industry group: Sales: 20   Profits:

Hardware:	Software:		Telecommunications:	Electronic Publishing:	Equipment:	Specialty Services:	
Computers:	Consumer:		Local:	Online Service:	Telecom:	Consulting:	Y
Accessories:	Corporate:	Y	Long Distance:	TV/Cable or Wireless:	Communication:	Contract Manufacturing:	
Network Equipment:	Telecom:		Cellular:	Games:	Distribution:	Processing:	
Chips/Circuits:	Internet:		Internet Service:	Financial Data:	VAR/Reseller:	Staff/Outsourcing:	Y
Parts/Drives:					Satellite Srv./Equip.:	Specialty Services:	

TYPES OF BUSINESS:

IT Consulting
Business Management Software
Software Development & Integration
System Design & Implementation
Applications Outsourcing
Health Care Consulting

BRANDS/DIVISIONS/AFFILIATES:

ShoreWise Adaptive Delivery
Keane Optimum
CyberFicient Technologies, Inc.
AMTEC Consulting plc

CONTACTS: Note: Officers with more than one job title may be intentionally listed here more than once.

John McCain, CEO
John McCain, Pres.
David Kaminsky, CFO/Exec. VP
David Vice, Chief Sales & Mktg. Officer/Exec. VP
Dean Williams, Sr. VP-Global Human Capital
Thomas S. Gary, CIO
John M. Dick, General Counsel
Leanne Orphanos, Sr. Dir.-Bus. Oper.
John M. Dick, Exec. VP-Corp. Dev.
Tara Jantzen, Sr. Dir.-Corp. Comm. & Public Rel.
Marv Mouchawar, Exec. VP-Global Delivery
James T. Milde, Exec. VP-Financial Svcs. & Insurance
Michael Thomas, Exec. VP-Healthcare & Life Science Svcs.
Robert W. Gray, Exec. VP-Commercial Svcs.
Mani Subramanian, Chmn.
Ian Miller, Exec. VP-EMEA

Phone: 617-241-9200	Fax: 617-241-9507
Toll-Free: 877-885-3263	
Address: 100 City Sq., Boston, MA 02129 US	

GROWTH PLANS/SPECIAL FEATURES:

Keane, Inc. is a global services company specializing in enabling the transformation of businesses and IT functions. The firm's global delivery approach, branded ShoreWise Adaptive Delivery, offers onsite, offsite, near shore and offshore options. In addition, the company offers Keane Optimum, a one-source solution intended to aid healthcare organizations improve patient care and financial performance. Keane has partnerships with several firms, including BMC Software; Business Objects; CIDEON; Compuware; Curam Software; Siemens; Ariba; Informatica; HP Software; IBM; Lombardi Software; Microsoft; Oracle; PlanetSoft; PlanView; SAP; and Vertica. The firm provides business services including consulting, process outsourcing, strategy and program and performance management services, and technology services including application, architecture, enterprise application, infrastructure, quality assurance and testing. The company serves the financial services, insurance, healthcare, manufacturing, public sector, telecom, life sciences, energy/utilities, hospitality, transportation and retail industries. Keane has operations in the U.S., Australia, Canada, China, France, India, New Zealand, Switzerland, Singapore, United Arab Emirates and the U.K. In April 2010, the firm acquired CyberFicient Technologies, Inc., a Texas-based provider of staffing services, enterprise Java consulting and human service solutions; and AMTEC Consulting plc, a U.K.-based independent advisory consulting firm.

Keane offers its employees tuition assistance; a 401(k); discounted home and auto insurance; an employee assistance program; adoption assistance; paid time off; a 529 College Savings Plan; mortgage discounts; and a variety of healthcare options.

FINANCIALS: Sales and profits are in thousands of dollars—add 000 to get the full amount. 2010 Note: Financial information for 2010 was not available for all companies at press time.

2010 Sales: $	2010 Profits: $	U.S. Stock Ticker: Private
2009 Sales: $1,200,000	2009 Profits: $	Int'l Ticker: Int'l Exchange:
2008 Sales: $1,200,000	2008 Profits: $	Employees: 13,000
2007 Sales: $1,100,000	2007 Profits: $	Fiscal Year Ends: 12/31
2006 Sales: $948,306	2006 Profits: $34,514	Parent Company:

SALARIES/BENEFITS:

Pension Plan:	ESOP Stock Plan:	Profit Sharing:	Top Exec. Salary: $	Bonus: $309,750
Savings Plan: Y	Stock Purch. Plan:		Second Exec. Salary: $	Bonus: $

OTHER THOUGHTS:

Apparent Women Officers or Directors: 2
Hot Spot for Advancement for Women/Minorities:

LOCATIONS: ("Y" = Yes)

West:	Southwest:	Midwest:	Southeast:	Northeast:	International:
Y	Y	Y	Y	Y	Y

KEMET CORP

www.kemet.com

Industry Group Code: 33441 Ranks within this company's industry group: Sales: 34 Profits: 49

Hardware:		Software:	Telecommunications:	Electronic Publishing:	Equipment:	Specialty Services:
Computers:		Consumer:	Local:	Online Service:	Telecom:	Consulting:
Accessories:		Corporate:	Long Distance:	TV/Cable or Wireless:	Communication:	Contract Manufacturing:
Network Equipment:		Telecom:	Cellular:	Games:	Distribution:	Processing:
Chips/Circuits:	Y	Internet:	Internet Service:	Financial Data:	VAR/Reseller:	Staff/Outsourcing:
Parts/Drives:					Satellite Srv./Equip.:	Specialty Services:

TYPES OF BUSINESS:

Electronic Equipment-Capacitors

BRANDS/DIVISIONS/AFFILIATES:

GROWTH PLANS/SPECIAL FEATURES:

KEMET Corp. is one of the world's largest manufacturers of tantalum, multilayer ceramic, film, electrolytic, paper and solid aluminum capacitors. These items are used as components in virtually all electronic applications and products, including communication systems, data processing equipment, personal computers, cellular phones, power management systems, automotive electronic systems and defense and aerospace systems, as well as most consumer electronics, providing KEMET with a wide customer base. KEMET also makes solid aluminum capacitors for high-frequency applications. The company is organized into three business divisions: the Tantalum business group, the ceramic business group and the film and electrolytic business group, with each group being responsible for the operations of their respective manufacturing sites as well as all related research and development efforts. The company's capacitors have been used in the Apollo moon landing, the Patriot missile and the Mir and International Space Stations. KEMET has manufacturing facilities and distribution centers in the Southeastern U.S., Mexico, China, Europe and Asia. In 2010, approximately 24% of the company's sales were in the Americas; 39% in Asia and the Pacific Rim; and 37% in Europe, the Middle East and Africa.

CONTACTS: Note: Officers with more than one job title may be intentionally listed here more than once.

Per-Olof Loof, CEO
William Lowe Jr., CFO/Exec. VP
Marc Kotelon, Sr. VP-Global Sales
Larry C. McAdams, VP-Human Resources
Daniel E. LaMorte, CIO/VP
Phil Lessner, CTO/VP
R. James Assaf, General Counsel/VP/Sec.
Robert Arguelles, Sr. VP-Operational Excellence
Daniel F. Persico, VP-Bus. Dev. & Strategic Mktg.
Donald Lung, VP-Sales, Asia-Pacific
Chuck Meeks, Jr., Sr. VP-Ceramic, Film & Electrolytics Bus. Group
Conrado Hinojosa, VP-Tantalum Bus. Group
Susan B. Barkal, Chief Compliance Officer/VP-Quality
Frank G. Brandenburg, Chmn.
Richard Curley, VP-Sales, EMEA

Phone: 864-963-6300	Fax: 864-963-6306
Toll-Free:	
Address: 2835 Kemet Way, Simpsonville, SC 29681 US	

FINANCIALS: Sales and profits are in thousands of dollars—add 000 to get the full amount. 2010 Note: Financial information for 2010 was not available for all companies at press time.

2010 Sales: $736,335	2010 Profits: $-69,447	U.S. Stock Ticker: KEM
2009 Sales: $804,385	2009 Profits: $-285,209	Int'l Ticker: Int'l Exchange:
2008 Sales: $850,120	2008 Profits: $-25,215	Employees: 10,400
2007 Sales: $658,714	2007 Profits: $6,897	Fiscal Year Ends: 3/31
2006 Sales: $490,106	2006 Profits: $ 375	Parent Company:

SALARIES/BENEFITS:

Pension Plan:	ESOP Stock Plan:	Profit Sharing:	Top Exec. Salary: $570,375	Bonus: $
Savings Plan:	Stock Purch. Plan:		Second Exec. Salary: $299,892	Bonus: $

OTHER THOUGHTS:

Apparent Women Officers or Directors:
Hot Spot for Advancement for Women/Minorities:

LOCATIONS: ("Y" = Yes)

West:	Southwest:	Midwest:	Southeast:	Northeast:	International:
				Y	Y

Note: Financial information, benefits and other data can change quickly and may vary from those stated here.

KEY TRONIC CORP
www.keytronic.com

Industry Group Code: 334419 Ranks within this company's industry group: Sales: 20 Profits: 15

Hardware:		Software:		Telecommunications:		Electronic Publishing:	Equipment:	Specialty Services:	
Computers:		Consumer:		Local:		Online Service:	Telecom:	Consulting:	
Accessories:	Y	Corporate:		Long Distance:		TV/Cable or Wireless:	Communication:	Contract Manufacturing:	Y
Network Equipment:		Telecom:		Cellular:		Games:	Distribution:	Processing:	
Chips/Circuits:		Internet:		Internet Service:		Financial Data:	VAR/Reseller:	Staff/Outsourcing:	
Parts/Drives:							Satellite Srv./Equip.:	Specialty Services:	

TYPES OF BUSINESS:
Contract Electronics Manufacturing
Keyboard & Mouse Manufacturing

BRANDS/DIVISIONS/AFFILIATES:
KeyTronic EMS Co

CONTACTS: Note: Officers with more than one job title may be intentionally listed here more than once.
Craig D. Gates, CEO
Craig D. Gates, Pres.
Ronald F. Klawitter, CFO/Treas.
Lawrence J. Bostwick, VP-Eng. & Quality
Ronald F. Klawitter, Exec. VP-Admin.
Kathleen L. Nemeth, Sec.
Douglas G. Burkhardt, VP-Worldwide Oper.
Philip S. Hochberg, VP-Bus. Dev.
Brett R. Larsen, VP-Finance/Controller
Donald R. Sincler, VP-Materials
Dale F. Pilz, Chmn.

Phone: 509-928-8000	Fax: 509-927-5383
Toll-Free:	
Address: N. 4424 Sullivan Rd., Spokane, WA 99216 US	

GROWTH PLANS/SPECIAL FEATURES:
Key Tronic Corp., doing business as KeyTronicEMS Co., is an electronics manufacturing services (EMS) provider. The firm manufactures keyboards and mice for personal computers, terminals and workstations for distributors and resellers. Its production capabilities include tool making, product design, liquid injection molding, printed screened silver flexible circuit membranes, automated tape winding and box build, or pre-built products. The firm's automated manufacturing processes enable it to work closely with its customers during design and prototype stages of production for new custom products and to jointly increase productivity and reduce response time to the marketplace. It uses computer-aided design techniques and unique software to assist in preparation of the tool design layout and fabrications, reduce costs, improve component and product quality, and accelerate turnaround time during product development. Key Tronic's current customer production programs include consumer electronics and plastics; specialty printers and sub-assemblies; household products; gaming devices; telecommunication satellite units; multimedia touch panels; digital control panels; computer accessories; medical devices; exercise equipment; educational toys; industrial tools; networking equipment; scientific instruments; and security surveillance devices. The firm's largest customers include Kaz Inc; Lexmark International, Inc.; and International Gaming Technology, Inc. Key Tronic operates facilities in the U.S., China and Mexico, engaged in production, testing, engineering and distribution.

The firm offers its employees life, disability, medical, dental and vision insurance.

FINANCIALS: Sales and profits are in thousands of dollars—add 000 to get the full amount. 2010 Note: Financial information for 2010 was not available for all companies at press time.
2010 Sales: $199,620	2010 Profits: $8,690	U.S. Stock Ticker: KTCC
2009 Sales: $184,924	2009 Profits: $1,063	Int'l Ticker: Int'l Exchange:
2008 Sales: $204,122	2008 Profits: $5,584	Employees: 2,036
2007 Sales: $201,712	2007 Profits: $5,230	Fiscal Year Ends: 6/30
2006 Sales: $187,699	2006 Profits: $9,753	Parent Company:

SALARIES/BENEFITS:
Pension Plan:	ESOP Stock Plan:	Profit Sharing:	Top Exec. Salary: $365,119	Bonus: $459,689
Savings Plan: Y	Stock Purch. Plan:		Second Exec. Salary: $283,749	Bonus: $318,930

OTHER THOUGHTS:
Apparent Women Officers or Directors: 1
Hot Spot for Advancement for Women/Minorities:

LOCATIONS: ("Y" = Yes)
West:	Southwest:	Midwest:	Southeast:	Northeast:	International:
Y	Y				Y

Note: Financial information, benefits and other data can change quickly and may vary from those stated here.

KLA TENCOR CORP

www.kla-tencor.com

Industry Group Code: 333295 Ranks within this company's industry group: Sales: 5 Profits: 11

Hardware:		Software:		Telecommunications:		Electronic Publishing:		Equipment:		Specialty Services:	
Computers:		Consumer:		Local:		Online Service:		Telecom:		Consulting:	
Accessories:		Corporate:	Y	Long Distance:		TV/Cable or Wireless:		Communication:		Contract Manufacturing:	
Network Equipment:		Telecom:		Cellular:		Games:		Distribution:		Processing:	
Chips/Circuits:	Y	Internet:		Internet Service:		Financial Data:		VAR/Reseller:		Staff/Outsourcing:	
Parts/Drives:								Satellite Srv./Equip.:		Specialty Services:	Y

TYPES OF BUSINESS:

Semiconductor Test Equipment
Process Control & Yield Management Software & Services
Support Services

BRANDS/DIVISIONS/AFFILIATES:

ICOS Vision Systems Corporation NV

CONTACTS: Note: Officers with more than one job title may be intentionally listed here more than once.

Richard P. Wallace, CEO
Richard P. Wallace, Pres.
Mark P. Dentinger, CFO/Exec. VP
Ben Tsai, CTO/Exec. VP
Robert P. Akins, Chmn.

Phone: 408-875-3000	Fax: 408-875-4144
Toll-Free:	
Address: 1 Technology Dr., Milpitas, CA 95035 US	

GROWTH PLANS/SPECIAL FEATURES:

KLA Tencor Corp. is one of the world's largest suppliers of process control and yield management products to the semiconductor and related nanoelectronics industries. The firm's portfolio of products, software, services and expertise is designed to help integrated circuit manufacturers manage yield throughout the entire fabrication process, from research and development to final volume production. The company markets and sells products to semiconductor, wafer, disk and reticle manufacturers worldwide. Its products are categorized into the following groups: chip manufacturing, wafer manufacturing, reticle manufacturing, complementary metal-oxide-semiconductor (CMOS) image sensor manufacturing, data storage media/head manufacturing, solar manufacturing, high-brightness LED manufacturing, microelectromechanical (MEMS) manufacturing and general purpose and lab applications. Chip manufacturing products and services encompass defect inspection, review, metrology, in-situ process monitoring and lithography modeling tools designed to help chip manufacturers manage yield. The company's wafer manufacturing tools include inspection, metrology and data-management systems. It offers inspection and metrology systems for reticle manufacturing and data storage media/ head manufacturing. The firm's CMOS sensors convert light to electrical signals and are primarily used in digital cameras. In the solar manufacturing category, the firm offers surface profilers and solar wafer and cell inspection modules, which are integrated in different stages of the solar wafer and cell production lines to increase yield and lower production costs. High Brightness LED manufacturing products include the ICOS wafer inspector for automated inspection of HB-LED wafers. KLA-Tencor's MEMS manufacturing products are tools and techniques for the manufacturing of complete systems-on-a-chip. The firm's general purpose and lab applications tools measure surface topography for a variety of industries. Subsidiaries include ICOS Vision Systems Corporation NV.

KLA-Tencor offers its employees medical, dental and vision coverage; life and disability insurance; flexible spending accounts; profit sharing; an employee stock purchase plan; a 401(k) plan; an employee assistance program; tuition reimbursement; pet insurance; and commuter assistance.

FINANCIALS: Sales and profits are in thousands of dollars—add 000 to get the full amount. 2010 Note: Financial information for 2010 was not available for all companies at press time.

2010 Sales: $1,820,760	2010 Profits: $212,300	U.S. Stock Ticker: KLAC
2009 Sales: $1,520,216	2009 Profits: $-523,368	Int'l Ticker: Int'l Exchange:
2008 Sales: $2,521,716	2008 Profits: $359,083	Employees: 5,000
2007 Sales: $2,731,229	2007 Profits: $528,098	Fiscal Year Ends: 6/30
2006 Sales: $2,070,627	2006 Profits: $380,452	Parent Company:

SALARIES/BENEFITS:

Pension Plan:	ESOP Stock Plan:	Profit Sharing: Y	Top Exec. Salary: $780,769	Bonus: $3,130,494
Savings Plan: Y	Stock Purch. Plan: Y		Second Exec. Salary: $400,000	Bonus: $891,000

OTHER THOUGHTS:

Apparent Women Officers or Directors: 1
Hot Spot for Advancement for Women/Minorities:

LOCATIONS: ("Y" = Yes)

West:	Southwest:	Midwest:	Southeast:	Northeast:	International:
Y	Y	Y		Y	Y

KONAMI CORP

www.konami.co.jp

Industry Group Code: 511210G Ranks within this company's industry group: Sales: 4 Profits: 1

Hardware:		Software:		Telecommunications:	Electronic Publishing:		Equipment:	Specialty Services:	
Computers:	Y	Consumer:	Y	Local:	Online Service:	Y	Telecom:	Consulting:	
Accessories:	Y	Corporate:		Long Distance:	TV/Cable or Wireless:		Communication:	Contract Manufacturing:	
Network Equipment:		Telecom:		Cellular:	Games:	Y	Distribution:	Processing:	
Chips/Circuits:		Internet:		Internet Service:	Financial Data:		VAR/Reseller:	Staff/Outsourcing:	
Parts/Drives:							Satellite Srv./Equip.:	Specialty Services:	Y

TYPES OF BUSINESS:

Software-Games
Toys
Arcade Games
Mobile Phone Media Content
Sports Clubs
Health & Fitness Products
Casino Games
Casino Management Systems

BRANDS/DIVISIONS/AFFILIATES:

Metal Gear
Castlevania
Silent Hill
Yu-Gi-Oh!
Konami Digital Entertainment Co., Ltd.
Konami Sports & Life Co., Ltd.
Konami Digital Entertainment, Inc.
Konami Gaming, Inc.

CONTACTS: Note: Officers with more than one job title may be intentionally listed here more than once.

Kagemasa Kozuki, CEO
Kagemasa Kozuki, Pres.
Noriaki Yamaguchi, CFO/Exec. VP
Sadaharu Kitaya, Gen. Mgr.-Sales & Mktg. Div.
Mineaki Yoshiba, Corp. Officer-Human Resources
Akira Tamai, Corp. Finance & Acct. Officer
Kazumi Kitaue, Chmn./Pres., Konami Digital Entertainment, Inc.
Toshimitsu Ohishi, Exec. VP-Konami Sports Corp.
Tetsu Sakamoto, Corp. Officer-Gaming & System Bus.
Kimihiko Higashio, Exec. VP
Kagemasa Kozuki, Chmn.

Phone: 81-3-5770-0573	Fax: 81-3-5412-3300
Toll-Free:	
Address: 9-7-2, Akasaka, Minato-ku, Tokyo, 107-8323 Japan	

GROWTH PLANS/SPECIAL FEATURES:

Konami Corp., founded in 1969, primarily produces entertainment products. It operates in three segments: Digital Entertainment, which accounts for 54.4% of revenues; Health & Fitness, 32.5%; and Gaming & Systems, 7.6%.; with the remaining 5.5% coming from other operations. The digital entertainment business produces video and computer games, as well as other entertainment products, including arcade games, game strategy guide books, action figures, mobile content and trading card games. Some of its game titles include the Metal Gear, Pro Evolution Soccer, Castlevania, Dance Dance Revolution and Silent Hill franchises; it also markets the Yu-Gi-Oh video game series and the related trading card game. The health and fitness segment operates health clubs in Japan and also manufactures and markets health-related products. During 2010, this segment owned and operated 211 fitness clubs with roughly 900,000 members, while managing 116 additional clubs owned by third parties. Its health-related products range from exercise machines to nutritional supplements. Lastly, the gaming and systems business manufactures gaming equipment (and slot machines in particular), and is licensed to sell these products to casinos in all Australian territories and states, as well as in various parts of the U.S. and Canada. This division also sells electronic casino management systems, which offer casinos real-time monitoring and management of slot machines and cash handling systems. The company maintains 20 domestic and international subsidiaries focused on different business areas. Japanese subsidiaries include Konami Digital Entertainment Co., Ltd.; Konami Sports & Life Co., Ltd.; and Konami Real Estate, Inc. Primary U.S.-based subsidiaries include Konami Digital Entertainment, Inc., which sells video games, toys and hobby products in North America, and Konami Gaming, Inc., which focuses on the production and sale of casino gaming machines. In 2010, the company released approximately 61 new software titles, mostly for leading home and portable game platforms.

FINANCIALS: Sales and profits are in thousands of dollars—add 000 to get the full amount. 2010 Note: Financial information for 2010 was not available for all companies at press time.

2010 Sales: $2,817,541	2010 Profits: $143,100	**U.S. Stock Ticker:** KNM
2009 Sales: $3,153,527	2009 Profits: $110,699	**Int'l Ticker:** 9766 Int'l Exchange: Tokyo-TSE
2008 Sales: $2,968,380	2008 Profits: $183,102	**Employees:** 13,136
2007 Sales: $2,374,240	2007 Profits: $137,323	**Fiscal Year Ends:** 3/31
2006 Sales: $2,231,523	2006 Profits: $195,863	**Parent Company:**

SALARIES/BENEFITS:

Pension Plan: Y	ESOP Stock Plan:	Profit Sharing:	Top Exec. Salary: $	Bonus: $
Savings Plan:	Stock Purch. Plan:		Second Exec. Salary: $	Bonus: $

OTHER THOUGHTS:

Apparent Women Officers or Directors:
Hot Spot for Advancement for Women/Minorities:

LOCATIONS: ("Y" = Yes)

West:	Southwest:	Midwest:	Southeast:	Northeast:	International:
Y					Y

KRONOS INC

www.kronos.com

Industry Group Code: 334111 Ranks within this company's industry group: Sales: Profits:

Hardware:	Software:		Telecommunications:	Electronic Publishing:	Equipment:	Specialty Services:	
Computers:	Consumer:		Local:	Online Service:	Telecom:	Consulting:	Y
Accessories:	Corporate:	Y	Long Distance:	TV/Cable or Wireless:	Communication:	Contract Manufacturing:	
Network Equipment:	Telecom:		Cellular:	Games:	Distribution:	Processing:	
Chips/Circuits:	Internet:		Internet Service:	Financial Data:	VAR/Reseller:	Staff/Outsourcing:	
Parts/Drives:					Satellite Srv./Equip.:	Specialty Services:	

TYPES OF BUSINESS:

Computer Hardware-Workplace Time & Attendance
Labor Management Software & Systems
Professional Services

BRANDS/DIVISIONS/AFFILIATES:

Hellman & Friedman LLC
Workforce HRMS
Kronos iSeries
Workforce Connect
Timekeeper
Automatic Data Processing Inc
Workforce Mobile Scheduler

CONTACTS: Note: Officers with more than one job title may be intentionally listed here more than once.

Aron J. Ain, CEO
Mark Julien, CFO
Jim Kizielewicz, Chief Mktg. Officer/Sr. VP
David Almeda, VP-Human Resources
Peter George, CTO/Sr. VP-Tech.
Peter George, Sr. VP-Prod.
Charlie Dickson, Chief Admin. Officer
Alyce Moore, General Counsel/VP
John O'Brien, VP-Sales, North America
Christopher Todd, VP-Svcs.
Michael Biery, VP-Support Svcs.
Mark S. Ain, Chmn.
Dick Cahill, VP/Gen. Mgr.-Int'l Oper.

Phone: 978-250-9800	Fax: 978-367-5900
Toll-Free: 800-225-1561	
Address: 297 Billerica Rd., Chelmsford, MA 01824 US	

GROWTH PLANS/SPECIAL FEATURES:

Kronos, Inc. is a single-source provider of human resources, payroll, scheduling, and time and labor solutions. The company develops, manufactures and markets frontline labor management (FLM) systems that improve productivity and labor resources by planning, tracking and analyzing time and activities information about employees, including hourly workers, hourly professionals and salaried professionals. These systems reduce the time needed to collect employee work-related information, improve payroll accuracy and provide time-sensitive labor information to frontline managers. The firm offers the Workforce HRMS (human resources management system) solution, an FLM system that captures information from all employees in the workplace using a variety of user interaction technologies, including the Internet, desktop applications, remote transmission applications and intelligent data collection terminals. Key products include the Workforce suite; the Kronos iSeries suite; the Timekeeper system; advance scheduling and data collection devices; and complementary products such as Workforce Connect. The firm's products are marketed through its own sales force and through an alliance with the payroll service company Automatic Data Processing, Inc. Kronos focuses on serving the hospitality, retail, government, manufacturing and health care industries. The company is owned by the private equity firm Hellman & Friedman LLC. The firm has offices located throughout North America, Africa, Europe, Middle East, Central America, South America and the Caribbean. In January 2010, the company released it new Workforce Mobile Scheduler application that will allow employers to advertise and fill open shift slots through text messages sent to qualified employees. In February 2010, Kronos opened a new office in Bangalore, India.

Employees of Kronos receive medical, dental, vision, disability, prescription drug and life insurance; flexible spending accounts; a group legal plan; tuition reimbursement; and a 401(k) plan.

FINANCIALS: Sales and profits are in thousands of dollars—add 000 to get the full amount. 2010 Note: Financial information for 2010 was not available for all companies at press time.

2010 Sales: $	2010 Profits: $	U.S. Stock Ticker: Private
2009 Sales: $	2009 Profits: $	Int'l Ticker: Int'l Exchange:
2008 Sales: $715,000	2008 Profits: $138,000	Employees: 3,300
2007 Sales: $662,000	2007 Profits: $111,000	Fiscal Year Ends: 9/30
2006 Sales: $578,203	2006 Profits: $41,439	Parent Company: HELLMAN & FRIEDMAN LLC

SALARIES/BENEFITS:

Pension Plan:	ESOP Stock Plan:	Profit Sharing:	Top Exec. Salary: $	Bonus: $
Savings Plan: Y	Stock Purch. Plan:		Second Exec. Salary: $	Bonus: $

OTHER THOUGHTS:

Apparent Women Officers or Directors: 1
Hot Spot for Advancement for Women/Minorities:

LOCATIONS: ("Y" = Yes)

West:	Southwest:	Midwest:	Southeast:	Northeast:	International:
Y	Y	Y	Y	Y	Y

L-3 COMMUNICATIONS HOLDINGS INC

www.l-3com.com

Industry Group Code: 3342 Ranks within this company's industry group: Sales: 1 Profits: 1

Hardware:		Software:		Telecommunications:		Electronic Publishing:		Equipment:		Specialty Services:	
Computers:	Y	Consumer:	Y	Local:	Y	Online Service:		Telecom:	Y	Consulting:	
Accessories:	Y	Corporate:	Y	Long Distance:	Y	TV/Cable or Wireless:	Y	Communication:	Y	Contract Manufacturing:	Y
Network Equipment:	Y	Telecom:	Y	Cellular:		Games:		Distribution:		Processing:	
Chips/Circuits:	Y	Internet:		Internet Service:		Financial Data:		VAR/Reseller:		Staff/Outsourcing:	
Parts/Drives:	Y							Satellite Srv./Equip.:	Y	Specialty Services:	Y

TYPES OF BUSINESS:

Electronic Equipment-Specialized Communications
Intelligence, Surveillance & Reconnaissance Systems
Aviation & Aerospace Products
Telemetry Products
Instrumentation Products
Microwave Components
Security Systems
Signal Intelligence Products

BRANDS/DIVISIONS/AFFILIATES:

L-3 Communications Corporation
Microdyne Outsourcing Inc.
L-3 Titan Group
Northrop Grumman
Chesapeake Sciences Corporation
HAS Systems Pty Limited
International Resources Group Ltd.
Insight Technology, Inc.

CONTACTS: Note: Officers with more than one job title may be intentionally listed here more than once.

Michael T. Strianese, CEO
Michael T. Strianese, Pres.
Ralph G. D'Ambrosio, CFO/Sr. VP
Steven M. Post, General Counsel/Sr. VP/Corp. Sec.
David T. Butler III, Sr. VP-Bus. Oper.
Curtis Brunson, Exec. VP-Corp. Strategy & Dev.
Dan Azmon, Controller/Principal Acct. Officer/VP
Steve Kantor, Sr. VP/Pres., L-3 Services Group
James W. Dunn, Sr. VP/Pres., Sensors & Simulation Group
Robert E. Leskow, Sr. VP/Pres., Marine & Power Systems Group
John McNellis, Sr. VP/Pres., Integrated Systems Group
Michael T. Strianese, Chmn.

Phone: 212-697-1111	Fax: 212-805-5477
Toll-Free:	
Address: 600 3rd Ave., New York, NY 10016 US	

GROWTH PLANS/SPECIAL FEATURES:

L-3 Communications Holdings, Inc., operating through its subsidiary L-3 Communications Corp., is a supplier of products and services used in various aerospace and defense platforms. The company operates through four business segments: C3ISR; Government Services; Aircraft Modernization and Maintenance (AM&M); and Electronic Systems. The C3ISR segment, which accounted for 20% of sales in 2009, specializes in signals intelligence and communications intelligence. Its products and services are used to connect a variety of airborne, space, ground and sea-based communication systems, and in the transmission, processing, recording, monitoring and dissemination functions of these systems. The Government Services division represented 27% of revenue in 2009 and provides training and operational support services; enterprise information technology solutions; intelligence solutions; support, command and control systems and software services; global security; and engineering solutions services. Through the AM&M segment, the company provides modernization, sustainment, maintenance and logistics services for military and various government aircraft. The AM&M segment represented 18% of sales in 2009. The Electronic Systems segment, which represented 35% of sales in 2009, provides aviation; security and detection; microwave RF, SATCOM and antenna; sensor and simulation; precision engagement; undersea warfare; and power and control system products. The company's customers include the U.S. Department of Defense, the U.S. Department of Homeland Security, U.S. Government intelligence agencies, aerospace and defense contractors, foreign governments and commercial customers. In April 2010, the firm acquired Insight Technology Inc., a firm that develops and manufactures night vision and electro-optical equipment.

L-3 Communications offers its employees medical, dental, vision and prescription insurance; flexible spending accounts; an employee assistance program; long-term care; short- and long-term disability; a 401(k) plan; an employee stock purchase plan; access to the L-3 Corporate Perks Program; and learning and developmental opportunities.

FINANCIALS: Sales and profits are in thousands of dollars—add 000 to get the full amount. 2010 Note: Financial information for 2010 was not available for all companies at press time.

2010 Sales: $	2010 Profits: $	U.S. Stock Ticker: LLL
2009 Sales: $15,615,000	2009 Profits: $911,000	Int'l Ticker: Int'l Exchange:
2008 Sales: $14,901,000	2008 Profits: $949,000	Employees: 67,000
2007 Sales: $13,960,500	2007 Profits: $756,100	Fiscal Year Ends: 12/31
2006 Sales: $12,476,900	2006 Profits: $526,100	Parent Company:

SALARIES/BENEFITS:

Pension Plan:	ESOP Stock Plan:	Profit Sharing:	Top Exec. Salary: $1,284,231	Bonus: $3,000,000
Savings Plan: Y	Stock Purch. Plan:		Second Exec. Salary: $562,846	Bonus: $700,000

OTHER THOUGHTS:

Apparent Women Officers or Directors:
Hot Spot for Advancement for Women/Minorities:

LOCATIONS: ("Y" = Yes)

West:	Southwest:	Midwest:	Southeast:	Northeast:	International:
Y	Y	Y	Y	Y	Y

Note: Financial information, benefits and other data can change quickly and may vary from those stated here.

LABARGE INC

www.labarge.com

Industry Group Code: 334419 Ranks within this company's industry group: Sales: 19 Profits: 12

Hardware:		Software:	Telecommunications:	Electronic Publishing:	Equipment:	Specialty Services:	
Computers:		Consumer:	Local:	Online Service:	Telecom:	Consulting:	
Accessories:		Corporate:	Long Distance:	TV/Cable or Wireless:	Communication:	Contract Manufacturing:	Y
Network Equipment:		Telecom:	Cellular:	Games:	Distribution:	Processing:	
Chips/Circuits:	Y	Internet:	Internet Service:	Financial Data:	VAR/Reseller:	Staff/Outsourcing:	
Parts/Drives:					Satellite Srv./Equip.:	Specialty Services:	

TYPES OF BUSINESS:

Contract Electronics Manufacturing
Printed Circuit Board Assemblies
Interconnect Systems
Turnkey Electro-Mechanical Assemblies

BRANDS/DIVISIONS/AFFILIATES:

CONTACTS: *Note: Officers with more than one job title may be intentionally listed here more than once.*

Craig E. LaBarge, CEO
Randy L. Buschling, COO/VP
Craig E. LaBarge, Pres.
Donald H. Nonnenkamp, CFO/VP
Tim LoGrasso, Dir.-Human Resources
George Hayward, Dir.-Info. Systems
Melanie Keenan, Dir.-Admin. & Finance
Donald H. Nonnenkamp, Sec.
William Bitner, VP-Oper.
Rick Parmley, VP-Bus. Dev.
Colleen P. Clements, Dir.-Corp. Comm.
Rue L. Pugh, Corp. Controller
Mark Teubert
Herbert Frye, Co-Dir.-Oper. Excellence
Brian Stewart, Co-Dir.-Oper. Excellence
Teresa K. Huber, VP-Oper.
Herbert Frye, Dir.-Finance
Robert G. Clark, Chmn.
John Piatak, Dir.-Corp. Supply Chain

Phone: 314-997-0800	Fax: 314-812-9438
Toll-Free:	
Address: 9900 Clayton Rd., St. Louis, MO 63124 US	

GROWTH PLANS/SPECIAL FEATURES:

LaBarge, Inc. manufactures and designs high-performance electronic, interconnect and electromechanical systems on a contract basis for customers in diverse technology-driven industries. The company produces electronic equipment for use in a variety of high-technology applications, including military communication, radar and weapons systems, industrial automation, military and commercial aircraft, satellites, space launch vehicles, oil and gas wells, mine automation equipment and medical devices. LaBarge provides complete electronic systems solutions, including the manufacturing, engineering and design of interconnect systems, circuit card assemblies and high-level assemblies for its customers' specialized applications. LaBarge maintains over 600,000 square feet of industrial space at 11 manufacturing facilities in Arkansas, Missouri, Wisconsin, Oklahoma, Pennsylvania and Texas. Approximately 42% of LaBarge's revenues are generated from customers in the defense market; approximately 22.6% from industrial customers; 19.9% from natural resources customers; 10.8% from medical customers; and 4.7% of revenues are derived from various customers in the aerospace, telecommunications and other industries. Sales contracts with original equipment manufacturers (OEMs) doing business with the U.S. government and its agencies account for 42% of total sales.

The company provides its employees with life, disability, AD&D, medical, dental and vision insurance; a 401(k); flexible spending accounts; a stock purchase plan; an assistance plan; paid time off, including nine paid holidays; and tuition assistance.

FINANCIALS: Sales and profits are in thousands of dollars—add 000 to get the full amount. 2010 Note: Financial information for 2010 was not available for all companies at press time.

2010 Sales: $289,303	2010 Profits: $14,888	**U.S. Stock Ticker:** LB
2009 Sales: $273,368	2009 Profits: $10,338	**Int'l Ticker:** Int'l Exchange:
2008 Sales: $279,485	2008 Profits: $14,827	**Employees:**
2007 Sales: $235,203	2007 Profits: $11,343	**Fiscal Year Ends:** 6/30
2006 Sales: $190,089	2006 Profits: $9,708	**Parent Company:**

SALARIES/BENEFITS:

Pension Plan:	ESOP Stock Plan:	Profit Sharing:	Top Exec. Salary: $527,306	Bonus: $305,000
Savings Plan: Y	Stock Purch. Plan:		Second Exec. Salary: $356,278	Bonus: $247,500

OTHER THOUGHTS:

Apparent Women Officers or Directors: 4
Hot Spot for Advancement for Women/Minorities: Y

LOCATIONS: ("Y" = Yes)

West:	Southwest:	Midwest:	Southeast:	Northeast:	International:
	Y	Y	Y	Y	

LAM RESEARCH CORP

www.lamrc.com

Industry Group Code: 333295 Ranks within this company's industry group: Sales: 6 Profits: 9

Hardware:		Software:		Telecommunications:		Electronic Publishing:		Equipment:		Specialty Services:	
Computers:		Consumer:		Local:		Online Service:		Telecom:		Consulting:	
Accessories:		Corporate:		Long Distance:		TV/Cable or Wireless:		Communication:		Contract Manufacturing:	
Network Equipment:		Telecom:		Cellular:		Games:		Distribution:		Processing:	
Chips/Circuits:	Y	Internet:		Internet Service:		Financial Data:		VAR/Reseller:		Staff/Outsourcing:	
Parts/Drives:								Satellite Srv./Equip.:		Specialty Services:	Y

TYPES OF BUSINESS:

Semiconductor Manufacturing Equipment
Etch Processing Systems
Chemical Mechanical Planarization Systems
Wafer Cleaning Equipment & Services
Support Services

BRANDS/DIVISIONS/AFFILIATES:

2300 Exelan Flex
2300 Versys Kiyo
Transformer Coupled Plasma
TCP 9400DSiE Deep Silicon Etch System
2300 Syndion Through-Silicon Via Etch System

CONTACTS: *Note: Officers with more than one job title may be intentionally listed here more than once.*

Stephen G. Newberry, CEO
Martin Anstice, COO
Martin Anstice, Pres.
Ernest E. Maddock, CFO/Sr. VP
Thomas J. Bondur, VP/Gen. Mgr.-Mktg. & Sales
Sarah A. O'Dowd, VP-Human Resources
Sarah A. O'Dowd, Chief Legal Officer
Ernest E. Maddock, Chief Acct. Officer
Richard A. Gottscho, VP/Gen. Mgr.-Etch Bus.
Jeffrey Marks, VP/Gen. Mgr.-Clean Bus.
James W. Bagley, Chmn.

Phone: 510-572-0200	Fax: 510-572-2935
Toll-Free: 800-526-7678	
Address: 4650 Cushing Pkwy., Fremont, CA 94538 US	

GROWTH PLANS/SPECIAL FEATURES:

Lam Research Corp. is a supplier of wafer fabrication equipment and services. The firm designs, manufactures, markets and services semiconductor processing equipment used in semiconductor device fabrication. The company's etch products are used to deposit special films on silicon wafers and to selectively etch away portions of various films, creating an integrated circuit. The firm also offers wafer cleaning services and equipment that employs proprietary technology and can be used throughout the semiconductor manufacturing process. Lam Research Corp.'s etch products selectively remove portions of various films from the wafer in the creation of semiconductor devices by utilizing various plasma-based technologies to create critical device features at current and future technology nodes. The firm's etch products include the 2300 Exelan Flex series for dielectric etch, the 2300 Versys Kiyo series for conductor etch, the Transformer Coupled Plasma (TCP) 9400DSiE Deep Silicon Etch System for micro-electromechanical systems and the 2300 Syndion Through-Silicon Via Etch System for three-dimensional integrated circuits. In addition, Lam provides technical support, training, spares and service. The company maintains more than 20 customer support centers in the U.S., Europe and the Asia-Pacific region. Lam developed several industry firsts including: the patented TCP source technology, the first inductive plasma source technology with a planar coil; introducing the dual frequency confined (DFC) technology for dielectric etch; developing the first 200/300mm capable etch product line with a 200mm comparable footprint; decoupling plasma density and bias power for conductor etch; and providing technologies to control parameters that impact critical dimension uniformity.

Employees are offered life, disability, AD&D, medical, dental and vision insurance; flexible spending accounts; group legal service plans; educational assistance; gym membership reimbursements; an employee assistance program; adoption aid; and a credit union.

FINANCIALS: Sales and profits are in thousands of dollars—add 000 to get the full amount. 2010 Note: Financial information for 2010 was not available for all companies at press time.

2010 Sales: $2,133,776	2010 Profits: $346,669	**U.S. Stock Ticker: LRCX**
2009 Sales: $1,115,946	2009 Profits: $-302,148	**Int'l Ticker:** Int'l Exchange:
2008 Sales: $2,474,911	2008 Profits: $439,349	Employees: 3,232
2007 Sales: $2,566,576	2007 Profits: $685,815	Fiscal Year Ends: 6/30
2006 Sales: $1,642,171	2006 Profits: $335,755	Parent Company:

SALARIES/BENEFITS:

Pension Plan:	ESOP Stock Plan:	Profit Sharing:	Top Exec. Salary: $737,473	Bonus: $3,211,287
Savings Plan: Y	Stock Purch. Plan: Y		Second Exec. Salary: $425,141	Bonus: $1,385,442

OTHER THOUGHTS:

Apparent Women Officers or Directors: 3
Hot Spot for Advancement for Women/Minorities: Y

LOCATIONS: ("Y" = Yes)

West:	Southwest:	Midwest:	Southeast:	Northeast:	International:
Y	Y	Y		Y	Y

LATTICE SEMICONDUCTOR CORP   www.latticesemi.com

Industry Group Code: 33441 Ranks within this company's industry group: Sales: 48   Profits: 34

Hardware:		Software:		Telecommunications:		Electronic Publishing:	Equipment:		Specialty Services:	
Computers:		Consumer:		Local:		Online Service:	Telecom:		Consulting:	
Accessories:		Corporate:	Y	Long Distance:		TV/Cable or Wireless:	Communication:		Contract Manufacturing:	
Network Equipment:		Telecom:		Cellular:		Games:	Distribution:		Processing:	
Chips/Circuits:	Y	Internet:		Internet Service:		Financial Data:	VAR/Reseller:		Staff/Outsourcing:	
Parts/Drives:							Satellite Srv./Equip.:		Specialty Services:	

TYPES OF BUSINESS:

Integrated Circuits-Programmable Logic Devices
Field Programmable Gate Arrays
Field Programmable System Chips
PLD Software

BRANDS/DIVISIONS/AFFILIATES:

ispLeverCORE
LatticeXP
MackXO
LatticeEC/ECP
LatticeSC
ispMACH
ispClock
Lattice SG Pte. Ltd.

CONTACTS: *Note: Officers with more than one job title may be intentionally listed here more than once.*

Darin Billerbeck, CEO
Darin Billerbeck, Pres.
Michael G. Potter, CFO/VP
Stacy Fender, VP-Worldwide Sales
David L. Rutledge, VP-R&D
Byron Milstead, General Counsel/VP/Sec.
William P. Bowman, VP-Product Oper./Gen. Mgr.-Lattice SG Pte Ltd
Brian Kiernan, Contact-Media
Christopher M. Fanning, VP/Gen. Mgr.-Low Density & Mixed Signal Solutions
Michael J. Gariepy, VP-Reliability & Quality Assurance
Sean Riley, VP/Gen. Mgr.-High Density Solutions
Douglas Hunter, VP-Mktg.
Patrick S. Jones, Chmn.

Phone: 503-268-8000	Fax: 503-268-8347
Toll-Free:	
Address: 5555 NE Moore Ct., Hillsboro, OR 97124-6421 US	

GROWTH PLANS/SPECIAL FEATURES:

Lattice Semiconductor Corp. (LSC) designs, develops and markets high performance programmable logic products (PLDs) and related software. PLDs are semiconductor components configured as specific logic circuits that allow shorter design cycle times and reduced development costs. The firm's PLDs are primarily used by original equipment manufacturers (OEMs) operating in the communications, computing, consumer, industrial, automotive, medical and military markets. The firm's products occur in two primary product families: field programmable gate arrays (FPGAs) and PLDs. FPGA products include the LatticeECP family of low-power high-value FPGAs, designed for customers who require digital signal processing, a large amount of memory and high-speed serial communications channels; non-volatile LatticeXP FPGAs, which incorporate an on-chip memory program to allow customers to reduce their board size; and the LatticeSC family of system level FPGAs, which offer high-speed serial communication channels, large memories and high-speed input/output. The PLD products, which generate 67% of revenue, include the MachXO, ispMACH 4000, Power Manager and ispClock product families. Of the three main breeds of digital integrated circuits (microprocessors, memory and logic), the logic market, which is LSC's focus, encompasses standard logic products, custom-designed application specific integrated circuits (ASICs) and PLDs. Company products are supported by the ispLEVER (software development tool suite) and PAC-Designer software, and the Windows, UNIX and LINUX platforms. Lattice's IP core program, ispLEVERCORE, assists customers' design efforts by providing pre-tested, reusable functions, allowing them to focus on their system architectures. Export sales, mainly to Europe and Asia, account for 85% of total revenue. In February 2010, LSC launched Lattice SG Pte. Ltd., its new Asian operations center, in Singapore.

Employees are offered medical, dental and vision coverage; flexible spending accounts; a 401(k) savings plan; an employee stock purchase plan; life insurance; credit union membership; and an on-site cafeteria and fitness center.

FINANCIALS: Sales and profits are in thousands of dollars—add 000 to get the full amount. 2010 Note: Financial information for 2010 was not available for all companies at press time.

2010 Sales: $	2010 Profits: $	U.S. Stock Ticker: LSCC
2009 Sales: $194,420	2009 Profits: $-6,957	Int'l Ticker: Int'l Exchange:
2008 Sales: $222,262	2008 Profits: $-38,206	Employees: 708
2007 Sales: $228,709	2007 Profits: $-239,816	Fiscal Year Ends: 12/31
2006 Sales: $245,459	2006 Profits: $3,093	Parent Company:

SALARIES/BENEFITS:

Pension Plan:	ESOP Stock Plan:	Profit Sharing:	Top Exec. Salary: $615,000	Bonus: $
Savings Plan: Y	Stock Purch. Plan: Y		Second Exec. Salary: $285,000	Bonus: $

OTHER THOUGHTS:

Apparent Women Officers or Directors:
Hot Spot for Advancement for Women/Minorities:

LOCATIONS: ("Y" = Yes)

West:	Southwest:	Midwest:	Southeast:	Northeast:	International:
Y		Y		Y	Y

LENOVO GROUP LIMITED

www.lenovo.com

Industry Group Code: 334111 Ranks within this company's industry group: Sales: 11   Profits: 23

Hardware:		Software:		Telecommunications:		Electronic Publishing:		Equipment:		Specialty Services:	
Computers:	Y	Consumer:		Local:		Online Service:		Telecom:	Y	Consulting:	
Accessories:	Y	Corporate:		Long Distance:		TV/Cable or Wireless:		Communication:		Contract Manufacturing:	
Network Equipment:	Y	Telecom:		Cellular:	Y	Games:		Distribution:		Processing:	
Chips/Circuits:		Internet:		Internet Service:	Y	Financial Data:		VAR/Reseller:		Staff/Outsourcing:	
Parts/Drives:	Y							Satellite Srv./Equip.:		Specialty Services:	

TYPES OF BUSINESS:

Manufacturing-PCs
Servers
Notebook Computers
Handheld Computers
Peripherals
Cellular Phones

BRANDS/DIVISIONS/AFFILIATES:

Legend Group Limited
Legend Group Holdings
International Business Machines Corp (IBM)
Thinkpad
ThinkVantage Toolbox
ThinkCentre
Innovation Design Center
Lenovo Mobile

CONTACTS: *Note: Officers with more than one job title may be intentionally listed here more than once.*

Yuanqing Yang, CEO
Rory Read, COO
Rory Read, Pres.
Wai Ming Wong, CFO/Sr. VP
David Roman, Chief Mktg. Officer/Sr. VP
Kenneth Dipietro, Sr. VP-Human Resources
Xiaoyan Wang, CIO/Sr. VP
Zhiqiang He, CTO/Sr. VP
Jun Liu, Sr. VP-Prod. Group
Michael O'Neill, General Counsel/Sr. VP
Robert Cones, Sr. VP-Oper.
Qiao Jian, VP-Corp. Strategy & Planning
Robert Cones, Sr. VP-Web Sales
Peter Bartolotta, Sr. VP-Global Svcs.
Milko Van Duijl, Sr. VP-Mature Markets
Shaopeng Chen, Sr. VP-Emerging Markets
Dion Weisler, VP-Bus. Oper.
Chuanzhi Liu, Chmn.
Rory Read, Acting Pres., Latin America
Gerry P. Smith, Sr. VP-Global Supply Chain

Phone:	Fax: 877-411-1329
Toll-Free: 866-458-4465	
Address: 1009 Think Pl., Morrisville, NC 27560 US	

GROWTH PLANS/SPECIAL FEATURES:

Lenovo Group Limited is one of the largest PC manufacturers in China, with 28.8% market share. The company manufactures its own line of PCs, notebook computers, printers, servers, handheld computers and cellular phones, marketing its products in 160 countries. Its key products continue to be notebook computers, sales of which accounted for 63% of its 2010 total. Desktop computers and other products represented 35% and 2%, respectively. Lenovo has major research centers in Yamato, Japan; Beijing, Shanghai and Shenzhen, China, and Morrisville, North Carolina. It has manufacturing centers in Beijing, Huiyang Shenzhen and Shanghai China, Greensboro North Carolina, Pondicherry India and Monterrey Mexico. Its principal operations are located in Morrisville, Beijing and Singapore. IBM has less than 5% interest in the firm. Under an agreement with IBM, Lenovo is the preferred supplier of PCs to IBM and is allowed to use the IBM brand, including the Think brand. Legend Group Holdings, which is controlled by the Chinese government, owns a 42% stake in the firm. In 2010, sales in China represented 47% of its total, while sales to mature markets (including Europe and North America) were 37% and sales to emerging markets (including India, Southeast Asia and Latin America) were 16%. In January 2010, the firm reacquired the shares of Lenovo Mobile, a leader in the Chinese mobile Internet market. In June 2010, it introduced the IdeaPad Y560d, its first laptop with a 3D display.

Employees are offered health plans; retirement and savings plans; discounts on fitness centers; and an employee discount program, which allows employees, as well as their friends and families to buy discounted Lenovo computers and accessories.

FINANCIALS: Sales and profits are in thousands of dollars—add 000 to get the full amount. 2010 Note: Financial information for 2010 was not available for all companies at press time.

2010 Sales: $16,604,800	2010 Profits: $129,400	**U.S. Stock Ticker: LNVGY**
2009 Sales: $14,901,400	2009 Profits: $-226,400	**Int'l Ticker:** Int'l Exchange:
2008 Sales: $16,352,000	2008 Profits: $2,450,000	Employees: 22,205
2007 Sales: $13,978,000	2007 Profits: $1,887,000	Fiscal Year Ends: 3/31
2006 Sales: $13,276,000	2006 Profits: $1,858,000	Parent Company:

SALARIES/BENEFITS:

Pension Plan: Y	ESOP Stock Plan:	Profit Sharing:	Top Exec. Salary: $	Bonus: $
Savings Plan: Y	Stock Purch. Plan:		Second Exec. Salary: $	Bonus: $

OTHER THOUGHTS:

Apparent Women Officers or Directors: 1
Hot Spot for Advancement for Women/Minorities:

LOCATIONS: ("Y" = Yes)

West:	Southwest:	Midwest:	Southeast:	Northeast:	International:
				Y	Y

LEXAR MEDIA INC

www.lexar.com

Industry Group Code: 334112 Ranks within this company's industry group: Sales: Profits:

Hardware:	Software:	Telecommunications:	Electronic Publishing:	Equipment:	Specialty Services:
Computers:	Consumer:	Local:	Online Service:	Telecom:	Consulting:
Accessories:	Corporate:	Long Distance:	TV/Cable or Wireless:	Communication:	Contract Manufacturing:
Network Equipment:	Telecom:	Cellular:	Games:	Distribution:	Processing:
Chips/Circuits:	Internet:	Internet Service:	Financial Data:	VAR/Reseller:	Staff/Outsourcing:
Parts/Drives: Y				Satellite Srv./Equip.:	Specialty Services:

TYPES OF BUSINESS:

Computer Storage Equipment-Digital Media
Flash-Based Storage Products
USB Flash Drives
Connectivity Products
Digital Camera Memory Cards
Card Readers
ATA Controller Technology
Software

BRANDS/DIVISIONS/AFFILIATES:

Micron Technology, Inc.
JumpDrive
Image Rescue
Crucial
Lexar Echo SE
Lexar ZE
Crucial Ballistix
Lexar Multi-Card 24-in-1 USB Reader

CONTACTS: *Note: Officers with more than one job title may be intentionally listed here more than once.*

Jeff Cable, Dir.-Mktg.
Scott Signore, Dir.-Public Rel.
Mark W. Adams, VP-Digital Media Group, Micron Technology

Phone: 510-413-1200	Fax: 510-440-3499
Toll-Free: 800-789-9418	
Address: 47300 Bayside Pkwy., Fremont, CA 94538 US	

GROWTH PLANS/SPECIAL FEATURES:

Lexar Media, Inc., a wholly-owned subsidiary of Micron Technology, Inc., designs, develops and manufactures high-performance digital media, flash based storage technology, card readers and ATA controller technology. These products can be used in digital photography, consumer electronics, industrial products and communications. The firm's JumpDrive products are high-speed, portable USB flash drives for consumer applications including floppy disk replacement. JumpDrive products allow customers to easily store, transfer and carry data. Lexar also offers a variety of connectivity products that link its media products to PCs and other electronic host devices. The company's digital film products are available in CompactFlash, SD and Memory Stick formats and enable customers to capture digital images and download them quickly to a personal computer for editing, distributing and printing. Lexar's flash memory controller technology can be applied to consumer electronic applications such as digital music players, laptop computers, personal digital assistants, telecommunications and network devices and digital video recorders. Additionally, the company offers Image Rescue brand recovery software for use with its memory cards, as well as USB and FireWire memory card readers. Lexar's Crucial brand memory upgrade supplies through the Crucial.com web site. The web site carries approximately 250,000 upgrades for over 40,000 systems, as well as tools to select compatible memory. The firm has selectively licensed its technologies to third parties in sectors including data communications, telecommunications, industrial, computing and embedded markets. It also sells memory cards under the Kodak brand. In 2010, Lexar Media introduced several new products, including Lexar Echo SE and Lexar ZE flash-based backup drives; Crucial Ballistix high-performance memory modules; and Lexar Multi-Card 24-in-1 USB Reader, which supports 24 memory card formats and has five slots.

FINANCIALS: Sales and profits are in thousands of dollars—add 000 to get the full amount. 2010 Note: Financial information for 2010 was not available for all companies at press time.

2010 Sales: $	2010 Profits: $	U.S. Stock Ticker: Subsidiary
2009 Sales: $	2009 Profits: $	Int'l Ticker: Int'l Exchange:
2008 Sales: $	2008 Profits: $	Employees:
2007 Sales: $	2007 Profits: $	Fiscal Year Ends: 12/31
2006 Sales: $	2006 Profits: $	Parent Company: MICRON TECHNOLOGY INC

SALARIES/BENEFITS:

Pension Plan:	ESOP Stock Plan:	Profit Sharing:	Top Exec. Salary: $	Bonus: $
Savings Plan:	Stock Purch. Plan:		Second Exec. Salary: $	Bonus: $

OTHER THOUGHTS:

Apparent Women Officers or Directors:
Hot Spot for Advancement for Women/Minorities:

LOCATIONS: ("Y" = Yes)

West:	Southwest:	Midwest:	Southeast:	Northeast:	International:
Y					Y

Note: Financial information, benefits and other data can change quickly and may vary from those stated here.

LEXMARK INTERNATIONAL INC

www.lexmark.com

Industry Group Code: 334119 Ranks within this company's industry group: Sales: 8 Profits: 4

Hardware:		Software:		Telecommunications:	Electronic Publishing:	Equipment:	Specialty Services:
Computers:		Consumer:		Local:	Online Service:	Telecom:	Consulting:
Accessories:	Y	Corporate:	Y	Long Distance:	TV/Cable or Wireless:	Communication:	Contract Manufacturing:
Network Equipment:		Telecom:		Cellular:	Games:	Distribution:	Processing:
Chips/Circuits:		Internet:		Internet Service:	Financial Data:	VAR/Reseller:	Staff/Outsourcing:
Parts/Drives:						Satellite Srv./Equip.:	Specialty Services:

TYPES OF BUSINESS:

Computer Accessories-Printers
Laser & Inkjet Printers
Printer Consumables
Typewriters & Supplies
Connectivity Products
Document Software
Managed Print Services Outsourcing

BRANDS/DIVISIONS/AFFILIATES:

Perceptive Software Inc

CONTACTS: *Note: Officers with more than one job title may be intentionally listed here more than once.*

Paul Rooke, CEO
Paul Rooke, Pres.
John W. Gamble Jr., CFO/Exec. VP
Jeri Isbell, VP-Human Resources
Robert J. Patton, General Counsel/Sec./VP
Gary Stromquist, Corp. Finance
Paul A. Rooke, Exec. VP/Pres., Imaging Solutions & Svcs.
Scott Coons, VP/CEO/Pres., Perceptive Software
Paul J. Curlander, Chmn.
Ronaldo Foresti, VP-Asia Pacific & Latin America

Phone: 859-232-2000	Fax: 859-232-2403
Toll-Free: 800-539-6275	
Address: 740 W. New Circle Rd., Lexington, KY 40550 US	

GROWTH PLANS/SPECIAL FEATURES:

Lexmark International, Inc. is a global developer, manufacturer and supplier of laser and inkjet printers and associated consumable supplies for the office and home markets. Its products are sold in over 150 countries across the Americas, Europe, the Middle East, Africa, Asia, the Pacific Rim and the Caribbean. The firm has four manufacturing sites and approximately 70 sales offices. Lexmark is divided into two segments: the Printing Solutions and Services Division, and the Imaging Solutions Division. The Printing Solutions and Services Division markets the company's lines of workgroup monochrome laser printers, color laser printers and laser multifunction printers to small and medium businesses, large corporations and the general public sector. The Imaging Solutions Division focuses on marketing inkjet and laser printers to the small office and home office (SOHO) markets. Lexmark also offers include outsourced managed print services, a service where Lexmark takes over ownership and/or operation of a client's printers, copiers and fax machines with the goal of savings substantial operating costs for the client. International sales, including exports from the U.S., accounted for approximately 57% of the firm's revenue. In June 2010, the company acquired Perceptive Software, Inc., a developer of enterprise content management software, for $280 million.

Employees are offered a 401(k) plan; flexible spending accounts; a stock purchase plan; and health benefits.

FINANCIALS: Sales and profits are in thousands of dollars—add 000 to get the full amount. 2010 Note: Financial information for 2010 was not available for all companies at press time.

2010 Sales: $	2010 Profits: $	U.S. Stock Ticker: LXK
2009 Sales: $3,879,900	2009 Profits: $145,900	Int'l Ticker: Int'l Exchange:
2008 Sales: $4,528,400	2008 Profits: $240,200	Employees: 11,900
2007 Sales: $4,973,900	2007 Profits: $300,800	Fiscal Year Ends: 12/31
2006 Sales: $5,108,100	2006 Profits: $338,400	Parent Company:

SALARIES/BENEFITS:

Pension Plan:	ESOP Stock Plan:	Profit Sharing:	Top Exec. Salary: $1,003,846	Bonus: $1,073,200
Savings Plan:	Stock Purch. Plan:		Second Exec. Salary: $572,192	Bonus: $552,520

OTHER THOUGHTS:

Apparent Women Officers or Directors: 3
Hot Spot for Advancement for Women/Minorities: Y

LOCATIONS: ("Y" = Yes)

West:	Southwest:	Midwest:	Southeast:	Northeast:	International:
		Y			Y

LG DISPLAY CO LTD

www.lgphilips-lcd.com

Industry Group Code: 334119 Ranks within this company's industry group: Sales: 2 Profits: 2

Hardware:		Software:	Telecommunications:	Electronic Publishing:	Equipment:	Specialty Services:
Computers:		Consumer:	Local:	Online Service:	Telecom:	Consulting:
Accessories:	Y	Corporate:	Long Distance:	TV/Cable or Wireless:	Communication:	Contract Manufacturing:
Network Equipment:		Telecom:	Cellular:	Games:	Distribution:	Processing:
Chips/Circuits:		Internet:	Internet Service:	Financial Data:	VAR/Reseller:	Staff/Outsourcing:
Parts/Drives:					Satellite Srv./Equip.:	Specialty Services:

TYPES OF BUSINESS:

LCD Panel Manufacturing

BRANDS/DIVISIONS/AFFILIATES:

L&I Electronic Technology (Dongguan) Limited

CONTACTS: Note: Officers with more than one job title may be intentionally listed here more than once.

Young Soo Kwon, CEO
Kim Jong Shik, COO
Jung Ho Young, CFO
Ha Hyun Hwoi, Exec. VP-IT Bus.
Chung In Jae, CTO
Han Sang Bum, VP/Mgr.-TV Bus. Unit
Yeo Sang Deok, Mgr.-Mobile & OLED Bus.
Young Soo Kwon, Chmn.

Phone: 82-2-3777-1665	Fax: 82-2-3777-0797

Toll-Free:

Address: LG Twin Towers, W. Wing, 17th Fl., 20 Yeouido-dong, Seoul, 150-721 Korea

GROWTH PLANS/SPECIAL FEATURES:

LG Display Co., Ltd., formerly LG Philips LCD, Inc., operates in the digital display business and is headquartered in Seoul, South Korea. LG Display develops and manufactures TFT-LCD panels for televisions, monitors, notebook PCs and emerging mobile applications such as WebPad, e-Book, car navigation, fingerprint recognition systems and online stock trading. LG Display is a member of the Philips Group, which spans a wide range of industries including consumer products, lighting, medical systems and semiconductors. The firm's international sales network is directed through locations in Germany, Japan, Taiwan, Hong Kong and China as well as LG Display America, Inc., with representatives and distributors in California. Some of the firms products include 27-inch full HDTV/monitor LCD panels with enhanced motion picture response time; 42-inch and 47-inch LCD TV panels with a thickness of 5.9 millimeters; a Full HD 23-inch 3D LCD panels with enhanced brightness for monitors; a thin-film solar cell featured for the e-Book to expand battery life; 23-inch 3D monitor LCD panels with full HD resolution; 2.6 millimeter 42-inch LCD TV panels; and 19-inch wide flexible e-paper. The company maintains a strategic partnership with Idemitsu Kosan Co. Ltd. to cooperatively develop organic light-emitting diode displays. In June 2010, the firm announced plans to develop joint venture L&I Electronic Technology (Dongguan) Limited with iriver Ltd., a Korea-based e-Book manufacturer, to develop e-Books. In May 2010, the company introduced a full HD 21.5-inch LCD monitor panel, which features optical touch technology.

FINANCIALS: Sales and profits are in thousands of dollars—add 000 to get the full amount. 2010 Note: Financial information for 2010 was not available for all companies at press time.

2010 Sales: $	2010 Profits: $	U.S. Stock Ticker: LPL
2009 Sales: $18,502,800	2009 Profits: $953,680	Int'l Ticker: 034220 Int'l Exchange: Seoul-KRX
2008 Sales: $12,410,800	2008 Profits: $829,320	Employees:
2007 Sales: $10,952,000	2007 Profits: $1,025,630	Fiscal Year Ends: 12/31
2006 Sales: $11,423,871	2006 Profits: $-744,923	Parent Company:

SALARIES/BENEFITS:

Pension Plan:	ESOP Stock Plan:	Profit Sharing:	Top Exec. Salary: $	Bonus: $
Savings Plan:	Stock Purch. Plan:		Second Exec. Salary: $	Bonus: $

OTHER THOUGHTS:

Apparent Women Officers or Directors:
Hot Spot for Advancement for Women/Minorities:

LOCATIONS: ("Y" = Yes)

West:	Southwest:	Midwest:	Southeast:	Northeast:	International:
Y					Y

LG ELECTRONICS INC

www.lge.com

Industry Group Code: 334220 Ranks within this company's industry group: Sales: 1   Profits: 2

Hardware:		Software:		Telecommunications:		Electronic Publishing:		Equipment:		Specialty Services:	
Computers:	Y	Consumer:		Local:		Online Service:		Telecom:	Y	Consulting:	
Accessories:	Y	Corporate:		Long Distance:		TV/Cable or Wireless:		Communication:	Y	Contract Manufacturing:	
Network Equipment:	Y	Telecom:		Cellular:		Games:		Distribution:		Processing:	
Chips/Circuits:	Y	Internet:		Internet Service:		Financial Data:		VAR/Reseller:		Staff/Outsourcing:	
Parts/Drives:	Y							Satellite Srv./Equip.:		Specialty Services:	

TYPES OF BUSINESS:

Manufacturing-Electronics
Cellular Handsets
Telecommunications Equipment
Computer Products
Home Appliances & Electronics
Security Systems
Displays
Audio Systems

BRANDS/DIVISIONS/AFFILIATES:

LG Corporation
LG-Shaker Air-Conditioning Co.
H.G. Ibrahim Shaker Co.

CONTACTS: *Note: Officers with more than one job title may be intentionally listed here more than once.*

Yong Nam, CEO/Vice Chmn.
Yu-Sig Kang, COO/Vice Chmn.
Hee-Gook Lee, Pres.
James Jeong, CFO
Woo Hyun Paik, CTO
Simon Kang, Pres./CEO-Home Entertainment Co.
Young-Ha Lee, Pres./CEO-Home Appliance Co.
Skott Ahn, Pres./CEO-Mobile Communications Co.
B.B Hwang, Exec. VP-Business Solutions Co.
Bon Moo Koo, Chmn.
James Kim, Pres./CEO-LG Electronics, Europe

Phone: 82-2-3777-3427	Fax: 82-2-3777-3428
Toll-Free:	
Address: LG Twin Towers, 20 Yeouido-dong, Yeoungdeungpo-gu, Seoul, 150-721 Korea	

GROWTH PLANS/SPECIAL FEATURES:

LG Electronics, Inc. is a Korean manufacturer of telecommunications equipment, home appliances, televisions, audio equipment, security systems and computer products. The company has five lines of business: Home Entertainment, Mobile Communications, Home Appliance, Air Conditioning and Business Solutions. The home entertainment division manufactures plasma screen, liquid crystal display (LCD), high definition, flat panel and projection TVs, as well as VCRs, notebook computers, optical storage devices, monitors, video tape and DVDs. LG's mobile communications division produces UMTS (WCDMA), CDMA and GSM mobile handsets. The division also manufactures wireline telephones, wireless telephone networking equipment, Voice-over Internet Protocol (VoIP) equipment and telecommunications mainframes. LG's home appliance division manufactures home appliances for home ubiquitous networking including refrigerators, dish washers, washers and dryers, ovens and vacuum cleaners. In addition, the company is a leading global supplier of home appliance components such as washing machine motors. The firm's air conditioner division manufactures air conditioners and dehumidifiers. LG's business solutions division offers office-related electronics such as computers, monitors and storage devices. The firm has offices throughout Asia, Europe, Africa, the Middle East, Latin America and North America. With 110 operating units worldwide, LG is a truly global firm. R&D is a focus here, with dozens of research centers worldwide, including the LG Electronics Institute of Technology in Seoul, Korea. The firm has partnered with Prada; GE; Siemens; Toyota; Google; Qualcomm; Hitachi; Nortel; Microsoft; Sun Microsystems; Dolby; and a variety of other companies. New products recently released by the company include a line of Internet-ready LED TVs; the Cosmos, Lotus Elite and Rumor Touch cell phones; and the LG X120 netbook.

FINANCIALS: Sales and profits are in thousands of dollars—add 000 to get the full amount. 2010 Note: Financial information for 2010 was not available for all companies at press time.

2010 Sales: $	2010 Profits: $	U.S. Stock Ticker:
2009 Sales: $65,780,900	2009 Profits: $1,855,860	Int'l Ticker: 066570 Int'l Exchange: Seoul-KRX
2008 Sales: $36,220,000	2008 Profits: $1,560,000	Employees:
2007 Sales: $25,298,000	2007 Profits: $1,315,000	Fiscal Year Ends: 12/31
2006 Sales: $24,263,000	2006 Profits: $223,000	Parent Company:

SALARIES/BENEFITS:

Pension Plan:	ESOP Stock Plan:	Profit Sharing:	Top Exec. Salary: $	Bonus: $
Savings Plan:	Stock Purch. Plan:		Second Exec. Salary: $	Bonus: $

OTHER THOUGHTS:

Apparent Women Officers or Directors:
Hot Spot for Advancement for Women/Minorities:

LOCATIONS: ("Y" = Yes)

West:	Southwest:	Midwest:	Southeast:	Northeast:	International:
					Y

LG ELECTRONICS INDIA PVT LTD

www.in.lge.com

Industry Group Code: 334310 Ranks within this company's industry group: Sales: Profits:

Hardware:		Software:	Telecommunications:	Electronic Publishing:	Equipment:	Specialty Services:
Computers:	Y	Consumer:	Local:	Online Service:	Telecom:	Consulting:
Accessories:	Y	Corporate:	Long Distance:	TV/Cable or Wireless:	Communication:	Contract Manufacturing:
Network Equipment:		Telecom:	Cellular:	Games:	Distribution:	Processing:
Chips/Circuits:		Internet:	Internet Service:	Financial Data:	VAR/Reseller:	Staff/Outsourcing:
Parts/Drives:					Satellite Srv./Equip.:	Specialty Services:

TYPES OF BUSINESS:

Consumer Durable Products

BRANDS/DIVISIONS/AFFILIATES:

LG Electronics Inc
PRADA Phone By LG
SolarDOM
Kompressor

CONTACTS: Note: Officers with more than one job title may be intentionally listed here more than once.

Moon B. Shin, Managing Dir.
Chandramani Singh, Chief Prod. Officer
Chandramani Singh, Head-Consumer Electronics

Phone:	Fax:
Toll-Free: 800-180-9999	
Address: Plot No. 51 Surajpur Kasna Rd., Greater Noida, 201306 India	

GROWTH PLANS/SPECIAL FEATURES:

LG Electronics India Pvt. Ltd., a wholly-owned subsidiary of LG Electronics, Inc., is a market leader in the manufacturing and marketing of consumer durable products. The company is organized into four business areas: Consumer electronics, home appliances, computer products and mobile communications. The consumer products segment encompasses LCD TVs, plasma display, color televisions, home theater systems, DVD players and recorders, and MP3 and MP4 players. The home appliances area offers room and commercial air conditioners, refrigerators, washing machines, dishwashers, microwaves and vacuum cleaners. Computer products include laptops, personal computers, LCD monitors, CRT monitors and optical storage devices. The mobile phone segment consists of premium trend setter phones, camera phones, music phones and color screen GSM handsets. Some of the firm's products include full HD LCD televisions with 1920 x 1080 resolution and a 6000:1 contrast ratio and a six millisecond response time; the PRADA Phone by LG; SolarDOM, a light wave oven; and the Kompressor vacuum cleaner.

FINANCIALS: Sales and profits are in thousands of dollars—add 000 to get the full amount. 2010 Note: Financial information for 2010 was not available for all companies at press time.

2010 Sales: $	2010 Profits: $	U.S. Stock Ticker: Subsidiary
2009 Sales: $	2009 Profits: $	Int'l Ticker: Int'l Exchange:
2008 Sales: $	2008 Profits: $	Employees:
2007 Sales: $	2007 Profits: $	Fiscal Year Ends: 12/31
2006 Sales: $	2006 Profits: $	Parent Company: LG ELECTRONICS INC

SALARIES/BENEFITS:

Pension Plan:	ESOP Stock Plan:	Profit Sharing:	Top Exec. Salary: $	Bonus: $
Savings Plan:	Stock Purch. Plan:		Second Exec. Salary: $	Bonus: $

OTHER THOUGHTS:

Apparent Women Officers or Directors:
Hot Spot for Advancement for Women/Minorities:

LOCATIONS: ("Y" = Yes)

West:	Southwest:	Midwest:	Southeast:	Northeast:	International:
					Y

LG ELECTRONICS USA INC

www.lg.com

Industry Group Code: 334220 Ranks within this company's industry group: Sales: Profits:

Hardware:		Software:	Telecommunications:	Electronic Publishing:	Equipment:		Specialty Services:	
Computers:		Consumer:	Local:	Online Service:	Telecom:	Y	Consulting:	
Accessories:	Y	Corporate:	Long Distance:	TV/Cable or Wireless:	Communication:		Contract Manufacturing:	
Network Equipment:		Telecom:	Cellular:	Games:	Distribution:		Processing:	
Chips/Circuits:		Internet:	Internet Service:	Financial Data:	VAR/Reseller:		Staff/Outsourcing:	
Parts/Drives:					Satellite Srv./Equip.:		Specialty Services:	Y

TYPES OF BUSINESS:

Consumer Electronics
Mobile Phones & Accessories
Home Appliances
Computer Products

BRANDS/DIVISIONS/AFFILIATES:

LG Electronics Inc
LG Electronics USA Inc
LG Electronics MobileComm U.S.A., Inc.

CONTACTS: Note: Officers with more than one job title may be intentionally listed here more than once.

Wayne Park, CEO
Wayne Parl, Pres.
James Shad, Pres., LG Electronics USA, Inc.

Phone:	Fax:
Toll-Free: 800-243-0000	
Address: 1000 Sylvan Ave., Englewood Cliffs, NJ 07632 US	

GROWTH PLANS/SPECIAL FEATURES:

LG Electronics USA, Inc. (LGE USA), a subsidiary of LG Electronics, Inc., sells consumer electronics products, mobile phones and digital applications in the U.S., Canada and Mexico. The firm sells its products in four categories: mobile phones, television, audio and video; appliances; and computer products. Subsidiary LG Electronics MobileComm U.S.A., Inc. (LGE MobileComm) is the firm's North American wireless division headquartered in San Diego, California. LGE MobileComm sells the LG signature dual internal/external LCD clamshell-style phones, featuring external organic electro-luminescent displays, embedded cameras, a variety of ringers and an icon-driven menu system. LGE USA's television, audio and video category includes plasma, LCD and digital video products. It offers one of the industry's widest ranges of flat-panel screen sizes, quiet fan-free cooling, special video processing technology and high-altitude plasma displays. It also offers 3D network Blu-ray disc players and portable DVD players. This segment features NetCast Entertainment Access, which brings Internet services such as Netflix, Roxio CinemaNow, Yahoo Widgets and Pandora directly to LG's televisions. The firm's appliances segment sells washers, dryers, refrigerators, built-in ovens, cooktops, dishwashers, microwave ovens, air conditioners, vacuums, dehumidifiers and accessories. Lastly, the computer products segment offers monitors, netbooks, optical media, network storage and USB aircards. In January 2010, the company entered into a strategic alliance with Viking Range Corporation to collaborate on areas such as expanded distribution, shared research and development resources and product cross-sourcing and joint procurement opportunities. In May 2010, LG Electronics MobileComm and AT&T announced the LG Vu Plus TM, the latest AT&T mobile TV-capable device.

The firm offers its employees medical insurance; holiday pay; company product discounts; and a retirement plan.

FINANCIALS: Sales and profits are in thousands of dollars—add 000 to get the full amount. 2010 Note: Financial information for 2010 was not available for all companies at press time.

2010 Sales: $	2010 Profits: $	**U.S. Stock Ticker: Subsidiary**
2009 Sales: $	2009 Profits: $	**Int'l Ticker:** Int'l Exchange:
2008 Sales: $	2008 Profits: $	Employees:
2007 Sales: $	2007 Profits: $	Fiscal Year Ends:
2006 Sales: $	2006 Profits: $	Parent Company: LG ELECTRONICS INC

SALARIES/BENEFITS:

Pension Plan:	ESOP Stock Plan:	Profit Sharing:	Top Exec. Salary: $	Bonus: $
Savings Plan: Y	Stock Purch. Plan:		Second Exec. Salary: $	Bonus: $

OTHER THOUGHTS:

Apparent Women Officers or Directors:
Hot Spot for Advancement for Women/Minorities:

LOCATIONS: ("Y" = Yes)

West:	Southwest:	Midwest:	Southeast:	Northeast:	International:
Y	Y	Y	Y	Y	

LIMELIGHT NETWORKS INC

www.limelightnetworks.com

Industry Group Code: 519130 Ranks within this company's industry group: Sales: 3 Profits: 3

Hardware:	Software:	Telecommunications:	Electronic Publishing:		Equipment:	Specialty Services:	
Computers:	Consumer:	Local:	Online Service:	Y	Telecom:	Consulting:	
Accessories:	Corporate:	Long Distance:	TV/Cable or Wireless:		Communication:	Contract Manufacturing:	
Network Equipment:	Telecom:	Cellular:	Games:		Distribution:	Processing:	
Chips/Circuits:	Internet:	Internet Service:	Financial Data:		VAR/Reseller:	Staff/Outsourcing:	
Parts/Drives:					Satellite Srv./Equip.:	Specialty Services:	Y

TYPES OF BUSINESS:

Online Media Distribution

BRANDS/DIVISIONS/AFFILIATES:

LimelightDELIVER
LimelightDELIVER XD
LimelightSUPPORT
LimelightSTREAM
LimelightSITE
LimelightREACH
EyeWonder, Inc.
Delve Networks

CONTACTS: Note: Officers with more than one job title may be intentionally listed here more than once.

Jeff Lunsford, CEO
Doug Lindroth, CFO
David Hatfield, Sr. VP-Mktg. & Sales
Nathan Raciborski, CTO
David Hatfield, Sr. VP-Prod.
Lonhyn Jasinskyj, Sr. VP-Software Eng.
Philip C. Maynard, Chief Legal Officer/Sr. VP/Corp. Sec.
John Vincent, CEO-EyeWonder
Jeff Lunsford, Chmn.

Phone: 602-850-5000	Fax: 602-850-5001
Toll-Free: 866-200-5463	
Address: 2220 W. 14th St., Tempe, AZ 85281 US	

GROWTH PLANS/SPECIAL FEATURES:

Limelight Networks, Inc. is a provider of high-performance content delivery network (CDN) services for traditional and emerging media companies, including businesses operating in the television, music, radio, newspaper, magazine, movie, videogame, software and social media industries. Limelight has operations in the U.S., Europe and Asia, with more than 1,370 customers worldwide. The CDN's global delivery capability exceeds three terabits per second, enabling quick response time to surges in end-user demand. The company's services are designed for the delivery of digital media to large, global audiences, and include LimelightDELIVER and LimelightDELIVER XD, which provide HTTP/web distribution of digital media files such as video, music, games, software and social media; LimelightSTREAM, which provides on-demand streaming for all major formats including Adobe Flash, MP3 audio, QuickTime, RealNetworks RealPlayer and Windows Media; LimelightSITE, a fast web site content delivery platform; LimelightHD, which streams video at high-definition resolution; LimelightREACH, which delivers content to mobile devices; LimelightADS, which provides advertising services; and LimelightSUPPORT, which provides customers with on-demand engineering resources. The firm's subsidiary EyeWonder, Inc. specializes in digital advertising and maintains locations all over the world. Customers of the company include Microsoft, Blue Cross, Facebook, Amazon, Oracle, University of Virginia, ABC Radio, Netflix, Sony PlayStation and Valve Corporation. In May 2010, the company completed its acquisition of EyeWonder, Inc. In August of the same year, the company acquired private firm Delve Networks, a cloud-based video publisher and a provider of analytics services.

The firm offered employees medical and dental insurance; disability coverage; life insurance; domestic partner insurance coverage; flexible spending accounts; and a 401(k) plan.

FINANCIALS: Sales and profits are in thousands of dollars—add 000 to get the full amount. 2010 Note: Financial information for 2010 was not available for all companies at press time.

2010 Sales: $	2010 Profits: $	U.S. Stock Ticker: LLNW
2009 Sales: $131,663	2009 Profits: $34,890	Int'l Ticker: Int'l Exchange:
2008 Sales: $129,530	2008 Profits: $-63,067	Employees: 238
2007 Sales: $103,111	2007 Profits: $-73,020	Fiscal Year Ends: 12/31
2006 Sales: $65,243	2006 Profits: $-3,377	Parent Company:

SALARIES/BENEFITS:

Pension Plan:	ESOP Stock Plan:	Profit Sharing:	Top Exec. Salary: $400,000	Bonus: $204,385
Savings Plan: Y	Stock Purch. Plan:		Second Exec. Salary: $300,000	Bonus: $74,322

OTHER THOUGHTS:

Apparent Women Officers or Directors:
Hot Spot for Advancement for Women/Minorities:

LOCATIONS: ("Y" = Yes)

West:	Southwest:	Midwest:	Southeast:	Northeast:	International:
Y	Y	Y	Y	Y	Y

LINEAR TECHNOLOGY CORP

www.linear.com

Industry Group Code: 33441 Ranks within this company's industry group: Sales: 30   Profits: 9

Hardware:		Software:	Telecommunications:	Electronic Publishing:	Equipment:	Specialty Services:
Computers:		Consumer:	Local:	Online Service:	Telecom:	Consulting:
Accessories:		Corporate:	Long Distance:	TV/Cable or Wireless:	Communication:	Contract Manufacturing:
Network Equipment:		Telecom:	Cellular:	Games:	Distribution:	Processing:
Chips/Circuits:	Y	Internet:	Internet Service:	Financial Data:	VAR/Reseller:	Staff/Outsourcing:
Parts/Drives:					Satellite Srv./Equip.:	Specialty Services:

TYPES OF BUSINESS:

Integrated Circuits-Linear
Amplifier Circuits
Buffers
Radio Frequency Circuits
Data Converters
Interface Circuits
Voltage References
Switched Capacitor Filters

BRANDS/DIVISIONS/AFFILIATES:

CONTACTS: Note: Officers with more than one job title may be intentionally listed here more than once.

Lothar Maier, CEO
Alexander R. McCann, COO/VP
Paul Coghlan, CFO
Richard E. Nickson, VP-Sales, North America
Robert C. Dobkin, CTO
Erik M. Soule, VP-Signal Conditioning Prod.
Robert C. Dobkin, VP-Eng.
Paul Coghlan, Sec.
Doug Dickinson, Mgr.-Media Rel.
Paul Coghlan, VP-Finance
Donald E. Paulus, VP/Gen. Mgr.-D Power Prod.
Paul V. Chantalat, VP-Quality & Reliability
Robert Reay, VP-Mixed Signal Prod.
John Hamburger, Dir.-Mktg. Comm.
Robert H. Swanson, Jr., Chmn.
David A. Quarles, VP-Sales, Int'l

Phone: 408-432-1900	Fax: 408-434-0507
Toll-Free:	
Address: 1630 McCarthy Blvd., Milpitas, CA 95035-7417 US	

GROWTH PLANS/SPECIAL FEATURES:

Linear Technology Corp. designs, manufactures and markets linear integrated circuits. Uses for these products include telecommunications; cellular telephones; networking products; satellite systems; notebook and desktop computers; computer peripherals; video and multimedia; industrial instrumentation; automotive electronics; factory automation; process control; and military and space systems. Linear Technology's over 7,500 products are sold to over 15,000 manufacturers worldwide. Although the types of linear products vary by application, the firm's principal product categories include amplifiers, high-speed amplifiers, voltage regulators, voltage references, interface circuits, radio frequency circuits, data converters, power over Ethernet controllers and signal chain modules. Amplifier circuits amplify the voltage or output current of a device. High-speed amplifiers are used to amplify signals above 5 MHz for applications such as video, fast data acquisition and data communication. Voltage regulators control the voltage of a device or circuit at a specified level. Voltage references serve as electronic benchmarks providing a constant voltage for system usage. Interface circuits act as an intermediary to transfer digital signals between or within electronic systems. Radio frequency circuits include mixers, modulators, demodulators, amplifiers, drivers and power detectors and controllers. Data converters change linear (analog) signals into digital signals, or vice versa, and are often referred to as data acquisition subsystems, A/D converters and D/A converters. Linear Technology's wafer fabrication facilities are located in Milpitas, California and Camas, Washington. The firm also maintains an assembly facility in Malaysia and a testing and distribution facility in Singapore.

Linear Technology offers its employees medical and dental plans; life and disability insurance; a profit sharing plan, sabbaticals; and tuition reimbursement.

FINANCIALS: Sales and profits are in thousands of dollars—add 000 to get the full amount. 2010 Note: Financial information for 2010 was not available for all companies at press time.

2010 Sales: $1,169,988	2010 Profits: $361,341	**U.S. Stock Ticker: LLTC**
2009 Sales: $968,498	2009 Profits: $313,510	**Int'l Ticker:** Int'l Exchange:
2008 Sales: $1,175,153	2008 Profits: $387,613	Employees: 4,191
2007 Sales: $1,083,078	2007 Profits: $411,675	Fiscal Year Ends: 6/30
2006 Sales: $1,092,977	2006 Profits: $428,680	Parent Company:

SALARIES/BENEFITS:

Pension Plan:	ESOP Stock Plan:	Profit Sharing: Y	Top Exec. Salary: $428,366	Bonus: $2,049,416
Savings Plan: Y	Stock Purch. Plan: Y		Second Exec. Salary: $375,553	Bonus: $1,456,901

OTHER THOUGHTS:

Apparent Women Officers or Directors:
Hot Spot for Advancement for Women/Minorities:

LOCATIONS: ("Y" = Yes)

West:	Southwest:	Midwest:	Southeast:	Northeast:	International:
Y	Y	Y	Y	Y	Y

Note: Financial information, benefits and other data can change quickly and may vary from those stated here.

LITE-ON TECHNOLOGY CORP

www.liteon.com

Industry Group Code: 334119 Ranks within this company's industry group: Sales: 6 Profits: 3

Hardware:		Software:	Telecommunications:	Electronic Publishing:	Equipment:		Specialty Services:
Computers:	Y	Consumer:	Local:	Online Service:	Telecom:		Consulting:
Accessories:	Y	Corporate:	Long Distance:	TV/Cable or Wireless:	Communication:	Y	Contract Manufacturing:
Network Equipment:	Y	Telecom:	Cellular:	Games:	Distribution:		Processing:
Chips/Circuits:		Internet:	Internet Service:	Financial Data:	VAR/Reseller:		Staff/Outsourcing:
Parts/Drives:	Y				Satellite Srv./Equip.:		Specialty Services:

TYPES OF BUSINESS:
Electronics & Computer Components
Computer Hardware
Computer Accessories
Networking Products
LED Lamps
Personal Digital Assistants
Portable Navigation Devices

BRANDS/DIVISIONS/AFFILIATES:
Lite-On Corp.
Silitech Technology Corporation
Actron Technology
Li Shin International Enterprise
Diodes, Inc.
Logah Technology, Inc.
DragonJet Corporation
Maxi Switch, Inc.

CONTACTS: Note: Officers with more than one job title may be intentionally listed here more than once.
K. C. Terng, CEO
Paul Lo, CTO
Raymond Soong, Chmn.-Lite-On Group

Phone: 886-2-8798-2888	Fax: 886-2-8798-2868
Toll-Free:	
Address: 392 Ruey Kuang Rd. 22F, Neihu, Taipei, 114 Taiwan	

GROWTH PLANS/SPECIAL FEATURES:

Lite-On Technology Corp. is a leading manufacturer of electronics products to the computer, digital home, consumer electronics, communications products and optoelectronic markets. Its products and services are divided into three categories: Components; Module; and System. The Components category is subdivided into power supply, including power switches, AC-DC and DC-DC converters and various power supplies; and opto electronics, which mainly produces various sizes of LED lamps and some infrared products. The Module category has three subdivisions: phone camera modules; network products, primarily modem and wireless products; and desktop computer cases. Lastly, the System category produces monitors; various portable entertaining systems (PES), including digital audio players, Bluetooth wireless speakers and FM transmitters and receivers; inkjet and laser printers; input devices, including keyboards, mice and webcams; network switches; wireless access points and Ethernet cards; personal digital assistants (PDAs); and portable navigation devices (PNDs). Based in Taiwan, the firm also has manufacturing facilities in China, Japan, Korea, the Philippines, Singapore, Thailand, Malaysia, Germany, France, the Netherlands, Italy, the U.K., the U.S. and Mexico. The company is the largest affiliate of electronics conglomerate Lite-On Group. The other 11 subsidiaries and affiliates that comprise the Lite-On Group are Silitech Technology Corporation; Actron Technology; Li Shin International Enterprise; Diodes, Inc.; Logah Technology; DragonJet Corporation; Maxi Switch, Inc.; Lite-On Automotive Corp.; Lite-On Semiconductor Corp.; Lite-On IT Corp.; and Lite-On Japan.

Lite-On offers its employees life, medical, accident, hospitalization and business travel insurance; on-site fitness and recreational facilities; subsidized domestic and overseas travel; staff cafeterias and stores; emergency assistance; subsidies for marriage, hospitalization, funerals and childbirth; and scholarships for employees and their children.

FINANCIALS: Sales and profits are in thousands of dollars—add 000 to get the full amount. 2010 Note: Financial information for 2010 was not available for all companies at press time.

2010 Sales: $	2010 Profits: $	**U.S. Stock Ticker:**
2009 Sales: $6,407,000	2009 Profits: $242,830	**Int'l Ticker: 2301** Int'l Exchange: Taipei-TPE
2008 Sales: $7,235,910	2008 Profits: $138,640	Employees:
2007 Sales: $8,215,200	2007 Profits: $266,340	Fiscal Year Ends: 12/31
2006 Sales: $	2006 Profits: $	Parent Company: LIGHT-ON GROUP CO LTD

SALARIES/BENEFITS:

Pension Plan: Y	ESOP Stock Plan:	Profit Sharing: Y	Top Exec. Salary: $	Bonus: $
Savings Plan:	Stock Purch. Plan:		Second Exec. Salary: $	Bonus: $

OTHER THOUGHTS:
Apparent Women Officers or Directors:
Hot Spot for Advancement for Women/Minorities:

LOCATIONS: ("Y" = Yes)

West:	Southwest:	Midwest:	Southeast:	Northeast:	International:
Y	Y		Y		Y

Note: Financial information, benefits and other data can change quickly and may vary from those stated here.

LIVEPERSON INC

www.liveperson.com

Industry Group Code: 511210K Ranks within this company's industry group: Sales: 7 Profits: 6

Hardware:	Software:		Telecommunications:	Electronic Publishing:	Equipment:	Specialty Services:	
Computers:	Consumer:		Local:	Online Service:	Telecom:	Consulting:	Y
Accessories:	Corporate:	Y	Long Distance:	TV/Cable or Wireless:	Communication:	Contract Manufacturing:	
Network Equipment:	Telecom:		Cellular:	Games:	Distribution:	Processing:	
Chips/Circuits:	Internet:		Internet Service:	Financial Data:	VAR/Reseller:	Staff/Outsourcing:	
Parts/Drives:					Satellite Srv./Equip.:	Specialty Services:	Y

TYPES OF BUSINESS:

E-Commerce Software
Customer Service Software
Sales & Marketing Service Software
Live Chat Applications

BRANDS/DIVISIONS/AFFILIATES:

LivePerson Enterprise for Sales
LivePerson Enterprise for Service
LivePerson Enterprise for Voice
LivePerson Pro
LivePerson Premier

CONTACTS: Note: Officers with more than one job title may be intentionally listed here more than once.

Robert LoCascio, CEO
Timothy Bixby, Pres.
Timothy Bixby, CFO
Jim Dicso, Exec. VP-Sales
Monica Greenberg, General Counsel/Sr. VP-Bus. Affairs
Peter K. Phillips, Exec. VP
Robert LoCascio, Chmn.
Eli Campo, Exec. VP/Gen. Mgr.-Tech. Oper., Israel

Phone: 212-609-4200	Fax:
Toll-Free:	
Address: 462 7th Ave., 3rd Fl., New York, NY 10018 US	

GROWTH PLANS/SPECIAL FEATURES:

LivePerson, Inc. is a facilitator of online e-commerce interaction, enhancing real-time sales, customer support and personalized expert advice through more than one billion chat interactions annually. The company offers real-time sales, marketing and customer service to online businesses with the aim of improving customer relationships. LivePerson's integrated multi-channel communication software platform combines a variety of features help companies manage online customer sales and support. The firm divides its products into two categories: small and midsize business services and enterprise services. Small and midsize business services include LivePerson Pro, which enables small business clients to economically increase online sales, and LivePerson Premier, an all-in-one platform encompassing live chat, e-mail, self-service and telephone logs. Enterprise products include LivePerson Enterprise for Sales, which combines online site traffic monitoring software with a sophisticated rules engine to enable LivePerson clients to proactively engage web site visitors; LivePerson Enterprise for Service, which utilizes a proactive customer care center to reduce attrition rates. These services are offered to a number of different specialties, such as financial services, retail, telecom, high tech, travel and automotive industries. The firm's professional services team offers consulting services to enterprise clients, helping to analyze their needs and implement appropriate strategies. In addition to its business services, LivePerson also hosts an online marketplace that allows experts and individual service providers to sell their information and knowledge via real-time chat with consumers. Users can seek advice in various categories including personal counseling; computers and programming; health and medicine; education; shopping; professional development; spirituality; legal services; and other topics. In December 2010, LivePerson opened new offices in San Francisco, California to take advantage of the Silicon Valley technology community.

FINANCIALS: Sales and profits are in thousands of dollars—add 000 to get the full amount. 2010 Note: Financial information for 2010 was not available for all companies at press time.

2010 Sales: $	2010 Profits: $	U.S. Stock Ticker: LPSN
2009 Sales: $87,490	2009 Profits: $7,763	Int'l Ticker: Int'l Exchange:
2008 Sales: $74,655	2008 Profits: $-23,837	Employees: 416
2007 Sales: $52,228	2007 Profits: $5,821	Fiscal Year Ends: 12/31
2006 Sales: $33,521	2006 Profits: $2,202	Parent Company:

SALARIES/BENEFITS:

Pension Plan:	ESOP Stock Plan:	Profit Sharing:	Top Exec. Salary: $325,000	Bonus: $325,000
Savings Plan:	Stock Purch. Plan:		Second Exec. Salary: $255,000	Bonus: $118,800

OTHER THOUGHTS:

Apparent Women Officers or Directors: 1
Hot Spot for Advancement for Women/Minorities:

LOCATIONS: ("Y" = Yes)

West:	Southwest:	Midwest:	Southeast:	Northeast:	International:
			Y	Y	Y

LOGICA PLC

www.logica.com

Industry Group Code: 541513 Ranks within this company's industry group: Sales: 10   Profits: 16

Hardware:	Software:		Telecommunications:	Electronic Publishing:	Equipment:	Specialty Services:	
Computers:	Consumer:		Local:	Online Service:	Telecom:	Consulting:	Y
Accessories:	Corporate:	Y	Long Distance:	TV/Cable or Wireless:	Communication:	Contract Manufacturing:	
Network Equipment:	Telecom:		Cellular:	Games:	Distribution:	Processing:	
Chips/Circuits:	Internet:		Internet Service:	Financial Data:	VAR/Reseller:	Staff/Outsourcing:	Y
Parts/Drives:					Satellite Srv./Equip.:	Specialty Services:	Y

TYPES OF BUSINESS:

IT Consulting
Systems Integration
Outsourced Services
Management Consulting

BRANDS/DIVISIONS/AFFILIATES:

Amstelveen Spark Innovation Center (The)

CONTACTS: Note: Officers with more than one job title may be intentionally listed here more than once.

Andy Green, CEO
Seamus Keating, COO/CEO-Benelux
Seamus Keating, CFO
Stephen Kelly, Chief People Officer
Serge Dubrana, CEO-Global Oper.
Patrick Guimbal, CEO-Strategic Programs
Karen Keyes, Head-Investor Rel.
Craig Boundy, CEO-U.K.
Joe Hemming, CEO-Outsourcing Svcs.
Joao Baptista, CEO-Northern & Central Europe
Jean-Marc Lazzari, CEO-France
David Tyler, Chmn.
Serge Dubrana, CEO-Int'l

Phone: 44-20-7637-9111	Fax: 44-20-7468-7006
Toll-Free:	
Address: 250 Brook Dr., Green Park, Reading, RG2 6UA UK	

GROWTH PLANS/SPECIAL FEATURES:

Logica plc is a business and technology service firm that operates in 36 countries. The firm is a provider of IT management and development, technology consulting, systems integration and business process outsourcing services. The company structures its business around five core industry sectors: energy and utilities (18% of revenues); financial services (15%); telecommunications and media (8%); industry, distribution and transport (27%); and the public sector (32%). Logica maintains partnerships with firms such as SAP, Microsoft, Metastorm and Oracle, implementing their software products into the system designs and updates that it offers its customers. The firm's customers are primarily headquartered in Europe, with sales in Europe accounting for approximately 62% of annual revenues. In order to serve the multinational needs of its European clients, and also to serve customers headquartered in other parts of the world, Logica maintains international offices and facilities in countries including Egypt, Kuwait, Lebanon, Morocco, Saudi Arabia, the United Arab Emirates, Australia, India, the Philippines, Taiwan, China, Indonesia, Singapore, Malaysia, Sri Lanka, Brazil, Canada and the U.S. The company's approach combines local, face-to-face client service teams with remote business process outsourcing centers in places like India, attempting to blend personalized service with the efficiencies afforded by offshore outsourcing and development. In April 2010, Logica opened The Amstelveen Spark Innovation Center in the Netherlands.

FINANCIALS: Sales and profits are in thousands of dollars—add 000 to get the full amount. 2010 Note: Financial information for 2010 was not available for all companies at press time.

2010 Sales: $	2010 Profits: $	U.S. Stock Ticker:
2009 Sales: $5,703,020	2009 Profits: $61,780	Int'l Ticker: LOG Int'l Exchange: London-LSE
2008 Sales: $5,322,940	2008 Profits: $57,710	Employees: 38,780
2007 Sales: $4,559,210	2007 Profits: $249,380	Fiscal Year Ends: 12/31
2006 Sales: $4,819,350	2006 Profits: $177,390	Parent Company:

SALARIES/BENEFITS:

Pension Plan:	ESOP Stock Plan:	Profit Sharing:	Top Exec. Salary: $1,129,520	Bonus: $1,355,424
Savings Plan:	Stock Purch. Plan:		Second Exec. Salary: $677,880	Bonus: $1,055,556

OTHER THOUGHTS:

Apparent Women Officers or Directors: 4
Hot Spot for Advancement for Women/Minorities: Y

LOCATIONS: ("Y" = Yes)

West:	Southwest:	Midwest:	Southeast:	Northeast:	International:
	Y		Y	Y	Y

LOGITECH INTERNATIONAL SA

www.logitech.com

Industry Group Code: 334119 Ranks within this company's industry group: Sales: 13 Profits: 8

Hardware:		Software:	Telecommunications:	Electronic Publishing:	Equipment:		Specialty Services:	
Computers:		Consumer:	Local:	Online Service:	Telecom:		Consulting:	
Accessories:	Y	Corporate:	Long Distance:	TV/Cable or Wireless:	Communication:	Y	Contract Manufacturing:	
Network Equipment:		Telecom:	Cellular:	Games:	Distribution:		Processing:	
Chips/Circuits:		Internet:	Internet Service:	Financial Data:	VAR/Reseller:		Staff/Outsourcing:	
Parts/Drives:					Satellite Srv./Equip.:		Specialty Services:	Y

TYPES OF BUSINESS:

Computer Accessories
Keyboards & Mice
Imaging Devices
Control Devices
Interface Devices
Cordless Technology
Video Conferencing

BRANDS/DIVISIONS/AFFILIATES:

3Dconnexion
Ultimate Ears
LifeSize Communications
Paradial AS
Logitech Revue

CONTACTS: *Note: Officers with more than one job title may be intentionally listed here more than once.*

Gerald P. Quindlen, CEO
Gerald P. Quindlen, Pres.
Eric K. Bardman, CFO
Werner Heid, Sr. VP-Worldwide Sales & Mktg.
Martha Tuma, VP-Human Resources
Junien Labrousse, Exec. VP-Prod.
Catherine Valentine, General Counsel/Sec./VP-Legal
L. Joseph Sullivan, Sr. VP-Worldwide Oper.
Eric K. Bardman, Sr. VP-Finance
Craig Malloy, Sr. VP/CEO-LifeSize Comm.
Guerrino de Luca, Chmn.
Junien Labrousse, Pres., Logitech Europe

Phone: 41-21-863-51-11	Fax: 41-21-863-53-11
Toll-Free:	
Address: Moulin du Choc, Romanel-sur-Morges, CH-1122 Switzerland	

GROWTH PLANS/SPECIAL FEATURES:

Logitech International S.A. is an industry leader in peripherals for personal computers and other digital platforms. It operates in two segments: personal peripherals, encompassing the design, development, production, and marketing of its personal peripheral products; and video conferencing. The firm's product offerings for PCs include mice, trackballs, keyboards, gaming controllers, multimedia speakers, headsets, webcams and 3D control devices. For digital music devices, the company's products include speakers, headphones, earphones and custom in-ear monitors. For gaming consoles, the company offers a range of controllers and other accessories. In addition, Logitech offers wireless music products for the home, advanced remote controls for home entertainment systems and PC based video security systems for a home or small business. The video conferencing segment, operated through LifeSize Communications, designs, develops and markets products for HD video communication and conferencing. Other subsidiaries include 3Dconnexions, a leading provider of mice for design and visualization professionals. Based in Switzerland, Logitech has manufacturing facilities in Asia, predominantly China, and maintains sales offices or sales representatives in 41 countries. In 2010, net sales divided geographically were as follows: EMEA (Europe, Middle East, Africa), 45%; Americas, 37%; and Asia Pacific, 18%. In July 2010, it acquired Paradial AS, a Norwegian firm specializing in video communications solutions. In October 2010, Logitech introduced the Logitech Revue with Google TV, a plug-and-play box that allows users to stream Internet content on their televisions.

Logitech's employees receive such benefits as medical, dental and vision insurance; flexible spending accounts; a 401(k); an employee stock purchase plan; tuition reimbursement; and employee referral bonuses.

FINANCIALS: Sales and profits are in thousands of dollars—add 000 to get the full amount. 2010 Note: Financial information for 2010 was not available for all companies at press time.

2010 Sales: $1,966,748	2010 Profits: $64,957	U.S. Stock Ticker: LOGI
2009 Sales: $2,208,832	2009 Profits: $107,032	Int'l Ticker: LOGN Int'l Exchange: Zurich-SWX
2008 Sales: $2,370,496	2008 Profits: $231,026	Employees: 9,944
2007 Sales: $2,066,569	2007 Profits: $229,848	Fiscal Year Ends: 3/31
2006 Sales: $1,796,715	2006 Profits: $181,105	Parent Company:

SALARIES/BENEFITS:

Pension Plan:	ESOP Stock Plan:	Profit Sharing:	Top Exec. Salary: $787,500	Bonus: $1,299,000
Savings Plan: Y	Stock Purch. Plan: Y		Second Exec. Salary: $680,000	Bonus: $680,000

OTHER THOUGHTS:

Apparent Women Officers or Directors: 2
Hot Spot for Advancement for Women/Minorities: Y

LOCATIONS: ("Y" = Yes)

West:	Southwest:	Midwest:	Southeast:	Northeast:	International:
Y	Y		Y		Y

LOGMELN INC

www.logmein.com

Industry Group Code: 511210C **Ranks within this company's industry group:** Sales: 4 Profits: 2

Hardware:	Software:		Telecommunications:	Electronic Publishing:	Equipment:	Specialty Services:	
Computers:	Consumer:	Y	Local:	Online Service:	Telecom:	Consulting:	
Accessories:	Corporate:	Y	Long Distance:	TV/Cable or Wireless:	Communication:	Contract Manufacturing:	
Network Equipment:	Telecom:		Cellular:	Games:	Distribution:	Processing:	
Chips/Circuits:	Internet:		Internet Service:	Financial Data:	VAR/Reseller:	Staff/Outsourcing:	
Parts/Drives:					Satellite Srv./Equip.:	Specialty Services:	Y

TYPES OF BUSINESS:

Computer Software, Remote Access

BRANDS/DIVISIONS/AFFILIATES:

LogMeIn Free
LogMeIn Central
LogMeIn Backup
LogMeIn Rescue
LogMeIn Ignition
LogMeIn Pro²
LogMeIn Hamachi²

CONTACTS: Note: Officers with more than one job title may be intentionally listed here more than once.

Michael Simon, CEO
Jim Kelliher, CFO
Kevin Harrison, Sr. VP-Sales
Scott Chase, VP-Human Resources
Marton Anka, CTO
Lee Weiner, VP-Support Prod.
Michael Donahue, General Counsel/VP
Sandeep Bajaj, VP-Network Oper.
Conan Reidy, VP-Bus. Dev.
Alan DiPietro, VP-eCommerce Sales
Craig VerColen, Contact-Media
Ed Herdiech, VP-Finance
Kevin Farrell, VP-Platforms & Core Tech.
Richard Redding, VP/Gen. Mgr.-Mobile
Kevin Bardos, VP-Support & Collaboration Tech.
Laura Pasquale, VP-Mktg. Comm.
Seth Shaw, VP-Mktg. & Sales, EMEA

Phone: 781-638-9050	Fax: 781-998-7792
Toll-Free:	
Address: 500 Unicorn Park Dr., Woburn, MA 01801 US	

GROWTH PLANS/SPECIAL FEATURES:

LogMeIn, Inc. is a provider of on-demand, remote-connectivity services to consumers, small/medium businesses and IT service providers. Consumers and mobile workers use the company's services to access computer resources remotely in order to facilitate mobility and increase productivity. Businesses and IT service providers use the firm's services to remotely access and manage computers and other Internet-enabled devices and to deliver end-user support. LogMeIn offers the following products specifically for personal use: LogMeIn Free, which offers individuals basic access to a remote PC or Mac; and LogMeIn Ignition, which provides direct one-click access to all of a customer's LogMeIn computers from a USB drive, iPhone, laptop or desktop. LogMeIn Ignition for iPhone connects an iPhone to all of a customer's computers with LogMeIn installed. The company's business products are LogMeIn Rescue, which provides clients with a connection to IT teams that can remotely support Macs, PCs and smartphones on-demand; and LogMeIn Central, an Internet-based management console that helps clients deliver and administer the firm's computer management, remote access and VPN connectivity services. LogMeIn also carries three application that are suitable for both personal and business use: LogMeIn Backup, which protects information with customer-controlled remote backup to storage devices; LogMeIn Hamachi², which offers on-demand network virtualization service and web-based access to home networked devices, including gaming consoles, printers and IP cameras; and LogMeIn Pro², which provides remote access to PC files and applications without disrupting end user operations. The company has more than 28 million registered users that have connected using its products to over 94 million Internet-enabled devices. LogMeIn has offices in the U.K., the Netherlands and Australia, as well as an office and a development facility in Hungary. In July 2010, the firm opened an office in London.

LogMeIn offers employees benefits including life, disability, AD&D, medical and dental insurance; flexible spending accounts; and a 401(k).

FINANCIALS: Sales and profits are in thousands of dollars—add 000 to get the full amount. 2010 Note: Financial information for 2010 was not available for all companies at press time.

2010 Sales: $	2010 Profits: $	**U.S. Stock Ticker:** LOGM
2009 Sales: $74,408	2009 Profits: $8,797	**Int'l Ticker:** Int'l Exchange:
2008 Sales: $51,723	2008 Profits: $-5,402	Employees: 338
2007 Sales: $	2007 Profits: $	Fiscal Year Ends: 12/31
2006 Sales: $	2006 Profits: $	Parent Company:

SALARIES/BENEFITS:

Pension Plan:	ESOP Stock Plan:	Profit Sharing:	Top Exec. Salary: $270,000	Bonus: $110,000
Savings Plan: Y	Stock Purch. Plan:		Second Exec. Salary: $230,000	Bonus: $69,000

OTHER THOUGHTS:

Apparent Women Officers or Directors: 1
Hot Spot for Advancement for Women/Minorities:

LOCATIONS: ("Y" = Yes)

West:	Southwest:	Midwest:	Southeast:	Northeast:	International:
				Y	Y

LSI CORPORATION

www.lsi.com

Industry Group Code: 33441 Ranks within this company's industry group: Sales: 20 Profits: 40

Hardware:	Software:	Telecommunications:	Electronic Publishing:	Equipment:	Specialty Services:
Computers:	Consumer:	Local:	Online Service:	Telecom:	Consulting:
Accessories:	Corporate:	Long Distance:	TV/Cable or Wireless:	Communication:	Contract Manufacturing:
Network Equipment:	Telecom:	Cellular:	Games:	Distribution:	Processing:
Chips/Circuits: Y	Internet:	Internet Service:	Financial Data:	VAR/Reseller:	Staff/Outsourcing:
Parts/Drives:				Satellite Srv./Equip.:	Specialty Services:

TYPES OF BUSINESS:

Integrated Circuits
Application-Specific Integrated Circuits (ASICs)
System-on-a-Chip Products
Storage Area Network Solutions

BRANDS/DIVISIONS/AFFILIATES:

Truestore
MegaRaid

CONTACTS: Note: Officers with more than one job title may be intentionally listed here more than once.

Abhi Talwalkar, CEO
Abhi Talwalkar, Pres.
Bryon Look, CFO/Exec. VP
Hayden Thomas, Sr. VP-Worldwide Mktg.
Guatam Srivastava, Sr. VP-Human Resources
Byron Look, Chief Admin. Officer
Jean F. Rankin, General Counsel/Exec. VP/Sec.
Hayden Thomas, Sr. VP-Oper.
Phil Bullinger, Sr. VP/Gen. Mgr.-Engenio Storage Group
Jeff Richardson, Exec. VP/Gen. Mgr.-Semiconductor Solutions Group
Gregorio Reyes, Chmn.

Phone: 408-433-8000	Fax: 408-954-3220
Toll-Free: 866-574-5741	
Address: 1621 Barber Ln., Milpitas, CA 95035 US	

GROWTH PLANS/SPECIAL FEATURES:

LSI Corporation designs, develops, manufactures and markets complex, high-performance semiconductors and storage systems. Its integrated circuits (ICs) are used in a wide range of communication devices, including devices used for wireless, broadband, data networking and set-top box applications. LSI provides IC products and board-level products for use in consumer applications, high-performance storage controllers and systems for storage area networks. The company operates in two segments: semiconductors and storage systems. The firm's semiconductor segment, accounting for 64.1% of the firm's 2009 revenue, develops complex integrated circuits for storage and networking applications. Its Truestore family of storage electronics products includes systems-on-a-chip, read channels, pre-amplifiers, serial physical interfaces, hard disk controllers and custom software. Storage standard product lines include the serial advanced technology attachment (SATA) and RAID-On-Chip integrated circuits. These products combine with the firm's Fusion-MPT firmware and drivers to form intelligent storage interface systems primarily for server and storage system motherboard applications. Other products in this segment include networking products such as, network processors, digital signal processors, content inspection processors, broadband aggregation devices and personal connectivity products. The storage systems segment, which represents 35.9% of revenue, offers a broad line of open, modular storage products comprised of complete systems and sub-assemblies configured from modular components, such as storage controller modules, disk drive enclosure modules, related management software and advanced data protection software for creating local and remote copies of critical data. The MegaRaid product family includes single-chip RAID-on-motherboard applications and software-based RAID products for entry level RAID protection.

Employees are offered medical insurance, as well as a 401(k) plan, a profit sharing plan and a stock purchase plan.

FINANCIALS: Sales and profits are in thousands of dollars—add 000 to get the full amount. 2010 Note: Financial information for 2010 was not available for all companies at press time.

2010 Sales: $	2010 Profits: $	U.S. Stock Ticker: LSI
2009 Sales: $2,219,159	2009 Profits: $-47,719	Int'l Ticker: Int'l Exchange:
2008 Sales: $2,677,077	2008 Profits: $-622,253	Employees: 5,397
2007 Sales: $2,603,643	2007 Profits: $-2,486,819	Fiscal Year Ends: 12/31
2006 Sales: $1,982,148	2006 Profits: $169,638	Parent Company:

SALARIES/BENEFITS:

Pension Plan:	ESOP Stock Plan:	Profit Sharing: Y	Top Exec. Salary: $803,087	Bonus: $
Savings Plan: Y	Stock Purch. Plan: Y		Second Exec. Salary: $428,660	Bonus: $

OTHER THOUGHTS:

Apparent Women Officers or Directors: 2
Hot Spot for Advancement for Women/Minorities: Y

LOCATIONS: ("Y" = Yes)

West:	Southwest:	Midwest:	Southeast:	Northeast:	International:
Y		Y			Y

LUCASARTS ENTERTAINMENT COMPANY LLC   www.lucasarts.com

Industry Group Code: 511210G Ranks within this company's industry group: Sales: Profits:

Hardware:	Software:		Telecommunications:	Electronic Publishing:		Equipment:		Specialty Services:
Computers:	Consumer:	Y	Local:	Online Service:		Telecom:		Consulting:
Accessories:	Corporate:		Long Distance:	TV/Cable or Wireless:		Communication:		Contract Manufacturing:
Network Equipment:	Telecom:		Cellular:	Games:	Y	Distribution:		Processing:
Chips/Circuits:	Internet:		Internet Service:	Financial Data:		VAR/Reseller:		Staff/Outsourcing:
Parts/Drives:						Satellite Srv./Equip.:		Specialty Services:

TYPES OF BUSINESS:
Computer Software-Games
Online Retail

BRANDS/DIVISIONS/AFFILIATES:
Lucasfilm Ltd
LEGO Indiana Jones
LEGO Star Wars
Indiana Jones and the Staff of Kings
Star Wars: The Force Unleashed
Fracture
Star Wars, The Clone Wars: Jedi Alliance Review
Monkey Island

CONTACTS: Note: Officers with more than one job title may be intentionally listed here more than once.
Paul Meegan, Pres.
Nell O'Donnell, Associate General Counsel
Kevin Parker, VP-Finance
Mary Bihr, VP-Global Publishing
George Lucas Jr., Chmn.

Phone: 415-746-8000	Fax:
Toll-Free:	
Address: 1110 Gorgas Ave., San Francisco, CA 94129 US	

GROWTH PLANS/SPECIAL FEATURES:
LucasArts Entertainment Company LLC, a subsidiary of Lucasfilm, Ltd., produces interactive entertainment software for personal computers (PC) and videogame consoles. The firm has developed and published more than 200 video game titles. The company was founded in 1982 by George Lucas to produce games with the Star Wars and Indiana Jones brand names. Today there are more than 150 game titles in these series. Current releases include Star Wars Battlefront: Elite Squadron and LEGO Indiana Jones 2: The Adventure Continues. Past titles include LEGO Star Wars; LEGO Indiana Jones; and Indiana Jones and the Staff of Kings. LucasArts' Star Wars franchise has been highly successful, particularly Star Wars: Knights of the Old Republic developed in collaboration with BioWare Corp. Following its success, the company released a slew of new titles, including Republic Commando; Knights of the Old Republic II; and Galaxies: Jump to Lightspeed, a massively multiplayer online (MMO) game. Other titles include Fracture; Thrillville; Armed and Dangerous; Secret Weapons Over Normandy; Lucidity; and The Secret of Monkey Island: Special Edition. The company offers its games and game paraphernalia for direct sale on its web site, Store.lucasarts.com. Titles released in 2010 include LEGO Star Wars III: The Clone Wars; Monkey Island 2 Special Edition: LeChuck's Revenge; and Star Wars: The Force Unleashed II.

FINANCIALS: Sales and profits are in thousands of dollars—add 000 to get the full amount. 2010 Note: Financial information for 2010 was not available for all companies at press time.

2010 Sales: $	2010 Profits: $	U.S. Stock Ticker: Subsidiary
2009 Sales: $	2009 Profits: $	Int'l Ticker: Int'l Exchange:
2008 Sales: $	2008 Profits: $	Employees:
2007 Sales: $	2007 Profits: $	Fiscal Year Ends: 4/30
2006 Sales: $	2006 Profits: $	Parent Company: LUCASFILM LTD

SALARIES/BENEFITS:

Pension Plan:	ESOP Stock Plan:	Profit Sharing:	Top Exec. Salary: $	Bonus: $
Savings Plan: Y	Stock Purch. Plan:		Second Exec. Salary: $	Bonus: $

OTHER THOUGHTS:
Apparent Women Officers or Directors: 2
Hot Spot for Advancement for Women/Minorities:

LOCATIONS: ("Y" = Yes)

West:	Southwest:	Midwest:	Southeast:	Northeast:	International:
Y					

MACRONIX INTERNATIONAL CO LTD

www.macronix.com

Industry Group Code: 33441 Ranks within this company's industry group: Sales: 33   Profits: 15

Hardware:		Software:		Telecommunications:		Electronic Publishing:		Equipment:		Specialty Services:	
Computers:		Consumer:		Local:		Online Service:		Telecom:		Consulting:	
Accessories:		Corporate:		Long Distance:		TV/Cable or Wireless:		Communication:		Contract Manufacturing:	Y
Network Equipment:		Telecom:		Cellular:		Games:		Distribution:		Processing:	
Chips/Circuits:	Y	Internet:		Internet Service:		Financial Data:		VAR/Reseller:		Staff/Outsourcing:	
Parts/Drives:								Satellite Srv./Equip.:		Specialty Services:	Y

TYPES OF BUSINESS:

Semiconductors-Memory Chips
Flash Memory Cards
Digital Voice Recorders
Digital Cameras
Flat Panel Displays
Design Services

BRANDS/DIVISIONS/AFFILIATES:

Magic Pixel, Inc.
Infomax Communication Co. Ltd.
Modiotek Co Ltd
Mxtran, Inc.
MaxRise, Inc.

CONTACTS: Note: Officers with more than one job title may be intentionally listed here more than once.

Miin Wu, CEO
Chih-Yuan Lu, Pres.
Dang-Hsing Yiu, Chief Mktg. Officer/Sr. VP
Ful-Long Ni, VP
Wen-Sen Pan, VP
Pei-Fu Yeh, VP
Miin Wu, Chmn.

Phone: 886-3-578-6688	Fax: 886-3-563-2888
Toll-Free:	
Address: 16 Li-Hsin Rd., Science Park, Hsinchu, F5 300 Taiwan	

GROWTH PLANS/SPECIAL FEATURES:

Macronix International Co. Ltd. designs, produces and supplies semiconductor products. Its portfolio includes mask ROM, flash, EPROM, logic and application-specific integrated circuit products, as well as highly integrated SOC (system-on-chip) products. The company's offerings include flash memory cards, digital voice recorders, sound generators, digital answering machines, digital still cameras and flat panel displays. The firm's family of Serial Flash products ranges in densities from 512 kilobytes to 256 megabytes. Macronix treats its clients as strategic partners and works closely with them from the early stages of product development to design silicon chips that meet their specific needs. Its partners include Nintendo Co., Ltd.; Hewlett-Packard, with whom it has had a relationship for over six years; Renesas; and LG Electronics. The firm operates five subsidiaries: Modiotek Co. Ltd, which offers the Mobile Audio platform and the Advanced Digital Answer Machine product family; Infomax Communication Co., Ltd., which offers baseband & smart phone turnkey products; Mxtran, Inc., which offers a SIM-based commerce device; MaxRise, Inc., which provides a mobile TV device; and Magic Pixel, Inc., whose offerings include a portable navigation device and a digital photo frame.

FINANCIALS: Sales and profits are in thousands of dollars—add 000 to get the full amount. 2010 Note: Financial information for 2010 was not available for all companies at press time.

2010 Sales: $	2010 Profits: $	**U.S. Stock Ticker:**
2009 Sales: $847,170	2009 Profits: $179,810	**Int'l Ticker: 2337** Int'l Exchange: Taipei-TPE
2008 Sales: $706,530	2008 Profits: $137,160	Employees:
2007 Sales: $738,310	2007 Profits: $141,380	Fiscal Year Ends: 12/31
2006 Sales: $683,700	2006 Profits: $61,000	Parent Company:

SALARIES/BENEFITS:

Pension Plan:	ESOP Stock Plan:	Profit Sharing:	Top Exec. Salary: $	Bonus: $
Savings Plan:	Stock Purch. Plan:		Second Exec. Salary: $	Bonus: $

OTHER THOUGHTS:

Apparent Women Officers or Directors:
Hot Spot for Advancement for Women/Minorities:

LOCATIONS: ("Y" = Yes)

West:	Southwest:	Midwest:	Southeast:	Northeast:	International:
Y					Y

MANHATTAN ASSOCIATES INC

www.manh.com

Industry Group Code: 511210A **Ranks within this company's industry group:** Sales: 5 Profits: 3

Hardware:		Software:		Telecommunications:	Electronic Publishing:	Equipment:	Specialty Services:	
Computers:	Y	Consumer:		Local:	Online Service:	Telecom:	Consulting:	Y
Accessories:	Y	Corporate:	Y	Long Distance:	TV/Cable or Wireless:	Communication:	Contract Manufacturing:	
Network Equipment:		Telecom:		Cellular:	Games:	Distribution:	Processing:	
Chips/Circuits:		Internet:		Internet Service:	Financial Data:	VAR/Reseller:	Staff/Outsourcing:	
Parts/Drives:						Satellite Srv./Equip.:	Specialty Services:	

TYPES OF BUSINESS:

Software-Supply Chain
Consulting & Support
RFID System Integration

BRANDS/DIVISIONS/AFFILIATES:

Manhattan SCOPE

CONTACTS: Note: Officers with more than one job title may be intentionally listed here more than once.

Peter Sinisgalli, CEO
Peter Sinisgalli, Pres.
Dennis Story, CFO/Sr. VP
Terrie O'Hanlon, Chief Mktg. Officer/Sr. VP
Terry Geraghty, Sr. VP-Global Human Resources
David Dabbiere, Chief Legal Officer/Sr. VP
Eddie Capel, Exec. VP-Global Oper.
Jeff Cashman, Sr. VP-Bus. Dev.
Jeff Mitchell, Exec. VP-Americas
Steve Smith, Sr. VP-EMEA
John J. Huntz, Jr., Chmn.
Jeff Baum, Sr. VP-Int'l

Phone: 770-955-7070	Fax: 770-955-0302
Toll-Free:	
Address: 2300 Windy Ridge Pkwy., 10th Fl., Atlanta, GA 30339 US	

GROWTH PLANS/SPECIAL FEATURES:

Manhattan Associates, Inc. develops and provides technology-based supply chain software service. Its products consist of software, services and hardware and are used for both the planning and execution of supply chain activities. All of the company's services also include services such as design, configuration, implementation, product assessment and training, as well as customer support and software enhancement subscriptions. The firm specializes in demand forecasting and inventory replenishment; warehouse and labor management; performance analysis and event planning. Manhattan Associates' software includes Manhattan SCOPE (Supply Chain Optimization, Planning through Execution), designed to reduce implementation cost and risk. Through several vendor partnerships, the company offers many hardware systems including bar code scanners, data collection terminals and document printers. The company's professional services provide clients with a team of consultants who offer training programs concerning the use of the firm's equipment, as well as 24-hour customer support and software enhancement subscriptions. The firm serves various industries including consumer goods, food, government, high-tech/electronics, industrial/wholesale, life science, logistics service providers, retail and transportation. Manhattan Associates operates in geographical segments covering the Americas; Europe, Middle East and Africa; and the Asia-Pacific Region. International sources typically make up about 24% of the company's revenues. Outside of the U.S., the firm has offices in Australia, China, France, India, Japan, the Netherlands, Singapore and the U.K., as well as representatives in Mexico and reseller partnerships in Latin America.

Manhattan Associates offers its employees medical, dental, vision and prescription drug coverage; flexible spending accounts; life and AD&D insurance; short- and long-term disability; a 401(k) plan; access to a credit union; discounted health club membership; and educational assistance.

FINANCIALS: Sales and profits are in thousands of dollars—add 000 to get the full amount. 2010 Note: Financial information for 2010 was not available for all companies at press time.

2010 Sales: $	2010 Profits: $	**U.S. Stock Ticker:** MANH
2009 Sales: $246,667	2009 Profits: $16,562	**Int'l Ticker:** Int'l Exchange:
2008 Sales: $337,201	2008 Profits: $22,798	Employees:
2007 Sales: $337,401	2007 Profits: $30,751	Fiscal Year Ends: 12/31
2006 Sales: $288,868	2006 Profits: $19,331	Parent Company:

SALARIES/BENEFITS:

Pension Plan:	ESOP Stock Plan:	Profit Sharing:	Top Exec. Salary: $460,000	Bonus: $238,050
Savings Plan: Y	Stock Purch. Plan:		Second Exec. Salary: $340,000	Bonus: $172,688

OTHER THOUGHTS:

Apparent Women Officers or Directors: 1
Hot Spot for Advancement for Women/Minorities:

LOCATIONS: ("Y" = Yes)

West:	Southwest:	Midwest:	Southeast:	Northeast:	International:
		Y	Y		Y

Note: Financial information, benefits and other data can change quickly and may vary from those stated here.

MANTECH INTERNATIONAL CORP

www.mantech.com

Industry Group Code: 541512 Ranks within this company's industry group: Sales: 4 Profits: 2

Hardware:	Software:		Telecommunications:	Electronic Publishing:	Equipment:	Specialty Services:	
Computers:	Consumer:		Local:	Online Service:	Telecom:	Consulting:	Y
Accessories:	Corporate:	Y	Long Distance:	TV/Cable or Wireless:	Communication:	Contract Manufacturing:	
Network Equipment:	Telecom:		Cellular:	Games:	Distribution:	Processing:	
Chips/Circuits:	Internet:		Internet Service:	Financial Data:	VAR/Reseller:	Staff/Outsourcing:	
Parts/Drives:					Satellite Srv./Equip.:	Specialty Services:	Y

TYPES OF BUSINESS:

Information Technology Services
Technology and Software Development

BRANDS/DIVISIONS/AFFILIATES:

MTSC, Inc.

CONTACTS: Note: Officers with more than one job title may be intentionally listed here more than once.

George J. Pedersen, CEO
Kevin M. Phillips, CFO/Exec. VP
Carlos S. Echalar, Exec. VP-Human Resources
Terry M. Ryan, Pres./COO-Eng. & Advanced Tech. Group
Jeffrey S. Brown, General Counsel/Exec./VP/Sec.
Matthew E. Candy, Sr. VP-Corp. Dev.
M. Stuart Davis, Exec. VP-Comm. & Strategy
Sherill I. Daily, Jr., VP-Portfolio Analysis
Sally Sullivan, VP-Bus. Dev.
Judith L. Bjornass, Sr. VP
George J. Pedersen, Chmn.

Phone: 703-218-6000	Fax: 703-218-8296
Toll-Free:	
Address: 12015 Lee Jackson Hwy., Fairfax, VA 22033 US	

GROWTH PLANS/SPECIAL FEATURES:

ManTech International Corp. is a provider of technologies and services for mission- critical security programs for the U.S. Intelligence Community, the U.S. Department of Defense, Homeland Security; and other U.S. federal government agencies. Services include engineering, systems integration, software services, cyber security, enterprise architecture, information operations and computer forensics, information technology, communications integration, engineering support and global logistics and supply chain management. The company operates in 40 countries. The company's services fall into three categories: Mission Support, Systems Engineering and Technical Services. The Mission Support category provides cyber warfare and cyber defense applications and services to the U.S. Department of Defense, agencies in the Intelligence Community, the Department of State and the Department of Justice. The firm also designs, develops, implements, tests and maintains security applications for information systems and network infrastructures. In addition, the Mission Support Category also offers enterprise systems engineering; intelligence operations and analysis support; and secrecy management and program security architecture services. The Systems Engineering segment in addition to providing systems engineering and support services, offers system analysis, modeling and testing of technologies and systems, particular those that are being deployed to identify and detect nuclear and radiological sources that are attempting entry into the U.S. The segment also performs certification tests of new and upgraded systems for confirmation of their operation in accordance with design requirements. The Technical Services division provides communication systems and infrastructure support; global and domestic mission-critical logistics support; global property management; and global IT modernization. In December 2010, the firm acquired MTSC, Inc., a provider of systems integration, cyber security and networking engineering services to U.S. government agencies, for $75 million.

The company offers employees medical, dental and vision insurance; flexible spending accounts; tuition assistance; life insurance; disability coverage; an employee assistance program; and a retail discount program.

FINANCIALS: Sales and profits are in thousands of dollars—add 000 to get the full amount. 2010 Note: Financial information for 2010 was not available for all companies at press time.

2010 Sales: $	2010 Profits: $	U.S. Stock Ticker: MANT
2009 Sales: $2,020,334	2009 Profits: $111,764	Int'l Ticker: Int'l Exchange:
2008 Sales: $1,870,879	2008 Profits: $90,292	Employees: 8,000
2007 Sales: $1,148,098	2007 Profits: $67,207	Fiscal Year Ends: 12/31
2006 Sales: $1,137,178	2006 Profits: $50,701	Parent Company:

SALARIES/BENEFITS:

Pension Plan:	ESOP Stock Plan: Y	Profit Sharing:	Top Exec. Salary: $1,666,394	Bonus: $1,056,250
Savings Plan: Y	Stock Purch. Plan:		Second Exec. Salary: $500,001	Bonus: $1,350,000

OTHER THOUGHTS:

Apparent Women Officers or Directors: 3
Hot Spot for Advancement for Women/Minorities: Y

LOCATIONS: ("Y" = Yes)

West:	Southwest:	Midwest:	Southeast:	Northeast:	International:
Y	Y		Y	Y	Y

MARKETLIVE INC

www.marketlive.com

Industry Group Code: 511210M Ranks within this company's industry group: Sales: Profits:

Hardware:	Software:		Telecommunications:	Electronic Publishing:		Equipment:	Specialty Services:	
Computers:	Consumer:		Local:	Online Service:	Y	Telecom:	Consulting:	
Accessories:	Corporate:	Y	Long Distance:	TV/Cable or Wireless:		Communication:	Contract Manufacturing:	
Network Equipment:	Telecom:		Cellular:	Games:		Distribution:	Processing:	
Chips/Circuits:	Internet:		Internet Service:	Financial Data:		VAR/Reseller:	Staff/Outsourcing:	
Parts/Drives:						Satellite Srv./Equip.:	Specialty Services:	Y

TYPES OF BUSINESS:

E-Commerce Software
Managed Support Services
Online Marketing Services
Search Engine Optimization

BRANDS/DIVISIONS/AFFILIATES:

MarketLive
Intelligent Insights
Intelligent Acquisition
MarketLive Intelligent Commerce
MarketLive Mobile
Intelligent Conversion

CONTACTS: Note: Officers with more than one job title may be intentionally listed here more than once.

Mark Pierce, CEO
Ralph VonSosen, VP-Mktg.
Marty Boos, CIO
Ralph VonSosen, VP-Prod. Mgmt.
Heather McKelvey, VP-Eng.
James Miller, Sr. VP-Client Svcs.
Ken Burke, Chief Evangelist
Ken Burke, Chmn.

Phone: 707-780-1600	Fax:
Toll-Free: 877-341-5729	
Address: 617 B 2nd St., Petaluma, CA 94952 US	

GROWTH PLANS/SPECIAL FEATURES:

MarketLive, Inc. provides e-commerce software and services for the retail and catalog industry, with a focus on midsize specialty retailers. The company's primary product is the MarketLive Intelligent Commerce Platform, its e-commerce platform, which provides merchandising, marketing, selling, mobile, customer care and analytics solutions. Services delivered by the Intelligent Commerce platform include interactive branding services, such as assistance with site design, brand expression, brand research and online design execution; site launch services, including training services and data flow services for product, pricing, order and inventory data; platform innovations services, which assists businesses with integrating new technologies into their web sites on an ongoing basis; and business solutions. The business solutions suite of software includes Intelligent Insights, through which customers can outsource e-commerce site analytics and insights processes to MarketLive; Intelligent Acquisition, which provides search engine optimization and traffic increase services; and Intelligent Conversion, which provides categorization and merchandising, testing and product content services. MarketLive's clients include Party City, Intermix, Neutrogena, John Deere, Gaiam and Sundance Catalog. The firm's e-commerce suite powers over 160 retail web sites. The company's recently developed products include Intelligent Insights and MarketLive Mobile, a program that makes the MarketLive Intelligent Commerce Platform available on mobile devices such as smart phones.

FINANCIALS: Sales and profits are in thousands of dollars—add 000 to get the full amount. 2010 Note: Financial information for 2010 was not available for all companies at press time.

2010 Sales: $	2010 Profits: $	U.S. Stock Ticker: Private
2009 Sales: $	2009 Profits: $	Int'l Ticker: Int'l Exchange:
2008 Sales: $	2008 Profits: $	Employees:
2007 Sales: $	2007 Profits: $	Fiscal Year Ends: 12/31
2006 Sales: $	2006 Profits: $	Parent Company:

SALARIES/BENEFITS:

Pension Plan:	ESOP Stock Plan:	Profit Sharing:	Top Exec. Salary: $	Bonus: $
Savings Plan:	Stock Purch. Plan:		Second Exec. Salary: $	Bonus: $

OTHER THOUGHTS:

Apparent Women Officers or Directors: 1
Hot Spot for Advancement for Women/Minorities:

LOCATIONS: ("Y" = Yes)

West:	Southwest:	Midwest:	Southeast:	Northeast:	International:
Y					

MARVELL TECHNOLOGY GROUP LTD

www.marvell.com

Industry Group Code: 33441 Ranks within this company's industry group: Sales: 17 Profits: 17

Hardware:		Software:		Telecommunications:		Electronic Publishing:		Equipment:		Specialty Services:	
Computers:		Consumer:		Local:		Online Service:		Telecom:	Y	Consulting:	
Accessories:		Corporate:		Long Distance:		TV/Cable or Wireless:		Communication:	Y	Contract Manufacturing:	
Network Equipment:		Telecom:		Cellular:		Games:		Distribution:		Processing:	
Chips/Circuits:	Y	Internet:		Internet Service:		Financial Data:		VAR/Reseller:		Staff/Outsourcing:	
Parts/Drives:								Satellite Srv./Equip.:		Specialty Services:	

TYPES OF BUSINESS:

Semiconductor Manufacturing
Storage Technology
Broadband Technology
Wireless Technology
Power Management Technology
Switching Technology

BRANDS/DIVISIONS/AFFILIATES:

Prestera
ARMADA
GalNet
Alaska
Libertas
Orion
Yukon
DS2

CONTACTS: Note: Officers with more than one job title may be intentionally listed here more than once.

Sehat Sutardja, CEO
Clyde R. Hosein, Interim COO
Sehat Sutardja, Pres.
Clyde R. Hosein, CFO/Sec.
Tom Hayes, VP-Corp. Mktg
Reid Linney, VP-Human Resources
Pantas Sutardja, Chief R&D Officer
Clyde R. Hosein, Interim CIO
Pantas Sutardja, CTO/VP
Gani Jusuf, VP-Prod. Dev. & Consumer Bus. Group
Roawen Chen, VP-Mfg.
James Laufman, General Counsel/VP
Albert Wu, VP-Oper.
Gani Jusuf, VP-Corp. Comm.
Jeff Palmer, VP-Investor Rel.
Nikhil Balram, VP/Gen. Mgr.-Digital Entertainment Bus. Group
Eliaz Lavi, Sr. VP/Gen. Mgr.-Marvell Israel
Weili Dai, VP/Gen. Mgr.-Comm. & Computing Bus.
Partho Mishra, VP/Gen. Mgr.-Embedded & Emerging Bus. Group
Sehat Sutardja, Chmn.
Hoo (H.K.) Kuong, VP/Gen. Mgr.-Marvell Asia Pte., Ltd.

Phone: 408-222-2500	Fax: 408-752-9028
Toll-Free:	
Address: 5488 Marvell Lane, Santa Clara, CA 95054 US	

GROWTH PLANS/SPECIAL FEATURES:

Marvell Technology Group Ltd. is a global semiconductor provider of high-performance analog, mixed-signal, digital signal processing and embedded microprocessor integrated circuits. Marvell makes products for computers, communications-related equipment and consumer devices that require the benefits of integrated mixed-signal devices for high-speed data storage, transmission and management. It also markets a broad range of electronic products that can utilize its power management solutions. The firm developments System-on-a-Chip (SoC) devices and has five key markets: storage solutions; mobile and wireless; networking; platforms; and digital entertainment. The storage products include hard disk drives and adaptors. The mobile and wireless market includes products for laptops and cellular phones, such as Wi-Fi and Bluetooth earpieces. The networking products include system controllers, Prestera switching architecture; Link Street SOHO multi-port integrated switches; and GalNet switch controllers. The platforms products include eReaders, plug computers and Smartphones. The digital entertainment products include DVRS, game consoles, hubs, switches, and routers. Marvell's other product offerings include Libertas wireless LAN chipsets; VoIP products; the Orion family of audiovisual streaming products; PC connectivity products such as Yukon Gigabit Ethernet controllers; gateway devices; communications controller products like Discovery system controllers and Horizon WAN controllers; and power management products like DSP Switcher integrated regulators and regulator modules. The firm has offices in the U.S., Israel, Singapore, Germany, China, Italy, Japan, Korea, Switzerland, Taiwan and the U.K. In January 2010, Marvell announced collaboration with AU Optronic Corp. to make the next generation of the eReader on a joint reference design. In August 2010, the company acquired the intellectual property and assets of Diseno de Sistemas en Silicio S.A. (DS2) a supplier of high speed semiconductor solutions for powerline communications. In September 2010, the firm introduced its ARMADA 628, a 1.5 Gigahertz tri-core application processor, which delivers dual stream 1080p 3D video for smartphones and tablets.

FINANCIALS: Sales and profits are in thousands of dollars—add 000 to get the full amount. 2010 Note: Financial information for 2010 was not available for all companies at press time.

2010 Sales: $2,807,687	2010 Profits: $353,456	**U.S. Stock Ticker:** MRVL
2009 Sales: $2,950,563	2009 Profits: $147,242	**Int'l Ticker:** **Int'l Exchange:**
2008 Sales: $2,894,693	2008 Profits: $-114,427	Employees: 5,241
2007 Sales: $2,237,553	2007 Profits: $-12,095	Fiscal Year Ends: 1/31
2006 Sales: $1,670,266	2006 Profits: $199,490	Parent Company:

SALARIES/BENEFITS:

Pension Plan: Y	ESOP Stock Plan: Y	Profit Sharing:	Top Exec. Salary: $657,000	Bonus: $985,000
Savings Plan: Y	Stock Purch. Plan:		Second Exec. Salary: $450,000	Bonus: $360,000

OTHER THOUGHTS:

Apparent Women Officers or Directors: 1
Hot Spot for Advancement for Women/Minorities:

LOCATIONS: ("Y" = Yes)

West:	Southwest:	Midwest:	Southeast:	Northeast:	International:
Y					Y

Note: Financial information, benefits and other data can change quickly and may vary from those stated here.

MAXIM INTEGRATED PRODUCTS INC

www.maxim-ic.com

Industry Group Code: 33441 **Ranks within this company's industry group:** Sales: 23 Profits: 32

Hardware:		Software:		Telecommunications:		Electronic Publishing:		Equipment:		Specialty Services:	
Computers:		Consumer:		Local:		Online Service:		Telecom:		Consulting:	
Accessories:		Corporate:		Long Distance:		TV/Cable or Wireless:		Communication:		Contract Manufacturing:	Y
Network Equipment:		Telecom:		Cellular:		Games:		Distribution:		Processing:	
Chips/Circuits:	Y	Internet:		Internet Service:		Financial Data:		VAR/Reseller:		Staff/Outsourcing:	
Parts/Drives:								Satellite Srv./Equip.:		Specialty Services:	

TYPES OF BUSINESS:

Integrated Circuits-Analog & Mixed Signal
High-Frequency Design Processes
Custom Manufacturing
Power Conversion Chips
Environmental Management & Monitoring Systems
Data Interface and Interconnection
Wireless & RF Receivers and Transmitters
Data Storage

BRANDS/DIVISIONS/AFFILIATES:

Mobilygen
Teridan Semiconductor Corporation
Phyworks Ltd.

CONTACTS: Note: Officers with more than one job title may be intentionally listed here more than once.

Tunc Doluca, CEO
Tunc Doluca, Pres.
Bruce E. Kiddoo, CFO/Sr. VP
Steve Yamasaki, VP-Human Resources
Pirooz Parvarandeh, CTO/Group Pres.
Vivek Jain, Sr. VP-Mfg. Oper.
Charles G. Rigg, Sr. VP-Admin.
Ed Medlin, General Counsel
Paresh Maniar, Exec. Dir.-Investor Rel.
Vijay Ullal, Group Pres.
Christopher J. Neil, Div. VP
B. Kipling Hagopian, Chmn.

Phone: 408-737-7600	Fax: 408-737-7194
Toll-Free:	
Address: 120 San Gabriel Dr., Sunnyvale, CA 94086 US	

GROWTH PLANS/SPECIAL FEATURES:

Maxim Integrated Products, Inc. designs, develops, manufactures and markets analog, mixed-signal, high frequency and digital circuits. Maxim's circuits connect the analog and digital world by detecting, measuring, amplifying and converting real-world signals into the digital signals necessary for computer processing. It produces electronic interface products to interact with people, through audio, video, touchpad, key pad and security devices; the physical world, through motion, time, temperature and humidity sensors; power sources, via conversion, charging, supervision and regulation systems; and other digital systems, including wireless, storage and fiber optic systems. Maxim's products serve four major end-markets: industrial, which includes automotive products, automatic test equipment, and military and medical equipment and instruments; communications, including base stations, networking/data communications and telecommunications; consumer products, specifically cell phones, digital cameras, GPS, handhelds and media players and home entertainment products; and computing, including notebook and desktop computers, peripherals, servers and workstations and storage. The company's video compression technology is provided by semiconductor subsidiary, Mobilygen. The company also offers custom design and manufacturing services. Some of Maxim's products include one of the industry's smallest VGA port protector; adjustable overvoltage protectors; quad/dual digital pulsers which enhance ultrasound imaging; and a hi-speed USB analogue switch that integrates the host-charger identification circuit. In May 2010, the firm acquired private company, Teridan Semiconductor Corporation. In September of the same year, Maxim acquired another private company, Phyworks Ltd., for $72.5 million.

The company offers employees medical, dental and vision insurance; an educational assistance program; health and dependent care flexible spending accounts; an employee assistance program; business travel accident insurance; transportation flexible spending accounts; health club membership discounts; wellness screenings; life and AD&D insurance; and disability coverage.

FINANCIALS: Sales and profits are in thousands of dollars—add 000 to get the full amount. 2010 Note: Financial information for 2010 was not available for all companies at press time.

2010 Sales: $1,997,603	2010 Profits: $125,139	**U.S. Stock Ticker: MXIM**
2009 Sales: $1,646,015	2009 Profits: $10,455	**Int'l Ticker:** Int'l Exchange:
2008 Sales: $2,052,783	2008 Profits: $317,725	Employees: 9,200
2007 Sales: $2,009,124	2007 Profits: $286,227	Fiscal Year Ends: 6/30
2006 Sales: $1,856,945	2006 Profits: $387,701	Parent Company:

SALARIES/BENEFITS:

Pension Plan:	ESOP Stock Plan:	Profit Sharing:	Top Exec. Salary: $480,769	Bonus: $321,429
Savings Plan:	Stock Purch. Plan:		Second Exec. Salary: $384,615	Bonus: $303,121

OTHER THOUGHTS:

Apparent Women Officers or Directors:
Hot Spot for Advancement for Women/Minorities:

LOCATIONS: ("Y" = Yes)

West:	Southwest:	Midwest:	Southeast:	Northeast:	International:
Y	Y	Y	Y	Y	Y

Note: Financial information, benefits and other data can change quickly and may vary from those stated here.

MCAFEE INC

www.mcafee.com

Industry Group Code: 511210E Ranks within this company's industry group: Sales: 2   Profits: 4

Hardware:	Software:		Telecommunications:	Electronic Publishing:	Equipment:	Specialty Services:	
Computers:	Consumer:		Local:	Online Service:	Telecom:	Consulting:	
Accessories:	Corporate:	Y	Long Distance:	TV/Cable or Wireless:	Communication:	Contract Manufacturing:	
Network Equipment:	Telecom:		Cellular:	Games:	Distribution:	Processing:	
Chips/Circuits:	Internet:		Internet Service:	Financial Data:	VAR/Reseller:	Staff/Outsourcing:	
Parts/Drives:					Satellite Srv./Equip.:	Specialty Services:	Y

TYPES OF BUSINESS:

Software-Security
Virus Protection Software
Network Management Software

BRANDS/DIVISIONS/AFFILIATES:

Intel Corp
McAfee Total Protection
Registry Power Cleaner
McAfee PCI Certifications Service
McAfee Network DPL Discovery
McAfee OK Mobile
LoJack for Laptops
Secure Computing Corporation

CONTACTS: Note: Officers with more than one job title may be intentionally listed here more than once.

David DeWalt, CEO
Albert A. Pimentel, COO
David DeWalt, Pres.
Jonathan Chadwick, CFO
David Milam, Chief Mktg. Officer/Exec. VP
Joseph Gabbert, Exec. VP-Human Resources
George Kurtz, CTO/Exec. VP
Bryan Reed Barney, Exec. VP-Prod. Oper.
Mark Cochran, General Counsel/Chief Legal Officer/Exec. VP
Gerhard Watzinger, Exec. VP-Corp. Strategy & Bus. Dev.
Keith Krzeminski, Chief Acct. Officer/Sr. VP-Finance
Michael DeCesare, Exec. VP-Worldwide Sales
Todd Gebhart, Exec. VP/Gen. Mgr.-Consumer, Mobile & Small Bus.
Barry McPherson, Exec. VP-Worldwide Tech Support & Customer Svcs.
Marc Olesen, Sr. VP/Gen. Mgr.-Content & Cloud Security
Charles J. Robel, Chmn.
Gert-Jan Schenk, Pres., EMEA

Phone: 408-988-3832	Fax: 408-970-9727
Toll-Free:	
Address: 3965 Freedom Cir., Santa Clara, CA 95054 US	

GROWTH PLANS/SPECIAL FEATURES:

McAfee, Inc. is a global developer and supplier of software-based computer security systems that prevent intrusions on networks and protect computer systems from attacks. It allows home users, businesses, government agencies, service providers and partners to block attacks, prevent disruptions and continuously track and improve their security. The company's products are categorized for Home and Home Office, Small Business, Medium Business and Large Enterprise. Home and Home Office products are geared toward users who work from home on one or multiple computers. Products consist of PC protection software such as McAfee Total Protection, which works as an anti-virus and maintains an enhanced firewall. LoJack for Laptops tracks and recovers lost or stolen computers and is supported by a professional theft recovery team. Registry Power Cleaner software repairs registry errors and protects data with automatic backups. Small Business products are designed for businesses with 10-50 computers. The McAfee PCI Certification Service offers analysis of compliance status, assisting companies in completing PCI DSS requirement. The McAfee Site Advisor reviews web site security and issues safety ratings before the user visits them. Medium Business products, targeted towards businesses with 100 to 1,000 computers, consist of data protection products such as the McAfee Network DLP Discovery; McAfee e-mail Security Service; and Total Protection for Secure Businesses, a complete network security product. Enterprise products are geared toward companies with hundreds to tens of thousands computers. McAfee OK Mobile and Content Safety inspects content and certification for mobile devices. The McAfee Policy Auditor provides automated manual audit processes. In August 2010, the company agreed to be acquired by Intel Corp. for $7.68 billion. In December 2010, the FTC approved Intel's proposed acquisition of McAfee.

FINANCIALS: Sales and profits are in thousands of dollars—add 000 to get the full amount. 2010 Note: Financial information for 2010 was not available for all companies at press time.

2010 Sales: $	2010 Profits: $	U.S. Stock Ticker: Subsidiary
2009 Sales: $1,927,332	2009 Profits: $173,420	Int'l Ticker: Int'l Exchange:
2008 Sales: $1,600,065	2008 Profits: $172,209	Employees: 6,100
2007 Sales: $1,308,220	2007 Profits: $166,980	Fiscal Year Ends: 12/31
2006 Sales: $1,142,327	2006 Profits: $137,529	Parent Company: INTEL CORP

SALARIES/BENEFITS:

Pension Plan:	ESOP Stock Plan:	Profit Sharing:	Top Exec. Salary: $950,000	Bonus: $1,000,000
Savings Plan: Y	Stock Purch. Plan:		Second Exec. Salary: $600,000	Bonus: $592,575

OTHER THOUGHTS:

Apparent Women Officers or Directors: 1
Hot Spot for Advancement for Women/Minorities:

LOCATIONS: ("Y" = Yes)

West:	Southwest:	Midwest:	Southeast:	Northeast:	International:
Y	Y	Y	Y	Y	Y

Note: Financial information, benefits and other data can change quickly and may vary from those stated here.

MEDIAPLATFORM INC

www.mediaplatform.com

Industry Group Code: 511210F Ranks within this company's industry group: Sales: Profits:

Hardware:	Software:		Telecommunications:	Electronic Publishing:	Equipment:	Specialty Services:	
Computers:	Consumer:		Local:	Online Service:	Telecom:	Consulting:	Y
Accessories:	Corporate:	Y	Long Distance:	TV/Cable or Wireless:	Communication:	Contract Manufacturing:	
Network Equipment:	Telecom:		Cellular:	Games:	Distribution:	Processing:	
Chips/Circuits:	Internet:		Internet Service:	Financial Data:	VAR/Reseller:	Staff/Outsourcing:	
Parts/Drives:					Satellite Srv./Equip.:	Specialty Services:	Y

TYPES OF BUSINESS:

Software-Interactive Video
Consulting Services

BRANDS/DIVISIONS/AFFILIATES:

MediaLauncher
WebCaster
PrimeTime
Interactive Video Technologies

CONTACTS: Note: Officers with more than one job title may be intentionally listed here more than once.

Jim McGovern, CEO
Greg Pulier, Pres.
Hugh Taylor, VP-Mktg.
Denis Khoo, CTO
Brett Law, VP-Prod. Dev.
Brett Law, VP-Eng.
Dena Kendros, VP-Admin.
Dena Kendros, VP-Finance
Ysette Witteveen, VP/Gen. Mgr.-Client Svcs.
Michael Grant, Dir.-Sales, Eastern Region
Mitchell Harper, Dir.-Sales, Western Region
Paul Wible, Dir.-Sales, Midwest Region
Mark Lieberman, Chmn.

Phone: 310-909-8410	Fax: 310-909-8410
Toll-Free: 888-488-2278	
Address: 8484 Wilshire Blvd., Ste. 515, Beverly Hills, CA 90211 US	

GROWTH PLANS/SPECIAL FEATURES:

MediaPlatform, Inc. provides e-communications software. The company's enterprise-scale mixed media software and services enable the creation, management, distribution and measurement of live and on-demand rich media presentations and training over the web. The firm partners with leading IT companies including Adobe, IBM, Cisco Systems and Oraclein order to provide seamless integration of its products into the latest media players and operating systems. Mediaplatofrm offers three software products: Webcaster, MediaLauncher and PrimeTime. Webcaster allows clients to produce, manage distribute and monitor live and on demand webcasts that feature streaming video, Microsoft PowerPoint slides, Adobe Flash animations, audio, surveys, polls and screen demos. core product, MediaPlatform, now available in version 4.0, enables business to create, produce, deliver and monitor live and on-demand webcasts. Webcaster is available as Software as a Service (SaaS) as well as in an on-site installation. MediaLauncher allows for customized webcasting interfaces that clients can utilize to match their brand standards. These templates, using MediaLauncher Template Editor, incorporate images, buttons, rollovers, Microsoft PowerPoint, tables of contents, Adobe Flash, video, polls, whiteboards and forms. Medialauncher also provide users with their choice of content distribution networks (CDN). PrimeTime is an enterprise rich media management and online video platform which allows clients to preserve, organize and centralize knowledge and corporate media. The company's clients include Dell, IBM, Mediaco, NEC, Rohm and Haas, Cramer and AT&T. Based in Los Angeles, California, MediaPlatform has satellite offices in New York, Chicago, and San Francisco. In May 2010, the company changed its named from Interactive Video Technologies to MediaPlatform, Inc.

FINANCIALS: Sales and profits are in thousands of dollars—add 000 to get the full amount. 2010 Note: Financial information for 2010 was not available for all companies at press time.

2010 Sales: $	2010 Profits: $	U.S. Stock Ticker: Private
2009 Sales: $	2009 Profits: $	Int'l Ticker: Int'l Exchange:
2008 Sales: $	2008 Profits: $	Employees:
2007 Sales: $	2007 Profits: $	Fiscal Year Ends: 12/31
2006 Sales: $	2006 Profits: $	Parent Company:

SALARIES/BENEFITS:

Pension Plan:	ESOP Stock Plan:	Profit Sharing:	Top Exec. Salary: $	Bonus: $60,000
Savings Plan:	Stock Purch. Plan:		Second Exec. Salary: $	Bonus: $

OTHER THOUGHTS:

Apparent Women Officers or Directors: 2
Hot Spot for Advancement for Women/Minorities: Y

LOCATIONS: ("Y" = Yes)

West:	Southwest:	Midwest:	Southeast:	Northeast:	International:
Y				Y	

Note: Financial information, benefits and other data can change quickly and may vary from those stated here.

MEDIATEK INC

www.mediatek.com.

Industry Group Code: 33441 Ranks within this company's industry group: Sales: 12 Profits: 5

Hardware:		Software:		Telecommunications:		Electronic Publishing:		Equipment:		Specialty Services:	
Computers:		Consumer:		Local:		Online Service:		Telecom:		Consulting:	
Accessories:		Corporate:		Long Distance:		TV/Cable or Wireless:		Communication:		Contract Manufacturing:	
Network Equipment:		Telecom:		Cellular:		Games:		Distribution:		Processing:	
Chips/Circuits:	Y	Internet:		Internet Service:		Financial Data:		VAR/Reseller:		Staff/Outsourcing:	
Parts/Drives:								Satellite Srv./Equip.:		Specialty Services:	

TYPES OF BUSINESS:

Semiconductor Manufacturing
Digital Media Products

BRANDS/DIVISIONS/AFFILIATES:

MDDi
PureEdge Engine

CONTACTS: *Note: Officers with more than one job title may be intentionally listed here more than once.*

Ming-Kai Tsai, CEO
Ching-Jiang Hsieh, Pres.
Mingto Yu, CFO
Wei-Fu Hsu, General Counsel/VP
Oliver Chow, Chief Strategy Officer/VP
Jyh-Jer Cho, Vice Chmn.
Ping-Hsing Lu, VP
Chwei-Huang Chang, VP
Kou-Hung Loh, VP
Ming-Kai Tsai, Chmn.

Phone: 886-3-567-0766	Fax: 886-3-578-7610
Toll-Free:	
Address: 1, Dusing Rd. 1, HsinChu Science Park, Hsinchu, 300 Taiwan	

GROWTH PLANS/SPECIAL FEATURES:

MediaTek, Inc., based in Taiwan, is a fables semiconductor company for wireless communications and digital media solutions. MediaTek develops, products and markets system-on-chip (SOC) systems for a variety of consumer devices. The firm's MDDi technology for progressive scan DVD players features the firm's proprietary PureEdge Engine edge processing technology, removing the saw-tooth effect in the interlace to progressive converters, and uses an architecture that combines the MPEG decoder, format converter and video enhancement unit. The company also offers low-power mobile device chips, all-in-one single-chip GPS units, integrated FM radio receivers, Bluetooth receivers, WiFI receivers, optical media for computers and digital television decoders. MediaTek's manufacturing operations are outsourced to third-party manufacturers. The firm has subsidiaries in Beijing, Hefei, Chengdu and Shenzhen China, as well as Japan, Korea, Singapore, India, the U.K and the U.S.

FINANCIALS: Sales and profits are in thousands of dollars—add 000 to get the full amount. 2010 Note: Financial information for 2010 was not available for all companies at press time.

2010 Sales: $	2010 Profits: $	U.S. Stock Ticker:
2009 Sales: $3,977,670	2009 Profits: $1,263,970	Int'l Ticker: 2454 Int'l Exchange: Taipei-TPE
2008 Sales: $2,835,960	2008 Profits: $602,000	Employees:
2007 Sales: $2,480,000	2007 Profits: $1,040,000	Fiscal Year Ends: 12/31
2006 Sales: $1,630,690	2006 Profits: $695,490	Parent Company:

SALARIES/BENEFITS:

Pension Plan:	ESOP Stock Plan:	Profit Sharing:	Top Exec. Salary: $	Bonus: $
Savings Plan:	Stock Purch. Plan:		Second Exec. Salary: $	Bonus: $

OTHER THOUGHTS:

Apparent Women Officers or Directors:
Hot Spot for Advancement for Women/Minorities:

LOCATIONS: ("Y" = Yes)

West:	Southwest:	Midwest:	Southeast:	Northeast:	International:
				Y	Y

Note: Financial information, benefits and other data can change quickly and may vary from those stated here.

MEDICAL INFORMATION TECHNOLOGY INC   www.meditech.com

Industry Group Code: 511210D Ranks within this company's industry group: Sales: Profits:

Hardware:	Software:		Telecommunications:	Electronic Publishing:	Equipment:	Specialty Services:
Computers:	Consumer:		Local:	Online Service:	Telecom:	Consulting:
Accessories:	Corporate:	Y	Long Distance:	TV/Cable or Wireless:	Communication:	Contract Manufacturing:
Network Equipment:	Telecom:		Cellular:	Games:	Distribution:	Processing:
Chips/Circuits:	Internet:		Internet Service:	Financial Data:	VAR/Reseller:	Staff/Outsourcing:
Parts/Drives:					Satellite Srv./Equip.:	Specialty Services:

TYPES OF BUSINESS:
Computer Software-Health Care

BRANDS/DIVISIONS/AFFILIATES:
MEDITECH
Health Care Information System
MEDITECH 6.0
MEDITECH Medication Management
Medical & Practice Management Solution

CONTACTS: Note: Officers with more than one job title may be intentionally listed here more than once.
Howard Messing, CEO
Howard Messing, Pres.
Barbara A. Manzolillo, CFO
Hoda Sayed-Friel, VP-Mktg.
Chris Anschuetz, VP-System Tech.
Robert Gale, Sr. VP-Prod. Dev.
Barbara A. Manzolillo, Treas.
Michelle O'Connor, VP-Prod. Dev.
Stu Lefthes, VP-Sales
Steve Koretz, VP-Implementation
Joanne Wood, VP-Client Svcs.
A. Neil Pappalardo, Chmn.

Phone: 781-821-3000	**Fax:** 781-821-2199
Toll-Free:	
Address: Meditech Cir., Westwood, MA 02090 US	

GROWTH PLANS/SPECIAL FEATURES:

Medical Information Technology, Inc. (MEDITECH) develops and markets information system software for the health care industry. MEDITECH's software products automate a variety of hospital functions, as well as providing products for long-term care facilities; ambulatory care centers; acute-care hospitals; emergency rooms; pharmacies; and imaging, therapeutic service and behavioral health facilities. MEDITECH specifies aggregate components for each hospital and suggests typical configurations from selected hardware vendors pertaining to its software needs. The firm's software products include MEDITECH 6.0 Release, an organizational interface tool; Health Care Information System, which provides health care groups with reporting tools for managing organizational performance quality; MEDITECH Medication Management, a closed loop system designed to aid in all aspects of medication delivery; Medical and Practice Management Solution software, which manages order entry, provides bedside medication verification, handles operating room management, provides nursing interface systems, creates enterprise medical records and provides patient education and discharge instructions; and software designed for long-term and home care needs. In addition, MEDITECH's corporate software can consolidate a hospital's human resources and general accounting needs, among others. The company's products are sold in all 50 states, the U.K., Latin America, Canada, Ireland, South Africa, Spain and Mexico. MEDITECH maintains a partnership with LS Data Systems, which develops administrative, financial, and clinical practice management software for the firm's facilities.

The firm offers employees benefits such as medical, dental, AD&D, life and long term disability insurance; travel stipends; child and elder care referral services; educational assistance; paid time off; profit sharing; and an annual bonus.

FINANCIALS: Sales and profits are in thousands of dollars—add 000 to get the full amount. 2010 Note: Financial information for 2010 was not available for all companies at press time.

2010 Sales: $	2010 Profits: $	**U.S. Stock Ticker:** Private
2009 Sales: $	2009 Profits: $	**Int'l Ticker:** Int'l Exchange:
2008 Sales: $	2008 Profits: $	Employees:
2007 Sales: $	2007 Profits: $	Fiscal Year Ends: 12/31
2006 Sales: $344,600	2006 Profits: $87,200	Parent Company:

SALARIES/BENEFITS:

Pension Plan: Y	ESOP Stock Plan:	Profit Sharing: Y	Top Exec. Salary: $	Bonus: $
Savings Plan:	Stock Purch. Plan: Y		Second Exec. Salary: $	Bonus: $

OTHER THOUGHTS:
Apparent Women Officers or Directors: 6
Hot Spot for Advancement for Women/Minorities: Y

LOCATIONS: ("Y" = Yes)

West:	Southwest:	Midwest:	Southeast:	Northeast:	International:
				Y	

MELLANOX TECHNOLOGIES LTD

www.mellanox.com

Industry Group Code: 334111 Ranks within this company's industry group: Sales: 29   Profits: 14

Hardware:		Software:	Telecommunications:	Electronic Publishing:	Equipment:	Specialty Services:
Computers:		Consumer:	Local:	Online Service:	Telecom:	Consulting:
Accessories:		Corporate:	Long Distance:	TV/Cable or Wireless:	Communication:	Contract Manufacturing:
Network Equipment:	Y	Telecom:	Cellular:	Games:	Distribution:	Processing:
Chips/Circuits:	Y	Internet:	Internet Service:	Financial Data:	VAR/Reseller:	Staff/Outsourcing:
Parts/Drives:					Satellite Srv./Equip.:	Specialty Services:

TYPES OF BUSINESS:
Ethernet & Switching Hardware

BRANDS/DIVISIONS/AFFILIATES:
InfiniBand
InfiniHost
InfiniScale
BridgeX
ConnectX
ConnectX-2
FabricIT
FabricIT BridgeX Manager

CONTACTS: Note: Officers with more than one job title may be intentionally listed here more than once.
Eyal Waldman, CEO
Michael Gray, CFO
Ron Aghazarian, VP-Worldwide Sales
Michael Kagan, CTO
Roni Ashuri, VP-Eng.
Ronnen Lovinger, VP-Mfg. Oper.
Matthew Gloss, VP-Legal Affairs
Shai Cohen, VP-Oper. & Eng.
Wayne Augsburger, VP-Bus. Dev.
Eyal Babish, VP-System Solutions
Ari Cohen, VP-Network Adapter Prod.
Dror Goldenberg, VP-Architecture
Evelyn Landman, VP-Back-End Eng.
Eyal Waldman, Chmn.

Phone: 408-970-3400	Fax: 408-370-3403
Toll-Free:	
Address: 350 Oakmead Pkwy., Ste. 100, Sunnyvale, CA 94085 US	

GROWTH PLANS/SPECIAL FEATURES:

Mellanox Technologies, Ltd. designs, develops and manufactures networking equipment, such as adapter, gateway and switch integrated circuits (ICs). The company's products are primarily semiconductor-based, high-performance equipment products that facilitate efficient data transmission between servers, communications infrastructure equipment and storage systems. The firm is a leading provider of InfiniBand-enabled products, which supports bandwidth ranging from 10 Gb/s (gigs per second) to 40 Gb/s for server-to-server communication and 10 Gb/s to 120 Gb/s for switch-to-switch communication. InfiniBand products include adapter ICs and cards (under the InfiniHost brand name); switch ICs (under the InfiniScale brand name); systems and gateway ICs (under the BridgeX brand name); and gateway systems. The company's newest adapters and cards, which use the ConnectX and ConnectX-2 brands, also support the Ethernet interconnect standard in addition to InfiniBand Mellanox supplies its OEM (original equipment manufacturer) customers with a suite of software tools to manage the equipment. The FabricIT program allows users to manage, optimize, test and verify the operation of InfiniBand switch fabrics, while the FabricIT BridgeX Manager works to manage input and output consolidation from an InfiniBand network to Ethernet and Fibre Channel for cluster, cloud and virtual environments. The firm's products are featured in servers built by companies including IBM, Hewlett-Packard, Dell, Sun Microsystems and Fujitsu-Siemens. In November 2010, the company entered into an agreement to acquire Voltaire, Ltd., a developer of network connectivity equipment, for about $218 million.

Mellanox offers its employees medical, health and dental coverage; life and AD&D insurance; a 401(k) plan; an employee stock purchase plan; long-term disability; and flexible spending accounts.

FINANCIALS: Sales and profits are in thousands of dollars—add 000 to get the full amount. 2010 Note: Financial information for 2010 was not available for all companies at press time.

2010 Sales: $	2010 Profits: $	**U.S. Stock Ticker: MLNX**
2009 Sales: $116,044	2009 Profits: $12,886	**Int'l Ticker:** Int'l Exchange:
2008 Sales: $107,701	2008 Profits: $22,371	Employees: 345
2007 Sales: $	2007 Profits: $	Fiscal Year Ends: 12/31
2006 Sales: $	2006 Profits: $	Parent Company:

SALARIES/BENEFITS:

Pension Plan:	ESOP Stock Plan:	Profit Sharing:	Top Exec. Salary: $301,171	Bonus: $142,000
Savings Plan: Y	Stock Purch. Plan: Y		Second Exec. Salary: $213,058	Bonus: $40,000

OTHER THOUGHTS:
Apparent Women Officers or Directors: 1
Hot Spot for Advancement for Women/Minorities:

LOCATIONS: ("Y" = Yes)

West:	Southwest:	Midwest:	Southeast:	Northeast:	International:
Y					Y

Note: Financial information, benefits and other data can change quickly and may vary from those stated here.

MEMC ELECTRONIC MATERIALS INC

www.memc.com

Industry Group Code: 33441 Ranks within this company's industry group: Sales: 28 Profits: 42

Hardware:		Software:	Telecommunications:	Electronic Publishing:	Equipment:	Specialty Services:	
Computers:		Consumer:	Local:	Online Service:	Telecom:	Consulting:	
Accessories:		Corporate:	Long Distance:	TV/Cable or Wireless:	Communication:	Contract Manufacturing:	
Network Equipment:		Telecom:	Cellular:	Games:	Distribution:	Processing:	
Chips/Circuits:	Y	Internet:	Internet Service:	Financial Data:	VAR/Reseller:	Staff/Outsourcing:	
Parts/Drives:					Satellite Srv./Equip.:	Specialty Services:	Y

TYPES OF BUSINESS:
Silicon Wafers Manufacturing
Intermediate Products Sales

BRANDS/DIVISIONS/AFFILIATES:
Sun Edison LLC
Eversol Corporation
Magic Denuded Zone
SunEdison LLC
Solaicx, Inc.

CONTACTS: *Note: Officers with more than one job title may be intentionally listed here more than once.*
Ahmad Chatila, CEO
Ahmad Chatila, Pres.
Mark Murphy, CFO/Sr. VP
John Kauffmann, Sr. VP-Mktg. & Sales
Scott Weisberg, Chief Human Resources Officer/Sr. VP
Brad Kohn, General Counsel/Sr. VP-Legal & Bus. Dev.
Stephen O'Rourke, Chief Strategy Officer/Sr. VP
Bill Michalek, Dir.-Corp. Comm.
Kurt Bruenning, Treas.
Ken Hannah, Exec. VP/Pres., Solar Materials
Shaker Sadasivam, Exec. VP/Pres., Semiconductor
Sean Hunkler, Sr. VP-Customer Advocacy
Carlos C. Domenech, Exec. VP/Pres., SunEdison
John Marren, Chmn.

Phone: 636-474-5000	Fax: 636-474-5158
Toll-Free:	
Address: 501 Pearl Dr., St. Peters, MO 63376 US	

GROWTH PLANS/SPECIAL FEATURES:
MEMC Electronic Materials, Inc. is a worldwide producer of silicon wafers for semiconductor device and solar cell manufacturers, with facilities in the U.S., Asia and Europe. The firm's semiconductors are manufactured using a proprietary Magic Denuded Zone technology, designed to produce a silicon wafer with ideal oxygen precipitation behavior. It operates in three segments: Semiconductor Materials, Solar Materials and Solar Energy. In the Semiconductor Materials division, the firm produces three main types of silicon wafers: prime polished, epitaxial wafers, and Silicon-on-Insulator (SOI) wafers. Its prime polished wafers are manufactured with a sophisticated chemical-mechanical polishing process that removes surface defects, producing extremely flat, mirror-like surfaces for use in various advanced integrated circuit applications. Epitaxial wafers consist of a thin, single-crystal silicon layer grown on the polished surface of a silicon wafer substrate. The epi layer is designed to have different compositional and electrical properties than the underlying wafer. SOI wafers are made up of three layers: a thin surface layer of silicon where the transistors are formed; a layer of insulating material and a support bulk silicon wafer; and an insulating layer typically made of silicon dioxide. The Solar Materials division fabricates multicrystalline and monocrystalline 156 mm wafers for solar capture applications. Through its acquisition of SunEdison LLC in 2009, the firm now engages in solar power project development. Its current portfolio includes over 250 solar energy systems operating under power purchase agreements and over 80 additional systems under SunEdison supervision. In May 2010, SunEdison and First Reserve established a joint venture for the acquisition of SunEdison's photovoltaic projects, up to a sum of $1.5 billion. In July 2010, MEMC acquired Solaicx, Inc., a supplier of silicon ingots to the solar industry.

Employees are offered medical and dental insurance; life insurance; flexible spending accounts; education reimbursement; and an employee assistance program.

FINANCIALS: Sales and profits are in thousands of dollars—add 000 to get the full amount. 2010 Note: Financial information for 2010 was not available for all companies at press time.

2010 Sales: $	2010 Profits: $	**U.S. Stock Ticker: WFR**
2009 Sales: $1,163,600	2009 Profits: $-68,300	Int'l Ticker: Int'l Exchange:
2008 Sales: $2,004,500	2008 Profits: $387,400	Employees: 4,568
2007 Sales: $1,921,800	2007 Profits: $826,200	Fiscal Year Ends: 12/31
2006 Sales: $1,540,584	2006 Profits: $369,288	Parent Company:

SALARIES/BENEFITS:
Pension Plan:	ESOP Stock Plan:	Profit Sharing:	Top Exec. Salary: $634,615	Bonus: $600,000
Savings Plan: Y	Stock Purch. Plan:		Second Exec. Salary: $463,223	Bonus: $226,688

OTHER THOUGHTS:
Apparent Women Officers or Directors:
Hot Spot for Advancement for Women/Minorities:

LOCATIONS: ("Y" = Yes)
West:	Southwest:	Midwest:	Southeast:	Northeast:	International:
Y	Y	Y		Y	Y

Note: Financial information, benefits and other data can change quickly and may vary from those stated here.

MENTOR GRAPHICS CORP

www.mentor.com

Industry Group Code: 511210N Ranks within this company's industry group: Sales: 6 Profits: 9

Hardware:	Software:		Telecommunications:	Electronic Publishing:	Equipment:	Specialty Services:	
Computers:	Consumer:		Local:	Online Service:	Telecom:	Consulting:	Y
Accessories:	Corporate:	Y	Long Distance:	TV/Cable or Wireless:	Communication:	Contract Manufacturing:	
Network Equipment:	Telecom:		Cellular:	Games:	Distribution:	Processing:	
Chips/Circuits:	Internet:		Internet Service:	Financial Data:	VAR/Reseller:	Staff/Outsourcing:	
Parts/Drives:					Satellite Srv./Equip.:	Specialty Services:	Y

TYPES OF BUSINESS:

Software-Component Design, Simulation & Testing
Electronic Design Automation Tools
Consulting Services

BRANDS/DIVISIONS/AFFILIATES:

Embedded Alley Solutions Inc
Calibre
Questa
ModelSim
Olympus-SoC
CodeSourcery Inc.
Expedition
Valor Computerized Systems Ltd.

CONTACTS: Note: Officers with more than one job title may be intentionally listed here more than once.

Walden C. Rhines, CEO
Gregory K. Hinckley, Pres.
Brian Derrick, VP-Corp. Mktg.
Alan Friedman, VP-Human Resources
Ananthan Thandri, CIO/VP
Dean Freed, General Counsel/VP
Joe Reinhart, Dir.-Investor Rel.
Ethan Manuel, Corp. Treas.
L. Don Maulsby, Sr. VP-World Trade
Robert Hum, VP/Gen. Mgr.-Deep Submicron Div.
Henry Potts, VP/Gen. Mgr.-System Design Div.
Simon Bloch, VP/Gen. Mgr.-Design & Synthesis Div.
Walden C. Rhines, Chmn.
Hanns Windele, VP-Europe

Phone: 503-685-7000	Fax: 503-685-1204
Toll-Free: 800-592-2210	
Address: 8005 SW Boeckman Rd., Wilsonville, OR 97070 US	

GROWTH PLANS/SPECIAL FEATURES:

Mentor Graphics Corp. is a supplier of electronic design automation (EDA) systems, advanced computer software and emulation hardware products used to automate the design, analysis and testing of electronic hardware and embedded systems and components. The products are primarily marketed to large companies in the military, aerospace, communications, computer, consumer electronics, semiconductor, networking, multimedia and transportation industries. The company's offerings include Functional Verification products, integrated circuit (IC) design and integrated system design. Functional Verification products are designed to help engineers verify that their IC designs function as needed. Products in this category include ModelSim software tools for Application-Specific ICs (ASICs), System-on-a-Chip (SoCs), Field-Programmable Gate Arrays (FPGAs) and other ICs as well as verification of entire systems; and Questa, a functional verification platform that includes support, simulation and verification technologies for extended verification of systems and ICs including ASICs, SoCs and FPGAs. IC design products consist of the Calibre and Olympus-SoC product lines. Calibre tools are designed to aid customers in the design process of ICs. Olympus-SoC products are designed for creating ICs with geometries of 65nm and below and address challenges such as manufacturing variability, design size, complexity and low power requirements. Integrated system design products support the PCB and FPGA design process with products such as The Board Station, Expedition, PADS, I/O Designer, Xtreme PCB and Xtreme AR. Mentor sells and licenses its products through its direct sales force as well as distributors and sales representatives. In March 2010, Mentor acquired Valor Computerized Systems, Ltd. for approximately $50 million. In December 2010, the company acquired CodeSourcery Inc., a provider of open source GNU-based toolchains and services for advanced systems development.

Employees of Mentor receive adoption assistance; employee assistance; medical, dental, vision and prescription drug coverage; life and AD&D insurance; and tuition reimbursement.

FINANCIALS: Sales and profits are in thousands of dollars—add 000 to get the full amount. 2010 Note: Financial information for 2010 was not available for all companies at press time.

2010 Sales: $802,727	2010 Profits: $-21,889	**U.S. Stock Ticker:** MENT
2009 Sales: $789,101	2009 Profits: $-88,802	**Int'l Ticker:** Int'l Exchange:
2008 Sales: $879,732	2008 Profits: $28,771	Employees: 4,400
2007 Sales: $802,839	2007 Profits: $27,204	Fiscal Year Ends: 1/31
2006 Sales: $802,839	2006 Profits: $27,204	Parent Company:

SALARIES/BENEFITS:

Pension Plan:	ESOP Stock Plan:	Profit Sharing:	Top Exec. Salary: $659,551	Bonus: $758,483
Savings Plan: Y	Stock Purch. Plan: Y		Second Exec. Salary: $539,111	Bonus: $566,067

OTHER THOUGHTS:

Apparent Women Officers or Directors: 1
Hot Spot for Advancement for Women/Minorities:

LOCATIONS: ("Y" = Yes)

West:	Southwest:	Midwest:	Southeast:	Northeast:	International:
Y	Y	Y	Y	Y	Y

MICROCHIP TECHNOLOGY INC

www.microchip.com

Industry Group Code: 33441 Ranks within this company's industry group: Sales: 32 Profits: 13

Hardware:		Software:		Telecommunications:		Electronic Publishing:		Equipment:		Specialty Services:	
Computers:		Consumer:		Local:		Online Service:		Telecom:		Consulting:	
Accessories:		Corporate:		Long Distance:		TV/Cable or Wireless:		Communication:		Contract Manufacturing:	
Network Equipment:		Telecom:		Cellular:		Games:		Distribution:		Processing:	
Chips/Circuits:	Y	Internet:		Internet Service:		Financial Data:		VAR/Reseller:		Staff/Outsourcing:	
Parts/Drives:								Satellite Srv./Equip.:		Specialty Services:	

TYPES OF BUSINESS:

Semiconductors-Specialized
Microcontrollers
Battery Management & Interface Devices
Development Tools
Memory Products

BRANDS/DIVISIONS/AFFILIATES:

PIC
dsPIC
Digital Signal Controllers
EEPROM
EPROM
Silicon Storage Technology Inc

CONTACTS: Note: Officers with more than one job title may be intentionally listed here more than once.

Steve Sanghi, CEO
Ganesh Moorthy, COO/Exec. VP
Steve Sanghi, Pres.
J. Eric Bjornholt, CFO/VP
Mitchell R. Little, VP-Worldwide Sales & Applications
Lauren A. Carr, VP-Human Resources
Robert H. Owen, VP-Info. Svcs.
Stephen V. Drehobl, VP-Tech, Security & Microcontroller Div.
Randall L. Drwinga, VP-Memory Prod. Div.
Kenneth N. Pye, VP-Worldwide Applications Eng.
David S. Lambert, VP-Fab Oper.
Kimberly van Herk, Corp. Sec.
Gordon W. Parnell, VP-Bus. Dev.
Gordon W. Parnell, VP-Investor Rel.
William Yang, VP-Pacific Rim Finance
Joseph R. Krawczyk, VP-Asia Sales
Mitchel Obolsky, VP-Advanced Microcontroller Architecture Div.
Dan L. Termer, VP-Vertical Markets Group
Steve Sanghi, Chmn.
Gary P. Marsh, VP-European Sales

Phone: 480-792-7200	Fax: 480-899-9210
Toll-Free:	
Address: 2355 W. Chandler Blvd., Chandler, AZ 85224-6199 US	

GROWTH PLANS/SPECIAL FEATURES:

Microchip Technology, Inc. develops and manufactures specialized semiconductor products used for a wide variety of embedded control applications. In addition, the company offers a broad spectrum of high-performance linear, mixed-signal, power management, thermal management, battery management and interface devices. The firm focuses on embedded control functions, including microcontrollers; development tools; analog and interface products; and memory products. Microchip offers a broad family of microcontroller products featuring the proprietary architecture PIC with a variety of memory technology configurations, low voltage and power and small footprint. The company targets the 8-bit , 16-bit and 32-bit microcontroller markets. Additionally, the scalable product architecture allows it to target both the entry-level of the 32-bit microcontroller markets, as well as the 4-bit microcontroller marketplace. The firm is able to incorporate non-volatile memory, such as Flash, EEPROM and EPROM Memory, into the microcontroller and offers reprogrammable microcontroller products. The development tools enable system designers to program a PIC microcontroller and dsPIC Digital Signal Controllers for specific applications. Microchip's family of development tools operate in the standard Windows environment on standard PC hardware. These tools range from entry-level systems, which include an assembler and programmer or in-circuit debugging hardware, to fully configured systems that provide in-circuit emulation hardware. Analog and interface products consist of several families with over 600 power management, linear, mixed-signal, thermal management and interface products. Memory products consists primarily of serial electrically erasable programmable read only memory, referred to as Serial EEPROMs. Serial EEPROM products are used for non-volatile program and data storage systems where such data must be either modified frequently or retained for long periods. In April 2010, the company acquired Silicon Storage Technology, Inc., a developer of memory and other similar products.

FINANCIALS: Sales and profits are in thousands of dollars—add 000 to get the full amount. 2010 Note: Financial information for 2010 was not available for all companies at press time.

2010 Sales: $947,729	2010 Profits: $217,005	**U.S. Stock Ticker: MCHP**
2009 Sales: $903,297	2009 Profits: $248,820	**Int'l Ticker:** Int'l Exchange:
2008 Sales: $1,035,737	2008 Profits: $297,748	Employees: 5,418
2007 Sales: $1,039,671	2007 Profits: $357,029	Fiscal Year Ends: 3/31
2006 Sales: $927,893	2006 Profits: $242,369	Parent Company:

SALARIES/BENEFITS:

Pension Plan:	ESOP Stock Plan:	Profit Sharing: Y	Top Exec. Salary: $505,762	Bonus: $1,378,720
Savings Plan: Y	Stock Purch. Plan: Y		Second Exec. Salary: $242,483	Bonus: $204,922

OTHER THOUGHTS:

Apparent Women Officers or Directors: 3
Hot Spot for Advancement for Women/Minorities: Y

LOCATIONS: ("Y" = Yes)

West:	Southwest:	Midwest:	Southeast:	Northeast:	International:
Y	Y	Y	Y	Y	Y

MICRON TECHNOLOGY INC

www.micron.com

Industry Group Code: 33441 Ranks within this company's industry group: Sales: 9 Profits: 53

Hardware:		Software:		Telecommunications:		Electronic Publishing:	Equipment:	Specialty Services:
Computers:		Consumer:		Local:		Online Service:	Telecom:	Consulting:
Accessories:	Y	Corporate:		Long Distance:		TV/Cable or Wireless:	Communication:	Contract Manufacturing:
Network Equipment:		Telecom:		Cellular:		Games:	Distribution:	Processing:
Chips/Circuits:	Y	Internet:		Internet Service:		Financial Data:	VAR/Reseller:	Staff/Outsourcing:
Parts/Drives:	Y						Satellite Srv./Equip.:	Specialty Services:

TYPES OF BUSINESS:

Components-Semiconductor Memory
PCs & Peripherals
Flash Memory Devices
CMOS Image Sensors
FLCOS Displays
Photovoltaic Solar Panels

BRANDS/DIVISIONS/AFFILIATES:

Lexar Media, Inc.
Crucial
Aptina Imaging Corporation
RealSSD
Numonyx BV

CONTACTS: Note: Officers with more than one job title may be intentionally listed here more than once.

Steven R. Appleton, CEO
D. Mark Durcan, COO
D. Mark Durcan, Pres.
Ronald C. Foster, CFO/VP-Finance
Mark W. Adams, VP-Worldwide Sales
Patrick T. Otte, VP-Human Resources
Scott J. DeBoer, VP-Process R&D
James E. Mahoney, VP-Info. Systems
Roderic W. Lewis, General Counsel/VP-Legal Affairs/Corp. Sec.
Brian J. Shields, VP-Worldwide Oper.
Michael W. Sadler, VP-Corp. Dev.
Kipp A. Bedard, VP-Investor Rel.
Philippe Morali, Treas.
John F. Schreck, VP-DRAM Dev.
Brian M. Shirley, VP-DRAM Solutions
Mario Licciardello, VP-Wireless Solutions
Frankie F. Roohparvar, VP-NAND Dev.
Steven R. Appleton, Chmn.
Steven L. Thorsen, Jr., Chief Procurement Officer/VP

Phone: 208-368-4000	Fax: 208-368-4435
Toll-Free:	
Address: 8000 S. Federal Way, Boise, ID 83707-0006 US	

GROWTH PLANS/SPECIAL FEATURES:

Micron Technology, Inc. designs, develops, manufactures and markets semiconductor memory products and personal computer systems. Its products are used in a range of electronic devices, including personal computers, workstations, servers, cell phones, digital cameras and other consumer and industrial products. Micron has three segments: Memory, producing dynamic random access memory (DRAM) and NAND flash memory, accounting for 89% of 2010 sales; Numonyx, acquired in May 2010 and representing 7% of 2010 sales; and all other, which includes various equity interests and joint developments. Micron offers double data rate (DDR), DDR2 and DDR3 DRAM, primarily used for the main system memory in computers; and synchronous DRAM (SDRAM), used in networking devices, servers, consumer electronics, communications equipment and computer peripherals. NAND products are re-writable, non-volatile semiconductor devices used in mobile devices such as digital cameras, MP3 players, USB Flash Drives and cellular phones. The firm also offers RealSSD solid-state drives for applications that require lower power consumption and higher reliability standards than traditional hard drives. Numonyx's chief products are NOR flash memory and Phase Change Memory (PCM) devices, which offer speed and other enhancements over earlier generations of memory drives. The all other segment includes its interest in Aptina Imaging Corp., which manufactures CMOS image sensors, as well as various development projects for FLCOS microdisplays and solar products. The company's Lexar Media, Inc. subsidiary markets digital media and flash-based products to retail and original equipment manufacturing markets, while the Crucial brand focuses on web-based direct sales. The firm's manufacturing facilities are located in the U.S., Italy, Japan, Puerto Rico, Singapore and China. In January 2010, the company established a joint venture with Origin Energy Ltd. to develop advanced photovoltaic technology. In May 2010, it acquired Numonyx BV for $1.2 billion.

Employees are offered medical, dental, vision and life insurance; short-and long-term disability coverage, business travel accident coverage; and educational assistance.

FINANCIALS: Sales and profits are in thousands of dollars—add 000 to get the full amount. 2010 Note: Financial information for 2010 was not available for all companies at press time.

2010 Sales: $8,482,000	2010 Profits: $1,850,000	**U.S. Stock Ticker: MU**
2009 Sales: $4,803,000	2009 Profits: $-1,882,000	**Int'l Ticker:** Int'l Exchange:
2008 Sales: $5,841,000	2008 Profits: $-1,655,000	Employees: 25,900
2007 Sales: $5,688,000	2007 Profits: $-320,000	Fiscal Year Ends: 8/31
2006 Sales: $5,272,000	2006 Profits: $408,000	Parent Company:

SALARIES/BENEFITS:

Pension Plan:	ESOP Stock Plan:	Profit Sharing:	Top Exec. Salary: $806,405	Bonus: $2,090,000
Savings Plan: Y	Stock Purch. Plan:		Second Exec. Salary: $507,692	Bonus: $1,068,000

OTHER THOUGHTS:

Apparent Women Officers or Directors:
Hot Spot for Advancement for Women/Minorities:

LOCATIONS: ("Y" = Yes)

West:	Southwest:	Midwest:	Southeast:	Northeast:	International:
Y				Y	Y

Note: Financial information, benefits and other data can change quickly and may vary from those stated here.

MICROS SYSTEMS INC

www.micros.com

Industry Group Code: 334111 Ranks within this company's industry group: Sales: 21 Profits: 8

Hardware:		Software:		Telecommunications:	Electronic Publishing:	Equipment:	Specialty Services:	
Computers:		Consumer:	Y	Local:	Online Service:	Telecom:	Consulting:	
Accessories:	Y	Corporate:	Y	Long Distance:	TV/Cable or Wireless:	Communication:	Contract Manufacturing:	
Network Equipment:		Telecom:		Cellular:	Games:	Distribution:	Processing:	
Chips/Circuits:		Internet:		Internet Service:	Financial Data:	VAR/Reseller:	Staff/Outsourcing:	
Parts/Drives:						Satellite Srv./Equip.:	Specialty Services:	Y

TYPES OF BUSINESS:

Computer Hardware-Point-of-Sale Systems
Hospitality & Retail Hardware
Hospitality Management Software
Retail Management Software
Online Reservation Services
Paging Systems
Consulting & Support Services

BRANDS/DIVISIONS/AFFILIATES:

MyFidelio.net
RedSky IT
MICROS-Retail
POS Depot
Fidelio Cruise
JTECH Communications Inc
Hospitality Solutions International
Fry Inc

CONTACTS: Note: Officers with more than one job title may be intentionally listed here more than once.

A.L. Giannopoulos, CEO
A.L. Giannopoulos, Pres.
Cynthia A. Russo, CFO/Exec. VP
Jennifer M. Kurdle, Chief Admin. Officer/Exec. VP
Peter J. Rogers, Jr., Exec. VP-Bus. Dev.
Peter J. Rogers, Jr., Exec. VP-Investor Rel.
Thomas L. Patz, Exec. VP-Strategic Initiatives
James T. Walsh, Chief Info. Security Officer
Bernard Jammet, Pres., MICROS-Fidelio, Latin America & Caribbean
Stefan Piringer, Pres., MICROS-Fidelio, Asia Pacific
A.L. Giannopoulos, Chmn.
Kaweh Niroomand, Pres., MICROS-Fidelio, EMEA

Phone: 443-285-6000	Fax:
Toll-Free: 800-638-0985	
Address: 7031 Columbia Gateway Dr., Columbia, MD 21046 US	

GROWTH PLANS/SPECIAL FEATURES:

MICROS Systems, Inc., is a worldwide enterprise applications provider to the specialty retail and hospitality industries. The firm designs, manufactures, markets and services information technology, specializing in point-of-sale systems. MICROS Systems provides complete IT management services and systems that include software, hardware, enterprise systems integration, consulting and support services. The company operates in two business segments: U.S. and international. Through its global markets subsidiary, MICROS-Fidelio International, the firm provides enterprise-wide information technologies for the hospitality and gaming industries on an international basis. MICROS offers services in three major areas: hotel information systems, restaurant information systems and retail information systems. The hotel information systems consist of software encompassing property based management systems, related property specific modules and applications and central reservation systems. The restaurant information systems consist of hardware and software for point-of-sale and operational applications; a suite of back-office applications, including inventory, labor and financial management; and certain centrally hosted enterprise applications. Retail systems consist of software for loss prevention, business analytics and enterprise applications. This segment is comprised entirely of subsidiary MICROS-Retail. The company also markets restaurant point-of-sale systems via its Hospitality Solutions International division. Additionally, MICROS offers an Internet-based reservation service through web-based subsidiary myfidelio.net. Moreover, the company markets paging and alert systems for its restaurant, retail and medical customers through JTECH Communications, Inc. MICROS has more than 330,000 installations around the world, including hotel chains such as Marriott and Hilton; table-service restaurant chains such as T.G.I. Friday's, Ruby Tuesday's and Hard Rock Cafe; and quick-service chains including Burger King, Subway, Krispy Kreme, Ben & Jerry's and Starbucks. MICROS subsidiaries include Fry, Inc., Fidelio Cruise, MyFidelio.net, Hospitality Solutions International, JTECH Communications, RedSky IT and POS Depot.

FINANCIALS: Sales and profits are in thousands of dollars—add 000 to get the full amount. 2010 Note: Financial information for 2010 was not available for all companies at press time.

2010 Sales: $914,319	2010 Profits: $114,353	U.S. Stock Ticker: MCRS
2009 Sales: $907,725	2009 Profits: $96,292	Int'l Ticker: Int'l Exchange:
2008 Sales: $953,950	2008 Profits: $100,737	Employees: 4,646
2007 Sales: $785,727	2007 Profits: $79,988	Fiscal Year Ends: 6/30
2006 Sales: $678,953	2006 Profits: $63,528	Parent Company:

SALARIES/BENEFITS:

Pension Plan:	ESOP Stock Plan:	Profit Sharing:	Top Exec. Salary: $2,000,000	Bonus: $4,166,944
Savings Plan: Y	Stock Purch. Plan:		Second Exec. Salary: $715,000	Bonus: $1,489,702

OTHER THOUGHTS:

Apparent Women Officers or Directors: 4
Hot Spot for Advancement for Women/Minorities: Y

LOCATIONS: ("Y" = Yes)

West:	Southwest:	Midwest:	Southeast:	Northeast:	International:
Y	Y	Y	Y	Y	Y

Note: Financial information, benefits and other data can change quickly and may vary from those stated here.

MICROSOFT CORP

www.microsoft.com

Industry Group Code: 511210I Ranks within this company's industry group: Sales: 1 Profits: 1

Hardware:		Software:		Telecommunications:		Electronic Publishing:	Equipment:		Specialty Services:	
Computers:		Consumer:	Y	Local:		Online Service:	Telecom:		Consulting:	
Accessories:	Y	Corporate:	Y	Long Distance:		TV/Cable or Wireless:	Communication:		Contract Manufacturing:	
Network Equipment:		Telecom:		Cellular:	Y	Games:	Distribution:		Processing:	
Chips/Circuits:		Internet:	Y	Internet Service:		Financial Data:	VAR/Reseller:		Staff/Outsourcing:	
Parts/Drives:							Satellite Srv./Equip.:		Specialty Services:	

TYPES OF BUSINESS:

Computer Software
Personal Communications Services
Video Games Systems
Mobile Communications
Voice-Enabled Mobile Search
Internet Search Engine
E-Mail Services
Instant Messaging

BRANDS/DIVISIONS/AFFILIATES:

Aquantive Inc
Tellme Networks
Microsoft Dynamics
Fast Search & Transfer ASA
Xbox
MSN Video
BigPark Inc.
Rosetta Biosoftware

CONTACTS: Note: Officers with more than one job title may be intentionally listed here more than once.

Steve Ballmer, CEO
B. Kevin Turner, COO
Peter Klein, CFO
Mich Mathews, Sr. VP-Central Mktg. Group
Lisa Brummel, Sr. VP-Human Resources
Rick Rashid, Sr. VP-Research
J. Allard, CTO
Brad Smith, General Counsel/Sr. VP-Legal/Sec.
Craig Mundie, Chief Research & Strategy Officer
Qi Lu, Pres., Online Svcs.
Brad Smith, Sr. VP-Corp. Affairs
Steven Sinofsky, Pres., Windows Div.
Bob Muglia, Pres., Server & Tools Bus.
Hank Vigil, Sr. VP-Consumer Strategy & Partnerships
Bill Gates, Chmn.
Jean-Philippe Courtois, Pres., Microsoft Int'l

Phone: 425-882-8080	Fax:
Toll-Free:	
Address: 1 Microsoft Way, Redmond, WA 98052-7329 US	

GROWTH PLANS/SPECIAL FEATURES:

Microsoft Corp. develops, manufactures and supports software for a wide range of computing devices. Microsoft operates in five segments: client; server and tools; online services business; Microsoft business division; and entertainment and devices division. The client segment provides premium and standard-edition Windows operating systems and manages the company's relationships with personal computer manufacturers. The company's latest operating system, introduced in 2009, is Windows 7. Other products that this segment includes are Windows Vista, Windows XP and Tablet PC Edition. The server and tools segment licenses products, applications, tools, content and services related to Windows server products and operating systems. The division offers Windows Server operating system, Microsoft SQL Server, Visual Studio and System Center products, among others. The online services business segment consists of an online advertising platform and provides personal services including Bing; Microsoft Media Network; MSN portals, channels and mobile services; and MSN Premium Web Services. The business division offers the Microsoft Office system and Microsoft Dynamics business solutions. The entertainment and devices division is responsible for developing, producing and marketing Xbox and Xbox 360 video game systems, including consoles and accessories; the Zune digital music and entertainment platform; PC software games; the Mediaroom Internet television software; the Surface computing system; and online games and services. In August 2009, the company announced plans to sell its interactive ad agency, Razorfish, Inc., to Paris-based Publicis Groupe for approximately $530 million. In May 2010, Microsoft introduced the Microsoft Dynamics ERP two-tier connector, a device that enables IT organizations to use Microsoft Dynamics AX throughout branch entities and subsidiaries to integrate SAP installations.

Microsoft offers its employees health, dental and vision coverage; health club memberships; autism therapy benefits; adoption assistance; a 401(k) plan; a stock purchase plan; charity gift matching; and tuition assistance.

FINANCIALS: Sales and profits are in thousands of dollars—add 000 to get the full amount. 2010 Note: Financial information for 2010 was not available for all companies at press time.

2010 Sales: $62,484,000	2010 Profits: $24,098,000	U.S. Stock Ticker: MSFT
2009 Sales: $58,437,000	2009 Profits: $14,569,000	Int'l Ticker: Int'l Exchange:
2008 Sales: $60,420,000	2008 Profits: $17,681,000	Employees: 89,000
2007 Sales: $51,122,000	2007 Profits: $14,065,000	Fiscal Year Ends: 6/30
2006 Sales: $44,282,000	2006 Profits: $12,599,000	Parent Company:

SALARIES/BENEFITS:

Pension Plan:	ESOP Stock Plan:	Profit Sharing:	Top Exec. Salary: $665,833	Bonus: $600,000
Savings Plan: Y	Stock Purch. Plan: Y		Second Exec. Salary: $641,667	Bonus: $2,840,008

OTHER THOUGHTS:

Apparent Women Officers or Directors: 4
Hot Spot for Advancement for Women/Minorities: Y

LOCATIONS: ("Y" = Yes)

West:	Southwest:	Midwest:	Southeast:	Northeast:	International:
Y	Y	Y	Y	Y	Y

MICROS-RETAIL

www.micros-retail.com

Industry Group Code: 511210K Ranks within this company's industry group: Sales: Profits:

Hardware:	Software:		Telecommunications:	Electronic Publishing:	Equipment:	Specialty Services:
Computers:	Consumer:		Local:	Online Service:	Telecom:	Consulting:
Accessories:	Corporate:	Y	Long Distance:	TV/Cable or Wireless:	Communication:	Contract Manufacturing:
Network Equipment:	Telecom:		Cellular:	Games:	Distribution:	Processing:
Chips/Circuits:	Internet:		Internet Service:	Financial Data:	VAR/Reseller:	Staff/Outsourcing:
Parts/Drives:					Satellite Srv./Equip.:	Specialty Services:

TYPES OF BUSINESS:

Software-Retail & E-Commerce
Supply Chain Software

BRANDS/DIVISIONS/AFFILIATES:

MICROS Systems Inc
Xstore Java POS
CommercialWare Inc
Store21
CWData & Analytics
XBR
CWSerenade
JTECH

CONTACTS: Note: Officers with more than one job title may be intentionally listed here more than once.

Chaz Napoli, COO
John E. Gularson, Pres.
Laura Martin, CFO
Michael Biliouris, Exec. VP-Sales & Mktg.
Shelley M. Sappet, Dir.-Human Resources
Jane Cannon, CTO
Jetemy Grunzweig, VP-Oper., Store Systems Group
Faruk Abdullah, VP-Strategy
Rudy Pataro, Exec. VP-eCommerce
Louise J. Casamento, VP-Customer Rel.
Carl Nemec, VP-Professional Svcs. Int'l
Louise J. Casament, VP-Mktg.
Drew Fyfe, VP-Asia Pacific
Jeremy Grunzweig, Exec. VP-Store Systems
Manfred Kaiser, VP-EMEA

Phone: 440-498-4414	Fax: 440-498-4430
Toll-Free:	
Address: 30500 Bruce Industrial Pkwy., Cleveland, OH 44139 US	

GROWTH PLANS/SPECIAL FEATURES:

MICROS-Retail, a subsidiary of MICROS Systems, Inc., designs software solutions for cross-channel retailers. The company was created through the combination of Datavantage; Fry, Inc.; CommercialWare; and the eOne Group. MICROS-Retail's products include point-of-sale (POS); loyalty and customer relationship management (CRM); eCommerce; order management; loss prevention; analytics software; merchandise and supplier management; and mobility applications. POS products include Xstore Java POS; Store21, enabling stores to communicate with a centralized database and sales associates to verify pricing, locate merchandise and validate returns, all in real-time; Tradewind, with capabilities including pricing, inventory management, store administration, labor management, shipping/receiving, customer portfolio and reporting; CWStore, a modular POS and back office solution, with real-time inventory management capabilities; and ARS POS, addressing the POS and back office needs of retailers and convenience stores in the Latin American market. MICROS-Retail's loyalty and customer relationship management (CRM) products include Relate Retail, which unifies marketing and planning management, and CW ValueCard, a card program capable of handling purchases, activations, reductions, refunds and merchandise store credits while making card balances, available amounts and historical activity accessible in real time. eCommerce is a business-to-business and business-to-consumer functionality; catalog browsing; ordering; customer service; promotions; feature product; check inventory; re-print invoices; browse order history; re-order from history; place new orders; update shipping and billing addresses; and get price and inventory information. XBR is the company's loss prevention product, which identifies trends associated with key performance indicators and automatically sends alerts. Additional products include CWSerenade, CWDirect, CWCollaborate and Locate for order management; Balance Sales Audit and CWData & Analytics for analytics; Enterprise Merchandising and CWCollaborate for merchandise and supplier management; and JTECH and Handheld POS for mobility.

FINANCIALS: Sales and profits are in thousands of dollars—add 000 to get the full amount. 2010 Note: Financial information for 2010 was not available for all companies at press time.

2010 Sales: $	2010 Profits: $	**U.S. Stock Ticker: Subsidiary**
2009 Sales: $	2009 Profits: $	**Int'l Ticker:** Int'l Exchange:
2008 Sales: $	2008 Profits: $	Employees:
2007 Sales: $7,600	2007 Profits: $	Fiscal Year Ends: 12/31
2006 Sales: $	2006 Profits: $	Parent Company: MICROS SYSTEMS INC

SALARIES/BENEFITS:

Pension Plan:	ESOP Stock Plan:	Profit Sharing:	Top Exec. Salary: $	Bonus: $
Savings Plan: Y	Stock Purch. Plan:		Second Exec. Salary: $	Bonus: $

OTHER THOUGHTS:

Apparent Women Officers or Directors: 3
Hot Spot for Advancement for Women/Minorities: Y

LOCATIONS: ("Y" = Yes)

West:	Southwest:	Midwest:	Southeast:	Northeast:	International:
		Y		Y	Y

MICRO-STAR INTERNATIONAL

www.msi.com

Industry Group Code: 334119 Ranks within this company's industry group: Sales: 10 Profits: 14

Hardware:		Software:		Telecommunications:		Electronic Publishing:		Equipment:		Specialty Services:	
Computers:	Y	Consumer:		Local:		Online Service:		Telecom:		Consulting:	
Accessories:	Y	Corporate:		Long Distance:		TV/Cable or Wireless:		Communication:	Y	Contract Manufacturing:	
Network Equipment:	Y	Telecom:		Cellular:		Games:		Distribution:		Processing:	
Chips/Circuits:	Y	Internet:		Internet Service:		Financial Data:		VAR/Reseller:		Staff/Outsourcing:	
Parts/Drives:	Y							Satellite Srv./Equip.:		Specialty Services:	

TYPES OF BUSINESS:

Computer Components
Motherboards
Graphics Cards
Optical Storage Drives
Server Systems
Barebones PCs
Communication Products

BRANDS/DIVISIONS/AFFILIATES:

GreenPower Center
MyECG E3-80

CONTACTS: Note: Officers with more than one job title may be intentionally listed here more than once.

Xiang Xu, Pres.
Baoyu Hong, Dir.-Finance
Jinqing Huang, Sr. VP-R&D
Qilong Lu, Chief Acct. Officer
Xianneng You, Sr. VP
Qilong Lu, Sr. VP-Bus.
Xiang Xu, Chmn.
Wentong Lin, Sr. VP-Purchasing

Phone: 886-2-3234-5599	Fax: 886-2-3234-5488
Toll-Free:	
Address: Li-De St. No. 69, Jung-He Dist., Taipei, Taiwan	

GROWTH PLANS/SPECIAL FEATURES:

Micro-Star International (MSI) is a leading manufacturer of electronic components and equipment. MSI specializes in cutting-edge performance-driven devices, especially in the manufacturing of motherboards and graphics cards. One of the top manufacturers of motherboards in the world, the company was among the first to make boards supporting 64-bit processors, as well as its new, industry-leading options such as server-class DrMOS, APS (Active Phase Switching) technology and Green Power Center power-saving technology. Some of its other products include notebook computers; consumer electronics, such as MP3 players, hard disks and USB storage devices; servers and workstations; industrial computers; medical products, such as MyECG E3-80, a 24-hour ECG recorder and analyzer; and multimedia equipment, such as TV tuners, webcams, mice and keyboards, card readers and accessories. It also manufactures vehicle entertainment and information equipment for movies, photos, music, games and USB playback; barebones systems, mainly computers without input or output devices such as monitors or keyboards; and communication products such as wireless LAN, Bluetooth and Ethernet cards. Its products are sold by regional partners worldwide through a network of distributors, retailers and web sites. It has subsidiaries in Taiwan, China, Japan, Korea, India, the U.S., Canada, Brazil, Germany, France, Italy, Australia, the Netherlands, Turkey, the U.K., Russia, Ukraine, Poland, the Czech Republic, Serbia and Saudi Arabia. MSI has offices in Europe, Asia, Australia, North America and South America.

FINANCIALS: Sales and profits are in thousands of dollars—add 000 to get the full amount. 2010 Note: Financial information for 2010 was not available for all companies at press time.

2010 Sales: $	2010 Profits: $	U.S. Stock Ticker:
2009 Sales: $2,830,720	2009 Profits: $8,310	Int'l Ticker: 2377　Int'l Exchange: Taipei-TPE
2008 Sales: $3,196,700	2008 Profits: $71,200	Employees: 17,000
2007 Sales: $3,018,330	2007 Profits: $91,370	Fiscal Year Ends: 12/31
2006 Sales: $	2006 Profits: $	Parent Company:

SALARIES/BENEFITS:

Pension Plan:	ESOP Stock Plan:	Profit Sharing:	Top Exec. Salary: $	Bonus: $
Savings Plan:	Stock Purch. Plan:		Second Exec. Salary: $	Bonus: $

OTHER THOUGHTS:

Apparent Women Officers or Directors:
Hot Spot for Advancement for Women/Minorities:

LOCATIONS: ("Y" = Yes)

West:	Southwest:	Midwest:	Southeast:	Northeast:	International:
Y					Y

Note: Financial information, benefits and other data can change quickly and may vary from those stated here.

MICROSTRATEGY INC

www.microstrategy.com

Industry Group Code: 511210K Ranks within this company's industry group: Sales: 5 Profits: 2

Hardware:	Software:		Telecommunications:	Electronic Publishing:	Equipment:	Specialty Services:	
Computers:	Consumer:		Local:	Online Service:	Telecom:	Consulting:	Y
Accessories:	Corporate:	Y	Long Distance:	TV/Cable or Wireless:	Communication:	Contract Manufacturing:	
Network Equipment:	Telecom:		Cellular:	Games:	Distribution:	Processing:	
Chips/Circuits:	Internet:		Internet Service:	Financial Data:	VAR/Reseller:	Staff/Outsourcing:	
Parts/Drives:					Satellite Srv./Equip.:	Specialty Services:	

TYPES OF BUSINESS:

Software-Data Analysis
Business Intelligence & Marketing Software
Customer Relationship Management Software
Consulting Services

BRANDS/DIVISIONS/AFFILIATES:

MicroStrategy 9
MicroStrategy Technical Support
MicroStrategy Consulting
MicroStrategy Education
Angel.com

CONTACTS: Note: Officers with more than one job title may be intentionally listed here more than once.

Michael J. Saylor, CEO
Sanju K. Bansal, COO/Exec. VP
Michael J. Saylor, Pres.
Douglas K. Thede, CFO
Paul Zolfaghari, VP-Worldwide Sales
Vincent M. Gabriele, Exec. VP-Human Resources
Peng Xiao, CIO/Exec. VP
Jeffrey A. Bedell, CTO/Exec. VP-Tech.
Jonathan F. Klein, General Counsel/Exec. VP-Law
Paul Zolfaghari, Exec. VP-Oper.
Eduardo S. Sanchez, Exec. VP-Strategic Dev.
Douglas K. Thede, Exec. VP-Finance
Sanju K. Bansal, Vice Chmn.
Michael J. Saylor, Chmn.
Bob Watts, Exec. VP-Worldwide Professional Svcs.

Phone: 703-848-8600	Fax: 703-848-8610
Toll-Free: 866-966-6787	
Address: 1850 Towers Crescent Plaza, Vienna, VA 22182 US	

GROWTH PLANS/SPECIAL FEATURES:

MicroStrategy, Inc. provides business intelligence software that analyzes raw enterprise data to spot trends, providing companies with opportunities to make informed business decisions. The firm's primary product, MicroStrategy 9 is an integrated, enterprise-class business intelligence software platform that enables organizations to consolidate business intelligence applications for reporting, analysis and report delivery applications. The platform allows companies to comb through databases, deliver customized information and develop numerous applications. The platform includes cashing technology, In-memory ROLAP, which provides a performance-optimized middle-tier database that can respond directly to data requests from reports, dashboards and OLAP analyses. MicroStrategy's interactive software delivers information to workgroups, enterprise and extranet communities via e-mail, web, fax, wireless and voice communication channels. MicroStrategy Technical Support provides a set of support options through a support team, an online support site and options to secure dedicated technical support. MicroStrategy Consulting offers a range of business intelligence and data warehousing expertise gathered from helping thousands of customers across diverse industries implement departmental, enterprise and extranet applications across various types of databases. The company's consulting staff identifies the optimal design and implementation strategy that includes detailed business requirements, user interface requirements and performance tuning. MicroStrategy Education offers goal-oriented, comprehensive education services for customers and partners, including self-tutorials, custom course development, joint training with customers' internal staff and standard course offerings. The company also offers technical advisory services, which provides subject matter expertise, project management, strategic consulting and expedited resources to enhance the success of customer deployments. MicroStrategy's non-core business, Angel.com, provides interactive voice response telephony systems.

FINANCIALS: Sales and profits are in thousands of dollars—add 000 to get the full amount. 2010 Note: Financial information for 2010 was not available for all companies at press time.

2010 Sales: $	2010 Profits: $	U.S. Stock Ticker: MSTR
2009 Sales: $377,788	2009 Profits: $74,837	Int'l Ticker: Int'l Exchange:
2008 Sales: $360,393	2008 Profits: $41,833	Employees:
2007 Sales: $335,373	2007 Profits: $58,468	Fiscal Year Ends: 12/31
2006 Sales: $313,823	2006 Profits: $70,876	Parent Company:

SALARIES/BENEFITS:

Pension Plan:	ESOP Stock Plan:	Profit Sharing:	Top Exec. Salary: $875,000	Bonus: $3,354,000
Savings Plan:	Stock Purch. Plan:		Second Exec. Salary: $400,000	Bonus: $542,233

OTHER THOUGHTS:

Apparent Women Officers or Directors:
Hot Spot for Advancement for Women/Minorities:

LOCATIONS: ("Y" = Yes)

West:	Southwest:	Midwest:	Southeast:	Northeast:	International:
Y	Y	Y	Y	Y	Y

MINDSPEED TECHNOLOGIES INC
www.mindspeed.com

Industry Group Code: 33441 Ranks within this company's industry group: Sales: 52 Profits: 38

Hardware:		Software:		Telecommunications:		Electronic Publishing:		Equipment:		Specialty Services:	
Computers:		Consumer:		Local:		Online Service:		Telecom:	Y	Consulting:	
Accessories:		Corporate:	Y	Long Distance:		TV/Cable or Wireless:		Communication:	Y	Contract Manufacturing:	
Network Equipment:	Y	Telecom:	Y	Cellular:		Games:		Distribution:		Processing:	
Chips/Circuits:	Y	Internet:		Internet Service:		Financial Data:		VAR/Reseller:		Staff/Outsourcing:	
Parts/Drives:								Satellite Srv./Equip.:		Specialty Services:	

TYPES OF BUSINESS:
Semiconductors-Communications
Networking Products
Software
Routers & Switches
VoIP Equipment

BRANDS/DIVISIONS/AFFILIATES:
Comcerto
Conexant Systems Inc

CONTACTS: Note: Officers with more than one job title may be intentionally listed here more than once.
Raouf Y. Halim, CEO
Bret W. Johnsen, CFO/Sr. VP
Gerald J. Hamilton, Sr. VP-Worldwide Sales
Allison K. Garcia, Sr. VP-Human Resources
Anil S. Mankar, Sr. VP-Eng.
Jing Cao, Sr. VP-Oper.
Andrea Williams, VP-Corp. Comm.
Bret W. Johnsen, Treas.
Kurt F. Busch, Sr. VP/Gen Mgr.-High Performance Analog
Thomas J. Medrek, Sr. VP/Gen. Mgr.-Comm. Convergence Processing
Hasnain Bajwa, Sr. VP/Gen. Mgr.-Lightspeed Connectivity Solutions
Dwight W. Decker, Chmn.

Phone: 949-579-3000	Fax: 949-579-3020
Toll-Free:	
Address: 4000 MacArthur Blvd., E. Tower, Newport Beach, CA 92660 US	

GROWTH PLANS/SPECIAL FEATURES:
Mindspeed Technologies, Inc., a spin-off of Conexant Systems, Inc., designs, develops and sells semiconductor networking products for communications applications in enterprise, access, metropolitan and wide area networks. The firm offers three product families: Communications Convergence Processing, High-Performance Analog and wide area networking (WAN) Communications. Communications Convergence Processing products include low-power multi-core digital signal processor (DSP) system-on-a-chip (SoC) products for carrier-class triple-play edge gateways, metro trunking gateways and other VoIP platforms. The Comcerto family of packet processors includes a full range of software-compatible solutions that enable OEMS to provide scalable systems with customized features for carrier, enterprise and customer premise applications. High-Performance Analog Products include transmission devices and switching products. Transmission products include laser drivers, transimpedance amplifiers, post amplifiers, clock and data recovery circuits and line equalizers. Switching products include a family of high-speed crosspoint switches capable of switching traffic beyond 8 gigabits per second (Gpbs) within various types of network switching equipment, as well as crosspoint switches optimized for standard and high-definition broadcast video routing and production switching applications. WAN Communications products also include T1/E1, T3/E3 and SONET carrier devices; high-performance ATM/MPLS network processors, which are designed to offer advanced protocol translation and traffic management capabilities; and Ethernet products such as Ethernet media access controllers and oversubscription aggregators. The company sells its products to original equipment manufacturers (OEMs) for use in a variety of network infrastructure equipment designed to process, transmit and switch voice, data and video traffic between and within the different segments of the communications network. Its network infrastructure equipment includes voice and media gateways, high-speed routers, switches, access multiplexers, cross-connect systems and add-drop multiplexers, digital loop carrier equipment and Internet protocol private branch exchanges.

Employees are offered health and life insurance; disability coverage; flexible spending accounts; a 401(k) plan; an employee stock purchase plan; adoption assistance; educational assistance; and an employee assistance program.

FINANCIALS: Sales and profits are in thousands of dollars—add 000 to get the full amount. 2010 Note: Financial information for 2010 was not available for all companies at press time.
2010 Sales: $178,179	2010 Profits: $21,070	**U.S. Stock Ticker: MSPD**
2009 Sales: $126,552	2009 Profits: $-25,114	**Int'l Ticker:** Int'l Exchange:
2008 Sales: $160,699	2008 Profits: $4,285	Employees: 519
2007 Sales: $127,805	2007 Profits: $-21,914	Fiscal Year Ends: 9/30
2006 Sales: $135,919	2006 Profits: $-24,514	Parent Company:

SALARIES/BENEFITS:
Pension Plan:	ESOP Stock Plan:	Profit Sharing:	Top Exec. Salary: $500,000	Bonus: $600,000
Savings Plan: Y	Stock Purch. Plan: Y		Second Exec. Salary: $308,077	Bonus: $

OTHER THOUGHTS:
Apparent Women Officers or Directors: 1
Hot Spot for Advancement for Women/Minorities:

LOCATIONS: ("Y" = Yes)
West:	Southwest:	Midwest:	Southeast:	Northeast:	International:
Y				Y	Y

MISYS PLC

www.misys.com

Industry Group Code: 511201 **Ranks within this company's industry group:** Sales: 3 Profits: 5

Hardware:		Software:		Telecommunications:		Electronic Publishing:		Equipment:		Specialty Services:	
Computers:		Consumer:	Y	Local:		Online Service:		Telecom:		Consulting:	Y
Accessories:	Y	Corporate:	Y	Long Distance:		TV/Cable or Wireless:		Communication:		Contract Manufacturing:	
Network Equipment:		Telecom:		Cellular:		Games:		Distribution:		Processing:	
Chips/Circuits:		Internet:		Internet Service:		Financial Data:		VAR/Reseller:		Staff/Outsourcing:	
Parts/Drives:								Satellite Srv./Equip.:		Specialty Services:	

TYPES OF BUSINESS:
Banking Software
Healthcare Software
Financial Advisory Software
Business Consulting

BRANDS/DIVISIONS/AFFILIATES:
Allscripts Healthcare Solutions Inc
Allscripts-Misys Healthcare Solutions Inc
Missys Tiger
Message Manager
Missys BankFusion Universal Banking
Missys Loan IQ
Misys International Banking Systems
Misys Open Source Solutions LLC

CONTACTS: Note: Officers with more than one job title may be intentionally listed here more than once.
Mike Lawrie, CEO
Stephen Wilson, CFO/Exec. VP
Harry Keegan, VP-Sales
Doreen Tyburski, Dir.-Human Resources
Ellen M. Clarke, CIO/Exec. VP
Robin Crewe, CTO
Tom Kilroy, General Counsel/Exec. VP/Sec.
Harry Keegan, VP-Field Oper.
Edward Taylor, Head-Public Rel.
Glen E. Tullman, Exec. VP/CEO-Allscripts-Misys Healthcare
Ed Ho, Exec. VP/Gen. Mgr.-Treasury & Capital Markets
Al-Noor Ramji, Exec. VP/Gen. Mgr.-Banking
Bob Barthelmes, Exec. VP/Gen. Mgr.-Open Source Solutions
James Crosby, Chmn.

Phone: 44-020-3320-5000	Fax: 44-020-3320-1771
Toll-Free:	
Address: 1 Kingdom St., London, W2 6BL UK	

GROWTH PLANS/SPECIAL FEATURES:
Misys plc is one of the largest developers of industry-specific software products in the world, with customers in the international banking and healthcare industries in more than 120 countries. The firm has over 1,200 banking customers. Misys International Banking Systems sells products such as Misys BankFusion Universal Banking, a packaged retail banking application for financial institutions of all sizes; Eagleye, for monitoring adherence to mandates, regulations, policies or any restriction; Loan IQ, accounting for half of all global traded loan volumes; Message Manager, an application for generating, routing and managing all financial messages; Summit, a multi-asset application for treasury and capital market participants; and Trade Portal software for e-business, trade processing and white labeling. Misys International Banking Systems operates in the U.K., the U.S., Australia, Luxembourg, Belgium, France, Canada, U.A.E., Germany, Hong Kong, Ireland, Japan, South Africa, Russia, Switzerland and Thailand. Misys' Global Services division offers business consulting services focusing on issues such as risk management and cost reduction through more than 500 consultants in over 30 countries. Subsidiary Misys Open Source Solutions, LLC offers consulting services focused on the management of carbon emissions. The subsidiary is also involved in the creation of an open source health care platform. In January 2010, the firm introduced Misys Personal Finance Portal, an Internet banking application designed for retail banking customers. In August 2010, the company merged its majority-owned subsidiary Allscripts-Misys Healthcare Solutions, Inc. with Eclipsys. Misys owns roughly 13% of the new company, Allscripts, which serves 180,000 physicians, 1,500 hospitals and 10,000 post-acute and homecare locations in 24 states, India, the Middle East, Canada and Asia. In November 2010, the firm agreed to acquire Sophis, a capital markets software vendor, for roughly $563.4 million.

FINANCIALS: Sales and profits are in thousands of dollars—add 000 to get the full amount. 2010 Note: Financial information for 2010 was not available for all companies at press time.

2010 Sales: $	2010 Profits: $	U.S. Stock Ticker:
2009 Sales: $1,109,220	2009 Profits: $13,140	Int'l Ticker: MSY Int'l Exchange: London-LSE
2008 Sales: $788,670	2008 Profits: $181,510	Employees: 5,411
2007 Sales: $752,460	2007 Profits: $24,030	Fiscal Year Ends: 5/31
2006 Sales: $1,154,900	2006 Profits: $421,900	Parent Company:

SALARIES/BENEFITS:

Pension Plan:	ESOP Stock Plan:	Profit Sharing:	Top Exec. Salary: $	Bonus: $
Savings Plan:	Stock Purch. Plan:		Second Exec. Salary: $	Bonus: $

OTHER THOUGHTS:
Apparent Women Officers or Directors: 2
Hot Spot for Advancement for Women/Minorities: Y

LOCATIONS: ("Y" = Yes)

West:	Southwest:	Midwest:	Southeast:	Northeast:	International:
				Y	Y

Note: Financial information, benefits and other data can change quickly and may vary from those stated here.

MITAC INTERNATIONAL CORP

www.mitac.com

Industry Group Code: 334111 Ranks within this company's industry group: Sales: 17 Profits: 12

Hardware:		Software:	Telecommunications:	Electronic Publishing:	Equipment:	Specialty Services:	
Computers:	Y	Consumer:	Local:	Online Service:	Telecom:	Consulting:	
Accessories:	Y	Corporate:	Long Distance:	TV/Cable or Wireless:	Communication:	Contract Manufacturing:	Y
Network Equipment:	Y	Telecom:	Cellular:	Games:	Distribution:	Processing:	
Chips/Circuits:		Internet:	Internet Service:	Financial Data:	VAR/Reseller:	Staff/Outsourcing:	
Parts/Drives:	Y				Satellite Srv./Equip.:	Specialty Services:	Y

TYPES OF BUSINESS:

Computer Manufacturing
Server Products
Mobile Communications Products
Storage Products

BRANDS/DIVISIONS/AFFILIATES:

MiTAC-SYNNEX Group
SYNNEX
Navman
Mio
Tyan
Magellan

CONTACTS: Note: Officers with more than one job title may be intentionally listed here more than once.

Billy Ho, Co-Pres.
C.J. Lin, Co-Pres.
Matthew Miau, Chmn.

Phone: 886-3-328-9000	Fax: 886-3-328-0926
Toll-Free:	
Address: No. 200 Wen Hwa 2nd Rd., Kuei Shan Hsiang, Taiwan	

GROWTH PLANS/SPECIAL FEATURES:

MiTAC International Corp., a member of the MiTAC-SYNNEX Group, is a Taiwanese computer hardware manufacturing company specializing in PCs, digital home products, liquid crystal displays, servers, workstations, GPS devices and smart phones. Its brands include Mio, Magellan and Navman, which focus on satellite navigation, as well as server/workstation platform producer, Tyan. The firm has production facilities in Taiwan that are responsible for introducing new products and manufacturing high-end items, and two factories in China that produce all the company's other assembly-line components. In addition, MiTAC has overseas assembly centers in the U.S., the U.K. Germany, Belgium and Japan as well as other oversea operations in those countries. The company operates research and development teams and an extensive customer service, warranty and repair division. In the U.S., MiTAC distributes its products exclusively through SYNNEX, a majority-owned subsidiary. Through SYNNEX, U.S. commercial or residential customers can order MiTAC components, barebone systems and complete, assembled systems.

FINANCIALS: Sales and profits are in thousands of dollars—add 000 to get the full amount. 2010 Note: Financial information for 2010 was not available for all companies at press time.

2010 Sales: $	2010 Profits: $	U.S. Stock Ticker:
2009 Sales: $1,974,730	2009 Profits: $18,700	Int'l Ticker: 2315 Int'l Exchange: Taipei-TPE
2008 Sales: $1,974,790	2008 Profits: $14,010	Employees:
2007 Sales: $2,743,134	2007 Profits: $177,810	Fiscal Year Ends: 12/31
2006 Sales: $2,785,880	2006 Profits: $173,140	Parent Company:

SALARIES/BENEFITS:

Pension Plan:	ESOP Stock Plan:	Profit Sharing:	Top Exec. Salary: $	Bonus: $
Savings Plan:	Stock Purch. Plan:		Second Exec. Salary: $	Bonus: $

OTHER THOUGHTS:

Apparent Women Officers or Directors:
Hot Spot for Advancement for Women/Minorities:

LOCATIONS: ("Y" = Yes)

West:	Southwest:	Midwest:	Southeast:	Northeast:	International:
Y	Y				Y

MITSUBISHI ELECTRIC CORPORATION

global.mitsubishielectric.com

Industry Group Code: 335 Ranks within this company's industry group: Sales: 2 Profits: 3

Hardware:	Software:	Telecommunications:	Electronic Publishing:	Equipment:	Specialty Services:
Computers:	Consumer:	Local:	Online Service:	Telecom:	Consulting:
Accessories:	Corporate:	Long Distance:	TV/Cable or Wireless:	Communication:	Contract Manufacturing:
Network Equipment:	Telecom:	Cellular:	Games:	Distribution:	Processing:
Chips/Circuits: Y	Internet:	Internet Service:	Financial Data:	VAR/Reseller:	Staff/Outsourcing:
Parts/Drives: Y				Satellite Srv./Equip.:	Specialty Services:

TYPES OF BUSINESS:

Electronic Equipment Manufacturer
Power Plant Manufacturing, Nuclear & Fossil
Wind & Solar Generation Systems
Consumer Electronics
Telecommunications & Computer Equipment
Industrial Automation Systems
Chips & Memory Devices
Semiconductors

BRANDS/DIVISIONS/AFFILIATES:

Mitsubishi Corp
Vincotech Holdings S.a r.l.

CONTACTS: Note: Officers with more than one job title may be intentionally listed here more than once.

Kenichiro Yamanishi, CEO
Takashi Sasakawa, Exec. Officer-Oper.
Kenichiro Yamanishi, Pres.
Hiroki Yoshimatsu, Exec. Officer-Acct. & Finance
Takashi Sasakawa, Exec. Officer-Global Strategic Mktg.
Noritomo Hashimoto, Exec. Officer-Human Resources
Kazuhiko Tsutsumi, Exec. Officer-R&D
Kenji Kuroda, Exec. Officer-Info. Systems & Network Service
Tsuyoshi Nakamura, Exec. Officer-Legal Affairs & Auditing
Masaki Sakuyama, Sr. VP-Strategy
Noritomo Hashimoto, Exec. Officer-Public Rel. & General Affairs
Kunio Oguchi, Exec. Officer-Advertising & Domestic Mktg.
Noboru Kurihara, Sr. Exec. Officer-Electronic Systems
Mitsuo Muneyuki, Exec. VP-Building Systems
Kenichiro Yamanishi, Sr. Exec. Officer-Semiconductor & Device
Setsuhiro Shimomura, Chmn.
Shoichi Sakata, Exec. Officer-Purchasing

Phone: 81-3-3218-2111 **Fax:** 81-3-3218-2185
Toll-Free:
Address: Tokyo Bldg. 2-7-3 Marunouchi, Chiyoda-ku, Tokyo, 100-8310 Japan

GROWTH PLANS/SPECIAL FEATURES:

Mitsubishi Electric Corporation, part of the Mitsubishi group of companies, is a global manufacturer, distributor and marketer of electrical and electronic equipment. This equipment is used in information processing and communications; space development and satellite communications; consumer electronics; industrial technology; energy; transportation; and building equipment. The company has five primary business segments: energy and electric systems; home appliances; information and communication systems; industrial automation systems; and electronic devices. The energy and electric systems segment manufactures nuclear and fossil fuel power generation plants and monitoring systems, as well as wind turbines, solar panels and other electricity generators; turbine generators and hydraulic turbine generators; proton beam radiation treatment systems; elevators; security systems; railway systems; and large scale display systems. This segment accounts for 27.3% of the firm's revenues. The home appliances segment (21.6% of revenues) manufactures home electronics such as air conditioners, flat-screen televisions, DVD players, computers and computer monitors. The industrial automation systems segment (19.2% of revenues) includes the manufacturing of programmable logic controllers, circuit breakers and robotics that are created and customized for multiple industrial uses. The information and communication systems segment (13.8% of revenues) includes mobile phones, satellites, aerospace communication systems, digital closed circuit television systems, enterprise information technology networks and Internet servers. The electronic devices segment (3.6% of revenues) makes power modules, high-frequency devices, optical devices, LCD devices and microcomputers. Other business activities (14.5% of revenues) include procurement, logistics, real estate, advertising and finance. Mitsubishi is among the largest solar power technology manufacturers in the world, and has invested approximately $113 million to construct a new solar cell factory in Nagano Prefecture, with the stated goal of tripling its overall photovoltaic cell production capacity by 2011. In November 2010, the company and The Gores Group agreed to acquire German electronic components manufacturer Vincotech Holdings S.a r.l.

FINANCIALS: Sales and profits are in thousands of dollars—add 000 to get the full amount. 2010 Note: Financial information for 2010 was not available for all companies at press time.

2010 Sales: $	2010 Profits: $	**U.S. Stock Ticker: MIELY.PK**
2009 Sales: $40,461,900	2009 Profits: $134,320	**Int'l Ticker: 6503** Int'l Exchange: Tokyo-TSE
2008 Sales: $40,498,200	2008 Profits: $1,579,800	Employees:
2007 Sales: $34,641,700	2007 Profits: $1,105,100	Fiscal Year Ends: 3/31
2006 Sales: $30,805,000	2006 Profits: $817,880	Parent Company: MITSUBISHI CORP

SALARIES/BENEFITS:

Pension Plan:	ESOP Stock Plan:	Profit Sharing:	Top Exec. Salary: $	Bonus: $
Savings Plan:	Stock Purch. Plan:		Second Exec. Salary: $	Bonus: $

OTHER THOUGHTS:

Apparent Women Officers or Directors:
Hot Spot for Advancement for Women/Minorities:

LOCATIONS: ("Y" = Yes)

West:	Southwest:	Midwest:	Southeast:	Northeast:	International:
Y	Y	Y	Y	Y	Y

Note: Financial information, benefits and other data can change quickly and may vary from those stated here.

MODUSLINK GLOBAL SOLUTIONS INC

www.moduslink.com

Industry Group Code: 511210A **Ranks within this company's industry group: Sales: 1   Profits: 6**

Hardware:		Software:		Telecommunications:		Electronic Publishing:		Equipment:		Specialty Services:	
Computers:		Consumer:		Local:		Online Service:	Y	Telecom:		Consulting:	Y
Accessories:		Corporate:	Y	Long Distance:		TV/Cable or Wireless:		Communication:		Contract Manufacturing:	
Network Equipment:		Telecom:		Cellular:		Games:		Distribution:		Processing:	
Chips/Circuits:		Internet:		Internet Service:		Financial Data:		VAR/Reseller:		Staff/Outsourcing:	
Parts/Drives:								Satellite Srv./Equip.:		Specialty Services:	Y

TYPES OF BUSINESS:
Software-Supply Chain Management
Web-Based Distribution & Fulfillment Services
Marketing Distribution Services
Consulting Services
Venture Capital

BRANDS/DIVISIONS/AFFILIATES:
Tech For Less, LCC
ModusLink Corporation
ModusLink PTS, Inc.
ModusLink Open Channel Solutions, Inc.

CONTACTS: *Note: Officers with more than one job title may be intentionally listed here more than once.*
Joseph C. Lawler, CEO
Joseph C. Lawler, Pres.
Steven G. Crane, CFO
Matthew J. Dattilo, CIO
Peter L. Gray, General Counsel/Sec./Exec. VP
Bill McLennan, Pres., Global Oper.
David J. Riley, Exec. VP-Corp Dev.
Joseph C. Lawler, Chmn.

Phone: 781-663-5001	Fax: 781-886-4884
Toll-Free: 888-996-6387	
Address: 1100 Winter St., Ste. 4600, Waltham, MA 02451 US	

GROWTH PLANS/SPECIAL FEATURES:
ModusLink Global Solutions, Inc. is a leading provider of global supply chain business process outsourcing to technology-based companies in the computing, software, consumer electronics, storage and communications markets. The company provides these services through its wholly owned subsidiaries, Moduslink Corporation; ModusLink Open Channel Solutions, Inc. (ModusLink OCS); ModusLink PTS, Inc. (ModusLink PTS); and Tech For Less, LCC (TFL). The company's services include supply chain, aftermarket services, e-business and entitlement management. Supply chain services, delivered by ModusLink Corporation, consist of factor supply and optimized configuration. Factor supply provides inbound supply of components into one or more of ModusLink's client's manufacturing or assembly operations on behalf of a client, and optimization configuration, which employs methods of determining the best time and place in the supply chain to perform final configuration, packaging and distribution of products. Aftermarket services, provided by Moduslink Corporation, ModusLink PTS and TFL, manage a range of post-sales activity including customer service, technical support and multi-channel returns management to testing, repair and asset disposition. Through its e-business services, such as e-commerce, customer support, financial transaction processing, physical shipment and returns processes, ModusLink provides a direct end-user revenue channel for its clients. E-business services are also conducted through ModusLink Corporation. The company's entitlement management services are designed to facilitate revenue generation for software publishers and related businesses by managing the complexities of multi-channel subscription and customer access rights inherent in software licensing. Entitlement management services are provided by ModusLink OCS. The company manages its supply chain operations through its technology infrastructure, which includes its Enterprise Resource Planning system. The company's capital venture business, @Ventures, invests in a variety of privately held companies. The firm's network consists of more than 25 facilities in 14 countries.

FINANCIALS: Sales and profits are in thousands of dollars—add 000 to get the full amount. 2010 Note: Financial information for 2010 was not available for all companies at press time.

2010 Sales: $923,996	2010 Profits: $-17,787	**U.S. Stock Ticker:** MLNK
2009 Sales: $1,008,554	2009 Profits: $-193,452	**Int'l Ticker:** **Int'l Exchange:**
2008 Sales: $1,068,207	2008 Profits: $9,128	Employees: 4,400
2007 Sales: $1,143,026	2007 Profits: $49,411	Fiscal Year Ends: 7/31
2006 Sales: $1,148,886	2006 Profits: $14,945	Parent Company:

SALARIES/BENEFITS:
Pension Plan:	ESOP Stock Plan:	Profit Sharing:	Top Exec. Salary: $645,000	Bonus: $974,337
Savings Plan: Y	Stock Purch. Plan:		Second Exec. Salary: $450,000	Bonus: $461,273

OTHER THOUGHTS:
Apparent Women Officers or Directors: 1
Hot Spot for Advancement for Women/Minorities:

LOCATIONS: ("Y" = Yes)
West:	Southwest:	Midwest:	Southeast:	Northeast:	International:
Y	Y	Y	Y	Y	Y

MOLEX INC

www.molex.com

Industry Group Code: 334119 Ranks within this company's industry group: Sales: 11 Profits: 22

Hardware:		Software:	Telecommunications:	Electronic Publishing:	Equipment:		Specialty Services:	
Computers:		Consumer:	Local:	Online Service:	Telecom:	Y	Consulting:	
Accessories:	Y	Corporate:	Long Distance:	TV/Cable or Wireless:	Communication:	Y	Contract Manufacturing:	
Network Equipment:		Telecom:	Cellular:	Games:	Distribution:		Processing:	
Chips/Circuits:		Internet:	Internet Service:	Financial Data:	VAR/Reseller:		Staff/Outsourcing:	
Parts/Drives:	Y				Satellite Srv./Equip.:		Specialty Services:	Y

TYPES OF BUSINESS:

Electronic Components
Transportation Products
Commercial Products
Micro Products
Automation & Electrical Products
Integrated Products
Global Sales & Marketing Organization

BRANDS/DIVISIONS/AFFILIATES:

CONTACTS: Note: Officers with more than one job title may be intentionally listed here more than once.

Martin P. Slark, CEO
Liam McCarthy, COO
Liam McCarthy, Pres.
David D. Johnson, CFO/Exec. VP
Graham C. Brock, Exec. VP/Pres., Global Sales & Mktg. Div.
Ana G. Rodriguez, Sr. VP-Global Human Resources
Gary J. Matula, CIO/Sr. VP-IS
David D. Johnson, Treas.
James E. Fleischhacker, Exec. VP/Pres., Global Commercial Prod. Div.
John H. Krehbiel, Jr., Co-Chmn.
J. Michael Nauman, Exec. VP/Pres., Global Integrated Prod. Div.
Katsumi Hirokawa, Exec. VP/Pres., Global Micro Prod. Div.
Frederick A. Krehbiel, Co-Chmn.

Phone: 630-969-4550	Fax: 630-968-8356
Toll-Free: 800-786-6539	
Address: 2222 Wellington Ct., Lisle, IL 60532-1682 US	

GROWTH PLANS/SPECIAL FEATURES:

Molex, Inc. is a manufacturer of electronic components. It designs, manufactures and sells more than 100,000 products, including terminals, connectors, planar cables, cable assemblies, interconnection systems, backplanes, integrated products and mechanical and electronic switches. The company also provides manufacturing services to integrate specific components into a customer's product. The firm is organized into four divisions: commercial products; micro products; integrated products; and global sales and marketing organization. The commercial products segment specializes in products that cater to multiple markets, especially to those that require high speed and quality parts, and components for engine and cockpit applications in the transportation industry. The micro products segment focuses on small-size connectors for portable electronics. The integrated products segment creates printed circuit boards and flexible circuits. Businesses that this division caters to include factories and automated facilities, as well as structured cabling for offices, universities and government buildings. The global sales and marketing organization segment comprises regional sales and industry marketing support teams, which provide customers with access to the Molex products. Molex operates 39 manufacturing facilities in 16 countries including Italy, Poland, Japan, South Korea, Vietnam, Thailand, China, the U.S. and Mexico. In 2009, the firm's Asia-Pacific segment was responsible for 60% of revenue, 24% was from the Americas and 16% from Europe.

FINANCIALS: Sales and profits are in thousands of dollars—add 000 to get the full amount. 2010 Note: Financial information for 2010 was not available for all companies at press time.

2010 Sales: $3,007,207	2010 Profits: $131,489	**U.S. Stock Ticker:** MOLX	
2009 Sales: $2,581,841	2009 Profits: $-321,287	**Int'l Ticker:** Int'l Exchange:	
2008 Sales: $3,328,347	2008 Profits: $215,437	**Employees:** 35,519	
2007 Sales: $3,265,874	2007 Profits: $240,768	**Fiscal Year Ends:** 6/30	
2006 Sales: $2,861,289	2006 Profits: $236,091	**Parent Company:**	

SALARIES/BENEFITS:

Pension Plan:	ESOP Stock Plan: Y	Profit Sharing:	Top Exec. Salary: $873,392	Bonus: $900,000
Savings Plan: Y	Stock Purch. Plan: Y		Second Exec. Salary: $565,250	Bonus: $500,000

OTHER THOUGHTS:

Apparent Women Officers or Directors: 1
Hot Spot for Advancement for Women/Minorities:

LOCATIONS: ("Y" = Yes)

West:	Southwest:	Midwest:	Southeast:	Northeast:	International:
Y		Y	Y	Y	Y

Note: Financial information, benefits and other data can change quickly and may vary from those stated here.

MOSER BAER INDIA LIMITED

www.moserbaer.in

Industry Group Code: 334112 Ranks within this company's industry group: Sales: 9 Profits: 10

Hardware:		Software:		Telecommunications:		Electronic Publishing:	Equipment:		Specialty Services:	
Computers:		Consumer:		Local:		Online Service:	Telecom:		Consulting:	
Accessories:	Y	Corporate:		Long Distance:		TV/Cable or Wireless:	Communication:		Contract Manufacturing:	Y
Network Equipment:		Telecom:		Cellular:		Games:	Distribution:		Processing:	
Chips/Circuits:		Internet:		Internet Service:		Financial Data:	VAR/Reseller:		Staff/Outsourcing:	
Parts/Drives:	Y						Satellite Srv./Equip.:		Specialty Services:	Y

TYPES OF BUSINESS:

Storage Products
Consumer Electronics
Photovoltaics
Entertainment
IT Peripherals

BRANDS/DIVISIONS/AFFILIATES:

Moser Baer Solar Limited
Photovoltaic Technologies India Ltd.
Media Masters LLC

CONTACTS: Note: Officers with more than one job title may be intentionally listed here more than once.

Deepak Puri, Managing Dir.
Yogesh B Mathur, CFO
Rakesh Govil, Pres., Corp. Strategy & Bus. Dev.
Ratul Puri, Controller/Exec. Dir.
Rajiv Arya, CEO-Moser Baer Photovoltaic Ltd.
V.C. Agerwal, COO-Moser Baer Photovoltaic Ltd.
Harish Dayani, CEO-Entertainment Div.
Bhaskar Sharma, CEO-Blank Optical Media & Consumer Prod.
Deepak Puri, Chmn.

Phone: 91-11-4059-4444	Fax: 91-11-4163-5211
Toll-Free:	
Address: 43B Okhla Industrial Estate, New Delhi, 110020 India	

GROWTH PLANS/SPECIAL FEATURES:

Moser Baer India Limited is an India-based technology company and a major worldwide provider of optical media products. The firm has four divisions: storage media; solar; entertainment; and IT peripherals and consumer electronics. The storage media division manufactures a wide range of optical storage products, such as recordable compact discs (CD-R); rewritable compact discs (CD-RW); recordable digital versatile discs (DVD-R); rewritable digital versatile discs (DVD-RW); and Blue-ray high-definition discs. The solar division encompasses the activities of subsidiaries Moser Baer Solar Limited and Photovoltaic Technologies India Ltd., which together are involved in the research, development and sale of solar energy products, with manufacturing efforts focused on crystalline solar cells, solar modules and thin-film photovoltaic technologies. The entertainment division is among the largest home video producers in India, offering movies, television programming and music videos in a diverse range of languages, including Hindi, English, Tamil, Telugu, Malayalam, Kannada, Marathi, Gujarati and Bengali. The entertainment division owns rights to a library of 10,000 film titles, with roughly 3,000 titles currently available. The IT peripherals and consumer electronics division offers a variety of products such as USB drives, memory cards, DVD writers, PC peripherals, thin-film transistor (TFT) monitors and external hard drives. Additionally, this segment manufactures a variety of consumer products including LCD TV's, DVD players, digital photo frames, digital music players and multimedia speakers. Moser Baer's products are sold in more than 80 countries, with sales and distribution operations overseen by offices in India, Japan and the U.S. The firm's manufacturing facilities are concentrated in India, while product distribution in the U.S. is facilitated through a partnership with South Dakota-based Media Masters LLC.

FINANCIALS: Sales and profits are in thousands of dollars—add 000 to get the full amount. 2010 Note: Financial information for 2010 was not available for all companies at press time.

2010 Sales: $532,760	2010 Profits: $-85,600	**U.S. Stock Ticker:**
2009 Sales: $537,350	2009 Profits: $-79,040	**Int'l Ticker: 517140** Int'l Exchange: Bombay-BSE
2008 Sales: $453,860	2008 Profits: $-43,960	Employees: 6,146
2007 Sales: $	2007 Profits: $	Fiscal Year Ends: 3/31
2006 Sales: $	2006 Profits: $	Parent Company:

SALARIES/BENEFITS:

Pension Plan:	ESOP Stock Plan:	Profit Sharing:	Top Exec. Salary: $	Bonus: $
Savings Plan:	Stock Purch. Plan:		Second Exec. Salary: $	Bonus: $

OTHER THOUGHTS:

Apparent Women Officers or Directors: 1
Hot Spot for Advancement for Women/Minorities:

LOCATIONS: ("Y" = Yes)

West:	Southwest:	Midwest:	Southeast:	Northeast:	International:
Y					Y

MSCSOFTWARE CORP

www.mscsoftware.com

Industry Group Code: 511210N Ranks within this company's industry group: Sales: Profits:

Hardware:	Software:		Telecommunications:	Electronic Publishing:	Equipment:	Specialty Services:	
Computers:	Consumer:		Local:	Online Service:	Telecom:	Consulting:	Y
Accessories:	Corporate:	Y	Long Distance:	TV/Cable or Wireless:	Communication:	Contract Manufacturing:	
Network Equipment:	Telecom:		Cellular:	Games:	Distribution:	Processing:	
Chips/Circuits:	Internet:		Internet Service:	Financial Data:	VAR/Reseller:	Staff/Outsourcing:	
Parts/Drives:					Satellite Srv./Equip.:	Specialty Services:	

TYPES OF BUSINESS:

Software-Computer-Aided Engineering
Engineering Consulting
Custom Software Development
Simulation Software
Product Lifecycle Management Software

BRANDS/DIVISIONS/AFFILIATES:

SimOffice
Fluid Connection
SimManager
Adams
SimXpert
Symphony Technology Group
Elliott Management Corporation
Maximus Holdings Inc

CONTACTS: Note: Officers with more than one job title may be intentionally listed here more than once.

Dominic Gallello, CEO
Dominic Gallello, Pres.
Jim Johnson, CFO
Ted Pawela, VP-Mktg.
Michele Langstaff, VP-Human Resources
Doug Neill, VP-Prod. Dev.
Doug Campbell, General Counsel/VP
John Janevic, VP-Strategic Oper.
Leslie Rickey, Contact-Media Rel.
Joanne Keates, Dir.-Investor Rel.
Eric Favre, VP-APAC
Albrecht Pfaff, VP-SimManager Bus. Unit
David J. Yuen, Sr. VP-Americas
Takehiko Kato, Pres., MSC Japan
Kais Bouchiba, Sr. VP-EMEA

Phone: 714-540-8900	Fax: 714-784-4056
Toll-Free: 800-328-4672	
Address: 2 MacArthur Pl., Santa Ana, CA 92707 US	

GROWTH PLANS/SPECIAL FEATURES:

MSC.Software Corp. (MSC) is a leading global provider of virtual product development tools using simulation software. Operating in approximately 30 countries, the company provides services and systems to optimize product design and quality and reduce costs and time-to-market as well as information systems and software integration systems through its product lifecycle management software. MSC's most popular software products include SimManager, SimDesigner, SimXpert, Sinda, EASY5, Marc, Dytran, MSC.Nastran, Patran, Fluid Connection and Adams.   The firm's solutions are intended to equip engineers with greater freedom to innovate design concepts, optimize complex solutions and exploit materials as a design variable. Computer-Aided Engineering (CAE) analysis is used to simulate the performance of a design before its physical manufacture, reducing the costly physical testing of prototypes and permitting a substantial increase in the number of design trade-offs and design cycles. Engineers use MSC's simulation software worldwide in industries including aerospace, automotive, defense, shipbuilding, consumer products and electronics. The company also provides strategic consulting services to customers to improve the integration and performance of its technologies. The firm's partners include ACUSIM Software, Inc.; VISTAGY; Free Field Technologies; Siemens PLM Software; Parametric Technology Corporation; Platform Computing, Inc.; LifeModeler, Inc.; FEV Motorentechnik GmbH; Dassault Systemes; Livermore Software Technology Corp.; and VI-grade GmbH. MSC is owned by Maximus Holdings, Inc., an investment group led by Symphony Technology Group and Elliott Management Corporation.

FINANCIALS: Sales and profits are in thousands of dollars—add 000 to get the full amount. 2010 Note: Financial information for 2010 was not available for all companies at press time.

2010 Sales: $	2010 Profits: $	**U.S. Stock Ticker:** Private
2009 Sales: $	2009 Profits: $	**Int'l Ticker:** Int'l Exchange:
2008 Sales: $254,386	2008 Profits: $-6,246	Employees:
2007 Sales: $246,651	2007 Profits: $-10,320	Fiscal Year Ends: 12/31
2006 Sales: $259,686	2006 Profits: $13,802	Parent Company: SYMPHONY TECHNOLOGY GROUP

SALARIES/BENEFITS:

Pension Plan:	ESOP Stock Plan:	Profit Sharing:	Top Exec. Salary: $	Bonus: $
Savings Plan: Y	Stock Purch. Plan: Y		Second Exec. Salary: $	Bonus: $

OTHER THOUGHTS:

Apparent Women Officers or Directors: 3
Hot Spot for Advancement for Women/Minorities: Y

LOCATIONS: ("Y" = Yes)

West:	Southwest:	Midwest:	Southeast:	Northeast:	International:
Y	Y	Y			Y

Note: Financial information, benefits and other data can change quickly and may vary from those stated here.

MULTI-FINELINE ELECTRONIX INC

www.mflex.com

Industry Group Code: 33441 Ranks within this company's industry group: Sales: 36 Profits: 30

Hardware:	Software:	Telecommunications:	Electronic Publishing:	Equipment:	Specialty Services:
Computers:	Consumer:	Local:	Online Service:	Telecom:	Consulting:
Accessories:	Corporate:	Long Distance:	TV/Cable or Wireless:	Communication:	Contract Manufacturing:
Network Equipment:	Telecom:	Cellular:	Games:	Distribution:	Processing:
Chips/Circuits: Y	Internet:	Internet Service:	Financial Data:	VAR/Reseller:	Staff/Outsourcing:
Parts/Drives:				Satellite Srv./Equip.:	Specialty Services:

TYPES OF BUSINESS:
Flexible Printed Circuit Boards
Flexible Printed Circuit Board Assemblies

BRANDS/DIVISIONS/AFFILIATES:
MFLEX U.K. Limited

CONTACTS: Note: Officers with more than one job title may be intentionally listed here more than once.
Reza Meshgin, CEO
Reza Meshgin, Pres.
Thomas Liguori, CFO/Exec. VP
Don Pucci, VP-Mktg. & Sales
Hedley Lawson, Jr., VP-Global Human Resources
Bill Beckenbaugh, CTO/VP
Christine Besnard, General Counsel/VP/Sec.
Thomas A. Lee, VP-Oper. & Program Mgmt.
Matthew Wolk, Chief Strategy Officer/VP-Corp. Dev.
Craig Riedel, Corp. Treas./VP
Philip A. Harding, Chmn.
Lance Jin, VP/Managing Dir.-China Oper.

Phone: 714-238-1488	Fax: 714-996-3834
Toll-Free:	
Address: 3140 E. Coronado St., Anaheim, CA 92806 US	

GROWTH PLANS/SPECIAL FEATURES:

Multi-Fineline Electronix, Inc. is one of the world's largest producers of flexible printed circuits and flexible printed circuit assemblies. Flexible printed circuits, which consist of copper conductive patterns that have been etched or printed while affixed to flexible substrate materials such as polyimide or polyester, are used to provide connections between electronic components and as a substrate to support these electronic devices. Flexible printed circuits can be enhanced by attaching electronic components, such as connectors, switches, resistors, capacitors, light emitting devices, integrated circuits, cameras and optical sensors, to the circuit. With operations in the U.S., China, Singapore, the U.K. and Malaysia, the firm offers a global service and support base for the design and manufacture of flexible interconnect products. The company has control over every aspect of its circuit production, from design and application engineering and prototyping through high-volume fabrication, component assembly and testing. The firm targets its efforts within the electronics market and focuses particularly on applications where flexible printed circuits facilitate human interaction with an electronic device and are the enabling technology in achieving a desired size, shape, weight or functionality of the device. Current applications for its products include mobile phones, consumer electronic devices, portable bar code scanners, computer storage devices and medical devices. Multi-Fineline Electronix provides its products to original equipment manufacturers (OEMs) such as Motorola, Inc. and Sony Ericsson; to electronic manufacturing services providers such as Foxconn Electronics, Inc. and Flextronics International, Ltd.; and to display manufacturers. The company also produces printed segmented electroluminescent displays and keyboards through its U.K. subsidiary, MFLEX U.K. Limited.

The firm offers employees in the U.S. medical, dental and vision insurance; life and AD&D insurance; disability coverage; a 401(k) plan; educational reimbursement; and an employee assistance program.

FINANCIALS: Sales and profits are in thousands of dollars—add 000 to get the full amount. 2010 Note: Financial information for 2010 was not available for all companies at press time.

2010 Sales: $791,339	2010 Profits: $29,775	U.S. Stock Ticker: MFLX
2009 Sales: $764,432	2009 Profits: $46,068	Int'l Ticker: Int'l Exchange:
2008 Sales: $728,805	2008 Profits: $40,479	Employees: 17,100
2007 Sales: $508,147	2007 Profits: $3,038	Fiscal Year Ends: 9/30
2006 Sales: $504,204	2006 Profits: $40,357	Parent Company:

SALARIES/BENEFITS:

Pension Plan:	ESOP Stock Plan:	Profit Sharing:	Top Exec. Salary: $570,000	Bonus: $601,113
Savings Plan: Y	Stock Purch. Plan:		Second Exec. Salary: $340,000	Bonus: $239,039

OTHER THOUGHTS:
Apparent Women Officers or Directors: 2
Hot Spot for Advancement for Women/Minorities:

LOCATIONS: ("Y" = Yes)

West:	Southwest:	Midwest:	Southeast:	Northeast:	International:
Y	Y				Y

NAN YA PCB CORP

www.nanyapcb.com.tw

Industry Group Code: 33441 Ranks within this company's industry group: Sales: Profits:

Hardware:		Software:	Telecommunications:	Electronic Publishing:	Equipment:	Specialty Services:	
Computers:		Consumer:	Local:	Online Service:	Telecom:	Consulting:	
Accessories:		Corporate:	Long Distance:	TV/Cable or Wireless:	Communication:	Contract Manufacturing:	Y
Network Equipment:		Telecom:	Cellular:	Games:	Distribution:	Processing:	
Chips/Circuits:	Y	Internet:	Internet Service:	Financial Data:	VAR/Reseller:	Staff/Outsourcing:	
Parts/Drives:					Satellite Srv./Equip.:	Specialty Services:	

TYPES OF BUSINESS:

Printed Circuit Board, Manufacture & Distribution

BRANDS/DIVISIONS/AFFILIATES:

CONTACTS: Note: Officers with more than one job title may be intentionally listed here more than once.

Jiafang Zhang, Gen. Mgr.
Otto Chang, Pres.
Jianfang Rao, Head-Finance
Wen-hui Huang, Head-Acct.
Andy Tang, Associate VP
Qinren Wu, Chmn.

Phone: 886-3-322-3751	Fax:
Toll-Free:	
Address: No. 338, Nankan Rd., Sec.1 Luchu Hsiang, Taoyuan, Taiwan	

GROWTH PLANS/SPECIAL FEATURES:

Nan Ya PCB (printed circuit board) Corp. manufactures and distributes printed circuit boards, which are the key component in electronics. Its products are used in desktop computers, notebook computers, work stations, mobile phones, central processing units (CPUs), radio frequency modules, servers and flat screen televisions. Its PCBs can be produced in conventional, HDI (high density interconnection) and Rigid-Flex configurations. The HDI structure allows for higher circuit density, better protection against signal distortion and higher speeds, while the Rigid-Flex structure offers a flexible form. The products can be produced as light, thin, small, long, soft or hard as the user wishes. Nan Ya also produces integrated circuit (IC) substrates, fuel cell and environmentally-friendly products. The IC substrates are used to connect processor and other similar chips to modules, such as graphics processing units, central processing units, memory and other computer motherboard units. Its fuel cell segment produces environmentally-friendly direct methanol and proton exchange membrane fuel cell, fuel stack and fuel pack products. All of the company's products are designed to be produced without hazardous materials like cadmium, lead, mercury and chromium.

Employees have access to an onsite convenience stores, delis, movie theater and gymnasium; discounts on medical treatment; and bonuses and gifts during national festivals.

FINANCIALS: Sales and profits are in thousands of dollars—add 000 to get the full amount. 2010 Note: Financial information for 2010 was not available for all companies at press time.

2010 Sales: $	2010 Profits: $	U.S. Stock Ticker:
2009 Sales: $	2009 Profits: $	Int'l Ticker: 8046 Int'l Exchange: Taipei-TPE
2008 Sales: $	2008 Profits: $	Employees:
2007 Sales: $	2007 Profits: $	Fiscal Year Ends:
2006 Sales: $	2006 Profits: $	Parent Company:

SALARIES/BENEFITS:

Pension Plan:	ESOP Stock Plan:	Profit Sharing:	Top Exec. Salary: $	Bonus: $
Savings Plan:	Stock Purch. Plan:		Second Exec. Salary: $	Bonus: $

OTHER THOUGHTS:

Apparent Women Officers or Directors:
Hot Spot for Advancement for Women/Minorities:

LOCATIONS: ("Y" = Yes)

West:	Southwest:	Midwest:	Southeast:	Northeast:	International: Y

Note: Financial information, benefits and other data can change quickly and may vary from those stated here.

NANYA TECHNOLOGY CORPORATION

www.nanya.com

Industry Group Code: 334111 Ranks within this company's industry group: Sales: 18 Profits: 25

Hardware:		Software:	Telecommunications:	Electronic Publishing:	Equipment:	Specialty Services:	
Computers:		Consumer:	Local:	Online Service:	Telecom:	Consulting:	
Accessories:		Corporate:	Long Distance:	TV/Cable or Wireless:	Communication:	Contract Manufacturing:	Y
Network Equipment:		Telecom:	Cellular:	Games:	Distribution:	Processing:	
Chips/Circuits:	Y	Internet:	Internet Service:	Financial Data:	VAR/Reseller:	Staff/Outsourcing:	
Parts/Drives:					Satellite Srv./Equip.:	Specialty Services:	

TYPES OF BUSINESS:
Computer Hardware, Manufacturing
Dynamic Random Access Memory Modules

BRANDS/DIVISIONS/AFFILIATES:
Elixir
Nanya Plastics Corp.
Formosa Plastics Corporation
Micron Technology Inc
MeiYa Technology Corporation

CONTACTS: Note: Officers with more than one job title may be intentionally listed here more than once.
Jih Lien, Pres.
Pei-Ing Lee, Sr. VP-Foundry & Tech. Dev.
Pei-Ing Lee, Sr. VP-Mfg.
Brian Donahue, Dir.-Sales, Nanya Tech. Corp. USA
David Dwyer, Dir.-Sales, Nanya Tech. Corp. USA
Carver Liu, Mgr.-Program
Chia Chau Wu, Chmn.
Ken Hurley, Pres., Nanya Tech. Corp. USA

Phone: 886-3-328-1688 **Fax:** 886-3-396-0997
Toll-Free:
Address: Hwa Ya Tech. Park 669, Fu Hsing 3rd Rd., Kueishan, Taoyuan, 333 Taiwan

GROWTH PLANS/SPECIAL FEATURES:
Nanya Technology Corporation (NTC) designs, manufactures and sells DRAM (Dynamic Random Access Memory) modules. It owns three fabrication facilities, two producing 8-inch wafers, located in Nan Kan and Hwa Ya Technology Park, in Taoyuan County, and one for 12-inch wafers, located in Taishan, Taipei County. The 12-inch manufacturing facility, which uses a 70 nm (nanometer) process technology, had a start-up monthly production capacity of 30,000 wafers and a planned capacity of more than 60,000 wafers. NTC's DRAM components and modules, sold primarily under the Elixir brand name, include DDR2 (Double Data Rate, 2nd generation) and DDR3 SDRAM (Synchronous DRAM) components, as well as 200-, 204- and 240-pin DDR, DDR2 and DDR3 SDRAM modules. Depending on the model, these products come in 256 Mb (megabyte), 512 Mb, 1 Gb (gigabyte), 2 Gb, 4 Gb or 8 Gb formats. NTC also manufactures specialty non-PC products, including 128 Mb DDR SDRAM chips. The firm has sales offices in the U.S., Europe, China, Taiwan and Japan. Its main shareholder is Nanya Plastics Corp., part of the Formosa Plastics Group. NTC maintains a joint venture with Micron Technology, MeiYa Technology Corporation. MeiYa produces 12-inch wafers using a 50 nm technology, with a maximum capacity of 45,000 wafers per month. In September 2010, the company invested approximately $106.5 million for the purchase of new fabrication equipment.

NTC's employee benefits include medical insurance; dormitories for single employees; an on-site cafeteria and store; birthday coupons; on-site medical assistance at the fabrication facilities; and cash stipends for employees who get married, have a new child, suffer a death in the family or need emergency financial assistance.

FINANCIALS: Sales and profits are in thousands of dollars—add 000 to get the full amount. 2010 Note: Financial information for 2010 was not available for all companies at press time.
2010 Sales: $	2010 Profits: $	**U.S. Stock Ticker:**
2009 Sales: $1,324,680	2009 Profits: $-642,720	**Int'l Ticker: 2408** Int'l Exchange: Taipei-TPE
2008 Sales: $1,631,600	2008 Profits: $-373,700	Employees:
2007 Sales: $2,244,300	2007 Profits: $522,000	Fiscal Year Ends: 12/31
2006 Sales: $1,503,200	2006 Profits: $69,800	Parent Company:

SALARIES/BENEFITS:
Pension Plan:	ESOP Stock Plan: Y	Profit Sharing:	Top Exec. Salary: $	Bonus: $
Savings Plan:	Stock Purch. Plan:		Second Exec. Salary: $	Bonus: $

OTHER THOUGHTS:
Apparent Women Officers or Directors:
Hot Spot for Advancement for Women/Minorities:

LOCATIONS: ("Y" = Yes)
West:	Southwest:	Midwest:	Southeast:	Northeast:	International:
Y					Y

Note: Financial information, benefits and other data can change quickly and may vary from those stated here.

NATIONAL INSTRUMENTS CORP

www.ni.com

Industry Group Code: 511210N Ranks within this company's industry group: Sales: 8 Profits: 7

Hardware:		Software:		Telecommunications:	Electronic Publishing:	Equipment:	Specialty Services:
Computers:		Consumer:		Local:	Online Service:	Telecom:	Consulting:
Accessories:	Y	Corporate:	Y	Long Distance:	TV/Cable or Wireless:	Communication:	Contract Manufacturing:
Network Equipment:		Telecom:		Cellular:	Games:	Distribution:	Processing:
Chips/Circuits:		Internet:		Internet Service:	Financial Data:	VAR/Reseller:	Staff/Outsourcing:
Parts/Drives:	Y					Satellite Srv./Equip.:	Specialty Services:

TYPES OF BUSINESS:

Software-Instrumentation
Virtual Instrumentation
Signal Conditioning Hardware
Test & Measurement Software
Motion Control Products
Analysis & Visualization Software
Automation Software
Image Acquisition Products

BRANDS/DIVISIONS/AFFILIATES:

LabVIEW
LabWindows
LabVIEW FPGA
TestStand
Measurement Studio
LabVIEW Real-Time
FieldPoint

CONTACTS: Note: Officers with more than one job title may be intentionally listed here more than once.

James Truchard, CEO
Alex Davern, COO/Exec. VP
James Truchard, Pres.
Alex Davern, CFO
Pete Zogas, Sr. VP-Sales & Mktg.
Mark Finger, VP-Human Resources
Phil Hester, Sr. VP-R&D
Arleene Porterfield, VP-Global IT
Tony Vento, VP-Systems & Applications Eng.
Rob Porterfield, VP-Mfg.
David Hugley, General Counsel/VP/Sec.
John Pasquarette, VP-eCommerce
John Roiko, VP-Finance
Ray Almgren, VP-Prod. Mktg., Core Platforms
Andrew Krupp, VP-Quality & Continuous Improvement
Ron Wolfe, VP-Semiconductor Test
Kevin Schultz, VP-R&D, Data Acquisition & Distributed I/O
James Truchard, Chmn.
Scott Rust, VP-R&D, NI Penang

Phone: 512-338-9119	Fax: 512-683-5759
Toll-Free: 800-433-3488	
Address: 11500 N. Mopac Expwy., Austin, TX 78759-3504 US	

GROWTH PLANS/SPECIAL FEATURES:

National Instruments Corp. (NI) supplies test, measurement and automation products used by engineers and scientists from numerous industries. Its key markets range from the automotive, aerospace, electronics, semiconductors and defense sectors, to the education, government, medical research and telecommunications industries, among others. The company provides flexible application software and modular, multifunction hardware that users combine with computers, networks and third party devices to create measurement, automation and embedded systems, or virtual instruments. Virtual instrumentation is a shift from traditional hardware-centered systems to software-centered systems that exploit the computational, display, productivity and connectivity capabilities of computers, networks and the Internet. NI's application software products include the LabVIEW, LabVIEW Real-Time, LabWindows and Measurement Studio programs that allow users to develop graphical user interfaces, control instruments and acquire, analyze and present data. Other applications include LabVIEW FPGA, which allows users to configure applications to execute directly in silicon via a field programmable gate array (FPGA); TestStand, targeted for T&M applications; and Multisim, a type of circuit simulation software used for electronic circuit design, board layout and electrical engineering training programs. The firm's hardware and related driver software products include data acquisition (DAQ), which help convert analog data into digital format; PCI hardware extensions for instrumentation chassis and controllers (PXI); and image acquisition and motion control products that integrate vision and motion into measurement applications. Additional products include the Compact FieldPoint distributed I/O application; modular instruments and embedded control hardware/software; industrial communications interfaces for communicating with serial devices; general purpose interface buses (GPIBs); and VXI computer controllers.

The firm offers its employees 401(k), stock purchase and profit sharing plans; health, dental and vision coverage; life and disability insurance; tuition assistance; and an on-site fitness center.

FINANCIALS: Sales and profits are in thousands of dollars—add 000 to get the full amount. 2010 Note: Financial information for 2010 was not available for all companies at press time.

2010 Sales: $	2010 Profits: $	U.S. Stock Ticker: NATI
2009 Sales: $676,594	2009 Profits: $17,085	Int'l Ticker: Int'l Exchange:
2008 Sales: $820,537	2008 Profits: $84,827	Employees: 5,120
2007 Sales: $740,378	2007 Profits: $107,033	Fiscal Year Ends: 12/31
2006 Sales: $660,407	2006 Profits: $72,708	Parent Company:

SALARIES/BENEFITS:

Pension Plan:	ESOP Stock Plan:	Profit Sharing: Y	Top Exec. Salary: $296,562	Bonus: $73,169
Savings Plan: Y	Stock Purch. Plan: Y		Second Exec. Salary: $237,250	Bonus: $37,741

OTHER THOUGHTS:

Apparent Women Officers or Directors: 1
Hot Spot for Advancement for Women/Minorities:

LOCATIONS: ("Y" = Yes)

West:	Southwest:	Midwest:	Southeast:	Northeast:	International:
Y	Y	Y	Y	Y	Y

NATIONAL SEMICONDUCTOR CORP

www.national.com

Industry Group Code: 33441 Ranks within this company's industry group: Sales: 24 Profits: 25

Hardware:		Software:	Telecommunications:	Electronic Publishing:	Equipment:	Specialty Services:	
Computers:		Consumer:	Local:	Online Service:	Telecom:	Consulting:	
Accessories:		Corporate:	Long Distance:	TV/Cable or Wireless:	Communication:	Contract Manufacturing:	Y
Network Equipment:	Y	Telecom:	Cellular:	Games:	Distribution:	Processing:	
Chips/Circuits:	Y	Internet:	Internet Service:	Financial Data:	VAR/Reseller:	Staff/Outsourcing:	
Parts/Drives:	Y				Satellite Srv./Equip.:	Specialty Services:	

TYPES OF BUSINESS:

Chips-Analog
Mixed-Signal Integrated Circuits
Information Appliances
Enterprise Networking Products
Display Products

BRANDS/DIVISIONS/AFFILIATES:

CONTACTS: Note: Officers with more than one job title may be intentionally listed here more than once.

Donald Macleod, CEO
Lewis Chew, CFO/Sr. VP
Suneil Parulekar, Sr. VP-Worldwide Mktg. & Sales
Edward Sweeney, Sr. VP-Worldwide Human Resources
Julie Wong, CIO/VP
Ahmad Bahai, CTO/Sr. VP
C.S. Liu, Sr. VP-Worldwide Mfg.
Todd DuChene, General Counsel/Sr. VP/Corp. Sec.
Mike Polacek, Sr. VP-Bus. Dev. & Key Market Segments
Detlev Kunz, Sr. VP/Gen. Mgr.-Prod. Group
Donald Macleod, Chmn.

Phone: 408-721-5000	Fax: 408-739-9803
Toll-Free: 800-272-9959	
Address: 2900 Semiconductor Dr., Santa Clara, CA 95052-8090 US	

GROWTH PLANS/SPECIAL FEATURES:

National Semiconductor Corp. is a leading semiconductor company focused on analog and mixed-signal integrated circuits (ICs) and sub-systems, particularly in the area of power management. It designs, develops, manufactures and markets analog intensive products, including a range of analog ICs that convert and regulate voltages to improve energy efficiency. It also designs ICs that handle the requisite analog technology for information or data as it travels from the point where it enters the electronic system, is conditioned, converted and processed to the point where it is sent out. National Semiconductor operates in five groups: products, worldwide marketing and sales, key market segments, technology research and manufacturing operations. The firm's products group is comprised of three broad categories: power management, signal path design and custom solutions. The power management business unit, which includes the subdivisions of infrastructure power, mobile devices power and performance power products, is concerned with the conversion and management of power consumption in electronic systems. The signal path design segment includes the precision signal path subdivision, which applies technology to the paths that information and data travel on; and the high speed product subdivision, which supplies ICs to the avionics, defense and aerospace markets. The custom solutions business unit supplies user-designed application specific products in the form of standard cells, gate arrays and full custom devices. The worldwide marketing and sales and key market segments groups are responsible for managing all aspects of the company's sales. The technology research group's primary task is the development of advanced process technologies. The manufacturing group manages all production, including outsourced manufacturing and global logistics, as well as quality assurance, purchasing and supply chain management.

The firm offers its employees a 401(k); profit-sharing; employee stock purchase plan; health and dental coverage; educational assistance; and an on-site fitness center.

FINANCIALS: Sales and profits are in thousands of dollars—add 000 to get the full amount. 2010 Note: Financial information for 2010 was not available for all companies at press time.

2010 Sales: $1,419,400	2010 Profits: $209,200	**U.S. Stock Ticker: NSM**
2009 Sales: $1,460,400	2009 Profits: $73,300	**Int'l Ticker:** Int'l Exchange:
2008 Sales: $1,885,900	2008 Profits: $332,300	Employees: 5,800
2007 Sales: $1,929,900	2007 Profits: $375,300	Fiscal Year Ends: 5/31
2006 Sales: $2,158,100	2006 Profits: $449,200	Parent Company:

SALARIES/BENEFITS:

Pension Plan: Y	ESOP Stock Plan:	Profit Sharing: Y	Top Exec. Salary: $911,407	Bonus: $3,893,768
Savings Plan:	Stock Purch. Plan: Y		Second Exec. Salary: $637,212	Bonus: $2,450,000

OTHER THOUGHTS:

Apparent Women Officers or Directors: 1
Hot Spot for Advancement for Women/Minorities:

LOCATIONS: ("Y" = Yes)

West:	Southwest:	Midwest:	Southeast:	Northeast:	International:
Y	Y	Y	Y	Y	Y

NAVISITE INC

www.navisite.com

Industry Group Code: 518210 Ranks within this company's industry group: Sales: 3 Profits: 5

Hardware:	Software:	Telecommunications:	Electronic Publishing:		Equipment:	Specialty Services:	
Computers:	Consumer:	Local:	Online Service:	Y	Telecom:	Consulting:	Y
Accessories:	Corporate:	Long Distance:	TV/Cable or Wireless:		Communication:	Contract Manufacturing:	
Network Equipment:	Telecom:	Cellular:	Games:		Distribution:	Processing:	
Chips/Circuits:	Internet:	Internet Service:	Financial Data:		VAR/Reseller:	Staff/Outsourcing:	Y
Parts/Drives:					Satellite Srv./Equip.:	Specialty Services:	Y

TYPES OF BUSINESS:

Web Site Hosting
Application Services Provider
Server & Application Management
Internet Application Solutions
e-Business Services
Electronic Software Distribution
Outsourcing Services

BRANDS/DIVISIONS/AFFILIATES:

NaviView
Alabanza
Jupiter Hosting
America's Job Exchange
NaviCloud MCS
Lawson / Kronos

CONTACTS: Note: Officers with more than one job title may be intentionally listed here more than once.

R. Brooks Borcherding, CEO
R. Brooks Borcherding, Pres.
Jim Pluntze, CFO
Claudine Bianchi, Chief Mktg. Officer
Denis Martin, CTO/Exec. VP
Mark Clayman, Sr. VP-Enterprise Sales
Sumeet Sabharwal, Sr. VP-Global Delivery
Mark Clayman, Sr. VP-Entreprise Sales
Roger Schwanhausser, Sr. VP-Service Delivery
Andrew Ruhan, Chmn.

Phone: 978-682-8300	Fax: 978-688-8100
Toll-Free: 877-485-9251	
Address: 400 Minuteman Rd., Andover, MA 01810 US	

GROWTH PLANS/SPECIAL FEATURES:

NaviSite, Inc. is an application services provider offering e-business-based Internet outsourcing, web hosting, server management, application management and Internet application services. Its clients are primarily middle-market organizations, such as mid-sized companies, divisions of large multinational companies and government agencies. The firm's services allow customers to outsource the hosting and management operations of their information technology infrastructure and applications, such as commerce systems, enterprise software applications and e-mail. Services include managed cloud services, enterprise hosting services, application management and NaviView. Managed cloud services are conducted through NaviCloud MCS, which provides computing, memory, storage, network, security and bandwidth services for the enterprise market. Enterprise hosting services offer managed hosting, software-as-a-service and co-location functions for secure IT infrastructure. The application management aspect encompasses monitoring, diagnosing and resolving problems, enabling software, eBusiness, content management and custom application management. Navisite's NaviView platform delivers services to customers and includes an event detection system, synthetic transaction monitoring, automated remediation, a component information manager, and an escalation manager. The company offers hosting services in state-of-the-art data centers in the U.S. and the U.K. Subsidiaries include Alabanza, Jupiter Hosting and America's Job Exchange. In February 2010, the firm sold its Lawson / Kronos application services business to Velocity Technology Solutions, Inc. for $56 million. In December 2010, NaviSite sold its Dallas Co-location business to Cologix Dallas, Inc. for $12.75 million.

The firm offers its employees medical and dental insurance; vision hardware reimbursement; life and AD&D insurance; short-and long term disability; flexible spending accounts; a 401(k) plan; an employee assistance program; and education assistance.

FINANCIALS: Sales and profits are in thousands of dollars—add 000 to get the full amount. 2010 Note: Financial information for 2010 was not available for all companies at press time.

2010 Sales: $126,147	2010 Profits: $13,473	U.S. Stock Ticker: NAVI
2009 Sales: $125,379	2009 Profits: $-15,111	Int'l Ticker: Int'l Exchange:
2008 Sales: $132,134	2008 Profits: $-8,684	Employees: 584
2007 Sales: $125,860	2007 Profits: $-25,910	Fiscal Year Ends: 7/31
2006 Sales: $108,844	2006 Profits: $-13,931	Parent Company:

SALARIES/BENEFITS:

Pension Plan:	ESOP Stock Plan:	Profit Sharing:	Top Exec. Salary: $350,000	Bonus: $254,625
Savings Plan: Y	Stock Purch. Plan: Y		Second Exec. Salary: $243,269	Bonus: $200,417

OTHER THOUGHTS:

Apparent Women Officers or Directors:
Hot Spot for Advancement for Women/Minorities:

LOCATIONS: ("Y" = Yes)

West:	Southwest:	Midwest:	Southeast:	Northeast:	International:
Y	Y	Y		Y	Y

NAVTEQ CORPORATION

www.navteq.com

Industry Group Code: 511210N Ranks within this company's industry group: Sales: Profits:

Hardware:	Software:		Telecommunications:	Electronic Publishing:	Equipment:	Specialty Services:
Computers:	Consumer:	Y	Local:	Online Service:	Telecom:	Consulting:
Accessories:	Corporate:	Y	Long Distance:	TV/Cable or Wireless:	Communication:	Contract Manufacturing:
Network Equipment:	Telecom:		Cellular:	Games:	Distribution:	Processing:
Chips/Circuits:	Internet:		Internet Service:	Financial Data:	VAR/Reseller:	Staff/Outsourcing:
Parts/Drives:					Satellite Srv./Equip.:	Specialty Services:

TYPES OF BUSINESS:

Digital Map Information
Route Planning Technology
Vehicle Navigation
Internet-Based Mapping
Location-Based Services
Geographic Information Systems

BRANDS/DIVISIONS/AFFILIATES:

Nokia Corporation
T-Systems Traffic GmbH
Motorway Junction Objects
Navteq LocationPoint

CONTACTS: Note: Officers with more than one job title may be intentionally listed here more than once.

Judson Green, CEO
Judson Green, Pres.
Jeff Mize, Exec. VP-Sales
Tiffany Treacy, VP-Global Prod. Mgmt.
Kirk Mitchell, Dir.-Bus. Dev.
Bob Richter, Public Rel.
Marc Naddell, VP-Partner & Dev. Programs
Roy Kolstad, VP/Gen. Mgr.-Enterprise North America
Christopher Rothey, VP-Market Dev. & Advertising
Cindy Paulauskas, VP-Map & Content Prod., Americas
Helder Azevedo, Gen. Dir.-Latin America

Phone: 312-894-7000	Fax: 312-894-7050
Toll-Free: 866-462-8837	
Address: 425 W. Randolph St., Chicago, IL 60606 US	

GROWTH PLANS/SPECIAL FEATURES:

Navteq Corporation, a subsidiary of Nokia Corp., is a provider of digital map, traffic and location data for automotive navigation systems, mobile navigation devices and Internet mapping applications. The firm maintains and continuously upgrading its geographical database, through 192 offices in 43 countries. The database covers millions of points of interest in 78 countries on six continents. Products are offered to both businesses and individuals and consist of a broad range of navigation tools, including databases of urban and rural transportation grids that are often incorporated into GPS products by systems manufacturers and mobile navigation device manufacturers. The firm also offers a route-planning tool that allows for driving directions and route optimization via the Internet and is used by web sites such as MapQuest, Microsoft/MSN, Autodesk, Toshiba and Yahoo!. In addition, location-based services provide geographic information about specific locations tailored to the proximity of a specific user, primarily utilized by mobile directory assistance services and emergency response systems. Geographic information systems (GIS) render geographic representations of information for use in infrastructure cataloging and tracking by government agencies and utility companies, as well as asset tracking and fleet management for commercial logistics companies. Navteq generally sells its products to mobile device and handset manufacturers, automobile manufacturers and dealers, navigation systems manufacturers, software developers, Internet portals, parcel and overnight delivery services companies and government entities. In January 2009, the firm completed its acquisition of T-Systems Traffic GmbH, a provider of traffic services in Germany. In May 2009, the company launched Navteq LocationPoint, a location-based advertising service, in Europe. In June 2009, Navteq released Motorway Junction Objects, an in-vehicle, three-dimensional display to assist drivers in navigating complex junctions and motorway rings, in Australia. In January 2010, the company was selected by United States Postal Service (USPS) to provide map data for eFMS (Electronic Facilities Management System).

FINANCIALS: Sales and profits are in thousands of dollars—add 000 to get the full amount. 2010 Note: Financial information for 2010 was not available for all companies at press time.

2010 Sales: $	2010 Profits: $	U.S. Stock Ticker: Subsidiary
2009 Sales: $	2009 Profits: $	Int'l Ticker: Int'l Exchange:
2008 Sales: $	2008 Profits: $	Employees:
2007 Sales: $853,387	2007 Profits: $172,950	Fiscal Year Ends: 12/31
2006 Sales: $581,619	2006 Profits: $109,970	Parent Company: NOKIA CORPORATION

SALARIES/BENEFITS:

Pension Plan:	ESOP Stock Plan:	Profit Sharing:	Top Exec. Salary: $	Bonus: $
Savings Plan:	Stock Purch. Plan:		Second Exec. Salary: $	Bonus: $

OTHER THOUGHTS:

Apparent Women Officers or Directors: 2
Hot Spot for Advancement for Women/Minorities:

LOCATIONS: ("Y" = Yes)

West:	Southwest:	Midwest:	Southeast:	Northeast:	International:
		Y			Y

NCR CORPORATION

www.ncr.com

Industry Group Code: 334111 Ranks within this company's industry group: Sales: 14 Profits: 21

Hardware:		Software:		Telecommunications:	Electronic Publishing:	Equipment:		Specialty Services:	
Computers:	Y	Consumer:		Local:	Online Service:	Telecom:		Consulting:	Y
Accessories:	Y	Corporate:	Y	Long Distance:	TV/Cable or Wireless:	Communication:	Y	Contract Manufacturing:	
Network Equipment:		Telecom:		Cellular:	Games:	Distribution:		Processing:	
Chips/Circuits:		Internet:		Internet Service:	Financial Data:	VAR/Reseller:		Staff/Outsourcing:	
Parts/Drives:						Satellite Srv./Equip.:		Specialty Services:	

TYPES OF BUSINESS:

Point-of-Sale Computer Systems
Barcode Scanning Equipment
Automatic Teller Machines (ATMs)
Transaction Processing Equipment
Point-of-Sale & Store Automation
Data Warehousing
Printer Consumables
Consulting Services

BRANDS/DIVISIONS/AFFILIATES:

NCI Ltd

CONTACTS: Note: Officers with more than one job title may be intentionally listed here more than once.

Bill Nuti, CEO
Bill Nuti, Pres.
Robert Fishman, CFO/Sr. VP
Peter Leav, Sr. VP-Global Sales
Andrea Ledford, Sr. VP-Human Resources
Ned F. Greene, Interim General Counsel/Sec./VP
Peter Dorsman, Sr. VP-Global Oper.
Richard Bravman, VP-Corp. Dev./Chief Mktg. Officer
Dan Bogan, Sr. VP/Gen. Mgr.-NCR Consumables
John G. Bruno, Exec. VP-Industry Solutions Group
Alex C. Camara, VP/Gen. Mgr.-NCR Entertainment Solutions
Stephen R. Crowley, VP-Continuous Improvement
Bill Nuti, Chmn.

Phone: 937-445-5000	Fax: 937-445-1682
Toll-Free: 800-225-5627	
Address: 2651 Satellite Blvd., Duluth, GA 30096 US	

GROWTH PLANS/SPECIAL FEATURES:

NCR Corporation provides information technology and related services to various industries, enabling client companies to interact more efficiently with customers. The company offers financial institutions, retailers and independent deployers financial-oriented self-service technologies, such as ATMs, cash dispensers, software solutions and consulting services relating to ATM security, software and bank branch optimization. Financial self-service solutions are designed to quickly and reliably process consumer transactions and incorporate advanced features such as automated check cashing/deposit, automated cash deposit, web-enablement, bill payment and the dispensing of non-cash items. NCR provides retail store automation solutions for the general merchandise, food, drug, travel, hospitality, health care, entertainment, gaming and public sector segments. The company has focused its investments and resources on self-service technologies with expanded offerings to include self-ticketing and self-check-in/out systems for the travel industry; self-service food ordering; and patient management check-in/out in the health care sector. The firm provides maintenance and support services for its products, including complete systems management and site assessment and site preparation, staging, installation and implementation. NCR is also involved in the resale and service of third-party computer hardware from select manufacturers, such as Cisco Systems. NCR Consumables develops, produces and markets a line of printer consumables for various print technologies, including paper rolls for receipts in ATMs and point of sale (POS) solutions; inkjet and laser printer supplies; thermal transfer and ink ribbons; labels; laser documents; business forms; and specialty media items such as photo and presentation papers and two-sided thermal paper. The firm's business segments are organized into three geographical groups: Americas; Europe, Middle East and Africa (EMEA); and Asia Pacific and Japan (APJ). In 2009, NCR opened a new manufacturing plant in Brail to support the market demand for ATMs in Brazil, the Caribbean and Latin America. In 2009, NCR acquired Netkey, Inc. and DVDPlay.

FINANCIALS: Sales and profits are in thousands of dollars—add 000 to get the full amount. 2010 Note: Financial information for 2010 was not available for all companies at press time.

2010 Sales: $	2010 Profits: $	U.S. Stock Ticker: NCR
2009 Sales: $4,612,000	2009 Profits: $-30,000	Int'l Ticker: Int'l Exchange:
2008 Sales: $5,315,000	2008 Profits: $228,000	Employees: 21,500
2007 Sales: $4,970,000	2007 Profits: $274,000	Fiscal Year Ends: 12/31
2006 Sales: $4,582,000	2006 Profits: $382,000	Parent Company:

SALARIES/BENEFITS:

Pension Plan:	ESOP Stock Plan:	Profit Sharing:	Top Exec. Salary: $1,000,000	Bonus: $
Savings Plan:	Stock Purch. Plan:		Second Exec. Salary: $750,000	Bonus: $650,000

OTHER THOUGHTS:

Apparent Women Officers or Directors: 2
Hot Spot for Advancement for Women/Minorities: Y

LOCATIONS: ("Y" = Yes)

West:	Southwest:	Midwest:	Southeast:	Northeast:	International:
Y		Y	Y	Y	Y

Note: Financial information, benefits and other data can change quickly and may vary from those stated here.

NEC CORPORATION

www.nec.com

Industry Group Code: 334111 Ranks within this company's industry group: Sales: 6 Profits: 29

Hardware:		Software:		Telecommunications:		Electronic Publishing:		Equipment:		Specialty Services:	
Computers:	Y	Consumer:		Local:		Online Service:		Telecom:	Y	Consulting:	Y
Accessories:	Y	Corporate:	Y	Long Distance:		TV/Cable or Wireless:		Communication:	Y	Contract Manufacturing:	
Network Equipment:	Y	Telecom:		Cellular:	Y	Games:		Distribution:		Processing:	
Chips/Circuits:	Y	Internet:		Internet Service:	Y	Financial Data:		VAR/Reseller:		Staff/Outsourcing:	Y
Parts/Drives:								Satellite Srv./Equip.:	Y	Specialty Services:	

TYPES OF BUSINESS:

Computer Hardware Manufacturing
Lithium-Ion Batteries
Servers & Supercomputers
Telecommunications & Wireless Equipment
Nanotube Research
Broadband & Networking Equipment
Operating Systems & Application Software
Cloud Computing

BRANDS/DIVISIONS/AFFILIATES:

BIGLOBE
TeleScouter
NEC Energy Devices, Ltd.
NEC CASIO Mobile Communications, Ltd.
NEC China Co., Ltd.

CONTACTS: Note: Officers with more than one job title may be intentionally listed here more than once.

Nobuhiro Endo, Pres.
Toshimitsu Iwanami, Sr. Exec. VP
Yukihiro Fujiyoshi, Sr. Exec. VP
Takao Ono, Exec. VP
Junji Yasui, Exec. VP
Kaoru Yano, Chmn.

Phone: 81-3-3454-1111	Fax: 81-3-3798-1510
Toll-Free: 800-268-3997	
Address: 7-1, Shiba 5-Chome, Minato-ku, Tokyo, 108-8001 Japan	

GROWTH PLANS/SPECIAL FEATURES:

NEC Corporation is a leading provider of Internet, broadband network and enterprise business solutions globally. The firm is divided into six business segments: IT services, platform, carrier network, social infrastructure, personal solutions and others. The IT services division will cover system integration, including construction and consulting; support services, such as maintenance; and outsourcing. The platform segment includes enterprise network systems, PC servers, mainframe computers, UNIX servers, supercomputers, storage products, professional workstations and computer software including operating systems, middleware and application software. The carrier network division provides network systems for communication service providers such as mobile communication systems and fixed-line communication systems. The social infrastructure unit offers broadcasting systems and video equipment; control systems; transportation systems; aerospace and defense systems; and fire and disaster prevention systems. The personal solutions business unit includes mobile handsets; PCs; personal communication equipment; BIGLOBE Internet services, a leading Internet service provider in Tokyo; monitors; and LCD projectors. The others segment includes certain miscellaneous businesses which include the production of lithium batteries, capacitors, LCD panels and lighting equipment. Notable products include the TeleScouter, a wearable computer terminal with spectacle-type retinal imaging displays, marketed as a business support system. Users of the TeleScouter can send and receive audio and video, access documents using wireless network connections, and view them through image projection technologies developed by Brother Industries that display virtual images on top of real objects. In February 2010, the company established NEC Energy Devices, Ltd., which specializes on the production of high-capacity laminate lithium-ion batteries. In June 2010, it completed the integration of its mobile terminal business with those of Casio Computer Co., Ltd. and Hitachi Ltd., formally establishing the joint venture NEC CASIO Mobile Communications, Ltd. In August 2010, the firm's subsidiary, NEC China Co., entered a joint venture agreement with Neusoft Corp. to develop cloud computing services in China.

FINANCIALS: Sales and profits are in thousands of dollars—add 000 to get the full amount. 2010 Note: Financial information for 2010 was not available for all companies at press time.

2010 Sales: $43,571,100	2010 Profits: $138,965	U.S. Stock Ticker: NIPNY
2009 Sales: $45,478,800	2009 Profits: $-3,200,280	Int'l Ticker: 6701 Int'l Exchange: Tokyo-TSE
2008 Sales: $46,171,500	2008 Profits: $226,800	Employees: 142,358
2007 Sales: $46,526,500	2007 Profits: $91,300	Fiscal Year Ends: 3/31
2006 Sales: $49,299,700	2006 Profits: $-100,600	Parent Company:

SALARIES/BENEFITS:

Pension Plan:	ESOP Stock Plan:	Profit Sharing:	Top Exec. Salary: $	Bonus: $
Savings Plan:	Stock Purch. Plan:		Second Exec. Salary: $	Bonus: $

OTHER THOUGHTS:

Apparent Women Officers or Directors:
Hot Spot for Advancement for Women/Minorities:

LOCATIONS: ("Y" = Yes)

West:	Southwest:	Midwest:	Southeast:	Northeast:	International:
Y	Y	Y		Y	Y

NETAPP INC

www.netapp.com

Industry Group Code: 334112 **Ranks within this company's industry group:** Sales: 5 Profits: 4

Hardware:		Software:		Telecommunications:	Electronic Publishing:	Equipment:	Specialty Services:
Computers:		Consumer:	Y	Local:	Online Service:	Telecom:	Consulting:
Accessories:	Y	Corporate:	Y	Long Distance:	TV/Cable or Wireless:	Communication:	Contract Manufacturing:
Network Equipment:	Y	Telecom:		Cellular:	Games:	Distribution:	Processing:
Chips/Circuits:		Internet:		Internet Service:	Financial Data:	VAR/Reseller:	Staff/Outsourcing:
Parts/Drives:	Y					Satellite Srv./Equip.:	Specialty Services:

TYPES OF BUSINESS:

Data Management Solutions
Storage Solutions
Data Protection Software Products
Data Protection Platform Products
Storage Security Products
Data Retention & Archive Software Products
Storage Management & Application Software
Management Tools

BRANDS/DIVISIONS/AFFILIATES:

Data ONTAP
Bycast, Inc.
NetCache
NetStore
NearStore
MetroCluster
FlexVol
DataFort

CONTACTS: *Note: Officers with more than one job title may be intentionally listed here more than once.*

Tom Georgens, CEO
Tom Georgens, Pres.
Steve Gomo, CFO/Exec. VP
Christine Heckart, Chief Mktg. Officer
Gwen McDonald, Exec. VP-Human Resources
Steve Kleiman, Chief Scientist/Sr. VP
Marina Levinson, CIO/Sr. VP
Brian Pawlowsku, CTO/Sr. VP
Manish Goel, Exec. VP-Product Oper.
Matthew Fawcett, General Counsel/Exec. VP/Sec.
Rob Salmon, Exec. VP-Field Oper.
Vic Mahadevan, Chief Strategy Officer
Tara Dhillon, VP-Investor Rel.
Eric Mann, Sr. VP-Americas Sales
Ed Deenihan, Exec. VP-Customer Advocacy
Tom Gerstenberger, Sr. VP-Bus. Oper.
Mark Jon Bluth, Sr. VP-Oper.
Dan Warmenhoven, Chmn.
Andreas Konig, Sr. VP/Gen. Mgr.-EMEA

Phone: 408-822-6000	Fax: 408-822-4501
Toll-Free: 877-263-8277	
Address: 495 E. Java Dr., Sunnyvale, CA 94089 US	

GROWTH PLANS/SPECIAL FEATURES:

NetApp, Inc. is a provider of storage and data management products. Its products include data management software; storage management and integration software; fabric-attached storage (FAS) products; V-Series products; virtual tape library (VTL) Data Protection Systems; data protection software products; data retention and archive products; storage security products; and the NetApp Performance Acceleration Module (PAM). The FAS and V-Series storage product lines are based on Data ONTAP, an optimized, scalable and flexible operating system that supports any mix of storage area network (SAN), network-attached storage (NAS) and Internet protocol SAN (IP SAN) environments concurrently in UNIX, Linux, Windows and Web environments. NetApp data management software includes FlexVol, FlexClone, Deduplication, FlexShare, FlexCache and MultiStore technology designed to enhance the efficiency of storage architecture. The company's storage management and application integration software is divided into four suites of products targeted to different IT administrative roles: Storage Suite, Server Suite, Database Suite and Application Suite. VTL Data Protection Systems is a disk-to-disk backup application that can be used by any heterogeneous primary storage environment. The company's data protection products include business continuance and disk backup solutions for enterprise customers including MetroCluster, SnapMirror, SyncMirror, SnapRestore, and SnapVault brands. Its data retention and archive products are designed to meet regulatory demands faced by enterprises and are marketed under the SnapLock brand name. Storage security products consist of the DataFort security appliance, which combines wire-speed encryption, access controls, authentication and automated key management tools. The PAM is designed to enhance the performance of random read intensive workloads such as file services and messaging. In May 2010, the company acquired Bycast, Inc., which specializes in mass data storage.

The firm offers its employees medical, dental and vision coverage; short- and long-term disability; a 401(k) plan; an employee stock purchase program; flexible spending accounts; an employee assistance program; and tuition reimbursement.

FINANCIALS: Sales and profits are in thousands of dollars—add 000 to get the full amount. 2010 Note: Financial information for 2010 was not available for all companies at press time.

2010 Sales: $3,931,400	2010 Profits: $400,400	**U.S. Stock Ticker:** NTAP
2009 Sales: $3,406,393	2009 Profits: $64,600	**Int'l Ticker:** Int'l Exchange:
2008 Sales: $3,303,167	2008 Profits: $309,738	**Employees:** 8,333
2007 Sales: $2,804,282	2007 Profits: $297,735	**Fiscal Year Ends:** 4/30
2006 Sales: $2,066,456	2006 Profits: $266,452	**Parent Company:**

SALARIES/BENEFITS:

Pension Plan:	ESOP Stock Plan:	Profit Sharing:	Top Exec. Salary: $754,038	Bonus: $2,001,750
Savings Plan: Y	Stock Purch. Plan: Y		Second Exec. Salary: $599,999	Bonus: $1,467,692

OTHER THOUGHTS:

Apparent Women Officers or Directors: 3
Hot Spot for Advancement for Women/Minorities: Y

LOCATIONS: ("Y" = Yes)

West:	Southwest:	Midwest:	Southeast:	Northeast:	International:
Y				Y	Y

NETGEAR INC

www.netgear.com

Industry Group Code: 33411 Ranks within this company's industry group: Sales: 4 Profits: 8

Hardware:	Software:	Telecommunications:	Electronic Publishing:	Equipment:	Specialty Services:
Computers:	Consumer:	Local:	Online Service:	Telecom:	Consulting:
Accessories:	Corporate:	Long Distance:	TV/Cable or Wireless:	Communication:	Contract Manufacturing:
Network Equipment:	Telecom:	Cellular:	Games:	Distribution:	Processing:
Chips/Circuits: Y	Internet:	Internet Service:	Financial Data:	VAR/Reseller:	Staff/Outsourcing:
Parts/Drives: Y				Satellite Srv./Equip.:	Specialty Services:

TYPES OF BUSINESS:

Networking Equipment
Wireless Networking Products
Broadband Products
Entertainment Management Software
Security Products
Wi-Fi Phones

BRANDS/DIVISIONS/AFFILIATES:

CONTACTS: Note: Officers with more than one job title may be intentionally listed here more than once.

Patrick C.S. Lo, CEO
Christine M. Gorjanc, CFO
Michael Werdann, VP-Americas Sales
Tamesa Rogers, VP-Human Resources
Mark Merrill, CTO
Charles T. Olson, Sr. VP-Eng.
Andrew Kim, General Counsel/Corp. Sec.
Michael Falcon, Sr. VP-Oper.
Andrew Kim, VP-Corp. Dev.
Patrick C.S. Lo, Chmn.
David Soares, Sr. VP-Worldwide Sales & SMB Business

Phone: 408-907-8000	Fax: 408-907-8097
Toll-Free: 888-638-4327	
Address: 350 E. Plumeria Dr., San Jose, CA 95134-1911 US	

GROWTH PLANS/SPECIAL FEATURES:

NETGEAR, Inc. designs, develops and markets networking products for home users and small businesses, defined as fewer than 250 employees. NETGEAR has offices in California in the U.S. and 23 other countries around the world. The firm's products allow users to share Internet access, peripherals, files, digital multimedia content and applications among multiple networked devices and other Internet-enabled devices. NETGEAR's products are grouped into three major lines: Ethernet networking products, broadband access products and network connectivity products. Ethernet products include switches, network interface cards, adapters and bridges and Internet Security Appliances; broadband products include routers, gateways, IP telephony products and products that include an integrated wireless access point, such as a wireless gateway; and networking connectivity products include wireless access points, wireless network interface cards, network attached storage, media adapters and powerline adapters and bridges. NETGEAR sells its products through multiple sales channels worldwide, including traditional retailers, online retailers, direct market resellers, value-added resellers and broadband service providers. International sales make up the majority of the company's net revenue, contributing 54% in 2009. Two of its significant customers include Ingram Micro, Inc. and Best Buy Co., Inc. In January 2010, NETGEAR unveiled a new line of routers that utilize 3G, 4G and WiMAX connections.

FINANCIALS: Sales and profits are in thousands of dollars—add 000 to get the full amount. 2010 Note: Financial information for 2010 was not available for all companies at press time.

2010 Sales: $	2010 Profits: $	U.S. Stock Ticker: NTGR
2009 Sales: $686,595	2009 Profits: $9,333	Int'l Ticker: Int'l Exchange:
2008 Sales: $743,344	2008 Profits: $17,719	Employees: 586
2007 Sales: $727,787	2007 Profits: $45,954	Fiscal Year Ends: 12/31
2006 Sales: $573,570	2006 Profits: $41,132	Parent Company:

SALARIES/BENEFITS:

Pension Plan:	ESOP Stock Plan:	Profit Sharing:	Top Exec. Salary: $567,693	Bonus: $55,000
Savings Plan:	Stock Purch. Plan:		Second Exec. Salary: $302,769	Bonus: $29,333

OTHER THOUGHTS:

Apparent Women Officers or Directors: 4
Hot Spot for Advancement for Women/Minorities: Y

LOCATIONS: ("Y" = Yes)

West:	Southwest:	Midwest:	Southeast:	Northeast:	International:
Y					Y

NETSCOUT SYSTEMS INC

www.netscout.com

Industry Group Code: 511210B Ranks within this company's industry group: Sales: 5 Profits: 4

Hardware:	Software:		Telecommunications:	Electronic Publishing:	Equipment:	Specialty Services:
Computers:	Consumer:		Local:	Online Service:	Telecom:	Consulting:
Accessories:	Corporate:	Y	Long Distance:	TV/Cable or Wireless:	Communication:	Contract Manufacturing:
Network Equipment:	Telecom:		Cellular:	Games:	Distribution:	Processing:
Chips/Circuits:	Internet:		Internet Service:	Financial Data:	VAR/Reseller:	Staff/Outsourcing:
Parts/Drives:					Satellite Srv./Equip.:	Specialty Services:

TYPES OF BUSINESS:

Performance Management Systems
Application Management Solutions

BRANDS/DIVISIONS/AFFILIATES:

nGenius
nGenius Service Assurance Solution
nGenius Analytics
nGenius K2
Sniffer

CONTACTS: Note: Officers with more than one job title may be intentionally listed here more than once.

Anil K. Singhal, CEO
Michael Szabados, COO
Anil K. Singhal, Pres.
David Sommers, CFO/Treas.
Steven Shalita, VP-Mktg.
Victor Becker, VP-Human Resources
Ashwani Singhal, Sr. VP-R&D
Ken Boyd, CIO/Sr. VP-Svcs.
Bruce Kelley, Jr., CTO/VP
Tracy Steele, VP-Mfg. & Bus. Oper.
David Sommers, Corp. Sec.
David Sommers, Sr. VP-Gen. Oper.
Bruce Sweet, VP-Bus. Dev.
Stephanie Xavier, Sr. Mgr.-Public Rel.
Jeff Wakely, VP-Finance/Chief Acct. Officer
Anil K. Singhal, Chmn.
John Downing, Sr. VP-Worldwide Sales Oper.

Phone: 978-614-4000	Fax: 978-614-4004
Toll-Free: 800-357-7666	
Address: 310 Littleton Rd., Westford, MA 01886-4105 US	

GROWTH PLANS/SPECIAL FEATURES:

NetScout Systems, Inc. designs, develops, manufactures, markets, sells and supports a family of products that assures the performance and availability of critical business applications and services in complex, high-speed networks. The company manufactures and markets these products as an integrated hardware and software solution that is used by enterprises, governmental agencies and service providers worldwide. The firm's nGenius Service Assurance Solution software product is a multi-function performance management solution implemented in a single, integrated application that monitors and reports on network, service and application traffic; troubleshoots performance problems; and provides precise information for capacity planning. It integrates real-time and historical information in a single management application. The system collects data from nGenius Probes, routers, switches and other flow-based information sources, such as NetFlow, and provides in-depth system-wide views of all applications on the network infrastructure. Other nGenius products include nGenius Performance Manager, which analyzes and correlates the meta-data delivered by an array of intelligent data sources; nGenius Analytics, one of the first intelligent early warning systems in the performance management marketplace; and nGenius K2, which principally offers IT professionals an at-a-glance overview of their network's health and overall performance. NetScout's Sniffer line of products offer more efficient troubleshooting and advanced network analysis. The firm sells its products to corporations, government agencies, other non-profit entities and other organizations with large- and medium-sized high-speed computer networks. The company's products have been sold to customers operating in industries such as financial services, technology, telecommunications, manufacturing, service provider, healthcare and retail.

FINANCIALS: Sales and profits are in thousands of dollars—add 000 to get the full amount. 2010 Note: Financial information for 2010 was not available for all companies at press time.

2010 Sales: $260,342	2010 Profits: $27,917	**U.S. Stock Ticker: NTCT**
2009 Sales: $267,604	2009 Profits: $20,048	**Int'l Ticker:** Int'l Exchange:
2008 Sales: $168,956	2008 Profits: $-2,088	Employees: 791
2007 Sales: $102,472	2007 Profits: $7,737	Fiscal Year Ends: 3/31
2006 Sales: $97,876	2006 Profits: $5,797	Parent Company:

SALARIES/BENEFITS:

Pension Plan:	ESOP Stock Plan:	Profit Sharing:	Top Exec. Salary: $318,747	Bonus: $750,000
Savings Plan:	Stock Purch. Plan:		Second Exec. Salary: $268,747	Bonus: $313,000

OTHER THOUGHTS:

Apparent Women Officers or Directors:
Hot Spot for Advancement for Women/Minorities:

LOCATIONS: ("Y" = Yes)

West:	Southwest:	Midwest:	Southeast:	Northeast:	International:
Y	Y			Y	Y

Note: Financial information, benefits and other data can change quickly and may vary from those stated here.

NETSUITE INC

www.netsuite.com

Industry Group Code: 511210H Ranks within this company's industry group: Sales: 15 Profits: 14

Hardware:		Software:		Telecommunications:		Electronic Publishing:		Equipment:		Specialty Services:	
Computers:		Consumer:		Local:		Online Service:		Telecom:		Consulting:	
Accessories:		Corporate:	Y	Long Distance:		TV/Cable or Wireless:		Communication:		Contract Manufacturing:	
Network Equipment:		Telecom:		Cellular:		Games:		Distribution:		Processing:	
Chips/Circuits:		Internet:		Internet Service:		Financial Data:		VAR/Reseller:		Staff/Outsourcing:	
Parts/Drives:								Satellite Srv./Equip.:		Specialty Services:	Y

TYPES OF BUSINESS:

Business Management Application Suites
Enterprise Resource Planning
Customer Relationship Management
E-Commerce Capabilities

BRANDS/DIVISIONS/AFFILIATES:

NetSuite
NetSuite CRM+
NetSuite OneWorld
OpenAir, Inc.
QuickArrow, Inc.

CONTACTS: *Note: Officers with more than one job title may be intentionally listed here more than once.*

Zach Nelson, CEO
Jim McGeever, COO
Zach Nelson, Pres.
Ron Gill, CFO
David Downing, Chief Mktg. Officer
Evan Goldberg, CTO
Gary Wiessinger, VP-Prod. Mgmt.
Douglas P. Solomon, General Counsel/Sr. VP/Corp. Sec.
Mei Li, Sr. VP-Corp. Comm.
Tim Dilley, Exec. VP-Worldwide Svcs./Chief Customer Officer
Evan Goldberg, Chmn.
James Ramsey, Sr. VP-Worldwide Sales & Dist.

Phone: 650-627-1000	Fax: 650-627-1001
Toll-Free:	
Address: 2955 Campus Dr., Ste. 100, San Mateo, CA 94403-2511 US	

GROWTH PLANS/SPECIAL FEATURES:

NetSuite, Inc. is a leading vendor of on-demand, integrated business management application suites for small and medium-sized businesses and large company divisions. It provides a suite of enterprise resource planning (ERP), customer relationship management (CRM) and e-commerce capabilities that enables customers to manage their back-office, front-office and web operations in a single application. The company's main offering is NetSuite, which is designed to provide the integrated core business management capabilities that most of its customers require. NetSuite, NetSuite CRM+ and NetSuite OneWorld are designed for use by most types of businesses. In addition, the firm offers industry-specific configurations for use by wholesale/distribution, services and software companies, as well as additional on-demand application modules that provide functionality for unique industry needs. All elements of the company's application suite share the same customer and transaction data, enabling cross-departmental business process automation and real-time monitoring of core business metrics. In addition, the integrated ERP, CRM and e-commerce capabilities provide users with real-time visibility and appropriate functionality through dashboards tailored to their particular job function and access rights. The firm delivers its suite over the Internet as a subscription service using the software-as-a-service (SaaS) model. NetSuite has customers in over 80 countries and derives roughly 20% of its revenues from sales outside of North America. Through its OpenAir and QuickArrow subsidiaries, the company offers professional services automation and project portfolio management services. In November 2010, NetSuite opened a cloud computing development center in the Czech Republic.

FINANCIALS: Sales and profits are in thousands of dollars—add 000 to get the full amount. 2010 Note: Financial information for 2010 was not available for all companies at press time.

2010 Sales: $	2010 Profits: $	**U.S. Stock Ticker: N**
2009 Sales: $165,540	2009 Profits: $-23,304	**Int'l Ticker:** Int'l Exchange:
2008 Sales: $152,476	2008 Profits: $-15,864	Employees:
2007 Sales: $108,541	2007 Profits: $-23,906	Fiscal Year Ends: 12/31
2006 Sales: $67,202	2006 Profits: $-35,722	Parent Company:

SALARIES/BENEFITS:

Pension Plan:	ESOP Stock Plan:	Profit Sharing:	Top Exec. Salary: $450,000	Bonus: $324,311
Savings Plan:	Stock Purch. Plan:		Second Exec. Salary: $375,000	Bonus: $140,647

OTHER THOUGHTS:

Apparent Women Officers or Directors: 3
Hot Spot for Advancement for Women/Minorities: Y

LOCATIONS: ("Y" = Yes)

West:	Southwest:	Midwest:	Southeast:	Northeast:	International:
Y	Y			Y	Y

NETWORK ENGINES INC

www.networkengines.com

Industry Group Code: 511210B Ranks within this company's industry group: Sales: 6 Profits: 6

Hardware:		Software:		Telecommunications:		Electronic Publishing:		Equipment:		Specialty Services:	
Computers:		Consumer:		Local:		Online Service:		Telecom:		Consulting:	
Accessories:		Corporate:	Y	Long Distance:		TV/Cable or Wireless:		Communication:		Contract Manufacturing:	
Network Equipment:	Y	Telecom:		Cellular:		Games:		Distribution:	Y	Processing:	
Chips/Circuits:		Internet:		Internet Service:		Financial Data:		VAR/Reseller:		Staff/Outsourcing:	
Parts/Drives:								Satellite Srv./Equip.:		Specialty Services:	Y

TYPES OF BUSINESS:

Server Applications
Storage & Security Software & Equipment
Supply Chain Services

BRANDS/DIVISIONS/AFFILIATES:

CONTACTS: Note: Officers with more than one job title may be intentionally listed here more than once.

Gregory A. Shortell, CEO
Gregory A. Shortell, Pres.
Doug Bryant, CFO
Rusty Cone, Sr. VP-Sales & Mktg.
Rich Graber, VP-Eng.
William O'Connell, VP-Mfg. Oper.
Doug Bryant, Sr. VP-Admin.
Rich Graber, Sr. VP-Oper.

Phone: 781-332-1000	Fax: 781-770-2000
Toll-Free:	
Address: 25 Dan Rd., Canton, MA 02021 US	

GROWTH PLANS/SPECIAL FEATURES:

Network Engines, Inc. (NEI) is a leading international developer, manufacturer and distributor of storage equipment, network security devices and services to original equipment manufacturers (OEM) and independent software vendors. The firm offers a comprehensive suite of services, including development, manufacturing, fulfillment and post-sale support. This enables customers to accelerate the time to market for their products, to optimize their server appliance solutions and in some cases enable them to utilize the company's infrastructure for fulfillment of server appliance solutions. The firm can fulfill orders from its software partners to their end-user base or to their channels. Network Engines produces equipment branded for its customers, who in turn resell the products to their own customers. Prominent clients include ArcSight, Inc.; Bradford Networks; Sepaton, Inc.; EMC Corporation; and Tektronix, Inc.

Employees are offered medical, dental, vision, life and disability insurance; and tuition reimbursement.

FINANCIALS: Sales and profits are in thousands of dollars—add 000 to get the full amount. 2010 Note: Financial information for 2010 was not available for all companies at press time.

2010 Sales: $221,620	2010 Profits: $1,529	U.S. Stock Ticker: NENG
2009 Sales: $148,722	2009 Profits: $-3,198	Int'l Ticker: Int'l Exchange:
2008 Sales: $197,495	2008 Profits: $-8,477	Employees: 226
2007 Sales: $119,627	2007 Profits: $2,502	Fiscal Year Ends: 9/30
2006 Sales: $118,696	2006 Profits: $-5,447	Parent Company:

SALARIES/BENEFITS:

Pension Plan:	ESOP Stock Plan:	Profit Sharing:	Top Exec. Salary: $375,000	Bonus: $
Savings Plan: Y	Stock Purch. Plan: Y		Second Exec. Salary: $331,886	Bonus: $

OTHER THOUGHTS:

Apparent Women Officers or Directors:
Hot Spot for Advancement for Women/Minorities:

LOCATIONS: ("Y" = Yes)

West:	Southwest:	Midwest:	Southeast:	Northeast:	International:
				Y	Y

NETWORK EQUIPMENT TECHNOLOGIES INC
www.net.com

Industry Group Code: 33411 Ranks within this company's industry group: Sales: 16 Profits: 15

Hardware:		Software:		Telecommunications:		Electronic Publishing:		Equipment:		Specialty Services:	
Computers:		Consumer:		Local:		Online Service:		Telecom:	Y	Consulting:	
Accessories:		Corporate:	Y	Long Distance:		TV/Cable or Wireless:		Communication:	Y	Contract Manufacturing:	
Network Equipment:	Y	Telecom:		Cellular:		Games:		Distribution:		Processing:	
Chips/Circuits:		Internet:		Internet Service:		Financial Data:		VAR/Reseller:		Staff/Outsourcing:	
Parts/Drives:								Satellite Srv./Equip.:		Specialty Services:	

TYPES OF BUSINESS:
Networking Systems-WAN Connectivity
VoIP Management Devices
Routers & Switching Modules

BRANDS/DIVISIONS/AFFILIATES:
Quintum Technologies LLC
Promina
VX Series
NX Series
netMS

CONTACTS: Note: Officers with more than one job title may be intentionally listed here more than once.
C. Nicholas Keating, Jr., CEO
C. Nicholas Keating, Jr., Pres.
David Wagenseller, CFO
Francois Le, VP-Global Sales
Caroline Strickler, VP-Human Resources
Talbot Harty, Chief Dev. Officer/VP
Talbot Harty, CIO/VP
John Fossett, VP-Mfg. Oper.
Frank Slattery, General Counsel/VP
Pete Patel, VP-Global Oper.
Matther Krueger, VP-Bus. Dev. & Corp. Mktg.
David Wagenseller, VP-Finance
James Fitzpatrick, VP/Pres., NET Federal
John P. Winters, VP-Federal Sales
Dixon R. Doll, Chmn.

Phone: 510-713-7300	Fax: 510-574-4000
Toll-Free: 800-234-4638	
Address: 6900 Paseo Padre Pkwy., Fremont, CA 94555 US	

GROWTH PLANS/SPECIAL FEATURES:
Network Equipment Technologies, Inc. (NET) develops and sells voice and data networking products and services. Its technology enables clients to integrate and migrate their existing networks to secure Internet protocol (IP) based networks, unify their communications platforms and secure their voice applications and high-speed multiservice wide area network (WAN). The company's voice applications include the VX series and the Quintum series of switching media gateways, offered through subsidiary Quintum Technologies, LLC. The VX series provides a voice over Internet protocol (VoIP)-based secure system for the U.S. Government. The VX product line consists of the VX1800, VX1200, VX900, VX900T and the VX400. The Quintum Series provides VoIP gateway technologies for small to mid-sized businesses. Multiservice products include the Promina, NX1000 and NX5010 platforms. The Promina product line consists of multi-service access platforms for managing voice, data, image and video traffic in a single network. These products are tailored to circuit-switched networks and provide support for a variety of communications applications and traffic types, including asynchronous transfer mode (ATM), frame relay, IP and ISDN signaling. The NX1000, an extension of the Promina product line, facilitates the migration of legacy traffic to IP. It also offers high-speed data interfaces, diskless data storage and an atomic clock module for synchronous applications over IP. The NX5000 Series of networking platforms provide data transfer between storage area networks (SANs) and WANs and secure grid computing. The firm also developed netMS, a management software application for its devices. NET divides its markets into two groups: government (accounting for 79% of 2010 revenue), serving U.S. defense and intelligence agencies, civilian agencies and international organizations; and enterprise (21%), which includes clients in the financial services, manufacturing, transportation and retail sectors.

Employees are offered medical, dental and vision insurance; a 401(k) plan; business travel insurance; short-and long-term disability; an employee assistance program; and credit union membership.

FINANCIALS: Sales and profits are in thousands of dollars—add 000 to get the full amount. 2010 Note: Financial information for 2010 was not available for all companies at press time.

2010 Sales: $74,494	2010 Profits: $-17,843	U.S. Stock Ticker: NWK
2009 Sales: $65,788	2009 Profits: $-53,503	Int'l Ticker: Int'l Exchange:
2008 Sales: $116,144	2008 Profits: $7,145	Employees: 247
2007 Sales: $84,094	2007 Profits: $-16,194	Fiscal Year Ends: 3/31
2006 Sales: $69,768	2006 Profits: $-27,235	Parent Company:

SALARIES/BENEFITS:
Pension Plan:	ESOP Stock Plan:	Profit Sharing:	Top Exec. Salary: $352,750	Bonus: $
Savings Plan: Y	Stock Purch. Plan:		Second Exec. Salary: $256,442	Bonus: $

OTHER THOUGHTS:
Apparent Women Officers or Directors:
Hot Spot for Advancement for Women/Minorities:

LOCATIONS: ("Y" = Yes)
West:	Southwest:	Midwest:	Southeast:	Northeast:	International:
Y		Y		Y	Y

NEXPRISE INC

www.nexprise.com

Industry Group Code: 511210I Ranks within this company's industry group: Sales: Profits:

Hardware:	Software:		Telecommunications:	Electronic Publishing:	Equipment:	Specialty Services:
Computers:	Consumer:		Local:	Online Service:	Telecom:	Consulting:
Accessories:	Corporate:	Y	Long Distance:	TV/Cable or Wireless:	Communication:	Contract Manufacturing:
Network Equipment:	Telecom:		Cellular:	Games:	Distribution:	Processing:
Chips/Circuits:	Internet:		Internet Service:	Financial Data:	VAR/Reseller:	Staff/Outsourcing:
Parts/Drives:					Satellite Srv./Equip.:	Specialty Services:

TYPES OF BUSINESS:

Software-Business Process Automation
Document & Project Management Software
Action Item Management Software

BRANDS/DIVISIONS/AFFILIATES:

WebSpace
WebSpace Project Manager
WebSpace Business Process Automation
WebSpace Document Manager
WebSpace Action Item Manager

CONTACTS: Note: Officers with more than one job title may be intentionally listed here more than once.

Ted Drysdale, CEO
Ted Drysdale, Pres.
John Lynch, Sr. VP-Sales & Service
Ted Drysdale, Chmn.

Phone: 760-804-1333	Fax: 760-804-1331
Toll-Free:	
Address: 5963 La Place Ct., Ste. 302, Carlsbad, CA 92008 US	

GROWTH PLANS/SPECIAL FEATURES:

NexPrise, Inc. develops and markets software that automates key business processes for manufacturers. The firm provides its products to customers in the automotive, aerospace, high tech manufacturing, education and medical device manufacturing industries. The NexPrise platform comprises over 25,000 users worldwide. The company's software platform covers four major lines of service: document management, project management, business process automation and action item management. NexPrise also offers collaboration services that help to organize total company or individual project data into one source for easy employee access and cooperation. NexPrise's solutions are all delivered through its WebSpace platform. Document management services, which are web-based, include archiving, querying, retrieval, access monitoring and version control. Project management, also web-based, helps business segments to track participants in their work, monitor task implementation and constantly update important information. In addition, NexPrise assists project management through a graphical interface that allows electronic mimicry of all company operations. The company's WebSpace business process automation solution provides the capability to streamline business processes, automating the collection of data and documents inside or across firewalls via workflow-driven Web forms. The WebSpace Platform also includes an Action Item Manager component designed to help manage activities across a geographically dispersed project team including suppliers, partners and/or offsite employees. WebSpace Action Items systematically collect and approve documents and other electronic deliverables related to a project, event or other activity. Some of the company's corporate clients include Novo Nordisk, Lockheed Martin, Subaru, Concept Rocket and Trelleborg.

The firm offers employees paid time off; stock options; and life, medical, dental and vision insurance.

FINANCIALS: Sales and profits are in thousands of dollars—add 000 to get the full amount. 2010 Note: Financial information for 2010 was not available for all companies at press time.

2010 Sales: $	2010 Profits: $	**U.S. Stock Ticker:** Private
2009 Sales: $	2009 Profits: $	**Int'l Ticker:** Int'l Exchange:
2008 Sales: $	2008 Profits: $	Employees:
2007 Sales: $	2007 Profits: $	Fiscal Year Ends: 12/31
2006 Sales: $	2006 Profits: $	Parent Company:

SALARIES/BENEFITS:

Pension Plan:	ESOP Stock Plan:	Profit Sharing:	Top Exec. Salary: $	Bonus: $71,000
Savings Plan: Y	Stock Purch. Plan:		Second Exec. Salary: $	Bonus: $

OTHER THOUGHTS:

Apparent Women Officers or Directors:
Hot Spot for Advancement for Women/Minorities:

LOCATIONS: ("Y" = Yes)

West:	Southwest:	Midwest:	Southeast:	Northeast:	International:
Y					

NIDEC CORPORATION

www.nidec.co.jp

Industry Group Code: 334112 Ranks within this company's industry group: Sales: 4 Profits: 3

Hardware:	Software:	Telecommunications:	Electronic Publishing:	Equipment:	Specialty Services:
Computers:	Consumer:	Local:	Online Service:	Telecom:	Consulting:
Accessories:	Corporate:	Long Distance:	TV/Cable or Wireless:	Communication:	Contract Manufacturing: Y
Network Equipment:	Telecom:	Cellular:	Games:	Distribution:	Processing:
Chips/Circuits: Y	Internet:	Internet Service:	Financial Data:	VAR/Reseller:	Staff/Outsourcing:
Parts/Drives: Y				Satellite Srv./Equip.:	Specialty Services:

TYPES OF BUSINESS:

Motor Manufacturing
Brushless DC Motors
Brushless DC Fans
Camera Shutters
Hard Drive Pivot Assemblies
Card Readers

BRANDS/DIVISIONS/AFFILIATES:

Nidec Brilliant Co Ltd
Sanyo Seimitsu Co., Ltd.
SC WADO Co., Ltd.
Nidec (Shaoguan) Limited
Sole Motors
SC WADO Co., Ltd.

CONTACTS: *Note: Officers with more than one job title may be intentionally listed here more than once.*

Shigenobu Nagamori, CEO
Hiroshi Kobe, COO/Exec. VP
Shigenobu Nagamori, Pres.
Masuo Yoshimatsu, CFO/Exec. VP
Takeaki Ishii, Dir.-Human Resources
Tsuyoshi Takahashi, Dir.-Central Dev. Tech. Research Institute
Toshinari Sato, CIO
Juntaro Fujii, Exec. VP-Corp. Strategy
Takuto Yasui, Dir.-Acct.
Kenji Sawamura, Exec. VP
Yasunobu Toriyama, Exec. VP
Yasuo Hamaguchi, Sr. VP
Tadaaki Hamada, Sr. VP/Dir.-Bus. Planning
Shigenobu Nagamori, Chmn.

Phone: 81-75-935-6140	Fax:
Toll-Free:	
Address: 338 Tonoshiro-cho, Kuze Minami-ku, Kyoto, 601-8205 Japan	

GROWTH PLANS/SPECIAL FEATURES:

Nidec Corporation, based in Japan, is a manufacturer of electric motors and related components, with a focus on brushless DC (Direct Current) motors. Brushless DC motors are a type of electric motor that use electronically controlled commutation systems, rather than mechanical commutation systems, which provide higher efficiency, longer operating life and higher dynamic response characteristics. The firm operates in five business groups, based on product type. Small precision motors include brushless DC motors for hard disk drives and laser printers; brushless DC fans for game machine consoles, personal computers and automobiles; and other small precision motors for mobile phones and DVD recorders. Mid-size motors include automotive motors for power steering systems and other applications; home appliances motors for air conditioners, washing machines and refrigerators; and industrial motors for machine tools and water heater systems. Machinery products include transfer robots (for LCD panels), card readers and power transmission systems. Electronic and optical components include shutters and lens units for digital cameras; precision plastic moldings; and plastic metal casings. The firm's other offerings include pivot assemblies for hard disk drives, control valves for automotive transmissions and logistics services. Nidec maintains 141 subsidiaries in 19 countries. Some of the firm's most recent international initiatives include the expansion of its China operations through the establishment of five new sales offices and the launch of manufacturing subsidiary Nidec (Shaoguan) Limited. Other recent company activities include the acquisition of Sole Motors, a manufacturer of motors for home appliances; the household appliances business of Appliances Components Companies S.p.A.; SC WADO Co., Ltd., a manufacturer of base plates; and the motors and controls business of Emerson Electric Co. In December 2010, Nidec agreed to acquire Sanyo Seimitsu Co., Ltd., a small precision motor manufacturer; and announced the establishment of a sales subsidiary in India, SC WADO Co., Ltd.

FINANCIALS: Sales and profits are in thousands of dollars—add 000 to get the full amount. 2010 Note: Financial information for 2010 was not available for all companies at press time.

2010 Sales: $6,314,048	2010 Profits: $558,480	**U.S. Stock Ticker: NJ**	
2009 Sales: $6,245,119	2009 Profits: $288,639	**Int'l Ticker:** Int'l Exchange:	
2008 Sales: $7,407,186	2008 Profits: $410,780	Employees: 96,482	
2007 Sales: $5,333,901	2007 Profits: $338,263	Fiscal Year Ends: 3/31	
2006 Sales: $4,570,171	2006 Profits: $348,591	Parent Company:	

SALARIES/BENEFITS:

Pension Plan:	ESOP Stock Plan:	Profit Sharing:	Top Exec. Salary: $	Bonus: $
Savings Plan:	Stock Purch. Plan:		Second Exec. Salary: $	Bonus: $

OTHER THOUGHTS:

Apparent Women Officers or Directors:
Hot Spot for Advancement for Women/Minorities:

LOCATIONS: ("Y" = Yes)

West:	Southwest:	Midwest:	Southeast:	Northeast:	International:
Y	Y	Y		Y	Y

NINTENDO CO LTD

www.nintendo.com

Industry Group Code: 334111 Ranks within this company's industry group: Sales: 8 Profits: 3

Hardware:	Software:		Telecommunications:	Electronic Publishing:		Equipment:	Specialty Services:
Computers:	Consumer:	Y	Local:	Online Service:		Telecom:	Consulting:
Accessories:	Corporate:		Long Distance:	TV/Cable or Wireless:		Communication:	Contract Manufacturing:
Network Equipment:	Telecom:		Cellular:	Games:	Y	Distribution:	Processing:
Chips/Circuits:	Internet:		Internet Service:	Financial Data:		VAR/Reseller:	Staff/Outsourcing:
Parts/Drives:						Satellite Srv./Equip.:	Specialty Services:

TYPES OF BUSINESS:

Video Games
Video Game Hardware & Software

BRANDS/DIVISIONS/AFFILIATES:

Nintendo DS
Nintendo DSi
Nintendo 3DS
Wii
Mario Brothers
Legend of Zelda (The)
Donkey Kong
Pokemon

CONTACTS:
Note: Officers with more than one job title may be intentionally listed here more than once.
Satoru Iwata, CEO
Yoshihiro Mori, Chief Dir.-Oper.
Satoru Iwata, Pres.
Masaharu Matsumoto, Chief Dir.-Finance
Shinji Hatano, Chief Dir.-Sales
Kaoru Takemura, Chief Dir.-Human Resources
Shigeru Miramoto, Chief Dir.-Info. Dev.
Nobuo Nagai, Chief Dir.-Mfg.
Kazuo Kawahara, Dir.-Admin.
Genyo Takeda, Chief Dir.-Gen. Dev.
Genyo Takeda, Chief Dir.-Total Dev.
Reginald Fils-Aime, COO/Pres., Nintendo of America, Inc.

Phone: 81-75-662-9600	Fax: 81-75-662-9601
Toll-Free:	
Address: 11-1 Kamitoba, Hokotate-cho, Minami-ku, Kyoto, 601-8116 Japan	

GROWTH PLANS/SPECIAL FEATURES:

Nintendo Co., Ltd. makes video game hardware and software, including the well-known video game titles Mario Brothers, Donkey Kong, Pokemon and The Legend of Zelda. Based in Kyoto, Japan, Nintendo owns subsidiaries in the U.S., Canada, Korea, Australia and several European countries, with overseas sales accounting for 84.1% of 2010 sales. Its main products are the video game systems and related software and merchandise for the Nintendo DS and DS Lite, which have sold approximately 128.9 million units cumulatively since it was introduced; with the Wii accounting for 70.9 million sales-to-date. Nintendo has recently increased focus on selling the DS line of portable devices. While its predecessor the Game Boy Advance was essentially a portable version of home-based video consoles, the DS sports a dual-screen format, an LCD touch screen, wireless connectivity and voice recognition capabilities. Nintendo's newest console and successor to the GameCube, the Wii, features a unique motion-sensitive controller, resembling a TV remote, which allows for point-and-click-style game play. The company's latest products include the Wii system and the new Touch! Generations software line, which includes Nintendo DS titles such as Nintendogs, a virtual pet program, and Brain Age. The worldwide top selling games for the Wii include Wii Sports with 63.5 million pieces sold, Wii Play with 27.4 million pieces sold and Wii Fit with 22.6 Million pieces sold. The top sellers for the Nintendo DS include Nintendogs, Super Mario Bros. and Brain Age with 23.3, 22.5 and 18.7 million pieces sold, respectively. In June 2010, the firm announced the Nintendo 3DS, a portable gaming device offering a 3-D playing experience.

FINANCIALS:
Sales and profits are in thousands of dollars—add 000 to get the full amount. 2010 Note: Financial information for 2010 was not available for all companies at press time.

2010 Sales: $17,441,900	2010 Profits: $2,780,200	**U.S. Stock Ticker:** NTDOY
2009 Sales: $19,933,000	2009 Profits: $3,025,680	**Int'l Ticker:** 7974 **Int'l Exchange:** Tokyo-TSE
2008 Sales: $16,724,230	2008 Profits: $2,573,426	Employees:
2007 Sales: $8,183,173	2007 Profits: $1,477,038	Fiscal Year Ends: 3/31
2006 Sales: $4,327,100	2006 Profits: $836,600	Parent Company:

SALARIES/BENEFITS:

Pension Plan:	ESOP Stock Plan:	Profit Sharing:	Top Exec. Salary: $	Bonus: $
Savings Plan:	Stock Purch. Plan:		Second Exec. Salary: $	Bonus: $

OTHER THOUGHTS:

Apparent Women Officers or Directors:
Hot Spot for Advancement for Women/Minorities:

LOCATIONS: ("Y" = Yes)

West:	Southwest:	Midwest:	Southeast:	Northeast:	International:
Y					Y

Note: Financial information, benefits and other data can change quickly and may vary from those stated here.

NOKIA CORPORATION

www.nokia.com

Industry Group Code: 334220 Ranks within this company's industry group: Sales: 2 Profits: 3

Hardware:		Software:		Telecommunications:		Electronic Publishing:	Equipment:		Specialty Services:	
Computers:		Consumer:	Y	Local:		Online Service:	Telecom:	Y	Consulting:	
Accessories:	Y	Corporate:	Y	Long Distance:		TV/Cable or Wireless:	Communication:	Y	Contract Manufacturing:	
Network Equipment:		Telecom:	Y	Cellular:		Games:	Distribution:		Processing:	
Chips/Circuits:		Internet:		Internet Service:		Financial Data:	VAR/Reseller:		Staff/Outsourcing:	
Parts/Drives:							Satellite Srv./Equip.:		Specialty Services:	Y

TYPES OF BUSINESS:

Telecommunications Equipment-Cellular Telephones
Network Systems & Services
Internet Software & Services
Multimedia Equipment
Digital Music
Digital Map Information

BRANDS/DIVISIONS/AFFILIATES:

Bit-side GmbH
Cellity
Nokia Siemens Networks
Symbian Ltd.
Troltech
NAVTEQ Corporation
Plazes
OZ Communications, Inc.

CONTACTS: Note: Officers with more than one job title may be intentionally listed here more than once.

Stephen Elop, CEO
Timo Ihamuotila, CFO/Exec. VP
Anssi Vanjoki, Exec. VP-Mktg.
Juha Akras, Exec. VP-Human Resources
Mary McDowell, Chief Dev. Officer/Exec. VP
Esko Aho, Exec. VP-Corp. Rel. & Responsibility
Tero Ojanpera, Exec. VP-Svcs.
Richard A. Simonson, Exec. VP-Mobile Phones & Devices
Niklas Savander, Exec. VP-Svcs.
Alberto Torres, Exec. VP-Solutions
Jorma Ollila, Chmn.

Phone: 358-7-1800-8000	Fax: 358-7-1803-4003
Toll-Free:	
Address: Keilalahdentie 2-4, Espoo, FIN-02150 Finland	

GROWTH PLANS/SPECIAL FEATURES:

Nokia Corporation is a leading supplier of mobile devices, services and software for the converging Internet and communications industries. The company consists of three business segments: devices and services; NAVTEQ; and Nokia Siemens Networks. The devices and services segment is responsible for developing and managing the company's portfolio of mobile devices, as well as designing and developing services, applications and content. This segment also manages the firm's supply chains, sales channels, and brand and marketing activities for mobile devices, services and their combinations. The NAVTEQ segment provides digital map information and related location-based content and services for automotive navigation systems; mobile navigation devices; Internet-based mapping applications; and government and business solutions. Nokia Siemens Networks is a 50/50 joint venture between Nokia and Siemens, combining Nokia's networks business and Siemens' carrier-related operations. It offers mobile and fixed network infrastructure, communications and service platforms, as well as professional services, to operators and service providers. Nokia Siemens Networks operates in three units: Business Solutions; Global Services; and Network Systems. Nokia has 10 manufacturing facilities in Finland, China, South Korea, the U.K., Hungary, Romania, India, Brazil and Mexico. In December 2009, Nokia partnered with New Alliance, an investment company, to form Nokia Alliance Internet Services Company Limited, a 50/50 joint venture company that will offer mobile services in China and support the local developer ecosystem. In May 2010, Nokia and Yahoo! announced a worldwide strategic alliance to extend online services. As part of the alliance, Nokia will be the exclusive provider of Yahoo!'s maps and navigation services, and Yahoo! will become the exclusive provider of Nokia's Ovi Mail and Chat services.

The firm offers its employees mobile working and teleworking options; health insurance; sporting events; social activities; laundry services; day care; on-site concierge services; training programs; on-site fitness facilities; and stock purchase options.

FINANCIALS: Sales and profits are in thousands of dollars—add 000 to get the full amount. 2010 Note: Financial information for 2010 was not available for all companies at press time.

2010 Sales: $	2010 Profits: $	U.S. Stock Ticker: NOK
2009 Sales: $55,759,100	2009 Profits: $1,212,210	Int'l Ticker: NOK1V Int'l Exchange: Helsinki-Euronext
2008 Sales: $66,957,600	2008 Profits: $9,284,190	Employees:
2007 Sales: $74,560,000	2007 Profits: $11,660,000	Fiscal Year Ends: 12/31
2006 Sales: $54,267,000	2006 Profits: $5,642,000	Parent Company:

SALARIES/BENEFITS:

Pension Plan:	ESOP Stock Plan:	Profit Sharing:	Top Exec. Salary: $	Bonus: $
Savings Plan:	Stock Purch. Plan:		Second Exec. Salary: $	Bonus: $

OTHER THOUGHTS:

Apparent Women Officers or Directors: 4
Hot Spot for Advancement for Women/Minorities: Y

LOCATIONS: ("Y" = Yes)

West:	Southwest:	Midwest:	Southeast:	Northeast:	International:
Y	Y	Y	Y	Y	Y

NOVATEK MICROELECTRONICS CORP

www.novatek.com.tw

Industry Group Code: 33441 Ranks within this company's industry group: Sales: 31 Profits: 18

Hardware:		Software:	Telecommunications:	Electronic Publishing:	Equipment:	Specialty Services:
Computers:		Consumer:	Local:	Online Service:	Telecom:	Consulting:
Accessories:		Corporate:	Long Distance:	TV/Cable or Wireless:	Communication:	Contract Manufacturing:
Network Equipment:		Telecom:	Cellular:	Games:	Distribution:	Processing:
Chips/Circuits:	Y	Internet:	Internet Service:	Financial Data:	VAR/Reseller:	Staff/Outsourcing:
Parts/Drives:	Y				Satellite Srv./Equip.:	Specialty Services:

TYPES OF BUSINESS:

Manufacturing-Semiconductors
Integrated Circuits
Products Design
Research & Development

BRANDS/DIVISIONS/AFFILIATES:

UMC Commercial Product Division

CONTACTS: Note: Officers with more than one job title may be intentionally listed here more than once.

Steve Wang, Pres.
J. H. Wang, Sr. VP
Tommy Chen, VP
David Chen, VP
Jeff Hsu, VP
Tai-Shung Ho, Chmn.

Phone: 886-3-567-0889	Fax: 886-3-577-0132
Toll-Free:	
Address: 2F, No. 13, Innovation Rd I, Hsinchu Science Park, Hsinchu, 300 Taiwan	

GROWTH PLANS/SPECIAL FEATURES:

Novatek Microelectronics Corp., spun off from the UMC Commercial Product Division, is a fabless chip design company. Based in Taiwan, the firm specializes in the research and development, design, manufacturing, management and sale of integrated circuits (ICs) for corporations and electronics manufacturers. Novatek splits its products into four categories: flat panel display drivers (FPDD), which aim to have high performance, high speed, high resolution, low power consumption, low EMI and high integration capacity; video display, which specializes in System-on-Chip (SoC); digital imaging; and digital AV multimedia. Novatek offers three types of FPDDs: large-size panels for television or notebook computer applications; mid-size panels for audio and video applications; and small-size panels for mobile devices. The firm's video display line includes TFT Timing Controller, which supports a variety of panel resolutions and supports ASIC and standard T-Con; monitor controller chips for LCD monitors and CRT monitors; and the TV product line, which features a video decoder, de-interlace capabilities and ADC/PLL. Digital imaging products include multi-standard audio and video decoders, cell-phone camera modules, portable multimedia players, digital image stabilizers, low power SoC design and digital scaling technology. The company's digital AV multimedia offerings use SoC technology to provide designers with versatile products for DVD players, set-top boxes and integrated digital TV sets.

Novatek offers its employees health insurance; physical check-ups every two years; wedding and childbirth subsidies; meal allowances; life and AD&D insurance; store discounts; an employee assistance program; free movies; and scholarships for children.

FINANCIALS: Sales and profits are in thousands of dollars—add 000 to get the full amount. 2010 Note: Financial information for 2010 was not available for all companies at press time.

2010 Sales: $	2010 Profits: $	**U.S. Stock Ticker:**
2009 Sales: $930,200	2009 Profits: $138,380	**Int'l Ticker: 3034** Int'l Exchange: Taipei-TPE
2008 Sales: $820,400	2008 Profits: $110,690	Employees:
2007 Sales: $1,132,510	2007 Profits: $237,660	Fiscal Year Ends: 12/31
2006 Sales: $	2006 Profits: $	Parent Company:

SALARIES/BENEFITS:

Pension Plan: Y	ESOP Stock Plan:	Profit Sharing:	Top Exec. Salary: $	Bonus: $
Savings Plan:	Stock Purch. Plan: Y		Second Exec. Salary: $	Bonus: $

OTHER THOUGHTS:

Apparent Women Officers or Directors:
Hot Spot for Advancement for Women/Minorities:

LOCATIONS: ("Y" = Yes)

West:	Southwest:	Midwest:	Southeast:	Northeast:	International:
					Y

NOVELL INC
www.novell.com

Industry Group Code: 511210B Ranks within this company's industry group: Sales: 3 Profits: 9

Hardware:	Software:		Telecommunications:	Electronic Publishing:	Equipment:	Specialty Services:	
Computers:	Consumer:	Y	Local:	Online Service:	Telecom:	Consulting:	Y
Accessories:	Corporate:	Y	Long Distance:	TV/Cable or Wireless:	Communication:	Contract Manufacturing:	
Network Equipment:	Telecom:		Cellular:	Games:	Distribution:	Processing:	
Chips/Circuits:	Internet:		Internet Service:	Financial Data:	VAR/Reseller:	Staff/Outsourcing:	
Parts/Drives:					Satellite Srv./Equip.:	Specialty Services:	Y

TYPES OF BUSINESS:
Computer Software-Networking & Application
Operational Strategy Consulting Services
E-Business Consulting
Open Source Software
Linux Support & Maintenance
Management Consulting
Workload Management Software

BRANDS/DIVISIONS/AFFILIATES:
SUSE Linux Enterprise
Intelligent Workload Management
Attachmate Corporation
Novell Identity Manager
Tencent, Inc.
Open Enterprise Server
ZENworks 11
Attachmate Corporation

CONTACTS: Note: Officers with more than one job title may be intentionally listed here more than once.
Ronald W. Hovsepian, CEO
Ronald W. Hovsepian, Pres.
Dana C. Russell, CFO
John Dragoon, Chief Mktg. Officer/Sr. VP/Chief-Channel
Russell Poole, Sr. VP-Human Resources
Jose Almandoz, CIO
Scott Semel, General Counsel/Sr. VP/Sec.
Jose Almandoz, VP-Global Field Oper.
Roger Levy, Sr. VP-Strategic Dev.
Bill Smith, VP-Finance
Scott Lewis, VP-Partner Mktg. & Enablement
Colleen O'Keefe, Sr. VP-Collaboration Solutions & Global Svcs.
Javier Colado, Sr. VP-Global Sales
Maarten Koster, Pres., Novell Asia Pacific
Rich Crandall, Chmn.
Javier Colado, Pres., EMEA

Phone: 781-464-8000	Fax:
Toll-Free: 800-529-3400	
Address: 404 Wyman St., Ste. 500, Waltham, MA 02451 US	

GROWTH PLANS/SPECIAL FEATURES:
Novell, Inc. develops, sells and installs enterprise-quality software focused on the operating system and infrastructure software sectors of the IT industry. The firm operates through two recently reorganized business segments: Security, Management and Operating Platforms (SMOP); and Collaboration Solutions (CS). The SMOP segment develops Intelligent Workload Management (IWM) solutions for the optimization of computing resources across physical, virtual and cloud computing environments. This segment's solutions include open platform solutions, consisting of products based on the SUSE Linux Enterprise platform, a leading distribution system; identity and security management solutions, including Novell Identity Manager, a data-sharing and synchronization product, and Novell Sentinel, which monitors IT effectiveness; and system and resource management solutions, such as PlateSpin, a workload mobility and protection product, and Novell Cloud Manager, for the creation and management of cloud computing environments. Novell's CS business segment provides infrastructure, management and security solutions for collaboration across multiple devise. Its solutions include Open Enterprise Server, a suite of services that provides networking, communication, collaboration and application services; NetWare, its proprietary operating system platform; and the Novell GroupWise suite of collaboration products, which provide personal e-mail, calendar and contact management in an integrated environment. The firm also provides professional services, including discovery workshops, strategy projects and solution implementations; phone-based, web-based and onsite technical support; and training services. Recently introduced products include Novell File Management Suite, an integrated file storage system; and ZENworks 11, an endpoint security management solution. In May 2010, the company announced a strategic alliance with Vodacom Business to integrate Novell's IWM solutions with Vodacom's cloud hosting offerings. In July 2010, Novell and Tencent, Inc. launched a joint research laboratory in China for the development of an Internet data center cloud computing platform. In November 2010, the firm agreed to be acquired by investor group Attachmate Corporation for $2.2 billion.

FINANCIALS: Sales and profits are in thousands of dollars—add 000 to get the full amount. 2010 Note: Financial information for 2010 was not available for all companies at press time.

2010 Sales: $811,871	2010 Profits: $377,976	**U.S. Stock Ticker: NOVL**
2009 Sales: $862,185	2009 Profits: $-212,736	**Int'l Ticker:** Int'l Exchange:
2008 Sales: $956,513	2008 Profits: $-8,745	Employees: 3,400
2007 Sales: $932,499	2007 Profits: $-44,460	Fiscal Year Ends: 10/31
2006 Sales: $919,331	2006 Profits: $18,656	Parent Company:

SALARIES/BENEFITS:

Pension Plan:	ESOP Stock Plan:	Profit Sharing:	Top Exec. Salary: $925,036	Bonus: $1,280,000
Savings Plan:	Stock Purch. Plan:		Second Exec. Salary: $450,018	Bonus: $450,000

OTHER THOUGHTS:
Apparent Women Officers or Directors: 2
Hot Spot for Advancement for Women/Minorities: Y

LOCATIONS: ("Y" = Yes)

West:	Southwest:	Midwest:	Southeast:	Northeast:	International:
Y	Y	Y	Y	Y	Y

NOVELLUS SYSTEMS INC

www.novellus.com

Industry Group Code: 333295 Ranks within this company's industry group: Sales: 9   Profits: 8

Hardware:		Software:	Telecommunications:	Electronic Publishing:	Equipment:	Specialty Services:	
Computers:		Consumer:	Local:	Online Service:	Telecom:	Consulting:	
Accessories:		Corporate:	Long Distance:	TV/Cable or Wireless:	Communication:	Contract Manufacturing:	Y
Network Equipment:		Telecom:	Cellular:	Games:	Distribution:	Processing:	Y
Chips/Circuits:	Y	Internet:	Internet Service:	Financial Data:	VAR/Reseller:	Staff/Outsourcing:	
Parts/Drives:					Satellite Srv./Equip.:	Specialty Services:	Y

TYPES OF BUSINESS:

Machinery-Semiconductor Manufacturing
Chemical Mechanical Planarization Products
Research & Development
Chemical Vapor Deposition
Physical Vapor Deposition
Ultraviolet Thermal Processing

BRANDS/DIVISIONS/AFFILIATES:

Semiconductor Group
Industrial Applications Group
Peter Wolters AG
Voumard Machines Co SA
Micron Machine Tools, Inc.

CONTACTS: Note: Officers with more than one job title may be intentionally listed here more than once.

Richard S. Hill, CEO
Timothy M. Archer, COO
John Hertz, CFO/VP
Gino Addiego, Chief Admin. Officer
Andrew Gottlieb, General Counsel/VP
Fusen Chen, Exec. VP-Semiconductor Systems Products
Richard S. Hill, Chmn.

Phone: 408-943-9700	Fax: 408-943-3422
Toll-Free:	
Address: 4000 N. First St., San Jose, CA 95134 US	

GROWTH PLANS/SPECIAL FEATURES:

Novellus Systems, Inc. develops, manufactures, sells and supports equipment used in the fabrication of integrated circuits (ICs). The firm also develops, manufactures, sells and supports grinding, lapping and polishing equipment for a broad spectrum of industrial applications. Novellus operates in two segments, the semiconductor group and the industrial applications group. The semiconductor group manufactures thin film deposition and surface preparation used in the fabrication of ICs. It is a leading supplier of chemical vapor deposition (CVD), electrochemical deposition (ECD), physical vapor deposition (PVD) technologies. High-Density Plasma CVD (HDP-CVD) and Plasma-Enhanced CVD (PECVD) systems employ chemical plasma to deposit dielectric material within the gaps formed by the etching of aluminum, or as a blanket film which can be etched with patterns for depositing conductive materials. These products are used to deposit thin films of insulating and conductive materials that create the wiring on a chip. The firm's Industrial Applications Group (IAG) operates through subsidiaries Peter Wolters AG, Voumard Machines, Co. SA and Micron Machine Tools, Inc. IAG is a supplier of high-precision machines for grinding, deburring, lapping, honing and polishing the outer surfaces of parts made from metal, silicon, ceramic and plastic. Products include single-side machines, double-side machines and thru-feed grinding machines and deburring systems.

Employees are offered medical, dental and vision insurance; life insurance; an employee assistance program; flexible spending accounts; a 401(k) retirement savings plan; educational assistance; business travel accident insurance; recreational and entertainment discounts; tech credit union membership; wellness programs; and group home, auto and pet insurance.

FINANCIALS: Sales and profits are in thousands of dollars—add 000 to get the full amount. 2010 Note: Financial information for 2010 was not available for all companies at press time.

2010 Sales: $	2010 Profits: $	**U.S. Stock Ticker:** NVLS
2009 Sales: $639,194	2009 Profits: $-85,235	**Int'l Ticker:** Int'l Exchange:
2008 Sales: $1,011,004	2008 Profits: $-115,710	Employees: 2,544
2007 Sales: $1,570,049	2007 Profits: $213,700	Fiscal Year Ends: 12/31
2006 Sales: $1,658,516	2006 Profits: $190,016	Parent Company:

SALARIES/BENEFITS:

Pension Plan:	ESOP Stock Plan:	Profit Sharing:	Top Exec. Salary: $648,707	Bonus: $
Savings Plan: Y	Stock Purch. Plan:		Second Exec. Salary: $356,903	Bonus: $

OTHER THOUGHTS:

Apparent Women Officers or Directors: 1
Hot Spot for Advancement for Women/Minorities:

LOCATIONS: ("Y" = Yes)

West:	Southwest:	Midwest:	Southeast:	Northeast:	International:
Y	Y	Y		Y	Y

NUANCE COMMUNICATIONS INC

www.nuance.com

Industry Group Code: 511210L Ranks within this company's industry group: Sales: 1 Profits: 3

Hardware:	Software:		Telecommunications:	Electronic Publishing:	Equipment:	Specialty Services:
Computers:	Consumer:	Y	Local:	Online Service:	Telecom:	Consulting:
Accessories:	Corporate:	Y	Long Distance:	TV/Cable or Wireless:	Communication:	Contract Manufacturing:
Network Equipment:	Telecom:		Cellular:	Games:	Distribution:	Processing:
Chips/Circuits:	Internet:		Internet Service:	Financial Data:	VAR/Reseller:	Staff/Outsourcing:
Parts/Drives:					Satellite Srv./Equip.:	Specialty Services:

TYPES OF BUSINESS:
Software-Digital Imaging
Document Automation & Management Software
Speech Recognition Software

BRANDS/DIVISIONS/AFFILIATES:
Dragon NaturallySpeaking
OmniPage Pro
PaperPort

CONTACTS: Note: Officers with more than one job title may be intentionally listed here more than once.
Paul Ricci, CEO
Tom Beaudoin, CFO/Exec. VP
Steve Chambers, Chief Mktg. Office/Exec. VP-Worldwide Sales
Dawn Howarth, Sr. VP-Human Resources
Jo-Anne Sinclair, General Counsel/Sr. VP
Richard Palmer, Sr. VP-Corp. Dev.
Janet Dillione, Exec. VP/Gen. Mgr.-Healthcare Div.
Thomas J. Chisholm, Sr. VP-Enterprise Prod. & Svcs.
Robert Weideman, Sr. VP/Gen. Mgr.-Imaging Div.
Paul Ricci, Chmn.

Phone: 781-565-5000	Fax: 781-565-5001
Toll-Free:	
Address: 1 Wayside Rd., Burlington, MA 01803 US	

GROWTH PLANS/SPECIAL FEATURES:

Nuance Communications, Inc. manufactures voice and language applications. The company offers products in five categories: healthcare; mobile and consumer; enterprise; and imaging. Healthcare applications offer dictation and transcription services that automate the input and management of medical information. The mobile and consumer category provides voice applications for mobile devices, text technologies, mobile messaging services and dictation applications. The company's desktop and portable computer dictation software is currently available in 11 languages. The Dragon NaturallySpeaking suite of products allows users to automatically convert speech into text at up to 160 words-per-minute, supporting a vocabulary of over 300,000 words that can be expanded to include specialized words and phrases. Enterprise products offer business intelligence and authentication services and provides consulting management, user-interface, speech science, and application development through a global professional services organization. Nuance's software supports 60 languages and dialects for speech recognition, as well as 39 languages in natural sounding synthesized speech. Imaging products include PDF applications designed for business users, and optical character recognition technology. Nuance's other key products are OmniPage Pro, used for scanning and editing images; and PaperPort, which manages scanned paper documents.

Employees are offered health coverage, a 401(k) plan and an employee stock purchase plan.

FINANCIALS: Sales and profits are in thousands of dollars—add 000 to get the full amount. 2010 Note: Financial information for 2010 was not available for all companies at press time.

2010 Sales: $	2010 Profits: $	U.S. Stock Ticker: NUAN
2009 Sales: $950,352	2009 Profits: $-12,202	Int'l Ticker: Int'l Exchange:
2008 Sales: $868,462	2008 Profits: $-30,068	Employees: 6,100
2007 Sales: $601,996	2007 Profits: $-14,015	Fiscal Year Ends: 12/31
2006 Sales: $388,596	2006 Profits: $-22,887	Parent Company:

SALARIES/BENEFITS:

Pension Plan:	ESOP Stock Plan:	Profit Sharing:	Top Exec. Salary: $575,000	Bonus: $460,000
Savings Plan: Y	Stock Purch. Plan: Y		Second Exec. Salary: $400,000	Bonus: $96,806

OTHER THOUGHTS:
Apparent Women Officers or Directors: 4
Hot Spot for Advancement for Women/Minorities: Y

LOCATIONS: ("Y" = Yes)

West:	Southwest:	Midwest:	Southeast:	Northeast:	International:
Y				Y	Y

Note: Financial information, benefits and other data can change quickly and may vary from those stated here.

NVIDIA CORP

www.nvidia.com

Industry Group Code: 334119 Ranks within this company's industry group: Sales: 9 Profits: 19

Hardware:		Software:		Telecommunications:		Electronic Publishing:		Equipment:		Specialty Services:	
Computers:		Consumer:	Y	Local:		Online Service:		Telecom:		Consulting:	
Accessories:	Y	Corporate:	Y	Long Distance:		TV/Cable or Wireless:		Communication:		Contract Manufacturing:	
Network Equipment:		Telecom:		Cellular:		Games:		Distribution:		Processing:	
Chips/Circuits:	Y	Internet:		Internet Service:		Financial Data:		VAR/Reseller:		Staff/Outsourcing:	
Parts/Drives:								Satellite Srv./Equip.:		Specialty Services:	

TYPES OF BUSINESS:
Computer Accessories-Graphics Cards
Graphics Processors
Graphics Software

BRANDS/DIVISIONS/AFFILIATES:
GeForce
GoForce
Quadro
nForce
Tegra
Tesla
PhysX
3DTV Play

CONTACTS: *Note: Officers with more than one job title may be intentionally listed here more than once.*
Jen-Hsun Huang, CEO
Jen-Hsun Huang, Pres.
David White, CFO/Exec. VP
Jay Puri, Exec. VP-Worldwide Sales
Scott P. Sullivan, Sr. VP-Human Resources
Bill Dally, Chief Scientist
Tony Tamasi, Sr. VP-Tech. & Content
Chris A. Malachowsky, Sr. VP-Eng. & Oper.
David M. Shannon, General Counsel/Exec. VP/Sec.
Debora Shoquist, Exec. VP-Oper.
Michael W. Hara, Sr. VP-Comm.
Michael W. Hara, Sr. VP-Investor Rel.
Jonah M. Alben, Sr. VP-GPU Eng.
Philip J. Carmack, Sr. VP-Mobile Bus. Unit
Dwight Diercks, Sr. VP-Software Eng.
Jeff Fisher, Sr. VP-GeForce Bus. Unit
Bernhard Gleissner, VP-EMEA & India

Phone: 408-486-2000	Fax: 408-615-2800
Toll-Free:	
Address: 2701 San Tomas Expressway, Santa Clara, CA 95050 US	

GROWTH PLANS/SPECIAL FEATURES:
NVIDIA Corp. designs, develops and markets a family of award-winning 3D graphics processors, graphics processing units (GPUs) and related software. The company serves virtually all markets that rely on good visual quality in PC applications, including manufacturing, science, e-business, entertainment and education. It has four product groups: GPU, PSB (Professional Solutions Business), MCP (Media and Communications Processor) and CPB (Consumer Products Business). The GPU segment, which produces the company's primary GeForce product line, creates graphics equipment for desktop and notebook platforms. These devices enable users to play visually-intensive video games or watch high-definition content. The products also include PhysX physics engine software technology incorporated from the firm's recent acquisition of AGEIA Technologies, Inc. The GeForce line can be implemented in traditional, mobile or multiple (SLI, or Scalable Link Interface) configurations. The PSB segment caters to professional companies, offering the Quadro and the Tesla processors for productivity and high-performance applications. The MCP segment focuses on the core logic market and includes the ION mGPU (motherboard GPU) lines. These products are designed to combine functional power with energy efficiency, and can be implemented in traditional or mobile configurations. The CPB is geared towards smaller, more mobile applications. Mobile products such as the Tegra processors are found in netbooks, music players, automotive navigation systems and phones, and are designed to have multimedia capabilities while limiting power consumption. NVIDIA also supplies the GPUs for Microsoft's Xbox 360 and Sony's PlayStation 3. In October 2010, the firm launched the 3DTV Play software, which allows users to connect NVIDIA 3D Vision-enabled computers to 3D HDTVs to view content from their computers in 3D.

NVIDIA offers its employees medical, dental and vision coverage; life and AD&D insurance; short- and long-term disability; a 401(k) plan; a college savings plan; flexible spending accounts; an employee stock purchase plan; access to a credit union; and more.

FINANCIALS: Sales and profits are in thousands of dollars—add 000 to get the full amount. 2010 Note: Financial information for 2010 was not available for all companies at press time.

2010 Sales: $3,326,445	2010 Profits: $-67,987	**U.S. Stock Ticker:** NVDA
2009 Sales: $3,424,859	2009 Profits: $-30,041	**Int'l Ticker:** Int'l Exchange:
2008 Sales: $4,097,860	2008 Profits: $797,645	Employees: 5,706
2007 Sales: $3,068,771	2007 Profits: $448,834	Fiscal Year Ends: 1/31
2006 Sales: $2,375,687	2006 Profits: $301,176	Parent Company:

SALARIES/BENEFITS:
Pension Plan:	ESOP Stock Plan:	Profit Sharing:	Top Exec. Salary: $348,855	Bonus: $326,640
Savings Plan: Y	Stock Purch. Plan: Y		Second Exec. Salary: $333,671	Bonus: $

OTHER THOUGHTS:
Apparent Women Officers or Directors: 1
Hot Spot for Advancement for Women/Minorities:

LOCATIONS: ("Y" = Yes)
West:	Southwest:	Midwest:	Southeast:	Northeast:	International:
Y	Y	Y	Y	Y	Y

NXP SEMICONDUCTORS NV

www.npx.com

Industry Group Code: 33441 Ranks within this company's industry group: Sales: Profits:

Hardware:		Software:	Telecommunications:	Electronic Publishing:	Equipment:	Specialty Services:
Computers:		Consumer:	Local:	Online Service:	Telecom:	Consulting:
Accessories:	Y	Corporate:	Long Distance:	TV/Cable or Wireless:	Communication:	Contract Manufacturing:
Network Equipment:	Y	Telecom:	Cellular:	Games:	Distribution:	Processing:
Chips/Circuits:		Internet:	Internet Service:	Financial Data:	VAR/Reseller:	Staff/Outsourcing:
Parts/Drives:					Satellite Srv./Equip.:	Specialty Services:

TYPES OF BUSINESS:
Semiconductor Research, Development & Manufacturing

GROWTH PLANS/SPECIAL FEATURES:

NPX Semiconductors NV is a global semiconductor firm. The company provides High-Performance Mixed-Signal and Standard Products solutions that utilize technologies such as radio frequency (RF), analog, power management, security and digital processing products. High-Performance Mixed-Signal solutions are an optimized mix of analog and digital functionality integrated into a system or sub-system. These solutions are fine-tuned to meet the specific performance, cost, power, size and quality requirements of applications. The firm's products are used in a wide range of automotive, identification, wireless infrastructure, lighting, industrial, mobile, consumer and computing applications. The company derives approximately 31% of its sales from China; 11% from Singapore; 8% from Germany; 7% from the U.S.; 5% from South Korea; 3% from Taiwan; 3% from the Netherlands; and 32% from other countries. NPX has approximately 28,000 full-time equivalent employees located in more than 25 countries, with research and development activities in Asia, Europe and the U.S., and manufacturing facilities in Asia and Europe. It has roughly 14,000 patents either issued or pending. Through distributors such as Arrow, Avnet, Digi-Key, Future, Mouser, Premier Farnell and World Peace Group, NPX sells its products to over 30,000 customers worldwide. Roughly 40 customers account for approximately half of the firm's direct sales. NPX's international joint ventures and investments include Systems on Silicon Manufacturing Company Pte. Ltd. (61%-owned); Jilin NXP Semiconductors Ltd. (60%); Trident Microsystems, Inc. (60%); NuTune, a joint venture with Technicolor (55%); Suzhou ASEN Semiconductors Co. Ltd. (40%); and Advanced Semiconductor Manufacturing Co. Ltd. (27%). In February 2010, NPX sold its television systems and set-box operation to Trident Microsystems, Inc. in exchange for 60% ownership of Trident. In May 2010, the firm opened a new facility in China. In June 2010, the company opened a new facility in Massachusetts. In July 2010, NPX acquired low-power radio frequency solutions developer Jennic.

BRANDS/DIVISIONS/AFFILIATES:
NuTune
Trident Microsystems, Inc.
Jilin NXP Semiconductors Ltd.
Systems on Silicon Manufacturing Company Pte. Ltd.
Suzhou ASEN Semiconductors Co. Ltd.
Advanced Semiconductor Manufacturing Co. Ltd.
Jennic
Arrow

CONTACTS: *Note: Officers with more than one job title may be intentionally listed here more than once.*
Richard L. Clemmer, CEO
Richard L. Clemmer, Pres.
Karl-Henrik Sundstrom, CFO/Exec. VP
Mike Noonen, Exec. VP-Global Sales
Peter Kleij, Sr. VP-Human Resources
Frans Scheper, Sr. VP/Gen. Mgr.-Standard Prod.
Guido Dierick, General Counsel/Sr. VP
Chris Belden, Exec. VP/Gen. Mgr.-Oper.
Alexander Everke, Exec. VP/Gen. Mgr.-High-Performance Mixed-Signals
Kurt Sievers, Sr. VP/Gen. Mgr.-High-Performance Mixed-Signals
Peter Bonfield, Chmn.

Phone: 31-40-27-29960	Fax: 31-40-27-26533
Toll-Free:	
Address: High Tech Campus 60, Eindhoven, 5656AG The Netherlands	

FINANCIALS: Sales and profits are in thousands of dollars—add 000 to get the full amount. 2010 Note: Financial information for 2010 was not available for all companies at press time.

2010 Sales: $	2010 Profits: $	U.S. Stock Ticker: NXPI
2009 Sales: $	2009 Profits: $	Int'l Ticker: Int'l Exchange:
2008 Sales: $	2008 Profits: $	Employees:
2007 Sales: $	2007 Profits: $	Fiscal Year Ends: 12/31
2006 Sales: $	2006 Profits: $	Parent Company:

SALARIES/BENEFITS:

Pension Plan:	ESOP Stock Plan:	Profit Sharing:	Top Exec. Salary: $	Bonus: $
Savings Plan:	Stock Purch. Plan:		Second Exec. Salary: $	Bonus: $

OTHER THOUGHTS:
Apparent Women Officers or Directors:
Hot Spot for Advancement for Women/Minorities:

LOCATIONS: ("Y" = Yes)

West:	Southwest:	Midwest:	Southeast:	Northeast:	International:
				Y	Y

OCZ TECHNOLOGY GROUP INC
www.ocztechnology.com

Industry Group Code: 334112 Ranks within this company's industry group: Sales: 11 Profits: 5

Hardware:		Software:		Telecommunications:		Electronic Publishing:		Equipment:		Specialty Services:	
Computers:		Consumer:	Y	Local:		Online Service:		Telecom:		Consulting:	
Accessories:	Y	Corporate:		Long Distance:		TV/Cable or Wireless:		Communication:		Contract Manufacturing:	
Network Equipment:		Telecom:		Cellular:		Games:		Distribution:		Processing:	
Chips/Circuits:	Y	Internet:		Internet Service:		Financial Data:		VAR/Reseller:		Staff/Outsourcing:	
Parts/Drives:	Y							Satellite Srv./Equip.:		Specialty Services:	

TYPES OF BUSINESS:
Solid State Hard Drive Research, Development & Manufacturing

BRANDS/DIVISIONS/AFFILIATES:
DDR3 Intel Extreme Memory
Z-Series
PC Power & Cooling, Inc.
OCZ Canada, Inc.
OCZ Technology Ireland Limited
Silencer Mk II Power Supply Unit
Enyo Portable SSD
Fatal1ty 750 Watt

CONTACTS: Note: Officers with more than one job title may be intentionally listed here more than once.
Ryan Petersen, CEO
Ryan Petersen, Pres.
Arthur Knapp, CFO
Alex Mei, Chief Mktg. Officer/Exec. VP
Michael Schuette, VP-Tech. Dev.
Ryan Edwards, Dir.-Prod. Mgmt.
John Apps, Sr. VP-Oper.
Bonnie Mott, Mgr.-Investor Rel.
Richard Singh, Sr. VP-Sales
Bob Roark, VP-Oper., Power Mgmt.
Eugene Chang, VP-Purchasing

Phone: 408-733-8400	Fax: 408-733-5200
Toll-Free:	
Address: 6373 San Ignacio Ave, San Jose, CA 95119 US	

GROWTH PLANS/SPECIAL FEATURES:
OCZ Technology Group, Inc. is a provider of high performance solid state drives (SSDs) and memory modules for computing devices and systems. In addition to its SSD and memory module product lines, the firm designs, develops, manufactures and distributes other high performance components for computing devices and systems, including thermal management solutions and AC/DC switching power supply units (PSUs). Its product names include DDR3 Intel Extreme Memory, Z-Series PSUs and Vertex. The company's solutions are interoperable and can be configured alone or in combination to make computers run faster, more reliably, efficiently and cost effectively. OCZ offers more than 450 products to 376 customers in 69 countries. These customers include leading retailers, original equipment manufacturers (OEMs), online retailers, and computer distributors. The firm's largest customer, NewEgg.com, accounts for approximately 19% of OCZ Technology Group's revenue; the company derives roughly 51% of its revenues from 10 customers. OCZ Technology Group's subsidiaries include PC Power and Cooling, Inc.; OCZ Canada, Inc., a Canadian corporation; and OCZ Technology Ireland Limited, an Irish corporation. OCZ Technology Group owns three U.S. patents, with 15 currently pending. The firm derives approximately 43.4% of its revenues from U.S. operations; 39.3% from those in Europe, the Middle East and Africa; 5.3% from Canadian operations; and 12% from the rest of the world. In 2010, OCZ Technology Group released several new products, including Silencer Mk II Power Supply Unit (through PC Power and Cooling), Enyo Portable SSD, the Fatal1ty 750 Watt power supply and the StealthXStream 2 Power Supply series. In November 2010, the company acquired certain intellectual properties from Solid Data, Inc.

FINANCIALS: Sales and profits are in thousands of dollars—add 000 to get the full amount. 2010 Note: Financial information for 2010 was not available for all companies at press time.

2010 Sales: $143,959	2010 Profits: $-13,534	U.S. Stock Ticker: OCZ
2009 Sales: $155,982	2009 Profits: $-11,724	Int'l Ticker: Int'l Exchange:
2008 Sales: $118,352	2008 Profits: $1,437	Employees: 312
2007 Sales: $	2007 Profits: $	Fiscal Year Ends: 2/28
2006 Sales: $	2006 Profits: $	Parent Company:

SALARIES/BENEFITS:

Pension Plan:	ESOP Stock Plan:	Profit Sharing:	Top Exec. Salary: $400,000	Bonus: $
Savings Plan:	Stock Purch. Plan:		Second Exec. Salary: $325,000	Bonus: $

OTHER THOUGHTS:
Apparent Women Officers or Directors: 1
Hot Spot for Advancement for Women/Minorities:

LOCATIONS: ("Y" = Yes)

West:	Southwest:	Midwest:	Southeast:	Northeast:	International:
Y					Y

OPEN TEXT CORP

www.opentext.com

Industry Group Code: 511210L Ranks within this company's industry group: Sales: 2 Profits: 2

Hardware:	Software:		Telecommunications:	Electronic Publishing:	Equipment:	Specialty Services:	
Computers:	Consumer:		Local:	Online Service:	Telecom:	Consulting:	Y
Accessories:	Corporate:	Y	Long Distance:	TV/Cable or Wireless:	Communication:	Contract Manufacturing:	
Network Equipment:	Telecom:		Cellular:	Games:	Distribution:	Processing:	
Chips/Circuits:	Internet:		Internet Service:	Financial Data:	VAR/Reseller:	Staff/Outsourcing:	Y
Parts/Drives:					Satellite Srv./Equip.:	Specialty Services:	Y

TYPES OF BUSINESS:

Enterprise Content Management
IT Hosting Services
Embedded Modules & Applications
Consulting Services

BRANDS/DIVISIONS/AFFILIATES:

Open Text ECM Suite
Vignette Corp
Vizible Corporation
Burntsand, Inc.
StreamServe, Inc.

CONTACTS: Note: Officers with more than one job title may be intentionally listed here more than once.

John Shackleton, CEO
John Shackleton, Pres.
Paul J. McFeeters, CFO
James Latham, Chief Mktg. Officer
Eugene Roman, CTO
Gordon A. Davies, Chief Legal Officer/Corp. Sec.
P. Thomas Jenkins, Chief Strategy Officer
Greg Secord, VP-Investor Rel.
P. Thomas Jenkins, Chmn.

Phone: 519-888-7111	Fax: 519-888-0677
Toll-Free: 800-499-6544	
Address: 275 Frank Tompa Dr., Waterloo, ON N2L 0A1 Canada	

GROWTH PLANS/SPECIAL FEATURES:

Open Text Corp. is a provider of enterprise content management (ECM) software. The firm's products help its customers manage enterprise information and allow users to access, view and manage all information related to a transaction or business process. The company's core product is its Open Text ECM Suite, which combines management capabilities for a range of enterprise content, including business documents, vital records, web content, digital assets (including images, audio and video), e-mail, forms and reports. The Open Text ECM Suite includes applications designed for tasks and requirements such as document management; project collaboration; social media collaboration; records management; e-mail management; information archiving; web content management; document capture and delivery; business process management; and content analysis and reporting. In addition, the company offers customers industry-specific solutions based on the Open Text ECM Suite and geared toward market sectors including government; high-technology and manufacturing; energy; financial services; pharmaceuticals and life sciences; legal; and media. The company also offers Open Text Everywhere, an application that allows users to access the ECM suite through mobile devices, which is available for Apple iPhone and iPad. Open Text also provides consulting, hosting and learning services, with training offered through a combination of mentoring, webinars and instructor-led courses for client employees. Open Text maintains strategic alliances with developers such as Microsoft Corporation; Oracle Corporation; and SAP AG, providing specialized software that integrates more easily with allied companies' products. In April 2010, Open Text an agreement to acquire all of the outstanding shares of Burntsand, Inc., a technology consulting services company. In October 2010, the company acquired StreamServe, Inc., a provider of business communication solutions.

Open Text offers employee benefits that include medical, dental and vision coverage; life insurance; educational assistance; and an employee assistance program.

FINANCIALS: Sales and profits are in thousands of dollars—add 000 to get the full amount. 2010 Note: Financial information for 2010 was not available for all companies at press time.

2010 Sales: $912,023	2010 Profits: $87,554	**U.S. Stock Ticker:** OTEX
2009 Sales: $785,665	2009 Profits: $56,938	**Int'l Ticker:** OTC Int'l Exchange: Toronto-TSX
2008 Sales: $725,532	2008 Profits: $53,006	Employees: 3,861
2007 Sales: $595,664	2007 Profits: $21,660	Fiscal Year Ends: 6/30
2006 Sales: $409,562	2006 Profits: $4,978	Parent Company:

SALARIES/BENEFITS:

Pension Plan:	ESOP Stock Plan:	Profit Sharing:	Top Exec. Salary: $500,000	Bonus: $387,500
Savings Plan: Y	Stock Purch. Plan: Y		Second Exec. Salary: $430,683	Bonus: $355,313

OTHER THOUGHTS:

Apparent Women Officers or Directors: 3
Hot Spot for Advancement for Women/Minorities: Y

LOCATIONS: ("Y" = Yes)

West:	Southwest:	Midwest:	Southeast:	Northeast:	International:
Y	Y	Y	Y	Y	Y

OPENTV CORP

www.opentv.com

Industry Group Code: 511210C Ranks within this company's industry group: Sales: 3 Profits: 3

Hardware:	Software:		Telecommunications:	Electronic Publishing:	Equipment:	Specialty Services:	
Computers:	Consumer:		Local:	Online Service:	Telecom:	Consulting:	
Accessories:	Corporate:	Y	Long Distance:	TV/Cable or Wireless:	Communication:	Contract Manufacturing:	
Network Equipment:	Telecom:		Cellular:	Games:	Distribution:	Processing:	
Chips/Circuits:	Internet:		Internet Service:	Financial Data:	VAR/Reseller:	Staff/Outsourcing:	
Parts/Drives:					Satellite Srv./Equip.:	Specialty Services:	Y

TYPES OF BUSINESS:

Software-Interactive Television

BRANDS/DIVISIONS/AFFILIATES:

OpenTV Core Middleware
OpenTV PVR
OpenTV Spyglass
OpenTV EclipsePlus
OpenTV iAd
Decentrix, Inc.
OpenTV Participate
Kudelski Group (The)

CONTACTS:
Note: Officers with more than one job title may be intentionally listed here more than once.

Christine Oury, Sr. Dir.-Comm.
Pierre Roy, COO-Digital TV, Kudelski Group
Paul Woidke, Sr. VP/Gen. Mgr.-Advanced Advertising, OpenTV
Andre Kudelski, Chmn.

Phone: 415-962-5000	Fax: 415-962-5300
Toll-Free:	
Address: 275 Sacramento St., San Francisco, CA 94111 US	

GROWTH PLANS/SPECIAL FEATURES:

OpenTV Corp. provides software, services and applications for digital interactive television (iTV). The company's software has been shipped with or installed in more than 145 million set-top boxes worldwide and has been selected by over 58 network operators worldwide. OpenTV licenses its set-top box software to more than 40 digital set-top box manufacturers and licenses its authoring tools to hundreds of independent developers and content and service providers. The firm operates in two segments: middleware and advertising. The middleware segment is composed of set-top box middleware and embedded browser technologies, as well as software components that are deployed at the network operator's headend. Its primary software technology is the OpenTV Core Middleware. Other products include OpenTV PVR, which enables network operators to deliver advanced personal video recording services to their subscribers; and OpenTV Spyglass, a customizable HTML browser designed specifically for information appliances. The advertising segment provides software for the creation and delivery of advertising for digital television systems. Services in this segment include OpenTV EclipsePlus, an advertising campaign management system; OpenTV iAd, a suite of products that allow customers to create, enable and display interactive advertising applications as an overlay to broadcast advertising content; OpenTV SpotOn, a service that allows customization of advertising deployment based on geographic, demographic or psychographic profiles; and OpenTV Participate, which allows viewers to interact with programming through competitions, quizzes, auctions, voting and games. In March 2010, OpenTV became a wholly-owned subsidiary of The Kudelski Group, a provider of content protection and related digital television technologies. In April 2010, the firm partnered with technology consulting firm Decentrix, Inc. to offer enhancements to OpenTV's EclipsePlus system that will provide operators with advertising analysis tools.

FINANCIALS:
Sales and profits are in thousands of dollars—add 000 to get the full amount. 2010 Note: Financial information for 2010 was not available for all companies at press time.

2010 Sales: $	2010 Profits: $	U.S. Stock Ticker: Subsidiary
2009 Sales: $120,012	2009 Profits: $6,242	Int'l Ticker: Int'l Exchange:
2008 Sales: $116,474	2008 Profits: $9,613	Employees: 521
2007 Sales: $109,977	2007 Profits: $-5,161	Fiscal Year Ends: 12/31
2006 Sales: $95,210	2006 Profits: $-10,818	Parent Company: KUDELSKI GROUP (THE)

SALARIES/BENEFITS:

Pension Plan:	ESOP Stock Plan:	Profit Sharing:	Top Exec. Salary: $475,000	Bonus: $
Savings Plan: Y	Stock Purch. Plan: Y		Second Exec. Salary: $334,223	Bonus: $

OTHER THOUGHTS:

Apparent Women Officers or Directors: 1
Hot Spot for Advancement for Women/Minorities:

LOCATIONS: ("Y" = Yes)

West:	Southwest:	Midwest:	Southeast:	Northeast:	International:
Y					Y

OPENWAVE SYSTEMS INC

www.openwave.com

Industry Group Code: 511210C Ranks within this company's industry group: Sales: 2 Profits: 5

Hardware:	Software:		Telecommunications:	Electronic Publishing:	Equipment:	Specialty Services:	
Computers:	Consumer:		Local:	Online Service:	Telecom:	Consulting:	
Accessories:	Corporate:	Y	Long Distance:	TV/Cable or Wireless:	Communication:	Contract Manufacturing:	
Network Equipment:	Telecom:	Y	Cellular:	Games:	Distribution:	Processing:	
Chips/Circuits:	Internet:		Internet Service:	Financial Data:	VAR/Reseller:	Staff/Outsourcing:	
Parts/Drives:					Satellite Srv./Equip.:	Specialty Services:	Y

TYPES OF BUSINESS:

Server Software
Client Software
Support Services

BRANDS/DIVISIONS/AFFILIATES:

CONTACTS: *Note: Officers with more than one job title may be intentionally listed here more than once.*

Ken Denman, CEO
Anne Brennan, CFO
Alan Park, Sr. VP-Worldwide Sales
Eileen Nelson, Sr. VP-Human Resources
John Giere, Sr. VP-Prod. & Mktg.
Martin McKendry, Sr. VP-Eng.
Bruce K. Posey, General Counsel/Sr. VP/Sec.
Heikki Makijarvi, VP-Bus. Dev.
Sean MacNeill, VP-Global Svcs. & Support
Charles E. Levine, Chmn.

Phone: 650-480-8000	Fax: 650-480-8100
Toll-Free:	
Address: 2100 Seaport Blvd., Redwood City, CA 94063 US	

GROWTH PLANS/SPECIAL FEATURES:

Openwave Systems, Inc. is a developer of software applications and infrastructure for mobile and broadband operators. Its products are designed to streamline costs and enable revenue-generating, personalized services, including mobile analytics; mobile access; content adaption; targeted mobile and broadband advertising; and a suite of unified messaging applications. Openwave's software also enables mobile and broadband operators to converge services, accelerating their time-to-market and reducing the cost and complexity associated with new service deployment. Currently, Openwave serves its customers through three product lines: service mediation products, to enable access and management of content and media and provide analytics services; messaging products, to enable enhanced, integrated mobile and broadband communications; location products, to enable high-accuracy location-based services. Openwave's products are modular and based on open standards, providing its customers with the ability to mix and match the right products and technologies to create differentiated mobile services. The company's technologies and products are designed to work on diverse mobile phones and platforms regardless of the brand or type of service that operators select to offer to their subscribers. The firm's professional services group works with customers during all stages of implementation of wireless services. Openwave's customer base has historically included a relatively limited number of large telecommunications service provides; in 2010, business conducted with Sprint-Nextel and AT&T accounted for approximately 31% and 8% of total revenues, respectively.

FINANCIALS: Sales and profits are in thousands of dollars—add 000 to get the full amount. 2010 Note: Financial information for 2010 was not available for all companies at press time.

2010 Sales: $183,304	2010 Profits: $-5,857	**U.S. Stock Ticker:** OPWV
2009 Sales: $191,698	2009 Profits: $-85,876	**Int'l Ticker:**　Int'l Exchange:
2008 Sales: $200,877	2008 Profits: $-21,862	Employees:　584
2007 Sales: $242,822	2007 Profits: $-196,637	Fiscal Year Ends: 6/30
2006 Sales: $296,336	2006 Profits: $5,236	Parent Company:

SALARIES/BENEFITS:

Pension Plan:	ESOP Stock Plan:	Profit Sharing:	Top Exec. Salary: $450,000	Bonus: $243,000
Savings Plan: Y	Stock Purch. Plan:		Second Exec. Salary: $300,000	Bonus: $162,000

OTHER THOUGHTS:

Apparent Women Officers or Directors: 2
Hot Spot for Advancement for Women/Minorities: Y

LOCATIONS: ("Y" = Yes)

West:	Southwest:	Midwest:	Southeast:	Northeast:	International:
Y			Y	Y	Y

OPERA SOFTWARE ASA

www.opera.com

Industry Group Code: 5112 Ranks within this company's industry group: Sales: 2 Profits: 2

Hardware:	Software:		Telecommunications:	Electronic Publishing:	Equipment:	Specialty Services:
Computers:	Consumer:	Y	Local:	Online Service:	Telecom:	Consulting:
Accessories:	Corporate:		Long Distance:	TV/Cable or Wireless:	Communication:	Contract Manufacturing:
Network Equipment:	Telecom:		Cellular:	Games:	Distribution:	Processing:
Chips/Circuits:	Internet:	Y	Internet Service:	Financial Data:	VAR/Reseller:	Staff/Outsourcing:
Parts/Drives:					Satellite Srv./Equip.:	Specialty Services:

TYPES OF BUSINESS:

Internet Browsers
Cell Phone Internet Browsers

BRANDS/DIVISIONS/AFFILIATES:

Opera Desktop
Opera Mini
Opera Mobile
Opera Device
Opera Dragonfly
Opera Unite
AdMarvel
FastMail.fm

CONTACTS: Note: Officers with more than one job title may be intentionally listed here more than once.

Lars Boilesen, CEO
Erik C. Harrell, COO
Erik C. Harrell, CFO
Andreas Thome, Exec. VP-Sales
Tove Selnes, Exec. VP-Human Resources
Hakon Wium Lie, CTO
Rikard Gillemyr, VP-Eng.
Rolf Assev, Chief Strategy Officer
Christen Krogh, Chief Dev. Officer
Lars Boilesen, Chief Commercial Officer
William J. Raduchel, Chmn.

Phone: 47-23-69-24-00	Fax: 47-23-69-24-01
Toll-Free:	
Address: Waldemar Thranes Gate 98, Oslo, 0175 Norway	

GROWTH PLANS/SPECIAL FEATURES:

Opera Software ASA is a Norwegian firm engaged in the production and distribution of various versions of its Opera web browser. The firm's products include Opera Desktop for Windows-, Mac- and Linux-based computers; Opera Mini and Opera Mobile for mobile phones; and Opera Device for various non-PC Internet-connected devices. The company also offers a number of add-ons for the Opera browser, including Opera Unite, a file sharing suite; Opera Widgets, which are small single-purpose programs that run independently from the browser but use the browser's engine; Opera Link, a multi-device synchronization tool; the Opera Mail e-mail suite; Opera Dragonfly, a JavaScript debugger; and Opera Turbo, which compresses web pages for devices with slow Internet connections. The company, which began providing PC-based web browser in 1997, has branched out beyond the PC and offers its products on an ever-increasing number of Internet-ready platforms, including Nintendo Co.'s DSi handheld gaming system and Wii gaming system; Usen Corporation's set-top boxes for televisions; and a wide variety of cell phones and personal digital assistants (PDAs). Most of the firm's products are offered free of charge, with the company earning revenue primarily through licensing, premium webmail and contracts with search engines such as Google, which is the default search engine of the PC browsers, and Yahoo!, which is the default search engine for its mobile browsers. Opera Software also charges for Opera Mobile, the premium version of its cell phone-based web browser, which offers increased functionality over the free Opera Mini. In January 2010, Opera acquired AdMarvel, a company specializing in mobile advertising. In April 2010, the company purchased FastMail.fm, an online e-mail provider.

FINANCIALS: Sales and profits are in thousands of dollars—add 000 to get the full amount. 2010 Note: Financial information for 2010 was not available for all companies at press time.

2010 Sales: $	2010 Profits: $	U.S. Stock Ticker:
2009 Sales: $95,160	2009 Profits: $4,800	Int'l Ticker: OPERA Int'l Exchange: Oslo-OBX
2008 Sales: $78,540	2008 Profits: $13,860	Employees: 757
2007 Sales: $62,517	2007 Profits: $2,470	Fiscal Year Ends: 12/31
2006 Sales: $42,356	2006 Profits: $-3,604	Parent Company:

SALARIES/BENEFITS:

Pension Plan:	ESOP Stock Plan:	Profit Sharing:	Top Exec. Salary: $	Bonus: $
Savings Plan:	Stock Purch. Plan:		Second Exec. Salary: $	Bonus: $

OTHER THOUGHTS:

Apparent Women Officers or Directors: 1
Hot Spot for Advancement for Women/Minorities:

LOCATIONS: ("Y" = Yes)

West:	Southwest:	Midwest:	Southeast:	Northeast:	International:
Y					Y

OPNET TECHNOLOGIES INC

www.opnet.com

Industry Group Code: 511210B Ranks within this company's industry group: Sales: 7 Profits: 5

Hardware:	Software:		Telecommunications:	Electronic Publishing:	Equipment:	Specialty Services:
Computers:	Consumer:		Local:	Online Service:	Telecom:	Consulting:
Accessories:	Corporate:	Y	Long Distance:	TV/Cable or Wireless:	Communication:	Contract Manufacturing:
Network Equipment:	Telecom:		Cellular:	Games:	Distribution:	Processing:
Chips/Circuits:	Internet:		Internet Service:	Financial Data:	VAR/Reseller:	Staff/Outsourcing:
Parts/Drives:					Satellite Srv./Equip.:	Specialty Services:

TYPES OF BUSINESS:
Networking Software

BRANDS/DIVISIONS/AFFILIATES:
ACE Analyst
ACE Live
OPNET nCompass for Service Providers
OPNET nCompass for Enterprises
OPNET Panorama
IT Guru Network Planner
DSAuditor
AppMapper Xpert

CONTACTS: Note: Officers with more than one job title may be intentionally listed here more than once.
Marc A. Cohen, CEO
Alain J. Cohen, Pres.
Melvin F. Wesley, CFO/VP
Joseph J. Lenz, Sr. VP-Int'l Sales
Alain J. Cohen, CTO
Eric Nudelman, Sr. VP-Applications Eng. & Training
Marc A. Cohen, Sec.
Todd Kaloudis, Sr. VP-Bus. Dev. & Global Channels
Susan S. Cole, Contact-Press
Marc A. Cohen, Chmn.

Phone: 240-497-3000	Fax: 240-497-3001
Toll-Free:	
Address: 7255 Woodmont Ave., Bethesda, MD 20814 US	

GROWTH PLANS/SPECIAL FEATURES:

OPNET Technologies, Inc. provides software products and related services for managing networks and applications. The firm offers software products related to network planning, engineering, operations, research and development; and application performance management. The company markets these products to network service providers, government/defense agencies, corporate enterprises and network equipment manufacturers. OPNET's applications include ACE Analyst, which enables application performance management through advanced analytics; ACE Live, which offers real-time network analytics and end-user experience monitoring; OPNET nCompass for Service Providers and Enterprises, a centralized data-unifying program; OPNET Panorama, which offers real-time system analytics for application performance management; IT Guru Network Planner, which offers predictive network capacity planning and design optimization; OPNET Modeler, a network modeling and simulation solution; and SP Sentinel, which offers automated and continuous network configuration integrity and security auditing. The company sells its products and related services through a variety of channels, including international subsidiaries, a direct sales force, third-party distributors, and several value-added resellers and original equipment manufacturers. In addition to its five U.S. locations, OPNET maintains offices in Singapore, India, Italy, Sweden, Germany, China, France, the U.K. and Belgium. In August 2010, the firm acquired the DSAuditor product line from software company, Embarcadero Technologies, Inc. In January 2011, the company launched AppMapper Xpert, an application mapping product that finds a production application's underlying infrastructure components and application.

The firm offers medical, dental and vision insurance; a 401(k) plan; an employee stock purchase plan; medical and dependent care flexible spending accounts; life and AD&D insurance; disability coverage; an employee assistance program; and transportation allowances.

FINANCIALS: Sales and profits are in thousands of dollars—add 000 to get the full amount. 2010 Note: Financial information for 2010 was not available for all companies at press time.

2010 Sales: $126,347	2010 Profits: $5,823	U.S. Stock Ticker: OPNT
2009 Sales: $122,879	2009 Profits: $4,732	Int'l Ticker: Int'l Exchange:
2008 Sales: $101,346	2008 Profits: $ 533	Employees: 579
2007 Sales: $43,186	2007 Profits: $7,965	Fiscal Year Ends: 3/31
2006 Sales: $	2006 Profits: $	Parent Company:

SALARIES/BENEFITS:

Pension Plan:	ESOP Stock Plan:	Profit Sharing:	Top Exec. Salary: $325,000	Bonus: $125,000
Savings Plan: Y	Stock Purch. Plan: Y		Second Exec. Salary: $325,000	Bonus: $125,000

OTHER THOUGHTS:
Apparent Women Officers or Directors: 1
Hot Spot for Advancement for Women/Minorities:

LOCATIONS: ("Y" = Yes)

West:	Southwest:	Midwest:	Southeast:	Northeast:	International:
Y	Y			Y	

ORACLE CORP

www.oracle.com

Industry Group Code: 511210H Ranks within this company's industry group: Sales: 1   Profits: 1

Hardware:		Software:		Telecommunications:		Electronic Publishing:		Equipment:		Specialty Services:	
Computers:		Consumer:	Y	Local:		Online Service:	Y	Telecom:		Consulting:	Y
Accessories:	Y	Corporate:	Y	Long Distance:		TV/Cable or Wireless:		Communication:		Contract Manufacturing:	
Network Equipment:	Y	Telecom:		Cellular:		Games:		Distribution:		Processing:	
Chips/Circuits:		Internet:		Internet Service:		Financial Data:		VAR/Reseller:		Staff/Outsourcing:	
Parts/Drives:								Satellite Srv./Equip.:		Specialty Services:	Y

TYPES OF BUSINESS:

Computer Software-Database Management
e-Business Applications Software
Internet-Based Software
Consulting Services
Human Resources Management Software
CRM Software
Middleware

BRANDS/DIVISIONS/AFFILIATES:

Oracle Database
Sun Microsystems
Solaris
Oracle Exadata
Oracle On Demand
Phase Forward, Inc.
Silver Creek Systems, Inc.
Art Technology Group Inc

CONTACTS: Note: Officers with more than one job title may be intentionally listed here more than once.

Lawrence J. Ellison, CEO
Safra A. Catz, Co-Pres.
Jeff Epstein, CFO/Exec. VP
Judith Sim, Chief Mktg. Officer/Sr. VP
Thomas Kurian, Exec. VP-Prod. Dev.
Dorian Daley, General Counsel/Sr. VP/Sec.
Cindy Reese, Sr. VP-Worldwide Oper.
William C. West, Chief Acct. Officer/Sr. VP/Corp. Controller
Mark V. Hurd, Co-Pres.
Mary Ann Davidson, Chief Security Officer
Luiz Meisler, Exec. VP-Latin America
Edward Screven, Chief Corp. Architect
Jeffrey O. Henley, Chmn.
Takao Endo, Pres./CEO-Oracle Japan

Phone: 650-506-7000	Fax: 650-506-7200
Toll-Free: 800-672-2531	
Address: 500 Oracle Pkwy., Redwood Shores, CA 94065 US	

GROWTH PLANS/SPECIAL FEATURES:

Oracle Corp. is one of the largest enterprise software companies in the world. The firm markets its software directly to corporations rather than dealing in the consumer market. Oracle's products can be categorized into three broad areas: software, which represented 77% of its 2010 revenue; hardware systems (through the acquisition of Sun Microsystems), 9%; and services, 14%. The company's core software business segment is based upon its prepackaged enterprise data management software and Internet applications including Oracle Database, Oracle Fusion Middleware, Oracle Enterprise Manager, Oracle Collaboration Suite, Oracle Developer Suite and Oracle E-Business Suite. The firm's flagship Oracle Database software is used to securely manage the retrieval and manipulation of all forms of data. Oracle Database is available in four different versions: Express Edition, which is the most basic offering; Standard Edition One, which includes Unix and 64-bit support; Standard Edition, which supports four CPU sockets and offers enhanced workload management; and the fully-loaded Enterprise Edition. The hardware systems segment consists of hardware products and systems support. Its offerings include a wide variety of innovative products, such as servers and storage products, networking components, the Solaris operating system and Oracle Exadata, a family of integrated software and hardware products. Oracle's services business is comprised of Oracle Consulting, specializing in the design, deployment and migration of database technology and applications software; and Oracle On Demand, which offers distributed application services including E-Business Suite On Demand, Technology On Demand and other Software-as-a-Service (SaaS) products. The services segment also provides education and training to its customers. Oracle actively acquires complimentary businesses and has made numerous acquisitions in recent years, including Sun Microsystems for $7.3 billion in January 2010. Other firms acquired in 2010 include Silver Creek Systems, Inc.; DataScaler; AmberPoint; Convergin; and Phase Forward, Inc. In January 2011, Oracle acquired Art Technology Group, Inc. for $1.1 billion.

FINANCIALS: Sales and profits are in thousands of dollars—add 000 to get the full amount. 2010 Note: Financial information for 2010 was not available for all companies at press time.

2010 Sales: $26,820,000	2010 Profits: $6,135,000	**U.S. Stock Ticker:** ORCL
2009 Sales: $23,252,000	2009 Profits: $5,593,000	**Int'l Ticker:** Int'l Exchange:
2008 Sales: $22,430,000	2008 Profits: $5,521,000	Employees: 105,000
2007 Sales: $17,996,000	2007 Profits: $4,274,000	Fiscal Year Ends: 5/31
2006 Sales: $14,380,000	2006 Profits: $3,381,000	Parent Company:

SALARIES/BENEFITS:

Pension Plan:	ESOP Stock Plan:	Profit Sharing:	Top Exec. Salary: $800,000	Bonus: $3,871,953
Savings Plan: Y	Stock Purch. Plan: Y		Second Exec. Salary: $800,000	Bonus: $3,871,953

OTHER THOUGHTS:

Apparent Women Officers or Directors: 5
Hot Spot for Advancement for Women/Minorities: Y

LOCATIONS: ("Y" = Yes)

West:	Southwest:	Midwest:	Southeast:	Northeast:	International:
Y	Y	Y	Y	Y	Y

OVERLAND STORAGE INC

www.overlandstorage.com

Industry Group Code: 334112 Ranks within this company's industry group: Sales: 13 Profits: 7

Hardware:		Software:		Telecommunications:	Electronic Publishing:	Equipment:	Specialty Services:
Computers:		Consumer:		Local:	Online Service:	Telecom:	Consulting:
Accessories:	Y	Corporate:	Y	Long Distance:	TV/Cable or Wireless:	Communication:	Contract Manufacturing:
Network Equipment:	Y	Telecom:		Cellular:	Games:	Distribution:	Processing:
Chips/Circuits:		Internet:		Internet Service:	Financial Data:	VAR/Reseller:	Staff/Outsourcing:
Parts/Drives:	Y					Satellite Srv./Equip.:	Specialty Services: Y

TYPES OF BUSINESS:

Computer Storage Equipment-Digital Linear Tape Products
Data Storage Systems
Interchange Software
Controller Cards
Storage Management Software
Tape Media

BRANDS/DIVISIONS/AFFILIATES:

GuardianOS
Snap Server
SnapSAN
REO
NEO
ARCvault
Dynamic Virtual Tape
MaxiScale

CONTACTS: Note: Officers with more than one job title may be intentionally listed here more than once.

Eric Kelly, CEO
Eric Kelly, Pres.
Kurt L. Kalbfleisch, CFO
Jillian Mansolf, VP-Global Sales & Mktg.
Geoff Barrall, CTO
Geoff Barrall, VP-Eng.
Kurt L. Kalbfleisch, Sec.
Christopher Gopal, VP-Worldwide Oper.
Kurt L. Kalbfleisch, VP-Finance
Scott McClendon, Chmn.

Phone: 858-571-5555	Fax: 858-571-3664
Toll-Free: 800-729-8725	
Address: 4820 Overland Ave., San Diego, CA 92123 US	

GROWTH PLANS/SPECIAL FEATURES:

Overland Storage, Inc. offers data protection appliances that help small- to mid-range and distributed enterprises ensure data is protected and readily available. The company's products reduce the backup window, improve data recovery speed, simplify short- and long-term data retention and provide cost-effective disaster recovery. Overland's network attached storage products (NAS) consist of Snap Server hardware and GuardianOS software management systems. The Snap Servers come in rack-mounted or desktop configurations. The SnapSAN storage area network (SAN) configurations provide block-based primary storage for virtual server environments. The company's disk backup and recovery portfolio consists of the REO Series, which includes the REO 4600, expandable to 120 TB raw capacity; and the REO 1500, with up to 4 TB raw capacity. All REO appliances come with Overland's REO Protection OS software, which delivers embedded data protection intelligence including sophisticated virtualization, management and connectivity features. The REO Series also includes patented Dynamic Virtual Tape (DVT) technology, which allows users to create virtual tape cartridges that automatically expand or shrink to match the exact capacity requirements of the backup operation. Overland's family of scalable libraries, the NEO Series, provides reliable data protection with nonstop operation, expansion on demand, investment protection, remote library management and one and two gigabyte per second serverless backup in a SAN environment. Other offerings include ARCvault, Overland's line of tape automation products. With over 300,000 installations, Overland's customer list is comprised of the financial services, education, healthcare, oil and gas, law enforcement and technology industries, among others. In October 2010, Overland acquired MaxiScale, a developer of scalable file serving and cloud-scale storage.

Overland offers its employees medical, dental and vision coverage; flexible spending accounts; life and AD&D insurance; short- and long-term disability coverage; a 401(k) plan; an employee stock purchase plan; an employee assistance program; discount entertainment tickets; and assistance for adoption, elderly care and financial counseling.

FINANCIALS: Sales and profits are in thousands of dollars—add 000 to get the full amount. 2010 Note: Financial information for 2010 was not available for all companies at press time.

2010 Sales: $77,662	2010 Profits: $-12,962	U.S. Stock Ticker: OVRL
2009 Sales: $105,621	2009 Profits: $-18,028	Int'l Ticker: Int'l Exchange:
2008 Sales: $127,700	2008 Profits: $-32,025	Employees: 190
2007 Sales: $160,443	2007 Profits: $-44,111	Fiscal Year Ends: 6/30
2006 Sales: $209,038	2006 Profits: $-19,486	Parent Company:

SALARIES/BENEFITS:

Pension Plan:	ESOP Stock Plan:	Profit Sharing:	Top Exec. Salary: $400,000	Bonus: $
Savings Plan: Y	Stock Purch. Plan: Y		Second Exec. Salary: $302,201	Bonus: $9,000

OTHER THOUGHTS:

Apparent Women Officers or Directors: 1
Hot Spot for Advancement for Women/Minorities:

LOCATIONS: ("Y" = Yes)

West:	Southwest:	Midwest:	Southeast:	Northeast:	International:
Y					Y

Note: Financial information, benefits and other data can change quickly and may vary from those stated here.

PALM INC

www.palm.com

Industry Group Code: 334111 Ranks within this company's industry group: Sales: 22   Profits: 26

Hardware:		Software:		Telecommunications:	Electronic Publishing:	Equipment:	Specialty Services:
Computers:	Y	Consumer:	Y	Local:	Online Service:	Telecom:	Consulting:
Accessories:	Y	Corporate:	Y	Long Distance:	TV/Cable or Wireless:	Communication:	Contract Manufacturing:
Network Equipment:		Telecom:		Cellular:	Games:	Distribution:	Processing:
Chips/Circuits:		Internet:		Internet Service:	Financial Data:	VAR/Reseller:	Staff/Outsourcing:
Parts/Drives:						Satellite Srv./Equip.:	Specialty Services:

TYPES OF BUSINESS:

Computer Hardware-Handheld Organizers
PDAs
Handheld Computer Accessories & Software

BRANDS/DIVISIONS/AFFILIATES:

Palm Pre
Palm Pixi
Palm webOS
Palm OS
webOS 2.0
Hewlett-Packard Co (HP)

CONTACTS: *Note: Officers with more than one job title may be intentionally listed here more than once.*

Todd Bradley, Exec. VP-Personal Systems Group, HP
Jon Rubinstein, Gen. Mgr.-Palm Global Bus. Unit/Sr. VP-HP

Phone: 408-617-7000	Fax: 408-617-0100
Toll-Free: 800-881-7256	
Address: 950 W. Maude Ave., Sunnyvale, CA 94085 US	

GROWTH PLANS/SPECIAL FEATURES:

Palm, Inc., a subsidiary of Hewlett-Packard Co. (HP), is a leading global provider of mobile electronics, primarily smartphones, related software, services and accessories for the consumer and business markets. Palm's products currently include the Palm Pre and Palm Pixi smartphones. Its products are sold through the Internet, retail, reseller, Palm online stores, and wireless carrier channels globally. In some cases, the company customizes its devices to meet individual needs. Palm smartphone features include wireless data applications such as e-mail and web browsing; wireless communication capabilities, such as Bluetooth, wireless fidelity or Wi-Fi; multimedia and productivity software; and non-volatile flash memory. The company's latest operating system, Palm webOS, is designed to run on a variety of hardware form factors and supports capabilities such as contacts, calendar, tasks, memos, phone, browser, e-mail, messaging, camera, photo viewer and audio/video player. The Centro smartphone was the last Palm device to run on the previous operating system, the Palm OS. In the U.S. wireless carriers offering Palm products include Sprint Nextel, Verizon Wireless and AT&T. Palm no longer manufactures handheld computers; however, it offers ongoing customer support to owners of these devices. In July 2010, the firm was acquired by HP for approximately $1 billion. Now operating as a subsidiary of HP, Palm will be responsible for webOS software development and webOS based hardware products, including smartphones and future development of slate PCs and netbooks. In October 2010, the company introduced webOS 2.0, an upgraded version of its operating system.

Employee benefits include medical, dental and vision insurance; flexible spending accounts; tuition reimbursement; a 401(k); disability programs; life insurance; and an on-site fitness center.

FINANCIALS: Sales and profits are in thousands of dollars—add 000 to get the full amount. 2010 Note: Financial information for 2010 was not available for all companies at press time.

2010 Sales: $	2010 Profits: $	U.S. Stock Ticker: Subsidiary
2009 Sales: $735,872	2009 Profits: $-732,188	Int'l Ticker: Int'l Exchange:
2008 Sales: $1,318,691	2008 Profits: $-105,419	Employees: 939
2007 Sales: $1,560,507	2007 Profits: $56,383	Fiscal Year Ends:
2006 Sales: $1,578,509	2006 Profits: $336,170	Parent Company: HEWLETT-PACKARD CO (HP)

SALARIES/BENEFITS:

Pension Plan:	ESOP Stock Plan:	Profit Sharing:	Top Exec. Salary: $800,000	Bonus: $
Savings Plan: Y	Stock Purch. Plan:		Second Exec. Salary: $600,000	Bonus: $

OTHER THOUGHTS:

Apparent Women Officers or Directors:
Hot Spot for Advancement for Women/Minorities:

LOCATIONS: ("Y" = Yes)

West:	Southwest:	Midwest:	Southeast:	Northeast:	International:
Y					Y

PANASONIC CORPORATION

www.panasonic.net

Industry Group Code: 334310 Ranks within this company's industry group: Sales: 3 Profits: 8

Hardware:		Software:	Telecommunications:	Electronic Publishing:	Equipment:	Specialty Services:
Computers:		Consumer:	Local:	Online Service:	Telecom:	Consulting:
Accessories:	Y	Corporate:	Long Distance:	TV/Cable or Wireless:	Communication:	Contract Manufacturing:
Network Equipment:	Y	Telecom:	Cellular:	Games:	Distribution:	Processing:
Chips/Circuits:	Y	Internet:	Internet Service:	Financial Data:	VAR/Reseller:	Staff/Outsourcing:
Parts/Drives:	Y				Satellite Srv./Equip.:	Specialty Services:

TYPES OF BUSINESS:

Audio & Video Equipment, Manufacturing
Batteries
Home Appliances
Electronic Components
Cellular Phones
Medical Equipment
Photovoltaic Equipment

BRANDS/DIVISIONS/AFFILIATES:

PanaHome
Technics
Panasonic Mobile Communications Co Ltd
Sanyo Electric Company Ltd.
Panasonic Electronic Devices Co., Ltd.
Panasonic Electric Works Co. Ltd.

CONTACTS:
Note: Officers with more than one job title may be intentionally listed here more than once.
Fumio Ohtsubo, Pres.
Shigeru Omori, Dir.-Corp. Industrial Mktg. & Sales Div.
Makoto Uenoyama, Dir.-Info. Systems
Tsuyoshi Nomura, Dir.-Corp. Mfg. Innovation Div.
Ikusaburo Kashima, Managing Dir.-Legal Affairs & Corp. Bus. Ethics
Yoshiaki Nakagawa, Gen. Mgr.-Corp. Planning
Hidetoshi Osawa, Dir.-Corp. Comm. Div.
Hideaki Kawai, Gen. Mgr.-Investor Rel.
Hideaki Kawai, Gen. Mgr.-Corp Finance
Masayuki Matsushita, Vice Chmn.
Ken Morita, Pres., AVC Networks Company
Osamu Waki, Pres., Panasonic Mobile Communications Co., Ltd.
Toshiaki Kobayashi, Pres., Panasonic Electronic Devices Co., Ltd.
Kunio Nakamura, Chmn.
Hitoshi Otsuki, Sr. Managing Dir.-Overseas Oper.
Koji Itazaki, Dir.-Corp. Procurement & Corp Logistics Div.

Phone: 81-6-6908-1121	Fax:
Toll-Free:	
Address: 1006 Oaza Kadoma, Kadoma City, Osaka, 571-8501 Japan	

GROWTH PLANS/SPECIAL FEATURES:

Panasonic Corporation, formerly Matsushita Electric Industrial Co., Ltd., produces consumer electronics products under brand names such as Panasonic, Technics and PanaHome. The company's business areas include audio, visual and communications (digital AVC Networks); home appliances; components and devices; Panasonic Electric Works and PanaHome, which are residential construction and home remodeling companies; business and professional products; and industrial products. Panasonic's Digital AVC Networks products include plasma and LCD TVs; DVD recorders; camcorders; computers; digital cameras; personal and home audio equipment; printers and fax machines; mobile phones; car AVC equipment; and memory cards and other recordable media. Home appliance products include refrigerators, air conditioners, washing machines and clothes dryers, vacuum cleaners, microwave ovens and other cooking appliances, dish washers, electric fans, electric lamps, compressors and vending machines. Components and devices include semiconductors; general components, such as capacitors, tuners, circuit boards, power supplies, circuit components, electromechanical components and speakers; electric motors; and batteries. The Panasonic Electric Works and PanaHome segment supplies lighting fixtures, wiring devices, personal-care products, modular kitchen systems, interior and exterior furnishing materials, automation controls, detached housing, rental apartment housing, medical and nursing care facilities and home remodeling products. The firm's business and professional products include Notebook PCs; office products such as digital imaging systems, network cameras, high-speed scanners, business fax machines and printers; broadcast and video products such as camcorders and monitors; security products such as network cameras, video recorders and iris recognition systems; and healthcare systems such as medical imaging products. The company's industrial products include motors, fans and compressors; semiconductors; and power supplies. Subsidiary, Sanyo Electric Co., Ltd., is a leading electronics company that also develops solar cells.

FINANCIALS:
Sales and profits are in thousands of dollars—add 000 to get the full amount. 2010 Note: Financial information for 2010 was not available for all companies at press time.

2010 Sales: $90,202,900	2010 Profits: $-2,079,360	U.S. Stock Ticker: PC
2009 Sales: $85,729,000	2009 Profits: $-4,183,620	Int'l Ticker: 6752 Int'l Exchange: Tokyo-TSE
2008 Sales: $93,428,320	2008 Profits: $2,905,150	Employees: 384,586
2007 Sales: $81,831,200	2007 Profits: $1,949,650	Fiscal Year Ends: 3/31
2006 Sales: $75,601,800	2006 Profits: $1,312,500	Parent Company:

SALARIES/BENEFITS:

Pension Plan:	ESOP Stock Plan:	Profit Sharing:	Top Exec. Salary: $	Bonus: $
Savings Plan:	Stock Purch. Plan:		Second Exec. Salary: $	Bonus: $

OTHER THOUGHTS:

Apparent Women Officers or Directors:
Hot Spot for Advancement for Women/Minorities:

LOCATIONS: ("Y" = Yes)

West:	Southwest:	Midwest:	Southeast:	Northeast:	International:
Y		Y	Y	Y	Y

Note: Financial information, benefits and other data can change quickly and may vary from those stated here.

PAR TECHNOLOGY CORPORATION

www.partech.com

Industry Group Code: 511210H Ranks within this company's industry group: Sales: 13   Profits: 13

Hardware:		Software:		Telecommunications:	Electronic Publishing:	Equipment:		Specialty Services:	
Computers:		Consumer:		Local:	Online Service:	Telecom:		Consulting:	Y
Accessories:	Y	Corporate:	Y	Long Distance:	TV/Cable or Wireless:	Communication:		Contract Manufacturing:	
Network Equipment:		Telecom:		Cellular:	Games:	Distribution:	Y	Processing:	
Chips/Circuits:		Internet:		Internet Service:	Financial Data:	VAR/Reseller:		Staff/Outsourcing:	
Parts/Drives:						Satellite Srv./Equip.:		Specialty Services:	Y

TYPES OF BUSINESS:

Point-of-Sale Systems
Technical Services
System Design & Engineering
Logistics Management Software
Research
Government Contract Services
Hospitality IT Services

BRANDS/DIVISIONS/AFFILIATES:

ParTech, Inc.
PAR Government Systems Corporation
Rome Research Corporation
PAR Logistics Management Systems

CONTACTS: *Note: Officers with more than one job title may be intentionally listed here more than once.*

John W. Sammon, Jr., CEO
John W. Sammon, Jr., Pres.
Ronald J. Casciano, CFO/VP
Gregory T. Cortese, General Counsel/Sec.
Gregory T. Cortese, Exec. VP-Strategic Initiatives
Christopher R. Byrnes, VP-Investor & Bus. Rel.
Ronald J. Casciano, Chief Acct. Officer/Treas.
Ed Soladay, Pres., ParTech, Inc.
Rick Franklin, VP-Global Client Svcs., ParTech, Inc.
Mike Todd, VP-Sales-Americas, ParTech, Inc.
Stephen P. Lynch, Pres., PAR Gov't Systems Corp. & Rome Research
John W. Sammon, Jr., Chmn.

Phone: 315-738-0600	Fax: 315-738-0411
Toll-Free: 800-448-6505	
Address: 8383 Seneca Turnpike, New Hartford, NY 13413 US	

GROWTH PLANS/SPECIAL FEATURES:

PAR Technology Corporation, through its subsidiaries, provides hardware, software and related services to the restaurant and hospitality markets, as well as applied technology and technical outsourcing services to certain government agencies. The company operates in two business segments, managed by three wholly-owned subsidiaries: Hospitality, managed by ParTech, Inc. and Government, managed by PAR Government Systems Corporation and Rome Research Corporation. ParTech, Inc. is a leading supplier of hospitality management technology systems to quick-service restaurants, with over 50,000 systems installed in more than 105 countries. It provides restaurant management technology solutions that combine software applications, an Intel-based hardware platform and installation and lifecycle support services. Its products include fixed and wireless order-entry terminals; self-service kiosks; printer and video monitor kitchen systems; food safety monitoring tools; back office applications; and enterprise business intelligence software. The firm also provides hospitality management technology for the needs of various hospitality enterprises, including five-star city-center hotel chains; destination spa and golf properties; timeshare properties; and five-star resorts worldwide. PAR Government Systems and Rome Research provide technical expertise in the development of advanced technology systems for the Department of Defense and other governmental agencies. Additionally, the firm provides information technology and communications support services to the U.S. Navy, U.S. Air Force and U.S. Army. Its technical services include experimental studies and advanced operational systems within such areas of research as radar, image and signal processing, logistics management systems, and geospatial services and products. PAR Logistics Management Systems, a subsidiary of PAR Government Systems, provides technical tracking systems focused on shipping and logistics for road, rail and transit markets.

FINANCIALS: Sales and profits are in thousands of dollars—add 000 to get the full amount. 2010 Note: Financial information for 2010 was not available for all companies at press time.

2010 Sales: $	2010 Profits: $	U.S. Stock Ticker: PAR
2009 Sales: $223,048	2009 Profits: $-5,186	Int'l Ticker: Int'l Exchange:
2008 Sales: $232,687	2008 Profits: $2,217	Employees: 1,649
2007 Sales: $209,484	2007 Profits: $-2,708	Fiscal Year Ends: 12/31
2006 Sales: $208,667	2006 Profits: $5,721	Parent Company:

SALARIES/BENEFITS:

Pension Plan:	ESOP Stock Plan:	Profit Sharing:	Top Exec. Salary: $355,591	Bonus: $71,900
Savings Plan:	Stock Purch. Plan:		Second Exec. Salary: $250,000	Bonus: $133,500

OTHER THOUGHTS:

Apparent Women Officers or Directors:
Hot Spot for Advancement for Women/Minorities:

LOCATIONS: ("Y" = Yes)

West:	Southwest:	Midwest:	Southeast:	Northeast:	International:
Y			Y	Y	Y

PARAMETRIC TECHNOLOGY CORP

www.ptc.com

Industry Group Code: 511210N Ranks within this company's industry group: Sales: 4 Profits: 6

Hardware:	Software:		Telecommunications:	Electronic Publishing:	Equipment:	Specialty Services:	
Computers:	Consumer:		Local:	Online Service:	Telecom:	Consulting:	Y
Accessories:	Corporate:	Y	Long Distance:	TV/Cable or Wireless:	Communication:	Contract Manufacturing:	
Network Equipment:	Telecom:		Cellular:	Games:	Distribution:	Processing:	
Chips/Circuits:	Internet:		Internet Service:	Financial Data:	VAR/Reseller:	Staff/Outsourcing:	
Parts/Drives:					Satellite Srv./Equip.:	Specialty Services:	Y

TYPES OF BUSINESS:

Computer Software-Engineering & Manufacturing
Engineering Consulting Services
Enterprise Publishing Software
Product Data Management

BRANDS/DIVISIONS/AFFILIATES:

Windchill
Arbortext
Creo Elements/View
Relex Reliability
InSight
Creo Elements/Pro
Creo Elements/Direct
Mathcad

CONTACTS: Note: Officers with more than one job title may be intentionally listed here more than once.

James E. Heppelmann, CEO
James E. Heppelmann, Pres.
Jeffrey D. Glidden, CFO/Exec. VP
Paul Cunningham, Exec. VP-Worldwide Sales
Tom Kearns, CIO/Sr. VP
Brian Shepherd, Exec. VP-Prod. Dev.
Aaron C. von Staats, General Counsel/Corp. VP
Barry F. Cohen, Exec. VP-Strategy
Rob Gremley, Exec. VP-Mktg.
Mark Hodges, Chief Customer Officer/Div. VP
Marc Diouane, Exec. VP-Global Svcs.
C. Richard (Dick) Harrison, Chmn.
Anthony Paul DiBona, Exec. VP-Global Maintenance Support
Paul Cunningham, Exec. VP-Dist.

Phone: 781-370-5000	Fax: 781-370-6000
Toll-Free: 877-275-4782	
Address: 140 Kendrick St., Needham, MA 02494 US	

GROWTH PLANS/SPECIAL FEATURES:

Parametric Technology Corp. (PTC) develops, markets and supports product development software and related services, designed to aid companies in designing products and managing product information. It competes in the product lifecycle management (PLM) market with product lines in product data management, collaboration and related fields. It also offers computer-aided design (CAD), manufacturing (CAM) and engineering (CAE) products that compete in the computer aided technologies (CAx) market. The company divides its product offerings into two categories: PLM and Desktop. PLM product lines include Windchill product content management, product development and project collaboration programs; Arbortext data management and delivery tools; Creo Elements/View visualization, verification, annotation and automated comparison tools for documents as well as MCAD (2D and 3D) and ECAD formats; Relex Reliability planning and safety management software; and InSight product analytics tools. Desktop software includes CAx products as well as document authoring tools, including Creo Elements/Pro, a line of three-dimensional design products; CreoElements/Direct CAD and collaboration software; Arbortext authoring and illustration tools; and Mathcad engineering calculation software. The firm also offers maintenance, consulting and training services. PTC serves customers in the aerospace and defense; airlines; automotive; consumer products; electronics; footwear & apparel; industrial equipment; medical devices; and retail industries.

The firm provides its employees with tuition reimbursement; medical, dental and vision plans; life insurance; a 401(k) plan; and short- and long-term disability coverage.

FINANCIALS: Sales and profits are in thousands of dollars—add 000 to get the full amount. 2010 Note: Financial information for 2010 was not available for all companies at press time.

2010 Sales: $1,010,049	2010 Profits: $24,368	**U.S. Stock Ticker: PMTC**
2009 Sales: $938,185	2009 Profits: $31,522	**Int'l Ticker:** Int'l Exchange:
2008 Sales: $1,070,330	2008 Profits: $79,702	Employees: 5,317
2007 Sales: $941,279	2007 Profits: $143,656	Fiscal Year Ends: 9/30
2006 Sales: $847,983	2006 Profits: $56,804	Parent Company:

SALARIES/BENEFITS:

Pension Plan:	ESOP Stock Plan:	Profit Sharing:	Top Exec. Salary: $600,000	Bonus: $
Savings Plan: Y	Stock Purch. Plan:		Second Exec. Salary: $521,650	Bonus: $

OTHER THOUGHTS:

Apparent Women Officers or Directors:
Hot Spot for Advancement for Women/Minorities:

LOCATIONS: ("Y" = Yes)

West:	Southwest:	Midwest:	Southeast:	Northeast:	International:
Y	Y	Y	Y	Y	Y

Note: Financial information, benefits and other data can change quickly and may vary from those stated here.

PC CONNECTION INC

www.pcconnection.com

Industry Group Code: 423430 **Ranks within this company's industry group:** Sales: 12 Profits: 12

Hardware:	Software:	Telecommunications:	Electronic Publishing:	Equipment:		Specialty Services:	
Computers:	Consumer:	Local:	Online Service:	Telecom:		Consulting:	
Accessories:	Corporate:	Long Distance:	TV/Cable or Wireless:	Communication:		Contract Manufacturing:	
Network Equipment:	Telecom:	Cellular:	Games:	Distribution:	Y	Processing:	
Chips/Circuits:	Internet:	Internet Service:	Financial Data:	VAR/Reseller:	Y	Staff/Outsourcing:	
Parts/Drives:				Satellite Srv./Equip.:		Specialty Services:	Y

TYPES OF BUSINESS:

Computer Products, Direct Selling
Computer Accessories
Software
IT Services
Online Sales
Catalog Sales

BRANDS/DIVISIONS/AFFILIATES:

MoreDirect, Inc.
GovConnection, Inc.
Traxx
ProConnection
PC Connection Express, Inc.

CONTACTS: *Note: Officers with more than one job title may be intentionally listed here more than once.*

Patricia Gallup, CEO
Timothy McGrath, COO
Timothy McGrath, Pres.
Jack Ferguson, CFO/Exec. VP/Treas.
Bradley Mousseau, Sr. VP-Human Resources
Steve Baldridge, Sr. VP-Finance/Corp. Controller
Patricia Gallup, Chmn.

Phone: 603-683-2000	Fax: 603-423-5748
Toll-Free: 800-800-0009	
Address: 730 Milford Rd., Merrimack, NH 03054-4631 US	

GROWTH PLANS/SPECIAL FEATURES:

PC Connection, Inc. is a direct marketer of information technology (IT) products and services, including computer systems, software and peripheral equipment, networking communications and other products and accessories. The company offers a selection of over 150,000 products, purchased from manufacturers, distributers and other suppliers, targeted for business use. It also offers a range of services including installation, configuration and repair, performed by company and third-party personnel. The company operates through three primary business segments: SMB, serving small- to medium-sized businesses and individual consumers; large accounts, responsible for sales to large enterprise customers and operating through MoreDirect, Inc.; and public sector, managing sales to federal, state and local governments and educational institutions through GovConnection, Inc. MoreDirect operates the Traxx Internet-based transaction system, an integrated application that provides sales order processing, supply chain visibility and full electronic data interchange (EDI) links. PC Connection sells products through a combination of outbound telemarketing, field sales, targeted direct mail catalogs, web sites, Internet advertising and through selected computer magazines. Its most frequently ordered products are carried in inventory and are typically shipped to customers the same day the order is received. Additionally, through ProConnection, the company provides complete IT solutions for its clients, including designing, developing, and managing the integration of products and services to implement IT projects. In 2009, net sales by business segment were as follows: 48% SMB; 27% large accounts; and 25% public sector. In 2010, the company established PC Connection Express, Inc., a new subsidiary targeted at the individual consumer and home office market.

PC Connection offers its employees medical, vision, dental, life and disability coverage; tuition reimbursement; adoption assistance; fitness reimbursement; legal services; computer loans; various product discounts; chair massages; and on-site dry cleaning services.

FINANCIALS: Sales and profits are in thousands of dollars—add 000 to get the full amount. 2010 Note: Financial information for 2010 was not available for all companies at press time.

2010 Sales: $	2010 Profits: $	U.S. Stock Ticker: PCCC
2009 Sales: $1,569,656	2009 Profits: $-1,222	Int'l Ticker: Int'l Exchange:
2008 Sales: $1,753,680	2008 Profits: $10,366	Employees: 1,625
2007 Sales: $1,785,379	2007 Profits: $22,995	Fiscal Year Ends: 12/31
2006 Sales: $1,635,651	2006 Profits: $13,776	Parent Company:

SALARIES/BENEFITS:

Pension Plan:	ESOP Stock Plan:	Profit Sharing:	Top Exec. Salary: $750,000	Bonus: $790,600
Savings Plan: Y	Stock Purch. Plan: Y		Second Exec. Salary: $500,000	Bonus: $527,100

OTHER THOUGHTS:

Apparent Women Officers or Directors: 2
Hot Spot for Advancement for Women/Minorities: Y

LOCATIONS: ("Y" = Yes)

West:	Southwest:	Midwest:	Southeast:	Northeast:	International:
	Y	Y	Y	Y	

PC MALL INC

www.pcmall.com

Industry Group Code: 423430 Ranks within this company's industry group: Sales: 13 Profits: 11

Hardware:	Software:	Telecommunications:	Electronic Publishing:	Equipment:		Specialty Services:
Computers:	Consumer:	Local:	Online Service:	Telecom:		Consulting:
Accessories:	Corporate:	Long Distance:	TV/Cable or Wireless:	Communication:		Contract Manufacturing:
Network Equipment:	Telecom:	Cellular:	Games:	Distribution:	Y	Processing:
Chips/Circuits:	Internet:	Internet Service:	Financial Data:	VAR/Reseller:	Y	Staff/Outsourcing:
Parts/Drives:				Satellite Srv./Equip.:		Specialty Services:

TYPES OF BUSINESS:

Computer & Software Products Retailer
Accessories & Supplies
Direct Marketing & Telemarketing
Catalog Sales
Online Sales

BRANDS/DIVISIONS/AFFILIATES:

PC Mall Gov, Inc.
SARCOM, Inc.
MacMall.com
PCMall.com
PCMallGov.com
GMRI.com
Abreon, Inc.
OnSale.com

CONTACTS: Note: Officers with more than one job title may be intentionally listed here more than once.

Frank F. Khulusi, CEO
Frank F. Khulusi, Pres.
Brandon H. LaVerne, CFO
Kristin M. Rogers, Exec. VP-Sales & Mktg.
Robert I. Newton, General Counsel/Exec. VP
Joseph B. Hayek, Exec. VP-Corp. Dev.
Joseph B. Hayek, Exec. VP-Investor Rel.
Daniel DeVries, Exec. VP-MacMall
Frank Khulusi, Chmn.

Phone: 310-354-5600	Fax: 310-225-6903
Toll-Free: 800-555-6255	
Address: 2555 W. 190th St., Ste. 201, Torrance, CA 90504 US	

GROWTH PLANS/SPECIAL FEATURES:

PC Mall, Inc. is a rapid response direct marketer of computer hardware, software, peripherals, electronics and other consumer products and services. It operates in four segments: the SMB (small and medium-sized businesses) segment, which markets common office devices to small businesses; the MME (mid-market and enterprise-sized businesses) which markets products under the SARCOM, DSW and Abreon brands and caters to larger corporate customers.; the public sector segment, which sells to federal, state and local governments, as well as educational institutions; and the consumer segment, which targets individuals and private citizens. The company sells more than 100,000 different products relating to systems needs, networking, software, software licensing, storage, audio/video, electronics and printers. PC Mall sells software packages in the business and personal productivity, utility, language, educational and entertainment categories, as well as spreadsheet and database software. The products sold are authorized through leading manufacturers such as Hewlett Packard (HP), Microsoft, Apple and Cisco. PC Mall offers its products and services through outbound and inbound telemarketing account executives, the Internet, direct marketing techniques, direct response catalogs, a direct sales force and three retail showrooms. In addition, it offers a broad selection of products through its distinctive full-color catalogs under the PC Mall, Mac Mall, and PC Mall Gov brands; its web sites, PCMall.com, MacMall.com, ClubMac.com, PCMallGov.com, GMRI.com (Government Micro Resources, Inc.), Sarcom.com, Abreon.com and OnSale.com. Through contracts, open market and procurement card purchases, the company's PC Mall Gov subsidiary makes products available to federal agencies, state and local governments and educational customers. Customer orders are filled by PC Mall's distribution center located near Memphis, Tennessee or through the firm's extensive network of distributors.

The firm offers employees medical, dental and vision insurance; life insurance; flexible spending accounts; a 401(k) plan; discounts on company products; discounted home and auto insurance; pet insurance; discounted health club memberships; an employee and an assistance program.

FINANCIALS: Sales and profits are in thousands of dollars—add 000 to get the full amount. 2010 Note: Financial information for 2010 was not available for all companies at press time.

2010 Sales: $	2010 Profits: $	U.S. Stock Ticker: MALL
2009 Sales: $1,138,061	2009 Profits: $3,357	Int'l Ticker: Int'l Exchange:
2008 Sales: $1,327,974	2008 Profits: $9,603	Employees: 2,344
2007 Sales: $1,215,433	2007 Profits: $12,443	Fiscal Year Ends: 12/31
2006 Sales: $1,005,820	2006 Profits: $3,956	Parent Company:

SALARIES/BENEFITS:

Pension Plan:	ESOP Stock Plan:	Profit Sharing:	Top Exec. Salary: $776,845	Bonus: $111,682
Savings Plan: Y	Stock Purch. Plan:		Second Exec. Salary: $326,360	Bonus: $35,268

OTHER THOUGHTS:

Apparent Women Officers or Directors: 1
Hot Spot for Advancement for Women/Minorities:

LOCATIONS: ("Y" = Yes)

West:	Southwest:	Midwest:	Southeast:	Northeast:	International:
Y		Y	Y		Y

PC-WARE INFORMATION TECHNOLOGIES AG   www.pc-ware.com

Industry Group Code: 541512 Ranks within this company's industry group: Sales: 6 Profits: 5

Hardware:	Software:		Telecommunications:	Electronic Publishing:	Equipment:		Specialty Services:	
Computers:	Consumer:		Local:	Online Service:	Telecom:		Consulting:	
Accessories:	Corporate:	Y	Long Distance:	TV/Cable or Wireless:	Communication:		Contract Manufacturing:	
Network Equipment:	Telecom:		Cellular:	Games:	Distribution:	Y	Processing:	
Chips/Circuits:	Internet:		Internet Service:	Financial Data:	VAR/Reseller:		Staff/Outsourcing:	
Parts/Drives:					Satellite Srv./Equip.:		Specialty Services:	Y

TYPES OF BUSINESS:

Information Technology Services
Software & Hardware Procurement
Software Asset Management
Remote Infrastructure Management
Software Security Services
Software Licensing

BRANDS/DIVISIONS/AFFILIATES:

Procerva
COMPAREX
PERUNI Holding GmbH

CONTACTS: *Note: Officers with more than one job title may be intentionally listed here more than once.*

Klaus Elsbacher, CEO
Hansjorg Egger, COO
Thomas Reich, CFO
Janine Stoye, Comm.
Wilfried Pruschak, Chmn.
Roger Sowerbutts, VP-Northern Europe

Phone: 49-341-25-68-000	**Fax:** 49-341-25-68-999
Toll-Free:	
Address: Blochstrasse 1, Leipzig, 04329 Germany	

GROWTH PLANS/SPECIAL FEATURES:

PC-Ware Information Technologies AG is an information and communication technology (ICT) solutions company that provides software licensing, licensing agreement consulting and software and IT asset management services across the EMEA region. The firm divides its operations into two segments: software, which includes all of its software licensing, software distribution, hardware reselling and software-as-a-service operations; and data center, which includes its entire infrastructure, consulting and managed service activities. The software segment handles a number of responsibilities, such as software procurement including the management of licenses and rights; software asset management (SAM); hosting solutions, including Service Provider License Agreement (SPLA) services; multivendor software services; and training courses. The data center segment, operated under the brand COMPAREX, offers solutions for IT hardware procurement management; IT consulting and implementation; infrastructure consolidation; communication and storage; and support and maintenance of IT infrastructure. Through the Procerva customer portal, the firm provides access to all its services online. PC-Ware maintains subsidiaries in 26 countries in Europe, Africa and Asia, and serves its customers in North and South America and Australia through corporate partnerships. The company is a Microsoft Large Account Reseller (LAR) in Europe, the Middle East, Africa and China. In January 2011, PERUNI Holding GmbH, through a squeeze-out transaction, acquired all the outstanding shares of PC-Ware, with PC-Ware becoming a wholly-owned subsidiary of PERUNI.

FINANCIALS: Sales and profits are in thousands of dollars—add 000 to get the full amount. 2010 Note: Financial information for 2010 was not available for all companies at press time.

2010 Sales: $1,121,490	2010 Profits: $ 540	**U.S. Stock Ticker:** Subsidiary
2009 Sales: $1,202,920	2009 Profits: $11,710	**Int'l Ticker:** PCW **Int'l Exchange:** Frankfurt-Euronext
2008 Sales: $1,287,570	2008 Profits: $12,530	**Employees:** 1,700
2007 Sales: $1,123,040	2007 Profits: $12,390	**Fiscal Year Ends:** 3/31
2006 Sales: $	2006 Profits: $	**Parent Company:** PERUNI HOLDING GMBH

SALARIES/BENEFITS:

Pension Plan:	ESOP Stock Plan:	Profit Sharing:	Top Exec. Salary: $	Bonus: $
Savings Plan:	Stock Purch. Plan:		Second Exec. Salary: $	Bonus: $

OTHER THOUGHTS:

Apparent Women Officers or Directors: 1
Hot Spot for Advancement for Women/Minorities:

LOCATIONS: ("Y" = Yes)

West:	Southwest:	Midwest:	Southeast:	Northeast:	International:
					Y

PEGASYSTEMS INC

www.pega.com

Industry Group Code: 511210H Ranks within this company's industry group: Sales: 11   Profits: 9

Hardware:	Software:		Telecommunications:	Electronic Publishing:	Equipment:	Specialty Services:	
Computers:	Consumer:		Local:	Online Service:	Telecom:	Consulting:	Y
Accessories:	Corporate:	Y	Long Distance:	TV/Cable or Wireless:	Communication:	Contract Manufacturing:	
Network Equipment:	Telecom:		Cellular:	Games:	Distribution:	Processing:	
Chips/Circuits:	Internet:		Internet Service:	Financial Data:	VAR/Reseller:	Staff/Outsourcing:	
Parts/Drives:					Satellite Srv./Equip.:	Specialty Services:	Y

TYPES OF BUSINESS:

Business Process Management Software
Consulting

BRANDS/DIVISIONS/AFFILIATES:

PegaRULES Process Commander (The)
Pegasystems SmartBPM Suite (The)
SmartPaaS
Chordiant Software Inc

CONTACTS: Note: Officers with more than one job title may be intentionally listed here more than once.

Alan Trefler, CEO
Craig A. Dynes, CFO/Sr. VP
Grant Johnson, Chief Mktg. Officer
Jeff Yanagi, Sr. VP-Human Capital
Mike Pyle, Sr. VP-Prod. Dev.
Mike Pyle, Sr. VP-Eng.
Shawn Hoyt, General Counsel/VP
Max Mayer, Sr. VP-Corp. Dev.
Brian Callahan, Dir.-Corp. Comm.
Douglas Kra, Sr. VP-Global Svcs.
Leon Trefler, Sr. VP-Sales
Alan Trefler, Chmn.

Phone: 617-374-9600	Fax: 617-374-9620
Toll-Free:	
Address: 101 Main St, Cambridge, MA 02142-1590 US	

GROWTH PLANS/SPECIAL FEATURES:

Pegasystems, Inc. develops, markets, licenses and supports business process management (BPM) software. The firm's Build for Change software technology directly captures business objectives, automating programming and automating work, enabling groups to build, deploy, and change enterprise applications. Build for Change is standards-based and can leverage existing technology investments to reduce implementation time. The PegaRULES Process Commander, a rules engine that offers features such as a business process application, browser-based graphical development environment, execution engine and management dashboard. The Pegasystems SmartBPM Suite adds content management, process simulation, enterprise integration, process analysis, portal integration and case management capabilities to the PegaRULES Process Commander. SmartPaaS is a cloud computing solution that allows for the quick development and deployment of dynamic business applications. Additionally, the firm's software supports secondary frameworks for industry specific purposes, such as financial services, healthcare and insurance, as well as exceptions management, including transactions that are not automatically processed by existing systems. The company also offers customer support and training/professional services. Pegasystems markets its products to customers in the financial services, healthcare, insurance, telecommunications, life sciences, travel, manufacturing and government sectors. The company maintains strategic partnerships with numerous companies, including IBM, Infosys, Wipro and Tata Consultancy Services. Its major clients include HSBC Holdings PLC, Citigroup, HealthNow New York, Inc., American National Insurance Group, Advanced Micro Devices, Inc., Novartis International AG and The British Airport Authority. In April 2010, the company acquired software developer Chordiant Software, Inc. for $161.5 million.

FINANCIALS: Sales and profits are in thousands of dollars—add 000 to get the full amount. 2010 Note: Financial information for 2010 was not available for all companies at press time.

2010 Sales: $	2010 Profits: $	**U.S. Stock Ticker: PEGA**
2009 Sales: $264,013	2009 Profits: $32,212	**Int'l Ticker:** Int'l Exchange:
2008 Sales: $211,647	2008 Profits: $10,977	Employees: 1,076
2007 Sales: $161,949	2007 Profits: $6,595	Fiscal Year Ends: 12/31
2006 Sales: $	2006 Profits: $	Parent Company:

SALARIES/BENEFITS:

Pension Plan:	ESOP Stock Plan:	Profit Sharing:	Top Exec. Salary: $288,000	Bonus: $220,205
Savings Plan:	Stock Purch. Plan:		Second Exec. Salary: $288,000	Bonus: $158,750

OTHER THOUGHTS:

Apparent Women Officers or Directors:
Hot Spot for Advancement for Women/Minorities:

LOCATIONS: ("Y" = Yes)

West:	Southwest:	Midwest:	Southeast:	Northeast:	International:
Y	Y	Y	Y	Y	Y

PHOENIX TECHNOLOGIES LTD   www.phoenix.com

Industry Group Code: 511210I Ranks within this company's industry group: Sales: 7 Profits: 6

Hardware:	Software:		Telecommunications:	Electronic Publishing:	Equipment:	Specialty Services:	
Computers:	Consumer:	Y	Local:	Online Service:	Telecom:	Consulting:	Y
Accessories:	Corporate:	Y	Long Distance:	TV/Cable or Wireless:	Communication:	Contract Manufacturing:	
Network Equipment:	Telecom:		Cellular:	Games:	Distribution:	Processing:	
Chips/Circuits:	Internet:		Internet Service:	Financial Data:	VAR/Reseller:	Staff/Outsourcing:	
Parts/Drives:					Satellite Srv./Equip.:	Specialty Services:	Y

TYPES OF BUSINESS:
Computer Software-Core System Software
Engineering & Support Services

BRANDS/DIVISIONS/AFFILIATES:
Phoenix CSS
Phoenix SecureCore
Phoenix TrustedCore
SecureCore
Marlin Equity Partners
Pharaoh Acquisition LLC

CONTACTS: *Note: Officers with more than one job title may be intentionally listed here more than once.*
Tom Lacey, CEO
Richard Arnold, COO
Tom Lacey, Pres.
Robert Andersen, CFO
Surendra Arora, VP-Mktg.
Babak Dehnad, VP-Human Resources
Stephen Jones, CTO
Surendra Arora, VP-Prod. Mgmt.
Srinivas Raman, VP-Eng.
Timothy Chu, General Counsel/Sec./VP
David Gibbs, Sr. VP/Gen. Mgr.-Worldwide Field Oper.
Apu Kumar, VP-Bus. Dev.
John Correia, VP/Gen. Mgr.-Core Systems Software
Jeffrey Smith, Chmn.

Phone: 408-570-1000	Fax: 408-570-1001
Toll-Free: 800-677-7305	
Address: 915 Murphy Ranch Rd., Milpitas, CA 95035 US	

GROWTH PLANS/SPECIAL FEATURES:
Phoenix Technologies Ltd. designs, develops and supports core system software (CSS, a modern form of BIOS) for personal computers and connected devices. This type of software, often referred to as firmware, is typically stored in a non-volatile memory chip that retains information even when the power is turned off, and is accessed and executed during the power-up process to test, initialize and manage the device's hardware. Its products are installed in approximately 125 million devices annually. The firm's offerings consist of the Phoenix CSS line. Phoenix SecureCore is the firm's primary CSS product and assists the compatibility, connectivity, security and manageability of components in modern desktop and notebook PCs; PC-based servers; and embedded computing systems. Phoenix TrustedCore is the predecessor to SecureCore, and is still offered for older model computers. Phoenix Award is utilized by high volume PC and digital device electronics design and manufacturing companies, offering standards-based features, simplicity and small code size. In April 2010, the company sold its FailSafe advanced theft-loss protection and prevention solution to Absolute Software Corporation. In June 2010, the firm sold its eSupport assets to eSupport.com, Inc. for roughly $1.6 million; and sold its HyperCore, HyperSpace and Phoenix Flip instant-on and client virtualization products to HP for approximately $12 million. In November 2010, Phoenix Technologies was acquired by Pharaoh Acquisition, LLC, an affiliate of Marlin Equity Partners. The firm is now an indirect subsidiary of Marlin Equity.

Employees are offered medical, dental and vision insurance; disability coverage; life insurance; an employee assistance program; flexible spending accounts and a fitness reimbursement program.

FINANCIALS: Sales and profits are in thousands of dollars—add 000 to get the full amount. 2010 Note: Financial information for 2010 was not available for all companies at press time.

2010 Sales: $	2010 Profits: $	**U.S. Stock Ticker:** Private
2009 Sales: $67,697	2009 Profits: $-75,272	**Int'l Ticker:** Int'l Exchange:
2008 Sales: $73,702	2008 Profits: $-6,223	Employees: 462
2007 Sales: $47,017	2007 Profits: $-16,409	Fiscal Year Ends: 9/30
2006 Sales: $60,495	2006 Profits: $-43,969	Parent Company: MARLIN EQUITY

SALARIES/BENEFITS:
Pension Plan:	ESOP Stock Plan:	Profit Sharing:	Top Exec. Salary: $450,000	Bonus: $86,592
Savings Plan: Y	Stock Purch. Plan: Y		Second Exec. Salary: $319,000	Bonus: $60,805

OTHER THOUGHTS:
Apparent Women Officers or Directors: 1
Hot Spot for Advancement for Women/Minorities:

LOCATIONS: ("Y" = Yes)
West:	Southwest:	Midwest:	Southeast:	Northeast:	International:
Y				Y	Y

PHOTRONICS INC

www.photronics.com

Industry Group Code: 333295 Ranks within this company's industry group: Sales: 11   Profits: 7

Hardware:		Software:	Telecommunications:	Electronic Publishing:	Equipment:	Specialty Services:	
Computers:		Consumer:	Local:	Online Service:	Telecom:	Consulting:	
Accessories:		Corporate:	Long Distance:	TV/Cable or Wireless:	Communication:	Contract Manufacturing:	Y
Network Equipment:		Telecom:	Cellular:	Games:	Distribution:	Processing:	
Chips/Circuits:	Y	Internet:	Internet Service:	Financial Data:	VAR/Reseller:	Staff/Outsourcing:	
Parts/Drives:					Satellite Srv./Equip.:	Specialty Services:	Y

TYPES OF BUSINESS:

Semiconductor Manufacturing Equipment
Photomasks

BRANDS/DIVISIONS/AFFILIATES:

PKL Ltd
Photronics Semiconductor Mask Corporation
CyberMask
MaskLink

CONTACTS: *Note: Officers with more than one job title may be intentionally listed here more than once.*

Constantine S. (Deno) Macricostas, CEO
Soo Hong Jeong, COO
Constantine S. (Deno) Macricostas, Pres.
Sean Smith, CFO/Sr. VP
Chris Progler, CTO/VP
Richelle E. Burr, General Counsel/Corp. Sec./VP
Scott J. Gish, VP-Corp. Comm.
Peter S. Kirlin, Sr. VP-U.S. & Europe
Constantine S. (Deno) Macricostas, Chmn.
Soo Hong Jeong, Pres., Asia Oper.

Phone: 203-775-9000	Fax: 203-740-5618
Toll-Free: 800-292-9396	
Address: 15 Secor Rd., Brookfield, CT 06804 US	

GROWTH PLANS/SPECIAL FEATURES:

Photronics, Inc. is one of the world's leading photomask manufactures. Photomasks, key elements in the production of semiconductors and flat panel displays (FPDs), are photographic quartz plates that contain microscopic images of electronic circuits. They are used as masters to transfer patterns onto semiconductor wafers and flat panel substrates during the fabrication of integrated circuits (ICs). The company's photomasks are manufactured using either electron beam or optical-based technologies, in accordance with circuit designs provided by its customers on a confidential basis. In addition to manufacturing, Photronics inspects, repairs and recycles photomasks. The company utilizes proprietary processes to clean the photomasks prior to shipment. Photronics also provides data services, through programs like MaskLink and CyberMask. MaskLink is a password-protected extranet that enables customers to check their mask product status online, giving customers access to production data and automated status reports. CyberMask is a program that automates the transmission, receipt and preparation of customer data and processes mask requirements. The company operates nine manufacturing facilities in the U.S., Europe and Asia. Its subsidiaries include PK, Ltd. in Korea and Photronics Semiconductor Mask Corporation in Taiwan. In early 2010, the firm sold its Shanghai manufacturing facility after stopping activities there in 2009.

FINANCIALS: Sales and profits are in thousands of dollars—add 000 to get the full amount. 2010 Note: Financial information for 2010 was not available for all companies at press time.

2010 Sales: $425,554	2010 Profits: $23,922	**U.S. Stock Ticker:** PLAB
2009 Sales: $361,353	2009 Profits: $-41,910	**Int'l Ticker:** Int'l Exchange:
2008 Sales: $422,548	2008 Profits: $-210,765	**Employees:** 1,300
2007 Sales: $421,479	2007 Profits: $24,523	**Fiscal Year Ends:** 10/31
2006 Sales: $454,875	2006 Profits: $29,332	**Parent Company:**

SALARIES/BENEFITS:

Pension Plan:	ESOP Stock Plan:	Profit Sharing:	Top Exec. Salary: $516,923	Bonus: $
Savings Plan: Y	Stock Purch. Plan:		Second Exec. Salary: $367,308	Bonus: $

OTHER THOUGHTS:

Apparent Women Officers or Directors:
Hot Spot for Advancement for Women/Minorities:

LOCATIONS: ("Y" = Yes)

West:	Southwest:	Midwest:	Southeast:	Northeast:	International:
Y	Y			Y	Y

PINNACLE SYSTEMS INC

www.pinnaclesys.com

Industry Group Code: 334310 Ranks within this company's industry group: Sales: Profits:

Hardware:		Software:		Telecommunications:	Electronic Publishing:	Equipment:	Specialty Services:
Computers:		Consumer:	Y	Local:	Online Service:	Telecom:	Consulting:
Accessories:	Y	Corporate:		Long Distance:	TV/Cable or Wireless:	Communication:	Contract Manufacturing:
Network Equipment:		Telecom:		Cellular:	Games:	Distribution:	Processing:
Chips/Circuits:		Internet:		Internet Service:	Financial Data:	VAR/Reseller:	Staff/Outsourcing:
Parts/Drives:						Satellite Srv./Equip.:	Specialty Services:

TYPES OF BUSINESS:

Video Editing Technology
Audio Editing Technology
DVD Recording Technology

BRANDS/DIVISIONS/AFFILIATES:

Avid Technology Inc
Dazzle
Pinnacle Studio
Pinnacle Studio Plus
Pinnacle Studio Ultimate
Pro Tools

CONTACTS: Note: Officers with more than one job title may be intentionally listed here more than once.
Sharad Rastogi, Gen. Mgr.

Phone: 650-526-1600	Fax: 650-526-1601
Toll-Free:	
Address: 280 N. Bernardo Ave., Mountain View, CA 94043 US	

GROWTH PLANS/SPECIAL FEATURES:

Pinnacle Systems, Inc., a consumer division of Avid Technologies, Inc., manufactures and distributes products designed to provide clients with digital video solutions. The company's hardware and software, used to create, edit, view and distribute media content using a personal computer, is generally sold to independent consumers. Pinnacle's flagship product line is the Pinnacle Studio suite of hardware and software, which allows entry-level users to capture, edit and produce video and photo. The product line is available in three configurations: Pinnacle Studio, Pinnacle Studio Plus and Pinnacle Studio Ultimate. Pinnacle Studio is designed for entry-level users to enhance and share their projects with others. Pinnacle Studio Plus and Pinnacle Studio Ultimate offer additional features such as high-definition editing and output that are intended for advanced video enthusiasts who require greater power, control and quality to create more professional looking results. The company offers additional third-party video plugins under the RedGiant, proDAD and NewBlue brand names, which are designed to give videos additional special effects. The firm also offers the Dazzle product line, which is designed to acquire video from video capture devices and apply minor edits, and the Pro Tools audio editing suite. Pinnacle's products are marketed around the world through retailers, distributors and the Internet.

FINANCIALS: Sales and profits are in thousands of dollars—add 000 to get the full amount. 2010 Note: Financial information for 2010 was not available for all companies at press time.

2010 Sales: $	2010 Profits: $	U.S. Stock Ticker: Subsidiary	
2009 Sales: $	2009 Profits: $	Int'l Ticker: Int'l Exchange:	
2008 Sales: $	2008 Profits: $	Employees:	
2007 Sales: $	2007 Profits: $	Fiscal Year Ends: 6/30	
2006 Sales: $	2006 Profits: $	Parent Company: AVID TECHNOLOGY INC	

SALARIES/BENEFITS:

Pension Plan:	ESOP Stock Plan:	Profit Sharing:	Top Exec. Salary: $	Bonus: $
Savings Plan: Y	Stock Purch. Plan:		Second Exec. Salary: $	Bonus: $

OTHER THOUGHTS:

Apparent Women Officers or Directors:
Hot Spot for Advancement for Women/Minorities:

LOCATIONS: ("Y" = Yes)

West:	Southwest:	Midwest:	Southeast:	Northeast:	International:
Y					

PIONEER CORPORATION

www.pioneer.jp

Industry Group Code: 334310 Ranks within this company's industry group: Sales: 7 Profits: 2

Hardware:		Software:	Telecommunications:	Electronic Publishing:	Equipment:		Specialty Services:
Computers:		Consumer:	Local:	Online Service:	Telecom:	Y	Consulting:
Accessories:	Y	Corporate:	Long Distance:	TV/Cable or Wireless:	Communication:		Contract Manufacturing:
Network Equipment:		Telecom:	Cellular:	Games:	Distribution:		Processing:
Chips/Circuits:		Internet:	Internet Service:	Financial Data:	VAR/Reseller:		Staff/Outsourcing:
Parts/Drives:	Y				Satellite Srv./Equip.:		Specialty Services:

TYPES OF BUSINESS:

Consumer Electronics
Audio/Video Equipment
CD/DVD Players
Automotive Electronics
Telecommunications Equipment
Research & Development
Software Development

BRANDS/DIVISIONS/AFFILIATES:

Pioneer Marketing Corp
Pioneer Sales & Marketing Corp.
Pioneer Digital Design & Manufacturing Corp.
Anyo Pioneer Motor Information Technology Co. Ltd.
NTT Docomo, Inc.
MicroVision, Inc.

CONTACTS: Note: Officers with more than one job title may be intentionally listed here more than once.

Susumu Kotani, Pres.
Satoshi Matsumoto, Managing Dir.-Pioneer Mktg. Corp.
Hideki Okayasu, Sr. Managing Dir.-Human Resources Div.
Masanori Koshoubu, Gen. Mgr.-R&D
Mikio Ono, Gen. Mgr.-IT Div.
Hideki Okayasu, Sr. Managing Dir.-Gen. Admin. Div.
Masanori Koshoubu, Managing Dir.-Legal & Intellectual Property Div.
Satoshi Matsumoto, Managing Dir.-New Bus. Dev.
Hideki Okayasu, Sr. Managing Dir.-Corp. Comm.
Hideki Okayasu, Sr. Managing Dir.-Finance & Acct. Div.
Satoshi Matsumoto, Managing Dir.-Quality Assurance Div.
Mikio Ono, Gen. Mgr.-Home Audiovisual Bus.
Satoshi Matsumoto, Managing Dir.-Pioneer Sales & Mktg. Corp.
Mikio Ono, Gen. Mgr.-Corp. Planning Div.
Tatsuo Takeuchi, Gen. Mgr.-Int'l Bus. Div.

Phone: 81-44-580-3211	Fax:
Toll-Free:	
Address: 1-1 Shin-ogura, Saiwai-ku, Kawasaki-shi, Kanagawa, 212-0031 Japan	

GROWTH PLANS/SPECIAL FEATURES:

Pioneer Corporation, headquartered in Japan, is a leading manufacturer of consumer electronics. The firm operates mainly in three segments: home electronics, car electronics and others. The home electronics segment manufactures home theater components such as Blu-ray disc players, DVD recorders, surround sound systems, audiovisual components, Blu-ray and DVD drives for computers, professional DJ equipment and professional speakers. The car electronics segment manufactures vehicle audiovisual and entertainment components such as car navigation systems that provide traffic congestion information, places of interest data and weather updates; Apple iPod connections; car theaters with DVD players and LCD monitors; speakers; and Handsfree mobile phone systems. The others segment focuses on researching organic light emitting diode (OLED)display applications in mobile phones and car stereos, as well as future applications in in-car panels, medical devices, measuring instruments, telephones and system integration solutions. Pioneer's operations also include patent licensing with regard to DVD recorders, car navigation systems and other products. During 2009, the firm announced plans to divest 30% of its international subsidiaries and reduce its workforce by approximately 10,000; released four new car navigation systems in Japan; and established two joint ventures: optical disk developer Pioneer Digital Design and Manufacturing Corporation (with Sharp Corporation); and Anyo Pioneer Motor Information Technology Co., Ltd., a Chinese car navigation systems developer (with Shanghai Automotive Industry Corporation Group). Also in late 2009, the firm moved its principal office to Kanagawa Prefecture. In February 2010, the company entered a business alliance with Mitsubishi Chemical Corporation related to the development of OLED lighting. In October 2010, Pioneer entered a business alliance with NTT Docomo, Inc. for the development of a wireless car navigation application for smartphones. In December 2010, the firm entered an agreement with MicroVision, Inc., to develop and manufacture projector modules.

FINANCIALS: Sales and profits are in thousands of dollars—add 000 to get the full amount. 2010 Note: Financial information for 2010 was not available for all companies at press time.

2010 Sales: $	2010 Profits: $	**U.S. Stock Ticker:**
2009 Sales: $6,022,370	2009 Profits: $1,408,170	**Int'l Ticker: 6773** Int'l Exchange: Tokyo-TSE
2008 Sales: $7,753,300	2008 Profits: $-179,900	Employees: 42,775
2007 Sales: $7,978,100	2007 Profits: $-67,600	Fiscal Year Ends: 3/31
2006 Sales: $7,549,600	2006 Profits: $-849,900	Parent Company:

SALARIES/BENEFITS:

Pension Plan:	ESOP Stock Plan:	Profit Sharing:	Top Exec. Salary: $	Bonus: $
Savings Plan:	Stock Purch. Plan:		Second Exec. Salary: $	Bonus: $

OTHER THOUGHTS:

Apparent Women Officers or Directors:
Hot Spot for Advancement for Women/Minorities:

LOCATIONS: ("Y" = Yes)

West:	Southwest:	Midwest:	Southeast:	Northeast:	International:
Y					Y

470 Plunkett Research, Ltd.

Note: Financial information, benefits and other data can change quickly and may vary from those stated here.

PITNEY BOWES SOFTWARE INC

www.pbinsight.com

Industry Group Code: 511210K Ranks within this company's industry group: Sales: Profits:

Hardware:	Software:		Telecommunications:	Electronic Publishing:	Equipment:	Specialty Services:	
Computers:	Consumer:		Local:	Online Service:	Telecom:	Consulting:	
Accessories:	Corporate:	Y	Long Distance:	TV/Cable or Wireless:	Communication:	Contract Manufacturing:	
Network Equipment:	Telecom: .		Cellular:	Games:	Distribution:	Processing:	
Chips/Circuits:	Internet:		Internet Service:	Financial Data:	VAR/Reseller:	Staff/Outsourcing:	
Parts/Drives:					Satellite Srv./Equip.:	Specialty Services:	Y

TYPES OF BUSINESS:

Software-Mass Mailing Marketing & Database Management
Electronic Document Systems
Business Geographics Products
Customer Communications Management Products
Data Quality Products
Data Integration Products
Support Services

BRANDS/DIVISIONS/AFFILIATES:

Ptiney Bowes Inc
Merge/Purge Plus
Data Flow
Address Now
Pitney Bowes Business Insight
DOC1
StreamWeaver
e2 Pay

CONTACTS: Note: Officers with more than one job title may be intentionally listed here more than once.

Ben Semmes, COO
John O'Hara, Pres.
Jeff Whiteside, CFO
David Newberry, Chief Mktg. Officer
Josette Valenti, Dir.-Human Resources
Jay Bourland, CTO
Angelo Chaclas, General Counsel/VP-Intellectual Property
Doug Gordon, VP-Bus. Planning
Luke McKeever, Exec. VP-Portrait Software
Jonathan Wright, VP/Gen. Mgr.-APAC
Brian Lantz, Exec. VP/Gen. Mgr.-Americas
Gary Roberts, Exec. VP-EMEA

Phone: 301-731-2300	Fax: 301-731-0360
Toll-Free: 800-327-8627	
Address: 1 Global View, Troy, NY 12180 US	

GROWTH PLANS/SPECIAL FEATURES:

Pitney Bowes Software, Inc. develops, manufactures, licenses, sells and supports software products for specialized marketing and mail management applications. It operates primarily through subsidiary Pitney Bowes Business Insight, and is itself a subsidiary of Pitney Bowes, Inc. Its software serves the needs of a wide variety of industries and clients, including financial services, retail, telecommunications, utilities, insurance, GIS/mapping and health care. Pitney Bowes Software also serves government agencies such as FEMA, the IRS, the U.S. Senate and Global Student Loan Corporation. The company offers three types of services: consulting, predictive analysis and business process outsourcing (BPO). The consulting services cover eight areas, which are: Data Integration, allowing for ease of information use through Data Flow software; Customer Data Quality, which allows for the management of customer data though a suite of software such as Merge/Purge Plus; Global Address Cleansing, which allows for the management of mailing addresses through software such as Address Now; Document Creation, though the DOC1 series of software; Distributed Output Management, which manages print streams through StreamWeaver and DOC1 applications; Electronic Document Management, including archiving and retrieval with products such as e2 Vault and OpenEDMS; Online Account Management, which gives customers ease of use on a company's web site with offerings e2 Present, e2 Online Account Management and e2 Pay; and Mailing Efficiency Software. Its predictive analysis services include predictive analytics models to predict performance drivers at new locations; strategic market planning; site selection research; sales transfer studies; customer profiling; applied research report packages; store budgeting; and problem store analysis. Pitney Bowes Software's BPO services include both full outsourcing and software licensing options.

FINANCIALS: Sales and profits are in thousands of dollars—add 000 to get the full amount. 2010 Note: Financial information for 2010 was not available for all companies at press time.

2010 Sales: $	2010 Profits: $	**U.S. Stock Ticker: Subsidiary**
2009 Sales: $	2009 Profits: $	**Int'l Ticker:** Int'l Exchange:
2008 Sales: $	2008 Profits: $	Employees:
2007 Sales: $37,800	2007 Profits: $	Fiscal Year Ends: 3/31
2006 Sales: $	2006 Profits: $	Parent Company: PITNEY BOWES INC

SALARIES/BENEFITS:

Pension Plan:	ESOP Stock Plan:	Profit Sharing:	Top Exec. Salary: $	Bonus: $
Savings Plan: Y	Stock Purch. Plan: Y		Second Exec. Salary: $	Bonus: $

OTHER THOUGHTS:

Apparent Women Officers or Directors: 1
Hot Spot for Advancement for Women/Minorities:

LOCATIONS: ("Y" = Yes)

West:	Southwest:	Midwest:	Southeast:	Northeast:	International:
Y	Y	Y	Y	Y	Y

PLANTRONICS INC

www.plantronics.com

Industry Group Code: 3342 Ranks within this company's industry group: Sales: 3 Profits: 7

Hardware:		Software:	Telecommunications:	Electronic Publishing:	Equipment:		Specialty Services:	
Computers:		Consumer:	Local:	Online Service:	Telecom:		Consulting:	
Accessories:	Y	Corporate:	Long Distance:	TV/Cable or Wireless:	Communication:	Y	Contract Manufacturing:	
Network Equipment:		Telecom:	Cellular:	Games:	Distribution:		Processing:	
Chips/Circuits:		Internet:	Internet Service:	Financial Data:	VAR/Reseller:		Staff/Outsourcing:	
Parts/Drives:					Satellite Srv./Equip.:		Specialty Services:	

TYPES OF BUSINESS:

Communications Headsets
Communications Accessories
Specialty Telephone Products
Wireless Headsets

BRANDS/DIVISIONS/AFFILIATES:

Clarity
Altec Lansing

CONTACTS: Note: Officers with more than one job title may be intentionally listed here more than once.

Ken Kannappan, CEO
Ken Kannappan, Pres.
Barbara Scherer, CFO
Donald Houston, Sr. VP-Sales
Mike Perkins, VP-Tech.
Mike Perkins, VP-Prod. Dev.
Barbara Scherer, Sr. VP-Admin.
Richard Pickard, General Counsel/VP-Legal/Corp. Sec.
Larry Wuerz, Sr. VP-Worldwide Oper.
Greg Klaben, VP-Investor Rel.
Barbara Scherer, Sr. VP-Finance
Barry Margerum, Chief Mktg. Officer
Renee Niemi, Sr. VP-Comm. Solutions
Carsten Trads, Pres., Clarity Div.
Greg Tyrrell, Dir.-Finance, EMEA/European Investor Rel.
Marvin Tseu, Chmn.
Philip Vanhoutte, Managing Dir.-EMEA

Phone: 831-426-5858	Fax: 831-426-6098
Toll-Free: 800-544-4660	
Address: 345 Encinal St., Santa Cruz, CA 95060 US	

GROWTH PLANS/SPECIAL FEATURES:

Plantronics, Inc. designs, manufactures, markets and sells lightweight communications headsets, telephone headset systems and accessories and other specialty products for the hearing impaired for the business and consumer markets. Its products, primarily marketed under the Plantronics brand, are designed for use in offices and contact centers, with mobile and cordless phones, and with computers and gaming consoles. The company's primary product categories include Office and Contact Center products, which include corded and cordless communication headsets, audio processors and telephone systems; Mobile products, which include Bluetooth and corded products for mobile phones; Gaming and Computer Audio products, including PC and gaming headsets; and Clarity products, comprised of specialty products marketed for hearing impaired individuals under the Clarity brand. Product accessories include batteries and chargers, cords, ear cushions and attachments and voice tubes. The company ships its communications products to over 65 countries through a worldwide network of distributors, original equipment manufacturers (OEMs), wireless carriers, retailers and telephony service providers. The firm has well-developed distribution channels in North America, Europe, Australia and New Zealand. In January 2009, the company announced plans to reduce its worldwide workforce by 18%. In December 2009, the firm sold Altec Lansing, its Audio Entertainment Group segment and a manufacturer of docking audio products, computer and home entertainment sound systems and headphones, to an affiliate of Prophet Equity LP, a private equity firm. Following this divestiture, the company reorganized its operations into one segment.

Employees are offered medical, dental and vision insurance; life insurance; business travel and accident insurance; short- and long-term disability coverage; access to company sponsored cafeterias; onsite credit union; onsite massage and dry cleaning services; discounts for exercise facility memberships; a 401(k) plan; profit sharing; a stock purchase plan; and educational assistance. The firm also hosts an annual Olympics event for its employees.

FINANCIALS: Sales and profits are in thousands of dollars—add 000 to get the full amount. 2010 Note: Financial information for 2010 was not available for all companies at press time.

2010 Sales: $613,837	2010 Profits: $57,378	**U.S. Stock Ticker:** PLT
2009 Sales: $674,590	2009 Profits: $-64,899	**Int'l Ticker:**　Int'l Exchange:
2008 Sales: $747,935	2008 Profits: $68,395	Employees: 3,200
2007 Sales: $800,154	2007 Profits: $50,143	Fiscal Year Ends: 9/30
2006 Sales: $750,394	2006 Profits: $81,150	Parent Company:

SALARIES/BENEFITS:

Pension Plan:	ESOP Stock Plan:	Profit Sharing: Y	Top Exec. Salary: $627,000	Bonus: $159,415
Savings Plan: Y	Stock Purch. Plan: Y		Second Exec. Salary: $375,000	Bonus: $79,523

OTHER THOUGHTS:

Apparent Women Officers or Directors: 2
Hot Spot for Advancement for Women/Minorities: Y

LOCATIONS: ("Y" = Yes)

West:	Southwest:	Midwest:	Southeast:	Northeast:	International:
Y			Y	Y	Y

PLATO LEARNING INC

www.plato.com

Industry Group Code: 511210P Ranks within this company's industry group: Sales: 3 Profits: 2

Hardware:	Software:		Telecommunications:	Electronic Publishing:	Equipment:	Specialty Services:	
Computers:	Consumer:	Y	Local:	Online Service:	Telecom:	Consulting:	
Accessories:	Corporate:		Long Distance:	TV/Cable or Wireless:	Communication:	Contract Manufacturing:	
Network Equipment:	Telecom:		Cellular:	Games:	Distribution:	Processing:	
Chips/Circuits:	Internet:		Internet Service:	Financial Data:	VAR/Reseller:	Staff/Outsourcing:	
Parts/Drives:					Satellite Srv./Equip.:	Specialty Services:	Y

TYPES OF BUSINESS:
Educational Software
E-Learning Services

BRANDS/DIVISIONS/AFFILIATES:
PLATO
Straight Curve
PLATO eduTest
PLATO Test Packs with Prescriptions
Academic Systems
PLATO Learning Environment
PLE 2.0

CONTACTS: Note: Officers with more than one job title may be intentionally listed here more than once.
Vincent (Vin) Riera, CEO
Vincent (Vin) Riera, Pres.
Robert J. Rueckl, CFO/VP/Corp. Sec.
Mary Schneider, Dir.-Mktg.
Stacey Herteux, Dir.-Human Resources
Mark Allen, CTO/VP
Jamie Candee, VP-Prod. & Mktg.
Ian Kees, Corp. Counsel/VP
Dave Adams, VP-Education Strategy & Content
Jennifer Morgans, VP-Customer Experience
David W. Smith, Chmn.

Phone: 952-832-1000	Fax: 952-832-1200
Toll-Free: 800-447-5286	
Address: 5600 W. 83rd St., Ste. 300, 8200 Tower, Bloomington, MN 55437 US	

GROWTH PLANS/SPECIAL FEATURES:
PLATO Learning, Inc. primarily develops and markets educational software and related services. It operates according to a SaaS (Software-as-a-Service) model, with the majority of its products delivered on a hosted, subscription service basis. The company provides online instruction, curriculum management, assessment and related professional development services K-12 schools, community colleges and other educational institutions across the U.S. Its flagship products are the PLATO brand Elementary Solutions and Secondary Solutions self-paced tutoring programs, which include coursework in reading, writing, language arts, mathematics, science and social studies. The firm also offers Straight Curve, providing a set of multimedia instructional materials designed to be integrated into normal classroom instruction. For assessment, the company offers PLATO eduTest, PLATO Test Packs with Prescriptions, Simulated Test Systems and Simulated Certification Tests. The firm also markets the Academic Systems brand of post-secondary materials, mainly products for students who have completed high school but are not yet ready for college classes. In addition to elementary and secondary education products, it offers post-secondary programs for college and adult students, such as developmental education courses, educator preparation and adult education. Through its web-based platform, the PLATO Learning Environment (PLE), the firm delivers all of the products mentioned above, while also allowing teachers to upload their own content. Besides products, the firm offers certain professional services, including consulting, professional development, curriculum and assessment management, funding recovery, data and support services and field engineering. In June 2010, the firm began offering PLATO AP online courses for advanced students. In July 2010, PLATO and Catapult Learning created a strategic partnership to offer PLATO's instructional technology through Catapult's programs.

The company offers its employees medical and dental insurance; flexible spending accounts; a stock purchase plan; a 401(k); and tuition reimbursement.

FINANCIALS: Sales and profits are in thousands of dollars—add 000 to get the full amount. 2010 Note: Financial information for 2010 was not available for all companies at press time.

2010 Sales: $	2010 Profits: $	U.S. Stock Ticker: TUTR
2009 Sales: $65,183	2009 Profits: $ 957	Int'l Ticker: Int'l Exchange:
2008 Sales: $68,401	2008 Profits: $-91,897	Employees: 300
2007 Sales: $69,632	2007 Profits: $-14,876	Fiscal Year Ends: 10/31
2006 Sales: $90,719	2006 Profits: $-22,480	Parent Company:

SALARIES/BENEFITS:

Pension Plan:	ESOP Stock Plan:	Profit Sharing:	Top Exec. Salary: $390,000	Bonus: $233,883
Savings Plan: Y	Stock Purch. Plan: Y		Second Exec. Salary: $262,080	Bonus: $104,780

OTHER THOUGHTS:
Apparent Women Officers or Directors: 4
Hot Spot for Advancement for Women/Minorities: Y

LOCATIONS: ("Y" = Yes)

West:	Southwest:	Midwest:	Southeast:	Northeast:	International:
		Y			

PLEXUS CORP
www.plexus.com

Industry Group Code: 334419 Ranks within this company's industry group: Sales: 14 Profits: 9

Hardware:	Software:	Telecommunications:	Electronic Publishing:	Equipment:	Specialty Services:	
Computers:	Consumer:	Local:	Online Service:	Telecom:	Consulting:	Y
Accessories:	Corporate:	Long Distance:	TV/Cable or Wireless:	Communication:	Contract Manufacturing:	Y
Network Equipment:	Telecom:	Cellular:	Games:	Distribution:	Processing:	
Chips/Circuits:	Internet:	Internet Service:	Financial Data:	VAR/Reseller:	Staff/Outsourcing:	
Parts/Drives:				Satellite Srv./Equip.:	Specialty Services:	Y

TYPES OF BUSINESS:
Contract Electronics Manufacturing-Diversified
Hardware & Software Design
Printed Circuit Board Design
Prototyping Services
Material Procurement & Management
Logistics Services

BRANDS/DIVISIONS/AFFILIATES:

CONTACTS:
Note: Officers with more than one job title may be intentionally listed here more than once.
Dean Foate, CEO
Dean Foate, Pres.
Ginger Jones, CFO/VP
Joe Mauthe, VP-Global Human Resources
Steve Frisch, Sr. VP-Global Eng. Svcs.
Mike Buseman, Sr. VP-Global Mfg. Oper.
Angelo Ninivaggi, General Counsel/VP/Sec.
Mike Verstegen, Sr. VP-Global Market Dev.
George Setton, Corp. Treas.
Todd Kelsey, Sr. VP-Global Customer Svcs.
John L. Nussbaum, Chmn.
Yong Jin Lim, Regional Pres., Plexus Asia Pacific

Phone: 920-722-3451	Fax: 920-751-5395
Toll-Free:	
Address: 1 Plexus Way, Neenah, WI 54957-0156 US	

GROWTH PLANS/SPECIAL FEATURES:
Plexus Corp. is a global provider of electronic manufacturing services (EMS). The company also provides global logistics management, aftermarket service and repair. It provides these services to original equipment manufacturers (OEMs) and other technology companies in the wireline and networking, wireless infrastructure, medical, industrial and commercial and defense, security and aerospace market sectors. The company's customers may outsource all stages of the product realization process, including product specifications; development, design and design verification; regulatory compliance support; prototyping and new product introduction; manufacturing test equipment development; materials sourcing, procurement and supply-chain management; product assembly, manufacturing, configuration and test; order fulfillment; logistics; and service and repair. Plexus's services include product development and design services, such as project management, feasibility studies, product conceptualization and product verification testing; prototyping and new product introduction services, including prototype assembly; test equipment development services, including testing for printed circuit assemblies, subassemblies, system assemblies and finished products; material sourcing and procurement services; agile manufacturing services, including printed circuit board assembly, basic assembly, system integration and mechatronic integration; fulfillment and logistic services; and aftermarket support. Plexus has 22 active facilities in 15 locations in the U.S., Europe and Asia. In November 2010, the firm announced plans to expand its engineering capacity in Germany. In December 2010, the company announced plans for the construction of a new manufacturing facility in China.

The company offers employees medical, dental and vision insurance; flexible spending accounts; life and AD&D insurance; travel accident insurance; disability coverage; a 401(k) plan; on-site financial planning free of charge; tuition reimbursement; relocation assistance; an employee assistance program; and employee discounts.

FINANCIALS:
Sales and profits are in thousands of dollars—add 000 to get the full amount. 2010 Note: Financial information for 2010 was not available for all companies at press time.

2010 Sales: $2,013,393	2010 Profits: $89,533	U.S. Stock Ticker: PLXS
2009 Sales: $1,616,622	2009 Profits: $46,327	Int'l Ticker: Int'l Exchange:
2008 Sales: $1,841,622	2008 Profits: $84,144	Employees: 8,700
2007 Sales: $1,546,264	2007 Profits: $65,718	Fiscal Year Ends: 9/30
2006 Sales: $1,460,557	2006 Profits: $100,025	Parent Company:

SALARIES/BENEFITS:
Pension Plan:	ESOP Stock Plan:	Profit Sharing:	Top Exec. Salary: $766,632	Bonus: $1,527,627
Savings Plan: Y	Stock Purch. Plan:		Second Exec. Salary: $349,537	Bonus: $347,308

OTHER THOUGHTS:
Apparent Women Officers or Directors: 1
Hot Spot for Advancement for Women/Minorities:

LOCATIONS: ("Y" = Yes)
West:	Southwest:	Midwest:	Southeast:	Northeast:	International:
Y		Y		Y	Y

PMC-SIERRA INC

www.pmc-sierra.com

Industry Group Code: 33441 Ranks within this company's industry group: Sales: 40 Profits: 28

Hardware:		Software:		Telecommunications:		Electronic Publishing:	Equipment:		Specialty Services:
Computers:		Consumer:		Local:		Online Service:	Telecom:	Y	Consulting:
Accessories:		Corporate:		Long Distance:		TV/Cable or Wireless:	Communication:		Contract Manufacturing:
Network Equipment:	Y	Telecom:		Cellular:		Games:	Distribution:		Processing:
Chips/Circuits:	Y	Internet:		Internet Service:		Financial Data:	VAR/Reseller:		Staff/Outsourcing:
Parts/Drives:							Satellite Srv./Equip.:		Specialty Services:

TYPES OF BUSINESS:
Broadband Networking Technology
Semiconductors

BRANDS/DIVISIONS/AFFILIATES:
Wintegra Inc

CONTACTS: Note: Officers with more than one job title may be intentionally listed here more than once.
Gregory S. Lang, CEO
Colin C. Harris, COO
Gregory S. Lang, Pres.
Michael W. Zellner, CFO/VP
Robert M. Liszt, VP-Worldwide Sales
Lee Rhodes, VP-Worldwide Human Resources
Brian Gerson, VP-R&D
Tom Snodgrass, VP-Tech. Office
Alinka Flaminia, General Counsel/VP/Corp. Sec.
Tom Snodgrass, VP-Corp. Strategy
O. Daryn Lau, VP/Gen. Mgr.-Comm. Prod. Div.
Ra'ed O. Elmurib, VP-Corp. Dev./Gen. Mgr.-Microprocessor Prod. Div.
Tom Sun, VP/Gen. Mgr.-Broadband Wireless Div.
Jared Peters, VP/Gen. Mgr.-Channel Storage Div.
Robert L. Bailey, Chmn.

Phone: 408-239-8000	Fax: 408-492-1157
Toll-Free:	
Address: 3975 Freedom Cir., Mission Towers 1, Santa Clara, CA 95054 US	

GROWTH PLANS/SPECIAL FEATURES:
PMC-Sierra, Inc. designs, develops, markets and supports broadband communications and storage semiconductors. The firm markets it products to the Wide Area Network Infrastructure, Enterprise Networking and Access Network markets. The company offers roughly 400 different semiconductor devices that are sold to leading equipment and design manufacturers, who in turn supply their equipment principally to communications network service providers and enterprises. PMC-Sierra's semiconductors are broadly divided into seven categories: line interface units; radio frequency transreceivers; framers and mappers; packet and cell processors; controllers; microprocessor-based system-on-chips; and serializers/deserializers. Line interface units, also referred to as transceivers, transmit and receive signals over a physical medium such as wire, cable or fiber. Radio frequency transreceivers transmit and receive broadband signals using orthogonal frequency-division multiple access-based protocols and multiple-input-multiple-output antenna technology. Framers and mappers covert data, before it's sent to the next destination, into a proper format for transmission in the network. Packet and cell processors examine the contents of cells, or packets, and perform various management and reporting functions. Controller products (based on Fibre Channel, Serial Attached SCSI and Serial ATA) are used to build network-attached storage system architecture. Microprocessors perform computations that help identify and control the flow of signals and data in many different types of network equipment used in the communications, enterprise and consumer markets. Serializers and deserializers convert networking traffic between slower speed parallel streams and higher speed serial streams. PMC-Sierra sells its semiconductors into three network infrastructure areas: Access, encompassing wired and wireless equipment that transmits data to central offices; Enterprise Storage, enabling large quantities of data to be stored, managed and moved securely; and Enterprise Networking, enabling data communications and other local area network applications. In June 2010, PMC-Sierra acquired the channel storage operations of Adaptec, Inc. In November 2010, the firm acquired network processor developer Wintegra, Inc.

FINANCIALS: Sales and profits are in thousands of dollars—add 000 to get the full amount. 2010 Note: Financial information for 2010 was not available for all companies at press time.
2010 Sales: $	2010 Profits: $	**U.S. Stock Ticker: PMCS**
2009 Sales: $496,139	2009 Profits: $46,877	**Int'l Ticker:** Int'l Exchange:
2008 Sales: $525,075	2008 Profits: $128,297	Employees: 1,079
2007 Sales: $449,381	2007 Profits: $-49,104	Fiscal Year Ends: 12/31
2006 Sales: $424,992	2006 Profits: $-99,892	Parent Company:

SALARIES/BENEFITS:
Pension Plan:	ESOP Stock Plan:	Profit Sharing:	Top Exec. Salary: $630,000	Bonus: $480,000
Savings Plan: Y	Stock Purch. Plan:		Second Exec. Salary: $365,000	Bonus: $175,200

OTHER THOUGHTS:
Apparent Women Officers or Directors: 1
Hot Spot for Advancement for Women/Minorities:

LOCATIONS: ("Y" = Yes)
West:	Southwest:	Midwest:	Southeast:	Northeast:	International:
Y	Y	Y		Y	Y

POMEROY IT SOLUTIONS
www.pomeroy.com

Industry Group Code: 541513 Ranks within this company's industry group: Sales: Profits:

Hardware:	Software:	Telecommunications:	Electronic Publishing:	Equipment:		Specialty Services:	
Computers:	Consumer:	Local:	Online Service:	Telecom:		Consulting:	Y
Accessories:	Corporate:	Long Distance:	TV/Cable or Wireless:	Communication:		Contract Manufacturing:	
Network Equipment:	Telecom:	Cellular:	Games:	Distribution:	Y	Processing:	
Chips/Circuits:	Internet:	Internet Service:	Financial Data:	VAR/Reseller:	Y	Staff/Outsourcing:	Y
Parts/Drives:				Satellite Srv./Equip.:		Specialty Services:	Y

TYPES OF BUSINESS:
Enterprise Consulting
Customer Relationship Management
Infrastructure Solutions
Staffing Services
Financial Consulting
Network Integration Services
Network Equipment & Software, Reselling

BRANDS/DIVISIONS/AFFILIATES:
Platinum Equity LLC
OAO Technology Solutions Inc

CONTACTS: Note: Officers with more than one job title may be intentionally listed here more than once.
Christopher C. Froman, CEO
Christopher C. Froman, Pres.
Craig Propst, CFO/Sr. VP/Treas.
Peter Thelen, Sr. VP-Sales
Kristi Nelson, Sr. VP-Human Resources
Keith M. Blachowiak, CIO
Kristi Nelson, General Counsel
Keith M. Blachowiak, Sr. VP-Oper.
John McKenna, Sr. VP-Corp. Dev. & Svcs.
Marcia Pfiester, Controller/VP
Matt McGee, VP-Alliances & Tech. Staffing Svcs.

Phone: 859-586-0600	Fax: 859-586-4414
Toll-Free: 800-846-8727	
Address: 1020 Petersburg Rd., Hebron, KY 41048 US	

GROWTH PLANS/SPECIAL FEATURES:
Pomeroy IT Solutions is a global provider of IT products and services. Its offerings include IT infrastructure services, professional services, procurement and logistics services and technical staffing services, in addition to IT hardware, software and consulting. Pomeroy delivers these services to enterprise clients, mid-size businesses and state and local government entities. The company's IT infrastructure services include cabling; data center services; IT hardware management and support; service desk development; print management; and network and server support. Professional services include a number of solutions designed to meet the changing IT needs of enterprises. These include asset management; data storage and data center infrastructure development; unified communications technology; and virtualization of IT infrastructure. Its procurement and logistics services are designed to help organizations procure and distribute IT systems and include order management, provisioning, configuration assistance; image management, systems integration, warehousing logistics and distribution. The technical staffing segment helps companies recruit and retain IT professionals. Leading technology vendors, such as Apple, HP, Dell, Microsoft and Cisco, supply Pomeroy's hardware and software products. The company is owned by private equity firm Platinum Equity, LLC. In February 2010, Platinum Equity announced plans to combine Pomeroy with international IT service provider OAO Technology Solutions, Inc. The combined company will operate under the Pomeroy name.

The firm offers its employees medical, dental and vision insurance; life insurance; disability coverage; flexible spending accounts; a 401(k) plan; and an employee stock purchase plan.

FINANCIALS: Sales and profits are in thousands of dollars—add 000 to get the full amount. 2010 Note: Financial information for 2010 was not available for all companies at press time.

2010 Sales: $	2010 Profits: $	U.S. Stock Ticker: Private
2009 Sales: $	2009 Profits: $	Int'l Ticker: Int'l Exchange:
2008 Sales: $565,830	2008 Profits: $-13,156	Employees: 2,013
2007 Sales: $586,907	2007 Profits: $-112,233	Fiscal Year Ends: 12/31
2006 Sales: $592,981	2006 Profits: $1,143	Parent Company: PLATINUM EQUITY LLC

SALARIES/BENEFITS:

Pension Plan:	ESOP Stock Plan:	Profit Sharing:	Top Exec. Salary: $	Bonus: $
Savings Plan: Y	Stock Purch. Plan: Y		Second Exec. Salary: $	Bonus: $

OTHER THOUGHTS:
Apparent Women Officers or Directors: 2
Hot Spot for Advancement for Women/Minorities: Y

LOCATIONS: ("Y" = Yes)

West:	Southwest:	Midwest:	Southeast:	Northeast:	International:
		Y	Y	Y	Y

POSITIVO INFORMATICA SA

www.positivoinformatica.com.br

Industry Group Code: 334111 Ranks within this company's industry group: Sales: Profits:

Hardware:		Software:		Telecommunications:	Electronic Publishing:	Equipment:	Specialty Services:	
Computers:	Y	Consumer:	Y	Local:	Online Service:	Telecom:	Consulting:	
Accessories:		Corporate:		Long Distance:	TV/Cable or Wireless:	Communication:	Contract Manufacturing:	
Network Equipment:		Telecom:		Cellular:	Games:	Distribution:	Processing:	
Chips/Circuits:		Internet:		Internet Service:	Financial Data:	VAR/Reseller:	Staff/Outsourcing:	
Parts/Drives:						Satellite Srv./Equip.:	Specialty Services:	Y

TYPES OF BUSINESS:
Computer Manufacturing
Educational Products

BRANDS/DIVISIONS/AFFILIATES:
POSITIVO Plus
POSITIVO PC da Familia
POSITIVO PCTV
POSITIVO Union
BGH Sociedad Anonima
Informatica Fueguina S.A.
Aurelio Online Dictionary
Kid Pix

CONTACTS: Note: Officers with more than one job title may be intentionally listed here more than once.
Helio B. Rotenberg, CEO
Marielva A. Dias, COO
Ariel L. Szwarc, CFO
Mauricio Roorda, Chief Mktg. Officer
Andre Caldeira, Pres., Educational Tech. Div.
Isar Mazer, Chief Officer-New Prod.
Roberta Ehlers, Mgr.-Investor Rel.
Guillermo A.D. Morales, Exec. Dir.-Outsourced Prod.
Elaine Guetter, Dir.-Educational Tech.
Claudio Rabinovitz, Commercial Dir.-Educational Tech.
Oriovisto Guimaraes, Chmn.
Isar Mazer, Chief Officer-Procurement

Phone: 55-41-3316-7991	Fax: 55-41-3316-7810
Toll-Free:	
Address: 5200 Joao Bettega Rd., Curitiba, 81350-000 Brazil	

GROWTH PLANS/SPECIAL FEATURES:
Positivo Informatica S.A. is a Brazilian manufacturer and marketer of computers. The firm accounts for approximately 14.1% of Brazil's total PC sales and holds a retail market share of approximately 20.4%. Positivo Informatica sells many of its computers through major retail chains. The company operates in two segments: hardware and educational technology. The hardware segment, which accounts for approximately 97.6% of Positivo Informatica's revenues, offers a complete line of personal computers, including desktop and portable computers, produced at the firm's plant in Curitiba, Parana. The company's desktop brands include POSITIVO Plus, POSITIVO PC da Familia, POSITIVO Faces, POSITIVO PCTV, POSITIVO PCTV Digital and POSITIVO Union; its portable computer brands include POSITIVO Mobo Black, POSITIVO Mobo Red, POSITIVO Mobo 3G, POSITIVO Premium, POSITIVO Platinum and POSITIVO Aureum. The company also maintains a technical assistance network of 450 firms across Brazil that provides support for government agencies and thousands of final consumers. Positivo Informatica's call center, CRP, receives approximately 4,000 calls per day. The firm's educational technology segment, which accounts for the remaining 2.4% of revenues, offers professional qualification services for teachers and users; complete systems; and software and education portals. The company's portals have over 1.6 million subscribers and receive over 4 million daily page views. Positivo Informatica's educational solutions are used in approximately 2,439 private teaching institutions, 11,790 public schools and over 900 retail points of sale. The firm's educational products include education/entertainment software, computer labs, translation pens, learning tables, simulators and multimedia authoring. Its brands include Aurelio Online Dictionary and Kid Pix; it is also the exclusive Brazilian distributor of Disney's interactive educational products. In December 2010, Positivo Informatica acquired 50%-interest in Argentina-based Informatica Fueguina S.A. from BGH Sociedad Anonima, making it a joint venture.

FINANCIALS: Sales and profits are in thousands of dollars—add 000 to get the full amount. 2010 Note: Financial information for 2010 was not available for all companies at press time.
2010 Sales: $	2010 Profits: $	U.S. Stock Ticker:
2009 Sales: $	2009 Profits: $	Int'l Ticker: POSI3 Int'l Exchange: Sao Paulo-SAO
2008 Sales: $	2008 Profits: $	Employees:
2007 Sales: $	2007 Profits: $	Fiscal Year Ends: 12/31
2006 Sales: $	2006 Profits: $	Parent Company:

SALARIES/BENEFITS:
Pension Plan:	ESOP Stock Plan:	Profit Sharing:	Top Exec. Salary: $	Bonus: $
Savings Plan:	Stock Purch. Plan:		Second Exec. Salary: $	Bonus: $

OTHER THOUGHTS:
Apparent Women Officers or Directors: 2
Hot Spot for Advancement for Women/Minorities:

LOCATIONS: ("Y" = Yes)
West:	Southwest:	Midwest:	Southeast:	Northeast:	International: Y

POWERCHIP TECHNOLOGY CORP

www.powerchip.com

Industry Group Code: 33441 Ranks within this company's industry group: Sales: 29 Profits: 50

Hardware:	Software:	Telecommunications:	Electronic Publishing:	Equipment:	Specialty Services:
Computers:	Consumer:	Local:	Online Service:	Telecom:	Consulting:
Accessories:	Corporate:	Long Distance:	TV/Cable or Wireless:	Communication:	Contract Manufacturing: Y
Network Equipment:	Telecom:	Cellular:	Games:	Distribution:	Processing:
Chips/Circuits: Y	Internet:	Internet Service:	Financial Data:	VAR/Reseller:	Staff/Outsourcing:
Parts/Drives:				Satellite Srv./Equip.:	Specialty Services: Y

TYPES OF BUSINESS:

Semiconductors (Microchips)/Integrated Circuits/Components, Mfg.

BRANDS/DIVISIONS/AFFILIATES:

Rexchip Electronics Corporation
Renesas SP Drivers, Inc.
Powerchip Semiconductor Corp.

CONTACTS: Note: Officers with more than one job title may be intentionally listed here more than once.

Alex Wang, Pres.
Peter Ting, Sr. VP-Sales & Mktg.
Su Lu, VP-R&D
K.T. Tong, Sr. VP-Admin.
Lico Li, VP-Foundry Oper.
Martin Chu, VP-Bus. Strategy & Planning
Eric Tang, VP-Public Rel.
Eric Tang, VP-Investor Rel.
Michael Tsai, Vice Chmn.
Stephen Chen, Sr. VP/Gen. Mgr.-Memory Prod. Group
Albert Wu, VP-DRAM Oper.
Frank Huang, Chmn.

Phone: 886-3-5795000	Fax: 886-3-5788565
Toll-Free:	
Address: No. 12, Li-Hsin 1st Rd., Hsinchu Science Park, Hsinchu, Taiwan	

GROWTH PLANS/SPECIAL FEATURES:

Powerchip Technology Corp. (PTC), formerly Powerchip Semiconductor Corp., is a manufacturer of Dynamic Random Access Memory (DRAM) products and a provider of foundry services. The company produces standard SDRAM (Synchronous DRAM) in 64 Mb (megabits), 128 Mb and 256 Mb formats; DDR (Double Data Rate) SDRAM, in 256 Mb and 512 Mb formats; DDR2 (DDR, 2nd generation) SDRAM in a 512 Mb format; and most recently, DDR III, with speeds up to 1600 MHz and a power requirement of 1.5 volts. SDRAM, DDR, DDR2 and DDR III perform successively faster than previous generations of DRAM, and consume less power during data transfer. Besides its core DRAM memory products, the firm offers foundry, or wafer process engineering services. These consist of manufacturing high voltage driver ICs (Integrated Circuits), mainly for advanced LEDs or LCDs, in 12 or 18-volt processes on 0.25 micrometer, 3.3 volt technology; and CMOS Image Sensors (CIS), which build upon the firm's DRAM technology to offer low power consumption in applications such as camera phones, digital cameras and PC camera sensor applications. It also offers custom DRAM chip manufacturing to client specifications. PTC's CIS process technology accommodates products from 0.5-0.13 micrometers, and also supports other custom designs. The company maintains a joint venture, Rexchip Electronics Corporation, with Tokyo-based Elpida Memory, Inc. Rexchip operates a 300 mm DRAM fabrication facility, located in the Central Taiwan Science Park Houli Site. Another joint venture, Renesas SP Drivers, Inc., a partnership with Renesas Technology Corp., focuses on the design, development and sale of LCD drivers and controllers.

Employees of PTC receive life, accident and medical insurance; access to the company coffee shop, convenience store, cafeteria and restaurant, as well as a complete gymnasium with various aerobics, fitness and sporting areas; a profit sharing plan; scholarships for children; and job-related training courses.

FINANCIALS: Sales and profits are in thousands of dollars—add 000 to get the full amount. 2010 Note: Financial information for 2010 was not available for all companies at press time.

2010 Sales: $	2010 Profits: $	**U.S. Stock Ticker:**
2009 Sales: $1,123,020	2009 Profits: $-648,490	**Int'l Ticker: 5346** Int'l Exchange: Taipei-TPE
2008 Sales: $1,639,900	2008 Profits: $-1,726,000	Employees:
2007 Sales: $2,325,700	2007 Profits: $-369,800	Fiscal Year Ends: 12/31
2006 Sales: $2,766,600	2006 Profits: $819,800	Parent Company:

SALARIES/BENEFITS:

Pension Plan: Y	ESOP Stock Plan: Y	Profit Sharing: Y	Top Exec. Salary: $	Bonus: $
Savings Plan:	Stock Purch. Plan:		Second Exec. Salary: $	Bonus: $

OTHER THOUGHTS:

Apparent Women Officers or Directors:
Hot Spot for Advancement for Women/Minorities:

LOCATIONS: ("Y" = Yes)

West:	Southwest:	Midwest:	Southeast:	Northeast:	International:
					Y

PRINTRONIX INC

www.printronix.com

Industry Group Code: 334119 **Ranks within this company's industry group:** Sales: Profits:

Hardware:	Software:		Telecommunications:	Electronic Publishing:	Equipment:	Specialty Services:	
Computers:	Consumer:		Local:	Online Service:	Telecom:	Consulting:	
Accessories: Y	Corporate:	Y	Long Distance:	TV/Cable or Wireless:	Communication:	Contract Manufacturing:	
Network Equipment:	Telecom:		Cellular:	Games:	Distribution:	Processing:	
Chips/Circuits:	Internet:		Internet Service:	Financial Data:	VAR/Reseller:	Staff/Outsourcing:	
Parts/Drives:					Satellite Srv./Equip.:	Specialty Services:	Y

TYPES OF BUSINESS:

Computer Accessories-Line Matrix Printers
Laser Printers
Thermal Printers
Printer Management Software
Maintenance Services
Radio Frequency Identification Printers

BRANDS/DIVISIONS/AFFILIATES:

AutoID Data Manager
LineMatrix
L7032 LaserLine
P7000 Line Matrix
SL5000r RFID
T5000r ENERGY STAR
TallyGenicom Laser
TN3270e

CONTACTS: Note: Officers with more than one job title may be intentionally listed here more than once.

Randy Eisenbach, CEO
Rhonda Longmore-Grund, CFO
Sreenath Pendyala, VP-Global Mktg.
Francince Meza, VP-Human Resources
Bill Mathewes, CTO
Bill Mathewes, VP-Worldwide Eng.
Sen-Yuan Ro, Sr. VP-Global Oper.
Clause Hinge, VP-Sales & Mktg., EMEA
Virginia Lee Williams, VP-Sales & Mktg., Americas & China
Albert Ching, VP-Sales & Mktg., APAC

Phone: 714-368-2300	Fax: 714-368-2600
Toll-Free: 800-665-6210	
Address: 14600 Myford Rd., Irvine, CA 92606 US	

GROWTH PLANS/SPECIAL FEATURES:

Printronix, Inc., owned by Vector Capital, Inc., offers printing technology products for the industrial marketplace and distribution supply.   The firm designs, manufactures and markets medium- and high-speed printers for industrial settings such as manufacturing plants and distribution centers, in addition to back office and information technology departments. Printronix has manufacturing and configuration sites located in the U.S., Europe, Singapore, China, India, Korea and Australia. The firm offers five types of applications-compatible printers: Line Matrix; Thermal bar code; RFID (radio-frequency identification); TallyGenicom Laser; and RJS scanners and verifiers.   The company also creates software solutions which manages these printers in an enterprise network.   Printronix's printers all have extensive graphics capabilities, allowing them to support graphics languages and print output types such as text, reports, tabular data, computer graphics, bar codes, forms, labels and logos. Printer and accessory product lines include: the P7000 Line Matrix family; SL5000r RFID printers; T5000r ENERGY STAR thermal bar code label printers; 9045 Mono and 9050 Mono laser printers; Laser Inspector 1000, which verifies hard to recognize bar codes. Software solutions include PrintNet Enterprise Suite, which offers remote management of networked printers around the world; TN3270e and TN5250e emulators; and AutoID Data Manager, which allows customers to manage industrial network printer systems while providing a safeguard against the bar code scanning and data accuracy failure costs. Printronix also sells consumables, such as ribbons, toner and spare parts to support the installed base of printers and verifiers.   The firm provides other customer services such as the Advanced Exchange spare parts logistics program, repairs and maintenance.   The company operates manufacturing facilities and sales and support locations in the Americas, Europe, the Middle East, Africa (EMEA) and the Asia Pacific Region (APAC).

Printronix offers its employees medical, dental and vision coverage; life insurance; long-term disability; a profit sharing plan; a 401(k) plan; educational assistance; corporate training; and an employee assistance program.

FINANCIALS: Sales and profits are in thousands of dollars—add 000 to get the full amount. 2010 Note: Financial information for 2010 was not available for all companies at press time.

2010 Sales: $	2010 Profits: $	**U.S. Stock Ticker:** Private	
2009 Sales: $	2009 Profits: $	**Int'l Ticker:** Int'l Exchange:	
2008 Sales: $	2008 Profits: $	Employees:	
2007 Sales: $128,416	2007 Profits: $2,880	Fiscal Year Ends: 3/31	
2006 Sales: $127,821	2006 Profits: $-7,959	Parent Company: VECTOR CAPITAL	

SALARIES/BENEFITS:

Pension Plan:	ESOP Stock Plan:	Profit Sharing: Y	Top Exec. Salary: $	Bonus: $
Savings Plan: Y	Stock Purch. Plan:		Second Exec. Salary: $	Bonus: $

OTHER THOUGHTS:

Apparent Women Officers or Directors: 3
Hot Spot for Advancement for Women/Minorities: Y

LOCATIONS: ("Y" = Yes)

West:	Southwest:	Midwest:	Southeast:	Northeast:	International:
Y					Y

PROGRESS SOFTWARE CORP

web.progress.com

Industry Group Code: 511210I Ranks within this company's industry group: Sales: 4   Profits: 4

Hardware:	Software:		Telecommunications:	Electronic Publishing:	Equipment:	Specialty Services:	
Computers:	Consumer:		Local:	Online Service:	Telecom:	Consulting:	Y
Accessories:	Corporate:	Y	Long Distance:	TV/Cable or Wireless:	Communication:	Contract Manufacturing:	
Network Equipment:	Telecom:		Cellular:	Games:	Distribution:	Processing:	
Chips/Circuits:	Internet:		Internet Service:	Financial Data:	VAR/Reseller:	Staff/Outsourcing:	
Parts/Drives:					Satellite Srv./Equip.:	Specialty Services:	Y

TYPES OF BUSINESS:

Software-Application Development & Integration
Application Management Software
Consulting & Technical Support Services
Data Connectivity Products
Data Management Software
Research & Development

BRANDS/DIVISIONS/AFFILIATES:

Progress OpenEdge
Progress Apama
Progress Sonic
Progress Actional
DataDirect Shadow
DataDirect Connect
Savvion, Inc.
FuseSource Corporation

CONTACTS: Note: Officers with more than one job title may be intentionally listed here more than once.

Richard D. Reidy, CEO
Richard D. Reidy, Pres.
Charles F. Wagner, CFO
Gary Conway, Chief Mktg. Officer/Exec. VP
Joseph A. Andrews, Sr. VP/Head-Human Resources
Dave Benson, CIO/Exec. VP
John Bates, CTO/Sr. VP
Robert Levy, Chief Prod. Officer/Sr. VP
Charles F. Wagner, Exec. VP-Admin.
James D. Freedman, General Counsel/Sr. VP
Christopher Larsen, Exec. VP-Global Field Oper.
John Bates, Sr. VP/Head-Corp. Dev.
John A. Stewart, Dir.-Corp. Public Rel.
John A. Stewart, Dir.-Investor Rel.
Charles F. Wagner, Exec. VP-Finance
John Goodson, Sr. VP-Prod.
Barry Bycoff, Chmn.

Phone: 781-280-4000	Fax:
Toll-Free: 800-477-6473	
Address: 14 Oak Park Dr., Bedford, MA 01730 US	

GROWTH PLANS/SPECIAL FEATURES:

Progress Software Corp. develops, markets and distributes application infrastructure software for the development, deployment, integration and management of business applications software. Its products are used by nearly 140,000 companies in over 180 countries. The company organizes its operations into three business units: Application Development Platforms (ADP), Enterprise Business Solutions (EBS) and Enterprise Data Solutions (EDS). The ADP segment consists primarily of the OpenEdge platform, comprised of development, management and integration tools; an embedded database and application servers; and EasyAsk products, which provide search navigation and merchandising for web sites. It also includes the Orbix and ObjectStore products. The Orbix product line is embedded in telephone switches, online brokerage systems, multimedia news delivery, airline front desk systems, rail and road traffic control, large scale banking systems, credit card clearance, subway management and CAD systems. Progress ObjectStore is a data management system that enables users to store data. The EBS segment includes the Apama complex event processing platform, the Actional business transaction management platform, the newly acquired Savvion business process management suite and Sonic integration products. The EDS segment is comprised of the Progress Data Services, Progress DataDirect Shadow and Progress DataDirect Connect product lines, which provide data management, data integration, replication, caching, access, and security capabilities. In January 2010, Progress acquired software developer Savvion, Inc. In October 2010, the firm established a new subsidiary, FuseSource Corporation, to provide professional open source integration and messaging software.

The company offers its employees medical and dental insurance; flexible spending accounts; computer discount purchase; an employee assistance program; and tuition reimbursement.

FINANCIALS: Sales and profits are in thousands of dollars—add 000 to get the full amount. 2010 Note: Financial information for 2010 was not available for all companies at press time.

2010 Sales: $	2010 Profits: $	**U.S. Stock Ticker: PRGS**
2009 Sales: $494,137	2009 Profits: $32,755	**Int'l Ticker:** Int'l Exchange:
2008 Sales: $515,560	2008 Profits: $46,296	Employees: 1,821
2007 Sales: $493,500	2007 Profits: $42,280	Fiscal Year Ends: 11/30
2006 Sales: $447,063	2006 Profits: $29,401	Parent Company:

SALARIES/BENEFITS:

Pension Plan:	ESOP Stock Plan:	Profit Sharing:	Top Exec. Salary: $351,461	Bonus: $167,400
Savings Plan: Y	Stock Purch. Plan: Y		Second Exec. Salary: $332,309	Bonus: $155,000

OTHER THOUGHTS:

Apparent Women Officers or Directors:
Hot Spot for Advancement for Women/Minorities:

LOCATIONS: ("Y" = Yes)

West:	Southwest:	Midwest:	Southeast:	Northeast:	International:
Y	Y	Y	Y	Y	Y

PROXIM WIRELESS CORP

www.proxim.com

Industry Group Code: 334220 Ranks within this company's industry group: Sales: 5 Profits: 5

Hardware:		Software:	Telecommunications:	Electronic Publishing:	Equipment:		Specialty Services:	
Computers:		Consumer:	Local:	Online Service:	Telecom:	Y	Consulting:	
Accessories:		Corporate:	Long Distance:	TV/Cable or Wireless:	Communication:	Y	Contract Manufacturing:	
Network Equipment:	Y	Telecom:	Cellular:	Games:	Distribution:		Processing:	
Chips/Circuits:		Internet:	Internet Service:	Financial Data:	VAR/Reseller:		Staff/Outsourcing:	
Parts/Drives:					Satellite Srv./Equip.:		Specialty Services:	

TYPES OF BUSINESS:

Wireless Networking Equipment
Home & Office Networking Equipment
Millimeter Wave Products

BRANDS/DIVISIONS/AFFILIATES:

Terabeam Inc
Tsunami
ORiNOCO
Lynx
GigaLink
MeshMAX

CONTACTS: Note: Officers with more than one job title may be intentionally listed here more than once.

Pankaj Manglik, CEO
Pankaj Manglik, Pres.
Tom Twerdahl, Interim CFO
Geoffrey L. Smith, Sr. VP-Sales
Kishore Gandham, VP-Eng.
David L. Renauld, General Counsel/Corp. Sec./VP-Corp. Affairs
Alan B. Howe, Chmn.
Kishore Gandham, Managing Dir.-Proxim India Dev. Center

Phone: 408-383-7600	Fax: 408-383-7680
Toll-Free: 800-229-1630	
Address: 1561 Buckeye Dr., Milpitas, CA 95035 US	

GROWTH PLANS/SPECIAL FEATURES:

Proxim Wireless Corp. (formerly Terabeam, Inc.) provides high-speed wireless communications equipment and services worldwide. Proxim products are often used for mobile enterprise, security and surveillance, last-mile access, voice and data backhaul, public hot spot and metropolitan area networks. Its products fall into five basic categories: Point-to-Multipoint (PtMP)/WiMAX; PtP/Wireless Backhaul; Wireless LAN; Wi-Fi Mesh; and Wireless NMS. The PtMP/WiMAX category provides outdoor wireless access technologies for high-speed, long-range broadband wireless distribution to both rural and metropolitan areas. It supports data, voice and video applications and includes the Tsunami brand. The PtP/Wireless Backhaul segment offers solutions for connecting telecommunications and corporate networks. The PTP/Wireless Backhaul category includes Lynx, Tsunami and GigaLink brand products, which are often used to bridge base stations or provide last-mile access for wireless cellular or Internet service providers; or to bridge building networks for universities and enterprises. The Wireless LAN segment offers the ORiNOCO wireless LANs, which provide organizations with networks with high reliability, upgradeability, security and flexibility. The Wi-Fi Mesh segment provides high capacity Wi-Fi mesh Access Points (APs) that deliver data, voice and video networks for large metropolitan and enterprise Wi-Fi deployments. This segment includes the Wi-Fi Mesh Series, with dual-radio architecture; and the Public Safety Wi-Fi Mesh Series, which supports both 2.4 GHz metropolitan networks and 4.9 GHz public safety networks through dual radios. Lastly, the Wireless NMS segment offers the ProximVision ES, which provides mobile configuration, rapid network deployment and a map overlay of a company's network with real-time status indicators. In May 2009, Proxim launched the OriNOCO 802.11a/b/g/n adapter, which exceeds 150 Mbps for laptops and desktops when used with the ORiNOCO AP-800 and AP-800 lines. In June 2009, the company launched the 6.4 GHz PtMP broadband wireless solutions for the Russian market.

The firm offers its employees medical, dental and vision insurance; short-and long-term disability coverage; flexible spending accounts; and a 401(k) plan.

FINANCIALS: Sales and profits are in thousands of dollars—add 000 to get the full amount. 2010 Note: Financial information for 2010 was not available for all companies at press time.

2010 Sales: $	2010 Profits: $	U.S. Stock Ticker: PRXM.PK
2009 Sales: $29,700	2009 Profits: $-7,400	Int'l Ticker: Int'l Exchange:
2008 Sales: $49,007	2008 Profits: $-10,045	Employees: 183
2007 Sales: $61,945	2007 Profits: $-19,064	Fiscal Year Ends: 12/31
2006 Sales: $68,169	2006 Profits: $-23,163	Parent Company:

SALARIES/BENEFITS:

Pension Plan:	ESOP Stock Plan:	Profit Sharing:	Top Exec. Salary: $345,548	Bonus: $58,056
Savings Plan: Y	Stock Purch. Plan:		Second Exec. Salary: $194,250	Bonus: $16,273

OTHER THOUGHTS:

Apparent Women Officers or Directors:
Hot Spot for Advancement for Women/Minorities:

LOCATIONS: ("Y" = Yes)

West:	Southwest:	Midwest:	Southeast:	Northeast:	International:
Y				Y	Y

Note: Financial information, benefits and other data can change quickly and may vary from those stated here.

PULSE ELECTRONICS CORPORATION   www.pulseelectronics.com

Industry Group Code: 334119 Ranks within this company's industry group: Sales: 21   Profits: 21

Hardware:		Software:	Telecommunications:	Electronic Publishing:	Equipment:		Specialty Services:
Computers:		Consumer:	Local:	Online Service:	Telecom:	Y	Consulting:
Accessories:		Corporate:	Long Distance:	TV/Cable or Wireless:	Communication:	Y	Contract Manufacturing:
Network Equipment:	Y	Telecom:	Cellular:	Games:	Distribution:		Processing:
Chips/Circuits:	Y	Internet:	Internet Service:	Financial Data:	VAR/Reseller:		Staff/Outsourcing:
Parts/Drives:	Y				Satellite Srv./Equip.:		Specialty Services:

TYPES OF BUSINESS:
Components-Electronic
Electrical Contact Products
Precious Metals & Refining

BRANDS/DIVISIONS/AFFILIATES:
Technitrol, Inc.
AMI Doduco

CONTACTS: Note: Officers with more than one job title may be intentionally listed here more than once.
Drew A. Moyer, Interim CEO/Sr. VP
Alan Benjamin, COO
Drew A. Moyer, CFO/Sr. VP
Roger Shahnazarian, Sr. VP-Prod. Oper.
Michael P. Ginnetti, Chief Acct. Officer
Michael J. McGrath, VP-Treasury & Tax
John Houston, Sr. VP-Network & Wireless Prod. Groups

Phone: 215-355-2900	Fax: 215-355-7397
Toll-Free:	
Address: 1210 Northbrook Dr., Ste. 470, Trevose, PA 19053 US	

GROWTH PLANS/SPECIAL FEATURES:

Pulse Electronics Corporation, formerly Technitrol, Inc., is a global producer of precision-engineered electronic components. The company offers three primary product lines: network products, power products and wireless products. The network products include a variety of magnetic and radio frequency components, modules and sub-assemblies such as connectors, filters, transformers and chokes. The firm's power products include power and signal transformers and inductors, automotive coils, military and aerospace products and other power magnetics products. Pulse's wireless products produce handset antenna products, non-cellular wireless products, antenna products and mobile speakers and receivers. The firm's products are used in mobile handsets, Internet-enabled devices, automobiles and other electronic and mechanical equipment. In September 2010, the company sold its AMI Doduco unit to Tinicum Capital Partners II, L.P. for about $44 million. In November 2010, the firm changed its name to Pulse Electronics Corp. from Technitrol, Inc.

FINANCIALS: Sales and profits are in thousands of dollars—add 000 to get the full amount. 2010 Note: Financial information for 2010 was not available for all companies at press time.

2010 Sales: $	2010 Profits: $	U.S. Stock Ticker: PULS
2009 Sales: $398,803	2009 Profits: $-193,837	Int'l Ticker: Int'l Exchange:
2008 Sales: $626,270	2008 Profits: $-275,758	Employees: 19,400
2007 Sales: $1,026,555	2007 Profits: $61,657	Fiscal Year Ends: 12/31
2006 Sales: $954,096	2006 Profits: $57,203	Parent Company:

SALARIES/BENEFITS:

Pension Plan:	ESOP Stock Plan:	Profit Sharing:	Top Exec. Salary: $707,200	Bonus: $
Savings Plan:	Stock Purch. Plan:		Second Exec. Salary: $339,900	Bonus: $

OTHER THOUGHTS:
Apparent Women Officers or Directors: 1
Hot Spot for Advancement for Women/Minorities:

LOCATIONS: ("Y" = Yes)

West:	Southwest:	Midwest:	Southeast:	Northeast:	International:
Y				Y	Y

Note: Financial information, benefits and other data can change quickly and may vary from those stated here.

QISDA CORPORATION

www.qisda.com

Industry Group Code: 334419 Ranks within this company's industry group: Sales: 11 Profits: 19

Hardware:		Software:	Telecommunications:	Electronic Publishing:	Equipment:		Specialty Services:	
Computers:		Consumer:	Local:	Online Service:	Telecom:	Y	Consulting:	
Accessories:	Y	Corporate:	Long Distance:	TV/Cable or Wireless:	Communication:	Y	Contract Manufacturing:	Y
Network Equipment:		Telecom:	Cellular:	Games:	Distribution:		Processing:	
Chips/Circuits:		Internet:	Internet Service:	Financial Data:	VAR/Reseller:		Staff/Outsourcing:	
Parts/Drives:	Y				Satellite Srv./Equip.:		Specialty Services:	

TYPES OF BUSINESS:

Contract Electronics Manufacturing
LCD Flat-Panel Displays
LCD TVs
Projectors
Multifunctional Printers
Mobile Phones
Portable Display Devices
Infotainment Displays

BRANDS/DIVISIONS/AFFILIATES:

BenQ Corporation

CONTACTS: Note: Officers with more than one job title may be intentionally listed here more than once.

Hui Hsiung, CEO
Hui Hsiung, Pres.
David Wang, CFO/VP
Hermit Huang, Exec. VP/Gen. Mgr.-Global Sales & Svcs.
Kelvin Lee, CTO/VP
Manfred Wang, VP/Chief Design Officer
C.M. Wu, Sr. VP/Gen. Mgr.-Global Mfg.
David Huang, Chief Legal Officer
David Wang, VP/Spokesperson
K.Y. Lee, Chmn.
Mark Hsiao, VP/Managing Dir.-China Oper.

Phone: 886-3-3595-000	Fax: 886-3-3599-000
Toll-Free:	
Address: 157 Shan-ying Rd., Gueishan, Taoyuan, 333 Taiwan	

GROWTH PLANS/SPECIAL FEATURES:

Qisda Corporation, formerly BenQ Corporation, is an original design manufacturer (ODM) and an original equipment manufacturer (OEM) of LCD monitors, commercial LCD TVs, projectors, multifunctional printers, mobile phones, car infotainment displays, medical electronics and portable display devices. The firm has four research and development centers in Taiwan and China as well as five manufacturing locations in China, the Czech Republic, Mexico and Taiwan. Qisda's in-house manufacturing capabilities include surface-mount technology (SMT), metal stamping, plastic injection and LCD module assembling. The firm's LCD monitors include wide format models from 15-27 inches; traditional format models from 15-20 inches; monitor-TVs; and pen/touch displays. Its LCD TVs include sizes ranging from 15-47 inches. Qisda's projectors include LCD projectors and home theater projectors and short-throw projectors for home and office settings. The firm's multifunctional printer offerings include color inkjet printers; color inkjet multifunctional printers; color laser printers (CLPs); color laser multifunctional printers (MFPs); high-speed inkjet and multifunctional printers; image scanners; mobile scanners; and medical electronics. Its mobile communications devices include mobile Internet devices (MIDs) and tablets, dual mode phones, wireless modules and USB modem modules. Qisda's infotainment products include car electronics, such as navigation systems, TFT-LCD displays and vehicle rear seat entertainment systems; portable display devices, such as mobile digital TVs,, e-readers, digital photo frames and GPS units; and general displays, such as professional displays, public displays, industrial displays and e-signage. In January 2011, the company announced plans to relocate certain of its LCD manufacturing activities from the Czech Republic to China.

Qisda offers its employees access to fitness facilities, employee seminars, a meal allowance, club activities and a patent bonus.

FINANCIALS: Sales and profits are in thousands of dollars—add 000 to get the full amount. 2010 Note: Financial information for 2010 was not available for all companies at press time.

2010 Sales: $	2010 Profits: $	U.S. Stock Ticker:
2009 Sales: $4,636,940	2009 Profits: $-55,830	Int'l Ticker: 2352 Int'l Exchange: Taipei-TPE
2008 Sales: $5,158,476	2008 Profits: $-107,277	Employees: 20,791
2007 Sales: $3,768,253	2007 Profits: $147,077	Fiscal Year Ends: 12/31
2006 Sales: $6,114,120	2006 Profits: $-850,130	Parent Company:

SALARIES/BENEFITS:

Pension Plan:	ESOP Stock Plan:	Profit Sharing:	Top Exec. Salary: $	Bonus: $
Savings Plan:	Stock Purch. Plan:		Second Exec. Salary: $	Bonus: $

OTHER THOUGHTS:

Apparent Women Officers or Directors:
Hot Spot for Advancement for Women/Minorities:

LOCATIONS: ("Y" = Yes)

West:	Southwest:	Midwest:	Southeast:	Northeast:	International:
					Y

QLIK TECHNOLOGIES INC

www.qlikview.com

Industry Group Code: 511210H Ranks within this company's industry group: Sales: Profits:

Hardware:	Software:		Telecommunications:	Electronic Publishing:	Equipment:	Specialty Services:	
Computers:	Consumer:	Y	Local:	Online Service:	Telecom:	Consulting:	
Accessories:	Corporate:	Y	Long Distance:	TV/Cable or Wireless:	Communication:	Contract Manufacturing:	
Network Equipment:	Telecom:		Cellular:	Games:	Distribution:	Processing:	
Chips/Circuits:	Internet:		Internet Service:	Financial Data:	VAR/Reseller:	Staff/Outsourcing:	
Parts/Drives:					Satellite Srv./Equip.:	Specialty Services:	Y

TYPES OF BUSINESS:

Business Software Development

BRANDS/DIVISIONS/AFFILIATES:

QlikView Publisher
QlikView Labs

CONTACTS: *Note: Officers with more than one job title may be intentionally listed here more than once.*

Lars Bjork, CEO
William G. Sorenson, CFO
Douglas Laird, VP-Mktg.
Jonas Nachmanson, CTO
Anthony Deighton, Sr. VP-Prod.
Leslie Bonney, Exec. VP-Global Field Oper.
Bruce Golden, Chmn.

Phone:	Fax: 610-975-5987
Toll-Free: 888-828-9768	
Address: 150 N. Radnor Chester Rd., Ste. E220, Radnor, PA 19087 US	

GROWTH PLANS/SPECIAL FEATURES:

Qlik Technologies, Inc. is engaged in the production of enterprise-class business informatics software that enables customers to navigate complex data sets and compile reports based on intelligent processes. The firm's software enables non-technical users to access data in a simple and streamlined format. Its software platform, QlikView, combines enterprise-class analytics and search functionality with the simplicity and ease-of-use found in office productivity software tools for a broad set of business users. Tools such as the associative search function operate much like the human brain, allowing users to interact with data more easily and intuitively. Once accessed, users can convert these complex data sets into attractive and readable graphs and tables. QlikView's in-memory scalable technology and load balancing allows the software to perform calculations in real time, even when dealing with larger datasets. Compatible data sources include Oracle, SAP, Cognos, Hyperion, SQL, and Excel formats. Once results are created, users can quickly deploy and distribute results by e-mail or to server databases using the QlikView Publisher. The QlikView application can be accessed locally on a computer, through mobile devices or through the cloud. Qlik Technologies gains revenue by licensing the program, performing maintenance and by providing professional services, such as training and support. The software is distributed directly, through OEM (original equipment manufacturers) and through resellers. The company also operates QlikView Labs, which allows customers and developers to brainstorm ideas and concepts. In July 2010, the firm held an initial public offering (IPO).

FINANCIALS: Sales and profits are in thousands of dollars—add 000 to get the full amount. 2010 Note: Financial information for 2010 was not available for all companies at press time.

2010 Sales: $	2010 Profits: $	**U.S. Stock Ticker:** QLIK
2009 Sales: $	2009 Profits: $	**Int'l Ticker:** Int'l Exchange:
2008 Sales: $	2008 Profits: $	Employees:
2007 Sales: $	2007 Profits: $	Fiscal Year Ends: 12/31
2006 Sales: $	2006 Profits: $	Parent Company:

SALARIES/BENEFITS:

Pension Plan:	ESOP Stock Plan:	Profit Sharing:	Top Exec. Salary: $	Bonus: $
Savings Plan:	Stock Purch. Plan:		Second Exec. Salary: $	Bonus: $

OTHER THOUGHTS:

Apparent Women Officers or Directors:
Hot Spot for Advancement for Women/Minorities:

LOCATIONS: ("Y" = Yes)

West:	Southwest:	Midwest:	Southeast:	Northeast:	International:
Y	Y	Y		Y	Y

QLOGIC CORP

www.qlogic.com

Industry Group Code: 33411 Ranks within this company's industry group: Sales: 5 Profits: 3

Hardware:		Software:		Telecommunications:	Electronic Publishing:	Equipment:	Specialty Services:
Computers:		Consumer:		Local:	Online Service:	Telecom:	Consulting:
Accessories:		Corporate:	Y	Long Distance:	TV/Cable or Wireless:	Communication:	Contract Manufacturing:
Network Equipment:	Y	Telecom:		Cellular:	Games:	Distribution:	Processing:
Chips/Circuits:	Y	Internet:		Internet Service:	Financial Data:	VAR/Reseller:	Staff/Outsourcing:
Parts/Drives:						Satellite Srv./Equip.:	Specialty Services:

TYPES OF BUSINESS:

Computer Networking Equipment
Storage Area Network Products
Controller Chips

BRANDS/DIVISIONS/AFFILIATES:

QLogic 2500 Series
QLogic 9000 Series
QLogic 6200 Series
QLogic 8200 Series
QLogic 3200 Series
QLogic 12400

CONTACTS: Note: Officers with more than one job title may be intentionally listed here more than once.

Simon Biddiscombe, CEO
Jeff W. Benck, COO
Simon Biddiscombe, Pres.
Phil A. Felando, VP-Human Resources
Rob Davis, CTO/VP
Michael L. Hawkins, General Counsel/VP/Sec.
Perry M. Mulligan, Sr. VP-Oper.
Roger J. Klein, VP/Gen. Mgr.-Host Solutions Group
Jesse L. Parker, VP/Gen. Mgr.-Network Solutions Group
Shishir Shah, VP/Gen. Mgr.-Storage Solutions Group
H. K. Desai, Chmn.

Phone: 949-389-6000	Fax: 949-389-6126
Toll-Free: 800-662-4471	
Address: 26650 Aliso Viejo Pkwy., Aliso Viejo, CA 92656 US	

GROWTH PLANS/SPECIAL FEATURES:

QLogic Corp. is a supplier of storage networking and network infrastructure products, which are sold primarily to original equipment manufacturers (OEMs) and distributors. The firm groups its products into three categories: Storage networking, converged networking and high performance computing (HPC) networking. Storage networking products include fibre channel adapters, fibre channel switches, Internet Small Computer Systems Interface (iSCSI) adapters and intelligent storage routers. QLogic's iSCSI products offer a cheaper alternative to fibre channel products for use in small and medium size businesses. Converged networking products include adapters that support both Ethernet data networking and fibre channel storage networking capabilities. HPC networking products include InfiniBand switches, including edge fabric switches and multi-protocol fabric directors; and InfiniBand host channel adapters for emerging high performance computer cluster (HPCC) environments. All of these product areas address the storage area network (SAN) or server fabric connectivity infrastructure requirements of small, medium and large enterprises. To ensure interoperability within the SAN, the firm works with independent hardware and software vendors, including Cisco Systems and Microsoft. Company products include the QLogic 2500 Series fibre channel adapters; the QLogic 9000 Series fibre channel switches; the QLogic 6200 Series intelligent storage routers; the QLogic 8200 Series converged network adapters; and the QLogic 3200 Series intelligent Ethernet adapters. In November 2010, the firm introduced QLogic 12400, a 26-port, QDR 40 Gigabit per second gateway that links InfiniBand clusters to the Ethernet cloud.

QLogic offers its employees medical, dental, vision and prescription drug coverage; life and AD&D insurance; short- and long-term disability; flexible spending accounts; a 401(k) plan; an employee stock purchase plan; education assistance; an employee referral program; discounted amusement tickets; a wellness program; and access to a credit union.

FINANCIALS: Sales and profits are in thousands of dollars—add 000 to get the full amount. 2010 Note: Financial information for 2010 was not available for all companies at press time.

2010 Sales: $549,070	2010 Profits: $54,948	U.S. Stock Ticker: QLGC
2009 Sales: $633,862	2009 Profits: $108,789	Int'l Ticker: Int'l Exchange:
2008 Sales: $597,866	2008 Profits: $96,210	Employees: 1,038
2007 Sales: $586,697	2007 Profits: $105,418	Fiscal Year Ends: 3/31
2006 Sales: $494,077	2006 Profits: $283,588	Parent Company:

SALARIES/BENEFITS:

Pension Plan:	ESOP Stock Plan:	Profit Sharing:	Top Exec. Salary: $700,003	Bonus: $375,000
Savings Plan: Y	Stock Purch. Plan: Y		Second Exec. Salary: $340,018	Bonus: $105,000

OTHER THOUGHTS:

Apparent Women Officers or Directors: 1
Hot Spot for Advancement for Women/Minorities:

LOCATIONS: ("Y" = Yes)

West:	Southwest:	Midwest:	Southeast:	Northeast:	International:
Y	Y	Y		Y	Y

Note: Financial information, benefits and other data can change quickly and may vary from those stated here.

QUALCOMM INC

www.qualcomm.com

Industry Group Code: 33441 Ranks within this company's industry group: Sales: 3 Profits: 3

Hardware:	Software:		Telecommunications:	Electronic Publishing:	Equipment:		Specialty Services:
Computers:	Consumer:		Local:	Online Service:	Telecom:	Y	Consulting:
Accessories:	Corporate:	Y	Long Distance:	TV/Cable or Wireless:	Communication:	Y	Contract Manufacturing:
Network Equipment:	Telecom:		Cellular:	Games:	Distribution:		Processing:
Chips/Circuits:	Internet:		Internet Service:	Financial Data:	VAR/Reseller:		Staff/Outsourcing:
Parts/Drives:					Satellite Srv./Equip.:		Specialty Services:

TYPES OF BUSINESS:

Telecommunications Equipment
Digital Wireless Communications Products
Integrated Circuits
Mobile Communications Systems
Wireless Software & Services
E-Mail Software
Code Division Multiple Access

BRANDS/DIVISIONS/AFFILIATES:

FLO TV Incoroporated
Qualcomm Flarion Technologies Inc
Qualcomm MEMS Technologies Inc
Qualcomm Innovation Center Inc
Qualcomm Austria Research Center GmbH
Atheros Communications Inc

CONTACTS:
Note: Officers with more than one job title may be intentionally listed here more than once.

Paul E. Jacobs, CEO
Steven R. Altman, Pres.
William E. Keitel, CFO/Exec. VP
William F. Davidson, Jr., Sr. VP-Global Mktg.
Daniel L. Sullivan, Exec. VP-Human Resources
Norm Fjeldheim, CIO/Sr. VP
Roberto Padovani, CTO/Exec. VP
Donald J. Rosenberg, General Counsel/Exec. VP/Corp. Sec.
William Bold, Sr. VP-Gov't Affairs
William F. Davidson, Jr., Sr. VP-Investor Rel.
Margaret L. Johnson, Exec. VP-Americas & India
Jing Wang, Exec. VP/Pres., Qualcomm Asia & Africa
Steve Mollenkopf, Exec. VP/Pres., Qualcomm CDMA Tech.
James Lederer, Exec. VP/Gen. Mgr.-Qualcomm CDMA Tech.
Paul E. Jacobs, Chmn.
Andrew Gilbert, Exec. VP/Pres., Qualcomm Europe & QIS

Phone: 858-587-1121	Fax: 858-658-2100
Toll-Free:	
Address: 5775 Morehouse Dr., San Diego, CA 92121 US	

GROWTH PLANS/SPECIAL FEATURES:

Qualcomm, Inc. provides digital wireless communications products, technologies and services. It designs application-specific integrated circuits based on Code Division Multiple Access (CDMA) technology and licenses its technology to domestic and international telecommunications equipment suppliers. CDMA technology is an industry standard for all forms of digital wireless communications networks. The company also sells Binary Runtime Environment for Wireless (BREW) software to network operators, handset manufacturers and application developers. BREW is an open-standard platform that can interface with many different wireless applications. The firm's wireless business services, which consist of satellite and terrestrial-based two-way data messaging and position reporting, serve transportation companies, private and construction equipment fleets and U.S. government agencies through its government technologies division. Subsidiary Qualcomm MEMS Technologies develops improved graphical systems for handheld devices. Subsidiary FLO TV Incorporated (formerly MediaFLO USA, Inc.) offers services over a nationwide multicast network based on the MediaFLO Media Distribution System (MDS) and Forward Link Only (FLO) technology. This network is utilized as a shared resource for wireless operators and partners. Subsidiary Qualcomm Flarion Technologies is a developer and provider of FLASH-OFDM (Orthogonal Frequency Division Multiplexing Access). The firm offers mobile entertainment services via partnerships with a variety of media networks including NBC, CBS, FOX, ESPN and MTV. In early 2009, Qualcomm acquired the handheld graphics and multimedia assets from Advanced Micro Devices. In July 2009, the company and Verizon Wireless agreed to form a machine-to-machine wireless communications joint venture to serve the utilities, healthcare, manufacturing, distribution and consumer product markets. In October 2009, the firm formed subsidiary Qualcomm Innovation Center, Inc., a provider of mobile open source platforms. In March 2010, Qualcomm established the Qualcomm Austria Research Center GmbH to design and develop augmented reality. In January 2011, the firm agreed to acquire technology company, Atheros Communications, Inc. for $3.1 billion.

Employees are offered medical, dental and vision insurance; dependent/health care reimbursement accounts; tuition reimbursement; and a 401(k).

FINANCIALS:
Sales and profits are in thousands of dollars—add 000 to get the full amount. 2010 Note: Financial information for 2010 was not available for all companies at press time.

2010 Sales: $10,991,000	2010 Profits: $3,247,000	**U.S. Stock Ticker:** QCOM
2009 Sales: $10,416,000	2009 Profits: $1,592,000	**Int'l Ticker:** Int'l Exchange:
2008 Sales: $11,142,000	2008 Profits: $3,160,000	Employees: 17,500
2007 Sales: $8,871,000	2007 Profits: $3,303,000	Fiscal Year Ends: 9/30
2006 Sales: $7,526,000	2006 Profits: $2,470,000	Parent Company:

SALARIES/BENEFITS:

Pension Plan:	ESOP Stock Plan:	Profit Sharing:	Top Exec. Salary: $964,427	Bonus: $3,606,750
Savings Plan: Y	Stock Purch. Plan: Y		Second Exec. Salary: $708,045	Bonus: $1,260,000

OTHER THOUGHTS:

Apparent Women Officers or Directors: 4
Hot Spot for Advancement for Women/Minorities: Y

LOCATIONS: ("Y" = Yes)

West:	Southwest:	Midwest:	Southeast:	Northeast:	International:
Y	Y	Y	Y	Y	Y

Note: Financial information, benefits and other data can change quickly and may vary from those stated here.

QUALITY SYSTEMS INC

www.qsii.com

Industry Group Code: 511210D Ranks within this company's industry group: Sales: 3 Profits: 2

Hardware:	Software:		Telecommunications:	Electronic Publishing:	Equipment:	Specialty Services:	
Computers:	Consumer:		Local:	Online Service:	Telecom:	Consulting:	Y
Accessories:	Corporate:	Y	Long Distance:	TV/Cable or Wireless:	Communication:	Contract Manufacturing:	
Network Equipment:	Telecom:		Cellular:	Games:	Distribution:	Processing:	
Chips/Circuits:	Internet:		Internet Service:	Financial Data:	VAR/Reseller:	Staff/Outsourcing:	
Parts/Drives:					Satellite Srv./Equip.:	Specialty Services:	

TYPES OF BUSINESS:

Software-Practice Management

BRANDS/DIVISIONS/AFFILIATES:

Practice Management Partners Inc
NextGen Healthcare Information Systems Inc
QSI Dental
NextGen Sphere LLC
Opus Healthcare Solutions Inc
Healthcare Strategic Initiatives
NextGen Electronic Health Records
NextGen Patient Portal

CONTACTS: Note: Officers with more than one job title may be intentionally listed here more than once.

Steven T. Plochocki, CEO
Patrick B. Cline, Pres.
Paul A. Holt, CFO
Paul A. Holt, Corp. Sec.
Scott D. Decker, Pres., NextGen Healthcare Info. Systems
Donn Neufeld, Exec. VP-EDI & Dental
Monte Sandler, Exec. VP-NextGen Practice Solutions
Sheldon Razin, Chmn.

Phone: 949-255-2600	Fax: 949-255-2605
Toll-Free: 800-888-7955	
Address: 18111 Von Karman, Ste. 600, Irvine, CA 92612 US	

GROWTH PLANS/SPECIAL FEATURES:

Quality Systems, Inc. develops and provides computer-based practice management, medical records, and e-business applications. The company is headquartered in Irvine, California, and has major facilities in Horsham, Pennsylvania, and Atlanta, Georgia; and additional facilities in Maryland, Missouri and Texas. Quality Systems operates through three divisions: QSI Dental, NextGen and Practice Solutions. All three develop and market products that streamline patient records and administrative functions such as billing and scheduling. They offer these services to medical and dental group practices, management service organizations, ambulatory care centers, community health centers and medical/dental schools. Quality Systems' QSI Dental division focuses on developing, marketing and supporting software suites for dental and niche medical practices. Its Clinical Product Suite is a UNIX-based medical practice management software suite that incorporates clinical tools including periodontal charting and digital imaging of x-ray and inter-oral camera images. The NextGen division, operated by NextGen Healthcare Information Systems, Inc., develops and sells proprietary electronic medical records software and practice management systems. Its NextGen product line includes NextGen Electronic Health Records; NextGen Patient Portal; NextGuard; NextGen Clinicals; and NextGen Financials. The group's EDI/Connectivity products automate a number of manual, often paper-based or telephony intensive communications between patients and providers, like as insurance claim forwards. NextGen products can operate in a client-server environment as well as via private intranet, the Internet or in an ASP environment. The firm's Practice Solutions segment, operated by subsidiaries Healthcare Strategic Initiatives and Practice Management Partners, primarily provides billing and collection services for medical practices through a combination of web-based software as a service (SaaS) and the NextGen software platform. In August 2009, Quality Systems acquired financial information systems provider NextGen Sphere, LLC. In February 2010, the firm acquired clinical information systems specialist Opus Healthcare Solutions, Inc. The company plans to incorporate both acquisitions into its NextGen division.

FINANCIALS: Sales and profits are in thousands of dollars—add 000 to get the full amount. 2010 Note: Financial information for 2010 was not available for all companies at press time.

2010 Sales: $291,811	2010 Profits: $48,379	U.S. Stock Ticker: QSII
2009 Sales: $245,515	2009 Profits: $46,119	Int'l Ticker: Int'l Exchange:
2008 Sales: $186,500	2008 Profits: $40,078	Employees: 1,502
2007 Sales: $157,165	2007 Profits: $33,232	Fiscal Year Ends: 3/31
2006 Sales: $119,287	2006 Profits: $23,322	Parent Company:

SALARIES/BENEFITS:

Pension Plan:	ESOP Stock Plan:	Profit Sharing:	Top Exec. Salary: $538,750	Bonus: $110,000
Savings Plan: Y	Stock Purch. Plan:		Second Exec. Salary: $296,875	Bonus: $

OTHER THOUGHTS:

Apparent Women Officers or Directors:
Hot Spot for Advancement for Women/Minorities:

LOCATIONS: ("Y" = Yes)

West:	Southwest:	Midwest:	Southeast:	Northeast:	International:
Y	Y	Y	Y	Y	

Note: Financial information, benefits and other data can change quickly and may vary from those stated here.

QUANTA COMPUTER INC

www.quantatw.com

Industry Group Code: 334419 Ranks within this company's industry group: Sales: 3   Profits: 3

Hardware:		Software:	Telecommunications:	Electronic Publishing:	Equipment:	Specialty Services:
Computers:	Y	Consumer:	Local:	Online Service:	Telecom:	Consulting:
Accessories:	Y	Corporate:	Long Distance:	TV/Cable or Wireless:	Communication:	Contract Manufacturing:
Network Equipment:		Telecom:	Cellular:	Games:	Distribution:	Processing:
Chips/Circuits:		Internet:	Internet Service:	Financial Data:	VAR/Reseller:	Staff/Outsourcing:
Parts/Drives:	Y				Satellite Srv./Equip.:	Specialty Services:

TYPES OF BUSINESS:

Contract Electronics Manufacturing
Server Systems
Optical Storage Hardware
LCD Displays
Smart Phones
Automotive Electronics
Notebook Computers

BRANDS/DIVISIONS/AFFILIATES:

Quanta Enterprise Solutions
Quanta Storage Inc
Quanta Microsystem Inc
RoyalTek Company Ltd
Quanta Research Institute
One Laptop Per Child Association
Quanta's Cloud Computing Business Unit
Chunghwa Telecom

CONTACTS: *Note: Officers with more than one job title may be intentionally listed here more than once.*

C.C. Leung, Pres.
T.J. Fang, CIO
Elton Yang, VP-Finance Center
C.C. Leung, Vice Chmn.
Barry Lam, Chmn.

Phone: 886-3-327-2345	Fax: 886-3-327-1511
Toll-Free:	
Address: 211 Wen Hwa 2nd. Rd., Kuei Shan Hsiang, Tao Yuan Shien, Taiwan	

GROWTH PLANS/SPECIAL FEATURES:

Quanta Computer Inc., based in Taiwan, specializes in the contract design and manufacture of computers and components. Its chief products are notebook computers. In addition to notebook computers, the firm produces additional products. Other categories include smart phones, including personal digital assistant (PDA) devices; servers; digital televisions; automotive electronics, a category encompassing car-mounted DVD players; and touch-panel LCD screens equipped with GPS (Global Positioning System) for navigation systems. Quanta's Enterprise Solution business unit collaborates with global systems integrators to offer server, storage, VoIP (Voice over Internet Protocol), networking and security solutions for companies of various sizes. Quanta's Cloud Computing Business Unit (CCBU) focuses on ODM/OEM business development providing server, server motherboard, VoIP and networking solutions for small to mid-level businesses. Quanta Research Institute collaborates with leading institutions around the globe to research new technologies, including a $200 million project with MIT Computer Science and Artificial Intelligence Laboratory (CSAIL) in designing new computing and communication platforms. Subsidiaries of the firm include Quanta Storage, Inc., focused on the development and manufacturing of slim optical disk drives; QMI, which designs and manufactures wireless devices and modules for both system integrators and end users; and RoyalTek, a provider of GPS-related components, including GPS receivers, Bluetooth GPS devices, active antennae and GPS data logging systems. Quanta is working with the U.S.-based non-profit One Laptop Per Child Association to develop inexpensive, sturdy laptop computers for educational purposes in developing nations. In May 2010, the firm collaborated with Chunghwa Telecom (CHT) to provide cloud computing-based services.

FINANCIALS: Sales and profits are in thousands of dollars—add 000 to get the full amount. 2010 Note: Financial information for 2010 was not available for all companies at press time.

2010 Sales: $	2010 Profits: $	U.S. Stock Ticker:
2009 Sales: $25,353,000	2009 Profits: $626,420	Int'l Ticker: 2382 Int'l Exchange: Taipei-TPE
2008 Sales: $25,019,670	2008 Profits: $843,740	Employees:
2007 Sales: $23,323,100	2007 Profits: $553,600	Fiscal Year Ends: 12/31
2006 Sales: $16,130,400	2006 Profits: $387,600	Parent Company:

SALARIES/BENEFITS:

Pension Plan:	ESOP Stock Plan:	Profit Sharing:	Top Exec. Salary: $	Bonus: $
Savings Plan:	Stock Purch. Plan:		Second Exec. Salary: $	Bonus: $

OTHER THOUGHTS:

Apparent Women Officers or Directors:
Hot Spot for Advancement for Women/Minorities:

LOCATIONS: ("Y" = Yes)

West:	Southwest:	Midwest:	Southeast:	Northeast:	International:
					Y

QUANTUM CORP

www.quantum.com

Industry Group Code: 334112 Ranks within this company's industry group: Sales: 8 Profits: 11

Hardware:		Software:		Telecommunications:		Electronic Publishing:	Equipment:		Specialty Services:	
Computers:		Consumer:		Local:		Online Service:	Telecom:		Consulting:	
Accessories:	Y	Corporate:		Long Distance:		TV/Cable or Wireless:	Communication:		Contract Manufacturing:	
Network Equipment:		Telecom:		Cellular:		Games:	Distribution:		Processing:	
Chips/Circuits:		Internet:		Internet Service:		Financial Data:	VAR/Reseller:		Staff/Outsourcing:	
Parts/Drives:	Y						Satellite Srv./Equip.:		Specialty Services:	

TYPES OF BUSINESS:

Data Storage Equipment
Tape Drives
Media Cartridges
Tape Automation Systems

BRANDS/DIVISIONS/AFFILIATES:

iLayer
SuperLoader 3
Scalar i500
Scalar i2000
DXi-Series
StorNext

CONTACTS: Note: Officers with more than one job title may be intentionally listed here more than once.

Rick Belluzzo, CEO
Jon Gacek, COO
Jon Gacek, CFO/Exec. VP
Bill Britts, Exec. VP-Sales & Mktg.
Barbara Barrett, Sr. VP-Human Resources
Jeffrey Tofano, CTO
Jerry Lopatin, Exec. VP-Eng.
Shawn Hall, General Counsel/Sr. VP/Sec.
Rick Belluzzo, Chmn.

Phone: 408-944-4000	Fax: 408-944-4040
Toll-Free: 800-677-6268	
Address: 1650 Technology Dr., Ste. 700, San Jose, CA 95110 US	

GROWTH PLANS/SPECIAL FEATURES:

Quantum Corp. is a global storage company specializing in backup, recovery and archive applications. It provides an integrated range of disk, tape and software products. The company aims to provide information technology (IT) departments with tools for protecting, retaining and accessing digital assets. The firm's products are divided into three categories: tape automation systems; data management software and disk-based backup systems; and devices and media. The tape automation systems portfolio includes autoloaders under the SuperLoader name and entry-level, midrange and enterprise libraries. These products integrate tape drives into a system with automation technology, advanced connectivity and management tools. These autoloaders range from products with one tape drive and up to 16 cartridges to large enterprise-class libraries with hundreds of drives and thousands of cartridges. The midrange and enterprise libraries leverage a common, integrated software management approach, iLayer, which provides monitoring, alerts and diagnostics. The disk-based backup system products include the DXi-Series disk-based backup appliances featuring data deduplication and replication technologies. Data deduplication technology increases effective disk capacity, enabling longer use of fast recovery disk. Data management software products, designed for open system computing environments, improve workflow efficiencies, storage consolidation and archive management. StorNext, Quantum's primary data management product, provides shared access to data across different operating systems and storage platforms, and automatically copies and moves data between different tiers of storage based on business value. Devices and media products include removable disk drives, standalone tape drives and media products in multiple tape technology formats. Quantum sells its products via its branded channels through more than 20 distributors and 5,000 resellers worldwide, and through original equipment manufacturers such as Dell, Inc.; Hewlett-Packard Co. (HP); EMC Corporation; International Business Machines Corp. (IBM); and Sun Microsystems, Inc. The company serves customers in approximately 100 countries, with multi-language technical support centers in North America, Europe and Asia.

FINANCIALS: Sales and profits are in thousands of dollars—add 000 to get the full amount. 2010 Note: Financial information for 2010 was not available for all companies at press time.

2010 Sales: $681,427	2010 Profits: $16,634	U.S. Stock Ticker: QTM
2009 Sales: $808,972	2009 Profits: $-358,264	Int'l Ticker: Int'l Exchange:
2008 Sales: $975,702	2008 Profits: $-60,234	Employees: 1,800
2007 Sales: $1,016,174	2007 Profits: $-64,094	Fiscal Year Ends: 3/31
2006 Sales: $834,287	2006 Profits: $-41,479	Parent Company:

SALARIES/BENEFITS:

Pension Plan:	ESOP Stock Plan:	Profit Sharing:	Top Exec. Salary: $700,000	Bonus: $
Savings Plan:	Stock Purch. Plan:		Second Exec. Salary: $386,639	Bonus: $80,000

OTHER THOUGHTS:

Apparent Women Officers or Directors: 2
Hot Spot for Advancement for Women/Minorities:

LOCATIONS: ("Y" = Yes)

West:	Southwest:	Midwest:	Southeast:	Northeast:	International:
Y	Y	Y	Y	Y	Y

QUARK INC

www.quark.com

Industry Group Code: 511210F **Ranks within this company's industry group: Sales: Profits:**

Hardware:	Software:		Telecommunications:	Electronic Publishing:	Equipment:	Specialty Services:	
Computers:	Consumer:	Y	Local:	Online Service:	Telecom:	Consulting:	Y
Accessories:	Corporate:	Y	Long Distance:	TV/Cable or Wireless:	Communication:	Contract Manufacturing:	
Network Equipment:	Telecom:		Cellular:	Games:	Distribution:	Processing:	
Chips/Circuits:	Internet:		Internet Service:	Financial Data:	VAR/Reseller:	Staff/Outsourcing:	
Parts/Drives:					Satellite Srv./Equip.:	Specialty Services:	Y

TYPES OF BUSINESS:
Multimedia Software
Publishing & Graphic Design Software

BRANDS/DIVISIONS/AFFILIATES:
QuarkXPress
QuarkXtensions
QuarkCopyDesk
Quark Labs
QuarkXPress Plus

CONTACTS: Note: Officers with more than one job title may be intentionally listed here more than once.
Raymond Schiavone, CEO
Raymond Schiavone, Pres.
Kevin Mammel, CFO
Gavin Drake, VP-Mktg.
Claire Hancock, VP-Human Resources
Jim Haggarty, CIO
Dave White, VP-Emerging Tech. & Alliances
P. G. Bartlett, Sr. VP-Prod. Mgmt.
Ronnie Thomson, Sr. VP-Eng.
Peter Jensen, General Counsel
Mark Benfer, Sr. VP-Sales, Americas, Pacific & Japan
Matthew Wallis, Sr. VP-Sales, EMEA & Asia

Phone: 308-894-8888	Fax: 303-894-3398
Toll-Free: 800-676-4575	
Address: 1800 Grant St., Ste. 800, Denver, CO 80203 US	

GROWTH PLANS/SPECIAL FEATURES:
Quark, Inc. is a global producer of desktop and enterprise publishing software. Its primary offerings are the QuarkXPress and QuarkCopyDesk products. QuarkXPress is a layout design program that allows complex print and picture manipulation used for authoring tools for Web and Flash. The software's key attributes include professional-grade collaborative sharing, typography, picture editing and printing capabilities. The QuarkXPress Plus edition offers extended support for Asian languages. Quark Xtensions is a line of plugin programs designed to enhance QuarkXPress, including improved word processing and document manipulation. QuarkCopyDesk facilitates coordination between the layout design established in QuarkXPress. Additionally, Quark offers professional services including integration, consulting and custom software development. The firm's online forum, Quark Labs, offers users free test versions of Quark XTensions and a community for online discussions. Quark's products are available for both Mac OSX and Windows 7.

FINANCIALS: Sales and profits are in thousands of dollars—add 000 to get the full amount. 2010 Note: Financial information for 2010 was not available for all companies at press time.
2010 Sales: $	2010 Profits: $	U.S. Stock Ticker: Private
2009 Sales: $	2009 Profits: $	Int'l Ticker: Int'l Exchange:
2008 Sales: $	2008 Profits: $	Employees:
2007 Sales: $	2007 Profits: $	Fiscal Year Ends: 12/31
2006 Sales: $	2006 Profits: $	Parent Company:

SALARIES/BENEFITS:
Pension Plan:	ESOP Stock Plan:	Profit Sharing:	Top Exec. Salary: $	Bonus: $
Savings Plan: Y	Stock Purch. Plan:		Second Exec. Salary: $	Bonus: $

OTHER THOUGHTS:
Apparent Women Officers or Directors: 1
Hot Spot for Advancement for Women/Minorities:

LOCATIONS: ("Y" = Yes)
West:	Southwest:	Midwest:	Southeast:	Northeast:	International:
Y			Y	Y	Y

QUEST SOFTWARE INC

www.quest.com

Industry Group Code: 511210I Ranks within this company's industry group: Sales: 2 Profits: 3

Hardware:	Software:		Telecommunications:	Electronic Publishing:	Equipment:	Specialty Services:
Computers:	Consumer:		Local:	Online Service:	Telecom:	Consulting:
Accessories:	Corporate:	Y	Long Distance:	TV/Cable or Wireless:	Communication:	Contract Manufacturing:
Network Equipment:	Telecom:		Cellular:	Games:	Distribution:	Processing:
Chips/Circuits:	Internet:		Internet Service:	Financial Data:	VAR/Reseller:	Staff/Outsourcing:
Parts/Drives:					Satellite Srv./Equip.:	Specialty Services:

TYPES OF BUSINESS:

Software-Corporate Enterprise Efficiency
Database Management Solutions
Customer Relationship Management
Windows Management Software

BRANDS/DIVISIONS/AFFILIATES:

Foglight
Jprobe
Quest Central
SharePlex
LiteSpeed
Vizioncore vFoglight
Vizioncore vRanger
MonoSphere

CONTACTS: Note: Officers with more than one job title may be intentionally listed here more than once.

Douglas F. Garn, CEO
Douglas F. Garn, Pres.
Scott Davidson, CFO/Sr. VP
Alan Fudge, Sr. VP-Worldwide Sales
John Ganley, VP-Human Resources
Carol Fawcett, VP-Global Info. Svcs.
Steve Dickson, Sr. VP-Prod. Mgmt. & Mktg.
David Cramer, General Counsel/Sec./VP
David Waugh, VP-Unified Comm.
Stephen Wideman, Dir.-Investor Rel.
Carl Eberling, VP/Gen. Mgr.-Virtualization & Monitoring
Steve Kahan, VP-Global Mktg.
Vincent C. Smith, Chmn.
Kim Kinnison, VP-Worldwide Support

Phone: 949-754-8000	Fax: 949-754-8999
Toll-Free:	
Address: 5 Polaris Way, Aliso Viejo, CA 92656 US	

GROWTH PLANS/SPECIAL FEATURES:

Quest Software, Inc. is an independent software vendor that designs, develops, markets, distributes and supports enterprise systems management software products. It provides its customers with products that improve the performance, productivity and reliability of their software applications and associated software infrastructure components such as databases, application servers and operating systems. Quest's primary focus is on identifying large and evolving markets and developing and acquiring new products and technologies. It generates revenues by licensing its products, principally on a perpetual basis, as well as by providing support, maintenance and implementation services for those products. The firm's product portfolio is grouped into four categories: Application Management, Database Management, Windows Management and Virtualization management. Application management software is predicated on ensuring performance and availability of mission-critical applications throughout their life cycle. Products in this category include Foglight, Spotlight, PerformaSure and JProbe. Database management software products support the needs of database developers and include TOAD, the Quest Central product line, SharePlex and LiteSpeed. Windows management tools enable IT personnel to simplify, automate and secure their infrastructure, and include the Quest Management product line, the Quest Migration product line, Quest in Trust, Quest Authentication Services and ScriptLogic Desktop Authority. Virtualization management products help companies safeguard and optimize their virtualized environments, and include Vizioncore vFoglight, Vizioncore vRanger Pro, and vWorkspace. Quest also provides services such as technical support, maintenance, consulting and training. The company markets and sells its products and services primarily through its direct sales organization, its telesales organization and via indirect sales channels with a group of value-added resellers (VARs) and distributors. In November 2010, the company announced an agreement to acquire Bakbone Software, Inc. for approximately $55 million.

The firm offers its employees medical, vision and dental benefits; short-and long-term disability and life insurance.

FINANCIALS: Sales and profits are in thousands of dollars—add 000 to get the full amount. 2010 Note: Financial information for 2010 was not available for all companies at press time.

2010 Sales: $	2010 Profits: $	**U.S. Stock Ticker: QSFT**
2009 Sales: $695,236	2009 Profits: $70,359	**Int'l Ticker:** Int'l Exchange:
2008 Sales: $735,377	2008 Profits: $68,043	Employees: 3,477
2007 Sales: $630,981	2007 Profits: $63,119	Fiscal Year Ends: 12/31
2006 Sales: $561,589	2006 Profits: $58,985	Parent Company:

SALARIES/BENEFITS:

Pension Plan:	ESOP Stock Plan:	Profit Sharing:	Top Exec. Salary: $1,000,000	Bonus: $963,364
Savings Plan: Y	Stock Purch. Plan:		Second Exec. Salary: $817,309	Bonus: $818,859

OTHER THOUGHTS:

Apparent Women Officers or Directors: 2
Hot Spot for Advancement for Women/Minorities: Y

LOCATIONS: ("Y" = Yes)

West:	Southwest:	Midwest:	Southeast:	Northeast:	International:
Y	Y	Y	Y	Y	Y

RADISYS CORP

www.radisys.com

Industry Group Code: 334111 Ranks within this company's industry group: Sales: 26   Profits: 22

Hardware:		Software:		Telecommunications:	Electronic Publishing:	Equipment:		Specialty Services:	
Computers:	Y	Consumer:		Local:	Online Service:	Telecom:	Y	Consulting:	
Accessories:		Corporate:	Y	Long Distance:	TV/Cable or Wireless:	Communication:	Y	Contract Manufacturing:	Y
Network Equipment:	Y	Telecom:	Y	Cellular:	Games:	Distribution:		Processing:	
Chips/Circuits:	Y	Internet:		Internet Service:	Financial Data:	VAR/Reseller:		Staff/Outsourcing:	
Parts/Drives:	Y					Satellite Srv./Equip.:		Specialty Services:	Y

TYPES OF BUSINESS:

Computer Hardware-Intel-Based Embedded Computers
DSP Modules & Algorithms
Network Interfaces & Protocols
Systems Platforms
Embedded Software
Systems Engineering
Integration Services

BRANDS/DIVISIONS/AFFILIATES:

Convedia
Promentum
Procelerant
Pactolus Communications Software Corporation

CONTACTS: Note: Officers with more than one job title may be intentionally listed here more than once.

Scott C. Grout, CEO
Scott C. Grout, Pres.
Brian Bronson, CFO
Christian Lepiane, VP-Global Sales, Service & Corp. Mktg.
Andrew Alleman, CTO
John Major, VP-Global Oper.
Grant Henderson, VP-Bus. Dev.
Lyn Pangares, Dir.-Corp. Mktg.
Holly Stephens, Mgr.-Investor Rel.
Holly Stephens, Mgr.-Finance
Anthony Ambrose, VP/Gen. Mgr.-Comm. Networks
David Smith, VP/Gen. Mgr.-Media Server Market
C. Scott Gibson, Chmn.

Phone: 503-615-1100	Fax: 503-615-1115
Toll-Free: 800-950-0044	
Address: 5445 NE Dawson Creek Dr., Hillsboro, OR 97124 US	

GROWTH PLANS/SPECIAL FEATURES:

RadiSys Corp. is a leading provider of advanced embedded technologies for the communications networking and commercial systems markets. The company's products are offered in three separate families: Convedia Media Servers; Advanced Telecommunications Computing Architecture (ATCA), under the brand Promentum; and the Procelerant commercial product line. Its products include embedded boards, application enabling platforms and turn-key systems, which are used in complex computing, processing and network intensive applications. The company primarily markets its products to original equipment manufacturers (OEMs) in the communication networks market and the commercial systems market. RadiSys' communication network products fall into two main divisions: wireless infrastructure; and IP networking and messaging. Applications in these markets include 2G, 2.5G, 3G and 4G wireless infrastructure products, IP media server platforms, packet-based switches, unified messaging applications, voice messaging, multimedia messaging, video distribution, network access, security and switching applications. RadiSys also serves the commercial systems market, encompassing submarkets such as medical imaging, test and measurement equipment, industrial automation and military. Applications in the commercial systems markets include X-ray machines; magnetic resonance imaging (MRI) scanners; computed tomography (CT) scan imaging equipment; ultrasound equipment; network and logic analyzers; network and production test equipment; and electronics assembly and semiconductor manufacturing equipment. In March 2010, the firm acquired Pactolus Communications Software Corporation, a developer of IP communication software.

RadiSys provides its employees with benefits including a 401(k) plan; financial planning assistance; an employee stock purchase plan; medical, dental and vision insurance with domestic partner coverage; flexible spending accounts; adoption assistance; subsidized health club memberships; a 24-hour-a-day nurse line; and an employee assistance program.

FINANCIALS: Sales and profits are in thousands of dollars—add 000 to get the full amount. 2010 Note: Financial information for 2010 was not available for all companies at press time.

2010 Sales: $	2010 Profits: $	U.S. Stock Ticker: RSYS
2009 Sales: $304,273	2009 Profits: $-42,567	Int'l Ticker: Int'l Exchange:
2008 Sales: $372,584	2008 Profits: $-65,950	Employees: 719
2007 Sales: $325,232	2007 Profits: $-17,552	Fiscal Year Ends: 12/31
2006 Sales: $292,481	2006 Profits: $-13,016	Parent Company:

SALARIES/BENEFITS:

Pension Plan:	ESOP Stock Plan:	Profit Sharing:	Top Exec. Salary: $478,570	Bonus: $375,917
Savings Plan: Y	Stock Purch. Plan: Y		Second Exec. Salary: $294,162	Bonus: $193,660

OTHER THOUGHTS:

Apparent Women Officers or Directors: 1
Hot Spot for Advancement for Women/Minorities:

LOCATIONS: ("Y" = Yes)

West:	Southwest:	Midwest:	Southeast:	Northeast:	International:
Y		Y	Y		Y

RADWARE LTD

www.radware.com

Industry Group Code: 511210B Ranks within this company's industry group: Sales: 8   Profits: 7

Hardware:	Software:		Telecommunications:	Electronic Publishing:	Equipment:	Specialty Services:
Computers:	Consumer:		Local:	Online Service:	Telecom:	Consulting:
Accessories:	Corporate:	Y	Long Distance:	TV/Cable or Wireless:	Communication:	Contract Manufacturing:
Network Equipment:	Telecom:		Cellular:	Games:	Distribution:	Processing:
Chips/Circuits:	Internet:		Internet Service:	Financial Data:	VAR/Reseller:	Staff/Outsourcing:
Parts/Drives:					Satellite Srv./Equip.:	Specialty Services:

TYPES OF BUSINESS:

Internet Management Software
Internet Security Software
e-Commerce Software
Connectivity Software

BRANDS/DIVISIONS/AFFILIATES:

RAD Group
APSolute Suite
AppDirector
AppXcel
DefensePro
LinkProof/LinkProof Branch
APSolute OS
Virtual Application Delivery Infrastructure (VADI)

CONTACTS: Note: Officers with more than one job title may be intentionally listed here more than once.

Roy Zisapel, CEO
Ilan Kinreich, COO
Roy Zisapel, Pres.
Meir Moshe, CFO
Sharon Trachtman, VP-Global Mktg.
Ilana Barak, VP-Global Human Resources
Amir Peles, CTO
Yaron Bielous, VP-Prod. Mgmt.
Udi Abramovic, VP-Global Oper.
Yossi Vardi, VP-Global Bus. Dev.
Shlomo Tenenberg, VP-EMEA
Avi Chesla, VP-Security Prod.
Christine Aruza, VP-Corp. Mktg.
Terence Ying, VP-APAC
Yehuda Zisapel, Chmn.
Ramesh Barasia, Pres., Americas

Phone: 972-3-766-8666	Fax: 972-3-766-8655
Toll-Free: 877-236-9807	
Address: 22 Raoul Wallenberg St., Tel Aviv, 69710 Israel	

GROWTH PLANS/SPECIAL FEATURES:

Radware, Ltd. is a leader in integrated application delivery and network security products. Radware is one of several independent companies that operate under the RAD Group. Nearly 10,000 enterprises and carriers worldwide use Radware applications to add security and improve performance of their IP infrastructure. Radware's APSolute Suite provides a complete set of IT infrastructure and security capabilities for application-smart networking to ensure faster, more secure business transactions. The APSolute family includes, among others: AppDirector, which serves as an intelligent application delivery controller for data centers, as well as providing for web compression and Hypertext Transfer Protocol; AppXcel, an application accelerator that provides end-to-end application-smart performance tuning for web-enabled and SSL-based applications; DefensePro intrusion prevention and denial of service products, which protect against worms, bots, viruses, malicious intrusions and denial of dervice attacks; and LinkProof/LinkProof Branch, an integrated application access solution that combines multi-homing, access control, connectivity management, remote office virtual private network (VPN) and wide area network (WAN) optimization. Additionally, the company offers APSolute OS, a modular operating system built around Radware's core software engines, which embeds common operating logic into each product. The common application management tool that runs across all Radware products is APSolute Insite. APSolute Insite is a unified management tool with an intuitive graphical user interface that provides end-to-end network visibility, control and policy management of all application switching devices. The company also offers a security update service, consisting of immediate and ongoing security updates to protect customers against the latest threats. The firm maintains a research and development center in Bangalore, India. In September 2010, Radware introduced its Virtual Application Delivery Infrastructure (VADI), an architecture that brings computing resources, application delivery and virtualization services together into an integrated package.

FINANCIALS: Sales and profits are in thousands of dollars—add 000 to get the full amount. 2010 Note: Financial information for 2010 was not available for all companies at press time.

2010 Sales: $	2010 Profits: $	**U.S. Stock Ticker: RDWR**
2009 Sales: $108,900	2009 Profits: $-5,900	**Int'l Ticker: RDWR** Int'l Exchange: Tel Aviv-TASE
2008 Sales: $94,581	2008 Profits: $-31,022	Employees: 534
2007 Sales: $88,631	2007 Profits: $-12,011	Fiscal Year Ends: 12/31
2006 Sales: $81,400	2006 Profits: $-1,300	Parent Company:

SALARIES/BENEFITS:

Pension Plan:	ESOP Stock Plan:	Profit Sharing:	Top Exec. Salary: $	Bonus: $
Savings Plan: Y	Stock Purch. Plan:		Second Exec. Salary: $	Bonus: $

OTHER THOUGHTS:

Apparent Women Officers or Directors: 4
Hot Spot for Advancement for Women/Minorities: Y

LOCATIONS: ("Y" = Yes)

West:	Southwest:	Midwest:	Southeast:	Northeast:	International:
				Y	Y

RAMBUS INC

www.rambus.com

Industry Group Code: 33441 Ranks within this company's industry group: Sales: 53   Profits: 43

Hardware:		Software:	Telecommunications:	Electronic Publishing:	Equipment:	Specialty Services:	
Computers:		Consumer:	Local:	Online Service:	Telecom:	Consulting:	
Accessories:		Corporate:	Long Distance:	TV/Cable or Wireless:	Communication:	Contract Manufacturing:	
Network Equipment:		Telecom:	Cellular:	Games:	Distribution:	Processing:	
Chips/Circuits:	Y	Internet:	Internet Service:	Financial Data:	VAR/Reseller:	Staff/Outsourcing:	
Parts/Drives:					Satellite Srv./Equip.:	Specialty Services:	Y

TYPES OF BUSINESS:

Chips-RAM
Memory & Logic Interfaces
Engineering Services

BRANDS/DIVISIONS/AFFILIATES:

XDR (eXtreme Data Rate)
XDR DRAM

CONTACTS: *Note: Officers with more than one job title may be intentionally listed here more than once.*

Harold Hughes, CEO
Harold Hughes, Pres.
Satish Rishi, CFO/Sr. VP
Michael Schroeder, VP-Human Resources
Thomas R. Lavelle, General Counsel/Sr. VP
Laura Stark, Sr. VP-Corp. Dev.
Satish Rishi, Sr. VP-Finance
Kevin S. Donnelly, Sr. VP-IP Strategy
Sharon Holt, Sr. VP/Gen. Mgr.-Semiconductor Bus. Group
Jeffery Parker, Sr. VP-Lighting & Display Tech.
Christopher M. Pickett, Sr. VP-Licensing
Bruce Dunlevie, Chmn.

Phone: 408-462-8000	Fax: 408-462-8001
Toll-Free:	
Address: 1050 Enterprise Way, Ste. 700, Sunnyvale, CA 94089 US	

GROWTH PLANS/SPECIAL FEATURES:

Rambus, Inc. designs, develops and licenses chip interface technologies and architectures for use in the manufacture of semiconductors. The company's line of products and patented inventions, including the XDR (eXtreme Data Rate) memory interface product family, are designed to enable higher performance, improved power efficiency, lower risk and greater cost-effectiveness for computing, gaming and graphics, consumer electronics and mobile applications. Devices that use Rambus' products include personal computers, servers, printers, video projectors, game consoles, digital TVs, set-top boxes and mobile phones. XDR DRAM (Dynamic Random Access Memory) is the main memory solution for Sony Computer Entertainment's PlayStation 3 as well as for Texas Instrument's latest generation of DLP front projectors. Other customers include Elpida, IBM, Intel, Qimonda, Panasonic, Sony and Toshiba. Rambus also offers custom memory and digital logic solutions for high-performance system applications. The company currently holds 950 U.S. and foreign patents and has about 600 patents pending on inventions in memory and logic chip interfaces. Rambus sells licenses to semiconductor and system companies, who then incorporate the interface products into their chips and systems. The company also performs engineering services for companies to help them successfully integrate its interface products into their semiconductor and system products. The firm operates in the U.S., Japan, Korea, China, Taiwan, India, France and Germany.

Rambus offers its employees medical, dental and vision coverage; an employee assistance plan; life and AD&D insurance; a 529 college savings plan; flexible spending accounts; a 401(k) program; an employee stock purchase plan; additional voluntary wellness plans; and Rambus University job training.

FINANCIALS: Sales and profits are in thousands of dollars—add 000 to get the full amount. 2010 Note: Financial information for 2010 was not available for all companies at press time.

2010 Sales: $	2010 Profits: $	U.S. Stock Ticker: RMBS
2009 Sales: $113,007	2009 Profits: $-92,186	Int'l Ticker: Int'l Exchange:
2008 Sales: $142,494	2008 Profits: $-195,923	Employees: 350
2007 Sales: $179,940	2007 Profits: $-27,664	Fiscal Year Ends: 12/31
2006 Sales: $195,324	2006 Profits: $-13,816	Parent Company:

SALARIES/BENEFITS:

Pension Plan:	ESOP Stock Plan:	Profit Sharing:	Top Exec. Salary: $440,000	Bonus: $242,000
Savings Plan: Y	Stock Purch. Plan: Y		Second Exec. Salary: $318,240	Bonus: $132,000

OTHER THOUGHTS:

Apparent Women Officers or Directors: 3
Hot Spot for Advancement for Women/Minorities: Y

LOCATIONS: ("Y" = Yes)

West:	Southwest:	Midwest:	Southeast:	Northeast:	International:
Y		Y		Y	Y

RDA MICROELECTRONICS INC

www.rdamicro.com

Industry Group Code: 33441 Ranks within this company's industry group: Sales: Profits:

Hardware:	Software:	Telecommunications:	Electronic Publishing:	Equipment:	Specialty Services:
Computers:	Consumer:	Local:	Online Service:	Telecom:	Consulting:
Accessories:	Corporate:	Long Distance:	TV/Cable or Wireless:	Communication:	Contract Manufacturing:
Network Equipment:	Telecom:	Cellular:	Games:	Distribution:	Processing:
Chips/Circuits: Y	Internet:	Internet Service:	Financial Data:	VAR/Reseller:	Staff/Outsourcing:
Parts/Drives:				Satellite Srv./Equip.:	Specialty Services:

TYPES OF BUSINESS:

Fabless Semiconductor

BRANDS/DIVISIONS/AFFILIATES:

CONTACTS:
Note: Officers with more than one job title may be intentionally listed here more than once.

Vincent Tai, CEO
Lily (Li) Dong, CFO
Dalei Fan, VP-Sales
Shuran Wei, CTO
Liang Zhang, Sr. VP-Eng.
Shun Lam Steven Tang, Sr. VP-Oper.
Jun Chen, Sr. VP-Eng.
Guoguang Zhao, VP-Oper.
Vincent Tai, Chmn.

Phone: 86-21-5027-1108	Fax: 86-21-5021-1099
Toll-Free:	
Address: 690 Bibo Rd., Bldg. 2, Ste. 302, Shanghai, 201203 China	

GROWTH PLANS/SPECIAL FEATURES:

RDA Microelectronics, Inc. is a fabless semiconductor company that designs and develops radio-frequency (RF) and mixed-signal semiconductors for use in a numerous products. The company is one of Asia's largest providers of analog application specific standard products (which include radio-frequency and mixed-signal semiconductors) for wireless communications. Products manufactured by the company are divided according to application into three groups: cellular, broadcast and connectivity. Its cellular line of products include GSM power amplifier modules, transceivers and front-end modules, 3G switch modules and RF switches. For the signal broadcast segment RDA offers FM radio receivers, analog mobile TV receiver systems-on-chip, DVB satellite tuners and LNB satellite down-converters used in set-top box tuners, digital video recorders and digital televisions. Connectivity chips include Bluetooth systems-on-chip for mobile handsets and walkie-talkie transceivers for consumer and professional applications. Its core competency is the design of highly integrated, high-performance radio-frequency and mixed-signal system-on-chip, which it developed through a combination of technical know-how, system and application level knowledge and expertise in mixed-signal integrated circuits. These circuits convert real-world analog signals, such as sound and radio waves, into digital signals that electronic products can process. Through internal development and licensing, the firm has assembled an extensive library of radio-frequency, mixed-signal, and digital signal processing building blocks, which enables it to develop comprehensive system-level intellectual property. RDA sells its products to OEMs in China through several independent distributors. Since its inception, over 800 million units of its products have been incorporated into mobile handsets, set-top boxes, MP3 players and other wireless and consumer electronic devices sold in China, Southeast Asia, India, the Middle East, Africa, Russia, and Latin America. In November 2010, the firm began trading on NASDAQ.

FINANCIALS:
Sales and profits are in thousands of dollars—add 000 to get the full amount. 2010 Note: Financial information for 2010 was not available for all companies at press time.

2010 Sales: $	2010 Profits: $	U.S. Stock Ticker: RDA
2009 Sales: $	2009 Profits: $	Int'l Ticker: Int'l Exchange:
2008 Sales: $	2008 Profits: $	Employees:
2007 Sales: $	2007 Profits: $	Fiscal Year Ends:
2006 Sales: $	2006 Profits: $	Parent Company:

SALARIES/BENEFITS:

Pension Plan:	ESOP Stock Plan:	Profit Sharing:	Top Exec. Salary: $	Bonus: $
Savings Plan:	Stock Purch. Plan:		Second Exec. Salary: $	Bonus: $

OTHER THOUGHTS:

Apparent Women Officers or Directors: 1
Hot Spot for Advancement for Women/Minorities:

LOCATIONS: ("Y" = Yes)

West:	Southwest:	Midwest:	Southeast:	Northeast:	International: Y

REALNETWORKS INC

www.realnetworks.com

Industry Group Code: 511210F Ranks within this company's industry group: Sales: 2 Profits: 6

Hardware:	Software:		Telecommunications:	Electronic Publishing:		Equipment:	Specialty Services:
Computers:	Consumer:	Y	Local:	Online Service:	Y	Telecom:	Consulting:
Accessories:	Corporate:	Y	Long Distance:	TV/Cable or Wireless:		Communication:	Contract Manufacturing:
Network Equipment:	Telecom:		Cellular:	Games:		Distribution:	Processing:
Chips/Circuits:	Internet:		Internet Service:	Financial Data:		VAR/Reseller:	Staff/Outsourcing:
Parts/Drives:						Satellite Srv./Equip.:	Specialty Services:

TYPES OF BUSINESS:

Digital Media Services
Computer Software-Streaming Audio & Video
Online Retail-Digital Media
Mobile Games
Mobile Music
Mobile Video

BRANDS/DIVISIONS/AFFILIATES:

RealPlayer
Backstage Technologies Inc
WiderThan Co Ltd
RealArcade
SuperPass
Gamehouse
Atrativa
Zylom

CONTACTS: Note: Officers with more than one job title may be intentionally listed here more than once.

Robert Kimball, CEO
Robert Kimball, Pres.
Michael Eggers, CFO/Sr. VP
Savino R. Ferrales, Sr. VP-Human Resources
Mike Lunsford, Exec. VP-Tech. Solutions
Tracy D. Daw, Chief Legal Officer/Corp. Sec.
Matt Hulett, Sr. VP-Game Div.
Mike Lunsford, Exec. VP-Music & Media
Hank Skorny, Sr. VP-Media Cloud Computing & Svcs.
Robert Glaser, Chmn.

Phone: 206-674-2700	Fax: 206-674-2699
Toll-Free:	
Address: 2601 Elliott Ave., Ste. 1000, Seattle, WA 98121 US	

GROWTH PLANS/SPECIAL FEATURES:

RealNetworks, Inc. is a creator of digital media services and software. The company operates in three segments: core products, games and emerging products. The firm's core products segment offers software as a service (SaaS) services, such as ringback tones, music on demand, video on demand, inter-carrier messages, professional services and system integration services to carriers and mobile handset firms. The core products segment also licenses its software products, including consumer subscriptions such as SuperPass, Helix for handsets and international radio subscriptions. RealNetworks' games segment creates, distributes and sells game licenses; advertising on game sites and social network sites; micro-transactions from online and social games; online games subscription services; games syndication services; and sales of mobile games. The company develops original content for these services through the game studios Gamehouse, RealArcade, Atrativa and Zylom. Its games include Scrabble, SuperCollapse, Uno and Sally's Salon. The emerging products division provides RealPlayer and its related products. RealPlayer enables consumers to discover, play and manage audio and video programming on the Internet. The emerging products segment also builds and develops new product offerings for the firm's consumers and corporate customers. Through subsidiary WiderThan Co., Ltd., RealNetworks develops digital entertainment services for wireless carriers, such as ringback tones, music-on-demand and video-on-demand services. In March 2010, the firm and MTV Networks spun off their former joint venture, digital music service provider Rhapsody America, LLC, into an independent company.

RealNetworks offers its employees medical, dental and vision coverage; a 401(k) plan; an employee stock purchase program; commuting subsidies; and charitable matching.

FINANCIALS: Sales and profits are in thousands of dollars—add 000 to get the full amount. 2010 Note: Financial information for 2010 was not available for all companies at press time.

2010 Sales: $	2010 Profits: $	**U.S. Stock Ticker:** RNWK
2009 Sales: $862,264	2009 Profits: $-212,264	**Int'l Ticker:** Int'l Exchange:
2008 Sales: $604,810	2008 Profits: $-243,878	Employees: 1,774
2007 Sales: $567,620	2007 Profits: $48,315	Fiscal Year Ends: 12/31
2006 Sales: $395,261	2006 Profits: $145,216	Parent Company:

SALARIES/BENEFITS:

Pension Plan:	ESOP Stock Plan:	Profit Sharing:	Top Exec. Salary: $450,000	Bonus: $288,631
Savings Plan: Y	Stock Purch. Plan: Y		Second Exec. Salary: $435,000	Bonus: $364,759

OTHER THOUGHTS:

Apparent Women Officers or Directors: 1
Hot Spot for Advancement for Women/Minorities:

LOCATIONS: ("Y" = Yes)

West:	Southwest:	Midwest:	Southeast:	Northeast:	International:
Y					Y

RED HAT INC

www.redhat.com

Industry Group Code: 511210I Ranks within this company's industry group: Sales: 3 Profits: 2

Hardware:	Software:		Telecommunications:	Electronic Publishing:	Equipment:	Specialty Services:	
Computers:	Consumer:		Local:	Online Service:	Telecom:	Consulting:	
Accessories:	Corporate:	Y	Long Distance:	TV/Cable or Wireless:	Communication:	Contract Manufacturing:	
Network Equipment:	Telecom:		Cellular:	Games:	Distribution:	Processing:	
Chips/Circuits:	Internet:		Internet Service:	Financial Data:	VAR/Reseller:	Staff/Outsourcing:	
Parts/Drives:					Satellite Srv./Equip.:	Specialty Services:	Y

TYPES OF BUSINESS:

Computer Software-Linux Operating Systems
Open-Source Software

BRANDS/DIVISIONS/AFFILIATES:

Red Hat Cloud Foundations
JBoss Enterprise Middleware Suite
Red Hat Network Satellite
JBoss Operations Network
Red Hat Enterprise Virtualization

CONTACTS: Note: Officers with more than one job title may be intentionally listed here more than once.

Jim Whitehurst, CEO
Jim Whitehurst, Pres.
Charlie Peters, CFO/Exec. VP
Alex Pinchev, Exec. VP/Pres., Global Sales, Svcs. & Field Mktg.
DeLisa Alexander, Sr. VP-People & Brand
Lee Congdon, CIO
Brian Stevens, CTO
Paul Cormier, Exec. VP/Pres., Prod. & Tech.
Brian Stevens, VP-Worldwide Eng.
Michael Cunningham, General Counsel/Exec. VP/Sec.
Tom Rabon, Exec. VP-Corp. Affairs
Jim Totton, VP-Platform Bus. Unit
Scott Crenshaw, VP-Cloud Bus. Unit
Michael Tiemann, VP-Open Source Affairs
Craig Muzilla, VP-Middleware Bus. Unit
Matthew J. Szulik, Chmn.

Phone: 919-754-3700	Fax: 919-754-3701
Toll-Free: 888-733-4281	
Address: 1801 Varsity Dr., Raleigh, NC 27606 US	

GROWTH PLANS/SPECIAL FEATURES:

Red Hat, Inc. is a provider of open source software solutions. The firm's solutions include its core enterprise operating system platform Red Hat Enterprise Linux, virtual solutions, the enterprise middleware platform JBoss Enterprise Middleware Suite and other Red Hat enterprise technologies. The company offers a choice of operating system platforms for servers, work stations and desktops that support multiple application areas, including the data center, edge-of-the-network applications, IT infrastructure, corporate desktop and technical/developer workstation. Red Hat Enterprise Linux 5 offers additional technology enhancements, including integrated virtualization. The enterprise middleware platform, JBoss Enterprise Middleware, delivers a suite of middleware products for service-oriented architectures, permitting web-enabled applications to run on open source and other platforms. JBoss Enterprise Middleware provides an application infrastructure for building and deploying distributed applications that are accessible via the Internet, corporate intranets, extranets and virtual private networks. Examples of applications deployed on JBoss include online e-business; hotel and airline reservations; online banking; credit card processing; securities trading; healthcare systems; customer and partner portals; retail and point of sale systems; telecommunications network infrastructure; and grid-based systems. The integrated management services, Red Hat Network Satellite and JBoss Operations Network, permit Red Hat enterprise technologies to be updated and configured and the performance of these and other technologies to be monitored and managed in an automated fashion. The firm's suite of training and other professional service offerings enable enterprise customers to adapt Red Hat's technologies to their needs. In June 2010, Red Hat introduced Red Hat Cloud Foundations, a series of comprehensive solutions for the planning, building and managing of and platform-as-a-service and infrastructure-as-a-service public and private clouds. Also in June 2010, the firm integrated its Red Hat Enterprise Virtualization product with Cisco's Virtual Network Link.

FINANCIALS: Sales and profits are in thousands of dollars—add 000 to get the full amount. 2010 Note: Financial information for 2010 was not available for all companies at press time.

2010 Sales: $748,236	2010 Profits: $87,253	**U.S. Stock Ticker: RHT**
2009 Sales: $652,572	2009 Profits: $78,721	**Int'l Ticker:** Int'l Exchange:
2008 Sales: $523,016	2008 Profits: $76,667	Employees: 3,200
2007 Sales: $400,624	2007 Profits: $59,907	Fiscal Year Ends: 2/28
2006 Sales: $278,330	2006 Profits: $79,685	Parent Company:

SALARIES/BENEFITS:

Pension Plan:	ESOP Stock Plan:	Profit Sharing:	Top Exec. Salary: $700,000	Bonus: $595,000
Savings Plan: Y	Stock Purch. Plan:		Second Exec. Salary: $425,000	Bonus: $270,938

OTHER THOUGHTS:

Apparent Women Officers or Directors: 3
Hot Spot for Advancement for Women/Minorities: Y

LOCATIONS: ("Y" = Yes)

West:	Southwest:	Midwest:	Southeast:	Northeast:	International:
Y	Y	Y	Y	Y	Y

Note: Financial information, benefits and other data can change quickly and may vary from those stated here.

REDINGTON (INDIA) LTD

www.redingtonindia.com

Industry Group Code: 423430 Ranks within this company's industry group: Sales: 10   Profits: 8

Hardware:	Software:	Telecommunications:	Electronic Publishing:	Equipment:		Specialty Services:	
Computers:	Consumer:	Local:	Online Service:	Telecom:		Consulting:	
Accessories:	Corporate:	Long Distance:	TV/Cable or Wireless:	Communication:		Contract Manufacturing:	
Network Equipment:	Telecom:	Cellular:	Games:	Distribution:	Y	Processing:	
Chips/Circuits:	Internet:	Internet Service:	Financial Data:	VAR/Reseller:		Staff/Outsourcing:	
Parts/Drives:				Satellite Srv./Equip.:		Specialty Services:	Y

TYPES OF BUSINESS:

Supply Chain Distribution
Logistics Services
Repair Services
Non-Banking Finance

BRANDS/DIVISIONS/AFFILIATES:

Redington Gulf FZE
Redington Distribution Private Ltd.
Easyaccess Financial Services Limited
Cadensworth (India) Limited
Arena Bilgisayar Sanayi Ve Ticaret Anonim Irketi

CONTACTS: Note: Officers with more than one job title may be intentionally listed here more than once.

S.V. Krishnan, CFO
Ramesh Natarajan, Head-National Sales
Clynton Almeida, CIO
M. Muthukumarasamy, Corp. Sec.
E.H. Kasturi Rangan, Pres., Consumer & Digital Prod. Div.
P.S. Neogi, Pres., IT Prod.
Anand Chakravarthy, Head-Networking & Power Prod.
S. Selvanayagam, Head-Components
J. Ramachandran, Chmn.
Vineeth Sebastian, VP-Middle East Oper.

Phone: 91-44-4224-3353	Fax: 91 44 2235 2790
Toll-Free:	
Address: SPL Guindy House, 95 Mount Rd., Guindy, Chennai, 600 032 India	

GROWTH PLANS/SPECIAL FEATURES:

Redington (India) Ltd. is an India-based IT distribution and supply chain management firm. The company focuses on delivering IT products, including peripherals, scanners, personal computer components, packaged software, storage tools and servers, as well as other products such as consumer electronics, video game consoles, mobile phones and household appliances. It also offers services such as replacement parts, logistics, reverse logistics for defective products and repair services. The company manages inventory from roughly 60 brands, encompassing over 6,000 individual stock-keeping units (SKUs). Redington serves over 18 countries, providing services to more than 75 manufacturers. Its distribution network includes over 12,000 channel partners in India and more than 2,800 channel partners in the Middle East and Africa. Redington Gulf FZE, the company's Middle East subsidiary, focuses on the wholesale distribution of IT products and after-sales service in 17 African and Middle Eastern countries. Redington Distribution Pte Ltd., the firm's Singapore-based subsidiary, oversees wholesale distribution of IT products in Bangladesh, Singapore and Sri Lanka. Subsidiary Cadensworth (India) Limited specializes in repairing motherboards, liquid crystal display (LCD) panels and wireless devices such as Bluetooth headsets. Easyaccess Financial Services Limited focuses on Redington's non-banking finance operations. Redington acts as an authorized service provider for a variety of technology brands, including HP, Intel, LG, Nortel, Sun Micro, IBM and Motorola. It offers both warranty and post-warranty repairs and product support directly to its major clients, as well as through a network of service centers located throughout India, some of which are operated through partnerships. In September 2010, the firm agreed to acquire a 49.4% stake in Turkish IT products distributor, Arena Bilgisayar Sanayi Ve Ticaret Anonim Irketi.

FINANCIALS: Sales and profits are in thousands of dollars—add 000 to get the full amount. 2010 Note: Financial information for 2010 was not available for all companies at press time.

2010 Sales: $	2010 Profits: $	**U.S. Stock Ticker: RDTNF.PK**
2009 Sales: $2,784,650	2009 Profits: $35,090	**Int'l Ticker: REDI** Int'l Exchange: Bombay-BSE
2008 Sales: $2,389,540	2008 Profits: $29,910	Employees:
2007 Sales: $1,991,480	2007 Profits: $22,350	Fiscal Year Ends: 3/31
2006 Sales: $1,386,370	2006 Profits: $15,180	Parent Company:

SALARIES/BENEFITS:

Pension Plan:	ESOP Stock Plan: Y	Profit Sharing:	Top Exec. Salary: $	Bonus: $
Savings Plan:	Stock Purch. Plan:		Second Exec. Salary: $	Bonus: $

OTHER THOUGHTS:

Apparent Women Officers or Directors:
Hot Spot for Advancement for Women/Minorities:

LOCATIONS: ("Y" = Yes)

West:	Southwest:	Midwest:	Southeast:	Northeast:	International:
					Y

Note: Financial information, benefits and other data can change quickly and may vary from those stated here.

RENAISSANCE LEARNING INC

www.renlearn.com

Industry Group Code: 511210P Ranks within this company's industry group: Sales: 2 Profits: 3

Hardware:	Software:		Telecommunications:	Electronic Publishing:	Equipment:	Specialty Services:
Computers:	Consumer:	Y	Local:	Online Service:	Telecom:	Consulting:
Accessories:	Corporate:	Y	Long Distance:	TV/Cable or Wireless:	Communication:	Contract Manufacturing:
Network Equipment:	Telecom:		Cellular:	Games:	Distribution:	Processing:
Chips/Circuits:	Internet:		Internet Service:	Financial Data:	VAR/Reseller:	Staff/Outsourcing:
Parts/Drives:					Satellite Srv./Equip.:	Specialty Services:

TYPES OF BUSINESS:

Educational Software
Support Services

BRANDS/DIVISIONS/AFFILIATES:

Accelerated Reader
2Know!
STAR Early Literacy
Read Now Power Up!
STAR Math
Accelerated Math
STAR Constellation
Successful Reader

CONTACTS: Note: Officers with more than one job title may be intentionally listed here more than once.

Glenn R. James, CEO
Steven A. Schmidt, COO
Steven A. Schmidt, Pres.
Mary T. Minch, CFO
Marian L. Staton, Exec. VP-Sales
Mary T. Minch, Corp. Sec.
Mary T. Minch, Exec. VP-Finance
Franklin L. Smith, Sr. VP-Urban Accounts
Roy E. Truby, Sr. VP-State & Federal Programs
Terrance D. Paul, Chmn.

Phone: 715-424-3636	Fax: 715-424-4242
Toll-Free: 800-338-4204	
Address: 2911 Peach St., Wisconsin Rapids, WI 54495-8036 US	

GROWTH PLANS/SPECIAL FEATURES:

Renaissance Learning, Inc. provides technology for personalizing reading, mathematics and writing practice for pre-kindergarten through senior high school districts. STAR Reading, STAR Early Literacy, Accelerated Reader and Read Now Power Up! are examples of the reading products. Math products include STAR Math, Accelerated Math, Accelerated Math for Intervention and Math Facts in a Flash. The AlphaSmart laptops and related software are the primary writing and keyboarding products. The company addresses language acquisition for English language learners with the English in a Flash software. In addition, the firm sells the 2Know! response system, which encourages classroom participation and provides instantaneous feedback to instructors in any educational setting. Renaissance Learning sells AccelScan, a patented optical-mark card scanner, which is primarily used with Accelerated Math to automate scoring and recordkeeping tasks. Other product offerings include supplemental resources for educators and classroom use such as handbooks, workbooks, learning card and motivational items. The company's educational software products are available on both the traditional desktop versions on local area networks of individual schools and the web-based Renaissance Place software platform. The Renaissance Place software platform meet the needs of district-wide installations such as scalability; remote access; centralized database and server for multiple campus use; statistical analysis; ease of administration and district support; and integration with student data from other district systems. Recent products include Successful Reader, a research-based reading intervention program for struggling readers in grades 4-12; and STAR Constellation, a comprehensive standards testing platform available to school districts on a statewide contract basis. Renaissance Learning also offers professional service and support solutions for its products. Sold separately or bundled with products, the service offerings include training workshops and seminar; report and data analysis; program evaluation; guide implementation; distance training; software support; software installation; database conversion and integration services; and application hosting.

FINANCIALS: Sales and profits are in thousands of dollars—add 000 to get the full amount. 2010 Note: Financial information for 2010 was not available for all companies at press time.

2010 Sales: $	2010 Profits: $	U.S. Stock Ticker: RLRN
2009 Sales: $121,513	2009 Profits: $-19,923	Int'l Ticker: Int'l Exchange:
2008 Sales: $115,223	2008 Profits: $-34,440	Employees: 888
2007 Sales: $107,932	2007 Profits: $7,567	Fiscal Year Ends: 12/31
2006 Sales: $111,528	2006 Profits: $11,993	Parent Company:

SALARIES/BENEFITS:

Pension Plan:	ESOP Stock Plan:	Profit Sharing:	Top Exec. Salary: $458,000	Bonus: $
Savings Plan:	Stock Purch. Plan:		Second Exec. Salary: $365,609	Bonus: $28,104

OTHER THOUGHTS:

Apparent Women Officers or Directors: 2
Hot Spot for Advancement for Women/Minorities:

LOCATIONS: ("Y" = Yes)

West:	Southwest:	Midwest:	Southeast:	Northeast:	International:
Y		Y			Y

RENESAS ELECTRONICS CORP

www.renesas.com

Industry Group Code: 33441 Ranks within this company's industry group: Sales: Profits:

Hardware:		Software:	Telecommunications:	Electronic Publishing:	Equipment:	Specialty Services:
Computers:		Consumer:	Local:	Online Service:	Telecom:	Consulting:
Accessories:		Corporate:	Long Distance:	TV/Cable or Wireless:	Communication:	Contract Manufacturing:
Network Equipment:		Telecom:	Cellular:	Games:	Distribution:	Processing:
Chips/Circuits:	Y	Internet:	Internet Service:	Financial Data:	VAR/Reseller:	Staff/Outsourcing:
Parts/Drives:					Satellite Srv./Equip.:	Specialty Services:

TYPES OF BUSINESS:

Semiconductor Systems
System in Package Technology
Microcontrollers
Smartcard Products

BRANDS/DIVISIONS/AFFILIATES:

Hitachi Ltd
Mitsubishi Electric Corporation
NEC Electronics Corporation
Renesas Technology Corp

CONTACTS: Note: Officers with more than one job title may be intentionally listed here more than once.

Yasushi Akao, Pres.
Kazuaki Ogura, Exec. VP
Masaki Kato, Sr. VP
Yoichi Yano, Exec. VP
Shozo Iwakuma, Exec. VP
Junshi Yamaguchi, Chmn.

Phone: 81-3-5201-5111	Fax: 81-3-3207-5003
Toll-Free:	
Address: Nippon Bldg., 2-6-2, Ote-machi, Chiyoda-ku, Tokyo, 100-0004 Japan	

GROWTH PLANS/SPECIAL FEATURES:

Renesas Electronics Corp., formerly Renesas Technology Corporation, is a provider of an array of semiconductor products. Renesas is headquartered in Tokyo and operates a group of 49 companies, including 23 in Japan and 26 overseas. The company is organized into seven business units: sales management, which studies, designs and carries out sales strategies; first SoC, conducting business in the industrial and imaging sectors; second SoC, producing SoCs for home multimedia use including consumer electronics and mobile devices; MCU, encompassing the company's microcontroller operations; analog and power devices, including power devices, mixed signal ICs, display systems and optical and microwave devices; technology development, in charge of the company's technological strategy; and production and technology, handling production, technology and investment plans as well as overseeing all manufacturing activities. Renesas's products include a variety of microprocessors and microcontrollers (MPUs and MCUs); a range of software and tools; memory products; standard ICs (integrated circuits); power MOS FETs (metal-oxide-semiconductor field-effect transistors) and diodes; key components with ASSPs (application specific standard products); system-on-chips (SoCs); USB devices; and more. The firm's products are primarily used in the following markets: automotive, for air bag control, cruise control and dashboard information; digital home electronics, for use in DVD players, LCD-TV and vacuum cleaners; inverter applications, for use in air conditioners and dishwashers; motor control, for use in fitness equipment and power tools; and communications, for mobile phones and Bluetooth technology. In April 2010, the merger between NEC Electronics Corporation and Renesas Technology Corp., a joint-venture between Hitachi Ltd. and Mitsubishi Electric Corporation, was completed and the company name was changed to Renesas Electronics Corporation.

FINANCIALS: Sales and profits are in thousands of dollars—add 000 to get the full amount. 2010 Note: Financial information for 2010 was not available for all companies at press time.

2010 Sales: $	2010 Profits: $	**U.S. Stock Ticker: Joint Venture**
2009 Sales: $	2009 Profits: $	**Int'l Ticker:** Int'l Exchange:
2008 Sales: $	2008 Profits: $	Employees:
2007 Sales: $	2007 Profits: $	Fiscal Year Ends: 3/31
2006 Sales: $	2006 Profits: $	Parent Company:

SALARIES/BENEFITS:

Pension Plan:	ESOP Stock Plan:	Profit Sharing:	Top Exec. Salary: $	Bonus: $
Savings Plan:	Stock Purch. Plan:		Second Exec. Salary: $	Bonus: $

OTHER THOUGHTS:

Apparent Women Officers or Directors:
Hot Spot for Advancement for Women/Minorities:

LOCATIONS: ("Y" = Yes)

West:	Southwest:	Midwest:	Southeast:	Northeast:	International:
Y		Y		Y	Y

RESEARCH IN MOTION LTD (RIM)

www.rim.com

Industry Group Code: 334220 Ranks within this company's industry group: Sales: 4 Profits: 1

Hardware:		Software:		Telecommunications:		Electronic Publishing:	Equipment:		Specialty Services:	
Computers:		Consumer:	Y	Local:		Online Service:	Telecom:	Y	Consulting:	
Accessories:	Y	Corporate:		Long Distance:		TV/Cable or Wireless:	Communication:	Y	Contract Manufacturing:	
Network Equipment:		Telecom:		Cellular:	Y	Games:	Distribution:		Processing:	
Chips/Circuits:		Internet:		Internet Service:		Financial Data:	VAR/Reseller:		Staff/Outsourcing:	
Parts/Drives:							Satellite Srv./Equip.:		Specialty Services:	Y

TYPES OF BUSINESS:
Wireless E-Mail Devices
Wireless Software & Services

BRANDS/DIVISIONS/AFFILIATES:
BlackBerry
BlackBerry Smartphone
Chalk Media Corp.
Certicom Corp.
Hewlett-Packard Co (HP)
QNX Software Systems

CONTACTS: Note: Officers with more than one job title may be intentionally listed here more than once.
James Balsillie, Co-CEO
Don Morrison, COO
Mike Lazaridis, Pres./Co-CEO
Brian Bidulka, CFO
Robin Bienfait, CIO
David Yach, CTO-Software

Phone: 519-888-7465	Fax: 519-888-7884
Toll-Free:	
Address: 295 Phillip St., Waterloo, ON N2L 3W8 Canada	

GROWTH PLANS/SPECIAL FEATURES:

Research In Motion Ltd. (RIM) is a leading designer, manufacturer and marketer of wireless applications for the worldwide mobile communications market. The company focuses on integrated hardware, software and services that support multiple wireless network standards and provide access to time-sensitive information, including e-mail, phone, text messaging, Internet and intranet applications. This is provided through various offerings, including the BlackBerry wireless platform, the BlackBerry smartphone, the RIM Wireless Handheld product line, software development tools, radio-modems and software and hardware licensing agreements. The BlackBerry wireless system is comprised of wireless handhelds, software and services. The product provides wireless extension of clients' work and personal e-mail accounts, including Microsoft Outlook, IBM Lotus Notes, Novell GroupWise and many Internet service provider (ISP) e-mail services. The BlackBerry subscription base includes over 40 million users. BlackBerry service is provided through a combination of the company's network operations center and more than 550 carriers and distribution channels in 175 countries. RIM technology also allows third-party developers to enhance their handsets with data connectivity solutions using the same wireless architecture and infrastructure as BlackBerry handheld customers. Recently, RIM introduced its BlackBerry products and services in several countries, including Korea, Kuwait, Denmark, Bosnia, Norway, Azerbaijan, Vietnam, Egypt, Cambodia, Malaysia, Ghana, Belgium, Thailand and Serbia. In April 2010, RIM announced plans to acquire QNX Software Systems. Also in April 2010, RIM and SK Telecom launched the Blackberry Bold 9700 smartphone in South Korea. In May 2010, RIM and China Telecom Corporation Limited launched the BlackBerry solution for China Telecom enterprise customers in China.

The firm offers its employees an employee assistance plan; a gym/fitness membership; a global travel program; a free BlackBerry smartphone; training and development programs; teambuilding sessions, summer picnics, RIM wear and holiday parties; and the Healthy RIM program.

FINANCIALS: Sales and profits are in thousands of dollars—add 000 to get the full amount. 2010 Note: Financial information for 2010 was not available for all companies at press time.

2010 Sales: $14,953,224	2010 Profits: $2,457,144	**U.S. Stock Ticker: RIMM**
2009 Sales: $11,065,186	2009 Profits: $1,892,616	**Int'l Ticker: RIM** Int'l Exchange: Toronto-TSX
2008 Sales: $6,009,395	2008 Profits: $1,293,867	Employees: 8,387
2007 Sales: $3,037,103	2007 Profits: $631,572	Fiscal Year Ends: 2/28
2006 Sales: $2,065,845	2006 Profits: $374,656	Parent Company:

SALARIES/BENEFITS:

Pension Plan:	ESOP Stock Plan:	Profit Sharing:	Top Exec. Salary: $1,081,900	Bonus: $1,178,102
Savings Plan:	Stock Purch. Plan:		Second Exec. Salary: $636,279	Bonus: $358,207

OTHER THOUGHTS:
Apparent Women Officers or Directors: 1
Hot Spot for Advancement for Women/Minorities:

LOCATIONS: ("Y" = Yes)

West:	Southwest:	Midwest:	Southeast:	Northeast:	International:
Y	Y	Y	Y	Y	Y

RESPONSYS INC
www.responsys.com

Industry Group Code: 511210K Ranks within this company's industry group: Sales: Profits:

Hardware:	Software:		Telecommunications:	Electronic Publishing:	Equipment:	Specialty Services:
Computers:	Consumer:		Local:	Online Service:	Telecom:	Consulting:
Accessories:	Corporate:	Y	Long Distance:	TV/Cable or Wireless:	Communication:	Contract Manufacturing:
Network Equipment:	Telecom:		Cellular:	Games:	Distribution:	Processing:
Chips/Circuits:	Internet:		Internet Service:	Financial Data:	VAR/Reseller:	Staff/Outsourcing:
Parts/Drives:					Satellite Srv./Equip.:	Specialty Services:

TYPES OF BUSINESS:
E-Mail Marketing Software & Services

BRANDS/DIVISIONS/AFFILIATES:
Responsys Interact Suite
Interact Campaign
Interact Program
Interact Team
Interact Insight
Interact Connect
Interact API
Eservices Group Pty Ltd

CONTACTS: *Note: Officers with more than one job title may be intentionally listed here more than once.*
Daniel D. Springer, CEO
Chris Paul, CFO
Scott Olrich, Chief Mktg. & Sales Officer
Don Smith, CIO
Antonio Casacuberta, CTO
Julian Ong, General Counsel
Ed Henrich, VP-Professional & Strategic Svcs.
Andrew Priest, Chief Customer Officer

Phone: 650-745-1700	Fax: 650-745-1701
Toll-Free: 888-219-7150	
Address: 900 Cherry Ave., 5th Fl., San Bruno, CA 94066 US	

GROWTH PLANS/SPECIAL FEATURES:
Responsys, Inc. provides e-mail marketing software under the Responsys Interact brand name. The company's suite of products and services integrates with customer relationship management applications, data warehouse and call center systems. The company's primary product is the Responsys Interact Suite software that consists of the Interact Campaign, which creates e-mail marketing campaigns; Interact Program that helps facilitate customer dialogue and interaction; Interact Team, which assists in project collaboration; Interact Insight, a marketing analytics program; Interact Connect helps to automate data transfers; and Interact API creates customized client applications. After installing its software, the firm can host and manage an e-mail, direct mail or mobile messaging campaign for its clients or teach them how to manage their own. The firm's e-mail campaigns usually start by tracking a user's web site experience and then sending them appropriate marketing e-mails. The company's e-mail marketing software can also be used to keep in contact with existing customers. Responsys has office locations throughout the U.S with additional international offices located in Singapore, Australia, Denmark, India and the U.K. In July 2010, the company acquired a majority stake in Eservices Group Pty Ltd., an Australian marketing firm. In December 2010, the firm announced plans to make an initial public offering (IPO).

FINANCIALS: Sales and profits are in thousands of dollars—add 000 to get the full amount. 2010 Note: Financial information for 2010 was not available for all companies at press time.

2010 Sales: $	2010 Profits: $	U.S. Stock Ticker: Private
2009 Sales: $	2009 Profits: $	Int'l Ticker: Int'l Exchange:
2008 Sales: $	2008 Profits: $	Employees:
2007 Sales: $16,700	2007 Profits: $	Fiscal Year Ends: 12/31
2006 Sales: $	2006 Profits: $	Parent Company:

SALARIES/BENEFITS:
Pension Plan:	ESOP Stock Plan:	Profit Sharing:	Top Exec. Salary: $	Bonus: $
Savings Plan:	Stock Purch. Plan:		Second Exec. Salary: $	Bonus: $

OTHER THOUGHTS:
Apparent Women Officers or Directors:
Hot Spot for Advancement for Women/Minorities:

LOCATIONS: ("Y" = Yes)
West:	Southwest:	Midwest:	Southeast:	Northeast:	International:
Y		Y		Y	Y

RICOH COMPANY LTD

www.ricoh.com

Industry Group Code: 333313 Ranks within this company's industry group: Sales: 1 Profits: 2

Hardware:		Software:		Telecommunications:		Electronic Publishing:		Equipment:		Specialty Services:	
Computers:		Consumer:		Local:		Online Service:		Telecom:		Consulting:	
Accessories:	Y	Corporate:	Y	Long Distance:		TV/Cable or Wireless:		Communication:		Contract Manufacturing:	
Network Equipment:	Y	Telecom:		Cellular:		Games:		Distribution:		Processing:	
Chips/Circuits:	Y	Internet:		Internet Service:		Financial Data:		VAR/Reseller:		Staff/Outsourcing:	Y
Parts/Drives:	Y							Satellite Srv./Equip.:		Specialty Services:	Y

TYPES OF BUSINESS:

Manufacturing-Business Machines
Network Systems
Printers, Copiers & Fax Machines
PCs & Servers
Accessories
Software
Electronic Devices
Managed Print Services

BRANDS/DIVISIONS/AFFILIATES:

Ricoh Logistics System Co., Ltd.
Savin
Lanier
Infotec
Ricoh Americas Corporation

CONTACTS: *Note: Officers with more than one job title may be intentionally listed here more than once.*

Shiro Kondo, CEO
Shiro Kondo, Pres.
Zenji Miura, CFO/Exec. VP
Kazunori Azuma, Chief Mktg. Officer/Exec. VP
Takashi Nakamura, Chief Human Resources Officer/Exec. VP
Terumoto Nonaka, Sr. VP-R&D
Zenji Miura, CIO/Exec. VP
Zenji Miura, Chief Strategy Officer
Shiro Sasaki, Exec. VP/Chmn.-Ricoh Europe
Kenji Hatanaka, Sr. VP-Mktg.
Hiroshi Kobayashi, Exec. VP/Chmn.-Ricoh Software Research Center
Nobuo Inaba, Pres., Ricoh Institute of Sustainability & Bus.
Masamitsu Sakurai, Chmn.
Kevin Togashi, CEO-Ricoh Americas Corp.

Phone: 81-3-6278-2111	Fax: 81-3-3543-9329
Toll-Free:	
Address: Ricoh Bldg., 8-13-1 Ginza, Chuo-ku, Tokyo, 104-8222 Japan	

GROWTH PLANS/SPECIAL FEATURES:

Ricoh Company, Ltd. is a global developer of office automation equipment. The firm manufactures and markets copiers, including plain paper copiers (PPCs); multi-functional printers (MFPs); scanners; fax machines; and media supplies and services. Ricoh has three business segments: Imaging and Solutions, generating 89% of 2010 sales; Industrial Products, 5%; and Other, 6%. The Imaging and Solutions segment consists of imaging and network systems, including monochrome and color digital copiers, MFPs, laser printers, digital duplicators, fax machines, analog PPCs and related items. The firm's services include managed print services, an outsourcing service whereby the company takes over ownership and/or operation of a client's desktop printers, faxes and copiers, with a goal of creating significant savings for the client. The Industrial Products segment consists of thermal media, optical equipment, semiconductor devices, electronic components and measuring equipment. The final segment offers digital cameras, financing and logistics services, the last through subsidiary Ricoh Logistics System Co., Ltd. The company has manufacturing facilities in Japan, China, Thailand, the U.K., France and the U.S. Products are marketed primarily under the Ricoh name, though internationally, brands such as Savin, Lanier and Infotec are used. The firm's North American operations include wholly-owned subsidiary Ricoh Americas Corporation, which oversees U.S. sales and manufacturing activities. Respectively, sales in Japan, the Americas and Europe accounted for 43%, 28% and 23% of 2010 sales, with the remaining 6% of sales generated in other parts of the world. In March 2010, Ricoh launched a new projection system business that aims to provide solution systems as well as projector units. In May 2010, the company signed global strategic alliances with software developers DirectSmile GmbH and Printable Technologies, Inc.

Ricoh offers its employees a variety of benefits, including medical and dental coverage; life and disability insurance; a 401(k) plan; flexible spending accounts; tuition assistance; and an employee assistance program.

FINANCIALS: Sales and profits are in thousands of dollars—add 000 to get the full amount. 2010 Note: Financial information for 2010 was not available for all companies at press time.

2010 Sales: $24,518,700	2010 Profits: $338,940	**U.S. Stock Ticker: RICOY**
2009 Sales: $21,395,000	2009 Profits: $70,450	**Int'l Ticker: 7752** Int'l Exchange: Tokyo-TSE
2008 Sales: $22,199,890	2008 Profits: $1,815,060	Employees: 108,525
2007 Sales: $17,533,263	2007 Profits: $946,814	Fiscal Year Ends: 3/31
2006 Sales: $16,368,291	2006 Profits: $829,547	Parent Company:

SALARIES/BENEFITS:

Pension Plan:	ESOP Stock Plan:	Profit Sharing:	Top Exec. Salary: $	Bonus: $
Savings Plan: Y	Stock Purch. Plan:		Second Exec. Salary: $	Bonus: $

OTHER THOUGHTS:

Apparent Women Officers or Directors:
Hot Spot for Advancement for Women/Minorities:

LOCATIONS: ("Y" = Yes)

West:	Southwest:	Midwest:	Southeast:	Northeast:	International:
Y	Y	Y	Y	Y	Y

Note: Financial information, benefits and other data can change quickly and may vary from those stated here.

RIGHTNOW TECHNOLOGIES INC

www.rightnow.com

Industry Group Code: 511210K Ranks within this company's industry group: Sales: 6   Profits: 7

Hardware:	Software:		Telecommunications:	Electronic Publishing:	Equipment:	Specialty Services:	
Computers:	Consumer:		Local:	Online Service:	Telecom:	Consulting:	Y
Accessories:	Corporate:	Y	Long Distance:	TV/Cable or Wireless:	Communication:	Contract Manufacturing:	
Network Equipment:	Telecom:		Cellular:	Games:	Distribution:	Processing:	
Chips/Circuits:	Internet:		Internet Service:	Financial Data:	VAR/Reseller:	Staff/Outsourcing:	
Parts/Drives:					Satellite Srv./Equip.:	Specialty Services:	Y

TYPES OF BUSINESS:

Software-Customer Relationship Management
Sales & Marketing Software
Professional Services

BRANDS/DIVISIONS/AFFILIATES:

RightNow Service
RightNow Sales
RightNow Marketing
RightNow Feedback
RightNow Voice
RightNow Analytics
RightNow CX

CONTACTS: Note: Officers with more than one job title may be intentionally listed here more than once.

Greg R. Gianforte, CEO
Wayne Huyard, COO
Wayne Huyard, Pres.
Jeffery C. Davison, CFO
Jason Mittelstaedt, Chief Mktg. Officer
Laef Olson, CIO
Mike A. Myer, CTO
Alan A. Rassaby, General Counsel/Sr. VP/Corp. Sec.
Brian Curran, VP-Web Solutions
Jeffery C. Davison, Treas.
David Vap, Chief Solutions Officer
Susan Carstensen, Sr. VP-Customer Experience
Marcus Bragg, Sr. VP-Global Sales
Steven D. Daines, VP/Gen. Mgr.-APAC
Greg R. Gianforte, Chmn.
Joseph Brown, VP/Gen. Mgr.-EMEA

Phone: 406-522-4200	Fax: 406-522-4227
Toll-Free: 877-363-5678	
Address: 136 Enterprise Blvd., Bozeman, MT 59718-9300 US	

GROWTH PLANS/SPECIAL FEATURES:

RightNow Technologies, Inc. is a major provider of on-demand customer relationship management (CRM) products and professional services that help organizations of all sizes build customer-focused businesses. RightNow's technology enables an organization's service, marketing and sales personnel to leverage a common application platform for phone, e-mail and chat functions. Additionally, through its on-demand delivery approach, RightNow's is able to reduce the complexity associated with traditional on-premise solutions and offer its products at lower prices than competitors. Products are designed to integrate with traditional enterprise applications, and are available in 33 languages and dialects. The firm's CRM products include several branded lines. RightNow Service, which generates between 80% and 90% of the company's software, hosting and support revenues, is a multi-channel product that handles customer interactions in both traditional and online channels. RightNow Sales, a sales automation solution, maximizes sales efficiency and productivity. RightNow Marketing reduces the complexity of marketing campaign administration. RightNow Voice offers businesses voice automation services such as call routing, survey tools and customer self-service options. RightNow Feedback increases a firm's real-time customer feedback capture and response options. RightNow CX, a suite aimed at aiding organizations to offer Internet, contact center and social customer experiences. RightNow Analytics offers service, sales, marketing and feedback analytics tools. The firm's professional services consist of business process optimization, integration services, customer development consultations and customer relations training for contact center staff. The company serves approximately 1,900 corporate customers worldwide, including firms in the following industries and sectors: travel and hospitality; telecommunications; retail and consumer goods; hi-tech; finance; education; civilian and defense agencies of the U.S. Federal Government; and U.S. and foreign state and local governments. Besides its several U.S. offices, the company has international locations in Australia, Japan, the U.K., the Netherlands and Germany.

FINANCIALS: Sales and profits are in thousands of dollars—add 000 to get the full amount. 2010 Note: Financial information for 2010 was not available for all companies at press time.

2010 Sales: $	2010 Profits: $	**U.S. Stock Ticker: RNOW**
2009 Sales: $152,700	2009 Profits: $5,900	**Int'l Ticker:** Int'l Exchange:
2008 Sales: $140,400	2008 Profits: $-7,300	Employees:
2007 Sales: $112,077	2007 Profits: $-18,641	Fiscal Year Ends: 12/31
2006 Sales: $110,388	2006 Profits: $-5,008	Parent Company:

SALARIES/BENEFITS:

Pension Plan:	ESOP Stock Plan:	Profit Sharing:	Top Exec. Salary: $325,000	Bonus: $253,942
Savings Plan: Y	Stock Purch. Plan:		Second Exec. Salary: $240,000	Bonus: $159,323

OTHER THOUGHTS:

Apparent Women Officers or Directors: 1
Hot Spot for Advancement for Women/Minorities:

LOCATIONS: ("Y" = Yes)

West:	Southwest:	Midwest:	Southeast:	Northeast:	International:
Y	Y	Y		Y	Y

RIGHTSCALE INC

www.rightscale.com

Industry Group Code: 518210 Ranks within this company's industry group: Sales: Profits:

Hardware:	Software:		Telecommunications:	Electronic Publishing:	Equipment:	Specialty Services:	
Computers:	Consumer:		Local:	Online Service:	Telecom:	Consulting:	
Accessories:	Corporate:	Y	Long Distance:	TV/Cable or Wireless:	Communication:	Contract Manufacturing:	
Network Equipment:	Telecom:		Cellular:	Games:	Distribution:	Processing:	
Chips/Circuits:	Internet:		Internet Service:	Financial Data:	VAR/Reseller:	Staff/Outsourcing:	
Parts/Drives:					Satellite Srv./Equip.:	Specialty Services:	Y

TYPES OF BUSINESS:
Online Software Hosting Services
Cloud Computing Management

BRANDS/DIVISIONS/AFFILIATES:
RightScale Cloud Management Platform (The)
RightScale Development & Test Solution Pack
RightScale Private Cloud Early Access Program

CONTACTS: Note: Officers with more than one job title may be intentionally listed here more than once.
Michael Crandell, CEO
Ida Kane, CFO
Betsy Zikakis, VP-Mktg.
Thorsten von Eicken, CTO
Rafael H. Saavedra, VP-Eng.
Mary Monaghan, VP-Admin.
Josh Fraser, VP-Bus. Dev.
Mary Monaghan, VP-Finance
Chris Fowler, VP-Svcs.

Phone: 805-500-4164	Fax:
Toll-Free:	
Address: 136 W. Canon Perdido St., Santa Barbara, CA 93101 US	

GROWTH PLANS/SPECIAL FEATURES:
RightScale, Inc. is a cloud computing management firm. The company operates the RightScale Cloud Management Platform, a fully automated Internet-based management platform that delivers cloud computing, while providing complete IT transparency and control. The firm's platform is available in several editions, including the free Developer and Social Gaming Editions; the $2,500 Grid and Web Site Editions; and the $4,000 Premium Edition. Some of the features on one or more of these versions include a management dashboard, lifecycle support, social gaming deployments, server templates, multi-server deployments, a multi-cloud engine, auditing, enterprise management services and monitoring. RightScale has launched more than 1,000,000 servers and several thousand deployments of its solution. Some of the company's major customers include Playfish, Sling Media, Animoto and TC3. Through its web site, the firm offers forums on both cloud computing and the RightScale Cloud Management Platform. RightScale maintains technological partnerships with independent software vendors such as Continuent, IBM, Jaspersoft, MySQL Enterprise and Talend; system integrators including Capgemini, CSS Corp., LTech, Full 360, Inc. and ELC Technologies; and cloud infrastructure providers such as Amazon Web Services, The Rackspace Cloud, VMware, Eucalyptus Systems and GoGrid. The firm has received the majority of its venture capital funding from Benchmark Capital and Index Ventures. In September 2010, Rightscale launched cloud management product RightScale Development & Test Solution Pack. In November 2010, the firm introduced RightScale Private Cloud Early Access Program, which aids firms to analyze building private clouds within their data centers.

FINANCIALS: Sales and profits are in thousands of dollars—add 000 to get the full amount. 2010 Note: Financial information for 2010 was not available for all companies at press time.

2010 Sales: $	2010 Profits: $	U.S. Stock Ticker: Private
2009 Sales: $	2009 Profits: $	Int'l Ticker: Int'l Exchange:
2008 Sales: $	2008 Profits: $	Employees:
2007 Sales: $	2007 Profits: $	Fiscal Year Ends:
2006 Sales: $	2006 Profits: $	Parent Company:

SALARIES/BENEFITS:
Pension Plan:	ESOP Stock Plan:	Profit Sharing:	Top Exec. Salary: $	Bonus: $
Savings Plan:	Stock Purch. Plan:		Second Exec. Salary: $	Bonus: $

OTHER THOUGHTS:
Apparent Women Officers or Directors: 2
Hot Spot for Advancement for Women/Minorities: Y

LOCATIONS: ("Y" = Yes)
West:	Southwest:	Midwest:	Southeast:	Northeast:	International:
Y					Y

RIVERBED TECHNOLOGY INC

www.riverbed.com

Industry Group Code: 33411 Ranks within this company's industry group: Sales: 7   Profits: 11

Hardware:	Software:		Telecommunications:	Electronic Publishing:	Equipment:	Specialty Services:
Computers:	Consumer:		Local:	Online Service:	Telecom:	Consulting:
Accessories:	Corporate:	Y	Long Distance:	TV/Cable or Wireless:	Communication:	Contract Manufacturing:
Network Equipment:	Telecom:		Cellular:	Games:	Distribution:	Processing:
Chips/Circuits:	Internet:		Internet Service:	Financial Data:	VAR/Reseller:	Staff/Outsourcing:
Parts/Drives:					Satellite Srv./Equip.:	Specialty Services:

TYPES OF BUSINESS:
Wide Area Data Services

BRANDS/DIVISIONS/AFFILIATES:
Application Streaming
Transport Streamlining
Data Streamlining
Steelhead
Riverbed Optimization System (RiOS)
Central Management Console (CMC)
Interceptor
Cloud Steelhead

CONTACTS: Note: Officers with more than one job title may be intentionally listed here more than once.
Jerry M. Kennelly, CEO
Randy S. Gottfried, CFO
Eric Wolford, Sr. VP-Mktg.
Mark Stuart Day, Chief Scientist
Steve McCanne, CTO
Gordon Chaffee, VP-Eng.
Brett A. Nissenberg, General Counsel/VP-Corp. & Legal Affairs
Stephen R. Smoot, VP-Tech. Oper.
Eric Wolford, Sr. VP-Bus. Dev.
Paul O'Farrell, VP-Corp. Dev. & Strategy
Jerry M. Kennelly, Chmn.
David M. Peranich, Sr. VP-Worldwide Sales

Phone: 415-247-8800	Fax: 415-247-8801
Toll-Free:	
Address: 199 Fremont St., San Francisco, CA 94105 US	

GROWTH PLANS/SPECIAL FEATURES:

Riverbed Technology, Inc. provides wide-area data services (WDS) products designed to enable organizations with more than one office to overcome such problems as poor application performance and insufficient bandwidth at remote sites. Riverbed's Steelhead appliances improve the performance of applications and access to data across wide area networks (WANs), typically increasing transmission speeds by 5-50 times, by reducing application protocol inefficiencies through its proprietary Application Streamlining techniques, reducing network protocol inefficiencies through its proprietary Transport Streamlining techniques and reducing bandwidth requirements through its proprietary Data Streamlining techniques and data compression. The company's Steelhead appliances, which consist of its Riverbed Optimization System (RiOS) software embedded on a general purpose hardware computing platform, are installed at both ends of a WAN connection and are designed to be more easily and transparently integrated into existing networks than alternative products. Riverbed's Central Management Console (CMC) is a complimentary product designed to centrally manage many Steelhead appliances distributed across a WAN, simplifying the tasks of deploying, configuring, monitoring, reporting and upgrading large numbers of Steelhead appliances. Another complimentary product, the Interceptor is designed to enable flexible and scalable deployment of a cluster of Steelhead appliances in complex, high traffic data center environments without requiring complex network reconfiguration. Riverbed's products have been sold to over 8,700 customers worldwide in such industries as manufacturing, finance, technology, government, architecture, engineering, professional services, utilities, healthcare, media and retail. In October 2010, the company acquired packet capture and analysis products developer CACE Technologies, Inc. In November 2010, the firm introduced Cloud Steelhead, which expedites migrating data and applications processes to the public cloud; and Riverbed Whitewater, a cloud storage accelerator that focuses on backup and select archive workloads. Also in November 2010, Riverbed acquired space communications protocol standards specialist Global Protocols, LLC.

FINANCIALS: Sales and profits are in thousands of dollars—add 000 to get the full amount. 2010 Note: Financial information for 2010 was not available for all companies at press time.

2010 Sales: $	2010 Profits: $	**U.S. Stock Ticker:** RVBD
2009 Sales: $394,146	2009 Profits: $7,085	**Int'l Ticker:** Int'l Exchange:
2008 Sales: $333,349	2008 Profits: $10,601	Employees: 1,013
2007 Sales: $236,406	2007 Profits: $14,798	Fiscal Year Ends: 12/31
2006 Sales: $90,207	2006 Profits: $-15,845	Parent Company:

SALARIES/BENEFITS:

Pension Plan:	ESOP Stock Plan:	Profit Sharing:	Top Exec. Salary: $435,000	Bonus: $486,441
Savings Plan: Y	Stock Purch. Plan: Y		Second Exec. Salary: $328,889	Bonus: $183,954

OTHER THOUGHTS:
Apparent Women Officers or Directors:
Hot Spot for Advancement for Women/Minorities:

LOCATIONS: ("Y" = Yes)

West:	Southwest:	Midwest:	Southeast:	Northeast:	International:
Y	Y	Y		Y	Y

ROCKET SOFTWARE

www.rocketsoftware.com

Industry Group Code: 511210B **Ranks within this company's industry group:** Sales: Profits:

Hardware:	Software:		Telecommunications:	Electronic Publishing:	Equipment:	Specialty Services:	
Computers:	Consumer:		Local:	Online Service:	Telecom:	Consulting:	
Accessories:	Corporate:	Y	Long Distance:	TV/Cable or Wireless:	Communication:	Contract Manufacturing:	
Network Equipment:	Telecom:	Y	Cellular:	Games:	Distribution:	Processing:	
Chips/Circuits:	Internet:		Internet Service:	Financial Data:	VAR/Reseller:	Staff/Outsourcing:	
Parts/Drives:					Satellite Srv./Equip.:	Specialty Services:	Y

TYPES OF BUSINESS:

Software Development
Data & Network Management Products
Security Software
Mobile & Wireless Software
Training & Maintenance Services

BRANDS/DIVISIONS/AFFILIATES:

Rocket Labs
BlueZone Software
Mainstar
UniData
UniVerse
U2 DataVu
CorVu
Rocket U2

CONTACTS: Note: Officers with more than one job title may be intentionally listed here more than once.

Andrew Youniss, CEO
Troy Heindel, COO
Brian Agle, CFO
Ron Bleakney, VP-Worldwide Sales
Karen Player, Dir.-Human Resources
Andre den Haan, CIO
Matt Kelley, CTO
Peter Kaes, Corp. Counsel
Simon Caddick, VP-Global Tech. Support
Mike Beasley, Chmn./Advisor
Keith McInish, VP-Worldwide Professional Svcs.

Phone: 617-614-4321	Fax: 617-630-7100
Toll-Free:	
Address: 275 Grove St., Newton, MA 02466-2272 US	

GROWTH PLANS/SPECIAL FEATURES:

Rocket Software develops and supports enterprise software products and technology components for hardware and software distributors in the U.S. and internationally. The firm's products are used within a variety of industries, including retail, agriculture, finance, health care, energy, chemicals, manufacturing and telecommunications. The company has produced over 100 software products for its reselling customers. The firm's array of software offerings addresses the areas of business intelligence; storage; networks and telecom; database and security; terminal emulation and filter transfer protocol; and integration, service-oriented architecture and modernization. The firm's brands include Arkivio, AS, BlueZone Software, CorVu, Mainstar, Seagull Software, Servergraph and U2. Products include Rocket Data Snap-Ins for Microsoft Office; Rocket Shuttle for WebSphere; Clone and Rename for IMS (ICR); which simplifies and automates the cloning IMS subsystems process; and Rocket NetCure, a flexible network management system framework and service assurance application for enterprises and service providers. Company development teams collaborate at the Rocket Labs to create software technology dealing with web, Linux and Windows applications and data, security, network and application management. Recently, the firm acquired the UniData and UniVerse and related tools business from IBM; and the Folio and NXT business from Microsoft Corporation. In November 2010, the company introduced U2 DataVu, which provides visual reports, graphic queries and interactive dashboards for UniData and UniVerse users.

The firm offers its employees medical, chiropractic, dental and prescription coverage; flexible spending accounts; life and disability insurance; and a 529 college savings plan.

FINANCIALS: Sales and profits are in thousands of dollars—add 000 to get the full amount. 2010 Note: Financial information for 2010 was not available for all companies at press time.

2010 Sales: $	2010 Profits: $	U.S. Stock Ticker: Private
2009 Sales: $	2009 Profits: $	Int'l Ticker: Int'l Exchange:
2008 Sales: $	2008 Profits: $	Employees:
2007 Sales: $	2007 Profits: $	Fiscal Year Ends: 12/31
2006 Sales: $	2006 Profits: $	Parent Company:

SALARIES/BENEFITS:

Pension Plan:	ESOP Stock Plan:	Profit Sharing:	Top Exec. Salary: $	Bonus: $
Savings Plan: Y	Stock Purch. Plan:		Second Exec. Salary: $	Bonus: $

OTHER THOUGHTS:

Apparent Women Officers or Directors: 1
Hot Spot for Advancement for Women/Minorities:

LOCATIONS: ("Y" = Yes)

West:	Southwest:	Midwest:	Southeast:	Northeast:	International:
Y	Y		Y	Y	Y

ROGUE WAVE SOFTWARE INC

www.roguewave.com

Industry Group Code: 511210I Ranks within this company's industry group: Sales: Profits:

Hardware:	Software:		Telecommunications:	Electronic Publishing:	Equipment:	Specialty Services:	
Computers:	Consumer:		Local:	Online Service:	Telecom:	Consulting:	Y
Accessories:	Corporate:	Y	Long Distance:	TV/Cable or Wireless:	Communication:	Contract Manufacturing:	
Network Equipment:	Telecom:		Cellular:	Games:	Distribution:	Processing:	
Chips/Circuits:	Internet:		Internet Service:	Financial Data:	VAR/Reseller:	Staff/Outsourcing:	
Parts/Drives:					Satellite Srv./Equip.:	Specialty Services:	

TYPES OF BUSINESS:

Software-Java-Based & C++
XML-Based Software
Terminal Emulation
GUI Application Development Software
Support Services
Application Consulting
Open Source Software

BRANDS/DIVISIONS/AFFILIATES:

Stingray Studio
TotalView Technologies Inc
Hydra Express
SourcePro C++
Acumem AB

CONTACTS: Note: Officers with more than one job title may be intentionally listed here more than once.

Brian Pierce, CEO
Steve McGee, CFO
Tom Gaunt, Sr. VP-Sales
Sean Fitzgerald, CTO
Sean Fitzgerald, Sr. VP-Eng.
Adam Schauer, VP-Finance
Scott Lasica, VP-Global Alliances

Phone: 303-473-9118	Fax: 303-473-9137
Toll-Free: 800-487-3217	
Address: 5500 Flatiron Pkwy., Ste. 200, Boulder, CO 80301 US	

GROWTH PLANS/SPECIAL FEATURES:

Rogue Wave Software, Inc. provides software applications that use object-oriented component technology, particularly C++ and Java.   The company offers software components for building distributed client-server, intranet and Internet applications that scale to the enterprise, honor legacy investments and are highly customizable. Rogue Wave also provides customers with proven object-oriented development technology so that they can better apply the principles of the software to their own software development efforts. The company's products are marketed to professional programmers in all industrial segments through multiple distribution channels and are designed to enable customers to customize useful applications quickly.   The products are also designed to support a broad range of development environments and methodologies.   Products offered by the company include Hydra Express, which provides a foundation for developing and hosting C++ Web services; Stingray Studio GUI application development software; and SourcePro C++, for comprehensive and elemental C++ application development. In addition, the company offers consulting services for all matters pertinent to its software, such as porting, company-specific service-oriented architecture (SOA) design, platform and database migrations and performance enhancements.   Rogue Wave provides telephone, e-mail, fax and Internet-based customer support for all of its products and services. `In January 2010, the firm acquired TotalView Technologies, Inc., which produces software built to provide memory analysis and advanced code debugging. In October 2010, the firm acquired Acumem AB, a memory optimization products provider.

FINANCIALS: Sales and profits are in thousands of dollars—add 000 to get the full amount. 2010 Note: Financial information for 2010 was not available for all companies at press time.

2010 Sales: $	2010 Profits: $	**U.S. Stock Ticker: Private**
2009 Sales: $	2009 Profits: $	Int'l Ticker: Int'l Exchange:
2008 Sales: $	2008 Profits: $	Employees:
2007 Sales: $15,800	2007 Profits: $	Fiscal Year Ends: 12/31
2006 Sales: $	2006 Profits: $	Parent Company:

SALARIES/BENEFITS:

Pension Plan:	ESOP Stock Plan:	Profit Sharing:	Top Exec. Salary: $	Bonus: $100,000
Savings Plan:	Stock Purch. Plan:		Second Exec. Salary: $	Bonus: $

OTHER THOUGHTS:

Apparent Women Officers or Directors:
Hot Spot for Advancement for Women/Minorities:

LOCATIONS: ("Y" = Yes)

West:	Southwest:	Midwest:	Southeast:	Northeast:	International:
Y					Y

ROHM CO LTD

www.rohm.com

Industry Group Code: 33441 Ranks within this company's industry group: Sales: 16 Profits: 20

Hardware:		Software:		Telecommunications:		Electronic Publishing:		Equipment:		Specialty Services:	
Computers:		Consumer:		Local:		Online Service:		Telecom:		Consulting:	
Accessories:		Corporate:		Long Distance:		TV/Cable or Wireless:		Communication:	Y	Contract Manufacturing:	Y
Network Equipment:		Telecom:		Cellular:		Games:		Distribution:		Processing:	
Chips/Circuits:	Y	Internet:		Internet Service:		Financial Data:		VAR/Reseller:		Staff/Outsourcing:	
Parts/Drives:	Y							Satellite Srv./Equip.:		Specialty Services:	Y

TYPES OF BUSINESS:

Electronic Components Manufacturing
Integrated Circuits
Discrete Semiconductor Devices
Passive Components
Resistors & Capacitors
Display Devices
LED Displays

BRANDS/DIVISIONS/AFFILIATES:

Kionix Inc

CONTACTS: Note: Officers with more than one job title may be intentionally listed here more than once.

Satoshi Sawamura, Pres.
Tadanobu Fujiwara, Chief Dir.-Eastern Japan Sales
Nobuo Hatta, Chief Dir.-Admin.
Kohei Nozato, Mgr.-Public Rel. Dept.
Kohei Nozato, Mgr.-Investor Rel. Dept.
Eiichi Sasayama, Chief Dir.-Acct.
Takahisa Yamaha, Co-Managing Dir.
Hidemi Takasu, Co-Managing Dir.
Osamu Hattori, Chief Dir.-Asia Sales & China Sales

Phone: 81-75-311-2121	Fax: 81-75-315-0172
Toll-Free:	
Address: 21 Saiin Mizosaki-cho, Ukyo-ku, Kyoto, 615-8585 Japan	

GROWTH PLANS/SPECIAL FEATURES:

Rohm Co., Ltd. is a Japanese manufacturer of electronic components and component systems. Rohm makes components for a number of applications, including car electronics; mobile phones; flat-panel display (FPD) TVs; and DVD players and recorders. The firm's product categories include integrated circuits (ICs), discrete semiconductor devices, passive components and display components. Rohm's ICs, which generate 56% of the firm's sales, include memory modules, voltage detectors, motor and display drivers, comparators, analog switches, digital converters, clock generators, audio amplifiers and other circuit types. Rohm's discrete semiconductor devices, 32% of sales, include bipolar and digital transistors, metal-oxide semiconductor field-effect (MOSFET) transistors, barrier diodes, rectifier diodes and switching diodes, among others. The firm's passive components, which generate 5% of sales, include chip resistors, chip attenuators, tantalum capacitors, polymer capacitors and electromagnetic interference (EMI) filters, along with other related products. Rohm's display components, 7% of sales, include light-emitting diodes (LEDs), LED displays, laser diodes, optical sensors, infrared communication modules and receiver modules for remote controls. Of the company's 2010 sales, Japan represented 38%; other Asian countries, 54%; Europe, 3%; and Americas, 5%. Rohm has 11 manufacturing centers in Japan and nine others located in Korea, China, Thailand, Malaysia and the Philippines. The company maintains 12 research and development centers worldwide, including two U.S. facilities, in San Jose and San Diego, California. Rohm's eight quality assurance centers are located in Europe, Asia and North America, including one in Novi, Michigan. The company also has over 50 sales offices worldwide, including 10 in the U.S. Recently, Rohm acquired Kionix, Inc., an Ithaca, New York-based company focused on MEMS (micro-electro-mechanical systems) and nanotechnology development.

FINANCIALS: Sales and profits are in thousands of dollars—add 000 to get the full amount. 2010 Note: Financial information for 2010 was not available for all companies at press time.

2010 Sales: $4,081,380	2010 Profits: $86,750	U.S. Stock Ticker: ROHCF
2009 Sales: $3,397,960	2009 Profits: $105,397	Int'l Ticker: 6963 Int'l Exchange: Tokyo-TSE
2008 Sales: $3,734,100	2008 Profits: $319,300	Employees:
2007 Sales: $3,950,800	2007 Profits: $474,500	Fiscal Year Ends: 3/31
2006 Sales: $3,877,900	2006 Profits: $483,000	Parent Company:

SALARIES/BENEFITS:

Pension Plan:	ESOP Stock Plan:	Profit Sharing:	Top Exec. Salary: $	Bonus: $
Savings Plan:	Stock Purch. Plan:		Second Exec. Salary: $	Bonus: $

OTHER THOUGHTS:

Apparent Women Officers or Directors:
Hot Spot for Advancement for Women/Minorities:

LOCATIONS: ("Y" = Yes)

West:	Southwest:	Midwest:	Southeast:	Northeast:	International:
Y	Y	Y	Y	Y	Y

ROVI CORPORATION

www.rovicorp.com

Industry Group Code: 511210L **Ranks within this company's industry group: Sales: 4 Profits: 4**

Hardware:	Software:		Telecommunications:	Electronic Publishing:	Equipment:	Specialty Services:
Computers:	Consumer:		Local:	Online Service:	Telecom:	Consulting:
Accessories:	Corporate:	Y	Long Distance:	TV/Cable or Wireless:	Communication:	Contract Manufacturing:
Network Equipment:	Telecom:		Cellular:	Games:	Distribution:	Processing:
Chips/Circuits:	Internet:		Internet Service:	Financial Data:	VAR/Reseller:	Staff/Outsourcing:
Parts/Drives:					Satellite Srv./Equip.:	Specialty Services:

TYPES OF BUSINESS:

Software-Video Copyright Protection
Digital Rights Management Technologies

BRANDS/DIVISIONS/AFFILIATES:

Macrovision Solutions Corporation
Analog Copy Protection (ACP)
RipGuard
BD+

CONTACTS:
Note: Officers with more than one job title may be intentionally listed here more than once.

Alfred J. Amoroso, CEO
Alfred J. Amoroso, Pres.
James Budge, CFO
Corey Ferengul, Exec. VP-Mktg. & Prod. Mgmt.
Eileen Schloss, Exec. VP-Human Resources
Stephen Yu, General Counsel/Exec. VP/Corp. Sec.
Jim Wickett, Exec. VP-Corp. Dev.
Tom Carson, Exec. VP-Sales & Svcs.
John Moakley, Exec. VP-Data Svcs.
Andrew K. Ludwick, Chmn.

Phone: 408-562-8400	Fax: 408-567-1800
Toll-Free:	
Address: 2830 De La Cruz Blvd., Santa Clara, CA 95050 US	

GROWTH PLANS/SPECIAL FEATURES:

Rovi Corporation provides a broad set of solutions that enable businesses to protect, enhance and distribute their digital goods to consumers across multiple channels. The company's offerings include embedded licensing technologies such as recommendations and search capability; interactive program guides (IPGs); digital rights management products and technologies; embedded licensing technologies; and licensing of the firm's extensive information database. Rovi Corporation also allows customers to license patents and deploy their own IPG or a third party IPG. The firm's products are deployed in three market divisions: CE manufacturers, including set-top box manufacturers, digital TV providers, DVD player manufacturers, PC DVD drive suppliers and network-attached storage device providers; service providers, such as satellite, cable, mobile, telecommunications and Internet service providers; and other. The other division includes the company's entertainment company content protection products and services such as Analog Copy Protection (ACP), RipGuard and BD+ for digital content owners and system operators. Its content security technology customers have included Columbia-TriStar, Twentieth Century Fox Home Entertainment, Buena Vista Home Video, HBO Studio Productions and Warner Home Video DVD. The other segment also handles the licensing of Rovi Corp.'s database of descriptive information about television, movie, music and game content. The database includes 400,000 movies; over 2.5 million television series episodes; searchable data on nearly every television show produced since 1960; and information regarding roughly 1.8 million music albums, 16 million music tracks, 62,000 video games and 7.5 million books. In 2009, Rovi Corporation sold TV Games Network to Betfair Group Ltd.; and sold TV Guide Networks and TVGuide.com to Lionsgate. In February 2010, Rovi Corporation sold it 49% interest in Guideworks LLC to Comcast Corporation. In September 2010, the company sold Canadian subsidiary Norpak Corporation.

Rovi employees receive life, disability, medical, dental and vision insurance; educational assistance; 11 paid holidays; and flexible spending accounts.

FINANCIALS:
Sales and profits are in thousands of dollars—add 000 to get the full amount. 2010 Note: Financial information for 2010 was not available for all companies at press time.

2010 Sales: $	2010 Profits: $	**U.S. Stock Ticker: ROVI**
2009 Sales: $483,911	2009 Profits: $-52,951	Int'l Ticker: Int'l Exchange:
2008 Sales: $330,045	2008 Profits: $-114,060	Employees: 1,200
2007 Sales: $155,685	2007 Profits: $31,500	Fiscal Year Ends: 12/31
2006 Sales: $121,328	2006 Profits: $33,043	Parent Company:

SALARIES/BENEFITS:

Pension Plan:	ESOP Stock Plan:	Profit Sharing:	Top Exec. Salary: $550,000	Bonus: $1,000,000
Savings Plan: Y	Stock Purch. Plan: Y		Second Exec. Salary: $447,352	Bonus: $332,120

OTHER THOUGHTS:

Apparent Women Officers or Directors: 2
Hot Spot for Advancement for Women/Minorities: Y

LOCATIONS: ("Y" = Yes)

West:	Southwest:	Midwest:	Southeast:	Northeast:	International:
Y	Y	Y		Y	Y

ROYAL PHILIPS ELECTRONICS NV
www.philips.com

Industry Group Code: 334310 Ranks within this company's industry group: Sales: 4 Profits: 3

Hardware:		Software:		Telecommunications:		Electronic Publishing:		Equipment:		Specialty Services:	
Computers:		Consumer:		Local:		Online Service:		Telecom:		Consulting:	Y
Accessories:	Y	Corporate:		Long Distance:		TV/Cable or Wireless:		Communication:		Contract Manufacturing:	
Network Equipment:		Telecom:		Cellular:		Games:		Distribution:		Processing:	
Chips/Circuits:	Y	Internet:		Internet Service:		Financial Data:		VAR/Reseller:		Staff/Outsourcing:	
Parts/Drives:								Satellite Srv./Equip.:		Specialty Services:	Y

TYPES OF BUSINESS:
Manufacturing-Electrical & Electronic Equipment
Consumer Electronics & Appliances
Lighting Systems
Medical Imaging Equipment
Semiconductors
Consulting Services
Nanotech Research
MEMS

BRANDS/DIVISIONS/AFFILIATES:
Koninklijke Philips Electronics N.V.
CDP Medical Ltd.
Gilde Healthcare III
NCW Holdings, Ltd.
Shanghai Apex Electronics Technology Co., Ltd.
TPV Technology Ltd.

CONTACTS: Note: Officers with more than one job title may be intentionally listed here more than once.
Gerard Kleisterlee, CEO
Gerard Kleisterlee, Pres.
Pierre-Jean Sivignon, CFO/Exec. VP
Hayko Kroese, Head-Global Human Resources Mgmt.
Maarten de Vries, CIO
Rick Harwig, CTO
Eric Coutinho, Chief Legal Officer/Sec.
Steve Rusckowski, Exec. VP/CEO-Philips Healthcare
Rudy Provoost, Exec. VP/CEO-Lighting
Gottfried Dutine, Exec. VP
Pieter Nota, CEO-Phillips Consumer Lifestyle
J-M. Hessels, Chmn.
Maarten de Vries, Head-Global Purchasing

Phone: 31-20-59-77-232	Fax: 31-20-59-77-070
Toll-Free: 877-248-4237	
Address: Breitner Center, Amstelplein 2, Amsterdam, 1096 BC The Netherlands	

GROWTH PLANS/SPECIAL FEATURES:
Royal Philips Electronics N.V. (Philips) is an electronics company organized into three divisions: Philips Healthcare, Philips Consumer Lifestyle and Philips Lighting. The Philips Healthcare division offers imaging systems, including x-ray, computed tomography, magnetic resonance imaging and nuclear medicine imaging equipment; clinical care systems, including ultrasound imaging, hospital respiratory systems, cardiac care systems and children's medical ventures; home healthcare solutions, such as sleep management and respiratory care; medical alert and remote cardiac services, healthcare informatics and patient monitoring systems; and customer services, including consultancy, clinical services, education, equipment financing, asset management and equipment maintenance and repair. The Philips Consumer Lifestyle division offers televisions; shaving and beauty products, including electric shavers, hair care and male grooming products; audio and video multimedia, including home and portable audio and video entertainment domes (Blu-ray Disc playback, MP3/MP4 players, etc.); tic appliances, such as kitchen appliances, floor care, garment care and water and air purifiers; health and wellness products; and peripherals and accessories, such as headphones, remote controls, PC peripherals, digital picture frames and cordless phones. The Philips Lighting division offers a range of products, including incandescent, halogen and fluorescent lighting, as well as fixtures and automotive headlights. The company has roughly 127 production sites in 29 countries, sales and service outlets in approximately 100 countries. In March 2010, Philips sold its majority of ownership of TPV Technology Ltd. to CEIEC (H.K.) Ltd. In July 2010, the firm agreed to acquire the street lighting controls business of Amplex A/S; and acquired Chinese ultrasound transducer manufacturer Shanghai Apex Electronics Technology Co., Ltd. In August 2010, the company acquired Israeli firm CDP Medical Ltd. and invested in venture capital fund Gilde Healthcare III. In late 2010, Philips agreed to acquire Discus Holdings, Inc. and sell Assembleon to H2 Equity Partners. In December 2010, the company acquired Hong Kong-based NCW Holdings, Ltd.

FINANCIALS: Sales and profits are in thousands of dollars—add 000 to get the full amount. 2010 Note: Financial information for 2010 was not available for all companies at press time.

2010 Sales: $	2010 Profits: $	U.S. Stock Ticker: PHG
2009 Sales: $33,389,000	2009 Profits: $611,000	Int'l Ticker: PHIA Int'l Exchange: Amsterdam-Euronext
2008 Sales: $37,183,000	2008 Profits: $-262,000	Employees: 115,924
2007 Sales: $39,459,000	2007 Profits: $6,138,000	Fiscal Year Ends: 12/31
2006 Sales: $35,537,000	2006 Profits: $7,091,000	Parent Company:

SALARIES/BENEFITS:
Pension Plan:	ESOP Stock Plan:	Profit Sharing:	Top Exec. Salary: $	Bonus: $
Savings Plan:	Stock Purch. Plan:		Second Exec. Salary: $	Bonus: $

OTHER THOUGHTS:
Apparent Women Officers or Directors:
Hot Spot for Advancement for Women/Minorities:

LOCATIONS: ("Y" = Yes)
West:	Southwest:	Midwest:	Southeast:	Northeast:	International:
Y	Y	Y	Y	Y	Y

RSA SECURITY INC

www.rsa.com

Industry Group Code: 511210E Ranks within this company's industry group: Sales: Profits:

Hardware:	Software:		Telecommunications:	Electronic Publishing:	Equipment:	Specialty Services:
Computers:	Consumer:		Local:	Online Service:	Telecom:	Consulting:
Accessories:	Corporate:	Y	Long Distance:	TV/Cable or Wireless:	Communication:	Contract Manufacturing:
Network Equipment:	Telecom:		Cellular:	Games:	Distribution:	Processing:
Chips/Circuits:	Internet:		Internet Service:	Financial Data:	VAR/Reseller:	Staff/Outsourcing:
Parts/Drives:					Satellite Srv./Equip.:	Specialty Services:

TYPES OF BUSINESS:

Computer Software-Security
Data Encryption Tools
Web Access Management Products

BRANDS/DIVISIONS/AFFILIATES:

Archer Technologies
RSA Authentication Manager
RSA BSAFE
RSA Certificate Manager
RSA Access Manager
RSA SecurID Token
RSA Data Security System
RSA Data Loss Prevention Suite

CONTACTS: Note: Officers with more than one job title may be intentionally listed here more than once.

Thomas P. Heiser, COO
Arthur W. Coviello, Jr., Pres./Exec. VP-EMC
Tom Corn, VP-Mktg.
Bret Hartman, CTO
Christopher Young, Sr. VP-Prod., Tech. & Markets
Mark Quigley, Sr. VP-Oper.
Bill Taylor, Sr. Dir.- Global Channels & Alliances
Mischel Kwon, VP-Public Sector Security Solutions
David Walter, Dir.-eGRC Solutions
Osamu Yamano, VP/Pres., RSA Japan

Phone: 781-515-5000	Fax: 781-515-5010
Toll-Free: 800-495-1095	
Address: 174 Middlesex Turnpike, Bedford, MA 01730 US	

GROWTH PLANS/SPECIAL FEATURES:

RSA Security, Inc., a subsidiary of EMC Corporation, is a provider of e-business security solutions in the telecommunications, pharmaceutical, financial and health care industries. RSA also caters to academic institutions, research laboratories and government organizations. The firm's secure mobile and remote access products include RSA SecurID authenticators and RSA Key Manager server software. They provide centrally managed two-factor user authentication systems for enterprise networks, operating systems, e-business web sites and other information technology infrastructures. SecurID software protects network resources by ensuring that only authorized users are granted access to information resources. RSA's secure enterprise access products manage and secure access to business-critical information resources within the enterprise. The company provides identity and access management capabilities through its RSA Access Manager, which provides a secure environment for web-based resources and centrally controls user access privileges to web-based resources. Other products include RSA BSAFE, a software security solution utilized by the U.S. Department of Defense; RSA enVision, a log, security and information event management solution; and RSA Certificate Manager, which enables organizations to issue, validate and manage digital certificates. The firm also uses its products to provide consumer identity protection and authentication services to the customers of online merchants and financial institutions. RSA Laboratories, which specializes in cryptography and data security, is the company's research center. Recent developments include new capabilities in the RSA Data Security System's encryption and key management suite, designed to secure sensitive data in file systems; the RSA SecurID Token for BlackBerry smartphones; RSA Entitlements Policy Manager for the security of branch offices and large infrastructures; and RSA Data Loss Prevention Suite, which protects sensitive data from loss and misuse. In January 2010, EMC Corporation acquired governance, risk and compliance software provider Archer Technologies and incorporated it into RSA's operations.

FINANCIALS: Sales and profits are in thousands of dollars—add 000 to get the full amount. 2010 Note: Financial information for 2010 was not available for all companies at press time.

2010 Sales: $	2010 Profits: $	**U.S. Stock Ticker: Subsidiary**
2009 Sales: $	2009 Profits: $	**Int'l Ticker:** Int'l Exchange:
2008 Sales: $	2008 Profits: $	Employees:
2007 Sales: $	2007 Profits: $	Fiscal Year Ends: 12/31
2006 Sales: $	2006 Profits: $	Parent Company: EMC CORP

SALARIES/BENEFITS:

Pension Plan:	ESOP Stock Plan:	Profit Sharing:	Top Exec. Salary: $	Bonus: $
Savings Plan:	Stock Purch. Plan:		Second Exec. Salary: $	Bonus: $

OTHER THOUGHTS:

Apparent Women Officers or Directors: 1
Hot Spot for Advancement for Women/Minorities:

LOCATIONS: ("Y" = Yes)

West:	Southwest:	Midwest:	Southeast:	Northeast:	International:
Y				Y	Y

S1 CORPORATION

www.s1.com

Industry Group Code: 511201 Ranks within this company's industry group: Sales: 6 Profits: 3

Hardware:	Software:		Telecommunications:	Electronic Publishing:	Equipment:	Specialty Services:
Computers:	Consumer:		Local:	Online Service:	Telecom:	Consulting:
Accessories:	Corporate:	Y	Long Distance:	TV/Cable or Wireless:	Communication:	Contract Manufacturing:
Network Equipment:	Telecom:		Cellular:	Games:	Distribution:	Processing:
Chips/Circuits:	Internet:		Internet Service:	Financial Data:	VAR/Reseller:	Staff/Outsourcing:
Parts/Drives:					Satellite Srv./Equip.:	Specialty Services:

TYPES OF BUSINESS:
Software-Financial Services
Internet Banking Applications

BRANDS/DIVISIONS/AFFILIATES:
Enterprise
Postilion

CONTACTS: Note: Officers with more than one job title may be intentionally listed here more than once.
Johann Dreyer, CEO
Paul Parrish, CFO
Greg Orenstein, Chief Legal Officer/Sec.
Greg Orenstein, Sr. VP-Corp. Dev.
Jan Kruger, Pres., Global Large Financial Institutions
Pierre Naude, Pres., Branch & Community Financial Bus.
Francois van Schoor, Pres., Global Payments Bus.
John W. Spiegel, Chmn.

Phone: 404-923-3500	Fax: 404-923-6727
Toll-Free: 888-457-2237	
Address: 705 Westech Dr., Norcross, GA 30092 US	

GROWTH PLANS/SPECIAL FEATURES:

S1 Corporation is a global provider of software and related services that automate the processing of financial transactions. The firm's solutions are designed for financial organizations including banks, credit unions, insurance companies, transaction processors, payment card associations and retailers. S1 operates in two segments: Enterprise and Postilion. The Enterprise segment represents global banking and insurance solutions primarily targeting larger financial institutions. It supports channels that a bank uses to interact with its customers, including self-service channels like the Internet for personal, business and corporate banking, as well as trade finance and mobile banking; and full service channels such as teller, branch, sales and service and call center. The Postilion segment represents the community financial, full service banking and lending businesses in North America and global payment processing and management solutions. It provides Internet personal and business banking, voice banking and mobile banking solutions to community banks and credit unions, as well as payment processing and management solutions that drive ATMs (automated teller machines) and point-of-sale (POS) devices, to financial institutions, retailers, third-party processors, payments associations and other transaction generating endpoints. S1 licenses its Postilion suite of online, telephone and mobile banking applications primarily on a subscription only basis. Postilion's payment processing and management and full service banking solutions are primarily licensed on a perpetual basis. In March 2010, the company acquired PM Systems Corp., which specializes in internet billing, banking and security for $28.9 million.

S1 offers its employees a 401(k) plan and medical, prescription, dental, disability, life, accidental death and travel accident insurance benefits.

FINANCIALS: Sales and profits are in thousands of dollars—add 000 to get the full amount. 2010 Note: Financial information for 2010 was not available for all companies at press time.

2010 Sales: $	2010 Profits: $	**U.S. Stock Ticker: SONE**
2009 Sales: $238,927	2009 Profits: $30,423	Int'l Ticker: Int'l Exchange:
2008 Sales: $228,435	2008 Profits: $21,850	Employees: 1,560
2007 Sales: $204,925	2007 Profits: $19,495	Fiscal Year Ends: 12/31
2006 Sales: $192,310	2006 Profits: $17,902	Parent Company:

SALARIES/BENEFITS:

Pension Plan:	ESOP Stock Plan:	Profit Sharing:	Top Exec. Salary: $415,000	Bonus: $251,714
Savings Plan: Y	Stock Purch. Plan:		Second Exec. Salary: $325,000	Bonus: $28,125

OTHER THOUGHTS:
Apparent Women Officers or Directors:
Hot Spot for Advancement for Women/Minorities:

LOCATIONS: ("Y" = Yes)

West:	Southwest:	Midwest:	Southeast:	Northeast:	International:
Y	Y			Y	Y

SAFENET INC

www.safenet-inc.com

Industry Group Code: 511210E **Ranks within this company's industry group:** Sales: Profits:

Hardware:	Software:		Telecommunications:	Electronic Publishing:	Equipment:	Specialty Services:
Computers:	Consumer:		Local:	Online Service:	Telecom:	Consulting:
Accessories:	Corporate:	Y	Long Distance:	TV/Cable or Wireless:	Communication:	Contract Manufacturing:
Network Equipment:	Telecom:		Cellular:	Games:	Distribution:	Processing:
Chips/Circuits: Y	Internet:		Internet Service:	Financial Data:	VAR/Reseller:	Staff/Outsourcing:
Parts/Drives:					Satellite Srv./Equip.:	Specialty Services:

TYPES OF BUSINESS:
Network Security Software
Security Chips

BRANDS/DIVISIONS/AFFILIATES:
Vector Capital
SafeNet Government Solutions, LLC
Aladdin Knowledge Systems Ltd

CONTACTS: Note: Officers with more than one job title may be intentionally listed here more than once.
Mark A. Floyd, CEO
Chris Fedde, COO
Chris Fedde, Pres.
Charles Neral, CFO/Sr. VP
Tsion Gonen, VP-Mktg. & Products
Diane Smith, VP-Human Resources
Jan Manning, CIO
Russell Dietz, CTO/VP
John Cetrone, VP-Worldwide Mfg.
Ken Siegel, General Counsel/Sec./VP
John Cetrone, VP-Oper.
James Hamilton, VP-Corp. Dev.
Prakash Panjwani, Sr. VP/Gen. Mgr.-Rights Mgmt.
Jim Summers, Sr. VP/Gen. Mgr.-Gov't Data Protection
Joseph J. Moorcones, VP-Cyber Security
Phil Saunders, Sr. VP-Worldwide Sales & Customer Svcs.

Phone: 410-931-7500	Fax: 410-931-7524
Toll-Free: 800-533-3958	
Address: 4690 Millennium Dr., Belcamp, MD 21017 US	

GROWTH PLANS/SPECIAL FEATURES:

SafeNet, Inc. develops, markets, sells and supports network security products and services, including hardware and software. The firm's specialized software targets the security needs of various governmental and commercial enterprises. For financial services companies, it offers applications for e-banking, compliance, data security and so-called green IT (information technology) initiatives. For hardware vendors, it supplies embedded security products for a wide range of devices, including mobile phones and semiconductors. For independent software vendors, it offers anti-piracy software protection and software license management services. For retailers, SafeNet offers various products, mostly transaction-related, such as secure digital communication products, secure login and authentication products, secure electronic transaction applications and digital identity management services; and other products such as compliance services and general database and application security. Finally, for governmental clients, the firm offers Type 1 Classified services for homeland security, network and voice encryption, space communications and net-centric abilities; and general services, such as application security and secure login and authentication products. Most of its governmental services are provided through subsidiary SafeNet Government Solutions, LLC. SafeNet holds over 100 patents. In December 2009, the company announced plans to acquire Assured Decisions, LLC, a cyber security consultancy firm. In April 2010, SafeNet combined with Aladdin Knowledge Systems Ltd., which provides information and content security for its customers. The two companies are owned by Vector Capital.

SafeNet offers its employees medical, dental, vision and prescription drug coverage; short- and long-term disability; life and AD&D insurance; profit sharing; a 401(k) plan; flexible spending accounts; and tuition reimbursement.

FINANCIALS: Sales and profits are in thousands of dollars—add 000 to get the full amount. 2010 Note: Financial information for 2010 was not available for all companies at press time.

2010 Sales: $	2010 Profits: $	**U.S. Stock Ticker: Private**
2009 Sales: $	2009 Profits: $	**Int'l Ticker:** Int'l Exchange:
2008 Sales: $	2008 Profits: $	Employees:
2007 Sales: $	2007 Profits: $	Fiscal Year Ends: 12/31
2006 Sales: $	2006 Profits: $	Parent Company: VECTOR CAPITAL

SALARIES/BENEFITS:

Pension Plan:	ESOP Stock Plan:	Profit Sharing: Y	Top Exec. Salary: $	Bonus: $
Savings Plan: Y	Stock Purch. Plan: Y		Second Exec. Salary: $	Bonus: $

OTHER THOUGHTS:
Apparent Women Officers or Directors: 1
Hot Spot for Advancement for Women/Minorities:

LOCATIONS: ("Y" = Yes)

West:	Southwest:	Midwest:	Southeast:	Northeast:	International:
Y		Y		Y	Y

SAGEM TELECOMMUNICATIONS

www.sagem.com

Industry Group Code: 334210 Ranks within this company's industry group: Sales: Profits:

Hardware:		Software:		Telecommunications:	Electronic Publishing:	Equipment:		Specialty Services:
Computers:		Consumer:		Local:	Online Service:	Telecom:		Consulting:
Accessories:	Y	Corporate:	Y	Long Distance:	TV/Cable or Wireless:	Communication:	Y	Contract Manufacturing:
Network Equipment:		Telecom:		Cellular:	Games:	Distribution:		Processing:
Chips/Circuits:	Y	Internet:		Internet Service:	Financial Data:	VAR/Reseller:		Staff/Outsourcing:
Parts/Drives:						Satellite Srv./Equip.:		Specialty Services:

TYPES OF BUSINESS:

Telecommunications Equipment
Electronics
Cellular Telephones
Broadband Products
Digital Kiosks
Digital TVs

BRANDS/DIVISIONS/AFFILIATES:

SAFRAN SA
Gradiente

CONTACTS: Note: Officers with more than one job title may be intentionally listed here more than once.

Thierry Buffenoir, CEO
Jerome Nadel, Exec. VP-Mktg.
Francois Guerineau, Exec. VP-R&D
Francois Guerineau, Exec.-Prod. Planning
Claude Vanacker, Exec. VP-Oper.
Yves Portalier, Exec. VP-Strategic Planning
Jerome Nadel, Exec. VP-User Experience
Giles Rees, VP-Exclusive Brands Bus.
Simon Gazikian, VP-Bus. Svcs.
Jean-Luc Guerit, VP-Sales & Brand Mgmt.
Thierry Buffenoir, Chmn.

Phone: 33-1-58-11-77-00	Fax: 33-1-58-11-77-50
Toll-Free:	
Address: 27 rue Leblanc, Paris, 75512 France	

GROWTH PLANS/SPECIAL FEATURES:

Sagem Telecommunications, the mobile communications subsidiary of Safran S.A., is a France-based designer, developer, manufacturer and marketer of mobile phones using advanced technologies such as fixed-mobile convergence, mobile TV and NFC (near field communication)/RFID (radio frequency identification) identification solutions. The company also develops and produces mobile phones for original design manufacturer offerings. Sagem Telecommunications sells mobile phones featuring 3G (third generation), MP3, Bluetooth, video, photo and USB functionality, as well as slim designs. Its Original Design Manufacturer (ODM) business segment develops mobile phone under the firm's partners' brand names. The company maintains research and development centers in Cergy, France and Ningbo, China. Sagem Telecommunications manages a Brazilian joint venture with Gradiente to handle the production and marketing of its mobile phones, as well as joint ventures with other firms globally. The firm maintains a web site, PlanetSagem.com, in which customers can download music, ringtones and logos. The site also offers screensavers; free ringtones; mobile and video games; and free mobile updating tools.

FINANCIALS: Sales and profits are in thousands of dollars—add 000 to get the full amount. 2010 Note: Financial information for 2010 was not available for all companies at press time.

2010 Sales: $	2010 Profits: $	U.S. Stock Ticker: Subsidiary
2009 Sales: $	2009 Profits: $	Int'l Ticker: Int'l Exchange:
2008 Sales: $	2008 Profits: $	Employees:
2007 Sales: $	2007 Profits: $	Fiscal Year Ends: 12/31
2006 Sales: $	2006 Profits: $	Parent Company: SAFRAN SA

SALARIES/BENEFITS:

Pension Plan:	ESOP Stock Plan:	Profit Sharing:	Top Exec. Salary: $	Bonus: $
Savings Plan:	Stock Purch. Plan:		Second Exec. Salary: $	Bonus: $

OTHER THOUGHTS:

Apparent Women Officers or Directors:
Hot Spot for Advancement for Women/Minorities:

LOCATIONS: ("Y" = Yes)

West:	Southwest:	Midwest:	Southeast:	Northeast:	International:
					Y

Note: Financial information, benefits and other data can change quickly and may vary from those stated here.

SAIC INC

www.saic.com

Industry Group Code: 541513 Ranks within this company's industry group: Sales: 6   Profits: 8

Hardware:		Software:		Telecommunications:		Electronic Publishing:	Equipment:	Specialty Services:	
Computers:		Consumer:		Local:		Online Service:	Telecom:	Consulting:	Y
Accessories:	Y	Corporate:	Y	Long Distance:		TV/Cable or Wireless:	Communication:	Contract Manufacturing:	
Network Equipment:		Telecom:		Cellular:		Games:	Distribution:	Processing:	
Chips/Circuits:		Internet:		Internet Service:		Financial Data:	VAR/Reseller:	Staff/Outsourcing:	
Parts/Drives:							Satellite Srv./Equip.:	Specialty Services:	Y

TYPES OF BUSINESS:

Systems Integration Services
Consulting Services
Research & Development
Software Development
Engineering
Cybersecurity
IT Infrastructure Management

BRANDS/DIVISIONS/AFFILIATES:

Atlan, Inc.
R.W. Beck Group, Inc.
Beck Disaster Recovery, Inc.
Spectrum San Diego
CloudShield Technologies, Inc.
Science, Engineering & Technology Associates Corp.
Reveal Imaging Technologies, Inc.
Science Applications International Corporation

CONTACTS: Note: Officers with more than one job title may be intentionally listed here more than once.

Walter P. Havenstein, CEO
Mark W. Sopp, CFO/Exec. VP
Brian F. Keenan, Exec. VP-Human Resources
Larry D. Cox, Gen. Mgr.-Info. Sys. & Intelligence Bus. Unit
Amy E. Alving, CTO
Vincent A. Maffio, General Counsel/Exec. VP-Audit
Anthony J. Moraco, Exec. VP-Oper. & Performance Excellence
James E. Cuff, Exec. VP-Bus. Dev. & Strategy
Deborah L. James, Exec. VP-Comm. & Gov't Affairs
Paul Levi, Sr. VP-Investor Rel.
K. Stuart Shea, Pres., Intelligence & Surveillance Group
Deborah H. Alderson, Pres., Defense Solutions Group
James E. Cuff, Exec. VP-Mergers & Acquisitions
Joseph W. Craver, III, Pres., Energy, Heath & Infrastructure Group
A. Thomas Young, Chmn.
Donald H. Foley, Exec. VP-Special Int'l Assignment

Phone: 703-676-4300	Fax: 703-676-2269
Toll-Free: 800-430-7629	
Address: 1710 SAIC Dr., McLean, VA 22102 US	

GROWTH PLANS/SPECIAL FEATURES:

SAIC, Inc., formerly Science Applications International Corporation, provides scientific, engineering, systems integration and technical services primarily to government customers. The company's clients include all branches of the U.S. military, the U.S. Department of Defense, intelligence agencies, the U.S. Department of Homeland Security, other U.S. government agencies, foreign governments and customers in select commercial markets. SAIC operates in three segments: government, commercial and corporate. The government segment, which generates 96% of the firm's revenues, offers services in the areas of systems integration; software development; IT outsourcing; cyber security; secure information sharing; data processing; communications; logistics; research and development; environmental consulting; energy and utilities; design and construction; homeland security; and geospatial solutions. SAIC's commercial segment, which generates 5% of its revenue, primarily targets commercial customers worldwide in the oil and gas; utilities; and life sciences industries. While the commercial segment provides a number of IT systems integration and advanced technical services, the focused offerings include applications and IT infrastructure management, data lifecycle management and business transformation services. The corporate segment handles issues relating to the company's internal real estate management subsidiary. SAIC's recent acquisitions includes Atlan, Inc., which provides cyber security product testing; R.W. Beck Group, Inc., a consulting firm; Beck Disaster Recovery, Inc., an emergency management consultant company; Spectrum San Diego, a producer of vehicle X-ray security scanners; CloudShield Technologies, Inc., a cyber security solutions company; Science, Engineering and Technology Associates Corporation, a technology company; and Reveal Imaging Technologies, Inc., a developer of threat detection products. In September 2010, the firm opened the Cyber Innovation Center in Maryland; the center is intended to help develop and deliver cyber security solutions.

SAIC offers its employees medical, dental and vision coverage; flexible spending accounts; life and disability insurance; a 401(k) plan; a wellness program; back-up childcare; an employee assistance program; tuition reimbursement; and a long-term care program.

FINANCIALS: Sales and profits are in thousands of dollars—add 000 to get the full amount. 2010 Note: Financial information for 2010 was not available for all companies at press time.

2010 Sales: $10,846,000	2010 Profits: $497,000	**U.S. Stock Ticker: SAI**
2009 Sales: $10,070,000	2009 Profits: $452,000	**Int'l Ticker:** Int'l Exchange:
2008 Sales: $8,926,000	2008 Profits: $416,000	Employees: 46,200
2007 Sales: $8,060,000	2007 Profits: $390,000	Fiscal Year Ends: 1/31
2006 Sales: $7,518,000	2006 Profits: $927,000	Parent Company:

SALARIES/BENEFITS:

Pension Plan:	ESOP Stock Plan:	Profit Sharing:	Top Exec. Salary: $1,000,000	Bonus: $1,444,500
Savings Plan: Y	Stock Purch. Plan:		Second Exec. Salary: $547,117	Bonus: $560,000

OTHER THOUGHTS:

Apparent Women Officers or Directors: 6
Hot Spot for Advancement for Women/Minorities: Y

LOCATIONS: ("Y" = Yes)

West:	Southwest:	Midwest:	Southeast:	Northeast:	International:
Y	Y	Y	Y	Y	Y

SALESFORCE.COM INC

www.salesforce.com

Industry Group Code: 511210K Ranks within this company's industry group: Sales: 3 Profits: 3

Hardware:	Software:		Telecommunications:	Electronic Publishing:	Equipment:	Specialty Services:	
Computers:	Consumer:		Local:	Online Service:	Telecom:	Consulting:	
Accessories:	Corporate:	Y	Long Distance:	TV/Cable or Wireless:	Communication:	Contract Manufacturing:	
Network Equipment:	Telecom:		Cellular:	Games:	Distribution:	Processing:	
Chips/Circuits:	Internet:		Internet Service:	Financial Data:	VAR/Reseller:	Staff/Outsourcing:	
Parts/Drives:					Satellite Srv./Equip.:	Specialty Services:	Y

TYPES OF BUSINESS:

Software-Sales & Marketing Automation
Customer Relationship Management Software
Software Subscription Services

BRANDS/DIVISIONS/AFFILIATES:

AppExchange
Force.com
Salesforce Chatter
Service Cloud
Heroku
Jigsaw
Premier Training
Vmforce

CONTACTS: Note: Officers with more than one job title may be intentionally listed here more than once.

Marc Benioff, CEO
Steve Cakebread, Pres.
Graham Smith, CFO/Exec. VP
George Hu, Exec. VP-Mktg. & Platform
J.P. Rangaswami, Chief Scientist
Parker Harris, Exec. VP-Tech.
David Schellhase, Exec. VP-Legal
Polly Sumner, Chief Adoption Officer
Jim Steele, Chief Customer Officer
Maria Martinez, Exec. VP-Customers For Life
Hilarie Koplow-McAdams, Exec. VP-Worldwide Sales
Marc Benioff, Chmn.
Frank van Veenendaal, Pres., Worldwide Sales & Svcs.

Phone: 415-901-7000	Fax: 415-901-7040
Toll-Free: 800-667-6389	
Address: 1 Market St., Ste. 300, The Landmark, San Francisco, CA 94105 US	

GROWTH PLANS/SPECIAL FEATURES:

SalesForce.com, Inc. builds and delivers customer relationship management (CRM) applications through an on-demand web services platform. The firm's web-based services enable clients to track sales and marketing by delivering enterprise software as an online service, making software purchases similar to paying for a utility as opposed to a packaged product. Its product suite provides integrated online sales force automation, customer service and support automation, partner relationship management and marketing automation applications. The company's AppExchange program allows businesses to access hundreds of on-demand business software applications developed by third parties. The company's products are scalable and can be mixed and matched with services such as system integration, data management, employee training and customer support. SalesForce.com also sponsors the Force.com online platform, which enables existing customers and third-party developers to develop and deliver software-as-a-service applications which they build within the platform's existing technology environment. Through Force.com, applications can be created, published, and run. In addition, these applications can be listed on the AppExchange marketplace. The firm also offers Premier Training, a subscription-based training model for the use of its platform; Service Cloud and Service Cloud 2, which are customer service solutions that uses cloud computing technology to capture the conversations and expertise of Google, Facebook and Amazon.com; and Contact Manager Edition, a subscription service aimed at individuals and small businesses. In 2010, SalesForce.com released several new products, including Force.com Visual Process Manager, a visual design tool; Salesforce Chatter, a real-time enterprise collaboration solution and platform; Chatter Mobile for mobile applications; Chatter Free, a free version of Salesforce Chatter; enterprise Java cloud VMforce; and crowd-sourced business data solution Jigsaw for Salesforce CRM. In May 2010, the company acquired crowd-sourced data services provider Jigsaw. In December 2010, SalesForce.com agreed to acquire Ruby-based cloud application platform Heroku for roughly $212 million.

FINANCIALS: Sales and profits are in thousands of dollars—add 000 to get the full amount. 2010 Note: Financial information for 2010 was not available for all companies at press time.

2010 Sales: $1,305,583	2010 Profits: $80,719	**U.S. Stock Ticker: CRM**
2009 Sales: $1,076,769	2009 Profits: $43,428	**Int'l Ticker:** Int'l Exchange:
2008 Sales: $748,700	2008 Profits: $18,356	Employees: 3,969
2007 Sales: $497,098	2007 Profits: $ 481	Fiscal Year Ends: 1/31
2006 Sales: $309,857	2006 Profits: $28,474	Parent Company:

SALARIES/BENEFITS:

Pension Plan:	ESOP Stock Plan:	Profit Sharing:	Top Exec. Salary: $750,000	Bonus: $600,000
Savings Plan:	Stock Purch. Plan:		Second Exec. Salary: $420,000	Bonus: $252,000

OTHER THOUGHTS:

Apparent Women Officers or Directors: 4
Hot Spot for Advancement for Women/Minorities: Y

LOCATIONS: ("Y" = Yes)

West:	Southwest:	Midwest:	Southeast:	Northeast:	International:
Y					Y

Note: Financial information, benefits and other data can change quickly and may vary from those stated here.

SAMSUNG ELECTRO-MECHANICS CO LTD   www.sem.samsung.co.kr

Industry Group Code: 335 Ranks within this company's industry group: Sales: Profits:

Hardware:		Software:	Telecommunications:	Electronic Publishing:	Equipment:	Specialty Services:
Computers:		Consumer:	Local:	Online Service:	Telecom:	Consulting:
Accessories:		Corporate:	Long Distance:	TV/Cable or Wireless:	Communication:	Contract Manufacturing:
Network Equipment:		Telecom:	Cellular:	Games:	Distribution:	Processing:
Chips/Circuits:	Y	Internet:	Internet Service:	Financial Data:	VAR/Reseller:	Staff/Outsourcing:
Parts/Drives:	Y				Satellite Srv./Equip.:	Specialty Services:

TYPES OF BUSINESS:

Electronic Components Manufacturing
Printed Circuit Boards
Capacitors
LED Products
Tuners
Network Modules
Crystal Devices

BRANDS/DIVISIONS/AFFILIATES:

SEMBrid

CONTACTS: Note: Officers with more than one job title may be intentionally listed here more than once.

Jong-Woo Park, CEO
Jong-Woo Park, Pres.
Byeong-Cheon Koh, Exec. VP
Jong-Hyouk Lee, Exec. VP

Phone: 82-31-210-5114	Fax: 82-31-210-6363
Toll-Free:	
Address: 314 Maetan-3-dong, Yeongtong-gu, Suwon, 443743 Korea	

GROWTH PLANS/SPECIAL FEATURES:

Samsung Electro-Mechanics Co., Ltd. (SEM) is a Korean-based manufacturer of electronic parts and components that are incorporated into televisions, personal computers, game systems, digital cameras, navigation systems, mobile devices, audio players and portable movie players. The company operates along three product lines: material technology, optic technology and radio frequency (RF) technology. Material technology products include printed circuit boards (PCB); multi-layer rigid-flex PCB (called SEMBrid); integrated circuit (IC) substrates; capacitors, resistors and inductors; electromagnetic compatibility (EMC) components, including chip beads and EMI (electromagnetic interference) filters; and low temperature co-fired ceramic (LTCC) components, such as diplexers and LC filters. Additionally, it manufactures a number of precision motors, including laser printer, hard disc and optical disc drive motors, as well as printing products, such as inkjet printheads, printing systems, functional ink and accessories. Optic technology products include camera modules, image sensors and photo sensors. RF technology products include digital and analog AV, audio and mobile device tuners; Bluetooth, wireless LAN and Zigbee network modules; power products, such as power drivers, inverters, adapters, LED lighting power and server power; and mobile RF components, including power amplifiers, antennas and crystal devices. The company maintains production and sales subsidiaries, research and development centers and other offices in the U.S., Europe, Japan, China and Southeast Asia.

SEM offers its employees a national pension; employment insurance; medical insurance; tuition fee support for employees' children; comprehensive medical testing for employees over 30 years old; on-site wellness clinics and wedding halls; nursery services; and heart surgery and leukemia treatment support for employees' children.

FINANCIALS: Sales and profits are in thousands of dollars—add 000 to get the full amount. 2010 Note: Financial information for 2010 was not available for all companies at press time.

2010 Sales: $	2010 Profits: $	U.S. Stock Ticker: Subsidiary	
2009 Sales: $	2009 Profits: $	Int'l Ticker: Int'l Exchange:	
2008 Sales: $	2008 Profits: $	Employees:	
2007 Sales: $	2007 Profits: $	Fiscal Year Ends:	
2006 Sales: $	2006 Profits: $	Parent Company: SAMSUNG GROUP	

SALARIES/BENEFITS:

Pension Plan: Y	ESOP Stock Plan:	Profit Sharing:	Top Exec. Salary: $	Bonus: $
Savings Plan:	Stock Purch. Plan:		Second Exec. Salary: $	Bonus: $

OTHER THOUGHTS:

Apparent Women Officers or Directors:
Hot Spot for Advancement for Women/Minorities:

LOCATIONS: ("Y" = Yes)

West:	Southwest:	Midwest:	Southeast:	Northeast:	International:
Y	Y	Y			Y

Note: Financial information, benefits and other data can change quickly and may vary from those stated here.

SAMSUNG ELECTRONICS CO LTD

www.samsung.com

Industry Group Code: 334310 Ranks within this company's industry group: Sales: 1 Profits: 1

Hardware:		Software:		Telecommunications:		Electronic Publishing:		Equipment:		Specialty Services:	
Computers:	Y	Consumer:		Local:		Online Service:		Telecom:	Y	Consulting:	
Accessories:	Y	Corporate:		Long Distance:		TV/Cable or Wireless:		Communication:	Y	Contract Manufacturing:	
Network Equipment:		Telecom:		Cellular:		Games:		Distribution:		Processing:	
Chips/Circuits:	Y	Internet:		Internet Service:		Financial Data:		VAR/Reseller:		Staff/Outsourcing:	
Parts/Drives:	Y							Satellite Srv./Equip.:		Specialty Services:	

TYPES OF BUSINESS:

Consumer Electronics
Semiconductors
Cellular Phones
Computers & Accessories
Digital Cameras
Fuel-Cell Technology
LCD Displays
Memory Products

BRANDS/DIVISIONS/AFFILIATES:

Samsung Group
Samsung NEC Mobile Displays Co., Ltd.
Samsung Austin Semiconductor
Samsung Electro-Mechanics
Samsung Opto-Electronics America, Inc.
Samsung Electronics America
Samsung SDS
Samsung Networks

CONTACTS: Note: Officers with more than one job title may be intentionally listed here more than once.

Yoon-Woo Lee, CEO
Ju-Hwa Yoon, Pres.
Ju-Hwa Yoon, CFO
Jon Kang, Pres., Samsung Semiconductor
Dale Sohn, Pres., Samsung Telecom America
Kun-Hee Lee, Chmn.
Gee-Sung Choi, Pres./CEO-Samsung Electronics America

Phone: 82-2-727-7114	Fax: 82-2-727-7892
Toll-Free:	
Address: 250, 2-ga, Taepyung-ro, Jung-gu, Seoul, 100-742 Korea	

GROWTH PLANS/SPECIAL FEATURES:

Samsung Electronics Co., Ltd., part of The Samsung Group, is a global leader in semiconductor, telecommunications and digital convergence technology. The company is organized into two segments: digital media and communications (DMC) or set business and device solutions (DS) or component business. The digital media and communications segment produces a wide array of specialties from mobile telephones to televisions to telecommunications systems. Samsung is a leading provider of cell phones utilizing its WiMax and High-Speed Downlink Packet Access (HSDPA) technologies to provide 3D and multimedia phones. It is also a leader in the HD Television market with its LED and LCD TV and monitor offerings. Samsung cameras and printers also enjoy a top market position as do its home appliances. This segment also includes its telecommunication networks business. The component business segment is a global leader in memory and LCD devices. The component business consists of semiconductors and LCDs. The semiconductor unit includes a memory division, which designs and manufactures ICs and is a leader in dynamic random access memory (DRAM), static random access memory (SRAM), flash memory and solid state drives (SSDs); the LSI division, which designs and manufactures logic and analog IC devices for applications in mobile, home, media and ASIC/foundry services; and the storage systems division, which is a leading manufacturer of hard disk drives for computers, camcorders, MP4 players and other digital devices. The LCD business produces panels for televisions, digital information displays and PCs such as LED backlit LCD panels. In February 2010, Samsung Electronics Co., Ltd. merged with Samsung Digital Imaging Co., Ltd.

FINANCIALS: Sales and profits are in thousands of dollars—add 000 to get the full amount. 2010 Note: Financial information for 2010 was not available for all companies at press time.

2010 Sales: $	2010 Profits: $	**U.S. Stock Ticker: SSNLF.PK**
2009 Sales: $123,691,000	2009 Profits: $8,587,090	**Int'l Ticker: 000830** Int'l Exchange: Seoul-KRX
2008 Sales: $97,035,500	2008 Profits: $4,420,700	Employees:
2007 Sales: $92,260,000	2007 Profits: $8,560,000	Fiscal Year Ends: 12/31
2006 Sales: $63,495,000	2006 Profits: $8,535,460	Parent Company: SAMSUNG GROUP

SALARIES/BENEFITS:

Pension Plan:	ESOP Stock Plan:	Profit Sharing:	Top Exec. Salary: $	Bonus: $
Savings Plan:	Stock Purch. Plan:		Second Exec. Salary: $	Bonus: $

OTHER THOUGHTS:

Apparent Women Officers or Directors:
Hot Spot for Advancement for Women/Minorities:

LOCATIONS: ("Y" = Yes)

West:	Southwest:	Midwest:	Southeast:	Northeast:	International:
Y	Y	Y	Y	Y	Y

Note: Financial information, benefits and other data can change quickly and may vary from those stated here.

SANDISK CORP

www.sandisk.com

Industry Group Code: 33441 Ranks within this company's industry group: Sales: 14 Profits: 7

Hardware:		Software:	Telecommunications:	Electronic Publishing:	Equipment:	Specialty Services:
Computers:		Consumer:	Local:	Online Service:	Telecom:	Consulting:
Accessories:	Y	Corporate:	Long Distance:	TV/Cable or Wireless:	Communication:	Contract Manufacturing:
Network Equipment:		Telecom:	Cellular:	Games:	Distribution:	Processing:
Chips/Circuits:	Y	Internet:	Internet Service:	Financial Data:	VAR/Reseller:	Staff/Outsourcing:
Parts/Drives:	Y				Satellite Srv./Equip.:	Specialty Services:

TYPES OF BUSINESS:

Flash-Based Data Storage Products
Flash Memory Cards

BRANDS/DIVISIONS/AFFILIATES:

SanDisk Ultra II
SanDisk Extreme
miniSD
microSD
CompactFlash
Flash Partners Ltd.
Flash Alliance Ltd.
Memory Stick PRO

CONTACTS: *Note: Officers with more than one job title may be intentionally listed here more than once.*

Eli Harari, CEO
Sanjay Mehrotra, COO
Sanjay Mehrotra, Pres.
Judy Bruner, CFO/Exec. VP
Yoram Cedar, CTO/Exec. VP
Yoram Cedar, Exec. VP-Corp. Eng.
Eli Harari, Chmn.

Phone: 408-801-1000	Fax: 408-801-8657
Toll-Free:	
Address: 601 McCarthy Blvd., Milpitas, CA 95035 US	

GROWTH PLANS/SPECIAL FEATURES:

SanDisk Corp. is a supplier of flash-based data storage products for the consumer, mobile communications and industrial markets. It designs, develops, markets and manufactures products in a variety of form factors using flash memory, controller and firmware technologies. The firm's products are used in a wide range of consumer electronics devices such as digital camera, mobile phones, gaming consoles, MP3 players and other digital devices. SanDisk's products are also embedded in a variety of systems for the enterprise, industrial, military and other markets. The company manufactures and sells every major flash card format including CompactFlash; Secure Digital (SD); MultiMediaCard; Reduced Size MultiMediaCard; Secure Digital High Capacity (SDHC); miniSD; microSD; Memory Stick PRO (which it co-owns with Sony Corp.); and other Memory Stick products such as USB flash drives. In addition to its standard grade products, SanDisk offers Ultra II and SanDisk Extreme memory cards, designed for faster write times and improved operation in harsh conditions. The company does not operate fabrication facilities but does control a significant portion of its flash memory wafer manufacturing through its Flash Partners Ltd. and Flash Alliance Ltd. joint ventures with Toshiba, as well as through sourcing agreements. SanDisk's customers include retailers such as Best Buy and original equipment manufacturers (OEMs) such as Canon. SanDisk also licenses its technologies to several companies, including Intel, Sony and Toshiba. The firm currently holds over 1,100 U.S. and 600 foreign patents. In July 2010, the company agreed to enter into a new joint venture with Toshiba Corporation to manufacture NAND flash memory. In August 2010, the firm introduced the SanDisk integrated solid slate drives (iSSD) for use in tablet PCs and ultra-thin notebooks.

SanDisk Corp. offers employees benefits including medical, dental, life, AD&D and vision insurance; an employee assistance program; tuition reimbursement; and a 401(k) savings plan.

FINANCIALS: Sales and profits are in thousands of dollars—add 000 to get the full amount. 2010 Note: Financial information for 2010 was not available for all companies at press time.

2010 Sales: $	2010 Profits: $	**U.S. Stock Ticker: SNDK**
2009 Sales: $3,566,806	2009 Profits: $519,390	**Int'l Ticker:** Int'l Exchange:
2008 Sales: $3,351,352	2008 Profits: $-1,973,480	Employees: 3,267
2007 Sales: $3,896,366	2007 Profits: $276,514	Fiscal Year Ends: 12/31
2006 Sales: $3,257,525	2006 Profits: $198,896	Parent Company:

SALARIES/BENEFITS:

Pension Plan:	ESOP Stock Plan:	Profit Sharing:	Top Exec. Salary: $848,000	Bonus: $1,696,000
Savings Plan: Y	Stock Purch. Plan: Y		Second Exec. Salary: $561,000	Bonus: $1,000,000

OTHER THOUGHTS:

Apparent Women Officers or Directors: 1
Hot Spot for Advancement for Women/Minorities:

LOCATIONS: ("Y" = Yes)

West:	Southwest:	Midwest:	Southeast:	Northeast:	International:
Y					Y

SANMINA-SCI CORPORATION
www.sanmina-sci.com

Industry Group Code: 334419 Ranks within this company's industry group: Sales: 9 Profits: 20

Hardware:	Software:	Telecommunications:	Electronic Publishing:	Equipment:	Specialty Services:
Computers:	Consumer:	Local:	Online Service:	Telecom:	Consulting:
Accessories:	Corporate:	Long Distance:	TV/Cable or Wireless:	Communication:	Contract Manufacturing: Y
Network Equipment:	Telecom:	Cellular:	Games:	Distribution:	Processing:
Chips/Circuits: Y	Internet:	Internet Service:	Financial Data:	VAR/Reseller:	Staff/Outsourcing:
Parts/Drives: Y				Satellite Srv./Equip.:	Specialty Services: Y

TYPES OF BUSINESS:
Contract Electronics Manufacturing
Assembly & Testing
Logistics Services
Support Services
Product Design & Engineering
Repair & Maintenance Services

BRANDS/DIVISIONS/AFFILIATES:
Viking Modular Solutions

CONTACTS:
Note: Officers with more than one job title may be intentionally listed here more than once.
Jure Sola, CEO
Hari Pillai, COO
Hari Pillai, Pres.
Bob Eulau, CFO/Exec. VP
Dennis Young, Exec. VP-Worldwide Sales & Mktg.
David Pulatie, Exec. VP-Human Resources
Michael R. Tyler, General Counsel/Corp. Sec./Exec. VP
Michael Kovacs, Dir.-Public Rel. & Worldwide Mktg.
Paige Bombino, Dir.-Investor Rel.
Hamid Shokrgozar, Pres., Viking Modular Solutions
Dave Dutkowsky, Exec. VP-Comm. Infrastructure
Jure Sola, Chmn.

Phone: 408-964-3500 **Fax:** 408-964-3636
Toll-Free:
Address: 2700 N. First St., San Jose, CA 95134 US

GROWTH PLANS/SPECIAL FEATURES:
Sanmina-SCI Corporation is an independent global provider of customized, integrated electronics manufacturing services (EMS). With production facilities in 18 countries, the firm is one of the largest global EMS providers. Its services include product design and engineering; manufacturing; final assembly and test; direct order fulfillment; and global supply chain management. The product design and engineering segment provides services for initial product development, detailed product design, prototyping, validation and pre-production services. The company designs high speed digital, analog, radio frequency, wired, wireless, optical and electro-mechanical products. Its manufacturing services are vertically integrated, allowing the company to manufacture key system components and subassemblies, such as circuit boards; printed circuit board assemblies; backplanes and backplane assemblies; enclosures; cable assemblies; precision machining; optical components and modules; and memory modules. This segment includes the operations of Viking Modular Solutions, a manufacturer of flash memory and related storage products. The final assembly and test unit combines the company's assemblies and modules to form finished products, and then tests these products for functionality, environmental impact, conformity to applicable industry, product integrity and regulatory standards. The direct order fulfillment segment receives customer orders, configures products to quickly fill the orders and delivers the products either to original equipment manufacturers (OEMs), a distribution channel (such as a retail outlet) or directly to the end customer. The global supply chain management segment plans, purchases and warehouses product components. It provides these services, as well as after-market support, primarily to OEMs in the communications; defense and aerospace; industrial and medical instrumentation; multimedia; computing and storage; and automotive technology sectors. In March 2010, the firm established a manufacturing facility in the Tamil Nadu state of India.

Sanmina-SCI offers its employees a 401(k) plan; tuition reimbursement; credit union membership; an employee assistance program; business travel accident insurance; and medical, dental, vision, life and AD&D insurance.

FINANCIALS:
Sales and profits are in thousands of dollars—add 000 to get the full amount. 2010 Note: Financial information for 2010 was not available for all companies at press time.

2010 Sales: $6,318,691	2010 Profits: $122,435	**U.S. Stock Ticker:** SANM
2009 Sales: $5,177,481	2009 Profits: $-136,222	**Int'l Ticker:** **Int'l Exchange:**
2008 Sales: $7,202,403	2008 Profits: $-486,349	**Employees:** 44,199
2007 Sales: $7,137,793	2007 Profits: $-1,134,657	**Fiscal Year Ends:** 9/30
2006 Sales: $7,645,118	2006 Profits: $-141,557	**Parent Company:**

SALARIES/BENEFITS:
Pension Plan:	ESOP Stock Plan:	Profit Sharing:	Top Exec. Salary: $804,385	Bonus: $1,401,918
Savings Plan: Y	Stock Purch. Plan:		Second Exec. Salary: $510,795	Bonus: $737,000

OTHER THOUGHTS:
Apparent Women Officers or Directors:
Hot Spot for Advancement for Women/Minorities:

LOCATIONS: ("Y" = Yes)
West:	Southwest:	Midwest:	Southeast:	Northeast:	International:
Y	Y	Y	Y	Y	Y

SANYO ELECTRIC COMPANY LTD   www.sanyo.com

Industry Group Code: 334310 Ranks within this company's industry group: Sales: 6 Profits: 5

Hardware:		Software:		Telecommunications:		Electronic Publishing:		Equipment:		Specialty Services:	
Computers:	Y	Consumer:		Local:		Online Service:		Telecom:	Y	Consulting:	
Accessories:	Y	Corporate:		Long Distance:		TV/Cable or Wireless:		Communication:	Y	Contract Manufacturing:	
Network Equipment:		Telecom:		Cellular:		Games:		Distribution:		Processing:	
Chips/Circuits:	Y	Internet:		Internet Service:		Financial Data:		VAR/Reseller:		Staff/Outsourcing:	
Parts/Drives:	Y							Satellite Srv./Equip.:		Specialty Services:	

TYPES OF BUSINESS:

Consumer Electronics
Fuel-Cell Technology
Communications Equipment
Industrial Equipment
Home Appliances
Batteries & Electronic Components
Photovoltaic Technology
Research & Development

BRANDS/DIVISIONS/AFFILIATES:

Sanyo Semiconductor Co Ltd
Panasonic Corporation

CONTACTS: *Note: Officers with more than one job title may be intentionally listed here more than once.*

Seiichiro Sano, Pres.
Hiroki Ohsaki, Chief Dir.-Finance
Hirokazu Teshima, Gen. Mgr.-Domestic Sales
Susumu Koike, Sr. Exec. VP/Head-IT
Akira Ibaraki, Exec. Dir.-New Prod.
Susumu Koike, Head-Prod. Eng.
Shigeharu Yoshii, Chief Dir.-Legal Affairs & Intellectual Property
Shinya Tsuda, Gen. Mgr.-Strategic Bus.
Mitsuru Homma, Exec. VP-Public Rel.
Susumu Koike, Gen. Mgr.-Corp. Planning
Tetsuhiro Maeda, Gen. Mgr.-Solar Div.
Masato Ito, Sr. VP/Pres., Mobile Energy Company
Mitsuru Homma, Exec. VP-Int'l Sales & Mktg.
Junji Esaka, Exec. VP/Head-Procurement

Phone: 81-6-6991-1181	Fax: 81-6-6992-0009
Toll-Free:	
Address: 2-5-5 Keihan-Hondori 2-Chome, Moriguchi City, 570-8677 Japan	

GROWTH PLANS/SPECIAL FEATURES:

Sanyo Electric Company, Ltd., a worldwide conglomerate with approximately 230 subsidiaries and affiliates, conducts manufacturing, sales, maintenance and service activities in five primary business segments: Consumer Electronics, Electronic Devices, Commercial, Digital Systems and Energy. The Consumer Electronics segment, which accounts for roughly 13.6% of the firm's revenues, offers audio, video and communications equipment, such as digital cameras, TVs and car navigation systems, as well as home appliances such as washing machines and air conditioners. The Electronic Devices division (18.7% of revenues) is a provider of semiconductors and electronic components such as optical pickups and capacitors. Sanyo's Commercial segment (23.8% of revenues) deals with commercial equipment, including showcases for supermarkets and convenience stores; commercial air conditioners, including package air conditioners; and computer systems for medical applications. The Digital Systems division (18.5% of revenues) offers televisions, digital cameras and projectors. The company's Energy segment (25.4% of revenues) covers electronic components, such as capacitors and motors, rechargeable batteries including lithium-ion batteries, photovoltaic systems, semiconductors, optical pickups and other products. Sanyo also invests heavily in research and development and is focused on a range of research areas, including solar cell technology; lithium-ion chemical batteries; electric hybrid batteries; photonics devices; flash memory; system-on-chip integrated circuit technology; secure digital content distribution; character and image recognition technologies; water treatment; biotechnologies; advanced fuel cells; and robotics. In October 2009, Sanyo sold certain subsidiaries focused on nickel hydride batteries and tubular-type lithium primary batteries to FDK Corporation for approximately $73.9 million. In December 2009, Panasonic Corporation acquired a 50.2% stake in the firm. In May 2010, the company sold its SANYO Electric Logistics Co., Ltd. subsidiary to LS Holdings Co., Ltd. In July 2010, Panasonic Corporation announced plans to buy up all remaining shares in Sanyo; and Sanyo agreed to sell subsidiary Sanyo Semiconductor Co., Ltd. to ON Semiconductor Corporation.

FINANCIALS: Sales and profits are in thousands of dollars—add 000 to get the full amount. 2010 Note: Financial information for 2010 was not available for all companies at press time.

2010 Sales: $20,327,200	2010 Profits: $-593,280	U.S. Stock Ticker: SANYY.PK
2009 Sales: $18,067,918	2009 Profits: $-951,286	Int'l Ticker: 6764 Int'l Exchange: Tokyo-TSE
2008 Sales: $20,389,900	2008 Profits: $287,000	Employees: 104,882
2007 Sales: $19,650,000	2007 Profits: $-390,000	Fiscal Year Ends: 3/31
2006 Sales: $21,804,658	2006 Profits: $-1,757,786	Parent Company: PANASONIC CORPORATION

SALARIES/BENEFITS:

Pension Plan:	ESOP Stock Plan:	Profit Sharing:	Top Exec. Salary: $	Bonus: $
Savings Plan: Y	Stock Purch. Plan:		Second Exec. Salary: $	Bonus: $

OTHER THOUGHTS:

Apparent Women Officers or Directors:
Hot Spot for Advancement for Women/Minorities:

LOCATIONS: ("Y" = Yes)

West:	Southwest:	Midwest:	Southeast:	Northeast:	International:
Y	Y		Y	Y	Y

SAP AG

www.sap.com

Industry Group Code: 511210H Ranks within this company's industry group: Sales: 2 Profits: 2

Hardware:	Software:		Telecommunications:	Electronic Publishing:	Equipment:	Specialty Services:	
Computers:	Consumer:		Local:	Online Service:	Telecom:	Consulting:	Y
Accessories:	Corporate:	Y	Long Distance:	TV/Cable or Wireless:	Communication:	Contract Manufacturing:	
Network Equipment:	Telecom:	Y	Cellular:	Games:	Distribution:	Processing:	
Chips/Circuits:	Internet:		Internet Service:	Financial Data:	VAR/Reseller:	Staff/Outsourcing:	
Parts/Drives:					Satellite Srv./Equip.:	Specialty Services:	Y

TYPES OF BUSINESS:

Enterprise Management Software
Consulting & Training Services
Hosting Services
Software Licensing
Software Development

BRANDS/DIVISIONS/AFFILIATES:

SAP Business Suite
SAP ERP
SAP Customer Relationship Management
SAP Product Lifecycle Management
SAP Business ByDesign
TechniData
Sybase Inc
Cundus AG

CONTACTS: Note: Officers with more than one job title may be intentionally listed here more than once.

Bill McDermott, Co-CEO
Gerhard Oswald, COO
Werner Brandt, CFO
Angelika Dammann, Chief Human Resources Officer/Dir.-Labor Rel.
Vishal Sikka, CTO
Hubertus Kuelps, Head-Global Comm.
Jim Hagemann Snabe, Co-CEO
Roger Bellis, Sr. VP-Talent, Leadership & Organizational Dev.
Hasso Plattner, Chmn.

Phone: 49-6227-7-47474	Fax: 49-6227-7-57575
Toll-Free: 800-872-1727	
Address: Dietmar-Hopp-Allee 16, Walldorf, 69190 Germany	

GROWTH PLANS/SPECIAL FEATURES:

SAP AG is a provider of enterprise software products and an independent software producer. The company's products include general-purpose applications as well as industry-specific applications. General-purpose applications include the SAP Business Suite family of applications, which consists of SAP ERP (an overarching enterprise resource planning application), SAP Customer Relationship Management, SAP Product Lifecycle Management, SAP Supply Chain Management and SAP Supplier Relationship Management. These applications, which can be licensed individually or together as a suite, are run on the firm's SAP NetWeaver technology platform, which allows customers to design, compose and adapt processes to address their unique industry and organizational needs. The firm's industry-specific applications perform defined business functions in particular industries, and are often delivered as add-ons to general-purpose applications. SAP offers more than 25 tailored software portfolios created by the company through the assembly of general-purpose applications, industry-specific applications, and, potentially, partner products. SAP's software portfolios encompass offerings for the following industry segments: process manufacturing, such as oil and gas, chemicals, mining and life sciences; discrete manufacturing, such as aerospace, high-tech and automotive; consumer industries, such as retail and wholesale distribution; and the telecommunications, financial and public services industries. For small and midsize enterprises, the firm offers the SAP Business One application, the SAP Business All-in-One package, and the SAP Business ByDesign package. SAP also offers services, including consulting, education, support, custom development, application management and hosting. The company, together with its 163 subsidiaries, serves more than 100,000 clients in 120 countries worldwide. Sales in Europe, the Middle East and Africa account for roughly 53% of annual revenues; the Americas represent 34%; and sales in the Asia Pacific region account for the remainder. In July 2010, the firm acquired enterprise software company Sybase, Inc. In September 2010, it acquired TechniData. In October 2010, SAP opened a Co-Innovation Lab in Brazil. In December 2010, it agreed to acquire disclosure management software from Cundus AG.

FINANCIALS: Sales and profits are in thousands of dollars—add 000 to get the full amount. 2010 Note: Financial information for 2010 was not available for all companies at press time.

2010 Sales: $	2010 Profits: $	U.S. Stock Ticker: SAP
2009 Sales: $14,499,400	2009 Profits: $2,374,900	Int'l Ticker: SAP Int'l Exchange: Frankfurt-Euronext
2008 Sales: $15,005,600	2008 Profits: $2,449,260	Employees: 51,500
2007 Sales: $16,387,200	2007 Profits: $3,070,400	Fiscal Year Ends: 12/31
2006 Sales: $15,028,800	2006 Profits: $2,993,600	Parent Company:

SALARIES/BENEFITS:

Pension Plan: Y	ESOP Stock Plan:	Profit Sharing: Y	Top Exec. Salary: $1,203,028	Bonus: $3,709,108
Savings Plan: Y	Stock Purch. Plan:		Second Exec. Salary: $1,002,100	Bonus: $6,497,777

OTHER THOUGHTS:

Apparent Women Officers or Directors: 1
Hot Spot for Advancement for Women/Minorities:

LOCATIONS: ("Y" = Yes)

West:	Southwest:	Midwest:	Southeast:	Northeast:	International:
Y	Y	Y	Y	Y	Y

Note: Financial information, benefits and other data can change quickly and may vary from those stated here.

SAS INSTITUTE INC

www.sas.com

Industry Group Code: 511210H Ranks within this company's industry group: Sales: 4   Profits:

Hardware:	Software:		Telecommunications:		Electronic Publishing:		Equipment:	Specialty Services:	
Computers:	Consumer:		Local:		Online Service:	Y	Telecom:	Consulting:	Y
Accessories:	Corporate:	Y	Long Distance:		TV/Cable or Wireless:		Communication:	Contract Manufacturing:	
Network Equipment:	Telecom:		Cellular:		Games:		Distribution:	Processing:	
Chips/Circuits:	Internet:		Internet Service:		Financial Data:		VAR/Reseller:	Staff/Outsourcing:	
Parts/Drives:							Satellite Srv./Equip.:	Specialty Services:	Y

TYPES OF BUSINESS:

Software-Statistical Analysis
Business Intelligence Software
Data Warehousing
Online Bookstore

BRANDS/DIVISIONS/AFFILIATES:

SAS 9.2
SAS Enterprise BI Server
DataFlux
IDeaS
JMP Software
Memex
RiskAdvisory
SAS Curriculum Pathways

CONTACTS: Note: Officers with more than one job title may be intentionally listed here more than once.

James Goodnight, CEO
James Goodnight, Pres.
Don Parker, CFO/Sr. VP
Jim Davis, Chief Mktg. Officer/Sr. VP
Jennifer Mann, VP-Human Resources
Suzanne Gordon, CIO/VP-IT
Keith Collins, CTO/Sr. VP
Carl Farrell, Exec. VP-SAS Americas
James Goodnight, Chmn.
Mikael Hagstrom, Exec. VP-EMEA & APAC

Phone: 919-677-8000	Fax: 919-677-4444
Toll-Free: 800-727-0025	
Address: 100 SAS Campus Dr., Cary, NC 27513-2414 US	

GROWTH PLANS/SPECIAL FEATURES:

SAS Institute, Inc. provides statistical analysis software. The company's products are designed to extract, manage and analyze large volumes of data, often assisting in financial reporting and credit analysis. Individual contracts can be tailored to specific global and local industries, such as banking, manufacturing and government. SAS's top products are SAS 9.2 and SAS Enterprise BI (Business Intelligence) Server. The SAS 9.2 platform is centered on providing extensive data management and analytics integration. It also features predictive applications, a highly adaptable interface and unique grid computing capabilities. SAS Enterprise BI Server is an enhanced reporting and analysis system for the organization and reporting of business intelligence. SAS also provides data warehousing services for large amounts of data, as well as consulting, training and technical support through its SAS Services unit. The company's DataFlux subsidiary helps it deliver quality capabilities in SAS Data Integration solutions. In addition, the firm operates an online bookstore offering a library of SAS-produced books, documentation and training materials. SAS serves more than 50,000 business, government and university sites in over 100 different countries, including 93 of the top 100 companies on the Fortune Global 500 list. The firm's software is used in a number of industries, including aerospace, defense, banking, government, financial services, insurance, manufacturing and retail. Other subsidiaries and divisions include IDeaS Revenue Optimization; JMP Software; DataFlux; RiskAdvisory; and SAS Curriculum Pathways. In June 2010, SAS Institute acquired intelligence management solutions provider Memex.

SAS offers its employees life, disability, medical, dental, auto, home and vision insurance; flexible spending accounts; on-site health care and fitness centers; an employee assistance program; adoption assistance; scholarship programs; and a casual work environment. The firm has been listed in Fortune's Top 100 Companies to Work For in America for 13 consecutive years, and was ranked number 1 in January 2010.

FINANCIALS: Sales and profits are in thousands of dollars—add 000 to get the full amount. 2010 Note: Financial information for 2010 was not available for all companies at press time.

2010 Sales: $	2010 Profits: $	U.S. Stock Ticker: Private
2009 Sales: $2,200,000	2009 Profits: $	Int'l Ticker: Int'l Exchange:
2008 Sales: $2,260,000	2008 Profits: $	Employees: 11,000
2007 Sales: $2,150,000	2007 Profits: $	Fiscal Year Ends: 12/31
2006 Sales: $1,900,000	2006 Profits: $	Parent Company:

SALARIES/BENEFITS:

Pension Plan:	ESOP Stock Plan:	Profit Sharing: Y	Top Exec. Salary: $	Bonus: $
Savings Plan: Y	Stock Purch. Plan:		Second Exec. Salary: $	Bonus: $

OTHER THOUGHTS:

Apparent Women Officers or Directors: 2
Hot Spot for Advancement for Women/Minorities: Y

LOCATIONS: ("Y" = Yes)

West:	Southwest:	Midwest:	Southeast:	Northeast:	International:
Y	Y	Y	Y	Y	Y

SCANSOURCE INC

www.scansourceinc.com

Industry Group Code: 423430 Ranks within this company's industry group: Sales: 11 Profits: 6

Hardware:	Software:	Telecommunications:	Electronic Publishing:	Equipment:		Specialty Services:	
Computers:	Consumer:	Local:	Online Service:	Telecom:		Consulting:	
Accessories:	Corporate:	Long Distance:	TV/Cable or Wireless:	Communication:		Contract Manufacturing:	
Network Equipment:	Telecom:	Cellular:	Games:	Distribution:	Y	Processing:	
Chips/Circuits:	Internet:	Internet Service:	Financial Data:	VAR/Reseller:		Staff/Outsourcing:	
Parts/Drives:				Satellite Srv./Equip.:		Specialty Services:	Y

TYPES OF BUSINESS:
Data Capture Products, Distribution
Bar Code & Point-of-Sale Products
Telephony Products Distribution
Business Communications Systems

BRANDS/DIVISIONS/AFFILIATES:
Catalyst Telecom
ScanSource Communications
ScanSource Security Distribution
ScanSource POS and Barcoding
ScanSource Communications GmbH

CONTACTS: Note: Officers with more than one job title may be intentionally listed here more than once.
Michael L. Baur, CEO
Richard P. Cleys, CFO
Marsha Madore, VP-Human Resources
John J. Ellsworth, General Counsel/VP/Corp. Sec.
Andrea D. Meade, Exec. VP-Oper.
Andrea D. Meade, Exec. VP-Corp. Dev.
Melissa Andrews, Contact-Media Rel.
Richard P. Cleys, VP-Finance
Scott Benbenek, Pres., Worldwide Oper.
John Black, Pres., Catalyst Telecom
Jeff Yelton, Pres., ScanSource POS & Barcoding
Buck Baker, Pres., ScanSource Comm.
Steven R. Fischer, Chmn.
Elias Botbol, Pres., Latin America

Phone: 864-288-2432	Fax: 864-288-1165
Toll-Free: 800-944-2439	
Address: 6 Logue Ct., Greenville, SC 29615 US	

GROWTH PLANS/SPECIAL FEATURES:
ScanSource, Inc. is a wholesale distributor of specialty technology products, providing value-added distribution sales to resellers in the specialty technology markets. The company has two geographic distribution segments: one segment serving North America from a Mississippi distribution center, the other serving Latin America (from distribution centers located in Florida and Mexico) and Europe (from the U.K. and Belgium). The North American distribution segment markets automatic identification and data capture (AIDC) and point-of-sale (POS) products through its ScanSource POS and Barcoding division (also utilized by the international segment); voice, data and converged communications equipment through its Catalyst Telecom sales unit; voice, data and converged communications products through its Paracon sales unit; and electronic security products through its ScanSource Security Distribution unit. AIDC and POS products interface with computer systems used to automate the collection, processing and communication of information for commercial and industrial applications, including retail sales, distribution, shipping, inventory control, materials handling and warehouse management. The Catalyst Telecom sales division is a distributor of Avaya communications products, including Small and Medium Enterprise, Avaya Aura Unified Communications, Avaya Global Communication Solutions and Internet protocol (IP) solutions; and Motorola wireless products. The ScanSource Communications sales division markets business converged communications and computer communication integration products from manufacturers including Dialogic, Polycom, Audiocodes, Plantronics and Quintum. Converged communications products combine traditional voice technologies with data technologies to deliver business communications solutions that combine computers, telecommunications and the Internet. In November 2009, ScanSource acquired Algol Europe, GmbH, a German distributor of convergence communications solutions; Algol is now known as ScanSource Communications GmbH.

ScanSource offers employees medical, dental, vision, disability, life and accident insurance; a 401(k) plan; an employee assistance program; an employee stock purchase plan; and other benefits.

FINANCIALS: Sales and profits are in thousands of dollars—add 000 to get the full amount. 2010 Note: Financial information for 2010 was not available for all companies at press time.

2010 Sales: $2,114,979	2010 Profits: $48,812	U.S. Stock Ticker: SCSC
2009 Sales: $1,847,969	2009 Profits: $47,688	Int'l Ticker: Int'l Exchange:
2008 Sales: $2,175,485	2008 Profits: $55,632	Employees: 1,074
2007 Sales: $1,986,927	2007 Profits: $42,626	Fiscal Year Ends: 6/30
2006 Sales: $1,665,600	2006 Profits: $39,816	Parent Company:

SALARIES/BENEFITS:
Pension Plan:	ESOP Stock Plan:	Profit Sharing:	Top Exec. Salary: $750,000	Bonus: $1,037,657
Savings Plan: Y	Stock Purch. Plan: Y		Second Exec. Salary: $323,908	Bonus: $233,475

OTHER THOUGHTS:
Apparent Women Officers or Directors: 1
Hot Spot for Advancement for Women/Minorities:

LOCATIONS: ("Y" = Yes)
West:	Southwest:	Midwest:	Southeast:	Northeast:	International:
	Y	Y	Y	Y	Y

SCENE7 INC

www.scene7.com

Industry Group Code: 511210F Ranks within this company's industry group: Sales: Profits:

Hardware:	Software:		Telecommunications:	Electronic Publishing:	Equipment:	Specialty Services:	
Computers:	Consumer:		Local:	Online Service:	Telecom:	Consulting:	Y
Accessories:	Corporate:	Y	Long Distance:	TV/Cable or Wireless:	Communication:	Contract Manufacturing:	
Network Equipment:	Telecom:		Cellular:	Games:	Distribution:	Processing:	
Chips/Circuits:	Internet:	•	Internet Service:	Financial Data:	VAR/Reseller:	Staff/Outsourcing:	
Parts/Drives:					Satellite Srv./Equip.:	Specialty Services:	Y

TYPES OF BUSINESS:
Software-Image Management
Interactive Web-Based Imaging
Visually Targeted, Personalized E-Mail Marketing Solutions

BRANDS/DIVISIONS/AFFILIATES:
Adobe Systems Inc
Scene7 On-Demand

CONTACTS: Note: Officers with more than one job title may be intentionally listed here more than once.
Shantanu Narayen, Pres./CEO-Adobe Systems, Inc.
Doug Mack, VP/Gen. Mgr.-Rich Media Solutions, Adobe Systems

Phone: 415-506-6000	Fax: 415-832-5301
Toll-Free: 877-723-6370	
Address: 601 Townsend St., San Francisco, CA 94103 US	

GROWTH PLANS/SPECIAL FEATURES:

Scene7, Inc., a subsidiary of Adobe Systems, Inc., produces a media-rich image management software platform that enables clients to enhance visual communications via the Internet, e-mail, displays and print, while automating media production and delivery. The Scene7 On-Demand platform allows customers to increase sales and marketing effectiveness, automate image management, generation and publishing and leverage image assets across various channels. Scene7's platform provides seven integrated enhancements: Web-to-Print; Multi-Media Viewers; eCatalogs; Visual Configurators; Dynamic Imaging; Dynamic Banners; and eVideos. Web-to-Print allows users to produce customized, branded and personalized documents. Multi-Media Viewers allows users to combine multiple image views, flash videos, color sets, animations, 360 spin and soundtrack to display all aspects of the featured product. The Targeted e-mail & Print segment delivers visually targeted, personalized e-mail and print campaigns. ECatalogs creates enhanced, interactive web-based versions of print marketing materials. Visual Configurators help users visualize custom-design items by applying product options, textures, fonts or logos. Dynamic Imaging enhances a product presentation by showing customers a variety of products, options, angles, zooms and details. Dynamic Banners provide targeted messages in promotional banners through real-time, image and Flash content. EVideos centrally manage videos and provide progressive download delivery. Scene7 offers its products with deployment flexibility, available as both licensed software and on-demand. The firm's clients include QVC; Harrods; Macy's; Office Depot; Polo Ralph Lauren; La-Z-Boy; Lands' End; VF Corporation; and Levi Strauss & Co. The firm sells its Scene7 On-Demand platform in the European market through U.K. services provider Intelligent Commerce Systems. Recently, the firm expanded its services into the Asia Pacific market.

FINANCIALS: Sales and profits are in thousands of dollars—add 000 to get the full amount. 2010 Note: Financial information for 2010 was not available for all companies at press time.

2010 Sales: $	2010 Profits: $	**U.S. Stock Ticker: Subsidiary**
2009 Sales: $	2009 Profits: $	**Int'l Ticker:** Int'l Exchange:
2008 Sales: $	2008 Profits: $	Employees:
2007 Sales: $	2007 Profits: $	Fiscal Year Ends: 12/31
2006 Sales: $	2006 Profits: $	Parent Company: ADOBE SYSTEMS INC

SALARIES/BENEFITS:

Pension Plan:	ESOP Stock Plan:	Profit Sharing:	Top Exec. Salary: $	Bonus: $
Savings Plan:	Stock Purch. Plan:		Second Exec. Salary: $	Bonus: $

OTHER THOUGHTS:
Apparent Women Officers or Directors:
Hot Spot for Advancement for Women/Minorities:

LOCATIONS: ("Y" = Yes)

West:	Southwest:	Midwest:	Southeast:	Northeast:	International:
Y					

SEACHANGE INTERNATIONAL INC

www.schange.com

Industry Group Code: 511210C Ranks within this company's industry group: Sales: 1 Profits: 1

Hardware:	Software:		Telecommunications:	Electronic Publishing:		Equipment:		Specialty Services:	
Computers:	Consumer:		Local:	Online Service:		Telecom:		Consulting:	
Accessories:	Corporate:	Y	Long Distance:	TV/Cable or Wireless:	Y	Communication:		Contract Manufacturing:	
Network Equipment: Y	Telecom:		Cellular:	Games:		Distribution:	Y	Processing:	
Chips/Circuits:	Internet:		Internet Service:	Financial Data:		VAR/Reseller:		Staff/Outsourcing:	
Parts/Drives:						Satellite Srv./Equip.:		Specialty Services:	Y

TYPES OF BUSINESS:

On Demand Video Systems & Services
Broadband & Broadcast Products
Media Content Services
Technical Support & Other Services

BRANDS/DIVISIONS/AFFILIATES:

Broadcast MediaCluster System
SPOT System
Axiom
On Demand Group Ltd
EventIS Group BV
SeaChange AdPulse On-Demand Advertising
VividLogic, Inc.

CONTACTS: Note: Officers with more than one job title may be intentionally listed here more than once.

William C. Styslinger, III, CEO
Yvette M. Kanouff, Pres.
Kevin M. Bisson, CFO
Ira Goldfarb, Sr. VP-Worldwide Sales
Steve Davi, Sr. VP-Advanced Tech.
Bruce Mann, Sr. VP-Network Storage Eng.
Kevin M. Bisson, Sr. VP-Admin.
Kevin M. Bisson, Sec.
Yvette M. Kanouff, Chief Strategy Officer
Jim Sheehan, Dir.-Public Rel.
Martha Schaefer, Dir.-Investor Rel.
Kevin M. Bisson, Sr. VP-Finance/Treas.
Erwin van Dommelen, Pres., SeaChange Software
Thomas Kracz, VP-Professional Svcs.
Maria Duquette, VP-Customer Svcs.
William C. Styslinger, III, Chmn.
Zheng Gao, Pres., SeaChange China & ZQ Interactive

Phone: 978-897-0100	Fax: 978-897-0132
Toll-Free:	
Address: 50 Nagog Pk., Acton, MA 01720 US	

GROWTH PLANS/SPECIAL FEATURES:

SeaChange International, Inc. develops, manufactures and markets digital video systems and services. The company operates in three segments: Software, which generated 65% of its 2010 revenue; Servers and Storage, 25%; and Media Services, 10%. The software segment includes the video-on-demand (VOD) platform suite, VODlink, which digitally manages, stores and distributes digital video. The system allows cable system operators and telecommunications companies to offer VOD and other interactive television services, including interactive electronic advertising and retrieval of Internet content. VODlink is comprised of hardware in the form of servers that store and deliver video content; and software that manages the video assets, the network and the back-office functions of the service. The division sells Axiom, its VOD software, independent of the hardware and offers subscription services for the software. The segment also includes the SPOT System for the insertion of advertisements and other short-form video into television network streams; and the SeaChange AdPulse On-Demand Advertising software platform, which allows operators to insert advertisements into on-demand content. Recently acquired subsidiaries, EventIS Group and VividLogic, Inc., have extended SeaChange's software capabilities. The Servers and Storage segment includes the MediaCluster System, which allows broadcast television companies to directly transmit content, such as commercials and other programming, to viewers through either single, multichannel or satellite delivery systems. The Media Services segment, through subsidiary On Demand Group Ltd. (ODG), offers development and interactive media services in Europe. ODG aggregates content for VOD and network VOD platforms and provides services to cable operators in several European countries. SeaChange's customers include Comcast, Cox Communications, Verizon Communications, ABC Disney, Clear Channel, Virgin Media and China Central Television. In February 2010, the company acquired software and services provider VividLogic, Inc. In April 2010, it sold its equity interest in Casa Systems, Inc.

FINANCIALS: Sales and profits are in thousands of dollars—add 000 to get the full amount. 2010 Note: Financial information for 2010 was not available for all companies at press time.

2010 Sales: $201,665	2010 Profits: $1,323	U.S. Stock Ticker: SEAC
2009 Sales: $201,836	2009 Profits: $9,974	Int'l Ticker: Int'l Exchange:
2008 Sales: $179,893	2008 Profits: $2,902	Employees: 1,223
2007 Sales: $161,334	2007 Profits: $-8,237	Fiscal Year Ends: 1/31
2006 Sales: $126,264	2006 Profits: $-12,199	Parent Company:

SALARIES/BENEFITS:

Pension Plan:	ESOP Stock Plan:	Profit Sharing:	Top Exec. Salary: $420,000	Bonus: $
Savings Plan: Y	Stock Purch. Plan:		Second Exec. Salary: $330,750	Bonus: $

OTHER THOUGHTS:

Apparent Women Officers or Directors: 3
Hot Spot for Advancement for Women/Minorities: Y

LOCATIONS: ("Y" = Yes)

West:	Southwest:	Midwest:	Southeast:	Northeast:	International:
Y		Y		Y	Y

SEAGATE TECHNOLOGY PLC

www.seagate.com

Industry Group Code: 334112 Ranks within this company's industry group: Sales: 2 Profits: 13

Hardware:		Software:		Telecommunications:		Electronic Publishing:		Equipment:		Specialty Services:	
Computers:		Consumer:		Local:		Online Service:		Telecom:		Consulting:	
Accessories:		Corporate:		Long Distance:		TV/Cable or Wireless:		Communication:		Contract Manufacturing:	Y
Network Equipment:		Telecom:		Cellular:		Games:		Distribution:		Processing:	
Chips/Circuits:		Internet:		Internet Service:		Financial Data:		VAR/Reseller:		Staff/Outsourcing:	
Parts/Drives:	Y							Satellite Srv./Equip.:		Specialty Services:	Y

TYPES OF BUSINESS:

Computer Storage Equipment-Disk & Tape Drives
Driver Components
Business Intelligence Software

BRANDS/DIVISIONS/AFFILIATES:

Maxtor Corp
Cheetah
Barracuda
Momentus
Seagate Technology, Inc.

CONTACTS: Note: Officers with more than one job title may be intentionally listed here more than once.

Stephen J. Luczo, CEO
Stephen J. Luczo, Pres.
Patrick O'Malley, CFO/Exec. VP
Dave Mosley, Exec. VP-Sales & Mktg.
Joy Nyberg, Sr. VP-Human Resources & Internal Comm.
Bob Whitmore, CTO/Exec. VP
Dave Mosley, Exec. VP-Prod. Line Mgmt.
Ken Massaroni, General Counsel/Corp. Sec.
Brian Ziel, Dir.-Corp. Comm.
Terry Cunningham, Pres./Gen. Mgr.-i365
David Richarz, Exec. VP-Sales
Stephen J. Luczo, Chmn.

Phone: 353-1-618-0517	Fax:
Toll-Free:	
Address: Arthur Cox Bldg., Earlsfort Terrace, Dublin, Ireland	

GROWTH PLANS/SPECIAL FEATURES:

Seagate Technology, plc, formerly Seagate Technology, Inc., manufactures rigid disk drives, often called disk drives or hard drives, used for storing electronic information in desktop and notebook computers, consumer electronic devices and data centers. Seagate sells its products primarily to original equipment manufacturers (OEMs), including Hewlett-Packard; Dell; IBM; EMC; and Lenovo Group Limited, as well as to independent distributors and retailers. Sales to OEMs accounted for 71% of company revenues in 2010. Its branded storage products are sold under the Seagate and Maxtor brand names. The company produces disk drive products used in enterprise servers, mainframes, workstations, PCs, digital video recorders, gaming platforms and digital music players. Its product lines include the Cheetah brand, used for Internet and e-commerce servers, data mining, transaction processing and medical imaging; the Barracuda brand, used in desktop storage, workstations and servers; and the Momentus brand of mobile computing products, used in notebook computers and digital audio equipment. Seagate also produces disk components for read/write heads, recording media, printed circuit boards, spindle motors, interface controllers and disc drive assemblies. Seagate's OEM customers typically enter into master purchase agreements with the firm, which provide for pricing, volume discounts, product support and other terms. Additionally, Seagate provides data storage services for small- to medium-sized businesses, including online backup, data protection and recovery. The firm maintains sales offices across the U.S., as well as in Asia and Europe. It has manufacturing facilities in the U.S., Ireland, China, Malaysia, Singapore and Thailand. In July 2010, the firm relocated its headquarters to Ireland. In August 2010, it entered into a joint development and licensing agreement with Samsung Electronics for the development of solid state drive (SSD) storage devices.

Seagate offers employees medical coverage; life insurance; a 401(k) plan; a stock purchase plan; and an employee assistance program, among other benefits.

FINANCIALS: Sales and profits are in thousands of dollars—add 000 to get the full amount. 2010 Note: Financial information for 2010 was not available for all companies at press time.

2010 Sales: $11,395,000	2010 Profits: $1,609,000	**U.S. Stock Ticker:** STX
2009 Sales: $9,805,000	2009 Profits: $-3,125,000	**Int'l Ticker:** Int'l Exchange:
2008 Sales: $12,708,000	2008 Profits: $1,251,000	**Employees:** 52,600
2007 Sales: $11,360,000	2007 Profits: $913,000	**Fiscal Year Ends:** 6/30
2006 Sales: $9,206,000	2006 Profits: $840,000	**Parent Company:**

SALARIES/BENEFITS:

Pension Plan:	ESOP Stock Plan:	Profit Sharing:	Top Exec. Salary: $870,182	Bonus: $1,550,000
Savings Plan: Y	Stock Purch. Plan: Y		Second Exec. Salary: $574,030	Bonus: $681,000

OTHER THOUGHTS:

Apparent Women Officers or Directors: 1
Hot Spot for Advancement for Women/Minorities:

LOCATIONS: ("Y" = Yes)

West:	Southwest:	Midwest:	Southeast:	Northeast:	International:
Y	Y	Y		Y	Y

Note: Financial information, benefits and other data can change quickly and may vary from those stated here.

SEGA SAMMY HOLDINGS INC

www.segasammy.co.jp

Industry Group Code: 511210G Ranks within this company's industry group: Sales: 1 Profits: 5

Hardware:	Software:	Telecommunications:	Electronic Publishing:	Equipment:	Specialty Services:
Computers:	Consumer:	Local:	Online Service:	Telecom:	Consulting:
Accessories:	Corporate:	Long Distance:	TV/Cable or Wireless:	Communication:	Contract Manufacturing:
Network Equipment:	Telecom:	Cellular:	Games: Y	Distribution:	Processing:
Chips/Circuits:	Internet:	Internet Service:	Financial Data:	VAR/Reseller:	Staff/Outsourcing:
Parts/Drives:				Satellite Srv./Equip.:	Specialty Services:

TYPES OF BUSINESS:

Computer Software-Games
Arcade Games
Amusement Centers
Toys
Ring Tones & Mobile Phone Media
Animation Production
Karaoke Machines
Display Design & Construction Services

BRANDS/DIVISIONS/AFFILIATES:

Sega Corporation
Sammy NetWorks Co., Ltd.
H-I System Corporation
Street Level, Inc
TMS Entertainment, Ltd.
SEGA Music Networks Co., Ltd.

CONTACTS: Note: Officers with more than one job title may be intentionally listed here more than once.

Hajime Satomi, CEO
Hajime Satomi, Pres.
Tomio Kazashi, Standing Corp. Auditor
Okitane Usui, Pres./CEO/COO-Sega Corporation
Keishi Nakayama, Exec. VP/Pres./CEO/COO-Sammy Corp.
Hisao Oguchi, Chief Creative Officer
Hideo Yoshizawa, Sr. Exec. Officer
Hajime Satomi, Chmn.

Phone: 81-3-621-59955	Fax: 81-3-5736-7066
Toll-Free:	
Address: Shiodome Sumitomo Bldg 21F,1-9-2 Higashi Shimbashi, Tokyo, 105-0021 Japan	

GROWTH PLANS/SPECIAL FEATURES:

Sega Sammy Holdings, Inc. (SSH), the product of a merger between Sega Corporation and Sammy Corporation, operates amusement centers and produces game software and arcade games. The company is organized into four principle segments: Pachislot and Pachinko Machines (PPM), similar to slot machines, which generated 41.7% of sales; Amusement Machine Sales (AMS), 11.7%; Amusement Center Operations (ACO), 14.2%; and Consumer Business, 31.6%. Other miscellaneous operations accounted for the remaining 0.7% of sales. In the PPM segment the company manufactures and maintains its Pachislot and Pachinko Machines. In the AMS segment, the company uses the ALL.Net P-ras business model, wherein it sells game hardware and provides mother board and software at no cost. SSH is paid by content use. This model allows operators of amusement centers to introduce new arcade machines with a small initial investment. The ACO segment owns and operates amusement centers, including those operated by Sega Corporation. Lastly, the Consumer Business segment manufactures software for home video game consoles (including producing the Incredible Hulk and Iron Man games for XBOX 360), Internet game play and mobile phones, as well as having operations in the traditional toy market. Some of the company's 27 domestic and 24 overseas subsidiaries and affiliates include Sega Corporation; Sammy NetWorks Co., LTD., a developer of ring tones and games for mobile phones; TMS Entertainment, LTD., an animation planning and production firm; H-I System Corporation, which makes amusement hall computers and prize POS systems; Street Level, Inc., which develops consumer games and game systems; and Sega Music Networks Co., Ltd., involved in the production and sales of karaoke machines.

FINANCIALS: Sales and profits are in thousands of dollars—add 000 to get the full amount. 2010 Note: Financial information for 2010 was not available for all companies at press time.

2010 Sales: $4,677,700	2010 Profits: $246,470	U.S. Stock Ticker: SGAMY.PK
2009 Sales: $4,630,230	2009 Profits: $-246,860	Int'l Ticker: 6460 Int'l Exchange: Tokyo-TSE
2008 Sales: $4,589,800	2008 Profits: $-524,700	Employees: 6,236
2007 Sales: $5,282,400	2007 Profits: $434,600	Fiscal Year Ends: 3/31
2006 Sales: $5,532,400	2006 Profits: $662,200	Parent Company:

SALARIES/BENEFITS:

Pension Plan:	ESOP Stock Plan:	Profit Sharing:	Top Exec. Salary: $	Bonus: $
Savings Plan:	Stock Purch. Plan:		Second Exec. Salary: $	Bonus: $

OTHER THOUGHTS:

Apparent Women Officers or Directors:
Hot Spot for Advancement for Women/Minorities:

LOCATIONS: ("Y" = Yes)

West:	Southwest:	Midwest:	Southeast:	Northeast:	International:
Y		Y	Y		Y

Note: Financial information, benefits and other data can change quickly and may vary from those stated here.

SEIKO EPSON CORPORATION

www.epson.com

Industry Group Code: 334119 Ranks within this company's industry group: Sales: 3 , Profits: 24

Hardware:		Software:		Telecommunications:	Electronic Publishing:	Equipment:		Specialty Services:	
Computers:	Y	Consumer:	Y	Local:	Online Service:	Telecom:	Y	Consulting:	
Accessories:	Y	Corporate:		Long Distance:	TV/Cable or Wireless:	Communication:		Contract Manufacturing:	Y
Network Equipment:		Telecom:		Cellular:	Games:	Distribution:		Processing:	
Chips/Circuits:	Y	Internet:		Internet Service:	Financial Data:	VAR/Reseller:		Staff/Outsourcing:	
Parts/Drives:	Y					Satellite Srv./Equip.:		Specialty Services:	

TYPES OF BUSINESS:
Electronic Device Manufacturing
Computers & Peripherals
Business Machines
Precision Components
Semiconductors
Industrial Robotics
Quartz Devices
Liquid Crystal Display Panels

BRANDS/DIVISIONS/AFFILIATES:
Seiko Group
Epson Imaging Devices Corp.
Epson Toyocom Corp.

CONTACTS: Note: Officers with more than one job title may be intentionally listed here more than once.
Minoru Usui, Pres.
Koichi Endo, Chmn.-Epson Singapore Pte. Ltd.
Hiromi Taba, Pres., Epson Europe B.V.
Kiyofumi Koike, Pres., Epson (China) Co., Ltd.
Yasuo Hattori, Vice Chmn.
Seiji Hanaoka, Chmn.
John Lang, CEO/Pres., Epson America, Inc.

Phone: 81-266-52-3131	Fax: 81-266-4844
Toll-Free:	
Address: 3-3-5 Owa, Suwa, Nagano, 392-8502 Japan	

GROWTH PLANS/SPECIAL FEATURES:
Seiko Epson Corporation, based in Japan, develops, markets, manufactures, sells and services information-related products, imaging products, electronic devices and precision products. Seiko's main product lines are computers and related peripherals, including printers, scanners and projectors; semiconductors, displays and quartz devices; and watches, plastic corrective lenses and factory automation equipment. The imaging products business markets printers, including inkjet printers and page printers; business systems, including serial impact dot matrix printers, miniprinters and point of sale (POS) systems; and visual instruments, consisting primarily of the 3LCD series of projectors. The firm's electronics devices business is comprised of the company's quartz device business, operating as Epson Toyocom Corporation, which manufactures crystal devices for the clock function in various applications; the high-temperature polysilicon (HTPS) thin film transistor (TFT) business, which manufactures HTPS TFT liquid crystal panels, 3LCD projector components; the semiconductor business; and the display business, operating as Epson Imaging Devices Corp., a manufacturer of small- to medium-sized displays. The company's precision products include watches, corrective lenses for eyeglasses and high-quality industrial robotics. The company has 25 domestic subsidiaries and 77 international subsidiaries.

FINANCIALS: Sales and profits are in thousands of dollars—add 000 to get the full amount. 2010 Note: Financial information for 2010 was not available for all companies at press time.

2010 Sales: $	2010 Profits: $	U.S. Stock Ticker:
2009 Sales: $12,109,700	2009 Profits: $-1,200,960	Int'l Ticker: 6724 Int'l Exchange: Tokyo-TSE
2008 Sales: $13,478,400	2008 Profits: $190,900	Employees:
2007 Sales: $14,160,300	2007 Profits: $-70,900	Fiscal Year Ends: 3/31
2006 Sales: $15,495,700	2006 Profits: $-179,200	Parent Company:

SALARIES/BENEFITS:
Pension Plan:	ESOP Stock Plan:	Profit Sharing:	Top Exec. Salary: $	Bonus: $
Savings Plan:	Stock Purch. Plan:		Second Exec. Salary: $	Bonus: $

OTHER THOUGHTS:
Apparent Women Officers or Directors:
Hot Spot for Advancement for Women/Minorities:

LOCATIONS: ("Y" = Yes)
West:	Southwest:	Midwest:	Southeast:	Northeast:	International:
Y	Y		Y	Y	Y

SELECTICA INC
www.selectica.com
Industry Group Code: 511210K Ranks within this company's industry group: Sales: 10 Profits: 10

Hardware:	Software:		Telecommunications:	Electronic Publishing:	Equipment:	Specialty Services:	
Computers:	Consumer:		Local:	Online Service:	Telecom:	Consulting:	Y
Accessories:	Corporate:	Y	Long Distance:	TV/Cable or Wireless:	Communication:	Contract Manufacturing:	
Network Equipment:	Telecom:	Y	Cellular:	Games:	Distribution:	Processing:	
Chips/Circuits:	Internet:		Internet Service:	Financial Data:	VAR/Reseller:	Staff/Outsourcing:	
Parts/Drives:					Satellite Srv./Equip.:	Specialty Services:	Y

TYPES OF BUSINESS:
Contract Lifecycle Management Software
Interactive Sales Software
Professional & Technical Services
Sales Execution Software
Pricing Management

BRANDS/DIVISIONS/AFFILIATES:
Selectica Sales Configuration
Selectica Contract Lifecycle Management
Selectica Deal Management Suite

CONTACTS: Note: Officers with more than one job title may be intentionally listed here more than once.
Jason Stern, COO
Jason Stern, Pres.
Todd Spartz, CFO
Allen Pogorzelski, VP-Mktg.
Leonard Rainow, CTO
Joe Lipple, VP-Prod. Mgmt.
Leonard Rainow, VP-Eng.
Marlene Bauer, VP-Professional Svcs.
Steven Gans, Chief Architect
David Knowlton, VP-Worldwide Sales
Alan Howe, Chmn.

Phone: 408-570-9700	Fax: 408-570-9705
Toll-Free: 877-712-9560	
Address: 1740 Technology Dr., Ste. 460, San Jose, CA 95110 US	

GROWTH PLANS/SPECIAL FEATURES:
Selectica, Inc. provides sales configuration and contract lifecycle management software. Its products and services include software, on-demand hosting and professional services that enable clients to manage the pricing and sale of complex business products. Selectica's Sales Configuration solution consolidates pricing, configuration and quoting functions into a single platform, enabling companies to streamline the opportunity-to-order process for service providers, manufacturers and financial services firms. The Selectica Contract Lifecycle Management solution is a contract authoring, analysis, repository and process automation product that helps companies take control of their contract management processes by converting from paper-based to electronic repositories and by unlocking multiple layers of critical business data. The firm's Deal Management Suite allows corporate departments to model specific contracting processes using its applications and to manage the lifecycle of the department's relationships with counterparties from creation through closure. Additionally, the company offers consulting, training and implementation services, as well as ongoing customer support and maintenance for its software. It serves a range of industries, including, telecommunications, high tech, manufacturing, healthcare and financial services. In October 2010, Selectica opened an operations and development center in Odessa, Ukraine.

FINANCIALS: Sales and profits are in thousands of dollars—add 000 to get the full amount. 2010 Note: Financial information for 2010 was not available for all companies at press time.

2010 Sales: $15,159	2010 Profits: $-4,644	U.S. Stock Ticker: SLTC
2009 Sales: $16,445	2009 Profits: $-8,422	Int'l Ticker: Int'l Exchange:
2008 Sales: $16,003	2008 Profits: $-23,901	Employees: 58
2007 Sales: $14,721	2007 Profits: $-20,944	Fiscal Year Ends: 3/31
2006 Sales: $23,433	2006 Profits: $-17,589	Parent Company:

SALARIES/BENEFITS:
Pension Plan:	ESOP Stock Plan:	Profit Sharing:	Top Exec. Salary: $201,421	Bonus: $1,150
Savings Plan: Y	Stock Purch. Plan:		Second Exec. Salary: $136,213	Bonus: $

OTHER THOUGHTS:
Apparent Women Officers or Directors: 1
Hot Spot for Advancement for Women/Minorities:

LOCATIONS: ("Y" = Yes)
West:	Southwest:	Midwest:	Southeast:	Northeast:	International:
Y					Y

SEMICONDUCTOR MANUFACTURING INTERNATIONAL CORP

www.smics.com

Industry Group Code: 333295 Ranks within this company's industry group: Sales: 7 Profits:

Hardware:		Software:		Telecommunications:		Electronic Publishing:		Equipment:		Specialty Services:	
Computers:		Consumer:		Local:		Online Service:		Telecom:		Consulting:	
Accessories:		Corporate:		Long Distance:		TV/Cable or Wireless:		Communication:		Contract Manufacturing:	Y
Network Equipment:		Telecom:		Cellular:		Games:		Distribution:		Processing:	
Chips/Circuits:	Y	Internet:		Internet Service:		Financial Data:		VAR/Reseller:		Staff/Outsourcing:	
Parts/Drives:	Y							Satellite Srv./Equip.:		Specialty Services:	

TYPES OF BUSINESS:

Semiconductor Manufacturing
Intellectual Property Licensing

BRANDS/DIVISIONS/AFFILIATES:

ARM Limited
Wuhan Xinxin Semiconductor Manufacturing Corp.
Brite Semiconductor

CONTACTS: Note: Officers with more than one job title may be intentionally listed here more than once.

David N.K. Wang, CEO
Simon Yang, COO
David N.K. Wang, Pres.
Gary Tseng, CFO
Samuel Tsou, VP-Human Resources
Zhou Mei Sheng, VP-Tech.
Barry Quan, Chief Admin. Officer
Anne Chen, Sec./Chief Compliance Officer
Zhou Mei Sheng, VP-Oper.
Chris Chi, Chief Bus. Officer
Jiang Shang Zhou, Chmn.

Phone: 86-21-3861-0000	Fax: 86-21-5080-2868
Toll-Free:	
Address: 18 Zhangjiang Rd., Pudong New Area, Shanghai, 201203 China	

GROWTH PLANS/SPECIAL FEATURES:

Semiconductor Manufacturing International Corp. (SMIC) is a leading Chinese semiconductor foundry. The firm operates three 8-inch wafer fabrication facilities in Shanghai; an 8-inch wafer fabrication facility in Tianjin; and a 12-inch wafer fabrication facility in Beijing. These facilities have an aggregate capacity of 162,050 8-inch wafer equivalents per month. In addition, the company has a 12-inch fabrication facility in Shanghai engaged primarily in research and development activities and an 8-inch wafer fabrication facility under construction in Shenzhen. The firm also manages the operations of certain wafer manufacturing facilities in Chengdu and Wuhan, China. SMIC provides semiconductor fabrication services using 0.35 micron to 45 nanometer process technology for logic technologies, including standard logic, mixed-signal, RF and high voltage circuits; memory technologies, including SRAM (Static Random Access Memory), DRAM (Dynamic Random Access Memory), Flash and EEPROM (Electrically Erasable Programmable Read-Only Memory); and specialty technologies, including liquid crystal on silicon (LCoS) and contact image sensors (CIS). In addition to wafer fabrication, the company owns and licenses intellectual property consisting of libraries and circuit design blocks, design support, mask-making, wafer probing, gold/solder bumping and redistribution layer manufacturing. Finally, SMIC offers assembly and testing services. Sales by geographic region in 2009 were as follows: U.S., 59%; Asia Pacific (excluding Taiwan and Japan), 23%; Taiwan, 15%; Europe, 2%; and Japan 1%. In October 2010, the company entered a collaboration agreement with ARM Limited for the development of ARM's physical IP library platform for process node applications. In the same month, it agreed to invest in 12-inch wafer production facilities operated by Wuhan Xinxin Semiconductor Manufacturing Corporation. In November 2010, SMIC agreed to invest in Brite Semiconductor, an IC design and turnkey service company based in Shanghai.

SMIC offers its employees a stock option plan, profit sharing, continuing education options and an insurance plan.

FINANCIALS: Sales and profits are in thousands of dollars—add 000 to get the full amount. 2010 Note: Financial information for 2010 was not available for all companies at press time.

2010 Sales: $	2010 Profits: $	U.S. Stock Ticker: SMI	
2009 Sales: $1,070,387	2009 Profits: $	Int'l Ticker: 0981 Int'l Exchange: Hong Kong-HKE	
2008 Sales: $1,353,711	2008 Profits: $-440,231	Employees: 10,598	
2007 Sales: $1,549,765	2007 Profits: $-19,468	Fiscal Year Ends: 12/31	
2006 Sales: $	2006 Profits: $	Parent Company:	

SALARIES/BENEFITS:

Pension Plan:	ESOP Stock Plan:	Profit Sharing: Y	Top Exec. Salary: $	Bonus: $
Savings Plan:	Stock Purch. Plan:		Second Exec. Salary: $	Bonus: $

OTHER THOUGHTS:

Apparent Women Officers or Directors: 1
Hot Spot for Advancement for Women/Minorities:

LOCATIONS: ("Y" = Yes)

West:	Southwest:	Midwest:	Southeast:	Northeast:	International:
Y					Y

SERENA SOFTWARE INC

www.serena.com

Industry Group Code: 511210I Ranks within this company's industry group: Sales: 6 Profits: 7

Hardware:	Software:		Telecommunications:	Electronic Publishing:	Equipment:	Specialty Services:
Computers:	Consumer:		Local:	Online Service:	Telecom:	Consulting:
Accessories:	Corporate:	Y	Long Distance:	TV/Cable or Wireless:	Communication:	Contract Manufacturing:
Network Equipment:	Telecom:		Cellular:	Games:	Distribution:	Processing:
Chips/Circuits:	Internet:		Internet Service:	Financial Data:	VAR/Reseller:	Staff/Outsourcing:
Parts/Drives:					Satellite Srv./Equip.:	Specialty Services:

TYPES OF BUSINESS:

Software-Systems Management
Web Content Management Software

BRANDS/DIVISIONS/AFFILIATES:

Silver Lake Partners
IT Process Management
Project and Portfolio Management
Serena Mariner
Application Development
Compliance Solutions
ChangeMan ZMF
Serena PVCS Professional Suite

CONTACTS: Note: Officers with more than one job title may be intentionally listed here more than once.

John Nugent, CEO
John Nugent, Pres.
Robert I. Pender, Jr., CFO
David Hurwitz, Sr. VP-Worldwide Mktg.
Carl Theobald, Sr. VP-Prod.
Robert I. Pender, Jr., Sr. VP-Admin.
Ed Malysz, General Counsel/Sr. VP
Robert I. Pender, Jr., Sr. VP-Finance
Kamran Kheirolomoom, Sr. VP-SBM Solutions
Peter Sianchuk, VP-Worldwide Customer Support
Mike deFisser, VP-Sales & Service, North America
John Wheeler, VP-Professional Svcs., North America
David Roux, Chmn.
Eric Driffort, VP-EMEA

Phone: 650-481-3400	Fax: 650-481-3700
Toll-Free: 800-457-3736	
Address: 1900 Seaport Blvd., Redwood City, CA 94063-5587 US	

GROWTH PLANS/SPECIAL FEATURES:

Serena Software, Inc. provides infrastructure software used to manage and control application change for organizations whose business operations are dependent on managing information technology. Its products are divided into five groups: Application Lifecycle Management software, which integrates multiple roles, existing tool investments, global locations and multiple platforms to optimize enterprise software development; IT Process Management, which streamline and more effectively coordinate project processes and communication; Project and Portfolio Management, which focuses on Serena Mariner, software that encompasses portfolio, project, resource, financial and demand management; Application Development; and Compliance Solutions, which allows companies to align and improve their software development processes with IT best practice methodologies. Other applications include ChangeMan ZMF mainframe development software and Serena PVCS Professional Suite, a software configuration management tool. The firm also provides clients with advisory and technical services, education and customer support. The company has more than 3,000 enterprise clients (nearly 1 million users) around the world in industry sectors such as finance, manufacturing, government, healthcare, technology and telecommunications. Serena Software has 29 offices in 14 countries worldwide. The firm's partners include SAP, immixGroup, Inc., Insight, Blue Turtle Technologies and SMG Co., Ltd. The company is owned by private investment firm Silver Lake Partners.

Serena Software offers its employees benefits including medical, dental, vision, life, AD&D, disability and long term care insurance; a 401(k) plan with company matching; flexible spending accounts; educational reimbursement; discounted auto and homeowners insurance; and an employee assistance program. In addition, employees enjoy a fully stocked kitchen and a referral bonus plan.

FINANCIALS: Sales and profits are in thousands of dollars—add 000 to get the full amount. 2010 Note: Financial information for 2010 was not available for all companies at press time.

2010 Sales: $	2010 Profits: $	U.S. Stock Ticker: Private
2009 Sales: $260,237	2009 Profits: $-339,506	Int'l Ticker: Int'l Exchange:
2008 Sales: $270,195	2008 Profits: $-27,110	Employees: 735
2007 Sales: $255,291	2007 Profits: $-47,212	Fiscal Year Ends: 1/31
2006 Sales: $255,772	2006 Profits: $35,267	Parent Company: SILVER LAKE PARTNERS

SALARIES/BENEFITS:

Pension Plan:	ESOP Stock Plan:	Profit Sharing:	Top Exec. Salary: $	Bonus: $
Savings Plan: Y	Stock Purch. Plan:		Second Exec. Salary: $	Bonus: $

OTHER THOUGHTS:

Apparent Women Officers or Directors: 1
Hot Spot for Advancement for Women/Minorities:

LOCATIONS: ("Y" = Yes)

West:	Southwest:	Midwest:	Southeast:	Northeast:	International:
Y				Y	Y

SERVEPATH

www.servepath.com

Industry Group Code: 518210 Ranks within this company's industry group: Sales: Profits:

Hardware:	Software:	Telecommunications:	Electronic Publishing:	Equipment:	Specialty Services:
Computers:	Consumer:	Local:	Online Service:	Telecom:	Consulting:
Accessories:	Corporate:	Long Distance:	TV/Cable or Wireless:	Communication:	Contract Manufacturing:
Network Equipment:	Telecom:	Cellular:	Games:	Distribution:	Processing:
Chips/Circuits:	Internet:	Internet Service:	Financial Data:	VAR/Reseller:	Staff/Outsourcing:
Parts/Drives:				Satellite Srv./Equip.:	Specialty Services: Y

TYPES OF BUSINESS:
Online Software Hosting Services

BRANDS/DIVISIONS/AFFILIATES:
GoGrid CDN
UpStream Networks

CONTACTS: Note: Officers with more than one job title may be intentionally listed here more than once.
John Keagy, CEO

Phone: 415-869-7000	Fax: 415-869-7001
Toll-Free: 866-321-7284	
Address: 2 Harrison St., Ste. 200, San Francisco, CA 94105 US	

GROWTH PLANS/SPECIAL FEATURES:

ServePath is a provider of data hosting and related information technology (IT) services. The company operates its own data center in San Francisco, California. The firm offers three primary specialties: dedicated hosting, hybrid hosting and managed services. Its dedicated hosting services provide server space for small businesses and corporations who need data stored in a central, secure location. ServePath provides server load balancing to maintain fast transmission speeds and prevent a single server from being overloaded by requests. In order to prevent potential downtime, its facility uses multiple network providers and generator backup systems along with other disaster prevention provisions. The company's hybrid hosting offers customers a scalable and secure network ideal for cloud computing and web hosting. If web traffic suddenly spikes, more servers will come online to help cope with the load in order to minimize potential bottlenecks. The firm also offers managed services, such as security through hardware firewalls and VPNs (virtual private networks); backup and recovery services through managed storage; networking services through dedicated private networks, load balancing and KVM (keyboard, video and mouse over IP); on-site network administrators; GoGrid CDN, which is a global content delivery network with 17 locations on four continents; and load balancing. ServePath offers multiple possible operating systems for client to run on their servers, including Windows Server 2008, Windows Server 2003, Microsoft SQL Server 2008, Red Hat Linux, Fedora Core Linux, Ubuntu Linux and FreeBSD. The company also offers on-demand media streaming for clients' websites through its UpStream Networks division.

ServePath offers its employees medical, dental and vision coverage; life insurance; a 401(k) program; discounted gym memberships; and free Friday lunches.

FINANCIALS: Sales and profits are in thousands of dollars—add 000 to get the full amount. 2010 Note: Financial information for 2010 was not available for all companies at press time.

2010 Sales: $	2010 Profits: $	U.S. Stock Ticker: Private
2009 Sales: $	2009 Profits: $	Int'l Ticker: Int'l Exchange:
2008 Sales: $	2008 Profits: $	Employees:
2007 Sales: $	2007 Profits: $	Fiscal Year Ends:
2006 Sales: $	2006 Profits: $	Parent Company:

SALARIES/BENEFITS:

Pension Plan:	ESOP Stock Plan:	Profit Sharing:	Top Exec. Salary: $	Bonus: $
Savings Plan: Y	Stock Purch. Plan:		Second Exec. Salary: $	Bonus: $

OTHER THOUGHTS:
Apparent Women Officers or Directors:
Hot Spot for Advancement for Women/Minorities:

LOCATIONS: ("Y" = Yes)

West:	Southwest:	Midwest:	Southeast:	Northeast:	International:
Y	Y	Y	Y	Y	Y

SHARP CORPORATION

www.sharp-world.com

Industry Group Code: 334310 **Ranks within this company's industry group:** Sales: 5 Profits: 7

Hardware:		Software:		Telecommunications:		Electronic Publishing:		Equipment:		Specialty Services:	
Computers:	Y	Consumer:		Local:		Online Service:		Telecom:		Consulting:	
Accessories:	Y	Corporate:		Long Distance:		TV/Cable or Wireless:		Communication:	Y	Contract Manufacturing:	
Network Equipment:		Telecom:		Cellular:		Games:		Distribution:		Processing:	
Chips/Circuits:	Y	Internet:		Internet Service:		Financial Data:		VAR/Reseller:		Staff/Outsourcing:	
Parts/Drives:	Y							Satellite Srv./Equip.:		Specialty Services:	

TYPES OF BUSINESS:

Audiovisual & Communications Equipment
Electronic Components
Solar Cells & Advanced Batteries
Home Appliances
Computers & Information Equipment
Consumer Electronics
LCD Flat Panel TVs, Monitors & Displays
Managed Print Services

BRANDS/DIVISIONS/AFFILIATES:

Sharp Electronics (Vietnam) Company Limited
LB-1085
Recurrent Energy LLC
Enel Green Power
ST Microelectronics

CONTACTS: *Note: Officers with more than one job title may be intentionally listed here more than once.*

Katsuhiko Machida, CEO
Mikio Katayama, COO
Mikio Katayama, Pres.
Moriyuki Okada, Group Gen. Mgr.-Domestic Sales & Mktg.
Nobuyuki Taniguchi, Group Gen. Mgr.-Human Resources
Shigeaki Mizushima, Group Gen. Mgr.-Corp. R&D
Masami Ohbatake, Gen. Mgr.-Info. Systems
Toshio Adachi, Chief Admin. Officer/Exec. VP
Toshio Adachi, Chief Legal Affairs Officer
Toshihiko Fujimoto, Gen. Mgr.-Corp. Strategy & Mgmt. Planning
Katsuaki Nomura, Group Gen. Mgr.-Corporate Acct. & Control
Kazutaka Ihori, Group Gen. Mgr.-Corp. Sales
Yoshiaki Ibuchi, Exec. VP-Electronic Components & Devices Bus.
Tetsuo Onishi, Group Gen. Mgr.-Solar Systems Group
Hiroshi Morimoto, Group Gen. Mgr.-Environmental Protection
Katsuhiko Machida, Chmn.
Toshishige Hamao, Exec. VP-Overseas Bus.

Phone: 81-6-6621-1221	Fax: 81-6-6625-0918
Toll-Free:	
Address: 22-22 Nagaike-cho, Abeno-ku, Osaka, 545-8522 Japan	

GROWTH PLANS/SPECIAL FEATURES:

Sharp Corporation designs, manufactures and distributes audiovisual and communication equipment, information system products and health and environment equipment. Its audiovisual and communication products include LCD color televisions, projectors, DVD recorders and players, Blu-ray Disc recorders and players, mobile communications handsets, mobile phones and PHS terminals. Sharp information system products include personal computers, electronic dictionaries, calculators, fax machines, telephones, POS systems, electronic cash registers, LCD color monitors, information displays, software and ultrasonic cleaners. The firm's health and environment equipment includes refrigerators, superheated steam ovens, microwave ovens, air conditioners, washing machines, vacuum cleaners, air purifiers, humidifiers, electric heaters, small cooking appliances, Plasmacluster Ion generators, LED lights and solar-powered LED lights. The Electronic Components business produces such items as CCD/CMOS imagers, LCD modules, microprocessors, flash memory, satellite broadcasting components, RF modules, network components, LEDs, optical sensors, optical communication components and regulators. The firm is also a leading manufacturer of crystalline and thin-film solar cells. Sharp offers managed print services outsourcing, where it can take over the complete operation of a client's desktop printers and copiers with the goal of creating significant savings. The company is also working on high-capacity lithium-ion battery technology. Sharp has 29 sales subsidiaries in 24 countries, 23 manufacturing bases in 14 countries and four research and development bases in three countries. In March 2010, Sharp began operations at its thin-film solar cell plant in Sakai City, Japan. In August 2010, the company announced a joint venture agreement with ST Microelectronics and Enel Green Power to produce thin-film solar cells. The joint venture will produce solar cells at a ST Microelectronics plant in Italy, with a production capacity of 160MW. In November 2010, the firm announced the acquisition of Recurrent Energy, LLC, a U.S. based developer of distributed solar project, for $305 million.

FINANCIALS: Sales and profits are in thousands of dollars—add 000 to get the full amount. 2010 Note: Financial information for 2010 was not available for all companies at press time.

2010 Sales: $33,512,300	2010 Profits: $53,470	**U.S. Stock Ticker:** SHCAY
2009 Sales: $31,432,600	2009 Profits: $-1,388,960	**Int'l Ticker:** 6753 **Int'l Exchange:** Tokyo-TSE
2008 Sales: $34,177,400	2008 Profits: $1,019,200	**Employees:** 53,999
2007 Sales: $26,620,000	2007 Profits: $870,000	**Fiscal Year Ends:** 3/31
2006 Sales: $24,113,009	2006 Profits: $764,405	**Parent Company:**

SALARIES/BENEFITS:

Pension Plan:	ESOP Stock Plan:	Profit Sharing:	Top Exec. Salary: $	Bonus: $
Savings Plan:	Stock Purch. Plan:		Second Exec. Salary: $	Bonus: $

OTHER THOUGHTS:

Apparent Women Officers or Directors:
Hot Spot for Advancement for Women/Minorities:

LOCATIONS: ("Y" = Yes)

West:	Southwest:	Midwest:	Southeast:	Northeast:	International:
Y		Y	Y	Y	Y

SHIN ZU SHING CO LTD

www.szs.com.tw

Industry Group Code: 334119 Ranks within this company's industry group: Sales: 22   Profits: 9

Hardware:	Software:	Telecommunications:	Electronic Publishing:	Equipment:	Specialty Services:
Computers:	Consumer:	Local:	Online Service:	Telecom:	Consulting:
Accessories:	Corporate:	Long Distance:	TV/Cable or Wireless:	Communication:	Contract Manufacturing:
Network Equipment:	Telecom:	Cellular:	Games:	Distribution:	Processing:
Chips/Circuits:	Internet:	Internet Service:	Financial Data:	VAR/Reseller:	Staff/Outsourcing:
Parts/Drives: Y				Satellite Srv./Equip.:	Specialty Services:

TYPES OF BUSINESS:

Manufacturing-Hinges, Springs
Manufacturing-Molded Plastic Computer Parts

BRANDS/DIVISIONS/AFFILIATES:

SZS Precision Electronics Co., Ltd.

GROWTH PLANS/SPECIAL FEATURES:

Shin Zu Shing Co. Ltd. (SZS), founded in 1965, manufactures components used in a wide variety of electrical and computer equipment. These products include hinges, springs and molded plastic pieces used in laptops, medical equipment and machinery. Notebook hinges generate the majority of its revenue. As an example of SZS's production capacity, the company has designed over 4,000 different spring models and can produce more than 100 million springs monthly. Additionally, for custom orders, the firm can typically produce a prototype for a client within days of receiving an order, and can produce the product on a large scale several weeks after that. The company has over 820 issued patents in 11 countries and over 115 pending patent applications. Its subsidiaries include SZS Precision Electronics Co., Ltd.

CONTACTS: *Note: Officers with more than one job title may be intentionally listed here more than once.*

Lin Ching-Cheng, Gen. Mgr.
Sheng-Nan Lu, Chmn.

Phone: 886-2-2681-3316	Fax: 886-2-2683-2116
Toll-Free:	
Address: No. 174, Jyunying St., Shulin City, 238 Taiwan	

FINANCIALS: Sales and profits are in thousands of dollars—add 000 to get the full amount. 2010 Note: Financial information for 2010 was not available for all companies at press time.

2010 Sales: $	2010 Profits: $	**U.S. Stock Ticker:**
2009 Sales: $242,050	2009 Profits: $49,670	**Int'l Ticker: 3376** Int'l Exchange: Taipei-TPE
2008 Sales: $220,580	2008 Profits: $40,830	Employees: 2,975
2007 Sales: $189,614	2007 Profits: $	Fiscal Year Ends: 12/31
2006 Sales: $	2006 Profits: $	Parent Company:

SALARIES/BENEFITS:

Pension Plan:	ESOP Stock Plan:	Profit Sharing:	Top Exec. Salary: $	Bonus: $
Savings Plan:	Stock Purch. Plan:		Second Exec. Salary: $	Bonus: $

OTHER THOUGHTS:

Apparent Women Officers or Directors:
Hot Spot for Advancement for Women/Minorities:

LOCATIONS: ("Y" = Yes)

West:	Southwest:	Midwest:	Southeast:	Northeast:	International:
					Y

SIEMENS AG

www.siemens.com

Industry Group Code: 335 Ranks within this company's industry group: Sales: 1 Profits: 1

Hardware:		Software:		Telecommunications:		Electronic Publishing:		Equipment:		Specialty Services:	
Computers:		Consumer:		Local:		Online Service:	Y	Telecom:	Y	Consulting:	Y
Accessories:		Corporate:	Y	Long Distance:		TV/Cable or Wireless:		Communication:	Y	Contract Manufacturing:	
Network Equipment:	Y	Telecom:		Cellular:		Games:		Distribution:		Processing:	
Chips/Circuits:		Internet:		Internet Service:		Financial Data:		VAR/Reseller:		Staff/Outsourcing:	
Parts/Drives:	Y							Satellite Srv./Equip.:		Specialty Services:	

TYPES OF BUSINESS:

Electrical Equipment Manufacturing
Energy & Power Plant Systems & Consulting
Medical and Health Care Services and Equipment
Lighting & Optical Systems
Automation Systems
Transportation & Logistics Systems
Photovoltaic Equipment

BRANDS/DIVISIONS/AFFILIATES:

CTI Molecular Imaging
Siemens Building Technologies
Siemens Canada
Siemens Corporate Technology
Siemens Energy & Automation Inc
Siemens Energy Services
Siemens Healthcare
Solel Solar Systems

CONTACTS: *Note: Officers with more than one job title may be intentionally listed here more than once.*

Peter H. Loscher, CEO
Peter H. Loscher, Pres.
Joe Kaeser, Head-Finance
Brigitte Ederer, Head-Corp. Human Resources
Joe Kaeser, Head-IT Solutions & Svcs.
Hermann Requardt, Head-Corp. Tech.
Peter Y. Solmssen, Head-Legal & Compliance
Joe Kaeser, Controller
Hermann Requardt, Sector CEO-Healthcare
Siegfried Russwurm, Sector CEO-Industry
Wolfgang Dehen, Sector CEO-Energy/Dir.-Asia & Australia
Eric Spiegel, CEO/Pres., Siemens Corp.
Gerhard Cromme, Chmn.
Peter Y. Solmssen, Dir.-The Americas
Barbara Kux, Head-Supply Chain Mgmt. & Sustainability

Phone: 49-69-797-6660	Fax:
Toll-Free:	
Address: Wittelsbacherplatz 2, Munich, 80333 Germany	

GROWTH PLANS/SPECIAL FEATURES:

Siemens AG is one of the largest electrical engineering and manufacturing companies in the world. Based in Germany, the firm sells products and services to approximately 190 countries around the globe, including all 50 states in the U.S. The company is organized in three primary sectors: industry, energy and healthcare. The industry sector's offerings range from industry automation products and services to building, lighting and mobility systems and services, as well as system integration for plant businesses. Additionally, this sector provides networking technology for transportation systems, including airport logistics, postal automation and railway electrification. The energy sector offers a broad range of products and services related to the generation, transmission and distribution of power, as well as for the extraction, conversion and transportation of oil and gas. The healthcare sector develops, manufactures and markets diagnostic and therapeutic systems, devices and consumables, as well as information technology systems for clinical and healthcare administration settings. Besides these activities, subsidiaries Siemens IT Solutions & Services (SIS) as well as Siemens Financial Services support sector activities as business partners, meanwhile continuing to build up their own business with external customers. In July 2009, the firm sold its 50% stake in Fujitsu Siemens Computers, an IT infrastructure provider, to Fujitsu Limited for roughly $670 million. In October 2009, Siemens announced that it would acquire Israel-based Solel Solar Systems Limited for $418 million. In October 2010, the company announced the further establishment of SIS as an independent limited liability company, operating under the Siemens IT Solutions and Services GmbH name. Later that month, Siemens also announced a strategic partnership with Masdar, Abu Dhabi's renewable energy company, in order to research and develop future energy technologies.

FINANCIALS: Sales and profits are in thousands of dollars—add 000 to get the full amount. 2010 Note: Financial information for 2010 was not available for all companies at press time.

2010 Sales: $103,974,000	2010 Profits: $5,566,940	**U.S. Stock Ticker: SI**
2009 Sales: $113,842,000	2009 Profits: $3,404,080	**Int'l Ticker: SIE** Int'l Exchange: Frankfurt-Euronext
2008 Sales: $107,580,000	2008 Profits: $8,189,070	Employees: 427,000
2007 Sales: $115,406,000	2007 Profits: $3,535,760	Fiscal Year Ends: 9/30
2006 Sales: $113,740,000	2006 Profits: $3,950,360	Parent Company:

SALARIES/BENEFITS:

Pension Plan:	ESOP Stock Plan:	Profit Sharing:	Top Exec. Salary: $4,618,982	Bonus: $
Savings Plan:	Stock Purch. Plan: Y		Second Exec. Salary: $2,098,621	Bonus: $

OTHER THOUGHTS:

Apparent Women Officers or Directors: 5
Hot Spot for Advancement for Women/Minorities: Y

LOCATIONS: ("Y" = Yes)

West:	Southwest:	Midwest:	Southeast:	Northeast:	International:
Y	Y	Y	Y	Y	Y

Note: Financial information, benefits and other data can change quickly and may vary from those stated here.

SIEMENS LIMITED

w1.siemens.com/entry/en/in/

Industry Group Code: 335 Ranks within this company's industry group: Sales: Profits:

Hardware:		Software:		Telecommunications:		Electronic Publishing:		Equipment:		Specialty Services:	
Computers:		Consumer:		Local:		Online Service:		Telecom:		Consulting:	Y
Accessories:		Corporate:	Y	Long Distance:		TV/Cable or Wireless:		Communication:		Contract Manufacturing:	Y
Network Equipment:	Y	Telecom:		Cellular:		Games:		Distribution:		Processing:	
Chips/Circuits:		Internet:		Internet Service:		Financial Data:		VAR/Reseller:		Staff/Outsourcing:	
Parts/Drives:								Satellite Srv./Equip.:		Specialty Services:	Y

TYPES OF BUSINESS:

Electrical & Electronics Engineering
Power Plants
Medical Technology
Industrial Automation
Lighting Products & Technology
Railway Rolling Stock

BRANDS/DIVISIONS/AFFILIATES:

Osram India Private Ltd.
Siemens Rolling Stock Pvt. Ltd.
Siemens Building Technologies Pvt. Ltd.
Siemens AG

CONTACTS: Note: Officers with more than one job title may be intentionally listed here more than once.

Armin Bruck, Managing Dir.
Sunil D. Mathur, CFO
Ajai Jain, VP-Legal/Company Sec.
Vijay V. Paranjape, Whole-time Dir.
Ajai Jain, Chief Compliance Officer
Deepak S. Parekh, Chmn.

Phone: 91-22-2498-7000	Fax: 91-22-2498-7500
Toll-Free:	
Address: 130, Pandurang Budhkar Marg, Mumbai, 400 018 India	

GROWTH PLANS/SPECIAL FEATURES:

Siemens Limited is an India-based company operating in the fields of electrical and electronics engineering. The company operates in several business segments, including Energy; Industry; Healthcare; Cross-Sector Business; Lighting; and Mobility. The energy segment focuses on both power generation and power transmission and distribution. The company builds power plants and power generating components, including coal and gas-based power plants, captive power plants, plants based on alternative energy sources, substations, medium voltage distribution networks and power system controls. The industry segment provides products and systems for industrial and building automation including project management, engineering, software, installation, commissioning, after-sales service, plant maintenance and training. Areas served by this segment include iron and steel making, waste water treatment, airports, postal automation, highway traffic management, shipbuilding and mining. The healthcare segment develops and produces medical technologies, such as hearing aids, X-ray systems, mammography equipment, ultrasound devices and hospital information systems. The cross-sector business segment offers consulting, systems integration and IT infrastructure management across a variety of government and industry sectors. The lighting segment, through subsidiary Osram India Private Ltd., produces lighting products, including general home and industrial lighting, automotive lighting, optical display technologies and LED systems. The mobility segment is involved in designing and manufacturing electrical systems for railway, mass transit and other transportation applications. Siemens Limited operates 19 manufacturing facilities and a network of sales and service offices throughout India. Wholly-owned subsidiaries include Siemens Rolling Stock Pvt. Ltd., a manufacturer of locomotives and railroad cars, and Siemens Building Technologies Pvt. Ltd., which provides products and services related to building automation, fire safety and security. In October 2010, the company announced that it would invest approximately $44 million to build two new manufacturing plants in the Indian state of Goa. German engineering giant Siemens AG holds approximately 55% of Siemens Limited.

FINANCIALS: Sales and profits are in thousands of dollars—add 000 to get the full amount. 2010 Note: Financial information for 2010 was not available for all companies at press time.

2010 Sales: $	2010 Profits: $	U.S. Stock Ticker: Subsidiary
2009 Sales: $	2009 Profits: $	Int'l Ticker: Int'l Exchange:
2008 Sales: $	2008 Profits: $	Employees:
2007 Sales: $	2007 Profits: $	Fiscal Year Ends: 9/30
2006 Sales: $	2006 Profits: $	Parent Company: SIEMENS AG

SALARIES/BENEFITS:

Pension Plan:	ESOP Stock Plan:	Profit Sharing:	Top Exec. Salary: $	Bonus: $
Savings Plan:	Stock Purch. Plan:		Second Exec. Salary: $	Bonus: $

OTHER THOUGHTS:

Apparent Women Officers or Directors:
Hot Spot for Advancement for Women/Minorities:

LOCATIONS: ("Y" = Yes)

West:	Southwest:	Midwest:	Southeast:	Northeast:	International:
					Y

SIEMENS PLM SOFTWARE

www.plm.automation.siemens.com

Industry Group Code: 511210N Ranks within this company's industry group: Sales: Profits:

Hardware:	Software:		Telecommunications:	Electronic Publishing:	Equipment:	Specialty Services:	
Computers:	Consumer:		Local:	Online Service:	Telecom:	Consulting:	
Accessories:	Corporate:	Y	Long Distance:	TV/Cable or Wireless:	Communication:	Contract Manufacturing:	
Network Equipment:	Telecom:		Cellular:	Games:	Distribution:	Processing:	
Chips/Circuits:	Internet:		Internet Service:	Financial Data:	VAR/Reseller:	Staff/Outsourcing:	Y
Parts/Drives:					Satellite Srv./Equip.:	Specialty Services:	

TYPES OF BUSINESS:

Software-Product Lifecycle Management
Engineering Outsourcing

BRANDS/DIVISIONS/AFFILIATES:

Solid Edge
D-Cubed Ltd
NX
Velocity Series
Tecnomatix
PLM Components
Teamcenter

CONTACTS: *Note: Officers with more than one job title may be intentionally listed here more than once.*

Anthony J. Affuso, CEO
Chuck Grindstaff, Pres.
Harry Volande, CFO/Exec. VP
Eric Sterling, Exec. VP-Global Mktg.
Dan Malliet, Sr. VP-Human Resources
Craig J. Berry, CIO/Sr. VP
Chuck Grindstaff, CTO
Chuck. Grindstaff, Exec. VP-Prod.
Rose Marie E. Glazer, General Counsel/Sec.
Mike Sayen, VP-Strategy
Paul Vogel, Exec. VP-Global Sales & Svcs.
Anthony J. Affuso, Chmn.

Phone: 972-987-3000	Fax: 972-987-3398
Toll-Free: 800-498-5351	
Address: 5800 Granite Pkwy., Ste. 600, Plano, TX 75024 US	

GROWTH PLANS/SPECIAL FEATURES:

Siemens PLM Software, (SPS) formerly UGS Corp., is a leading global provider of product lifecycle management (PLM) products and services, with more than 6.7 million licensed seats of its technology in use and 69,500 clients worldwide. PLM products help customers accelerate their time to market, improve quality and increase revenue by allowing organizations to digitally manage a product's complete lifecycle, from its concept and design to its retirement. The firm's portfolio of software and service solutions includes: product development; enterprise collaboration; data management; and factory and manufacturing planning tools. SPS's six primary product suites and business initiatives are Teamcenter, which focuses on economizing business operations by helping employees communicate more effectively; NX, which contains primarily Computer Aided Design (CAD) software and other design software; Tecnomatix, which aids in industrial design and assembly; Velocity Series, which is a modular set of solutions to assist small and medium businesses with PLM; Solid Edge, a core feature of Velocity Series and a complete, history-free feature-based 2D/3D CAD software system; and PLM Components, which helps companies share data with customers and partners. The firm's subsidiary D-Cubed, Ltd. is a U.K. engineering outsourcer.

FINANCIALS: Sales and profits are in thousands of dollars—add 000 to get the full amount. 2010 Note: Financial information for 2010 was not available for all companies at press time.

2010 Sales: $	2010 Profits: $	U.S. Stock Ticker: Private
2009 Sales: $	2009 Profits: $	Int'l Ticker: Int'l Exchange:
2008 Sales: $	2008 Profits: $	Employees:
2007 Sales: $	2007 Profits: $	Fiscal Year Ends: 12/31
2006 Sales: $1,218,747	2006 Profits: $-10,338	Parent Company:

SALARIES/BENEFITS:

Pension Plan:	ESOP Stock Plan:	Profit Sharing:	Top Exec. Salary: $	Bonus: $
Savings Plan:	Stock Purch. Plan:		Second Exec. Salary: $	Bonus: $

OTHER THOUGHTS:

Apparent Women Officers or Directors: 1
Hot Spot for Advancement for Women/Minorities:

LOCATIONS: ("Y" = Yes)

West:	Southwest:	Midwest:	Southeast:	Northeast:	International:
Y	Y	Y	Y	Y	Y

SIGMA DESIGNS INC

www.sigmadesigns.com

Industry Group Code: 33441 Ranks within this company's industry group: Sales: 46   Profits: 31

Hardware:		Software:		Telecommunications:		Electronic Publishing:	Equipment:	Specialty Services:
Computers:		Consumer:		Local:		Online Service:	Telecom:	Consulting:
Accessories:		Corporate:	Y	Long Distance:		TV/Cable or Wireless:	Communication:	Contract Manufacturing:
Network Equipment:		Telecom:		Cellular:		Games:	Distribution:	Processing:
Chips/Circuits:	Y	Internet:		Internet Service:		Financial Data:	VAR/Reseller:	Staff/Outsourcing:
Parts/Drives:							Satellite Srv./Equip.:	Specialty Services:

TYPES OF BUSINESS:
Digital Media Processing Hardware & Software

BRANDS/DIVISIONS/AFFILIATES:
SMP8650 (The)
SMP8640 (The)
SMP8630 (The)
Windeo
GF9450
ZW0301
SD3402 Z-Wave
CopperGate Communications, Ltd.

CONTACTS: Note: Officers with more than one job title may be intentionally listed here more than once.
Thinh Q. Tran, CEO
Thinh Q. Tran, Pres.
Thomas E. Gay III, CFO
Sal Cobar, VP-Worldwide Sales
Jacques Martinella, VP-Eng.
Thomas E. Gay III, Sec.
Sal Cobar, VP-Bus. Dev.
Kenneth A. Lowe, VP-Strategic Mktg.
David Baum, VP-Corp. Dev.
David Lynch, VP/Gen. Mgr.-Media Processor Group
Thinh Q. Tran, Chmn.
Kit Tsui, Managing Dir.-Sigma Designs Tech. Singapore

Phone: 408-262-9003	Fax: 408-957-9740
Toll-Free:	
Address: 1778 McCarthy Blvd., Milpitas, CA 95035 US	

GROWTH PLANS/SPECIAL FEATURES:
Sigma Designs, Inc. is a fabless semiconductor firm that provides system-on-chip (SoC) products used to deliver digital media, generally in the home. Its SoC products, combining semiconductors and software, are critical components of digital video/audio processing equipment, including Internet Protocol television (IPTV) set-top boxes, high definition (HD) DVD players, HDTVs and portable media players. Generally, the semiconductors function as the central processing unit (CPU) for the media system, providing HD video decoding for various compression standards, graphics acceleration, audio decoding and display control. The software provides control of the media processing and system security management. Specific products include Sigma's latest generation SoC media processor, the SMP8650, primarily serving the IPTV set-top box markets; the SMP8640, which serves the IPTV and Blu-ray markets; the SMP8630, which serves the IPTV, Blu-ray and HDTV markets; the Windeo, which uses an ultra wideband chip for IPTV, Blu-ray, HDTV and digital media applications; the GF9450 for use in home theater and high-end HDTV settings; and the ZW0301 for home security. The company's two biggest markets are IPTV set-top boxes and HD DVD players. Sigma serves customers in Asia, Europe and North America, including telecommunications carriers such as AT&T, Deutsche Telekom and Freebox; and consumer electronics producers such as Netgear, Sharp, and Sony. Customers outside North America generate approximately 97% of the firm's revenue. Recently, the firm acquired CopperGate Communications, Ltd., which develops multimedia home networking equipment for original equipment manufacturers (OEMs). In 2010, Sigma Designs released SD3402 Z-Wave, a chip that adds Z-Wave wireless control and status capabilities to set-top boxes, radio frequency remote controls and consumer electronic products; and the SMP8656 media processor SoC, which features enhanced security and 3D graphics. In April 2010, the firm established three new divisions: Media Processor Business Group, Home Connectivity Business Group and Worldwide Sales Group.

FINANCIALS: Sales and profits are in thousands of dollars—add 000 to get the full amount. 2010 Note: Financial information for 2010 was not available for all companies at press time.
2010 Sales: $206,083	2010 Profits: $2,455	U.S. Stock Ticker: SIGM
2009 Sales: $209,160	2009 Profits: $26,423	Int'l Ticker: Int'l Exchange:
2008 Sales: $221,206	2008 Profits: $70,209	Employees: 499
2007 Sales: $91,218	2007 Profits: $6,244	Fiscal Year Ends: 1/31
2006 Sales: $33,320	2006 Profits: $-1,561	Parent Company:

SALARIES/BENEFITS:
Pension Plan:	ESOP Stock Plan:	Profit Sharing:	Top Exec. Salary: $550,000	Bonus: $
Savings Plan: Y	Stock Purch. Plan: Y		Second Exec. Salary: $265,000	Bonus: $

OTHER THOUGHTS:
Apparent Women Officers or Directors: 1
Hot Spot for Advancement for Women/Minorities:

LOCATIONS: ("Y" = Yes)
West:	Southwest:	Midwest:	Southeast:	Northeast:	International:
Y					Y

SIGMATRON INTERNATIONAL INC

www.sigmatronintl.com

Industry Group Code: 334419 Ranks within this company's industry group: Sales: 22 Profits: 14

Hardware:		Software:	Telecommunications:	Electronic Publishing:	Equipment:		Specialty Services:	
Computers:		Consumer:	Local:	Online Service:	Telecom:		Consulting:	
Accessories:		Corporate:	Long Distance:	TV/Cable or Wireless:	Communication:		Contract Manufacturing:	Y
Network Equipment:		Telecom:	Cellular:	Games:	Distribution:		Processing:	
Chips/Circuits:	Y	Internet:	Internet Service:	Financial Data:	VAR/Reseller:		Staff/Outsourcing:	
Parts/Drives:	Y				Satellite Srv./Equip.:		Specialty Services:	Y

TYPES OF BUSINESS:

Contract Electronics Manufacturing
Printed Circuit Boards & Components
Design & Testing Services (ODM)
Logistics Services

BRANDS/DIVISIONS/AFFILIATES:

CONTACTS: Note: Officers with more than one job title may be intentionally listed here more than once.

Gary R. Fairhead, CEO
Gary R. Fairhead, Pres.
Linda K. Frauendorfer, CFO/Sec.
Stephen H. McNulty, VP-Sales
Thomas F. Rovtar, VP-IT
Yousef M. Heidari, VP-Eng.
Henry J. Underwood, Corp. Counsel
Donald G. Madsen, VP-Customer Service Hayward Oper.
Keith D. Wheaton, VP-Bus. Dev., West Coast
Linda K. Frauendorfer, VP-Finance/Treas.
Raj B. Upadhyaya, Exec. VP-West Coast Oper.
Daniel P. Camp, VP-Acuna Oper.
Curtis W. Campbell, VP-Sales, West Coast Oper.
Gregory A. Fairhead, Exec. VP/Assistant Sec.
John P. Chen, Chmn.
Hom-Ming Chang, VP-China Oper.
John P. Sheehan, VP/Dir.-Supply Chain/Assistant Sec.

Phone: 847-956-8000	Fax: 847-640-4528
Toll-Free: 800-700-9095	
Address: 2201 Landmeier Rd., Elk Grove Village, IL 60007 US	

GROWTH PLANS/SPECIAL FEATURES:

SigmaTron International, Inc. is a provider of electronic manufacturing services (EMS). The firm's EMS include printed circuit board assemblies and completely assembled (box-build) electronic products. The company is primarily a turnkey manufacturer, sourcing its own raw materials, though it also has some consignment operations where the customer provides the materials. SigmaTron International offers five basic kinds of services: supply chain management; assembly and manufacturing; manufacturing and related services; product testing; and warehousing and distribution. The supply chain management services include purchasing, managing, storing and delivering raw components of a customer's product. Raw materials are purchased from a select group of vendors with which the firm contracts on a customer-by-customer basis to provide greater flexibility. Assembly and manufacturing services are the firm's core business and include both automated and manual insertion of components onto raw printed circuit boards. The company offers both pin-through-hole and surface mount interconnect technologies at all of its manufacturing facilities. Manufacturing and related services include LCD/touch screen assembly services, parylene coating services, repair and rework services and DC-to-AC inverter manufacturing. Product testing offerings include both in-circuit and functional testing of assemblies and finished products. In-circuit testing verifies that all the necessary components of a product have been properly inserted, while functional testing ensures that the product is performing to the customer's specifications. The warehousing and distribution operations provide in-house warehousing, shipping and receiving and customer brokerage services through the firm's center in Del Rio, Texas. SigmaTron serves roughly 105 customers in the appliance, gaming, consumer electronics, industrial electronics, fitness, life sciences, semiconductor, telecommunications and automotive industries.

FINANCIALS: Sales and profits are in thousands of dollars—add 000 to get the full amount. 2010 Note: Financial information for 2010 was not available for all companies at press time.

2010 Sales: $122,476	2010 Profits: $2,245	U.S. Stock Ticker: SGMA
2009 Sales: $133,745	2009 Profits: $1,956	Int'l Ticker: Int'l Exchange:
2008 Sales: $167,811	2008 Profits: $-6,456	Employees: 1,700
2007 Sales: $165,909	2007 Profits: $1,698	Fiscal Year Ends: 4/30
2006 Sales: $124,786	2006 Profits: $1,882	Parent Company:

SALARIES/BENEFITS:

Pension Plan:	ESOP Stock Plan:	Profit Sharing:	Top Exec. Salary: $156,000	Bonus: $40,000
Savings Plan: Y	Stock Purch. Plan:		Second Exec. Salary: $153,600	Bonus: $40,000

OTHER THOUGHTS:

Apparent Women Officers or Directors: 1
Hot Spot for Advancement for Women/Minorities:

LOCATIONS: ("Y" = Yes)

West:	Southwest:	Midwest:	Southeast:	Northeast:	International:
Y		Y			Y

SILICON LABORATORIES INC

www.silabs.com

Industry Group Code: 33441 Ranks within this company's industry group: Sales: 41 Profits: 26

Hardware:		Software:		Telecommunications:		Electronic Publishing:		Equipment:		Specialty Services:	
Computers:		Consumer:		Local:		Online Service:		Telecom:		Consulting:	
Accessories:	Y	Corporate:		Long Distance:		TV/Cable or Wireless:		Communication:		Contract Manufacturing:	Y
Network Equipment:	Y	Telecom:		Cellular:		Games:		Distribution:		Processing:	
Chips/Circuits:	Y	Internet:		Internet Service:		Financial Data:		VAR/Reseller:		Staff/Outsourcing:	
Parts/Drives:								Satellite Srv./Equip.:		Specialty Services:	

TYPES OF BUSINESS:

Integrated Circuits
Mixed-Signal Integrated Circuits
Microcontrollers
Radio USB Products

BRANDS/DIVISIONS/AFFILIATES:

ISOmodem
ProSLIC
EZRadio
Silicon Clocks
Si3217x ProSLIC
Si84xx ISOpro
Si2170
Si85xx ac

CONTACTS: Note: Officers with more than one job title may be intentionally listed here more than once.

Necip Sayiner, CEO
Necip Sayiner, Pres.
William Bock, CFO/Sr. VP-Finance
Kurt Hoff, VP-Worldwide Sales
Diane Williams, VP-Human Resources
Everett G. Plante, Jr., CIO
Tyson Tuttle, CTO
Mark Thompson, VP/Gen. Mgr.-Embedded Mixed Signal Prod.
William Bock, Sr. VP-Admin.
Jon Ivester, Sr. VP-Worldwide Oper.
Mark Downing, VP-Bus. Dev. & Strategy
Paul Walsh, Chief Acct. Officer/VP
David Bresemann, VP-Broadcast Prod.
Carlos Garcia, VP-Wireline Prod.
Navdeep S. Sooch, Chmn.

Phone: 512-416-8500	Fax: 512-416-9669
Toll-Free: 877-444-3032	
Address: 400 W. Cesar Chavez, Austin, TX 78701 US	

GROWTH PLANS/SPECIAL FEATURES:

Silicon Laboratories, Inc. designs and develops proprietary, analog-intensive mixed-signal integrated circuits (ICs). Mixed-signal ICs are electronic components that convert real-world analog signals, such as sound and radio waves, into digital signals that electronic products are able to process. The firm's mixed-signal ICs are utilized as components in a variety of industries, including the medical, industrial, automotive, communications, consumer and power management markets. Silicon Laboratories' products use standard complementary metal oxide semiconductor technology to dramatically reduce the cost, size and system power requirements of devices that its customers sell to end-users. Its product applications include portable devices; motor control and sensors; satellite set top boxes; industrial monitoring and control; central office telephone equipment; FM/AM radios; customer premises equipment; test and measurement equipment; personal video recorders; and networking equipment. The company groups its products into the following categories: broad-based products, including EZRadio short-range wireless transceivers, 8-bit mixed-signal microcontrollers, ProSLIC subscriber line interface circuits, ISOmodem embedded modems and voice direct access arrangement (DAA); broadcast products, including video demodulators, broadcast radio receivers/ transmitters, satellite set-top box receivers and satellite radio tuners; mature products, including DSL analog front end ICs, silicon DAA for PC modems, optical physical layer transceivers and RF Synthesizers; and broad-based products, including clocks, recovery ICs/oscillators, isolators and current sensors. Silicon Laboratories' largest customers include Huawei, Philips, Samsung, Sony Ericsson, LG Electronics, 2Wire, Apple, Nokia, Thomson and Varian Medical Systems.. The company maintains sales offices in North America, Europe and Asia. Recently released Silicon products include the EZRadioPRO embedded wireless radio series; the Si84xx ISOpro series of digital isolators; the Si3217x ProSLIC family of single-channel foreign exchange station solutions; the Si2170 hybrid television tuner; and the Si85xx ac current sensor. In April 2010, the firm acquired microelectromechanical system developer Silicon Clocks.

FINANCIALS: Sales and profits are in thousands of dollars—add 000 to get the full amount. 2010 Note: Financial information for 2010 was not available for all companies at press time.

2010 Sales: $	2010 Profits: $	**U.S. Stock Ticker:** SLAB
2009 Sales: $441,020	2009 Profits: $73,092	**Int'l Ticker:** Int'l Exchange:
2008 Sales: $415,630	2008 Profits: $32,935	Employees: 736
2007 Sales: $337,461	2007 Profits: $204,836	Fiscal Year Ends: 12/31
2006 Sales: $288,156	2006 Profits: $31,158	Parent Company:

SALARIES/BENEFITS:

Pension Plan:	ESOP Stock Plan:	Profit Sharing:	Top Exec. Salary: $525,000	Bonus: $1,226,191
Savings Plan:	Stock Purch. Plan:		Second Exec. Salary: $312,000	Bonus: $564,747

OTHER THOUGHTS:

Apparent Women Officers or Directors: 1
Hot Spot for Advancement for Women/Minorities:

LOCATIONS: ("Y" = Yes)

West:	Southwest:	Midwest:	Southeast:	Northeast:	International:
Y	Y			Y	Y

SILICONWARE PRECISION INDUSTRIES CO LTD   www.spil.com.tw

Industry Group Code: 333295 Ranks within this company's industry group: Sales: 4 Profits: 1

Hardware:		Software:		Telecommunications:		Electronic Publishing:		Equipment:		Specialty Services:	
Computers:		Consumer:		Local:		Online Service:		Telecom:		Consulting:	
Accessories:		Corporate:		Long Distance:		TV/Cable or Wireless:		Communication:		Contract Manufacturing:	Y
Network Equipment:		Telecom:		Cellular:		Games:		Distribution:	Y	Processing:	
Chips/Circuits:	Y	Internet:		Internet Service:		Financial Data:		VAR/Reseller:		Staff/Outsourcing:	
Parts/Drives:	Y							Satellite Srv./Equip.:		Specialty Services:	Y

TYPES OF BUSINESS:
Integrated Circuit Assembly & Testing
Wafer Packages
Wafer Bumping
Flash Memory Cards
Drop-Shipping

BRANDS/DIVISIONS/AFFILIATES:
Flex-On-Cap
Flip Chip International LLC
Siliconware Technology (Suzhou) Limited

CONTACTS: *Note: Officers with more than one job title may be intentionally listed here more than once.*
Chi-Wen Tsai, CEO
Chi-Wen Tsai, Pres./Vice Chmn.
C.Y. Lin, Sr. VP-Mktg. & Sales Group
Carl Chen, VP-R&D Center
C.S Hsiao, VP-Eng. Center
Yen-Chun Chang, Sr. VP-Mfg. Group
Kun-Yi Chien, VP-Admin. Center
Eva Chen, Dir.-Financial Div.
Yu Hu Liu, VP-Chang Hua Site
Johnson Tai, VP-Quality & Reliability
Michael Chang, VP-Hsinchu Branch
Kuo-Jui Tai, VP
Bough Lin, Chmn.
Jack Chen, VP-North American Customer Service & Europe Sales

Phone: 886-4-2534-1525	Fax: 886-4-2534-2025
Toll-Free: 888-215-8632	
Address: No. 123, Sec. 3, Da Fong Rd., Tan Tzu, Taichung, 427 Taiwan	

GROWTH PLANS/SPECIAL FEATURES:

Siliconware Precision Industries Co., Ltd. (SPIL) is a supplier of integrated circuits (ICs) and semiconductor packaging and testing services to the consumer electronics and communications industries. It has four manufacturing facilities in Taiwan and a fifth in Suzhou, China, from which it provides consultation; packaging foundry services; assembly; wafer sorting and bumping; final testing; burn-in; and drop shipping. The Suzhou operations are overseen by subsidiary Siliconware Technology (Suzhou) Limited. The company also maintains customer support offices in China, Japan, Germany and the U.S. SPIL's wafer packaging capabilities encompass substrate packages, including ball grid array and system-in-packages (incorporating multiple semiconductor chips), as well as lead-frame packages and flip-chip ball grid array packages, the latter based on proprietary Flex-On-Cap wafer bumping technologies licensed from Flip Chip International, LLC. Testing services provided by SPIL include wafer probing, which involves sorting the processed wafers for defects; final testing for both logic and mixed signal packages; system-level testing, which evaluates the chip's functionality in a motherboard environment; dynamic burn-in testing to screen out faulty devices; laser repair and trimming, to modify device connection structure for specific product applications; and others. Assembly and packaging services generate approximately 87% of the firm's revenues, with testing and other services generating the remaining 13%. Geographically, the U.S. and Canada generate 50% of the company's sales; Taiwan, 34%; while the remaining 16% comes from other countries, principally Singapore, Japan, Germany and Korea.

SPIL provides its employees with health, life and disability insurance; a profit-sharing plan; an onsite recreation center and dining room; and a variety of employee clubs, among other benefits.

FINANCIALS: Sales and profits are in thousands of dollars—add 000 to get the full amount. 2010 Note: Financial information for 2010 was not available for all companies at press time.

2010 Sales: $	2010 Profits: $	U.S. Stock Ticker: SPIL
2009 Sales: $1,855,856	2009 Profits: $275,112	Int'l Ticker: 2325 Int'l Exchange: Taipei-TPE
2008 Sales: $1,904,851	2008 Profits: $192,721	Employees:
2007 Sales: $2,040,600	2007 Profits: $403,900	Fiscal Year Ends: 12/31
2006 Sales: $1,752,900	2006 Profits: $409,000	Parent Company:

SALARIES/BENEFITS:
Pension Plan:	ESOP Stock Plan:	Profit Sharing: Y	Top Exec. Salary: $	Bonus: $
Savings Plan:	Stock Purch. Plan:		Second Exec. Salary: $	Bonus: $

OTHER THOUGHTS:
Apparent Women Officers or Directors: 1
Hot Spot for Advancement for Women/Minorities:

LOCATIONS: ("Y" = Yes)
West:	Southwest:	Midwest:	Southeast:	Northeast:	International:
Y	Y				Y

SIMPLO TECHNOLOGY CO LTD

www.simplo.com.tw

Industry Group Code: 33591 Ranks within this company's industry group: Sales: Profits:

Hardware:		Software:	Telecommunications:	Electronic Publishing:	Equipment:	Specialty Services:	
Computers:		Consumer:	Local:	Online Service:	Telecom:	Consulting:	
Accessories:	Y	Corporate:	Long Distance:	TV/Cable or Wireless:	Communication:	Contract Manufacturing:	Y
Network Equipment:		Telecom:	Cellular:	Games:	Distribution:	Processing:	
Chips/Circuits:		Internet:	Internet Service:	Financial Data:	VAR/Reseller:	Staff/Outsourcing:	
Parts/Drives:					Satellite Srv./Equip.:	Specialty Services:	

TYPES OF BUSINESS:
Lithium Battery Manufacturing

BRANDS/DIVISIONS/AFFILIATES:

GROWTH PLANS/SPECIAL FEATURES:

Simplo Technology Co., Ltd. is a manufacturer and distributor of lithium-ion battery packs. Its products include battery packs for consumer electronics such as notebook computers, PDAs (personal digital assistants), mobile phones and power wheelchairs, as well as for other specialized applications. Additional products manufactured by the firm include protection circuit boards for lithium-ion battery packs, smart charge units for smart battery packs and battery pack automatic manufacturing equipment. The Simplo markets its technology to prominent technology firms like Acer, Dell, Hewlett-Packard, Apple, LG and MSI. The company also provides technical support and design services for lithium-ion battery packs.

CONTACTS: Note: Officers with more than one job title may be intentionally listed here more than once.
Fuxiang Song, Gen. Mgr.
Liman Zhou, Mgr.-Finance
Zongcheng Cai, Deputy Gen. Mgr.-R&D
Fuzhi Xie, Deputy Gen. Mgr.-Info. & Materials
Zhaofeng Li, Deputy Gen. Mgr.-Tech. Dev.
Huimin Ding, Deputy Gen. Mgr.-Admin.
Jianguo Yan, Deputy Gen. Mgr.-Bus.
Zhiyun Song, Deputy Gen. Mgr.-Optoelectronics
Dayun Liu, Deputy Gen. Mgr.
Xiude Zhang, Deputy Gen. Mgr.-Quality Assurance
Fuxiang Song, Chmn.

Phone: 886-3-5695920	Fax: 886-3-5695931
Toll-Free:	
Address: No. 471, Section 2, Pa Teh Rd., Hu Kou Township, Hsin Chu Hsien, Taiwan	

FINANCIALS: Sales and profits are in thousands of dollars—add 000 to get the full amount. 2010 Note: Financial information for 2010 was not available for all companies at press time.

2010 Sales: $	2010 Profits: $	U.S. Stock Ticker: SPLOF.PK
2009 Sales: $	2009 Profits: $	Int'l Ticker: 6121 Int'l Exchange: Taipei-TPE
2008 Sales: $	2008 Profits: $	Employees:
2007 Sales: $	2007 Profits: $	Fiscal Year Ends:
2006 Sales: $	2006 Profits: $	Parent Company:

SALARIES/BENEFITS:

Pension Plan:	ESOP Stock Plan:	Profit Sharing:	Top Exec. Salary: $	Bonus: $
Savings Plan:	Stock Purch. Plan:		Second Exec. Salary: $	Bonus: $

OTHER THOUGHTS:
Apparent Women Officers or Directors:
Hot Spot for Advancement for Women/Minorities:

LOCATIONS: ("Y" = Yes)

West:	Southwest:	Midwest:	Southeast:	Northeast:	International:
					Y

SIMTROL INC

www.simtrol.com

Industry Group Code: 511210F Ranks within this company's industry group: Sales: 6 Profits: 2

Hardware:	Software:		Telecommunications:	Electronic Publishing:	Equipment:	Specialty Services:
Computers:	Consumer:		Local:	Online Service:	Telecom:	Consulting:
Accessories:	Corporate:	Y	Long Distance:	TV/Cable or Wireless:	Communication:	Contract Manufacturing:
Network Equipment:	Telecom:		Cellular:	Games:	Distribution:	Processing:
Chips/Circuits:	Internet:		Internet Service:	Financial Data:	VAR/Reseller:	Staff/Outsourcing:
Parts/Drives:					Satellite Srv./Equip.:	Specialty Services:

TYPES OF BUSINESS:

Software-Videoconferencing
Software-Judicial Arraignment
Software-Emergency Response

BRANDS/DIVISIONS/AFFILIATES:

Justice Digital Solutions
Device Manager
Curiax Visitor
Arraigner

CONTACTS: Note: Officers with more than one job title may be intentionally listed here more than once.

Oliver M. Cooper III, CEO
Oliver M. Cooper III, Pres.
Stephen N. Samp, CFO
Stephen N. Samp, Sec.
Dallas S. Clement, Chmn.

Phone: 678-533-1200	Fax: 770-441-1823
Toll-Free: 800-423-0769	
Address: 520 Guthridge Ct., Ste. 250, Norcross, GA 30092 US	

GROWTH PLANS/SPECIAL FEATURES:

Simtrol, Inc. develops, markets and supports software-based audiovisual control systems and videoconferencing products that operate on PC platforms. The firm's Device Management Platform supports Device Manager, its principal product, which streamlines the management of devices through management, monitoring and control; diagnostics and troubleshooting; network asset administration; reporting and predictive analysis; document management and workflow; and energy efficient management services. This system is designed to manage otherwise incompatible electronic devices across three target markets: Education, government and corporate. Simtrol offers control software for educational devices in the 21st century classroom such as interactive whiteboards, computers, projectors, DVD players and digital displays. Through its subsidiary, Justice Digital Solutions, it develops and markets its Curiax and Arraigner software for government and law enforcement agencies. The company's Curiax Video Visitation software allows correctional facilities to effectively schedule and manage visitations, observe a live grid of video visitations, record sessions, send messages to participants and start and stop visitation sessions automatically. Simtrol's Arraigner pre-trial process management software is an integrated multipoint videoconferencing, digital document management, workflow and device control solution that allows judges, prosecutors and other law enforcement officials to efficiently manage the criminal justice process from inception through pre-trial proceedings. Products for the corporate market include digital signage, a communications platform for content creation, scheduling and distribution across electronic devices and digital kiosks, primarily for the retail and hospitality industries.

FINANCIALS: Sales and profits are in thousands of dollars—add 000 to get the full amount. 2010 Note: Financial information for 2010 was not available for all companies at press time.

		U.S. Stock Ticker: SMRL
2010 Sales: $	2010 Profits: $	Int'l Ticker: Int'l Exchange:
2009 Sales: $ 591	2009 Profits: $-2,674	Employees: 11
2008 Sales: $ 295	2008 Profits: $-4,880	Fiscal Year Ends: 12/31
2007 Sales: $ 191	2007 Profits: $-4,905	Parent Company:
2006 Sales: $ 225	2006 Profits: $-1,462	

SALARIES/BENEFITS:

Pension Plan:	ESOP Stock Plan:	Profit Sharing:	Top Exec. Salary: $126,600	Bonus: $
Savings Plan:	Stock Purch. Plan:		Second Exec. Salary: $105,881	Bonus: $

OTHER THOUGHTS:

Apparent Women Officers or Directors:
Hot Spot for Advancement for Women/Minorities:

LOCATIONS: ("Y" = Yes)

West:	Southwest:	Midwest:	Southeast:	Northeast:	International:
			Y		

Note: Financial information, benefits and other data can change quickly and may vary from those stated here.

SKILLSOFT PLC

www.skillsoft.com

Industry Group Code: 511210P Ranks within this company's industry group: Sales: 1 Profits: 1

Hardware:	Software:		Telecommunications:	Electronic Publishing:		Equipment:	Specialty Services:	
Computers:	Consumer:	Y	Local:	Online Service:	Y	Telecom:	Consulting:	
Accessories:	Corporate:	Y	Long Distance:	TV/Cable or Wireless:		Communication:	Contract Manufacturing:	
Network Equipment:	Telecom:		Cellular:	Games:		Distribution:	Processing:	
Chips/Circuits:	Internet:		Internet Service:	Financial Data:		VAR/Reseller:	Staff/Outsourcing:	
Parts/Drives:						Satellite Srv./Equip.:	Specialty Services:	Y

TYPES OF BUSINESS:

Software-Educational
Online Courses & Seminars
Online Mentoring Program

BRANDS/DIVISIONS/AFFILIATES:

Books24x7, Inc.
GoTrain Corp.
Referenceware
SkillPort
Roleplay
Search-and-Learn
NetUniversity
Accelerated Path

CONTACTS: Note: Officers with more than one job title may be intentionally listed here more than once.

Chuck Moran, CEO
Jerry Nine, COO
Chuck Moran, Pres.
Thomas McDonald, CFO
Lee Ritze, Sr. VP-Mktg.
Mark Townsend, Exec. VP-Tech.
Tom McDonald, Exec. VP-Oper.
John Ambrose, Sr. VP-Corp. Dev., Strategy & Emerging Bus.
Colm Darcy, Exec. VP-Content Dev.
Kevin Young, VP/Managing Dir.-EMEA
Glenn Nott, VP/Managing Dir.-Asia Pacific

Phone: 603-324-3000	Fax: 603-324-3009
Toll-Free: 877-545-5763	
Address: 107 Northeastern Blvd., Nashua, NH 03062 US	

GROWTH PLANS/SPECIAL FEATURES:

SkillSoft plc provides comprehensive, integrated e-learning software and services which help businesses deploy knowledge across their extended enterprise of employees, customers, suppliers, distributors and other business partners. SkillSoft offers courseware, simulations, online books, reference materials and online test preparation. It focuses on a variety of professional effectiveness, IT and business topics representing the critical skills required of employees in differing work environments. The company's platform allows organizations to customize their e-learning environment to meet corporate objectives and to efficiently train their employees and business partners. SkillSoft's products include Business Skill Library and IT SkillSoft Corp. provides comprehensive, integrated e-learning software and services which help businesses deploy knowledge across their entire organization of employees, customers, suppliers, distributors and other business partners. SkillSoft offers courseware, simulations, online books, reference materials and online test preparation. It focuses on a variety of professional effectiveness, IT and business topics representing the critical skills required of employees in differing work environments. The company's platform allows organizations to customize their e-learning environment to meet corporate objectives and to efficiently train their employees and business partners. SkillSoft's products include Business Skill Library and IT Skills and Certification Library; subsidiary Books24x7, Inc. offers ITPro, BusinessPro and FinancePro; and subsidiary GoTrain Corp. offers health and safety compliance courseware. Additional offerings include the Referenceware brand, a service-mark of Books24x7, as are SkillPort and Search-and-Learn all which are trademarked by SkillSoft. Lastly, the firm's SkillSoft Dialogue is a virtual classroom solution for creating and delivering effective live and on-demand learning. SkillSoft has partnered with leaders in learning management, such as Oracle, Plateau and SumTotal, to insure that SkillSoft can be integrated with those systems for joint customers.

Employees are offered medical, dental and vision insurance; flexible spending accounts; an employee assistance program; short-and long-term disability coverage; life insurance; a 401(k) plan; an employee stock purchase program; and tuition reimbursement.

FINANCIALS: Sales and profits are in thousands of dollars—add 000 to get the full amount. 2010 Note: Financial information for 2010 was not available for all companies at press time.

2010 Sales: $314,968	2010 Profits: $71,368	**U.S. Stock Ticker: SKIL**
2009 Sales: $328,494	2009 Profits: $50,789	**Int'l Ticker:** Int'l Exchange:
2008 Sales: $281,223	2008 Profits: $59,998	Employees: 1,085
2007 Sales: $225,172	2007 Profits: $24,153	Fiscal Year Ends: 1/31
2006 Sales: $215,567	2006 Profits: $35,215	Parent Company:

SALARIES/BENEFITS:

Pension Plan:	ESOP Stock Plan:	Profit Sharing:	Top Exec. Salary: $372,000	Bonus: $590,806
Savings Plan: Y	Stock Purch. Plan:		Second Exec. Salary: $282,000	Bonus: $281,648

OTHER THOUGHTS:

Apparent Women Officers or Directors:
Hot Spot for Advancement for Women/Minorities:

LOCATIONS: ("Y" = Yes)

West:	Southwest:	Midwest:	Southeast:	Northeast:	International:
				Y	Y

SKYWORKS SOLUTIONS INC

www.skyworksinc.com

Industry Group Code: 33441 Ranks within this company's industry group: Sales: 35 Profits: 21

Hardware:		Software:		Telecommunications:		Electronic Publishing:		Equipment:		Specialty Services:	
Computers:		Consumer:		Local:		Online Service:		Telecom:	Y	Consulting:	
Accessories:		Corporate:		Long Distance:		TV/Cable or Wireless:		Communication:	Y	Contract Manufacturing:	
Network Equipment:		Telecom:		Cellular:		Games:		Distribution:		Processing:	
Chips/Circuits:	Y	Internet:		Internet Service:		Financial Data:		VAR/Reseller:		Staff/Outsourcing:	
Parts/Drives:								Satellite Srv./Equip.:		Specialty Services:	

TYPES OF BUSINESS:

Semiconductor Manufacturing
Radio Frequency & Cellular Systems

BRANDS/DIVISIONS/AFFILIATES:

Intera
Breakthrough Simplicity
Trans-Tech
Skyworks

CONTACTS: Note: Officers with more than one job title may be intentionally listed here more than once.

David J. Aldrich, CEO
David J. Aldrich, Pres.
Donald W. Palette, CFO/VP
Liam K. Griffin, VP-Mktg. & Sales
George M. LeVan, VP-Human Resources
Mark V.B. Tremallo, General Counsel/VP/Sec.
Bruce J. Freyman, VP-Worldwide Oper.
Thomas S. Schiller, VP-Corp. Dev.
David C. Stasey, VP-Analog Components
Nien-Tsu Shen, VP-Quality
Gregory L. Waters, Exec. VP/Gen. Mgr.-Front-End Solutions
David J. McLachlan, Chmn.

Phone: 781-376-3000	Fax:
Toll-Free:	
Address: 20 Sylvan Rd., Woburn, MA 01801 US	

GROWTH PLANS/SPECIAL FEATURES:

Skyworks Solutions, Inc. is a creator of high reliability analog and mixed signal semiconductors. The company offers diverse standard and custom linear products supporting automotive, broadband, cellular infrastructure, energy management, industrial, medical, military and cellular handset applications. The firm's portfolio includes amplifiers, attenuators, detectors, diodes, directional couplers, front-end modules, hybrids, infrastructure RF subsystems, mixers/demodulators, phase shifters, receivers, switchers and technical ceramics. Skyworks' products revolve around two broad markets: cellular handsets and analog semiconductors. Its handset products include customizes power amplifiers that are found in many cellular devices, such as smart phones, with products that enable CDMA, EDGE, 3G and 4G reception. The firm also offers more than 2,500 different catalog and custom linear products to its non-handset customer base. Skyworks's brands include Intera, Skyworks, Breakthrough Simplicity, and Trans-Tech. The firm has design, engineering, manufacturing, marketing, sales and service facilities throughout North America, Europe and the Asia-Pacific region. The company's products are primarily sold through a direct sales force.

The firm offers its employees medical, dental and vision insurance; life insurance; disability coverage; flexible spending accounts; an education assistance program; a 401(k) plan; a 529 college savings program; and an employee stock purchase plan.

FINANCIALS: Sales and profits are in thousands of dollars—add 000 to get the full amount. 2010 Note: Financial information for 2010 was not available for all companies at press time.

2010 Sales: $1,071,849	2010 Profits: $137,294	**U.S. Stock Ticker: SWKS**
2009 Sales: $802,577	2009 Profits: $94,983	**Int'l Ticker:** Int'l Exchange:
2008 Sales: $860,017	2008 Profits: $111,006	Employees: 3,700
2007 Sales: $741,744	2007 Profits: $57,650	Fiscal Year Ends: 9/30
2006 Sales: $773,750	2006 Profits: $-88,152	Parent Company:

SALARIES/BENEFITS:

Pension Plan:	ESOP Stock Plan: Y	Profit Sharing:	Top Exec. Salary: $598,077	Bonus: $653,750
Savings Plan: Y	Stock Purch. Plan:		Second Exec. Salary: $378,846	Bonus: $270,085

OTHER THOUGHTS:

Apparent Women Officers or Directors: 4
Hot Spot for Advancement for Women/Minorities: Y

LOCATIONS: ("Y" = Yes)

West:	Southwest:	Midwest:	Southeast:	Northeast:	International:
Y		Y		Y	Y

SMART MODULAR TECHNOLOGIES INC

www.smartm.com

Industry Group Code: 334111 Ranks within this company's industry group: Sales: 25 Profits: 18

Hardware:	Software:	Telecommunications:	Electronic Publishing:	Equipment:	Specialty Services:
Computers:	Consumer:	Local:	Online Service:	Telecom:	Consulting:
Accessories:	Corporate:	Long Distance:	TV/Cable or Wireless:	Communication:	Contract Manufacturing:
Network Equipment:	Telecom:	Cellular:	Games:	Distribution:	Processing:
Chips/Circuits: Y	Internet:	Internet Service:	Financial Data:	VAR/Reseller:	Staff/Outsourcing:
Parts/Drives: Y				Satellite Srv./Equip.:	Specialty Services: Y

TYPES OF BUSINESS:

Computer Hardware, Manufacturing
Logistics Services
Design Services

BRANDS/DIVISIONS/AFFILIATES:

Xceed

CONTACTS: Note: Officers with more than one job title may be intentionally listed here more than once.

Iain MacKenzie, CEO
Iain MacKenzie, Pres.
Barry Zwarenstein, CFO/Sr. VP
Wayne Eisenberg, VP-Worldwide Sales
Jack Moyer, VP-Human Resources
Alan Gulachenski, VP-Storage Prod. Dev.
Mike Rubino, VP-Eng.
Bruce Goldberg, General Counsel/VP/Chief Compliance Officer
Alan Marten, Sr. VP/Gen. Mgr.-Memory Bus. Unit
John Scaramuzzo, Sr. VP/Gen. Mgr.-Storage Bus. Unit
Frank Perezalonso, VP/Gen. Mgr.-SSD Defense Prod. Line
Ajay Shah, Chmn.
Kiwan Kim, Pres., SMART Brazil/Sr. VP-Emerging Markets

Phone: 510-623-1231	Fax: 510-623-1434
Toll-Free:	
Address: 39870 Eureka Dr., Newark, CA 94560 US	

GROWTH PLANS/SPECIAL FEATURES:

SMART Modular Technologies, Inc. (SMART) is an independent designer, manufacturer and supplier of value added subsystems to original equipment manufacturers (OEMs). The company offers an array of standard and custom products to such OEMs as Cisco Systems; Dell; and Hewlett-Packard, which together accounted for over 50% of the company's 2010 net sales. Its products fall into two principal categories: Memory products and services and solid state storage products. Memory products include Dynamic Random Access Memory (DRAM) modules, flash memory cards and modules; Static Random Access Memory (SRAM)-based single in-line memory modules (SIMMs), dual in-line memory modules (DIMMs) and small outline dual in-line memory modules (SO-DIMMs). It also offers product-related logistics and supply chain services. Solid state storage products include solid state drives (SSDs) and embedded storage products. SSDs are offered to multiple markets under the Xceed brand name and range in capacity from 4GB to 400GB. Embedded storage products, such as flash memory cards and modules, are manufactured in a variety of form factors and capacities, ranging from CompactFlash, PC Card and Key Drives to Embedded USB (EUSB), iSATA Drives and uSATA Drives, among other form factors. SMART has manufacturing facilities in the U.S., Malaysia, Brazil and Puerto Rico. Historically, the firm offered embedded computing products and TFT-LCD display products, which it ceased to manufacture in 2010 to focus on core memory and data storage products.

The firm offers its employees health benefits as well as a 401(k) plan.

FINANCIALS: Sales and profits are in thousands of dollars—add 000 to get the full amount. 2010 Note: Financial information for 2010 was not available for all companies at press time.

2010 Sales: $703,090	2010 Profits: $52,571	**U.S. Stock Ticker:** SMOD
2009 Sales: $441,317	2009 Profits: $-11,403	**Int'l Ticker:** Int'l Exchange:
2008 Sales: $670,151	2008 Profits: $8,974	Employees: 1,223
2007 Sales: $844,627	2007 Profits: $57,733	Fiscal Year Ends: 8/31
2006 Sales: $727,206	2006 Profits: $32,309	Parent Company:

SALARIES/BENEFITS:

Pension Plan:	ESOP Stock Plan:	Profit Sharing:	Top Exec. Salary: $416,770	Bonus: $675,000
Savings Plan: Y	Stock Purch. Plan:		Second Exec. Salary: $335,769	Bonus: $368,040

OTHER THOUGHTS:

Apparent Women Officers or Directors: 1
Hot Spot for Advancement for Women/Minorities:

LOCATIONS: ("Y" = Yes)

West:	Southwest:	Midwest:	Southeast:	Northeast:	International:
Y	Y			Y	Y

SMTC CORP

www.smtc.com

Industry Group Code: 334419 Ranks within this company's industry group: Sales: 21 Profits: 16

Hardware:		Software:		Telecommunications:	Electronic Publishing:	Equipment:	Specialty Services:
Computers:		Consumer:		Local:	Online Service:	Telecom:	Consulting:
Accessories:		Corporate:		Long Distance:	TV/Cable or Wireless:	Communication:	Contract Manufacturing:
Network Equipment:		Telecom:		Cellular:	Games:	Distribution:	Processing:
Chips/Circuits:		Internet:		Internet Service:	Financial Data:	VAR/Reseller:	Staff/Outsourcing:
Parts/Drives:	Y					Satellite Srv./Equip.:	Specialty Services:

TYPES OF BUSINESS:

Contract Electronics Manufacturing

BRANDS/DIVISIONS/AFFILIATES:

SMTC China
SMTC de Chihuahua S.A. de C.V.
SMTC Manufacturing Corporation of California
SMTC Manufacturing Corporation of Wisconsin
SMTC Ontario

CONTACTS: Note: Officers with more than one job title may be intentionally listed here more than once.

John Caldwell, CEO
John Caldwell, Pres.
Jane Todd, CFO
Betsy Smith, VP-Human Resources
Don Simpson, Sr. VP-Eng.
Don Simpson, Sr. VP-Mfg.
Steve Hoffrogge, Sr. VP-Bus. Dev.
Jane Todd, Sr. VP-Finance
Wayne McLeod, Chmn.
Paul Blom, Sr. VP-Supply Chain

Phone: 905-479-1810	Fax: 905-479-1877
Toll-Free:	
Address: 635 Hood Rd., Markham, ON L3R 4N6 Canada	

GROWTH PLANS/SPECIAL FEATURES:

SMTC Corp., based in Toronto, Canada, is a mid-tier provider of end-to-end electronics manufacturing services. These services include product design, sustained engineering services, printed circuit board assembly, production, enclosure fabrication, systems integration, comprehensive testing services, configuration to order and end customer fulfillment. The company's maintains a number of facilities in the U.S., Canada, Mexico and China, totaling approximately 400,000 square feet with over 50 manufacturing and assembly lines. The firm's services extend over the entire electronic product lifecycle, from the development and introduction of new products through to growth, maturity and end-of-life phases. SMTC offers fully integrated contract manufacturing services to global original equipment manufacturers (OEMs) and technology companies, primarily within the industrial; networking and computing; and communications market segments. The company works through its T.O.P.S. (Team-Oriented Production System) business model, which enables SMTC to create individual applications through dedicated product teams and unique manufacturing units assigned to each individual customer. The firm's assembly locations are all designed according to the same model, employing the same basic equipment and software systems, allowing clients to transfer production easily to the most suitable facility. The Ontario site serves as the company's primary technical center, with particular emphasis on assisting current and new customers to develop, prototype and bring new products to full production. This site also continues to manufacture lower volume, higher complexity printed circuit board assemblies. The company's Chinese operations offers box build, assembly, testing, final product integration, and worldwide customer logistics through 40,000 square feet of facility space. Its Mexico facility services as the largest assembly operation. SMTC's facility in San Jose, California, specializes in printed board circuit board assemblies, system integration/configuration and other related activities. Its facility in Appleton, Wisconsin, serves as a technical center for product design and development. In mid-2009, SMTC closed its manufacturing facility in Boston, Massachusetts.

FINANCIALS: Sales and profits are in thousands of dollars—add 000 to get the full amount. 2010 Note: Financial information for 2010 was not available for all companies at press time.

2010 Sales: $	2010 Profits: $	**U.S. Stock Ticker: SMTX**
2009 Sales: $179,509	2009 Profits: $-3,595	**Int'l Ticker: SMX** Int'l Exchange: Toronto-TSX
2008 Sales: $206,879	2008 Profits: $-5,895	Employees: 1,000
2007 Sales: $200,977	2007 Profits: $2,672	Fiscal Year Ends: 12/31
2006 Sales: $262,782	2006 Profits: $10,461	Parent Company:

SALARIES/BENEFITS:

Pension Plan:	ESOP Stock Plan:	Profit Sharing:	Top Exec. Salary: $501,003	Bonus: $
Savings Plan:	Stock Purch. Plan:		Second Exec. Salary: $257,538	Bonus: $

OTHER THOUGHTS:

Apparent Women Officers or Directors: 2
Hot Spot for Advancement for Women/Minorities: Y

LOCATIONS: ("Y" = Yes)

West:	Southwest:	Midwest:	Southeast:	Northeast:	International:
Y		Y			Y

SOFTWARE AG

www.softwareag.com

Industry Group Code: 5112 Ranks within this company's industry group: Sales: 1 Profits: 1

Hardware:	Software:		Telecommunications:	Electronic Publishing:	Equipment:	Specialty Services:
Computers:	Consumer:		Local:	Online Service:	Telecom:	Consulting:
Accessories:	Corporate:	Y	Long Distance:	TV/Cable or Wireless:	Communication:	Contract Manufacturing:
Network Equipment:	Telecom:		Cellular:	Games:	Distribution:	Processing:
Chips/Circuits:	Internet:		Internet Service:	Financial Data:	VAR/Reseller:	Staff/Outsourcing:
Parts/Drives:					Satellite Srv./Equip.:	Specialty Services:

TYPES OF BUSINESS:
Business Infrastructure Software

BRANDS/DIVISIONS/AFFILIATES:
WebMethods
CentraSite
Adabas
Natural
Tamino
ApplinX
Data Foundations, Inc.
IDS Sheer AG

CONTACTS: *Note: Officers with more than one job title may be intentionally listed here more than once.*
Karl-Heinz Streibich, CEO
Arnd Zinnhardt, CFO
Wolfram Jost, CTO
Kamyar Niroumand, COO-Germany, Austria & Switzerland
Mark Edwards, CEO-Americas, Asia Pacific & Japan
Ivo Totev, Chief Service Officer
Andreas Bereczky, Chmn.
David Broadbent, COO-EMEA

Phone: 49-6151-92-3100	Fax: 49-6151-92-3223
Toll-Free:	
Address: Uhlandstrasse 9, Darmstadt, 64297 Germany	

GROWTH PLANS/SPECIAL FEATURES:

Software AG is an enterprise IT systems enhancement software company with offices in 50 countries worldwide. Following the acquisition and integration of its rival, webMethods, Inc., the combined company has over 4,000 customers spread across 70 countries. The firm operates through three business divisions: a product suite called webMethods, the Enterprise Transactions Systems (ETS) business line and the Enterprise Process Innovation business line. Products in the webMethods suite include CentraSite, an IT monitoring and control system; Tamino, a multi-channel XML information delivery system; ApplinX, a product designed to modernize older systems without rewriting code; and EntireX, a systems interoperability enhancement program. The Enterprise Transactions Systems (ETS) business line includes Adabas, a database management system, and Natural, a user friendly programming language. The Enterprise Process Innovation Platform business line includes the ARIS platform, an integrated product portfolio that offers business process strategy, analysis, design, implementation and control. Software AG offers products for the following industries and sectors: Banking, Energy & Utilities, Government, Insurance, Manufacturing, Retail and Telecommunications. In October 2010, the firm acquired U.S. company Data Foundations, Inc., utilizing its Master Data Management (MDM) software to enhance its webMethods suite. In December of the same year, the company merged with IDS Sheer AG.

FINANCIALS: Sales and profits are in thousands of dollars—add 000 to get the full amount. 2010 Note: Financial information for 2010 was not available for all companies at press time.

2010 Sales: $	2010 Profits: $	**U.S. Stock Ticker:**
2009 Sales: $1,140,130	2009 Profits: $189,710	**Int'l Ticker: SOWG** Int'l Exchange: Frankfurt-Euronext
2008 Sales: $1,045,120	2008 Profits: $168,090	Employees: 3,526
2007 Sales: $978,600	2007 Profits: $140,500	Fiscal Year Ends: 12/31
2006 Sales: $762,000	2006 Profits: $115,900	Parent Company:

SALARIES/BENEFITS:

Pension Plan:	ESOP Stock Plan:	Profit Sharing:	Top Exec. Salary: $	Bonus: $
Savings Plan:	Stock Purch. Plan:		Second Exec. Salary: $	Bonus: $

OTHER THOUGHTS:
Apparent Women Officers or Directors: 1
Hot Spot for Advancement for Women/Minorities:

LOCATIONS: ("Y" = Yes)

West:	Southwest:	Midwest:	Southeast:	Northeast:	International:
Y	Y		Y	Y	Y

SOLARWINDS

www.solarwinds.com

Industry Group Code: 511210B Ranks within this company's industry group: Sales: 9 Profits: 3

Hardware:	Software:		Telecommunications:		Electronic Publishing:	Equipment:	Specialty Services:
Computers:	Consumer:		Local:		Online Service:	Telecom:	Consulting:
Accessories:	Corporate:	Y	Long Distance:		TV/Cable or Wireless:	Communication:	Contract Manufacturing:
Network Equipment:	Telecom:		Cellular:		Games:	Distribution:	Processing:
Chips/Circuits:	Internet:	Y	Internet Service:		Financial Data:	VAR/Reseller:	Staff/Outsourcing:
Parts/Drives:						Satellite Srv./Equip.:	Specialty Services:

TYPES OF BUSINESS:
Network Management Software

BRANDS/DIVISIONS/AFFILIATES:
ipMonitor
Orion Network Performance Monitor
Orion Network Configuration Manager
Kiwi Syslog Server
Kiwi CatTools
LANsurveyor
LANsurveyor Express

CONTACTS:
Note: Officers with more than one job title may be intentionally listed here more than once.
Kevin B. Thompson, CEO
Kevin B. Thompson, Pres.
Michael J. Berry, CFO
Rita J. Selvaggi, Sr. VP-Mktg.
Garry D. Strop, VP-Human Resources
Doug G. Hibbard, Sr. VP-Eng.
Bryan A. Sims, General Counsel/Sec./VP
Jason Ream, VP-Corp. & Bus. Dev.
Jason Ream, VP-Investor Rel.
J. Barton Kalsu, VP-Finance
Paul Strelzick, Sr. VP-Worldwide Sales
David Owens, VP-Finance & Oper., EMEA

Phone: 512-682-9300	**Fax:** 512-682-9301
Toll-Free: 866-530-8100	
Address: 3711 S. MoPac Expressway, Bldg. 2, Austin, TX 78746 US	

GROWTH PLANS/SPECIAL FEATURES:
SolarWinds is a provider of enterprise-class network management software. The firm's software offerings range from individual software tools to more comprehensive software products designed to serve networks and implementations of varying sizes and levels of complexity, ranging from a single device to over 100,000 installed devices. SolarWinds' products fall under four broad categories: enterprise-class network management, entry level network monitoring, software for engineers and free software. SolarWinds' enterprise-class network management software consists of its Orion line of products. These include the firm's flagship products, the Orion Network Performance Monitor and Orion Network Configuration Manager, formerly known as Cirrus Configuration Manager. The company's entry-level product is ipMonitor, which delivers basic up/down monitoring for network devices and servers. The firm's software for engineers includes Engineer's Toolset, Standard Toolset, Kiwi Syslog Server, Kiwi CatTools, LANsurveyor and LANsurveyor Express. SolarWinds' free tools for network monitoring include a network configuration generator, an IP address tracker, an exchange monitor and a TFTP server, among others. The firm's products can be downloaded directly from its web site, SolarWinds.com and installed and configured by end-users in a matter of hours. In December 2010, the company established a headquarters for its Asia-Pacific operations in Brisbane, Australia.

FINANCIALS:
Sales and profits are in thousands of dollars—add 000 to get the full amount. 2010 Note: Financial information for 2010 was not available for all companies at press time.

2010 Sales: $	2010 Profits: $	**U.S. Stock Ticker:** SWI
2009 Sales: $62,378	2009 Profits: $29,509	**Int'l Ticker:** **Int'l Exchange:**
2008 Sales: $55,461	2008 Profits: $11,383	**Employees:** 354
2007 Sales: $	2007 Profits: $	**Fiscal Year Ends:** 12/31
2006 Sales: $	2006 Profits: $	**Parent Company:**

SALARIES/BENEFITS:
Pension Plan:	ESOP Stock Plan:	Profit Sharing:	Top Exec. Salary: $400,000	Bonus: $245,950
Savings Plan:	Stock Purch. Plan:		Second Exec. Salary: $300,000	Bonus: $232,500

OTHER THOUGHTS:
Apparent Women Officers or Directors:
Hot Spot for Advancement for Women/Minorities:

LOCATIONS: ("Y" = Yes)
West:	Southwest:	Midwest:	Southeast:	Northeast:	International:
	Y				Y

Note: Financial information, benefits and other data can change quickly and may vary from those stated here.

SONIC SOLUTIONS

www.sonic.com

Industry Group Code: 511210F **Ranks within this company's industry group:** Sales: 4   Profits: 5

Hardware:	Software:		Telecommunications:	Electronic Publishing:	Equipment:	Specialty Services:
Computers:	Consumer:	Y	Local:	Online Service:	Telecom:	Consulting:
Accessories:	Corporate:	Y	Long Distance:	TV/Cable or Wireless:	Communication:	Contract Manufacturing:
Network Equipment:	Telecom:		Cellular:	Games:	Distribution:	Processing:
Chips/Circuits:	Internet:		Internet Service:	Financial Data:	VAR/Reseller:	Staff/Outsourcing:
Parts/Drives:					Satellite Srv./Equip.:	Specialty Services:

TYPES OF BUSINESS:

Video Software Authoring Tools
Consumer Digital Media Software
Audio & Video Encoders

BRANDS/DIVISIONS/AFFILIATES:

Scenarist
CineVision
CinemaNow Inc
DivX Inc
MainConcept
CinePlayer Navigator
Roxio
AuthorScript

CONTACTS: Note: Officers with more than one job title may be intentionally listed here more than once.

Dave Habiger, CEO
Clay Leighton, COO
Dave Habiger, Pres.
Paul Norris, CFO/Exec. VP
Paul Norris, General Counsel
Clay Leighton, Pres., Oper.
Mark Ely, Pres., Strategy
Robert J. Doris, Chmn.

Phone: 415-893-8000	Fax: 415-893-8008
Toll-Free: 888-766-4297	
Address: 7250 Redwood Blvd., Ste. 300, Novato, CA 94945 US	

GROWTH PLANS/SPECIAL FEATURES:

Sonic Solutions develops and markets digital media software based primarily on the CD-Audio, DVD, HD DVD and Blu-ray Disc formats. The firm makes software for creating digital audio and video titles; recording data files; editing video programs; playing discs; managing digital media on the file system of a computer or other consumer electronic device; editing and adjusting digital photographs and other images; and backing up the information on hard disks. Sonic also sells computer-hosted hardware with its software to professional clients, and licenses the software technology underlying its tools to other companies. The firm is divided into three operating units. The Premium Products segment offers software authoring tools for skilled content creation customers, high-end authoring houses, motion picture studios and disc replicators. These tools include the Scenarist, DVDit, and the CineVision series for video and audio encoding. The Consumer Products segment, operated by subsidiary Roxio, is focused on consumer digital media software applications. Its products include CD and DVD burning software; VHS to DVD transfer software; audio converters; and backup systems under the Roxio brand. The segment also offers converts and disc burning software for Mac under the Toast and Popcorn brands. These products are sold and marketed through product bundling agreements with original equipment manufacturers (OEM) suppliers. The Advanced Technology Group develops software/software components, including AuthorScript and CinePlayer Navigator, which it licenses to PC application and consumer electronics developers; and provides Sonic's DVD-On-Demand platform, which allows consumers to burn movies and TV programs securely, in compliance with the program owner's copyright protection. Subsidiary CinemaNow sells, rents, and distributes premium entertainment content to consumers over the Internet. In April 2010, the firm introduced RoxioNow, a broad technology platform focused on simplifying the access to media outlets. In October 2010, Sonic Solutions acquired DivX, Inc. and formed new division Professional Technology from the assets of MainConcept.

FINANCIALS: Sales and profits are in thousands of dollars—add 000 to get the full amount. 2010 Note: Financial information for 2010 was not available for all companies at press time.

2010 Sales: $72,489	2010 Profits: $-1,213	**U.S. Stock Ticker:** SNIC
2009 Sales: $67,478	2009 Profits: $-118,123	**Int'l Ticker:** Int'l Exchange:
2008 Sales: $99,723	2008 Profits: $-5,537	Employees: 490
2007 Sales: $148,649	2007 Profits: $6,250	Fiscal Year Ends: 3/31
2006 Sales: $147,608	2006 Profits: $19,334	Parent Company:

SALARIES/BENEFITS:

Pension Plan:	ESOP Stock Plan:	Profit Sharing:	Top Exec. Salary: $350,000	Bonus: $56,753
Savings Plan:	Stock Purch. Plan:		Second Exec. Salary: $300,000	Bonus: $35,471

OTHER THOUGHTS:

Apparent Women Officers or Directors: 1
Hot Spot for Advancement for Women/Minorities:

LOCATIONS: ("Y" = Yes)

West:	Southwest:	Midwest:	Southeast:	Northeast:	International:
Y					Y

SONICWALL INC

www.sonicwall.com

Industry Group Code: 33411 Ranks within this company's industry group: Sales: 11 Profits: 7

Hardware:		Software:		Telecommunications:	Electronic Publishing:	Equipment:	Specialty Services:	
Computers:		Consumer:	Y	Local:	Online Service:	Telecom:	Consulting:	
Accessories:	Y	Corporate:		Long Distance:	TV/Cable or Wireless:	Communication:	Contract Manufacturing:	
Network Equipment:		Telecom:		Cellular:	Games:	Distribution:	Processing:	
Chips/Circuits:		Internet:		Internet Service:	Financial Data:	VAR/Reseller:	Staff/Outsourcing:	
Parts/Drives:						Satellite Srv./Equip.:	Specialty Services:	Y

TYPES OF BUSINESS:

Computer Peripherals-Security
Content Filtering Services
Anti-Virus Protection
Security Software

BRANDS/DIVISIONS/AFFILIATES:

Global Management System
Global VPN Client
CDP Backup and Recovery
Network Security Appliance Series
SonicWALL Security Content Management

CONTACTS: Note: Officers with more than one job title may be intentionally listed here more than once.

Matt Medeiros, CEO
Matt Medeiros, Pres.
Robert D. Selvi, CFO
Steve Franzese, VP-Worldwide Mktg.
Dawn Thompson, VP-Human Resources
John Gmuender, CTO
Patrick Sweeney, VP-Prod. Mgmt.
John Gmuender, VP-Eng.
Frederick M. Gonzalez, General Counsel/VP/Sec.
Colleen Nichols, Sr. Dir.-Public Rel.
Robert B. Knauff, VP-Finance/Corp. Controller
Douglas Brockett, VP/Gen. Mgr.
Robert B. Knauff, Chief Acct. Officer
John C. Shoemaker, Chmn.
Marvin Blough, VP-Worldwide Sales

Phone: 408-745-9600	Fax: 408-745-9300
Toll-Free: 888-557-6642	
Address: 2001 Logic Dr., San Jose, CA 95124-3452 US	

GROWTH PLANS/SPECIAL FEATURES:

SonicWALL, Inc. designs, develops, manufactures and sells integrated network security, content security and business continuity solutions. It caters to networks in the commercial, healthcare, education and governmental sectors. The company's products are designed to enable secure Internet-based connectivity for distributed organizations against inbound and outbound e-mail threats; provide secure Internet access to both wired and wireless broadband customers; and provide business continuity during data connectivity loss. SonicWALL offers security appliances that provide robust Internet firewall security. The company also sells, on a subscription basis, value-added services for its security appliances, including anti-spam protection; content filtering through the SonicWALL Security Content Management series; offsite backup through its Continuous Data Protection (CDP) Backup and Recovery solution; anti-virus protection; and intrusion prevention. In addition, SonicWALL's enterprise-grade unified threat management (UTM) solutions include the Network Security Appliance (NSA) Series; SSL VPN solutions; and e-mail security offerings. SonicWALL also licenses software packages such as Global Management System (GMS) and Global VPN Client. GMS enables distributed enterprises and service providers to manage and monitor a large number of SonicWALL Internet security appliances and deploy its security software and services from a central location to reduce staffing requirements, speed deployment and lower costs. Global VPN Client provides mobile users with a simple solution for securely accessing the network. SonicWALL's products and services are primarily sold, and its software is licensed, on an indirect basis through two-tiered distribution, first to distributors and then to value-added resellers, who sell to customers. In September 2009, the firm opened a new customer support center in the U.K. In June 2010, the company agreed to be acquired by private equity firm Thomas Bravo, LLC for roughly $717 million.

FINANCIALS: Sales and profits are in thousands of dollars—add 000 to get the full amount. 2010 Note: Financial information for 2010 was not available for all companies at press time.

2010 Sales: $	2010 Profits: $	**U.S. Stock Ticker:** SNWL
2009 Sales: $200,575	2009 Profits: $13,154	**Int'l Ticker:** Int'l Exchange:
2008 Sales: $218,644	2008 Profits: $4,881	Employees: 819
2007 Sales: $199,199	2007 Profits: $28,621	Fiscal Year Ends: 12/31
2006 Sales: $175,538	2006 Profits: $-10,753	Parent Company:

SALARIES/BENEFITS:

Pension Plan:	ESOP Stock Plan:	Profit Sharing:	Top Exec. Salary: $441,346	Bonus: $393,750
Savings Plan: Y	Stock Purch. Plan: Y		Second Exec. Salary: $279,519	Bonus: $106,875

OTHER THOUGHTS:

Apparent Women Officers or Directors: 1
Hot Spot for Advancement for Women/Minorities:

LOCATIONS: ("Y" = Yes)

West:	Southwest:	Midwest:	Southeast:	Northeast:	International:
Y					Y

SONUS NETWORKS INC

www.sonusnet.com

Industry Group Code: 3342 Ranks within this company's industry group: Sales: 4 Profits: 5

Hardware:		Software:		Telecommunications:		Electronic Publishing:		Equipment:		Specialty Services:	
Computers:		Consumer:		Local:		Online Service:		Telecom:	Y	Consulting:	
Accessories:		Corporate:		Long Distance:		TV/Cable or Wireless:		Communication:		Contract Manufacturing:	
Network Equipment:	Y	Telecom:	Y	Cellular:		Games:		Distribution:		Processing:	
Chips/Circuits:		Internet:		Internet Service:		Financial Data:		VAR/Reseller:		Staff/Outsourcing:	
Parts/Drives:								Satellite Srv./Equip.:		Specialty Services:	

TYPES OF BUSINESS:
Manufacturing-Networking Equipment
Voice Infrastructure Products
Switching Equipment & Software

BRANDS/DIVISIONS/AFFILIATES:
GSX9000 Open Services Switch
GSX4000 Open Services Switch
SGX Signaling Gateway
PSX Call Routing Server
ASX Call Feature Server
NBS Network Border Switch
Sonus Insight Management System
IMX Application Platform

CONTACTS: Note: Officers with more than one job title may be intentionally listed here more than once.
Richard N. Nottenburg, CEO
Richard N. Nottenburg, Pres.
Wayne Pastore, CFO
David Tipping, VP-Mktg. & Prod. Mgmt.
Kathy Harris, VP-Human Resources
Bill Scudder, CIO/VP
Gale England, VP-Prod. Oper.
Kumar Vishwanathan, VP-Eng./Chief Architect
Jeffrey M. Snider, General Counsel/VP
Mehdi Ghasem, VP-Strategy & Bus. Dev.
Howard E. Janzen, Chmn.
Matt Dillon, VP-Global Svcs.

Phone: 978-614-8100	Fax: 978-614-8101
Toll-Free:	
Address: 7 Technology Park Dr., Westford, MA 01886 US	

GROWTH PLANS/SPECIAL FEATURES:
Sonus Networks, Inc. is a leading provider of voice infrastructure products for wireline and wireless service providers. Its products consist of carrier-class switching equipment and software that enable voice services to be delivered over Internet Protocol (IP) packet-based networks. The company's target customers include communications service providers such as long-distance carriers, local exchange carriers, Internet service providers, wireless operators, cable operators, international telephone companies and carriers that provide service to other carriers. Sonus' suite of voice infrastructure solutions allows wireline and wireless operators to build converged voice over IP (VoIP) networks. Its products are built on the same distributed, IP-based principles embraced by the IP Multimedia Subsystem (IMS) architecture, as defined by the Third Generation Partnership Project (3GPP). This IMS architecture is being accepted by network operators globally as the common approach for building converged voice, data, wireline and wireless networks. Sonus' IMS-based solution product suite includes the GSX9000 Open Services Switch, GSX4000 Open Services Switch, SGX Signaling Gateway, the PSX Call Routing Server, the ASX Call Feature Server, the ASX Access Gateway Control Function, the NBS Network Border Switch, the Sonus Insight Management System and the IMX Service Delivery Platform. These products, designed for deployment as the platform of a service provider's voice network, can reduce the cost to build and operate voice services compared to traditional alternatives. They offer an open platform for network providers to increase their revenues through the creation and delivery of new voice and data services. Sonus also offers support and professional services including installation, systems integration and testing, technical support, maintenance and training services.

FINANCIALS: Sales and profits are in thousands of dollars—add 000 to get the full amount. 2010 Note: Financial information for 2010 was not available for all companies at press time.
2010 Sales: $	2010 Profits: $	U.S. Stock Ticker: SONS
2009 Sales: $227,496	2009 Profits: $-4,932	Int'l Ticker: Int'l Exchange:
2008 Sales: $313,145	2008 Profits: $-121,382	Employees: 879
2007 Sales: $319,415	2007 Profits: $-24,213	Fiscal Year Ends: 12/31
2006 Sales: $279,483	2006 Profits: $102,854	Parent Company:

SALARIES/BENEFITS:
| Pension Plan: | ESOP Stock Plan: | Profit Sharing: | Top Exec. Salary: $500,000 | Bonus: $380,310 |
| Savings Plan: Y | Stock Purch. Plan: Y | | Second Exec. Salary: $285,010 | Bonus: $139,003 |

OTHER THOUGHTS:
Apparent Women Officers or Directors: 1
Hot Spot for Advancement for Women/Minorities:

LOCATIONS: ("Y" = Yes)
West:	Southwest:	Midwest:	Southeast:	Northeast:	International:
	Y			Y	Y

SONY CORPORATION

www.sony.net

Industry Group Code: 334310 **Ranks within this company's industry group: Sales: 2 Profits: 6**

Hardware:		Software:		Telecommunications:	Electronic Publishing:		Equipment:		Specialty Services:
Computers:	Y	Consumer:	Y	Local:	Online Service:		Telecom:	Y	Consulting:
Accessories:	Y	Corporate:		Long Distance:	TV/Cable or Wireless:		Communication:		Contract Manufacturing:
Network Equipment:		Telecom:		Cellular:	Games:	Y	Distribution:		Processing:
Chips/Circuits:	Y	Internet:		Internet Service:	Financial Data:		VAR/Reseller:		Staff/Outsourcing:
Parts/Drives:							Satellite Srv./Equip.:		Specialty Services:

TYPES OF BUSINESS:
Consumer Electronics Manufacturer
Film & Television Production
Music Production
Personal Computers
Semiconductors
Technology Research
Video Games
Financial Services

BRANDS/DIVISIONS/AFFILIATES:
Columbia Tristar Motion Picture Group
Sony Canada
Sony Financial Holdings Inc
Sony Music Entertainment Inc
Sony Pictures Entertainment
Sony R&D
Sony Ericsson Mobile Communications AB
Sony Computer Entertainment, Inc.

CONTACTS: *Note: Officers with more than one job title may be intentionally listed here more than once.*
Howard Stringer, CEO
Howard Stringer, Pres.
Masaru Kato, CFO/Exec. VP
Yutaka Nakagawa, Exec. Deputy Pres., Mfg.
Nicole Seligman, General Counsel/Exec. VP
Ryoji Chubachi, Vice Chmn.
Hiroshi Yoshioka, Exec. Deputy Pres., Consumer Prod. & Devices
Keiji Kimura, Exec. VP-Intellectual Property & Disc Mfg.
Kazuo Hirai, Exec. VP-Networked Prod. & Svcs. Bus.
Howard Stringer, Chmn.
Yutaka Nakagawa, Exec. Deputy Pres., Logistics & Procurement

Phone: 81-3-6748-2111	Fax: 81-3-6748-2244
Toll-Free:	
Address: 7-1-1 Konan, Minato-Ku, Tokyo, 108-0075 Japan	

GROWTH PLANS/SPECIAL FEATURES:
Sony Corporation, a leading consumer electronics firm, produces consumer and industrial electronic products and entertainment. The firm operates through three primary divisions, the Consumer Products & Devices group, the Networked Products & Services group and the B2B & Disc Manufacturing group, in addition to several secondary segments: Music, Pictures, Financial Services, Sony Ericsson and Other. The Consumer Products & Devices group comprises the firm's television, digital imaging, audio and video, semiconductor and component businesses. The Networked Products & Services group comprises Sony Computer Entertainment, Inc., the firm's game business; and its personal computer and personal audio player businesses. The B2B & Disc group includes the company's broadcast- and professional-use products and its Blu-ray, DVD and CD disc manufacturing operations. The Music segment includes subsidiaries Sony Music Entertainment, a developer, producer and distributer of recorded music; Sony Music Entertainment Japan, a Japanese domestic recorded music business; and Sony/ATV Music Publishing LLC, a 50%-owned U.S.-based music publishing business. The Pictures segment, operating through Sony Pictures Entertainment, is engaged in motion picture production and distribution; television production; home entertainment distribution; a global channel network; and digital content creation. The Financial Services group is composed of Sony Financial Holdings, Inc., which operates through three subsidiaries: Sony Life Insurance Co., Ltd.; Sony Assurance, Inc.; and Sony Bank, Inc. Sony Ericsson Mobile Communications AB is a 50-50 joint venture between consumer electronics giants Sony Corp. and Telefonaktiebolaget LM Ericsson (Ericsson AB) that provides product research, development, design, marketing, production and distribution for mobile phones, accessories, services and applications. The Other segment includes the group's mobile phone original equipment manufacturing (OEM) business in Japan; and So-net, an Internet-related service business subsidiary. In May 2010, Sony and Google, Inc. formed a strategic alliance to deliver cloud computing-based products and services on Google's Android platform.

FINANCIALS: Sales and profits are in thousands of dollars—add 000 to get the full amount. 2010 Note: Financial information for 2010 was not available for all companies at press time.
2010 Sales: $87,722,300	2010 Profits: $-496,150	U.S. Stock Ticker: SNE
2009 Sales: $86,711,870	2009 Profits: $-1,109,850	Int'l Ticker: 6758 Int'l Exchange: Tokyo-TSE
2008 Sales: $88,714,100	2008 Profits: $3,694,400	Employees: 167,900
2007 Sales: $70,513,400	2007 Profits: $1,073,800	Fiscal Year Ends: 3/31
2006 Sales: $64,021,000	2006 Profits: $1,047,270	Parent Company:

SALARIES/BENEFITS:
Pension Plan:	ESOP Stock Plan:	Profit Sharing:	Top Exec. Salary: $	Bonus: $
Savings Plan:	Stock Purch. Plan:		Second Exec. Salary: $	Bonus: $

OTHER THOUGHTS:
Apparent Women Officers or Directors: 1
Hot Spot for Advancement for Women/Minorities:

LOCATIONS: ("Y" = Yes)
West:	Southwest:	Midwest:	Southeast:	Northeast:	International:
Y		Y	Y	Y	Y

SOURCEFIRE INC

www.sourcefire.com

Industry Group Code: 511210E Ranks within this company's industry group: Sales: 9 Profits: 8

Hardware:	Software:		Telecommunications:	Electronic Publishing:	Equipment:	Specialty Services:	
Computers:	Consumer:		Local:	Online Service:	Telecom:	Consulting:	
Accessories:	Corporate:	Y	Long Distance:	TV/Cable or Wireless:	Communication:	Contract Manufacturing:	
Network Equipment:	Telecom:		Cellular:	Games:	Distribution:	Processing:	
Chips/Circuits:	Internet:		Internet Service:	Financial Data:	VAR/Reseller:	Staff/Outsourcing:	
Parts/Drives:					Satellite Srv./Equip.:	Specialty Services:	Y

TYPES OF BUSINESS:
Security Software

BRANDS/DIVISIONS/AFFILIATES:
Sourcefire IPS
Sourcefire RUA
Sourcefire NetFlow Analysis
Sourcefire RNA
ClamAV
Snort
Sourcefire Defense Center

CONTACTS: Note: Officers with more than one job title may be intentionally listed here more than once.
John Burris, CEO
Tom McDonough, COO
Tom McDonough, Pres.
Todd Headley, CFO
Greg Fitzgerald, Sr. VP-Mktg.
Leslie Pendergrast, Chief People Officer
Martin Roesch, CTO
Tom Ashoff, Sr. VP-Eng. & Customer Support
Douglas McNitt, General Counsel/Sec.
John Czupak, Sr. VP-Bus. Dev.
John Negron, Sr. VP-Sales, Americas
Chris Peterson, Sr. VP-Worldwide Channels, Svcs. & Support
Steven R. Polk, Chmn.
John Czupak, Sr. VP-Int'l Sales

Phone: 410-290-1616	Fax: 410-290-0024
Toll-Free: 800-917-4134	
Address: 9770 Patuxent Woods Dr., Columbia, MD 21046 US	

GROWTH PLANS/SPECIAL FEATURES:
Sourcefire, Inc. offers intelligent cybersecurity solutions for the IT environments of commercial enterprises. The firm's customers include energy, financial services, healthcare, manufacturing, education, retail and telecommunications companies. It also serves federal, state and local government organizations around the world. Sourcefire's products are comprised of multiple hardware and software product and service offerings. Its security solutions provide customers with an efficient and effective network security defense of assets and applications before, during and after an attack. The firm's Sourcefire Defense Center unifies critical network security functions including event correlation, monitoring and prioritization with network and user intelligence for forensic analysis, trends analysis, reporting and alerting. The company also carries four intrusion detection and prevention sensors, with processing speeds ranging from 5 megabytes per second to 10 gigabytes per second: Sourcefire IPS (Intrusion Prevention System), Sourcefire RUA (Real-time User Awareness), Sourcefire NetFlow Analysis and Sourcefire RNA (Real-time Network Awareness). These sensors are responsible for detecting, blocking and analyzing network traffic. Sourcefire manages two open source projects: ClamAV, an anti-malware product downloaded from over 1.4 million unique IP addresses daily from 121 mirror servers in 43 countries; and Snort, a traffic inspection engine used in the firm's intrusion prevention system that has been downloaded roughly 4 million times. The firm offers customer support services such as online technical support, over-the-phone support, hardware repair/advanced replacement, and ongoing software updates; professional services for the planning, installing, configuring and managing all components of the Sourcefire security system; and several training programs to help security professionals using Sourcefire products. In March 2010, Sourcefire partnered with Immunet to release a free Windows-based version of ClamAV.

FINANCIALS: Sales and profits are in thousands of dollars—add 000 to get the full amount. 2010 Note: Financial information for 2010 was not available for all companies at press time.

2010 Sales: $	2010 Profits: $	U.S. Stock Ticker:
2009 Sales: $103,465	2009 Profits: $8,878	Int'l Ticker: Int'l Exchange:
2008 Sales: $75,673	2008 Profits: $-6,071	Employees: 307
2007 Sales: $	2007 Profits: $	Fiscal Year Ends: 12/31
2006 Sales: $	2006 Profits: $	Parent Company:

SALARIES/BENEFITS:
Pension Plan:	ESOP Stock Plan:	Profit Sharing:	Top Exec. Salary: $400,000	Bonus: $600,000
Savings Plan:	Stock Purch. Plan:		Second Exec. Salary: $290,000	Bonus: $225,000

OTHER THOUGHTS:
Apparent Women Officers or Directors: 1
Hot Spot for Advancement for Women/Minorities:

LOCATIONS: ("Y" = Yes)
West:	Southwest:	Midwest:	Southeast:	Northeast:	International:
				Y	Y

Note: Financial information, benefits and other data can change quickly and may vary from those stated here.

SPANLINK COMMUNICATIONS

www.spanlink.com

Industry Group Code: 511210C Ranks within this company's industry group: Sales: Profits:

Hardware:	Software:		Telecommunications:	Electronic Publishing:	Equipment:		Specialty Services:
Computers:	Consumer:		Local:	Online Service:	Telecom:	Y	Consulting:
Accessories:	Corporate:	Y	Long Distance:	TV/Cable or Wireless:	Communication:		Contract Manufacturing:
Network Equipment:	Telecom:		Cellular:	Games:	Distribution:		Processing:
Chips/Circuits:	Internet:		Internet Service:	Financial Data:	VAR/Reseller:		Staff/Outsourcing:
Parts/Drives:					Satellite Srv./Equip.:		Specialty Services:

TYPES OF BUSINESS:

Software-Customer Management
IP Products
Call Center Software
VoIP Products
Speech Recognition Software

BRANDS/DIVISIONS/AFFILIATES:

Concentric Customer Interaction Network
Calabrio, Inc.

CONTACTS: Note: Officers with more than one job title may be intentionally listed here more than once.

Scott Christian, CEO
Scott Christian, Pres.
Rosemary Friedrichs, VP-Human Resources
Mark Langanki, VP-Customer Eng. & Support
Anna Sunderman, Senior Counsel
Eric LeBow, VP-Professional Svcs.

Phone: 763-971-2000	Fax: 763-971-2300
Toll-Free:	
Address: 605 Highway 169 N., Minneapolis, MN 55441 US	

GROWTH PLANS/SPECIAL FEATURES:

Spanlink Communications provides unified communications, workforce management and system management products and customer interaction solutions through its Voice over Internet Protocol (VoIP) network infrastructure. The firm's software provides call center agents and administrators with information management systems to process customers and route calls efficiently. The company's use of Cisco's technologies allows Spanlink to provide single-source vendor solutions through Cisco Unified CallManager and Cisco Internet Protocol (IP) phones. Through the firm's partnership with Cisco Unified Contact Center, Spanlink is certified to provide call routing, CTI and multi-channel contact management for IP networks and has deployed more than 1,000 contact center site solutions and software to thousands of desktops. In addition, Spanlink's workforce optimization software allows voice and screen recording and software solutions for multi-site staff forecasting and scheduling. Spanlink's Concentric Customer Interaction Network allows organizations to manage virtual sites independently and integrates necessary tools within a unified desktop. The firm also manufactures a variety of products for IP phone applications, system administration, billing and reporting, IP communications, IP contact centers, monitoring, recording and natural language speech recognition. Additionally, Spanlink provides consulting, training, support, and systems integration services. The firm's software division, Calabrio, Inc., focuses on the development and distribution of customer interaction and workforce optimization software for IP-based contact centers. Spanlink has alliances with Adobe Systems, Inc.; Austin Logistics, Inc.; Datria Systems, Inc.; eGain Communications Corp.; ISI Telemanagement Solutions, Inc.; Netformx; and RISC Networks, Inc.

Spanlink provides employees with medical, dental and life insurance; a 401(k) plan; a pre-tax reimbursement plan; stock options; short- and long-term disability; and educational assistance.

FINANCIALS: Sales and profits are in thousands of dollars—add 000 to get the full amount. 2010 Note: Financial information for 2010 was not available for all companies at press time.

2010 Sales: $	2010 Profits: $	U.S. Stock Ticker: Private
2009 Sales: $	2009 Profits: $	Int'l Ticker: Int'l Exchange:
2008 Sales: $	2008 Profits: $	Employees:
2007 Sales: $11,700	2007 Profits: $	Fiscal Year Ends: 12/31
2006 Sales: $	2006 Profits: $	Parent Company:

SALARIES/BENEFITS:

Pension Plan:	ESOP Stock Plan:	Profit Sharing:	Top Exec. Salary: $	Bonus: $
Savings Plan: Y	Stock Purch. Plan:		Second Exec. Salary: $	Bonus: $

OTHER THOUGHTS:

Apparent Women Officers or Directors: 2
Hot Spot for Advancement for Women/Minorities: Y

LOCATIONS: ("Y" = Yes)

West:	Southwest:	Midwest:	Southeast:	Northeast:	International:
Y		Y		Y	

SPANSION

www.spansion.com

Industry Group Code: 334112 Ranks within this company's industry group: Sales: 7 Profits: 12

Hardware:		Software:	Telecommunications:	Electronic Publishing:	Equipment:	Specialty Services:
Computers:		Consumer:	Local:	Online Service:	Telecom:	Consulting:
Accessories:		Corporate:	Long Distance:	TV/Cable or Wireless:	Communication:	Contract Manufacturing:
Network Equipment:		Telecom:	Cellular:	Games:	Distribution:	Processing:
Chips/Circuits:	Y	Internet:	Internet Service:	Financial Data:	VAR/Reseller:	Staff/Outsourcing:
Parts/Drives:					Satellite Srv./Equip.:	Specialty Services:

TYPES OF BUSINESS:
Flash Memory Semiconductors

BRANDS/DIVISIONS/AFFILIATES:
MirrorBit
Nihon Spansion Ltd.
Elpida Memory, Inc.
Freescale Semiconductor

CONTACTS: Note: Officers with more than one job title may be intentionally listed here more than once.
John H. Kispert, CEO
John H. Kispert, Pres.
Randy Furr, CFO/Exec. VP
Jim Reid, Exec. VP-Sales & Mktg.
Carmine Renzulli, Sr. VP-Worldwide Human Resources
Saied Tehrani, Sr. VP-R&D
Ali Pourkeramati, CTO
Joe Rauschmayer, Sr. VP-Prod. Eng.
Nancy Richardson, Sr. VP-Legal
Joe Rauschmayer, Sr. VP-Wafer Fabrication Oper. & Corp. Quality
Thomas T. Eby, Exec. VP-Strategy
Thomas T. Eby, Exec. VP-Corp. Comm.
Ahmed Nawaz, Exec. VP-Wireless Solutions Group
Ray Bingham, Chmn.
S. L. Chan, VP-Sales & Field Mktg., Asia

Phone: 408-962-2500	Fax:
Toll-Free: 866-772-6746	
Address: 915 DeGuigne Dr., Sunnyvale, CA 94085 US	

GROWTH PLANS/SPECIAL FEATURES:

Spansion is a semiconductor device company that designs, manufactures, develops and markets NOR Flash memory products and related solutions. The firm is focused on the embedded Flash market, providing its software solutions to more than 4,500 customers worldwide. Its Flash memory products primarily store data and software code for microprocessors, controllers and other programmable semiconductors that run applications in a broad range of electronics systems. These electronic systems include automotive electronics, such as navigation systems and engine control systems; PC and peripheral computing equipment, such as printers; set top boxes; home networking; communication equipment, such as enterprise networking and cellular infrastructure; arcade gaming equipment; industrial control equipment; and mobile phones. Spansion's Flash memory products are based on one of two technologies: single-bit-per-cell floating gate technology, the conventional memory cell technology; and one-, two- or more-bit-per-cell MirrorBit technology, Spansion's proprietary charge trapping non-volatile memory technology. Compared to the conventional technology, MirrorBit systems have simpler cell architecture, which helps reduce costs by simplifying the manufacturing process. Spansion operates product design centers in Texas and California and internationally in Japan, Germany, Israel and Malaysia, with additional international facilities in Thailand, Italy, Sweden, the U.K., China, Singapore and Korea. The firm holds over 2,100 patents. In May 2010, Spansion emerged from Chapter 11 bankruptcy reorganization. In the same month, it formed a new, wholly-owned subsidiary, Nihon Spansion Ltd., from the acquisition of the distribution business of Spansion Japan. In September 2010, the firm announced the development, in collaboration with Elpida Memory, Inc., a Japanese integrated circuits manufacturer, of a 4 gigabit Flash memory device. Also in September 2010, it began a co-development agreement with Freescale Semiconductor to produce memory subsystems in next-generation dashboards for the auto industry.

FINANCIALS: Sales and profits are in thousands of dollars—add 000 to get the full amount. 2010 Note: Financial information for 2010 was not available for all companies at press time.

2010 Sales: $	2010 Profits: $	**U.S. Stock Ticker:** CODE
2009 Sales: $1,630,573	2009 Profits: $-514,059	**Int'l Ticker:** Int'l Exchange:
2008 Sales: $1,627,253	2008 Profits: $-2,435,012	Employees: 3,200
2007 Sales: $	2007 Profits: $	Fiscal Year Ends: 12/31
2006 Sales: $	2006 Profits: $	Parent Company:

SALARIES/BENEFITS:

Pension Plan:	ESOP Stock Plan:	Profit Sharing:	Top Exec. Salary: $796,155	Bonus: $
Savings Plan:	Stock Purch. Plan:		Second Exec. Salary: $600,000	Bonus: $

OTHER THOUGHTS:
Apparent Women Officers or Directors: 1
Hot Spot for Advancement for Women/Minorities:

LOCATIONS: ("Y" = Yes)

West:	Southwest:	Midwest:	Southeast:	Northeast:	International:
Y	Y				Y

Note: Financial information, benefits and other data can change quickly and may vary from those stated here.

SPECTRIS

www.spectris.com

Industry Group Code: 3345 Ranks within this company's industry group: Sales: 3 Profits: 3

Hardware:	Software:	Telecommunications:	Electronic Publishing:	Equipment:	Specialty Services:
Computers:	Consumer:	Local:	Online Service:	Telecom:	Consulting:
Accessories:	Corporate:	Long Distance:	TV/Cable or Wireless:	Communication:	Contract Manufacturing:
Network Equipment:	Telecom:	Cellular:	Games:	Distribution:	Processing:
Chips/Circuits:	Internet:	Internet Service:	Financial Data:	VAR/Reseller:	Staff/Outsourcing:
Parts/Drives:				Satellite Srv./Equip.:	Specialty Services: Y

TYPES OF BUSINESS:

Instrumentation & Controls Manufacturing

BRANDS/DIVISIONS/AFFILIATES:

Malvern Instruments
HBM
BTG
Microscan Systems, Inc.
PANalytical
Particle Measuring Systems
N-TRON Corp.
Fusion UV Systems

CONTACTS: Note: Officers with more than one job title may be intentionally listed here more than once.

John O'Higgins, CEO
Clive Watson, Dir.-Finance
Roger Stephens, Sec.
Jim Webster, Dir.-Bus.
Roger Stephens, Head-Commercial
John Hughes, Chmn.

Phone: 44-1784-470470	Fax: 44-1784-470848
Toll-Free:	
Address: Station Rd., Egham, TW20 9NP UK	

GROWTH PLANS/SPECIAL FEATURES:

Spectris, based in the U.K., is a developer and marketer of instruments and controls designed to increase productivity, reduce downtime and increase yield. The company operates through 14 subsidiaries, divided by business into four segments: Materials Analysis; Test and Measurement; In-Line Instrumentation; and Industrial Controls. Materials Analysis provides analytical instrumentation, with applications in material characterization, contamination detection and quality control, to the life sciences, mining, electronics and semiconductor industries. Subsidiaries operating in this business include Malvern Instruments, PANalytical and Particle Measuring Systems. The Test and Measurement business provides test, measurement and analysis equipment, with applications in data acquisition and processing, measurement and simulation, to the automotive, aerospace, electronics and environmental market segments. Subsidiaries in this business include Bruel & Kjaer Sound & Vibration and HBM. In-Line Instrumentation provides asset monitoring, analytical management and online controls, used in quality control, process technology and safety applications, to the process and converting industries, including pulp and paper. Subsidiaries operating in this business include Beta LaserMike, BTG, Bruel & Kjaer Vibrio, Fusion UV Systems, NDC Infrared Engineering and Servomex. Finally, the Industrial Controls business supplies automation and control products for product tracking, machine interface and industrial networking to the general manufacturing, machine building and distribution market segments. Subsidiaries in this business include Microscan and Red Lion. The largest percentage of Spectris' sales (approximately 37%) is derived from Europe, while Asia accounts for 29%, North America for 23%, the U.K. accounts for 4% and the rest of the world accounts for 7%. In recent years Spectris acquired software and data instrument supplier nCode International (through HBM); and the assets of Siemens' Machine Vision Business (through Microscan Systems); and the LDS Test & Measurement business of SPX Corporation. In October 2010, the firm acquired N-TRON Corporation, a manufacturer of industrial networking components, for $51 million.

FINANCIALS: Sales and profits are in thousands of dollars—add 000 to get the full amount. 2010 Note: Financial information for 2010 was not available for all companies at press time.

2010 Sales: $	2010 Profits: $	**U.S. Stock Ticker:**
2009 Sales: $1,275,060	2009 Profits: $68,130	**Int'l Ticker:** SXS Int'l Exchange: London-LSE
2008 Sales: $1,268,310	2008 Profits: $130,680	Employees: 5,764
2007 Sales: $1,077,040	2007 Profits: $138,900	Fiscal Year Ends: 12/31
2006 Sales: $	2006 Profits: $	Parent Company:

SALARIES/BENEFITS:

Pension Plan:	ESOP Stock Plan:	Profit Sharing:	Top Exec. Salary: $713,040	Bonus: $578,920
Savings Plan:	Stock Purch. Plan:		Second Exec. Salary: $466,846	Bonus: $353,106

OTHER THOUGHTS:

Apparent Women Officers or Directors:
Hot Spot for Advancement for Women/Minorities:

LOCATIONS: ("Y" = Yes)

West:	Southwest:	Midwest:	Southeast:	Northeast:	International:
Y	Y	Y		Y	Y

Note: Financial information, benefits and other data can change quickly and may vary from those stated here.

SPSS INC

www.spss.com

Industry Group Code: 511210K Ranks within this company's industry group: Sales: Profits:

Hardware:	Software:		Telecommunications:	Electronic Publishing:	Equipment:	Specialty Services:	
Computers:	Consumer:		Local:	Online Service:	Telecom:	Consulting:	
Accessories:	Corporate:	Y	Long Distance:	TV/Cable or Wireless:	Communication:	Contract Manufacturing:	
Network Equipment:	Telecom:		Cellular:	Games:	Distribution:	Processing:	
Chips/Circuits:	Internet:		Internet Service:	Financial Data:	VAR/Reseller:	Staff/Outsourcing:	
Parts/Drives:					Satellite Srv./Equip.:	Specialty Services:	Y

TYPES OF BUSINESS:

Software-Statistics
Business Performance Management Software
Data Mining Software
Fraud Detection Software
Sales Forecasting
Market Research

BRANDS/DIVISIONS/AFFILIATES:

International Business Machines (IBM)
IBM SPSS Data Collection Author
IBM SPSS Data Collection Interviewer Web
IBM SPSS 19
IBM SPSS Statistics Professional
IBM SPSS Statistics Premium
IBM SPSS Modeler
IBM SPSS Collaboration & Deployment Services

CONTACTS: *Note: Officers with more than one job title may be intentionally listed here more than once.*

Deepak Avanti, CEO

Phone: 312-651-3000	Fax:
Toll-Free:	
Address: 233 S. Wacker Dr., 11th Fl., Chicago, IL 60606 US	

GROWTH PLANS/SPECIAL FEATURES:

SPSS, Inc., a subsidiary of IBM, is a major global provider of predictive analytics software and services. Its software products provide statistical analysis, data mining, performance measurement and fraud detection. The company's business intelligence products help organizations to make decisions using predictive analytics software to identify and predict consumer behavior especially in such areas as sales and targeted marketing. SPSS software is used in over 100 countries, by all 50 U.S. state governments, national newspapers, and many top U.S. universities. The firm's customers include research analysts; software vendors; and banking, telecom, health care, education and retail firms. The company's software is organized into four categories: data collection, statistics, modeling and deployment. Data collection includes phone, online and written surveys; survey management and reporting and data entry. Data products include the IBM SPSS Data Collection Author series and the Data Collection Interviewer Web. Statistics programs allow business users to coordinate with statistical analysts, protect and publish data. Statistical products include IBM SPSS 19, Statistics Professional and Statistics Premium. Modeling programs allow businesses to access, organize and model several types of data using a single visual interface. Modeling products include the IBM SPSS Modeler, Modeler Server and SPSS Premium. Deployment tools apply analytics to business practices, automating certain decisions for speed and consistency. Deployment products include IBM SPSS Collaboration and Deployment Services, and Decision Management Tools.

FINANCIALS: Sales and profits are in thousands of dollars—add 000 to get the full amount. 2010 Note: Financial information for 2010 was not available for all companies at press time.

2010 Sales: $	2010 Profits: $	**U.S. Stock Ticker:** Subsidiary
2009 Sales: $	2009 Profits: $	**Int'l Ticker:** Int'l Exchange:
2008 Sales: $302,913	2008 Profits: $36,046	Employees: 1,203
2007 Sales: $291,000	2007 Profits: $33,725	Fiscal Year Ends: 12/31
2006 Sales: $261,532	2006 Profits: $15,140	Parent Company: INTERNATIONAL BUSINESS MACHINES CORP (IBM)

SALARIES/BENEFITS:

Pension Plan:	ESOP Stock Plan:	Profit Sharing:	Top Exec. Salary: $	Bonus: $
Savings Plan:	Stock Purch. Plan:		Second Exec. Salary: $	Bonus: $

OTHER THOUGHTS:

Apparent Women Officers or Directors:
Hot Spot for Advancement for Women/Minorities:

LOCATIONS: ("Y" = Yes)

West:	Southwest:	Midwest:	Southeast:	Northeast:	International:
Y	Y	Y	Y	Y	Y

SRA INTERNATIONAL INC

www.sra.com

Industry Group Code: 541513 Ranks within this company's industry group: Sales: 19 Profits: 17

Hardware:	Software:	Telecommunications:	Electronic Publishing:	Equipment:	Specialty Services:	
Computers:	Consumer:	Local:	Online Service:	Telecom:	Consulting:	Y
Accessories:	Corporate:	Long Distance:	TV/Cable or Wireless:	Communication:	Contract Manufacturing:	
Network Equipment:	Telecom:	Cellular:	Games:	Distribution:	Processing:	
Chips/Circuits:	Internet:	Internet Service:	Financial Data:	VAR/Reseller:	Staff/Outsourcing:	Y
Parts/Drives:				Satellite Srv./Equip.:	Specialty Services:	Y

TYPES OF BUSINESS:

Technology Consulting
Strategic Consulting
Systems Design
Systems Integration
Managed Services
Outsourcing

BRANDS/DIVISIONS/AFFILIATES:

RABA Technologies, LLC
NetOwl
ORIONMagic
Era Systems Corporation
Interface & Control Systems, Inc.
Perrin Quarles Associates (PQA), Inc.

CONTACTS: Note: Officers with more than one job title may be intentionally listed here more than once.

Stanton D. Sloane, CEO
Timothy J. Atkin, COO/Exec. VP
Stanton D. Sloane, Pres.
Richard J. Nadeau, CFO/Exec. VP
Jeffrey Rydant, Sr. VP-Mktg. & Sales
Mary E. Good, Sr. VP-Human Resources
Brian Michl, CIO
David L. Matthews, Sr. VP-Tech. Oper.
Mark D. Schultz, General Counsel
Sheila S. Blackwell, VP-Comm. & Public Affairs
David Keffer, VP-Investor Rel.
Stewart Simonson, VP-Gov't Affairs
Patrick Burke, Sr. VP-Offerings & Prod.
Max N. Hall, Sr. VP-Civil Sector
Gordon K. McElroy, Sr. VP-National Security Sector
Ernst Volgenau, Chmn.
Jim McClave, VP-EMEA

Phone: 703-803-1500	Fax: 703-803-1509
Toll-Free:	
Address: 4300 Fair Lakes Ct., Fairfax, VA 22033 US	

GROWTH PLANS/SPECIAL FEATURES:

SRA International, Inc. provides technology and strategic consulting services and solutions to a broad range of clients involved in national security, civil government and global health. The firm's business strategy focuses primarily on the U.S. federal government, with a portfolio of clients in national security, including defense, homeland security, intelligence and law enforcement; and civil government, including health, environmental, aviation and other domestic customers. The company's services across all sectors include strategic consulting; systems design, development and integration; cyber security and information assurance; outsourcing and managed services; and business solutions. The strategic consulting service helps clients form and execute business plans. The systems design, development and integration service includes security engineering, software development, and database design. The cyber security and information assurance service offers various cyber security approaches such as security architecture, information operations, and training services. The outsourcing and managed services segment helps clients consolidate infrastructures and reduce operational costs. The business solutions segment includes text and data mining; enterprise resource planning; control systems; disaster planning; and business intelligence. SRA also develops and sells software and hardware products in each market. Some of the firm's software products include ORIONMagic, NetOwl and GangNet. ORIONMagic helps clients sift through gigabytes of information, store the most relevant pieces and search through each piece. NetOwl applies advanced natural language understanding technologies to Chinese, English, Arabic, Farsi, French, Korean and Spanish texts to extract content. The GangNet database system helps law enforcement officials record and track gang member information and activities. In February 2010, SRA acquired Virginia-based Perrin Quarles Associates (PQA), Inc., an environmental consulting firm.

Employees are offered medical, vision and dental insurance; a 401(k) plan; life insurance; disability coverage; health and dependent care flexible spending programs; a stock purchase program; educational assistance; commuter expense reimbursement; college savings plans; and financial planning assistance.

FINANCIALS: Sales and profits are in thousands of dollars—add 000 to get the full amount. 2010 Note: Financial information for 2010 was not available for all companies at press time.

2010 Sales: $1,666,629	2010 Profits: $18,415	U.S. Stock Ticker: SRX
2009 Sales: $1,540,556	2009 Profits: $58,000	Int'l Ticker: Int'l Exchange:
2008 Sales: $1,506,933	2008 Profits: $73,264	Employees: 7,100
2007 Sales: $1,268,872	2007 Profits: $63,430	Fiscal Year Ends: 6/30
2006 Sales: $1,179,267	2006 Profits: $62,520	Parent Company:

SALARIES/BENEFITS:

Pension Plan:	ESOP Stock Plan:	Profit Sharing:	Top Exec. Salary: $677,500	Bonus: $528,136
Savings Plan: Y	Stock Purch. Plan: Y		Second Exec. Salary: $361,667	Bonus: $219,000

OTHER THOUGHTS:

Apparent Women Officers or Directors: 3
Hot Spot for Advancement for Women/Minorities: Y

LOCATIONS: ("Y" = Yes)

West:	Southwest:	Midwest:	Southeast:	Northeast:	International:
Y	Y	Y	Y	Y	Y

STANDARD MICROSYSTEMS CORPORATION   www.smsc.com

Industry Group Code: 33441 Ranks within this company's industry group: Sales: 43   Profits: 41

Hardware:		Software:		Telecommunications:		Electronic Publishing:		Equipment:		Specialty Services:	
Computers:		Consumer:		Local:		Online Service:		Telecom:		Consulting:	
Accessories:		Corporate:		Long Distance:		TV/Cable or Wireless:		Communication:		Contract Manufacturing:	
Network Equipment:	Y	Telecom:		Cellular:		Games:		Distribution:		Processing:	
Chips/Circuits:	Y	Internet:		Internet Service:		Financial Data:		VAR/Reseller:		Staff/Outsourcing:	
Parts/Drives:								Satellite Srv./Equip.:		Specialty Services:	Y

TYPES OF BUSINESS:

Integrated Circuits-Input/Output
Networking Products
Thermal Management
Capacitive Sensing Technology

BRANDS/DIVISIONS/AFFILIATES:

Smart Mixed-Signal Connectivity
Media Oriented Systems Transport
Kleer Semiconductor Corporation
Wireless Audio IP B.V.
Symwave, Inc.
Tallika Corporation

CONTACTS: *Note: Officers with more than one job title may be intentionally listed here more than once.*

Christine King, CEO
Christine King, Pres.
Kris Sennesael, CFO/VP
Roger Wendelken, VP-Worldwide Sales
Walter Siegel, General Counsel/Sr. VP
David Coller, Sr. VP-Oper.
Steven J. Bilodeau, Chmn.

Phone: 631-435-6000	Fax: 631-435-6110
Toll-Free:	
Address: 80 Arkay Dr., Hauppauge, NY 11788 US	

GROWTH PLANS/SPECIAL FEATURES:

Standard Microsystems Corporation (SMSC) designs and sells a range of silicon-based integrated circuits (IC) that utilize analog and mixed-signal semiconductor products, also known under the company's trademark brand, Smart Mixed-Signal Connectivity products, for a broad range of high-speed communications and computing applications. The firm's products are used in connectivity, networking and input/output control solutions for a variety of high-speed communication, computer, consumer electronics, industrial control systems and automotive information applications. Its products are applied across a wide range of technologies, including USB, Ethernet, wireless audio and Media Oriented Systems Transport (MOST), as well as embedded control, capacitive sensing and thermal management technologies. Products include USB hub controllers, memory card readers, network multimedia processing engines, embedded Ethernet switches, radio frequency integrated circuits (RFIC), biometric sensors, temperature sensors and fan controllers. End products that incorporate SMSC's technology primarily serve the personal computing, consumer electronics, industrial and automotive markets. Customers include Toshiba, Sony, Audi, BMW, Dell, Hewlett-Packard, Intel and Fujitsu, among others. The company also provides a range of support services and tools, including valuation boards, diagnostics programs, sample schematics, driver programs and datasheets. Besides its U.S. offices, in New York, North Carolina, Arizona, Texas and California, the firm has operations in Canada, Germany, China, India, Singapore, Japan, Bulgaria, the Netherlands and Sweden. The company recently acquired the Tallika Corporation for $3.4 million. In February 2010, the company acquired Kleer Semiconductor Corporation, a developer of wireless audio technology. In June 2010, SMSC acquired Wireless Audio IP B.V. (known as STS), a plug-and-play wireless technology developer. In November 2010, the firm acquired Symwave, Inc., a semiconductor company that delivers analog/mixed signal connectivity solutions.

Employees are offered medical, dental and vision insurance; life insurance; long-term disability coverage; a 401(k) plan; tuition reimbursement; a 529 college savings plan; and an employee assistance program.

FINANCIALS: Sales and profits are in thousands of dollars—add 000 to get the full amount. 2010 Note: Financial information for 2010 was not available for all companies at press time.

2010 Sales: $307,778	2010 Profits: $-7,978	**U.S. Stock Ticker: SMSC**
2009 Sales: $325,496	2009 Profits: $-49,409	**Int'l Ticker:** Int'l Exchange:
2008 Sales: $377,849	2008 Profits: $32,906	Employees: 916
2007 Sales: $370,594	2007 Profits: $27,015	Fiscal Year Ends: 7/31
2006 Sales: $319,118	2006 Profits: $12,030	Parent Company:

SALARIES/BENEFITS:

Pension Plan:	ESOP Stock Plan:	Profit Sharing:	Top Exec. Salary: $625,000	Bonus: $1,144,688
Savings Plan: Y	Stock Purch. Plan:		Second Exec. Salary: $308,942	Bonus: $317,001

OTHER THOUGHTS:

Apparent Women Officers or Directors: 1
Hot Spot for Advancement for Women/Minorities:

LOCATIONS: ("Y" = Yes)

West:	Southwest:	Midwest:	Southeast:	Northeast:	International:
Y	Y			Y	Y

STERLING COMMERCE INC

www.sterlingcommerce.com

Industry Group Code: 511210L Ranks within this company's industry group: Sales: Profits:

Hardware:	Software:		Telecommunications:	Electronic Publishing:	Equipment:	Specialty Services:	
Computers:	Consumer:		Local:	Online Service:	Telecom:	Consulting:	Y
Accessories:	Corporate:	Y	Long Distance:	TV/Cable or Wireless:	Communication:	Contract Manufacturing:	
Network Equipment:	Telecom:		Cellular:	Games:	Distribution:	Processing:	Y
Chips/Circuits:	Internet:		Internet Service:	Financial Data:	VAR/Reseller:	Staff/Outsourcing:	
Parts/Drives:					Satellite Srv./Equip.:	Specialty Services:	Y

TYPES OF BUSINESS:

Intranet Communities
Multi-Enterprise Collaboration Software

BRANDS/DIVISIONS/AFFILIATES:

International Business Machines Corp (IBM)
Sterling Business Integration Suite
Sterling Total Payments

CONTACTS: *Note: Officers with more than one job title may be intentionally listed here more than once.*

Bob Irwin, CEO
Bob Irwin, Pres.
Donna Angiulo, CFO
Joel Reed, Sr. VP-Mktg.
Steven Aulds, Sr. VP-Tech.
Joel Reed, Sr. VP-Prod. Mgmt.
Deborah Surrette, Sr. VP-Americas Field Oper.
Phil Galati, Sr. VP-Global Svcs.
Robert Prigge, VP-Global Sales
Dave Robinson, Sr. VP-European Field Oper.

Phone: 614-793-7000	Fax: 614-793-4040
Toll-Free: 800-876-9772	
Address: 4600 Lakehurst Ct., Dublin, OH 43016-2000 US	

GROWTH PLANS/SPECIAL FEATURES:

Sterling Commerce, Inc., a subsidiary of IBM, provides multi-enterprise collaboration solutions. Through the construction of collaborative, multi-enterprise communities, the firm provides business process integration, secure file transfers, multi-channel selling, supply chain fulfillment and payment management solutions to companies in the communications, media, distribution and logistics, financial services, retail, services and manufacturing industries. These communities consist of integrated applications and network services, including e-mail, e-business transactions, file transfers and electronic libraries, as well as offering customer support services, education services and implementation services. Two of Sterling's software packages are IBMSterling Business Integration Suite, a diversified application that enables data movement, business visibility, business process integration, secure file transfer and other solutions; and IBMSterling Total Payments, a secure, streamlining solution for financial services institutions. The firm partners with several other companies to develop its service packages, including Infosoft Global Private Limited, iWay Software and ChoiceStream. Sterling has approximately 18,000 corporate customers worldwide, including large companies like Boston Market, Honeywell, Monsanto and Pitney Bowes. In August 2010, the company was acquired by IBM from AT&T for approximately $1.4 billion.

Sterling offers its employees medical and dental insurance, life insurance, tuition reimbursement, fitness facilities and concierge services.

FINANCIALS: Sales and profits are in thousands of dollars—add 000 to get the full amount. 2010 Note: Financial information for 2010 was not available for all companies at press time.

2010 Sales: $	2010 Profits: $	U.S. Stock Ticker: Subsidiary
2009 Sales: $	2009 Profits: $	Int'l Ticker: Int'l Exchange:
2008 Sales: $	2008 Profits: $	Employees:
2007 Sales: $	2007 Profits: $	Fiscal Year Ends: 12/31
2006 Sales: $	2006 Profits: $	Parent Company: INTERNATIONAL BUSINESS MACHINES CORP (IBM)

SALARIES/BENEFITS:

Pension Plan:	ESOP Stock Plan:	Profit Sharing:	Top Exec. Salary: $	Bonus: $
Savings Plan: Y	Stock Purch. Plan:		Second Exec. Salary: $	Bonus: $

OTHER THOUGHTS:

Apparent Women Officers or Directors: 3
Hot Spot for Advancement for Women/Minorities: Y

LOCATIONS: ("Y" = Yes)

West:	Southwest:	Midwest:	Southeast:	Northeast:	International:
Y	Y	Y	Y	Y	Y

Note: Financial information, benefits and other data can change quickly and may vary from those stated here.

STMICROELECTRONICS NV

www.st.com

Industry Group Code: 33441 Ranks within this company's industry group: Sales: 5 Profits: 52

Hardware:		Software:	Telecommunications:	Electronic Publishing:	Equipment:	Specialty Services:
Computers:		Consumer:	Local:	Online Service:	Telecom:	Consulting:
Accessories:		Corporate:	Long Distance:	TV/Cable or Wireless:	Communication:	Contract Manufacturing:
Network Equipment:		Telecom:	Cellular:	Games:	Distribution:	Processing:
Chips/Circuits:	Y	Internet:	Internet Service:	Financial Data:	VAR/Reseller:	Staff/Outsourcing:
Parts/Drives:					Satellite Srv./Equip.:	Specialty Services:

TYPES OF BUSINESS:

Semiconductor Manufacturing
Integrated Circuits
Transistors & Diodes

BRANDS/DIVISIONS/AFFILIATES:

ST-Ericsson
Enel Green Power
Sharp Corporation

CONTACTS: Note: Officers with more than one job title may be intentionally listed here more than once.

Carlo Bozotti, CEO
Didier Lamouche, COO
Carlo Bozotti, Pres.
Carlo Ferro, CFO/Exec. VP
Andrea Cuomo, Exec. VP-Sales & Mktg., EMEA
Patrice Chastagner, VP-Human Resources
Jean-Marc Chery, CTO/Exec. VP
Orio Bellezza, Exec. VP/Gen. Mgr.-Front-End Mfg.
Tjerk Hooghiemstra, Chief Admin. Officer/Exec. VP
Pierre Ollivier, General Counsel/VP
Loic Lietar, Chief Strategic Officer/VP
Carlo Emanuele Ottaviani, VP-Corp. Comm.
Celine Berthier, Dir.-Investor Rel.
Otto Kosgalwies, Exec. VP-Infrastructure & Svcs.
Georges Auguste, Exec. VP-Quality, Education & Sustainable Dev.
Alisia Grenville, Chief Compliance Officer/VP
Jeffrey See, Exec. VP-Packaging & Test Mfg.
Antonino Turicchi, Chmn.
Marco Luciano Cassis, VP-Japan

Phone: 41-22-929-29-29	Fax: 41-22-929-29-88
Toll-Free:	
Address: 39 Chemin du Champ des Filles, Plan-Les-Ouates, 1228 Switzerland	

GROWTH PLANS/SPECIAL FEATURES:

STMicroelectronics N.V. (STM) is one of the world's largest semiconductor companies. It is a leading chip manufacturer in Europe, as well as a top maker of analog chips globally. STM operates across three primary product segments: Automotive, Consumer, Computer and Communication Infrastructure (ACCCI); Industrial and Multi-Segment (IMS); and Wireless Products (WP). The ACCCI segment encompasses the design, development and manufacture of application-specific products, as well as mixed analog/digital semi-custom devices, using advanced bipolar, CMOS, BiCMOS mixed-signal and power technologies. This segment offers product lines for use in satellite and cable television boxes; Blu-Ray Disc players; televisions; audio amplifiers and speakers; digital cameras; radios; and automotive electronics systems. The IMS segment comprises two product groups: one that produces discrete power devices, standard analog devices and sensors, and another that focuses on 8- and 32-bit microcontrollers, read-only memory (ROM) devices and Smartcards for a variety of applications. The WP segment, encompassing subsidiary ST-Ericsson (a joint venture with Swedish telecom firm Ericsson formed during 2009), is responsible for the design, development and manufacture of semiconductors and platforms for mobile applications. The firm sells to manufacturers in the telecommunications, computer, consumer electronics, industrial and automotive markets. One of STM's top clients in recent years, Nokia, accounts for over 15% of annual revenues. Other notable customers include Research in Motion; Dell; Siemens; Apple; Samsung; Sony; GE; LG; Sharp; Hyundai; HP; Motorola; Microsoft; and Nintendo. STM operates 15 main manufacturing sites worldwide, as well as numerous research and development centers. Sales and marketing offices are located across Europe, as well as in North America, Latin America, the Middle East, Africa and Asia. In January 2010, the firm entered an agreement with Enel Green Power and Sharp Corporation to manufacture thin-film photovoltaic solar panels at is plant in Catania, Italy. In May 2010, it sold its 48.6% stake in Numonyx to Micron Technology.

FINANCIALS: Sales and profits are in thousands of dollars—add 000 to get the full amount. 2010 Note: Financial information for 2010 was not available for all companies at press time.

2010 Sales: $	2010 Profits: $	**U.S. Stock Ticker: STM**
2009 Sales: $8,465,000	2009 Profits: $-1,131,000	**Int'l Ticker: STM** Int'l Exchange: Paris-Euronext
2008 Sales: $9,792,000	2008 Profits: $-786,000	Employees: 51,560
2007 Sales: $9,966,000	2007 Profits: $-477,000	Fiscal Year Ends: 12/31
2006 Sales: $9,854,000	2006 Profits: $782,000	Parent Company:

SALARIES/BENEFITS:

Pension Plan:	ESOP Stock Plan:	Profit Sharing:	Top Exec. Salary: $933,474	Bonus: $649,755
Savings Plan:	Stock Purch. Plan:		Second Exec. Salary: $	Bonus: $

OTHER THOUGHTS:

Apparent Women Officers or Directors: 1
Hot Spot for Advancement for Women/Minorities:

LOCATIONS: ("Y" = Yes)

West:	Southwest:	Midwest:	Southeast:	Northeast:	International:
Y	Y	Y	Y	Y	Y

SUN MICROSYSTEMS INC

www.oracle.com/us/sun/index.html

Industry Group Code: 334111 **Ranks within this company's industry group:** Sales: 12 Profits: 28

Hardware:		Software:		Telecommunications:	Electronic Publishing:	Equipment:		Specialty Services:	
Computers:	Y	Consumer:		Local:	Online Service:	Telecom:		Consulting:	Y
Accessories:		Corporate:	Y	Long Distance:	TV/Cable or Wireless:	Communication:		Contract Manufacturing:	
Network Equipment:		Telecom:		Cellular:	Games:	Distribution:		Processing:	
Chips/Circuits:	Y	Internet:		Internet Service:	Financial Data:	VAR/Reseller:		Staff/Outsourcing:	
Parts/Drives:	Y					Satellite Srv./Equip.:		Specialty Services:	Y

TYPES OF BUSINESS:

Computer Hardware
UNIX-Based Workstation Computers
Multiprocessing Servers
Operating System Software
Systems Integration
Office Application Software
Network Products
Consulting Services

BRANDS/DIVISIONS/AFFILIATES:

Oracle
UltraSPARC
Sun Fire
Solaris OS
Java
Sun Open Cloud Platform
SunSpectrum
Tarantella Inc

CONTACTS: Note: Officers with more than one job title may be intentionally listed here more than once.

Dorian Daley, CEO
Dorian Daley, Pres.
Leslie Maher, VP-Sales
James Hollingshead, VP-Global Sales Eng.
Michael A. Dillon, General Counsel/Exec. VP/Corp. Sec.
Mary Beth Walker, VP-Global Bus. Oper.
Brady Mickelsen, VP

Phone: 650-960-1300	Fax: 408-276-3804
Toll-Free: 800-786-0404	
Address: 4150 Network Cir., Santa Clara, CA 95054 US	

GROWTH PLANS/SPECIAL FEATURES:

Sun Microsystems, Inc. is a provider of scalable computer systems, networks, storage systems, software, microprocessors and support services. The products segment includes computer systems and data storage products. The firm's services segment offers maintenance contracts; client solutions; and educational services, which consist of technical consulting to help customers plan, implement, and manage distributed network computing environments and developing integrated learning solutions for enterprises, IT organizations and individual IT professionals. Sun's desktops and workstations, including the Sun Ray series, facilitate a wide range of activities such as software development, mechanical design, scientific visualization, and electronic design automation. Sun's proprietary microprocessor, the 64-bit UltraSPARC, powers most Sun platforms, including the Sun Fire series. The software segment of the computer systems group consists of Solaris Operating System (OS) and Java, Sun's universal software platform. Java is one of the computer industry's most widely-used software development languages. The platform is designed to allow developers and vendors to write software on one platform and run it on many different platforms, independent of operating system and hardware architecture. Solaris OS is a secure operating system for Sun platforms. Sun's storage systems segment includes the StorEdge system and StorEdge software, offering multi-level storage solutions. Sun Microsystems also offers MySQL, one of the world's most popular open source database management systems, designed to offer developers a simple-to-use, horizontally-scalable database often used to power applications such as web sites and web-based applications. Additionally, the firm offers Sun Oracle Database Machine, a fast database warehousing machine that runs online transaction processing applications. The company, which does not currently sell its products directly, employs independent distributors in over 100 countries; however, it has announced plans to engage in direct sales. In January 2010, Sun was acquired by Oracle Corporation for approximately $7 billion. Following the acquisition, Sun was integrated into Oracle's newly created hardware systems business.

FINANCIALS: Sales and profits are in thousands of dollars—add 000 to get the full amount. 2010 Note: Financial information for 2010 was not available for all companies at press time.

2010 Sales: $	2010 Profits: $	**U.S. Stock Ticker: Subsidiary**
2009 Sales: $11,449,000	2009 Profits: $-2,234,000	**Int'l Ticker:** Int'l Exchange:
2008 Sales: $13,880,000	2008 Profits: $403,000	Employees: 29,000
2007 Sales: $13,873,000	2007 Profits: $473,000	Fiscal Year Ends: 6/30
2006 Sales: $13,068,000	2006 Profits: $-864,000	Parent Company: ORACLE CORP

SALARIES/BENEFITS:

Pension Plan: Y	ESOP Stock Plan:	Profit Sharing:	Top Exec. Salary: $1,000,000	Bonus: $
Savings Plan: Y	Stock Purch. Plan: Y		Second Exec. Salary: $800,000	Bonus: $73,040

OTHER THOUGHTS:

Apparent Women Officers or Directors: 14
Hot Spot for Advancement for Women/Minorities: Y

LOCATIONS: ("Y" = Yes)

West:	Southwest:	Midwest:	Southeast:	Northeast:	International:
Y	Y	Y	Y	Y	Y

SUNGARD DATA SYSTEMS INC

www.sungard.com

Industry Group Code: 511201 Ranks within this company's industry group: Sales: 1 Profits: 6

Hardware:	Software:		Telecommunications:		Electronic Publishing:	Equipment:	Specialty Services:	
Computers:	Consumer:		Local:		Online Service:	Telecom:	Consulting:	
Accessories:	Corporate:	Y	Long Distance:		TV/Cable or Wireless:	Communication:	Contract Manufacturing:	
Network Equipment:	Telecom:		Cellular:	Y	Games:	Distribution:	Processing:	Y
Chips/Circuits:	Internet:		Internet Service:		Financial Data:	VAR/Reseller:	Staff/Outsourcing:	Y
Parts/Drives:						Satellite Srv./Equip.:	Specialty Services:	Y

TYPES OF BUSINESS:

Outsourced Information Processing & Services

BRANDS/DIVISIONS/AFFILIATES:

ICE Risk Solution
Performance Pathways, Inc.
Genix Systems AG
GL Trade
Ambit Enterprise Banking Suite
SunGard Transaction Network
Inmatrix
Fox River Execution

CONTACTS: Note: Officers with more than one job title may be intentionally listed here more than once.

Cristobal Conde, CEO
Cristobal Conde, Pres.
Robert Woods, CFO
Brian Robins, Chief Mktg. Officer/Sr. VP
Kathleen Asser Weslock, Chief Human Resources Officer
Victoria E. Silbey, General Counsel/VP-Legal
Richard C. Tarbox, Sr. VP-Corp. Dev.
Karen Mullane, Controller/VP
Jim Ashton, Div. CEO-Financial Systems
Harold Finders, Div. CEO-Financial Systems
Gil Santos, CEO-Public Sector
Ron Lang, CEO-Higher Education
Glenn H. Hutchins, Chmn.

Phone: 484-582-2000	Fax:
Toll-Free: 800-825-2518	
Address: 680 E. Swedesford Rd., Wayne, PA 19087 US	

GROWTH PLANS/SPECIAL FEATURES:

SunGard Data Systems, Inc. is a leading global provider of integrated software and information technology services for financial services companies, higher education and the public sector. The firm serves more than 25,000 clients in over 70 countries. SunGard is organized into four business segments: Financial Systems, Higher Education, Public Sector and Availability Services. SunGard Financial Systems serves financial services companies specializing in alternative investments; banking; benefit administration; brokerage and clearance; capital markets and investment banking; energy trading and risk management; institutional asset management; insurance; trading; treasury management; and wealth management. The Higher Education segment provides specialized enterprise resource planning and administrative software to over 1,600 higher education institutions. SunGard Public Sector serves school districts, nonprofit organizations and local, state and federal government agencies, with solutions for accounting; human resources; payroll; utility billing; land management; public safety and criminal justice; and grant and project management. The Availability Services segment provides solutions to information-dependent companies across virtually all industries protecting against breaches of security; network or hardware failures; data loss; power failure; and extreme events, such as natural disaster and terrorism. In 2009, the firm launched several new products, including the Ambit Enterprise Banking Suite, a front-to-middle-office retail banking solution; and SunGard Transaction Network, an Internet-based portal for the management of stock repurchase transactions and reporting. In January 2010, SunGard introduced MyWealthSeries, a web-based financial planning solution. In February 2010, the company acquired credit risk analysis and business forecasting solutions provider Inmatrix. In July 2010, SunGard acquired broker dealer Fox River Execution; and agreed to sell its high-volume financial messaging product, Ambit Messaging Hub, to Society for Worldwide Interbank Financial Telecommunication (SWIFT).

SunGard offers its employees medical, dental and vision insurance; an employee assistance program; a flexible compensation plan; short- and long-term disability; life and AD&D insurance; a retirement savings plan; a college tuition savings plan; tuition reimbursement; and adoption assistance.

FINANCIALS: Sales and profits are in thousands of dollars—add 000 to get the full amount. 2010 Note: Financial information for 2010 was not available for all companies at press time.

2010 Sales: $	2010 Profits: $	U.S. Stock Ticker: Private
2009 Sales: $5,508,000	2009 Profits: $-576,000	Int'l Ticker: Int'l Exchange:
2008 Sales: $5,596,000	2008 Profits: $470,000	Employees: 20,700
2007 Sales: $4,901,000	2007 Profits: $-60,000	Fiscal Year Ends: 12/31
2006 Sales: $4,323,000	2006 Profits: $-118,000	Parent Company:

SALARIES/BENEFITS:

Pension Plan:	ESOP Stock Plan:	Profit Sharing:	Top Exec. Salary: $	Bonus: $1,517,972
Savings Plan: Y	Stock Purch. Plan:		Second Exec. Salary: $	Bonus: $

OTHER THOUGHTS:

Apparent Women Officers or Directors: 3
Hot Spot for Advancement for Women/Minorities: Y

LOCATIONS: ("Y" = Yes)

West:	Southwest:	Midwest:	Southeast:	Northeast:	International:
Y	Y	Y	Y	Y	Y

SUPER MICRO COMPUTER INC

www.supermicro.com

Industry Group Code: 334111 Ranks within this company's industry group: Sales: 23 Profits: 13

Hardware:		Software:	Telecommunications:	Electronic Publishing:	Equipment:	Specialty Services:
Computers:		Consumer:	Local:	Online Service:	Telecom:	Consulting:
Accessories:	Y	Corporate:	Long Distance:	TV/Cable or Wireless:	Communication:	Contract Manufacturing:
Network Equipment:		Telecom:	Cellular:	Games:	Distribution:	Processing:
Chips/Circuits:		Internet:	Internet Service:	Financial Data:	VAR/Reseller:	Staff/Outsourcing:
Parts/Drives:	Y				Satellite Srv./Equip.:	Specialty Services:

TYPES OF BUSINESS:
Server Systems & Components

BRANDS/DIVISIONS/AFFILIATES:

CONTACTS: Note: Officers with more than one job title may be intentionally listed here more than once.
Charles Liang, CEO
Charles Liang, Pres.
Howard Hideshima, CFO
Phidias Chou, VP-Worldwide Sales
Wally Liaw, Sec.
Sara Liu, VP-Oper.
Sara Liu, Treas.
Charles Liang, Chmn.
Wally Liaw, VP-Int'l Sales

Phone: 408-503-8000	Fax: 408-503-8008
Toll-Free:	
Address: 980 Rock Ave., San Jose, CA 95131 US	

GROWTH PLANS/SPECIAL FEATURES:

Super Micro Computer, Inc. designs, develops, manufactures and sells application optimized, high performance server systems based on modular and open-standard x86 architecture. Its products include a range of complete rackmount and blade server systems, as well as components, including serverboards, chassis, power supplies and system accessories such as microprocessors and memory and disk drives. The firm offers its clients a high degree of flexibility and customization by providing a broad array of server components, which are interoperable and can be configured to create complete server systems. The company bases its offerings on open-standard components, such as processors from Intel and AMD. Its products are compatible with both Linux and Windows operating systems. The firm sells server systems in rack-mounted, standalone tower and blade form factors. It currently offers a complete range of server options with single, dual and quad CPU capability, supporting Intel Pentium and Xeon multi-core architectures in 1U, 2U, 3U and 4U, tower and blade form factors. Additionally, the firm offers complete server systems for AMD dual and quad Opteron in 1U, 2U, 4U and blade form factors. Super Micro Computer offers over 900 different server systems, and for each system it provides multiple chassis designs and power supply options. The company also offers Supermicro Intelligent Management (SIM) card solutions to provide remote access and system monitoring. Super Micro Computer sells its server systems and components primarily through distributors, which include value added resellers and systems integrators, and, to a lesser extent, original equipment manufacturers (OEMs) as well as a direct sales force.

The company offers its employees benefits that include health, dental, vision, life AD&D and disability insurance, as well as a 401(k) plan.

FINANCIALS: Sales and profits are in thousands of dollars—add 000 to get the full amount. 2010 Note: Financial information for 2010 was not available for all companies at press time.

2010 Sales: $721,438	2010 Profits: $26,915	U.S. Stock Ticker: SMCI
2009 Sales: $505,609	2009 Profits: $16,107	Int'l Ticker: Int'l Exchange:
2008 Sales: $540,503	2008 Profits: $25,419	Employees: 1,012
2007 Sales: $420,393	2007 Profits: $19,339	Fiscal Year Ends: 6/30
2006 Sales: $302,541	2006 Profits: $16,947	Parent Company:

SALARIES/BENEFITS:

Pension Plan:	ESOP Stock Plan:	Profit Sharing:	Top Exec. Salary: $286,598	Bonus: $4,823
Savings Plan: Y	Stock Purch. Plan:		Second Exec. Salary: $253,331	Bonus: $3,638

OTHER THOUGHTS:
Apparent Women Officers or Directors: 1
Hot Spot for Advancement for Women/Minorities:

LOCATIONS: ("Y" = Yes)

West:	Southwest:	Midwest:	Southeast:	Northeast:	International:
Y					Y

SUPPORT.COM INC

www.support.com

Industry Group Code: 511210K Ranks within this company's industry group: Sales: 9 Profits: 11

Hardware:	Software:		Telecommunications:	Electronic Publishing:	Equipment:	Specialty Services:
Computers:	Consumer:	Y	Local:	Online Service:	Telecom:	Consulting:
Accessories:	Corporate:	Y	Long Distance:	TV/Cable or Wireless:	Communication:	Contract Manufacturing:
Network Equipment:	Telecom:		Cellular:	Games:	Distribution:	Processing:
Chips/Circuits:	Internet:		Internet Service:	Financial Data:	VAR/Reseller:	Staff/Outsourcing:
Parts/Drives:					Satellite Srv./Equip.:	Specialty Services:

TYPES OF BUSINESS:

Software-Service & Support Automation
Real-Time Service Management Software

BRANDS/DIVISIONS/AFFILIATES:

CONTACTS: Note: Officers with more than one job title may be intentionally listed here more than once.

Josh Pickus, CEO
Anthony Rodio, COO/Exec. VP
Joshua Pickus, Pres.
Shelly Schaffer, CFO/Exec. VP
James Morehead, VP-Prod. Mgmt.
Rich Matta, VP-Eng.
Greg Wrenn, General Counsel/VP
Paul Vaillancourt, VP-Contact Center Oper.
Tim Krozek, Sr. VP-Bus. Dev.
Barak Ben-Gal, VP-Finance/Controller
Allen Nieman, VP/Gen. Mgr.
Jim Stephens, Chmn.

Phone: 650-556-9440	Fax: 650-556-1195
Toll-Free: 877-493-2778	
Address: 1900 Seaport Blvd., 3rd Fl., Redwood City, CA 94063 US	

GROWTH PLANS/SPECIAL FEATURES:

Support.com, Inc. is a leading provider of software and services designed to assist small businesses and end-users in solving technology problems. The firm delivers its services online and by telephone through work-from-home agents, as well as provides software products for personal computers. The company's services include repair and maintenance; virus removal; computer security; data recovery and backup; file management; computer networking, such as wireless internet and connecting two computers; connecting and installing peripherals such as Bluetooth; and installing operating systems, software and applications. Services can be purchased on a subscription basis, on a one-time incident basis, through small business plans or with prepaid service and gift cards. The company sells its products through direct sales to consumers and indirectly through channel partners, such as brick-and-mortar and online retailers, anti-virus providers, PC/CE manufacturers and others.

The company offers employees life and AD&D insurance; a 401(k) plan; an employee stock options program (ESOP); medical, dental and vision insurance; emergency travel insurance; an employee assistance program; and an educational reimbursement program.

FINANCIALS: Sales and profits are in thousands of dollars—add 000 to get the full amount. 2010 Note: Financial information for 2010 was not available for all companies at press time.

2010 Sales: $	2010 Profits: $	U.S. Stock Ticker: SPRT
2009 Sales: $17,495	2009 Profits: $-14,577	Int'l Ticker: Int'l Exchange:
2008 Sales: $6,811	2008 Profits: $-19,106	Employees: 420
2007 Sales: $47,802	2007 Profits: $-21,369	Fiscal Year Ends: 12/31
2006 Sales: $45,028	2006 Profits: $-8,235	Parent Company:

SALARIES/BENEFITS:

Pension Plan:	ESOP Stock Plan: Y	Profit Sharing:	Top Exec. Salary: $337,500	Bonus: $221,655
Savings Plan: Y	Stock Purch. Plan:		Second Exec. Salary: $260,000	Bonus: $108,122

OTHER THOUGHTS:

Apparent Women Officers or Directors: 2
Hot Spot for Advancement for Women/Minorities:

LOCATIONS: ("Y" = Yes)

West:	Southwest:	Midwest:	Southeast:	Northeast:	International:
Y					Y

Note: Financial information, benefits and other data can change quickly and may vary from those stated here.

SYBASE INC

www.sybase.com

Industry Group Code: 511210H Ranks within this company's industry group: Sales: 7 Profits: 6

Hardware:	Software:		Telecommunications:	Electronic Publishing:	Equipment:	Specialty Services:	
Computers:	Consumer:		Local:	Online Service:	Telecom:	Consulting:	Y
Accessories:	Corporate:	Y	Long Distance:	TV/Cable or Wireless:	Communication:	Contract Manufacturing:	
Network Equipment:	Telecom:	Y	Cellular:	Games:	Distribution:	Processing:	
Chips/Circuits:	Internet:		Internet Service:	Financial Data:	VAR/Reseller:	Staff/Outsourcing:	
Parts/Drives:					Satellite Srv./Equip.:	Specialty Services:	

TYPES OF BUSINESS:

Software-Database Management
Enterprise Portal Products
Consulting Services
Wireless Software Solutions

BRANDS/DIVISIONS/AFFILIATES:

Infrastructure Platform Group
iAnywhere Solutions
Sybase 365
Adaptive Server Enterprise
Sybase IQ
PowerDesigner
PowerBuilder
SAP AG

CONTACTS: Note: Officers with more than one job title may be intentionally listed here more than once.

John S. Chen, CEO
John S. Chen, Pres.
Jeff G. Ross, CFO/Sr. VP
Raj Nathan, Chief Mktg. Officer/Sr. VP-Worldwide Mktg. Oper.
Nita C. White-Ivy, VP-Human Resources
Billy Ho, Sr. VP-Tech. Oper.
Billy Ho, Sr. VP-Prod. Oper.
Dan R. Carl, General Counsel/Sec./VP
Raj Nathan, Sr. VP-Bus. Solutions Oper.
Keith F. Jensen, Corp. Controller/VP
Marty J. Beard, Pres., Sybase 365
Terry Stepien, Pres., Sybase iAnywhere
John S. Chen, Chmn.
Steve Capelli, Pres., Worldwide Field Oper.

Phone: 925-236-5000	Fax: 925-236-4468
Toll-Free: 800-792-2735	
Address: 1 Sybase Dr., Dublin, CA 94568 US	

GROWTH PLANS/SPECIAL FEATURES:

Sybase, Inc., a subsidiary of SAP AG, is a global enterprise software and services company exclusively focused on managing and mobilizing information from the data-center to the point of action. The firm operates through three segments: Infrastructure Platform Group (IPG), iAnywhere Solutions (iAS) and Sybase 365. IPG focuses on information management, offering two lines of enterprise class data servers: Adaptive Server Enterprise (ASE), a relational database management system for mission-critical transactions, and Sybase IQ, a specialized column-based analytic server, for business intelligence applications such as accelerated reporting, advanced analytics and analytics services. IPG also produces solutions for business continuity, including the Sybase Replication Server and the Sybase Mirror Activator for very high availability data environments. Products include PowerDesigner, a modeling tool; PowerBuilder, a Rapid Application Development tool; and WorkSpace for integrated development environments. IPG generates approximately 73% of Sybase's revenue. iAS, which generates approximately 27% of the firm's revenue, provides mobile and embedded databases; mobile management and security; mobile middleware and synchronization; and Bluetooth and infrared protocol technologies. iAS's technologies include SQL Anywhere, Afaria and iAnywhere Mobile Office. Sybase 365 provides mobile messaging interoperability; the delivery and settlement of Short Message Service (SMS) and Multimedia Messaging Service (MMS) content; mobile commerce; and enterprise-class messaging services. Sybase 365 utilizes an operator-grade, secure messaging platform connected by a global private network of IP and SS7 connections to more than 700 mobile operators worldwide. Sybase 365 processed over 1 billion messages per day with approximately 4 billion subscribers. In July 2010, the firm was acquired by German software development company SAP AG for $5.8 billion

Sybase Inc. offers employee benefits including medical, dental, vision, AD&D, life and disability insurance; a 401(k) plan; paid time off; an adoption assistance program; and onsite child care at some locations.

FINANCIALS: Sales and profits are in thousands of dollars—add 000 to get the full amount. 2010 Note: Financial information for 2010 was not available for all companies at press time.

2010 Sales: $	2010 Profits: $	**U.S. Stock Ticker: Subsidiary**
2009 Sales: $1,170,569	2009 Profits: $164,059	**Int'l Ticker:** Int'l Exchange:
2008 Sales: $1,131,930	2008 Profits: $128,238	Employees: 3,819
2007 Sales: $1,025,530	2007 Profits: $139,139	Fiscal Year Ends: 12/31
2006 Sales: $876,163	2006 Profits: $95,064	Parent Company: SAP AG

SALARIES/BENEFITS:

Pension Plan:	ESOP Stock Plan:	Profit Sharing:	Top Exec. Salary: $990,000	Bonus: $2,352,000
Savings Plan: Y	Stock Purch. Plan:		Second Exec. Salary: $440,748	Bonus: $321,903

OTHER THOUGHTS:

Apparent Women Officers or Directors: 1
Hot Spot for Advancement for Women/Minorities:

LOCATIONS: ("Y" = Yes)

West:	Southwest:	Midwest:	Southeast:	Northeast:	International:
Y	Y	Y	Y	Y	Y

SYMANTEC CORP

www.symantec.com

Industry Group Code: 511210E　Ranks within this company's industry group: Sales: 1　Profits: 12

Hardware:	Software:		Telecommunications:	Electronic Publishing:	Equipment:	Specialty Services:
Computers:	Consumer:	Y	Local:	Online Service:	Telecom:	Consulting:
Accessories:	Corporate:	Y	Long Distance:	TV/Cable or Wireless:	Communication:	Contract Manufacturing:
Network Equipment:	Telecom:		Cellular:	Games:	Distribution:	Processing:
Chips/Circuits:	Internet:	Y	Internet Service:	Financial Data:	VAR/Reseller:	Staff/Outsourcing:
Parts/Drives:					Satellite Srv./Equip.:	Specialty Services:

TYPES OF BUSINESS:
Software-Security
Remote Management Products
IT Consulting Services

BRANDS/DIVISIONS/AFFILIATES:
Norton360
Norton Utilities
Norton AntiVirus
Norton Internet Security
GuardianEdge
PGP Corporation
Symantec Data Insight for Storage
Ubiquity

CONTACTS: Note: Officers with more than one job title may be intentionally listed here more than once.
Enrique T. Salem, CEO
Enrique T. Salem, Pres.
James Beer, CFO/Exec. VP
Carine Clark, Chief Mktg. Officer/Sr. VP
Rebecca Ranninger, Chief Human Resources Officer/Exec. VP
Deepak Mohan, Sr. VP-Info. Mgmt. Group
Mark Bregman, CTO/Exec. VP
Scott Taylor, General Counsel/Exec. VP/Sec.
Ken Berryman, Sr. VP-Strategy
Genevieve Haldeman, VP-Corp. Comm.
Bill Robbins, Exec. VP-Worldwide Sales
Janice Chaffin, Pres., Consumer Bus. Unit
Bernard Kwok, Sr. VP-APAC & Japan
Francis deSouza, Sr. VP-Enterprise Security Group
John W. Thompson, Chmn.
John Brigden, Sr. VP-EMEA

Phone: 650-527-8000	Fax:
Toll-Free:	
Address: 350 Ellis St., Mountain View, CA 94043 US	

GROWTH PLANS/SPECIAL FEATURES:
Symantec Corp. provides a range of software, appliances and services designed to secure and manage information technology (IT) infrastructure. The company provides customers worldwide with software and services that protect, manage and control information risks related to security, data protection, storage, compliance, and systems management. The firm has five operating segments: consumer products; security and compliance; storage and service management; services; and other. The consumer products segment delivers Internet security, PC tuneup and backup products. The company's Norton brand provides protection for Windows and Macintosh platforms. Primary consumer products include Norton Antivirus, Norton360, and Norton Internet Security, which help defend home and home office users by blocking online identity theft, detecting and eliminating spyware and protecting against hackers from entering a user's system. The security and compliance segment provides solutions for compliance and security management, endpoint security, messaging management and data protection management software solutions that allow customers to secure, provision, backup and remotely access laptops, PCs, mobile devices and servers. The storage and service management division provides storage and server management, data protection, and application performance services that manage IT risk on an ongoing basis. Symantec's services division offers technical support, managed services, consulting, support and education. The other segment includes sunset products and products nearing the end of their life cycle. Symantec Corp. operates in over 40 countries and maintains more than 40,000 partnerships worldwide. In January 2010, the firm agreed to acquire information security solutions provider Gideon Technologies, Inc. In June 2010, the company acquired email and data encryption firms GuardianEdge and PGP Corporation. In August 2010, Symantec Corp. acquired the identity and authentication operations of VeriSign. In late 2010, the company released evolving malware fighting product Ubiquity. In December 2010, the firm launched new unstructured data organizing tool Symantec Data Insight for Storage.

FINANCIALS: Sales and profits are in thousands of dollars—add 000 to get the full amount. 2010 Note: Financial information for 2010 was not available for all companies at press time.

2010 Sales: $5,985,000	2010 Profits: $714,000	**U.S. Stock Ticker: SYMC**
2009 Sales: $6,149,854	2009 Profits: $-6,728,870	**Int'l Ticker:**　Int'l Exchange:
2008 Sales: $5,874,419	2008 Profits: $463,850	Employees: 17,400
2007 Sales: $5,199,370	2007 Profits: $404,380	Fiscal Year Ends: 3/31
2006 Sales: $4,143,392	2006 Profits: $156,852	Parent Company:

SALARIES/BENEFITS:

Pension Plan:	ESOP Stock Plan:	Profit Sharing:	Top Exec. Salary: $660,000	Bonus: $747,120
Savings Plan: Y	Stock Purch. Plan: Y		Second Exec. Salary: $625,000	Bonus: $3,092,969

OTHER THOUGHTS:
Apparent Women Officers or Directors: 4
Hot Spot for Advancement for Women/Minorities: Y

LOCATIONS: ("Y" = Yes)

West:	Southwest:	Midwest:	Southeast:	Northeast:	International:
Y					Y

Note: Financial information, benefits and other data can change quickly and may vary from those stated here.

SYMMETRICOM INC

www.symmetricom.com

Industry Group Code: 334210 Ranks within this company's industry group: Sales: 15 Profits: 8

Hardware:	Software:	Telecommunications:	Electronic Publishing:	Equipment:		Specialty Services:	
Computers:	Consumer:	Local:	Online Service:	Telecom:	Y	Consulting:	Y
Accessories:	Corporate:	Long Distance:	TV/Cable or Wireless:	Communication:	Y	Contract Manufacturing:	
Network Equipment:	Telecom:	Cellular:	Games:	Distribution:		Processing:	
Chips/Circuits:	Internet:	Internet Service:	Financial Data:	VAR/Reseller:		Staff/Outsourcing:	
Parts/Drives:				Satellite Srv./Equip.:		Specialty Services:	Y

TYPES OF BUSINESS:

Telecommunications Equipment
Business DSL Products
Network Synchronization & Timing Equipment
Atomic Clocks
Test & Measurement Equipment
Consulting Services

BRANDS/DIVISIONS/AFFILIATES:

Infrastructure Platform Group
iAnywhere Solutions
Sybase 365
Sybase IQ
Sybase Replication Server
Sybase Mirror Activator
PowerDesigner
PowerBuilder

CONTACTS: Note: Officers with more than one job title may be intentionally listed here more than once.

Dave Cote, CEO
Dave Cote, Pres.
Justin Spencer, CFO
Phil Bourekas, Exec. VP-Mktg.
Bill Minor, Exec. VP-Global Human Resources
Samuel Stein, CTO
Greg Ruebusch, Exec. VP-Global Mfg. Oper.
Justin Spencer, Corp. Sec.
William Slater, Exec. VP-Finance
Bruce Bromage, Exec. VP/Gen. Mgr.-TT&M Div.
James Armstrong, Exec. VP/Gen. Mgr.-Telecom Solutions Div.
Robert T. Clarkson, Chmn.
Juan Dewar, Exec. VP-Global Sales & Svcs.

Phone: 408-433-0910	Fax: 408-428-6960
Toll-Free:	
Address: 2300 Orchard Pkwy., San Jose, CA 95131-1017 US	

GROWTH PLANS/SPECIAL FEATURES:

Symmetricom, Inc. (SYMM) supplies timing and synchronization hardware, software and services to government agencies, enterprises and research facilities in over 90 countries. Its products include global positioning system (GPS) time and frequency receivers and time and frequency distribution systems. SYMM operates through five segments, four of which are organized under the Telecom Solutions Division (TSD): Wireline products, Wireless/OEM (original equipment manufacturer) Products, Global Services and Quality of Experience Assurance Products. The fifth segment is the Timing, Test and Measurement (TT&M) division. SYMM's TSD supplies network synchronization and timing solutions to global communications companies. Its products control or synchronize the flow of information, voice, video or data that enable customers to maximize network efficiency and quality of service in narrowband and broadband networks. This division also provides hardware/software-based probes and/or embedded agents that are distributed throughout an IP network in order to monitor network and application performance. The TT&M division provides precision time and frequency instruments and reference standards for a variety of applications to the aerospace, defense, enterprise, and metrology marketplaces. Its products include network timeservers, synchronized clocks, network displays, time code generators, computer plug-in cards and primary reference standards such as cesium frequency standards and active hydrogen masers. In 2009, SYMM introduced several new products, including 5125A Allan Deviation Test Set (ADEV), a digital solution for phase noise and stability characterization of frequency sources up to 400 megahertz (MHz); XLi IEEE 1588 PTP v2 Grandmaster, a GPS referenced grandmaster clock and measurement/validation solution; and TimeAnalyzer, a comprehensive packet-timing data all-in-one test and measurement tool. In March 2010, the firm sold its video Quality of Experience operations to Cheetah Technologies, L.P. for roughly $2.25 million.

The company offers its employees life, AD&D, business travel accident, medical, dental and vision insurance; a 401(k); education assistance; and a stock grant options plan.

FINANCIALS: Sales and profits are in thousands of dollars—add 000 to get the full amount. 2010 Note: Financial information for 2010 was not available for all companies at press time.

2010 Sales: $221,316	2010 Profits: $2,526	U.S. Stock Ticker: SYMM
2009 Sales: $219,746	2009 Profits: $-45,757	Int'l Ticker: Int'l Exchange:
2008 Sales: $206,386	2008 Profits: $-17,747	Employees: 700
2007 Sales: $208,380	2007 Profits: $6,105	Fiscal Year Ends: 6/30
2006 Sales: $176,112	2006 Profits: $ 819	Parent Company:

SALARIES/BENEFITS:

Pension Plan:	ESOP Stock Plan:	Profit Sharing:	Top Exec. Salary: $500,000	Bonus: $296,625
Savings Plan: Y	Stock Purch. Plan: Y		Second Exec. Salary: $290,000	Bonus: $164,695

OTHER THOUGHTS:

Apparent Women Officers or Directors: 1
Hot Spot for Advancement for Women/Minorities:

LOCATIONS: ("Y" = Yes)

West:	Southwest:	Midwest:	Southeast:	Northeast:	International:
Y				Y	Y

Note: Financial information, benefits and other data can change quickly and may vary from those stated here.

SYMPHONY TECHNOLOGY GROUP

www.symphonytg.com

Industry Group Code: 5112 Ranks within this company's industry group: Sales: Profits:

Hardware:	Software:		Telecommunications:	Electronic Publishing:	Equipment:	Specialty Services:	
Computers:	Consumer:		Local:	Online Service:	Telecom:	Consulting:	Y
Accessories:	Corporate:	Y	Long Distance:	TV/Cable or Wireless:	Communication:	Contract Manufacturing:	
Network Equipment:	Telecom:		Cellular:	Games:	Distribution:	Processing:	
Chips/Circuits:	Internet:		Internet Service:	Financial Data:	VAR/Reseller:	Staff/Outsourcing:	
Parts/Drives:					Satellite Srv./Equip.:	Specialty Services:	Y

TYPES OF BUSINESS:

Enterprise Management Software
Retail Industry Software
Analytic Services
Outsourcing

BRANDS/DIVISIONS/AFFILIATES:

Netik Inc
Lawson Software Inc
Aldata Software Management Inc
First Advantage Corporation
MSC.Software Corporation
Teleca AB
Symphony Services Corporation
Symphony Information Resources Inc

CONTACTS: Note: Officers with more than one job title may be intentionally listed here more than once.

Romesh Wadhwani, CEO
Brad MacMillin, CFO
Chris Langone, VP-Bus. Dev.
Stephen Combs, Chief Recruiting Officer
Romesh Wadhwani, Chmn.

Phone: 650-935-9500	Fax: 650-935-9501
Toll-Free:	
Address: 2475 Hanover St., Palo Alto, CA 94304 US	

GROWTH PLANS/SPECIAL FEATURES:

Symphony Technology Group (STG) is a private equity firm that focuses its investments in the enterprise software and service markets. STG's major portfolio companies include Aldata; EYC; First Advantage; Lawson; MSC.Software; Netik; Symphony Services; Symphony Information Resources, Inc. (IRI); and Teleca. Aldata is a global leader in supply chain software for retail, wholesale and logistics with over 300 customers across 50 countries. EYC specializes in consumer data, especially data generated by grocery store loyalty card programs. First Advantage provides workplace information services, such as talent acquisition and behavioral assessments. Lawson is a global enterprise application provider serving mid-market companies in the manufacturing, maintenance and distribution sectors. Its Movex application suite includes supplier relationship management, customer relationship management, value chain collaboration, e-business, enterprise asset management, enterprise performance management and supply chain management applications. MSC.Software develops and designs computer aided engineering software. Netik provides data warehouse solutions, particularly in financial information automation. Symphony Services is a global business services outsourcing partner comprising three business groups: the commercial software group, which uses its proprietary development framework to provide increased productivity and faster time-to-market for commercial-grade software products and solutions; the cost management group, which provides a full suite of telecommunications and IT expense management outsourcing and software solutions; and the demand analytics group, which combines high-volume data factory services with analytic skills. Symphony IRI provides market content applications, analytic services and business performance management solutions to the consumer goods and retail industries. Teleca is a global software services provider and has locations in 11 countries. In February 2010, STG sold its Symphony Marketing Solutions business to GenPact. In October 2010, the firm agreed to sell its Capco consulting business to Fidelity National Information Systems for $300 million. In January 2011, the company acquired First Advantage from CoreLogic for $265 million.

FINANCIALS: Sales and profits are in thousands of dollars—add 000 to get the full amount. 2010 Note: Financial information for 2010 was not available for all companies at press time.

2010 Sales: $	2010 Profits: $	**U.S. Stock Ticker: Private**
2009 Sales: $	2009 Profits: $	**Int'l Ticker:** Int'l Exchange:
2008 Sales: $	2008 Profits: $	Employees:
2007 Sales: $	2007 Profits: $	Fiscal Year Ends: 12/31
2006 Sales: $	2006 Profits: $	Parent Company:

SALARIES/BENEFITS:

Pension Plan:	ESOP Stock Plan:	Profit Sharing:	Top Exec. Salary: $	Bonus: $
Savings Plan:	Stock Purch. Plan:		Second Exec. Salary: $	Bonus: $

OTHER THOUGHTS:

Apparent Women Officers or Directors:
Hot Spot for Advancement for Women/Minorities:

LOCATIONS: ("Y" = Yes)

West:	Southwest:	Midwest:	Southeast:	Northeast:	International:
Y					

SYNAPTICS INC

www.synaptics.com

Industry Group Code: 334119 Ranks within this company's industry group: Sales: 19 Profits: 10

Hardware:		Software:		Telecommunications:	Electronic Publishing:	Equipment:	Specialty Services:
Computers:		Consumer:		Local:	Online Service:	Telecom:	Consulting:
Accessories:	Y	Corporate:		Long Distance:	TV/Cable or Wireless:	Communication:	Contract Manufacturing:
Network Equipment:		Telecom:		Cellular:	Games:	Distribution:	Processing:
Chips/Circuits:		Internet:		Internet Service:	Financial Data:	VAR/Reseller:	Staff/Outsourcing:
Parts/Drives:	Y					Satellite Srv./Equip.:	Specialty Services:

TYPES OF BUSINESS:

Electronic Components
User Interface Systems

BRANDS/DIVISIONS/AFFILIATES:

TouchPad
TouchStyk
OneTouch
LightTouch
QuickStroke
TouchStyk
ScrollStrip
MobileTouch

CONTACTS: Note: Officers with more than one job title may be intentionally listed here more than once.

Tom Tiernan, CEO
Tom Tiernan, Pres.
Kathleen Bayless, CFO
Gopal Garg, Sr. VP-Mktg. & Handheld Bus.
James Harrington, VP-Global Human Resources
Joe Montalbo, Sr. VP-Platform Research & Dev.
Shawn Day, CTO/VP
Kathleen Bayless, Sec.
Alex Wong, VP-Worldwide Oper.
Kathleen Bayless, Treas.
Ruth Lutes, VP-Customer Care & Quality
Dave Long, VP-Worldwide Sales
Mark Vena, VP-PC Bus. Unit
Francis Lee, Chmn.

Phone: 408-454-5100	Fax: 408-454-5200

Toll-Free:

Address: 3120 Scott Blvd., Ste. 130, Santa Clara, CA 95054 US

GROWTH PLANS/SPECIAL FEATURES:

Synaptics, Inc. (SYNA) is a worldwide developer of custom-designed user interface products for mobile computing, communications, entertainment and other electronic devices. These products emphasize ease of use, small size, low power consumption, advanced functionality, durability and reliability, making them applicable to a multitude of markets, including notebook computers, PC peripherals, mobile phones and portable entertainment devices such as MP3 players. SYNA's original equipment manufacturer (OEM) customers include most of the tier one PC OEMs and many of the world's largest OEMs for mobile smartphones and portable digital music players. The firm's OneTouch product enables customers to access the company's other technologies to develop their own interface designs for capacitive button and scrolling applications. Products for the PC market include the TouchPad, a touch-sensitive pad that senses movement of a person's finger on its surface; TouchStyk, a self-contained pointing stick module; and dual pointing solutions, a combination of a TouchPad and a pointing stick into a single notebook computer. The company also addresses the growing market of new mobile computing and communications devices, called information appliances (or iAppliances), as well as other electronic devices. Products in this market sector include the Scroll Strip and TouchRing, which are scrolling applications allowing users to navigate efficiently through menus and content; LightTouch capacitive buttons, which provide illuminated button functionality; as well as MobileTouch, NavPoint, ClearPad and TouchScreen products.

The firm offers its employees medical, dental and vision insurance; flexible spending accounts; an employee stock purchase plan; a 401(k) plan; and an educational assistance program.

FINANCIALS: Sales and profits are in thousands of dollars—add 000 to get the full amount. 2010 Note: Financial information for 2010 was not available for all companies at press time.

2010 Sales: $514,890	2010 Profits: $52,965	U.S. Stock Ticker: SYNA
2009 Sales: $473,302	2009 Profits: $48,079	Int'l Ticker: Int'l Exchange:
2008 Sales: $361,057	2008 Profits: $26,363	Employees: 586
2007 Sales: $266,787	2007 Profits: $26,534	Fiscal Year Ends: 6/30
2006 Sales: $184,557	2006 Profits: $13,701	Parent Company:

SALARIES/BENEFITS:

Pension Plan:	ESOP Stock Plan:	Profit Sharing:	Top Exec. Salary: $375,000	Bonus: $466,498
Savings Plan: Y	Stock Purch. Plan: Y		Second Exec. Salary: $326,914	Bonus: $232,000

OTHER THOUGHTS:

Apparent Women Officers or Directors: 2
Hot Spot for Advancement for Women/Minorities:

LOCATIONS: ("Y" = Yes)

West:	Southwest:	Midwest:	Southeast:	Northeast:	International:
Y					Y

SYNNEX CORP

www.synnex.com

Industry Group Code: 423430 Ranks within this company's industry group: Sales: 6 Profits: 4

Hardware:	Software:	Telecommunications:	Electronic Publishing:	Equipment:		Specialty Services:	
Computers:	Consumer:	Local:	Online Service:	Telecom:		Consulting:	
Accessories:	Corporate:	Long Distance:	TV/Cable or Wireless:	Communication:		Contract Manufacturing:	Y
Network Equipment:	Telecom:	Cellular:	Games:	Distribution:	Y	Processing:	
Chips/Circuits:	Internet:	Internet Service:	Financial Data:	VAR/Reseller:		Staff/Outsourcing:	Y
Parts/Drives:				Satellite Srv./Equip.:		Specialty Services:	Y

TYPES OF BUSINESS:
IT Supply Chain Services
Distribution Services
Contract Assembly Services
Outsourcing Services

BRANDS/DIVISIONS/AFFILIATES:
Synnex Canada Ltd
SYNNEX de Mexico, S.A. de C.V.

CONTACTS:
Note: Officers with more than one job title may be intentionally listed here more than once.
Kevin Murai, CEO
Dennis Polk, COO
Kevin Murai, Pres.
Thomas C. Alsborg, CFO
Steve Jow, Sr. VP-Sales
Gary Gulmon, CIO/Sr. VP
Gary Palenbaum, Sr. VP-Prod. Mgmt.
Simon Leung, General Counsel/Sr. VP/Corp. Sec.
Tim Rush, Sr. VP-Oper.
Pradip Madan, Sr. VP-Corp. Strategy & Dev.
Mike Vaishnav, Corp. Controller/Sr. VP
Robert Stegner, Sr. VP-Mktg., North America
Christopher Caldwell, Sr. VP/Gen. Mgr.-Global Bus. Svcs.
Adam Carroll, Pres., New Age Electronics
Stephen Ichinaga, Sr. VP/Gen. Mgr.-Systems
Dwight Steffensen, Chmn.
Peter Larocque, Pres., U.S. Distribution

Phone: 510-656-3333	Fax: 510-668-3777
Toll-Free: 800-756-9888	
Address: 44201 Nobel Dr., Fremont, CA 94538 US	

GROWTH PLANS/SPECIAL FEATURES:
SYNNEX Corp. is a leading business process services company, serving resellers, retailers and original equipment manufacturers (OEMs) around the world. The firm operates in two segments: distribution services and global business services (GBS). The distribution services segment distributes computer systems and complimentary products to a variety of customers, including value-added resellers, system integrators and retailers. This segment also provides assembly services to OEMs, including integrated supply chain management, build-to-order and configure-to-order system configurations, materials and management and logistics. The GBS segment offers a range of services, including customer management, software development, web hosting, hosted software, domain name registration and back office processing. SYNNEX delivers these services through various methods, including voice, chat, web, e-mail and digital print. The firm also offers value-added support services such as demand generation, pre-sales support, product marketing, print and fulfillment, back office outsourcing, post-sales technical support, web hosting and domain name registration services. The company purchases IT systems from OEM suppliers such as Hewlett-Packard Company; Panasonic; Lenovo; and Seagate, and sells them to its reseller and retail customers. It currently distributes over 15,000 technology products from over 100 OEM suppliers to more than 15,000 resellers. The firm operates more than 20 distribution facilities in the U.S., Canada, China and Mexico. Foreign subsidiaries include SYNNEX Canada Ltd. and SYNNEX de Mexico, S.A. de C.V. In 2010, the company acquired a controlling interest in Marubeni Infotec Corp. Also in 2010, the firm announced plans to purchase Aspire Technology, Ltd.; Encover, Inc.; and the tech support, customer service and telesales divisions of e4e, Inc.

The company offers its employees medical, dental and vision insurance; flexible spending accounts; a 401(k) plan; life and AD&D insurance; short- and long-term disability insurance; an employee stock purchase plan; an emergency travel program; an employee assistance program and product purchase plan; pet insurance; and tuition reimbursement.

FINANCIALS:
Sales and profits are in thousands of dollars—add 000 to get the full amount. 2010 Note: Financial information for 2010 was not available for all companies at press time.

2010 Sales: $	2010 Profits: $	U.S. Stock Ticker: SNX
2009 Sales: $7,719,197	2009 Profits: $92,088	Int'l Ticker: Int'l Exchange:
2008 Sales: $7,736,726	2008 Profits: $83,797	Employees: 6,330
2007 Sales: $6,986,714	2007 Profits: $63,127	Fiscal Year Ends: 11/30
2006 Sales: $6,343,514	2006 Profits: $51,385	Parent Company:

SALARIES/BENEFITS:
Pension Plan:	ESOP Stock Plan:	Profit Sharing:	Top Exec. Salary: $498,076	Bonus: $1,100,000
Savings Plan: Y	Stock Purch. Plan: Y		Second Exec. Salary: $322,938	Bonus: $870,000

OTHER THOUGHTS:
Apparent Women Officers or Directors: 1
Hot Spot for Advancement for Women/Minorities:

LOCATIONS: ("Y" = Yes)
West:	Southwest:	Midwest:	Southeast:	Northeast:	International:
Y	Y	Y	Y	Y	Y

SYNOPSYS INC

www.synopsys.com

Industry Group Code: 511210N Ranks within this company's industry group: Sales: 3 Profits: 4

Hardware:	Software:		Telecommunications:	Electronic Publishing:	Equipment:	Specialty Services:	
Computers:	Consumer:		Local:	Online Service:	Telecom:	Consulting:	Y
Accessories:	Corporate:	Y	Long Distance:	TV/Cable or Wireless:	Communication:	Contract Manufacturing:	
Network Equipment:	Telecom:		Cellular:	Games:	Distribution:	Processing:	
Chips/Circuits:	Internet:		Internet Service:	Financial Data:	VAR/Reseller:	Staff/Outsourcing:	
Parts/Drives:					Satellite Srv./Equip.:	Specialty Services:	

TYPES OF BUSINESS:

Computer Software-Electronic Design Automation
Consulting & Support Services

BRANDS/DIVISIONS/AFFILIATES:

Galaxy Design Platform
Discovery Verification Platform
VaST Systems Technology Corporation
CoWare, Inc.
Optical Research Associates
Virage Logic Corporation
SuperSpeed USB 3.0.
Lynx

CONTACTS: Note: Officers with more than one job title may be intentionally listed here more than once.

Aart de Geus, CEO
Chi-Foon Chan, COO
Chi-Foon Chan, Pres.
Brian Beattie, CFO
John Chilton, Sr. VP-Mktg.
Jan Collinson, Sr. VP-Human Resources & Facilities
Dierdre Hanford, Sr. VP-Global Tech. Svcs.
Howard Ko, Sr. VP/Gen. Mgr.-Silicon Eng. Group
Brian Cabrera, General Counsel/VP/Corp. Sec.
John Chilton, Sr. VP-Strategic Dev.
Joachim Kunkel, Sr. VP/Gen. Mgr.-Solutions Group
Antun Domic, Sr. VP/Gen. Mgr.-Implementation Group
Manoj Gandhi, Sr. VP/Gen. Mgr.-Verification Group
Aart de Geus, Chmn.
Joe Logan, Sr. VP-Worldwide Sales

Phone: 650-584-5000	Fax:
Toll-Free: 800-541-7737	
Address: 700 E. Middlefield Rd., Mountain View, CA 94043 US	

GROWTH PLANS/SPECIAL FEATURES:

Synopsys, Inc. is a supplier of electronic design automation (EDA) software and related services for the design, creation and testing of integrated circuits (IC). The firm also offers pre-designed circuits used as components in larger chip designs; and technical and support services. Synopsys' products and services are divided into four groups: Core EDA, which includes the Galaxy Design Platform, the Discovery Verification Platform and the FPGA (Field Programmable Gate Array) design products; intellectual property (IP) and system-level solutions; manufacturing solutions; and professional services. The company's Core EDA products are used by semiconductor manufactures to automate the integrated circuit design process and reduce errors. The Galaxy Design Platform provides a single, integrated IC design platform, while the Discovery Verification Platform combines simulation and verification products and design-for-verification methodologies. FPGA design products are complex chips that can be programmed to perform a specific function. The IP and systems-level solutions group includes IP products and components. The manufacturing solutions group addresses the mask-making and yield enhancement of very small geometry IC, as well as very high-level modeling of physical effects within the ICs. The professional services group provides consulting and design services. Recently, the company acquired the analog business group of MIPS Technologies, Inc.; and introduced Lynx, a new semiconductor design system. In January 2010, Synopsys announced the SuperSpeed USB 3.0., a DesignWare System-on-Chip Development product. During 2010, the firm made a number of acquisitions, including: VaST Systems Technology Corporation; CoWare, Inc., an electronic systems design service provider; certain synthesis technology assets from Synfora, Inc.; Virage Logic Corporation, a developer of semiconductor IP; and Optical Research Associates, an optical design software provider.

The firm offers its employees medical, dental and vision coverage; life, AD&D and disability insurance; an employee assistance program; educational assistance; adoption benefits; shopping discounts; a wellness program; and telecommuting options.

FINANCIALS: Sales and profits are in thousands of dollars—add 000 to get the full amount. 2010 Note: Financial information for 2010 was not available for all companies at press time.

2010 Sales: $1,380,661	2010 Profits: $237,063	**U.S. Stock Ticker:** SNPS
2009 Sales: $1,360,045	2009 Profits: $167,681	**Int'l Ticker:** Int'l Exchange:
2008 Sales: $1,336,951	2008 Profits: $189,978	Employees: 6,707
2007 Sales: $1,212,469	2007 Profits: $130,491	Fiscal Year Ends: 10/31
2006 Sales: $1,095,560	2006 Profits: $24,742	Parent Company:

SALARIES/BENEFITS:

Pension Plan:	ESOP Stock Plan:	Profit Sharing:	Top Exec. Salary: $500,000	Bonus: $1,247,000
Savings Plan: Y	Stock Purch. Plan: Y		Second Exec. Salary: $450,000	Bonus: $894,726

OTHER THOUGHTS:

Apparent Women Officers or Directors: 4
Hot Spot for Advancement for Women/Minorities: Y

LOCATIONS: ("Y" = Yes)

West:	Southwest:	Midwest:	Southeast:	Northeast:	International:
Y	Y	Y	Y	Y	Y

576

Plunkett Research, Ltd.

TAIWAN SEMICONDUCTOR MANUFACTURING CO LTD (TSMC)

www.tsmc.com

Industry Group Code: 33441 Ranks within this company's industry group: Sales: 4 Profits: 2

Hardware:		Software:		Telecommunications:		Electronic Publishing:		Equipment:		Specialty Services:	
Computers:		Consumer:		Local:		Online Service:		Telecom:		Consulting:	
Accessories:		Corporate:	Y	Long Distance:		TV/Cable or Wireless:		Communication:		Contract Manufacturing:	Y
Network Equipment:		Telecom:		Cellular:		Games:		Distribution:		Processing:	
Chips/Circuits:	Y	Internet:		Internet Service:		Financial Data:		VAR/Reseller:		Staff/Outsourcing:	
Parts/Drives:								Satellite Srv./Equip.:		Specialty Services:	Y

TYPES OF BUSINESS:
Contract Manufacturing-Semiconductors
Assembly & Testing Services
CAD Software Products

BRANDS/DIVISIONS/AFFILIATES:
WaferTech LLC
eFoundry
CyberShuttle
Motech Industries Inc

CONTACTS: Note: Officers with more than one job title may be intentionally listed here more than once.
Morris Chang, CEO
Rick Tsai, Pres.
Lora Ho, CFO/VP
Jason C.S. Chen, VP-Worldwide Sales & Mktg.
L.C. Tu, VP-Human Resources
Shang-Yi Chiang, Sr. VP-R&D
Stephen T. Tso, CIO/Sr. VP
Jack Sun, CTO/VP-R&D
Richard Thurston, General Counsel/VP
Mark Liu, Sr. VP-Oper.
C.C. Wei, Sr. VP-Bus. Dev.
Elizabeth Sun, Dir.-Corp. Comm.
M.C. Tzeng, VP-Mainstream Fab Oper. & Affiliates
Y.P. Chin, VP-Oper.
Fu-Chieh Hsu, VP-Design & Tech. Platform/Deputy Head-R&D
N.S.Tsai, VP-Quality & Reliability
Morris Chang, Chmn.
Rick Cassidy, Pres., TSMC North America

Phone: 886-3-563-6688	Fax: 886-3-563-7000
Toll-Free:	
Address: No. 8, Li-Hsin Rd. 6, Hsinchu Science Park, Hsinchu, 300 Taiwan	

GROWTH PLANS/SPECIAL FEATURES:
Taiwan Semiconductor Manufacturing Co., Ltd. (TSMC) is one of the world's largest dedicated semiconductor foundries. Using a variety of advanced and mainstream manufacturing processes, the company produces semiconductors for its customers based on their own designs or based on proprietary third party integrated circuit designs. TSMC offers a range of wafer fabrication processes, including processes to manufacture CMOS logic, mixed-signal, radio frequency, embedded memory, BiCMOS mixed-signal and other semiconductors. The company also provides design, mask making, probing, testing and assembly services. TSMC operates one 150 mm wafer fabrication facility, six 200 mm wafer fabrication facilities and two 300 mm wafer fabrication facilities. Operations are primarily centralized in Taiwan near the firm's headquarters, with additional production facilities located in Shanghai and in the U.S. Subsidiary WaferTech LLC oversees its U.S. operations. The company also maintains service offices in Taiwan, Japan, China, India, Korea, the Netherlands and the U.S. TSMC offers a software program called eFoundry, which aids the semiconductor manufacturing process from design to completion, as well as CyberShuttle, a service that allows a number of customers to share design and prototyping processes, thus reducing production costs. Sales to fabless semiconductor and system companies accounted for approximately 80% of 2009 sales, while integrated device manufacturers accounted for 20%. Recently, TSMC acquired a 20% stake in Motech Industries, Inc., a manufacturer of solar cells. In March 2010, it began constructing a LED lighting R&D facility in Taiwan. In April 2010, TSMC announced it would commence manufacturing processes using 20 nanometer technology. In July 2010, the company began construction on a third 300 mm wafer fabrication center, and in September 2010, it started construction on a thin-film solar photovoltaic design and fabrication building.
TSMC offers its employees health and fitness programs; incentive plans; tuition reimbursement; and an employee assistance program.

FINANCIALS: Sales and profits are in thousands of dollars—add 000 to get the full amount. 2010 Note: Financial information for 2010 was not available for all companies at press time.

2010 Sales: $	2010 Profits: $	U.S. Stock Ticker: TSM
2009 Sales: $9,366,340	2009 Profits: $2,825,580	Int'l Ticker: 2330 Int'l Exchange: Taipei-TPE
2008 Sales: $10,608,000	2008 Profits: $3,201,000	Employees: 26,390
2007 Sales: $9,967,000	2007 Profits: $2,210,000	Fiscal Year Ends: 12/31
2006 Sales: $9,739,400	2006 Profits: $3,902,900	Parent Company:

SALARIES/BENEFITS:
Pension Plan:	ESOP Stock Plan:	Profit Sharing: Y	Top Exec. Salary: $	Bonus: $
Savings Plan:	Stock Purch. Plan:		Second Exec. Salary: $	Bonus: $

OTHER THOUGHTS:
Apparent Women Officers or Directors: 2
Hot Spot for Advancement for Women/Minorities: Y

LOCATIONS: ("Y" = Yes)
West:	Southwest:	Midwest:	Southeast:	Northeast:	International:
Y					Y

Note: Financial information, benefits and other data can change quickly and may vary from those stated here.

TAKE-TWO INTERACTIVE SOFTWARE INC   www.take2games.com

Industry Group Code: 511210G Ranks within this company's industry group: Sales: 5 Profits: 4

Hardware:	Software:		Telecommunications:	Electronic Publishing:		Equipment:	Specialty Services:
Computers:	Consumer:	Y	Local:	Online Service:		Telecom:	Consulting:
Accessories:	Corporate:		Long Distance:	TV/Cable or Wireless:		Communication:	Contract Manufacturing:
Network Equipment:	Telecom:		Cellular:	Games:	Y	Distribution:	Processing:
Chips/Circuits:	Internet:		Internet Service:	Financial Data:		VAR/Reseller:	Staff/Outsourcing:
Parts/Drives:						Satellite Srv./Equip.:	Specialty Services:

TYPES OF BUSINESS:
Computer Software-Video Games
Software Distribution

BRANDS/DIVISIONS/AFFILIATES:
Rockstar Games
Red Dead Redemption
2K Games
2K Sports
2K Play
Carnival Games
Civilization
Grand Theft Auto IV: Complete Edition.

CONTACTS: *Note: Officers with more than one job title may be intentionally listed here more than once.*
Benjamin Feder, CEO
Karl Slatoff, COO
Lainie Goldstein, CFO
Seth Krauss, General Counsel/Exec. VP
Strauss Zelnick, Chmn.

Phone: 646-536-2842	Fax: 646-536-2926
Toll-Free:	
Address: 622 Broadway, New York, NY 10012 US	

GROWTH PLANS/SPECIAL FEATURES:

Take-Two Interactive Software, Inc. is a global publisher, developer and distributor of interactive entertainment software, hardware and accessories. Its publishing segment consists of Rockstar Games, 2K Games, 2K Sports and 2K Play publishing labels. The firm develops, markets and publishes software titles for the leading gaming and entertainment hardware platforms, including Sony's PlayStation 3; Sony's PSP system; Microsoft's Xbox 360; Nintendo's Wii; Nintendo's DS handheld system; personal computer (PC) games using Windows; and Apple iPhone, iPad and iPod Touch. The company digitally distributes some of its games for distribution through the Playstation Network for Playstation 3 games, Xbox LIVE Marketplace and Xbox LIVE Arcade for Xbox 360 games. The interactive software that it develops and publishes is broken down into two major categories: games developed by internal development studios, and games that it publishes with, or markets and distributes on behalf of, third party developers. The firm has internal development studios located in the U.S., Canada, the U.K., the Czech Republic, Australia and China. The Rockstar Games titles are primarily internally developed and include the Grand Theft Auto series. Most of the firms third party developed titles are published by its 2K Games label. 2K Games has actively secured rights to publish popular entertainment properties including The Elder Scrolls IV: Oblivion, and its internally developed BioShock and Civilization franchises. Its 2K Sports titles include Major League Baseball 2K and NBA 2K. Its 2K Play publishes casual and family-friendly titles, including Carnival Games and Dora the Explorer. In 2010, Take-Two Interactive released several new games, including Grand Theft Auto: Chinatown Wars; The Lost and Damned; The Ballad of Gay Tony; Red Dead Redemption and Red Dead Redemption's Legends and Killers Pack; the newest version of Carnival Games; Nickelodeon Fit for Wii; NHL 2K11; Civilization V; and Grand Theft Auto IV: Complete Edition.

FINANCIALS: Sales and profits are in thousands of dollars—add 000 to get the full amount. 2010 Note: Financial information for 2010 was not available for all companies at press time.

2010 Sales: $	2010 Profits: $	**U.S. Stock Ticker: TTWO**
2009 Sales: $968,488	2009 Profits: $-137,930	**Int'l Ticker:** Int'l Exchange:
2008 Sales: $1,537,530	2008 Profits: $97,097	Employees: 2,263
2007 Sales: $981,791	2007 Profits: $-138,406	Fiscal Year Ends: 10/31
2006 Sales: $1,037,840	2006 Profits: $-184,889	Parent Company:

SALARIES/BENEFITS:

Pension Plan:	ESOP Stock Plan:	Profit Sharing:	Top Exec. Salary: $500,000	Bonus: $
Savings Plan: Y	Stock Purch. Plan:		Second Exec. Salary: $247,636	Bonus: $

OTHER THOUGHTS:
Apparent Women Officers or Directors: 1
Hot Spot for Advancement for Women/Minorities:

LOCATIONS: ("Y" = Yes)

West:	Southwest:	Midwest:	Southeast:	Northeast:	International:
				Y	Y

TANDBERG

www.tandberg.net

Industry Group Code: 334119 Ranks within this company's industry group: Sales: 16   Profits: 6

Hardware:		Software:		Telecommunications:	Electronic Publishing:	Equipment:		Specialty Services:
Computers:		Consumer:	Y	Local:	Online Service:	Telecom:	Y	Consulting:
Accessories:	Y	Corporate:	Y	Long Distance:	TV/Cable or Wireless:	Communication:	Y	Contract Manufacturing:
Network Equipment:	Y	Telecom:	Y	Cellular:	Games:	Distribution:		Processing:
Chips/Circuits:		Internet:		Internet Service:	Financial Data:	VAR/Reseller:		Staff/Outsourcing:
Parts/Drives:						Satellite Srv./Equip.:		Specialty Services:

TYPES OF BUSINESS:
Video Conferencing Systems
Video Systems & Software

BRANDS/DIVISIONS/AFFILIATES:
TANBERG Telepresence Server
Telepresence T3
Content Server
Cisco Systems Inc

CONTACTS: *Note: Officers with more than one job title may be intentionally listed here more than once.*
Fredrik Halvorsen, CEO
Marjorie Lao, CFO
Jean Rosauer, Sr. VP-Global Mktg.
Hakon Dahle, Chief Technologist
Odd Johnny (OJ) Winge, Exec. VP-Prod.
Steven Peri, General Counsel/Sr. VP
Johan Jemdahl, Sr. VP-Global Oper.
Hakon Dahle, Dir.-Strategic Planning
Jean Rosauer, Contact-Public Rel.
Jean Rosauer, Contact-Investor Rel.
Rick Snyder, Pres., Global Bus.
Larry Satterfield, Pres., Americas Commercial Sector
Joel S. Brunson, Pres., Americas Public Sector
Wayne McAllister, Sr. VP-Global Svcs.
Jan C. Opsahl, Chmn.
Geir Langfeldt Olsen, Pres., EMEA

Phone: 47-67-125-125	Fax: 47-67-125-234
Toll-Free:	
Address: Philip Pedersens vei 20, Lysaker, 1366 Norway	

GROWTH PLANS/SPECIAL FEATURES:
TANDBERG, a subsidiary of Cisco Systems, Inc., is a leading global provider of video systems and services, focused on supplying companies and organizations with visual communication. Its systems enable user-friendly two-way video communication and media presentation, with automatic encryption, between up to six sites. TANDBERG's product line includes video system products for various-sized meeting rooms, mobile applications and field use, as well as standard television set-top units, secure web conferencing systems, Internet Protocol-(IP) based video telephony systems and software for scheduling, corporate instant messaging and other business needs. It also offers TANBERG Telepresence Server, which consists of the Telepresence T3 server, additional hardware and a host of related services. The Telepresence Server is capable of bridging multiple platforms, including connecting HD (high-definition) to standard definition feeds from a PC. The displays feature an eye height tailored to insure eye-contact, enhancing the feeling that the other participants are in the same room, and integrated touch-screen controls. The company designs its products to support a broad range of protocols and to be usable on multiple networks including IP, wireless and ISDN (Integrated Services Digital Network). TANDBERG offers support services for its systems including deployment, installation and training. The firm serves health care providers, colleges and universities, government agencies, retail and financial businesses, manufacturers and legal institutions. The company has offices and representatives in 34 countries and customer installations in over 90 countries worldwide. In March 2010, Tandberg launched the EX90 desktop video conferencing system, which is a comprised of a 24-inch HD screen and a small interface console, with inTouch touch screen capability, to manage calls. In April 2010, Cisco acquired Tandberg for $3.3 billion.

FINANCIALS: Sales and profits are in thousands of dollars—add 000 to get the full amount. 2010 Note: Financial information for 2010 was not available for all companies at press time.

2010 Sales: $	2010 Profits: $	U.S. Stock Ticker: Subsdiary
2009 Sales: $902,600	2009 Profits: $122,200	Int'l Ticker: Int'l Exchange:
2008 Sales: $808,800	2008 Profits: $134,600	Employees: 1,451
2007 Sales: $630,500	2007 Profits: $102,400	Fiscal Year Ends: 12/31
2006 Sales: $419,700	2006 Profits: $61,100	Parent Company: CISCO SYSTEMS INC

SALARIES/BENEFITS:
Pension Plan:	ESOP Stock Plan:	Profit Sharing:	Top Exec. Salary: $641,305	Bonus: $191,008
Savings Plan:	Stock Purch. Plan:		Second Exec. Salary: $392,349	Bonus: $118,153

OTHER THOUGHTS:
Apparent Women Officers or Directors: 4
Hot Spot for Advancement for Women/Minorities: Y

LOCATIONS: ("Y" = Yes)
West:	Southwest:	Midwest:	Southeast:	Northeast:	International:
	Y			Y	Y

TATA CONSULTANCY SERVICES (TCS)
www.tcs.com

Industry Group Code: 541513 Ranks within this company's industry group: Sales: 9 Profits: 4

Hardware:	Software:		Telecommunications:	Electronic Publishing:	Equipment:	Specialty Services:	
Computers:	Consumer:		Local:	Online Service:	Telecom:	Consulting:	Y
Accessories:	Corporate:	Y	Long Distance:	TV/Cable or Wireless:	Communication:	Contract Manufacturing:	
Network Equipment:	Telecom:		Cellular:	Games:	Distribution:	Processing:	
Chips/Circuits:	Internet:		Internet Service:	Financial Data:	VAR/Reseller:	Staff/Outsourcing:	Y
Parts/Drives:					Satellite Srv./Equip.:	Specialty Services:	Y

TYPES OF BUSINESS:
IT Consulting
Software Engineering
Business Process Outsourcing
Research

BRANDS/DIVISIONS/AFFILIATES:
Tata America International Corporation
Tata Consultancy Services Asia Pacific Pte Limited
Diligenta Limited
TCS e-Serve Limited
JDA Software Group Inc

CONTACTS: Note: Officers with more than one job title may be intentionally listed here more than once.
Natarajan Chandrasekaran, CEO/Managing Dir.
Seturaman Mahalingam, CFO/Exec. VP
John Lenzen, Head-Mktg.
Ajoyendra Mukherjee, VP/Head-Global Human Resources
K. Ananth Krishnan, Head-R&D
Satya Hegde, Head-Legal
Pradipta Bagchi, Head-Corp. Comm.
Surya Kant, Regional Head-North America
A.S. Lakshminarayanan, Regional Head-Europe
Phiroz Vandrevala, Exec. Dir./Head-Global Corp. Affairs
Suprakash Mukhopadhyay, Company Sec.
Ratan Tata, Chmn.
Henry Manzano, Regional Head-Latin America

Phone: 91-22-6778-9999   Fax: 91-22-6778-9000
Toll-Free:
Address: TCS House, Raveline St., Mumbai, 400 001 India

GROWTH PLANS/SPECIAL FEATURES:
Tata Consultancy Services (TCS) is one of India's largest consulting companies and one of Asia's largest independent software and services organizations, with a presence in 42 countries. TCS primarily provides IT consulting, services and business process outsourcing (BPO) for international businesses. The firm is a subsidiary of the TATA Group, one of Asia's largest conglomerates with interests in energy, telecommunications, financial services, chemicals, engineering and materials. TCS' services are divided into several divisions, including consulting; IT services; business intelligence; performance management; IT infrastructure; engineering and industrial services; and platform BPO solutions. The company focuses on software engineering practices and standards, software quality assurance, software project management, software processes, and research and development in software engineering and technology. Core research areas include systems and software engineering, process engineering, embedded systems, very large scale integration (VLSI), bioinformatics and security. The firm has formed alliances with some of the world's leading technology companies, academic institutions and consulting firms to provide customers with expertise in technology fields in which it does not specialize. Development of new strategies and technologies occurs in the firm's global centers of excellence, located in several nations. The firm has roughly 30 offices in North America, with a regional headquarters in New York City. A few of the company's international subsidiaries include Tata America International Corporation; Tata Consultancy Services Asia Pacific Pte Limited, in Singapore; Diligenta Limited, in the U.K.; and TCS e-Serve Limited, in India. In August 2010, TCS announced a strategic alliance with Arizona-based JDA Software Group, Inc. In December 2010, the company opened a new BPO center located in the Philippines.

The firm offers its employees holiday homes across India; on-site gym and recreation facilities; medical insurance for children and dependant parents; office banks; and personal loans for housing, computers and automobiles.

FINANCIALS: Sales and profits are in thousands of dollars—add 000 to get the full amount. 2010 Note: Financial information for 2010 was not available for all companies at press time.
2010 Sales: $
2009 Sales: $6,015,700
2008 Sales: $4,597,100
2007 Sales: $4,320,000
2006 Sales: $4,300,000

2010 Profits: $
2009 Profits: $1,136,700
2008 Profits: $
2007 Profits: $970,000
2006 Profits: $950,000

U.S. Stock Ticker: Subsidiary
Int'l Ticker: Int'l Exchange:
Employees: 180,000
Fiscal Year Ends: 3/31
Parent Company: TATA GROUP

SALARIES/BENEFITS:
Pension Plan: ESOP Stock Plan: Profit Sharing: Top Exec. Salary: $ Bonus: $
Savings Plan: Stock Purch. Plan: Second Exec. Salary: $ Bonus: $

OTHER THOUGHTS:
Apparent Women Officers or Directors: 1
Hot Spot for Advancement for Women/Minorities:

LOCATIONS: ("Y" = Yes)
West:	Southwest:	Midwest:	Southeast:	Northeast:	International:
Y	Y	Y	Y	Y	Y

TECH DATA CORP

www.techdata.com

Industry Group Code: 423430 Ranks within this company's industry group: Sales: 2 Profits: 3

Hardware:	Software:	Telecommunications:	Electronic Publishing:	Equipment:		Specialty Services:
Computers:	Consumer:	Local:	Online Service:	Telecom:		Consulting:
Accessories:	Corporate:	Long Distance:	TV/Cable or Wireless:	Communication:		Contract Manufacturing:
Network Equipment:	Telecom:	Cellular:	Games:	Distribution:	Y	Processing:
Chips/Circuits:	Internet:	Internet Service:	Financial Data:	VAR/Reseller:		Staff/Outsourcing:
Parts/Drives:				Satellite Srv./Equip.:		Specialty Services:

TYPES OF BUSINESS:
Computer & Software Products, Distribution
Training
Assembly Services

BRANDS/DIVISIONS/AFFILIATES:
Cisco Solutions Group
Triade Holding BV

CONTACTS: Note: Officers with more than one job title may be intentionally listed here more than once.
Robert M. Dutkowsky, CEO
Jeffery P. Howells, CFO/Exec. VP
John O'Shea, VP-Network Prod. Mktg.
John Tonnison, CIO/Exec. VP
David R. Vetter, General Counsel/Sr. VP/Sec.
Jarred LeFebvre, Mgr.-Public Rel.
Charles V. Dannewitz, Treas./Sr. VP
Joseph B. Trepani, Sr. VP/Controller
Murray Wright, Pres., The Americas
Steven A. Raymund, Chmn.
Nestor Cano, Pres., Europe
Darryl Branch, Sr. VP-Logistics & Integration Svcs.

Phone: 727-539-7429	Fax: 727-538-5860
Toll-Free: 800-292-7906	
Address: 5350 Tech Data Dr., Clearwater, FL 33760 US	

GROWTH PLANS/SPECIAL FEATURES:

Tech Data Corp. is a worldwide distributor of information technology (IT) products, logistics management and other value-added services. The company serves more than 125,000 value-added resellers (VARs), direct marketers, retailers and corporate resellers in over 100 countries throughout Europe, Latin America and North America. It offers a variety of products from manufacturers and publishers including Fujitsu-Siemens, Apple, Autodesk, Symantec, Hewlett-Packard, Canon, Nortel Networks, Cisco Systems, Acer, Adobe, IBM, Intel, Kingston, McAfee, Lexmark, Microsoft, Samsung, Sony, Toshiba, Western Digital and Xerox. Products are typically purchased directly from manufacturers or software publishers on a non-exclusive basis, and then shipped to customers from one of Tech Data's 24 regionally located logistics centers. The company's vendor agreements do not restrict it from selling similar products manufactured by competitors. The firm also provides resellers with extensive pre- and post-sale training, service and support, as well as configuration and assembly services and e-commerce tools. Tech Data provides products and services to the online reseller channel and does business with thousands of resellers through its web site. The firm's entire electronic catalog is available online, and its electronic software distribution initiative allows resellers and vendors to easily access software titles directly from a secure location on the web site. Tech Data's Cisco Solutions Group business unit supports the firm's entire solutions offering from networking firm Cisco Systems. In October 2010, the firm acquired electronics and information technology company Triade Holding B.V.

FINANCIALS: Sales and profits are in thousands of dollars—add 000 to get the full amount. 2010 Note: Financial information for 2010 was not available for all companies at press time.

2010 Sales: $22,099,876	2010 Profits: $180,155	**U.S. Stock Ticker: TECD**
2009 Sales: $24,080,484	2009 Profits: $117,278	**Int'l Ticker:** Int'l Exchange:
2008 Sales: $23,423,078	2008 Profits: $102,129	Employees: 7,600
2007 Sales: $21,440,445	2007 Profits: $-96,981	Fiscal Year Ends: 1/31
2006 Sales: $20,482,851	2006 Profits: $26,586	Parent Company:

SALARIES/BENEFITS:

Pension Plan:	ESOP Stock Plan:	Profit Sharing:	Top Exec. Salary: $957,000	Bonus: $1,914,000
Savings Plan: Y	Stock Purch. Plan: Y		Second Exec. Salary: $709,500	Bonus: $993,300

OTHER THOUGHTS:
Apparent Women Officers or Directors: 1
Hot Spot for Advancement for Women/Minorities:

LOCATIONS: ("Y" = Yes)

West:	Southwest:	Midwest:	Southeast:	Northeast:	International:
Y	Y	Y	Y	Y	Y

TECH MAHINDRA LIMITED

www.techmahindra.com

Industry Group Code: 541513 Ranks within this company's industry group: Sales: 23 Profits: 13

Hardware:	Software:		Telecommunications:	Electronic Publishing:	Equipment:	Specialty Services:	
Computers:	Consumer:		Local:	Online Service:	Telecom:	Consulting:	Y
Accessories:	Corporate:	Y	Long Distance:	TV/Cable or Wireless:	Communication:	Contract Manufacturing:	
Network Equipment:	Telecom:	Y	Cellular:	Games:	Distribution:	Processing:	
Chips/Circuits:	Internet:		Internet Service:	Financial Data:	VAR/Reseller:	Staff/Outsourcing:	Y
Parts/Drives:					Satellite Srv./Equip.:	Specialty Services:	

TYPES OF BUSINESS:

Business Intelligence Consulting
Software Provider
Business Process Outsourcing Services

BRANDS/DIVISIONS/AFFILIATES:

Tech Mahindra (Beijing) IT Services Limited
Tech Mahindra (Americas), Inc.
Tech Mahindra GmbH
Tech Mahindra (Singapore) Pte. Limited
Satyam Computer Services Ltd (Mahindra Satyam)

CONTACTS: Note: Officers with more than one job title may be intentionally listed here more than once.

Vineet Nayyar, CEO/Managing Dir.
Sonjoy Anand, CFO
L. Ravichandran, Pres., IT Svcs.
Sujit Baksi, Pres., Corp. Affairs
Vineet Nayyar, Vice Chmn.
Anand G. Mahindra, Chmn.

Phone: 91-20-6601-8100	Fax: 91-20-2542-4466
Toll-Free:	
Address: Sharda Center, Karve Rd., Pune, 411004 India	

GROWTH PLANS/SPECIAL FEATURES:

Tech Mahindra Limited is an India-based firm working primarily with the communications industry and offering IT and technology consulting and global systems integration. The firm provides telecom software and telecommunications services from locations in India, Singapore, Thailand, Malaysia, Indonesia, the Philippines, China, the United Arab Emirates, Egypt, Nigeria, South Africa, the U.S., Canada, the U.K., Germany, the Netherlands, Sweden, Australia and New Zealand. The firm's services are divided into three segments: IT services; research and development services; and business process outsourcing. The IT services segment encompasses systems integration; software development and management; consulting; managed services; and infrastructure management. The research and development division provides IT and technology research services to telecom equipment manufacturers worldwide. Service offerings consist of product lifecycle management; testing; NMS/EMS software development, for systems management; hardware board development; network offerings; technology updating; customer support; and modeling and post deployment of IT infrastructure. Business process outsourcing offerings include customer relationship management (CRM); finance and accounting; human resources and training; data analytics; procurement; contract management; service provisioning; inventory management; and invoice validation. The company has partnerships with firms such as Microsoft, HP, IBM, Oracle, BroadSoft and Openwave Systems. Tech Mahindra is majority owned by Mahindra & Mahindra in partnership with British Telecommunications plc. A few of the company's international subsidiaries include Tech Mahindra (Beijing) IT Services Limited; Tech Mahindra (Americas), Inc.; Tech Mahindra GmbH; and Tech Mahindra (Singapore) Private Limited. In November 2010, the firm announced plans to merge subsidiary Satyam Computer Services Limited into the parent company over the course of 2011.

Employees are offered wellness programs with visiting doctors, nutritionists and wellness consultants; on-site gym access; banking, insurance and tax planning help desks; tuition assistance; and discounts on a variety of products and services.

FINANCIALS: Sales and profits are in thousands of dollars—add 000 to get the full amount. 2010 Note: Financial information for 2010 was not available for all companies at press time.

2010 Sales: $1,005,050	2010 Profits: $152,210	**U.S. Stock Ticker:**
2009 Sales: $979,020	2009 Profits: $222,460	**Int'l Ticker:** TEML Int'l Exchange: Bombay-BSE
2008 Sales: $934,700	2008 Profits: $205,300	Employees: 33,524
2007 Sales: $648,000	2007 Profits: $163,300	Fiscal Year Ends: 3/31
2006 Sales: $280,100	2006 Profits: $60,200	Parent Company: MAHINDRA & MAHINDRA LIMITED

SALARIES/BENEFITS:

Pension Plan:	ESOP Stock Plan:	Profit Sharing:	Top Exec. Salary: $	Bonus: $
Savings Plan:	Stock Purch. Plan:		Second Exec. Salary: $	Bonus: $

OTHER THOUGHTS:

Apparent Women Officers or Directors:
Hot Spot for Advancement for Women/Minorities:

LOCATIONS: ("Y" = Yes)

West:	Southwest:	Midwest:	Southeast:	Northeast:	International:
Y	Y		Y	Y	Y

TEKELEC

www.tekelec.com

Industry Group Code: 334210 Ranks within this company's industry group: Sales: 11   Profits: 4

Hardware:	Software:	Telecommunications:	Electronic Publishing:	Equipment:		Specialty Services:	
Computers:	Consumer:	Local:	Online Service:	Telecom:	Y	Consulting:	
Accessories:	Corporate:	Long Distance:	TV/Cable or Wireless:	Communication:		Contract Manufacturing:	
Network Equipment:	Telecom:	Cellular:	Games:	Distribution:		Processing:	
Chips/Circuits:	Internet:	Internet Service:	Financial Data:	VAR/Reseller:		Staff/Outsourcing:	
Parts/Drives:				Satellite Srv./Equip.:		Specialty Services:	

TYPES OF BUSINESS:

Network Switching Equipment
Diagnostics Systems
Contact Center Products
IP Network Equipment
Mobile Messaging

BRANDS/DIVISIONS/AFFILIATES:

Blueslice Network
Camiant
EAGLE 5
EAGLE XG

CONTACTS: Note: Officers with more than one job title may be intentionally listed here more than once.

Frank Plastina, CEO
Frank Plastina, Pres.
Gregory Rush, CFO/Sr. VP
Susie Kim Riley, Chief Mktg. Officer
Marykay Wells, CIO/VP-IT
Vince Lesch, CTO
Stuart H. Kupinsky, General Counsel
David K. Rice, Sr. VP-Oper.
Stuart H. Kupinsky, Sr. VP-Corp. Affairs
Gregory S. Rush, Chief Acct. Officer/VP/Corp. Controller
Ronald J. de Lange, Exec. VP-Global Prod. Solutions
Mark A. Floyd, Chmn.
Wolrad Claudy, Exec. VP-Global Sales

Phone: 919-460-5500	Fax: 919-460-0877
Toll-Free: 888-628-5521	
Address: 5200 Paramount Pkwy., Morrisville, NC 27560 US	

GROWTH PLANS/SPECIAL FEATURES:

Tekelec is an international provider of telecommunications network systems and software applications. The majority of the firm's customers are traditional landline (wireline) telecommunications carriers and mobile (wireless) communications operators; however, the company also caters to emerging competitive service providers and cable television service providers who are offering communication services. These customers, including many of the largest service providers in the world, have deployed over 1,800 Tekelec systems and software applications in 107 countries. The network applications are designed to increase network efficiency and performance; provide basic and enhanced voice and data services to subscribers; and aid the transition from traditional networks to Internet Protocol- (IP) based networks. The firm's software and network solutions include signaling network applications, number portability applications and performance management and monitoring applications. The network signaling product portfolio enables service providers to establish, control and terminate voice and data communications calls or sessions. It utilizes EAGLE 5, a product family which offers flexible routing applications and voice, short message, multimedia message and prepaid services, and EAGLE XG, a platform which offers corrective dialing, number portability, SIP signaling routers, IP multimedia call control and electronic number mapping. Tekelec's performance management and monitoring applications work with EAGLE 5 and assist customers in measuring network and service performance, managing network and service efficiency and monetizing their networks and service offerings through the reduction of revenue loss. Tekelec's mobile messaging segment, which includes both 2G/3G and SIP-based networks, offers products and services such as SMS Personalized Services, SMS Advertising, Application Gateway, SMS Store, SMS Routing, SMS Security and a SIP Messaging Gateway. In May 2010, the firm acquired Blueslice Networks, a marketer of evolved Subscriber Data Management (eSDM) solutions, and Camiant, a provider of policy control solutions to broadband service providers.

Tekelec offers employees a bonus plan and business accident insurance.

FINANCIALS: Sales and profits are in thousands of dollars—add 000 to get the full amount. 2010 Note: Financial information for 2010 was not available for all companies at press time.

2010 Sales: $	2010 Profits: $	**U.S. Stock Ticker:** TKLC
2009 Sales: $469,261	2009 Profits: $47,402	**Int'l Ticker:** Int'l Exchange:
2008 Sales: $460,564	2008 Profits: $55,039	Employees: 1,101
2007 Sales: $431,800	2007 Profits: $-35,336	Fiscal Year Ends: 12/31
2006 Sales: $443,346	2006 Profits: $86,056	Parent Company:

SALARIES/BENEFITS:

Pension Plan:	ESOP Stock Plan:	Profit Sharing:	Top Exec. Salary: $570,000	Bonus: $766,080
Savings Plan:	Stock Purch. Plan: Y		Second Exec. Salary: $627,099	Bonus: $

OTHER THOUGHTS:

Apparent Women Officers or Directors: 2
Hot Spot for Advancement for Women/Minorities: Y

LOCATIONS: ("Y" = Yes)

West:	Southwest:	Midwest:	Southeast:	Northeast:	International:
	Y	Y		Y	Y

TEKTRONIX INC

www.tek.com

Industry Group Code: 3345 Ranks within this company's industry group: Sales: Profits:

Hardware:		Software:	Telecommunications:	Electronic Publishing:	Equipment:	Specialty Services:	
Computers:		Consumer:	Local:	Online Service:	Telecom:	Consulting:	
Accessories:	Y	Corporate:	Long Distance:	TV/Cable or Wireless:	Communication:	Contract Manufacturing:	
Network Equipment:		Telecom:	Cellular:	Games:	Distribution:	Processing:	
Chips/Circuits:		Internet:	Internet Service:	Financial Data:	VAR/Reseller:	Staff/Outsourcing:	
Parts/Drives:	Y				Satellite Srv./Equip.:	Specialty Services:	Y

TYPES OF BUSINESS:

Test & Measurement Equipment
Support Services
Oscilloscopes
Logic analyzers
Video test equipment
Communications test equipment

BRANDS/DIVISIONS/AFFILIATES:

MAXTEK
TEKTRONIX
Danaher Corp
Arantech
Scope Central

CONTACTS: Note: Officers with more than one job title may be intentionally listed here more than once.

James A. Lico, Pres.
Chuck McLaughlin, CFO/VP
Robert W. Blaskowsky, CIO/VP
Neil Huddlestone, Pres., Tektronix China
Fuki Yoneyama, Pres., Japan Region/VP-Japan Sales

Phone: 503-627-7111	Fax: 503-627-6108
Toll-Free:	
Address: 14200 SW Karl Braun Dr., Beaverton, OR 97077 US	

GROWTH PLANS/SPECIAL FEATURES:

Tektronix, Inc. develops, manufactures and markets test, measurement and monitoring products to a wide variety of customers in the computing, communications semiconductors, education, computer, military/aerospace, research and consumer electronics industries. The company provides general purpose testing products and video test, measurement and monitoring products, which includes oscilloscopes, logic analyzers, signal sources and spectrum analyzers. Additional video products include waveform monitors, video signal generators, compressed digital video test products and other test and measurement for video equipment manufacturers, content developers and traditional television broadcasters. The general testing products are designed to capture, display and analyze streams of electrical data, while video products ensure the delivery of the best possible video experience to the viewer. The firm also offers telecommunications network management and network diagnostics products. Network management products consist of network monitoring systems that actively test networks and provide troubleshooting, provisioning and automated service quality monitoring. The firm's products are sold under the TEKTRONIX and MAXTEK brand names. The company is a subsidiary of Danaher Corporation, a designer and manufacturer of a variety of professional, medical, industrial and consumer products. In early 2009, the company acquired Arantech, an Ireland-based provider of Customer Experience Management (CEM) solutions. In November 2009, Tektronix introduced Scope Central, an Internet community for oscilloscope users. In December 2009, the firm launched the DPO4USB module, an oscilloscope that triggers and analyzes USB serial buses. In April 2010, the company acquired integrity test and measurement instrument manufacturer SyntheSys Research, Inc. In May 2010, Tektronix acquired digital content monitoring firm Mixed Signals, Inc.

Employees are offered medical and dental insurance; disability coverage; life insurance; and retirement plans.

FINANCIALS: Sales and profits are in thousands of dollars—add 000 to get the full amount. 2010 Note: Financial information for 2010 was not available for all companies at press time.

2010 Sales: $	2010 Profits: $	U.S. Stock Ticker: Subsidiary	
2009 Sales: $	2009 Profits: $	Int'l Ticker: Int'l Exchange:	
2008 Sales: $	2008 Profits: $	Employees: 4,400	
2007 Sales: $1,105,172	2007 Profits: $90,408	Fiscal Year Ends: 12/31	
2006 Sales: $1,039,870	2006 Profits: $92,355	Parent Company: DANAHER CORP	

SALARIES/BENEFITS:

Pension Plan:	ESOP Stock Plan:	Profit Sharing:	Top Exec. Salary: $	Bonus: $472,900
Savings Plan:	Stock Purch. Plan:		Second Exec. Salary: $	Bonus: $

OTHER THOUGHTS:

Apparent Women Officers or Directors:
Hot Spot for Advancement for Women/Minorities:

LOCATIONS: ("Y" = Yes)

West:	Southwest:	Midwest:	Southeast:	Northeast:	International:
Y	Y			Y	Y

TELCORDIA TECHNOLOGIES

www.telcordia.com

Industry Group Code: 511210B　Ranks within this company's industry group: Sales:　Profits:

Hardware:	Software:		Telecommunications:	Electronic Publishing:	Equipment:	Specialty Services:	
Computers:	Consumer:		Local:	Online Service:	Telecom:	Consulting:	Y
Accessories:	Corporate:	Y	Long Distance:	TV/Cable or Wireless:	Communication:	Contract Manufacturing:	
Network Equipment:	Telecom:	Y	Cellular:	Games:	Distribution:	Processing:	
Chips/Circuits:	Internet:		Internet Service:	Financial Data:	VAR/Reseller:	Staff/Outsourcing:	
Parts/Drives:					Satellite Srv./Equip.:	Specialty Services:	Y

TYPES OF BUSINESS:

Telecommunications Software Services
Consulting & Professional Services
Network Systems & Services
Engineering & Research Services
Systems Integration Services

BRANDS/DIVISIONS/AFFILIATES:

Network Engineer
Telcordia Next Generation OSS
Telcordia Activator
Telcordia Test Expert
Providence Equity Partners
Warburg Pincus
TIRKS
Telcordia Personalized Advertising

CONTACTS: *Note: Officers with more than one job title may be intentionally listed here more than once.*

Mark Greenquist, CEO
Mark Greenquist, Pres.
Steve Noonan, CFO
Linda DeLukey, Exec. VP-Human Resources
Adam Drobot, CTO/Pres., Advanced Tech. Solutions
Steve Noonan, Exec. VP-Admin.
Joseph Giordano, General Counsel/Corp. Sec.
Rich Marano, Exec. VP-Oper.
Adan Pope, Chief Strategy Officer
Sharon Oddy, Exec. Dir.-Corp. Comm. & Public Rel.
Steve Noonan, Exec. VP-Finance
Richard Jacowleff, Pres., Interconnection Solutions
William J. Wanke, Pres., Oper. Solutions
Mike Wojcik, Pres., Service Delivery Solutions
Linda DeLukey, Exec. VP-Corp. Security
Anil Pandey, Head-Telcordia India Labs

Phone: 732-699-2000	Fax: 732-336-2320
Toll-Free: 800-521-2673	
Address: 1 Telcordia Dr., Piscataway, NJ 08854-4151 US	

GROWTH PLANS/SPECIAL FEATURES:

Telcordia Technologies, a holding of private equity firms Providence Equity Partners and Warburg Pincus, is a global leader in network systems, operations support systems, business support systems and related services for communications carriers. It is one of the largest employee-owned research and engineering firms in the U.S. The company serves wireless/wireline service providers, cable operators and large enterprises. Telcordia Technologies holds approximately 1,800 patents, and serves over 800 clients in 55 countries. The firm helps customers use technology to streamline operations; advance network flexibility; add new services; reduce operating and capital expenditures; and increase profits. Telcordia Technologies' products include Telcordia Converged Application Server, a service delivery platform for mobile, cable, fixed, IP, IMS and converged networks; Telcordia Activator, an activation solution for communication service providers; Telcordia Personalized Advertising, a permission-based marketing solution for broadband and mobile networks; Telcordia Test Expert, a test and analysis program intended to reduce the cost of supporting advanced broadband services; Network Engineer, which manages company information through spatial representation; TIRKS, which provides clients with inventory management and order control processing; and the Telcordia Next Generation OSS software system, which addresses issues relating to planning, engineering, service assurance and more. In addition, the firm offers consulting and testing services for a variety of software applications and software training courses. Telcordia Technologies maintains partnerships with several firms, including Nokia Siemens Networks; IBM; GlobalLogic, Inc.; Accenture; Swisscom IT; and Sun.

Telcordia offers its employees a benefits package that includes medical, dental, life, disability and accident insurance; a 401(k); a cash balance pension; an employee assistance program; work-life resources and referrals; adoption benefits; flexible spending accounts; and educational assistance.

FINANCIALS: Sales and profits are in thousands of dollars—add 000 to get the full amount. 2010 Note: Financial information for 2010 was not available for all companies at press time.

2010 Sales: $	2010 Profits: $	**U.S. Stock Ticker:** Private
2009 Sales: $	2009 Profits: $	**Int'l Ticker:**　Int'l Exchange:
2008 Sales: $	2008 Profits: $	Employees:
2007 Sales: $	2007 Profits: $	Fiscal Year Ends: 1/31
2006 Sales: $	2006 Profits: $	Parent Company: PROVIDENCE EQUITY PARTNERS

SALARIES/BENEFITS:

Pension Plan: Y	ESOP Stock Plan:	Profit Sharing:	Top Exec. Salary: $	Bonus: $
Savings Plan: Y	Stock Purch. Plan:		Second Exec. Salary: $	Bonus: $

OTHER THOUGHTS:

Apparent Women Officers or Directors: 2
Hot Spot for Advancement for Women/Minorities: Y

LOCATIONS: ("Y" = Yes)

West:	Southwest:	Midwest:	Southeast:	Northeast:	International:
Y	Y		Y	Y	Y

TELECA AB

www.teleca.com

Industry Group Code: 511210C Ranks within this company's industry group: Sales: Profits:

Hardware:	Software:		Telecommunications:	Electronic Publishing:	Equipment:	Specialty Services:
Computers:	Consumer:	Y	Local:	Online Service:	Telecom:	Consulting:
Accessories:	Corporate:		Long Distance:	TV/Cable or Wireless:	Communication:	Contract Manufacturing:
Network Equipment:	Telecom:	Y	Cellular:	Games:	Distribution:	Processing:
Chips/Circuits:	Internet:		Internet Service:	Financial Data:	VAR/Reseller:	Staff/Outsourcing:
Parts/Drives:					Satellite Srv./Equip.:	Specialty Services:

TYPES OF BUSINESS:

Software for Mobile Devices
Consulting

BRANDS/DIVISIONS/AFFILIATES:

Symphony Technology Group

CONTACTS: Note: Officers with more than one job title may be intentionally listed here more than once.

Rene Svendsen-Tune, CEO
Rene Svendsen-Tune, Pres.
Leif Norgaard, CFO/Sr. VP
Anette Gregow, Sr. VP-Mktg.
Lisbeth Hald, Sr. VP-Human Resources
Magnus Rimvall, CIO/VP
Kristian Jonsson, General Counsel/VP
Tomi Rantakari, VP-Global Sales Oper.
Anette Gregow, Sr. VP-Corp. Comm.
Valery Kalachev, Sr. VP-Russia
John Trobough, Sr. VP/Head-Americas
Markku Hollstrom, VP-Large Accounts
Ben Salama, VP-Large Accounts
Pallab Chatterjee, Chmn.
Edwin Moses, Sr. VP/Head-Europe & APAC

Phone: 46-40-25-3000	Fax: 46-40-25-3001
Toll-Free:	
Address: 13 Hallenborgs St., Malmo, 211 19 Sweden	

GROWTH PLANS/SPECIAL FEATURES:

Teleca AB is a Swiss company that produces and distributes software for mobile phones and offers mobile consulting services. Working with firms such as Microsoft, Adobe Nokia, SVOX and Imagination Technologies Group, Teleca offers tailored solutions, software development, customization/testing, integration and solutions related to browser and messenger software platforms for mobile phones. The company uses technology from its clients and its reserve of intellectual property to create products. Additionally, the firm is increasingly integrating open source software (OSS) into its products. Teleca supplies its products and services to original equipment manufacturers (OEMs), original design manufacturers (ODMs), carriers, content providers and services providers. The firm's products are designed to work across a wide variety of platforms, including Windows Mobile, Adobe, Android, MeeGo, BREW, Symbian, UIQ, Linux and OSS. Teleca also offers consulting services to its working partners. In addition to its headquarters and locations in Sweden, the company maintains offices in 10 other countries: the U.K., Finland, Japan, Germany, Poland, Russia, India, Korea, China and the U.S. North American offices are located in Seattle, Washington; Plano, Texas; and Menlo Park, California. Teleca is owned by Symphony Technology Group, a California-based private equity firm focused on software and technology investments. In February 2010, the firm became a development partner of Antix Labs Ltd., a gaming infrastructure specialist.

FINANCIALS: Sales and profits are in thousands of dollars—add 000 to get the full amount. 2010 Note: Financial information for 2010 was not available for all companies at press time.

2010 Sales: $	2010 Profits: $	U.S. Stock Ticker: Private
2009 Sales: $	2009 Profits: $	Int'l Ticker: Int'l Exchange:
2008 Sales: $	2008 Profits: $	Employees:
2007 Sales: $220,123	2007 Profits: $-54,923	Fiscal Year Ends: 12/31
2006 Sales: $250,264	2006 Profits: $ 335	Parent Company: SYMPHONY TECHNOLOGY GROUP

SALARIES/BENEFITS:

Pension Plan:	ESOP Stock Plan:	Profit Sharing:	Top Exec. Salary: $	Bonus: $
Savings Plan:	Stock Purch. Plan:		Second Exec. Salary: $	Bonus: $

OTHER THOUGHTS:

Apparent Women Officers or Directors: 2
Hot Spot for Advancement for Women/Minorities:

LOCATIONS: ("Y" = Yes)

West:	Southwest:	Midwest:	Southeast:	Northeast:	International:
Y	Y				Y

TELEFON AB LM ERICSSON (ERICSSON)

www.ericsson.com

Industry Group Code: 334220 Ranks within this company's industry group: Sales: 3 Profits: 4

Hardware:		Software:		Telecommunications:		Electronic Publishing:		Equipment:		Specialty Services:	
Computers:		Consumer:		Local:		Online Service:		Telecom:	Y	Consulting:	Y
Accessories:	Y	Corporate:		Long Distance:		TV/Cable or Wireless:		Communication:	Y	Contract Manufacturing:	
Network Equipment:	Y	Telecom:	Y	Cellular:		Games:		Distribution:		Processing:	
Chips/Circuits:		Internet:		Internet Service:		Financial Data:		VAR/Reseller:		Staff/Outsourcing:	
Parts/Drives:								Satellite Srv./Equip.:		Specialty Services:	Y

TYPES OF BUSINESS:

Telecommunications Equipment
Mobile Phones
Pagers
Networking Equipment
Defense Electronics
Telecommunications Software
Professional Services
Research & Development

BRANDS/DIVISIONS/AFFILIATES:

Sony Ericsson Mobile Communications
Drutt Corporation
Redback Networks, Inc.
LHS
Tandberg Television
Entrisphere
HyC Group
Bizitek

CONTACTS: Note: Officers with more than one job title may be intentionally listed here more than once.

Hans Vestberg, CEO
Hans Vestberg, Pres.
Jan Frykhammar, CFO/Exec. VP
Torbjorn Possne, Sr. VP-Sales & Mktg.
Marita Hellberg, Sr. VP-Human Resources & Organization
Hakan Eriksson, CTO/Sr. VP
Carl Olof Blomqvist, General Counsel/Sr. VP-Legal Affairs
Henry Stenson, Sr. VP-Comm.
Cesare Avenia, Chief Brand Officer
Jan Wareby, Sr. VP-Multimedia
Rima Qureshi, Sr. VP-CDMA Mobile Systems
Magnus Mandersson, Sr. VP/Head-Global Svcs.
Michael Treschow, Chmn.
Mats H. Olsson, Head-Region Greater China & Northeast Asia

Phone: 46-10-719-00-00	Fax:
Toll-Free:	
Address: Torshamnsgatan 23, Kista, Stockholm, 164 83 Sweden	

GROWTH PLANS/SPECIAL FEATURES:

Telefon AB LM Ericsson (Ericsson) is a leading global supplier of mobile phone handsets and equipment for mobile and fixed-line telecommunications operators. The company is structured into three business units: networks, professional services and multimedia. The networks unit, which accounted for 66% of sales in 2009, is grouped into mobile and fixed access, core and transmission networks and next generation IP-networks. The mobile networks division provides radio base stations, base station controllers and radio network controllers, mobile switching centers, service application nodes and other nodes for billing and operations support for GSM, CDMA and EDGE networks. Fixed network operators are moving from single-service networks toward new multi-service networks that have the ability to simultaneously handle multiple services, such as voice, text and images. The professional services unit accounted for 27% of revenues in 2009 and consists of customer support services, managed services, systems integration and consulting. The multimedia unit accounted for 6% of 2009's revenues and consists of media and messaging applications, services delivery platforms and mobile platforms. It also includes Sony Ericsson Mobile Communications, a 50/50 joint venture with Sony Corporation; and ST-Ericsson, a subsidiary that develops wireless platforms and semiconductors. Subsidiaries include HyC Group, a leading Spanish TV consultancy and systems integration company; Entrisphere, a company providing fiber access technology; Drutt Corporation, a Service Delivery Platform (SDP) solutions provider; Redback Networks, Inc., a U.S. supplier of multi-service routing platform for broadband services; LHS, a German provider of post-paid billing and customer care systems for wireless markets; Tandberg Television, a Norwegian global provider of digital TV products; and Mobeon AB, a supplier of IP-messaging components. In May 2010, the firm entered a managed services deal with Telefonica, in which it will operate Telefonica's network operations center in Sao Paulo.

FINANCIALS: Sales and profits are in thousands of dollars—add 000 to get the full amount. 2010 Note: Financial information for 2010 was not available for all companies at press time.

2010 Sales: $	2010 Profits: $	U.S. Stock Ticker: ERIC
2009 Sales: $28,758,200	2009 Profits: $511,440	Int'l Ticker: ERIC Int'l Exchange: Stockholm-SSE
2008 Sales: $26,120,660	2008 Profits: $1,412,940	Employees: 82,500
2007 Sales: $31,375,900	2007 Profits: $3,698,510	Fiscal Year Ends: 12/31
2006 Sales: $30,046,000	2006 Profits: $4,417,150	Parent Company:

SALARIES/BENEFITS:

Pension Plan:	ESOP Stock Plan:	Profit Sharing:	Top Exec. Salary: $	Bonus: $
Savings Plan:	Stock Purch. Plan:		Second Exec. Salary: $	Bonus: $

OTHER THOUGHTS:

Apparent Women Officers or Directors: 8
Hot Spot for Advancement for Women/Minorities: Y

LOCATIONS: ("Y" = Yes)

West:	Southwest:	Midwest:	Southeast:	Northeast:	International:
Y	Y	Y	Y	Y	Y

TELEX COMMUNICATIONS INC

www.telex.com

Industry Group Code: 3342 Ranks within this company's industry group: Sales: Profits:

Hardware:	Software:	Telecommunications:	Electronic Publishing:	Equipment:		Specialty Services:
Computers:	Consumer:	Local:	Online Service:	Telecom:		Consulting:
Accessories:	Corporate:	Long Distance:	TV/Cable or Wireless:	Communication:	Y	Contract Manufacturing:
Network Equipment:	Telecom:	Cellular:	Games:	Distribution:		Processing:
Chips/Circuits:	Internet:	Internet Service:	Financial Data:	VAR/Reseller:		Staff/Outsourcing:
Parts/Drives:				Satellite Srv./Equip.:		Specialty Services:

TYPES OF BUSINESS:

Professional Audio & Communications Equipment
Wireless Communications Equipment
Life Safety Equipment

BRANDS/DIVISIONS/AFFILIATES:

Electro-Voice
FMR-500
Telex Legacy
RoadKing 56 CB
Bosch Security Systems
Robert Bosch GmbH

CONTACTS: Note: Officers with more than one job title may be intentionally listed here more than once.

Raymond V. Malpocher, CEO
Raymond V. Malpocher, Pres.
Gregory W. Richter, CFO/VP
Gregory W. Richter, Corp. Sec.
Kamil Swobodzinski, Dir.-Sales, EMEA

Phone: 952-884-4051	Fax:
Toll-Free: 877-863-4166	
Address: 12000 Portland Ave. S., Burnsville, MN 55337 US	

GROWTH PLANS/SPECIAL FEATURES:

Telex Communications, Inc. is part of the Bosch Group. The company designs, manufactures and markets professional audio, wireless, life safety and communications equipment to commercial, professional and industrial customers. As the result of the recent acquisition of Telex by Robert Bosch GmbH, the company is a division of Bosch Security Systems. Telex manufactures a comprehensive range of products worldwide for professional audio systems and wireless product markets, including the Electro-Voice line of speakers, microphones and electronics; the RoadKing 56 CB microphone; Telex Legacy football headsets; and the FMR-500 wireless microphone. Professional communication systems include both advanced digital matrix intercoms, used by broadcasters to control production communications, and intercoms, headsets and wireless communications systems used by utilities, aerospace/industrial organizations and sports teams and stadiums. Telex generates most of its revenue from sales of professional audio products. In addition, the company sells audio and wireless products such as military and aviation headsets.

FINANCIALS: Sales and profits are in thousands of dollars—add 000 to get the full amount. 2010 Note: Financial information for 2010 was not available for all companies at press time.

2010 Sales: $	2010 Profits: $	U.S. Stock Ticker: Subsidiary
2009 Sales: $	2009 Profits: $	Int'l Ticker: Int'l Exchange:
2008 Sales: $	2008 Profits: $	Employees:
2007 Sales: $	2007 Profits: $	Fiscal Year Ends: 12/31
2006 Sales: $	2006 Profits: $	Parent Company: BOSCH GROUP (THE)

SALARIES/BENEFITS:

Pension Plan:	ESOP Stock Plan:	Profit Sharing:	Top Exec. Salary: $	Bonus: $
Savings Plan: Y	Stock Purch. Plan:		Second Exec. Salary: $	Bonus: $

OTHER THOUGHTS:

Apparent Women Officers or Directors:
Hot Spot for Advancement for Women/Minorities:

LOCATIONS: ("Y" = Yes)

West:	Southwest:	Midwest:	Southeast:	Northeast:	International:
	Y	Y			

TELLABS INC

www.tellabs.com

Industry Group Code: 334210 Ranks within this company's industry group: Sales: 4 Profits: 2

Hardware:	Software:	Telecommunications:	Electronic Publishing:	Equipment:		Specialty Services:	
Computers:	Consumer:	Local:	Online Service:	Telecom:	Y	Consulting:	
Accessories:	Corporate:	Long Distance:	TV/Cable or Wireless:	Communication:	Y	Contract Manufacturing:	
Network Equipment:	Telecom:	Cellular:	Games:	Distribution:		Processing:	
Chips/Circuits:	Internet:	Internet Service:	Financial Data:	VAR/Reseller:		Staff/Outsourcing:	
Parts/Drives:				Satellite Srv./Equip.:		Specialty Services:	Y

TYPES OF BUSINESS:
Wireline & Wireless Products & Services
Consulting

BRANDS/DIVISIONS/AFFILIATES:
Tellabs 1000
Tellabs SmartCore 9100
Tellabs 8600
Tellabs 8000
Tellabs 3000
Tellabs 5000
Tellabs 7100

CONTACTS: Note: Officers with more than one job title may be intentionally listed here more than once.
Robert W. Pullen, CEO
Robert W. Pullen, Pres.
Timothy J. Wiggins, CFO/Exec. VP
Rizwan Khan, Exec. VP-Global Mktg.
Jean K. Holley, CIO/Exec. VP
Vikram Saksena, CTO/Exec. VP
Daniel P. Kelly, Exec. VP-Prod. Dev.
James M. Sheehan, Chief Admin. Officer
James M. Sheehan, General Counsel/Exec. VP/Sec.
John M. Brots, Exec. VP-Global Oper.
Rehan Jalil, Sr. VP-Mobile Internet
Ariana Nikitas, Contact-Media
Tom Scottino, Sr. Mgr.-Investor Rel.
Roger J. Heinz, Exec. VP-Global Sales & Svcs.
Michael J. Birck, Chmn.

GROWTH PLANS/SPECIAL FEATURES:
Tellabs, Inc. provides products and services that enable customers to deliver wireline and wireless voice, data and video services to business and residential customers. It operates in three segments: broadband, transport and services. Within the broadband segment, the company markets its products in three areas: access, which includes products that enable service providers to deliver bundled voice, video and high-speed Internet/data services over copper or fiber networks; managed access, which includes aggregation and transport products that deliver wireless and business services outside of North America; and data, which includes packet-switched products that enable wireline and wireless carriers to deliver business services and wireless services to their customers. This division's products include the Tellabs 1000 series, the Tellabs SmartCore 9100 platform, the Tellabs 8600 system and the Tellabs 8000 network manager. The transport segment includes applications that enable service providers to transport services and manage bandwidth by adding capacity when and where it is needed. Products include the Tellabs 3000 voice-quality enhancement products, the Tellabs 5000 series of digital cross-connect systems and the Tellabs 7100 optical transport system. The services division delivers deployment, training, support services and professional consulting to Tellabs' customers. Through these offerings, the firm supports its customers through all phases of running a network (planning, building and operating). Tellabs' customers are primarily communication service providers, including local exchange carriers; national post, telephone and telegraph administrators; wireless service providers; multi system operators; and competitive service providers. The customer base also includes distributors, original equipment manufacturers, system integrators and government agencies.

Phone: 630-798-8800	Fax: 630-798-2000
Toll-Free:	
Address: 1415 W. Diehl Rd., Naperville, IL 60563 US	

FINANCIALS: Sales and profits are in thousands of dollars—add 000 to get the full amount. 2010 Note: Financial information for 2010 was not available for all companies at press time.

2010 Sales: $	2010 Profits: $	U.S. Stock Ticker: TLAB
2009 Sales: $1,526,000	2009 Profits: $114,000	Int'l Ticker: Int'l Exchange:
2008 Sales: $1,729,000	2008 Profits: $-930,000	Employees: 3,295
2007 Sales: $1,913,400	2007 Profits: $65,000	Fiscal Year Ends: 12/31
2006 Sales: $2,041,200	2006 Profits: $194,100	Parent Company:

SALARIES/BENEFITS:
Pension Plan:	ESOP Stock Plan:	Profit Sharing:	Top Exec. Salary: $600,000	Bonus: $543,925
Savings Plan:	Stock Purch. Plan:		Second Exec. Salary: $400,000	Bonus: $192,000

OTHER THOUGHTS:
Apparent Women Officers or Directors: 4
Hot Spot for Advancement for Women/Minorities: Y

LOCATIONS: ("Y" = Yes)
West:	Southwest:	Midwest:	Southeast:	Northeast:	International:
Y	Y	Y		Y	Y

Note: Financial information, benefits and other data can change quickly and may vary from those stated here.

TELVENT GIT SA

www.telvent.com

Industry Group Code: 541513 Ranks within this company's industry group: Sales: 21 Profits: 18

Hardware:	Software:		Telecommunications:	Electronic Publishing:	Equipment:	Specialty Services:	
Computers:	Consumer:		Local:	Online Service:	Telecom:	Consulting:	
Accessories:	Corporate:	Y	Long Distance:	TV/Cable or Wireless:	Communication:	Contract Manufacturing:	
Network Equipment:	Telecom:		Cellular:	Games:	Distribution:	Processing:	
Chips/Circuits:	Internet:		Internet Service:	Financial Data:	VAR/Reseller:	Staff/Outsourcing:	
Parts/Drives:					Satellite Srv./Equip.:	Specialty Services:	Y

TYPES OF BUSINESS:
IT Outsourcing

BRANDS/DIVISIONS/AFFILIATES:
Abengoa Group
Telvent DTN

CONTACTS: Note: Officers with more than one job title may be intentionally listed here more than once.
Ignacio Gonzalez Dominguez, CEO
Javier Garoz, COO
Manuel Fernandez Maza, CFO
Amy Eggen, Sr. VP-Mktg.
Aranzazu Caja, Dir.-Human Resources
Travis Richardson, Sr. VP-Tech.
Travis Richardson, Sr. VP-Prod.
Lidia Garcia, General Counsel
Javier Garoz, Chief Corp. Dev. Officer
Manuel Fernandez Maza, Head-Investor Rel.
Tom Dilworth, Chief Acct. Officer
Larry Stack, Pres., Energy
Jose Ignacio del Barrio, Pres., Transportation
Cristobal Ramos, Exec. VP-Environment
Dai Yue, Chmn.-China
Ignacio Gonzalez Dominguez, Chmn.
Dave Jardine, Chmn./Pres., North America

Phone: 34-902-335-599	Fax: 34-917-147-001
Toll-Free:	
Address: 6 Valgrande, Alcobendas, Madrid, 28108 Spain	

GROWTH PLANS/SPECIAL FEATURES:

Telvent GIT S.A. is an information technology (IT) solutions and business information services provider targeting customers in several industrial sectors primarily in Europe, North America, Latin America, the Asia-Pacific region, the Middle East and Africa. The company operates in five segments: Energy, Transportation, Environment, Agriculture and Global Services. Energy focuses on real-time IT solutions to better manage energy delivery efficiency. It offers measurement and control systems and services that help manage critical infrastructures and data through highly available and secure solutions in three primary areas: electricity, oil and gas. Transportation provides solutions and services for traffic information and control systems; freeway information and management applications; and automatic fare collection solutions. Environment focuses on the observation and forecasting of the weather, the climate, air quality and hydrology and its impact on the different economic sectors, together with the provision of technology oriented to improve the use and management of water resources by water utilities. Agriculture provides information services, including critical business information and trading services, which support the agriculture supply chain, including producers, originators, traders and food processors in the U.S. and Canada. Global Services comprises consulting, integration and outsourcing and IT infrastructure management services. The firm's products and services include systems integration; consulting services; design and engineering services; maintenance services; real-time business-to-business information services; and business process and management software. Through Telvent DTN, it also delivers business-critical market intelligence, commercial weather, trading, and supply-chain services supporting the production, trading and distribution of agriculture and energy commodities. Additionally, the firm offers its proprietary weather technologies to serve weather-sensitive businesses in key sectors including aviation, transportation and public safety. Telvent GIT is a member of the Abengoa Group. In November 2010, the company began a partnership with Microsoft to create more efficient smart grid solutions for the utilities industry.

FINANCIALS: Sales and profits are in thousands of dollars—add 000 to get the full amount. 2010 Note: Financial information for 2010 was not available for all companies at press time.

2010 Sales: $	2010 Profits: $	**U.S. Stock Ticker: TLVT**
2009 Sales: $1,039,480	2009 Profits: $51,580	**Int'l Ticker:** Int'l Exchange:
2008 Sales: $1,008,588	2008 Profits: $42,050	Employees: 5,707
2007 Sales: $911,690	2007 Profits: $36,328	Fiscal Year Ends: 12/31
2006 Sales: $	2006 Profits: $	Parent Company:

SALARIES/BENEFITS:

Pension Plan:	ESOP Stock Plan:	Profit Sharing:	Top Exec. Salary: $	Bonus: $
Savings Plan:	Stock Purch. Plan:		Second Exec. Salary: $	Bonus: $

OTHER THOUGHTS:
Apparent Women Officers or Directors: 3
Hot Spot for Advancement for Women/Minorities: Y

LOCATIONS: ("Y" = Yes)

West:	Southwest:	Midwest:	Southeast:	Northeast:	International:
Y	Y	Y	Y	Y	Y

TERADATA CORPORATION

www.teradata.com

Industry Group Code: 511210J Ranks within this company's industry group: Sales: 1 Profits: 1

Hardware:	Software:		Telecommunications:	Electronic Publishing:	Equipment:	Specialty Services:	
Computers:	Consumer:		Local:	Online Service:	Telecom:	Consulting:	Y
Accessories:	Corporate:	Y	Long Distance:	TV/Cable or Wireless:	Communication:	Contract Manufacturing:	
Network Equipment:	Telecom:		Cellular:	Games:	Distribution:	Processing:	
Chips/Circuits:	Internet:		Internet Service:	Financial Data:	VAR/Reseller:	Staff/Outsourcing:	
Parts/Drives: Y					Satellite Srv./Equip.:	Specialty Services:	Y

TYPES OF BUSINESS:

Data Warehousing
Database & Data Mining Software
Consulting Services

BRANDS/DIVISIONS/AFFILIATES:

Aprimo
Cloudera

CONTACTS: *Note: Officers with more than one job title may be intentionally listed here more than once.*

Michael F. Koehler, CEO
Bruce A. Langos, COO
Michael F. Koehler, Pres.
Stephen Scheppmann, CFO
Darryl D. McDonald, Exec. VP-Mktg.
Saundra Davis, VP-Human Resources
Stephen Brobst, CTO
Laura Nyquist, General Counsel/Sec.
Robert A. Young, VP-Oper.
Darryl D. McDonald, Exec. VP-Bus. Dev.
Robert A. Young, VP-Financial Planning
Rocky J. Blanton, Pres., Americas Region
Bob Fair, Exec. VP-Global Field Oper.
Alan Chow, Chief Customer Officer
Dan Harrington, Exec. VP-Tech. & Support Svcs.
James R. Ringler, Chmn.
Hermann Wimmer, Pres., EMEA Region

Phone: 937-445-5993	Fax:
Toll-Free: 866-548-8348	
Address: 10000 Innovation Dr., Dayton, OH 45342 US	

GROWTH PLANS/SPECIAL FEATURES:

Teradata Corporation is a provider of data warehousing services and analytical applications. It is managed along three geographic regions, which are also its operating segments: the North America and Latin America (Americas) region; the Europe, Middle East and Africa region; and the Asia Pacific and Japan region. The company's fully scalable warehousing services include hardware; database, data mining and application software; professional consulting services; and customer support. Data warehousing provides customers with a single, accurate view of their business, which allows for deeper analysis of detailed data and information delivery. The firm's professional service consultants aid in customer data delivery, while the company's customer services organization provides maintenance and support. Teradata's services are focused around major industries, including retail, financial services, telecommunications, travel, transportation, insurance, manufacturing and government entities. The company's data warehousing solutions are delivered through a combination of direct and indirect channels. The firm's revenue is primarily generated through direct sales, with the remaining revenues coming through indirect channels such as alliances with value-added resellers, distributors and original equipment manufacturers. Approximately 60% of Teradata's revenues are derived from the North America and Latin America segment; 22% from the Europe, Middle East and Africa region; and 18% from the Asia Pacific and Japan division. The firm has over 900 enterprise customers worldwide (more than half of which have at least one system over one terabyte in size) and operates offices in approximately 40 countries. In September 2010, Teradata formed a partnership with Cloudera, allowing the company's customers to utilize Cloudera's Distribution for Hadoop solution. In December 2010, the firm agreed to acquire cloud-based integrated marketing software provider Aprimo for roughly $525 million.

Teradata offers benefits including medical, dental, vision, life and disability insurance; a 401(k); flexible work hours; and bonuses.

FINANCIALS: Sales and profits are in thousands of dollars—add 000 to get the full amount. 2010 Note: Financial information for 2010 was not available for all companies at press time.

2010 Sales: $	2010 Profits: $	**U.S. Stock Ticker: TDC**
2009 Sales: $1,709,000	2009 Profits: $254,000	**Int'l Ticker:** Int'l Exchange:
2008 Sales: $1,762,000	2008 Profits: $250,000	Employees: 6,400
2007 Sales: $1,702,000	2007 Profits: $200,000	Fiscal Year Ends: 12/31
2006 Sales: $1,547,000	2006 Profits: $192,000	Parent Company:

SALARIES/BENEFITS:

Pension Plan:	ESOP Stock Plan:	Profit Sharing:	Top Exec. Salary: $700,000	Bonus: $769,790
Savings Plan: Y	Stock Purch. Plan:		Second Exec. Salary: $412,000	Bonus: $339,807

OTHER THOUGHTS:

Apparent Women Officers or Directors: 4
Hot Spot for Advancement for Women/Minorities: Y

LOCATIONS: ("Y" = Yes)

West:	Southwest:	Midwest:	Southeast:	Northeast:	International:
Y		Y	Y		Y

TEXAS INSTRUMENTS INC (TI)

www.ti.com

Industry Group Code: 33441 Ranks within this company's industry group: Sales: 2 Profits: 4

Hardware:		Software:		Telecommunications:		Electronic Publishing:		Equipment:		Specialty Services:	
Computers:		Consumer:		Local:		Online Service:		Telecom:		Consulting:	
Accessories:	Y	Corporate:		Long Distance:		TV/Cable or Wireless:		Communication:		Contract Manufacturing:	
Network Equipment:		Telecom:		Cellular:		Games:		Distribution:		Processing:	
Chips/Circuits:	Y	Internet:		Internet Service:		Financial Data:		VAR/Reseller:		Staff/Outsourcing:	
Parts/Drives:								Satellite Srv./Equip.:		Specialty Services:	

TYPES OF BUSINESS:

Chips-Digital Signal Processors
Semiconductors
Calculators
Educational Software

BRANDS/DIVISIONS/AFFILIATES:

DLP
Luminary Micro

CONTACTS: Note: Officers with more than one job title may be intentionally listed here more than once.

Richard K. (Rich) Templeton, CEO
Richard K. (Rich) Templeton, Pres.
Kevin P. March, CFO/Sr. VP
John Szczsponik, Sr. VP/Pres., Sale & Mktg.
Darla Whitaker, Sr. VP/Dir.-Worldwide Human Resources
Kevin Ritchie, Sr. VP-Tech.
Kevin Ritchie, Sr. VP-Mfg.
Joseph F. Hubach, General Counsel/Sec./Sr. VP
Terri West, Sr. VP/Mgr.-Comm. & Investor Rel.
Ron Slaymaker, VP-Investor Rel.
Steve Anderson, Sr. VP/Worldwide Mgr.-Power Mgmt.
Greg Delagi, Sr. VP/Gen. Mgr.-Wireless Bus. Unit
Art George, Sr. VP/Mgr.-High-Performance Analog
Mike Hames, Sr. VP/Pres., Application Specific Prod.
Richard K. (Rich) Templeton, Chmn.

Phone: 972-995-3773	Fax: 972-927-6377
Toll-Free: 800-336-5236	
Address: 12500 TI Blvd., P.O. Box 660199, Dallas, TX 75266-0199 US	

GROWTH PLANS/SPECIAL FEATURES:

Texas Instruments, Inc. (TI), founded in 1930, is a technology company with design, sales and manufacturing operations in more than 30 countries. It operates in four segments: analog semiconductors (generating 40% of TI's total 2009 sales), embedded processing (15%), wireless (25%) and other (20%). Analog semiconductors process real world inputs (such as sound, temperature, pressure and visual images), conditions them, amplifies them and converts them into digital signals. They also assist in the management of power distribution and consumption. Embedded processing includes digital signal processing (DSP) products, which use complex algorithms and compression techniques to alter and improve a data stream instantaneously and power-efficiently. These products are ideal for applications that require precise, real-time processing of real-world analog signals that have been converted into digital form. TI's wireless semiconductors are mainly used in mobile phones, including standard voice-centric and more advanced multimedia-rich data handsets. Lastly, other includes semiconductors such as the firm's proprietary DLP optical semiconductor products, which enable clear video and microprocessors that serve as the brains of everything from high-end computer servers to high definition televisions (HDTVs). Other also includes educational products, such as handheld graphing calculators, business calculators and scientific calculators, as well as a wide range of advanced classroom tools and professional development resources, including educational software, to help students and teachers interactively explore math and science. Some of the firm's latest products include a multicore system-on-a-chip (SoC); a quad-radio chip that integrates WLAN 802.11n, GPS, FM transmit/receive and Bluetooth technologies; and a megapixel IP camera SoC equipped with smart analytics. In March 2009, the company acquired Luminary Micro.

Texas Instruments offers its employees medical, dental, vision and life insurance; AD&D, business travel accident and short- and long-term disability insurance; an employee assistance program; and educational assistance.

FINANCIALS: Sales and profits are in thousands of dollars—add 000 to get the full amount. 2010 Note: Financial information for 2010 was not available for all companies at press time.

2010 Sales: $	2010 Profits: $	U.S. Stock Ticker: TXN
2009 Sales: $10,427,000	2009 Profits: $1,470,000	Int'l Ticker: Int'l Exchange:
2008 Sales: $12,501,000	2008 Profits: $1,920,000	Employees: 26,584
2007 Sales: $13,835,000	2007 Profits: $2,657,000	Fiscal Year Ends: 12/31
2006 Sales: $14,255,000	2006 Profits: $4,341,000	Parent Company:

SALARIES/BENEFITS:

Pension Plan:	ESOP Stock Plan:	Profit Sharing: Y	Top Exec. Salary: $963,120	Bonus: $1,788,084
Savings Plan: Y	Stock Purch. Plan: Y		Second Exec. Salary: $535,020	Bonus: $810,044

OTHER THOUGHTS:

Apparent Women Officers or Directors: 7
Hot Spot for Advancement for Women/Minorities: Y

LOCATIONS: ("Y" = Yes)

West:	Southwest:	Midwest:	Southeast:	Northeast:	International:
Y	Y	Y	Y	Y	Y

Note: Financial information, benefits and other data can change quickly and may vary from those stated here.

THQ INC

www.thq.com

Industry Group Code: 511210G Ranks within this company's industry group: Sales: 6 Profits: 7

Hardware:	Software:	Telecommunications:	Electronic Publishing:		Equipment:	Specialty Services:
Computers:	Consumer:	Local:	Online Service:		Telecom:	Consulting:
Accessories:	Corporate:	Long Distance:	TV/Cable or Wireless:		Communication:	Contract Manufacturing:
Network Equipment:	Telecom:	Cellular:	Games:	Y	Distribution:	Processing:
Chips/Circuits:	Internet:	Internet Service:	Financial Data:		VAR/Reseller:	Staff/Outsourcing:
Parts/Drives:					Satellite Srv./Equip.:	Specialty Services:

TYPES OF BUSINESS:

Software-Video Games
Mobile Gaming Software

BRANDS/DIVISIONS/AFFILIATES:

Vigil Games
WWE SmackDown vs. Raw 2010
THQ Partners
Kaos Studios
THQ Digital Studios Warrington
THQ Wireless Inc
THQ Digital Studio UK
THQ Digital Studio Phoenix

CONTACTS: *Note: Officers with more than one job title may be intentionally listed here more than once.*

Brian J. Farrell, CEO
Brian J. Farrell, Pres.
Paul J. Pucino, CFO/Exec. VP
Germaine Gioia, Sr. VP-Merch. & Licensing
Edward L. Kaufman, Corp. Sec./Exec. VP-Bus. & Legal Affairs
Martin J. Good, Exec. VP-Global Online Svcs.
Julie MacMedan, VP-Corp. Comm.
Julie MacMedan, VP-Investor Rel.
Teri J. Manby, Chief Acct. Officer
Danny Bilson, Exec. VP-Core Games
Martin J. Good, Exec. VP-Kids, Family & Casual Games
Brian J. Farrell, Chmn.
Ian Curran, Exec. VP-Global Publishing

Phone: 818-871-5000	Fax: 818-871-7590
Toll-Free:	
Address: 29903 Agoura Rd., Agoura Hills, CA 91301 US	

GROWTH PLANS/SPECIAL FEATURES:

THQ, Inc. is a worldwide publisher, marketer and developer of proprietary and licensed video game software. Its games are featured on the Sony PSP, PlayStation 2 and PlayStation 3; Microsoft Xbox and Xbox 360; Nintendo GameCube, Game Boy Advance, DS and Wii; PCs; and mobile devices such as iPad, iPhone and iTouch. It develops titles through company-owned development studios located in the U.S. and Canada; and through Studio System, a group of third-party software developers, artists, voice-over actors and composers in Australia and the U.K. THQ's studios include Relic Entertainment; Vigil Games; Volition, Inc.; Kaos Studios; THQ Digital Studios Warrington; THQ Digital Studio U.K.; THQ Digital Studio Phoenix; and THQ San Diego. Games based on the company's own intellectual property include Company of Heroes, Darksiders, Frontlines, Red Faction, de Blob and Saints Row. Its games based on properties it licenses from third parties include SpongeBob SquarePants, WWE Smackdown vs. Raw, Bratz, Warhammer 40,000 and several Disney/Pixar properties, including WALL-E, Up and Ratatouille. The firm also has software and artwork developed for it by third parties. Subsidiary THQ Wireless, Inc., produces ringtones and videogames for mobile phones, including products related to the Star Wars franchise, which the firm only develops for wireless applications. THQ's corporate strategy focuses on improving its internal development capabilities and technology base, increasing its international presence and exploring the potential of the mobile interactive entertainment segment. Approximately 62% of the company's sales are derived from the U.S. THQ's most profitable games released in 2010 were UFC 2009 Undisputed and WWE SmackDown vs. Raw 2010. Other 2010 releases include All Star Karate, JEOPARDY!, Wheel of Fortune and Star Wars: The Battle for Hoth (through subsidiary THQ Wireless, Inc.). In May 2010, the firm established THQ Partners. In October 2010, THQ opened a new studio in Montreal, Canada.

FINANCIALS: Sales and profits are in thousands of dollars—add 000 to get the full amount. 2010 Note: Financial information for 2010 was not available for all companies at press time.

2010 Sales: $899,137	2010 Profits: $-9,017	**U.S. Stock Ticker:** THQI	
2009 Sales: $829,963	2009 Profits: $-431,112	**Int'l Ticker:** Int'l Exchange:	
2008 Sales: $1,030,467	2008 Profits: $-35,337	Employees: 1,680	
2007 Sales: $1,026,856	2007 Profits: $68,038	Fiscal Year Ends: 3/31	
2006 Sales: $806,560	2006 Profits: $32,106	Parent Company:	

SALARIES/BENEFITS:

Pension Plan:	ESOP Stock Plan:	Profit Sharing:	Top Exec. Salary: $677,131	Bonus: $1,137,580
Savings Plan: Y	Stock Purch. Plan:		Second Exec. Salary: $382,981	Bonus: $448,000

OTHER THOUGHTS:

Apparent Women Officers or Directors: 2
Hot Spot for Advancement for Women/Minorities: Y

LOCATIONS: ("Y" = Yes)

West:	Southwest:	Midwest:	Southeast:	Northeast:	International:
Y	Y				Y

Note: Financial information, benefits and other data can change quickly and may vary from those stated here.

TIBCO SOFTWARE INC

www.tibco.com

Industry Group Code: 511210H Ranks within this company's industry group: Sales: 9 Profits: 8

Hardware:	Software:		Telecommunications:	Electronic Publishing:	Equipment:	Specialty Services:	
Computers:	Consumer:		Local:	Online Service:	Telecom:	Consulting:	Y
Accessories:	Corporate:	Y	Long Distance:	TV/Cable or Wireless:	Communication:	Contract Manufacturing:	
Network Equipment:	Telecom:		Cellular:	Games:	Distribution:	Processing:	
Chips/Circuits:	Internet:	Y	Internet Service:	Financial Data:	VAR/Reseller:	Staff/Outsourcing:	
Parts/Drives:					Satellite Srv./Equip.:	Specialty Services:	Y

TYPES OF BUSINESS:

Software-Business Process
Data Management Software
Consulting & Support Services

BRANDS/DIVISIONS/AFFILIATES:

Netrics, Inc.
Proginet Corp.
OpenSpirit Corp.
Loyalty Lab, Inc.

CONTACTS: Note: Officers with more than one job title may be intentionally listed here more than once.

Vivek Y. Ranadive, CEO
Murray Rode, COO
Sydney Carey, CFO/Exec. VP
Ram Menon, Exec. VP-Worldwide Mktg.
Tom Laffey, Exec. VP-Tech.
Tom Laffey, Exec. VP-Prod. Dev.
William Hughes, General Counsel/Exec. VP/Corp. Sec.
Murat Sonmez, Exec. VP-Global Field Oper.
Vivek Y. Ranadive, Chmn.

Phone: 650-846-1000	**Fax:** 650-846-1005
Toll-Free: 800-420-8450	
Address: 3303 Hillview Ave., Palo Alto, CA 94304 US	

GROWTH PLANS/SPECIAL FEATURES:

TIBCO Software, Inc. is a provider of infrastructure software, focused on creating and marketing software for use in the integration of business information, processes and applications. The company offers a range of standards-based infrastructure software products that help customers to streamline business process management by offering real-time access to information. TIBCO's software products are capable of instantly correlating information about an organization's operations and performance with information about expected behavior and business rules, allowing customers to anticipate and respond to business developments. While its products can be sold individually to address specific technical challenges, the overall emphasis of the firm's development and sales efforts is to create products that interoperate and can be sold together as a suite. TIBCO's products are designed to address three primary areas of operational efficiency: Service Oriented Architecture (SOA), Business Process Management (BPM) and Business Optimization. The firm's SOA offerings enable organizations to migrate their IT infrastructure to a common framework by turning information and functions into discrete and reusable components that can be invoked from across the business and aggregated with other such services to create composite applications. BPM products enable the automation and coordination of the assets and tasks that make up business processes. The firm's Business Optimization software automatically converts and analyzes data, and can also initiate appropriate notifications or adaptation of business processes. The company also offers professional services, including consulting, planning, maintenance and support of information systems. In 2010, TIBCO acquired Netrics, Inc., which specializes in data matching algorithms; Proginet Corp., which focuses on file transfer technologies; OpenSpirit Corp., which develops oil and gas software; and Loyalty Lab, Inc., which produces marketing software.

TIBCO offers its employees medical, dental and vision coverage; life and AD&D insurance; a 401(k) program; short- and long-term disability; an employee assistance program; and tuition reimbursement.

FINANCIALS: Sales and profits are in thousands of dollars—add 000 to get the full amount. 2010 Note: Financial information for 2010 was not available for all companies at press time.

2010 Sales: $	2010 Profits: $	**U.S. Stock Ticker:** TIBX
2009 Sales: $621,388	2009 Profits: $62,302	**Int'l Ticker:** Int'l Exchange:
2008 Sales: $644,471	2008 Profits: $52,411	Employees: 2,097
2007 Sales: $577,386	2007 Profits: $51,888	Fiscal Year Ends: 11/30
2006 Sales: $517,279	2006 Profits: $72,864	Parent Company:

SALARIES/BENEFITS:

Pension Plan:	ESOP Stock Plan:	Profit Sharing:	Top Exec. Salary: $488,750	Bonus: $488,750
Savings Plan: Y	Stock Purch. Plan:		Second Exec. Salary: $355,416	Bonus: $277,974

OTHER THOUGHTS:

Apparent Women Officers or Directors:
Hot Spot for Advancement for Women/Minorities:

LOCATIONS: ("Y" = Yes)

West:	Southwest:	Midwest:	Southeast:	Northeast:	International:
Y					Y

TII NETWORK TECHNOLOGIES INC

www.tiinettech.com

Industry Group Code: 335 Ranks within this company's industry group: Sales: 5 Profits: 5

Hardware:		Software:		Telecommunications:		Electronic Publishing:		Equipment:		Specialty Services:	
Computers:		Consumer:		Local:		Online Service:		Telecom:		Consulting:	
Accessories:	Y	Corporate:		Long Distance:		TV/Cable or Wireless:		Communication:	Y	Contract Manufacturing:	
Network Equipment:	Y	Telecom:		Cellular:		Games:		Distribution:		Processing:	
Chips/Circuits:		Internet:		Internet Service:		Financial Data:		VAR/Reseller:		Staff/Outsourcing:	
Parts/Drives:								Satellite Srv./Equip.:		Specialty Services:	

TYPES OF BUSINESS:
Overvoltage & Lightning Protection Devices
Network Interface Devices
Telecommunications Equipment
Station Electronics Products

BRANDS/DIVISIONS/AFFILIATES:
HomePlug
Copper Products Division

CONTACTS: Note: Officers with more than one job title may be intentionally listed here more than once.
Kenneth A. Paladino, CEO
Kenneth A. Paladino, Pres.
Jennifer E. Katsch, CFO
Walter Fay, VP-Mktg. & Sales
Nisar A. Chaudhry, Chief Scientist/VP
David E. Foley, VP-Tech. Dev.
Thomas Smith, VP-Eng. & Materials
Jennifer E. Katsch, Sec.
Jennifer E. Katsch, Head-Investor Rel.
Jennifer E. Katsch, VP-Finance/Treas.
Christopher James, VP-Quality
Monica Gonzalez-Greer, VP-Sales, Latin America & Caribbean
Brian J. Kelley, Chmn.
Michael Dawe, VP-Sales-U.K., Europe & Asia

Phone: 631-789-5000	Fax: 631-789-5063
Toll-Free: 888-844-4720	
Address: 141 Rodeo Dr., Edgewood, NY 11717 US	

GROWTH PLANS/SPECIAL FEATURES:

TII Network Technologies, Inc. designs, manufactures and markets network interface devices (NID), broadband products, over-voltage surge protection and connectivity solutions for the communications industry. The company's NIDs connect and make use of surge protection technologies, electronics and DSL and fiber components. Along with its NIDs, TII also markets station electronic products that are installed with an NID. These products include a line of DSL station electronic items; for example, splitters that isolate the voice and data signals on a line to provide separate outputs for phone and data services, allowing for DSL services. Broadband products include Outrigger, the firm's intelligent NID that facilitates delivery of digital telephone, television and Internet data by telephone or cable service providers; and HomePlug, a technology that enables networking of voice, data and audio devices through the consumer's AC powerlines. The company's overvoltage products include gas tubes, which are the principal component of all of its overvoltage surge protectors; modular station protectors, the firm's most advanced overvoltage surge protectors; broadband coaxial protectors, which protect network powered coaxial lines that bring telephony and broadband services to homes and businesses; and AC powerline and dataline protectors for personal computers and home entertainment systems. TII's connectivity products include aerial and buried terminals as well as various VoIP (Voice over Internet Protocol) products. The company's principal VoIP products are a collection of passive products, which allow clients to consolidate multiple phone lines in one location in order to provide VoIP telephony to cable subscribers. TII sells its products through a network of multiple sales channels, principally to telecommunications providers, multi-system operators of communications services, including cable satellite service providers and original equipment manufacturers (OEMs). In May 2010, the company acquired Porta Systems Corp.'s Copper Products Division for roughly $8.2 million.

FINANCIALS: Sales and profits are in thousands of dollars—add 000 to get the full amount. 2010 Note: Financial information for 2010 was not available for all companies at press time.

2010 Sales: $	2010 Profits: $	U.S. Stock Ticker: TII
2009 Sales: $27,437	2009 Profits: $ 73	Int'l Ticker: Int'l Exchange:
2008 Sales: $35,190	2008 Profits: $ 578	Employees: 46
2007 Sales: $46,486	2007 Profits: $6,440	Fiscal Year Ends: 12/31
2006 Sales: $39,104	2006 Profits: $2,681	Parent Company:

SALARIES/BENEFITS:

Pension Plan:	ESOP Stock Plan:	Profit Sharing:	Top Exec. Salary: $300,000	Bonus: $
Savings Plan:	Stock Purch. Plan:		Second Exec. Salary: $195,000	Bonus: $

OTHER THOUGHTS:
Apparent Women Officers or Directors: 2
Hot Spot for Advancement for Women/Minorities:

LOCATIONS: ("Y" = Yes)

West:	Southwest:	Midwest:	Southeast:	Northeast:	International:
				Y	

TOKYO ELECTRON LIMITED

www.tel.com

Industry Group Code: 33441 Ranks within this company's industry group: Sales: 6 Profits: 23

Hardware:		Software:		Telecommunications:		Electronic Publishing:		Equipment:		Specialty Services:	
Computers:		Consumer:		Local:		Online Service:		Telecom:	Y	Consulting:	
Accessories:	Y	Corporate:		Long Distance:		TV/Cable or Wireless:		Communication:		Contract Manufacturing:	
Network Equipment:	Y	Telecom:		Cellular:		Games:		Distribution:	Y	Processing:	
Chips/Circuits:	Y	Internet:		Internet Service:		Financial Data:		VAR/Reseller:		Staff/Outsourcing:	
Parts/Drives:								Satellite Srv./Equip.:		Specialty Services:	

TYPES OF BUSINESS:

Semiconductor & Electronic Components Manufacturing
Photovoltaic Production Equipment
Electronic Component Sales & Distribution

BRANDS/DIVISIONS/AFFILIATES:

Tokyo Electron Device Ltd.
Tokyo Electron PV Ltd.
Tel U.S. Holdings, Inc.
Tokyo Electron Europe Ltd.
Tokyo Electron Israel Ltd.
Tokyo Electron Korea Ltd.
Tokyo Electron Taiwan Ltd.
Tokyo Electron (Shanghai) Ltd.

CONTACTS: *Note: Officers with more than one job title may be intentionally listed here more than once.*

Hiroshi Takenaka, CEO
Hiroshi Takenaka, Pres.
Chiaki Yamaguchi, Sr. VP/Gen. Mgr.-Sales & Svcs.
Yutaka Nanasawa, Gen. Mgr.-Human Resources
Hirofumi Kitayama, Exec VP/Gen. Mgr.-Mfg.
Takashi Nakamura, Sr. VP/Gen. Mgr.-Corp. Admin.
Tetsuro Hori, Gen. Mgr.-Legal & Intellectual Property
Kenji Washino, Exec. VP/Gen. Mgr.-Corp. Bus. Strategy
Yutaka Nanasawa, Gen. Mgr.-Finance
Hikaru Ito, Exec. VP/Gen. Mgr.-SPE Div.
Mitsuru Onozato, Exec. VP/Gen. Mgr.-FPD Div.
Masami Akimoto, Sr. VP/Gen. Mgr.-System Dev.
Takashi Ito, Sr. VP/Gen. Mgr.-PVE Div.
Tetsuro Higashi, Chmn.
Yutaka Nanasawa, Gen. Mgr.-Export & Logistics

Phone: 813-556-17000	Fax: 813-556-17400

Toll-Free:

Address: 3-1 Akasaka 5-chome, Minato-ku, Tokyo, 107-8481 Japan

GROWTH PLANS/SPECIAL FEATURES:

Tokyo Electron Limited (TEL) is a global supplier of electronics for industrial use. TEL serves customers through 30 subsidiaries in approximately 90 locations, covering 12 countries in Europe, Asia and the U.S. Its products include production equipment for semiconductors, LCD flat panel displays (FPDs) used for personal computers and TVs and photovoltaic (PV) cells, as well as computer network-related products and electronic components. The firm is divided into three divisions: semiconductor production equipment, accounting for 63% of net sales; FPD/PV production equipment, 17% of net sales; and electronic components and computer networks, 20% of net sales. Through the semiconductor production equipment division, TEL offers a wide range of equipment for producing semiconductors, along with superior technical support and service. Its product lineup consists of six groups: coaters/developers, plasma etch systems, thermal processing systems, single wafer deposition systems, cleaning systems and wafer probers used in wafer testing processes. The FPD/PV production equipment segment produces the components and equipment required by manufacturers of LCD displays and PV cells. Subsidiary Tokyo Electron Device Ltd. manages the operations of the electronic components and computer networks division, which acts as a distributor of a wide array of components and network equipment. In January 2010, the firm began construction on a new plant in the Miyagi Prefecture. In October 2010, TEL announced plans to establish a new FPD production site in the Jiangsu province of China. In November 2010, the firm entered a joint development agreement with Seiko Epson Corp. to integrate organic light-emitting diode (OLED) TV display manufacturing technologies using Seiko Epson's inkjet method with its production equipment technology.

FINANCIALS: Sales and profits are in thousands of dollars—add 000 to get the full amount. 2010 Note: Financial information for 2010 was not available for all companies at press time.

2010 Sales: $5,090,620	2010 Profits: $-109,840	**U.S. Stock Ticker:** TOELF
2009 Sales: $5,504,560	2009 Profits: $81,720	**Int'l Ticker:** 8035 Int'l Exchange: Tokyo-TSE
2008 Sales: $9,816,590	2008 Profits: $1,151,340	**Employees:**
2007 Sales: $9,230,300	2007 Profits: $988,733	**Fiscal Year Ends:** 3/31
2006 Sales: $	2006 Profits: $	**Parent Company:**

SALARIES/BENEFITS:

Pension Plan:	ESOP Stock Plan:	Profit Sharing:	Top Exec. Salary: $	Bonus: $
Savings Plan:	Stock Purch. Plan:		Second Exec. Salary: $	Bonus: $

OTHER THOUGHTS:

Apparent Women Officers or Directors:
Hot Spot for Advancement for Women/Minorities:

LOCATIONS: ("Y" = Yes)

West:	Southwest:	Midwest:	Southeast:	Northeast:	International:
Y	Y			Y	Y

TOMTOM NV

www.tomtom.com

Industry Group Code: 3345 Ranks within this company's industry group: Sales: 2 Profits: 2

Hardware:		Software:		Telecommunications:		Electronic Publishing:	Equipment:	Specialty Services:
Computers:	Y	Consumer:	Y	Local:		Online Service:	Telecom:	Consulting:
Accessories:	Y	Corporate:		Long Distance:		TV/Cable or Wireless:	Communication:	Contract Manufacturing:
Network Equipment:		Telecom:		Cellular:		Games:	Distribution:	Processing:
Chips/Circuits:		Internet:		Internet Service:		Financial Data:	VAR/Reseller:	Staff/Outsourcing:
Parts/Drives:							Satellite Srv./Equip.:	Specialty Services:

TYPES OF BUSINESS:

Communications Equipment-GPS-Based
Navigation Services
Mapping Technology
PDA & Smartphone Software

BRANDS/DIVISIONS/AFFILIATES:

Tele Atlas
TomTom, Inc.
TomTom Asia Ltd.
Phonetic Topographics NV
Tele Atlas GmbH
Tele Atlas Polska Sp. z o.o.
TomTom Gox50 series
TomTom NAVIGATOR 7

CONTACTS: Note: Officers with more than one job title may be intentionally listed here more than once.

Harold Goddijn, CEO
Marina Wyatt, CFO
Peter-Frans Pauwels, CTO
Richard Piekaar, Mgr.-Investor Rel.
Karel Vuursteen, Chmn.

Phone: 31-20-850-0800	Fax: 31-20-850-1099
Toll-Free:	
Address: Rembrandtplein 35, Amsterdam, 1017 CT The Netherlands	

GROWTH PLANS/SPECIAL FEATURES:

TomTom NV is a manufacturer of portable navigation devices for the consumer market. The company's line of navigation products focus on digital mapping and routing using GPS technology to pinpoint a user's precise location and produce directions to the user's destination. TomTom's products include windshield-mounted and in-dash navigation systems in cars and trucks, as well as software for handheld devices like PDAs and smartphones. TomTom also offers navigation solutions for bicycles. In addition to portable and built-in navigation devices for vehicles, the company sells digital maps through its Tele Atlas division, covering 80 countries in North and South America, Europe, Australia, Africa and Asia. The company maintains a fleet of surveying vehicles to keep its growing map database up-to-date. TomTom sells its products, primarily through third-party retailers, in over 30 countries in more than 20 languages around the world, and maintains offices in Europe, North America, Asia and Australia. The company's subsidiaries include TomTom, Inc.; TomTom Asia Ltd.; Phonetic Topographics NV; Tele Atlas GmbH; and Tele Atlas Polska Sp. z o.o. Some of the company's recently launched products include the TomTom GO x40 LIVE series, which incorporates a variety of live services (such as traffic information and historical travel times) into the device's planned routes, and the TomTom NAVIGATOR 7, its navigation software solution for selected smartphones. In September 2009, the firm introduced the TomTom Gox50 series, which feature the portable navigation devices TomTom GO 950, TomTom GO 550 and TomTom GO 750. In December 2009, the company acquired Netherlands-based business listings firm Ilocal. In early 2010, the firm began offering products in Mexico and Morocco. In April 2010, TomTom introduced two new real-time government solutions: HD Route Times, which offers travel and delay updates for all possible routes; and HD Flow, which offers European standard traffic flow information.

FINANCIALS: Sales and profits are in thousands of dollars—add 000 to get the full amount. 2010 Note: Financial information for 2010 was not available for all companies at press time.

2010 Sales: $	2010 Profits: $	U.S. Stock Ticker:
2009 Sales: $1,806,050	2009 Profits: $105,940	Int'l Ticker: TOM2 Int'l Exchange: Amsterdam-Euronext
2008 Sales: $2,427,870	2008 Profits: $-1,265,570	Employees: 3,089
2007 Sales: $2,519,390	2007 Profits: $460,050	Fiscal Year Ends: 12/31
2006 Sales: $	2006 Profits: $	Parent Company:

SALARIES/BENEFITS:

Pension Plan:	ESOP Stock Plan:	Profit Sharing:	Top Exec. Salary: $	Bonus: $
Savings Plan:	Stock Purch. Plan:		Second Exec. Salary: $	Bonus: $

OTHER THOUGHTS:

Apparent Women Officers or Directors:
Hot Spot for Advancement for Women/Minorities:

LOCATIONS: ("Y" = Yes)

West:	Southwest:	Midwest:	Southeast:	Northeast:	International:
				Y	Y

TOSHIBA CORPORATION

www.toshiba.co.jp

Industry Group Code: 334111 Ranks within this company's industry group: Sales: 3 Profits: 30

Hardware:		Software:		Telecommunications:	Electronic Publishing:	Equipment:		Specialty Services:	
Computers:	Y	Consumer:	Y	Local:	Online Service:	Telecom:	Y	Consulting:	
Accessories:	Y	Corporate:		Long Distance:	TV/Cable or Wireless:	Communication:	Y	Contract Manufacturing:	
Network Equipment:	Y	Telecom:		Cellular:	Games:	Distribution:		Processing:	
Chips/Circuits:	Y	Internet:		Internet Service:	Financial Data:	VAR/Reseller:		Staff/Outsourcing:	
Parts/Drives:	Y					Satellite Srv./Equip.:		Specialty Services:	

TYPES OF BUSINESS:

Electronics Manufacturing
Computers & Accessories
Telecommunications Equipment
Semiconductors
Consumer Electronics
Medical & Industrial Equipment
Satellite Radio
Internet Services

BRANDS/DIVISIONS/AFFILIATES:

Mobile Communications Company
Digital Media Network Company
Personal Computer & Network Company
Semiconductor Company
Industrial Systems Company
Westinghouse Electric Company LLC
Toshiba Thailand Co Ltd
Toshiba Corporate R&D Center

CONTACTS: Note: Officers with more than one job title may be intentionally listed here more than once.

Norio Sasaki, CEO
Norio Sasaki, Pres.
Kosei Okamoto, VP/Pres./CEO-Mobile Comm. Co.
Masaaki Oosumi, Sr. VP/Pres./CEO-Visual Prod. Co.
Kazuyoshi Yamamori, Sr. VP/Pres./CEO-Storage Prod. Co.
Shozo Saito, Sr. VP/Pres./CEO-Semiconductor Co.
Atsutoshi Nishida, Chmn.

Phone: 81-3-3457-4511	Fax: 81-3-3456-1631
Toll-Free:	
Address: 1-1, Shibaura 1-chome, Minato-ku, Tokyo, 105-8001 Japan	

GROWTH PLANS/SPECIAL FEATURES:

Toshiba Corporation is a diversified technology firm. It has 537 consolidated subsidiaries and eight in-house companies that are active in four business segments: Digital Products; Electronic Devices; Social Infrastructure; and Home Appliances. Digital Products consists of the Mobile Communications Company, which develops mobile phones, Smartphones and data terminals; Digital Media Network Company, which manufactures LCD TVs, surveillance cameras and hard disk drives; and Personal Computer & Network Company, which mainly manufactures notebook PCs. It also works with Toshiba TEC Corporation, which creates peripheral equipment such as fax machines and cash registers. Electronic Devices consists of the Semiconductor Company, which manufactures circuits such as NAND flash memory, power devices and cell phone components. It also works with the Display Devices & Components Control Center, which manufactures direct methanol fuel cells and various materials and components; and Toshiba Mobile Display Co., Ltd., which manufactures low-temperature polysilicon TFT technology and supplies displays for mobile phones, car navigation systems and mobile PCs. The Social Infrastructure segment includes the Power Systems Company, which develops nuclear, hydroelectric and thermal power plants and related equipment; Transmission Distribution and Industrial Systems Company, which provides power transmission and distribution systems, transportation systems and industrial systems; and Social Infrastructure Systems Company, which manufactures broadcasting systems, air-traffic control systems and power distribution systems. It also works with Toshiba Elevator and Building Systems Corporation; Toshiba Solutions Corporation, an IT company; and Toshiba Medical Systems Corporation, developing CT scanners, ultrasound equipment and X-ray systems. The Home Appliances & Other division works with Toshiba Consumer Electronics Holding Corporation supplying home appliances, lighting solutions and batteries. In April 2010, the company and Westinghouse Electric Company, LLC formed a new joint venture, Advance Uranium Asset Management Ltd.

Employees are offered medical and dental insurance; a pension program; retirement allowance; life insurance; a housing loan support program; recreational facilities; and medical and health care facilities.

FINANCIALS: Sales and profits are in thousands of dollars—add 000 to get the full amount. 2010 Note: Financial information for 2010 was not available for all companies at press time.

2010 Sales: $74,288,300	2010 Profits: $-229,530	U.S. Stock Ticker: TOSBF
2009 Sales: $72,732,800	2009 Profits: $-3,755,040	Int'l Ticker: 6502 Int'l Exchange: Tokyo-TSE
2008 Sales: $76,680,800	2008 Profits: $1,274,100	Employees:
2007 Sales: $64,330,700	2007 Profits: $1,242,340	Fiscal Year Ends: 3/31
2006 Sales: $53,945,200	2006 Profits: $664,900	Parent Company:

SALARIES/BENEFITS:

Pension Plan: Y	ESOP Stock Plan:	Profit Sharing:	Top Exec. Salary: $	Bonus: $
Savings Plan:	Stock Purch. Plan:		Second Exec. Salary: $	Bonus: $

OTHER THOUGHTS:

Apparent Women Officers or Directors:
Hot Spot for Advancement for Women/Minorities:

LOCATIONS: ("Y" = Yes)

West:	Southwest:	Midwest:	Southeast:	Northeast:	International:
Y	Y			Y	Y

Note: Financial information, benefits and other data can change quickly and may vary from those stated here.

TPV TECHNOLOGY LTD

www.tpvholdings.com

Industry Group Code: 334119 Ranks within this company's industry group: Sales: 5 Profits: 5

Hardware:		Software:	Telecommunications:	Electronic Publishing:	Equipment:	Specialty Services:	
Computers:		Consumer:	Local:	Online Service:	Telecom:	Consulting:	
Accessories:	Y	Corporate:	Long Distance:	TV/Cable or Wireless:	Communication:	Contract Manufacturing:	Y
Network Equipment:		Telecom:	Cellular:	Games:	Distribution:	Processing:	
Chips/Circuits:		Internet:	Internet Service:	Financial Data:	VAR/Reseller:	Staff/Outsourcing:	
Parts/Drives:					Satellite Srv./Equip.:	Specialty Services:	

TYPES OF BUSINESS:

Computer Accessories-Monitors
LCD Television Manufacturing

BRANDS/DIVISIONS/AFFILIATES:

Top Victory Investments, Ltd.
Envision Peripherals, Inc.
P-Harmony Monitors Hong Kong Holding, Ltd.
MMD-Monitors & Displays Holding, Ltd.
Envision
AOC
L&T Display Technology (Xiamen), Ltd.
BriVictory Display Technology (Labuan) Co., Ltd.

CONTACTS: Note: Officers with more than one job title may be intentionally listed here more than once.

Jason Hsuan, CEO
Houng Yu-Te, CFO/Sr. VP
Lu Being-Chang, CTO/Sr. VP
Jason Hsuan, Chmn.
Hsieh Chi Tsung, Chief Procurement Officer/Sr. VP

Phone: 852-2858-5736	Fax: 852-2546-8884
Toll-Free:	
Address: 5 Canton Rd., 10th Fl., Ste. 1023, Harbour City, Tsim Sha Tsui, Kowloon, Hong Kong China	

GROWTH PLANS/SPECIAL FEATURES:

TPV Technology, Ltd. is a leading contract manufacturer of television and computer display monitors. The firm targets both the PC and TV markets, with PC displays representing 81% of total production units and TVs the remaining 19%. Products include CRT (cathode ray tube) PC monitors and TFT-LCD monitors, which generate the vast majority of the firm's revenue. The company also sells its own CRT monitors in over 30 countries worldwide under the Envision brand name, as well as both CRT and LCD monitors under the AOC (Admiral Overseas Corporation) brand name. It is incorporated in Bermuda, but conducts its manufacturing operations primarily in China and sells to Europe, the Americas, China and other Asian countries. Major subsidiaries include Top Victory Investments, Ltd.; Envision Peripherals, Inc.; P-Harmony Monitors Hong Kong Holding, Ltd.; and MMD-Monitors & Displays Holding, Ltd. During 2010, about 30% of the company's sales were in China; 32% in Europe; 18% in North America; and 20% throughout the rest of the world. The company maintains several joint ventures, including two with LG Display Co., L&T Display Technology (Xiamen), Ltd. and L&T Display Technology (Fujian), Ltd., which manufacture and sell LCD products. In March 2010, it formed BriVictory Display Technology (Labuan) Co., Ltd., a joint venture with AU Optronics Corp., to assemble TFT-LCD modules at a factory in Poland.

FINANCIALS: Sales and profits are in thousands of dollars—add 000 to get the full amount. 2010 Note: Financial information for 2010 was not available for all companies at press time.

2010 Sales: $	2010 Profits: $	U.S. Stock Ticker:
2009 Sales: $8,032,000	2009 Profits: $141,200	Int'l Ticker: T18 Int'l Exchange: Singapore-SIN
2008 Sales: $9,247,020	2008 Profits: $97,580	Employees:
2007 Sales: $8,455,151	2007 Profits: $183,396	Fiscal Year Ends: 12/31
2006 Sales: $7,176,300	2006 Profits: $154,400	Parent Company:

SALARIES/BENEFITS:

Pension Plan:	ESOP Stock Plan:	Profit Sharing:	Top Exec. Salary: $	Bonus: $
Savings Plan:	Stock Purch. Plan:		Second Exec. Salary: $	Bonus: $

OTHER THOUGHTS:

Apparent Women Officers or Directors:
Hot Spot for Advancement for Women/Minorities:

LOCATIONS: ("Y" = Yes)

West:	Southwest:	Midwest:	Southeast:	Northeast:	International:
					Y

TRANSCEND INFORMATION INC

www.transcend.com.tw

Industry Group Code: 334111   Ranks within this company's industry group: Sales: 19   Profits: 7

Hardware:		Software:		Telecommunications:		Electronic Publishing:		Equipment:		Specialty Services:	
Computers:		Consumer:		Local:		Online Service:		Telecom:		Consulting:	
Accessories:	Y	Corporate:		Long Distance:		TV/Cable or Wireless:		Communication:		Contract Manufacturing:	Y
Network Equipment:		Telecom:		Cellular:		Games:		Distribution:		Processing:	
Chips/Circuits:		Internet:		Internet Service:		Financial Data:		VAR/Reseller:		Staff/Outsourcing:	
Parts/Drives:	Y							Satellite Srv./Equip.:		Specialty Services:	

TYPES OF BUSINESS:

Computer Memory Devices Manufacturing
Digital Music Players
USB Memory Devices
Portable Computer Hard Drives

BRANDS/DIVISIONS/AFFILIATES:

CONTACTS: Note: Officers with more than one job title may be intentionally listed here more than once.

Peter Shu, CEO
Lydia Lee, CFO
Steve Chang, VP-Sales & Mktg.
Frankie Chiu, VP-R&D
Peter Shu, Chmn.

Phone: 886-2-2792-8000	Fax: 886-2-2793-2222
Toll-Free:	
Address: No. 70, Xing Zhong Rd., Nei Hu District, Taipei, Taiwan	

GROWTH PLANS/SPECIAL FEATURES:

Transcend Information, Inc. is a Taiwan-based company that designs, develops, manufactures and markets electronic memory devices. The firm's products include over 2,000 types of memory modules, including flash memory cards for digital cameras and mobile phones, USB flash drives, MP3 players, digital photo frames, portable hard drives, multimedia products and accessories. Some of its products are compatible with proprietary equipment while others are designed to be used with mass marketed personal computers of various brands. The company creates proprietary memory modules for companies such as Acer, Apple, Dell, LG Electronics, ASUS, Toshiba and Intel. Transcend operates a chain of retail stores in Taiwan, as well as an e-commerce web site for its products. In addition to its operations in Taiwan, the company maintains sales and logistics offices in Germany, the Netherlands, Japan, Hong Kong, China, the U.K., Korea and the U.S. Offices in the U.S. are located near Los Angeles, California and Baltimore, Maryland.

Transcend offers its employees a variety of benefits that vary by location; U.S. employees have access to benefits such as medical and dental plans; life and disability insurance; a 401(k) plan; and a bonus program.

FINANCIALS: Sales and profits are in thousands of dollars—add 000 to get the full amount. 2010 Note: Financial information for 2010 was not available for all companies at press time.

2010 Sales: $	2010 Profits: $	U.S. Stock Ticker:
2009 Sales: $1,185,150	2009 Profits: $149,840	Int'l Ticker: 2451 Int'l Exchange: Taipei-TPE
2008 Sales: $1,082,660	2008 Profits: $70,700	Employees:
2007 Sales: $1,191,610	2007 Profits: $84,970	Fiscal Year Ends: 12/31
2006 Sales: $	2006 Profits: $	Parent Company:

SALARIES/BENEFITS:

Pension Plan:	ESOP Stock Plan:	Profit Sharing:	Top Exec. Salary: $	Bonus: $
Savings Plan: Y	Stock Purch. Plan:		Second Exec. Salary: $	Bonus: $

OTHER THOUGHTS:

Apparent Women Officers or Directors: 1
Hot Spot for Advancement for Women/Minorities:

LOCATIONS: ("Y" = Yes)

West:	Southwest:	Midwest:	Southeast:	Northeast:	International:
Y				Y	Y

TREND MICRO INC
www.trendmicro.com

Industry Group Code: 511210E Ranks within this company's industry group: Sales: 3 Profits: 3

Hardware:	Software:		Telecommunications:	Electronic Publishing:	Equipment:	Specialty Services:
Computers:	Consumer:	Y	Local:	Online Service:	Telecom:	Consulting:
Accessories:	Corporate:	Y	Long Distance:	TV/Cable or Wireless:	Communication:	Contract Manufacturing:
Network Equipment:	Telecom:		Cellular:	Games:	Distribution:	Processing:
Chips/Circuits:	Internet:		Internet Service:	Financial Data:	VAR/Reseller:	Staff/Outsourcing:
Parts/Drives:					Satellite Srv./Equip.:	Specialty Services:

TYPES OF BUSINESS:
Software-Security
Antivirus Software

BRANDS/DIVISIONS/AFFILIATES:
humyo
Smart Protection Network
Worry Free Business Security
InterScan

CONTACTS: Note: Officers with more than one job title may be intentionally listed here more than once.
Eva Chen, CEO
Mahendra Negi, COO
Mahendra Negi, CFO
Jenny Chang, Chief Culture Officer
Steve Chang, Chmn.

Phone: 81-3-5334-3650	Fax: 81-3-5334-2651
Toll-Free: 800-228-5651	
Address: Shinjuku Maynds Tower, 2-1-1 Yoyogi, Shibuya, Tokyo, 151-0053 Japan	

GROWTH PLANS/SPECIAL FEATURES:
Trend Micro, Inc. develops and markets endpoint, messaging and web security software and services to protect against threats such as viruses, spam, phishing, spyware and other malware. The company offers a broad range of applications for enterprises, small and medium businesses, individuals, service providers and original equipment manufacturers (OEMs). The firm's premier security application, the Trend Micro Smart Protection Network, is a cloud-client content security infrastructure product that combines cloud-based reputation technology, feedback loops and Trend Micro threat research, product services and support centers to provide real-time protection and prevent threats from reaching the target network or endpoint. The Smart Protection Network infrastructure powers the company's enterprise products for endpoint, datacenter, web, messaging, data protection and central management security, as well as its threat discovery, remediation and proactive planning applications. For small business customers, Trend Micro offers Worry Free Business Security antivirus and anti-spam products; InterScan Messaging hosted security for e-mail protection; and the SecureSite web site vulnerability scanning service. The firm also offers Internet security, anti-spam and antivirus and home network defense products for home and home office customers. The company has a presence in 23 countries around the world. The company's key subsidiaries include Trend Micro, Inc. (Taiwan); Trend Micro, Inc. (U.S.); Trend Micro Australia Pty. Ltd.; Trend Micro Ireland Ltd; and Trend Micro EMEA Ltd. In 2010 the firm acquired U.K. online storage company, humyo. In January 2011, the company launched Mobile Security for Android devices, an application designed to protect digital files, filter texts and calls and provide download protection.

FINANCIALS: Sales and profits are in thousands of dollars—add 000 to get the full amount. 2010 Note: Financial information for 2010 was not available for all companies at press time.

2010 Sales: $	2010 Profits: $	U.S. Stock Ticker: TMICY
2009 Sales: $1,171,570	2009 Profits: $214,478	Int'l Ticker: 4704 Int'l Exchange: Tokyo-TSE
2008 Sales: $1,101,890	2008 Profits: $208,520	Employees: 4,434
2007 Sales: $1,081,290	2007 Profits: $255,260	Fiscal Year Ends: 12/31
2006 Sales: $804,800	2006 Profits: $181,700	Parent Company:

SALARIES/BENEFITS:

Pension Plan:	ESOP Stock Plan:	Profit Sharing:	Top Exec. Salary: $	Bonus: $
Savings Plan:	Stock Purch. Plan:		Second Exec. Salary: $	Bonus: $

OTHER THOUGHTS:
Apparent Women Officers or Directors: 2
Hot Spot for Advancement for Women/Minorities: Y

LOCATIONS: ("Y" = Yes)

West:	Southwest:	Midwest:	Southeast:	Northeast:	International:
Y					Y

TRILOGY INC

www.trilogy.com

Industry Group Code: 511210K Ranks within this company's industry group: Sales: Profits:

Hardware:	Software:		Telecommunications:	Electronic Publishing:	Equipment:	Specialty Services:
Computers:	Consumer:		Local:	Online Service:	Telecom:	Consulting:
Accessories:	Corporate:	Y	Long Distance:	TV/Cable or Wireless:	Communication:	Contract Manufacturing:
Network Equipment:	Telecom:	Y	Cellular:	Games:	Distribution:	Processing:
Chips/Circuits:	Internet:	Y	Internet Service:	Financial Data:	VAR/Reseller:	Staff/Outsourcing:
Parts/Drives:					Satellite Srv./Equip.:	Specialty Services:

TYPES OF BUSINESS:

Business-to-Business Software
Enterprise Software
E-Commerce Software

BRANDS/DIVISIONS/AFFILIATES:

Trinity Enterprises, Inc.
Versata Software, Inc.
SmartLeads
CarBuy.com
YourBillBuddy.com
Versata Distribution Channel Management
Versata Benefit Payment Control

CONTACTS: Note: Officers with more than one job title may be intentionally listed here more than once.

Joe Liemandt, CEO
Scott Brighton, Pres.
Jim Abolt, VP-Human Resources

Phone: 512-874-3100	Fax: 512-874-8900
Toll-Free:	
Address: 6011 W. Courtyard Dr., Austin, TX 78730 US	

GROWTH PLANS/SPECIAL FEATURES:

Trilogy, Inc is a privately held enterprise software company that assists its clients in collecting consumer data. Trilogy operates via two primary subsidiaries: Trinity Enterprises, Inc. and Versata Software, Inc., (formerly Trilogy Software Inc). Trinity Enterprises' program suites and services amass data and analyze consumer behavior, which allows the company's clients to focus their marketing on the consumers with the highest propensity for purchase. The company offers several products and services for its clients. These include the company's SmartLeads program, which is a predictive modeling program that analyses consumer data and assigns that information into one of four SmartScore categories. These categories allow clients to focus their marketing strategies on the consumers with the highest score, those most likely to buy. The company's CarBuy.com is a direct marketing program that allows car manufacturers to target consumers through the web site of the same name. CarBuy uses a lead scoring engine to help manufacturers prioritize the leads with a strong likelihood of purchase. The company's telecom suite, YourBillBuddy.com allows wireless service providers to analyze consumer mobile usage behavior and present competitive plans based on that data. The software suite also provides clients with services for tariff plan management, customer retention and acquisition. Versata Software Inc. provides its clients with business applications that run rule-based code engines; these allow clients to translate updated company policy into usable software codes. Some of the services Versata offers include Versata Distribution Channel Management (DCM), tailored for the insurance and brokerage industries. DCM allows for more efficient production of compensation plans and policy administration. Versata government services include Benefit Payment Control (BPC), which allows states to administer paperless unemployment benefits. Versata also offers services for the automotive, retail, banking, manufacturing and high-tech industries.

FINANCIALS: Sales and profits are in thousands of dollars—add 000 to get the full amount. 2010 Note: Financial information for 2010 was not available for all companies at press time.

2010 Sales: $	2010 Profits: $	U.S. Stock Ticker: Private
2009 Sales: $	2009 Profits: $	Int'l Ticker: Int'l Exchange:
2008 Sales: $	2008 Profits: $	Employees:
2007 Sales: $	2007 Profits: $	Fiscal Year Ends: 12/31
2006 Sales: $	2006 Profits: $	Parent Company:

SALARIES/BENEFITS:

Pension Plan:	ESOP Stock Plan:	Profit Sharing:	Top Exec. Salary: $	Bonus: $
Savings Plan:	Stock Purch. Plan:		Second Exec. Salary: $	Bonus: $

OTHER THOUGHTS:

Apparent Women Officers or Directors:
Hot Spot for Advancement for Women/Minorities:

LOCATIONS: ("Y" = Yes)

West:	Southwest:	Midwest:	Southeast:	Northeast:	International:
	Y				Y

TRIMBLE NAVIGATION LTD

www.trimble.com

Industry Group Code: 3345 Ranks within this company's industry group: Sales: 4 Profits: 4

Hardware:		Software:		Telecommunications:	Electronic Publishing:	Equipment:		Specialty Services:
Computers:		Consumer:		Local:	Online Service:	Telecom:		Consulting:
Accessories:	Y	Corporate:	Y	Long Distance:	TV/Cable or Wireless:	Communication:	Y	Contract Manufacturing:
Network Equipment:		Telecom:		Cellular:	Games:	Distribution:		Processing:
Chips/Circuits:		Internet:		Internet Service:	Financial Data:	VAR/Reseller:		Staff/Outsourcing:
Parts/Drives:						Satellite Srv./Equip.:		Specialty Services:

TYPES OF BUSINESS:

GPS Technologies
Surveying & Mapping Equipment
Navigation Tools
Autopilot Systems
Data Collection Products
Fleet Management Systems
Outdoor Recreation Information Service
Telecommunications & Automotive Components

BRANDS/DIVISIONS/AFFILIATES:

NTech Industries
QuickPen International
Accutest Engineering Solutions Ltd
CTN Data Service LLC
Farm Works
Pondera Engineers LLC
Copernicus GPS Receiver
LET Systems

CONTACTS: Note: Officers with more than one job title may be intentionally listed here more than once.

Steven W. Berglund, CEO
Steven W. Berglund, Pres.
Rajat Bahri, CFO
Mary Kay Strangis, VP-Human Resources
Bruce Peetz, VP-Advanced Tech. & Systems
James A. Kirkland, General Counsel/VP
Jurgen Kliem, VP-Bus. Dev. & Strategy
Lea Ann McNabb, Head-Corp. Public Rel.
Julie Shepard, Chief Acct. Officer/VP-Finance
Mark Harrington, VP
Bryn Fosburgh, VP
Ann Ciganer, VP-Strategic Policy
Rick Beyer, VP
Ulf Johansson, Chmn.

Phone: 408-481-8000	Fax: 408-481-7781
Toll-Free: 800-874-6253	
Address: 935 Stewart Dr., Sunnyvale, CA 94085 US	

GROWTH PLANS/SPECIAL FEATURES:

Trimble Navigation, Ltd. provides global positioning products to industrial, commercial, governmental and agricultural customers. With offices in 11 states and 19 countries, the firm operates in four segments: engineering/construction, field solutions, mobile solutions and advanced devices. Engineering and construction products incorporate global positioning systems (GPS), optical, global navigation satellite systems (GNSS), radio, laser and cellular technologies to facilitate precise surveying, site preparation and interior measurement by small crews. The field solutions segment offers handheld geographic information system (GIS) data collectors for fieldwork and manual and automated navigation systems for tractors and other agricultural equipment. The mobile solutions segment offers a fleet management tool for large enterprise clients, consisting of vehicle-mounted hardware together with a web-based subscription service. The advanced devices segment combines the company's previously reported component technologies and portfolio segments. The combined businesses within this division share several characteristics: they are hardware centric, generally rely on original equipment manufacturer (OEM) distribution and have products that can be utilized in a number of different end-user markets. Products sold by this segment include the Copernicus, Lassen, Panda and Condor GPS Receivers; Applanix POS/AV; Applanix DSS Digital Sensor System; Force 524D Module; and Trimble Outdoors. Trimble holds roughly 750 U.S. patents and about 140 non-U.S. patents, the majority of which cover GPS technology and other applications such as optical and laser technology. In 2009, Trimble Navigation acquired QuickPen International, a building information modeling provider; NTech Industries, a crop sensing technology developer; Accutest Engineering Solutions Ltd., a U.K.-based provider of vehicle diagnostics and telematics technologies; and CTN Data Service, LLC, developer of integrated office and mobile software solution Farm Works. In January 2010, the company acquired the assets of engineering and development firm Pondera Engineers LLC. In March 2010, the company acquired LET Systems, an Irish incident and outage management system solutions developer.

FINANCIALS: Sales and profits are in thousands of dollars—add 000 to get the full amount. 2010 Note: Financial information for 2010 was not available for all companies at press time.

2010 Sales: $	2010 Profits: $	U.S. Stock Ticker: TRMB
2009 Sales: $1,126,259	2009 Profits: $63,446	Int'l Ticker: Int'l Exchange:
2008 Sales: $1,329,234	2008 Profits: $141,472	Employees: 3,794
2007 Sales: $1,222,270	2007 Profits: $117,374	Fiscal Year Ends: 12/31
2006 Sales: $940,150	2006 Profits: $103,658	Parent Company:

SALARIES/BENEFITS:

Pension Plan:	ESOP Stock Plan:	Profit Sharing:	Top Exec. Salary: $618,000	Bonus: $243,338
Savings Plan:	Stock Purch. Plan:		Second Exec. Salary: $297,400	Bonus: $78,078

OTHER THOUGHTS:

Apparent Women Officers or Directors: 4
Hot Spot for Advancement for Women/Minorities: Y

LOCATIONS: ("Y" = Yes)

West:	Southwest:	Midwest:	Southeast:	Northeast:	International:
Y	Y	Y	Y	Y	Y

TRIZETTO GROUP INC (THE)

www.trizetto.com

Industry Group Code: 511210D Ranks within this company's industry group: Sales: Profits:

Hardware:	Software:		Telecommunications:	Electronic Publishing:		Equipment:	Specialty Services:	
Computers:	Consumer:		Local:	Online Service:	Y	Telecom:	Consulting:	Y
Accessories:	Corporate:	Y	Long Distance:	TV/Cable or Wireless:		Communication:	Contract Manufacturing:	
Network Equipment:	Telecom:		Cellular:	Games:		Distribution:	Processing:	
Chips/Circuits:	Internet:		Internet Service:	Financial Data:		VAR/Reseller:	Staff/Outsourcing:	Y
Parts/Drives:						Satellite Srv./Equip.:	Specialty Services:	Y

TYPES OF BUSINESS:

Software-Medical Billing & Administration
Health Care Internet Portal
IT Staffing & Consulting Services
Hosted Services
Consulting Services

BRANDS/DIVISIONS/AFFILIATES:

Facets
QicLink
CareAdvance Enterprise
QNXT
NetworX Suite
Apax Partners
Tela Sourcing Inc

CONTACTS: Note: Officers with more than one job title may be intentionally listed here more than once.

Trace Devanny, CEO
Tony Bellomo, Pres.
Regina Paolillo, CFO/Exec. VP-Enterprise Svcs.
Dan Spirek, Chief Mktg. Officer
Alan Ross, Sr. VP-Human Capital Mgmt.
Jeff Rideout, Chief Medical Officer/Sr. VP-Cost & Care Mgmt.
Alan Cullop, CIO/Sr. VP
Rich Kerian, Sr. VP-Prod. Dev. & Support
Jim Sullivan, General Counsel/Sr. VP/Sec.
Dan Spirek, Chief Strategy Officer
John Jordan, Pres., Regional Healthcare Market
Rob Scavo, Pres., Emerging Market
J. Michael Jenner, Exec. VP-TriZetto Svcs.
Dan Spirek, Exec. VP-Enterprise Strategy & Comm.
Jeffrey H. Margolis, Chmn.

Phone: 303-495-7000	Fax: 303-495-7001
Toll-Free: 800-569-1222	
Address: 6061 S. Willow Dr., Ste. 310, Greenwood Village, CO 80111 US	

GROWTH PLANS/SPECIAL FEATURES:

The TriZetto Group, Inc. provides software application services to the health care industry. The company's software solutions include enterprise core administration, care management, network management, consumer retail healthcare and government programs. Software packages include the Facets, QicLink, CareAdvance Enterprise, QNXT and NetworX Suite. Facets is a scalable, enterprise-wide core administration product for healthcare payors, allowing them to meet various business requirements, including claims processing, claims re-pricing, risk fund accounting, referral management and customer service. QicLink is one of the most widely-used automated claims administration technologies in the U.S. It allows benefits administrators to handle enrollment, customer service, claims adjudication, billing, accounts receivable, re-pricing and payment processes. The CareAdvance Enterprise suite of applications allows health plans to automate various aspects of care management, including member identification and assessment, guideline-based care planning, member and provider communications, task and team management, ongoing member monitoring and personalized health content. The QNXT enterprise application system is a user-configurable system that aids healthcare payers in adapting to market changes in a rapid and efficient manner. NetworX Suite is a group of software applications that provide execution, claims pricing, network operations and complete automation of contract modeling. TriZetto also offers applications focused on Medicare Advantage and managed Medicaid plans. The company can host and manage customer applications from its own data center or remotely manage on-site applications; and allows customers to outsource non-critical functions, including claims administration, enrollment and rules configuration. TriZetto's consulting staff provides project management, technology consulting and other customer-specific solutions to health plans and benefits administrators. The company is owned by global private equity advisory firm Apax Partners. In August 2010, the firm acquired business process outsourcing company Tela Sourcing, Inc.

TriZetto offers employees benefits including life, disability, medical, dental and vision insurance; tuition reimbursement; a group legal plan; and an employee assistance program.

FINANCIALS: Sales and profits are in thousands of dollars—add 000 to get the full amount. 2010 Note: Financial information for 2010 was not available for all companies at press time.

2010 Sales: $	2010 Profits: $	U.S. Stock Ticker: Private
2009 Sales: $	2009 Profits: $	Int'l Ticker: Int'l Exchange:
2008 Sales: $	2008 Profits: $	Employees:
2007 Sales: $451,791	2007 Profits: $28,230	Fiscal Year Ends: 12/31
2006 Sales: $347,937	2006 Profits: $15,115	Parent Company: APAX PARTNERS INC

SALARIES/BENEFITS:

Pension Plan:	ESOP Stock Plan:	Profit Sharing:	Top Exec. Salary: $	Bonus: $
Savings Plan: Y	Stock Purch. Plan:		Second Exec. Salary: $	Bonus: $

OTHER THOUGHTS:

Apparent Women Officers or Directors: 2
Hot Spot for Advancement for Women/Minorities: Y

LOCATIONS: ("Y" = Yes)

West:	Southwest:	Midwest:	Southeast:	Northeast:	International:
Y	Y	Y		Y	

TTM TECHNOLOGIES INC

www.ttmtech.com

Industry Group Code: 334419 Ranks within this company's industry group: Sales: 15   Profits: 13

Hardware:		Software:		Telecommunications:		Electronic Publishing:	Equipment:		Specialty Services:	
Computers:		Consumer:		Local:		Online Service:	Telecom:		Consulting:	
Accessories:		Corporate:		Long Distance:		TV/Cable or Wireless:	Communication:		Contract Manufacturing:	Y
Network Equipment:		Telecom:		Cellular:		Games:	Distribution:		Processing:	
Chips/Circuits:	Y	Internet:		Internet Service:		Financial Data:	VAR/Reseller:		Staff/Outsourcing:	
Parts/Drives:							Satellite Srv./Equip.:		Specialty Services:	Y

TYPES OF BUSINESS:

Printed Circuit Board Manufacturing
Backplane Assemblies
Quick-Turn Manufacturing Services

BRANDS/DIVISIONS/AFFILIATES:

CONTACTS:
Note: Officers with more than one job title may be intentionally listed here more than once.

Kenton K. Alder, CEO
Shane Whiteside, COO/Exec. VP
Kenton K. Alder, Pres.
Steven W. Richards, CFO/Exec. VP
Grace Lee, Sr. VP-Human Resources
Dale Knecht, VP-IT
Douglas L. Soder, Exec. VP
Robert Klatell, Chmn.
Canice T. K. Chung, CEO-Asia Pacific Region

Phone: 714-241-0300	Fax: 714-241-0708
Toll-Free:	
Address: 2630 S. Harbor Blvd., Santa Ana, CA 92704 US	

GROWTH PLANS/SPECIAL FEATURES:

TTM Technologies, Inc. is a provider of complex printed circuit boards (PCBs) used in electronic equipment and provides backplane assembly services for both standard and specialty products in defense and commercial operations. The primary raw materials that the firm uses in PCB manufacturing include copper-clad laminate; chemical solutions such as copper and gold for plating operations; photographic film; carbide drill bits; and plastic for testing fixtures. The firm is capable of manufacturing high-layer count PCBs, stacked microvias (small conducting pathways between layers of a circuit board), copper and epoxy-filled vias, flex and rigid flex circuits, multiple surface finishes, fine line traces, embedded passives and oversize panel formats, among others. TTM also offers thermal management and custom assembly services, as well as design, modeling and simulation services. The company can function as a one-stop manufacturing service because its facilities are specialized and integrated, each focusing on a different stage of an electronic product's life cycle. TTM's specialty is quick-turn services, which enable customers to shorten the time required to develop new products and bring them to market. The company serves high-end commercial markets and aerospace markets, providing PCBs and backplane assemblies for applications including networking/communications infrastructure; high-end computing; defense systems; industrial controls; and medical testing equipment. Customers include both OEMs and electronic manufacturing services (EMS) providers. In March 2010, the firm combined its business with Meadville Holdings Limited's PCB business.

TTM offers its employees medical, dental and vision coverage; life and AD&D insurance; short- and long-term disability; a 401(k) plan; and access to a credit union.

FINANCIALS:
Sales and profits are in thousands of dollars—add 000 to get the full amount. 2010 Note: Financial information for 2010 was not available for all companies at press time.

2010 Sales: $	2010 Profits: $	**U.S. Stock Ticker: TTMI**	
2009 Sales: $582,476	2009 Profits: $4,857	**Int'l Ticker:** Int'l Exchange:	
2008 Sales: $680,981	2008 Profits: $-35,270	Employees: 3,037	
2007 Sales: $669,458	2007 Profits: $34,683	Fiscal Year Ends: 12/31	
2006 Sales: $369,316	2006 Profits: $35,039	Parent Company:	

SALARIES/BENEFITS:

Pension Plan:	ESOP Stock Plan:	Profit Sharing:	Top Exec. Salary: $586,000	Bonus: $324,058
Savings Plan: Y	Stock Purch. Plan:		Second Exec. Salary: $345,000	Bonus: $149,903

OTHER THOUGHTS:

Apparent Women Officers or Directors: 1
Hot Spot for Advancement for Women/Minorities:

LOCATIONS: ("Y" = Yes)

West:	Southwest:	Midwest:	Southeast:	Northeast:	International:
Y		Y		Y	Y

TXCOM-AXIOHM

www.axiohm.com

Industry Group Code: 334119 Ranks within this company's industry group: Sales: Profits:

Hardware:		Software:		Telecommunications:	Electronic Publishing:	Equipment:		Specialty Services:	
Computers:		Consumer:		Local:	Online Service:	Telecom:		Consulting:	
Accessories:	Y	Corporate:		Long Distance:	TV/Cable or Wireless:	Communication:		Contract Manufacturing:	
Network Equipment:		Telecom:		Cellular:	Games:	Distribution:		Processing:	
Chips/Circuits:		Internet:		Internet Service:	Financial Data:	VAR/Reseller:		Staff/Outsourcing:	
Parts/Drives:						Satellite Srv./Equip.:		Specialty Services:	

TYPES OF BUSINESS:

Computer Accessories-Printers
Thermal Printing Systems
Controller Boards
Receipt Printers

BRANDS/DIVISIONS/AFFILIATES:

Axiohm Transaction Solutions, Inc.
Axiohm USA
Astrium
Compact Board II
TPSK
VLTK
Sens'n Print Solution
KRMG

CONTACTS: Note: Officers with more than one job title may be intentionally listed here more than once.

Phone: 33-01-4601-0506	Fax: 33-01-4601-4948
Toll-Free:	
Address: 10 Ave. Descartes, Le Plessis Robinson, 92350 France	

GROWTH PLANS/SPECIAL FEATURES:

TXCOM-Axiohm is a global leader in the design, manufacture and marketing of a wide range of thermal printing solutions, including thermal printing mechanisms and controller boards; thermal receipt and label printers; and kiosk printers (which are generally placed in unattended terminals such as gas pumps, cash dispensers, transportation terminals and video-gaming machines) and electronic boards with embedded firmware. The company's products provide records such as receipts, tickets, register journals, checks and other documents. Axiohm is one of the world's leading manufacturers of thermal printing mechanisms for electronic funds transfer terminals (ETFs). The firm's thermal printers include A630, A631, A632, A711 TPOS, TPOS couponing and PCPR. Its thermal printer mechanisms include Electron, Asteron, CM/RM, CM Thick Paper Series, CM/RM Premium, MHTA, MGTA, XA/XB, XA/XB Premium and Sens'n Print Solution. The company's kiosk printers include the KMGA, KRMG, TPSK, KPSx and Sens'n Print Solution. Its controller boards include TPSB and Compact Board II. Axiohm provides its products to a variety of markets including EFT, gaming/lottery, gas pump, hospitality, transportation and other point-of-service (POS) venues. The company makes approximately 71% of its sales outside of France, and approximately 40% in the U.S., where it operates through subsidiary Axiohm USA.

FINANCIALS: Sales and profits are in thousands of dollars—add 000 to get the full amount. 2010 Note: Financial information for 2010 was not available for all companies at press time.

2010 Sales: $	2010 Profits: $	**U.S. Stock Ticker: Subsidiary**
2009 Sales: $	2009 Profits: $	**Int'l Ticker:** Int'l Exchange:
2008 Sales: $	2008 Profits: $	Employees:
2007 Sales: $	2007 Profits: $	Fiscal Year Ends:
2006 Sales: $	2006 Profits: $	Parent Company: TXCOM SA

SALARIES/BENEFITS:

Pension Plan:	ESOP Stock Plan:	Profit Sharing:	Top Exec. Salary: $	Bonus: $
Savings Plan:	Stock Purch. Plan:		Second Exec. Salary: $	Bonus: $

OTHER THOUGHTS:

Apparent Women Officers or Directors: 1
Hot Spot for Advancement for Women/Minorities:

LOCATIONS: ("Y" = Yes)

West:	Southwest:	Midwest:	Southeast:	Northeast:	International:
		Y			Y

ULTICOM INC

www.ulticom.com

Industry Group Code: 511210C Ranks within this company's industry group: Sales: 5   Profits: 4

Hardware:	Software:		Telecommunications:	Electronic Publishing:	Equipment:	Specialty Services:
Computers:	Consumer:		Local:	Online Service:	Telecom:	Consulting:
Accessories:	Corporate:		Long Distance:	TV/Cable or Wireless:	Communication:	Contract Manufacturing:
Network Equipment:	Telecom:	Y	Cellular:	Games:	Distribution:	Processing:
Chips/Circuits:	Internet:		Internet Service:	Financial Data:	VAR/Reseller:	Staff/Outsourcing:
Parts/Drives:					Satellite Srv./Equip.:	Specialty Services:

TYPES OF BUSINESS:
Network Signaling Software

BRANDS/DIVISIONS/AFFILIATES:
Signalware

CONTACTS:
Note: Officers with more than one job title may be intentionally listed here more than once.
Shawn K. Osbourne, CEO
Shawn K. Osbourne, Pres.
Mark Kissman, CFO/Sr. VP
Jamie McArdle, VP-Sales
Shila Roohi, Sr. VP-Eng.
James Johnston, Sr. VP-Oper.
Andre Dahan, Chmn.

Phone: 856-787-2700	Fax: 856-866-2033
Toll-Free:	
Address: 1020 Briggs Rd., Mt. Laurel, NJ 08054 US	

GROWTH PLANS/SPECIAL FEATURES:

Ulticom, Inc. is a global provider of signaling software that enables telecommunications network equipment and service providers to deploy mobility, location, payment, switching and messaging services. The firm's Signalware software product is based on the international signaling protocol standard, SS7, and is utilized by equipment manufacturers, application developers and communication service providers to deploy such services as voice and text messaging, prepaid calling, virtual private networks, global roaming, Voice over Internet Protocol (VoIP) and Internet call waiting. Its application-ready products include its Signalware SP signaling services platform; Signalware TC thin client application server; and Signalware SF server farm suite. Signalware network-ready products perform routing functions for SS7 and Sigtran/IP signaling networks and include its Signalware SG signaling gateway; Signalware ES edge signal transfer point; and Signalware CS core signal transfer. Over 5,000 Signalware products have been deployed in over 300 carrier networks and 100 countries. Ulticom's products target wireless, IP and wireline networks. Wireless network components built with Signalware include base station systems, home/visitor location registers, mobile switching centers, short message service centers, equipment identity registers and authentication centers. Wireless services enabled by Signalware include global roaming, prepaid calling, text messaging, mobile switching, location based services and public WLAN (wireless local area network) access. IP network components built with Signalware include signaling gateways, media gateway controllers and SIP (session initiation protocol) servers. IP network services enabled by Signalware include Internet offload, multimedia session control, unified messaging and click to talk. Wireline network components built with Signalware include service control points, service switching points and intelligent peripherals. Wireline services enabled by Signalware include local number portability and voice mail.

Ulticom offers its employees tuition assistance; an employee assistance program; discounted health club membership; flexible spending accounts; and medical, dental, vision, prescription, life and disability insurance.

FINANCIALS:
Sales and profits are in thousands of dollars—add 000 to get the full amount. 2010 Note: Financial information for 2010 was not available for all companies at press time.

2010 Sales: $	2010 Profits: $	**U.S. Stock Ticker: ULCM**
2009 Sales: $53,047	2009 Profits: $-3,136	**Int'l Ticker: ULCM** Int'l Exchange:
2008 Sales: $59,010	2008 Profits: $3,887	Employees: 164
2007 Sales: $63,632	2007 Profits: $12,553	Fiscal Year Ends: 12/31
2006 Sales: $	2006 Profits: $	Parent Company:

SALARIES/BENEFITS:

Pension Plan:	ESOP Stock Plan:	Profit Sharing:	Top Exec. Salary: $327,104	Bonus: $70,290
Savings Plan: Y	Stock Purch. Plan:		Second Exec. Salary: $325,000	Bonus: $173,609

OTHER THOUGHTS:
Apparent Women Officers or Directors: 2
Hot Spot for Advancement for Women/Minorities:

LOCATIONS: ("Y" = Yes)

West:	Southwest:	Midwest:	Southeast:	Northeast:	International:
	Y	Y		Y	Y

ULTIMATE SOFTWARE GROUP INC
www.ultimatesoftware.com

Industry Group Code: 511210H Ranks within this company's industry group: Sales: 14 Profits: 11

Hardware:	Software:		Telecommunications:	Electronic Publishing:	Equipment:	Specialty Services:
Computers:	Consumer:		Local:	Online Service:	Telecom:	Consulting:
Accessories:	Corporate:	Y	Long Distance:	TV/Cable or Wireless:	Communication:	Contract Manufacturing:
Network Equipment:	Telecom:		Cellular:	Games:	Distribution:	Processing:
Chips/Circuits:	Internet:		Internet Service:	Financial Data:	VAR/Reseller:	Staff/Outsourcing:
Parts/Drives:					Satellite Srv./Equip.:	Specialty Services:

TYPES OF BUSINESS:
Employee Management Software

BRANDS/DIVISIONS/AFFILIATES:
UltiPro
Intersourcing
UltiPro Workplace
Ultimate Software Group of Canada, Inc. (The)
Ultimate Software Group UK Limited (The)
UltiPro Enterprises

CONTACTS: Note: Officers with more than one job title may be intentionally listed here more than once.
Scott Scherr, CEO
Marc D. Scherr, COO/Vice Chmn.
Scott Scherr, Pres.
Mitchell K. Dauerman, CFO/Exec. VP
Darlene Marcroft, Dir.-Public Rel.
Mitchell K. Dauerman, Treas.
Scott Scherr, Chmn.

Phone: 954-331-7000	Fax: 954-331-7300
Toll-Free: 800-432-1729	
Address: 2000 Ultimate Way, Weston, FL 33326 US	

GROWTH PLANS/SPECIAL FEATURES:

The Ultimate Software Group, Inc. designs, markets, implements and supports human resources (HR), payroll and talent management solutions principally in the U.S. and Canada. The company main product is UltiPro, a web-based employee management program offered in two suites: UltiPro Enterprise, designed for large enterprises, defined as companies with more than 1,000 employees; and UltiPro Workplace, developed for medium-sized and smaller companies with less than 1,000 employees. Ultimate also offers Intersourcing, a software-as-a-service (SaaS) version of UltiPro, meaning it is available on-demand as a subscription service, rather than being purchased outright. To manage Intersourcing, the company contracts three data centers in Miami, Florida; Toronto, Ontario; and Atlanta, Georgia. The two in the United States are owned and operated by a third-party company, Quality Technology Services (QTS), while the data center in Toronto is owned and operated by Verizon. In addition to standard UltiPro services, customers have the option to purchase optional features on a per-employee-per-month basis. These optional services include talent management products, benefits enrollment, time, attendance and scheduling, time management, tax filing, wage attachments and other features. The firm has two wholly-owned subsidiaries: The Ultimate Software Group of Canada, Inc. and The Ultimate Software Group UK Limited. The firm serves over 1,900 businesses. Company customers include Adobe Systems Incorporated, Inc.; Nikon, Inc.; Popeyes Chicken & Biscuits; Teavana; the Chicago Cubs; the San Diego Convention Center; the City of Ann Arbor; and Bryant University.

Ultimate offers its employees medical and dental benefits, tuition reimbursement, life insurance, flexible spending accounts and credit union membership.

FINANCIALS: Sales and profits are in thousands of dollars—add 000 to get the full amount. 2010 Note: Financial information for 2010 was not available for all companies at press time.

2010 Sales: $	2010 Profits: $	U.S. Stock Ticker: ULTI
2009 Sales: $196,579	2009 Profits: $-1,142	Int'l Ticker: Int'l Exchange:
2008 Sales: $178,572	2008 Profits: $-2,897	Employees: 933
2007 Sales: $151,464	2007 Profits: $33,129	Fiscal Year Ends: 12/31
2006 Sales: $114,811	2006 Profits: $4,133	Parent Company:

SALARIES/BENEFITS:
Pension Plan:	ESOP Stock Plan:	Profit Sharing:	Top Exec. Salary: $700,000	Bonus: $33,339
Savings Plan: Y	Stock Purch. Plan:		Second Exec. Salary: $625,000	Bonus: $25,004

OTHER THOUGHTS:
Apparent Women Officers or Directors:
Hot Spot for Advancement for Women/Minorities:

LOCATIONS: ("Y" = Yes)
West:	Southwest:	Midwest:	Southeast:	Northeast:	International:
		Y	Y		Y

UNISYS CORP   www.unisys.com

Industry Group Code: 541513 Ranks within this company's industry group: Sales: 13   Profits: 14

Hardware:	Software:		Telecommunications:	Electronic Publishing:	Equipment:	Specialty Services:	
Computers:	Consumer:		Local:	Online Service:	Telecom:	Consulting:	Y
Accessories:	Corporate:	Y	Long Distance:	TV/Cable or Wireless:	Communication:	Contract Manufacturing:	
Network Equipment:	Telecom:		Cellular:	Games:	Distribution:	Processing:	
Chips/Circuits:	Internet:		Internet Service:	Financial Data:	VAR/Reseller:	Staff/Outsourcing:	Y
Parts/Drives:					Satellite Srv./Equip.:	Specialty Services:	Y

TYPES OF BUSINESS:

Consulting-Systems Integration & Technology Support
Enterprise Systems & Servers
Outsourcing Services
Infrastructure Services
Security Technology
Server Software & Middleware

BRANDS/DIVISIONS/AFFILIATES:

ClearPath Plus
ES7000 Server
SmartSource Micro

CONTACTS: Note: Officers with more than one job title may be intentionally listed here more than once.

J. Edward Coleman, CEO
Janet B. Haugen, CFO/Sr. VP
Patricia A. Bradford, Sr. VP-Human Resources
Suresh Mathews, CIO/Sr. VP
Dominick Cavuoto, Sr. VP/Pres., Tech., Consulting & Integration
Nancy S. Sundheim, General Counsel/Corp. Sec./Sr. VP
M. Lazane Smith, Sr. VP-Corp. Dev.
Jack F. McHale, VP-Investor Rel.
Scott W. Hurley, Corp. Controller/VP
Scott A. Battersby, VP/Treas.
Ted Davies, Sr. VP/Pres., Federal Systems
Ron Frankenfield, Pres., Global Outsourcing & Infrastructure Svcs.
J. Edward Coleman, Chmn.
Dominick Cavuoto, Sr. VP/Pres., Worldwide Strategic Svcs.

Phone: 215-986-4011	Fax: 215-986-6850
Toll-Free:	
Address: Unisys Way, Blue Bell, PA 19424 US	

GROWTH PLANS/SPECIAL FEATURES:

Unisys Corp. is a worldwide information technology services company. The firm offers services for systems integration, outsourcing, infrastructure, server technology and consulting to commercial businesses and governments. Unisys operates in two business segments: services and technology. The services unit provides end-to-end services designed to help clients improve their competitiveness and efficiency in four main categories: systems integration and consulting; outsourcing; infrastructure services; and core maintenance. Systems integration and consulting services include check processing systems, public welfare systems, airline reservations and messaging technology. Outsourcing services provide for the management of a customer's internal information systems and its specific business processes, such as insurance claims processing, mortgage administration and cargo management. Infrastructure services involve the design and support of customers' IT infrastructure and enterprise-wide security software. Core maintenance services include the maintenance of Unisys proprietary products. In the technology segment, the company designs and develops servers and related products. Major technology offerings include enterprise-class servers based on Cellular Multi-Processing architecture, such as the ClearPath family of servers, and the ES7000 family of servers, providing enterprise-class attributes on Intel-based servers; operating system software and middleware; and specialized technologies such as payment systems and third-party products. Primary markets served by Unisys include the financial services, communications, transportation, commercial and public sectors. Unisys owns over 1,350 U.S. patents and over 200 patents outside the U.S. The company maintains working partnerships with leading technology companies, including Dell, Intel, Microsoft and Oracle, among others. In February 2010, Unisys sold its check and cash automation equipment and related U.S. maintenance, printer and direct supply business. In May 2010, it completed the sale of its health information management business, and in September 2010, Unisys sold its U.K.-based insurance and pension processing business, Unisys Insurance Services Limited.

Employees are offered medical and dental insurance; flexible spending accounts; disability coverage; life insurance; an employee assistance program; and a 401(k) plan.

FINANCIALS: Sales and profits are in thousands of dollars—add 000 to get the full amount. 2010 Note: Financial information for 2010 was not available for all companies at press time.

2010 Sales: $	2010 Profits: $	U.S. Stock Ticker: UIS
2009 Sales: $4,597,700	2009 Profits: $189,300	Int'l Ticker: Int'l Exchange:
2008 Sales: $5,233,200	2008 Profits: $-130,100	Employees: 25,600
2007 Sales: $5,652,500	2007 Profits: $-79,100	Fiscal Year Ends: 12/31
2006 Sales: $5,757,200	2006 Profits: $-278,700	Parent Company:

SALARIES/BENEFITS:

Pension Plan:	ESOP Stock Plan:	Profit Sharing:	Top Exec. Salary: $972,000	Bonus: $1,579,500
Savings Plan: Y	Stock Purch. Plan:		Second Exec. Salary: $558,428	Bonus: $653,361

OTHER THOUGHTS:

Apparent Women Officers or Directors: 4
Hot Spot for Advancement for Women/Minorities: Y

LOCATIONS: ("Y" = Yes)

West:	Southwest:	Midwest:	Southeast:	Northeast:	International:
Y	Y	Y		Y	Y

UNITED MICROELECTRONICS CORP

www.umc.com

Industry Group Code: 33441 Ranks within this company's industry group: Sales: 18 Profits: 19

Hardware:		Software:		Telecommunications:		Electronic Publishing:	Equipment:		Specialty Services:	
Computers:		Consumer:		Local:		Online Service:	Telecom:		Consulting:	
Accessories:		Corporate:		Long Distance:		TV/Cable or Wireless:	Communication:		Contract Manufacturing:	Y
Network Equipment:		Telecom:		Cellular:		Games:	Distribution:		Processing:	
Chips/Circuits:	Y	Internet:		Internet Service:		Financial Data:	VAR/Reseller:		Staff/Outsourcing:	
Parts/Drives:							Satellite Srv./Equip.:		Specialty Services:	

TYPES OF BUSINESS:

Chips/Semiconductors

BRANDS/DIVISIONS/AFFILIATES:

UMC Japan

CONTACTS: Note: Officers with more than one job title may be intentionally listed here more than once.

Shih Wei Sun, CEO
Wen Yang Chen, COO
Chitung Liu, CFO
S. C. Chien, VP/Head-Advanced Tech. Dev.
Peter Courture, General Counsel
Po Wen Yen, Sr. VP-12-inch Oper.
Peter Courture, Sr. VP-Strategy
Ih Chin Chen, VP-Advanced Tech. Dev.
Stan Hung, Chmn.

Phone: 886-3-578-2258	Fax: 886-3-577-9392
Toll-Free:	
Address: 3 Li-Hsin 2nd Rd., Hsinchu Science Park, Hsinchu, Taiwan	

GROWTH PLANS/SPECIAL FEATURES:

United Microelectronics Corp. (UMC), based in Taiwan, is one of the world's largest semiconductor foundries, providing comprehensive wafer fabrication services and technologies to customers based on their designs. The company has 10 manufacturing facilities in Taiwan, Singapore and Japan. It works closely with customers through each of the five steps required to produce viable products: circuit design, mask tooling, wafer fabrication, assembly and testing. At the initial step, circuit design, UMC engineers work with clients to ensure their designs can be manufactured successfully and cost effectively in the company's facilities. During the mask tooling process, UMC engineers assist in the design or purchase of masks that work best with UMC equipment. During the wafer fabrication stage, a photosensitive material is deposited on the wafer and exposed to light through the mask to form a transistor and other circuit elements, then tested, generally on-site to ensure quality. It also offers turnkey services, providing UMC with subcontracted assembly and testing services at its manufacturing facilities. UMC's products include a range of advanced processes, such as 65 nanometer (nm), 45/40nm, embedded memories and Mixed Signal/RF CMOS. In December 2009, UMC acquired the outstanding shares of its partially-owned subsidiary UMC Japan, which operates a semiconductor manufacturing plant in Japan. In June 2010, the firm entered into a three-way cooperation with Elpida Memory, Inc. and Powertech Technology, Inc. to advance 28nm integrated circuit (IC) process technology.

UMC offers its employees counseling services and the use of a recreation center at its Hsinchu headquarters, which features sports facilities, an art gallery, a performance venue and meeting spaces.

FINANCIALS: Sales and profits are in thousands of dollars—add 000 to get the full amount. 2010 Note: Financial information for 2010 was not available for all companies at press time.

2010 Sales: $	2010 Profits: $	U.S. Stock Ticker: UMC
2009 Sales: $2,894,370	2009 Profits: $122,690	Int'l Ticker: 2303 Int'l Exchange: Taipei-TPE
2008 Sales: $2,824,000	2008 Profits: $-681,000	Employees:
2007 Sales: $3,440,000	2007 Profits: $1,000,000	Fiscal Year Ends: 12/31
2006 Sales: $3,437,000	2006 Profits: $1,001,000	Parent Company:

SALARIES/BENEFITS:

Pension Plan: Y	ESOP Stock Plan:	Profit Sharing:	Top Exec. Salary: $	Bonus: $
Savings Plan:	Stock Purch. Plan:		Second Exec. Salary: $	Bonus: $

OTHER THOUGHTS:

Apparent Women Officers or Directors:
Hot Spot for Advancement for Women/Minorities:

LOCATIONS: ("Y" = Yes)

West:	Southwest:	Midwest:	Southeast:	Northeast:	International:
Y					Y

UTSTARCOM INC

www.utstar.com

Industry Group Code: 334210 Ranks within this company's industry group: Sales: 12 Profits: 10

Hardware:	Software:	Telecommunications:	Electronic Publishing:	Equipment:		Specialty Services:
Computers:	Consumer:	Local:	Online Service:	Telecom:	Y	Consulting:
Accessories:	Corporate:	Long Distance:	TV/Cable or Wireless:	Communication:	Y	Contract Manufacturing:
Network Equipment:	Telecom:	Cellular:	Games:	Distribution:	Y	Processing:
Chips/Circuits:	Internet:	Internet Service:	Financial Data:	VAR/Reseller:		Staff/Outsourcing:
Parts/Drives:				Satellite Srv./Equip.:		Specialty Services:

TYPES OF BUSINESS:

Telecommunications Equipment
Voice, Data & Broadband Networking Equipment
Network Access Systems
Wireless Network Equipment
Handsets
Telecommunications Software & Hardware
Optical Products

BRANDS/DIVISIONS/AFFILIATES:

Stage Smart Ltd.
RollingStream
mStream

CONTACTS: *Note: Officers with more than one job title may be intentionally listed here more than once.*

Jack Lu, CEO
Jack Lu, Pres.
Edmond Cheng, CFO/Sr. VP
Yanya Sheng, Sr. VP-R&D
Susan Marsch, General Counsel/Sr. VP/Sec.
K.P. Lim, VP/Chief Quality Officer
Thomas J. Toy, Chmn.

Phone: 86-8520-5588	Fax: 86-8520-5599
Toll-Free:	
Address: No. 1 E. Chang An Ave., 20F, Tower E1, Beijing, 100738 China	

GROWTH PLANS/SPECIAL FEATURES:

UTStarcom, Inc. designs, manufactures and sells telecommunications infrastructure, handsets and customer premise equipment. It also provides services associated with their installation, operation and maintenance. The company operates in four segments: broadband infrastructure, multimedia communications, handsets and services. The broadband infrastructure segment (representing approximately 21% of UTStarcom's revenues) is responsible for software and hardware products that enable end users to access high-speed wireless data, voice and media communications. Products within each of these categories include multiple hardware and software subsystems that can be offered in various combinations to suit individual carrier needs. The multimedia communications division (36% of revenues) develops and manages the IPTV and related technologies (such as surveillance) plus the core NGN software. The RollingStream IPTV solution includes storage and streaming device products for combining different video signals onto a unified distribution system. The mSwitch NGN solution provides voice communications over an IP network. UTStarcom's Personal Access System (PAS) is a wireless core infrastructure product series; it is utilized in the UTStarcom IP-Based PAS wireless access network, which allows operators to transfer their current wireline network to an IP-based PHS wireless network that provides wireless voice and data services within a city or community. The firm's handset segment (27% of revenues) designs, builds and sells consumer handset devices that allow customers to access wireless services. The services division (16% of revenues) assists customers with activities ranging from network planning, circuit-to-packet network migration planning, systems integration, program management, operations management and knowledge transfer. In May 2010, UTStarcom sold its IP Messaging and US PSDN operations to NewNet Communication Technologies LLC, a telecommunications infrastructure company. Also in May 2010, the company sold its manufacturing and research and development facility in Hangzhou, China for about $140 million. In November 2010, the firm acquired Stage Smart Ltd.

FINANCIALS: Sales and profits are in thousands of dollars—add 000 to get the full amount. 2010 Note: Financial information for 2010 was not available for all companies at press time.

2010 Sales: $	2010 Profits: $	**U.S. Stock Ticker: UTSI**
2009 Sales: $386,344	2009 Profits: $-225,688	**Int'l Ticker:** Int'l Exchange:
2008 Sales: $1,640,449	2008 Profits: $-150,316	Employees: 2,400
2007 Sales: $2,466,970	2007 Profits: $-195,575	Fiscal Year Ends: 12/31
2006 Sales: $2,458,861	2006 Profits: $-117,345	Parent Company:

SALARIES/BENEFITS:

Pension Plan:	ESOP Stock Plan:	Profit Sharing:	Top Exec. Salary: $676,667	Bonus: $1,059,200
Savings Plan: Y	Stock Purch. Plan: Y		Second Exec. Salary: $385,417	Bonus: $

OTHER THOUGHTS:

Apparent Women Officers or Directors: 1
Hot Spot for Advancement for Women/Minorities:

LOCATIONS: ("Y" = Yes)

West:	Southwest:	Midwest:	Southeast:	Northeast:	International:
Y					Y

Note: Financial information, benefits and other data can change quickly and may vary from those stated here.

VARIAN SEMICONDUCTOR EQUIPMENT ASSOCIATES INC

www.vsea.com

Industry Group Code: 33441 Ranks within this company's industry group: Sales: 42   Profits: 39

Hardware:		Software:	Telecommunications:	Electronic Publishing:	Equipment:	Specialty Services:
Computers:		Consumer:	Local:	Online Service:	Telecom:	Consulting:
Accessories:		Corporate:	Long Distance:	TV/Cable or Wireless:	Communication:	Contract Manufacturing:
Network Equipment:		Telecom:	Cellular:	Games:	Distribution:	Processing:
Chips/Circuits:	Y	Internet:	Internet Service:	Financial Data:	VAR/Reseller:	Staff/Outsourcing:
Parts/Drives:					Satellite Srv./Equip.:	Specialty Services:

TYPES OF BUSINESS:

Semiconductor Manufacturing Equipment

BRANDS/DIVISIONS/AFFILIATES:

VIISta
Varian Control System (VCS)
Varian Positioning System (VPS)

CONTACTS: Note: Officers with more than one job title may be intentionally listed here more than once.

Gary E. Dickerson, CEO
Robert J. Halliday, CFO/Exec. VP
Gary J. Rosen, VP-Eng.
Robert J. Perlmutter, Exec. VP-Implant Bus. Units
Richard A. Aurelio, Chmn.
Yong-Kil Kim, Exec. VP/Gen. Mgr.-Asia Oper.

Phone: 978-281-2000	Fax:
Toll-Free:	
Address: 35 Dory Rd., Gloucester, MA 01930 US	

GROWTH PLANS/SPECIAL FEATURES:

Varian Semiconductor Equipment Associates, Inc. (VSEA) is a leading supplier of ion implantation systems used to build the transistors in semiconductor chips. It designs, manufactures, markets and services semiconductor processing equipment for virtually all of the major semiconductor manufacturers worldwide. Ion implanters work by creating ions, which are electrically charged particles, of a given atomic element, called the dopant, and shooting those ions a given depth into a silicon wafer according to the circuit pattern. The amount of dopant, or dose, together with the depth of the implant into the wafer, or energy, constitutes the two variables that characterize VSEA's implanters. The company offers four implanters: high current, with high dose and low energy; ultra high dose, with very high dose and very low energy; medium current, with low dose and medium energy; and high energy, with low dose and very high energy. High current and medium current implanters are used in logic, memory and foundry manufacturers. Ultra high dose implanters are used in memory manufacturers and certain new flash memory applications. High energy implanters are predominantly used by memory manufacturers, as well as in most wafer fabrication facilities. All of the firm's implanters are built upon the same technology platform and are sold under the VIISta brand name. Additionally, they all feature the Varian Control System (VCS), the Varian Positioning System (VPS) and the VIISta single wafer end station. The VCS monitors and maintains the precise conditions required for semiconductor manufacturing; the VPS increases beam accuracy, allowing for smaller, more compact semiconductor design; and the single wafer end station enhances the final processing of the wafer. The firm has more than 3,300 implanters installed worldwide, which combined implant 5 million wafers daily. Besides its locations in the U.S., the firm has offices in Israel and seven European countries.

FINANCIALS: Sales and profits are in thousands of dollars—add 000 to get the full amount. 2010 Note: Financial information for 2010 was not available for all companies at press time.

2010 Sales: $831,780	2010 Profits: $159,584	**U.S. Stock Ticker:** VSEA
2009 Sales: $362,081	2009 Profits: $-37,998	**Int'l Ticker:** Int'l Exchange:
2008 Sales: $834,061	2008 Profits: $99,516	**Employees:** 1,462
2007 Sales: $1,054,864	2007 Profits: $144,409	**Fiscal Year Ends:** 9/30
2006 Sales: $730,714	2006 Profits: $94,684	**Parent Company:**

SALARIES/BENEFITS:

Pension Plan:	ESOP Stock Plan:	Profit Sharing:	Top Exec. Salary: $628,617	Bonus: $1,266,840
Savings Plan: Y	Stock Purch. Plan: Y		Second Exec. Salary: $356,846	Bonus: $642,218

OTHER THOUGHTS:

Apparent Women Officers or Directors:
Hot Spot for Advancement for Women/Minorities:

LOCATIONS: ("Y" = Yes)

West:	Southwest:	Midwest:	Southeast:	Northeast:	International:
Y	Y			Y	Y

VASCO DATA SECURITY INTERNATIONAL INC   www.vasco.com

Industry Group Code: 511210E   Ranks within this company's industry group: Sales: 10   Profits: 6

Hardware:		Software:		Telecommunications:		Electronic Publishing:		Equipment:		Specialty Services:	
Computers:		Consumer:	Y	Local:		Online Service:		Telecom:		Consulting:	
Accessories:	Y	Corporate:	Y	Long Distance:		TV/Cable or Wireless:		Communication:		Contract Manufacturing:	
Network Equipment:		Telecom:		Cellular:		Games:		Distribution:		Processing:	
Chips/Circuits:		Internet:		Internet Service:		Financial Data:		VAR/Reseller:		Staff/Outsourcing:	
Parts/Drives:								Satellite Srv./Equip.:		Specialty Services:	

TYPES OF BUSINESS:

Security Software
Authentication Devices
Banking Transaction Support Products
Credit Card Verification Products
Remote Verification Products
Anti-Fraud Services

BRANDS/DIVISIONS/AFFILIATES:

Digipass
VACMAN Controller
VACMAN Middleware
aXs GUARD
Identikey
DigipassPlus
DIGIPASS KEY 200
DIGIPASS KEY 860

CONTACTS: Note: Officers with more than one job title may be intentionally listed here more than once.

T. Kendall Hunt, CEO
Jan Valcke, COO
Jan Valcke, Pres.
Clifford K. Bown, CFO/Exec. VP
Clifford K. Brown, Sec.
T. Kendall Hunt, Chmn.

Phone: 630-932-8844	Fax: 630-932-8852
Toll-Free:	
Address: 1901 S. Meyers Rd., Ste. 210, Oakbrook Terrace, IL 60181 US	

GROWTH PLANS/SPECIAL FEATURES:

VASCO Data Security International, Inc. designs, develops, markets and supports open-standards-based hardware and software security systems that manage and secure access to information assets. The company's products provide mission-critical security to corporate customers' internal and external infrastructures. The firm also secures financial transactions made over private enterprise networks and the Internet. VASCO's primary product line is the VACMAN Controller, which supports all VASCO authentication technologies including passwords, dynamic password technology (Digipass), certificates and biometrics. Other products include VACMAN Middleware security software; aXs GUARD, an authentication appliance; Digipass, a suite of over 50 multi-application client e-signature software products based on the world's most widely spread electronic client platforms; and DigipassPlus, an authentication service that combines all VASCO products in an outsourced service offering; Digipass is used in a wide variety of applications, the largest of which is banking, both corporate and retail banking. Another application of the Digipass is to secure access to corporate networks for home-based, traveling and other remote users. Digipass 110, a zero-footprint e-signature application, is aimed at the large volume e-commerce and retail e-banking markets. Another key product is IdentiKey. With this product, a credit card customer is given a small token on which a password constantly changes. The password can be used to securely authorize ATM transactions or credit card purchases, including online purchases. Targeted markets are the applications that use fixed passwords as security. In 2009, the company's top 10 customers accounted for 34% of worldwide revenue. The firm currently serves 9,500 companies in over 100 countries, including 1,450 international financial institutions.

FINANCIALS: Sales and profits are in thousands of dollars—add 000 to get the full amount. 2010 Note: Financial information for 2010 was not available for all companies at press time.

2010 Sales: $	2010 Profits: $	U.S. Stock Ticker: VDSI
2009 Sales: $101,695	2009 Profits: $12,632	Int'l Ticker: Int'l Exchange:
2008 Sales: $132,977	2008 Profits: $24,291	Employees: 310
2007 Sales: $119,980	2007 Profits: $20,963	Fiscal Year Ends: 12/31
2006 Sales: $76,062	2006 Profits: $12,587	Parent Company:

SALARIES/BENEFITS:

Pension Plan:	ESOP Stock Plan:	Profit Sharing:	Top Exec. Salary: $446,080	Bonus: $536,407
Savings Plan:	Stock Purch. Plan:		Second Exec. Salary: $375,000	Bonus: $407,763

OTHER THOUGHTS:

Apparent Women Officers or Directors: 1
Hot Spot for Advancement for Women/Minorities:

LOCATIONS: ("Y" = Yes)

West:	Southwest:	Midwest:	Southeast:	Northeast:	International:
		Y		Y	Y

VENTYX INC

www.ventyx.com

Industry Group Code: 511210A Ranks within this company's industry group: Sales: Profits:

Hardware:	Software:		Telecommunications:	Electronic Publishing:	Equipment:	Specialty Services:	
Computers:	Consumer:		Local:	Online Service:	Telecom:	Consulting:	Y
Accessories:	Corporate:	Y	Long Distance:	TV/Cable or Wireless:	Communication:	Contract Manufacturing:	
Network Equipment:	Telecom:		Cellular:	Games:	Distribution:	Processing:	
Chips/Circuits:	Internet:		Internet Service:	Financial Data:	VAR/Reseller:	Staff/Outsourcing:	
Parts/Drives:					Satellite Srv./Equip.:	Specialty Services:	Y

TYPES OF BUSINESS:

Software-Enterprise Asset Management
Consulting Services
Supply Chain Software
Business Application Software
Support & Hosting Services

BRANDS/DIVISIONS/AFFILIATES:

ABB Group (The)
NewEnergy Associates
Tech-Assist, Inc.
EPM Operations Suite
eSOMS Suite
Performance Suite
Service Suite
Velocity Suite

CONTACTS: Note: Officers with more than one job title may be intentionally listed here more than once.

Peter Leupp, Head-Power Systems Div., ABB Group
Hubertus von Grunberg, Chmn.

Phone: 770-952-8444	Fax: 770-989-4231
Toll-Free: 800-868-0497	
Address: 3301 Windy Ridge Pkwy. SE, Atlanta, GA 30339-5618 US	

GROWTH PLANS/SPECIAL FEATURES:

Ventyx, Inc., a subsidiary of the ABB Group, develops, markets and supports integrated enterprise asset management, supply chain software and service products for capital-intensive industries worldwide. The company offers solutions in the areas of asset management, mobile workforce management, customer care, energy trading, energy risk management, energy operations and energy analytics. The company also focuses on database management, data warehousing, data mining, web development, geographic information systems, telecommunications and data security. Ventyx offers customers several software applications that include the Asset Suite, Customer Suite, EPM Operations Suite, eSOMS Suite, Performance Suite, Service Suite, the Velocity Suite as well as energy planning and analytics software. The Asset Management Suite allows users to keep real-time asset records. The Customer Suite is tailored to call centers and other segments dedicated to strengthening a customer base. The asset suite allows companies to manage their inventory and maximize returns on assets. The EPM Operations Suite allows portfolio optimization by generating reports on operating restraints and market conditions. The eSOMS Suite helps clients integrate and manage plant operations. The Performance Suite assists clients in data warehousing and works in conjunction with the company's other optimization software. The Service Suite helps to tie together elements of a client's service supply chain (namely the customers, the assets and the workforce) to maximize consumer satisfaction and lower the costs of services. The Velocity Suite allows for data sharing between EV Power, EV Fuels, EV Market Operations, EV Energy Map and EV Weather data. This suite also includes Virtual Analysts, which allows users to retrieve data reports directly from their desktop. The company's energy planning and analytics software includes market based supply forecasts, market price forecasting, risk analysis, geographic solutions and simulations to help determine uncertain market demand. In May 2010, the company was acquired by ABB, a power and automation company, for approximately $1 billion. Ventyx operates as part of ABB's Power Systems Division.

FINANCIALS: Sales and profits are in thousands of dollars—add 000 to get the full amount. 2010 Note: Financial information for 2010 was not available for all companies at press time.

2010 Sales: $	2010 Profits: $	U.S. Stock Ticker: Subsidiary
2009 Sales: $	2009 Profits: $	Int'l Ticker: Int'l Exchange:
2008 Sales: $	2008 Profits: $	Employees:
2007 Sales: $	2007 Profits: $	Fiscal Year Ends: 3/31
2006 Sales: $133,156	2006 Profits: $8,180	Parent Company: ABB GROUP (THE)

SALARIES/BENEFITS:

Pension Plan:	ESOP Stock Plan:	Profit Sharing:	Top Exec. Salary: $	Bonus: $
Savings Plan:	Stock Purch. Plan:		Second Exec. Salary: $	Bonus: $

OTHER THOUGHTS:

Apparent Women Officers or Directors: 1
Hot Spot for Advancement for Women/Minorities:

LOCATIONS: ("Y" = Yes)

West:	Southwest:	Midwest:	Southeast:	Northeast:	International:
Y			Y	Y	Y

VERISIGN INC

www.verisign.com

Industry Group Code: 511210E Ranks within this company's industry group: Sales: 4 Profits: 2

Hardware:	Software:		Telecommunications:	Electronic Publishing:		Equipment:	Specialty Services:	
Computers:	Consumer:		Local:	Online Service:	Y	Telecom:	Consulting:	Y
Accessories:	Corporate:	Y	Long Distance:	TV/Cable or Wireless:		Communication:	Contract Manufacturing:	
Network Equipment:	Telecom:		Cellular:	Games:		Distribution:	Processing:	Y
Chips/Circuits:	Internet:		Internet Service:	Financial Data:		VAR/Reseller:	Staff/Outsourcing:	
Parts/Drives:						Satellite Srv./Equip.:	Specialty Services:	Y

TYPES OF BUSINESS:

Software-Security
Domain Name Registration

BRANDS/DIVISIONS/AFFILIATES:

VeriSign iDefense

CONTACTS: Note: Officers with more than one job title may be intentionally listed here more than once.

Mark D. McLaughlin, CEO
Mark D. McLaughlin, Pres.
Brian G. Robins, CFO/Exec. VP
Christine C. Brennan, Sr. VP-Worldwide Human Resources
Kenneth J. Silva, CTO/Sr. VP
Richard H. Goshorn, General Counsel/Sr. VP/Corp. Sec.
Kevin A. Werner, Sr. VP-Corp. Dev. & Strategy
Russell S. Lewis, Exec. VP-Strategic Dev.
D. James Bidzos, Chmn.

Phone: 650-961-7500	Fax: 650-961-7300
Toll-Free:	
Address: 487 E. Middlefield Rd., Mountain View, CA 94043 US	

GROWTH PLANS/SPECIAL FEATURES:

VeriSign, Inc. operates infrastructure services that enable and protect billions of interactions every day across worldwide voice, video and data networks. It offers a variety of Internet services that are marketed through web site sales, direct field sales, channel sales, telesales and member organizations in its global affiliate network. Following the sale of its Authentication Services business to Symantec Corp. in August 2010, the company's two operating segments are naming services and other services. The naming services division consists of registry services and network intelligence and availability (NIA) services. The registry services segment is the authoritative directory provider of all .com, .net, .name, .cc and .tv domain names, as well as the provider of back-end systems for all .jobs and .edu domains. It has roughly 103.5 million domain names registered under its principal .com and .net registries. The NIA Services segment provides infrastructure assurance to organizations. It is comprised of VeriSign iDefense security intelligence services, managed domain name system services and distributed denial of service mitigation. VeriSign's other services segment includes the continuing operations of its content portal services, its remaining non-core business, and legacy products and services from divested businesses. In August 2010, VeriSign sold its Authentication Services business, including certain trademarks and intellectual property, to Symantec Corp. for approximately $1.14 billion.

Employees of VeriSign receive a flexible benefits package that includes health and welfare coverage; a 401(k); a discount stock purchase plan; tuition reimbursement; and health club membership reimbursement.

FINANCIALS: Sales and profits are in thousands of dollars—add 000 to get the full amount. 2010 Note: Financial information for 2010 was not available for all companies at press time.

2010 Sales: $	2010 Profits: $	**U.S. Stock Ticker: VRSN**
2009 Sales: $1,030,619	2009 Profits: $249,239	**Int'l Ticker:** Int'l Exchange:
2008 Sales: $964,748	2008 Profits: $-390,260	Employees: 2,328
2007 Sales: $847,457	2007 Profits: $-149,328	Fiscal Year Ends: 12/31
2006 Sales: $982,734	2006 Profits: $382,930	Parent Company:

SALARIES/BENEFITS:

Pension Plan:	ESOP Stock Plan:	Profit Sharing:	Top Exec. Salary: $751,154	Bonus: $
Savings Plan: Y	Stock Purch. Plan: Y		Second Exec. Salary: $579,807	Bonus: $499,885

OTHER THOUGHTS:

Apparent Women Officers or Directors: 2
Hot Spot for Advancement for Women/Minorities: Y

LOCATIONS: ("Y" = Yes)

West:	Southwest:	Midwest:	Southeast:	Northeast:	International:
Y	Y			Y	Y

VIA TECHNOLOGIES INC

www.via.com.tw

Industry Group Code: 33441 Ranks within this company's industry group: Sales: 49 Profits: 44

Hardware:		Software:	Telecommunications:	Electronic Publishing:	Equipment:	Specialty Services:
Computers:		Consumer:	Local:	Online Service:	Telecom:	Consulting:
Accessories:		Corporate:	Long Distance:	TV/Cable or Wireless:	Communication:	Contract Manufacturing:
Network Equipment:	Y	Telecom:	Cellular:	Games:	Distribution:	Processing:
Chips/Circuits:	Y	Internet:	Internet Service:	Financial Data:	VAR/Reseller:	Staff/Outsourcing:
Parts/Drives:	Y				Satellite Srv./Equip.:	Specialty Services:

TYPES OF BUSINESS:

Chips-PCs & Internet
Core Logic Chipsets
Microprocessors
Multimedia Chips
Audio Chips
Graphics Products
Networking Controllers
CDMA Chipsets

BRANDS/DIVISIONS/AFFILIATES:

S3 Graphics Inc
Centaur Technology Inc
VIA Vinyl Audio
VIA Nano
VIA C7
VIA Eden
VIA CoreFusion
Chrome

CONTACTS: *Note: Officers with more than one job title may be intentionally listed here more than once.*

WenChi Chen, CEO
WenChi Chen, Pres.
TzuMu Lin, Sr. VP-R&D
TzuMu Lin, Sr. VP-Eng.
Cher Wang, Chmn.

Phone: 886-2-2218-5452	Fax: 886-2-2218-5453
Toll-Free:	
Address: 531 Zhongzheng Rd., 1st. Fl., New Taipei City, 231 Taiwan	

GROWTH PLANS/SPECIAL FEATURES:

VIA Technologies, Inc. provides PC core logic chipsets, microprocessors and mainboards as well as multimedia and communications chips. The company offers processors for the PC, client, ultra mobile and embedded markets, including the VIA Nano, the VIA C7, the VIA Eden and the VIA CoreFusion. Processors are designed and developed by the firm's subsidiary, Centaur Technology, Inc. VIA chipsets include standard use, high performance chips, as well as a wide range of multimedia chipsets that integrate graphics for desktops and notebooks. S3 Graphics, Inc., the company's computer graphics subsidiary, has developed the Chrome line of graphics cores aimed at the mid-range consumer graphics market. VIA Technologies is a leading developer of Ethernet networking controllers, network switch controllers and PHY receivers, delivering Fast and Gigabit Ethernet networking connectivity. The VIA embedded platform division combines the VIA processor and VIA chipset groups into a single autonomous business unit focused on designing, developing and distributing highly integrated, low-power x86 platforms. Other technologies, such as VIA Vinyl Audio, boost sound, while still others enhance high definition video displays. The company also designs and manufactures fanless touchscreen LCD displays. VIA's client base includes many of the world's leading computer distributors and resellers, which integrate its products into computer systems sold in the PC retail market.

FINANCIALS: Sales and profits are in thousands of dollars—add 000 to get the full amount. 2010 Note: Financial information for 2010 was not available for all companies at press time.

2010 Sales: $	2010 Profits: $	**U.S. Stock Ticker:**
2009 Sales: $193,820	2009 Profits: $-97,580	**Int'l Ticker: 2388** Int'l Exchange: Taipei-TPE
2008 Sales: $285,120	2008 Profits: $-138,300	Employees: 2,774
2007 Sales: $522,410	2007 Profits: $-26,110	Fiscal Year Ends: 12/31
2006 Sales: $725,070	2006 Profits: $3,450	Parent Company:

SALARIES/BENEFITS:

Pension Plan:	ESOP Stock Plan:	Profit Sharing:	Top Exec. Salary: $	Bonus: $
Savings Plan:	Stock Purch. Plan:		Second Exec. Salary: $	Bonus: $

OTHER THOUGHTS:

Apparent Women Officers or Directors: 1
Hot Spot for Advancement for Women/Minorities:

LOCATIONS: ("Y" = Yes)

West:	Southwest:	Midwest:	Southeast:	Northeast:	International:
Y	Y				Y

VIASYSTEMS GROUP INC

www.viasystems.com

Industry Group Code: 334419 Ranks within this company's industry group: Sales: 18   Profits: 18

Hardware:		Software:	Telecommunications:	Electronic Publishing:	Equipment:		Specialty Services:	
Computers:		Consumer:	Local:	Online Service:	Telecom:		Consulting:	
Accessories:		Corporate:	Long Distance:	TV/Cable or Wireless:	Communication:		Contract Manufacturing:	Y
Network Equipment:		Telecom:	Cellular:	Games:	Distribution:		Processing:	
Chips/Circuits:	Y	Internet:	Internet Service:	Financial Data:	VAR/Reseller:		Staff/Outsourcing:	Y
Parts/Drives:					Satellite Srv./Equip.:		Specialty Services:	

TYPES OF BUSINESS:

Contract Electronics Manufacturing
Assembly, Integration & Testing
Manufacturing Outsourcing Services

BRANDS/DIVISIONS/AFFILIATES:

Merix Corp
Viasystems Guangzhou
Viasystems Zhongshan
Viasystems Juarez
Viasystems Qingdao
Viasystems Shanghai
Viasystems Shenzhen
Viasystems Inc

CONTACTS: Note: Officers with more than one job title may be intentionally listed here more than once.

David M. Sindelar, CEO
Tim L. Conlon, COO
Tim L. Conlon, Pres.
Gerald G. Sax, CFO/Sr. VP
Richard B. Kampf, Sr. VP-Mktg. & Sales
Daniel J. Weber, General Counsel/VP
Brian W. Barber, Sr. VP-Oper., Printed Circuit Boards
Christopher J. Steffen, Chmn.
Brian W. Barber, Sr. VP-Supply Chain Mgmt.

Phone: 314-727-2087	Fax: 314-746-2233
Toll-Free:	
Address: 101 S. Hanley Rd., Ste. 400, St. Louis, MO 63105 US	

GROWTH PLANS/SPECIAL FEATURES:

Viasystems Group, Inc., formerly known as Viasystems, Inc., is a leading international provider of printed circuit boards and electro-mechanical products, primarily in the telecommunications and automotive industries. The company offers services to original equipment manufacturers in five primary markets: automotive; industrial and instrumentation, medical, consumer and other; telecommunications; computer and data communications; and military and aerospace. These services include design and prototyping; fabrication of printed circuit boards, backpanels, custom cable assemblies, thermal management equipment and electromechanical enclosure systems such as equipment racks, cabinets, shelters and walk-in cabinets; manufacture of custom backpanel assemblies; procurement and management of materials; sheet metal fabrication; and comprehensive product testing. The firm specializes in quick turnaround times for contracted printed circuit boards with the ability to manufacture products within 24-72 hours. Viasystems operates 10 manufacturing facilities that are located in the U.S., Mexico, Hong Kong and China. International manufacturing subsidiaries include Viasystems Guangzhou; Viasystems Zhongshan; Viasystems Juarez; Viasystems Qingdao; Viasystems Shanghai; and Viasystems Shenzhen. The firm recently completed a restructuring operation that shuttered manufacturing plants in Milwaukee, Wisconsin and Newberry, South Carolina. In February 2010, the company merged with Merix Corporation, a manufacturer of printed circuit boards.

FINANCIALS: Sales and profits are in thousands of dollars—add 000 to get the full amount. 2010 Note: Financial information for 2010 was not available for all companies at press time.

2010 Sales: $	2010 Profits: $	U.S. Stock Ticker: VIAS
2009 Sales: $496,447	2009 Profits: $-54,717	Int'l Ticker: Int'l Exchange:
2008 Sales: $712,830	2008 Profits: $-5,703	Employees: 13,783
2007 Sales: $714,343	2007 Profits: $17,317	Fiscal Year Ends: 12/31
2006 Sales: $734,992	2006 Profits: $202,437	Parent Company:

SALARIES/BENEFITS:

Pension Plan:	ESOP Stock Plan:	Profit Sharing:	Top Exec. Salary: $954,354	Bonus: $460,000
Savings Plan:	Stock Purch. Plan:		Second Exec. Salary: $572,663	Bonus: $275,000

OTHER THOUGHTS:

Apparent Women Officers or Directors:
Hot Spot for Advancement for Women/Minorities:

LOCATIONS: ("Y" = Yes)

West:	Southwest:	Midwest:	Southeast:	Northeast:	International:
Y	Y	Y		Y	Y

VICORP GROUP PLC

www.vicorp.com

Industry Group Code: 511210C Ranks within this company's industry group: Sales: Profits:

Hardware:	Software:		Telecommunications:	Electronic Publishing:	Equipment:	Specialty Services:
Computers:	Consumer:		Local:	Online Service:	Telecom:	Consulting:
Accessories:	Corporate:	Y	Long Distance:	TV/Cable or Wireless:	Communication:	Contract Manufacturing:
Network Equipment:	Telecom:	Y	Cellular:	Games:	Distribution:	Processing:
Chips/Circuits:	Internet:		Internet Service:	Financial Data:	VAR/Reseller:	Staff/Outsourcing:
Parts/Drives:					Satellite Srv./Equip.:	Specialty Services:

TYPES OF BUSINESS:

Computer Software-Call Processing

BRANDS/DIVISIONS/AFFILIATES:

xMP
xMP Reporter
xMP Director
xMP Console
xMP Studio
xMP Campaign Master

CONTACTS: Note: Officers with more than one job title may be intentionally listed here more than once.

Brendan Treacy, CEO
Tim Hearley, Chmn.

Phone: 44-1753-838-420	Fax: 44-1753-838-421
Toll-Free:	
Address: 119-120 High St., Eton, Berkshire, SL4 6AN UK	

GROWTH PLANS/SPECIAL FEATURES:

Vicorp Group plc is a leading independent provider of service creation software and professional services for automated voice solutions. The company serves the telecommunications, wireless and ISP (Internet service provider) industries through its xMP platform. xMP provides a suite of tools and a methodology that enables Vicorp customers to create and modify their own interactive services to manage customer calls. These services include voicemail, voice authentication, text-to-speech, automated speech recognition, bilingual speech interfaces and video streaming. The xMP product includes xMP Director, a drag-and-drop service creation tool that enables applications to be designed and created quickly; xMP Studio, which customizes template services and manages content; xMP Console, which deploys and manages services and platform resources; and xMP Reporter, providing data on every aspect of xMP applications. Customers include Banque SofinCo; Littlewoods; Centrica; Barclaycard; Rogers AT&T; Faber; Land Rover; and HBOS. The company also has partnerships with Genesys; HP; Holly Connects; HTK; IBM; Avaya; Nuance; Oracle; Vox Pilot; and Telisma. In March 2010, the company launched xMP Campaign Master, an outbound communication platform that is designed to open self-service into the mobile channel and across all forms of outbound communication channels. In April 2010, the firm partnered with Vodafone Egypt to launch advanced speech self-service applications with Vicorp's xMP software.

FINANCIALS: Sales and profits are in thousands of dollars—add 000 to get the full amount. 2010 Note: Financial information for 2010 was not available for all companies at press time.

2010 Sales: $	2010 Profits: $	U.S. Stock Ticker:
2009 Sales: $	2009 Profits: $	Int'l Ticker: VICP Int'l Exchange: London-LSE
2008 Sales: $	2008 Profits: $	Employees:
2007 Sales: $3,400	2007 Profits: $-1,400	Fiscal Year Ends: 12/31
2006 Sales: $1,100	2006 Profits: $-5,100	Parent Company:

SALARIES/BENEFITS:

Pension Plan:	ESOP Stock Plan:	Profit Sharing:	Top Exec. Salary: $	Bonus: $
Savings Plan:	Stock Purch. Plan:		Second Exec. Salary: $	Bonus: $

OTHER THOUGHTS:

Apparent Women Officers or Directors:
Hot Spot for Advancement for Women/Minorities:

LOCATIONS: ("Y" = Yes)

West:	Southwest:	Midwest:	Southeast:	Northeast:	International:
					Y

VIDEOCON INDUSTRIES LTD

www.videoconworld.com

Industry Group Code: 334310 Ranks within this company's industry group: Sales: 8 Profits: 4

Hardware:	Software:	Telecommunications:	Electronic Publishing:	Equipment:	Specialty Services:
Computers:	Consumer:	Local:	Online Service:	Telecom:	Consulting:
Accessories:	Corporate:	Long Distance:	TV/Cable or Wireless:	Communication:	Contract Manufacturing:
Network Equipment:	Telecom:	Cellular: Y	Games:	Distribution:	Processing:
Chips/Circuits:	Internet:	Internet Service:	Financial Data:	VAR/Reseller:	Staff/Outsourcing:
Parts/Drives:				Satellite Srv./Equip.:	Specialty Services:

TYPES OF BUSINESS:

Consumer Electronics & Appliances
Consumer Electronics and Appliances
Color Picture Tube Glass and Display Manufacturing

BRANDS/DIVISIONS/AFFILIATES:

Paramount GlobalLimited
Middle East Appliances LLC
Videocon Electronic (Shenzhen) Limited
Pipavav Energy Private Limited
Videocon Energy Brazil Limited
Godavari Consumer Electronics Appliances Pvt Ltd
Videocon Careen

CONTACTS: *Note: Officers with more than one job title may be intentionally listed here more than once.*

K. R. Kim, CEO
Shekhar Jyoti, VP-Corp. Human Resources
Vinod Kumar Bohra, Corp. Sec.
Venugopal N. Dhoot, Chmn.

Phone: 91-24-3125-1501	Fax:
Toll-Free:	
Address: 14 Kms Stone, Aurangabad-Paithan Rd., Paithan, 431 105 India	

GROWTH PLANS/SPECIAL FEATURES:

Videocon Industries Ltd. is an India-based company engaged in the production of consumer electronics, appliances and glass, as well as energy exploration and production. The company operates in four primary sectors: consumer durables; color picture tube (CPT) displays; CPT glass; and oil and gas. In the consumer durables sector, the company is a leading provider of a variety of products, including color televisions, washing machines, air conditioners, refrigerators, microwave ovens and other home appliances, sold through one of India's largest sales and service networks. The company's refrigerator manufacturing is further supported by its in-house compressor manufacturing facility in Bangalore. The CPT display segment is one of the largest color picture tube manufacturers in the world. The firm's CPT Glass sector is one of the world's largest manufacturers of glass for color picture tubes, with operations centered in India. It produces a range of panels and funnels to meet the growing demand for large-size, flat and slim CRT display products. The operations of this sector also support the company's CPT display sector. Videocon's oil and gas business has interests in exploration, production and distribution in India, Oman, Australia and the Timor Sea near Indonesia. The firm's subsidiaries include Paramount GlobalLimited; Middle East Appliances, LLC; Videocon Electronic (Shenzhen) Limited; Pipavav Energy Private Limited; Videocon Energy Brazil Limited; and Godavari Consumer Electronics Appliances Pvt. Ltd. In July 2010, the company introduced Videocon Careen, a series of tilt-tub washing machines.

FINANCIALS: Sales and profits are in thousands of dollars—add 000 to get the full amount. 2010 Note: Financial information for 2010 was not available for all companies at press time.

2010 Sales: $	2010 Profits: $	U.S. Stock Ticker:
2009 Sales: $2,263,400	2009 Profits: $111,520	Int'l Ticker: 511389 Int'l Exchange: Bombay-BSE
2008 Sales: $2,682,350	2008 Profits: $240,880	Employees:
2007 Sales: $2,670,350	2007 Profits: $154,730	Fiscal Year Ends: 9/30
2006 Sales: $	2006 Profits: $	Parent Company:

SALARIES/BENEFITS:

Pension Plan:	ESOP Stock Plan:	Profit Sharing:	Top Exec. Salary: $	Bonus: $
Savings Plan:	Stock Purch. Plan:		Second Exec. Salary: $	Bonus: $

OTHER THOUGHTS:

Apparent Women Officers or Directors:
Hot Spot for Advancement for Women/Minorities:

LOCATIONS: ("Y" = Yes)

West:	Southwest:	Midwest:	Southeast:	Northeast:	International: Y

Note: Financial information, benefits and other data can change quickly and may vary from those stated here.

VITESSE SEMICONDUCTOR CORP

www.vitesse.com

Industry Group Code: 33441 Ranks within this company's industry group: Sales: 51 Profits: 47

Hardware:		Software:	Telecommunications:	Electronic Publishing:	Equipment:	Specialty Services:
Computers:		Consumer:	Local:	Online Service:	Telecom:	Consulting:
Accessories:		Corporate:	Long Distance:	TV/Cable or Wireless:	Communication:	Contract Manufacturing:
Network Equipment:	Y	Telecom:	Cellular:	Games:	Distribution:	Processing:
Chips/Circuits:	Y	Internet:	Internet Service:	Financial Data:	VAR/Reseller:	Staff/Outsourcing:
Parts/Drives:					Satellite Srv./Equip.:	Specialty Services:

TYPES OF BUSINESS:

Integrated Circuits
Optoelectronics
Network Processors
Traffic Management Products
Switch Fabrics
Media Access Controllers
Storage Products

BRANDS/DIVISIONS/AFFILIATES:

SimpliPHY
Crosspoint
VSC3144-11
LynX
E-StaX-III
EcoEthernet

CONTACTS: Note: Officers with more than one job title may be intentionally listed here more than once.

Christopher R. Gardner, CEO
Christopher R. Gardner, Pres.
Rich Yonker, CFO
Steve Perna, VP-Prod. Mktg.
Martin Nuss, VP-Tech.
Roy Carew, VP-Quality, Prod. & Test Eng.
Paul Browne, VP-Eng.
Michael Green, General Counsel/Corp. Sec./VP
Martin Nuss, VP-Strategy
Edward Rogas, Jr., Chmn.

Phone: 805-388-3700	Fax: 805-389-7188
Toll-Free: 800-848-3773	
Address: 741 Calle Plano, Camarillo, CA 93012-8543 US	

GROWTH PLANS/SPECIAL FEATURES:

Vitesse Semiconductor Corp. designs, develops and markets semiconductor products. The company is a leading provider of advanced integrated circuits (ICs) that are utilized primarily by manufacturers of networking systems for carrier, enterprise and storage communications applications. Specializing in Ethernet networking, a dominant networking protocol in both carrier and enterprise networks, it offers products in the following segments: transport processing; Ethernet switches, media access controllers (MACs) and transceivers; physical media devices, physical layer devices (PHYs) and signal integrity devices; and Intellectual Property (IP) licensing. Products include Ethernet and Carrier Ethernet MACs with speeds up to 14 gigabytes per second (Gbps); SimpliPHY Ethernet transceivers that provide low power operation; and the Crosspoint switch family of products. Vitesse markets its products directly to original equipment manufacturers (OEMs) and original design manufacturers (ODMs), as well as through third-party electronic component distributors and manufacturing service providers. Top direct customers include Cisco, Nokia Siemens and Huawei Technologies. Vitesse has 89 U.S. patents, 20 foreign patents, and 18 patent applications pending in the U.S. In 2010, the firm added 30 new products to its portfolio, including Jaguar and LynX Carrier Ethernet switch engines; E-StaX-III Gigabit Ethernet switch engines; and three new SimpliPHY copper PHYs, using its energy saving EcoEthernet technology.

Employees are offered medical, dental, vision and life insurance; disability coverage; a 401(k) savings plan; and health club reimbursements.

FINANCIALS: Sales and profits are in thousands of dollars—add 000 to get the full amount. 2010 Note: Financial information for 2010 was not available for all companies at press time.

2010 Sales: $165,990	2010 Profits: $-20,181	**U.S. Stock Ticker:** VTSS.PK
2009 Sales: $168,177	2009 Profits: $-194,041	**Int'l Ticker:** Int'l Exchange:
2008 Sales: $228,536	2008 Profits: $16,554	Employees: 467
2007 Sales: $221,948	2007 Profits: $-21,647	Fiscal Year Ends: 9/30
2006 Sales: $203,289	2006 Profits: $-67,285	Parent Company:

SALARIES/BENEFITS:

Pension Plan:	ESOP Stock Plan:	Profit Sharing:	Top Exec. Salary: $410,676	Bonus: $206,250
Savings Plan: Y	Stock Purch. Plan:		Second Exec. Salary: $288,799	Bonus: $33,915

OTHER THOUGHTS:

Apparent Women Officers or Directors:
Hot Spot for Advancement for Women/Minorities:

LOCATIONS: ("Y" = Yes)

West:	Southwest:	Midwest:	Southeast:	Northeast:	International:
Y	Y			Y	Y

VMWARE INC

www.vmware.com

Industry Group Code: 511210B Ranks within this company's industry group: Sales: 1 Profits: 1

Hardware:	Software:		Telecommunications:	Electronic Publishing:	Equipment:	Specialty Services:	
Computers:	Consumer:		Local:	Online Service:	Telecom:	Consulting:	Y
Accessories:	Corporate:	Y	Long Distance:	TV/Cable or Wireless:	Communication:	Contract Manufacturing:	
Network Equipment:	Telecom:		Cellular:	Games:	Distribution:	Processing:	
Chips/Circuits:	Internet:		Internet Service:	Financial Data:	VAR/Reseller:	Staff/Outsourcing:	
Parts/Drives:					Satellite Srv./Equip.:	Specialty Services:	Y

TYPES OF BUSINESS:

Virtualization Solutions
Virtual Infrastructure Automation
Virtual Infrastructure Management

BRANDS/DIVISIONS/AFFILIATES:

VMware Global Support Services
VMware Professional Services
EMC Corp.
SpringSource
Zimbra
Integrien
TriCipher

CONTACTS: *Note: Officers with more than one job title may be intentionally listed here more than once.*

Paul Maritz, CEO
Tod Nielsen, COO
Paul Maritz, Pres.
Mark Peek, CFO
Rick Jackson, Chief Mktg. Officer
Betsy Sutter, Sr. VP-Human Resources
Stephen Herrod, Sr. VP-R&D
Mark Egan, CIO
Stephen Herrod, CTO
Raghu Raghuram, VP-Prod. & Solutions
Dawn Smith, General Counsel/Sr. VP
Carl Eschenbach, Exec. VP-Worldwide Field Oper.
Richard McAniff, Chief Dev. Officer
Scott Bajtos, Sr. VP-Global Support Svcs.
Raghu Raghuram, Sr. VP/Gen. Mgr.-Virtualization & Cloud Platforms
Jocelyn Goldfein, VP/Gen Mgr.-Desktop Bus. Unit
Brian Byun, VP/Gen. Mgr.-Cloud Applications & Svcs.
Joseph M. Tucci, Chmn.
Maurizio Carli, Gen. Mgr.-EMEA

Phone: 650-427-5000	Fax: 650-427-5001
Toll-Free: 877-486-9273	
Address: 3401 Hillview Ave., Palo Alto, CA 94304 US	

GROWTH PLANS/SPECIAL FEATURES:

VMware, Inc. is a provider of virtual infrastructure software, which offers virtualization capabilities ranging from server consolidation and infrastructure optimization to business continuity, virtual lab automation and enterprise desktop management. VMware's software runs on industry-standard desktops and servers and support a wide range of operating system and application environments, as well as networking and storage infrastructures. Products fall into two categories: datacenter products and desktop products. Datacenter products include datacenter virtualization technology, such as VMware Infrastructure, that increase hardware utilization, lower power consumption and reduce capital and operating costs; and datacenter applications and infrastructure management tools, which automate IT processes to provide more efficient, reliable and available virtual datacenter operations. Desktop products are focused on providing user-centric services, as opposed to device-centric. Desktop virtualization allows users to use local hardware and peripherals or remotely access a machine using a display protocol. The services allow a user to manipulate multiple different virtual machines from a single source or interact with applications that require different operating systems. The company's Fusion application allows Apple users to run Windows applications, and vice-versa. VMware Global Support Services, the firm's global customer support organization, offers services including customization and onsite support. VMware also provides a range of professional services through VMware Professional Services, which include VMware consulting services and VMware education services. The firm collaborates with over 900 technology vendors, both hardware and software, in order to achieve greater interoperability between systems. EMC Corporation owns approximately 81% of the company's outstanding stock. In February 2010, VMWare acquired Zimbra, an open source email and collaboration software vendor, from Yahoo! Inc. In August 2010, the company acquired Integrien, a vendor of real time application and infrastructure performance analytics software; as well as TriCipher, a software company that produce secure access management and Software as a Service (SaaS) applications.

FINANCIALS: Sales and profits are in thousands of dollars—add 000 to get the full amount. 2010 Note: Financial information for 2010 was not available for all companies at press time.

2010 Sales: $	2010 Profits: $	**U.S. Stock Ticker: VMW**
2009 Sales: $2,023,937	2009 Profits: $197,098	Int'l Ticker: Int'l Exchange:
2008 Sales: $1,881,027	2008 Profits: $290,133	Employees: 7,100
2007 Sales: $1,325,811	2007 Profits: $218,137	Fiscal Year Ends: 12/31
2006 Sales: $703,904	2006 Profits: $85,890	Parent Company:

SALARIES/BENEFITS:

Pension Plan:	ESOP Stock Plan:	Profit Sharing:	Top Exec. Salary: $778,518	Bonus: $925,125
Savings Plan: Y	Stock Purch. Plan: Y		Second Exec. Salary: $612,829	Bonus: $733,470

OTHER THOUGHTS:

Apparent Women Officers or Directors: 3
Hot Spot for Advancement for Women/Minorities: Y

LOCATIONS: ("Y" = Yes)

West:	Southwest:	Midwest:	Southeast:	Northeast:	International:
Y	Y	Y	Y	Y	Y

VSE CORP

www.vsecorp.com

Industry Group Code: 541330 Ranks within this company's industry group: Sales: 1 Profits: 1

Hardware:	Software:	Telecommunications:	Electronic Publishing:	Equipment:	Specialty Services:	
Computers:	Consumer:	Local:	Online Service:	Telecom:	Consulting:	Y
Accessories:	Corporate:	Long Distance:	TV/Cable or Wireless:	Communication:	Contract Manufacturing:	
Network Equipment:	Telecom:	Cellular:	Games:	Distribution:	Processing:	Y
Chips/Circuits:	Internet:	Internet Service:	Financial Data:	VAR/Reseller:	Staff/Outsourcing:	
Parts/Drives:				Satellite Srv./Equip.:	Specialty Services:	Y

TYPES OF BUSINESS:

Technical Services to Government
Engineering Services
Logistics Services
Technology Research & Development
Equipment Maintenance, Refurbishment & Implementation
Information Technology Support

BRANDS/DIVISIONS/AFFILIATES:

Energetics, Inc.
BAV
Integrated Concepts and Research Corporation
Akimedia LLC
G&B Solutions, Inc.

CONTACTS: Note: Officers with more than one job title may be intentionally listed here more than once.

Maurice Gauthier, CEO
Maurice Gauthier, COO
Maurice Gauthier, Pres.
Thomas R. Loftus, CFO/Exec. VP
Randy Hollstein, VP-Sales & Mktg.
Tina Bailey, VP-Human Resources
Thomas M. Kiernan, General Counsel/Sec./VP
James W. Lexo, Jr., Exec. VP-Strategic Planning & Bus. Initiatives
Thomas G. Dacus, Exec. VP/Pres., Federal Group
Nancy Margolis, Pres., Energetics, Inc.
Carl E. Williams, Pres., Integrated Concepts & Research Corp.
Linda Berdine, Pres., G&B Solutions, Inc.
Donald M. Ervine, Chmn.
Michael E. Hamerly, Pres., Int'l Group
William J. Jonas, VP-Procurement

Phone: 703-960-4600	Fax: 703-960-2688
Toll-Free:	
Address: 2550 Huntington Ave., Alexandria, VA 22303-1499 US	

GROWTH PLANS/SPECIAL FEATURES:

VSE Corp. is a contract provider of services and equipment to U.S. Department of Defense legacy systems and federal civilian agencies. Its businesses are organized into four groups: Federal; International; IT, Energy and Management Consulting; and Infrastructure. The Federal Group provides engineering, technical, management, integrated logistics support and IT services to all U.S. military branches and to other government agencies. The group consists of the following divisions: communications and electronics; engineering and logistics; field support services; and systems engineering. The International Group provides engineering, industrial, logistics and foreign military sales services to similar groups. It consists of three divisions: BAV, Coast Guard and fleet maintenance. The IT, Energy and Management Consulting Group, which encompasses wholly-owned subsidiaries, Energetics, Inc. and G&B Solutions, Inc., provides technical and consulting services primarily to various civilian government agencies. Energetics, Inc. provides technical and management support in the areas of nuclear energy, technology research, development and demonstration, and consulting services in the energy and environmental management fields. G&B is an IT company. The Infrastructure Group includes Integrated Concepts and Research Corporation (ICRC), a wholly-owned subsidiary, and is engaged in providing technical and management services to the U.S. government, including transportation infrastructure services, advanced vehicle technology, aerospace services and engineering and information technology. In August 2010, VSE acquired Akimedia LLC, a Hawaii-based health services information technology consulting company, for approximately $33 million.

FINANCIALS: Sales and profits are in thousands of dollars—add 000 to get the full amount. 2010 Note: Financial information for 2010 was not available for all companies at press time.

2010 Sales: $	2010 Profits: $	U.S. Stock Ticker: VSEC
2009 Sales: $1,014,639	2009 Profits: $24,024	Int'l Ticker: Int'l Exchange:
2008 Sales: $1,043,735	2008 Profits: $19,040	Employees: 2,534
2007 Sales: $653,164	2007 Profits: $14,102	Fiscal Year Ends: 12/31
2006 Sales: $363,734	2006 Profits: $7,789	Parent Company:

SALARIES/BENEFITS:

Pension Plan:	ESOP Stock-Plan:	Profit Sharing:	Top Exec. Salary: $415,000	Bonus: $415,000
Savings Plan: Y	Stock Purch. Plan:		Second Exec. Salary: $235,000	Bonus: $235,000

OTHER THOUGHTS:

Apparent Women Officers or Directors: 3
Hot Spot for Advancement for Women/Minorities: Y

LOCATIONS: ("Y" = Yes)

West:	Southwest:	Midwest:	Southeast:	Northeast:	International:
Y	Y	Y	Y	Y	Y

Note: Financial information, benefits and other data can change quickly and may vary from those stated here.

WATCHGUARD TECHNOLOGIES INC
www.watchguard.com

Industry Group Code: 511210E Ranks within this company's industry group: Sales: Profits:

Hardware:	Software:		Telecommunications:	Electronic Publishing:		Equipment:	Specialty Services:	
Computers:	Consumer:		Local:	Online Service:	Y	Telecom:	Consulting:	
Accessories:	Corporate:	Y	Long Distance:	TV/Cable or Wireless:		Communication:	Contract Manufacturing:	
Network Equipment:	Telecom:		Cellular:	Games:		Distribution:	Processing:	
Chips/Circuits:	Internet:		Internet Service:	Financial Data:		VAR/Reseller:	Staff/Outsourcing:	
Parts/Drives:						Satellite Srv./Equip.:	Specialty Services:	Y

TYPES OF BUSINESS:
Internet Security Software
Firewall & VPN Appliances
Training & Technical Support
Online Services

BRANDS/DIVISIONS/AFFILIATES:
WatchGuard XTM
WatchGuard XCS
WatchGuard SSL
Francisco Partners
Vector Capital

CONTACTS: *Note: Officers with more than one job title may be intentionally listed here more than once.*
Joe Wang, CEO
Richard Barber, CFO
Eric Aarrestad, VP-Mktg.
Sin-Yaw Wang, VP-Eng.
Matt Deichman, VP-Bus. Dev.
Bill Smith, VP-Sales, Americas
Shari McLaren, VP-Customer Svcs. & Support
Terry Haas, VP-Int'l Sales

Phone: 206-613-6600	Fax: 206-521-8342
Toll-Free:	
Address: 505 5th Ave. S., Ste. 500, Seattle, WA 98104 US	

GROWTH PLANS/SPECIAL FEATURES:

WatchGuard Technologies, Inc. develops and implements network security services designed to protect small- to medium-sized enterprises that use the Internet for e-commerce and secure communications. WatchGuard offers three primary lines of hardware that can be used to protect connections of businesses ranging from small offices to corporate headquarters. The company's XTM (Extensible Threat Management) products features built-in firewall and VPN (Virtual Private Networks) services to protect against malicious attacks and security breaches. Its XCS (Extensible Content Security) hardware is designed to protect against e-mail spam, viruses and other malware. The firm's SSL products allow remote users to access a private network securely, even if they are logging in from a public source. The company's security subscriptions protect users against spam, viruses and web sites with poor reputations. WatchGuard also offers 3G wireless connection extensions, product support and training services. The company has offices located in Europe, Africa, Latin America and North America. The company was recently acquired by California-based private equity firms Francisco Partners and Vector Capital.

FINANCIALS: Sales and profits are in thousands of dollars—add 000 to get the full amount. 2010 Note: Financial information for 2010 was not available for all companies at press time.

2010 Sales: $	2010 Profits: $	**U.S. Stock Ticker: Private**
2009 Sales: $	2009 Profits: $	**Int'l Ticker:** Int'l Exchange:
2008 Sales: $	2008 Profits: $	Employees:
2007 Sales: $	2007 Profits: $	Fiscal Year Ends: 12/31
2006 Sales: $	2006 Profits: $	Parent Company: FRANCISCO PARTNERS

SALARIES/BENEFITS:
Pension Plan:	ESOP Stock Plan:	Profit Sharing:	Top Exec. Salary: $	Bonus: $
Savings Plan: Y	Stock Purch. Plan: Y		Second Exec. Salary: $	Bonus: $

OTHER THOUGHTS:
Apparent Women Officers or Directors: 1
Hot Spot for Advancement for Women/Minorities:

LOCATIONS: ("Y" = Yes)
West:	Southwest:	Midwest:	Southeast:	Northeast:	International:
Y					Y

Note: Financial information, benefits and other data can change quickly and may vary from those stated here.

WEB.COM GROUP INC

www.web.com

Industry Group Code: 518210 Ranks within this company's industry group: Sales: 4 Profits: 3

Hardware:	Software:		Telecommunications:	Electronic Publishing:		Equipment:	Specialty Services:	
Computers:	Consumer:		Local:	Online Service:	Y	Telecom:	Consulting:	Y
Accessories:	Corporate:	Y	Long Distance:	TV/Cable or Wireless:		Communication:	Contract Manufacturing:	
Network Equipment:	Telecom:		Cellular:	Games:		Distribution:	Processing:	
Chips/Circuits:	Internet:		Internet Service:	Financial Data:		VAR/Reseller:	Staff/Outsourcing:	
Parts/Drives:						Satellite Srv./Equip.:	Specialty Services:	Y

TYPES OF BUSINESS:
Web Hosting Products & Services
Web Design Services

BRANDS/DIVISIONS/AFFILIATES:
Website Pros, Inc.
eWorks! XL
SmartClicks
Register.com
1ShoppingCart.com
Renex
LEADS.com
Web.com Search Agency

CONTACTS: Note: Officers with more than one job title may be intentionally listed here more than once.
David L. Brown, CEO
David L. Brown, Pres.
Kevin Carney, CFO
Roseann Duran, Chief Mktg. Officer
Chris Nowlin, Sr. VP-Human Resources
Vikas Rijsinghani, CTO
Matthew P. McClure, Chief Legal Officer/Sec.
Joel Williamson, Sr. VP-Oper.
Robert C. Wiegand, Sr. VP-Bus. Dev.
Gonzalo Troncoso, Pres., Web Svcs.
Peter Delgrosso, Sr. VP-Bus. Dev & Corp. Comm.
William H. Borzage, Sr. VP-Mktg. & Lead Generation
Gregory Wong, Sr. VP-Corp. Dev.
David L. Brown, Chmn.

Phone: 904-680-6600	Fax: 904-880-0350
Toll-Free:	
Address: 12808 Gran Bay Pkwy. W., Jacksonville, FL 32258 US	

GROWTH PLANS/SPECIAL FEATURES:
Web.com Group, Inc. is a provider of Do-It-For-Me and Do-It-Yourself web site building, Internet marketing, lead generation and technology solutions that enable small and mid-sized businesses to build and maintain an Internet presence. Web.com's primary service offerings, eWorks! XL and SmartClicks, include web site design and publishing; Internet marketing and advertising; search engine optimization; search engine submission; lead generation; logo design and web analytics. In addition to its primary service offerings, Web.com provides a variety of services to customers who desire more advanced capabilities, such as e-commerce solutions and other sophisticated Internet marketing services and online lead generation. Through its Web.com product, the company offers a variety of Do-It-Yourself web site building and marketing solutions for small and mid-sized businesses that are more technically savvy. It offers standardized, scalable managed hosting services that place numerous customers on a single shared server. Web.com offers complete custom web site design services that provide sophisticated functionality and interactivity beyond those available under eWorks! XL and SmartClicks. Through 1ShoppingCart.com and Solid Cactus, Web.com offers a set of sales and marketing tools for businesses selling products and services online. It offers targeted lead generation services through Renex, matching homeowners in need of remodeling services with qualified contractors, and LEADS.com, offering leads in other home services categories. Web.com Search Agency offers search engine optimization and placement services. Additionally, LogoYes, allows users to create custom design logos. In order to increase subscription-based revenue the company sold its NetObjects Fusion software and acquired Register.com, which provides global domain name registration and site design services. Likewise, the announcement of an exclusive partnership with the National Federation of Independent Business, with its 350,000 members, sees Web.com expanding.

Web.com offers its employees a 401(k) plan; a health and dependent care flexible spending account; and life, medical, dental, vision and disability insurance.

FINANCIALS: Sales and profits are in thousands of dollars—add 000 to get the full amount. 2010 Note: Financial information for 2010 was not available for all companies at press time.

2010 Sales: $	2010 Profits: $	U.S. Stock Ticker: WWWW
2009 Sales: $106,489	2009 Profits: $2,609	Int'l Ticker: Int'l Exchange:
2008 Sales: $122,488	2008 Profits: $-96,210	Employees: 700
2007 Sales: $82,521	2007 Profits: $1,358	Fiscal Year Ends: 12/31
2006 Sales: $52,041	2006 Profits: $8,597	Parent Company:

SALARIES/BENEFITS:

Pension Plan:	ESOP Stock Plan:	Profit Sharing:	Top Exec. Salary: $487,500	Bonus: $292,500
Savings Plan: Y	Stock Purch. Plan: Y		Second Exec. Salary: $385,000	Bonus: $300,000

OTHER THOUGHTS:
Apparent Women Officers or Directors: 1
Hot Spot for Advancement for Women/Minorities:

LOCATIONS: ("Y" = Yes)

West:	Southwest:	Midwest:	Southeast:	Northeast:	International:
Y	Y		Y	Y	Y

WEBSENSE INC

www.websense.com

Industry Group Code: 511210E Ranks within this company's industry group: Sales: 7 Profits: 11

Hardware:	Software:		Telecommunications:	Electronic Publishing:	Equipment:	Specialty Services:
Computers:	Consumer:		Local:	Online Service:	Telecom:	Consulting:
Accessories:	Corporate:	Y	Long Distance:	TV/Cable or Wireless:	Communication:	Contract Manufacturing:
Network Equipment:	Telecom:		Cellular:	Games:	Distribution:	Processing:
Chips/Circuits:	Internet:		Internet Service:	Financial Data:	VAR/Reseller:	Staff/Outsourcing:
Parts/Drives:					Satellite Srv./Equip.:	Specialty Services:

TYPES OF BUSINESS:
Software-Employee Internet Management

BRANDS/DIVISIONS/AFFILIATES:
Websense Web Security Gateway
Websense Data Security Suite
Websense Hosted Email Security
Websense TRITION
Websense Web Security Gateway Anywhere
SurfControl
Websense Secutiry Labs

CONTACTS: Note: Officers with more than one job title may be intentionally listed here more than once.
Gene Hodges, CEO
Douglas C. Wride, COO
John R. McCormack, Pres.
Arthur S. Locke, CFO/Sr. VP
Didier Guibal, Sr. VP-Worldwide Sales
Michael Newman, General Counsel/Sr. VP
Kate Patterson, VP-Investor Rel.
John B. Carrington, Chmn.

Phone: 858-320-8000	Fax: 858-458-2950
Toll-Free: 800-723-1166	
Address: 10240 Sorrento Valley Rd., San Diego, CA 92121 US	

GROWTH PLANS/SPECIAL FEATURES:
Websense, Inc. is a leading provider of Web filtering and security, data loss prevention (DLP), and e-mail anti-spam and security products to over 44 million employees at organizations worldwide. It organizes its offerings into three categories: web security; e-mail and messaging; and data security products, available as server-based software or hosted (on-demand) solutions. The company's products are designed to provide web, data and e-mail security by preventing employee access to unwanted and dangerous web elements, such as sites that contain inappropriate content or sites that download malicious code; filtering unwanted e-mails out of incoming traffic; filtering viruses and other malicious attachments out of e-mails and instant messages; managing the use of non-web Internet traffic, such as peer-to-peer communications and instant messaging; restricting the unauthorized use and loss of sensitive data, such as customer or employee information; and controlling misuse of computing resources, including the unauthorized download of high-bandwidth content. Some of the company's products include Websense Web Filter, which allows employers to analyze, report and manage employee access to the Internet; Websense Web Security Gateway, which secures Web traffic while enabling web-based applications; the Websense Data Security Suite, which discovers, protects and monitors information on a network; and Websense Hosted E-mail Security, which blocks inbound and outbound e-mail threats. Websense maintains research and development facilities in San Diego and Los Gatos, California; Reading, England; Beijing, China; and Ra'anana, Israel. In February 2010, the company announced the new Websense TRITON unified security architecture, which combines the three categories of security (web, e-mail and data) into one platform that provides analysis and management of all three. In May 2010, the company released Web Security Gateway Anywhere, a component of the TRITON system, which provides data loss prevention, advanced persistent threat prevention and hybrid Software as a Service (SaaS).

FINANCIALS: Sales and profits are in thousands of dollars—add 000 to get the full amount. 2010 Note: Financial information for 2010 was not available for all companies at press time.

2010 Sales: $	2010 Profits: $	U.S. Stock Ticker: WBSN
2009 Sales: $262,907	2009 Profits: $-10,697	Int'l Ticker: Int'l Exchange:
2008 Sales: $288,274	2008 Profits: $-26,779	Employees: 1,452
2007 Sales: $210,307	2007 Profits: $-16,481	Fiscal Year Ends: 12/31
2006 Sales: $178,814	2006 Profits: $32,093	Parent Company:

SALARIES/BENEFITS:

Pension Plan:	ESOP Stock Plan:	Profit Sharing:	Top Exec. Salary: $578,423	Bonus: $561,070
Savings Plan: Y	Stock Purch. Plan:		Second Exec. Salary: $415,383	Bonus: $276,116

OTHER THOUGHTS:
Apparent Women Officers or Directors: 2
Hot Spot for Advancement for Women/Minorities: Y

LOCATIONS: ("Y" = Yes)

West:	Southwest:	Midwest:	Southeast:	Northeast:	International:
Y	Y				Y

WESTELL TECHNOLOGIES INC

www.westell.com

Industry Group Code: 334210 Ranks within this company's industry group: Sales: 16   Profits: 6

Hardware:		Software:		Telecommunications:	Electronic Publishing:	Equipment:		Specialty Services:	
Computers:		Consumer:		Local:	Online Service:	Telecom:	Y	Consulting:	
Accessories:		Corporate:	Y	Long Distance:	TV/Cable or Wireless:	Communication:		Contract Manufacturing:	
Network Equipment:	Y	Telecom:		Cellular:	Games:	Distribution:		Processing:	
Chips/Circuits:		Internet:		Internet Service:	Financial Data:	VAR/Reseller:		Staff/Outsourcing:	
Parts/Drives:						Satellite Srv./Equip.:		Specialty Services:	Y

TYPES OF BUSINESS:

Telecommunications Equipment-High-Speed Data Transmission
Broadband & DSL Solutions
Modems, Switches, Routers & Gateways
Home Networking Equipment
Data Conferencing Services

BRANDS/DIVISIONS/AFFILIATES:

ConferencePlus Inc
OSPlant Systems
LiteLine
ProLine
VersaLink Gateway
Noran Tel
UltraLine Series3 Wireless Broadband Home Router

CONTACTS: *Note: Officers with more than one job title may be intentionally listed here more than once.*

Richard S. Gilbert, CEO
Richard S. Gilbert, Pres.
Brian S. Cooper, CFO/Sr. VP/Treas.
Mark Skurla, VP-Sales & Customer Service
Brian S. Cooper, Sec.
Amy Forster, Chief Acct. Officer/Sr. VP
Timothy J. Reedy, CEO/Pres., Conference Plus
Christopher J. Shaver, VP/Gen. Mgr.-CNS Div.
Brian Powers, VP/Mgr.-OSPlant Systems Div.
Richard S. Gilbert, Chmn.
Mark Skowronski, VP-Supply Chain Oper. & Quality

Phone: 630-898-2500	Fax: 630-375-4940
Toll-Free:	
Address: 750 N. Commons Dr., Aurora, IL 60504 US	

GROWTH PLANS/SPECIAL FEATURES:

Westell Technologies, Inc. is a holding company involved in broadband and telecommunications products. The firm operates through three segments: Customer Networking Solutions (CNS) equipment, Outside Plant Systems (OPS) equipment (together known as Combined Equipment Segments) and ConferencePlus Services. The CNS equipment allows small businesses, residential customers and small office/home office users to access and share broadband services on networked computers, media players, cell phones, televisions, telephones and other networked devices. CNS products include LiteLine and ProLine ADSL2+ Modems, enabling residential and small office/home office (SOHO) customers to connect one or more PCs and networking equipment to the ADSL (Asymmetric Digital Subscriber Line) service; VersaLink Gateway, enabling residential, SOHO and small businesses to network their broadband service to multiple PCs and other networked devices with wired and wireless access; and UltraLine Series3 Wireless Broadband Home Router, supporting a variety of wired and wireless broadband applications. The OSP division is a provider of next-generation outdoor cabinets, enclosures, power distribution panels, flexible edge connectors, remote monitoring solutions, DS1 and DS3 transmission plugs. The power distribution and remote monitoring solutions are provided through Westell's Noran Tel subsidiary. The ConferencePlus segment, which is operated by the firm's wholly-owned subsidiary ConferencePlus, Inc., is a provider of audio, video and web conferencing services. In March 2010, Westell formed a joint development agreement with fiber management solutions provider Clearfield, Inc., thereby incorporating Clearfield's Clearview Cassette into its outside plant enclosure operations.

FINANCIALS: Sales and profits are in thousands of dollars—add 000 to get the full amount. 2010 Note: Financial information for 2010 was not available for all companies at press time.

2010 Sales: $181,485	2010 Profits: $10,327	**U.S. Stock Ticker: WSTL**
2009 Sales: $185,916	2009 Profits: $-16,594	**Int'l Ticker:** Int'l Exchange:
2008 Sales: $205,729	2008 Profits: $-76,230	Employees: 380
2007 Sales: $256,533	2007 Profits: $8,694	Fiscal Year Ends: 3/31
2006 Sales: $283,171	2006 Profits: $12,847	Parent Company:

SALARIES/BENEFITS:

Pension Plan:	ESOP Stock Plan:	Profit Sharing:	Top Exec. Salary: $500,000	Bonus: $334,500
Savings Plan: Y	Stock Purch. Plan: Y		Second Exec. Salary: $286,200	Bonus: $170,595

OTHER THOUGHTS:

Apparent Women Officers or Directors: 2
Hot Spot for Advancement for Women/Minorities:

LOCATIONS: ("Y" = Yes)

West:	Southwest:	Midwest:	Southeast:	Northeast:	International:
		Y			Y

WESTERN DIGITAL CORP

www.westerndigital.com

Industry Group Code: 334112 Ranks within this company's industry group: Sales: 3   Profits: 2

Hardware:	Software:	Telecommunications:	Electronic Publishing:	Equipment:	Specialty Services:
Computers:	Consumer:	Local:	Online Service:	Telecom:	Consulting:
Accessories:	Corporate:	Long Distance:	TV/Cable or Wireless:	Communication:	Contract Manufacturing:
Network Equipment:	Telecom:	Cellular:	Games:	Distribution:	Processing:
Chips/Circuits:	Internet:	Internet Service:	Financial Data:	VAR/Reseller:	Staff/Outsourcing:
Parts/Drives: Y				Satellite Srv./Equip.:	Specialty Services:

TYPES OF BUSINESS:

Data Storage Hardware
Hard Drives

BRANDS/DIVISIONS/AFFILIATES:

SiliconEdge
Caviar
S25
SiliconDrive
VelociRaptor
My Passport
My Book
GreenPower

CONTACTS: *Note: Officers with more than one job title may be intentionally listed here more than once.*

John F. Coyne, CEO
Timothy M. Leyden, COO
John F. Coyne, Pres.
Wolfgang U. Nickl, CFO/Sr. VP
James J. Murphy, Exec. VP-Worldwide Sales & Sales Oper.
James D. Morris, Exec. VP/Gen. Mgr.-Storage Prod.
James K. Welsh, Exec. VP/Gen. Mgr.-Branded Prod.
Thomas E. Pardun, Chmn.

Phone: 949-672-7000	Fax: 949-672-5490
Toll-Free:	
Address: 20511 Lake Forest Dr., Lake Forest, CA 92630-7741 US	

GROWTH PLANS/SPECIAL FEATURES:

Western Digital Corp. (WD) designs, develops, manufactures and sells hard drives. Hard drives are storage devices that are key components of computers including desktop and notebook computers; data storage subsystems; and other consumer electronic devices. WD hard drives include 3.5-inch and 2.5-inch form factor drives and have capacities ranging from 80 gigabytes to 3 terabytes with nominal rotation speeds up to 10,000 RPM. The company also sells external hard drives, stand alone storage products, compatible with most new PC systems, which allow users to supplement the storage space of their computers. Hard drive products include desktop hard drives, designed for desktop PCs; mobile hard drives, designed for use with notebook computers; enterprise hard drive products, designed for business use and the high-end PC market; consumer electronics, hard drives that may be used in products such as DVRs and karaoke systems; and other branded products. The company has recently expanded its offerings to include solid state drives and media players. Solid-state drives, constructed with semiconductor material and marketed under the SiliconEdge and SiliconDrive brands, are used in embedded systems markets, which include network-communications; industrial, embedded-computing; medical; military; aerospace; media appliance and data streaming applications. WD media players can be used to play digital movies music and photos from WD storage devices. WD brand names include the WD S25, WD RE, WD Velociraptor, WD Scorpio, My Passport, My Book, My DVR Expander and WD Greenpower Technology, designed to consume substantially less power than standard drives. In June 2010, the company acquired Hoya Corporation's magnetic media business for about $233 million. In October 2010, the firm commenced manufacturing operations in Brazil.

The firm offers its employees a 401(k) plan; health, dental and vision coverage; life and AD&D insurance; educational reimbursements; adoption assistance; and an employee assistance program.

FINANCIALS: Sales and profits are in thousands of dollars—add 000 to get the full amount. 2010 Note: Financial information for 2010 was not available for all companies at press time.

2010 Sales: $9,850,000	2010 Profits: $1,382,000	U.S. Stock Ticker: WDC
2009 Sales: $7,453,000	2009 Profits: $470,000	Int'l Ticker: Int'l Exchange:
2008 Sales: $8,074,000	2008 Profits: $867,000	Employees: 62,500
2007 Sales: $5,468,000	2007 Profits: $564,000	Fiscal Year Ends: 6/30
2006 Sales: $4,341,300	2006 Profits: $395,900	Parent Company:

SALARIES/BENEFITS:

Pension Plan:	ESOP Stock Plan:	Profit Sharing:	Top Exec. Salary: $807,692	Bonus: $3,645,673
Savings Plan: Y	Stock Purch. Plan:		Second Exec. Salary: $507,692	Bonus: $1,122,275

OTHER THOUGHTS:

Apparent Women Officers or Directors: 1
Hot Spot for Advancement for Women/Minorities:

LOCATIONS: ("Y" = Yes)

West:	Southwest:	Midwest:	Southeast:	Northeast:	International:
Y					Y

WIND RIVER SYSTEMS INC

www.windriver.com

Industry Group Code: 511210I Ranks within this company's industry group: Sales: Profits:

Hardware:	Software:		Telecommunications:	Electronic Publishing:	Equipment:	Specialty Services:	
Computers:	Consumer:		Local:	Online Service:	Telecom:	Consulting:	Y
Accessories:	Corporate:	Y	Long Distance:	TV/Cable or Wireless:	Communication:	Contract Manufacturing:	
Network Equipment:	Telecom:		Cellular:	Games:	Distribution:	Processing:	
Chips/Circuits:	Internet:		Internet Service:	Financial Data:	VAR/Reseller:	Staff/Outsourcing:	
Parts/Drives:					Satellite Srv./Equip.:	Specialty Services:	Y

TYPES OF BUSINESS:

Computer Software-Embedded Systems
Consulting Services
Operating Systems
Device Software Optimization

BRANDS/DIVISIONS/AFFILIATES:

Intel Corporation
Wind River Workbench
VxWorks
Wind River Network Acceleration Platform
Wind River Test Management

CONTACTS: Note: Officers with more than one job title may be intentionally listed here more than once.

Barry Mainz, COO
Ken Klein, Pres.
Ian Halifax, CFO
Jim Douglas, Sr. VP-Mktg.
Jeff Loehr, Sr. VP-Human Resources
Tomas Evensen, CTO/Gen. Mgr.-Common Tech. Prod. Div.
Scot Morrison, Sr. VP-Prod.
Ian Halifax, Sr. VP-Admin.
Ian Halifax, Sec.
Roger Williams, VP-Bus. Dev. & Alliances
Vincent Rerolle, Chief Strategy Officer
Ian Halifax, Sr. VP-Finance
Tomas Evensen, VP/Gen. Mgr.-Wind River Tools
Amit Ronen, VP/Gen. Mgr.-Device Mgmt. Prod. Div.
Damian Artt, VP-Worldwide Sales & Svcs.

Phone: 510-748-4100	Fax: 510-749-2010
Toll-Free: 800-545-9463	
Address: 500 Wind River Way, Alameda, CA 94501 US	

GROWTH PLANS/SPECIAL FEATURES:

Wind River Systems, Inc., a leader in device software optimization (DSO), is a wholly-owned subsidiary of Intel Corporation. The firm develops, markets and sells operating systems, middleware and software development tools for embedded systems to be used in a diverse range of products, including set-top boxes; automobile braking and navigation systems; mobile handsets; Internet routers; avionics control panels; and coronary pacemakers. Because the company's solutions are hardware-agnostic, they may bedeployed on several architectures, including Intel, ARM, PowerPC, Freescale, MIPS and others. Wind River offers five primary services: VxWorks, which consists of the firm's proprietary VxWorks real-time operating system and related products; Linux, which comprises Wind River's open-source-based, commercial-grade Linux operating systems and related products; Windriver Workbench, an Eclipse-based software development suite, which allows customers to manage the design, development, debugging and testing of their device software systems; Industry solutions, which offers solutions to the consumer electronics, automotive, aerospace/defense, network infrastructure, and industrial markets; and on-chip debugging tools, which simplify the hardware development process and integrate firmware, hardware, and software debugging. Wind River technology is deployed in more than 500 million devices worldwide. The company offers solutions to the aerospace and defense, automotive, consumer, industrial and network equipment industries. In April 2010, the firm launched Wind River Network Acceleration Platform, a fast packet acceleration solution that provides multiple Gigabit Ethernet wire-speed performance managed by either Wind River Linux or VxWorks.

FINANCIALS: Sales and profits are in thousands of dollars—add 000 to get the full amount. 2010 Note: Financial information for 2010 was not available for all companies at press time.

2010 Sales: $	2010 Profits: $	U.S. Stock Ticker: Subsidiary
2009 Sales: $	2009 Profits: $	Int'l Ticker: Int'l Exchange:
2008 Sales: $328,631	2008 Profits: $-2,358	Employees: 1,507
2007 Sales: $285,298	2007 Profits: $ 573	Fiscal Year Ends: 1/31
2006 Sales: $266,323	2006 Profits: $29,295	Parent Company: INTEL CORP

SALARIES/BENEFITS:

Pension Plan:	ESOP Stock Plan:	Profit Sharing:	Top Exec. Salary: $650,000	Bonus: $280,000
Savings Plan:	Stock Purch. Plan:		Second Exec. Salary: $350,000	Bonus: $98,000

OTHER THOUGHTS:

Apparent Women Officers or Directors:
Hot Spot for Advancement for Women/Minorities:

LOCATIONS: ("Y" = Yes)

West:	Southwest:	Midwest:	Southeast:	Northeast:	International:
Y	Y	Y	Y	Y	Y

WIPRO LTD
www.wipro.com

Industry Group Code: 541513 Ranks within this company's industry group: Sales: 11   Profits: 6

Hardware:		Software:		Telecommunications:		Electronic Publishing:	Equipment:		Specialty Services:	
Computers:	Y	Consumer:		Local:		Online Service:	Telecom:		Consulting:	Y
Accessories:		Corporate:	Y	Long Distance:		TV/Cable or Wireless:	Communication:		Contract Manufacturing:	
Network Equipment:	Y	Telecom:	Y	Cellular:		Games:	Distribution:		Processing:	
Chips/Circuits:	Y	Internet:		Internet Service:		Financial Data:	VAR/Reseller:		Staff/Outsourcing:	Y
Parts/Drives:	Y						Satellite Srv./Equip.:		Specialty Services:	Y

TYPES OF BUSINESS:
IT Consulting & Outsourcing
Computer Hardware & Software Design
Hydraulic Equipment
Medical Electronics
Lighting Equipment
Soaps & Toiletries

BRANDS/DIVISIONS/AFFILIATES:
Wipro Technologies
Wipro Infotech
Wipro Consumer Care and Lighting
Wipro EcoEnergy
Wipro GE Medical Systems Ltd
Wipro Infrastructure Engineering

CONTACTS: *Note: Officers with more than one job title may be intentionally listed here more than once.*
Azim Premji, CEO
Suresh C. Senapaty, CFO
Rajan Kohli, Chief Mktg. Officer
Pratik Kumar, Exec. VP-Human Resources
Suresh Vaswani, Joint CEO/Exec. Dir.-IT Business
I. Vijaya Kumar, CTO
Pratik Kumar, Pres., Wipro Infrastructure Eng.
N. S. Bala, Sr. VP-Mfg.
Martha Bejar, Pres., Global Oper. & Sales
Pratik Kumar, Exec. VP-Brand & Corp. Comm.
Girish S. Paranipe, Joint CEO/Exec. Dir.-IT Business
Jagdish Ramaswamy, Chief Quality Officer
Vineet Agrawal, Pres., Wipro Consumer Care & Lighting
T.K. Kurien, Pres., Wipro EcoEnergy
Azim Premji, Chmn.
Sid Nair, Chief Sales & Oper. Officer-North America

Phone: 91-80-2844-0055	Fax: 91-80-2844-0104
Toll-Free:	
Address: Doddakannelli, Sarjapur Rd., Bangalore, 560035 India	

GROWTH PLANS/SPECIAL FEATURES:
Wipro, Ltd. is a leading global IT services company. The company provides software programs; IT consulting; business process outsourcing (BPO) services; and research and development services in the areas of hardware and software design to companies around the world. Additional offerings include IT products and consumer care and lighting which account for a small percentage of its business. Wipro operates through multiple subsidiaries, including Wipro Technologies; Wipro Infotech; Wipro Consumer Care and Lighting; Wipro EcoEnergy; Wipro Infrastructure Engineering Limited; and Wipro GE Medical Systems, Ltd. Wipro Technologies is a premier technology company and one of the world's first SEI CMM Level 5 certified IT services firms, a certification given by the Software Engineering Institute in association with Carnegie Mellon University that is widely accepted as an industry standard of software maturity and effectiveness. Wipro Technologies and Wipro Infotech are responsible for the firm's IT, BPO, R&D and Consulting services. Wipro Infotech operates in India and the Middle-East, and Wipro Technologies serves customers in the U.S., Europe, Japan, Australia and South-East Asia. Wipro Consumer Care and Lighting focuses on niche markets and offers a mix of consumer products, including soaps and toiletries; baby care products; light bulbs, fluorescent tubes and other lighting accessories; furniture; and hydrogenated oil. Wipro EcoEnergy provides equipment and services that aid clients in increasing energy efficiency and implementing renewable energy systems. Wipro Infrastructure Engineering develops and delivers hydraulic cylinders, water treatment systems and clean energy systems to original equipment manufacturers (OEMs) worldwide. Wipro GE Medical Systems, a joint venture with General Electric (GE), provides South-Asian markets with GE products and after-sales services for all GE medical products sold to them. In November 2010, the company announced plans to convert a recently purchased facility in North Carolina into a state of the art IT infrastructure data center.

FINANCIALS: Sales and profits are in thousands of dollars—add 000 to get the full amount. 2010 Note: Financial information for 2010 was not available for all companies at press time.

2010 Sales: $6,050,000	2010 Profits: $1,026,000	**U.S. Stock Ticker: WIT**
2009 Sales: $5,004,000	2009 Profits: $677,000	**Int'l Ticker: 507685** Int'l Exchange: Bombay-BSE
2008 Sales: $4,933,000	2008 Profits: $806,000	Employees: 108,000
2007 Sales: $3,467,000	2007 Profits: $677,000	Fiscal Year Ends: 3/31
2006 Sales: $2,385,500	2006 Profits: $455,710	Parent Company:

SALARIES/BENEFITS:
Pension Plan:	ESOP Stock Plan:	Profit Sharing:	Top Exec. Salary: $416,167	Bonus: $354,631
Savings Plan:	Stock Purch. Plan:		Second Exec. Salary: $257,276	Bonus: $186,017

OTHER THOUGHTS:
Apparent Women Officers or Directors: 2
Hot Spot for Advancement for Women/Minorities:

LOCATIONS: ("Y" = Yes)
West:	Southwest:	Midwest:	Southeast:	Northeast:	International:
Y	Y	Y	Y	Y	Y

WYSE TECHNOLOGY INC

www.wyse.com

Industry Group Code: 518210 Ranks within this company's industry group: Sales: Profits:

Hardware:		Software:		Telecommunications:	Electronic Publishing:	Equipment:		Specialty Services:	
Computers:		Consumer:		Local:	Online Service:	Telecom:		Consulting:	
Accessories:		Corporate:	Y	Long Distance:	TV/Cable or Wireless:	Communication:	Y	Contract Manufacturing:	
Network Equipment:	Y	Telecom:		Cellular:	Games:	Distribution:		Processing:	
Chips/Circuits:		Internet:	Y	Internet Service:	Financial Data:	VAR/Reseller:		Staff/Outsourcing:	
Parts/Drives:						Satellite Srv./Equip.:		Specialty Services:	Y

TYPES OF BUSINESS:
Cloud Computing Services
Virtualization Services
Thin Client Manufacturing
Software Development

BRANDS/DIVISIONS/AFFILIATES:
Wyse ThinOS
Wyse Zero
Wyse Mobile Cloud Software
Wyse Cloud PC Software

CONTACTS: *Note: Officers with more than one job title may be intentionally listed here more than once.*
Tarkan Maner, CEO
Phil Underwood, COO
Tarkan Maner, Pres.
Lumin Chang, CFO
Maryam Alexandrian, Sr. VP-Worldwide Sales & Channels
Jamie Horejs, Dir.-People Dev.
Curt Schwebke, CTO
Anthony Armenta, Sr. VP-Prod. Dev.
Cheree McAlpine, General Counsel/VP
Ricardo Antuna, Sr. VP-Bus. Dev. & Alliances
Ricardo Antuna, Sr. VP-Prod. Mgmt.
Daniel Barreto, Gen. Mgr.-Mobile Cloud Bus. Unit
Jeff McNaught, Chief Mktg. & Strategy Officer

Phone: 408-473-1200	Fax:
Toll-Free: 800-438-9973	
Address: 3471 North First St., San Jose, CA 95134-1801 US	

GROWTH PLANS/SPECIAL FEATURES:

Wyse Technology, Inc. is a global provider of cloud client computing services. Wyse provides clients with networked data storage and access to a wide variety of software applications as an alternative to storing data and software on individual PCs. It does so through cloud client computing, thin computing and zero client computing, which allows users to find, enter and analyze data through thin or zero client terminals (including desktop and mobile units) connected to the Internet. Wyse's software, hardware and network systems securely store data across a broad network of servers which relay data on demand to thin or zero clients. The firm has shipped more than 20 million client terminals and has over 200 million users interacting with Wyse products on a daily basis. Wyse partners with leading InfoTech firms including Citrix, IBM, Microsoft and VMware. Products and services are organized into three areas: Cloud Clients, Cloud Software and Service and Support. Cloud Clients focuses on hardware such as desktop and laptop units, handheld units and Wyse ThinOS which connects users to necessary applications and data. Cloud Software is segmented into a number of connection tools such as Wyse Zero, Wyse Mobile Cloud Software and Wyse Cloud PC Software, in addition to data management and virtualization software. Service and Support provides software services such as customized imaging, deployment services, on-site maintenance and training. In addition to its California headquarters, the company maintains offices around the world.

FINANCIALS: Sales and profits are in thousands of dollars—add 000 to get the full amount. 2010 Note: Financial information for 2010 was not available for all companies at press time.

2010 Sales: $	2010 Profits: $	**U.S. Stock Ticker:** Private
2009 Sales: $	2009 Profits: $	**Int'l Ticker:** Int'l Exchange:
2008 Sales: $	2008 Profits: $	Employees:
2007 Sales: $	2007 Profits: $	Fiscal Year Ends:
2006 Sales: $	2006 Profits: $	Parent Company:

SALARIES/BENEFITS:

Pension Plan:	ESOP Stock Plan:	Profit Sharing:	Top Exec. Salary: $	Bonus: $
Savings Plan:	Stock Purch. Plan:		Second Exec. Salary: $	Bonus: $

OTHER THOUGHTS:
Apparent Women Officers or Directors: 4
Hot Spot for Advancement for Women/Minorities: Y

LOCATIONS: ("Y" = Yes)

West:	Southwest:	Midwest:	Southeast:	Northeast:	International:
Y					Y

XEROX CORP

www.xerox.com

Industry Group Code: 333313 Ranks within this company's industry group: Sales: 2   Profits: 1

Hardware:		Software:		Telecommunications:	Electronic Publishing:	Equipment:	Specialty Services:
Computers:		Consumer:		Local:	Online Service:	Telecom:	Consulting:
Accessories:	Y	Corporate:	Y	Long Distance:	TV/Cable or Wireless:	Communication:	Contract Manufacturing:
Network Equipment:		Telecom:		Cellular:	Games:	Distribution:	Processing:
Chips/Circuits:		Internet:		Internet Service:	Financial Data:	VAR/Reseller:	Staff/Outsourcing:
Parts/Drives:						Satellite Srv./Equip.:	Specialty Services:

TYPES OF BUSINESS:

Business Machines-Copiers, Printers & Scanners
Managed Print Services Outsourcing
Software
Multipurpose Office Machines
Consulting Services
Desktop Printers

BRANDS/DIVISIONS/AFFILIATES:

Fuji Xerox
DocuColor
Global Imaging Systems Inc
ColorQube
WorkCentre
Phaser
iGen
Affiliated Computer Services

CONTACTS: *Note: Officers with more than one job title may be intentionally listed here more than once.*

Ursula M. Burns, CEO
Ursula M. Burns, Pres.
Lawrence A. Zimmerman, CFO/Vice Chmn.
Christa Carone, Chief Mktg. Officer/VP
Tom Maddison, VP-Human Resources
John E. McDermott, CIO/VP
Sophie V. Vandebroek, CTO/VP/Pres., Xerox Innovation Group
Anthony M. Federico, Chief Engineer/VP
Don H. Liu, General Counsel/Sr. VP/Sec.
James A. Firestone, Exec. VP-Corporate Oper.
Uta Werner, Chief Strategy Officer/VP
James H. Lesko, VP-Investor Rel.
Gary R. Kabureck, Chief Acct. Officer/VP
John M. Kelly, Corp. VP-Xerox Global Services North America
Leslie F. Varon, VP-Finance/Controller
Jule Limoli, Pres., North American Agent Oper.
Rhonda L. Seegal, VP/Treas.
Ursula M. Burns, Chmn.
Jacques Guers, VP-Europe

Phone: 203-968-3000	Fax: 203-968-3218
Toll-Free:	
Address: 45 Glober Ave., Norwalk, CT 06856 US	

GROWTH PLANS/SPECIAL FEATURES:

Xerox Corp. is a document systems and services company operating in the global document market. It operates in three segments: Production, Office, and Other. The Production segment manufactures high-end digital monochrome and color systems designed for customers in the graphic communications industry and for large enterprises. These products enable digital on-demand printing, digital full-color printing and enterprise printing. The division offers a complete family of monochrome production systems from 65-288 pages per minute (ppm) and color production systems from 40-110 ppm. Additionally, it offers a variety of pre-press and post-press options, as well as workflow software. Key products in this segment include FreeFlow digital workflow software, the iGen family of digital production presses and the DocuColor digital presses. The Office segment develops and manufactures a range of color and black-and-white multifunction, printer, copier and fax products used by global, national, and small to mid-size commercial customers, as well as government, education and other public sectors. Office systems and services, which include monochrome devices at speeds up to 95 ppm and color devices up to 85 ppm, include the family of ColorQube, WorkCentre multifunction printers and Phaser desktop printers and multifunction printers. The Other segment primarily includes revenue from paper sales, value-added services, wide-format systems and Global Imaging Systems (GIS) network integration and electronic presentation systems. The firm receives about 50% of its revenues from services such as managed printing. Fuji Xerox, an unconsolidated entity of which Xerox owns 25%, develops, manufactures and distributes document management system, supplies and services. In February 2010, the company acquired Affiliated Computer Services, a leading provider of business process outsourcing and information technology services.

The company offers employees medical, dental and vision insurance; health care and dependent care accounts; life insurance; disability coverage; a 401(k) plan; an employee assistance program; childcare assistance; mortgage assistance; tuition assistance; and credit union membership.

FINANCIALS: Sales and profits are in thousands of dollars—add 000 to get the full amount. 2010 Note: Financial information for 2010 was not available for all companies at press time.

2010 Sales: $	2010 Profits: $	U.S. Stock Ticker: XRX
2009 Sales: $15,179,000	2009 Profits: $485,000	Int'l Ticker: Int'l Exchange:
2008 Sales: $17,608,000	2008 Profits: $230,000	Employees: 53,600
2007 Sales: $17,228,000	2007 Profits: $1,135,000	Fiscal Year Ends: 12/31
2006 Sales: $15,895,000	2006 Profits: $1,210,000	Parent Company:

SALARIES/BENEFITS:

Pension Plan:	ESOP Stock Plan:	Profit Sharing:	Top Exec. Salary: $1,160,000	Bonus: $2,331,350
Savings Plan: Y	Stock Purch. Plan:		Second Exec. Salary: $900,000	Bonus: $1,884,375

OTHER THOUGHTS:

Apparent Women Officers or Directors: 12
Hot Spot for Advancement for Women/Minorities: Y

LOCATIONS: ("Y" = Yes)

West:	Southwest:	Midwest:	Southeast:	Northeast:	International:
Y	Y	Y	Y	Y	Y

XILINX INC

www.xilinx.com

Industry Group Code: 33441 Ranks within this company's industry group: Sales: 22 Profits: 8

Hardware:		Software:		Telecommunications:		Electronic Publishing:		Equipment:		Specialty Services:	
Computers:		Consumer:		Local:		Online Service:		Telecom:		Consulting:	Y
Accessories:		Corporate:	Y	Long Distance:		TV/Cable or Wireless:		Communication:		Contract Manufacturing:	
Network Equipment:		Telecom:		Cellular:		Games:		Distribution:		Processing:	
Chips/Circuits:	Y	Internet:		Internet Service:		Financial Data:		VAR/Reseller:		Staff/Outsourcing:	
Parts/Drives:								Satellite Srv./Equip.:		Specialty Services:	Y

TYPES OF BUSINESS:

Integrated Circuits
Development System Software
Engineering & Technical Services
Design Services & Field Engineering
Customer Training & Tech. Support

BRANDS/DIVISIONS/AFFILIATES:

Virtex
Spartan
CoolRunner

CONTACTS: Note: Officers with more than one job title may be intentionally listed here more than once.

Moshe Gavrielov, CEO
Moshe Gavrielov, Pres.
Jon Olson, CFO/Sr. VP
Vin Ratford, Sr. VP-Worldwide Mktg.
Marilyn Stiborek, VP-Worldwide Human Resources
Kevin Cooney, CIO/VP
Ivo Bolsens, CTO/Sr. VP
Scott Hover-Smoot, General Counsel/VP/Sec.
Raja Petrakian, Sr. VP-Worldwide Oper.
Krishna Rangasayee, VP-Corp. Strategic Planning
Frank Tornaghi, Sr. VP-Worldwide Sales
Vincent Tong, Sr. VP-Worldwide Quality & New Prod. Introductions
Victor Peng, Sr. VP-Programmable Platforms Dev.
Philip T. Gianos, Chmn.
Sam Rogan, Pres., Xilinx Japan

Phone: 408-559-7778	Fax: 408-559-7114
Toll-Free:	
Address: 2100 Logic Dr., San Jose, CA 95124-3400 US	

GROWTH PLANS/SPECIAL FEATURES:

Xilinx, Inc. is a leading developer and provider of programmable logic devices (PLDs) and related products, competing in the semiconductor industry. Logic devices are used to manage the interchange and manipulation of digital signals within an electronic system. PLDs have an advantage over alternative devices, such as custom gate arrays and application specific integrated circuits (ASICs), because PLDs can be programmed to perform whatever function the user requires, whereas the operations of other devices are fixed. Types of PLDs manufactured by the company include field programmable gate arrays (FPGAs) and complex programmable devices (CPLDs), which have applications in a variety of industries including wired and wireless communications; industrial; scientific and medical; aerospace and defense; audio, video and broadcast; consumer; automotive; and data processing. The firm's leading FPGA brands are the Virtex series, including the Virtex-II, Virtex-E, Virtex-4, Virtex-5 and Virtex-6, and Spartan Products, including the Spartan-II, Spartan-3 and Spartan-6. CoolRunner is the company's main CPLD brand. In addition to PLDs, Xilinx offerings include software design tools to program the PLDs, intellectual property, design services, customer training, field engineering and technical support. The firm has also developed a technology that enables the hardware in Xilinx-based systems to be upgraded remotely over any kind of private or public network, including the Internet, even after the equipment has been shipped to a customer. This upgradable system allows equipment manufacturers to add new features and capabilities remotely to installed systems or repair problems without having to buy new hardware.

The company offers its employees stock options; medical, dental and vision insurance; tuition reimbursement; short- and long-term disability insurance; life and AD&D insurance; auto and home insurance; and pet insurance.

FINANCIALS: Sales and profits are in thousands of dollars—add 000 to get the full amount. 2010 Note: Financial information for 2010 was not available for all companies at press time.

2010 Sales: $1,833,554	2010 Profits: $357,484	**U.S. Stock Ticker: XLNX**
2009 Sales: $1,825,184	2009 Profits: $375,640	**Int'l Ticker:** Int'l Exchange:
2008 Sales: $1,841,372	2008 Profits: $374,047	Employees: 2,948
2007 Sales: $1,842,739	2007 Profits: $350,672	Fiscal Year Ends: 3/31
2006 Sales: $1,726,250	2006 Profits: $354,149	Parent Company:

SALARIES/BENEFITS:

Pension Plan:	ESOP Stock Plan:	Profit Sharing:	Top Exec. Salary: $606,667	Bonus: $656,250
Savings Plan: Y	Stock Purch. Plan: Y		Second Exec. Salary: $414,000	Bonus: $323,438

OTHER THOUGHTS:

Apparent Women Officers or Directors: 1
Hot Spot for Advancement for Women/Minorities:

LOCATIONS: ("Y" = Yes)

West:	Southwest:	Midwest:	Southeast:	Northeast:	International:
Y	Y				Y

YAHOO! INC

www.yahoo.com

Industry Group Code: 519130 Ranks within this company's industry group: Sales: 2   Profits: 2

Hardware:	Software:	Telecommunications:	Electronic Publishing:		Equipment:	Specialty Services:	
Computers:	Consumer:	Local:	Online Service:	Y	Telecom:	Consulting:	
Accessories:	Corporate:	Long Distance:	TV/Cable or Wireless:		Communication:	Contract Manufacturing:	
Network Equipment:	Telecom:	Cellular:	Y	Games:	Distribution:	Processing:	
Chips/Circuits:	Internet:	Internet Service:	Financial Data:		VAR/Reseller:	Staff/Outsourcing:	
Parts/Drives:					Satellite Srv./Equip.:	Specialty Services:	Y

TYPES OF BUSINESS:

Online Portal-Search Engine
Broadcast Media
Job Placement Services
Paid Positioning Services
Advertising Services
Online Business & Consumer Information
Search Technology Licensing
E-Commerce

BRANDS/DIVISIONS/AFFILIATES:

Yahoo.com
Yahoo! Hotjobs
Citizen Sports
Maktoob
Associate Content
Koprol
Yahoo! Finance
Yahoo! Sports

CONTACTS: Note: Officers with more than one job title may be intentionally listed here more than once.

Carol Bartz, CEO
Timothy R. Morse, CFO/Exec. VP
Elisa Steele, Chief Mktg. Officer/Exec. VP
David Windley, Chief Human Resources Officer/Exec. VP
Prabhakar Raghavan, Chief Scientist/Head-Yahoo Labs/Sr. VP
Blake Irving, Chief Products Officer/Exec. VP
David Dibble, Exec. VP-Service Eng.
Michael J. Callahan, General Counsel/Exec. VP/Sec.
David Dibble, Exec. VP-Oper.
Eric C. Brown, Sr. VP-Global Comm.
Michael A. Murray, Sr. VP-Finance/Chief Acct. Officer
Jerry Yang, Co-Founder/Chief Yahoo
Hilary Schneider, Exec. VP-Americas Region
David Filo, Co-founder/Chief Yahoo
Rose Tsou, Sr. VP-APAC Region
Roy J. Bostock, Chmn.
Rich Riley, Sr. VP-Europe & Canada

Phone: 408-349-3300	Fax: 408-349-3301
Toll-Free:	
Address: 701 First Ave., Sunnyvale, CA 94089 US	

GROWTH PLANS/SPECIAL FEATURES:

Yahoo! Inc. is a provider of online products and services to consumers and businesses worldwide. For users, the company's offerings fall into four categories: Integrated Consumer Experiences, Applications, Search, and Media Products and Solutions. Integrated Consumer Experiences includes the Yahoo! Home page, My Yahoo!, the Yahoo! Toolbar, Yahoo! Local and Connected TV. The Applications segment further breaks down into Communications, including Yahoo! Mail and Yahoo! Messenger, and Communities, which includes Yahoo! Groups, Yahoo! Answers, and Flickr. The Company's Search offering is the company's widely-recognized and proprietary Yahoo! Search engine. Its Media Products and Solutions segment includes Yahoo! News, Yahoo! Finance, Yahoo! Sports and Yahoo! Entertainment & Lifestyles. For advertisers and publishers, Yahoo! provides a range of marketing solutions and tools that enable businesses to reach users who visit Yahoo! Properties and its Affiliate sites. For developers, Yahoo provides an innovative and easily accessible array of Web Services and Application Programming Interfaces (APIs), technical resources, tools, and channels to market. Yahoo! is present in over 50 countries in Europe, Latin America, Asia Pacific and North America. The company also operates Yahoo! HotJobs.com, Ltd., a leading Internet job placement and recruiting company. In August 2009, the company announced an agreement to acquire Maktoob.com, the largest online community in the Arab world. In December 2009, Yahoo announced an agreement with Microsoft in which Microsoft provides the algorithmic technology and paid search services for Yahoo! Search while Yahoo serves as the sales force for advertising for both. In March 2010, Yahoo announced an agreement to acquire Citizen Sports, a sports content provider for social networking sites and mobile devices. In May 2010, the firm announced an agreement to acquire Associated Content, a major online content provider. In May 2010, Yahoo announced the acquisition of Koprol, an Indonesian-based social community.

FINANCIALS: Sales and profits are in thousands of dollars—add 000 to get the full amount. 2010 Note: Financial information for 2010 was not available for all companies at press time.

2010 Sales: $	2010 Profits: $	U.S. Stock Ticker: YHOO
2009 Sales: $6,460,315	2009 Profits: $605,289	Int'l Ticker: Int'l Exchange:
2008 Sales: $7,208,502	2008 Profits: $424,298	Employees: 13,900
2007 Sales: $6,969,274	2007 Profits: $660,000	Fiscal Year Ends: 12/31
2006 Sales: $6,425,679	2006 Profits: $751,391	Parent Company:

SALARIES/BENEFITS:

Pension Plan:	ESOP Stock Plan:	Profit Sharing:	Top Exec. Salary: $969,872	Bonus: $1,500,000
Savings Plan: Y	Stock Purch. Plan: Y		Second Exec. Salary: $600,000	Bonus: $1,113,333

OTHER THOUGHTS:

Apparent Women Officers or Directors: 6
Hot Spot for Advancement for Women/Minorities: Y

LOCATIONS: ("Y" = Yes)

West:	Southwest:	Midwest:	Southeast:	Northeast:	International:
Y					Y

ZEBRA TECHNOLOGIES CORP

www.zebra.com

Industry Group Code: 334119 Ranks within this company's industry group: Sales: 17   Profits: 11

Hardware:		Software:		Telecommunications:	Electronic Publishing:	Equipment:	Specialty Services:
Computers:		Consumer:		Local:	Online Service:	Telecom:	Consulting:
Accessories:	Y	Corporate:	Y	Long Distance:	TV/Cable or Wireless:	Communication:	Contract Manufacturing:
Network Equipment:		Telecom:		Cellular:	Games:	Distribution:	Processing:
Chips/Circuits:		Internet:		Internet Service:	Financial Data:	VAR/Reseller:	Staff/Outsourcing:
Parts/Drives:						Satellite Srv./Equip.:	Specialty Services:

TYPES OF BUSINESS:

Computer Accessories-Bar Code & Plastic Card Printers
Printer-Related Software
RFID Products

BRANDS/DIVISIONS/AFFILIATES:

Specialty Printing Group
Zebra Enterprise Solutions Group
Zebralink Multiplatform Software Development Kit

CONTACTS: Note: Officers with more than one job title may be intentionally listed here more than once.

Anders Gustafsson, CEO
Michael C. Smiley, CFO/Treas.
Tara Ryan, Sr. VP-Corp. Mktg.
Joanne Townsend, VP-Human Resources
Jim L. Kaput, General Counsel/Sr. VP/Sec.
Hugh K Gagnier, Sr. VP-Oper.
Philip Gerskovich, VP-Corp. Dev.
Douglas A. Fox, Dir.-Investor Rel.
Todd Naughton, VP-Finance
Michael H. Terzich, Sr. VP-Specialty Printer
Gerhard Cless, Exec. VP
Bill Walsh, Sr. VP/Gen. Mgr.-Zebra Enterprise Solutions
Michael A. Smith, Chmn.

Phone: 847-634-6700	Fax: 847-913-8766
Toll-Free: 866-230-9494	
Address: 333 Corporate Woods Pkwy., Vernon Hills, IL 60061-3109 US	

GROWTH PLANS/SPECIAL FEATURES:

Zebra Technologies Corp. and its subsidiaries deliver products that help businesses identify, track and manage assets, transactions and people. Through its subsidiary, Zebra Specialty Printing Group (SPG), the company designs, manufactures and sells specialty printing devices that dispense labels, tickets, receipts, plastic identification cards, wristbands and tags. Its products include direct thermal and thermal bar code label and receipt printers and supplies; plastic card printers; passive radio frequency identification (RFID) printer/encoders; dye sublimation card printers; and digital photo printers. Its products are designed to operate at the user's location or on a mobile basis to produce and dispense labels and plastic cards in time-sensitive applications. A subsidiary, Zebra Enterprise Solutions Group (ESG), offers asset tracking and management services to optimize the flow of goods in complex logistical operations such as cargo shipping. The firm also provides maintenance and repair services. A substantial majority of ESG's business consists of software licenses and related service including maintenance, support and consulting services. It also sells Zebra's proprietary real time asset management hardware. Zebra products are sold primarily through distributors, resellers and original equipment manufacturers, but products are also sold directly to select customers and through the company's Internet and telesales operations. The firm has customers in more than 100 countries that include manufacturing and service organizations, Fortune 500 companies and governments, for use in automatic identification, data collection and personal identification systems. The ZebraLink Multiplatform Software Development Kit and Smart Phone Utility allows users to print field service records, tracking tags, point-of-sale receipts and more from their BlackBerry smartphones. In April 2010, the company opened a thermal printer accesory research and development center in Guangzhou, China.

Zebra offers its employees benefits including medical, dental and prescription drug plans; life, disability and AD&D insurance; flexible spending accounts; tuition assistance; and an on-site cafeteria.

FINANCIALS: Sales and profits are in thousands of dollars—add 000 to get the full amount. 2010 Note: Financial information for 2010 was not available for all companies at press time.

2010 Sales: $	2010 Profits: $	U.S. Stock Ticker: ZBRA
2009 Sales: $803,585	2009 Profits: $47,104	Int'l Ticker: Int'l Exchange:
2008 Sales: $976,700	2008 Profits: $-38,421	Employees: 2,700
2007 Sales: $868,279	2007 Profits: $110,113	Fiscal Year Ends: 12/31
2006 Sales: $759,524	2006 Profits: $70,946	Parent Company:

SALARIES/BENEFITS:

Pension Plan:	ESOP Stock Plan:	Profit Sharing:	Top Exec. Salary: $700,000	Bonus: $146,468
Savings Plan: Y	Stock Purch. Plan: Y		Second Exec. Salary: $378,000	Bonus: $39,546

OTHER THOUGHTS:

Apparent Women Officers or Directors: 2
Hot Spot for Advancement for Women/Minorities:

LOCATIONS: ("Y" = Yes)

West:	Southwest:	Midwest:	Southeast:	Northeast:	International:
Y		Y	Y	Y	Y

Note: Financial information, benefits and other data can change quickly and may vary from those stated here.

ZOOM TECHNOLOGIES INC

www.zoomleimone.com

Industry Group Code: 3342 Ranks within this company's industry group: Sales: 5 Profits: 3

Hardware:		Software:	Telecommunications:	Electronic Publishing:	Equipment:	Specialty Services:
Computers:		Consumer:	Local:	Online Service:	Telecom:	Consulting:
Accessories:	Y	Corporate:	Long Distance:	TV/Cable or Wireless:	Communication:	Contract Manufacturing:
Network Equipment:	Y	Telecom:	Cellular:	Games:	Distribution:	Processing:
Chips/Circuits:		Internet:	Internet Service:	Financial Data:	VAR/Reseller:	Staff/Outsourcing:
Parts/Drives:					Satellite Srv./Equip.:	Specialty Services:

TYPES OF BUSINESS:

Mobile Phone Manufacturing

BRANDS/DIVISIONS/AFFILIATES:

Gold Lion Holding Ltd
TCB Digital
Profit Harvest
Jiangsu Leimone
China Telecom
China UNICOM
China Mobile

CONTACTS: *Note: Officers with more than one job title may be intentionally listed here more than once.*

Lei Gu, CEO
Anthony K. Chan, CFO
Anthony K. Chan, Corp. Sec.
Zuohua Yin, Gen. Mgr.
Lei Gu, Chmn.

Phone:	Fax:
Toll-Free:	
Address: No.6 Zhongguancun South St., Rm. 608, CEC Bldg., Beijing, 100086 China	

GROWTH PLANS/SPECIAL FEATURES:

Zoom Technologies, Inc. is a tech company engaged primarily in the development, manufacture and sale of wireless communications technology and related software products. The firm operates via wholly-owned subsidiary Gold Lion Holding Limited. Gold Lion owns 100% of Jiangsu Leimone Electronics Co., Ltd.; 51% of Tianjin Tong Guang Group Digital Communication Co., Ltd. (TCB Digital); and 100% of Profit Harvest Corporation Ltd. Jiangsu Leimone produces electronic components for 3rd generation mobile phones, wireless communication circuitry, GPS equipment and related software products. TCB Digital has two main business operations: providing Electronic Manufacturing Service for OEM (Original Equipment Manufacturer) customers, and designing and producing mobile phone products. TCB Digital's major products include mobile phones, wireless telecommunication modules, digital cameras, cable TV set-up boxes and GPS equipment. In addition, TCB Digital develops various state-of-art feature mobile phones and Smartphones based on TD-SCDMA, GSM, WCDMA and CDMA technologies. Profit Harvest is the sales and marketing arm of TCB Digital. Through Profit Harvest, the company markets its mobile phone products through retail distributors in China and supplies to major operator customers such as China Mobile (CMCC), China UNICOM and China Telecom. In 2009, TCB Digital custom made two models of CDMA mobile phone for China Telecom. These models are sold through China Telecom's retail network and carry both logos of China Telecom and the LEIMONE brand. In September 2009, the company acquired Gold Lion; pursuant to this transaction, the company's Zoom Telephonics, Inc. subsidiary, which consolidated Zoom Technology's former business operations, was spun off into a separate, publicly traded company. In April 2010, the firm unveiled the LEIMONE E63, its first in a series of 3G brand phones.

FINANCIALS: Sales and profits are in thousands of dollars—add 000 to get the full amount. 2010 Note: Financial information for 2010 was not available for all companies at press time.

2010 Sales: $	2010 Profits: $	**U.S. Stock Ticker: ZOOM**
2009 Sales: $189,056	2009 Profits: $6,243	**Int'l Ticker:** Int'l Exchange:
2008 Sales: $80,612	2008 Profits: $3,067	Employees: 1,400
2007 Sales: $18,478	2007 Profits: $-3,503	Fiscal Year Ends: 12/31
2006 Sales: $18,322	2006 Profits: $1,030	Parent Company:

SALARIES/BENEFITS:

Pension Plan:	ESOP Stock Plan:	Profit Sharing:	Top Exec. Salary: $107,616	Bonus: $
Savings Plan:	Stock Purch. Plan:		Second Exec. Salary: $94,468	Bonus: $

OTHER THOUGHTS:

Apparent Women Officers or Directors:
Hot Spot for Advancement for Women/Minorities:

LOCATIONS: ("Y" = Yes)

West:	Southwest:	Midwest:	Southeast:	Northeast:	International:
				Y	Y

ADDITIONAL INDEXES

Contents:

INDEX OF FIRMS NOTED AS HOT SPOTS FOR ADVANCEMENT FOR WOMEN & MINORITIES

ACCENTURE PLC
ADC TELECOMMUNICATIONS INC
ADOBE SYSTEMS INC
AFFILIATED COMPUTER SERVICES INC
AKAMAI TECHNOLOGIES INC
ALCATEL-LUCENT
ALLSCRIPTS HEALTHCARE SOLUTIONS INC
ANALYSTS INTERNATIONAL CORP
ANSYS INC
APPLIED MATERIALS INC
ARCSIGHT INC
ARM HOLDINGS PLC
ART TECHNOLOGY GROUP INC
ASPECT SOFTWARE INC
ASPEN TECHNOLOGY INC
ATHEROS COMMUNICATIONS INC
ATMI INC
AUTODESK INC
AVIAT NETWORKS INC
AVID TECHNOLOGY INC
AVNET INC
BELDEN INC
BLUE COAT SYSTEMS INC
BMC SOFTWARE INC
BOE TECHNOLOGY GROUP CO LTD
CA INC (CA TECHNOLOGIES)
CACI INTERNATIONAL INC
CDW CORPORATION
CELESTICA INC
CGI GROUP INC
CHECK POINT SOFTWARE TECHNOLOGIES LTD
CHIMEI INNOLUX CORPORATION
CIBER INC
CISCO SYSTEMS INC
COMMTOUCH SOFTWARE LTD
COMPUWARE CORP
COREL CORPORATION
CRAY INC
CSG SYSTEMS INTERNATIONAL INC
DASSAULT SYSTEMES SA
DIEBOLD INC
DIGITAL ANGEL CORP
DIGITAL CHINA HOLDINGS LIMITED
DIMENSION DATA HOLDINGS PLC
DRS TECHNOLOGIES INC
ECHELON CORP
ELECTRONIC ARTS INC
FORCE10 NETWORKS INC
FORRESTER RESEARCH INC
GARTNER INC
GSI COMMERCE INC
GUIDEWIRE SOFTWARE INC
HARRIS CORPORATION
HEWLETT-PACKARD CO (HP)

IKON OFFICE SOLUTIONS INC
IMATION CORP
IMMERSION CORP
INDRA SISTEMAS SA
INDUSTRIAL & FINANCIAL SYSTEMS (IFS) AB
INFOR GLOBAL SOLUTIONS
INGRAM MICRO INC
INSIGHT ENTERPRISES INC
INTEL CORP
INTERMEC INC
INTERNATIONAL BUSINESS MACHINES CORP (IBM)
INTUIT INC
JABIL CIRCUIT INC
JDS UNIPHASE CORPORATION
JUNIPER NETWORKS INC
LABARGE INC
LAM RESEARCH CORP
LEXMARK INTERNATIONAL INC
LOGICA PLC
LOGITECH INTERNATIONAL SA
LSI CORPORATION
MANTECH INTERNATIONAL CORP
MEDIAPLATFORM INC
MEDICAL INFORMATION TECHNOLOGY INC
MICROCHIP TECHNOLOGY INC
MICROS SYSTEMS INC
MICROSOFT CORP
MICROS-RETAIL
MISYS PLC
MSCSOFTWARE CORP
NCR CORPORATION
NETAPP INC
NETGEAR INC
NETSUITE INC
NOKIA CORPORATION
NOVELL INC
NUANCE COMMUNICATIONS INC
OPEN TEXT CORP
OPENWAVE SYSTEMS INC
ORACLE CORP
PC CONNECTION INC
PLANTRONICS INC
PLATO LEARNING INC
POMEROY IT SOLUTIONS
PRINTRONIX INC
QUALCOMM INC
QUEST SOFTWARE INC
RADWARE LTD
RAMBUS INC
RED HAT INC
RIGHTSCALE INC
ROVI CORPORATION
SAIC INC
SALESFORCE.COM INC
SAS INSTITUTE INC
SEACHANGE INTERNATIONAL INC
SIEMENS AG

SKYWORKS SOLUTIONS INC
SMTC CORP
SPANLINK COMMUNICATIONS
SRA INTERNATIONAL INC
STERLING COMMERCE INC
SUN MICROSYSTEMS INC
SUNGARD DATA SYSTEMS INC
SYMANTEC CORP
SYNOPSYS INC
TAIWAN SEMICONDUCTOR MANUFACTURING CO
LTD (TSMC)
TANDBERG
TEKELEC
TELCORDIA TECHNOLOGIES
TELEFON AB LM ERICSSON (ERICSSON)
TELLABS INC
TELVENT GIT SA
TERADATA CORPORATION
TEXAS INSTRUMENTS INC (TI)
THQ INC
TREND MICRO INC
TRIMBLE NAVIGATION LTD
TRIZETTO GROUP INC (THE)
UNISYS CORP
VERISIGN INC
VMWARE INC
VSE CORP
WEBSENSE INC
WYSE TECHNOLOGY INC
XEROX CORP
YAHOO! INC

INDEX OF SUBSIDIARIES, BRAND NAMES AND AFFILIATIONS

Brand or subsidiary, followed by the name of the related corporation

1ShoppingCart.com; **WEB.COM GROUP INC**
2300 Exelan Flex; **LAM RESEARCH CORP**
2300 Syndion Through-Silicon Via Etch System; **LAM RESEARCH CORP**
2300 Versys Kiyo; **LAM RESEARCH CORP**
2K Games; **TAKE-TWO INTERACTIVE SOFTWARE INC**
2K Play; **TAKE-TWO INTERACTIVE SOFTWARE INC**
2K Sports; **TAKE-TWO INTERACTIVE SOFTWARE INC**
2Know!; **RENAISSANCE LEARNING INC**
360 Scheduling Ltd; **INDUSTRIAL & FINANCIAL SYSTEMS (IFS) AB**
3Dconnexion; **LOGITECH INTERNATIONAL SA**
3DTV Play; **NVIDIA CORP**
3DVIA; **DASSAULT SYSTEMES SA**
3GPP Long Term Evolution; **INTERDIGITAL INC**
3Tera, Inc.; **CA INC (CA TECHNOLOGIES)**
4G RF; **HUAWEI TECHNOLOGIES CO LTD**
ABB Group (The); **VENTYX INC**
Abend-AID; **COMPUWARE CORP**
Abengoa Group; **TELVENT GIT SA**
Abreon, Inc.; **PC MALL INC**
Academic Systems; **PLATO LEARNING INC**
Accelerated Math; **RENAISSANCE LEARNING INC**
Accelerated Path; **SKILLSOFT PLC**
Accelerated Reader; **RENAISSANCE LEARNING INC**
Accenture Mobility Operated Services; **ACCENTURE PLC**
Acceria; **ACCENTURE PLC**
Access Manager; **INDUSTRIAL DEFENDER INC**
ACCESS NetFront Browser v4 1; **ACCESS CO LTD**
ACCESS Systems Americas, Inc.; **ACCESS CO LTD**
Accton Wireless Broadband; **ACCTON TECHNOLOGY CORP**
Accudose; **ATMI INC**
Accutest Engineering Solutions Ltd; **TRIMBLE NAVIGATION LTD**
AccuTouch; **IMMERSION CORP**
ACE Analyst; **OPNET TECHNOLOGIES INC**
ACE Live; **OPNET TECHNOLOGIES INC**
Acer Inc; **GATEWAY INC**
ACI Automated Case Management; **ACI WORLDWIDE INC**
ACI Enterprise Banker; **ACI WORLDWIDE INC**
ACI Global Banker; **ACI WORLDWIDE INC**
ACI Proactive Risk Manager; **ACI WORLDWIDE INC**
Acsience; **ALTRAN TECHNOLOGIES SA**
ActivEdge 3000 Series; **CIENA CORP**
ActivEdge 5000 Series; **CIENA CORP**

ActivFlex 5400 Series; **CIENA CORP**
ActivFlex 6500; **CIENA CORP**
Activision Publishing, Inc.; **ACTIVISION BLIZZARD INC**
ActivSpan 4200 Series; **CIENA CORP**
ActivSpan 5100/5200; **CIENA CORP**
Actron Technology; **LITE-ON TECHNOLOGY CORP**
Acumem AB; **ROGUE WAVE SOFTWARE INC**
Acute Corporation; **ACCTON TECHNOLOGY CORP**
Acxiom Access-X Express; **ACXIOM CORP**
Acxiom Information Security Services (AISS); **ACXIOM CORP**
Ad Network; **BUZZ TECHNOLOGIES INC**
Adabas; **SOFTWARE AG**
Adams; **MSCSOFTWARE CORP**
Adaptive Server Enterprise; **SYBASE INC**
Address Now; **PITNEY BOWES SOFTWARE INC**
Adept ActiveV; **ADEPT TECHNOLOGY INC**
Adept Python; **ADEPT TECHNOLOGY INC**
Adept Quattro; **ADEPT TECHNOLOGY INC**
AdMarvel; **OPERA SOFTWARE ASA**
Adobe Acrobat; **ADOBE SYSTEMS INC**
Adobe Air; **ADOBE SYSTEMS INC**
Adobe Creative Suite; **ADOBE SYSTEMS INC**
Adobe Flash Player; **ADOBE SYSTEMS INC**
Adobe LiveCycle; **ADOBE SYSTEMS INC**
Adobe Photoshop; **ADOBE SYSTEMS INC**
Adobe Systems Inc; **SCENE7 INC**
Advanced Micro Devices Inc (AMD); **GLOBALFOUNDRIES**
Advanced Semiconductor Manufacturing Co. Ltd.; **NXP SEMICONDUCTORS NV**
Advanced Technology Investment Co; **GLOBALFOUNDRIES**
Advanced Technology Investment Company; **ADVANCED MICRO DEVICES INC (AMD)**
Advantest (Europe) GmbH; **ADVANTEST CORPORATION**
Advantest America Inc; **ADVANTEST CORPORATION**
Advantest Finance Inc; **ADVANTEST CORPORATION**
Advantest Laboratories Ltd; **ADVANTEST CORPORATION**
Advantest Manufacturing Inc; **ADVANTEST CORPORATION**
Affiliated Computer Services; **XEROX CORP**
AFPD Pte.; **AU OPTRONICS CORP**
AgigaTech, Inc.; **CYPRESS SEMICONDUCTOR CORP**
AhnLab HackShield Pro; **AHNLAB INC**
Aisino Bill Master; **AISINO CORPORATION INC**
Aisino Finance & Taxation Security Card; **AISINO CORPORATION INC**
Akimedia LLC; **VSE CORP**
Akita Elpida Memory Inc; **ELPIDA MEMORY INC**
Alabanza; **NAVISITE INC**
Aladdin Knowledge Systems Ltd; **SAFENET INC**
Alaska; **MARVELL TECHNOLOGY GROUP LTD**

INDEX OF SUBSIDIARIES, BRAND NAMES AND AFFILIATIONS, CONT.

Alcatel-Lucent Wireless Network Optimization;
ALCATEL-LUCENT
Aldata Software Management Inc; **SYMPHONY TECHNOLOGY GROUP**
Alienware; **DELL INC**
AllegroSystem Interconnect Platform; **CADENCE DESIGN SYSTEMS INC**
Allied Panels Entwicklungs-und Produktions Gmbh; **CELESTICA INC**
Alliente, Inc.; **ARIBA INC**
Allison Transmission, Inc.; **DRS TECHNOLOGIES INC**
Allscripts Healthcare Solutions Inc; **MISYS PLC**
Allscripts- Misys Healthcare Solutions, Inc.; **ALLSCRIPTS HEALTHCARE SOLUTIONS INC**
Allscripts-Misys Healthcare Solutions Inc; **MISYS PLC**
Alone in the Dark; **ATARI INC**
Alpine; **EXTREME NETWORKS INC**
Alps Green Device; **ALPS ELECTRIC CO LTD**
Altec Lansing; **PLANTRONICS INC**
Altran Europe; **ALTRAN TECHNOLOGIES SA**
Altran Foundation; **ALTRAN TECHNOLOGIES SA**
Altran GmbH & Co KG; **ALTRAN TECHNOLOGIES SA**
Altran India; **ALTRAN TECHNOLOGIES SA**
Altran Solutions Corp; **ALTRAN TECHNOLOGIES SA**
Altran Technologies Korea; **ALTRAN TECHNOLOGIES SA**
Ambit Enterprise Banking Suite; **SUNGARD DATA SYSTEMS INC**
Amdocs CES; **AMDOCS LTD**
American Consumer Satisfaction Index; **FORESEE RESULTS INC**
American Software ERP; **AMERICAN SOFTWARE INC**
American Software UK, Ltd.; **AMERICAN SOFTWARE INC**
American Software USA, Inc.; **AMERICAN SOFTWARE INC**
American Technical Ceramics Corp; **AVX CORPORATION**
America's Job Exchange; **NAVISITE INC**
AMI Doduco; **PULSE ELECTRONICS CORPORATION**
Ampex Data Systems Corp.; **AMPEX CORP**
Ampex Great Britain Ltd.; **AMPEX CORP**
Ampex Japan Ltd.; **AMPEX CORP**
Amstelveen Spark Innovation Center (The); **LOGICA PLC**
AMTEC Consulting plc; **KEANE INC**
Analog Copy Protection (ACP); **ROVI CORPORATION**
Android; **GOOGLE INC**
Angel.com; **MICROSTRATEGY INC**
Anix; **AFFILIATED COMPUTER SERVICES INC**
ANSYS 12.0; **ANSYS INC**
ANSYS AUTODYN; **ANSYS INC**
ANSYS DesignModeler; **ANSYS INC**

ANSYS Engineering Knowledge Manager; **ANSYS INC**
ANSYS FLUENT; **ANSYS INC**
ANSYS Workbench; **ANSYS INC**
Any2; **CORESITE REALTY CORP**
Anyo Pioneer Motor Information Technology Co. Ltd.; **PIONEER CORPORATION**
AOC; **TPV TECHNOLOGY LTD**
Apax Partners; **TRIZETTO GROUP INC (THE)**
Apax Partners, Inc; **ALTRAN TECHNOLOGIES SA**
Apex Precision Power; **CIRRUS LOGIC INC**
AppDirector; **RADWARE LTD**
AppExchange; **SALESFORCE.COM INC**
Application Development; **SERENA SOFTWARE INC**
Application Security Manager; **F5 NETWORKS INC**
Application Store; **COMVERSE TECHNOLOGY INC**
Application Streaming; **RIVERBED TECHNOLOGY INC**
ApplinX; **SOFTWARE AG**
AppMapper Xpert; **OPNET TECHNOLOGIES INC**
AppServer; **BORLAND SOFTWARE CORPORATION**
AppXcel; **RADWARE LTD**
Aprimo; **TERADATA CORPORATION**
APSolute OS; **RADWARE LTD**
APSolute Suite; **RADWARE LTD**
Aptina Imaging Corporation; **MICRON TECHNOLOGY INC**
Aquantive Inc; **MICROSOFT CORP**
Arantech; **TEKTRONIX INC**
Arbortext; **PARAMETRIC TECHNOLOGY CORP**
Arcadyan; **ACCTON TECHNOLOGY CORP**
Archer Technologies; **RSA SECURITY INC**
ArcSight Compliance; **ARCSIGHT INC**
ArcSight Connectors; **ARCSIGHT INC**
ArcSight ESM; **ARCSIGHT INC**
ArcSight Express; **ARCSIGHT INC**
ArcSight Identity View; **ARCSIGHT INC**
ArcSight Inc; **HEWLETT-PACKARD CO (HP)**
ArcSight Logger; **ARCSIGHT INC**
ArcSight Security Information and Event Management; **ARCSIGHT INC**
ARCvault; **OVERLAND STORAGE INC**
Arena Bilgisayar Sanayi Ve Ticaret Anonim Irketi; **REDINGTON (INDIA) LTD**
Arete Sistemas; **INGRAM MICRO INC**
Arkenova Sistemas; **INGRAM MICRO INC**
ARM Cortex; **ARM HOLDINGS PLC**
ARM Limited; **SEMICONDUCTOR MANUFACTURING INTERNATIONAL**
ARM Securcore; **ARM HOLDINGS PLC**
ARM11; **ARM HOLDINGS PLC**
ARM7; **ARM HOLDINGS PLC**
ARM9; **ARM HOLDINGS PLC**
ARMADA; **MARVELL TECHNOLOGY GROUP LTD**
Arraigner; **SIMTROL INC**
Arrow; **NXP SEMICONDUCTORS NV**

INDEX OF SUBSIDIARIES, BRAND NAMES AND AFFILIATIONS, CONT.

INDEX OF SUBSIDIARIES, BRAND NAMES AND AFFILIATIONS, CONT.

INDEX OF SUBSIDIARIES, BRAND NAMES AND AFFILIATIONS, CONT.

CalAmp Wireless Networks Corporation; **CALAMP CORP**
CalAmp Wireless Networks, Inc.; **CALAMP CORP**
CaliberRM; **BORLAND SOFTWARE CORPORATION**
Calibre; **MENTOR GRAPHICS CORP**
California Amplifier SARL; **CALAMP CORP**
California Amplifier, Inc.; **CALAMP CORP**
Call of Duty; **ACTIVISION BLIZZARD INC**
Call Tracking; **ART TECHNOLOGY GROUP INC**
Cambridge Entertainment Software Limited; **GIGAMEDIA LTD**
Cambridge Interactive Development Corporation; **GIGAMEDIA LTD**
Camiant; **TEKELEC**
CAMIO; **CHYRON CORP**
Campaign Director; **CONCURRENT COMPUTER CORP**
Canon Ecology Industry Inc; **CANON INC**
Canon Information Systems Co Ltd; **CANON INC**
Canon Machinery, Inc.; **CANON INC**
Canon Marketing Japan Inc; **CANON INC**
Canon Singapore PTE Ltd; **CANON INC**
CapSense; **CYPRESS SEMICONDUCTOR CORP**
Captiva Software Corp; **EMC CORP**
CarBuy.com; **TRILOGY INC**
Cardiff; **AUTONOMY CORP PLC**
CARDplus; **INDRA SISTEMAS SA**
CareAdvance Enterprise; **TRIZETTO GROUP INC (THE)**
Carlyle Group (The); **FREESCALE SEMICONDUCTOR INC**
Carnival Games; **TAKE-TWO INTERACTIVE SOFTWARE INC**
Casio America, Inc.; **CASIO COMPUTER CO LTD**
Casio Techno Co., Ltd.; **CASIO COMPUTER CO LTD**
Castlevania; **KONAMI CORP**
Catalyst Telecom; **SCANSOURCE INC**
CathLabVR; **IMMERSION CORP**
CATIA; **DASSAULT SYSTEMES SA**
Caviar; **WESTERN DIGITAL CORP**
CBS Technologies Corp.; **BLACK BOX CORPORATION**
CDC Front Office; **CDC SOFTWARE CORP**
CDC Manufacturing; **CDC SOFTWARE CORP**
CDC SaaS; **CDC SOFTWARE CORP**
CDC Solutions; **CDC SOFTWARE CORP**
CDC Solutions for Microsoft; **CDC SOFTWARE CORP**
CDC Supply Chain; **CDC SOFTWARE CORP**
CDG Systems; **CDG GROUP**
CDMA; **INTERDIGITAL INC**
CDP Backup and Recovery; **SONICWALL INC**
CDP Medical Ltd.; **ROYAL PHILIPS ELECTRONICS NV**
CDW Canada Inc; **CDW CORPORATION**

CDW Government Inc; **CDW CORPORATION**
Cegedim Dendrite; **CEGEDIM SA**
Cegedim Strategic Data; **CEGEDIM SA**
Cegers; **CEGEDIM SA**
Cellity; **NOKIA CORPORATION**
Centaur Technology Inc; **VIA TECHNOLOGIES INC**
Center for Development of Telemetics; **ITI LIMITED**
CenterVision; **BANCTEC INC**
Central Management Console (CMC); **RIVERBED TECHNOLOGY INC**
CentraSite; **SOFTWARE AG**
Certicom Corp.; **RESEARCH IN MOTION LTD (RIM)**
CGI Federal, Inc.; **CGI GROUP INC**
CGI Technologies and Solutions, Inc.; **CGI GROUP INC**
Chalk Media Corp.; **RESEARCH IN MOTION LTD (RIM)**
ChangeMan ZMF; **SERENA SOFTWARE INC**
Changepoint; **COMPUWARE CORP**
Changsha Digital China Co., Ltd.; **DIGITAL CHINA HOLDINGS LIMITED**
Check Point Full Disk Encryption; **CHECK POINT SOFTWARE TECHNOLOGIES LTD**
Check Point Power-1; **CHECK POINT SOFTWARE TECHNOLOGIES LTD**
Check Point Software Blades; **CHECK POINT SOFTWARE TECHNOLOGIES LTD**
Checker; **COGNEX CORP**
Cheetah; **SEAGATE TECHNOLOGY PLC**
Chesapeake Sciences Corporation; **L-3 COMMUNICATIONS HOLDINGS INC**
Chi Mei Optoelectronics; **CHIMEI INNOLUX CORPORATION**
Chicony America Inc; **CHICONY ELECTRONICS CO LTD**
Chicony Electronics CEZ SRO; **CHICONY ELECTRONICS CO LTD**
Chicony Electronics GmbH; **CHICONY ELECTRONICS CO LTD**
Chillingo Ltd; **ELECTRONIC ARTS INC**
China Mobile; **ZOOM TECHNOLOGIES INC**
China Telecom; **ZOOM TECHNOLOGIES INC**
China UNICOM; **ZOOM TECHNOLOGIES INC**
Chordiant Software Inc; **PEGASYSTEMS INC**
Chrome; **GOOGLE INC**
Chrome; **VIA TECHNOLOGIES INC**
Chunghwa Telecom; **QUANTA COMPUTER INC**
CIBER International; **CIBER INC**
Cicero Integrator; **CICERO INC**
Cicero XM Desktop; **CICERO INC**
Cicero XM Enterprise; **CICERO INC**
Cicero XM Integrator; **CICERO INC**
Cicero XM Studio; **CICERO INC**
Ciena One Software Suite; **CIENA CORP**
CIF 20/20; **JACK HENRY & ASSOCIATES INC**
CinemaNow Inc; **SONIC SOLUTIONS**

INDEX OF SUBSIDIARIES, BRAND NAMES AND AFFILIATIONS, CONT.

INDEX OF SUBSIDIARIES, BRAND NAMES AND AFFILIATIONS, CONT.

INDEX OF SUBSIDIARIES, BRAND NAMES AND AFFILIATIONS, CONT.

INDEX OF SUBSIDIARIES, BRAND NAMES AND AFFILIATIONS, CONT.

INDEX OF SUBSIDIARIES, BRAND NAMES AND AFFILIATIONS, CONT.

INDEX OF SUBSIDIARIES, BRAND NAMES AND AFFILIATIONS, CONT.

INDEX OF SUBSIDIARIES, BRAND NAMES AND AFFILIATIONS, CONT.

INDEX OF SUBSIDIARIES, BRAND NAMES AND AFFILIATIONS, CONT.

Indra bmb; **INDRA SISTEMAS SA**
Indra Systems, Inc.; **INDRA SISTEMAS SA**
Industrial Applications Group; **NOVELLUS SYSTEMS INC**
Industrial Defender Managed Security Services; **INDUSTRIAL DEFENDER INC**
Industrial Systems Company; **TOSHIBA CORPORATION**
iNews Instinct; **AVID TECHNOLOGY INC**
Infineon Technologies Asia Pacific Pte Ltd; **INFINEON TECHNOLOGIES AG**
Infineon Technologies Japan KK; **INFINEON TECHNOLOGIES AG**
Infineon Technologies North America Corp; **INFINEON TECHNOLOGIES AG**
InfiniBand; **MELLANOX TECHNOLOGIES LTD**
InfiniHost; **MELLANOX TECHNOLOGIES LTD**
InfiniScale; **MELLANOX TECHNOLOGIES LTD**
Infinity Engine; **BIOWARE CORP**
InfoBase-X; **ACXIOM CORP**
Infogrames Entertainment S.A.; **ATARI INC**
Infomax Communication Co. Ltd.; **MACRONIX INTERNATIONAL CO LTD**
Infopharm; **CEGEDIM SA**
Informatica Fueguina S.A.; **POSITIVO INFORMATICA SA**
InfoSante; **CEGEDIM SA**
Infosys BPO; **INFOSYS TECHNOLOGIES LTD**
Infosys China; **INFOSYS TECHNOLOGIES LTD**
Infosys Consulting; **INFOSYS TECHNOLOGIES LTD**
Infosys Leadership Institute; **INFOSYS TECHNOLOGIES LTD**
Infosys Mexico; **INFOSYS TECHNOLOGIES LTD**
Infotec; **RICOH COMPANY LTD**
InfoWay 3D; **ITAUTEC SA**
InfoWay Net W7020; **ITAUTEC SA**
InfoWay Note N8645; **ITAUTEC SA**
InfoWay Note W7415; **ITAUTEC SA**
InfoWay SM3322; **ITAUTEC SA**
InfoWay ST4254; **ITAUTEC SA**
InfoWay ST4262; **ITAUTEC SA**
Infrastructure Platform Group; **SYBASE INC**
Infrastructure Platform Group; **SYMMETRICOM INC**
Inmatrix; **SUNGARD DATA SYSTEMS INC**
InMoTx; **ADEPT TECHNOLOGY INC**
Innolux Display Corp.; **CHIMEI INNOLUX CORPORATION**
Innovation Design Center; **LENOVO GROUP LIMITED**
INPHI Design Center; **INPHI CORPORATION**
InSight; **PARAMETRIC TECHNOLOGY CORP**
In-Sight; **COGNEX CORP**
Insight Technology, Inc.; **L-3 COMMUNICATIONS HOLDINGS INC**
InSpeed; **EMULEX CORP**
Inspiron; **DELL INC**

InstantService; **ART TECHNOLOGY GROUP INC**
Institute for Quality Management, Inc.; **CACI INTERNATIONAL INC**
Intec Telecom Systems PLC; **CSG SYSTEMS INTERNATIONAL INC**
Intechra; **ARROW ELECTRONICS INC**
Integrated Concepts and Research Corporation; **VSE CORP**
Integrien; **VMWARE INC**
Integrity PadReactor; **ATMI INC**
Intel Corp; **MCAFEE INC**
Intel Corporation; **WIND RIVER SYSTEMS INC**
Intel Research Labs; **INTEL CORP**
Intelec Geomatique; **FUJITSU NETWORK COMMUNICATIONS INC**
Intelliden, Inc.; **INTERNATIONAL BUSINESS MACHINES CORP (IBM)**
Intelligent Acquisition; **MARKETLIVE INC**
Intelligent Conversion; **MARKETLIVE INC**
Intelligent Insights; **MARKETLIVE INC**
Intelligent Workload Management; **NOVELL INC**
IntelliScan; **BANCTEC INC**
Intellon Corporation; **ATHEROS COMMUNICATIONS INC**
Intera; **SKYWORKS SOLUTIONS INC**
Interact API; **RESPONSYS INC**
Interact Campaign; **RESPONSYS INC**
Interact Connect; **RESPONSYS INC**
Interact Insight; **RESPONSYS INC**
Interact Program; **RESPONSYS INC**
Interact Team; **RESPONSYS INC**
Interactive Video Technologies; **MEDIAPLATFORM INC**
Interceptor; **RIVERBED TECHNOLOGY INC**
InterDigital Communications Corp; **INTERDIGITAL INC**
Interface & Control Systems, Inc.; **SRA INTERNATIONAL INC**
International Business Machines (IBM); **SPSS INC**
International Business Machines Corp (IBM); **COGNOS INC**
International Business Machines Corp (IBM); **IBM GLOBAL SERVICES**
International Business Machines Corp (IBM); **STERLING COMMERCE INC**
International Business Machines Corp (IBM); **INTERNET SECURITY SYSTEMS INC**
International Business Machines Corp (IBM); **LENOVO GROUP LIMITED**
International Business Machines Corp (IBM); **COREMETRICS INC**
International Bussiness Machines Corp (IBM); **IBM INDIA PVT LTD**
International Resources Group Ltd.; **L-3 COMMUNICATIONS HOLDINGS INC**

INDEX OF SUBSIDIARIES, BRAND NAMES AND AFFILIATIONS, CONT.

INDEX OF SUBSIDIARIES, BRAND NAMES AND AFFILIATIONS, CONT.

INDEX OF SUBSIDIARIES, BRAND NAMES AND AFFILIATIONS, CONT.

LonWorks; **ECHELON CORP**
LonWorks 2.0; **ECHELON CORP**
Lottery Technology Services; **ACER INC**
Loyalty Lab, Inc.; **TIBCO SOFTWARE INC**
LS Power Semitech Co Ltd; **INFINEON TECHNOLOGIES AG**
LTK Wiring Co., Ltd.; **BELDEN INC**
Lucasfilm Ltd; **LUCASARTS ENTERTAINMENT COMPANY LLC**
Luminary Micro; **TEXAS INSTRUMENTS INC (TI)**
Lynx; **PROXIM WIRELESS CORP**
LynX; **VITESSE SEMICONDUCTOR CORP**
Lynx; **SYNOPSYS INC**
Lyric; **CHYRON CORP**
Lyric Pro; **CHYRON CORP**
Mac OS X; **APPLE INC**
MacBook Air; **APPLE INC**
MackXO; **LATTICE SEMICONDUCTOR CORP**
MacMall.com; **PC MALL INC**
Macrovision Solutions Corporation; **ROVI CORPORATION**
Madden NFL; **ELECTRONIC ARTS INC**
Madison Dearborn Partners LLC; **CDW CORPORATION**
Magellan; **DATALOGIC SCANNING INC**
Magellan; **MITAC INTERNATIONAL CORP**
Magellan 3300HSi; **DATALOGIC SCANNING INC**
Magenta Computacion S.A.; **DIMENSION DATA HOLDINGS PLC**
Magic Denuded Zone; **MEMC ELECTRONIC MATERIALS INC**
Magic Pixel, Inc.; **MACRONIX INTERNATIONAL CO LTD**
MainConcept; **SONIC SOLUTIONS**
Mainstar; **ROCKET SOFTWARE**
Maktoob; **YAHOO! INC**
Malvern Instruments; **SPECTRIS**
Manhattan SCOPE; **MANHATTAN ASSOCIATES INC**
MAPA; **INDRA SISTEMAS SA**
Marine Enterprise; **INTERGRAPH CORP**
Mario Brothers; **NINTENDO CO LTD**
MarketLive; **MARKETLIVE INC**
MarketLive Intelligent Commerce; **MARKETLIVE INC**
MarketLive Mobile; **MARKETLIVE INC**
Marlin Equity Partners; **PHOENIX TECHNOLOGIES LTD**
MaskLink; **PHOTRONICS INC**
Mass Effect; **BIOWARE CORP**
Master B+; **DATALOGIC SCANNING INC**
Master BB+; **DATALOGIC SCANNING INC**
Math Made Easy; **INSTRUCTIVISION INC**
Mathcad; **PARAMETRIC TECHNOLOGY CORP**
Matrix; **ENTERASYS NETWORKS INC**
Maxi Switch, Inc.; **LITE-ON TECHNOLOGY CORP**
Maximus Holdings Inc; **MSCSOFTWARE CORP**

MaxiScale; **OVERLAND STORAGE INC**
MAXLink; **HARMONIC INC**
MaxRise, Inc.; **MACRONIX INTERNATIONAL CO LTD**
MAXTEK; **TEKTRONIX INC**
Maxtor Corp; **SEAGATE TECHNOLOGY PLC**
maXTouch; **ATMEL CORP**
McAfee Network DPL Discovery; **MCAFEE INC**
McAfee OK Mobile; **MCAFEE INC**
McAfee PCI Certifications Service; **MCAFEE INC**
McAfee Total Protection; **MCAFEE INC**
MDDA-860; **BLONDER TONGUE LABORATORIES INC**
MDDi; **MEDIATEK INC**
Measurement Studio; **NATIONAL INSTRUMENTS CORP**
Medfusion; **INTUIT INC**
Media Composer; **AVID TECHNOLOGY INC**
Media Masters LLC; **MOSER BAER INDIA LIMITED**
Media Oriented Systems Transport; **STANDARD MICROSYSTEMS CORPORATION**
MediaLauncher; **MEDIAPLATFORM INC**
Medical & Practice Management Solution; **MEDICAL INFORMATION TECHNOLOGY INC**
MEDITECH; **MEDICAL INFORMATION TECHNOLOGY INC**
MEDITECH 6.0; **MEDICAL INFORMATION TECHNOLOGY INC**
MEDITECH Medication Management; **MEDICAL INFORMATION TECHNOLOGY INC**
MegaRaid; **LSI CORPORATION**
MeiYa Technology Corporation; **NANYA TECHNOLOGY CORPORATION**
Memcorp; **IMATION CORP**
Memex; **SAS INSTITUTE INC**
Memorex; **IMATION CORP**
Memory Stick PRO; **SANDISK CORP**
Memova; **CRITICAL PATH INC**
Memova Anti-Abuse; **CRITICAL PATH INC**
Memova Messaging; **CRITICAL PATH INC**
Memova Mobile; **CRITICAL PATH INC**
Merchants; **DIMENSION DATA HOLDINGS PLC**
Merge/Purge Plus; **PITNEY BOWES SOFTWARE INC**
Meridio; **AUTONOMY CORP PLC**
Merix Corp; **VIASYSTEMS GROUP INC**
MeshMAX; **PROXIM WIRELESS CORP**
MeshNetics ZigBee; **ATMEL CORP**
Message Manager; **MISYS PLC**
Messaging Interaction Center; **INTERACTIVE INTELLIGENCE**
Metal Gear; **KONAMI CORP**
MetroCluster; **NETAPP INC**
METROLink; **HARMONIC INC**
MFLEX U.K. Limited; **MULTI-FINELINE ELECTRONIX**

INDEX OF SUBSIDIARIES, BRAND NAMES AND AFFILIATIONS, CONT.

Micro Focus International Plc; **BORLAND SOFTWARE CORPORATION**
Micro Logistics; **INGRAM MICRO INC**
Microdyne Outsourcing Inc.; **L-3 COMMUNICATIONS HOLDINGS INC**
Micron Machine Tools, Inc.; **NOVELLUS SYSTEMS INC**
Micron Technology Inc; **NANYA TECHNOLOGY CORPORATION**
Micron Technology, Inc.; **LEXAR MEDIA INC**
MicroPress; **ELECTRONICS FOR IMAGING INC**
MICROS Systems Inc; **MICROS-RETAIL**
Microscan Systems, Inc.; **SPECTRIS**
microSD; **SANDISK CORP**
Microsoft Corp.; **DIMENSION DATA HOLDINGS PLC**
Microsoft Dynamics; **MICROSOFT CORP**
MICROS-Retail; **MICROS SYSTEMS INC**
MicroStrategy 9; **MICROSTRATEGY INC**
MicroStrategy Consulting; **MICROSTRATEGY INC**
MicroStrategy Education; **MICROSTRATEGY INC**
MicroStrategy Technical Support; **MICROSTRATEGY INC**
MicroVision, Inc.; **PIONEER CORPORATION**
Middle East Appliances LLC; **VIDEOCON INDUSTRIES LTD**
MIMO; **INTERDIGITAL INC**
MindVision, Inc.; **DIGITAL RIVER INC**
miniSD; **SANDISK CORP**
Mint.com; **INTUIT INC**
Mio; **MITAC INTERNATIONAL CORP**
MirrorBit; **SPANSION**
Missys BankFusion Universal Banking; **MISYS PLC**
Missys Loan IQ; **MISYS PLC**
Missys Tiger; **MISYS PLC**
Misys International Banking Systems; **MISYS PLC**
Misys Open Source Solutions LLC; **MISYS PLC**
MiTAC-SYNNEX Group; **MITAC INTERNATIONAL CORP**
Mitsubishi Corp; **MITSUBISHI ELECTRIC CORPORATION**
Mitsubishi Electric Corporation; **RENESAS ELECTRONICS CORP**
MMD-Monitors & Displays Holding, Ltd.; **TPV TECHNOLOGY LTD**
Mobile Communications Company; **TOSHIBA CORPORATION**
MobileRobots, Inc.; **ADEPT TECHNOLOGY INC**
MobileTouch; **SYNAPTICS INC**
Mobilygen; **MAXIM INTEGRATED PRODUCTS INC**
ModelSim; **MENTOR GRAPHICS CORP**
Modiotek Co Ltd; **MACRONIX INTERNATIONAL CO LTD**
ModusLink Corporation; **MODUSLINK GLOBAL SOLUTIONS INC**

ModusLink Open Channel Solutions, Inc.; **MODUSLINK GLOBAL SOLUTIONS INC**
ModusLink PTS, Inc.; **MODUSLINK GLOBAL SOLUTIONS INC**
Moldflow Corp; **AUTODESK INC**
Momentus; **SEAGATE TECHNOLOGY PLC**
Monkey Island; **LUCASARTS ENTERTAINMENT COMPANY LLC**
MonoSphere; **QUEST SOFTWARE INC**
MoreDirect, Inc.; **PC CONNECTION INC**
Moser Baer Solar Limited; **MOSER BAER INDIA LIMITED**
Motech Industries Inc; **TAIWAN SEMICONDUCTOR MANUFACTURING CO LTD (TSMC)**
Motherboard Intelligent BIOS II; **ELITEGROUP COMPUTER SYSTEMS CO LTD**
Motorola Inc; **HCL INFOSYSTEMS LIMITED**
Motorway Junction Objects; **NAVTEQ CORPORATION**
Mototech; **ACCTON TECHNOLOGY CORP**
MSC.Software Corporation; **SYMPHONY TECHNOLOGY GROUP**
M-Series; **JUNIPER NETWORKS INC**
MSN Video; **MICROSOFT CORP**
mStream; **UTSTARCOM INC**
MTSC, Inc.; **MANTECH INTERNATIONAL CORP**
mvision; **DIMENSION DATA HOLDINGS PLC**
MX Telecom; **AMDOCS LTD**
MX-Series; **JUNIPER NETWORKS INC**
Mxtran, Inc.; **MACRONIX INTERNATIONAL CO LTD**
My Book; **WESTERN DIGITAL CORP**
My Passport; **WESTERN DIGITAL CORP**
MyECG E3-80; **MICRO-STAR INTERNATIONAL**
MyFidelio.net; **MICROS SYSTEMS INC**
Nakaya Microdevices Corporation; **AMKOR TECHNOLOGY INC**
Nanhai Chi Mei Optoelectronics Ltd.; **CHIMEI INNOLUX CORPORATION**
Nanomanufacturing Technologies; **APPLIED MATERIALS INC**
Nanya Plastics Corp.; **NANYA TECHNOLOGY CORPORATION**
Natural; **SOFTWARE AG**
NaviCloud MCS; **NAVISITE INC**
NaviView; **NAVISITE INC**
Navman; **MITAC INTERNATIONAL CORP**
NAVTEQ Corporation; **NOKIA CORPORATION**
Navteq LocationPoint; **NAVTEQ CORPORATION**
NBS Network Border Switch; **SONUS NETWORKS INC**
NCAA Football; **ELECTRONIC ARTS INC**
NCI Ltd; **NCR CORPORATION**
NCW Holdings, Ltd.; **ROYAL PHILIPS ELECTRONICS NV**

INDEX OF SUBSIDIARIES, BRAND NAMES AND AFFILIATIONS, CONT.

INDEX OF SUBSIDIARIES, BRAND NAMES AND AFFILIATIONS, CONT.

INDEX OF SUBSIDIARIES, BRAND NAMES AND AFFILIATIONS, CONT.

INDEX OF SUBSIDIARIES, BRAND NAMES AND AFFILIATIONS, CONT.

INDEX OF SUBSIDIARIES, BRAND NAMES AND AFFILIATIONS, CONT.

INDEX OF SUBSIDIARIES, BRAND NAMES AND AFFILIATIONS, CONT.

INDEX OF SUBSIDIARIES, BRAND NAMES AND AFFILIATIONS, CONT.

INDEX OF SUBSIDIARIES, BRAND NAMES AND AFFILIATIONS, CONT.

INDEX OF SUBSIDIARIES, BRAND NAMES AND AFFILIATIONS, CONT.

INDEX OF SUBSIDIARIES, BRAND NAMES AND AFFILIATIONS, CONT.

INDEX OF SUBSIDIARIES, BRAND NAMES AND AFFILIATIONS, CONT.

INDEX OF SUBSIDIARIES, BRAND NAMES AND AFFILIATIONS, CONT.

INDEX OF SUBSIDIARIES, BRAND NAMES AND AFFILIATIONS, CONT.

CPSIA information can be obtained at www.ICGtesting.com
228643LV00001B/2/P